INFORMATION PRIVACY LAW

ASPEN CASEBOOK SERIES

INFORMATION PRIVACY LAW

Sixth Edition

Daniel J. Solove

John Marshall Harlan Research Professor of Law
George Washington University Law School

Paul M. Schwartz

Jefferson E. Peyser Professor of Law
U.C. Berkeley School of Law
Faculty Director, Berkeley Center for Law & Technology

 Wolters Kluwer

Published by Wolters Kluwer in New York.

Wolters Kluwer Legal & Regulatory U.S. serves customers worldwide with CCH, Aspen Publishers, and Kluwer Law International products. (www.WKLegaledu.com)

To contact Customer Service, e-mail customer.service@wolterskluwer.com, call 1-800-234-1660, fax 1-800-901-9075, or mail correspondence to:

Wolters Kluwer
Attn: Order Department
PO Box 990
Frederick, MD 21705

Printed in the United States of America.

1 2 3 4 5 6 7 8 9 0

ISBN 978-1-4548-9275-5

Library of Congress Cataloging-in-Publication Data

Library of Congress Cataloging-in-Publication Data

Names: Solove, Daniel J., 1972- author. | Schwartz, Paul M., 1959- author.
Title: Information privacy law / Daniel J. Solove, John Marshall Harlan
    Research Professor of Law, George Washington University Law School; Paul
    M. Schwartz, Jefferson E. Peyser Professor of Law, U.C. Berkeley School of
    Law, Faculty Director, Berkeley Center for Law & Technology.
Description: Sixth edition. | New York : Wolters Kluwer Law & Business,
    [2018] | Series: Aspen casebook series | Includes bibliographical
    references and index.
Identifiers: LCCN 2017045456 | ISBN 9781454892755
Subjects: LCSH: Privacy, Right of--United States. | Data protection--Law and
    legislation--United States. | Confidential communications--United States.
    | Personality (Law)--United States. | LCGFT: Casebooks.
Classification: LCC KF1262 .S66 2018 | DDC 342.7308/58--dc23 LC record
    available at https://lccn.loc.gov/2017045456

About Wolters Kluwer Legal & Regulatory U.S.

Wolters Kluwer Legal & Regulatory U.S. delivers expert content and solutions in the areas of law, corporate compliance, health compliance, reimbursement, and legal education. Its practical solutions help customers successfully navigate the demands of a changing environment to drive their daily activities, enhance decision quality and inspire confident outcomes.

Serving customers worldwide, its legal and regulatory portfolio includes products under the Aspen Publishers, CCH Incorporated, Kluwer Law International, ftwilliam.com and MediRegs names. They are regarded as exceptional and trusted resources for general legal and practice-specific knowledge, compliance and risk management, dynamic workflow solutions, and expert commentary.

To Pamela and Griffin—DJS

To Steffie, Clara, and Leo—PMS

SUMMARY OF CONTENTS

CONTENTS

4 PRIVACY AND LAW ENFORCEMENT   253

PREFACE

The rapid growth of the Internet, coupled with new business practices and new efforts by government to deploy technology for law enforcement and the administration of programs, has raised far-reaching questions about the future of privacy.

The role of law is central to many of these debates. To what extent can the law safeguard the right of privacy in an era of rapidly evolving technology? What competing interests must be considered? What is the appropriate role of the courts and the legislatures? These questions are not new, but they have acquired greater urgency as the law is asked to evaluate an increasingly complex array of privacy matters.

For lawyers, these developments have raised both new challenges and new opportunities. In the private sector, attorneys now routinely advise business clients about the development of privacy policies, compliance with privacy statutes, and privacy regulations in new markets. Attorneys litigate on behalf of clients who believe that their privacy has been violated, while others defend against these allegations. State attorneys general have become leading champions of privacy rights. Policymakers in government evaluate new legislative proposals both to expand and to limit privacy claims. Legal advisors on trade policy, technology development, consumer protection, and national security all consider privacy issues in the course of their work.

Clearly, privacy has emerged as one of the critical legal subjects in the modern era. Since the first edition of this book was published in 2003, the field of information privacy has grown tremendously. Many new laws have been passed, countless cases have been decided, and a litany of fascinating new issues has arisen. Courses in information privacy law are being offered at law schools around the country, and many lawyers devote their practice to information privacy issues.

This text provides a cornerstone for the study of information privacy law. Our goal is to provide a comprehensive and accessible introduction for the student and an authoritative reference for the practitioner. We have organized the book around the general topics and themes of this area of law. Information privacy law is a complicated and vast body of different types of legal protections, and our organizational choices reflect our aim of producing a clear and coherent synthesis of the field. When selecting cases, we have included the leading cases as well as endeavored to provide a solid historical background and a timely and fresh perspective on the major privacy issues facing lawyers in the twenty-first century. Important majority opinions are followed by equally important dissents. The text includes extensive notes and commentary, and it integrates cases and statutes with policy and jurisprudential perspectives. To facilitate discussion and debate, we have included excerpts from commentators with a wide range of viewpoints. Technical terms are clearly explained.

Information Privacy Law also draws heavily on recent developments in the high-tech field as well as international law. We anticipate that these factors will contribute significantly to the development of privacy law in the near future. The text also explores the major themes in the development of the field — the meaning of privacy, the reasonable expectation of privacy, the application of constitutional principles to new technologies, and the transformation of norms into legal frameworks. We hope that this text provides a useful introduction to the challenges of the field of information privacy now and in the future.

A Note on the Casebook Website. We strive to keep the book up to date between editions, and we maintain a web page for the book with downloadable updates and other useful information. We invite you to visit the website:

https://informationprivacylaw.com

The website contains links to useful news sites, blogs, and online resources pertaining to information privacy law issues. We also provide a list of recommended books that can be read in conjunction with this book.

A Note on Privacy Law Fundamentals. Students may find our short volume, *Privacy Law Fundamentals,* to be a useful companion to the casebook. *Privacy Law Fundamentals* is designed to be a distilled overview of information privacy law for both practitioners and students. More information about this book can be found at https://informationprivacylaw.com.

A Note on the Editing. We have deleted many citations and footnotes from the cases to facilitate readability. The footnotes that have been retained in the cases have been renumbered. We have also included many citations to additional works in the footnotes that may be of interest to the reader.

Daniel J. Solove
Paul M. Schwartz

November 2017

ACKNOWLEDGMENTS

Daniel J. Solove: I would like to thank Carl Coleman, Scott Forbes, Susan Freiwald, Tomás Gómez-Arostegui, Stephen Gottlieb, Marcia Hofmann, Chris Hoofnagle, John Jacobi, Orin Kerr, Raymond Ku, Peter Raven-Hansen, Joel Reidenberg, Neil Richards, Michael Risinger, Lior Strahilevitz, Peter Swire, William Thompson, and Peter Winn for helpful comments and suggestions. Charlie Sullivan and Jake Barnes provided indispensable advice about how to bring this project to fruition. Special thanks to Richard Mixter at Aspen Publishers for his encouragement and faith in this project. Thanks as well to the other folks at Aspen who have contributed greatly to the editing and development of this book: John Devins, Christine Hannan, Carmen Reid, Jessica Barmack, John Burdeaux, and Sandra Doherty. I would like to thank my research assistants Peter Choy, Monica Contreras, Carly Grey, Maeve Miller, James Murphy, Poornima Ravishankar, Vladimir Semendyai, Sheerin Shahinpoor, John Spaccarotella, Tiffany Stedman, Lourdes Turrecha, Eli Weiss, and Kate Yannitte. I would also like to thank Dean Blake Morant for providing the resources I needed. And thanks to my wife Pamela Solove and son Griffin Solove, who kept me in good cheer throughout this project.

Paul M. Schwartz: For their suggestions, encouragement, and insights into information privacy law, I would like to thank Ken Bamberger, Fred Cate, Malcolm Crompton, Christopher Gulotta, Andrew Guzman, Chris Hoofnagle, Ted Janger, Ronald D. Lee, Lance Liebman, Viktor Mayer-Schönberger, Steven McDonald, Deirdre Mulligan, Karl-Nikolaus Peifer, Joel Reidenberg, Ira Rubinstein, Pam Samuelson, Lior Strahilevitz, Peter Swire, William M. Treanor, and Peter Winn. I benefited as well from the help of my talented research assistants: Cesar Alvarez, Henry Becker, Benedikt Burger, Sarah Chai, Kai-Dieter Classen, Leah Duranti, Sarah Haji, Anne Hilby, Thaddeus Houston, Jesse Koehler, Leah Mekhneche, Devon Mongeluzzi, Joseph Mornin, Alpa Patel, Karl Saddlemire, Brian St. John, Malvika Sinha, Laura Sullivan, and Sebastian Zimmeck. Many thanks to my co-author, Daniel Solove. Many thanks as well to my mother, Nancy Schwartz, and to Laura Schwartz and Ed Holden; David Schwartz and Kathy Smith; and Daniel Schwartz.

A profound debt is owed Spiros Simitis. My interest in the subject of information privacy began in 1985 with his suggestion that I visit his office of the Hessian Data Protection Commissioner in Wiesbaden and sit in on meetings there. Through his scholarship, example, and friendship, Professor Simitis has provided essential guidance during the decades since that initial trip to Wiesbaden. My portion of the book is dedicated to Steffie, Clara, and Leo, with my gratitude and love.

Finally, both of us would like to thank Marc Rotenberg, who helped us shape the book in its first two editions and provided invaluable input.

We are grateful to the following sources for their permission to reprint excerpts of their scholarship:

Anita L. Allen, *Coercing Privacy*, 40 William & Mary L. Rev. 723 (1999). Used by permission. © 1999 by William & Mary Law Review and Anita L. Allen.

William C. Banks & M.E. Bowman, *Executive Authority For National Security Surveillance,* 50 Am. U. L. Rev. 1 (2000). Reprinted with permission.

Fred H. Cate, *The Privacy Problem: A Broader View of Information Privacy and the Costs and Consequences of Protecting It*, 4 First Reports 1 (March 2003). Reprinted with permission.

Julie E. Cohen, *Examined Lives: Informational Privacy*, 52 Stan. L. Rev. 1371 (2000). © 2000. Reprinted by permission of the Stanford Law Review in the format textbook via Copyright Clearance Center and Julie Cohen.

Mary DeRosa, *Data Mining and Data Analysis for Counterterrorism,* Center for Strategic and International Studies 6-8 (CSIS) (2004). Reprinted with permission.

Richard Epstein, *The Legal Regulation of Genetic Discrimination: Old Responses to New Technology,* 74 B.U. L. Rev. 1, 2-4, 8-13, 18-19 (1994). Reprinted with permission of Richard Epstein.

Eric Goldman, *The Privacy Hoax,* Forbes (Oct. 14, 2002) available at http://www.ericgoldman.org/Articles/privacyhoax.htm. Reprinted with permission.

Lawrence O. Gostin, Health Information Privacy, 80 Cornell L. Rev. 451 (1995). Reprinted with permission.

Steven Hetcher, *The FTC as Internet Privacy Norm Entrepreneur*, 53 Vand. L. Rev. 2041 (2000). Reprinted with the permission of Steven Hetcher.

Orin S. Kerr, *A User's Guide to the Stored Communications Act — and a Legislator's Guide to Amending It,* 72 Geo. Wash. L. Rev. 1208 (2004). Reprinted with permission.

Orin S. Kerr, *The Fourth Amendment and New Technologies: Constitutional Myths and the Case for Caution*, 102 Mich. L. Rev. 801 (2004). © 2004 by the Michigan Law Review Association. Reprinted with permission.

Pauline T. Kim, *Privacy Rights, Public Policy, and the Employment Relationship*, 57 Ohio St. L.J. 671 (1996). Reprinted with permission.

Catharine A. MacKinnon, Toward a Feminist Theory of the State 190-193 (1989). © 1989 by Harvard University Press. Reprinted with permission.

Richard A. Posner, *The Right of Privacy,* 12 Ga. L. Rev. 393 (1978). Reprinted with permission.

Radhika Rao, *Property, Privacy and the Human Body,* 80 B.U. L Rev. 359 (2000). Reprinted with permission of the Boston University Law Review and Radhika Rao.

Joel Reidenberg, *E-Commerce and Trans-Atlantic Privacy,* 38 Hous. L. Rev. 717 (2001). Reprinted with permission.

Marc Rotenberg, *Fair Information Practices and the Architecture of Privacy (What Larry Doesn't Get)*, 2001 Stan. Tech. L. Rev. 1, 43 (2001). Reprinted with permission.

Paul M. Schwartz, *Privacy and Democracy in Cyberspace*, 52 Vand. L. Rev. 1609 (1999). Reprinted with the permission of Paul Schwartz.

Paul M. Schwartz, *Privacy and the Economics of Health Care Information*, 76 Tex. L. Rev. 1 (1997). © 1997 the Texas Law Review. Reprinted with permission.

Reva B. Seigel, *The Rule of Love: Wife Beating as Prerogative of Privacy*, 105 Yale L.J. 2117 (1996). Reprinted by permission of the *Yale Law Journal* Company and the William S. Hein Company, from the *Yale Law Journal,* vol. 105, pages 2117-2207.

Spiros Simitis, *Reviewing Privacy in an Informational Society*, 135 U. Pa. L. Rev. 707, 709-710, 724-726, 732-738, 746 (1987). © 1987 by the University of Pennsylvania Law Review. Reprinted by permission of the University of Pennsylvania Law Review and Spiros Simitis.

Richard Sobel, *The Degradation of the Moral Economy of Political Identity Under a Computerized National Identification System*, 8 B.U. J. Sci. & Tech. L. 37 (2002). Reprinted with permission.

Daniel J. Solove, *Conceptualizing Privacy,* 90 California Law Review 1087 (2002). © 2002 by the California Law Review.

Daniel J. Solove, *Reconstructing Electronic Surveillance Law*, 72 George Washington Law Review 1264 (2004). © 2004 by Daniel J. Solove.

Jeff Sovern, *Opting In, Opting Out, or No Options at All: The Fight for Control of Personal Information,* 74 Wash. L. Rev. 1033 (1999). Reprinted with permission.

Michael E. Staten & Fred H. Cate, *The Impact of Opt-In Privacy Rules on Retail Markets: A Case Study of MBNA*, 52 Duke L.J. 745 (2003). Reprinted with permission.

Alan Westin, Privacy and Freedom 7, 31-38 (1967). A study sponsored by the Association of the Bar of the City of New York. Reprinted with permission.

James Q. Whitman, *The Two Western Cultures of Privacy: Dignity Versus Liberty,* 113 Yale L.J. 1151 (2004). Reprinted with permission.

Peter A. Winn, *Online Court Records: Balancing Judicial Accountability and Privacy in an Age of Electronic Information*, 79 Wash. L. Rev. 307 (2004). Reprinted with permission.

INFORMATION PRIVACY LAW

CHAPTER 1

INTRODUCTION

CHAPTER OUTLINE

A. INFORMATION PRIVACY, TECHNOLOGY, AND THE LAW

We live in a world shaped by technology and fueled by information. Technological devices — such as mobile phones, video and audio recording devices, computers, and the Internet — have revolutionized our ability to capture information about the world and to communicate with each other. Information is the lifeblood of today's society. Increasingly, our everyday activities involve the transfer and recording of information. The government collects vast quantities of personal information in records pertaining to an individual's birth, marriage, divorce, property, court proceedings, motor vehicles, voting activities, criminal transgressions, professional licensing, and other activities. Private sector entities also amass gigantic databases of personal information for marketing purposes or to prepare credit histories. Wherever we go, whatever we do, we could easily leave behind a trail of data that is recorded and gathered together.

These new technologies, coupled with the increasing use of personal information by business and government, pose new challenges for the protection of privacy. This book is about the law's response to new challenges to privacy. A significant amount of law regulates information privacy in the United States and around the world. Is this law responsive to the present and future dangers to privacy? Can information privacy itself endanger other important values? What duties and responsibilities must corporations, government agencies, and other private and public sector entities have with regard to personal data? What rights do individuals have to prevent and redress invasions to their privacy? When and how should privacy rights be limited? Does the war on terrorism require less privacy and more sharing of information? How should the law respond to an age of rapid technological change? Has the meaning of privacy changed in the age of social media and powerful search engines? How does privacy change when refrigerators, automobiles, thermostats, and many other devices generate information about their users? These are some of the questions that this text will address.

This book's topic is information privacy law. Information privacy concerns the collection, use, and disclosure of personal information. Information privacy is often contrasted with "decisional privacy," which concerns the freedom to make decisions about one's body and family. Decisional privacy involves matters such as contraception, procreation, abortion, and child rearing, and is at the center of a series of Supreme Court cases often referred to as "substantive due process" or "the constitutional right to privacy." But information privacy increasingly incorporates elements of decisional privacy as the use of data both expands and limits individual autonomy.

Information privacy law is an interrelated web of tort law, federal and state constitutional law, federal and state statutory law, evidentiary privileges, property law, contract law, and criminal law. Information privacy law is relatively new, although its roots reach far back. It is developing coherence as privacy doctrines in one area are being used to inform and structure legal responses in other areas. Information privacy law raises a related set of political, policy, and philosophical questions: What is privacy? Why is privacy important? What is the impact of technology on privacy? How does privacy affect the efforts of law enforcement and national security agencies to protect the public? What is the role of the courts, the legislatures, and the law in safeguarding, or in placing limits on, privacy?

Furthermore, one might wonder: Why study information privacy law? There are a number of answers to this question. First, in today's Information Age, privacy is an issue of paramount significance for freedom, democracy, and security. One of the central issues of information privacy concerns the power of commercial and government entities over individual autonomy and decision making. Privacy also concerns the drawing of rules that may limit this autonomy and decision making by necessarily permitting commercial and government entities access to personal information. Understood broadly, information privacy plays an important role in the society we are constructing in today's Information Age.

Second, information privacy is an issue of growing public concern. Information privacy has become a priority on the legislative agenda of Congress and many state legislatures. Information privacy problems are also timely, frequently in the news, and often the subject of litigation.

Third, there are many new laws and legal developments regarding information privacy. It is a growth area in the law. Increased litigation, legislation, regulation, as well as public concern over privacy are spurring corporations in a variety of businesses to address privacy. Lawyers are drafting privacy policies, litigating privacy issues, and developing ways for dot-com companies, corporations, hospitals, insurers, and banks to conform to privacy regulations. A new position, the Chief Privacy Officer, is a mainstay at most corporations. The leading organization of these officers, the International Association of Privacy Professionals (IAPP), boasts thousands of members. Attorneys increasingly are grappling with privacy issues — either through litigation of privacy violations or through measures to comply with privacy regulations and to prevent litigation. All of these developments demand lawyers who are well-versed in the grand scheme and subtle nuances of information privacy law.

Fourth, information privacy law is an engaging and fascinating topic. The issues are controversial, complex, relevant, and current. Few areas of law are more closely intertwined with our world of rapid technological innovation. Moreover, concerns regarding information privacy play an important role in debates regarding security in post-9/11 America. The study of privacy law also helps us understand how our legal institutions respond to change and may help prepare us for other challenges ahead.

SIDIS V. F-R PUBLISHING CORP.

113 F.2d 806 (2d Cir. 1940)

[William James Sidis (1898–1944) was perhaps the most famous child prodigy of his day. According to Amy Wallace's biography of Sidis, *The Prodigy*, he was able to read the *New York Times* at the age of 18 months.[1] By the time he was three, William had learned to operate a typewriter and used it to compose a letter to Macy's to order toys. At that age, he also learned Latin "as a birthday present for his father." That year, after his father taught him the Greek alphabet, he taught himself to read Homer with the aid of a Greek primer. By the time he started elementary school, at the age of six, he could speak and read at least eight languages. At the age of five, he had already devised a method for calculating the day of the week on which any given date occurred, and when he was seven years old, he wrote a book about calendars. At that time, he had already prepared manuscripts about anatomy, astronomy, grammar, linguistics, and mathematics. At the age of eight, he created a new table of logarithms, which used a base of 12 instead of the conventional ten. From early childhood on, Sidis was also passionately interested in politics and world events. According to Wallace, Sidis was one of the few child prodigies in world history whose talents were not limited to a single field.

In 1909, Harvard University permitted Sidis to enroll in it; he was 11 years old and the youngest student in the history of Harvard. Sidis also made the front pages

---

[1] Amy Wallace, *The Prodigy* (1986).

of newspapers around the nation when on January 5, 1910, he delivered a two-hour lecture to the Harvard Mathematics Club. The *New York Times* featured Sidis on its front page of October 11, 1909, as "Harvard's Child Prodigy."[2]

Boris Sidis, William's father, was a distinguished physician, early pioneer of American psychology (and opponent of Sigmund Freud), and prolific author. In 1911, Boris published a book about his educational theories and his virulent opposition to the educational institutions of the day. At the time of the publication of this book, *Philistine and Genius*, William was 13, and in Wallace's description, "teetering on the edge of his endurance to public exposure." Although the book did not mention his son by name, it did discuss him and his accomplishments, which brought William additional publicity. Sarah Sidis, William's mother and herself a physician, had a domineering and deeply troubled relationship with her son. Neither she nor Boris did anything to shelter William from the great publicity that followed him from an early age and the tremendous stress that it created in his life.

When he graduated from Harvard at age 16, William told reporters: "I want to live the perfect life. The only way to live the perfect life is to live it in seclusion. I have always hated crowds." After graduating from college, Sidis accepted a teaching position at the Rice University in Houston. After a difficult eight months as a professor of mathematics there, William returned to Boston and enrolled in Harvard Law School in 1916. He left the law school in his last semester there without taking a degree.

From 1918 until a *New Yorker* article about him in 1937, Sidis engaged in socialist and other radical politics, published numerous newsletters, lived an active social life, addressed a monthly study group, wrote a treatise about the classification of streetcar transfers, and financed his life through a series of modest clerical jobs and sales of his patented "perpetual calendar." During this period, in 1925, Sidis also published *The Animate and the Inanimate*. In Wallace's view, this book is the first work on the subject of "black holes" in space as well as an extraordinary work in the field of cosmogony, or the study of the origins of the universe. The book did not receive a single review at the time and was ignored by academia.

Before 1937, Sidis had done an excellent job of avoiding publicity for a decade. In that year, however, a local paper, the *Boston Sunday Advertiser*, published an article about him. This was followed by the August 14, 1937, issue of the *New Yorker*, which contained a brief biographical sketch about Sidis, his life following his graduation from Harvard, and the subsequent decades during which he lived in obscurity.[3] The article was part of a regular feature of the magazine called "Where Are They Now?," which provided brief updates on the lives of famous figures of the past. The article was printed under the subtitle *April Fool*, a reference to the fact that Sidis was born on April Fool's Day. The article recounted the history of Sidis's life and his current whereabouts: "William James Sidis lives today, at the age of thirty-nine, in a hall bedroom of Boston's shabby south end." The article also contained numerous errors about Sidis's life.

[2] *Harvard's Child Prodigy: All Amazed at Mathematical Grasp of Youngest Matriculate, Aged 13 Years*, N.Y. Times, Oct. 10, 1909, at A1.

[3] J.L. Manley, *Where Are They Now?: April Fool!*, New Yorker 22 (Aug. 14, 1937).

A mystery still exists regarding the interview at the basis of this article. According to Wallace, Sidis's contemporary biographer, a member of the monthly study group, whom she refers to only as "John," had brought along a friend to one meeting. Several members of this group suspected that this woman, who was the daughter of a publisher at a large company, served as the basis for the *New Yorker*'s report. Yet, the mystery remains as this individual did not interview Sidis at the time of the monthly meeting. Wallace writes: "William always maintained that the entire article was a combination of imagination and old stories about him, and no strangers had gained access to his room." Another possibility is that Sidis spoke to someone without knowing that she was a reporter, which seems unlikely due to his aversion to publicity.

The *New Yorker* article described Sidis's famous childhood and then recounted his subsequent career as an insignificant clerk: "He seems to get a great and ironic enjoyment out of leading a life of wandering irresponsibility after a childhood of scrupulous regimentation." Sidis never remained at one job for too long because "his employers or fellow-workers [would] soon find out that he is the famous boy wonder, and he can't tolerate a position after that." According to Sidis: "The very sight of a mathematical formula makes me physically ill. . . . All I want to do is run an adding machine, but they won't let me alone." The article also described Sidis's dwelling, a small bedroom in a poor part of Boston and his personal activities, interests, and habits.

In his legal action against the *Boston Sunday Advertiser*, Sidis won a settlement of $375. Sidis also sued F-R Publishing Corporation, the publisher of the *New Yorker*. Among his claims were a violation of his privacy rights under §§ 50-51 of the N.Y. Civil Rights Law.]

CLARK, C.J. . . . It is not contended that any of the matter printed is untrue. Nor is the manner of the author unfriendly; Sidis today is described as having "a certain childlike charm." But the article is merciless in its dissection of intimate details of its subject's personal life, and this in company with elaborate accounts of Sidis' passion for privacy and the pitiable lengths to which he has gone in order to avoid public scrutiny. The work possesses great reader interest, for it is both amusing and instructive; but it may be fairly described as a ruthless exposure of a once public character, who has since sought and has now been deprived of the seclusion of private life.

The article of December 25, 1937, was a biographical sketch of another former child prodigy, in the course of which William James Sidis and the recent account of him were mentioned. The advertisement published in the New York World-Telegram of August 13, 1937, read: "Out Today. Harvard Prodigy. Biography of the man who astonished Harvard at age 11. Where are they now? by J.L. Manley. Page 22. The New Yorker."

The complaint contains a general allegation, repeated for all the claims, of publication by the defendant of *The New Yorker*, "a weekly magazine of wide circulation throughout the United States." Then each separate "cause" contains an allegation that the defendant publicly circulated the articles or caused them to be circulated in the particular states upon whose law that cause is assumed to be founded. Circulation of the New York World-Telegram advertisement is, however, alleged only with respect to the second "cause," for asserted violation of New York law.

Under the first "cause of action" we are asked to declare that this exposure transgresses upon plaintiff's right of privacy, as recognized in California, Georgia, Kansas, Kentucky, and Missouri. Each of these states except California grants to the individual a common law right, and California a constitutional right, to be let alone to a certain extent. The decisions have been carefully analyzed by the court below, and we need not examine them further. None of the cited rulings goes so far as to prevent a newspaper or magazine from publishing the truth about a person, however intimate, revealing, or harmful the truth may be. Nor are there any decided cases that confer such a privilege upon the press. . . .

It must be conceded that under the strict standards suggested by [Warren and Brandeis in their article, *The Right to Privacy*] plaintiff's right of privacy has been invaded. Sidis today is neither politician, public administrator, nor statesman. Even if he were, some of the personal details revealed were of the sort that Warren and Brandeis believed "all men alike are entitled to keep from popular curiosity."

But despite eminent opinion to the contrary, we are not yet disposed to afford to all of the intimate details of private life an absolute immunity from the prying of the press. Everyone will agree that at some point the public interest in obtaining information becomes dominant over the individual's desire for privacy. Warren and Brandeis were willing to lift the veil somewhat in the case of public officers. We would go further, though we are not yet prepared to say how far. At least we would permit limited scrutiny of the "private" life of any person who has achieved, or has had thrust upon him, the questionable and indefinable status of a "public figure."

William James Sidis was once a public figure. As a child prodigy, he excited both admiration and curiosity. Of him great deeds were expected. In 1910, he was a person about whom the newspapers might display a legitimate intellectual interest, in the sense meant by Warren and Brandeis, as distinguished from a trivial and unseemly curiosity. But the precise motives of the press we regard as unimportant. And even if Sidis had loathed public attention at that time, we think his uncommon achievements and personality would have made the attention permissible. Since then Sidis has cloaked himself in obscurity, but his subsequent history, containing as it did the answer to the question of whether or not he had fulfilled his early promise, was still a matter of public concern. The article in *The New Yorker* sketched the life of an unusual personality, and it possessed considerable popular news interest.

We express no comment on whether or not the newsworthiness of the matter printed will always constitute a complete defense. Revelations may be so intimate and so unwarranted in view of the victim's position as to outrage the community's notions of decency. But when focused upon public characters, truthful comments upon dress, speech, habits, and the ordinary aspects of personality will usually not transgress this line. Regrettably or not, the misfortunes and frailties of neighbors and "public figures" are subjects of considerable interest and discussion to the rest of the population. And when such are the mores of the community, it would be unwise for a court to bar their expression in the newspapers, books, and magazines of the day.

Plaintiff in his first "cause of action" charged actual malice in the publication, and now claims that an order of dismissal was improper in the face of such an allegation. We cannot agree. If plaintiff's right of privacy was not invaded by the article, the existence of actual malice in its publication would not change that result. Unless made so by statute, a truthful and therefore non-libelous statement will not become libelous when uttered maliciously. A similar rule should prevail on invasions of the right of privacy. "Personal ill-will is not an ingredient of the offence, any more than in an ordinary case of trespass to person or to property." Warren and Brandeis, supra at page 218. Nor does the malice give rise to an independent wrong based on an intentional invasion of the plaintiff's interest in mental and emotional tranquility.

If the article appearing in the issue of August 14, 1937, does not furnish grounds for action, then it is clear that the brief and incidental reference to it contained in the article of December 25, 1937, is not actionable. . . .

[The court concluded that the second cause of action under N.Y. Civil Rights Law was properly dismissed as well. The second cause of action charged invasion of the rights conferred on plaintiff by §§ 50 and 51 of the N.Y. Civil Rights Law. Section 50 states: "A person, firm or corporation that uses for advertising purposes, or for the purposes of trade, the name, portrait or picture of any living person without having first obtained the written consent of such person, or if a minor of his or her parent or guardian, is guilty of a misdemeanor." Section 51 gives the injured person an injunction remedy and damages. The court found: "Though a publisher sells a commodity, and expects to profit from the sale of his product, he is immune from the interdict of Secs. 50 and 51 so long as he confines himself to the unembroidered dissemination of facts. . . . *The New Yorker* articles limit themselves to the unvarnished, unfictionalized truth."]

NOTES & QUESTIONS

1. *Involuntary Public Figures.* After losing his privacy suit against the *New Yorker*, Sidis sued it for libel for the false information in the story. Among his charges, he claimed that a reader of the article would think that he was a reprehensible character, disloyal to his country, a loathsome and filthy person in personal habits, suffered a mental breakdown, and was a fool, who lived in misery and poverty. The *New Yorker* settled this case out of court for a small amount of money, which Wallace estimates in her biography of Sidis at between $500 and $600.

   Sidis suffered from high blood pressure, and, approximately three months after receiving the settlement from the *New Yorker*, on July 17, 1944, he died from a cerebral hemorrhage and pneumonia. He was 46 years old and had $652.81 in his bank account.

   The life of William Sidis illustrates a man profoundly disturbed by being thrust by his parents into the limelight as a child and by the media hounding him. He tried to spend his adult life fleeing from being the focus of any public attention. If he had been an involuntary public figure in the past, should this affect whether he should be able to retreat from the public eye in the future?

Does it matter that he became a public figure as a child, that is, that he did not voluntarily choose this status as an adult?

The *Sidis* case suggests the principle that once one is a public figure, one is always a public figure. Can people who were once famous ever retreat into obscurity?

2. ***Who Was J.L. Manley? What Did He Try to Convey in His Article?*** The Sidis article was written by a "J.L. Manley." In a biography of James Thurber, the famous American humorist, Burton Bernstein reveals that Thurber used Jared L. Manley as a pseudonym.[4] Under this signature, Thurber wrote 24 profiles of onetime celebrities, including the Sidis piece. All pieces were based on the research of other reporters at the *New Yorker*, including the unnamed reporter who actually interviewed Sidis.

   In Thurber's own account of his time at the *New Yorker*, he faulted the *Sidis* court on one matter: "[N]owhere was there any indication of what I thought had stood out all through my story, implicit though it was — my feeling that the piece would help to curb the great American thrusting of talented children into the glare of fame or notoriety, a procedure in so many cases disastrous to the later career and happiness of the exploited youngsters."[5]

3. ***J.D. Salinger's Letters.*** In 1998, Joyce Maynard wrote an autobiography, *At Home in the World*, that describes her romance with J.D. Salinger in the 1970s. J.D. Salinger, an acclaimed author who wrote *The Catcher in the Rye*, had long ago completely retreated from public life and adopted a highly secluded existence in New Hampshire. In 1999, Maynard auctioned the letters J.D. Salinger wrote to her. She received $156,500 for the letters from the auction at Sotheby's. CNN reported at that time, "California philanthropist Peter Norton, who bought the letters, said he plans to return them to Salinger." Should Salinger have a right to privacy in the disclosure of the letters? Copyright law does create a copyright interest in unpublished letters — which prevents not only the publication of the entire contents of the letters, but a paraphrase of the letters that is too close to the actual text of the letters. *See Salinger v. Random House, Inc.*, 811 F.2d 90 (2d Cir. 1987). Should privacy law provide Salinger with the right to sue over the writing of Maynard's book?

4. ***Girls Gone Wild.*** A company markets videotapes of young college women at spring break or Mardi Gras flashing and undressing. The women, often intoxicated, reveal their nudity in public and give their permission to use the video footage on the company's videotapes, which are called "Girls Gone Wild." Later on, when sober, some of the women regret their decision to be in

---

[4] *See* Burton Bernstein, *Thurber* 261 (1975). Bernstein writes:

> For all the distractions of city life and his sleepless schedule, Thurber was getting a lot of good work done. In early 1936, he began to write (really rewrite, since some of the New Yorker's best reporters, like Eugene Kinkead, were doing the research) a number of short, retrospective Profiles. His nonfiction craft rose to a new high in these excellent pieces, which lent themselves to his human approach.

Id. Bernstein also reveals that Jared L. Manley was a name that Thurber cobbled together when writing his first piece about an old boxer based on the initials of the boxer John L. Sullivan and "Manley" based on "the manly art of self-defense."

[5] James Thurber, *My Years with Ross* (1959).

the video. Have they waived all privacy rights to their nude images on the video if they sign a consent form? Or should they be entitled to have some time to reconsider? Should they not be able to sign away these rights even when sober? Others have sued claiming that they were just filmed in public without signing a consent form. Do they have a valid privacy claim even when they exposed themselves in public?

5. *Privacy Inalienability.* Do we care whether or not Sidis knew he was talking to a reporter as opposed to a new neighbor? Can we assume that anyone who talks to a reporter has abandoned a privacy interest in the information that she shares with the journalist? More broadly, to what extent should privacy interests be tradable, waiveable, or otherwise alienable?[6]

6. *Googleization.* The Internet makes the preservation and dissemination of information much easier. Information about a person can be easily discovered by "Googling" them. Google will pull up dozens, sometimes hundreds of thousands, of information fragments about a person. It is becoming increasingly difficult for people to hide their personal information, which once would fade into obscurity but is now preserved forever on the Internet. Youthful indiscretions become permanent baggage. Consider the plight of one Michael, who was briefly imprisoned as a minor. The information comes up on a Google search, and Michael finds that it is inhibiting his ability to date, since many of the women he dates inquire about his time in prison. They have obviously Googled him:

> "When you meet someone," Michael says, "you don't say, 'I had an affair one time,' or 'I was arrested for DUI once,' or 'I cheated on my taxes in 1984.' "... [W]hat Michael finds most disturbing are the sudden silences. "Instead of thinking, 'Was I curt last week?' or 'Did I insult this political party or that belief?' I have to think about what happened when I was 17."[7]

Is Sidis's claim to privacy quaint by today's standards? How do we protect privacy in a post-Google world?

7. *The* Star Wars *Kid and the Numa Numa Dance.* An overweight, awkward 15-year-old kid videotaped himself pretending to be a character from a *Star Wars* movie.[8] He swung around a golf ball retriever pretending that it was a light saber and made his own sound effects. Somebody found the video, digitized it, and posted it on the Internet. The video created a buzz, and it was downloaded millions of times around the world. Versions of the video with music and special effects were soon posted. People made fun of the kid in various discussions throughout the Internet.

---

[6] Paul M. Schwartz, *Property, Privacy, and Personal Data,* 117 Harv. L. Rev. 2055, 2074 (2004).

[7] Neil Swidey, *A Nation of Voyeurs: How the Internet Search Engine Google Is Changing What We Can Find Out About Each Other and Raising Questions About Whether We Should,* Boston Globe Mag., Feb. 2, 2003, at 10.

[8] Amy Harmon, *Fame Is No Laughing Matter for the "Star Wars" Kid,* N.Y. Times, May 19, 2003, at C3.

In December 2005, Gary Brolsma placed on the Internet a clip of himself lip-synching and dancing in a chair to a Romanian pop song.[9] He called his performance the "Numa Numa Dance." The video was featured on newsgrounds.com, a website devoted to animation and videos, as well as elsewhere on the Internet. Newsgrounds.com alone soon received almost two million hits for the "Numa Numa Dance." Brolsma appeared on Good Morning America, and CNN and VH1 showed his clip.

Suddenly, however, he decided that he disliked the attention. The *New York Times* reported that Brolsma "has now sought refuge from his fame in his family's small house on a gritty street in Saddle Brook." The article added: "According to his relatives, he mopes around the house. . . . He is distraught, embarrassed." His grandmother quoted him as saying: "I just want this to end."

Is this simply life in the Internet Age? Does it matter that the parents of the "*Star Wars* kid" alleged that the clip of their son was placed online without his permission? In contrast, Brolsma posted the video of his dance himself. Is there something that the law can do to protect people like the *Star Wars* kid or the Numa Numa dancer? If so, what?

Ultimately, Brolsma moved beyond any anguish at his fame or notoriety. In September 2006, he released a second video, "New Numa," with corporate sponsorship at newnuma.com. The new video features Brolsma and members of a rock band, the Nowadays, and a new song. The video was released along with a promotion that allowed the public to submit their own videos and win a share of $45,000 in prizes. Brolsma also offered a selection of t-shirts and a coffee mug for sale to the public. In 2008, he started a website, the Numa Network, which has grown to include a YouTube channel and a Facebook presence.

B. INFORMATION PRIVACY LAW: ORIGINS AND TYPES

Information privacy law is a wide-ranging body of law, encompassing common law, constitutional law, statutory law, and international law. This section will provide a brief introduction to the various strands of information privacy law that will be covered throughout this book. It begins by looking in detail at the most important article ever written about privacy.

1. COMMON LAW

(a) The Warren and Brandeis Article

The common law's development of tort remedies to protect privacy is one of the most significant chapters in the history of privacy law. In the late nineteenth century, considerable concerns about privacy captured the public's attention,

---

[9] Alan Feuer & Jason George, *Internet Fame Is Cruel Mistress for Dancer of the Numa Numa,* N.Y. Times, Feb. 26, 2005, at A1.

ultimately resulting in the 1890 publication of Samuel Warren and Louis Brandeis's pathbreaking article, *The Right to Privacy*.[10] According to Roscoe Pound, the article did "nothing less than add a chapter to our law."[11] Harry Kalven even hailed it as the "most influential law review article of all."[12] The clearest indication of the article's ongoing vitality can be found in the Supreme Court's decision *Kyllo v. United States*, 533 U.S. 27 (2001). The Brandeis and Warren article is cited by the majority, those in concurrence, and even those in dissent.

Several developments in the late nineteenth century created a growing interest in privacy. First, the press became increasingly sensationalistic. Prior to the Civil War, wide-circulation newspapers were rare. However, the development of a new form of sensationalistic journalism, known as "yellow journalism," made newspapers wildly successful. In 1833, Benjamin Day began publishing a newspaper called *The Sun* patterned after the "penny presses" in London (so named because they sold for a penny). The *Sun* contained news of scandals, such as family squabbles, public drunkenness, and petty crimes. In about four months, the *Sun* had a circulation of 4,000, almost the same as the existing New York daily papers. Just two months later, the *Sun* was reaching 8,000 in circulation. Other penny press papers soon followed. In reporting on his travels in America, Charles Dickens observed that New York newspapers were "pulling off the roofs of private houses."[13] In his great novel of 1844, *The Life and Adventures of Martin Chuzzlewit*, he listed (imaginary) New York newspapers called *The Sewer, The Stabber, The Family Spy, The Private Listener, The Peeper, The Plunderer*, and *The Keyhole Reporter*.[14]

Between 1850 and 1890, newspaper circulation increased about 1,000 percent — from 100 papers with 800,000 readers to 900 papers with more than 8 million readers. Joseph Pulitzer and William Randolph Hearst became the leading rivals in the newspaper business, each amassing newspaper empires. Their highly sensationalistic journalism became the paradigm for yellow journalism.[15]

Second, technological developments caused great alarm for privacy. In their article, Warren and Brandeis pointed to the invention of "instantaneous photography" as a new challenge to privacy. Photography had been around for many years before Warren and Brandeis penned their article. However, the equipment was expensive, cumbersome, and complicated to use. In 1884, the Eastman Kodak Company introduced the "snap camera," a handheld camera that was small and cheap enough for use by the general public. The snap camera allowed people to take candid photographs in public places for the first time. In the late nineteenth century, few daily newspapers even printed drawings, let alone photographs. Warren and Brandeis, however, astutely recognized the potential for the new technology of cameras to be used by the sensationalistic press.

---

[10] Samuel Warren & Louis Brandeis, *The Right to Privacy*, 4 Harv. L. Rev. 193 (1890).

[11] Quoted in Alpheus Mason, *Brandeis: A Free Man's Life* 70 (1946).

[12] Harry Kalven, Jr., *Privacy in Tort Law — Were Warren and Brandeis Wrong?*, 31 Law & Contemp. Probs. 326, 327 (1966).

[13] Charles Dickens, *American Notes* (1842).

[14] Charles Dickens, *The Life and Adventures of Martin Chuzzlewit* (1844).

[15] For more information about yellow journalism, *see generally* Gini Graham Scott, *Mind Your Own Business: The Battle for Personal Privacy* 37-38 (1995); Robert Ellis Smith, *Ben Franklin's Web Site: Privacy and Curiosity from Plymouth Rock to the Internet* 102-20 (2000).

The question of the origin of Warren and Brandeis's article has led to considerable debate. Some scholars suggest that Warren and Brandeis were strongly influenced by an article written in 1890 by E.L. Godkin, a famous social commentator in his day.[16] In the article, Godkin observed:

> . . . Privacy is a distinctly modern product, one of the luxuries of civilization, which is not only unsought for but unknown in primitive or barbarous societies.
> . . .
>
> The chief enemy of privacy in modern life is that interest in other people and their affairs known as curiosity, which in the days before newspapers created personal gossip. . . . [A]s long as gossip was oral, it spread, as regarded any one individual, over a very small area, and was confined to the immediate circle of his acquaintants. It did not reach, or but rarely reached, those who knew nothing of him. It did not make his name, or his walk, or his conversation familiar to strangers. . . . [G]ossip about private individuals is now printed, and makes its victim, with all his imperfections on his head, known to hundreds or thousands miles away from his place of abode; and, what is worst of all, brings to his knowledge exactly what is said about him, with all its details. It thus inflicts what is, to many men, the great pain of believing that everybody he meets in the street is perfectly familiar with some folly, or misfortune, or indiscretion, or weakness, which he had previously supposed had never got beyond his domestic circle. . . .
>
> In truth, there is only one remedy for the violations of the right to privacy within the reach of the American public, and that is but an imperfect one. It is to be found in attaching social discredit to invasions of it on the part of conductors of the press. At present this check can hardly be said to exist. It is to a large extent nullified by the fact that the offence is often pecuniarily profitable.[17]

Warren and Brandeis referred to Godkin's essay, and their article does bear some similarities to his work. One difference is that Godkin, although recognizing the growing threats to privacy, remained cynical about the possibility of a solution, expressing only the hope that attitudes would change to be more respectful of privacy. Warren and Brandeis had a different view. In their judgment, the law could and should provide protection for privacy.

Another theory suggests that incursions by journalists into the privacy of Samuel Warren inspired the article. Warren, a wealthy and powerful attorney in Boston, practiced law with Louis Brandeis, who later went on to become a U.S. Supreme Court Justice. In 1883, Samuel Warren married Mabel Bayard, the daughter of a prominent senator from Delaware, and set up house in Boston's Back Bay. The Warrens were among the Boston elite and were frequently reported on in the *Saturday Evening Gazette*, "which specialized in 'blue blood items,' " and "reported their activities in lurid detail."[18]

According to William Prosser, Warren was motivated to write the article because reporters intruded upon his daughter's wedding. However, this certainly

---

[16] *See* Elbridge L. Adams, *The Right to Privacy and Its Relation to the Law of Libel*, 39 Am. L. Rev. 37 (1905); Dorothy J. Glancy, *The Invention of the Right to Privacy*, 21 Ariz. L. Rev. 1 (1979).

[17] E.L. Godkin, *The Rights of the Citizen: To His Own Reputation*, Scribner's Mag. (1890); *see also* E.L. Godkin, *The Right to Privacy*, The Nation (Dec. 25, 1890).

[18] Mason, *Brandeis, supra*, at 46.

could not have been the reason because in 1890, Warren's oldest daughter was not even ten years old![19] Most likely, the impetus for writing the article was Warren's displeasure about a number of stories in the *Gazette* about his dinner parties.[20]

Whatever inspired them to write, Warren and Brandeis published an article that profoundly shaped the development of the law of privacy.

SAMUEL D. WARREN AND LOUIS D. BRANDEIS, *THE RIGHT TO PRIVACY*

4 Harv. L. Rev. 193 (1890)

It could be done only on principles of private justice, moral fitness, and public convenience, which, when applied to a new subject, make common law without a precedent; much more when received and approved by usage.

— Willes, J., in *Millar v. Taylor,* 4 Burr. 2303, 2312

That the individual shall have full protection in person and in property is a principle as old as the common law; but it has been found necessary from time to time to define anew the exact nature and extent of such protection. Political, social, and economic changes entail the recognition of new rights, and the common law, in its eternal youth, grows to meet the demands of society. Thus, in very early times, the law gave a remedy only for physical interference with life and property, for trespasses *vi et armis*.[21] Then the "right to life" served only to protect the subject from battery in its various forms; liberty meant freedom from actual restraint; and the right to property secured to the individual his lands and his cattle. Later, there came a recognition of man's spiritual nature, of his feelings and his intellect. Gradually the scope of these legal rights broadened; and now the right to life has come to mean the right to enjoy life, — the right to be let alone; the right to liberty secures the exercise of extensive civil privileges; and the term "property" has grown to comprise every form of possession — intangible, as well as tangible.

Thus, with the recognition of the legal value of sensations, the protection against actual bodily injury was extended to prohibit mere attempts to do such injury; that is, the putting another in fear of such injury. From the action of battery grew that of assault. Much later there came a qualified protection of the individual against offensive noises and odors, against dust and smoke, and excessive vibration. The law of nuisance was developed. So regard for human emotions soon extended the scope of personal immunity beyond the body of the individual. His reputation, the standing among his fellow-men, was considered, and the law of slander and libel arose. Man's family relations became a part of the legal

---

[19] *See* James H. Barron, *Warren and Brandeis*, The Right to Privacy, 4 Harv. L. Rev. 193 (1890): *Demystifying a Landmark Citation*, 13 Suffolk L. Rev. 875 (1979).

[20] *See* Smith, *Ben Franklin's Web Site, supra*, at 118-19. For further discussion of the circumstances surrounding the publication of the article, see Martin Burgess Green, *The Mount Vernon Street Warrens: A Boston Story, 1860–1910* (1989); Morris L. Ernst & Alan U. Schwartz, *Privacy: The Right to Be Let Alone* 45-46 (1962); Philippa Strum, *Brandeis: Beyond Progressivism* (1993); Lewis J. Paper, *Brandeis* (1983); Irwin R. Kramer, *The Birth of Privacy Law: A Century Since Warren and Brandeis*, 39 Cath. U. L. Rev. 703 (1990); Dorothy Glancy, *The Invention of the Right to Privacy*, 21 Ariz. L. Rev. 1, 25-27 (1979); Symposium, *The Right to Privacy One Hundred Years Later*, 41 Case W. Res. L. Rev. 643-928 (1991).

[21] Editors' Note: Latin — By or with force and arms.

conception of his life, and the alienation of a wife's affections was held remediable. Occasionally the law halted, — as in its refusal to recognize the intrusion by seduction upon the honor of the family. But even here the demands of society were met. A mean fiction, the action *per quod servitium amisit*,[22] was resorted to, and by allowing damages for injury to the parents' feelings, an adequate remedy was ordinarily afforded. Similar to the expansion of the right to life was the growth of the legal conception of property. From corporeal property arose the incorporeal rights issuing out of it; and then there opened the wide realm of intangible property, in the products and processes of the mind, as works of literature and art, goodwill, trade secrets, and trademarks.

This development of the law was inevitable. The intense intellectual and emotional life, and the heightening of sensations which came with the advance of civilization, made it clear to men that only a part of the pain, pleasure, and profit of life lay in physical things. Thoughts, emotions, and sensations demanded legal recognition, and the beautiful capacity for growth which characterizes the common law enabled the judges to afford the requisite protection, without the interposition of the legislature.

Recent inventions and business methods call attention to the next step which must be taken for the protection of the person, and for securing to the individual what Judge Cooley calls the right "to be let alone."[23] Instantaneous photographs and newspaper enterprise have invaded the sacred precincts of private and domestic life; and numerous mechanical devices threaten to make good the prediction that "what is whispered in the closet shall be proclaimed from the house-tops." For years there has been a feeling that the law must afford some remedy for the unauthorized circulation of portraits of private persons; and the evil of invasion of privacy by the newspapers, long keenly felt, has been but recently discussed by an able writer. The alleged facts of a somewhat notorious case brought before an inferior tribunal in New York a few months ago, directly involved the consideration of the right of circulating portraits; and the question whether our law will recognize and protect the right to privacy in this and in other respects must soon come before our courts for consideration.

Of the desirability — indeed of the necessity — of some such protection, there can, it is believed, be no doubt. The press is overstepping in every direction the obvious bounds of propriety and of decency. Gossip is no longer the resource of the idle and of the vicious, but has become a trade, which is pursued with industry as well as effrontery. To satisfy a prurient taste the details of sexual relations are spread broadcast in the columns of the daily papers. To occupy the indolent, column upon column is filled with idle gossip, which can only be procured by intrusion upon the domestic circle. The intensity and complexity of life, attendant upon advancing civilization, have rendered necessary some retreat from the world, and man, under the refining influence of culture, has become more sensitive to publicity, so that solitude and privacy have become more essential to the individual; but modern enterprise and invention have, through invasions upon his privacy, subjected him to mental pain and distress, far greater than could be inflicted by mere bodily injury. Nor is the harm wrought by such invasions

---

[22] Editors' Note: Latin — Whereby he lost the services (of his servant).

[23] Cooley on Torts, 2d ed., p. 29.

confined to the suffering of those who may be made the subjects of journalistic or other enterprise. In this, as in other branches of commerce, the supply creates the demand. Each crop of unseemly gossip, thus harvested, becomes the seed of more, and, in direct proportion to its circulation, results in a lowering of social standards and of morality. Even gossip apparently harmless, when widely and persistently circulated, is potent for evil. It both belittles and perverts. It belittles by inverting the relative importance of things, thus dwarfing the thoughts and aspirations of a people. When personal gossip attains the dignity of print, and crowds the space available for matters of real interest to the community, what wonder that the ignorant and thoughtless mistake its relative importance. Easy of comprehension, appealing to that weak side of human nature which is never wholly cast down by the misfortunes and frailties of our neighbors, no one can be surprised that it usurps the place of interest in brains capable of other things. Triviality destroys at once robustness of thought and delicacy of feeling. No enthusiasm can flourish, no generous impulse can survive under its blighting influence.

It is our purpose to consider whether the existing law affords a principle which can properly be invoked to protect the privacy of the individual; and, if it does, what the nature and extent of such protection is.

Owing to the nature of the instruments by which privacy is invaded, the injury inflicted bears a superficial resemblance to the wrongs dealt with by the law of slander and of libel, while a legal remedy for such injury seems to involve the treatment of mere wounded feelings, as a substantive cause of action. The principle on which the law of defamation rests, covers, however, a radically different class of effects from those for which attention is now asked. It deals only with damage to reputation, with the injury done to the individual in his external relations to the community, by lowering him in the estimation of his fellows. The matter published of him, however widely circulated, and however unsuited to publicity, must, in order to be actionable, have a direct tendency to injure him in his intercourse with others, and even if in writing or in print, must subject him to the hatred, ridicule, or contempt of his fellow-men, — the effect of the publication upon his estimate of himself and upon his own feelings not forming an essential element in the cause of action. In short, the wrongs and correlative rights recognized by the law of slander and libel are in their nature material rather than spiritual. That branch of the law simply extends the protection surrounding physical property to certain of the conditions necessary or helpful to worldly prosperity. On the other hand, our law recognizes no principle upon which compensation can be granted for mere injury to the feelings. However painful the mental effects upon another of an act, though purely wanton or even malicious, yet if the act itself is otherwise lawful, the suffering inflicted is *damnum absque injuria*.[24] Injury of feelings may indeed be taken account of in ascertaining the amount of damages when attending what is recognized as a legal injury; but our system, unlike the Roman law, does not afford a remedy even for mental suffering which results from mere contumely and insult, from an intentional and unwarranted violation of the "honor" of another.

It is not however necessary, in order to sustain the view that the common law recognizes and upholds a principle applicable to cases of invasion of privacy, to

---

[24] Editors' Note: Latin — Loss or harm from something other than a wrongful act and which occasions no legal remedy.

invoke the analogy, which is but superficial, to injuries sustained, either by an attack upon reputation or by what the civilians called a violation of honor; for the legal doctrines relating to infractions of what is ordinarily termed the common-law right to intellectual and artistic property are, it is believed, but instances and applications of a general right to privacy, which properly understood afford a remedy for the evils under consideration.

The common law secures to each individual the right of determining, ordinarily, to what extent his thoughts, sentiments, and emotions shall be communicated to others. Under our system of government, he can never be compelled to express them (except when upon the witness-stand); and even if he has chosen to give them expression, he generally retains the power to fix the limits of the publicity which shall be given them. The existence of this right does not depend upon the particular method of expression adopted. It is immaterial whether it be by word or by signs, in painting, by sculpture, or in music. Neither does the existence of the right depend upon the nature or value of the thought or emotion, nor upon the excellence of the means of expression. The same protection is accorded to a casual letter or an entry in a diary and to the most valuable poem or essay, to a botch or daub and to a masterpiece. In every such case the individual is entitled to decide whether that which is his shall be given to the public. No other has the right to publish his productions in any form, without his consent. This right is wholly independent of the material on which, or the means by which, the thought, sentiment, or emotion is expressed. It may exist independently of any corporeal being, as in words spoken, a song sung, a drama acted. Or if expressed on any material, as in a poem in writing, the author may have parted with the paper, without forfeiting any proprietary right in the composition itself. The right is lost only when the author himself communicates his production to the public, — in other words, publishes it. It is entirely independent of the copyright laws, and their extension into the domain of art. The aim of those statutes is to secure to the author, composer, or artist the entire profits arising from publication; but the common-law protection enables him to control absolutely the act of publication, and in the exercise of his own discretion, to decide whether there shall be any publication at all. The statutory right is of no value, *unless* there is a publication; the common-law right is lost *as soon as* there is a publication.

What is the nature, the basis, of this right to prevent the publication of manuscripts or works of art? It is stated to be the enforcement of a right of property; and no difficulty arises in accepting this view, so long as we have only to deal with the reproduction of literary and artistic compositions. They certainly possess many of the attributes of ordinary property: they are transferable; they have a value; and publication or reproduction is a use by which that value is realized. But where the value of the production is found not in the right to take the profits arising from publication, but in the peace of mind or the relief afforded by the ability to prevent any publication at all, it is difficult to regard the right as one of property, in the common acceptation of that term. A man records in a letter to his son, or in his diary, that he did not dine with his wife on a certain day. No one into whose hands those papers fall could publish them to the world, even if possession of the documents had been obtained rightfully; and the prohibition would not be confined to the publication of a copy of the letter itself, or of the diary entry; the restraint extends also to a publication of the contents. What is the thing which is protected?

Surely, not the intellectual act of recording the fact that the husband did not dine with his wife, but that fact itself. It is not the intellectual product, but the domestic occurrence. A man writes a dozen letters to different people. No person would be permitted to publish a list of the letters written. If the letters or the contents of the diary were protected as literary compositions, the scope of the protection afforded should be the same secured to a published writing under the copyright law. But the copyright law would not prevent an enumeration of the letters, or the publication of some of the facts contained therein. The copyright of a series of paintings or etchings would prevent a reproduction of the paintings as pictures; but it would not prevent a publication of list or even a description of them. Yet in the famous case of *Prince Albert v. Strange*, the court held that the common-law rule prohibited not merely the reproduction of the etchings which the plaintiff and Queen Victoria had made for their own pleasure, but also "the publishing (at least by printing or writing), though not by copy or resemblance, a description of them, whether more or less limited or summary, whether in the form of a catalogue or otherwise." Likewise, an unpublished collection of news possessing no element of a literary nature is protected from piracy.

That this protection cannot rest upon the right to literary or artistic property in any exact sense, appears the more clearly when the subject-matter for which protection is invoked is not even in the form of intellectual property, but has the attributes of ordinary tangible property. Suppose a man has a collection of gems or curiosities which he keeps private: it would hardly be contended that any person could publish a catalogue of them, and yet the articles enumerated are certainly not intellectual property in the legal sense, any more than a collection of stoves or of chairs.

The belief that the idea of property in its narrow sense was the basis of the protection of unpublished manuscripts led an able court to refuse, in several cases, injunctions against the publication of private letters, on the ground that "letters not possessing the attributes of literary compositions are not property entitled to protection;" and that it was "evident the plaintiff could not have considered the letters as of any value whatever as literary productions, for a letter cannot be considered of value to the author which he never would consent to have published." But those decisions have not been followed, and it may now be considered settled that the protection afforded by the common law to the author of any writing is entirely independent of its pecuniary value, its intrinsic merits, or of any intention to publish the same and, of course, also, wholly independent of the material, if any, upon which, or the mode in which, the thought or sentiment was expressed.

Although the courts have asserted that they rested their decisions on the narrow grounds of protection to property, yet there are recognitions of a more liberal doctrine. Thus in the case of *Prince Albert v. Strange*, already referred to, the opinions both of the Vice-Chancellor and of the Lord Chancellor, on appeal, show a more or less clearly defined perception of a principle broader than those which were mainly discussed, and on which they both placed their chief reliance. Vice-Chancellor Knight Bruce referred to publishing of a man that he had "written to particular persons or on particular subjects" as an instance of possibly injurious disclosures as to private matters, that the courts would in a proper case prevent; yet it is difficult to perceive how, in such a case, any right of privacy, in the narrow sense, would be drawn in question, or why, if such a publication would be restrained when it threatened to expose the victim not merely to sarcasm, but to ruin, it should not equally be enjoined, if it threatened to embitter his life. To deprive a man of the potential profits to be realized by publishing a catalogue of his gems cannot *per se* be a wrong to him. The possibility of future profits is not a right of property which the law ordinarily recognizes; it must, therefore, be an infraction of other rights which constitutes the wrongful act, and that infraction is equally wrongful, whether its results are to forestall the profits that the individual himself might secure by giving the matter a publicity obnoxious to him, or to gain an advantage at the expense of his mental pain and suffering. . . .

These considerations lead to the conclusion that the protection afforded to thoughts, sentiments, and emotions, expressed through the medium of writing or of the arts, so far as it consists in preventing publication, is merely an instance of the enforcement of the more general right of the individual to be let alone. It is like the right not [to] be assaulted or beaten, the right not [to] be imprisoned, the right not to be maliciously prosecuted, the right not to be defamed. In each of these rights, as indeed in all other rights recognized by the law, there inheres the quality of being owned or possessed — and (as that is the distinguishing attribute of property) there may be some propriety in speaking of those rights as property. But, obviously, they bear little resemblance to what is ordinarily comprehended under that term. The principle which protects personal writings and all other personal productions, not against theft and physical appropriation, but against publication in any form, is in reality not the principle of private property, but that of an inviolate personality.

If we are correct in this conclusion, the existing law affords a principle which may be invoked to protect the privacy of the individual from invasion either by the too enterprising press, the photographer, or the possessor of any other modern device for recording or reproducing scenes or sounds. For the protection afforded is not confined by the authorities to those cases where any particular medium or form of expression has been adopted, not to products of the intellect. The same protection is afforded to emotions and sensations expressed in a musical composition or other work of art as to a literary composition; and words spoken, a pantomime acted, a sonata performed, is no less entitled to protection than if each had been reduced to writing. The circumstance that a thought or emotion has been recorded in a permanent form renders its identification easier, and hence may be important from the point of view of evidence, but it has no significance as a matter of substantive right. If, then, the decisions indicate a general right to privacy for thoughts, emotions, and sensations, these should receive the same protection, whether expressed in writing, or in conduct, in conversation, in attitudes, or in facial expression.

It may be urged that a distinction should be taken between the deliberate expression of thoughts and emotions in literary or artistic compositions and the casual and often involuntary expression given to them in the ordinary conduct of life. In other words, it may be contended that the protection afforded is granted to the conscious products of labor, perhaps as an encouragement to effort. This contention, however plausible, has, in fact, little to recommend it. If the amount of labor involved be adopted as the test, we might well find that the effort to conduct one's self properly in business and in domestic relations had been far greater than that involved in painting a picture or writing a book; one would find that it was far easier to express lofty sentiments in a diary than in the conduct of a noble life. If the test of deliberateness of the act be adopted, much casual correspondence which is now accorded full protection would be excluded from the beneficent operation of existing rules. After the decisions denying the distinction attempted to be made between those literary productions which it was intended to publish and those which it was not, all considerations of the amount of labor involved, the degree of deliberation, the value of the product, and the intention of publishing must be abandoned, and no basis is discerned upon which the right to restrain publication and reproduction of such so-called literary and artistic works can be rested, except the right to privacy, as a part of the more general right to the immunity of the person, — the right to one's personality.

It should be stated that, in some instances where protection has been afforded against wrongful publication, the jurisdiction has been asserted, not on the ground of property, or at least not wholly on that ground, but upon the ground of an alleged breach of an implied contract or of a trust or confidence. . . .

This process of implying a term in a contract, or of implying a trust (particularly where the contract is written, and where there is no established usage or custom), is nothing more nor less than a judicial declaration that public morality, private justice, and general convenience demand the recognition of such a rule, and that the publication under similar circumstances would be considered an intolerable abuse. So long as these circumstances happen to present a contract upon which such a term can be engrafted by the judicial mind, or to supply relations upon which a trust or confidence can be erected, there may be no objection to working out the desired protection through the doctrines of contract or of trust. But the court can hardly stop there. The narrower doctrine may have satisfied the demands of society at a time when the abuse to be guarded against could rarely have arisen without violating a contract or a special confidence; but now that modern devices afford abundant opportunities for the perpetration of such wrongs without any participation by the injured party, the protection granted by the law must be placed upon a broader foundation. While, for instance, the state of the photographic art was such that one's picture could seldom be taken without his consciously "sitting" for the purpose, the law of contract or of trust might afford the prudent man sufficient safeguards against the improper circulation of his portrait; but since the latest advances in photographic art have rendered it possible to take pictures surreptitiously, the doctrines of contract and of trust are inadequate to support the required protection, and the law of tort must be resorted to. The right of property in its widest sense, including all possession, including all rights and privileges, and hence embracing the right to an inviolate personality, affords alone that broad basis upon which the protection which the individual demands can be rested.

Thus, the courts, in searching for some principle upon which the publication of private letters could be enjoined, naturally came upon the ideas of a breach of confidence, and of an implied contract; but it required little consideration to discern that this doctrine could not afford all the protection required, since it would not support the court in granting a remedy against a stranger; and so the theory of property in the contents of letters was adopted. Indeed, it is difficult to conceive on what theory of the law the casual recipient of a letter, who proceeds to publish it, is guilty of a breach of contract, express or implied, or of any breach of trust, in the ordinary acceptation of that term. Suppose a letter has been addressed to him without his solicitation. He opens it, and reads. Surely, he has not made any contract; he has not accepted any trust. He cannot, by opening and reading the letter, have come under any obligation save what the law declares; and, however expressed, that obligation is simply to observe the legal right of the sender, whatever it may be, and whether it be called his right or property in the contents of the letter, or his right to privacy. . . .

We must therefore conclude that the rights, so protected, whatever their exact nature, are not rights arising from contract or from special trust, but are rights as against the world; and, as above stated, the principle which has been applied to protect these rights is in reality not the principle of private property, unless that word be used in an extended and unusual sense. The principle which protects personal writings and any other productions of the intellect of or the emotions, is the right to privacy, and the law has no new principle to formulate when it extends this protection to the personal appearance, sayings, acts, and to personal relation, domestic or otherwise.

If the invasion of privacy constitutes a legal *injuria*, the elements for demanding redress exist, since already the value of mental suffering, caused by an act wrongful in itself, is recognized as a basis for compensation.

The right of one who has remained a private individual, to prevent his public portraiture, presents the simplest case for such extension; the right to protect one's self from pen portraiture, from a discussion by the press of one's private affairs, would be a more important and far-reaching one. If casual and unimportant statements in a letter, if handiwork, however inartistic and valueless, if possessions of all sorts are protected not only against reproduction, but against description and enumeration, how much more should the acts and sayings of a man in his social and domestic relations be guarded from ruthless publicity. If you may not reproduce a woman's face photographically without her consent, how much less should be tolerated the reproduction of her face, her form, and her actions, by graphic descriptions colored to suit a gross and depraved imagination.

The right to privacy, limited as such right must necessarily be, has already found expression in the law of France.

It remains to consider what are the limitations of this right to privacy, and what remedies may be granted for the enforcement of the right. To determine in advance of experience the exact line at which the dignity and convenience of the individual must yield to the demands of the public welfare or of private justice would be a difficult task; but the more general rules are furnished by the legal analogies already developed in the law of slander and libel, and in the law of literary and artistic property.

1. The right to privacy does not prohibit any publication of matter which is of public or general interest.

In determining the scope of this rule, aid would be afforded by the analogy, in the law of libel and slander, of cases which deal with the qualified privilege of comment and criticism on matters of public and general interest. There are of course difficulties in applying such a rule; but they are inherent in the subject-matter, and are certainly no greater than those which exist in many other branches of the law, — for instance, in that large class of cases in which the reasonableness or unreasonableness of an act is made the test of liability. The design of the law must be to protect those persons with whose affairs the community has no legitimate concern, from being dragged into an undesirable and undesired publicity and to protect all persons, whatsoever; their position or station, from having matters which they may properly prefer to keep private, made public against their will. It is the unwarranted invasion of individual privacy which is reprehended, and to be, so far as possible, prevented. The distinction, however, noted in the above statement is obvious and fundamental. There are persons who may reasonably claim as a right, protection from the notoriety entailed by being made the victims of journalistic enterprise. There are others who, in varying degrees, have renounced the right to live their lives screened from public observation. Matters which men of the first class may justly contend, concern themselves alone, may in those of the second be the subject of legitimate interest to their fellow-citizens. Peculiarities of manner and person, which in the ordinary individual should be free from comment, may acquire a public importance, if found in a candidate for public office. Some further discrimination is necessary, therefore, than to class facts or deeds as public or private according to a standard to be applied to the fact or deed *per se*. To publish of a modest and retiring individual that he suffers from an impediment in his speech or that he cannot spell correctly, is an unwarranted, if not an unexampled, infringement of his rights, while to state and comment on the same characteristics found in a would-be congressman could not be regarded as beyond the pale of propriety.

The general object in view is to protect the privacy of private life, and to whatever degree and in whatever connection a man's life has ceased to be private, before the publication under consideration has been made, to that extent the protection is to be withdrawn. Since, then, the propriety of publishing the very same facts may depend wholly upon the person concerning whom they are published, no fixed formula can be used to prohibit obnoxious publications. Any rule of liability adopted must have in it an elasticity which shall take account of the varying circumstances of each case, — a necessity which unfortunately renders such a doctrine not only more difficult of application, but also to a certain extent uncertain in its operation and easily rendered abortive. Besides, it is only the more flagrant breaches of decency and propriety that could in practice be reached, and it is not perhaps desirable even to attempt to repress everything which the nicest taste and keenest sense of the respect due to private life would condemn.

In general, then, the matters of which the publication should be repressed may be described as those which concern the private life, habits, acts, and relations of an individual, and have no legitimate connection with his fitness for a public office which he seeks or for which he is suggested, or for any public or quasi public position which he seeks or for which he is suggested, and have no legitimate relation to or bearing upon any act done by him in a public or quasi public capacity. The foregoing is not designed as a wholly accurate or exhaustive definition, since that which must ultimately in a vast number of cases become a question of individual judgment and opinion is incapable of such definition; but it is an attempt to indicate broadly the class of matters referred to. Some things all men alike are entitled to keep from popular curiosity, whether in public life or not, while others are only private because the persons concerned have not assumed a position which makes their doings legitimate matters of public investigation.

2. The right to privacy does not prohibit the communication of any matter, though in its nature private, when the publication is made under circumstances which would render it a privileged communication according to the law of slander and libel.

Under this rule, the right to privacy is not invaded by any publication made in a court of justice, in legislative bodies, or the committees of those bodies; in municipal assemblies, or the committees of such assemblies, or practically by any communication made in any other public body, municipal or parochial, or in any body quasi public, like the large voluntary associations formed for almost every purpose of benevolence, business, or other general interest; and (at least in many jurisdictions) reports of any such proceedings would in some measure be accorded a like privilege. Nor would the rule prohibit any publication made by one in the discharge of some public or private duty, whether legal or moral, or in conduct of one's own affairs, in matters where his own interest is concerned.

3. The law would probably not grant any redress for the invasion of privacy by oral publication in the absence of special damage.

The same reasons exist for distinguishing between oral and written publications of private matters, as is afforded in the law of defamation by the restricted liability for slander as compared with the liability for libel. The injury resulting from such oral communications would ordinarily be so trifling that the law might well, in the interest of free speech, disregard it altogether.

4. The right to privacy ceases upon the publication of the facts by the individual, or with his consent.

This is but another application of the rule which has become familiar in the law of literary and artistic property. The cases there decided establish also what should be deemed a publication, — the important principle in this connection being that a private communication of circulation for a restricted purpose is not a publication within the meaning of the law.

5. The truth of the matter published does not afford a defence. Obviously this branch of the law should have no concern with the truth or falsehood of the matters published. It is not for injury to the individual's character that redress or prevention is sought, but for injury to the right of privacy. For the former, the law of slander and libel provides perhaps a sufficient safeguard. The latter implies the right not merely to prevent inaccurate portrayal of private life, but to prevent its being depicted at all.

6. The absence of "malice" in the publisher does not afford a defence.

Personal ill-will is not an ingredient of the offence, any more than in an ordinary case of trespass to person or to property. Such malice is never necessary to be shown in an action for libel or slander at common law, except in rebuttal of some defence, *e.g.*, that the occasion rendered the communication privileged, or, under the statutes in this State and elsewhere, that the statement complained of was true. The invasion of the privacy that is to be protected is equally complete and equally injurious, whether the motives by which the speaker or writer was actuated are, taken by themselves, culpable or not; just as the damage to character, and to some extent the tendency to provoke a breach of the peace, is equally the result of defamation without regard to the motives leading to its publication. Viewed as a wrong to the individual, this rule is the same pervading the whole law of torts, by which one is held responsible for his intentional acts, even though they are committed with no sinister intent; and viewed as a wrong to society, it is the same principle adopted in a large category of statutory offences.

The remedies for an invasion of the right of privacy are also suggested by those administered in the law of defamation, and in the law of literary and artistic property, namely: —

1. An action of tort for damages in all cases. Even in the absence of special damages, substantial compensation could be allowed for injury to feelings as in the action of slander and libel.

2. An injunction, in perhaps a very limited class of cases.

It would doubtless be desirable that the privacy of the individual should receive the added protection of the criminal law, but for this, legislation would be required. Perhaps it would be deemed proper to bring the criminal liability for such publication within narrower limits; but that the community has an interest in preventing such invasions of privacy, sufficiently strong to justify the introduction of such a remedy, cannot be doubted. Still, the protection of society must come mainly through a recognition of the rights of the individual. Each man is responsible for his own acts and omissions only. If he condones what he reprobates, with a weapon at hand equal to his defence, he is responsible for the results. If he resists, public opinion will rally to his support. Has he then such a weapon? It is believed that the common law provides him with one, forged in the slow fire of the centuries, and to-day fitly tempered to his hand. The common law has always recognized a man's house as his castle, impregnable, often, even to its own officers engaged in the execution of its command. Shall the courts thus close the front entrance to constituted authority, and open wide the back door to idle or prurient curiosity?

NOTES & QUESTIONS

1. *The Need for a New Right.* The article argued for the creation of a new right — the right to privacy. Why did the authors believe that other legal claims were inadequate? For example, why does the law of defamation or the law of contracts not provide a sufficient remedy for the harm described by the authors? Why do Warren and Brandeis reject property rights and copyright as tools to protect privacy?

2. *Deriving a Right to Privacy in the Common Law.* How do Warren and Brandeis derive a right to privacy from the common law? Under what principle do they locate this right? In a footnote in the article, Warren and Brandeis observe:

> The application of an existing principle to a new state of facts is not judicial legislation. To call it such is to assert that the existing body of law consists practically of the statutes and decided cases, and to deny that the principles (of which these cases are ordinarily said to be evidence) exist at all. It is not the application of an existing principle to new cases, but the introduction of a new principle, which is properly termed judicial legislation.
>
> But even the fact that a certain decision would involve judicial legislation should not be taken against the property of making it. This power has been commonly exercised by our judges, when applying to a new subject principles of private justice, moral fitness, and public convenience. Indeed, the elasticity

of our law, its adaptability to new conditions, the capacity for growth, which has enabled it to meet the wants of an ever changing society and to apply immediate relief for every recognized wrong, have been its greatest boast. . . .

Why do they include this footnote? Do you agree with their argument?

3. *Inviolate Personality in the United States and Germany.* The authors describe privacy as not "the principle of private property but that of inviolate personality." What does that mean? James Whitman traces the idea of the personality right from Warren and Brandeis back to nineteenth-century German legal philosophy:

> . . . [N]ineteenth-century Germans often thought of "freedom" as opposed primarily to determinism. To be free was, in the first instance, not to be free from government control, nor to be free to engage in market transactions. Instead, to be free was to exercise free will, and the defining characteristic of creatures with free will was that they were unpredictably individual, creatures whom no science of mechanics or biology could ever capture in their full richness. For Germans who thought of things in this way, the purpose of "freedom" was to allow each individual fully to realize his potential as an individual: to give full expression to his peculiar capacities and powers.[25]

Although the Warren and Brandeis article has been highly influential, their concept of a personality right has failed to gain traction in U.S. privacy law. Nonetheless, the idea of a personality right has formed the basis of modern German information privacy law. As Paul Schwartz and Karl-Nikolaus Peifer state, it is "a 'source right' that has proven a fertile source for the creation of a related series of legal rights" in Germany.[26] More specifically, they note that "the right has been used to protect honor and reputation, privacy in a spatial sense (a '*Privatsphäre*,' or a private area), individuality, and commercial uses of personality." Why do you think the concept of a "right of personality" has been unsuccessful as a legal concept for privacy in the United States?

4. *"The Right to Be Let Alone."* Warren and Brandeis refer to privacy as "the right to be let alone." This phrase was coined by Judge Thomas Cooley earlier in his famous treatise on torts.[27] Do Warren and Brandeis define what privacy is or elaborate upon what being "let alone" consists of? If so, what do they say privacy is? Is this a good account of what constitutes privacy?

5. *The Scope of the Right to Privacy.* Brandeis and Warren were careful not to describe privacy as an absolute right. They set out six limitations on the right to privacy. Consider the first limitation and the relationship between the right to privacy and the need for publication on matters of public concern. What conclusions do the authors reach about these competing claims? According to Warren and Brandeis, would the reporting that a public official engaged in illegal business practices be protected by a right to privacy? What about illicit

---

[25] James Q. Whitman, *The Two Western Cultures of Privacy: Dignity Versus Liberty*, 113 Yale L.J. 1151, 1181 (2004).

[26] Paul M. Schwartz & Karl-Nikolaus Peifer, *Prosser's Privacy and the German Right of Personality*, 98 Cal. L. Rev. 1925, 1952 (2010).

[27] Thomas M. Cooley, *Law of Torts* 29 (2d ed. 1888).

sexual activity? Consider the holding of the *Sidis* court regarding a person who was once of public interest due to his great achievements. Do you think that Warren and Brandeis would agree with the conclusion of *Sidis*?

6. ***The Economics of Gossip.*** Warren and Brandeis begin with a startling observation about the economics of gossip: "In this, as in other branches of commerce, the supply creates the demand." Have Warren and Brandeis inverted the normal concept in which demand drives supply? Note that already in the early nineteenth century, Jean-Baptiste Say, the French economist, famously expressed the idea, henceforth known as Say's Law, that the supply of a product would inherently create demand for it. Is gossip such a product?

7. ***The Nature of the Injury Caused by Privacy Invasions.*** Warren and Brandeis argue that privacy invasions are more harmful than bodily injuries. Do you agree? Warren and Brandeis characterize the injury caused by the violation of privacy as an injury to the feelings. Do you agree? Or do you think that the injury extends beyond an injury to the feelings?

8. ***Remedies.*** Brandeis and Warren suggest two remedies for an invasion of privacy — an action in tort and injunction. These remedies are similar to those in defamation and copyright. What do the authors say about a criminal remedy?

9. ***Criticisms.*** Some have argued that the article is a defense of bourgeois values, i.e., the freedom of an elite group to avoid public scrutiny.[28] Which aspects of the article support this view? Do parts of the article suggest otherwise? Is privacy, as described in the Warren and Brandeis article, a class-based right?

10. ***Did Brandeis Change His Mind?*** Neil Richards argues that Brandeis's views about the importance of publicity and free speech eventually eclipsed the views he set forth in his article with Warren. According to Richards, the First Amendment views that Brandeis developed in the 1920s are "inconsistent with many aspects of the right to privacy that he called for in 1890." As a further matter, Richard contends that "to the extent [Brandeis] retained a belief in tort privacy to the end of his life, it was a narrow category subordinated to the interests of publicity and free speech." At a normative level, Richards builds on Brandeis to develop a "concept of intellectual privacy" — a more focused concept that views privacy as a paramount value when it "is relevant to the activities of thinking, reading, and discussing safeguarded by the First Amendment."[29]

(b) The Recognition of Warren and Brandeis's Privacy Torts

Warren and Brandeis's 1890 article suggested that the existing causes of action under the common law did not adequately protect privacy but that the legal concepts in the common law could be modified to achieve the task. As early as 1903, courts and legislatures responded to the Warren and Brandeis article by creating a number of privacy torts to redress the harms that Warren and Brandeis had noted. In *Roberson v. Rochester Folding Box Co.*, 64 N.E. 442 (N.Y. 1902),

---

[28] *See* Donald R. Pember, *Privacy and the Press* (1972).

[29] Neil Richards, *The Puzzle of Brandeis, Privacy, and Speech*, 63 Vand. L. Rev. 1295, 1312 (2010).

the New York Court of Appeals refused to recognize a common law tort action for privacy invasions. Franklin Mills Flour displayed a lithograph of Abigail Roberson (a teenager) on 25,000 advertisement flyers without her consent. The lithograph printed her photograph with the advertising pun: "Flour of the Family." Roberson claimed that the use of her image on the flyer caused her great humiliation and resulted in illness requiring medical help. The court, however, concluded:

> . . . There is no precedent for such an action to be found in the decisions of this court. . . . Mention of such a right is not to be found in Blackstone, Kent, or any other of the great commentators upon the law; nor, so far as the learning of counsel or the courts in this case have been able to discover, does its existence seem to have been asserted prior to about the year 1890. . . .
>
> The legislative body could very well interfere and arbitrarily provide that no one should be permitted for his own selfish purpose to use the picture or the name of another for advertising purposes without his general consent. In such event no embarrassment would result to the general body of law, for the law would be applicable only to cases provided for by statute. The courts, however, being without authority to legislate, are required to decide cases upon principle, and so are necessarily embarrassed by precedents created by an extreme, and therefore unjustifiable, application of an old principle. . . . [W]hile justice in a given case may be worked out by a decision of the court according to the notions of right which govern the individual judge or body of judges comprising the court, the mischief which will finally result may be almost incalculable under our system, which makes a decision in one case a precedent for decisions in all future cases which are akin to it in the essential facts. . . .

Shortly after the decision, a note in the *Yale Law Journal* criticized the *Roberson* decision because it enabled the press "to pry into and grossly display before the public matters of the most private and personal concern."[30] One of the judges in the majority defended the opinion in the *Columbia Law Review*.[31]

In 1903, the New York legislature responded to the explicit invitation in *Roberson* to legislate by creating a privacy tort action by statute. *See* N.Y. Civ. Rights Act § 51. This statute is still in use today. As you will see again later in this text, courts are frequently engaged in a dialogue with legislatures about the scope of privacy rights.

In the 1905 case *Pavesich v. New England Life Insurance Co.*, 50 S.E. 68 (Ga. 1905), Georgia became the first state to recognize a common law tort action for privacy invasions. There, a newspaper published a life insurance advertisement with a photograph of the plaintiff without the plaintiff's consent. The court held:

> . . . The right of privacy has its foundation in the instincts of nature. It is recognized intuitively, consciousness being the witness that can be called to establish its existence. Any person whose intellect is in a normal condition recognizes at once that as to each individual member of society there are matters private, and there are matters public so far as the individual is concerned. Each individual as instinctively resents any encroachment by the public upon his rights which are of a private nature as he does the withdrawal of those of his rights which

---

[30] *An Actionable Right to Privacy?*, 12 Yale L.J. 34 (1902).
[31] Denis O'Brien, *The Right to Privacy*, 2 Colum. L. Rev. 486 (1902).

are of a public nature. A right of privacy in matters purely private is therefore derived from natural law. . . .

All will admit that the individual who desires to live a life of seclusion cannot be compelled against his consent, to exhibit his person in any public place, unless such exhibition is demanded by the law of the land. He may be required to come from his place of seclusion to perform public duties — to serve as a juror and to testify as a witness and the like; but, when the public duty is once performed, if he exercises his liberty to go again into seclusion, no one can deny him the right. One who desires to live a life of partial seclusion has a right to choose the times, places, and manner in which and at which he will submit himself to the public gaze. Subject to the limitation above referred to, the body of a person cannot be put on exhibition at any time or at any place without his consent. . . .

It therefore follows from what has been said that a violation of the right of privacy is a direct invasion of a legal right of the individual. . . .

In 1960, Dean William Prosser wrote his famous article, *Privacy*, examining the over 300 privacy tort cases decided in the 70 years since the Warren and Brandeis article.

WILLIAM PROSSER, *PRIVACY*

48 Cal. L. Rev. 383 (1960)

. . . The law of privacy comprises four distinct kinds of invasion of four different interests of the plaintiff, which are tied together by the common name, but otherwise have almost nothing in common except that each represents an interference with the right of the plaintiff, in the phrase coined by Judge Cooley, "to be let alone." Without any attempt at exact definition, these four torts may be described as follows:

1. Intrusion upon the plaintiff's seclusion or solitude, or into his private affairs.
2. Public disclosure of embarrassing private facts about the plaintiff.
3. Publicity which places the plaintiff in a false light in the public eye.
4. Appropriation, for the defendant's advantage, of the plaintiff's name or likeness. . . .

Judge Briggs has described the present state of the law of privacy as "still that of a haystack in a hurricane." Disarray there certainly is; but almost all of the confusion is due to a failure to separate and distinguish these four forms of invasion and to realize that they call for different things. . . .

Taking them in order — intrusion, disclosure, false light, and appropriation — the first and second require the invasion of something secret, secluded or private pertaining to the plaintiff; the third and fourth do not. The second and third depend upon publicity, while the first does not, nor does the fourth, although it usually involves it. The third requires falsity or fiction; the other three do not. The fourth involves a use for the defendant's advantage, which is not true of the rest. Obviously this is an area in which one must tread warily and be on the lookout for bogs. Nor is the difficulty decreased by the fact that quite often two or more of these forms of invasion may be found in the same case, and quite conceivably in all four.

NOTES & QUESTIONS

1. ***The Restatement of Torts.*** Prosser's analytical framework imposed order and clarity on the jumbled line of cases that followed the Warren and Brandeis article. The Restatement of Torts recognizes the four torts Prosser described in his article. These torts are known collectively as "invasion of privacy." The torts are: (1) intrusion upon seclusion, (2) public disclosure of private facts, (3) false light, and (4) appropriation.

2. ***The Interests Protected by the Privacy Torts.*** In response to Prosser's assertion that the privacy torts have almost "nothing in common," Edward Bloustein replied that "what provoked Warren and Brandeis to write their article was a fear that a rampant press feeding on the stuff of private life would destroy individual dignity and integrity and emasculate individual freedom and independence." This underlying principle is a protection of "human dignity" and "personality."[32]

   In contrast to Bloustein, Robert Post contends that the privacy torts do "not simply uphold the interests of individuals against the demands of the community, but instead safeguard[ ] rules of civility that in some significant measure constitute both individuals and community." Post argues that the torts establish boundaries between people, which when violated create strife. The privacy torts promote "forms of respect [for other people] by which we maintain a community."[33]

3. ***Prosser's Privacy at 50.*** In 2010, the *California Law Review* held a symposium at Berkeley Law School to celebrate the fiftieth anniversary of the publication of Prosser's *Privacy*. The verdict on the momentous article is mixed. Lior Strahilevitz advocates abandoning the Prosser categories and replacing them with a unitary tort for invasion of privacy. The key under the recast privacy tort would simply be whether "the gravity of the harm to the plaintiff's privacy interest [is] outweighed by a paramount public policy interest."[34]

   Along similar negative lines, Neil Richards and Daniel Solove concluded that Prosser's view of the privacy tort has been "rigid and ossifying." Dean Prosser "stunted [privacy law's] development in ways that have limited its ability to adapt to the problems of the Information Age." The authors conclude that tort law should look beyond the narrow categories Prosser proposed in order for it to "regain the creative spirit it once possessed." One way for tort law to do so, in their view, would be to adopt the English approach to the tort of confidentiality.[35]

---

[32] Edward J. Bloustein, *Privacy as an Aspect of Human Dignity: An Answer to Dean Prosser*, 39 N.Y.U. L. Rev. 962, 974, 1000-01 (1964).

[33] Robert C. Post, *The Social Foundations of Privacy: Community and Self in the Common Law Tort*, 77 Cal. L. Rev. 957 (1989).

[34] Lior Strahilevitz, *Reunifying Privacy Law*, 98 Cal. L. Rev. 2007 (2010).

[35] Neil Richards & Daniel Solove, *Prosser's Privacy Law: A Mixed Legacy*, 98 Cal. L. Rev. 1887, 1924 (2010).

In contrast, Paul Schwartz and Karl-Nikolaus Peifer praised Prosser: "Prosser pragmatically assessed the kind and amount of privacy that the American legal system was willing to accommodate." In their summary, "Prosser's contribution generated useful doctrinal categories where previously had been unclassified cases and a lingering air of skepticism towards the tort."[36]

Would it be useful to extend the four privacy torts as Richards and Solove propose? Or would a better approach be to replace Prosser's four torts with pure balancing as Strahilevitz advocates? Or do Prosser's categories adequately capture the various privacy interests that should be addressed by tort law?

LAKE V. WAL-MART STORES, INC.

582 N.W.2d 231 (Minn. 1998)

BLATZ, C.J. . . . Elli Lake and Melissa Weber appeal from a dismissal of their complaint for failure to state a claim upon which relief may be granted. The district court and court of appeals held that Lake and Weber's complaint alleging intrusion upon seclusion, appropriation, publication of private facts, and false light publicity could not proceed because Minnesota does not recognize a common law tort action for invasion of privacy. We reverse as to the claims of intrusion upon seclusion, appropriation, and publication of private facts, but affirm as to false light publicity.

Nineteen-year-old Elli Lake and 20-year-old Melissa Weber vacationed in Mexico in March 1995 with Weber's sister. During the vacation, Weber's sister took a photograph of Lake and Weber naked in the shower together. After their vacation, Lake and Weber brought five rolls of film to the Dilworth, Minnesota Wal-Mart store and photo lab. When they received their developed photographs along with the negatives, an enclosed written notice stated that one or more of the photographs had not been printed because of their "nature."

In July 1995, an acquaintance of Lake and Weber alluded to the photograph and questioned their sexual orientation. Again, in December 1995, another friend told Lake and Weber that a Wal-Mart employee had shown her a copy of the photograph. By February 1996, Lake was informed that one or more copies of the photograph were circulating in the community.

Lake and Weber filed a complaint against Wal-Mart Stores, Inc. and one or more as-yet unidentified Wal-Mart employees on February 23, 1996, alleging the four traditional invasion of privacy torts — intrusion upon seclusion, appropriation, publication of private facts, and false light publicity. . . . The district court granted Wal-Mart's motion to dismiss, explaining that Minnesota has not recognized any of the four invasion of privacy torts. The court of appeals affirmed.

Whether Minnesota should recognize any or all of the invasion of privacy causes of action is a question of first impression in Minnesota. . . .

This court has the power to recognize and abolish common law doctrines. The common law is not composed of firmly fixed rules. Rather, as we have long recognized, the common law:

---

[36] Paul M. Schwartz & Karl-Nikolaus Peifer, *Prosser's Privacy and the German Right of Personality*, 98 Cal. L. Rev. 1925, 1982 (2010).

is the embodiment of broad and comprehensive unwritten principles, inspired by natural reason, an innate sense of justice, adopted by common consent for the regulation and government of the affairs of men. It is the growth of ages, and an examination of many of its principles, as enunciated and discussed in the books, discloses a constant improvement and development in keeping with advancing civilization and new conditions of society. Its guiding star has always been the rule of right and wrong, and in this country its principles demonstrate that there is in fact, as well as in theory, a remedy for all wrongs.

As society changes over time, the common law must also evolve:

It must be remembered that the common law is the result of growth, and that its development has been determined by the social needs of the community which it governs. It is the resultant of conflicting social forces, and those forces which are for the time dominant leave their impress upon the law. It is of judicial origin, and seeks to establish doctrines and rules for the determination, protection, and enforcement of legal rights. Manifestly it must change as society changes and new rights are recognized. To be an efficient instrument, and not a mere abstraction, it must gradually adapt itself to changed conditions.

To determine the common law, we look to other states as well as to England.

The tort of invasion of privacy is rooted in a common law right to privacy first described in an 1890 law review article by Samuel Warren and Louis Brandeis. The article posited that the common law has always protected an individual's person and property, with the extent and nature of that protection changing over time. The fundamental right to privacy is both reflected in those protections and grows out of them:

Thus, in the very early times, the law gave a remedy only for physical interference with life and property, for trespass vi et armis. Then the "right to life" served only to protect the subject from battery in its various forms; liberty meant freedom from actual restraint; and the right to property secured to the individual his lands and his cattle. Later, there came a recognition of a man's spiritual nature, of his feelings and his intellect. Gradually the scope of these legal rights broadened; and now the right to life has come to mean the right to enjoy life, — the right to be let alone; the right to liberty secures the exercise of extensive civil privileges; and the term "property" has grown to comprise every form of possession — intangible, as well as tangible.

Although no English cases explicitly articulated a "right to privacy," several cases decided under theories of property, contract, or breach of confidence also included invasion of privacy as a basis for protecting personal violations. The article encouraged recognition of the common law right to privacy, as the strength of our legal system lies in its elasticity, adaptability, capacity for growth, and ability "to meet the wants of an ever changing society and to apply immediate relief for every recognized wrong.". . .

Today, the vast majority of jurisdictions now recognize some form of the right to privacy. Only Minnesota, North Dakota, and Wyoming have not yet recognized any of the four privacy torts. Although New York and Nebraska courts have declined to recognize a common law basis for the right to privacy and instead provide statutory protection, we reject the proposition that only the legislature may establish new causes of action. The right to privacy is inherent in the English protections of individual property and contract rights and the "right to be let alone" is recognized as part of the common law across this country. Thus, it is within the province of the judiciary to establish privacy torts in this jurisdiction.

Today we join the majority of jurisdictions and recognize the tort of invasion of privacy. The right to privacy is an integral part of our humanity; one has a public persona, exposed and active, and a private persona, guarded and preserved. The heart of our liberty is choosing which parts of our lives shall become public and which parts we shall hold close. . . .

We decline to recognize the tort of false light publicity at this time. We are concerned that claims under false light are similar to claims of defamation, and to the extent that false light is more expansive than defamation, tension between this tort and the First Amendment is increased.

False light is the most widely criticized of the four privacy torts and has been rejected by several jurisdictions. . . .

Thus we recognize a right to privacy present in the common law of Minnesota, including causes of action in tort for intrusion upon seclusion, appropriation, and publication of private facts, but we decline to recognize the tort of false light publicity. . . .

TOMLJANOVICH, J. dissenting. I would not recognize a cause of action for intrusion upon seclusion, appropriation or publication of private facts. . . .

An action for an invasion of the right to privacy is not rooted in the Constitution. "[T]he Fourth Amendment cannot be translated into a general constitutional 'right to privacy.' " *Katz v. United States*, 389 U.S. 347, 350 (1967). Those privacy rights that have their origin in the Constitution are much more fundamental rights of privacy — marriage and reproduction. *See Griswold v. Connecticut*, 381 U.S. 479, 485 (1965) (penumbral rights of privacy and repose protect notions of privacy surrounding the marriage relationship and reproduction).

We have become a much more litigious society since 1975 when we acknowledged that we have never recognized a cause of action for invasion of privacy. We should be even more reluctant now to recognize a new tort.

In the absence of a constitutional basis, I would leave to the legislature the decision to create a new tort for invasion of privacy.

NOTES & QUESTIONS

1. *Other Remedies?* If the Minnesota Supreme Court had rejected the privacy tort, what other legal remedies might be available to Elli Lake?
2. *Postscript.* What happened in *Lake* after the Minnesota Supreme Court's decision? In response to a query from the casebook authors, the lead attorney for the *Lake* plaintiff, Keith L. Miller of Miller, Norman & Associates, Ltd., explained that his client lost at the trial that followed the remand. He writes: "The jury found that an invasion of Ms. Lake's privacy had occurred, but that it did not happen 'in the course and scope' of a Wal-Mart worker's employment." In other words, tort notions of agency were found to apply, and a privacy tort violation could be attributed to Wal-Mart only if the employee had carried out the tort in the course and scope of employment. Miller added:

"Our proof was problematic because, expectedly, no employee could specifically be identified as the culprit. It was all circumstantial." Finally, he summarized his experience litigating this case: "Gratifying? Certainly. Remunerative? Not so much."

3. ***Legislatures vs. Courts.*** The dissent in *Lake* contends, in a similar way as *Roberson*, that it should be the legislature, not the courts, that recognizes new tort actions to protect privacy. In New York, the statute passed in response to *Roberson* remains the state's source for privacy tort remedies. Like New York, some states have recognized the privacy torts legislatively; other states, like Georgia in *Pavesich* and Minnesota in *Lake*, have recognized them judicially. Which means of recognizing the torts do you believe to be most justifiable? Why? Does the legislature have expertise that courts lack? Are courts more or less sensitive to civil rights issues, such as privacy?

(c) Privacy Protection in Tort Law

The Privacy Torts. Prosser's classification of these torts survives to this day. The Restatement (Second) of Torts recognizes four privacy torts:

(1) *Public Disclosure of Private Facts.* This tort creates a cause of action for one who publicly discloses a private matter that is "highly offensive to a reasonable person" and "is not of legitimate concern to the public." Restatement (Second) of Torts § 652D (1977).

(2) *Intrusion upon Seclusion.* This tort provides a remedy when one intrudes "upon the solitude or seclusion of another or his private affairs or concerns" if the intrusion is "highly offensive to a reasonable person." Restatement (Second) of Torts § 652B (1977).

(3) *False Light.* This tort creates a cause of action when one publicly discloses a matter that places a person "in a false light" that is "highly offensive to a reasonable person." Restatement (Second) of Torts § 652E (1977).

(4) *Appropriation.* Under this tort, a plaintiff has a remedy against one "who appropriates to his own use or benefit the name or likeness" of the plaintiff. Restatement (Second) of Torts § 652C (1977).

Today, most states recognize some or all of these torts.

Breach of Confidentiality. The tort of breach of confidentiality provides a remedy when a professional (i.e., doctor, lawyer, banker) divulges a patient's or client's confidential information.

Defamation. The law of defamation existed long before Warren and Brandeis's article. Defamation law, consisting of the torts of libel and slander, creates liability when one makes a false statement about a person that harms the person's reputation. The Supreme Court has held that the First Amendment places certain limits on defamation law.

Infliction of Emotional Distress. The tort of intentional infliction of emotional distress can also serve as a remedy for certain privacy invasions. This tort provides a remedy when one "by extreme and outrageous conduct intentionally or recklessly causes severe emotional distress to another." Restatement (Second) of Torts § 46 (1977). Since privacy invasions can often result in severe emotional distress, this tort may provide a remedy. However, it is limited by the requirement of "extreme and outrageous conduct."

(d) Privacy Protection in Evidence Law

The law of evidence has long recognized privacy as an important goal that can override the truth-seeking function of the trial. Under the common law, certain communications are privileged, and hence cannot be inquired into during a legal proceeding. The law of evidence has recognized the importance of protecting the privacy of communications between attorney and client, priest and penitent, husband and wife, physician and patient, and psychotherapist and patient.

(e) Privacy Protection via Property Rights

Property Rights. Although there are few property laws specifically governing privacy, these laws often implicate privacy. The appropriation tort is akin to a property right, and some commentators suggest that personal information should be viewed as a form of property.[37] If personal information is understood as a form of property, the tort of conversion might apply to those who collect and use a person's private data. Recall, however, that Warren and Brandeis rejected property as an adequate protection for privacy. What kind of market structures might be needed if personal data is to be traded or sold?

Trespass. The law of trespass, which provides tort remedies and criminal penalties for the unauthorized entry onto another's land, can protect privacy. There is some overlap between the torts of intrusion and trespass, as many forms of intrusion involve a trespass as well.

(f) Privacy Protection in Contract Law

Sometimes specific contractual provisions protect against the collection, use, or disclosure of personal information. In certain contexts, courts have entertained actions for breach of implied contract or tort actions based on implicit duties once certain relationships are established, such as physician-patient relationships, which have been analogized to fiduciary relationships. Privacy policies as well as terms of service containing privacy provisions can sometimes be analogized to a contract.

Contract can also function as a way of sidestepping state and federal privacy laws. Many employers make employees consent to drug testing as well as e-mail and workplace surveillance in their employment contracts.

---

[37] *See, e.g.,* Alan Westin, *Privacy and Freedom* 324 (1967); *see also* Richard S. Murphy, *Property Rights in Personal Information: An Economic Defense of Privacy*, 84 Geo. L.J. 2381 (1996); Richard A. Posner, *The Economics of Justice* (1981); Lawrence Lessig, *Code and Other Laws of Cyberspace* 154-62 (1999); Paul M. Schwartz, *Property, Privacy, and Personal Data*, 117 Harv. L. Rev. 2055 (2004).

(g) Privacy Protection in Criminal Law

Warren and Brandeis noted that under certain circumstances, criminal law would be appropriate to protect privacy. The criminal law protects bodily invasions, such as assault, battery, and rape. The privacy of one's home is also protected by criminal sanctions for trespass. Stalking and harassing can give rise to criminal culpability. The crime of blackmail prohibits coercing an individual by threatening to expose her personal secrets. Many of the statutes protecting privacy also contain criminal penalties, such as the statutes pertaining to wiretapping and identity theft.

2. CONSTITUTIONAL LAW

Federal Constitutional Law. Although the United States Constitution does not specifically mention privacy, it has a number of provisions that protect privacy, and it has been interpreted as providing a right to privacy. In some instances the First Amendment serves to safeguard privacy. For example, the First Amendment protects the right to speak anonymously. *See McIntyre v. Ohio Election Comm'n*, 514 U.S. 334 (1995). The First Amendment's Freedom of Association Clause protects individuals from being compelled to disclose the groups to which they belong or contribute. Under the First Amendment "Congress shall make no law . . . abridging . . . the right of the people peaceably to assemble. . . ." For example, the Court has struck down the compulsory disclosure of the names and addresses of an organization's members, *see NAACP v. Alabama*, 357 U.S. 449 (1958), as well as a law requiring public teachers to list all organizations to which they belong or contribute. *See Shelton v. Tucker*, 364 U.S. 479 (1960).

The Third Amendment protects the privacy of the home by preventing the government from requiring soldiers to reside in people's homes: "No Soldier shall, in time of peace be quartered in any house, without the consent of the Owner, nor in time of war, but in a manner to be prescribed by law."

The Fourth Amendment provides that people have the right "to be secure in their persons, houses, papers, and effects, against unreasonable searches and seizures. . . ." Almost 40 years after writing *The Right to Privacy*, Brandeis, then a Supreme Court Justice, wrote a dissent that has had a significant influence on Fourth Amendment law. The case was *Olmstead v. United States*, 277 U.S. 438 (1928), where the Court held that wiretapping was not an invasion of privacy under the Fourth Amendment because it was not a physical trespass into the home. Justice Brandeis dissented, contending that the central interest protected by the Fourth Amendment was not property but the "right to be let alone":

> The protection guaranteed by the amendments is much broader in scope. The makers of our Constitution undertook to secure conditions favorable to the pursuit of happiness. They recognized the significance of man's spiritual nature, of his feelings and of his intellect. They knew that only a part of the pain, pleasure and satisfactions of life are to be found in material things. They sought to protect Americans in their beliefs, their thoughts, their emotions and their sensations. They conferred, as against the government, the right to be let alone — the most comprehensive of rights and the right most valued by civilized men. To protect that right, every unjustifiable intrusion by the government upon the privacy of the

individual, whatever the means employed, must be deemed a violation of the Fourth Amendment.

Brandeis's dissent demonstrated that the "right to be let alone" did not merely have common law roots (as he had argued in *The Right to Privacy*) but also had constitutional roots as well in the Fourth Amendment.

Modern Fourth Amendment law incorporates much of Brandeis's view. In *Katz v. United States*, 389 U.S. 347 (1967), the Court held that the Fourth Amendment "protects people, not places" and said that the police must obtain a warrant when a search takes place in a public pay phone on a public street. The Court currently determines a person's right to privacy by the "reasonable expectations of privacy" test, a standard articulated in Justice Harlan's concurrence to *Katz*. First, a person must "have exhibited an actual (subjective) expectation of privacy" and, second, "the expectation [must] be one that society is prepared to recognize as 'reasonable.' "

The Fifth Amendment guarantees that: "No person . . . shall be compelled in any criminal case to be a witness against himself. . . ." This right, commonly referred to as the "privilege against self-incrimination," protects privacy by restricting the ability of the government to force individuals to divulge certain information about themselves.

In the landmark 1965 case *Griswold v. Connecticut*, 318 U.S. 479 (1965), the Court declared that an individual has a constitutional right to privacy. The Court located this right within the "penumbras" or "zones" of freedom created by an expansive interpretation of the Bill of Rights. Subsequently, the Court has handed down a line of cases protecting certain fundamental life choices such as abortion and aspects of one's intimate sexual life.

In *Whalen v. Roe*, 429 U.S. 589 (1977), the Court extended its substantive due process privacy protection to information privacy, holding that the "zone of privacy" protected by the Constitution encompasses the "individual interest in avoiding disclosure of personal matters." This offshoot of the right to privacy has become known as the "constitutional right to information privacy."

State Constitutional Law. A number of states have directly provided for the protection of privacy in their constitutions. For example, the Alaska Constitution provides: "The right of the people to privacy is recognized and shall not be infringed." Alaska Const. art. I, § 22. According to the California Constitution: "All people are by their nature free and independent and have inalienable rights. Among these are enjoying and defending life and liberty, acquiring, possessing, and protecting property, and pursuing and obtaining safety, happiness, and privacy." Cal. Const. art. I, § 1. Unlike most state constitutional provisions, the California constitutional right to privacy applies not only to state actors but also to private parties. *See, e.g., Hill v. NCAA*, 865 P.2d 638 (Cal. 1994). The Florida Constitution provides: "Every natural person has the right to be let alone and free from governmental intrusion into his private life except as otherwise provided herein." Fla. Const. art. I, § 23.[38]

---

[38] For more examples, see Ariz. Const. art. II, § 8; Mont. Const. art. II, § 10; Haw. Const. art. I, § 6; Ill. Const. art. I, §§ 6, 12; La. Const. art. I, § 5; S.C. Const. art. I, § 10; Wash. Const. art. I, § 7. For a further discussion of state constitutional protections of privacy, see Timothy O. Lenz, *"Rights*

3. STATUTORY LAW

Federal Statutory Law. From the mid-1960s to the mid-1970s, privacy emerged as a central political and social concern. In tune with the heightened attention to privacy, philosophers, legal scholars, and others turned their focus on privacy, raising public awareness about the growing threats to privacy from technology.[39]

In the mid-1960s, electronic eavesdropping erupted into a substantial public issue, spawning numerous television news documentaries as well as receiving significant attention in major newspapers. A proposal for a National Data Center in 1965 triggered public protest and congressional hearings. At this time, the computer was a new and unexplored technological tool that raised risks of unprecedented data collection about individuals, with potentially devastating effects on privacy. Indeed, toward the end of the 1960s, the issue of the collection of personal information in databases had become one of the defining social issues of American society.

During this time the Supreme Court announced landmark decisions regarding the right to privacy, including *Griswold v. Connecticut* in 1965 and *Roe v. Wade* in 1973, which were landmark decisions regarding the right to decisional/reproductive privacy and autonomy. The famous reasonable expectations of privacy test in Fourth Amendment jurisprudence emerged in 1967 with *Katz v. United States*.

Due to growing fears about the ability of computers to store and search personal information, Congress devoted increasing attention to the issue of privacy. As Priscilla Regan observes:

> In 1965, a new problem was placed on the congressional agenda by subcommittee chairs in both the House and the Senate. The problem was defined as the invasion of privacy by computers and evoked images of *1984*, the "Computerized Man," and a dossier society. Press interest was high, public concern was generated and resulted in numerous letters being sent to members of Congress, and almost thirty days of congressional hearings were held in the late 1960s and early 1970s.[40]

In 1973, in a highly influential report, the United States Department of Health, Education, and Welfare (HEW) undertook an extensive review of data processing in the United States. Among many recommendations, the HEW report proposed that a Code of Fair Information Practices be established. The Fair Information Practices consist of a number of basic information privacy principles that allocate rights and responsibilities in the collection and use of personal information:

Talk" About Privacy in State Courts, 60 Alb. L. Rev. 1613 (1997); Mark Silverstein, Note, *Privacy Rights in State Constitutions: Models for Illinois?*, 1989 U. Ill. L. Rev. 215.

[39] *See, e.g.,* Vance Packard, *The Naked Society* (1964); Myron Brenton, *The Privacy Invaders* (1964); Alan Westin, *Privacy and Freedom* (1967); Arthur Miller, *The Assault on Privacy* (1971); *Nomos XII: Privacy* (J. Ronald Pennock & J.W. Chapman eds., 1971); Alan Westin & Michael A. Baker, *Databanks in a Free Society: Computers, Record-Keeping and Privacy* (1972); Aryeh Neier, *The Secret Files They Keep on You* (1975); Kenneth L. Karst, *"The Files": Legal Controls over the Accuracy and Accessibility of Stored Personal Data*, 31 Law & Contemp. Probs. 342 (1966); Symposium, *Computers, Data Banks, and Individual Privacy*, 53 Minn. L. Rev. 211-45 (1968); Symposium, *Privacy*, 31 Law & Contemp. Probs. 251-435 (1966).

[40] Priscilla M. Regan, *Legislating Privacy: Technology, Social Values, and Public Policy* 82 (1995).

- There must be no personal-data record-keeping systems whose very existence is secret.

- There must be a way for an individual to find out what information about him is in a record and how it is used.

- There must be a way for an individual to prevent information about him obtained for one purpose from being used or made available for other purposes without his consent.

- There must be a way for an individual to correct or amend a record of identifiable information about him.

- Any organization creating, maintaining, using, or disseminating records of identifiable personal data must ensure the reliability of the data for their intended use and must take reasonable precautions to prevent misuse of the data.[41]

As Marc Rotenberg observes, the Fair Information Practices have "played a significant role in framing privacy laws in the United States."[42]

Beginning in the 1970s, Congress has passed a number of laws protecting privacy in various sectors of the information economy:

- Fair Credit Reporting Act of 1970, Pub. L. No. 90-32, 15 U.S.C. §§ 1681 et seq. — provides citizens with rights regarding the use and disclosure of their personal information by credit reporting agencies.

- Privacy Act of 1974, Pub. L. No. 93-579, 5 U.S.C. § 552a — provides individuals with a number of rights concerning their personal information maintained in government record systems, such as the right to see one's records and to ensure that the information in them is accurate.

- Family Educational Rights and Privacy Act of 1974, Pub. L. No. 93-380, 20 U.S.C. §§ 1221 note, 1232g — protects the privacy of school records.

- Right to Financial Privacy Act of 1978, Pub. L. No. 95-630, 12 U.S.C. §§ 3401–3422 — requires a subpoena or search warrant for law enforcement officials to obtain financial records.

- Foreign Intelligence Surveillance Act of 1978, Pub. L. No. 95-511, 15 U.S.C. §§ 1801-1811 — regulates foreign intelligence gathering within the U.S.

- Privacy Protection Act of 1980, Pub. L. No. 96-440, 42 U.S.C. § 2000aa — restricts the government's ability to search and seize the work product of the press and the media.

- Cable Communications Policy Act of 1984, Pub. L. No. 98-549, 47 U.S.C. § 551 — mandates privacy protection for records maintained by cable companies.

---

[41] *See* U.S. Dep't of Health, Education, and Welfare, *Secretary's Advisory Committee on Automated Personal Data Systems, Records, Computers, and Rights of Citizens* viii (1973).

[42] Marc Rotenberg, *Fair Information Practices and the Architecture of Privacy (What Larry Doesn't Get),* Stan. Tech. L. Rev. 1, 44 (2001).

- Electronic Communications Privacy Act of 1986, Pub. L. No. 99-508 and Pub. L. No. 103-414, 18 U.S.C §§ 2510–2522, 2701–2709 — updates federal electronic surveillance law to respond to the new developments in technology.

- Computer Matching and Privacy Protection Act of 1988, Pub. L. No. 100-503, 5 U.S.C. §§ 552a — regulates automated investigations conducted by government agencies comparing computer files.

- Employee Polygraph Protection Act of 1988, Pub. L. No. 100-347, 29 U.S.C. §§ 2001–2009 — governs the use of polygraphs by employers.

- Video Privacy Protection Act of 1988, Pub. L. No. 100-618, 18 U.S.C. §§ 2710–2711 — protects the privacy of videotape rental information.

- Telephone Consumer Protection Act of 1991, Pub. L. No. 102-243, 47 U.S.C. § 227 — provides certain remedies from repeat telephone calls by telemarketers.

- Driver's Privacy Protection Act of 1994, Pub. L. No. 103-322, 18 U.S.C. §§ 2721–2725 — restricts the states from disclosing or selling personal information in their motor vehicle records.

- Health Insurance Portability and Accountability Act of 1996, Pub. L. No. 104-191 — gives the Department of Health and Human Services (HHS) the authority to promulgate regulations governing the privacy of medical records.

- Identity Theft and Assumption Deterrence Act of 1998, Pub. L. No. 105-318, 18 U.S.C. § 1028 — criminalizes the transfer or use of fraudulent identification with the intent to commit unlawful activity.

- Children's Online Privacy Protection Act of 1998, Pub. L. No. 106-170, 15 U.S.C. §§ 6501–6506 — restricts the use of information gathered from children under age 13 by Internet websites.

- Gramm-Leach-Bliley Act of 1999, Pub. L. No. 106-102, 15 U.S.C. §§ 6801–6809 — requires privacy notices and provides opt-out rights when financial institutions seek to disclose personal data to other companies.

- CAN-SPAM Act of 2003, Pub. L. No. 108-187 — provides penalties for the transmission of unsolicited e-mail.

- Fair and Accurate Credit Transactions Act of 2003, Pub. L. No. 108-159 — amends and updates the Fair Credit Reporting Act, providing (among other things) additional protections against identity theft.

- Video Voyeurism Prevention Act of 2004, Pub. L. No. 108-495, 18 U.S.C. § 1801 — criminalizes the capturing of nude images of people (when on federal property) under circumstances where they have a reasonable expectation of privacy.

- Health Information Technology for Economic and Clinical Health Act (HITECH Act) of 2009, Pub. L. No. 111-5 — expands HIPAA's coverage, strengthens penalties for HIPAA violations, and provides for data breach notification under HIPAA.

Not all of Congress's legislation regarding privacy has been protective of privacy. A number of statutes have mandated the government collection of sensitive personal data or facilitated government investigation techniques:

- Bank Secrecy Act of 1970, Pub. L. No. 91-508 — requires banks to maintain reports of people's financial transactions to assist in government white collar investigations.

- Communications Assistance for Law Enforcement Act of 1994, Pub. L. No. 103-414 — requires telecommunication providers to help facilitate government interceptions of communications and surveillance.

- Personal Responsibility and Work Opportunity Reconciliation Act of 1996, Pub. L. No. 104-193 — requires the collection of personal information (including Social Security numbers, addresses, and wages) of all people who obtain a new job anywhere in the nation, which will be placed into a national database to help track down deadbeat parents.

- USA-PATRIOT Act of 2001, Pub. L. No. 107-56 — amends a number of electronic surveillance statutes and other statutes to facilitate law enforcement investigations and access to information.

State Statutory Law. The states have passed statutes protecting privacy in many contexts, regulating both the public and private sectors. These laws cover a wide range of subjects, from employment records and medical records to library records and student records.

States have led the way in the area of breach notification. Following California's enactment of such a statute, more than 90 percent of the states have now enacted statutes that require organizations to let the affected party know when there is a data leak involving personal data. Many states also have enacted data disposal statutes, and an increasing number of state statutes are setting substantive requirements for data security.

4. INTERNATIONAL LAW

Privacy is a global concern. International law and, more precisely, the privacy laws of other countries and international privacy norms, implicate privacy interests in the United States. For example, commercial firms in the United States must comply with the various standards for global commerce. The Organization of Economic Cooperation and Development (OECD) developed an extensive series of privacy guidelines in 1980 that formed the basis for privacy laws in North America, Europe, and East Asia.

In 1995, the European Union issued the *European Community Directive on Data Protection*, which outlined the basic principles for privacy legislation for European Union member countries.[43] The Directive became effective on October 25, 1998. It will be replaced by the sweeping General Data Protection Regulation

---

[43] *See* Directive of the European Parliament and the Council of Europe on the Protection of Individuals with Regard to the Processing of Personal Data and on the Free Movement of Such Data (1996).

(GDPR) on May 25, 2018. The GDPR will be immediately binding as law in all EU Member States.[44]

In November 2004, an Asian-Pacific Economic Cooperative (APEC) Privacy Framework was endorsed by the ministers of the APEC countries. The APEC countries are more than 20 nations, mostly in Asia, but also including the United States.

---

[44] European Commission, Regulation 2016/670 of the European Parliament and of the Council of 27 April 2016 on the protection of individuals with regard to the processing of personal data and on the free movement of such data, and repealing Directive 95/46/EC, O.J. L119, 1 (May 4, 2016).

CHAPTER 2

PERSPECTIVES ON PRIVACY

CHAPTER OUTLINE

A. THE PHILOSOPHICAL DISCOURSE ABOUT PRIVACY

1. THE CONCEPT OF PRIVACY AND THE RIGHT TO PRIVACY

At the outset, it is important to distinguish between the concept of privacy and the right of privacy. As Hyman Gross observed, "[t]he law does not determine what privacy is, but only what situations of privacy will be afforded legal protection."[1] Privacy as a concept involves what privacy entails and how it is to be valued. Privacy as a right involves the extent to which privacy is (and should be) legally protected.

While instructive and illuminative, law cannot be the exclusive material for constructing a concept of privacy. Law is the product of the weighing of competing values, and it sometimes embodies difficult trade-offs. In order to determine what the law *should* protect, we cannot merely look to what the law *does* protect.

---

[1] Hyman Gross, *The Concept of Privacy*, 42 N.Y.U. L. Rev. 34, 36 (1967).

2. THE PUBLIC AND PRIVATE SPHERES

A long-standing distinction in philosophical discourse is between the public and private spheres. Some form of boundary between public and private has been maintained throughout the history of Western civilization.[2]

Generally, the public sphere is the realm of life experienced in the open, in the community, and in the world of politics. The private sphere is the realm of life where one retreats to isolation or to one's family. At its core is the world of the home. The private sphere, observes Edward Shils, is a realm where the individual "is not bound by the rules that govern public life. . . . The 'private life' is a secluded life, a life separated from the compelling burdens of public authority."[3]

According to Hannah Arendt, both spheres are essential dimensions of human life:

> . . . In ancient feeling, the privative trait of privacy, indicated in the word itself, was all-important; it meant literally a state of being deprived of something, and even of the highest and most human of man's capacities. A man who lived only a private life, who like the slave was not permitted to enter the public realm, or like the barbarian had chosen not to establish such a realm, was not fully human. We no longer think primarily of deprivation when we use the word "privacy," and this is partly due to the enormous enrichment of the private sphere through modern individualism. . . .
>
> To live an entirely private life means above all to be deprived of things essential to a truly human life: to be deprived of the reality that comes from being seen and heard by others, to be deprived of an "objective" relationship with them that comes from being related to and separated from them through the intermediary of a common world of things, to be deprived of the possibility of achieving something more permanent than life itself. . . .
>
> . . . [T]he four walls of one's private property offer the only reliable hiding place from the common public world, not only from everything that goes on in it but also from its very publicity, from being seen and being heard. A life spent entirely in public, in the presence of others, becomes, as we would say, shallow. While it retains visibility, it loses the quality of rising into sight from some darker ground which must remain hidden if it is not to lose its depth in a very real, non-subjective sense. . . . [4]

John Stuart Mill relied upon a notion of the public/private dichotomy to determine when society should regulate individual conduct. Mill contended that there was a realm where people had social responsibilities and where society could properly restrain people from acting or punish them for their deeds. This realm consisted in acts that were hurtful to others or to which people "may rightfully be compelled to perform; such as to give evidence in a court of justice; to bear his fair share in the common defence, or in any other joint work necessary to the interest of the society of which he enjoys the protection." However, "there is a sphere of action in which society, as distinguished from the individual, has, if any, only an

---

[2] *See* Georges Duby, *Foreword,* in *A History of the Private Life I: From Pagan Rome to Byzantium* viii (Paul Veyne ed. & Arthur Goldhammer trans., 1987); *see also* Jürgen Habermas, *The Structural Transformation of the Public Sphere* (Thomas Burger trans., 1991).

[3] Edward Shils, *Privacy: Its Constitution and Vicissitudes,* 31 Law & Contemp. Probs. 281, 283 (1966).

[4] Hannah Arendt, *The Human Condition* (1958).

indirect interest; comprehending all that portion of a person's life and conduct which affects only himself, or if it also affects others, only with their free, voluntary, and undeceived consent and participation." Conduct within this sphere consists of "self-regarding" acts, and society should not interfere with such acts. As Mill further elaborated:

> . . . I fully admit that the mischief which a person does to himself may seriously affect, both through their sympathies and their interests, those nearly connected with him and, in a minor degree, society at large. When, by conduct of this sort, a person is led to violate a distinct and assignable obligation to any other person or persons, the case is taken out of the self-regarding class, and becomes amenable to moral disapprobation in the proper sense of the term. . . . Whenever, in short, there is a definite damage, or a definite risk of damage, either to an individual or to the public, the case is taken out of the province of liberty, and placed in that of morality or law.
>
> But with regard to the merely contingent, or, as it may be called, constructive injury which a person causes to society, by conduct which neither violates any specific duty to the public, nor occasions perceptible hurt to any assignable individual except himself; the inconvenience is one which society can afford to bear, for the sake of the greater good of human freedom. . . . [5]

B. THE DEFINITION AND THE VALUE OF PRIVACY

The following excerpts explore the definition and value of privacy. Those who attempt to define privacy seek to describe what privacy constitutes. Over the past four decades, academics have defined privacy as a right of personhood, intimacy, secrecy, limited access to the self, and control over information. However, defining privacy has proven to be quite complicated, and many commentators have expressed great difficulty in defining precisely what privacy is. In the words of one commentator, "even the most strenuous advocate of a right to privacy must confess that there are serious problems of defining the essence and scope of this right."[6] According to Robert Post, "[p]rivacy is a value so complex, so entangled in competing and contradictory dimensions, so engorged with various and distinct meanings, that I sometimes despair whether it can be usefully addressed at all."[7]

Conceptualizing privacy not only involves defining privacy but articulating the value of privacy. The value of privacy concerns its importance — how privacy is to be weighed relative to other interests and values. The excerpts that follow attempt to grapple with the complicated task of defining privacy and explaining why privacy is worth protecting.

---

[5] John Stuart Mill, *On Liberty* 12, 13, 74-75 (1859).

[6] William M. Beaney, *The Right to Privacy and American Law*, 31 Law & Contemp. Probs. 253, 255 (1966).

[7] Robert C. Post, *Three Concepts of Privacy*, 89 Geo. L.J. 2087, 2087 (2001).

ALAN WESTIN, *PRIVACY AND FREEDOM*

(1967)

. . . Privacy is the claim of individuals, groups, or institutions to determine for themselves when, how, and to what extent information about them is communicated to others. Viewed in terms of the relation of the individual to social participation, privacy is the voluntary and temporary withdrawal of a person from the general society through physical or psychological means, either in a state of solitude or small-group intimacy or, when among larger groups, in a condition of anonymity or reserve. The individual's desire for privacy is never absolute, since participation in society is an equally powerful desire. Thus each individual is continually engaged in a personal adjustment process in which he balances the desire for privacy with the desire for disclosure and communication of himself to others, in light of the environmental conditions and social norms set by the society in which he lives. The individual does so in the face of pressures from the curiosity of others and from the processes of surveillance that every society sets in order to enforce its social norms. . . .

Recognizing the differences that political and sensory cultures make in setting norms of privacy among modern societies, it is still possible to describe the general functions that privacy performs for individuals and groups in Western democratic nations. Before describing these, it is helpful to explain in somewhat greater detail the four basic states of individual privacy [solitude, intimacy, anonymity, and reserve.] . . .

The first state of privacy is solitude; here the individual is separated from the group and freed from the observation of other persons. He may be subjected to jarring physical stimuli, such as noise, odors, and vibrations. His peace of mind may continue to be disturbed by physical sensations of heat, cold, itching, and pain. He may believe that he is being observed by God or some supernatural force, or fear that some authority is secretly watching him. Finally, in solitude he will be especially subject to that familiar dialogue with the mind or conscience. But, despite all these physical or psychological intrusions, solitude is the most complete state of privacy that individuals can achieve.

In the second state of privacy, the individual is acting as part of a small unit that claims and is allowed to exercise corporate seclusion so that it may achieve a close, relaxed, and frank relationship between two or more individuals. Typical units of intimacy are husband and wife, the family, a friendship circle, or a work clique. Whether close contact brings relaxed relations or abrasive hostility depends on the personal interaction of the members, but without intimacy a basic need of human contact would not be met.

The third state of privacy, anonymity, occurs when the individual is in public places or performing public acts but still seeks, and finds, freedom from identification and surveillance. He may be riding a subway, attending a ball game, or walking the streets; he is among people and knows that he is being observed; but unless he is a well-known celebrity, he does not expect to be personally identified and held to the full rules of behavior and role that would operate if he were known to those observing him. In this state the individual is able to merge into the "situational landscape." Knowledge or fear that one is under systematic observation in public places destroys the sense of relaxation and freedom that men seek in open spaces and public arenas. . . .

Still another kind of anonymity is the publication of ideas anonymously. Here the individual wants to present some idea publicly to the community or to a segment of it, but does not want to be universally identified at once as the author — especially not by the authorities, who may be forced to take action if they "know" the perpetrator. The core of each of these types of anonymous action is the desire of individuals for times of "public privacy."

Reserve, the fourth and most subtle state of privacy, is the creation of a psychological barrier against unwanted intrusion; this occurs when the individual's need to limit communication about himself is protected by the willing discretion of those surrounding him. Most of our lives are spent not in solitude or anonymity but in situations of intimacy and in group settings where we are known to others. Even in the most intimate relations, communication of self to others is always incomplete and is based on the need to hold back some parts of one's self as either too personal and sacred or too shameful and profane to express. This circumstance gives rise to what Simmel called "reciprocal reserve and indifference," the relation that creates "mental distance" to protect the personality. This creation of mental distance — a variant of the concept of "social distance" — takes place in every sort of relationship under rules of social etiquette; it expresses the individual's choice to withhold or disclose information — the choice that is the dynamic aspect of privacy in daily interpersonal relations. . . .

This analysis of the various states of privacy is useful in discussing the basic question of the functions privacy performs for individuals in democratic societies. These can also be grouped conveniently under four headings — personal autonomy, emotional release, self-evaluation, and limited and protected communication. . . .

Personal Autonomy. . . . Each person is aware of the gap between what he wants to be and what he actually is, between what the world sees of him and what he knows to be his much more complex reality. In addition, there are aspects of himself that the individual does not fully understand but is slowly exploring and shaping as he develops. Every individual lives behind a mask in this manner; indeed, the first etymological meaning of the word "person" was "mask," indicating both the conscious and expressive presentation of the self to a social audience. If this mask is torn off and the individual's real self bared to a world in which everyone else still wears his mask and believes in masked performances, the individual can be seared by the hot light of selective, forced exposure. . . .

The autonomy that privacy protects is also vital to the development of individuality and consciousness of individual choice in life. . . . This development of individuality is particularly important in democratic societies, since qualities of independent thought, diversity of views, and non-conformity are considered desirable traits for individuals. Such independence requires time for sheltered experimentation and testing of ideas, for preparation and practice in thought and conduct, without fear of ridicule or penalty, and for the opportunity to alter opinions before making them public. The individual's sense that it is he who decides when to "go public" is a crucial aspect of his feeling of autonomy. Without such time for incubation and growth, through privacy, many ideas and positions would be launched into the world with dangerous prematurity. . . .

Emotional Release. Life in society generates such tensions for the individual that both physical and psychological health demand periods of privacy for various types of emotional release. At one level, such relaxation is required from the pressure of playing social roles. Social scientists agree that each person constantly plays a series of varied and multiple roles, depending on his audience and behavioral situation. On any given day a man may move through the roles of stern father, loving husband, car-pool comedian, skilled lathe operator, union steward, water-cooler flirt, and American Legion committee chairman — all psychologically different roles that he adopts as he moves from scene to scene on the social stage. Like actors on the dramatic stage, Goffman has noted, individuals can sustain roles only for reasonable periods of time, and no individual can play indefinitely, without relief, the variety of roles that life demands. There have to be moments "off stage" when the individual can be "himself": tender, angry, irritable, lustful, or dream-filled. . . .

Another form of emotional release is provided by the protection privacy gives to minor non-compliance with social norms. Some norms are formally adopted — perhaps as law — which society really expects many persons to break. This ambivalence produces a situation in which almost everyone does break some social or institutional norms — for example, violating traffic laws, breaking sexual mores, cheating on expense accounts, overstating income-tax deductions, or smoking in rest rooms when this is prohibited. Although society will usually punish the most flagrant abuses, it tolerates the great bulk of the violations as "permissible" deviations. If there were no privacy to permit society to ignore these deviations — if all transgressions were known — most persons in society would be under organizational discipline or in jail, or could be manipulated by threats of such action. The firm expectation of having privacy for permissible deviations is a distinguishing characteristic of life in a free society. At a lesser but still important level, privacy also allows individuals to deviate temporarily from social etiquette when alone or among intimates, as by putting feet on desks, cursing, letting one's face go slack, or scratching wherever one itches.

Another aspect of release is the "safety-valve" function afforded by privacy. Most persons need to give vent to their anger at "the system," "city hall," "the boss," and various others who exercise authority over them, and to do this in the intimacy of family or friendship circles, or in private papers, without fear of being held responsible for such comments. . . . Without the aid of such release in accommodating the daily abrasions with authorities, most people would experience serious emotional pressure. . . .

Limited and Protected Communication. The greatest threat to civilized social life would be a situation in which each individual was utterly candid in his communications with others, saying exactly what he knew or felt at all times. The havoc done to interpersonal relations by children, saints, mental patients, and adult "innocents" is legendary. . . .

Privacy for limited and protected communication has two general aspects. First, it provides the individual with the opportunities he needs for sharing confidences and intimacies with those he trusts — spouse, "the family," personal friends, and close associates at work. The individual discloses because he knows that his confidences will be held, and because he knows that breach of confidence violates social norms in a civilized society. "A friend," said Emerson, "is someone before . . . [whom] I can think aloud." In addition, the individual often wants to secure counsel from persons with whom he does not have to live daily after disclosing his confidences. He seeks professionally objective advice from persons whose status in society promises that they will not later use his distress to take advantage of him. To protect freedom of limited communication, such relationships — with doctors, lawyers, ministers, psychiatrists, psychologists, and others — are given varying but important degrees of legal privilege against forced disclosure. . . .

NOTES & QUESTIONS

1. ***Privacy as Control over Information.*** A number of theorists, including Westin, conceive of privacy as a form of control over personal information.[8] Consider Charles Fried's definition of privacy:

> At first approximation, privacy seems to be related to secrecy, to limiting the knowledge of others about oneself. This notion must be refined. It is not true, for instance, that the less that is known about us the more privacy we have. Privacy is not simply an absence of information about what is in the minds of others; rather it is the *control* we have over information about ourselves.
>
> To refer for instance to the privacy of a lonely man on a desert island would be to engage in irony. The person who enjoys privacy is able to grant or deny access to others. . . .
>
> Privacy, thus, is control over knowledge about oneself. But it is not simply control over the quantity of information abroad; there are modulations in the quality of the knowledge as well. We may not mind that a person knows a general fact about us, and yet feel our privacy invaded if he knows the details.[9]

Is this a compelling definition of privacy?

In contrast to privacy-as-control, Christena Nippert-Eng, a sociologist, talks about the managerial dimension of privacy. Based on her wide-reaching field interviews, Nippert-Eng concludes that "participants find it incumbent upon themselves to create their own pockets of uninterruptible time and space, or take make decisions without letting anyone else unduly pressure them into a particular choice."[10] She adds that "a need to *manage* one's privacy" runs through all the definitions of privacy offered by her interview participants.

2. ***Privacy as Limited Access to the Self.*** Another group of theorists view privacy as a form of limited access to the self. Consider Ruth Gavison:

> . . . Our interest in privacy . . . is related to our concern over our accessibility to others: the extent to which we are known to others, the extent to which others have physical access to us, and the extent to which we are the subject of others' attention. This concept of privacy as concern for limited accessibility enables us to identify when losses of privacy occur. Furthermore, the reasons for which

---

[8] *See* Adam Carlyle Breckenridge, *The Right to Privacy* 1 (1970); Randall P. Bezanson, *The Right to Privacy Revisited: Privacy, News, and Social Change, 1810–1990*, 80 Cal. L. Rev. 1133 (1992). For a critique of privacy as control, see Anita L. Allen, *Privacy as Data Control: Conceptual, Practical, and Moral Limits of the Paradigm*, 32 Conn. L. Rev. 861 (2000).

[9] Charles Fried, *Privacy*, 77 Yale L.J. 475 (1968).

[10] Christena Nippert-Eng, *Islands of Privacy* 7 (2010).

we claim privacy in different situations are similar. They are related to the functions privacy has in our lives: the promotion of liberty, autonomy, selfhood, and human relations, and furthering the existence of a free society. . . .

The concept of privacy suggested here is a complex of these three independent and irreducible elements: secrecy, anonymity, and solitude. Each is independent in the sense that a loss of privacy may occur through a change in any one of the three, without a necessary loss in either of the other two. The concept is nevertheless coherent because the three elements are all part of the same notion of accessibility, and are related in many important ways.[11]

How does this theory of privacy differ from the notion of privacy as "the right to be let alone"? How does it differ from privacy as control over information? How much control should individuals have over access to themselves? Should the decision depend upon each particular person's desires? Or should there be an objective standard — a reasonable degree of control over access?

3. ***Privacy as Intimacy.*** A number of theorists argue that "intimacy" appropriately defines what information or matters are private. For example, Julie Inness argues that "intimacy" is the common denominator in all the matters that people claim to be private. Privacy is "the state of the agent having control over decisions concerning matters that draw their meaning and value from the agent's love, caring, or liking. These decisions cover choices on the agent's part about access to herself, the dissemination of information about herself, and her actions."[12]

Jeffrey Rosen adopts a similar view when he writes:

> . . . Privacy protects us from being misdefined and judged out of context in a world of short attention spans, a world in which information can easily be confused with knowledge. True knowledge of another person is the culmination of a slow process of mutual revelation. It requires the gradual setting aside of social masks, the incremental building of trust, which leads to the exchange of personal disclosures. It cannot be rushed; this is why, after intemperate self-revelation in the heat of passion, one may feel something close to self-betrayal. True knowledge of another person, in all of his or her complexity, can be achieved only with a handful of friends, lovers, or family members. In order to flourish, the intimate relationships on which true knowledge of another person depends need space as well as time: sanctuaries from the gaze of the crowd in which slow mutual self-disclosure is possible.

---

[11] Ruth Gavison, *Privacy and the Limits of Law*, 89 Yale L.J. 421 (1980); *see also* Edward Shils, *Privacy: Its Constitution and Vicissitudes*, 31 Law & Contemp. Probs. 281, 281 (1996); Sissela Bok, *Secrets: On the Ethics of Concealment and Revelation* 10-11 (1982); Ernest Van Den Haag, *On Privacy*, in *Nomos XII: Privacy* 149 (J. Ronald Pennock & J.W. Chapman eds., 1971); Sidney M. Jourard, *Some Psychological Aspects of Privacy*, 31 L. & Contemp. Probs. 307, 307 (1966); David O'Brien, *Privacy, Law, and Public Policy* 16 (1979); Hyman Gross, *The Concept of Privacy*, 42 N.Y.U. L. Rev. 34 (1967).

[12] Julie C. Inness, *Privacy, Intimacy, and Isolation* 56, 58, 63, 64, 67 (1992). For other proponents of privacy as intimacy, see Robert S. Gerstein, *Intimacy and Privacy*, in *Philosophical Dimensions of Privacy: An Anthology* 265, 265 (Ferdinand David Schoeman ed., 1984); James Rachels, *Why Privacy Is Important*, in *Philosophical Dimensions of Privacy: An Anthology* 290, 292 (Ferdinand David Schoeman ed., 1984); Tom Gerety, *Redefining Privacy*, 12 Harv. C.R.-C.L. L. Rev. 233 (1977).

When intimate personal information circulates among a small group of people who know us well, its significance can be weighed against other aspects of our personality and character. By contrast, when intimate information is removed from its original context and revealed to strangers, we are vulnerable to being misjudged on the basis of our most embarrassing, and therefore most memorable, tastes and preferences. . . . In a world in which citizens are bombarded with information, people form impressions quickly, based on sound bites, and these impressions are likely to oversimplify and misrepresent our complicated and often contradictory characters.[13]

Does "intimacy" adequately separate private matters from public ones? Can something be private but not intimate? Can something be intimate but not private?

In reaction to Rosen's views on privacy, Lawrence Lessig restates the problem of short attention spans in this fashion: "Privacy, the argument goes, would remedy such a problem by concealing those things that would not be understood with the given attention span. Privacy's function . . . is not to protect the presumptively innocent from true but damaging information, but rather to protect the actually innocent from damaging conclusions drawn from misunderstood information."[14] Lessig notes his skepticism regarding this approach: privacy will not alone solve the problem with the information market. Moreover, there "are possible solutions to this problem of attention span. But what should be clear is that there is no guarantee that a particular problem of attention span will have any solution at all."

JULIE E. COHEN, *EXAMINED LIVES: INFORMATIONAL PRIVACY AND THE SUBJECT AS OBJECT*

52 Stan. L. Rev. 1373 (2000)

Prevailing market-based approaches to data privacy policy — including "solutions" in the form of tradable privacy rights or heightened disclosure requirements before consent — treat preferences for informational privacy as a matter of individual taste, entitled to no more (and often much less) weight than preferences for black shoes over brown or red wine over white. But the values of informational privacy are far more fundamental. A degree of freedom from scrutiny and categorization by others promotes important noninstrumental values, and serves vital individual and collective ends.

First, informational autonomy comports with important values concerning the fair and just treatment of individuals within society. From Kant to Rawls, a central strand of Western philosophical tradition emphasizes respect for the fundamental dignity of persons, and a concomitant commitment to egalitarianism in both principle and practice. Advocates of strong data privacy protection argue that these principles have clear and very specific implications for the treatment of personally-identified data: They require that we forbid data-processing practices that treat individuals as mere conglomerations of transactional data, or that rank people as prospective customers, tenants, neighbors, employees, or insureds based on their financial or genetic desirability. . . .

---

[13] Jeffrey Rosen, *The Unwanted Gaze: The Destruction of Privacy in America* 8-9 (2000).

[14] Lawrence Lessig, *Privacy and Attention Span*, 89 Geo. L.J. 2063, 2065 (2001).

Autonomous individuals do not spring full-blown from the womb. We must learn to process information and to draw our own conclusions about the world around us. We must learn to choose, and must learn something before we can choose anything. Here, though, information theory suggests a paradox: "Autonomy" connotes an essential independence of critical faculty and an imperviousness to influence. But to the extent that information shapes behavior, autonomy is radically contingent upon environment and circumstance. . . . Autonomy in a contingent world requires a zone of relative insulation from outside scrutiny and interference — a field of operation within which to engage in the conscious construction of self. The solution to the paradox of contingent autonomy, in other words, lies in a second paradox: To exist in fact as well as in theory, autonomy must be nurtured.

A realm of autonomous, unmonitored choice, in turn, promotes a vital diversity of speech and behavior. The recognition that anonymity shelters constitutionally-protected decisions about speech, belief, and political and intellectual association — decisions that otherwise might be chilled by unpopularity or simple difference — is part of our constitutional tradition. . . .

The benefits of informational privacy are related to, but distinct from, those afforded by seclusion from visual monitoring. It is well-recognized that respite from visual scrutiny affords individuals an important measure of psychological repose. Within our society, at least, we are accustomed to physical spaces within which we can be unobserved, and intrusion into those spaces is experienced as violating the boundaries of self. But the scrutiny, and the repose, can be informational as well as visual, and this does not depend entirely on whether the behavior takes place "in private." The injury, here, does not lie in the exposure of formerly private behaviors to public view, but in the dissolution of the boundaries that insulate different spheres of behavior from one another. The universe of all information about all record-generating behaviors generates a "picture" that, in some respects, is more detailed and intimate than that produced by visual observation, and that picture is accessible, in theory and often in reality, to just about anyone who wants to see it. In such a world, we all may be more cautious.

The point is not that people will not learn under conditions of no-privacy, but that they will learn differently, and that the experience of being watched will constrain, ex ante, the acceptable spectrum of belief and behavior. Pervasive monitoring of every first move or false start will, at the margin, incline choices toward the bland and the mainstream. The result will be a subtle yet fundamental shift in the content of our character, a blunting and blurring of rough edges and sharp lines. . . . The condition of no-privacy threatens not only to chill the expression of eccentric individuality, but also, gradually, to dampen the force of our aspirations to it. . . .

. . . [T]he insulation provided by informational privacy also plays a subtler, more conservative role in reinforcing the existing social fabric. Sociologist Erving Goffman demonstrated that the construction of social facades to mediate between self and community is both instinctive and expected. Alan Westin describes this social dimension of privacy as "reserve." This characterization, though, seems incomplete. On Goffman's account, the construction of social personae isn't just about withholding information that we don't want others to have. It is about defining the parameters of social interaction in ways that maximize social ease, and thus is about collective as well as individual comfort. We do not need, or even want, to know each other that well. Less information makes routine interactions easier; we are then free to choose, consensually and without embarrassment, the interactions that we wish to treat as less routine. Informational privacy, in short, is a constitutive element of a civil society in the broadest sense of that term. . . .

NOTES & QUESTIONS

1. *Privacy and Respect for Persons.* Julie Cohen's theory locates the purpose of privacy as promoting the development of autonomous individuals and, more broadly, civil society. Compare her theory to the following theory by Stanley Benn:

> Finding oneself an object of scrutiny, as the focus of another's attention, brings one to a new consciousness of oneself, as something seen through another's eyes. According to [Jean-Paul] Sartre, indeed, it is a necessary condition for knowing oneself as anything at all that one should conceive oneself as an object of scrutiny. It is only through the regard of the other that the observed becomes aware of himself as an object, knowable, having a determinate character, in principle predictable. His consciousness of pure freedom as subject, as originator and chooser, is at once assailed by it; he is fixed as *something* — with limited probabilities rather than infinite, indeterminate possibilities. . . .
>
> The underpinning of a claim not to be watched without leave will be more general if it can be grounded in this way on the principle of respect for persons than on a utilitarian duty to avoid inflicting suffering. . . . But respect for persons will sustain an objection even to secret watching, which may do no actual harm at all. Covert observation — spying — is objectionable because it deliberately deceives a person about his world, thwarting, for reasons that *cannot* be his reasons, his attempts to make a rational choice. One cannot be said to respect a man as engaged on an enterprise worthy of consideration if one knowingly and deliberately alters his conditions of action, concealing the fact from him. . . .[15]

How is Cohen's theory similar to and/or different from Benn's?

Benn argues that privacy is a form of respect for persons. By being watched, Benn contends, the observed becomes "fixed as *something* — with limited probabilities rather than infinite indeterminate possibilities." Does Benn adequately capture why surveillance is harmful? Is Benn really concerned about the negative consequences of surveillance on a person's behavior? Or is Benn more concerned about the violation of respect for another?

2. *Privacy as an Individual Right and as a Social Value.* Consider the following argument from Priscilla Regan:

> . . . [The] emphasis of privacy as an individual right or an individual interest provides a weak basis for formulating policy to protect privacy. When privacy is defined as an individual right, policy formulation entails a balancing of the individual right to privacy against a competing interest or right. In general, the competing interest is recognized as a social interest. . . . It is also assumed that the individual has a stake in these societal interests. As a result, privacy has

---

[15] Stanley I. Benn, *Privacy, Freedom, and Respect for Persons*, from *Nomos XIII: Privacy* (J. Ronald Pennock & J.W. Chapman eds., 1971).

been on the defensive, with those alleging a privacy invasion bearing the burden of proving that a certain activity does indeed invade privacy and that the "social" benefit to be gained from the privacy invasion is less important than the individual harm incurred. . . .

Privacy is a *common value* in that all individuals value some degree of privacy and have some common perceptions about privacy. Privacy is also a *public value* in that it has value not just to the individual as an individual or to all individuals in common but also to the democratic political system. . . .

A public value of privacy derives not only from its protection of the individual as an individual but also from its usefulness as a restraint on the government or on the use of power. . . .[16]

DANIEL J. SOLOVE, *CONCEPTUALIZING PRIVACY*

90 Cal. L. Rev. 1087 (2002)

Despite what appears to be a welter of different conceptions of privacy, I argue that they can be dealt with under six general headings, which capture the recurrent ideas in the discourse. These headings include: (1) the right to be let alone — Samuel Warren and Louis Brandeis's famous formulation for the right to privacy; (2) limited access to the self — the ability to shield oneself from unwanted access by others; (3) secrecy — the concealment of certain matters from others; (4) control over personal information — the ability to exercise control over information about oneself; (5) personhood — the protection of one's personality, individuality, and dignity; and (6) intimacy — control over, or limited access to, one's intimate relationships or aspects of life. Some of the conceptions concentrate on means to achieve privacy; others focus on the ends or goals of privacy. Further, there is overlap between conceptions, and the conceptions discussed under different headings are by no means independent from each other. For example, control over personal information can be seen as a subset of limited access to the self, which in turn bears significant similarities to the right to be let alone. . . .

The most prevalent problem with the conceptions is that they are either too narrow or too broad. The conceptions are often too narrow because they fail to include the aspects of life that we typically view as private, and are often too broad because they fail to exclude matters that we do not deem private. Often, the same conceptions can suffer from being both too narrow and too broad. I contend that these problems stem from the way that the discourse goes about the task of conceptualizing privacy. . . .

Most attempts to conceptualize privacy thus far have followed the traditional method of conceptualizing. The majority of theorists conceptualize privacy by defining it *per genus et differentiam*. In other words, theorists look for a common set of necessary and sufficient elements that single out privacy as unique from other conceptions. . . .

[Philosopher Ludwig] Wittgenstein suggests that certain concepts might not share one common characteristic; rather they draw from a common pool of similar characteristics, "a complicated network of similarities overlapping and criss-

---

[16] Priscilla M. Regan, *Legislating Privacy: Technology, Social Values, and Public Policy* 213, 225 (1995).

crossing: sometimes overall similarities, sometimes similarities of detail." . . . Wittgenstein uses the term "family resemblances," analogizing to the overlapping and crisscrossing characteristics that exist between members of a family, such as "build, features, colour of eyes, gait, temperament, etc." For example, in a family, each child has certain features similar to each parent; and the children share similar features with each other; but they may not all resemble each other in the same way. Nevertheless, they all bear a resemblance to each other. . . .

When we state that we are protecting "privacy," we are claiming to guard against disruptions to certain practices. Privacy invasions disrupt and sometimes completely annihilate certain practices. Practices can be disrupted in certain ways, such as interference with peace of mind and tranquility, invasion of solitude, breach of confidentiality, loss of control over facts about oneself, searches of one's person and property, threats to or violations of personal security, destruction of reputation, surveillance, and so on.

There are certain similarities in particular types of disruptions as well as in the practices that they disrupt; but there are differences as well. We should conceptualize privacy by focusing on the specific types of disruption and the specific practices disrupted rather than looking for the common denominator that links all of them. If privacy is conceptualized as a web of interconnected types of disruption of specific practices, then the act of conceptualizing privacy should consist of mapping the typography of the web. . . .

It is reductive to carve the world of social practices into two spheres, public and private, and then attempt to determine what matters belong in each sphere. First, the matters we consider private change over time. While some form of dichotomy between public and private has been maintained throughout the history of Western civilization, the matters that have been considered public and private have metamorphosed throughout history due to changing attitudes, institutions, living conditions, and technology. The matters we consider to be private are shaped by culture and history, and have differed across cultures and historical epochs.

Second, although certain matters have moved from being public to being private and vice versa, the change often has been more subtle than a complete transformation from public to private. Particular matters have long remained private but in different ways; they have been understood as private but because of different attributes; or they have been regarded as private for some people or groups but not for others. In other words, to say simply that something is public or private is to make a rather general claim; what it means for something to be private is the central question. We consider our Social Security number, our sexual behavior, our diary, and our home private, but we do not consider them private in the same way. A number of aspects of life have commonly been viewed as private: the family, body, and home to name a few. To say simply that these things are private is imprecise because what it means for them to be private is different today than it was in the past. . . .

. . . [P]rivacy is not simply an empirical and historical question that measures the collective sense in any given society of what is and has long been considered to be private. Without a normative component, a conception of privacy can only provide a status report on existing privacy norms rather than guide us toward shaping privacy law and policy in the future. If we focus simply on people's current expectations of privacy, our conception of privacy would continually shrink given the increasing surveillance in the modern world. Similarly, the government could gradually condition people to accept wiretapping or other privacy incursions, thus altering society's expectations of privacy. On the other hand, if we merely seek to preserve those activities and matters that have historically been considered private, then we fail to adapt to the changing realities of the modern world. . . .

NOTES & QUESTIONS

1. *Core Characteristics vs. Family Resemblances.* Is there a core characteristic common in all the things we understand as being "private"? If so, what do you think it is? Can privacy be more adequately conceptualized by shifting away from the quest to find the common core characteristics of privacy?

2. *Context.* Solove contends that the meaning of privacy depends upon context, that there is no common denominator to all things we refer to as "privacy." Does this make privacy too amorphous a concept?

   Consider Helen Nissenbaum:

   > Specifically, whether a particular action is determined a violation of privacy is a function of several variables, including the nature of the situation, or context; the nature of the information in relation to that context; the roles of agents receiving information; their relationships to information subjects; on what terms the information is shared by the subject; and the terms of further dissemination.
   > . . .
   > [N]orms of privacy in fact vary considerably from place to place, culture to culture, period to period; this theory not only incorporates this reality but systematically pinpoints the sources of variation. A second consequence is that, because questions about whether particular restrictions on flow are acceptable call for investigation into the relevant contextual details, protecting privacy will be a messy task, requiring a grasp of concepts and social institutions as well as knowledge of facts of the matter.[17]

3. *Revising the Prosser Taxonomy.* Daniel Solove contends that the taxonomy of four privacy interests identified by William Prosser, *supra,* must be revised as well as expanded beyond tort law. Solove identifies 16 different kinds of activity that create privacy harms or problems:

   > The first group of activities that affect privacy involve information collection. *Surveillance* is the watching, listening to, or recording of an individual's activities. *Interrogation* consists of various forms of questioning or probing for information.
   > A second group of activities involves the way information is stored, manipulated, and used — what I refer to collectively as "information processing." *Aggregation* involves the combination of various pieces of data about a person. *Identification* is linking information to particular individuals. *Insecurity* involves carelessness in protecting stored information from being leaked or improperly accessed. *Secondary use* is the use of information collected for one purpose for a different purpose without a person's consent. *Exclusion* concerns

---

[17] Helen Nissenbaum, *Privacy as Contextual Integrity,* 79 Wash. L. Rev. 119, 155-56 (2004). For a more complete account of Nissenbaum's theory, see Helen Nissenbaum, *Privacy in Context: Technology, Policy, and the Integrity of Social Life* (2010).

the failure to allow people to know about the data that others have about them and participate in its handling and use. These activities do not involve the gathering of data, since it has already been collected. Instead, these activities involve the way data is maintained and used.

The third group of activities involves the dissemination of information. *Breach of confidentiality* is breaking the promise to keep a person's information confidential. *Disclosure* involves the revelation of truthful information about a person which impacts the way others judge that person's character. *Exposure* involves revealing another's nudity, grief, or bodily functions. *Increased accessibility* is amplifying the accessibility of information. *Blackmail* is the threat to disclose personal information. *Appropriation* involves the use of another's identity to serve the aims and interests of another. *Distortion* consists of the dissemination of false or misleading information about individuals. Information dissemination activities all involve the spreading or transfer of personal data — or the threat to do so.

The fourth and final group of activities involves invasions into people's private affairs. Invasion, unlike the other groupings, need not involve personal information (although in numerous instances, it does). *Intrusion* concerns invasive acts that disturb one's tranquility or solitude. *Decisional interference* involves the government's incursion into people's decisions regarding their private affairs.[18]

4. ***Reductionists.*** Some theorists, referred to as "reductionists," assert that privacy can be reduced to other concepts and rights. For example, Judith Jarvis Thomson contends that there is nothing particularly distinctive about privacy and to talk about things as violating the "right to privacy" is not all that useful. Privacy is really a cluster of other rights, such as the right to liberty, property rights, and the right not to be injured: "[T]he right to privacy is everywhere overlapped by other rights."[19] Is there something distinctive about privacy? Or can privacy be explained in terms of other, more primary rights and interests? What does privacy capture that these other rights and interests (autonomy, property, liberty, etc.) do not?

ANITA L. ALLEN, *COERCING PRIVACY*

40 Wm. & Mary L. Rev. 723 (1999)

. . . The final decades of the twentieth century could be remembered for the rapid erosion of expectations of personal privacy and of the taste for personal privacy in the United States. . . . I sense that people expect increasingly little physical, informational, and proprietary privacy, and that people seem to prefer less of these types of privacy relative to other goods. . . .

One way to address the erosion would be to stop the avalanche of technology and commercial opportunity responsible for the erosion. We could stop the avalanche of technology, but we will not, if the past is any indication. . . . In the

---

[18] Daniel J. Solove, *A Taxonomy of Privacy,* 154 U. Pa. L. Rev. 477 (2006). For a more complete account of Solove's theory, see Daniel J. Solove, *Understanding Privacy* (2008).
[19] Judith Jarvis Thomson, *The Right to Privacy*, 4 Phil. & Pub. Aff. 295 (1975).

United States, with a few exceptions like government-funded human cloning and fetal tissue research, the rule is that technology marches on.

We could stop the avalanche of commercial opportunity by intervening in the market for privacy; that is, we could (some way or another) increase the costs of consuming other people's privacy and lower the profits of voluntarily giving up one's own privacy. The problem with this suggested strategy is that, even without the details of implementation, it raises the specter of censorship, repression, paternalism, and bureaucracy. Privacy is something we think people are supposed to want; if it turns out that they do not, perhaps third parties should not force it on them, decreasing both their utility and that of those who enjoy disclosure, revelation, and exposure.

Of course, we force privacy on people all the time. Our elected officials criminalize public nudity, even to the point of discouraging breastfeeding. . . . It is one thing, the argument might go, to force privacy on someone by criminalizing nude sun-bathing and topless dancing. These activities have pernicious third-party effects and attract vice. It would be wrong, the argument might continue, to force privacy on someone, in the absence of harm to others, solely on the grounds that one ought not say too much about one's thoughts, feelings, and experiences; one ought not reveal in detail how one spends one's time at home; and one ought not live constantly on display. Paternalistic laws against extremes of factual and physical self-revelation seem utterly inconsistent with liberal self-expression, and yet such laws are suggested by the strong claims liberal theorists make about the value of privacy. Liberal theorists claim that we need privacy to be persons, independent thinkers, free political actors, and citizens of a tolerant democracy. . .

.

For people under forty-five who understand that they do not, and cannot, expect to have many secrets, informational privacy may now seem less important. As a culture, we seem to be learning how to be happy and productive — even spiritual — knowing that we are like open books, our houses made of glass. Our parents may appear on the television shows of Oprah Winfrey or Jerry Springer to discuss incest, homosexuality, miscegenation, adultery, transvestitism, and cruelty in the family. Our adopted children may go on television to be reunited with their birth parents. Our law students may compete with their peers for a spot on the MTV program The Real World, and a chance to live with television cameras for months on end and be viewed by mass audiences. Our ten-year-olds may aspire to have their summer camp experiences — snits, fights, fun, and all — chronicled by camera crews and broadcast as entertainment for others on the Disney Channel.

Should we worry about any of this? What values are at stake? Scholars and other commentators associate privacy with several important clusters of value. Privacy has value relative to normative conceptions of spiritual personality, political freedom, health and welfare, human dignity, and autonomy. . . .

To speak of "coercing" privacy is to call attention to privacy as a foundation, a precondition of a liberal egalitarian society. Privacy is not an optional good, like a second home or an investment account. . . .

A hard task seems to lay before us — namely, deciding which forms of privacy are so critical that they should become matters of coercion. . . .

As liberals, we should not want people to sell all their freedom, and, as liberals, we should not want people to sell all their privacy and capacities for private choices. This is, in part, because the liberal conceptions of private choice as freedom from governmental and other outside interference with decision-making closely link privacy and freedom. The liberal conception of privacy as freedom from unwanted disclosures, publicity, and loss of control of personality also closely links privacy to freedom. . . .

Government will have to intervene in private lives for the sake of privacy and values associated with it. . . . The threat to liberalism is not that individuals sometimes expose their naked bodies in public places, display affection with same-sex partners in public, or broadcast personal information on national television. The threat to liberalism is that in an increasing variety of ways our lives are being emptied of privacy on a daily basis, especially physical and informational privacy. . . .

NOTES & QUESTIONS

1. ***Should Privacy Be an Inalienable Right?*** Allen argues that people regularly surrender their privacy and that we should "coerce" privacy. In other words, privacy must be seen as an inalienable right, one that people cannot give away. What if a person wants to live in the spotlight or to give away her personal information? Why shouldn't she be allowed to do so? Recall those who defined privacy as control over information. One aspect of control is that an individual can decide for herself how much privacy she desires. What would Allen say about such a definition of privacy?

2. ***Privacy and Publicity.*** Consider also whether a desire for publicity and a desire for privacy can coexist. Does the person who "tells it all" on the Jerry Springer talk show have any less expectation of privacy when she returns home to be with her family and friends or picks up the telephone to make a private call?

3. ***Eroding Expectations of Privacy and Privacy Paternalism.*** Allen contends that our society is changing by becoming more exhibitionistic and voyeuristic. The result is that expectations of privacy are eroding. In 2011, Allen further develops these themes in a book, *Unpopular Privacy*. She argues that "privacy is so important and so neglected in contemporary life that democratic states, though liberal and feminist, could be justified in undertaking a rescue mission that includes enacting paternalistic privacy laws for the benefit of uneager beneficiaries."[20]

   If people no longer expect privacy in many situations, then why should the law continue to protect it? If people no longer desire privacy, should the law force privacy upon them? Under what circumstances?

---

[20] Anita L. Allen, *Unpopular Privacy* (2011).

PAUL M. SCHWARTZ, *PRIVACY AND DEMOCRACY IN CYBERSPACE*

52 Vand. L. Rev. 1609 (1999)

. . . Self-determination is a capacity that is embodied and developed through social forms and practices. The threat to this quality arises when private or government action interferes with a person's control of her reasoning process. . . . [P]erfected surveillance of naked thought's digital expression short-circuits the individual's own process of decisionmaking. . . .

The maintenance of a democratic order requires both deliberative democracy and an individual capacity for self-determination. . . . [T]he emerging pattern of information use in cyberspace poses a risk to these two essential values. Our task now is to develop privacy standards that are capable of structuring the right kind of information use. . . .

Most scholars, and much of the law in this area, work around a liberal paradigm that we can term "privacy-control." From the age of computer mainframes in the 1960s to the current reign of the Internet's decentralized networks, academics and the law have gravitated towards the idea of privacy as a personal right to control the use of one's data. . . .

. . . [One flaw with the "privacy-control" paradigm is the "autonomy trap."] [T]he organization of information privacy through individual control of personal data rests on a view of autonomy as a given, preexisting quality. . . .

As a policy cornerstone, however, the idea of privacy-control falls straight into the "autonomy trap." The difficulty with privacy-control in the Information Age is that individual self-determination is itself shaped by the processing of personal data. . . .

To give an example of an autonomy trap in cyberspace, the act of clicking through a "consent" screen on a Web site may be considered by some observers to be an exercise of self-reliant choice. Yet, this screen can contain boilerplate language that permits all further processing and transmission of one's personal data. Even without a consent screen, some Web sites place consent boilerplate within a "privacy statement" on their home page or elsewhere on their site. For example, the online version of one New York newspaper states, "By using this site, you agree to the Privacy Policy of the New York Post." This language presents the conditions for data processing on a take-it-or-leave-it basis. It seeks to create the legal fiction that all who visit this Web site have expressed informed consent to its data processing practices. An even more extreme manifestation of the "consent trap" is a belief that an initial decision to surf the Web itself is a self-reliant choice to accept all further use of one's personal data generated by this activity. . . .

The liberal ideal views autonomous individuals as able to interact freely and equally so long as the government or public does not interfere. The reality is, however, that individuals can be trapped when such glorification of freedom of action neglects the actual conditions of choice. Here, another problem arises with self-governance through information-control: the "data seclusion deception." The idea of privacy as data seclusion is easy to explain: unless the individual wishes to surrender her personal information, she is to be free to use her privacy right as a trump to keep it confidential or to subject its release to conditions that she alone wishes to set. The individual is to be at the center of shaping data anonymity. Yet, this right to keep data isolated quickly proves illusory because of the demands of the Information Age. . . .

NOTES & QUESTIONS

1. **Privacy and Personhood.** Like Schwartz, a number of theorists argue that privacy is essential for self-development. According to Jeffrey Reiman, privacy "protects the individual's interest in becoming, being, and remaining a person."[21] The notion that privacy protects personhood or identity is captured in Warren and Brandeis's notion of "inviolate personality." How does privacy promote self-development?

   Consider the following: "Every acceptance of a public role entails the repression, channelizing, and deflection of 'private' or personal attention, motives, and demands upon the self in order to address oneself to the expectations of others."[22] Can we really be ourselves in the public sphere? Is our "public self" any less part of our persona than our "private self"?

2. **Privacy and Democracy.** Schwartz views privacy as essential for a democratic society. Why is privacy important for political participation?

3. **Privacy and Role Playing.** Recall Westin's view of selfhood:

   > Each person is aware of the gap between what he wants to be and what he actually is, between what the world sees of him and what he knows to be his much more complex reality. In addition, there are aspects of himself that the individual does not fully understand but is slowly exploring and shaping as he develops. Every individual lives behind a mask in this manner; indeed, the first etymological meaning of the word "person" was "mask," indicating both the conscious and expressive presentation of the self to a social audience. If this mask is torn off and the individual's real self bared to a world in which everyone else still wears his mask and believes in masked performances, the individual can be seared by the hot light of selective, forced exposure.

   Is there a "true" or "core" or "authentic" self? Or do we perform many roles and perhaps have multiple selves? Is there a self beneath the roles that we play? Daniel Solove contends that "[s]ociety accepts that public reputations will be groomed to some degree. . . . Society protects privacy because it wants to provide individuals with some degree of influence over how they are judged in the public arena."[23] To what extent should the law allow people to promote a polished public image and hide the dirt in private?

4. **Individual Autonomy, Democratic Order, and Data Trade.** In a later article, Schwartz argues from the premise that "[p]ersonal information is an important currency in the new millennium."[24] He rejects arguments that opposed

---

[21] Jeffrey H. Reiman, *Privacy, Intimacy, and Personhood*, in *Philosophical Dimensions of Privacy: An Anthology* 300, 308 (Ferdinand David Schoeman ed., 1984).

[22] Joseph Bensman & Robert Lilienfeld, *Between Public and Private: Lost Boundaries of the Self* 174 (1979).

[23] Daniel J. Solove, *The Virtues of Knowing Less: Justifying Privacy Protections Against Disclosure*, 53 Duke L.J. 957 (2003).

[24] Paul M. Schwartz, *Property, Privacy, and Personal Data*, 117 Harv. L. Rev. 2055 (2004).

propertization of personal data, and developed a model to permit data trade consistent with individual autonomy and the maintenance of a democratic order. A key concept in this model is that of the "privacy commons," where privacy is viewed "as a social and not merely an individual good." As a result, Schwartz states, "If sound rules for the use of personal data are not established and enforced, society as a whole will suffer because people will decline to engage in a range of different social interactions due to concerns about use of personal information. A public good — the privacy commons — will be degraded." Do you think that property is a sound concept for building a public goods approach to information privacy?

SPIROS SIMITIS, *REVIEWING PRIVACY IN AN INFORMATION SOCIETY*

135 U. Pa. L. Rev. 707 (1987)

. . . The increased access to personal information resulting from modern, sophisticated techniques of automated processing has sharpened the need to abandon the search for a "neutral" concept in favor of an understanding free of abstractions and fully aware of the political and societal background of all privacy debates. Modern forms of data collection have altered the privacy discussion in three principal ways. First, privacy considerations no longer arise out of particular individual problems; rather, they express conflicts affecting everyone. The course of the privacy debate is neither determined by the caricature of a prominent golfer with a chocolate packet protruding out of his pocket, nor by the hints at the use of a sexual stimulant by a respected university professor, but by the intensive retrieval of personal data of virtually every employee, taxpayer, patient, bank customer, welfare recipient, or car driver. Second, smart cards and videotex make it possible to record and reconstruct individual activities in minute detail.[25] Surveillance has thereby lost its exceptional character and has become a more and more routine practice. Finally, personal information is increasingly used to enforce standards of behavior. Information processing is developing, therefore, into an essential element of long-term strategies of manipulation intended to mold and adjust individual conduct. . . .

. . . [B]ecause of both the broad availability of personal data and the elaborate matching procedures, individual activities can be accurately reconstructed through automated processing. Surveillance becomes the order of the day. Significantly enough, security agencies were among the first to discover the advantages of automated retrieval. They not only quickly computerized their own data collections but also sought and obtained access to state and private data banks. Entirely new investigation techniques, such as computer profiling, were developed, enabling the agencies to trace wanted persons by matching a presumptive pattern of consumption habits against, for instance, the records of utility companies. The

[25] Editors' Note: Smart cards are also known as "chip cards" or "integrated circuit cards." These devices, generally the size of a credit card, feature an embedded circuit for the processing of data. A precursor of the Internet, Videotex enjoyed its heyday from the late 1970s to mid-1980s. Videotex was typically deployed through a centralized system with one provider of information and involved the display of text on a television screen or dedicated terminal. France Telecom's Minitel was the most successful videotext system in the world.

successful attempts at computer-based voice and picture identification will probably influence the work of security agencies even more. . . .

Both the quest for greater transparency and the defense of free speech are legitimated by the goal of allowing the individual to understand social reality better and thus to form a personal opinion on its decisive factors as well as on possible changes. The citizen's right to be "a participator in the government of affairs," to use Jefferson's terms, reflects a profoundly rational process. It presupposes individuals who not only disperse the necessary information but also have the capacity to transform the accessible data into policy expectations. Transparency is, in other words, a basic element of competent communicative action and consequently remains indispensable as long as social discourse is to be promoted, not inhibited.

Inhibition, however, tends to be the rule once automated processing of personal data becomes a normal tool of both government and private enterprises. The price for an undoubted improvement in transparency is a no less evident loss in competence of communication. Habits, activities, and preferences are compiled, registered, and retrieved to facilitate better adjustment, not to improve the individual's capacity to act and to decide. Whatever the original incentive for computerization may have been, processing increasingly appears as the ideal means to adapt an individual to a predetermined, standardized behavior that aims at the highest possible degree of compliance with the model patient, consumer, taxpayer, employee, or citizen. Furthermore, interactive systems do not, despite all contrary assertions, restore a long lost individuality by correcting the effects of mass production in a mass society. On the contrary, the telematic integration forces the individual once more into a preset scheme. The media supplier dictates the conditions under which communication takes place, fixes the possible subjects of the dialogue, and, due to the personal data collected, is in an increasingly better position to influence the subscriber's behavior. Interactive systems, therefore, suggest individual activity where in fact no more than stereotyped reactions occur.

In short, the transparency achieved through automated processing creates possibly the best conditions for colonization of the individual's lifeworld.[26] Accurate, constantly updated knowledge of her personal history is systematically incorporated into policies that deliberately structure her behavior. The more routinized automated processing augments the transparency, however, the more privacy proves to be a prerequisite to the capacity to participate in social discourse. Where privacy is dismantled, both the chance for personal assessment of the political and societal process and the opportunity to develop and maintain a particular style of life fade. . . .

The processing of personal data is not unique to a particular society. On the contrary, the attractiveness of information technology transcends political boundaries, particularly because of the opportunity to guide the individual's behavior. For a democratic society, however, the risks are high: labeling of individuals, manipulative tendencies, magnification of errors, and strengthening of social

---

[26] For both the colonization process and the impact of the individual's lifeworld on communicative action, see Jürgen Habermas, 1 *The Theory of Communicative Action* 70-71 (1983) (defining "lifeworld" as shared understandings about what will be treated as a fact, valid norms, and subjective experience). . . .

control threaten the very fabric of democracy. Yet, despite the incontestable importance of its technical aspects, informatization, like industrialization, is primarily a political and social challenge. When the relationship between information processing and democracy is understood, it becomes clear that the protection of privacy is the price necessary to secure the individual's ability to communicate and participate. Regulations that create precisely specified conditions for personal data processing are the decisive test for discerning whether society is aware of this price and willing to pay it. If the signs of experience are correct, this payment can be delayed no further. There is, in fact, no alternative to the advice of Horace: Seize the day, put not trust in the morrow. . . .

NOTES & QUESTIONS

1. *Privacy and Democracy.* As Simitis and other authors in this section observe, privacy is an issue about social structure. What is the relationship between privacy and democracy according to Simitis?

2. *Privacy Law and Information Flow.* Generally, one would assume that greater information flow facilitates democracy — it enables more expression, more political discourse, more information about the workings of government. Simitis, however, contends that privacy is "necessary to secure the individual's ability to communicate and participate." How are these two notions about information flow to be reconciled? Consider Joel Reidenberg:

> Data privacy rules are often cast as a balance between two basic liberties: fundamental human rights on one side and the free flow of information on the other side. Yet, because societies differ on how and when personal information should be available for private and public sector needs, the treatment and interaction of these liberties will express a specific delineation between the state, civil society, and the citizen.[27]

Privacy, according to Reidenberg, involves establishing a balance between protecting the rights of individuals and enabling information flow. Do you think these interests always exist in opposition? Consider financial services, communications networks, and medical care. Does privacy impair or enable information flow?[28]

---

[27] Joel R. Reidenberg, *Resolving Conflicting International Data Privacy Rules in Cyberspace,* 52 Stan. L. Rev. 1315 (2000).

[28] For additional reading about philosophical theories of privacy, see Judith W. DeCew, *In Pursuit of Privacy: Law, Ethics, and the Rise of Technology* (1997) (surveying and critiquing various theories of privacy); Anita L. Allen, *Uneasy Access: Privacy for Women in a Free Society* (1988) (same); Ferdinand David Schoeman, ed., *Philosophical Dimensions of Privacy* (1984) (anthology of articles about the concept of privacy).

C. CRITICS OF PRIVACY

RICHARD A. POSNER, *THE RIGHT OF PRIVACY*
12 Ga. L. Rev. 393 (1978)

People invariably possess information, including facts about themselves and contents of communications, that they will incur costs to conceal. Sometimes such information is of value to others: that is, others will incur costs to discover it. Thus we have two economic goods, "privacy" and "prying." . . .

[M]uch of the casual prying (a term used here without any pejorative connotation) into the private lives of friends and colleagues that is so common a feature of social life is also motivated, to a greater extent than we may realize, by rational considerations of self-interest. Prying enables one to form a more accurate picture of a friend or colleague, and the knowledge gained is useful in one's social or professional dealings with him. For example, in choosing a friend one legitimately wants to know whether he will be discreet or indiscreet, selfish or generous, and these qualities are not always apparent on initial acquaintance. Even a pure altruist needs to know the (approximate) wealth of any prospective beneficiary of his altruism in order to be able to gauge the value of a transfer to him.

The other side of the coin is that social, like business, dealings present opportunities for exploitation through misrepresentation. Psychologists and sociologists have pointed out that even in every day life people try to manipulate by misrepresentation other people's opinion of them. As one psychologist has written, the "wish for privacy expresses a desire . . . to control others' perceptions and beliefs vis-à-vis the self-concealing person." Even the strongest defenders of privacy describe the individual's right to privacy as the right to "control the flow of information about him." A seldom remarked corollary to a right to misrepresent one's character is that others have a legitimate interest in unmasking the deception.

Yet some of the demand for private information about other people is not self-protection in the foregoing sense but seems mysteriously disinterested — for example, that of the readers of newspaper gossip columns, whose "idle curiosity" Warren and Brandeis deplored, groundlessly in my opinion. Gossip columns recount the personal lives of wealthy and successful people whose tastes and habits offer models — that is, yield information — to the ordinary person in making consumption, career, and other decisions. . . . Gossip columns open people's eyes to opportunities and dangers; they are genuinely informational. . . .

Warren and Brandeis attributed the rise of curiosity about people's lives to the excesses of the press. The economist does not believe, however, that supply creates demand. A more persuasive explanation for the rise of the gossip column is the secular increase in personal incomes. There is apparently very little privacy in poor societies, where, consequently, people can easily observe at first hand the intimate lives of others. Personal surveillance is costlier in wealthier societies both because people live in conditions that give them greater privacy from such observation and because the value (and hence opportunity cost) of time is greater—too great to make a generous allotment of time to watching neighbors worthwhile. People in wealthier societies sought an alternative method of informing themselves about how others live and the press provided it. A legitimate and important function of the press is to provide specialization in prying in societies where the costs of obtaining information have become too great for the Nosey Parker. . . .

Transaction-cost considerations may also militate against the assignment of a property right to the possessor of a secret. . . . Consider, for example, . . . whether the law should allow a magazine to sell its subscriber list to another magazine without obtaining the subscribers' consent. . . . [T]he costs of obtaining subscriber approval would be high relative to the value of the list. If, therefore, we believe that these lists are generally worth more to the purchasers than being shielded from possible unwanted solicitations is worth to the subscribers, we should assign the property right to the magazine; and the law does this. . . .

Much of the demand for privacy . . . concerns discreditable information, often information concerning past or present criminal activity or moral conduct at variance with a person's professed moral standards. And often the motive for concealment is, as suggested earlier, to mislead those with whom he transacts. Other private information that people wish to conceal, while not strictly discreditable, would if revealed correct misapprehensions that the individual is trying to exploit, as when a worker conceals a serious health problem from his employer or a prospective husband conceals his sterility from his fiancée. It is not clear why society should assign the property right in such information to the individual to whom it pertains; and the common law, as we shall see, generally does not. . . .

We think it wrong (and inefficient) that the law should permit a seller in hawking his wares to make false or incomplete representations as to their quality. But people "sell" themselves as well as their goods. They profess high standards of behavior in order to induce others to engage in social or business dealings with them from which they derive an advantage but at the same time they conceal some of the facts that these acquaintances would find useful in forming an accurate picture of their character. There are practical reasons for not imposing a general legal duty of full and frank disclosure of one's material. . . .

. . . [E]veryone should be allowed to protect himself from disadvantageous transactions by ferreting out concealed facts about individuals which are material to the representations (implicit or explicit) that those individuals make concerning their moral qualities.

It is no answer that such individuals have "the right to be let alone." Very few people want to be let alone. They want to manipulate the world around them by selective disclosure of facts about themselves. Why should others be asked to take their self-serving claims at face value and be prevented from obtaining the information necessary to verify or disprove these claims?

NOTES & QUESTIONS

1. ***Posner's Conception of Privacy.*** What is Posner's definition of privacy? How does Posner determine the value of privacy (i.e., how it should be weighed relative to other interests and values)? In what circumstances is Posner likely to defend a privacy claim?

2. *Irrational Judgments.* One economic argument for privacy is that sometimes people form irrational judgments based upon learning certain information about others. For example, an employer may not hire certain people based on their political views or associations, sexual orientation, mental illness, and prior criminal convictions — even though these facts may have no relevance to a potential employee's abilities to do the job. These judgments decrease efficiency. In *The Economics of Justice*, Posner offers a response:

> This objection overlooks the opportunity costs of shunning people for stupid reasons, or, stated otherwise, the gains from dealing with someone whom others shun irrationally. If ex-convicts are good workers but most employers do not know this, employers who do know will be able to hire them at a below-average wage because of their depressed job opportunities and will thereby obtain a competitive advantage over the bigots. In a diverse, decentralized, and competitive society, irrational shunning will be weeded out over time. . . [29]

Will the market be able to eradicate irrational judgments?

3. *The Dangers of the "Masquerade Ball."* Consider Dennis Bailey:

> . . . [I]t is interesting to consider the ways in which the world has become like a giant masquerade ball. Far removed from the tight knit social fabric of the village of the past, we've lost the ability to recognize the people we pass on the street. People might as well be wearing masks because we are likely to know very little about them. In other words, these strangers are anonymous to us, anonymous in the sense that not only their names, but their entire identities, are unknown to us — the intimate details of who they are, where they have come from, and how they have lived their lives. [30]

Are we living in a "masquerade ball"? Businesses and the government have unprecedented new technologies to engage in surveillance and gather information. Should the law facilitate or restrict anonymity?

Also consider Steven Nock:

> Any method of social control depends, immediately, on information about individuals. . . . There can be no social control without such information. . . .
>
> Modern Americans enjoy vastly more privacy than did their forebears because ever and ever larger numbers of strangers in our lives are legitimately denied access to our personal affairs. . . . Privacy, however, makes it difficult to form reliable opinions of one another. Legitimately shielded from other's regular scrutiny, we are thereby more immune to the routine monitoring that once formed the basis of our individual reputations. [31]

Does too much privacy erode trust and lessen social control in detrimental ways?

---

[29] Richard A. Posner, *The Economics of Justice* (1981). Posner further develops his theories about privacy in Richard A. Posner, *Overcoming Law* 531-51 (1995). Posner first set out his views on privacy in Richard A. Posner, *An Economic Theory of Privacy*, Regulations (May/June 1978).

[30] Dennis Bailey, *The Open Society Paradox* 26-27 (2004).

[31] Steven L. Nock, *The Costs of Privacy: Surveillance and Reputation in America* (1993).

4. ***Information Dissemination and Economic Efficiency.*** Does economic theory necessarily lead to the conclusion that more personal information is generally preferable? Consider the following critique of Posner by Edward Bloustein:

> We must remember that Posner stated in *Economic Analysis of Law* that economics "cannot prescribe social change"; it can only tell us about the economic costs of managing it one way or another. . . . [Posner's] characterization of the privacy of personal information as a species of commercial fraud . . . [is an] extension[ ] of a social value judgment rather than implications or conclusions of economic theory. . . .Our society, in fact, places a very high value on maintaining individual privacy, even to the extent of concealing "discreditable" information. . . .[32]

Also consider Richard Murphy's critique of Posner:

> [D]emarcating a relatively large sphere for the private self creates an opportunity for discovery or actualization of a "true" nature, which may have a value beyond the utility of satisfying preferences. . . . As Roger Rosenblatt put it, "Out of our private gropings and self-inspections grow our imaginative values — private language, imagery, memory. In the caves of the mind one bats about to discover a light entirely of one's own which, though it should turn out to be dim, is still worth a life." Unless a person can investigate without risk of reproach what his own preferences are, he will not be able to maximize his own happiness.[33]

When can the circulation of less personal information be more economically efficient than greater information flow?

5. ***Why Don't Individuals Protect Their Privacy?*** Empirical studies frequently report on growing privacy concerns across the United States. Yet, individuals seem willing to exchange privacy for services or small rewards and generally fail to adopt technologies and techniques that would protect their privacy. If people are willing to sell their privacy for very little in return, isn't this evidence that they do not really value privacy as much as they say they do?

Alessandro Acqusiti and Jens Grossklags have pointed to a number of reasons for this divergence between stated privacy preferences and actual behavior:

> First, incomplete information affects privacy decision making because of externalities (when third parties share personal information about an individual, they might affect that individual without his being part of the transaction between those parties), information asymmetries (information relevant to the privacy decision process — for example, how personal information will be used — might be known only to a subset of the parties making decisions), risk (most privacy related payoffs are not deterministic), and uncertainties (payoffs might not only be stochastic, but dependent on unknown random distributions). Benefits and costs associated with privacy intrusions and protection are

---

[32] Edward J. Bloustein, *Privacy Is Dear at Any Price: A Response to Professor Posner's Economic Theory*, 12 Ga. L. Rev. 429, 441 (1978). For another critique of Posner's approach, see Kim Lane Scheppele, *Legal Secrets: Equality and Efficiency in the Common Law* (1988).

[33] Richard S. Murphy, *Property Rights in Personal Information: An Economic Defense of Privacy*, 84 Geo. L.J. 2381 (1996).

complex, multifaceted, and context-specific. They are frequently bundled with other products and services (for example, a search engine query can prompt the desired result but can also give observers information about the searcher's interests), and they are often recognized only after privacy violations have taken place. They can be monetary but also immaterial and, thus, difficult to quantify.

Second, even if individuals had access to complete information, they would be unable to process and act optimally on vast amounts of data. Especially in the presence of complex, ramified consequences associated with the protection or release of personal information, our innate bounded rationality limits our ability to acquire, memorize and process all relevant information, and it makes us rely on simplified mental models, approximate strategies, and heuristics. . . .

Third, even if individuals had access to complete information and could successfully calculate optimization strategies for their privacy sensitive decisions, they might still deviate from the rational strategy. A vast body of economic and psychological literature has revealed several forms of systematic psychological deviations from rationality that affect individual decision making. . . . Research in psychology . . . documents how individuals mispredict their own future preferences or draw inaccurate conclusions from past choices. In addition, individuals often suffer from self-control problems — in particular, the tendency to trade off costs and benefits in ways that damage their future utility in favor of immediate gratification. Individuals' behavior can also be guided by social preferences or norms, such as fairness or altruism. Many of these deviations apply naturally to privacy-sensitive scenarios.[34]

FRED H. CATE, *PRINCIPLES OF INTERNET PRIVACY*

32 Conn. L. Rev. 877 (2000)

Perhaps the most important consideration when balancing restrictions on information is the historical importance of the free flow of information. The free flow concept is one that is not only enshrined in the First Amendment, but frankly in any form of democratic or market economy. In the United States, we have placed extraordinary importance on the open flow of information. As the Federal Reserve Board noted in its report to Congress on data protection in financial institutions, "it is the freedom to speak, supported by the availability of information and the free-flow of data, that is the cornerstone of a democratic society and market economy."

The significance of open data flows is reflected in the constitutional provisions not only for freedom of expression, but for copyrights — to promote the creation and dissemination of expression, and for a post office — to deliver the mail and the news. Federal regulations demonstrate a sweeping preference for openness, reflected in the Freedom of Information Act, Government in the Sunshine Act, and dozens of other laws applicable to the government. There are even more laws requiring disclosure by private industry, such as the regulatory disclosures required by securities and commodities laws, banking and insurance laws, and many others. This is a very basic tenet of the society in which we live. Laws that restrict that free flow almost always conflict with this basic principle. That does not mean that

[34] Alessandro Acquisti & Jens Grossklags, *Privacy and Rationality in Decision Making*, IEEE, Security and Privacy 24 (2005).

such laws are never upheld, but merely that they face a considerable constitutional hurdle.

This is done with good reason. Open information flows are not only essential to self-governance; they have also generated significant, practical benefits. The ready availability of personal information helps businesses "deliver the right products and services to the right customers, at the right time, more effectively and at lower cost," Fred Smith, founder and President of the Competitive Enterprise Institute, has written. Federal Reserve Board Governor Edward Gramlich testified before Congress in July 1999 that "[i]nformation about individuals' needs and preferences is the cornerstone of any system that allocates goods and services within an economy." The more such information is available, he continued, "the more accurately and efficiently will the economy meet those needs and preferences."

Federal Reserve Board Chairman Alan Greenspan has been perhaps the most articulate spokesperson for the extraordinary value of accessible personal information. In 1998, he wrote to Congressman Ed Markey (D-Mass.):

> A critical component of our ever more finely hewn competitive market system has been the plethora of information on the characteristics of customers both businesses and individuals. Such information has enabled producers and marketers to fine tune production schedules to the ever greater demands of our consuming public for diversity and individuality of products and services. Newly devised derivative products, for example, have enabled financial institutions to unbundle risk in a manner that enables those desirous of taking on that risk (and potential reward) to do so, and those that chose otherwise, to be risk averse. It has enabled financial institutions to offer a wide variety of customized insurance and other products.
>
> Detailed data obtained from consumers as they seek credit or make product choices help engender the whole set of sensitive price signals that are so essential to the functioning of an advanced information based economy such as ours. . . .

In a recent report on public record information, Richard Varn, Chief Information Officer of the State of Iowa, and I examined the critical roles played by public record information in our economy and society. We concluded that such information constitutes part of this nation's "essential infrastructure," the benefits of which are "so numerous and diverse that they impact virtually every facet of American life. . . ." The ready availability of public record data "facilitates a vibrant economy, improves efficiency, reduces costs, creates jobs, and provides valuable products and services that people want."

Perhaps most importantly, widely accessible personal information has helped to create a democratization of opportunity in the United States. Anyone can go almost anywhere, make purchases from vendors they will never see, maintain accounts with banks they will never visit, and obtain credit far from home all because of open information flows. Americans can take advantage of opportunities based on their records, on what they have done rather than who they know, because access to consumer information makes it possible for distant companies and creditors to make rational decisions about doing business with individuals. The open flow of information gives consumers real choice. This is what the open flow of information principle reflects, not just the constitutional importance of information flows, but their significant economic and social benefits as well.

NOTES & QUESTIONS

1. ***The Pros and Cons of the Free Flow of Information.*** In a striking passage, Cate points out that free flows of information create a "democratization of opportunity in the United States." With this phrase, he reminds us that part of the equality at the basis of American life concerns economic opportunity, and that, in his view, a certain kind of flow of personal information will contribute to this goal. While privacy can be problematic, can open access to information also raise difficulties? How should one establish a baseline for open access or restricted access to personal information?

2. ***The Costs of Privacy.*** Can you think of some of the other important values with which privacy might conflict and the costs that privacy can impose? What should be the baseline in measuring costs?

3. ***The Business of Data Trade.*** The trade in personal information is now a valuable part of the U.S. economy. As a single example, Google reached an agreement on April 14, 2007, to purchase DoubleClick, an online advertising company, for $3.1 billion. The deal was driven by Google's interest in behavioral advertising, in which companies use digital data collection techniques to track individuals around the Internet and serve them targeted ads. Should consumers be allowed to sign up for a National Do Not Track List?

4. ***The Benefits of Information Collection and Use.*** Consider Kent Walker:

> Having some information about yourself out there in the world offers real convenience that goes beyond dollars and cents. Many people benefit from warehousing information — billing and shipping addresses, credit card numbers, individual preferences, and the like — with trustworthy third parties. Such storage of information can dramatically simplify the purchasing experience, ensure that you get a nonsmoking room, or automate the task of ordering a kiddie meal every time your child boards a plane. Likewise, most people prefer to use a credit card rather than a debit card, trading confidentiality of purchases for the convenience of deferred payment. . . .
>
> While there's often little individual incentive to participate in the aggregation of information about people, a great collective good results from the default participation of most people. The aggregation of information often requires a critical mass to be worth doing, or for the results to be worth using. (A phone book with only one out of ten numbers would hardly be worth using, let alone printing.) . . .
>
> Another example is Caller ID, which pits different privacy claims against one another. Many people like the notion of an electronic peephole, letting them know who's at the electronic door before they decide whether to pick up the phone. Yet many people block transmission of their own numbers, valuing protection of their privacy. Neither choice is necessarily right, but it's worth recognizing that the assertion of the privacy claim affects the contending desires of others. The classic Tragedy of the Commons aspects are clear. From my selfish perspective, I want access to information about everyone else — the identity of who's calling me, their listed phone number, etc. I want to be able to intrude on others without their knowing who I am (which I can accomplish by blocking Caller ID), and don't want others to be able to intrude on me unbidden

(which I can accomplish by unlisting my phone number). The gain in privacy makes it harder to find the people you want to reach, and harder to know who's calling you.[35]

D. THE FEMINIST PERSPECTIVE ON PRIVACY

Has the legal concept of privacy hurt or helped women throughout history? What is the impact of privacy on women today?

STATE V. RHODES

1868 WL 1278 (N.C. 1868)

[The defendant was indicted for an assault and battery upon his wife, Elizabeth Rhodes. The jury returned the following special verdict: "We find that the defendant struck Elizabeth Rhodes, his wife, three licks, with a switch about the size of one of his fingers (but not as large as a man's thumb) without any provocation except some words uttered by her and not recollected by the witness." The lower court found that the defendant "had a right to whip his wife with a switch no larger than his thumb, and that upon the facts found in the special verdict he was not guilty in law." Judgment in favor of the defendant was entered from which the State appealed.]

The laws of this State do not recognize *the right of the husband to whip his wife,* but our Courts will not interfere to punish him for moderate correction of her, even if there had been no provocation for it.

Family government being in its nature as complete in itself as the State government is in itself, the Courts will not attempt to control, or interfere with it, in favor of either party, except in cases where permanent or malicious injury is inflicted or threatened, or the condition of the party is intolerable.

In determining whether the husband has been guilty of an indictable assault and battery upon his wife, the criterion is the *effect produced,* and not the manner of producing it or the instrument used. . . .

READE J. The violence complained of would without question have constituted a battery if the subject of it had not been the defendant's wife. The question is how far that fact affects the case.

The courts have been loath to take cognizance of trivial complaints arising out of the domestic relations — such as master and apprentice, teacher and pupil, parent and child, husband and wife. Not because those relations are not subject to the law, but because the evil of publicity would be greater than the evil involved in the trifles complained of; and because they ought to be left to family government. . . .

In this case no provocation worth the name was proved. The fact found was that it was "without any provocation except some words which were not

---

[35] Kent Walker, *Where Everybody Knows Your Name: A Pragmatic Look at the Costs of Privacy and the Benefits of Information Exchange,* 2000 Stan. Tech. L. Rev. 2, 39, 46, 48 (2000).

recollected by the witness." The words must have been of the slightest import to have made no impression on the memory. We must therefore, consider the violence as unprovoked. The question is therefore plainly presented, whether the court will allow a conviction of the husband for moderate correction of the wife without provocation.

Our divorce laws do not compel a separation of husband and wife, unless the conduct of the husband be so cruel as to render the wife's condition intolerable, or her life burdensome. What sort of conduct on the part of the husband, would be allowed to have that effect, has been repeatedly considered. And it has not been found easy to lay down any iron rule upon the subject. In some cases it has been held that actual and repeated violence to the person, was not sufficient. In others that insults, indignities and neglect without any actual violence, were quite sufficient. So much does each case depend upon its peculiar surroundings.

We have sought the aid of the experience and wisdom of other times, and of other countries.

Blackstone says "that the husband, by the old law, might give the wife moderate correction, for as he was to answer for her misbehavior, he ought to have the power to control her; but that in the polite reign of Charles the Second, this power of correction began to be doubted." . . . The old law of moderate correction has been questioned even in England, and has been repudiated in Ireland and Scotland. The old rule is approved in Mississippi, but it has met with but little favor elsewhere in the United States. In looking into the discussions of the other States we find but little uniformity. . . .

Our conclusion is that family government is recognized by law as being as complete in itself as the State government is in itself, and yet subordinate to it; and that we will not interfere with or attempt to control it, in favor of either husband or wife, unless in cases where permanent or malicious injury is inflicted or threatened, or the condition of the party is intolerable. For, however great are the evils of ill temper, quarrels, and even personal conflicts inflicting only temporary pain, they are not comparable with the evils which would result from raising the curtain, and exposing to public curiosity and criticism, the nursery and the bed chamber. Every household has and must have, a government of its own, modeled to suit the temper, disposition and condition of its inmates. Mere ebullitions of passion, impulsive violence, and temporary pain, affection will soon forget and forgive; and each member will find excuse for the other in his own frailties. But when trifles are taken hold of by the public, and the parties are exposed and disgraced, and each endeavors to justify himself or herself by criminating the other, that which ought to be forgotten in a day, will be remembered for life.

It is urged in this case, that as there was no provocation the violence was of course excessive and malicious; that every one in whatever relation of life should be able to purchase immunity from pain, by obedience to authority and faithfulness in duty. . . . Take the case before us. The witness said, there was no provocation except some slight words. But then who can tell what significance the trifling words may have had to the husband? Who can tell what had happened an hour before, and every hour for a week? To him they may have been sharper than a sword. And so in every case, it might be impossible for the court to appreciate what might be offered as an excuse, or no excuse might appear at all, when a complete justification exists. Or, suppose the provocation could in every case be known, and the court should undertake to weigh the provocation in every trifling family broil, what would be the standard? Suppose a case coming up to us from a hovel, where neither delicacy of sentiment nor refinement of manners is appreciated or known. The parties themselves would be amazed, if they were to be held responsible for rudeness or trifling violence. What do they care for insults and indignities? In such cases what end would be gained by investigation or punishment? Take a case from the middle class, where modesty and purity have their abode but nevertheless have not immunity from the frailties of nature, and are sometimes moved by the mysteries of passion. What could be more harassing to them, or injurious to society, than to draw a crowd around their seclusion. Or take a case from the higher ranks, where education and culture have so refined nature, that a look cuts like a knife, and a word strikes like a hammer; where the most delicate attention gives pleasure, and the slightest neglect pain; where an indignity is disgrace and exposure is ruin. Bring all these cases into court side by side, with the same offence charged and the same proof made; and what conceivable charge of the court to the jury would be alike appropriate to all the cases, except, That they all have domestic government, which they have formed for themselves, suited to their own peculiar conditions, and that those governments are supreme, and from them there is no appeal except in cases of great importance requiring the strong arm of the law, and that to those governments they must submit themselves.

It will be observed that the ground upon which we have put this decision, is not, that the husband has the *right* to whip his wife much or little; but that we will not interfere with family government in trifling cases. We will no more interfere where the husband whips the wife, than where the wife whips the husband; and yet we would hardly be supposed to hold, that a wife has a *right* to whip her husband. We will not inflict upon society the greater evil of raising the curtain upon domestic privacy, to punish the lesser evil of trifling violence. Two boys under fourteen years of age fight upon the play-ground, and yet the courts will take no notice of it, not for the reason that boys have the *right* to fight, but because the interests of society require that they should be left to the more appropriate discipline of the school room and of home. . . . The standard is the *effect produced,* and not the manner of producing it, or the instrument used.

Because our opinion is not in unison with the decisions of some of the sister States, or with the philosophy of some very respectable law writers, and could not be in unison with all, because of their contrariety, — a decent respect for the opinions of others has induced us to be very full in stating the reasons for our conclusion.

REVA B. SIEGEL, *"THE RULE OF LOVE": WIFE BEATING AS PREROGATIVE AND PRIVACY*

105 Yale L.J. 2117 (1996)

. . . The Anglo-American common law originally provided that a husband, as master of his household, could subject his wife to corporal punishment or "chastisement" so long as he did not inflict permanent injury upon her. During the nineteenth century, an era of feminist agitation for reform of marriage law, authorities in England and the United States declared that a husband no longer had the right to chastise his wife. Yet, for a century after courts repudiated the right of chastisement, the American legal system continued to treat wife beating differently from other cases of assault and battery. While authorities denied that a husband had the right to beat his wife, they intervened only intermittently in cases of marital violence: Men who assaulted their wives were often granted formal and informal immunities from prosecution, in order to protect the privacy of the family and to promote "domestic harmony." In the late 1970s, the feminist movement began to challenge the concept of family privacy that shielded wife abuse, and since then, it has secured many reforms designed to protect women from marital violence. . .

Until the late nineteenth century, Anglo-American common law structured marriage to give a husband superiority over his wife in most aspects of the relationship. By law, a husband acquired rights to his wife's person, the value of her paid and unpaid labor, and most property she brought into the marriage. A wife was obliged to obey and serve her husband, and the husband was subject to a reciprocal duty to support his wife and represent her within the legal system. . . .

As master of the household, a husband could command his wife's obedience, and subject her to corporal punishment or "chastisement" if she defied his authority. In his treatise on the English common law, Blackstone explained that a husband could "give his wife moderate correction." . . .

During the 1850s, woman's rights advocates organized numerous conventions throughout the Northeast and Midwest, published newspapers, and conducted petition campaigns seeking for women the right to vote and demanding various reforms of marriage law. And in time the movement did elicit a response. Legislatures and courts began to modify the common law of marital status — first giving wives the right to hold property in marriage, and then the right to their earnings and the rudiments of legal agency: the right to file suit in their own names and to claim contract and tort damages. . . .

. . . By the 1880s, prominent members of the American Bar Association advocated punishing wife beaters at the whipping post, and campaigned vigorously for legislation authorizing the penalty. Between 1876 and 1906, twelve states and the District of Columbia considered enacting legislation that provided for the punishment of wife beaters at the whipping post. The bills were enacted in Maryland (1882), Delaware (1901), and Oregon (1906). . . .

We are left with a striking portrait of legal change. Jurists and lawmakers emphatically repudiated the doctrine of marital chastisement, yet responded to marital violence erratically — often condoning it, and condemning it in circumstances suggesting little interest in the plight of battered wives. Given this record, how are we to make sense of chastisement's demise? . . .

A key concept in the doctrinal regime that emerged from chastisement's demise was the notion of marital privacy. During the antebellum era, courts began to invoke marital privacy as a supplementary rationale for chastisement, in order to justify the common law doctrine within the discourse of companionate marriage, when rationales rooted in authority-based discourses of marriage had begun to lose their persuasive power. . . .

To quote a North Carolina chastisement opinion:

> We know that a slap on the cheek, let it be as light as it may, indeed any touching of the person of another in a rude or angry manner — is in law an assault and battery. In the nature of things it cannot apply to persons in the marriage state, it would break down the great principle of mutual confidence and dependence; throw open the bedroom to the gaze of the public; and spread discord and misery, contention and strife, where peace and concord ought to reign. It must be remembered that rules of law are intended to act in all classes of society. . . .

In *Rhodes*, the defendant whipped his wife "three licks, with a switch about the size of one of his fingers (but not as large as a man's thumb)"; the trial court ruled that a husband had the right to chastise his wife and so was not guilty of assault and battery. On appeal, the North Carolina Supreme Court upheld the verdict but justified it on different grounds. Opening its opinion with the blunt observation that "[t]he violence complained of would without question have constituted a battery if the subject of it had not been the defendant's wife," the court explained why it would not find the defendant guilty:

> The courts have been loath to take cognizance of trivial complaints arising out of the domestic relations — such as master and apprentice, teacher and pupil, parent and child, husband and wife. Not because those relations are not subject to law, but because the evil of publicity would be greater than the evil involved in the trifles complained of; and because they ought to be left to family government. . .

. . . By now it should be clear enough how privacy talk was deployed in the domestic violence context to enforce and preserve authority relations between man and wife. . . .

. . . By the early twentieth century, numerous state supreme courts had barred wives from suing their husbands for intentional torts — typically on the grounds that "the tranquility of family relations" would be "disturb[ed]." . . .

It was not until the late 1970s that the contemporary women's rights movement mounted an effective challenge to this regime. Today, after numerous protest activities and law suits, there are shelters for battered women and their children, new arrest procedures for police departments across the country, and even federal legislation making gender-motivated assaults a civil rights violation. . . .

There is remarkably little scholarship on the social history of privacy discourses; consequently, we know very little about the ways in which conceptions of privacy shaped popular understandings of marriage, or marital violence, in the nineteenth century. But there is no reason to assume that, before demise of the chastisement prerogative, married persons understood a traditional prerogative of marriage, rooted in notions of a husband's authority as master and head of his household, in a framework of "privacy" and "domestic harmony." It seems just as likely that legal elites devised the story linking "privacy" and "domestic harmony" to wife beating in the wake of chastisement's demise (or in anticipation of it). . . .

CATHARINE A. MACKINNON, *TOWARD A FEMINIST THEORY OF THE STATE*

(1989)

The liberal ideal of the private holds that, as long as the public does not interfere, autonomous individuals interact freely and equally. Privacy is the ultimate value of the negative state. Conceptually, this private is hermetic. It means that which is inaccessible to, unaccountable to, unconstructed by, anything beyond itself. By definition, it is not part of or conditioned by anything systematic outside it. It is personal, intimate, autonomous, particular, individual, the original source and final outpost of the self, gender neutral. It is defined by everything that feminism reveals women have never been allowed to be or to have, and by everything that women have been equated with and defined in terms of men's ability to have. To complain in public of inequality within the private contradicts the liberal definition of the private. . . . Its inviolability by the state, framed as an individual right, presupposes that the private is not already an arm of the state. In this scheme, intimacy is implicitly thought to guarantee symmetry of power. Injuries arise through violation of the private sphere, not within and by and because of it.

In private, consent tends to be presumed. Showing coercion is supposed to avoid this presumption. But the problem is getting anything private to be perceived as coercive. This is an epistemic problem of major dimensions and explains why privacy doctrine is most at home at home, the place women experience the most force, in the family, and why it centers on sex. Why a person would "allow" force in private (the "why doesn't she leave" question raised to battered women) is a question given its insult by the social meaning of the private as a sphere of choice. For women the measure of the intimacy has been the measure of oppression. This is why feminism has seen the personal as the political. The private is public for those for whom the personal is political. In this sense, for women there is no private, either normatively or empirically. Feminism confronts the fact that women have no privacy to lose or to guarantee. Women are not inviolable. Women's sexuality is not only violable, it is — hence, women are — seen in and as their violation. To confront the fact that women have no privacy is to confront the intimate degradation of women as the public order. . . .

When the law of privacy restricts intrusions into intimacy, it bars changes in control over that intimacy through law. The existing distribution of power and resources within the private sphere are precisely what the law of privacy exists to protect. . . . [T]he legal concept of privacy can and has shielded the place of battery, marital rape, and women's exploited domestic labor. It has preserved the central institutions whereby women are deprived of identity, autonomy, control, and self-definition. It has protected a primary activity through which male supremacy is expressed and enforced. . . .

This right to privacy is a right of men "to be let alone" to oppress women one at a time. . . .

ANITA L. ALLEN, *UNEASY ACCESS: PRIVACY FOR WOMEN IN A FREE SOCIETY*
(1988)

Critiques of privacy such as MacKinnon's go wrong at the point where the historic unequal treatment of women and the misuse of the private household to further women's domination is taken as grounds for rejecting either the condition of privacy itself or the long-overdue legal rights to effective decision-making that promote and protect that condition. Privacy, here broadly defined as the inaccessibility of persons, their mental states, or information about them to the senses and surveillance devices of others . . . does not pose an inherent threat to women. Nor do sex, love, marriage, and children any longer presume the total abrogation of the forms of privacy a woman might otherwise enjoy. On the contrary, women today are finally in a position to expect, experience, and exploit real privacy within the home and within heterosexual relationships. The women's movement, education, access to affordable birth control, liberalized divorce laws, and the larger role for women in politics, government, and the economy have expanded women's opinions and contributed to the erosion of oppressively nonegalitarian styles of home life. These advances have enhanced the capacity of American men and women, but especially and for the first time women, to secure conditions of adequate and meaningful privacy at home paramount to moral personhood and responsible participation in families and larger segments of society. Instead of rejecting privacy as "male ideology" and subjugation, women can and ought to embrace opportunities for privacy and the exercise of reproductive liberty in their private lives.

NOTES & QUESTIONS

1. *Privacy and Gender.* As the *Rhodes* court stated in 1868: "We will not interfere with family government in trifling cases. We will no more interfere where the husband whips the wife, than where the wife whips the husband; and yet we would hardly be supposed to hold, that a wife has a *right* to whip her husband." Is this decision really a neutral one? Does the right to privacy described by Warren and Brandeis apply equally to men and women?[36]

2. *The Uses of the Public/Private Distinction.* Reva Siegel points out the troubling use of privacy to protect the oppression of women in the home, which Catharine MacKinnon has discussed at length elsewhere. Is MacKinnon's negative response to the public/private distinction justifiable given the prior uses of this distinction? Or do you agree with Anita Allen that privacy should not be abandoned as a value despite its checkered past?[37]

---

[36] For a feminist critique of the Warren and Brandeis article, see Anita L. Allen & Erin Mack, *How Privacy Got Its Gender*, 10 N. Ill. U. L. Rev. 441 (1990).

[37] For an overview of the feminist critique of privacy, see generally Judith W. DeCew, *In Pursuit of Privacy: Law, Ethics, and the Rise of Technology* 81-94 (1997); Patricia Boling, *Privacy and the Politics of Intimate Life* (1996); Frances Olsen, *Constitutional Law: Feminist Critiques of the Public/Private Distinction*, 10 Const. Commentary 327 (1993); Ruth Gavison, *Feminism and the Public/Private Distinction*, 45 Stan. L. Rev. 21 (1992).

3. ***To What Extent Can Law Change Social Practices?*** According to Frances Olsen, "The notion of noninterference in the family depends upon some shared conception of proper family roles, and 'neutrality' [of the State] can be understood only with reference to such roles."[38] This idea suggests that privacy, within or without the family, might also depend on shared views as to proper social roles. Do you agree?

Olsen also notes: "The theory of the private family, like free market theory, includes the assertion that particularized adjustments of seemingly unfair or inhumane results will not actually serve anybody's long run interests." Specifically, "it is claimed that state intervention to protect the weaker family members from abuse by the stronger is ineffective because powerful, underlying 'real' relations between family members will inevitably reassert themselves." This argument, which one might term the argument from futility, was rejected in the course of the twentieth century by the powerful social movement to stop spousal abuse and mistreatment of children. Are similar arguments from futility being made today about the "inevitable" erosion of privacy?

---

[38] Frances Olsen, *The Family and the Market: A Study of Ideology and Legal Reform*, 96 Harv. L. Rev. 1497, 1506 (1983).

CHAPTER 3

PRIVACY AND THE MEDIA

CHAPTER OUTLINE

4. Connection to Matters of Public Interest

5. First Amendment Limitations

E. PRIVACY PROTECTIONS FOR ANONYMITY AND RECEIPT OF IDEAS

1. Anonymity

(a) Anonymous Speech

(b) Reporter's Privilege

2. Privacy of Reading and Intellectual Exploration

In 1890, Samuel Warren and Louis Brandeis wrote about the increasing proliferation of gossip in newspapers.[1] Today, the problems Warren and Brandeis were concerned about are dramatically magnified by the vast expansion of the media. In addition to newspapers, there are magazines, movies, television, and the Internet. From marketers to moviemakers, from tabloids to 24-hour news channels, from talk shows to reality TV, we are witnessing an explosion in the demand for images, video, and stories about the personal lives of individuals, both famous and obscure. Further, anybody with a website can now disseminate information instantly around the world.

Warren and Brandeis were also concerned with photography, a new technology that had the potential to greatly facilitate information gathering by the media. Today, technologies of gathering data are significantly more sophisticated. Video cameras are in widespread use and exist in miniature forms for easy concealment; high-powered telephoto lenses can enable one to film or photograph from large distances. Moreover, almost every cell phone now contains a small built-in camera.

This chapter focuses on legal remedies for the gathering and dissemination of personal information by media entities. "Media" is understood broadly in this chapter to include people and businesses that gather and disseminate information to inform, advertise, or entertain. The chapter then explores four general types of privacy incursion by the media: (1) intrusions and harassment in the course of gathering information; (2) the disclosure of truthful information, (3) the dissemination of misleading or false information; and (4) the appropriation of name or likeness. The principal remedies for media incursions into privacy are the four privacy torts inspired by Warren and Brandeis's article. The privacy torts are not the only remedies for privacy invasions. The tort of defamation, discussed at length in this chapter, is an older remedy for a particular type of privacy intrusion — the dissemination of false information. Another remedy is the tort of infliction of emotional distress, which is discussed briefly in section C. Additionally, a number of states have enacted statutes that protect against particular forms of disclosure.

---

[1] Samuel D. Warren & Louis D. Brandeis, *The Right to Privacy,* 4 Harv. L. Rev. 193 (1890).

A. INFORMATION GATHERING

In order to report the news, journalists must gather information. This task often involves being nosy, inquisitive, and aggressive. Given the vast proliferation of media and the tremendous competition to get breaking information and live video or photographs, there is great potential for media information gathering to become intrusive and harassing, especially when a person becomes the subject of a prominent story. In response to such intrusions by information gatherers, an injured party has available a number of remedies. The primary remedy is the tort of intrusion upon seclusion. Some states, such as California, have passed statutes providing remedies from aggressive photographers, known as "paparazzi." These two types of remedies will be the focus of this section. Other remedies include trespass (if the newsgatherer wrongfully entered one's home or property) and fraud (if the newsgatherer lied or used deceitful methods to obtain information). Additionally, the electronic surveillance laws of many states provide remedies when one records the conversations of others without their consent. In a number of states, consent is required from all participants to a conversation. In some states and under federal electronic surveillance law, consent is only required from one of the parties. As a consequence of such one-party consent statutes, a journalist can secretly record a conversation in which she participates.

1. INTRUSION UPON SECLUSION

INTRUSION UPON SECLUSION

Restatement (Second) of Torts § 652B

One who intentionally intrudes, physically or otherwise, upon the solitude or seclusion of another or his private affairs or concerns, is subject to liability to the other for invasion of his privacy, if the intrusion would be highly offensive to a reasonable person.

NOTES & QUESTIONS

1. *Intrusion upon Seclusion vs. Public Disclosure of Private Facts.* The tort of intrusion concerns the way that the information is obtained. In contrast, for the tort of public disclosure of private facts, liability does not depend upon how the information is obtained. Consider the following commentary to the Restatement:

> Comment (a): Intrusion "does not depend upon any publicity given to the person whose interest is invaded or to his affairs."
> Comment (b): "The intrusion itself makes the defendant subject to liability, even though there is no publication or other use of any kind of the photograph or information outlined."

NADER V. GENERAL MOTORS CORP.

255 N.E.2d 765 (N.Y. Ct. App. 1970)

FULD, C.J. . . . The plaintiff [Ralph Nader], an author and lecturer on automotive safety, has, for some years, been an articulate and severe critic of General Motors' products from the standpoint of safety and design. According to the complaint — which, for present purposes, we must assume to be true — the appellant [General Motors Corporation], having learned of the imminent publication of the plaintiff's book "Unsafe at Any Speed," decided to conduct a campaign of intimidation against him in order to "suppress plaintiff's criticism of and prevent his disclosure of information" about its products. To that end, the appellant authorized and directed the other defendants to engage in a series of activities which, the plaintiff claims in his first two causes of action, violated his right to privacy.

Specifically, the plaintiff alleges that the appellant's agents (1) conducted a series of interviews with acquaintances of the plaintiff, "questioning them about, and casting aspersions upon (his) political . . . racial and religious views. . . ; his integrity; his sexual proclivities and inclinations; and his personal habits"; (2) kept him under surveillance in public places for an unreasonable length of time; (3) caused him to be accosted by girls for the purpose of entrapping him into illicit relationships; (4) made threatening, harassing and obnoxious telephone calls to him; (5) tapped his telephone and eavesdropped, by means of mechanical and electronic equipment, on his private conversations with others; and (6) conducted a "continuing" and harassing investigation of him. [Nader's complaint, among other things, contained a cause of action for intrusion.]

. . . It should be emphasized that the mere gathering of information about a particular individual does not give rise to a cause of action under [the intrusion tort]. Privacy is invaded only if the information sought is of a confidential nature and the defendant's conduct was unreasonably intrusive. Just as a common-law copyright is lost when material is published, so, too, there can be no invasion of privacy where the information sought is open to public view or has been voluntarily revealed to others. In order to sustain a cause of action for invasion of privacy, therefore, the plaintiff must show that the appellant's conduct was truly "intrusive" and that it was designed to elicit information which would not be available through normal inquiry or observation. . . .

. . . At most, only two of the activities charged to the appellant are, in our view, actionable as invasions of privacy under the law of the District of Columbia. . . .

Turning, then, to the particular acts charged in the complaint, we cannot find any basis for a claim of invasion of privacy, under District of Columbia law, in the allegations that the appellant, through its agents or employees, interviewed many persons who knew the plaintiff, asking questions about him and casting aspersions on his character. Although those inquiries may have uncovered information of a personal nature, it is difficult to see how they may be said to have invaded the plaintiff's privacy. Information about the plaintiff which was already known to others could hardly be regarded as private to the plaintiff. Presumably, the plaintiff had previously revealed the information to such other persons, and he would necessarily assume the risk that a friend or acquaintance in whom he had confided might breach the confidence. If, as alleged, the questions tended to disparage the plaintiff's character, his remedy would seem to be by way of an action for defamation, not for breach of his right to privacy.

Nor can we find any actionable invasion of privacy in the allegations that the appellant caused the plaintiff to be accosted by girls with illicit proposals, or that it was responsible for the making of a large number of threatening and harassing telephone calls to the plaintiff's home at odd hours. Neither of these activities, howsoever offensive and disturbing, involved intrusion for the purpose of gathering information of a private and confidential nature. . . .

Apart, however, from the foregoing allegations which we find inadequate to spell out a cause of action for invasion of privacy under District of Columbia law, the complaint contains allegations concerning other activities by the appellant or its agents which do satisfy the requirements for such a cause of action. The one which most clearly meets those requirements is the charge that the appellant and its codefendants engaged in unauthorized wiretapping and eavesdropping by mechanical and electronic means. . . .

There are additional allegations that the appellant hired people to shadow the plaintiff and keep him under surveillance. In particular, he claims that, on one occasion, one of its agents followed him into a bank, getting sufficiently close to him to see the denomination of the bills he was withdrawing from his account. From what we have already said, it is manifest that the mere observation of the plaintiff in a public place does not amount to an invasion of his privacy. But, under certain circumstances, surveillance may be so "overzealous" as to render it actionable. Whether or not the surveillance in the present case falls into this latter category will depend on the nature of the proof. A person does not automatically make public everything he does merely by being in a public place, and the mere fact that Nader was in a bank did not give anyone the right to try to discover the amount of money he was withdrawing. On the other hand, if the plaintiff acted in such a way as to reveal that fact to any casual observer, then, it may not be said that the appellant intruded into his private sphere. In any event, though, it is enough for present purposes to say that the surveillance allegation is not insufficient as a matter of law. . . .

BRIETEL, J. concurring in the result. . . . [S]cholars, in trying to define the elusive concept of the right of privacy, have, as of the present, subdivided the common law right into separate classifications, most significantly distinguishing between unreasonable intrusion and unreasonable publicity. This does not mean, however, that the classifications are either frozen or exhausted, or that several of the classifications may not overlap.

Concretely applied to this case, it is suggested, for example, that it is premature to hold that the attempted entrapment of plaintiff in a public place by seemingly promiscuous ladies is no invasion of any of the categories of the right to privacy and is restricted to a much more limited cause of action for intentional infliction of mental distress. Moreover, it does not strain credulity or imagination to conceive of the systematic "public" surveillance of another as being the implementation of a plan to intrude on the privacy of another. Although acts performed in "public," especially if taken singly or in small numbers, may not be confidential, at least arguably a right to privacy may nevertheless be invaded through extensive or exhaustive monitoring and cataloguing of acts normally disconnected and anonymous.

These are but illustrations of the problems raised in attempting to determine issues of relevancy and allocability of evidence in advance of a trial record. The other allegations so treated involve harassing telephone calls, and investigatory interviews. It is just as important that while allegations treated singly may not constitute a cause of action, they may do so in combination, or serve to enhance other violations of the right to privacy.

It is not unimportant that plaintiff contends that a giant corporation had allegedly sought by surreptitious and unusual methods to silence an unusually effective critic. If there was such a plan, and only a trial would show that, it is unduly restrictive of the future trial to allocate the evidence beforehand based only on a pleader's specification of overt acts on the bold assumption that they are not connected causally or do not bear on intent and motive.

It should be observed, too, that the right to privacy, even as thus far developed, does not always refer to that which is not known to the public or is confidential. Indeed, the statutory right of privacy in this State and perhaps the most traditional right of privacy in the "common law sense" relates to the commercialized publicity of one's face or name, perhaps the two most public aspects of an individual. . . .

Accordingly, because of the prematurity of ruling on any other question but the sufficiency of the causes of action, I concur in result only.

NOTES & QUESTIONS

1. *Postscript.* General Motors eventually settled the case with Nader for $425,000. It also made a public apology to Nader.[2]

2. *Intrusion Liability Only for Confidential Information?* The *Nader* court finds that mere information gathering is not actionable under the intrusion tort. It states: "Privacy is invaded only if the information sought is of a confidential nature and the defendant's conduct was unreasonably intrusive." Hence, GM's interviewing of Nader's acquaintances, harassing phone calls, and use of "girls with illicit proposals" did not constitute an intrusion on his privacy. Note, however, the text of Restatement (Second) Torts, § 652B. Does this text require the court's holding in this regard? Is the text consistent with this holding?

3. *Surveillance in Public Places.* The Restatement of Torts adopts a similar approach to the majority in *Nader*:

> The defendant is subject to liability under the rule stated in this Section only when he has intruded into a private place, or has otherwise invaded a private seclusion that the plaintiff has thrown about his person or affairs. Thus there is no liability for the examination of a public record concerning the plaintiff, or of documents that the plaintiff is required to keep and make available for public inspection. Nor is there liability for observing him or even taking his photograph while he is walking on the public highway, since he is not then in seclusion, and his appearance is public and open to the public eye. Even in a public place, however, there may be some matters about the plaintiff, such as

---

[2] For more background about case, see Stuart M. Speiser, *Lawsuit* (1980).

his underwear or lack of it, that are not exhibited to the public gaze; and there may still be invasion of privacy when there is intrusion upon these matters. Restatement (Second) of Torts § 652B comment (c).

Judge Breitel's concurrence goes even further than the majority: "Although acts performed in 'public,' especially if taken singly or in small numbers, may not be confidential, at least arguably a right to privacy may nevertheless be invaded through extensive or exhaustive monitoring and cataloguing of acts normally disconnected and anonymous." How does Breitel's approach differ from the majority's approach and that of the Restatement?

Also consider *Summers v. Bailey*, 55 F.3d 1564 (11th Cir. 1995), where the court held:

> Traditionally, watching or observing a person in a public place is not an intrusion upon one's privacy. However, Georgia courts have held that surveillance of an individual on public thoroughfares, where such surveillance aims to frighten or torment a person, is an unreasonable intrusion upon a person's privacy.

4. ***Harassing Phone Calls.*** *Nader* holds that there is no actionable invasion of privacy caused by a "large number of threatening and harassing telephone calls . . . at odd hours." The Restatement of Torts (Second) takes a different view. It first concedes that "there is no liability for knocking at the plaintiff's door, or calling him to the telephone on one occasion or even two or three, to demand payment of a debt." But the Restatement then states: "It is only when the telephone calls are repeated with such persistence and frequency as to amount to a course of hounding the plaintiff, that becomes a substantial burden to his existence, that his privacy is invaded." Restatement (Second) of Torts § 652B comment (d).

Courts have also found that harassing a person by telephone can support a tort privacy claim. In *Donnel v. Lara*, 703 S.W.2d 257 (Tex. App. 1985), the court held that excessive telephone harassment "by placing repeated phone calls to [a person's] residence at unreasonable hours" can be actionable. In *Harms v. Miami Daily News, Inc.,* 127 So. 2d 715 (Fla. App. 1961), the defendant published in the newspaper the following statement: "Wanna hear a sexy telephone voice? Call [number] and ask for Louise." As a result, the plaintiff was "flooded with hundreds of telephone calls by various and sundry persons." The court concluded that the plaintiff had an actionable claim against the defendant, and that there was sufficient evidence for the jury to decide whether it was highly offensive.

5. ***Wiretapping and Electronic Surveillance.*** In *Hamberger v. Eastman*, 206 A.2d 239 (N.H. 1964), a husband and wife brought an intrusion action against their landlord for installing a secret recording device in their bedroom. The device had wires going into the landlord's residence. The court sided with the plaintiffs:

> The defendant contends that the right of privacy should not be recognized on the facts of the present case as they appear in the pleadings because there are no allegations that anyone listened or overheard any sounds or voices originating from the plaintiffs' bedroom. The tort of intrusion on the plaintiffs' solitude or

seclusion does not require publicity and communication to third persons although this would affect the amount of damages, as Prosser makes clear. The defendant also contends that the right of privacy is not violated unless something has been published, written or printed and that oral publicity is not sufficient. Recent cases make it clear that this is not a requirement.

If the peeping Tom, the big ear and the electronic eavesdropper (whether ingenious or ingenuous) have a place in the hierarchy of social values, it ought not to be at the expense of a married couple minding their own business in the seclusion of their bedroom who have never asked for or by their conduct deserved a potential projection of their private conversations and actions to their landlord or to others. Whether actual or potential such "publicity with respect to private matters of purely personal concern is an injury to personality. It impairs the mental peace and comfort of the individual and may produce suffering more acute than that produced by a mere bodily injury." III Pound, Jurisprudence 58 (1959). The use of parabolic microphones and sonic wave devices designed to pick up conversations in a room without entering it and at a considerable distance away makes the problem far from fanciful.

6. ***The Highly Offensive Requirement.*** What intrusions are "highly offensive to a reasonable person" as required by the tort? Courts have held that trespasses into places where people have reasonable expectations of privacy are actionable, as are unjustified searches. *See, e.g., Gerard v. Parish of Jefferson*, 424 So. 2d 440 (La. App. 1982) (dog catcher entered plaintiff's property without authorization); *K-Mart Corp. v. Trotti*, 677 S.W.2d 632 (Tex. App. 1984) (unauthorized search of employee's personal locker). In *Klebanoff v. McMongale*, 552 A.2d 677 (Pa. Super. 1988), about 20 to 30 pro-life demonstrators picketed noisily on the public street directly outside of an abortion doctor's home. This had a "devastating effect . . . on the [doctor and his family's] quiet enjoyment of their home," and the family was "figuratively, and perhaps literally, trapped within the home, and held captive." The court held that the protestors could be enjoined.

As illustrated by *Hamberger* and *Nader,* non-physical activities such as wiretapping and overzealous surveillance can amount to highly offensive intrusions. Peering into a person's home windows can be actionable according to the court in *Pinkerton Nat'l Detective Agency, Inc. v. Stevens*, 132 S.E.2d 119 (Ga. App. 1963). In *Pulla v. Amoco Oil Co.*, 882 F. Supp. 836 (S.D. Iowa 1994), the court held that it was actionable when the defendant illegally accessed the plaintiff's credit card records to determine if he abused his sick leave at work.

DIETEMANN V. TIME, INC.

449 F.2d 245 (9th Cir. 1971)

HUFSTEDLER, C.J. . . . Plaintiff, a disabled veteran with little education, was engaged in the practice of healing with clay, minerals, and herbs — as practiced, simple quackery.

Defendant, Time, Incorporated, a New York corporation, publishes Life Magazine. Its November 1, 1963 edition carried an article entitled "Crackdown on Quackery." The article depicted plaintiff as a quack and included two pictures of him. One picture was taken at plaintiff's home on September 20, 1963, previous to his arrest on a charge of practicing medicine without a license, and the other taken at the time of his arrest.

Life Magazine entered into an arrangement with the District Attorney's Office of Los Angeles County whereby Life's employees would visit plaintiff and obtain facts and pictures concerning his activities. Two employees of Life, Mrs. Jackie Metcalf and Mr. William Ray, went to plaintiff's home on September 20, 1963. When they arrived at a locked gate, they rang a bell and plaintiff came out of his house and was told by Mrs. Metcalf and Ray that they had been sent there by a friend, a Mr. Johnson. The use of Johnson's name was a ruse to gain entrance. Plaintiff admitted them and all three went into the house and into plaintiff's den.

The plaintiff had some equipment which could at best be described as gadgets, not equipment which had anything to do with the practice of medicine. Plaintiff, while examining Mrs. Metcalf, was photographed by Ray with a hidden camera without the consent of plaintiff. One of the pictures taken by him appeared in Life Magazine showing plaintiff with his hand on the upper portion of Mrs. Metcalf's breast while he was looking at some gadgets and holding what appeared to be a wand in his right hand. Mrs. Metcalf had told plaintiff that she had a lump in her breast. Plaintiff concluded that she had eaten some rancid butter 11 years, 9 months, and 7 days prior to that time. Other persons were seated in the room during this time.

The conversation between Mrs. Metcalf and plaintiff was transmitted by radio transmitter hidden in Mrs. Metcalf's purse to a tape recorder in a parked automobile occupied by Joseph Bride, Life employee, John Miner of the District Attorney's Office, and Grant Leake, an investigator of the State Department of Public Health. While the recorded conversation was not quoted in the article in Life, it was mentioned that Life correspondent Bride was making notes of what was being received via the radio transmitter, and such information was at least referred to in the article.

The foregoing events were photographed and recorded by an arrangement among Miner of the District Attorney's Office, Leake of the State Department of Public Health, and Bride, a representative of Life. It had been agreed that Life would obtain pictures and information for use as evidence, and later could be used by Life for publication. . . .

Plaintiff, although a journeyman plumber, claims to be a scientist. Plaintiff had no listings and his home had no sign of any kind. He did not advertise, nor did he have a telephone. He made no charges when he attempted to diagnose or to prescribe herbs and minerals. He did accept contributions.

[The plaintiff was arrested at his home on a charge of practicing medicine without a license. After the plaintiff entered a plea of nolo contendere to the charges, *Life*'s article was published. The plaintiff sued *Life* in federal district court. The district court concluded that the defendant had invaded the plaintiff's privacy and awarded $1,000 in damages.]

. . . In jurisdictions other than California in which a common law tort for invasion of privacy is recognized, it has been consistently held that surreptitious electronic recording of a plaintiff's conversation causing him emotional distress is actionable. Despite some variations in the description and the labels applied to the tort, there is agreement that publication is not a necessary element of the tort, that the existence of a technical trespass is immaterial, and that proof of special damages is not required. . . .[3]

. . . [W]e have little difficulty in concluding that clandestine photography of the plaintiff in his den and the recordation and transmission of his conversation without his consent resulting in his emotional distress warrants recovery for invasion of privacy in California. . . .

Plaintiff's den was a sphere from which he could reasonably expect to exclude eavesdropping newsmen. He invited two of defendant's employees to the den. One who invites another to his home or office takes a risk that the visitor may not be what he seems, and that the visitor may repeat all he hears and observes when he leaves. But he does not and should not be required to take the risk that what is heard and seen will be transmitted by photograph or recording, or in our modern world, in full living color and hi-fi to the public at large or to any segment of it that the visitor may select. A different rule could have a most pernicious effect upon the dignity of man and it would surely lead to guarded conversations and conduct where candor is most valued, e.g., in the case of doctors and lawyers.

The defendant claims that the First Amendment immunizes it from liability for invading plaintiff's den with a hidden camera and its concealed electronic instruments because its employees were gathering news and its instrumentalities "are indispensable tools of investigative reporting." We agree that newsgathering is an integral part of news dissemination. We strongly disagree, however, that the hidden mechanical contrivances are "indispensable tools" of newsgathering. Investigative reporting is an ancient art; its successful practice long antecedes the invention of miniature cameras and electronic devices. The First Amendment has never been construed to accord newsmen immunity from torts or crimes committed during the course of newsgathering. The First Amendment is not a license to trespass, to steal, or to intrude by electronic means into the precincts of another's home or office. It does not become such a license simply because the person subjected to the intrusion is reasonably suspected of committing a crime.

Defendant relies upon the line of cases commencing with *New York Times Co. v. Sullivan* and extending through *Rosenbloom v. Metromedia, Inc.* to sustain its contentions that (1) publication of news, however tortiously gathered, insulates defendant from liability for the antecedent tort, and (2) even if it is not thus shielded

---

[3] Editors' Note: Special damages, or "consequential" damages, are damages that follow from the initial harm. They include lost profits and other diminishments of the plaintiff's income, such as increased expenses.

from liability, those cases prevent consideration of publication as an element in computing damages. . . .

No interest protected by the First Amendment is adversely affected by permitting damages for intrusion to be enhanced by the fact of later publication of the information that the publisher improperly acquired. Assessing damages for the additional emotional distress suffered by a plaintiff when the wrongfully acquired data are purveyed to the multitude chills intrusive acts. It does not chill freedom of expression guaranteed by the First Amendment. A rule forbidding the use of publication as an ingredient of damages would deny to the injured plaintiff recovery for real harm done to him without any countervailing benefit to the legitimate interest of the public in being informed. The same rule would encourage conduct by news media that grossly offends ordinary men. . . .

DESNICK V. AMERICAN BROADCASTING CO., INC.

44 F.3d 1345 (7th Cir. 1995)

[Dr. Desnick owned an ophthalmic clinic known as the Desnick Eye Center. The Eye Center had 25 offices in four states and performed over 10,000 cataract operations each year, mainly on elderly persons under Medicare. In 1993, Entine, the producer of ABC's news program *Primetime Live*, telephoned Dr. Desnick and told him that the show wanted to do a segment on cataract practices. Entine told Desnick that the segment would be "fair and balanced" and that it would not include undercover surveillance. Desnick permitted an ABC crew to videotape the Eye Center's Chicago office, to film a cataract operation, and to interview doctors and patients. However, unknown to Desnick, Entine sent seven people with concealed cameras to the Eye Center's Wisconsin and Indiana offices. These seven people posed as patients and requested eye operations. Glazer and Simon are among the employees who were secretly videotaped examining these "test patients."

When the program aired, it was introduced by Sam Donaldson, who began by stating: "We begin tonight with the story of a so-called 'big cutter,' Dr. James Desnick. . . . [I]n our undercover investigation of the big cutter you'll meet tonight, we turned up evidence that he may also be a big charger, doing unnecessary cataract surgery for the money." As part of the segment, brief interviews with four patients of the Desnick Eye Center were shown. While one of the patients was satisfied ("I was blessed"), the other three were not. Indeed, one of them commented, "If you got three eyes, he'll get three eyes." Donaldson then reported on the experiences of the seven test patients. The two who were under 65 and therefore ineligible for Medicare reimbursement were found by the clinic not to need cataract surgery. The Desnick eye clinic told four of the other five that they did need this operation.

Donaldson told the viewer that *Primetime Live* hired a professor of ophthalmology to examine the test patients who had been told they needed cataract surgery. The professor not only said that these patients did not need it, but with regard to one, he stated, "I think it would be near malpractice to do surgery on him." Later in the segment he denies that this could just be an honest difference of opinion between professionals. The show also mentioned that the Illinois Medical

Board had charged Dr. Desnick with malpractice and deception. Additionally, the show contained an "ambush interview" of Dr. Desnick while he was at an airport, with Donaldson shouting out allegations of fraud to Desnick.

Among a number of causes of action raised by the plaintiffs, who included the Desnick Eye Clinic, and Simon and Glazer as individual plaintiffs, is an action for intrusion upon seclusion.]

POSNER, C.J. . . . To enter upon another's land without consent is a trespass. The force of this rule has, it is true, been diluted somewhat by concepts of privilege and of implied consent. But there is no journalists' privilege to trespass. And there can be no implied consent in any nonfictitious sense of the term when express consent is procured by a misrepresentation or a misleading omission. The Desnick Eye Center would not have agreed to the entry of the test patients into its offices had it known they wanted eye examinations only in order to gather material for a television expose of the Center and that they were going to make secret videotapes of the examinations. Yet some cases, illustrated by *Martin v. Fidelity & Casualty Co.*, 421 So. 2d 109, 111 (Ala. 1982), deem consent effective even though it was procured by fraud. There must be *something* to this surprising result. Without it a restaurant critic could not conceal his identity when he ordered a meal, or a browser pretend to be interested in merchandise that he could not afford to buy. Dinner guests would be trespassers if they were false friends who never would have been invited had the host known their true character, and a consumer who in an effort to bargain down an automobile dealer falsely claimed to be able to buy the same car elsewhere at a lower price would be a trespasser in the dealer's showroom. Some of these might be classified as privileged trespasses, designed to promote competition. Others might be thought justified by some kind of implied consent — the restaurant critic for example might point by way of analogy to the use of the "fair use" defense by book reviewers charged with copyright infringement and argue that the restaurant industry as a whole would be injured if restaurants could exclude critics. But most such efforts at rationalization would be little better than evasions. The fact is that consent to an entry is often given legal effect even though the entrant has intentions that if known to the owner of the property would cause him for perfectly understandable and generally ethical or at least lawful reasons to revoke his consent.

The law's willingness to give effect to consent procured by fraud is not limited to the tort of trespass. The *Restatement* gives the example of a man who obtains consent to sexual intercourse by promising a woman $100, yet (unbeknownst to her, of course) he pays her with a counterfeit bill and intended to do so from the start. The man is not guilty of battery, even though unconsented-to sexual intercourse is a battery. Yet we know that to conceal the fact that one has a venereal disease transforms "consensual" intercourse into battery. Seduction, standardly effected by false promises of love, is not rape; intercourse under the pretense of rendering medical or psychiatric treatment is, at least in most states. It certainly is battery. Trespass presents close parallels. If a homeowner opens his door to a purported meter reader who is in fact nothing of the sort — just a busybody curious about the interior of the home — the homeowner's consent to his entry is not a defense to a suit for trespass. And likewise if a competitor gained entry to a business firm's premises posing as a customer but in fact hoping to steal the firm's trade secrets.

How to distinguish the two classes of case — the seducer from the medical impersonator, the restaurant critic from the meter-reader impersonator? The answer can have nothing to do with fraud; there is fraud in all the cases. It has to do with the interest that the torts in question, battery and trespass, protect. The one protects the inviolability of the person, the other the inviolability of the person's property. The woman who is seduced wants to have sex with her seducer, and the restaurant owner wants to have customers. The woman who is victimized by the medical impersonator has no desire to have sex with her doctor; she wants medical treatment. And the homeowner victimized by the phony meter reader does not want strangers in his house unless they have authorized service functions. The dealer's objection to the customer who claims falsely to have a lower price from a competing dealer is not to the physical presence of the customer, but to the fraud that he is trying to perpetuate. The lines are not bright — they are not even inevitable. They are the traces of the old forms of action, which have resulted in a multitude of artificial distinctions in modern law. But that is nothing new.

There was no invasion in the present case of any of the specific interests that the tort of trespass seeks to protect. The test patients entered offices that were open to anyone expressing a desire for ophthalmic services and videotaped physicians engaged in professional, not personal, communications with strangers (the testers themselves). The activities of the offices were not disrupted. . . . Nor was there any "inva[sion of] a person's private space," as in our hypothetical meter-reader case, as in the famous case of *De May v. Roberts*, 9 N.W. 146 (Mich. 1881) (where a doctor, called to the plaintiff's home to deliver her baby, brought along with him a friend who was curious to see a birth but was not a medical doctor, and represented the friend to be his medical assistant), as in one of its numerous modern counterparts, . . . and as in *Dietemann v. Time, Inc.*, 449 F.2d 245 (9th Cir. 1971), on which the plaintiffs in our case rely. *Dietemann* involved a home. True, the portion invaded was an office, where the plaintiff performed quack healing of nonexistent ailments. The parallel to this case is plain enough, but there is a difference. Dietemann was not in business, and did not advertise his services or charge for them. His quackery was private.

No embarrassingly intimate details of anybody's life were publicized in the present case. There was no eavesdropping on a private conversation; the testers recorded their own conversations with the Desnick Eye Center's physicians. There was no violation of the doctor-patient privilege. There was no theft, or intent to steal, trade secrets; no disruption of decorum, of peace and quiet; no noisy or distracting demonstrations. Had the testers been undercover FBI agents, there would have been no violation of the Fourth Amendment, because there would have been no invasion of a legally protected interest in property or privacy. . . .

What we have said largely disposes of [the claim of] infringement of the right of privacy. . . . The right of privacy embraces several distinct interests, but the only ones conceivably involved here are the closely related interests in concealing intimate personal facts and in preventing intrusion into legitimately private activities, such as phone conversations. As we have said already, no intimate personal facts concerning the two individual plaintiffs . . . were revealed; and the only conversations that were recorded were conversations with the testers themselves.

NOTES & QUESTIONS

1. *Investigative Reporting.* As is illustrated by *Dietemann* and *Desnick*, investigative reporting often depends upon deception. Those cases are split on the issue of whether such investigative techniques can give rise to intrusion. Recall the *Dietemann* court's statement:

> Investigative reporting is an ancient art; its successful practice long antecedes the invention of miniature cameras and electronic devices. The First Amendment has never been construed to accord newsmen immunity from torts or crimes committed during the course of newsgathering. The First Amendment is not a license to trespass, to steal, or to intrude by electronic means into the precincts of another's home or office. It does not become such a license simply because the person subjected to the intrusion is reasonably suspected of committing a crime.

However, investigative reporting has served an important function throughout history. In 1887, a reporter named Nellie Bly pretended to be mentally ill to gain access to a mental asylum. Her portrayal of the brutal conditions led to significant reforms. Upton Sinclair went undercover as a meatpacker to expose conditions in slaughterhouses for his book *The Jungle* in 1904. C. Thomas Dienes argues:

> . . . Undercover journalism often serves the public interest. In the public sector, it allows the media to perform its role as the eyes and ears of the people, to perform a checking function on government. Especially at a time when citizens are often unable or unwilling to supervise government, this media role is critical to self-government. In the private sector, when the government fails in its responsibility to protect the public against fraudulent and unethical business and professional practices, whether because of lack of resources or unwillingness, media exposure of such practices can and often does provide the spur forcing government action.[4]

2. *Posner's Analogies in* **Desnick.** Judge Posner draws an analogy between (1) seduction with false promises of love in order to have sexual intercourse and (2) the deceitful trespass in *Desnick.* Are these situations really analogous?

3. *Trespass: The* **Food Lion Case.** The tort of trespass is related to the tort of intrusion. To commit a trespass, one must enter upon another's land without consent. To what extent does trespass overlap with intrusion? In many respects, it has fewer requirements — no requirement that solitude or seclusion be invaded, that a private matter be involved, or that the invasion be highly offensive. On the other hand, intrusion can be committed without entering upon another's land.

---

[4] C. Thomas Dienes, *Protecting Investigative Journalism*, 67 Geo. Wash. L. Rev. 1139, 1141, 1143 (1999). For further background about investigative journalism and the use of deception, see Bernard W. Bell, *Secrets and Lies: News Media and Law Enforcement Use of Deception as an Investigative Tool*, 60 U. Pitt. L. Rev. 745 (1999).

Can one trespass if one obtains consent through deception? And can a person trespass if she is present upon another's land with consent but secretly engages in activities that the landowner would likely not authorize? Consider *Food Lion, Inc. v. ABC*, 194 F.3d 505 (4th Cir. 2001). ABC reporters investigated allegations of unsanitary food-handling practices at supermarkets operated by Food Lion, Inc. According to the allegations, "Food Lion employees ground out-of-date beef together with new beef, bleached rank meat to remove its odor, and re-dated (and offered for sale) products not sold before their printed expiration date." Two reporters submitted fake resumes to obtain jobs at Food Lion supermarkets. The reporters secretly videotaped the food-handling practices at the stores. The reporters quit their jobs within a few weeks. The video was broadcast on the show *Primetime Live*. "The broadcast included, for example, videotape that appeared to show Food Lion employees repackaging and redating fish that had passed the expiration date, grinding expired beef with fresh beef, and applying barbeque sauce to chicken past its expiration date in order to mask the smell and sell it as fresh in the gourmet food section." Food Lion sued for fraud, breach of duty of loyalty, trespass, and unfair trade practices. Food Lion won at trial — $1,400 on the fraud claim, $1 each for the duty of loyalty and trespass claims, and $1,500 on the unfair trade practices claim. The jury awarded approximately $5.5 million in punitive damages on the fraud claim, which the court reduced to $315,000.

On appeal, the court dismissed the fraud and unfair trade practices claims but affirmed the duty of loyalty and trespass claims.

Regarding the trespass claim, the court reasoned:

> [I]t is a trespass to enter upon another's land without consent. Accordingly, consent is a defense to a claim of trespass. Even consent gained by misrepresentation is sometimes sufficient. *See Desnick v. American Broad. Cos.*, 44 F.3d 1345 (7th Cir. 1995). The consent to enter is canceled out, however, "if a wrongful act is done in excess of and in abuse of authorized entry." . . .
>
> [W]e have not found any case suggesting that consent based on a resume misrepresentation turns a successful job applicant into a trespasser the moment she enters the employer's premises to begin work. . . .
>
> There is a problem, however, with what Dale and Barnett did after they entered Food Lion's property. The jury also found that the reporters committed trespass by breaching their duty of loyalty to Food Lion "as a result of pursuing [their] investigation for ABC." We affirm the finding of trespass on this ground because the breach of duty of loyalty — triggered by the filming in non-public areas, which was adverse to Food Lion — was a wrongful act in excess of Dale and Barnett's authority to enter Food Lion's premises as employees. . . .
>
> [S]ecretly installing a video camera in someone's private home can be a wrongful act in excess of consent given to enter. In the trespass case of *Miller v. Brooks* the (defendant) wife, who claimed she had consent to enter her estranged husband's (the plaintiff's) house, had a private detective place a video camera in the ceiling of her husband's bedroom. The court noted that "[e]ven an authorized entry can be trespass if a wrongful act is done in excess of and in abuse of authorized entry." . . . We recognize that *Miller* involved a private home, not a grocery store, and that it involved some physical alteration to the plaintiff's property (installation of a camera). Still, we believe the general

principle is applicable here, at least in the case of Dale, who worked in a Food Lion store in North Carolina. Although Food Lion consented to Dale's entry to do her job, she exceeded that consent when she videotaped in non-public areas of the store and worked against the interests of her second employer, Food Lion, in doing so. . . .

The court only affirmed the duty of loyalty and trespass claims. As a result, Food Lion could only collect $2 in damages because the punitive damages were based on the fraud claim. Although *Food Lion* did not involve the tort of intrusion, to what extent is its holding regarding the tort of trespass applicable to intrusion cases? Is its holding consistent with *Dietemann* and *Desnick*?

4. ***Intrusion Liability for the Receipt of Data Obtained by Intrusion.*** In *Pearson v. Dodd*, 410 F.2d 701 (D.C. Cir. 1969), two former employees of Senator Thomas Dodd of Connecticut, with the assistance of two of Dodd's active staff members, entered Dodd's office without authorization and surreptitiously made copies of many documents in his files. These documents related to Dodd's relationship to lobbyists for foreign interests. Newspaper columnists Drew Pearson and Jack Anderson published articles containing information from these documents. Pearson and Anderson did not participate in or order the illegal copying; they only received copies of the documents knowing that they had been copied without authorization. Dodd sued Pearson and Anderson for invasion of privacy. The court held that intrusion could not extend to those who merely received the information:

> If we were to hold appellants liable for invasion of privacy on these facts, we would establish the proposition that one who receives information from an intruder, knowing it has been obtained by improper intrusion, is guilty of a tort. In an untried and developing area of tort law, we are not prepared to go so far. A person approached by an eavesdropper with an offer to share in the information gathered through the eavesdropping would perhaps play the nobler part should he spurn the offer and shut his ears. However, it seems to us that at this point it would place too great a strain on human weakness to hold one liable in damages who merely succumbs to temptation and listens.

SHULMAN V. GROUP W PRODUCTIONS, INC.

955 P.2d 469 (Cal. 1998)

WERDEGAR, J. . . . On June 24, 1990, plaintiffs Ruth and Wayne Shulman, mother and son, were injured when the car in which they and two other family members were riding on interstate 10 in Riverside County flew off the highway and tumbled down an embankment into a drainage ditch on state-owned property, coming to rest upside down. Ruth, the most seriously injured of the two, was pinned under the car. Ruth and Wayne both had to be cut free from the vehicle by the device known as "the jaws of life."

A rescue helicopter operated by Mercy Air was dispatched to the scene. The flight nurse, who would perform the medical care at the scene and on the way to the hospital, was Laura Carnahan. Also on board were the pilot, a medic and Joel Cooke, a video camera operator employed by defendants Group W Productions,

Inc., and 4MN Productions. Cooke was recording the rescue operation for later broadcast.

Cooke roamed the accident scene, videotaping the rescue. Nurse Carnahan wore a wireless microphone that picked up her conversations with both Ruth and the other rescue personnel. Cooke's tape was edited into a piece approximately nine minutes long, which, with the addition of narrative voice-over, was broadcast on September 29, 1990, as a segment of *On Scene: Emergency Response.*

The segment begins with the Mercy Air helicopter shown on its way to the accident site. The narrator's voice is heard in the background, setting the scene and describing in general terms what has happened. . . .

The videotape shows only a glimpse of Wayne, and his voice is never heard. Ruth is shown several times, either by brief shots of a limb or her torso, or with her features blocked by others or obscured by an oxygen mask. She is also heard speaking several times. Carnahan calls her "Ruth" and her last name is not mentioned on the broadcast.

While Ruth is still trapped under the car, Carnahan asks Ruth's age. Ruth responds, "I'm old." On further questioning, Ruth reveals she is 47, and Carnahan observes that "it's all relative. You're not that old." During her extrication from the car, Ruth asks at least twice if she is dreaming. At one point she asks Carnahan, who has told her she will be taken to the hospital in a helicopter: "Are you teasing?" At another point she says: "This is terrible. Am I dreaming?" She also asks what happened and where the rest of her family is, repeating the questions even after being told she was in an accident and the other family members are being cared for. While being loaded into the helicopter on a stretcher, Ruth says: "I just want to die." Carnahan reassures her that she is "going to do real well," but Ruth repeats: "I just want to die. I don't want to go through this."

Ruth and Wayne are placed in the helicopter, and its door is closed. The narrator states: "Once airborne, Laura and [the flight medic] will update their patients' vital signs and establish communications with the waiting trauma teams at Loma Linda." Carnahan, speaking into what appears to be a radio microphone, transmits some of Ruth's vital signs and states that Ruth cannot move her feet and has no sensation. The video footage during the helicopter ride includes a few seconds of Ruth's face, covered by an oxygen mask. Wayne is neither shown nor heard.

The helicopter lands on the hospital roof. With the door open, Ruth states while being taken out: "My upper back hurts." Carnahan replies: "Your upper back hurts. That's what you were saying up there." Ruth states: "I don't feel that great." Carnahan responds: "You probably don't."

Finally, Ruth is shown being moved from the helicopter into the hospital. . . .

The accident left Ruth a paraplegic. When the segment was broadcast, Wayne phoned Ruth in her hospital room and told her to turn on the television because "Channel 4 is showing our accident now." Shortly afterward, several hospital workers came into the room to mention that a videotaped segment of her accident was being shown. Ruth was "shocked, so to speak, that this would be run and I would be exploited, have my privacy invaded, which is what I felt had happened." She did not know her rescue had been recorded in this manner and had never consented to the recording or broadcast. Ruth had the impression from the broadcast "that I was kind of talking non-stop, and I remember hearing some of the things I said, which were not very pleasant." Asked at deposition what part of the broadcast material she considered private, Ruth explained: "I think the whole scene was pretty private. It was pretty gruesome, the parts that I saw, my knee sticking out of the car. I certainly did not look my best, and I don't feel it's for the public to see. I was not at my best in what I was thinking and what I was saying and what was being shown, and it's not for the public to see this trauma that I was going through."

Ruth and Wayne sued the producers of *On Scene: Emergency Response*, as well as others. The first amended complaint included two causes of action for invasion of privacy, one based on defendants' unlawful intrusion by videotaping the rescue in the first instance and the other based on the public disclosure of private facts, i.e., the broadcast. . . .

The trial court granted the media defendants' summary judgment motion, basing its ruling on plaintiffs' admissions that the accident and rescue were matters of public interest and public affairs. Those admissions, in the trial court's view, showed as a matter of law that the broadcast material was newsworthy, thereby vesting the media defendants' conduct with First Amendment protection. The court entered judgment for defendants on all causes of action. . . .

[T]he action for intrusion has two elements: (1) intrusion into a private place, conversation or matter, (2) in a manner highly offensive to a reasonable person. We consider the elements in that order.

We ask first whether defendants "intentionally intrude[d], physically or otherwise, upon the solitude or seclusion of another," that is, into a place or conversation private to Wayne or Ruth. . . .

Cameraman Cooke's mere presence at the accident scene and filming of the events occurring there cannot be deemed either a physical or sensory intrusion on plaintiffs' seclusion. Plaintiffs had no right of ownership or possession of the property where the rescue took place, nor any actual control of the premises. Nor could they have had a reasonable expectation that members of the media would be excluded or prevented from photographing the scene; for journalists to attend and record the scenes of accidents and rescues is in no way unusual or unexpected.

Two aspects of defendants' conduct, however, raise triable issues of intrusion on seclusion. First, a triable issue exists as to whether both plaintiffs had an objectively reasonable expectation of privacy in the interior of the rescue helicopter, which served as an ambulance. Although the attendance of reporters and photographers at the scene of an accident is to be expected, we are aware of no law or custom permitting the press to ride in ambulances or enter hospital rooms during treatment without the patient's consent. Other than the two patients and Cooke, only three people were present in the helicopter, all Mercy Air staff. As the Court of Appeal observed, "[i]t is neither the custom nor the habit of our society that any member of the public at large or its media representatives may hitch a ride in an ambulance and ogle as paramedics care for an injured stranger."

Second, Ruth was entitled to a degree of privacy in her conversations with Carnahan and other medical rescuers at the accident scene, and in Carnahan's conversations conveying medical information regarding Ruth to the hospital base. Cooke, perhaps, did not intrude into that zone of privacy merely by being present at a place where he could hear such conversations with unaided ears. But by placing a microphone on Carnahan's person, amplifying and recording what she said and heard, defendants may have listened in on conversations the parties could reasonably have expected to be private. . . .

We turn to the second element of the intrusion tort, offensiveness. . . .

On this summary judgment record, we believe a jury could find defendants' recording of Ruth's communications to Carnahan and other rescuers, and filming in the air ambulance, to be "'highly offensive to a reasonable person.'" With regard to the depth of the intrusion, a reasonable jury could find highly offensive the placement of a microphone on a medical rescuer in order to intercept what would otherwise be private conversations with an injured patient. In that setting, as defendants could and should have foreseen, the patient would not know her words were being recorded and would not have occasion to ask about, and object or consent to, recording. Defendants, it could reasonably be said, took calculated advantage of the patient's "vulnerability and confusion." Arguably, the last thing an injured accident victim should have to worry about while being pried from her wrecked car is that a television producer may be recording everything she says to medical personnel for the possible edification and entertainment of casual television viewers.

For much the same reason, a jury could reasonably regard entering and riding in an ambulance — whether on the ground or in the air — with two seriously injured patients to be an egregious intrusion on a place of expected seclusion. Again, the patients, at least in this case, were hardly in a position to keep careful watch on who was riding with them, or to inquire as to everyone's business and consent or object to their presence. A jury could reasonably believe that fundamental respect for human dignity requires the patients' anxious journey be taken only with those whose care is solely for them and out of sight of the prying eyes (or cameras) of others.

Nor can we say as a matter of law that defendants' motive — to gather usable material for a potentially newsworthy story — necessarily privileged their intrusive conduct as a matter of common law tort liability. A reasonable jury could conclude the producers' desire to get footage that would convey the "feel" of the event — the real sights and sounds of a difficult rescue — did not justify either placing a microphone on Nurse Carnahan or filming inside the rescue helicopter. Although defendants' purposes could scarcely be regarded as evil or malicious (in the colloquial sense), their behavior could, even in light of their motives, be thought to show a highly offensive lack of sensitivity and respect for plaintiffs' privacy. A reasonable jury could find that defendants, in placing a microphone on an emergency treatment nurse and recording her conversation with a distressed, disoriented and severely injured patient, without the patient's knowledge or consent, acted with highly offensive disrespect for the patient's personal privacy. . . .

Turning to the question of constitutional protection for newsgathering, one finds the decisional law reflects a general rule of *nonprotection*: the press in its newsgathering activities enjoys no immunity or exemption from generally applicable laws. . . .

As should be apparent from the above discussion, the constitutional protection accorded newsgathering, if any, is far narrower than the protection surrounding the publication of truthful material; consequently, the fact that a reporter may be seeking "newsworthy" material does not in itself privilege the investigatory

activity. The reason for the difference is simple: the intrusion tort, unlike that for publication of private facts, does not subject the press to liability for the contents of its publications. Newsworthiness . . . is a complete bar to liability for publication of private facts and is evaluated with a high degree of deference to editorial judgment. The same deference is not due, however, when the issue is not the media's right to publish or broadcast what they choose, but their right to intrude into secluded areas or conversations in pursuit of publishable material. At most, the Constitution may preclude tort liability that would "place an impermissible burden on newsgatherers" by depriving them of their " 'indispensable tools' " . . .
.

NOTES & QUESTIONS

1. **Intrusion in Public Places.** Consider *Sanders v. ABC*, 978 P.2d 67 (Cal. 1999), decided by the same court one year after *Shulman*. In *Sanders*, a reporter obtained a job with a telephone psychics company that gave "readings" to callers for a fee. The psychics worked in a large room with rows of cubicles. The reporter secretly videotaped conversations of the plaintiff, an employee, with others at his cubicle or other cubicles. The plaintiff sued for intrusion upon seclusion. The defendants argued that the employee lacked a reasonable expectation of privacy in his conversations because they could be seen and overheard by co-workers. The court sided with the plaintiff:

> . . . [W]e adhere to the view suggested in *Shulman*: privacy, for purposes of the intrusion tort, is not a binary, all-or-nothing characteristic. There are degrees and nuances to societal recognition of our expectations of privacy: the fact that the privacy one expects in a given setting is not complete or absolute does not render the expectation unreasonable as a matter of law. Although the intrusion tort is often defined in terms of "seclusion" the seclusion referred to need not be absolute. "Like 'privacy,' the concept of 'seclusion' is relative. The mere fact that a person can be seen by someone does not automatically mean that he or she can legally be forced to be subject to being seen by everyone."

2. PARAZZI

Paparazzi are aggressive photographers who often harass celebrities to take candid photographs to sell to newspapers, tabloids, and magazines. Fueling the behavior of the paparazzi are the exorbitant prices that photographs of celebrities command. For example, a photo of Princess Diana embracing Dodi Al-Fayed was sold for over $3 million. According to the *New York Times*, "A growing constellation of Web sites, magazines and television programs serve [gossip] up minute by minute, creating a river of cash for secrets of the stars, or near stars."[5] It estimated the revenue stream of the "new world of round-the-clock" gossip at $3 billion annually.

Paparazzi have a reputation for being very invasive into the privacy of celebrities. For example, paparazzi flew over Michael J. Fox's wedding in helicopters to take photographs. Disguised photographers took photographs of

---

[5] Jim Rutenberg, *The Gossip Machine, Churning Out Cash*, N.Y. Times, May 22, 2011.

Paul Reiser's baby in the hospital. Paparazzi also camped outside Reiser's backyard taking photographs with telephoto lenses. Paparazzi chased Arnold Schwarzenegger and Maria Shriver off the road to take the first photos of him leaving the hospital after heart surgery. In 2005, paparazzi followed Lindsey Lohan as she drove onto a dead end street. When she tried to make a U-turn, one photographer drove his automobile into her vehicle. Lohan suffered cuts and bruises from the accident. To what extent does the law of privacy restrict the behavior of paparazzi?

GALELLA V. ONASSIS

487 F.2d 986 (2d Cir. 1973)

SMITH, J. . . . Galella is a free-lance photographer specializing in the making and sale of photographs of well-known persons. Defendant Onassis is the widow of the late President, John F. Kennedy, mother of the two Kennedy children, John and Caroline, and is the wife of Aristotle Onassis, widely known shipping figure and reputed multimillionaire. John Walsh, James Kalafatis and John Connelly are U.S. Secret Service agents assigned to the duty of protecting the Kennedy children under 18 U.S.C. § 3056, which provides for protection of the children of deceased presidents up to the age of 16.

Galella fancies himself as a "paparazzo" (literally a kind of annoying insect, perhaps roughly equivalent to the English "gadfly.") Paparazzi make themselves as visible to the public and obnoxious to their photographic subjects as possible to aid in the advertisement and wide sale of their works.[6]

Some examples of Galella's conduct brought out at trial are illustrative. Galella took pictures of John Kennedy riding his bicycle in Central Park across the way from his home. He jumped out into the boy's path, causing the agents concern for John's safety. The agents' reaction and interrogation of Galella led to Galella's arrest and his action against the agents; Galella on other occasions interrupted Caroline at tennis, and invaded the children's private schools. At one time he came uncomfortably close in a power boat to Mrs. Onassis swimming. He often jumped and postured around while taking pictures of her party notably at a theater opening but also on numerous other occasions. He followed a practice of bribing apartment house, restaurant and nightclub doormen as well as romancing a family servant to keep him advised of the movements of the family.

After detention and arrest following complaint by the Secret Service agents protecting Mrs. Onassis' son and his acquittal in the state court, Galella filed suit in state court against the agents and Mrs. Onassis. Galella claimed that under orders from Mrs. Onassis, the three agents had falsely arrested and maliciously prosecuted him, and that this incident in addition to several others described in the complaint constituted an unlawful interference with his trade.

Mrs. Onassis answered denying any role in the arrest or any part in the claimed interference with his attempts to photograph her, and counterclaimed for damages and injunctive relief, charging that Galella had invaded her privacy, assaulted and

---

[6] The newspapers report a recent incident in which one Marlon Brando, annoyed by Galella, punched Galella, breaking Galella's jaw and infecting Brando's hand.

battered her, intentionally inflicted emotional distress and engaged in a campaign of harassment. . . .

After a six-week trial the court dismissed Galella's claim and granted relief to both the defendant and the intervenor. Galella was enjoined from (1) keeping the defendant and her children under surveillance or following any of them; (2) approaching within 100 yards of the home of defendant or her children, or within 100 yards of either child's school or within 75 yards of either child or 50 yards of defendant; (3) using the name, portrait or picture of defendant or her children for advertising; (4) attempting to communicate with defendant or her children except through her attorney.

We conclude that grant of summary judgment and dismissal of Galella's claim against the Secret Service agents was proper. . . .

Evidence offered by the defense showed that Galella had on occasion intentionally physically touched Mrs. Onassis and her daughter, caused fear of physical contact in his frenzied attempts to get their pictures, followed defendant and her children too closely in an automobile, endangered the safety of the children while they were swimming, water skiing and horseback riding. Galella cannot successfully challenge the court's finding of tortious conduct.

Finding that Galella had "insinuated himself into the very fabric of Mrs. Onassis' life . . ." the court framed its relief in part on the need to prevent further invasion of the defendant's privacy. Whether or not this accords with present New York law, there is no doubt that it is sustainable under New York's proscription of harassment.

Of course legitimate countervailing social needs may warrant some intrusion despite an individual's reasonable expectation of privacy and freedom from harassment. However the interference allowed may be no greater than that necessary to protect the overriding public interest. Mrs. Onassis was properly found to be a public figure and thus subject to news coverage. Nonetheless, Galella's action went far beyond the reasonable bounds of news gathering. When weighed against the de minimis public importance of the daily activities of the defendant, Galella's constant surveillance, his obtrusive and intruding presence, was unwarranted and unreasonable. If there were any doubt in our minds, Galella's inexcusable conduct toward defendant's minor children would resolve it.

Galella does not seriously dispute the court's finding of tortious conduct. Rather, he sets up the First Amendment as a wall of immunity protecting newsmen from any liability for their conduct while gathering news. There is no such scope to the First Amendment right. Crimes and torts committed in news gathering are not protected. There is no threat to a free press in requiring its agents to act within the law. . . .

CALIFORNIA ANTI-PAPARAZZI ACT

Cal. Civ. Code § 1708.8

Princess Diana's death in 1997 precipitated calls for anti-paparazzi legislation in the United States. On the evening of August 30, Princess Diana and Dodi Al-Fayed were being chauffeured in a Mercedes from the Ritz Hotel in Paris. Paparazzi followed the Mercedes on motorcycles and in cars. A chase developed, and according to eyewitnesses, the motorcycles were swarming around the Mercedes as it entered a tunnel. The Mercedes crashed in the tunnel, killing both Princess Diana and Dodi Al-Fayed. About 10 to 15 photographers gathered around the Mercedes after the crash and continued to take pictures at the scene of the accident.

In the United States, anti-paparazzi legislation was introduced in Congress but failed to be passed. In 1998, California became the first state to adopt anti-paparazzi legislation. In 2005, California amended the existing statute to add enhanced penalties for violations of the statute by paparazzi who engage in an "assault" to capture a photograph. Further amendments to the statute followed in 2009 and 2010.

California's Anti-Paparazzi Act does not supplant the state's existing privacy torts. Rather, it provides rights and remedies "in addition to any other rights and remedies provided by law." § 1708.8(h).

The Act recognizes two forms of invasion of privacy. First, it defines liability for "physical invasion of privacy":

> (a) A person is liable for physical invasion of privacy when the defendant knowingly enters onto the land of another without permission or otherwise committed a trespass, in order to physically invade the privacy of the plaintiff with the intent to capture any type of visual image, sound recording, or other physical impression of the plaintiff engaging in a personal or familial activity and the physical invasion occurs in a manner that is offensive to a reasonable person.

"Personal or familial activity" is defined as including but not limited to "intimate details of the plaintiff's personal life, interactions with the plaintiff's family or significant others, or other aspects of plaintiff's private affairs or concerns." § 1708.8(k).

Second, the Act defines liability for "constructive invasion of privacy":

> (b) A person is liable for constructive invasion of privacy when the defendant attempts to capture, in a manner that is offensive to a reasonable person, any type of visual image, sound recording, or other physical impression of the plaintiff engaging in a personal or familial activity under circumstances in which the plaintiff had a reasonable expectation of privacy, through the use of a visual or auditory enhancing device, regardless of whether there is a physical trespass, if this image, sound recording, or other physical impression could not have been achieved without a trespass unless the visual or auditory enhancing device was used.

The Act provides for increased damages for the two types of privacy violations defined above:

> (c) A person who commits physical invasion of privacy or constructive invasion of privacy, or both, is liable for up to three times the amount of any general and special damages that are proximately caused by the violation of this section. This person may also be liable for punitive damages, subject to proof according to Section 3294. If the plaintiff proves that the invasion of privacy was committed for a commercial purpose, the defendant shall also be subject to disgorgement to the plaintiff of any proceeds or other consideration obtained as a result of the violation of this section.

Equitable relief is also available. § 1708.8(g).

Further, the Act punishes a person who "directs, solicits, actually induces, or actually causes" a person to violate the law. § 1708.8(d). However, the Act does not punish the sale or dissemination of images or recordings in violation of the Act. § 1708.8(e).

Since the Act is aimed at limiting the intrusive activities of paparazzi, not merely the invasion of privacy caused by having one's photograph taken or voice recorded, the Act applies even if no image or recording is ever captured or sold. § 1708.8(i).

NOTES & QUESTIONS

1. ***"Papa Paparazzo": Ron Galella Post-Onassis.*** According to the *New Yorker*, Galella repeatedly violated the terms of the court order in the *Onassis* litigation, which led to a settlement in which he agreed to stop photographing Onassis.[7] Nonetheless, Galella lost little time in publishing a volume, *Jacqueline* (1978), containing his Onassis photographs. Remaining productive, Galella has published numerous other volumes of his candid photographs. He is considered as the father of the modern celebrity industry as well as a celebrity himself.[8] In 2010, Galella was the subject of a documentary, *Smash His Camera.*

2. ***Collective Actions by Different Journalists.*** Suppose a person is accosted by throngs of reporters. At any moment, there is always one or more reporters on her trail. Groups of reporters camp outside her home. The impact from the collective actions of all the reporters is extremely disruptive to the person's life. Can she sue the reporters collectively? Bruce Sanford argues that each reporter should only be liable for his or her own behavior: "A stake-out by a group of unrelated reporters should be viewed as no more than the sum of its separate parts."[9]

3. ***The Anti-Paparazzi Act vs. the Intrusion Tort.*** How does California's Anti-Paparazzi Act differ from the ordinary intrusion upon seclusion tort?

4. ***The Anti-Paparazzi Act and the First Amendment.*** Is California's Anti-Paparazzi Act constitutional?

    Erwin Chemerinsky contends that newsgathering, although currently not protected by the First Amendment, should be protected by intermediate scrutiny because the "very notion of a marketplace of ideas rests on the availability of information. Aggressive newsgathering, such as by undercover reporters, is often the key to gathering the information." However, Chemerinsky goes on to argue that the California Anti-Paparazzi Act would survive intermediate scrutiny:

    > Despite strongly believing in First Amendment protection for newsgathering, I believe that this law is constitutional. The government has an important interest in protecting the privacy of the home. Fourth Amendment cases have recognized the special privacy interests surrounding the home. . . .

---

[7] Tad Friend, *No Pictures!*, 86 The New Yorker 24-25 (May 31, 2010). The article described the photographer as "a tireless stalker with an Elmer Fudd laugh."

[8] Jacqueline Mroz, *Papa Paparazzo*, New Jersey Monthly (June 15, 2010).

[9] Bruce W. Sanford, *Libel and Privacy* § 11.2, at 541 (2d ed. 1991).

The California Privacy Protection Act says that people, no matter how famous, should be able to shut their door and close out the media and the world. If the image could not have been gained except through a trespass, the media should not be able to obtain it through technological enhancement equipment. Simply put, the law is constitutional because it substantially advances the government's interest in safeguarding privacy in the home.[10]

Consider the following argument by C. Thomas Dienes:

The antipaparazzi laws, by focusing only on taking photographs and making sound recordings when done for commercial purposes and on the defendant photographer's profits, clearly target the press. Liability for photographing or recording the same event will depend on whether the photographer is a private individual or a for-profit photojournalist whose work is intended for public distribution. Statements made at legislative hearings by proponents of these laws leave no doubt that the press is the focus of the antipaparazzi legislation.

The taking of photographs or the making of sound recordings is not itself speech. . . . [T]he sale or trade of a photo or recording is probably not a form of expression. . . .

Nevertheless the antipaparazzi legislation singles out press photography and sound recording for significant and discriminatory burdens. Even if such acts do not themselves constitute speech, they are protected means of newsgathering vital to press publication. If the photographs and sound recordings cannot be made, they cannot be published. As the Supreme Court said in *Arcara v. Cloud Books, Inc.*, laws are subject to heightened scrutiny "although directed at activity with no expressive component, [if they] impose a disproportionate burden upon those engaged in protected First Amendment activities." Because media speech-related activity is significantly and disproportionately burdened, the antipaparazzi laws should be treated as presumptively unconstitutional, subject to strict scrutiny review.[11]

3. VIDEO VOYEURISM

Cameras are everywhere today. Warren and Brandeis wrote about the perils of small accessible cameras; one wonders what they would have thought about the proliferation of cell phone cameras, which millions of people now carry around with them at all times. Some people are posting their cell phone snapshots on the Web. The dark underbelly of these practices is the rise of what is referred to as "video voyeurism," the use of video or photography to capture people naked without their consent. Websites have been popping up with "upskirt" photos — pictures taken up women's skirts. There are more than 100 websites with images of unsuspecting people who are caught in the act of showering or undressing.[12] Indeed, it is relatively easy to snap photos in locker rooms with a cell phone camera. Several states have passed video voyeurism laws, some with criminal penalties. *See, e.g.,* La. Rev. Stat. Ann. § 14:283; N.J. Stat. Ann. § 2C:18-3; N.Y. Penal Law § 250.45.

---

[10] Erwin Chemerinsky, *Protect the Press: A First Amendment Standard for Safeguarding Aggressive Newsgathering*, 33 U. Rich. L. Rev. 1143, 1159, 1163-64 (2000).

[11] C. Thomas Dienes, *Protecting Investigative Journalism,* 67 Geo. Wash. L. Rev. 1139 (1999).

[12] Clay Calvert, *Voyeur Nation: Media, Privacy, and Peering in Modern Culture* (2000).

The state of Washington passed a video voyeurism law that provided that

> [a] person commits the crime of voyeurism if, for the purpose of arousing or gratifying the sexual desire of any person, he or she knowingly views, photographs, or films another person, without that person's knowledge and consent, while the person being viewed, photographed, or filmed is in a place where he or she would have a reasonable expectation of privacy.

RCW 9A.44.115. The statute defined the place where people have a reasonable expectation of privacy as:

> (i) A place where a reasonable person would believe that he or she could disrobe in privacy, without being concerned that his or her undressing was being photographed or filmed by another; *or*
> (ii) A place where one may reasonably expect to be safe from casual or hostile intrusion or surveillance. . . .

In *Washington v. Glas,* 54 P.3d 147 (Wash. 2002), Sean Glas was convicted under the statute for taking photos up women's skirts in a shopping mall without their consent. The court dismissed Glas's conviction because "although the Legislature may have intended to cover intrusions of privacy in public places, the plain language of the statute does not accomplish this goal." The court reasoned that "[c]asual surveillance frequently occurs in public. Therefore, public places could not logically constitute locations where a person could reasonably expect to be safe from casual or hostile intrusion or surveillance."

Shortly after this opinion, in 2003, Washington revised its statute to include "intimate areas of another person without that person's knowledge and consent and under circumstances where the person has a reasonable expectation of privacy, whether in a public or private place." RCW 9A.44.115.

Consider the following law enacted by the U.S. Congress in 2004:

VIDEO VOYEURISM PREVENTION ACT

18 U.S.C. § 1801

(a) Whoever, in the special maritime and territorial jurisdiction of the United States, having the intent to capture an improper image of an individual, knowingly does so and that individual's naked or undergarment clad genitals, pubic area, buttocks, or female breast is depicted in the improper image under circumstances in which that individual has a reasonable expectation of privacy regarding such body part or parts, shall be fined under this title or imprisoned not more than one year, or both.

(b) In this section —

> (1) the term "captures," with respect to an image, means videotapes, photographs, films, or records by any means or broadcasts;
> (2) the term "female breast" means any portion of the female breast below the top of the areola;
> (3) the term "improper image," with respect to an individual, means an image, captured without the consent of that individual, of the naked or

undergarment clad genitals, pubic area, buttocks, or female breast of that individual; and

(4) the term "under circumstances in which that individual has a reasonable expectation of privacy" means —

(A) circumstances in which a reasonable person would believe that he or she could disrobe in privacy, without being concerned that his or her image was being videotaped, photographed, filmed, broadcast, or otherwise recorded by any means; or

(B) circumstances in which a reasonable person would believe that his or her naked or undergarment-clad pubic area, buttocks, genitals, or female breast would not be visible to the public, regardless of whether that person is in a public or private area.

(c) This section shall not apply to any person engaged in lawful law enforcement or intelligence activities.

NOTES & QUESTIONS

1. *The Washington Statute vs. the Video Voyeurism Protection Act.* How does the federal statute compare with the Washington statute? Does the federal statute violate the First Amendment?

2. *Privacy in Public.* Clay Calvert contends that because the Act "applies in public areas, not merely those that are private . . . [t]his would be a radical change for the legal system's conception of privacy, but surely one that is necessary to preserve human dignity from offensive intrusions."[13] Consider again *Nader v. General Motors,* where the court held that "a person does not automatically make public everything he does merely by being in a public place." In what circumstances might a person have an expectation of privacy in a public place?

3. *The Burning Man Festival Video.* The Burning Man Festival, held annually in the Nevada desert, has nearly 25,000 participants, including a large contingent of technology professionals. There is significant nudity at the festival, as people are encouraged to engage in "radical self-expression." Videos for personal use are permitted with prior approval by the festival organizers. In 2002, 12 videos of nude participants at the festival appeared for sale on a pornographic website called Video Voyeur. Video Voyeur had sought permission to videotape the event, but was denied.[14] Does Video Voyeur's videotaping, which captures naked people, including breasts and genitals, violate the Video Voyeurism Prevention Act?

---

[13] Clay Calvert, *Revisiting the Voyeurism Value in the First Amendment: From the Sexually Sordid to the Details of Death,* 27 Seattle U. L. Rev. 721, 731 (2004); *see also* Helen Nissenbaum, *Protecting Privacy in the Information Age: The Problem of Privacy in Public,* 17 Law & Phil. 559 (1998) (arguing that being in public should not eliminate one's privacy interest).

[14] Evelyn Nieves, *A Festival With Nudity Sues a Sex Web Site,* N.Y. Times, July 5, 2002. The Burning Man Festival's suit was filed prior to the Video Voyeurism Prevention Act. Among the claims were intrusion, appropriation, public disclosure, breach of contract, and trespass. The suit was settled when Video Voyeur agreed to stop selling the videos, to turn them over to the festival organizers, and to cease from videotaping the event in the future.

B. DISCLOSURE OF TRUTHFUL INFORMATION

In certain circumstances, the law provides remedies for individuals who suffer harm as a result of the disclosure of their personal information. One of the primary remedies is the tort of public disclosure of private facts. Other remedies include statutes passed by states and the federal government that restrict the disclosure of specific information. For example, a number of states have laws prohibiting the disclosure of the identities of sexual offense victims. *See, e.g.*, N.Y. Civ. Rights L. § 50-b; 42 Pa. Comp. Stat. § 5988. States have also provided statutory remedies for the disclosure that a person has AIDS. *See, e.g.*, 410 Ill. Comp. Stat. 305/9; Fla. Stat. § 381.004. Federal wiretap law prohibits the disclosure of a communication that one has reason to know was obtained through an illegal wiretap. *See* 18 U.S.C. § 2511(1)(c). This provision of federal wiretap law is the subject of *Bartnicki v. Vopper*, discussed below. What types of disclosures of personal information can and should give rise to civil liability? How can liability for the disclosure of true information coexist with the First Amendment's protection of free speech?

1. PUBLIC DISCLOSURE OF PRIVATE FACTS

(a) Introduction

PUBLICITY GIVEN TO PRIVATE LIFE

Restatement (Second) of Torts § 652D

One who gives publicity to a matter concerning the private life of another is subject to liability to the other for invasion of his privacy, if the matter publicized is of a kind that
    (a) would be highly offensive to a reasonable person, and
    (b) is not of legitimate concern to the public

NOTES & QUESTIONS

1. ***Publicity.*** "Publicity" means that the matter is communicated to the "public at large" or "to so many persons that the matter must be regarded as substantially certain to become one of public knowledge." The Restatement (comment b) notes that communicating "a fact concerning the plaintiff's private life to a single person or even to a small group of persons" is not sufficient to establish publicity. The Restatement commentary goes on to explain:

> On the other hand, any publication in a newspaper or a magazine, even of small circulation, or in a handbill distributed to a large number of persons, or any broadcast over the radio, or statement made in an address to a large audience, is sufficient to give publicity within the meaning of the term as it is used in this Section. The distinction, in other words, is one between private and public communication.

Most courts have followed the Restatement and concluded that disclosure to a small group of individuals does not constitute publicity. For example, in *Yoder v. Smith*, 112 N.W.2d 862 (Iowa 1962), the court held that the publicity element was not satisfied when the defendant disclosed the plaintiff's debts to the plaintiff's employer. In *Wells v. Thomas*, 569 F. Supp. 426 (E.D. Pa. 1983), the court held that disclosure to a plaintiff's co-workers at a hospital was not sufficient to establish the publicity element.

In contrast, posting information in public places constitutes sufficient publicity. In *Brents v. Morgan*, 299 S.W. 967 (Ky. 1927), the court held that there was sufficient publicity when the owner of an automobile garage posted a large sign on a show window of his garage stating that the plaintiff owed him a debt. In *Biederman's of Springfield, Inc. v. Wright*, 322 S.W.2d 892 (Mo. 1959), the court concluded that making loaded comments to a person "in a public restaurant with numerous customers present satisfies any reasonable requirement as to publicity."

However, consider *Miller v. Motorola, Inc.*, 560 N.E2d 900 (Ill. App. 1990). The plaintiff shared information that with her employer's nurse that she was undergoing a mastectomy and reconstructive surgeries. The information was disclosed to other employees. The court held that although the information was made to a small group, "in circumstances where a special relationship exists between the plaintiff and the 'public' to whom the information has been disclosed, the disclosure may be just as devastating to the person even though the disclosure was made to a limited number of people." The court in *Miller* followed an earlier case, *Beaumont v. Brown*, 257 N.W.2d 522 (Mich. 1977), which explained: "An invasion of a plaintiff's right to privacy is important if it exposes private facts to a public whose knowledge of those facts would be embarrassing to the plaintiff."

Which approach to publicity do you agree with? Consider Jonathan Mintz:

> A person loses some sense of privacy the moment a second person divulges a private fact to a third person, particularly when the third person is a member of the same community as the first person. Thus, the degree of publicity, and the corresponding degree of injury to a person's dignity, is a factor better addressed in damage calculations than in summary judgments or motions to dismiss.[15]

Why does the publicity requirement exist? As one court observed, the requirement of widespread publicity "singles out the print, film, and broadcast media for legal restraints that will not be applied to gossip-mongers in neighborhood taverns or card-parties, to letter writers or telephone tattlers." *Anderson v. Fisher Broadcasting Co.*, 712 P.2d 803, 805 (Or. 1986). A major function of the publicity requirement is to prevent lawsuits for a wide array of gossip, which often occurs between just a few people. The publicity requirement attempts to exclude mere gossip from the tort. Would the public disclosure tort apply too widely without the publicity requirement?

2. ***Highly Offensive.*** The disclosure must be highly offensive. According to the Restatement (comment c):

---

[15] Jonathan B. Mintz, *The Remains of Privacy's Disclosure Tort: An Exploration of the Private Domain*, 55 Md. L. Rev. 425, 438 (1996).

Complete privacy does not exist in this world except in a desert, and anyone who is not a hermit must expect and endure the ordinary incidents of the community life of which he is a part. Thus he must expect the more or less casual observation of his neighbors as to what he does, and that his comings and goings and his ordinary daily activities, will be described in the press as a matter of casual interest to others. The ordinary reasonable man does not take offense at a report in a newspaper that he has returned from a visit, gone camping in the woods or given a party at his house for his friends. Even minor and moderate annoyance, as for example through public disclosure of the fact that the plaintiff has clumsily fallen downstairs and broken his ankle, is not sufficient to give him a cause of action under the rule stated in this Section. It is only when the publicity given to him is such that a reasonable person would feel justified in feeling seriously aggrieved by it, that the cause of action arises.

Note the irony. The Restatement commentary suggests that the ordinary person does not take offense of a newspaper report that he has "given a party at his house for his friends." Indeed, it was such a newspaper report that some suggest inspired Samuel Warren to write the law review article with Louis Brandeis that gave rise to this very tort.

3. *Newsworthiness.* As stated by Restatement (comment f): "When the subject-matter of the publicity is of legitimate public concern, there is no invasion of privacy." Recall that the first exception to the right to privacy proposed by Brandeis and Warren was for "any publication of matter which is of general public interest."

4. *Recognition of the Tort by the States.* Most states recognize the public disclosure tort.[16] There are some states that have not recognized the tort: Nebraska, New York, North Carolina, North Dakota, Rhode Island, Utah, and Virginia.[17] As you read in *Lake v. Wal-Mart*, Minnesota, a long time holdout on recognizing the public disclosure tort, finally recognized the tort in 1998.

(b) Private Matters

GILL V. HEARST PUBLISHING CO.

253 P.2d 441 (Cal. 1953)

SPENCE, J. . . . [P]laintiffs, husband and wife, sought damages for an alleged invasion of their right of privacy. . . . Plaintiffs' original complaint was predicated solely on the charge that in the October, 1947, issue of Harper's Bazaar, a

---

[16] For more background about the public disclosure tort, see Jonathan B. Mintz, *The Remains of Privacy's Disclosure Tort: An Exploration of the Private Domain,* 55 Md. L. Rev. 425 (1996); Robert C. Post, *The Social Foundations of Privacy: Community and Self in the Common Law Tort,* 77 Cal. L. Rev. 957 (1989); Peter L. Felcher & Edward L. Rubin, *Privacy, Publicity, and the Portrayal of Real People by the Media,* 88 Yale L.J. 1577 (1979); Dorsey D. Ellis, Jr., *Damages and the Privacy Tort: Sketching a "Legal Profile,"* 64 Iowa L. Rev. 1111 (1979); Randall Bezanson, *Public Disclosure as News: Injunctive Relief and Newsworthiness in Privacy Actions Involving the Press,* 64 Iowa L. Rev. 1061 (1979); John W. Wade, *Defamation and the Right to Privacy,* 15 Vand. L. Rev. 1093 (1962).

[17] *See* Geoff Dendy, Note, *The Newsworthiness Defense to the Public Disclosure Tort,* 85 Ky. L.J. 147, 158 (1997).

magazine published and distributed by the corporate defendants, there appeared an unauthorized photograph of plaintiffs taken by defendants' employee while plaintiffs were seated in an affectionate pose at their place of business, a confectionery and ice cream concession in the Farmers' Market in Los Angeles. This photograph was used to illustrate an article entitled "And So the World Goes Round," a short commentary reaffirming "the poet's conviction that the world could not revolve without love," despite "vulgarization" of the sentiment by some, and that ballads may still be written about everyday people in love. . . .

Plaintiffs . . . amended their complaint to allege that the same photograph was republished with defendants' consent in the May, 1949, issue of the Ladies' Home Journal, a monthly magazine published and distributed by the Curtis Publishing Company. . . . Specifically, it is here alleged that the "picture" was republished with the "knowledge, permission and consent" of defendants and that "credit" for the publication was given to and required by defendants; that the published photograph depicts plaintiffs in an "uncomplimentary" pose; that plaintiffs' right of privacy was thereby invaded and plaintiffs were subjected to humiliation and annoyance to their damage in the sum of $25,000. . . .

. . . [M]ere publication of the photograph standing alone does not constitute an actionable invasion of plaintiffs' right of privacy. The right "to be let alone" and to be protected from undesired publicity is not absolute but must be balanced against the public interest in the dissemination of news and information consistent with the democratic processes under the constitutional guaranties of freedom of speech and of the press. The right of privacy may not be extended to prohibit any publication of matter which may be of public or general interest, but rather the "general object in view is to protect the privacy of private life, and to whatever degree and in whatever connection a man's life has ceased to be private, before the publication under consideration has been made, to that extent the protection is to be withdrawn." Brandeis-Warren Essay, 4 Harvard Law Rev., 193, 215. Moreover, the right of privacy is determined by the norm of the ordinary man; that is to say, the alleged objectionable publication must appear offensive in the light of "ordinary sensibilities." . . .

The picture allegedly was taken at plaintiffs' "place of business," a confectionery and ice cream concession in the Farmers' Market, Los Angeles. It shows plaintiffs, a young man and young woman, seated at a counter near a cash register, the young woman apparently in intent thought, with a notebook and pencil in her hands, which rest on the counter. Plaintiffs are dressed informally and are in a romantic pose, the young man having one arm about the young woman. There are at least five other persons plainly visible in the photograph in positions in close proximity to plaintiffs as the central figures. Apparently the picture has no particular news value but is designed to serve the function of entertainment as a matter of legitimate public interest. However, the constitution guaranties of freedom of expression apply with equal force to the publication whether it be a news report or an entertainment feature, and defendants' liability accrues only in the event that it can be said that there has been a wrongful invasion of plaintiffs' right of privacy.

In considering the nature of the picture in question, it is significant that it was not surreptitiously snapped on private grounds, but rather was taken of plaintiffs in a pose voluntarily assumed in a public market place. . . . Here plaintiffs, photographed at their concession allegedly "well known to persons and travelers throughout the world" as conducted for "many years" in the "world-famed" Farmers' Market, had voluntarily exposed themselves to public gaze in a pose open to the view of any persons who might then be at or near their place of business. By their own voluntary action plaintiffs waived their right of privacy so far as this particular public pose was assumed, for "There can be no privacy in that which is already public." *Melvin v. Reid*, 297 P. 91, 93. The photograph of plaintiffs merely permitted other members of the public, who were not at plaintiffs' place of business at the time it was taken, to see them as they had voluntarily exhibited themselves. Consistent which their own voluntary assumption of this particular pose in a public place, plaintiffs' right to privacy as to this photographed incident ceased and it in effect became a part of the public domain, as to which they could not later rescind their waiver in an attempt to assert a right of privacy. In short, the photograph did not disclose anything which until then had been private, but rather only extended knowledge of the particular incident to a somewhat larger public then had actually witnessed it at the time of occurrence.

Nor does there appear to be anything "uncomplimentary" or discreditable in the photograph itself, so that its publication might be objectionable as going "beyond the limits of decency" and reasonably indicate defendants' conduct to be such that they "should have realized it would be offensive to persons of ordinary sensibilities." Here the picture of plaintiffs, sitting romantically close to one another, the man with his arm around the woman, depicts no more than a portrayal of an incident which may be seen almost daily in ordinary life couples in a sentimental mood on public park benches, in railroad depots or hotel lobbies, at public games, the beaches, the theatres. Such situation is readily distinguishable from cases where the right of privacy has been enforced with regard to the publication of a picture which was shocking, revolting or indecent in its portrayal of the human body. In fact, here the photograph may very well be said to be complimentary and pleasing in its pictorial representation of plaintiffs.

Plaintiffs have failed to cite, and independent research has failed to reveal, any case where the publication of a mere photograph under the circumstances here prevailing a picture (1) taken in a pose voluntarily assumed in a public place and (2) portraying nothing to shock the ordinary sense of decency or propriety has been held an actionable invasion of the right of privacy. To so hold would mean that plaintiffs "under all conceivable circumstances had an absolute legal right to (prevent publication of) any photograph of them taken without their permission. If every person has such a right, no (periodical) could lawfully publish a photograph of a parade or a street scene. We are not prepared to sustain the assertion of such a right." . . .

CARTER, J. dissenting. I dissent, however, from the holding that the publication of the photograph alone did not violate plaintiffs' right of privacy. . . .

[F]irst, it should be quite obvious that there is no news or educational value whatsoever in the photograph alone. It depicts two persons (plaintiffs) in an amorous pose. There is nothing to show whether they are or are not married. While some remote news significance might be attached to persons in such a pose on the theory that the public likes and is entitled to see persons in such a pose, there is no reason why the publisher need invade the privacy of John and Jane Doe for his purpose. He can employ models for that purpose and the portion of the public interested will never know the difference but its maudlin curiosity will be appeased.

For the same reasons the discussion in the majority opinion to the effect that plaintiffs consented to the publication because they assumed the pose in a public place is fallacious. But in addition, such a theory is completely at odds with the violation of the right of privacy. By plaintiffs doing what they did in view of a tiny fraction of the public, does not mean that they consented to observation by the millions of readers of the defendant's magazine. In effect, the majority holding means that anything anyone does outside of his own home is with consent to the publication thereof, because, under those circumstances he waives his right of privacy even though there is no news value in the event. If such were the case, the blameless exposure of a portion of the naked body of a man or woman in a public place as the result of inefficient buttons, hooks or other clothes-holding devices could be freely photographed and widely published with complete immunity. The majority opinion confuses the situation, as have some of the other cases, with the question of newsworthiness. It has been said that when a person is involved in either a public or private event, voluntarily or involuntarily, of news value, that he has waived his right of privacy. Plainly such is not the case where the event is involuntary such as the victim of a holdup. . . . There is no basis for the conclusion that the second a person leaves the portals of his home he consents to have his photograph taken under all circumstances thereafter. There being no legitimate public interest, there is no excuse for the publication.

The [argument] that the picture would not offend the senses of an ordinary person is equally untenable. It is alleged in plaintiffs' complaint, and admitted by the demurrer that it so offended them. It is then a matter of proof at the trial. Certainly reasonable men could view the picture as showing plaintiffs in a sultry or sensual pose. For this Court to say as a matter of law that such portrayal would not seriously offend the feelings of an ordinary man is to take an extreme view to say the least. The question is one for the trier of fact. If it is in part a question of law it is so only to the extent that the right does not extend to "supersensitiveness or agoraphobia." An examination of the photograph shows that it would offend the feelings of persons other than oversensitive ones. . . .

In announcing a rule of law defining the right of a private citizen to be left alone, and not have his photograph published to the four winds, especially when he is depicted in an uncomplimentary pose, courts should consider the effect of such publication upon the sensibility of the ordinary private citizen, and not upon the sensibility of those persons who seek and enjoy publicity and notoriety and seeing their pictures on public display, or those who are in the "public eye" such as public officials, clergymen, lecturers, actors and others whose professional career brings them in constant contact with the public and in whom the public or some segment thereof is interested. Obviously anything the latter group may do or say has news or educational value such cannot be said of the persons engaged in private business or employment who constitute more that 90% of our population. These private citizens, who desire to be left alone, should have and enjoy a right of privacy so long as they do nothing which can reasonably be said to have news value. Certainly this right is entitled to protection. It seems to me that the law should be so molded as to protect the right of the 90% who do not desire publicity

or notoriety and who may be offended by publications such as that here involved.
. . .

NOTES & QUESTIONS

1. *Privacy in Public.* Similar to *Gill,* many courts hold that matters cease to be "private" when occurring in public. Appearing in public "necessarily involves doffing the cloak of privacy which the law protects." *Cefalu v. Globe Newspaper Co.*, 391 N.E.2d 935, 939 (Mass. App. 1979). In *Penwell v. Taft Broadcasting*, 469 N.E.2d 1025 (Ohio App. 1984), a husband and wife were arrested in a bar, handcuffed, and taken to the police station, where it was discovered that they had been arrested due to mistaken identity. A television film crew that arrived at the bar with the police filmed the plaintiff's arrest and removal from the bar, and the footage was later broadcast by the television station. The court dismissed the plaintiff's public disclosure action because the arrest was filmed in public and was "left open to the public eye." Does appearing in public extinguish a person's claim to privacy?

2. *Google Street View.* Google Street View allows Web surfers to see images of each street at street level. In the United States, Google provides an opt-out option for individuals who do not wish to have an image of their residence included in the Street View database. The Borings, who live on a private road outside of Pittsburgh, sued Google for taking Street View pictures without their permission. In an unpublished opinion, the Third Circuit affirmed a lower court's granting of Google's motion to dismiss. *Boring v. Google*, 38 Media L. Rep. 1306 (2010). On the intrusion upon seclusion claim, the Third Circuit declared, "No person of ordinary sensibility would be shamed, humiliated, or have suffered mentally as a result of a vehicle entering into his or her ungated driveway and photographing the view from there." As for publicity given to private life, it also found that the Borings failed to establish that the publicity would be highly offensive to a reasonable person. As an international comparison, protests in Germany against Google's introduction of this same service led the company to permit individuals, including persons who live in apartment buildings, to opt out their residence from the database *before* it went live. Which version of opt-out is preferable?

3. *Photography of Public Scenes.* Judge Carter, in dissent, argues that there is a difference between engaging in public displays of affection "in view of a tiny fraction of the public" and being observed by millions of magazine readers. Thus, the prior public exposure of the plaintiffs did not extinguish their privacy claim. How is the law to draw the appropriate line? At what point does the public exposure of the plaintiff's activities become too great to sustain a claim that the activities are private? Suppose, for example, a photographer is taking photos of people in the park. How is that photographer to know if she can publish the photos? Should she obtain the consent of everyone captured in the photos? According to the majority opinion, if Judge Carter's view were the law, this "would mean that plaintiffs under all conceivable circumstances had an

absolute legal right to (prevent publication of) any photograph of them taken without their permission. If every person has such a right, no (periodical) could lawfully publish a photograph of a parade or a street scene." How would Judge Carter respond?

4. ***Take Me Out to the Ball Game***. In July 2014, a Yankees fan sued Major League Baseball, the Yankees, and ESPN after announcers made allegedly disparaging comments about him as he slept soundly through a baseball game.[18] Among his claims was that Major League Baseball was responsible for "vituperative utterances" about him after it posted a clip of him sleeping on its website. For example, Twitter users inserted the sleeping fan's picture in various situations, including one that featured him in "Sleeping Beauty." Should the rise of social media and the ability of video clips and photography to "go viral" necessarily alter the analysis regarding photography and broadcasting of images captured in public? Does it matter for the analysis that the Yankees fan attended a publicly broadcast game?

DAILY TIMES DEMOCRAT V. GRAHAM

162 So. 2d 474 (Ala. 1964)

HARWOOD, J. This is an appeal from a judgment in favor of the plaintiff in an action charging an invasion by the defendant of the plaintiff's right of privacy. Damages were assessed by the jury at $4,166.00. . . .

Appellee is a woman 44 years of age who has lived in Cullman County, Alabama her entire life. She is married and has two sons, ages 10 and 8. The family resides in a rural community where her husband is engaged in the business of raising chickens. . . .

On 9 October 1961, the Cullman County Fair was in progress. On that day the appellee took her two children to the Fair. After going on some of the rides, the boys expressed a wish to go through what is called in the record the "Fun House." The boys were afraid to enter alone so the appellee accompanied them. She testified she had never been through a Fun House before and had no knowledge that there was a device that blew jets of air up from the platform of the Fun House upon which one exited therefrom.

The appellee entered the Fun House with her two boys and as she was leaving her dress was blown up by the air jets and her body was exposed from the waist down, with the exception of that portion covered by her "panties."

At this moment the appellant's photographer snapped a picture of the appellee in this situation. This was done without the appellee's knowledge or consent. Four days later the appellant published this picture on the front page of its newspaper.

The appellant publishes about five thousand newspapers daily which are delivered to homes, mailed to subscribers, and displayed on racks in various locations in the city of Cullman and elsewhere.

---

[18] James C. McKinley, Jr., *Fan Sues After Untimely Nap Brings Unwanted Attention*, N.Y. Times (July 8, 2014).

On the Sunday following the publication of the picture, the appellee went into the city of Cullman. There she saw the appellant's newspaper display with her picture on the front page in one of the appellant's newspaper racks, and she also saw copies of the said newspaper in other places.

While the appellee's back was largely towards the camera in the picture, her two sons are in the picture, and the photograph was recognized as being of her by other people with whom she was acquainted. The matter of her photograph was mentioned to the appellee by others on several occasions. Evidence offered by the appellee during the trial tended to show that the appellee, as a result of the publication of the picture, became embarrassed, self-conscious, upset and was known to cry on occasions. . . .

. . . Counsel contends that as a matter of law the publication of the photograph was a matter of legitimate news of interest to the public; that the publishing of the picture was in connection with a write-up of the Fair, which was a matter of legitimate news. If this be so, then of course the appellant would have been privileged to have published the picture.

Counsel has quoted from an array of cases as to what constitutes news. We see no need to refer to these cases in that their applicability to the facts now before us is negligible. We can see nothing of legitimate news value in the photograph. Certainly it discloses nothing as to which the public is entitled to be informed. . . .

Not only was this photograph embarrassing to one of normal sensibilities, we think it could properly be classified as obscene, in that "obscene" means "offensive to modesty or decency"; or expressing to the mind or view something which delicacy, purity, or decency forbid to be expressed.

The appellant's insistence of error in this aspect is therefore without merit.

Counsel further argues that the court erred in refusal of appellant's requested affirmative charges in that appellee's picture was taken at the time she was a part of a public scene, and the publication of the photograph could not therefore be deemed an invasion of her privacy as a matter of law.

The proposition for which appellant contends is probably best illustrated by the following quotation from *Forster v. Manchester*, 410 Pa. 192, 189 A.2d 147:

> On the public street, or in any other public place, the plaintiff has no right to be alone, and it is no invasion of his privacy to do no more than follow him about. Neither is it such an invasion to take his photograph in such a place, since this amounts to nothing more than making a record, not differing essentially from a full written description of a public sight which anyone present would be free to see.

Admittedly this principle is established by the cases. As well stated in *Hinish v. Meir & Frank Co., Inc.*, 113 P.2d 438:

> When a legal principle is pushed to an absurdity, the principle is not abandoned, but the absurdity avoided.

In other words, a purely mechanical application of legal principles should not be permitted to create an illogical conclusion.

To hold that one who is involuntarily and instantaneously enmeshed in an embarrassing pose forfeits her right of privacy merely because she happened at the moment to be part of a public scene would be illogical, wrong, and unjust.

One who is a part of a public scene may be lawfully photographed as an incidental part of that scene in his ordinary status. Where the status he expects to occupy is changed without his volition to a status embarrassing to an ordinary person of reasonable sensitivity, then he should not be deemed to have forfeited his right to be protected from an indecent and vulgar intrusion of his right of privacy merely because misfortune overtakes him in a public place. . . .

NOTES & QUESTIONS

1. *The Focus of the News Article.* Would a change in the focus of the news article change the outcome? What if the article appeared in a journal devoted to amusement parks, the (hypothetical) *Fun House Journal*?

2. *Voluntary vs. Involuntary Exposure.* The court holds that although Graham was in public, the exposure of her body was involuntary, and hence a private matter. Does whether a matter is public or private depend upon voluntary or involuntary disclosure or upon one's expectation? Is *Graham* consistent with *Gill v. Hearst Publishing Co.*? Can these cases be reconciled?

   Also consider *McNamara v. Freedom Newspapers, Inc.*, 802 S.W.2d 901 (Tex. Ct. App. 1991). A newspaper published a photo of a high school soccer player's inadvertently exposed genitalia while running on a soccer field. The plaintiff, McNamara, relied on *Daily Times Democrat v. Graham*, but the court found *Graham* unpersuasive and concluded:

   > The uncontroverted facts in this case establish that the photograph of McNamara was taken by a newspaper photographer for media purposes. The picture accurately depicted a public event and was published as part of a newspaper article describing the game. At the time the photograph was taken, McNamara was voluntarily participating in a spectator sport at a public place. None of the persons involved in the publishing procedure actually noticed that McNamara's genitals were exposed.

   Can *McNamara* be reconciled with *Graham*?

3. *Retracting Statements Made to the Media.* In *Virgil v. Time, Inc.*, 527 F.2d 1122 (9th Cir. 1975), a well-known body surfer was interviewed by *Sports Illustrated*, and photographs of the surfer were taken for the story. The surfer revoked his consent to publishing the story when he discovered that the article was not going to be exclusively about his surfing but was also going to discuss some of his personal eccentricities and incidents about his life in order to explain the psychological profile of those who engage in such a dangerous sport. The story was published, and the surfer sued for public disclosure. The court held that the information about the surfer's life was private:

   > It is not the manner in which information has been obtained that determines whether it is public or private. Here it is undisputed that the information was obtained without commission of a tort and in a manner wholly unobjectionable. However, that is not determinative as to this particular tort. The offense with which we are here involved is not the intrusion by means of which information is obtained; it is the publicizing of that which is private in character. The question, then, is whether the information disclosed was public rather than

private — whether it was generally known and, if not, whether the disclosure by appellant can be said to have been to the public at large.

Talking freely to someone is not in itself . . . making public the substance of the talk. There is an obvious and substantial difference between the disclosure of private facts to an individual — a disclosure that is selective and based on a judgment as to whether knowledge by that person would be felt to be objectionable — and the disclosure of the same facts to the public at large. . . .

Talking freely to a member of the press, knowing the listener to be a member of the press, is not then in itself making public. Such communication can be said to anticipate that what is said will be made public since making public is the function of the press, and accordingly such communication can be construed as a consent to publicize. Thus if publicity results it can be said to have been consented to. However, if consent is withdrawn prior to the act of publicizing, the consequent publicity is without consent. . . .

4. ***Privacy and Communication to Other People.*** Generally, a fact widely known about a person is not considered private; however, certain limited disclosures of information do not destroy its private nature. In *Times Mirror Co. v. Superior Court*, 244 Cal. Rptr. 556 (Cal. Ct. App. 1988), the plaintiff (Doe) discovered the murdered body of her roommate lying on the floor of her apartment and saw the perpetrator before she fled the apartment. Doe's identity was withheld from the public by the police to protect her safety (since the murderer was still at large), but her identity was leaked to a reporter and published in a newspaper article about the incident. Doe sued for public disclosure, and the newspaper argued that the matter was not private because Doe revealed it to certain neighbors, friends, family members, and investigating officials. The court, however, concluded that Doe had not "rendered otherwise private information public by cooperating in the criminal investigation and seeking solace from friends and relatives."

How many people must a person tell a secret to before it ceases to become private? In *Y.G. v. Jewish Hospital*, 795 S.W.2d 488 (Mo. Ct. App. 1990), a couple used in vitro fertilization at a hospital to become pregnant. While people at the hospital knew about their use of in vitro fertilization, the couple kept this hidden from others because it was against the teachings of their church. At a party in this hospital for in vitro couples, a camera crew from a television station filmed the plaintiffs (despite their making reasonable efforts to not be filmed). The court held that the plaintiffs retained an expectation of privacy because "attending this limited gathering . . . did not waive their right to keep their condition and the process of in vitro private, in respect to the general public." In *Multimedia WMAZ, Inc. v. Kubach*, 443 S.E.2d 491 (Ga. 1994), an HIV-positive plaintiff disclosed that he had the disease to about 60 people — family, friends, doctors, and members of an HIV support group. The plaintiff agreed to appear on a television show with his face obscured, but the obscuring process was botched, and the plaintiff was identifiable. He sued, and the court concluded that his telling his HIV-positive status to 60 people did not extinguish his privacy interest because these people "cared about him . . . or because they also had AIDS."

In contrast, consider *Duran v. Detroit News, Inc.,* 504 N.W.2d 715 (Mich. Ct. App. 1993). A Colombian judge, who indicted the violent drug lord Pablo Escobar, fled to Detroit after receiving death threats. She told a few people about her identity. Reporters, however, revealed her address and discussed the million-dollar bounty on her head. The court rejected Duran's public disclosure claim because she had exposed her identity "to the public eye." In *Fisher v. Ohio Dep't of Rehabilitation and Correction,* 578 N.E.2d 901 (Ohio Ct. Cl. 1988), the plaintiff told just four co-workers about encounters with her child that had "sexual overtones." The court concluded that the information was no longer private because the plaintiff "publicly and openly" told it to her co-workers.

Can you articulate a coherent approach to guide courts when analyzing how sharing information with other people affects the privacy of that information?

5. *Social Networks and Boundaries of Information Flow.* Lior Strahilevitz concludes that "courts are not being terribly explicit or precise about why particular disclosures waive privacy expectations and others do not. Certainly, a simple head-counting approach does not reconcile the precedents. After all, Kubach's disclosure of facts to sixty people did not render them public, but Fisher's disclosure to three people did." Strahilevitz suggests that looking to the number of people who are exposed to a secret is not the right approach. Instead, he uses social network theory.

Network theory describes how information flows between people. In particular, network theory seeks to assess the probability that information disclosed to one member of a particular group or community will be disseminated to others outside of that realm. According to Strahilevitz, the analysis should not focus on how many people already know a person's secret but how likely the secret is to be widely disseminated beyond the group of people who already know it. Information should be deemed private so long as it remains within a confined group — even if that group is rather large. The law should recognize that a particular person expects information to stay within these boundaries.

Strahilevitz identifies three key factors that affect the likelihood of data staying within a particular group: (1) how interesting the information is (the more interesting, the more likely it is to spread beyond the group); (2) the norms that a particular group has with regard to spreading the kind of information at issue; and (3) the way the group is structured and how information generally flows within and beyond the group. Strahilevtiz agrees with the *Kubach* court's decision that the plaintiff still retained a privacy interest in his HIV-positive status even though 60 others knew about it:

> [An empirical] study of HIV disclosure suggests that information about HIV status is frequently shared with some parts of an individual's social network, while other members, who might know the HIV positive person well and be interested in her health status, remain in the dark. Information about HIV status, therefore, seems not to flow through social networks readily, at least in the case of private figures. . . . Kubach had a reasonable expectation that his disclosure to some people who knew him would not result in the information being

revealed to others who knew him, let alone thousands of people in his local community.

Strahilevitz argues that the holding in *Duran* is inconsistent with social network theory:

> According to the court, Duran used her real name when shopping in stores or eating in restaurants, which waived an expectation of privacy in her identity. Under a network theory approach, these acts, combined with her notoriety in Colombia, would not have eliminated her reasonable expectation of privacy in her identity. . . . [When shopping or at a restaurant, at] most, Duran would have come into fleeting contact with other customers or service sector employees. There was nothing interesting about Duran's shopping or eating out. In order to generate interest in the story, the defendant had to connect Duran's presence in Detroit to her past notoriety in Colombia and the bounty that had been placed on her head. Such information was quite unlikely to be aggregated through the kinds of weak ties that Duran established in Detroit's public spaces. Perhaps a Colombian waiter put two-and-two together, but this would have been a highly improbable turn of events. Duran's general obscurity in Detroit properly engendered a reasonable expectation of privacy with respect to her shopping and visiting restaurants.[19]

6. ***Closed Communities.*** Woodrow Hartzog notes that there are certain closed communities where a strong expectation of confidentiality has developed, such as Alcoholics Anonymous. Closed communities also exist online — indeed, Alcoholics Anonymous has an online group. Hartzog contends: "Members of these closed communities have not disclosed their personal information to the world. Rather, they have revealed their information to other members of the community based on that community's norms and expectations of confidentiality."[20]

Suppose a person shares information with a group of 300 Facebook friends on her profile, which is set to be seen by "friends only." One of that person's friends reveals the information on a publicly accessible media site. In a lawsuit for public disclosure of private facts, the friend argues that the person's information was not private because it was available to 300 individuals on Facebook. How should a court rule on whether the information was private?

7. ***Further Dissemination of Previously Disclosed Information.*** Media entities that further disseminate information already disclosed by another media entity are not liable for public disclosure. *Ritzmann v. Weekly World News*, 614 F. Supp. 1336 (N.D. Tex. 1985) (giving further publicity to information contained in news stories already published is not actionable because the information is no longer private); *Heath v. Playboy Enterprises, Inc.*, 732 F. Supp. 1145 (S.D. Fla. 1990) ("Republication of facts already publicized elsewhere cannot provide a basis for an invasion of privacy claim.").

However, when only partial facts are revealed, the disclosure of more information can give rise to a viable action for public disclosure. For example, in

---

[19] Lior Jacob Strahilevitz, *A Social Networks Theory of Privacy,* 72 U. Chi. L. Rev. 919 (2005).

[20] Woodrow Hartzog, *Promises and Privacy: Promissory Estoppel and Confidential Disclosures in Online Communities*, 82 Temple L. Rev. 891 (2009).

Michaels v. Internet Entertainment Group, Inc., 5 F. Supp. 2d 823 (C.D. Cal. 1998), Bret Michaels, the former lead singer for the rock band Poison, and Pamela Anderson Lee, a celebrity, sought a preliminary injunction to prevent the defendant from making a videotape of the two having sex available on the Internet. The defendant argued that the plaintiffs lacked a privacy interest in the tape because a part of the tape had already been released by a foreign Internet source. The court, however, concluded that "plaintiffs' privacy interest in the unreleased portions of the Tape is undiminished." Further, another videotape depicting Lee having sex with her husband, Tommy Lee, had been widely distributed, and the defendant contended that this negated Lee's privacy interest. The court rejected the defendant's argument: "The Court is not prepared to conclude that public exposure of one sexual encounter forever removes a person's privacy interest in all subsequent and previous sexual encounters." The defendant also contended that Lee lacked a privacy interest because she had previously appeared nude in magazines and on video, but the court concluded that the defendant's "contention unreasonably blurs the line between fiction and reality. Lee is a professional actor. She has played roles involving sex and sexual appeal. The fact that she has performed a role involving sex does not, however, make her real sex life open to the public."

8. ***Obscurity.*** Woodrow Hartzog and Fred Stutzman argue that the law often fails to grasp the concept of obscurity and that the law should better integrate obscurity into its fabric. They contend:

> Perhaps more than anything else, Internet users rely on obscurity for protection of their online information. Obscurity allows Internet users to be genuine by disclosing information that they would not otherwise share in "public." Yet this concept, which is at the very heart of the social web, is largely undeveloped in privacy law. . .
>
> Obscurity could serve as a continuum when courts are asked to determine if information is eligible for privacy protections. Obscurity could be used as a benefit or protection—instead of forcing websites to remove information, a compromise could be some form of mandated obscurity. Finally, obscurity could serve as a metric for the boundary of allowable disclosure by information recipients. Internet users who were bound to a "duty to maintain obscurity" would be allowed to further disclose information, so long as they kept the information as generally obscure as they received it.[21]

Could locating a publicly available yet obscure piece of information about a person and writing about it in a widely read media outlet constitute a violation of privacy? Suppose a reporter finds information online in a blog that has only a handful of readers. The reporter writes about it on a major news media website. Is this a violation of privacy? If not, is anything appearing online and accessible to the public no longer able to be deemed private?

---

[21] Woodrow Hartzog & Fred Stutzman, *The Case for Online Obscurity,* 101 Cal. L. Rev. 1, 48 (2013).

(c) The Newsworthiness Test

SIPPLE V. CHRONICLE PUBLISHING CO.

201 Cal. Rptr. 665 (Cal. Ct. App. 1984)

CALDECOTT, J. On September 22, 1975, Sara Jane Moore attempted to assassinate President Gerald R. Ford while the latter was visiting San Francisco, California. Plaintiff Oliver W. Sipple (hereafter appellant or Sipple) who was in the crowd at Union Square, San Francisco, grabbed or struck Moore's arm as the latter was about to fire the gun and shoot at the President. Although no one can be certain whether or not Sipple actually saved the President's life, the assassination attempt did not succeed and Sipple was considered a hero for his selfless action and was subject to significant publicity throughout the nation following the assassination attempt.

Among the many articles concerning the event was a column, written by Herb Caen and published by the San Francisco Chronicle on September 24, 1975. The article read in part as follows: "One of the heroes of the day, Oliver 'Bill' Sipple, the ex-Marine who grabbed Sara Jane Moore's arm just as her gun was fired and thereby may have saved the President's life, was the center of midnight attention at the Red Lantern, a Golden Gate Ave. bar he favors. The Rev. Ray Broshears, head of Helping Hands, and Gay Politico, Harvey Milk, who claim to be among Sipple's close friends, describe themselves as 'proud — maybe this will help break the stereotype.' Sipple is among the workers in Milk's campaign for Supervisor."

Thereafter, the Los Angeles Times and numerous out-of-state newspapers published articles which referring to the primary source, (i.e., the story published in the San Francisco Chronicle) mentioned both the heroic act shown by Sipple and the fact that he was a prominent member of the San Francisco gay community. Some of those articles speculated that President Ford's failure to promptly thank Sipple for his heroic act was a result of Sipple's sexual orientation.[22]

. . . Sipple filed an action against the [newspapers]. The complaint was predicated upon the theory of invasion of privacy and alleged in essence that defendants without authorization and consent published private facts about plaintiff's life by disclosing that plaintiff was homosexual in his personal and private sexual orientation; that said publications were highly offensive to plaintiff inasmuch as his parents, brothers and sisters learned for the first time of his homosexual orientation; and that as a consequence of disclosure of private facts about his life plaintiff was abandoned by his family, exposed to contempt and ridicule causing him great mental anguish, embarrassment and humiliation.

---

[22] For example, the September 25, 1975, issue of the *Los Angeles Times* wrote inter alia as follows: "A husky ex-marine who was a hero in the attempted assassination of President Ford emerged Wednesday as a prominent figure in the gay community. And questions were raised in the gay community if Oliver (Bill) Sipple, 32, was being shunned by the White House because of his associations. Sipple, who lunged at Sara Jane Moore and deflected her revolver as she fired at the President, conceded that he is a member of the 'court' of Mike Caringi, who was elected 'emperor of San Francisco' by the gay community. A column item in a morning newspaper here strongly implied Wednesday that Sipple is gay. . . . Harvey Milk, a prominent member of this city's large homosexual community and a longtime friend of Sipple, speculated Wednesday that the absence of a phone call or telegram of gratitude from the White House might not be just an oversight."

Plaintiff finally alleged that defendants' conduct amounted to malice and oppression calling for both compensatory and punitive damages.

Appellant's principal contention on appeal is that the trial court prejudicially erred in granting summary judgment in favor of respondents. More precisely, appellant argues that the individual elements of the invasion of privacy (i.e., public disclosure of private facts; the offensiveness of the public disclosure; and the newsworthiness of the publication as an exception to tort liability) constituted a factual determination which could not be resolved or adjudicated by way of summary procedure.

Before discussing appellant's contentions on the merits, as an initial matter we set out the legal principles governing the case. It is well settled that there are three elements of a cause of action predicated on tortious invasion of privacy. First, the disclosure of the private facts must be a public disclosure. Second, the facts disclosed must be private facts, and not public ones. Third, the matter made public must be one which would be offensive and objectionable to a reasonable person of ordinary sensibilities. It is likewise recognized, however, that due to the supreme mandate of the constitutional protection of freedom of the press even a tortious invasion of one's privacy is exempt from liability if the publication of private facts is truthful and newsworthy. . . .

When viewed in light of the aforegoing principles, the summary judgment in this case must be upheld on two grounds. First, as appears from the record properly considered for the purposes of summary judgment, the facts disclosed by the articles were not private facts within the meaning of the law. Second, the record likewise reveals on its face that the publications in dispute were newsworthy and thus constituted a protective shield from liability based upon invasion of privacy. . . .

[Regarding the first ground,] the cases explain that there can be no privacy with respect to a matter which is already public or which has previously become part of the "public domain." Moreover, it is equally underlined that there is no liability when the defendant merely gives further publicity to information about the plaintiff which is already public or when the further publicity relates to matters which the plaintiff leaves open to the public eye.

The case at bench falls within the aforestated rules. The undisputed facts reveal that prior to the publication of the newspaper articles in question appellant's homosexual orientation and participation in gay community activities had been known by hundreds of people in a variety of cities, including New York, Dallas, Houston, San Diego, Los Angeles and San Francisco. Thus, appellant's deposition shows that prior to the assassination attempt appellant spent a lot of time in "Tenderloin" and "Castro," the well-known gay sections of San Francisco; that he frequented gay bars and other homosexual gatherings in both San Francisco and other cities; that he marched in gay parades on several occasions; that he supported the campaign of Mike Caringi for the election of "Emperor"; that he participated in the coronation of the "Emperor" and sat at Caringi's table on that occasion; that his friendship with Harvey Milk, another prominent gay, was well-known and publicized in gay newspapers; and that his homosexual association and name had been reported in gay magazines (such as Data Boy, Pacific Coast Times, Male Express, etc.) several times before the publications in question. In fact, appellant quite candidly conceded that he did not make a secret of his being a homosexual and that if anyone would ask, he would frankly admit that he was gay. In short, since appellant's sexual orientation was already in public domain and since the articles in question did no more than to give further publicity to matters which appellant left open to the eye of the public, a vital element of the tort was missing rendering it vulnerable to summary disposal. . . .

[Turning to the second ground — newsworthiness,] our courts have recognized a broad privilege cloaking the truthful publication of all newsworthy matters. . . . [T]he cases and authorities further explain that the paramount test of newsworthiness is whether the matter is of legitimate public interest which in turn must be determined according to the community mores. As pointed out in *Virgil v. Time, Inc.*, "In determining what is a matter of legitimate public interest, account must be taken of the customs and conventions of the community; and in the last analysis what is proper becomes a matter of the community mores. The line is to be drawn when the publicity ceases to be the giving of information to which the public is entitled, and becomes a morbid and sensational prying into private lives for its own sake, with which a reasonable member of the public, with decent standards, would say that he had no concern."

In the case at bench the publication of appellant's homosexual orientation which had already been widely known by many people in a number of communities was not so offensive even at the time of the publication as to shock the community notions of decency. Moreover, and perhaps even more to the point, the record shows that the publications were not motivated by a morbid and sensational prying into appellant's private life but rather were prompted by legitimate political considerations, i.e., to dispel the false public opinion that gays were timid, weak and unheroic figures and to raise the equally important political question whether the President of the United States entertained a discriminatory attitude or bias against a minority group such as homosexuals. . . .

Appellant's contention that by saving the President's life he did not intend to enter into the limelight and become a public figure, can be easily answered. In elaborating on involuntary public figures, Restatement Second of Torts section 625D, comment f, sets out in part as follows: "There are other individuals who have not sought publicity or consented to it, but through their own conduct or otherwise have become a legitimate subject of public interest. They have, in other words, become 'news.' "

NOTES & QUESTIONS

1. ***The Sad Fate of a Hero.*** Sipple passed away in January 1989, alone in a cluttered apartment with half-gallon bottles of bourbon within reach of his bed. A story in the *Los Angeles Times* almost a month after he passed away detailed the sad circumstances of his death and filled in some details of his life. Sipple had been wounded twice in Vietnam, lived on a veteran's disability pension, and, despite his lack of funds and poor health, was remembered by friends as a generous person who would readily give money to charity or to help a derelict.

The *L.A. Times* also noted that a framed letter hung in the apartment where Sipple had died — it was a letter of "heartfelt appreciation," signed "Jerry Ford," which thanked Sipple for his "selfless actions" in acting quickly and without fear and averting danger to the President and the crowd. The letter was sent three days after Sipple had knocked away the gun of the would-be assassin in San Francisco.

The *L.A. Times* article also stressed how much Sipple had suffered after the press outed him. It quoted George Sipple, Bill's brother: "His personal life never should have made it back to Detroit" (his hometown). Sipple's parents were shocked by the revelation of their son's sexual orientation; as the *L.A. Times* states: "The estrangement between Sipple and his father was so deep that when his mother died in 1979, his father made it clear that he was not welcome."[23] Sipple remained in San Francisco and did not attend his mother's funeral.

Taking a break from cleaning his brother's apartment, George Sipple noted that his brother was pleased that he left a mark and remembered that his brother once said that long after he died, "somebody will pick up a book and see Oliver Sipple saved President Ford's life."

2. ***Group Privacy.*** The court rejects Sipple's claim in part because Sipple's homosexuality and participation in the gay community were known by hundreds of people in many cities. But Sipple's argument is that he wanted to keep his homosexuality a secret from certain people — namely his parents and siblings. Can Sipple legitimately claim that something known widely to many people can still remain private?

3. ***President Ford's Prejudice.*** In *Sipple*, the newsworthiness of the story did not just turn on exposing the background of a hero who prevented an assassination. The story also exposed President Ford's possible prejudice against homosexuals. Does this fact alone establish that the story was newsworthy?

4. ***Outing.*** There has been extensive debate about the propriety of outing gays. Is the fact that a prominent individual is gay newsworthy? John Elwood observes that there are three rationales advanced for outing gays:

> According to its advocates, outing serves three basic purposes: (1) to expose the illogic of governmental policies that discriminate against homosexuals and of the hypocrisy of gay public officials who publicly support such policies; (2) to provide positive examples of gays, as role models to other gays and as ambassadors to mainstream America; and (3) to break down the stigma surrounding homosexuality by making it commonplace.

Elwood contends: "Even under the best of circumstances, the relationship between outing a particular figure and effecting a societal change is simply too attenuated to override the outing target's privacy rights." However, "a closeted government official who made disparaging public remarks about homosexuals or who enforced discriminatory programs might be a valid target for outing. Her hypocrisy calls into question her honesty and motivation, and thus information about her sexuality is relevant to the question of her fitness for office."[24] How would this argument apply in the *Sipple* case?

---

[23] Dean Morain, *Sorrow Trailed a Veteran Who Saved a President's Life and Then Was Cast in an Unwanted Spotlight*, L.A. Times, Feb. 13, 1989, at Part 5, 1.

[24] John P. Elwood, Note, *Outing, Privacy, and the First Amendment*, 102 Yale L.J. 747, 748-49, 773-74 (1992).

In contrast to Elwood, Kathleen Guzman disagrees with the hypocrisy justification for outing:

> . . . [T]his justification presupposes two potentially invalid assumptions. Presuming that the outers are even correct in asserting someone's orientation, one wonders whether there is such a thing as a "gay viewpoint." While abstract generalization may be made regarding the tendency of a group member to sympathize with in-group concerns, it is absurd to attribute to an individual a pre-packaged set of opinions merely because that individual is gay. One's views should no more be determined by sexual orientation than by being Caucasian or agnostic or underweight or female. . . .
>
> Second, what is orientation hypocrisy and at what level of conduct should it be penalized? Hypocrisy is a broad term which can encompass a range of activity: merely keeping same-sex orientation a secret; actively asserting heterosexuality; failing to vote for or affirmatively and publicly support pro-gay legislation; actively opposing similar legislation. The (non)actor whose conduct contravenes the mythical "gay viewpoint" need not necessarily be driven by "hypocrisy," but is equally likely to act through privacy, self-preservation, cowardice, or merely a different belief. A smoker who supports legislation restricting cigarette sales to minors is no more a hypocrite than a non-smoker who does so. A woman who votes against equal rights legislation is no more a hypocrite than a man who does so. To assert that she or he must be a hypocrite anathematizes individuality and accords insufficient weight to the myriad reasons that impel behavior or decision making.[25]

After Sipple's death, Fred Friendly, a journalism professor and former head of CBS News, wrote that journalists did not act fairly in Sipple's case and should not have written about his sexuality.[26] Friendly argued that the right to privacy should prevail unless the "individual's private conduct becomes relevant in assessing his integrity or validity in a public role." Do you agree with this approach? Does it resolve the *Sipple* case?

Barney Frank, a prominent gay politician, offered another perspective on outing. A member of the House of Representatives from 1981-2013, he articulated the approach that is now known as the "Frank Rule." He said: "I think there's a right to privacy. But the right to privacy should not be a right to hypocrisy. And people who want to demonize other people shouldn't then be able to go home and close the door and do it themselves." By this, he meant that a closeted politician who uses power to harm LGBT individuals should be outed. Do you agree with the Frank Rule, and, if so, should it be limited to politicians or also extended to other individuals with influence on society, such as CEOs, television or movie stars, or even novelists?

5. *Newsworthiness Tests.* Courts use at least three newsworthiness tests.[27] First is the "leave it to the press" approach, where courts defer to editorial judgment

---

[25] Kathleen Guzman, *About Outing: Public Discourse, Private Lives*, 73 Wash. U. L.Q. 1531, 1536-37, 1555-56 (1995). For further arguments against outing, see Jean L. Cohen, *Is Privacy a Legal Duty?*, in *Public and Private: Legal, Political, and Philosophical Perspectives* 117, 125 (Maurizio Passerin d'Entreves & Ursula Vogel eds., 2000).

[26] Fred W. Friendly, *Gays, Privacy and a Free Press*, Wash. Post, Apr. 8, 1990, at B7.

[27] *See* Geoff Dendy, Note, *The Newsworthiness Defense to the Public Disclosure Tort*, 85 Ky. L.J. 147 (1997).

and do not attempt to distinguish between what is news and what is entertainment. Second, the Restatement looks to the "customs and conventions of the community" and draws a line between the "giving of information to which the public is entitled" and "morbid and sensational prying into private lives for its own sake." A third approach is the "nexus test," which involves the Restatement approach but also requires a "logical nexus (or relationship) . . . between the complaining individual and the matter of legitimate public interest." Which test do you find most appropriate?

6. *What Is Newsworthy?* Many of the cases applying the newsworthiness test do so to avoid First Amendment problems. Keep in mind that the newsworthiness test is an element of the tort of public disclosure. Applications of the tort — involving possibly even non-newsworthy facts — can still be subject to an independent First Amendment challenge. This issue will be discussed later in this chapter.

How are courts to determine what is newsworthy? According to the Restatement of Torts § 652D (comment h), adopting language from *Virgil v. Time*, 527 F.2d 1122, 1129 (9th Cir. 1975), courts are to look to the "customs and conventions of the community."

Consider the case of *Diaz v. Oakland Tribune*, 188 Cal. Rptr. 762 (Ct. App. 1983). Diaz was the first woman student body president elected at a community college. The *Oakland Tribune* published the fact that Diaz was a transsexual. Diaz sued for public disclosure, and the court held that the suit could proceed to the jury, which would determine whether the fact that Diaz was a transsexual was newsworthy. The court noted: "[W]e find little if any connection between the information disclosed and Diaz's fitness for office. The fact that she is a transsexual does not adversely reflect on her honesty or judgment." Eugene Volokh, who opposes the tort of public disclosure altogether, argues:

> Now I agree with the [*Diaz*] court's factual conclusion; people's gender identity strikes me as irrelevant to their fitness for office. But other voters take a different view. Transsexuality, in their opinion, may say various things about politicians (even student body politicians): It may say that they lack attachment to traditional values, that they are morally corrupt, or even just that they have undergone an unnatural procedure and therefore are somehow tainted by it. These views may be wrong and even immoral, but surely it is not for government agents — whether judges or jurors — to dictate the relevant criteria for people's political choices, and to use the coercive force of law to keep others from informing them of things that they may consider relevant to those choices. I may disagree with what you base your vote on, but I must defend your right to base your vote on it, and the right of others to tell you about it.[28]

If Volokh is right, then what isn't relevant for fitness for office? Do public figures have any claim to privacy, or is everything about them newsworthy?

In *Neff v. Time, Inc.*, 406 F. Supp. 858 (W.D. Pa. 1976), a *Sports Illustrated* photographer printed a photograph of John W. Neff, a teacher, with the front zipper of his pants open in *Sports Illustrated*. The photograph was used in a

---

[28] Eugene Volokh, *Freedom of Speech and Information Privacy: The Troubling Implications of a Right to Stop People from Speaking About You*, 52 Stan. L. Rev. 1049, 1090 (2000).

story about Pittsburgh Steelers fans, and the article was entitled: "A Strange Kind of Love." The photograph was taken while Neff was with a group of fans at a football game between the Cleveland Browns and Pittsburgh Steelers. The fans were waving Steeler banners, drinking beer, and appeared slightly intoxicated. When the *Sports Illustrated* photographer approached them and the group found out that the photographer was covering the game for *Sports Illustrated*, the group "hammed it up" while the photographer snapped the pictures. Of the 30 pictures of the group that were taken, a committee of five employees at *Sports Illustrated* selected the photograph of Neff with his fly open for inclusion in the issue. According to the court, "[a]lthough Neff's fly was not open to the point of being revealing, the selection was deliberate and surely in utmost bad taste; subjectively, as to Neff, the published picture could have been embarrassing, humiliating and offensive to his sensibilities." According to Neff, the photograph implied "that he is a 'crazy, drunken slob,' and combined with the title of the article, 'a sexual deviate.'" Neff asserted that the article invaded his right to privacy, caused him reputational injury, subjected him to public ridicule, destroyed his peace of mind, and caused him severe emotional distress. The court, however, rejected Neff's claim:

> . . . It seems to us that art directors and editors should hesitate to deliberately publish a picture which most likely would be offensive and cause embarrassment to the subject when many other pictures of the same variety are available. Notwithstanding, "(t)he courts are not concerned with establishing canons of good taste for the press or the public." . . .
>
> The article about Pittsburgh Steeler fans was of legitimate public interest; the football game in Cleveland was of legitimate public interest; Neff's picture was taken in a public place with his knowledge and with his encouragement; he was catapulted into the news by his own actions; nothing was falsified; a photograph taken at a public event which everyone present could see, with the knowledge and implied consent of the subject, is not a matter concerning a private fact. A factually accurate public disclosure is not tortious when connected with a newsworthy event even though offensive to ordinary sensibilities. The constitutional privilege protects all truthful publications relevant to matters of public interest. . . .

Graham involved a photograph taken of a woman who was in an embarrassing position in public. How does the situation in *Neff* differ from that in *Graham*? *Graham* did not focus much on newsworthiness, but suppose that the case were being decided by the *Neff* court — would the photograph in *Graham* be newsworthy?

7. ***The Privacy of Public Figures.*** To what extent can a public figure's life be private? Consider the Restatement of Torts (Second) § 652D (comment h):

> The extent of the authority to make public private facts is not, however, unlimited. There may be some intimate details of [a celebrity actress's] life, such as sexual relations, which even the actress is entitled to keep to herself. In determining what is a matter of legitimate public interest, account must be taken of the customs and conventions of the community; and in the last analysis what is proper becomes a matter of the community mores. The line is to be drawn when the publicity ceases to be the giving of information to which the public is entitled, and becomes a morbid and sensational prying into private lives for its

own sake, with which a reasonable member of the public, with decent standards, would say that he had no concern. The limitations, in other words, are those of common decency, having due regard to the freedom of the press and its reasonable leeway to choose what it will tell the public, but also due regard to the feelings of the individual and the harm that will be done to him by the exposure. Some reasonable proportion is also to be maintained between the event or activity that makes the individual a public figure and the private facts to which publicity is given.

J.M. Balkin argues that by creating media events that show the politician "with his or her family, participating in casual activities or in a seemingly unguarded and intimate moment," politicians have been "willing accomplices in the creation of a new political culture that sees private aspects of a person's life as politically relevant, that collapses older boundaries between public and private." Moreover, Balkin argues, the media plays a role in shaping the boundaries between public and private: "Journalists do not simply respect the existing boundaries of the public and the private but actively reshape them: Merely by talking about sexual scandal and encouraging others to do so journalists make these topics part of public discourse and public comment."[29]

8. *The Disclosure of Identifying Information.* In *Barber v. Time, Inc.*, 159 S.W.2d 291 (Mo. 1942), the plaintiff's photograph taken in a hospital was published in a *Time* magazine article about the plaintiff's unusual disease. The article, "Starving Glutton," described the plaintiff's rare disorder where no matter how much she ate, she continued to lose weight. The photograph showed the plaintiff in her hospital bed. The court held that "[w]hile plaintiff's ailment may have been a matter of some public interest because unusual, certainly the identity of the person who suffered this ailment was not." In other words, the matter about the rare disorder was newsworthy, but the plaintiff's identity was not of public concern.

In contrast, consider *Haynes v. Alfred A. Knopf, Inc.*, 8 F.3d 1222 (7th Cir. 1993). In 1991, Alfred A. Knopf, Inc. published Nicholas Lemann's best-selling historical book entitled *The Promised Land: The Great Black Migration and How It Changed America*. The book chronicled the migration of 5 million African Americans from the rural areas in the South to urban areas in the North from 1940 to 1970. The book focuses centrally around the story of one individual, Ruby Lee Daniels. The book recounts Ruby's troubled marriage to Luther Haynes. Luther had a well-paying factory job but began to drink too much, waste money, and get into bitter fights with Ruby. The book recounts the couple's financial struggles, Luther's squandering of their money, their spiral into poverty, and their difficulties in providing for their children. When the couple was finally able to buy a home, Luther purchased a new car, and as a result, they couldn't meet their house payments and lost the home. Luther would frequently lose jobs and would often fail to come home. Luther then

---

[29] J.M. Balkin, *How Mass Media Stimulate Political Transparency*, 3 Cultural Values 393 (1999). For a discussion of when public figures should be entitled to privacy, see Anita L. Allen, *Lying to Protect Privacy*, 44 Vill. L. Rev. 161, 177 (1999); Anita L. Allen, *Privacy and the Public Official: Talking About Sex as a Dilemma for Democracy*, 67 Geo. Wash. L. Rev. 1165 (1999).

began to have an affair with their neighbor Dorothy Johnson, which was discovered by the children. Ruby and Luther got a divorce.

Subsequently, Luther married Dorothy. He turned his life around and began acting more responsibly. In their new community, nobody knew of Luther's past behavior toward Ruby. As Luther stated: "I know I haven't been no angel, but since almost 30 years ago I have turned my life completely around. I stopped the drinking and all this bad habits and stuff like that. . . . I look good in the eyes of my church members and my community. Now . . . all this is going to go down the drain. And I worked like a son of a gun to build myself up in a good reputation and he has torn it down."

Luther and Dorothy Haynes sued Lemann and his publisher Knopf under the public disclosure tort. Judge Posner, writing for the Seventh Circuit, rejected their claim: "No detail in the book claimed to invade the Hayneses' privacy is not germane to the story that the author wanted to tell, a story not only of legitimate but of transcendent public interest."

Was Luther Haynes's actual name really necessary for telling the story? The court concluded:

> The details of the Hayneses' lives recounted in the book would identify them unmistakably to anyone who has known the Hayneses well for a long time (members of their families, for example), or who knew them before they got married; and no more is required for liability either in defamation law or in privacy law. Lemann would have had to change some, perhaps many, of the details. But then he would no longer have been writing history. He would have been writing fiction. The nonquantitative study of living persons would be abolished as a category of scholarship, to be replaced by the sociological novel. That is a genre with a distinguished history punctuated by famous names, such as Dickens, Zola, Stowe, Dreiser, Sinclair, Steinbeck, and Wolfe, but we do not think that the law of privacy makes it (or that the First Amendment would permit the law of privacy to make it) the exclusive format for a social history of living persons that tells their story rather than treating them as data points in a statistical study. Reporting the true facts about real people is necessary to "obviate any impression that the problems raised in the [book] are remote or hypothetical."

Also consider *Gilbert v. Medical Economics Co.*, 665 F.2d 305 (10th Cir. 1981). An article describing a doctor's malpractice and arguing that hospitals and other physicians were not adequately self-policing included the doctor's name and photograph and discussed her psychiatric and marital problems. The doctor sued, contending that her photo, name, and personal life "add[ed] nothing to the concededly newsworthy topic of policing failures in the medical profession." The court disagreed, concluding:

> . . . [T]hese truthful representations are substantially relevant to a newsworthy topic because they strengthen the impact and credibility of the article. They obviate any impression that the problems raised in the article are remote or hypothetical, thus providing an aura of immediacy and even urgency that might not exist had plaintiff's name and photograph been suppressed. Similarly, we find the publication of plaintiff's psychiatric and marital problems to be substantially relevant to the newsworthy topic [because] . . . they are connected

to the newsworthy topic by the rational inference that plaintiff's personal problems were the underlying cause of the acts of alleged malpractice.

In *Howard v. Des Moines Register & Tribune Co.*, 870 F.2d 271 (5th Cir. 1989), the identities of victims of involuntary sterilization were disclosed in a report about abuses by a mental institution. The court rejected the argument that the identities were unnecessarily disclosed because they were needed to "strengthen the accuracy of the public perception of the merits of the controversy." In *Ross v. Midwest Communications, Inc.*, 870 F.2d 271 (5th Cir. 1989), the court held that the disclosure of a rape victim's name in an article about the potential innocence of the man convicted of the rape was of "unique importance to the credibility and persuasive force of the story."

Daniel Solove argues in favor of the approach taken in *Barber*. He contends that the use of initials or pseudonyms is a workable compromise between the interests of reporting the news and of protecting privacy: "Journalists generally do not include the names of rape victims or whistleblowers in their stories. On television, the media sometimes obscures the faces of particular people in video footage. With minimal effort, the media can report stories and also protect privacy."[30] In response to arguments about the importance of identifying people to help make the story more verifiable, Solove argues:

> [S]tories of paramount importance have not identified the critical parties; for example, in exposing Watergate, Bob Woodward and Carl Bernstein relied on the well-known pseudonymous source "Deep Throat." Certainly, it affects verifiability when a story does not identify a party. However, when the journalists protect confidential sources, they engage in a balancing determination, sacrificing the public's ability to verity for the importance of protecting confidentiality. Public verifiability is not sacrosanct, but can be outweighed by privacy interests.[31]

9. ***Who Decides What Is Newsworthy?*** Who ought to determine the proper subject for news? Courts? Journalists? The market? Juries? A number of courts defer to the judgment of the press for newsworthiness: "[W]hat is newsworthy is primarily a function of the publisher, not the courts." *Heath v. Playboy Enterprises, Inc.*, 732 F. Supp. 1145, 1149 (S.D. Fla. 1990); *see also Jenkins v. Dell Publishing Co.*, 251 F.2d 447, 451-52 (3d Cir. 1958); *Wagner v. Fawcett Publications*, 307 F.2d 409, 410 (7th Cir. 1962). If courts are not to second guess the judgment of the press, how are courts to determine newsworthiness? Is anything not newsworthy?

Daniel Solove contends that the deference to the media approach is a poor one. He argues that although the media might be a capable decision maker for assessing public interest in a story, "[w]hat is of interest to most of society is not the same question as what is of legitimate public concern. . . . [Public] interest can stem from a desire for entertainment or sexual pleasure just as much as it can from wanting to learn about the news and current events." Therefore, Solove concludes, "the media should not have a monopoly on determining what

---

[30] Daniel J. Solove, *The Virtues of Knowing Less: Justifying Privacy Protections Against Disclosure*, 53 Duke L.J. 967, 1018-19 (2003).
[31] *Id.* at 1018.

is of public concern."[32] In contrast, consider Eugene Volokh, who contends: "Under the First Amendment, it's generally not the government's job to decide what subjects speakers and listeners should concern themselves with."[33]

10. ***Is the Newsworthiness Test Necessary or Desirable?*** Lior Strahilevitz argues that the newsworthiness test is not the best way to reconcile the public disclosure tort with free speech. He contends that the First Amendment already provides a sufficient constraint on the tort and a newsworthiness test is not needed:

> The fact that the First Amendment may constrain the state's ability to impose damages on those who publish private facts does not mean that the underlying tort causes of action need to look any different. Rather, it simply means that once tort liability is found, the courts should conduct an independent inquiry as to whether imposing liability on that defendant (or class of defendants) will undermine fundamental expressive or self-governance interests. Indeed, such a textured inquiry better coheres with First Amendment doctrine than does the public disclosure tort's binary newsworthiness/non-newsworthiness distinction.[34]

If the newsworthiness test is merely designed to protect First Amendment interests, then why not just have the First Amendment provide the protection? Is there a good reason to keep the newsworthiness test?

SHULMAN V. GROUP W PRODUCTIONS, INC.

955 P.2d 469 (Cal. 1998)

[Recall the facts of this case earlier in this chapter. The plaintiffs, Ruth and Wayne Shulman, mother and son, were injured in a car accident. A medical transport and rescue helicopter crew came to their assistance along with a video camera operator, who filmed the plaintiffs' rescue from the car, the flight nurse and medic's medical aid during the rescue, as well as their medical aid in the helicopter en route to the hospital. The flight nurse wore a small microphone that picked up her conversations with Ruth and other rescue workers. The segment was broadcast on a television show called *On Scene: Emergency Response*. Ruth, a paraplegic from the accident, watched the episode in her hospital room in shock. Neither Ruth nor Wayne Shulman consented to the filming or broadcasting. They sued the producers of the show, and their complaint included causes of action for public disclosure of private facts and intrusion upon seclusion. The trial court granted the defendants' motion for summary judgment on all causes of action.

On the intrusion claim, the California Supreme Court held that the activities of the defendants in recording the events in the helicopter constituted a valid cause of action for intrusion upon seclusion. The court's decision on the public disclosure claim is excerpted below.]

---

[32] Daniel J. Solove, *The Virtues of Knowing Less: Justifying Privacy Protections Against Disclosure*, 53 Duke L.J. 967, 1001, 1006 (2003).

[33] Eugene Volokh, *Freedom of Speech and Information Privacy: The Troubling Implications of a Right to Stop People from Speaking About You*, 52 Stan. L. Rev. 1049, 1089 (2000).

[34] Lior Strahilevitz, *Reunifying Privacy Law*, 98 Cal. L. Rev. 2007, 2033 (2010).

WERDEGAR, J. . . . [U]nder California common law the dissemination of truthful, newsworthy material is not actionable as a publication of private facts. If the contents of a broadcast or publication are of legitimate public concern, the plaintiff cannot establish a necessary element of the tort action, the lack of newsworthiness. . . .

Although we speak of the lack of newsworthiness as an element of the private facts tort, newsworthiness is at the same time a constitutional defense to, or privilege against, liability for publication of truthful information. . . . Tort liability, obviously, can extend no further than the First Amendment allows; conversely, we see no reason or authority for fashioning the newsworthiness element of the private facts tort to *preclude* liability where the Constitution would allow it. . . .

Newsworthiness — constitutional or common law — is also difficult to define because it may be used as either a descriptive or a normative term. "Is the term 'newsworthy' a descriptive predicate, intended to refer to the fact there is widespread public interest? Or is it a value predicate, intended to indicate that the publication is a meritorious contribution and that the public's interest is praise-worthy?" A position at either extreme has unpalatable consequences. If "news-worthiness" is completely descriptive — if all coverage that sells papers or boosts ratings is deemed newsworthy — it would seem to swallow the publication of private facts tort, for "it would be difficult to suppose that publishers were in the habit of reporting occurrences of little interest." At the other extreme, if newsworthiness is viewed as a purely normative concept, the courts could become to an unacceptable degree editors of the news and self-appointed guardians of public taste. . . .

Courts balancing these interests in cases similar to this have recognized that, when a person is involuntarily involved in a newsworthy incident, not all aspects of the person's life, and not everything the person says or does, is thereby rendered newsworthy. . . . This principle is illustrated in the decisions holding that, while a particular event was newsworthy, identification of the plaintiff as the person involved, or use of the plaintiff's identifiable image, added nothing of significance to the story and was therefore an unnecessary invasion of privacy. . .

Consistent with the above, courts have generally protected the privacy of otherwise private individuals involved in events of public interest "by requiring that a logical nexus exist between the complaining individual and the matter of legitimate public interest." . . .

Intensely personal or intimate revelations might not, in a given case, be considered newsworthy, especially where they bear only slight relevance to a topic of legitimate public concern. . . .

Turning now to the case at bar, we consider whether the possibly private facts complained of here — broadly speaking, Ruth's appearance and words during the rescue and evacuation — were of legitimate public interest. If so, summary judgment was properly entered. . . .

We agree at the outset with defendants that the subject matter of the broadcast as a whole was of legitimate public concern. Automobile accidents are by their nature of interest to that great portion of the public that travels frequently by automobile. The rescue and medical treatment of accident victims is also of legitimate concern to much of the public, involving as it does a critical service that any member of the public may someday need. The story of Ruth's difficult extrication from the crushed car, the medical attention given her at the scene, and her evacuation by helicopter was of particular interest because it highlighted some of the challenges facing emergency workers dealing with serious accidents.

The more difficult question is whether Ruth's appearance and words as she was extricated from the overturned car, placed in the helicopter and transported to the hospital were of legitimate public concern. Pursuant to the analysis outlined earlier, we conclude the disputed material was newsworthy as a matter of law. One of the dramatic and interesting aspects of the story as a whole is its focus on flight nurse Carnahan, who appears to be in charge of communications with other emergency workers, the hospital base and Ruth, and who leads the medical assistance to Ruth at the scene. Her work is portrayed as demanding and important and as involving a measure of personal risk (e.g., in crawling under the car to aid Ruth despite warnings that gasoline may be dripping from the car). The broadcast segment makes apparent that this type of emergency care requires not only medical knowledge, concentration and courage, but an ability to talk and listen to severely traumatized patients. One of the challenges Carnahan faces in assisting Ruth is the confusion, pain and fear that Ruth understandably feels in the aftermath of the accident. For that reason the broadcast video depicting Ruth's injured physical state (which was not luridly shown) and audio showing her disorientation and despair were substantially relevant to the segment's newsworthy subject matter.

Plaintiffs argue that showing Ruth's "intimate private, medical facts and her suffering was not *necessary* to enable the public to understand the significance of the accident or the rescue as a public event." The standard, however, is not necessity. That the broadcast *could* have been edited to exclude some of Ruth's words and images and still excite a minimum degree of viewer interest is not determinative. Nor is the possibility that the members of this or another court, or a jury, might find a differently edited broadcast more to their taste or even more interesting. The courts do not, and constitutionally could not, sit as superior editors of the press. . . .

BROWN, J. concurring and dissenting. . . . I respectfully dissent . . . from the conclusion that summary judgment was proper as to plaintiff Ruth Shulman's cause of action for publication of private facts. . . .

. . . The private facts broadcast had little, if any, social value. The public has no legitimate interest in witnessing Ruth's disorientation and despair. Nor does it have any legitimate interest in knowing Ruth's personal and innermost thoughts immediately after sustaining injuries that rendered her a paraplegic and left her hospitalized for months — "I just want to die. I don't want to go through this." The depth of the broadcast's intrusion into ostensibly private affairs was substantial. . . . There was nothing voluntary about Ruth's position of public notoriety. She was involuntarily caught up in events of public interest, all the more so because defendants appear to have surreptitiously and unlawfully recorded her private conversations with nurse Laura Carnahan. . . .

NOTES & QUESTIONS

1. *Voluntariness and Public Exposure.* Is this case consistent with *Graham*?
2. *Grief and Newsworthiness.* Reality television shows and "caught on film" docudramas frequently capture people in moments of profound trauma and grief. Is it newsworthy to display footage of grieving relatives after a disaster or personal tragedy occurs?
3. *Post-Mortem Privacy Rights?* Generally, privacy rights are said to expire when the subject of this interest dies. The traditional exception to this doctrine is the right of publicity. Another exception is that courts recognize actions for privacy torts such as public disclosure and intrusion upon seclusion for family members of a decedent in autopsy or death-scene photos. In *Catsouras v. Department of the California Highway Patrol (CHP)*, 104 Cal. Rptr. 3d 352 (2010), 18-year-old Nicole Catsouras "was decapitated in an automobile accident." Police officers took multiple photographs of her corpse. According to allegations in a lawsuit filed by her family, the photos were e-mailed by these police officers to some members of the public.

   The *Catsouras* court found that the decedent's family had a cognizable claim for an invasion of privacy based on the public disclosure tort. The court reasoned that "family members do have their own privacy rights in death images." The court noted that the images were "allegedly disseminated out of sheer morbidity or gossip, as opposed to any official law enforcement purpose or genuine public interest."

   Would it be significant if the Catsouras family had attempted to sue the media and not the police? Would it matter to the outcome of this litigation if the leaked photographs accompanied an article on driving safety?

BONOME V. KAYSEN

17 Mass. L. Rptr. 695 (Mass. Supp. 2004)

MUSE, J. Joseph Bonome filed this action alleging invasion of privacy against Susana Kaysen, the author of a memoir at the center of this case, and Random House, Inc., the publisher. . . .

In the early 1990s, Bonome owned and operated a tree surgery and landscaping business primarily in the Cambridge, Massachusetts area. At the time, he was living in New Hampshire and was married with step-children. Kaysen was an author living in Cambridge. She had gained success and notoriety for her book *Girl, Interrupted* which was made into what has been described to be a critically acclaimed film. In 1994, Bonome met Kaysen and the two began having an affair, including a physical relationship. Kaysen pressured Bonome to leave his wife, and Bonome ultimately succumbed to that pressure. Bonome divorced his wife in 1996 and shortly thereafter moved into Kaysen's home, where they continued the relationship.

Within six months or a year into the relationship, Kaysen began to experience severe vaginal pain. She began to regularly see doctors for her problem, but over the course of several years was unable to receive sufficient curative treatment.

During this time period, she began working on a new book, which book is the subject of this case. Despite Bonome's inquiries, Kaysen would not reveal the subject of the book to him.

The fact of their relationship was well-known to Bonome's family, friends, and clientele. However, the details of their physical relationship were private. Bonome's parents and three brothers all spent time, including some holidays, with the couple. However, in July 1998, the relationship "ended" when Kaysen asked Bonome to move out, which he did. Despite the breakup, their physical relationship continued for at least three months longer.

In 2001, Random House published the book [*The Camera My Mother Gave Me*]. The book only refers to Bonome as Kaysen's "boyfriend" and alters details about his life — such as where he was from, and his occupation. The book is an autobiographical memoir chronicling the effects of Kaysen's seemingly undiagnosable vaginal pain in a series of ruminations about the condition's effects on many aspects of her life, including her overall physical and emotional state, friendships, and her relationship with her boyfriend. It details her intense pain and discomfort and her many fruitless attempts to obtain an accurate medical diagnosis and effective treatment.

One of the central themes of the book concerns the impact of her chronic pain on the emotional and physical relationship with Kaysen's boyfriend. To that end, the book details, graphically on a few occasions, several sexual encounters between them. It portrays the boyfriend as becoming increasingly frustrated and impatient with Kaysen's condition and her reluctance and/or refusal to engage in physical intimacy. The boyfriend is described as "always bugging [her] for sex" and "whining and pleading" for sex, as well as being ignorant and insensitive to her emotional and physical state. In this vein, it attributes many aggressive and overtly offensive sexual quotes to him. Ultimately, the development of this theme culminates in a scene where the boyfriend is physically forceful in an attempt to engage her in sex. This scene is followed by ruminations about whether the relationship had exceeded the bounds of consensual sexual relations into the realm of coerced non-consensual sex. . . .

After publication of the book, Bonome learned that many local friends and family had read the book and understood the portrayal of the "boyfriend" to be a depiction of him. In addition, Bonome's business clientele included friends of Kaysen who also understood that Bonome was the "boyfriend." As a result of the publication, Bonome has suffered severe personal humiliation, and his reputation has been severely damaged among a substantial percentage of his clients and acquaintances. . . .

General Laws chapter 214 Section 1B provides that: "[a] person shall have a right against unreasonable, substantial or serious interference with his privacy." Section 1B has been interpreted to include the common-law tort of "public disclosure of private facts" as articulated in the Restatement (Second) of Torts. . . .

[T]his case presents an additional challenge in that it pits Kaysen's right of publicity — her own right to disclose intimate facts about herself — directly in conflict Bonome's right to control the dissemination of private information about himself. . . .

Undoubtedly, the information revealed was of an intensely intimate and personal nature. Indeed, commentators and courts have almost universally

recognized one's sexual affairs as falling squarely within the sphere of private life.
. . .

[O]therwise private information may properly be published when it is sufficiently related to a broader topic of legitimate public concern. In this case, a critical issue is whether the personal information concerning Bonome is in the book for its relevance to issues of legitimate public concern or is merely "morbid and sensational plying into [Bonome's] private [life] for its own sake."

After examining the statements concerning the boyfriend and their relevance to the broader themes of the book, it is clear that the details are included to develop and explore those themes. Specifically, the book explores the way in which Kaysen's undiagnosed physical condition impacted her physical and emotional relationship with "her boyfriend." Moreover, it explores the issue of when undesired physical intimacy crosses the line into non-consensual sexual relations in the context of her condition. These broader topics are all matters of legitimate public concern, and it is within this specific context that the explicit and highly personal details of the relationship are discussed. Thus, the defendants had a legitimate and protected interest to publish these facts.

As noted above, there is an additional interest in this case: Kaysen's right to disclose her own intimate affairs. In this case, it is critical that Kaysen was not a disinterested third party telling Bonome's personal story in order to develop the themes in her book. Rather, she is telling *her own* personal story — which inextricably involves Bonome in an intimate way. In this regard, several courts have held that where an autobiographical account related to a matter of legitimate public interest reveals private information concerning a third party, the disclosure is protected so long as there is a sufficient nexus between those private details and the issue of public concern.

Where one's own personal story involves issues of legitimate public concern, it is often difficult, if not impossible, to separate one's intimate and personal experiences from the people with whom those experiences are shared. Thus, it is within the context of Bonome and Kaysen's lives being inextricably bound together by their intimate relationship that the disclosures in this case must be viewed. Because the First Amendment protects Kaysen's ability to contribute *her own* personal experiences to the public discourse on important and legitimate issues of public concern, disclosing Bonome's involvement in those experiences is a necessary incident thereto.

. . . [T]he privilege to disclose private information is limited by the requirement that the disclosure bear the necessary nexus (both logical and proportional) to the issue of legitimate public concern. In this regard, it is of importance that Kaysen did not use Bonome's name in the book. The defendants did not subject Bonome to unnecessary publicity or attention. The realm of people that could identify Bonome as the boyfriend are those close personal friends, family, and business clients that knew of the relationship. This is not to overlook or discount the impact this disclosure may have had on Bonome, or his substantial claim that Kaysen breached a fundamental trust of their relationship. However arguably odious, the defendants did not exercise the right of disclosure in a manner offensive to the balance of those interests. See Restatement (Second) Torts § 652D, comment a ("Publicity . . . means that the matter is made public, by communicating it to the public at large, or to so many persons that the matter must be regarded as substantially certain to become one of public knowledge"). . . .

This court is not unmindful of the injury claimed by Bonome, who alleges to have suffered personal humiliation within his familial circle, as well as with friends and business clientele as a result of the book's publication. Nonetheless, Kaysen's own personal story — insofar as it relates to matters of legitimate public concern — is hers to contribute to the public discourse. This right is protected by the First Amendment. Inasmuch as the book does not exceed the bounds of that constitutional privilege, Bonome's claim for invasion of privacy under G.L.c. 214, § 1B is *DISMISSED*.

NOTES & QUESTIONS

1. ***The Right to Tell One's Story.*** The newsworthiness test examines whether a disclosure is of "legitimate concern to the public." It does not matter who is making the disclosure for the purposes of the test. However, the court suggests that "there is an additional interest in this case: Kaysen's right to disclose her own intimate affairs." The court states that "it is critical that Kaysen was not a disinterested third party telling Bonome's personal story in order to develop the themes in her book. Rather, she is telling *her own* personal story — which inextricably involves Bonome in an intimate way." Does the autobiographical nature of the disclosure change the newsworthiness analysis? Should it?

 Sonja West contends that when autobiographical speech is involved, courts should not look to whether it is of legitimate public interest: "The power to decide what is of consequence in a person's life story should ultimately lie with that person alone. As long as the content and intention of the speech is truly autobiographical, its perceived importance by others should not affect its constitutional protection."[35] Should a person have increased latitude when revealing private information about others when it also involves her own autobiographical details?

 Suppose Kaysen told her story to a journalist, who wrote about it in an article. Should the journalist receive less protection for making the disclosure than Kaysen would receive for revealing the same facts?

2. ***Blogs, Social Network Websites, and Gossip.*** In *Steinbuch v. Cutler*, 463 F. Supp. 2d 1 (D.D.C. 2006), Jessica Cutler, a staff member for a U.S. senator, wrote a blog about her relationships with several men, including a man she was dating who also worked for the senator. In her blog, The Washingtonienne, she recounted in vivid detail their budding romance. Specifically, Cutler described their sexual practices, personal conversations, and other intimate details. Cutler did not identify Steinbuch directly, but she used his real initials and disclosed other personally identifiable information that made it possible for him to be identified. For a few weeks, only a handful of people knew about Cutler's blog. Then Wonkette, a very popular political gossip blog, linked to her blog and tens of thousands began flocking to the site. The story was written about in many

---

[35] Sonja West, *The Story of Me: The Underprotection of Autobiographical Speech,* 84 Wash. U. L. Rev. 905, 966 (2006).

major newspapers. Steinbuch sued Cutler for violating his privacy. The case never proceeded to trial because Cutler declared bankruptcy.

One of Cutler's arguments was that the blog was only read by a handful of her friends until Wonkette linked to it. Cutler contended that she never gave widespread publicity to the information — Wonkette did. When information is disclosed on the Internet, but only a few people read it, is disclosure sufficiently widespread for the publicity element to be satisfied?

Cutler also argued that her account of her relationships was newsworthy. According to her motion to dismiss: "Cutler's Blog makes a shocking and disturbing portrayal of casual and even reckless sexual encounters between young, entry-level Capitol Hill staffers like Cutler and more senior staffers like Steinbuch. . . . The interrelationship between youth, beauty, sex, money, and power in Washington has long been a matter of legitimate and sometimes *pressing* public interest." Is Cutler's blog newsworthy? What are the best arguments on each side of the issue?

In his book, *The Future of Reputation,* Daniel Solove observes that people are increasingly expressing themselves in blogs and social network websites. People are revealing information about their private lives as well as gossip and rumors about their friends, family, co-workers, and others. Solove notes:

> The Internet is transforming the nature and effects of gossip. It is making gossip more permanent and widespread, but less discriminating in the appropriateness of audience. . . . The problem with Internet gossip is that it can so readily be untethered from its context.

More broadly, Solove observes, the transformation of gossip from the fleeting and forgettable to the permanent and searchable might have significant social effects:

> We may find it increasingly difficult to have a fresh start, a second chance, or a clean slate. We might find it harder to engage in self-exploration if every false step and foolish act is chronicled forever in a permanent record. This record will affect our ability to define our identities, to obtain jobs, to participate in public life, and more. Ironically, the unconstrained flow of information on the Internet might impede our freedom.[36]

Are the privacy torts a viable way to protect people from having their personal lives written about online?

3. *The Breach of Confidentiality Tort.* The breach of confidentiality tort protects against the nonconsensual disclosures of confidential information. To establish liability under the tort, a plaintiff must prove that the defendant owed the plaintiff a duty of confidentiality and that the defendant breached that duty.[37]

---

[36] Daniel J. Solove, *The Future of Reputation: Gossip, Rumor, and Privacy on the Internet* (2007). For more background about applying the privacy torts to blogs and social network sites, see Patricia Sánchez Abril, *Recasting Privacy Torts in a Spaceless World,* 21 Harv. J.L. & Tech. 1 (2007).

[37] For more background about the tort, see Alan B. Vickery, Note, *Breach of Confidence: An Emerging Tort,* 82 Colum. L. Rev. 1426 (1982); G. Michael Harvey, Comment, *Confidentiality: A Measured Response to the Failure of Privacy,* 140 U. Pa. L. Rev. 2385 (1992); Susan M. Gilles, *Promises Betrayed: Breach of Confidence as a Remedy for Invasion of Privacy,* 43 Buff. L. Rev. 1 (1995).

Unlike the tort of public disclosure, the breach of confidentiality tort does not have the elements of highly offensive, publicity, or the newsworthiness test. In America, the breach of confidentiality tort has been applied to doctors and other professionals. In contrast, in England, which rejects the Warren and Brandeis privacy torts, including the public disclosure tort, has a robust breach of confidentiality tort. As Neil Richards and Daniel Solove observe:

> The law of confidentiality in England also has attributes that the American privacy torts lack. In America, the prevailing belief is that people assume the risk of betrayal when they share secrets with each other. But in England, spouses, ex-spouses, friends, and nearly anyone else can be liable for divulging confidences. As one English court noted: "The fact is that when people kiss and later one of them tells, that second person is almost certainly breaking a confidential arrangement." Confidentiality thus recognizes that nondisclosure expectations emerge not just from norms of individual dignity, but also from norms of relationships, trust, and reliance on promises. American privacy law has never fully embraced privacy within relationships; it typically views information exposed to others as no longer private. Although a tort remedying breach of confidence would emerge later on in American law, it has developed slowly in comparison to the Warren and Brandeis privacy torts.[38]

Should a person accept the risk of betrayal when sharing confidential information with another?

Suppose the breach of confidentiality tort were applied more broadly to situations where friends, spouses, and others disclosed the secrets of others. Andrew McClurg notes that the First Amendment implications of the breach of confidentiality tort are different from those of the public disclosure tort:

> If one accepts the proposition that a party to an intimate relationship impliedly agrees not the breach the other party's confidence by publishing private, embarrassing information about them via an instrument of mass communication, the speech restriction is one that is self-imposed, rather than state-imposed.[39]

How might a broader application of the breach of confidentiality tort impact bloggers like Jessica Cutler who write about their sexual activities with others? Would the tort impair free speech too much? Note that there is no newsworthiness test under the tort, so information of public concern is not protected. On the other hand, as McClurg notes, the breach of confidentiality tort understands that parties have made an implicit contract of confidentiality. Is it a violation of free speech to enforce a person's explicit or implicit promise not to speak about something?

4. *Reputation-Tracking Technologies.* Lior Strahilevitz argues that reputation-tracking technologies can yield beneficial results. He points to programs such as "How's My Driving?" (HMD) programs in which some commercial vehicles have stickers with a number to call to complain about bad driving. Insurance

---

[38] Neil M. Richards & Daniel J. Solove, *Privacy's Other Path: Recovering the Law of Confidentiality,* 96 Geo. L.J. 123 (2007).

[39] Andrew J. McClurg, *Kiss and Tell: Protecting Intimate Relationship Privacy Through Implied Contracts of Confidentiality,* 74 U. Cin. L. Rev. 887, 938 (2006).

company statistics reveal significant reductions in crash costs and accidents (declines of well over 30 percent) following the implementation of HMD programs. Strahilevitz argues that the reason for the effectiveness of HMD programs is that they reduce driver anonymity:

> The problems associated with urban and suburban driving are, by and large, creatures of motorist anonymity. That statement may seem too bold to readers accustomed to hearing about drunken driving, drowsy driving, and road rage. But a review of the literature on driving suggests that these problems largely stem from roadway anonymity. If society were able to monitor its roadways around the clock and to analyze this data immediately to identify and punish problematic motorists, many of the traffic accident deaths that occur every year would be averted. A dangerous driving environment is the almost inevitable consequence of sporadic traffic law enforcement by the police combined with rare traffic norm enforcement by motorists.[40]

Strahilevitz points out that various websites such as Amazon.com, Tripadvisor.com, and eBay.com harness user feedback, where people can leave comments about a particular merchant or individual: "Though eBay's reputation system is admittedly imperfect, it has been extraordinarily successful at preventing fraud among auction participants." He proposes that more measures like HMD programs in other contexts might be beneficial. In what other situations would reputation-tracking technologies be useful? What are the potential problems with such technologies? Is there a way to implement these technologies that minimize these problems?

5. **_Practical Limitations on the Public Disclosure Tort._** Consider Jacqueline Lipton:

> Individuals who have faced shame, humiliation, or embarrassment as a result of the public dissemination of truthful information may have a variety of practical reasons for declining to bring a legal action, even if a cause of action is technically available. Many individual plaintiffs may not have the financial wherewithal or the time to litigate to protect their privacy. More worrisome, the private individual would have to relive the shame and embarrassment of the damaging information being entered into the public record during the course of court proceedings. On top of this, bringing a privacy-based action is effectively an admission by the plaintiff that the information in question is true. . . . [A] privacy action — unlike a defamation suit, which can have a restorative nature by publicly disclaiming the information in question and by imposing a monetary penalty for the disclosure — emphasizes the truth of the information.[41]

Are there ways to reduce these impediments to plaintiffs who desire to vindicate their privacy rights in court?

---

[40] Lior Strahilevitz, _"How's My Driving?" For Everyone (and Everything?),_ 81 N.Y.U. L. Rev. 1699, 1706 (2006).

[41] Jacqueline D. Lipton, _Mapping Online Privacy,_ 104 Nw. U. L. Rev. 477, 505-06 (2010).

2. FIRST AMENDMENT LIMITATIONS

The First Amendment has a complex relationship to privacy. In many instances, the First Amendment and privacy are mutually reinforcing. Privacy is often essential to freedom of assembly. The Supreme Court has noted that there is a "vital relationship between freedom to associate and privacy in one's associations." *NAACP v. Alabama*, 357 U.S. 449 (1958). Privacy is also essential for freedom of speech, as the Supreme Court has recognized the importance of protecting the anonymity of speakers. *See McIntyre v. Ohio Elections Commission*, 514 U.S. 334 (1995).

However, privacy can come into conflict with the First Amendment. The privacy torts exist in an uneasy tension with the First Amendment. Indeed, Warren and Brandeis's article was aimed at the excesses of the press. Recall the authors' strong criticism of the press: "The press is overstepping in every direction the obvious bounds of propriety and of decency. Gossip is no longer the resource of the idle and of the vicious, but has become a trade, which is pursued with industry as well as effrontery."[42]

Although Brandeis was interested in privacy and skeptical of the press's trade in gossip, as a Supreme Court Justice, Brandeis was one of the champions of free speech.[43] Consider Brandeis's concurrence in *Whitney v. California*, 274 U.S. 357, 375 (1927):

> Those who won our independence believed that the final end of the state was to make men free to develop their faculties, and that in its government the deliberative forces should prevail over the arbitrary. They valued liberty both as an end and as a means. They believed liberty to be the secret of happiness and courage to be the secret of liberty. They believed that freedom to think as you will and to speak as you think are means indispensable to the discovery and spread of political truth; that without free speech and assembly discussion would be futile; that with them, discussion affords ordinarily adequate protection against the dissemination of noxious doctrine; that the greatest menace to freedom is an inert people; that public discussion is a political duty; and that this should be a fundamental principle of the American government. They recognized the risks to which all human institutions are subject. But they knew that order cannot be secured merely through fear of punishment for its infraction; that it is hazardous to discourage thought, hope and imagination; that fear breeds repression; that repression breeds hate; that hate menaces stable government; that the path of safety lies in the opportunity to discuss freely supposed grievances and proposed remedies; and that the fitting remedy for evil counsels is good ones. Believing in the power of reason as applied through public discussion, they eschewed silence coerced by law — the argument of force in its worst form. Recognizing the occasional tyrannies of governing majorities, they amended the Constitution so that free speech and assembly should be guaranteed.

---

[42] Samuel D. Warren & Louis D. Brandeis, *The Right to Privacy*, 4 Harv. L. Rev. 193 (1890).

[43] Neil Richards contends that Brandeis actually changed his views on privacy and free speech: "Although he never repudiated tort privacy, by the end of his life, Brandeis had moved to a position on publicity and free speech that was inconsistent with a broad reading of the tort theory of *The Right to Privacy*." Neil M. Richards, *The Puzzle of Brandeis, Privacy, and Speech,* 63 Vand. L. Rev. 1295, 1298 (2010).

Although the privacy torts are litigated by private parties, they employ the machinery of the state (its tort law and legal system) to impose costs on the press for gathering, producing, and disseminating news. The danger is that the threat of lawsuits will chill the press from running certain stories. Further, the threat of lawsuits alone might chill the press, because even if the press ultimately prevails in such suits, the lawsuits cost money to defend.

The public disclosure tort raises complicated tensions with the First Amendment, for it permits liability for the publication of truthful information. Built into the tort, however, is the newsworthiness test, which a number of courts have stated is required to square the tort with the First Amendment. The newsworthiness test, however, is a limitation *within* the tort. Does the First Amendment provide any additional limitations upon the tort?[44] The cases in this section address this question. In order to understand the cases, some basic background about First Amendment analysis is necessary.

Unprotected Forms of Expression. The Court has held that certain forms of expression receive no First Amendment protection. Such categories include obscenity, *Miller v. California,* 413 U.S. 15 (1973); fighting words, *Chaplinsky v. New Hampshire,* 315 U.S. 568 (1942); and child pornography, *New York v. Ferber,* 458 U.S. 747 (1982).

Strict and Intermediate Scrutiny. Most restrictions on speech are reviewed under either strict or intermediate scrutiny. Under strict scrutiny, a law must be the "least restrictive means" to achieve a "compelling" government interest. *Sable Communications, Inc. v. FCC,* 492 U.S. 115, 116 (1989). Strict scrutiny is very difficult to withstand, and most laws subject to it are struck down. In contrast, under intermediate scrutiny, a law must be narrowly tailored to a "substantial government interest." *United States v. O'Brien,* 391 U.S. 467, 377 (1968).

Content-Based vs. Content-Neutral Regulation. Under First Amendment analysis, the Court first analyzes whether a speech restriction is content-based or content-neutral. A content-based regulation targets particular messages. Content-neutral regulation restricts speech regardless of its message, such as regulating the time, place, or manner of the speech. If a speech restriction is content-based, then strict scrutiny is generally applied. There are some exceptions. For example, the Court has held that the government may single out content if the purpose is to prevent certain secondary effects caused by such speech. In *City of Renton v. Playtime Theatres,* 475 U.S. 41 (1986), the Court did not apply strict scrutiny to an ordinance restricting the location of adult movie theaters because the purpose

---

[44] For more background on the First Amendment and the privacy torts, see Peter B. Edelman, *Free Press v. Privacy: Haunted by the Ghost of Justice Black,* 68 Tex. L. Rev. 1195 (1990); Thomas I. Emerson, *The Right of Privacy and Freedom of Press,* 14 Harv. CR-CL L. Rev. 329 (1979); Edward Bloustein, *The First Amendment and Privacy: The Supreme Court Justice and the Philosopher,* 28 Rutgers L. Rev. 41 (1974); Melville B. Nimmer, *The Right to Speak from Times to Time: First Amendment Theory Applied to Libel and Misapplied to Privacy,* 56 Cal. L. Rev. 935 (1968); Harry Kalven, Jr., *Privacy in Tort Law — Were Warren and Brandeis Wrong?,* 31 Law & Contemp. Probs. 326 (1966); Marc A. Franklin, *A Constitutional Problem in Privacy Protection: Legal Inhibitions on Reporting of Fact,* 16 Stan. L. Rev. 107 (1963; Rodney A. Smolla, *Accounting for the Slow Growth of American Privacy Law,* 27 Nova L. Rev. 289 (2002).

was to prevent crime — a secondary effect. Content-neutral speech regulation is generally subject to intermediate scrutiny.

In *R.A.V. v. City of St. Paul,* 505 U.S. 377 (1992), the Court held that a content-based regulation of expression that falls in an unprotected category will be subject to strict scrutiny. The Court struck down a hate speech law because it regulated the content of "fighting words" — it applied to fighting words based on "race, color, creed, religion, or gender." Unprotected categories of expression, such as fighting words, may be regulated so long as they are not "made the vehicle for content discrimination unrelated to their distinctively proscribable content. Thus, the government may proscribe libel; but it may not make the further content discrimination of proscribing only libel critical of the government." Content-based regulation on an unprotected category of expression is permissible if "based on the very reasons why the particular class of speech . . . is proscribable."

COX BROADCASTING CORP. V. COHN

420 U.S. 469 (1975)

WHITE, J. . . . In August 1971, appellee's 17-year-old daughter was the victim of a rape and did not survive the incident. Six youths were soon indicted for murder and rape. Although there was substantial press coverage of the crime and of subsequent developments, the identity of the victim was not disclosed pending trial, perhaps because of Ga. Code Ann. § 26-9901 (1972),[45] which makes it a misdemeanor to publish or broadcast the name or identity of a rape victim. In April 1972, some eight months later, the six defendants appeared in court. Five pleaded guilty to rape or attempted rape, the charge of murder having been dropped. The guilty pleas were accepted by the court, and the trial of the defendant pleading not guilty was set for a later date.

In the course of the proceedings that day, appellant Wasell, a reporter covering the incident for his employer, learned the name of the victim from an examination of the indictments which were made available for his inspection in the courtroom. That the name of the victim appears in the indictments and that the indictments were public records available for inspection are not disputed. Later that day, Wassell broadcast over the facilities of station WSB-TV, a television station owned by appellant Cox Broadcasting Corp., a news report concerning the court proceedings. The report named the victim of the crime and was repeated the following day.

In May 1972, appellee brought an action for money damages against appellants, relying on § 26-9901 and claiming that his right to privacy had been invaded by the television broadcasts giving the name of his deceased daughter. . . .

---

[45] "It shall be unlawful for any news media or any other person to print and publish, broadcast, televise, or disseminate through any other medium of public dissemination or cause to be printed and published, broadcast, televised, or disseminated in any newspaper, magazine, periodical or other publication published in this State or through any radio or television broadcast originating in the State the name or identity of any female who may have been raped or upon whom an assault with intent to commit rape may have been made. Any person or corporation violating the provisions of this section shall, upon conviction, be punished as for a misdemeanor." Three other States have similar statutes. . . .

Georgia stoutly defends both § 26-9901 and the State's common-law privacy action challenged here. Its claims are not without force, for powerful arguments can be made, and have been made, that however it may be ultimately defined, there is a zone of privacy surrounding every individual, a zone within which the State may protect him from intrusion by the press, with all its attendant publicity. Indeed, the central thesis of the root article by Warren and Brandeis, *The Right to Privacy*, 4 Harv. L. Rev. 193 (1890), was that the press was overstepping its prerogatives by publishing essentially private information and that there should be a remedy for the alleged abuses.

More compellingly, the century has experienced a strong tide running in favor of the so-called right of privacy. In 1967, we noted that "[it] has been said that a 'right of privacy' has been recognized at common law in 30 States plus the District of Columbia and by statute in four States." *Time, Inc. v. Hill*, 385 U.S. 374, 383 n.7. We there cited the 1964 edition of Prosser's *Law of Torts*. The 1971 edition of that same source states that "[in] one form or another, the right of privacy is by this time recognized and accepted in all but a very few jurisdictions." . . .

These are impressive credentials for a right of privacy, but we should recognize that we do not have at issue here an action for the invasion of privacy involving the appropriation of one's name or photograph, a physical or other tangible intrusion into a private area, or a publication of otherwise private information that is also false although perhaps not defamatory. The version of the privacy tort now before us — termed in Georgia "the tort of public disclosure," — is that in which the plaintiff claims the right to be free from unwanted publicity about his private affairs, which, although wholly true, would be offensive to a person of ordinary sensibilities. Because the gravamen of the claimed injury is the publication of information, whether true or not, the dissemination of which is embarrassing or otherwise painful to an individual, it is here that claims of privacy most directly confront the constitutional freedoms of speech and press. The face-off is apparent, and the appellants urge upon us the broad holding that the press may not be made criminally or civilly liable for publishing information that is neither false nor misleading but absolutely accurate, however damaging it may be to reputation or individual sensibilities. . . .

It is true that in defamation actions, where the protected interest is personal reputation, the prevailing view is that truth is a defense. . . .

The Court has nevertheless carefully left open the question whether the First and Fourteenth Amendments require that truth be recognized as a defense in a defamation action brought by a private person as distinguished from a public official or public figure. . . . In similar fashion, *Time, Inc. v. Hill*, expressly saved the question whether truthful publication of very private matters unrelated to public affairs could be constitutionally proscribed. . . .

Those precedents, as well as other considerations, counsel similar caution here. In this sphere of collision between claims of privacy and those of the free press, the interests on both sides are plainly rooted in the traditions and significant concerns of our society. Rather than address the broader question whether truthful publications may ever be subjected to civil or criminal liability consistently with the First and Fourteenth Amendments, or to put it another way, whether the State may ever define and protect an area of privacy free from unwanted publicity in the press, it is appropriate to focus on the narrower interface between press and privacy that this case presents, namely, whether the State may impose sanctions on the accurate publication of the name of a rape victim obtained from public records — more specifically, from judicial records which are maintained in connection with a public prosecution and which themselves are open to public inspection. We are convinced that the State may not do so.

In the first place, in a society in which each individual has but limited time and resources with which to observe at first hand the operations of his government, he relies necessarily upon the press to bring to him in convenient form the facts of those operations. Great responsibility is accordingly placed upon the news media to report fully and accurately the proceedings of government, and official records and documents open to the public are the basic data of governmental operations. Without the information provided by the press most of us and many of our representatives would be unable to vote intelligently or to register opinions on the administration of government generally. With respect to judicial proceedings in particular, the function of the press serves to guarantee the fairness of trials and to bring to bear the beneficial effects of public scrutiny upon the administration of justice. . . .

. . . By placing the information in the public domain on official court records, the State must be presumed to have concluded that the public interest was thereby being served. Public records by their very nature are of interest to those concerned with the administration of government, and a public benefit is performed by the reporting of the true contents of the records by the media. The freedom of the press to publish that information appears to us to be of critical importance to our type of government in which the citizenry is the final judge of the proper conduct of public business. In preserving that form of government the First and Fourteenth Amendments command nothing less than that the States may not impose sanctions on the publication of truthful information contained in official court records open to public inspection.

We are reluctant to embark on a course that would make public records generally available to the media but forbid their publication if offensive to the sensibilities of the supposed reasonable man. Such a rule would make it very difficult for the media to inform citizens about the public business and yet stay within the law. The rule would invite timidity and self-censorship and very likely lead to the suppression of many items that would otherwise be published and that should be made available to the public. At the very least, the First and Fourteenth Amendments will not allow exposing the press to liability for truthfully publishing information released to the public in official court records. If there are privacy interests to be protected in judicial proceedings, the States must respond by means which avoid public documentation or other exposure of private information. Their political institutions must weigh the interests in privacy with the interests of the public to know and of the press to publish. Once true information is disclosed in public court documents open to public inspection, the press cannot be sanctioned for publishing it. In this instance as in others reliance must rest upon the judgment of those who decide what to publish or broadcast.

NOTES & QUESTIONS

1. *Justifications for the* **Cox** *Holding.* There are two potential justifications for the rule in *Cox.* The first is that the information in public records is not private because it is in the public domain, and once that information falls into the public domain, the First Amendment prohibits restrictions on speaking about it. The other justification is that the press must be able to report on public records dealing with the criminal justice system to permit greater accountability and transparency in government. Which justification does the Court's opinion rely upon most heavily? Under the second justification, would the state be permitted to keep rape victims' names confidential?

2. *The* **Oklahoma Publishing** *and* **Daily Mail** *Cases.* After *Cox,* the Supreme Court held in *Oklahoma Publishing Co. v. Oklahoma County District Court,* 430 U.S. 308 (1977), that a state court violated the First Amendment by prohibiting the media from publishing the name or photograph of an 11-year-old boy in a juvenile proceeding which members of the media attended. A few years later, the Court confronted the issue of whether a state could prohibit the press from publishing the name of a juvenile offender. In *Smith v. Daily Mail Publishing Co.,* 443 U.S. 97 (1979), two newspapers published the name and photograph of a 15-year-old who had shot and killed his 14-year-old classmate. The newspapers were indicted with the misdemeanor offense of publishing the name of a juvenile offender without a court order. The Court stated: "At issue is simply the power of a state to punish the truthful publication of an alleged juvenile delinquent's name lawfully obtained by a newspaper. The asserted state interest [to protect the anonymity of juvenile offenders] cannot justify the statute's imposition of criminal sanctions on this type of publication."

3. **Melvin v. Reid.** One of the earliest cases to recognize the tort of public disclosure is *Melvin v. Reid,* 297 P. 91 (Cal. 1931). Gabrielle Darley was a prostitute who was tried for murder but was acquitted. She abandoned her life as a prostitute, married Bernard Melvin, and became a housewife. In 1925, *The Red Kimono,* a motion picture based on her past life, was released. The film used her maiden name of Darley. As a result, some of her friends learned "for the first time of the unsavory incidents of her early life." Gabrielle sued. The California Supreme Court concluded that she had a cause of action:

> One of the major objectives of society as it is now constituted, and of the administration of our penal system, is the rehabilitation of the fallen and the reformation of the criminal. Under these theories of sociology, it is our object to lift up and sustain the unfortunate rather than tear him down. Where a person has by his own efforts rehabilitated himself, we, as right-thinking members of society, should permit him to continue in the path of rectitude rather than throw him back into a life of shame or crime. Even the thief on the cross was permitted to repent during the hours of his final agony.

According to Lawrence Friedman, who has examined the history of the case, the facts surrounding Gabrielle's murder trial were sensational. Gabrielle was on trial for murdering her lover, who was also her pimp. Gabrielle had given him money to buy her a wedding ring, but instead he used the money to buy a ring to wed another woman. Gabrielle confronted him in the street with a gun and shot him dead. Gabrielle was charged with murder. Gabrielle was acquitted. But the lurid details surrounding the incident attracted attention:

> Rogers's daughter, Adela Rogers St. John, a writer, covered the trial. Later, she wrote a short story based on the case and called it "The Red Kimono." It used incidents from Gabrielle's life, and it used her actual name. Dorothy Reid bought the story and produced a movie based on it. The film also was called *The Red Kimono*. It was shown in theaters in 1927. The movie identified the heroine as Gabrielle Darley. The next year, Gabrielle, now calling herself Gabrielle Darley Melvin, brought suit against Reid and Reid's motion picture company.

Friedman believes that Gabrielle's claim that she had reformed herself was fake:

> There is good evidence that she was, in fact, as phony as a three dollar bill. A journalist in Arizona argues that she was still working as a prostitute and madam at the time of the trial in a town in Arizona. During her lifetime she had several husbands, but they had the distressing habit of turning up dead.[46]

After Gabrielle won in the California Supreme Court, she moved to dismiss the case in 1933 prior to trial. Evidence suggests that she settled the case, which caused Reid to lose her home in West Hollywood. Today, Reid is considered as an important pioneering woman producer and director. The film, *The Red Kimono*, is available on DVD in a series devoted to "Early Women Filmmakers." Paul Schwartz has noted that the film itself "is a protofeminist account, a morality play, regarding the difficulty faced by a former prostitute in finding a life free of shame notoriety."[47] In this regard, as Friedman also notes, the film makes a point similar to the *Melvin* court.

Are the facts about Gabrielle in *The Red Kimono* newsworthy? Should the interest in allowing people like Gabrielle to start a new life trump people like Reid's right to make her movie or the public's right to know about a person's past?

4. ***Information About Past Crimes.*** In *Briscoe v. Reader's Digest*, 483 P.2d 34 (Cal. 1971), a magazine article about hijacking discussed the plaintiff's hijacking of a truck 11 years earlier. Since then, the plaintiff had rehabilitated himself, and many people did not know of his previous crime. Similar to *Melvin v. Reid*, the court held that the article was newsworthy, but that the use of the plaintiff's real name had no relevance to the article.

> We have no doubt that reports of the facts of past crimes are newsworthy. . . . However, identification of the Actor in reports of long past crimes usually serves little independent public purpose. Once legal proceedings have terminated, and a suspect or offender has been released, identification of the individual will not usually aid the administration of justice. Identification will

---

[46] Lawrence M. Friedman, *Guarding Life's Dark Secrets: Legal and Social Controls over Reputation, Propriety, and Privacy* 216-18 (2007).

[47] Paul M. Schwartz, *From Victorian Secrets to Cyberspace Shaming*, 76 U. Chi. L. Rev. 1407, 1416 (2009).

no longer serve to bring forth witnesses or obtain succor for victims. Unless the individual has reattracted the public eye to himself in some independent fashion, the only public "interest" that would usually be served is that of curiosity. . . .

Another factor militating in favor of protecting the individual's privacy here is the state's interest in the integrity of the rehabilitative process. . . .

One of the premises of the rehabilitative process is that the rehabilitated offender can rejoin that great bulk of the community from which he has been ostracized for his anti-social acts. In return for becoming a "new man," he is allowed to melt into the shadows of obscurity. . . .

Plaintiff is a man whose last offense took place 11 years before, who has paid his debt to society, who has friends and an 11-year-old daughter who were unaware of his early life—a man who assumed a position in "respectable" society. Ideally, his neighbors should recognize his present worth and forget his past life of shame. But men are not so divine as to forgive the past trespasses of others, and plaintiff therefore endeavored to reveal as little as possible of his past life. Yet, as if in some bizarre canyon of echoes, petitioner's past life pursues him through the pages of Reader's Digest, now published in 13 languages and distributed in 100 nations, with a circulation in California alone of almost 2,000,000 copies. . . .

Consider Eugene Volokh's criticism of the *Briscoe* case:

[S]ome people do take a view that differs from that of the *Briscoe* judges: While criminals can change their character, this view asserts, they often don't. Someone who was willing to fight a gun battle with the police eleven years ago may be more willing than the average person to do something bad today, even if he has led a blameless life since then. . . .

Under this ideology, it's perfectly proper to keep this possibility in mind in one's dealings with the supposedly "reformed" felon. While the government may want to give him a second chance by releasing him from prison, restoring his right to vote and possess firearms, and even erasing its publicly accessible records related to the conviction, his friends, acquaintances, and business associates are entitled to adopt a different attitude. Most presumably wouldn't treat him as a total pariah, but they might use extra caution in dealing with him, especially when it comes to trusting their business welfare or even their physical safety (or that of their children) to his care. . . .[48]

According to Richard Posner, the *Briscoe* case improperly assumes that people will behave irrationally toward rehabilitated people:

Remote past criminal activity is less relevant to a prediction of future misconduct than recent — and those who learn of it will discount it accordingly — but such information is hardly irrelevant to people considering whether to enter into or continue social or business relations with the individual; if it were irrelevant, publicizing it would not injure the individual. People conceal past criminal acts not out of bashfulness but because potential acquaintances quite sensibly regard a criminal past as negative evidence of the value of associating with a person.[49]

---

[48] Eugene Volokh, *Freedom of Speech and Information Privacy: The Troubling Implications of a Right to Stop People from Speaking About You*, 52 Stan. L. Rev. 1049, 1091-92 (2000). For another critique, see T. Markus Funk, *The Dangers of Hiding Criminal Pasts*, 66 Tenn. L. Rev. 287 (1998).

[49] Richard A. Posner, *The Economics of Justice* 260-61 (1983).

In *Gates v. Discovery Communications, Inc.,* 101 P.3d 552 (Cal. 2004), the California Supreme Court held that the U.S. Supreme Court's "decision in *Cox* and its subsequent pronouncements . . . have fatally undermined *Briscoe*'s holding that a media defendant may be held liable in tort for recklessly publishing true but not newsworthy facts concerning a rehabilitated former criminal, insofar as that holding applies to facts obtained from public official court records."

To what extent does *Gates* overturn *Melvin* or *Briscoe*? In both cases, the information about them was available in public records. But do *Cox* and its progeny turn on the *availability* of the information in public records or whether the media actually *obtained* the information from public records? In other words, if the information was obtained elsewhere, would plaintiffs in *Melvin* and *Briscoe* still have a cause of action?

5. ***The Right to Be Forgotten.*** In 2014, a Spanish man requested that Google search results stop including links to a 1998 article in a newspaper about an auction for his foreclosed house. The EU Court of Justice (ECJ) ruled in favor of the plaintiff. Under what has become known as the "right to be forgotten," EU citizens have a right to the deletion of certain personal data under the EU Data Protection Directive. The ECJ concluded that "the operator of a search engine is obliged to remove from the list of results displayed following a search made on the basis of a person's name links to web pages, published by third parties and containing information relating to that person, also in a case where that name or information is not erased beforehand or simultaneously from those web pages, and even, as the case may be, when its publication in itself on those pages is lawful." *Google Spain, S.L., Google Inc. y Agencia Española de Protección de Datos (AEPD)*, European Court of Justice, EU:C:2014:317. This case is excerpted and covered in more detail in Chapter 13.

The ECJ noted that the invasion of privacy search engines create for individuals "cannot be justified by merely the economic interest which the operator of such an engine has in that processing." Moreover, the court noted that "the removal of links from the list of results could, depending on the information at issue, have effects upon the legitimate interest of internet users potentially interested in having access to that information." Thus, the court stated, "a fair balance should be sought in particular between that interest and the data subject's fundamental [privacy] rights." The court went on to state: "Whilst it is true that the data subject's rights protected by those articles also override, as a general rule, that interest of internet users, that balance may however depend, in specific cases, on the nature of the information in question and its sensitivity for the data subject's private life and on the interest of the public in having that information, an interest which may vary, in particular, according to the role played by the data subject in public life."

Although the ECJ decision was referred to as enforcing the right to be forgotten, the ECJ did not technically require forgetting. Instead, the information remained online in the original articles. Google just could not show these articles in search results. Should Google be forced to remove search results when the newspapers can continue to keep the information on their websites?

As Evan Selinger and Woodrow Hartzog note, the use of the word "forgetting" is misleading: "This debate is not and should not be about forgetting or disappearing in the traditional sense. Instead, let's recognize that the talk about forgetting and disappearing is really concern about the concept of obscurity in the protection of our personal information."[50]

In the United States, the First Amendment would very likely restrict any attempt to force the newspapers to remove the personal data from their websites. But to what extent does the First Amendment protect linking to information, especially when those links are generated by a computer algorithm?

6. **Anti-SLAPP.** When lawsuits implicate a defendant's speech, 30 states and the District of Columbia provide special anti-SLAPP protections. A SLAPP lawsuit — or a "strategic lawsuit against public participation" — is a lawsuit designed to censor or retaliate against a person for their speech. Fearing significant legal defense costs, defendants might retract their speech or stop engaging in new speech about a matter. SLAPP suits can successfully silence people engaging in protected speech even when the suit is without merit because the costs of getting the suit dismissed can still be significant.

Nearly all anti-SLAPP legislation shares important common elements, which include: (1) requirements that the plaintiff demonstrate early that the case has merit; (2) provisions that allow the defendant to seek an expedited hearing; (3) limits on long costly discovery; (4) the right of a prevailing defendant to recover attorney fees and costs.

THE FLORIDA STAR V. B.J.F.

491 U.S. 524 (1989)

MARSHALL, J. Florida Stat. § 794.03 (1987) makes it unlawful to "print, publish, or broadcast . . . in any instrument of mass communication" the name of the victim of a sexual offense. Pursuant to this statute, appellant The Florida Star was found civilly liable for publishing the name of a rape victim which it had obtained from a publicly released police report. The issue presented here is whether this result comports with the First Amendment. We hold that it does not. . . .

The Florida Star is a weekly newspaper which serves the community of Jacksonville, Florida, and which has an average circulation of approximately 18,000 copies. A regular feature of the newspaper is its "Police Reports" section. That section, typically two to three pages in length, contains brief articles describing local criminal incidents under police investigation.

On October 20, 1983, appellee B.J.F.[51] reported to the Duval County, Florida, Sheriff's Department (Department) that she had been robbed and sexually

---

[50] Evan Seligner & Woodrow Hartzog, *Google Can't Forget You, But It Should Make You Hard to Find,* Wired, May 20, 2014,http://www.wired.com/2014/05/google-cant-forget-you-but-it-should-make-you-hard-to-find/.

[51] In filing this lawsuit, appellee used her full name in the caption of the case. On appeal, the Florida District Court of Appeal sua sponte revised the caption, stating that it would refer to the appellee by her initials, "in order to preserve [her] privacy interests." Respecting those interests, we, too, refer to appellee by her initials, both in the caption and in our discussion.

assaulted by an unknown assailant. The Department prepared a report on the incident which identified B.J.F. by her full name. The Department then placed the report in its pressroom. The Department does not restrict access either to the pressroom or to the reports made available therein.

A Florida Star reporter-trainee sent to the pressroom copied the police report verbatim, including B.J.F.'s full name, on a blank duplicate of the Department's forms. A Florida Star reporter then prepared a one-paragraph article about the crime, derived entirely from the trainee's copy of the police report. The article included B.J.F.'s full name. It appeared in the "Robberies" subsection of the "Police Reports" section on October 29, 1983, one of 54 police blotter stories in that day's edition. . . .

In printing B.J.F.'s full name, The Florida Star violated its internal policy of not publishing the names of sexual offense victims.

On September 26, 1984, B.J.F. filed suit in the Circuit Court of Duval County against the Department and The Florida Star, alleging that these parties negligently violated § 794.03. Before trial, the Department settled with B.J.F. for $2,500. The Florida Star moved to dismiss, claiming, inter alia, that imposing civil sanctions on the newspaper pursuant to § 794.03 violated the First Amendment. The trial judge rejected the motion.

At the ensuing daylong trial, B.J.F. testified that she had suffered emotional distress from the publication of her name. She stated that she had heard about the article from fellow workers and acquaintances; that her mother had received several threatening phone calls from a man who stated that he would rape B.J.F. again; and that these events had forced B.J.F. to change her phone number and residence, to seek police protection, and to obtain mental health counseling. In defense, The Florida Star put forth evidence indicating that the newspaper had learned B.J.F.'s name from the incident report released by the Department, and that the newspaper's violation of its internal rule against publishing the names of sexual offense victims was inadvertent.

At the close of B.J.F.'s case, and again at the close of its defense, The Florida Star moved for a directed verdict. On both occasions, the trial judge denied these motions. He ruled from the bench that § 794.03 was constitutional because it reflected a proper balance between the First Amendment and privacy rights, as it applied only to a narrow set of "rather sensitive . . . criminal offenses." . . . The jury awarded B.J.F. $75,000 in compensatory damages and $25,000 in punitive damages. . . .

Appellant takes the position that this case is indistinguishable from *Cox Broadcasting*. Alternatively, it urges that our decisions . . . can be distilled to yield a broader First Amendment principle that the press may never be punished, civilly or criminally, for publishing the truth. . . .

We conclude that imposing damages on appellant for publishing B.J.F.'s name violates the First Amendment, although not for either of the reasons appellant urges. Despite the strong resemblance this case bears to *Cox Broadcasting*, that case cannot fairly be read as controlling here. The name of the rape victim in that case was obtained from courthouse records that were open to public inspection. . . . Significantly, one of the reasons we gave in *Cox Broadcasting* for invalidating the challenged damages award was the important role the press plays in subjecting trials to public scrutiny and thereby helping guarantee their fairness. That role is not directly compromised where, as here, the information in question comes from a police report prepared and disseminated at a time at which not only had no adversarial criminal proceedings begun, but no suspect had been identified.

Nor need we accept appellant's invitation to hold broadly that truthful publication may never be punished consistent with the First Amendment. Our cases have carefully eschewed reaching this ultimate question, mindful that the future may bring scenarios which prudence counsels our not resolving anticipatorily. . . . We continue to believe that the sensitivity and significance of the interests presented in clashes between First Amendment and privacy rights counsel relying on limited principles that sweep no more broadly than the appropriate context of the instant case.

In our view, this case is appropriately analyzed with reference to such a limited First Amendment principle. It is the one, in fact, which we articulated in *Daily Mail* in our synthesis of prior cases involving attempts to punish truthful publication: "[I]f a newspaper lawfully obtains truthful information about a matter of public significance then state officials may not constitutionally punish publication of the information, absent a need to further a state interest of the highest order." According the press the ample protection provided by that principle is supported by at least three separate considerations, in addition to, of course, the overarching "'public interest, secured by the Constitution, in the dissemination of truth.'" . . .

First, because the *Daily Mail* formulation only protects the publication of information which a newspaper has "lawfully obtain[ed]," the government retains ample means of safeguarding significant interests upon which publication may impinge, including protecting a rape victim's anonymity. . . . Where information is entrusted to the government, a less drastic means than punishing truthful publication almost always exists for guarding against the dissemination of private facts.[52]

A second consideration undergirding the *Daily Mail* principle is the fact that punishing the press for its dissemination of information which is already publicly available is relatively unlikely to advance the interests in the service of which the State seeks to act. . . . [W]here the government has made certain information publicly available, it is highly anomalous to sanction persons other than the source of its release. . . . As *Daily Mail* observed in its summary of Oklahoma Publishing, "once the truthful information was 'publicly revealed' or 'in the public domain' the court could not constitutionally restrain its dissemination."

A third and final consideration is the "timidity and self-censorship" which may result from allowing the media to be punished for publishing certain truthful information. . . . A contrary rule, depriving protection to those who rely on the government's implied representations of the lawfulness of dissemination, would force upon the media the onerous obligation of sifting through government press releases, reports, and pronouncements to prune out material arguably unlawful for publication. . . .

---

[52] The *Daily Mail* principle does not settle the issue whether, in cases where information has been acquired unlawfully by a newspaper or by a source, government may ever punish not only the unlawful acquisition, but the ensuing publication as well. This issue was raised but not definitively resolved in *New York Times Co. v. United States*, 403 U.S. 713 (1971), and reserved in *Landmark Communications*, 435 U.S., at 837. We have no occasion to address it here.

Applied to the instant case, the *Daily Mail* principle clearly commands reversal. The first inquiry is whether the newspaper "lawfully obtain[ed] truthful information about a matter of public significance." It is undisputed that the news article describing the assault on B.J.F. was accurate. In addition, appellant lawfully obtained B.J.F.'s name. Appellee's argument to the contrary is based on the fact that under Florida law, police reports which reveal the identity of the victim of a sexual offense are not among the matters of "public record" which the public, by law, is entitled to inspect. But the fact that state officials are not required to disclose such reports does not make it unlawful for a newspaper to receive them when furnished by the government. . . . It is, clear, furthermore, that the news article concerned "a matter of public significance," in the sense in which the *Daily Mail* synthesis of prior cases used that term. That is, the article generally, as opposed to the specific identity contained within it, involved a matter of paramount public import: the commission, and investigation, of a violent crime which had been reported to authorities.

The second inquiry is whether imposing liability on appellant pursuant to § 794.03 serves "a need to further a state interest of the highest order." Appellee argues that a rule punishing publication furthers three closely related interests: the privacy of victims of sexual offenses; the physical safety of such victims, who may be targeted for retaliation if their names become known to their assailants; and the goal of encouraging victims of such crimes to report these offenses without fear of exposure.

At a time in which we are daily reminded of the tragic reality of rape, it is undeniable that these are highly significant interests. . . . For three independent reasons, however, imposing liability for publication under the circumstances of this case is too precipitous a means of advancing these interests to convince us that there is a "need" within the meaning of the *Daily Mail* formulation for Florida to take this extreme step.

First is the manner in which appellant obtained the identifying information in question. As we have noted, where the government itself provides information to the media, it is most appropriate to assume that the government had, but failed to utilize, far more limited means of guarding against dissemination than the extreme step of punishing truthful speech. That assumption is richly borne out in this case. B.J.F.'s identity would never have come to light were it not for the erroneous, if inadvertent, inclusion by the Department of her full name in an incident report made available in a pressroom open to the public. Florida's policy against disclosure of rape victims' identities, reflected in § 794.03, was undercut by the Department's failure to abide by this policy. Where, as here, the government has failed to police itself in disseminating information, it is clear under *Cox Broadcasting*, *Oklahoma Publishing*, and *Landmark Communications* that the imposition of damages against the press for its subsequent publication can hardly be said to be a narrowly tailored means of safeguarding anonymity. . . .

A second problem with Florida's imposition of liability for publication is the broad sweep of the negligence per se standard applied under the civil cause of action implied from § 794.03. Unlike claims based on the common law tort of invasion of privacy, civil actions based on § 794.03 require no case-by-case findings that the disclosure of a fact about a person's private life was one that a reasonable person would find highly offensive. On the contrary, under the per se theory of negligence adopted by the courts below, liability follows automatically from publication. This is so regardless of whether the identity of the victim is already known throughout the community; whether the victim has voluntarily called public attention to the offense; or whether the identity of the victim has otherwise become a reasonable subject of public concern — because, perhaps, questions have arisen whether the victim fabricated an assault by a particular person. Nor is there a scienter requirement of any kind under § 794.03, engendering the perverse result that truthful publications challenged pursuant to this cause of action are less protected by the First Amendment than even the least protected defamatory falsehoods. . . .

Third, and finally, the facial underinclusiveness of § 794.03 raises serious doubts about whether Florida is, in fact, serving, with this statute, the significant interests which appellee invokes in support of affirmance. Section 794.03 prohibits the publication of identifying information only if this information appears in an "instrument of mass communication," a term the statute does not define. Section 794.03 does not prohibit the spread by other means of the identities of victims of sexual offenses. An individual who maliciously spreads word of the identity of a rape victim is thus not covered, despite the fact that the communication of such information to persons who live near, or work with, the victim may have consequences as devastating as the exposure of her name to large numbers of strangers.

When a State attempts the extraordinary measure of punishing truthful publication in the name of privacy, it must demonstrate its commitment to advancing this interest by applying its prohibition evenhandedly, to the smalltime disseminator as well as the media giant. Where important First Amendment interests are at stake, the mass scope of disclosure is not an acceptable surrogate for injury. . . .

Our holding today is limited. We do not hold that truthful publication is automatically constitutionally protected, or that there is no zone of personal privacy within which the State may protect the individual from intrusion by the press, or even that a State may never punish publication of the name of a victim of a sexual offense. We hold only that where a newspaper publishes truthful information which it has lawfully obtained, punishment may lawfully be imposed, if at all, only when narrowly tailored to a state interest of the highest order, and that no such interest is satisfactorily served by imposing liability under § 794.03 to appellant under the facts of this case. . . .

WHITE, J. joined by REHNQUIST, C.J. and O'CONNOR, J. dissenting. . . . *Cox Broadcasting* reversed a damages award entered against a television station, which had obtained a rape victim's name from public records maintained in connection with the judicial proceedings brought against her assailants. While there are similarities, critical aspects of that case make it wholly distinguishable from this one. First, in *Cox Broadcasting*, the victim's name had been disclosed in the hearing where her assailants pleaded guilty; and, as we recognized, judicial records have always been considered public information in this country. . . . Second, unlike the incident report at issue here, which was meant by state law to be withheld from public release, the judicial proceedings at issue in *Cox Broadcasting* were open as a matter of state law. . . .

Cox Broadcasting stands for the proposition that the State cannot make the press its first line of defense in withholding private information from the public — it cannot ask the press to secrete private facts that the State makes no effort to safeguard in the first place. In this case, however, the State has undertaken "means which avoid [but obviously, not altogether prevent] public documentation or other exposure of private information." . . .

More importantly, at issue in *Daily Mail* was the disclosure of the name of the perpetrator of an infamous murder of a 15-year-old student. Surely the rights of those accused of crimes and those who are their victims must differ with respect to privacy concerns. That is, whatever rights alleged criminals have to maintain their anonymity pending an adjudication of guilt — and after *Daily Mail*, those rights would seem to be minimal — the rights of crime victims to stay shielded from public view must be infinitely more substantial. . . .

Consequently, I cannot agree that *Cox Broadcasting*, or *Oklahoma Publishing*, or *Daily Mail* requires — or even substantially supports — the result reached by the Court today. . . .

We are left, then, to wonder whether the . . . "independent reasons" the Court cites for reversing the judgment for B.J.F. support its result.

The first of these reasons relied on by the Court is the fact "appellant gained access to [B.J.F.'s name] through a government news release." "The government's issuance of such a release, without qualification, can only convey to recipients that the government considered dissemination lawful," the Court suggests. So described, this case begins to look like the situation in *Oklahoma Publishing*, where a judge invited reporters into his courtroom, but then tried to prohibit them from reporting on the proceedings they observed. But this case is profoundly different. Here, the "release" of information provided by the government was not, as the Court says, "without qualification." As the Star's own reporter conceded at trial, the crime incident report that inadvertently included B.J.F.'s name was posted in a room that contained signs making it clear that the names of rape victims were not matters of public record, and were not to be published. The Star's reporter indicated that she understood that she "[was not] allowed to take down that information" (i.e., B.J.F.'s name) and that she "[was] not supposed to take the information from the police department." Thus, by her own admission the posting of the incident report did not convey to the Star's reporter the idea that "the government considered dissemination lawful"; the Court's suggestion to the contrary is inapt. . . .

. . . By amending its public records statute to exempt rape victims names from disclosure, and forbidding its officials to release such information, the State has taken virtually every step imaginable to prevent what happened here. This case presents a far cry, then, from *Cox Broadcasting* or *Oklahoma Publishing*, where the State asked the news media not to publish information it had made generally available to the public: here, the State is not asking the media to do the State's job in the first instance. Unfortunately, as this case illustrates, mistakes happen: even when States take measures to "avoid" disclosure, sometimes rape victims' names are found out. As I see it, it is not too much to ask the press, in instances such as this, to respect simple standards of decency and refrain from publishing a victims' name, address, and/or phone number. . . .

. . . By holding that only "a state interest of the highest order" permits the State to penalize the publication of truthful information, and by holding that protecting a rape victim's right to privacy is not among those state interests of the highest order, the Court accepts appellant's invitation to obliterate one of the most noteworthy legal inventions of the 20th century: the tort of the publication of private facts. Even if the Court's opinion does not say as much today, such obliteration will follow inevitably from the Court's conclusion here. . . .

NOTES & QUESTIONS

1. *The Government's Responsibility for Leaking the Information.* What more could the state have done to protect the information? Florida made it a crime to disseminate the information. The state recognized that the police might make a mistake in certain cases and accidentally fail to redact a rape victim's name from the report. To protect against this, signs were put up outside the room notifying the press not to record a rape victim's name that was inadvertently left on the report. The Court did not dispute that the government could refuse to divulge the rape victim's name. If the government is not required to divulge the name, what is the problem with the government making it available and then punishing its further disclosure?

2. *The Legality of How the Information Was Obtained.* The Court relies in part on the fact that the information was "legally available." If the journalist had stolen a confidential police report and published the information, would the Court's holding have been different? Since the Florida law proscribed both the government dissemination of the information and the press publication of it, was the information "legally available"?

3. *The Future of the Public Disclosure Tort After* **Florida Star.** What effect does *Florida Star* have on the public disclosure tort? Rodney Smolla writes that the public disclosure tort exists "more 'in the books' than in practice."[53] Commentators describe the tort as "alive, but on life support"[54] and as "a phantom tort."[55] According to Jacqueline Rolfs: "Given the narrow class of information that fulfills the *Florida Star* requirements, the tort can no longer be an effective tool for protecting individual privacy."[56] Peter Edelman contends: "The Court paid lip service to the possibility that a private fact plaintiff may

---

[53] Rodney A. Smolla, *Privacy and the First Amendment Right to Gather News*, 67 Geo. Wash. L. Rev. 1097 (1999).

[54] Richard S. Murphy, *Property Rights in Personal Information: An Economic Defense of Privacy*, 84 Geo. L.J. 2381, 2388 (1996). *But see* John A. Jurata, Jr., *Comment, The Tort That Refuses to Go Away: The Subtle Reemergence of Public Disclosure of Private Facts*, 36 San Diego L. Rev. 489 (1999).

[55] Phillip E. DeLaTorre, *Resurrecting a Sunken Ship: An Analysis of Current Judicial Attitudes Toward Public Disclosure Claims*, 38 Sw. L.J. 1151, 1184 (1985).

[56] Jacqueline K. Rolfs, The Florida Star v. B.J.F.: *The Beginning of the End for the Tort of Public Disclosure*, 1990 Wis. L. Rev. 1107, 1128.

recover in some cases, but its decisions leave little hope for vindication of such a plaintiff's rights."[57] Do you agree with these characterizations?

Consider Daniel Solove:

> Many have read *Florida Star* as a broad indication that restrictions on the disclosure of true information are unconstitutional. Nevertheless, this case can be read very narrowly. The Court suggested that the Florida statute was far too broad. The statute applied "regardless of whether the identity of the victim is already known throughout the community; whether the victim has voluntarily called public attention to the offense; or whether the identity of the victim [had] otherwise become a reasonable subject of public concern." The law focused only on the nature of the information, rather than on whether each particular use of a rape victim's name in a specific context would be of public or private concern. *Florida Star* can be construed to suggest that a law adopting a less categorical approach—by addressing the use of the identifying data more contextually—might not be subject to strict scrutiny under the First Amendment.[58]

Under this analysis, how could the Florida statute be rewritten to pass constitutional muster?

4. ***Free Speech and Privacy: Weighing the Values.*** Eugene Volokh argues that both normatively and doctrinally, free speech considerations outweigh privacy:

> . . . [T]he speech vs. privacy and speech vs. speech tensions are not tensions between constitutional rights on both sides. The Constitution presumptively prohibits government restrictions on speech and perhaps some government revelation of personal information, but it says nothing about interference with speech or revelation of personal information by nongovernmental speakers. . .
>
> [I]s it constitutional for the government to suppress certain kinds of speech in order to protect dignity, prevent disrespectful behavior, prevent emotional distress, or to protect a supposed civil right not to be talked about? Under current constitutional doctrine, the answer seems to be no. . . . Even offensive, outrageous, disrespectful, and dignity-assaulting speech is constitutionally protected.
>
> And there is good reason for this approach. All of us can imagine some speech that is so offensive and at the same time so valueless that we would feel no loss if it were restricted, but the trouble is that each of us has a somewhat different vision of which speech should qualify. . . .
>
> . . . [A] good deal of speech that reveals information about people, including speech that some describe as being of merely "private concern," is actually of eminently legitimate interest. Some of it is directly relevant to the formation of general social and political opinions; most of it is of interest to people deciding how to behave in their daily lives, whether daily business or daily personal lives — whom to approach to do business, whom to trust with their money, and the like.[59]

---

[57] Peter B. Edelman, *Free Press v. Privacy: Haunted by the Ghost of Justice Black*, 68 Tex. L. Rev. 1195, 1207 (1990).

[58] Solove, *Virtues of Knowing Less, supra.*

[59] Eugene Volokh, *Freedom of Speech and Information Privacy: The Troubling Implications of a Right to Stop People from Speaking About You*, 52 Stan. L. Rev. 1049, 1089, 1092-93, 1107, 1112-15 (2000). For other free speech critiques of privacy protections, see Thomas I. Emerson, *The System*

In contrast to Volokh, Daniel Solove argues that privacy fares quite well when balanced against free speech. Solove argues that "speech of private concern does not strongly further the interests justifying free speech. If society wants to promote the interests justifying free speech, a vigorous protection of speech at the expense of privacy can, in fact, impair these interests." Free speech is often justified as essential for individual autonomy, but Solove contends that "[t]here is no clear reason why the autonomy of speakers or listeners should prevail over that of the harmed individuals." Regarding the theory that free speech is valued because it promotes democratic self-governance, Solove argues:

> [S]peech of private concern often does not promote democratic self-governance. For example, it is difficult to justify how the sale from one company to another of mailing lists about people's hobbies and incomes promotes democratic self-governance. Additionally, the reporting of one's personal secrets often does not illuminate the sphere of politics. In fact, privacy protections against disclosure strongly promote democratic self-governance. . . .
>
> Privacy encourages uninhibited speech by enabling individuals to direct frank communication to those people they trust and who will not cause them harm because of what they say. Important discourse, especially communication essential for democratic participation, often takes place in microlevel contexts (between two people or in small groups) rather than in macrolevel contexts (public rallies or nationwide television broadcasts). Indeed, a significant amount of political discussion occurs not on soapboxes or street corners, but within private conversations. . . . Therefore, privacy protections do not just inhibit free speech; they can promote it as well.

Solove argues that the value of speech of private concern is significantly less than that of public concern: "Privacy regulations that promote speech should not simply be viewed in terms of their speech-restrictive elements; they should be understood holistically, in terms of their overall purpose in the protection of free speech. We protect free speech to promote certain ends. Volokh loses sight of the ends of the First Amendment by focusing too heavily on the means."[60]

5. ***The First Amendment and Threats to People's Private Lives.*** In *Planned Parenthood v. American Coalition of Life Activists*, 290 F.3d 1058 (9th Cir. 2002) (en banc), the American Coalition of Life Activists (ACLA), an antiabortion advocacy group, provided a series of dossiers it assembled on doctors, clinic employees, politicians, judges, and other abortion rights supporters to Neal Horsley, an antiabortion activist, who posted the information on his website entitled the "Nuremberg Files." The "Nuremberg Files" dossiers included doctors' names, photos, Social Security numbers, home addresses, descriptions of their cars, and information about their families. The website

---

of Freedom of Expression (1970); Solveig Singleton, *Privacy Versus the First Amendment: A Skeptical Approach,* 11 Fordham Intell. Prop. Media & Ent. L.J. 97 (2000); Harry Kalven, Jr., *Privacy in Tort Law — Were Warren and Brandeis Wrong?*, 31 Law & Contemp. Probs. 326 (1966); Diane L. Zimmerman, *Requiem for a Heavyweight: A Farewell to Warren and Brandeis's Privacy Tort,* 68 Cornell L. Rev. 291 (1983).

[60] Daniel J. Solove, *The Virtues of Knowing Less: Justifying Privacy Protections Against Disclosure,* 53 Duke L.J. 967, 988-98 (2003).

marked the names of doctors who had been killed with a black line through them and the names of wounded doctors shaded in gray. The website did not contain any explicit threats against the doctors. The website caused the doctors great fear, and several protected themselves by wearing bulletproof vests, closing all the curtains to the windows of their homes, and even asking for the protection of the U.S. Marshals. Some of the doctors sued ACLA alleging a variety of causes of action including the Freedom of Access to Clinic Entrances Act of 1994 (FACE), 18 U.S.C. § 248.

A jury awarded the doctors $107 million in actual and punitive damages. The Ninth Circuit, en banc, affirmed the actual damages and reversed on punitive damages. The court held that the "Nuremberg Files" (in combination with "wanted" posters of various doctors) constituted a "true threat" to the doctors' lives under FACE, and such true threats were not protected under the First Amendment. Although speech advocating violence is protected, speech "directed to inciting or producing imminent lawless action" is not. "Violence is not a protected value. Nor is a *true threat* of violence *with intent to intimidate*. . . . ACLA was not staking out a position of debate but of threatened demise." According to a dissent by Judge Kozinski: "The Nuremberg Files website is clearly an expression of a political point of view. . . . [S]peech, including the intimidating message, does not constitute a direct threat because there is no evidence other than the speech itself that the speakers intend to resort to physical violence if their threat is not heeded." Would the doctors have a cause of action for public disclosure of private facts? Would the First Amendment prohibit liability on this basis?

Recently, antiabortion protesters have begun to photograph individuals entering abortion clinics. A loose network of activists across the country photographs women and places the photos on websites. Sometimes personal information, such as license plate numbers or medical records, is posted next to the photograph. Should these activities be actionable? What does the Restatement suggest? Based on the *American Coalition of Life Activists* case above, would liability for this activity run afoul of the First Amendment?

6. ***Restricting Speech to Protect Speech: Cyber Civil Rights.*** Danielle Citron argues that online attacks, especially those against women, can have the effect of silencing them. In one incident, a group of anonymous people engaged in extensive online harassment of blogger Kathy Sierra. They threatened to rape and strangle her, and posted doctored photos of her with a noose near her neck. She stopped blogging and canceled public speaking appearances out of fear. Citron argues:

> One of free speech's most important functions is promoting individual autonomy. This view urges that people be free to choose their own path. Free speech facilitates self-mastery, allowing people to author their own narratives.
>
> . . .
>
> Restraining a mob's most destructive assaults is essential to defending the expressive autonomy and equality of its victims. Preventing mobs from driving vulnerable people offline would "advance the reasons why we protect free speech in the first place," even though it would inevitably chill some speech of online mobs. Free from mob attacks, victims might continue to blog, join online

discussions, and generally express themselves on public issues. Protecting them from grotesque defamation, threats, invasions of privacy, and technological attacks would allow them to be candid about their ideas.

Although online mobs express themselves and their autonomy through their assaults, their actions also implicate their victims' autonomy and ability to participate in political and social discourse. Self-expression should receive no protection if its sole purpose is to extinguish the self-expression of another. . . . Rarely is that more true than when one group of voices consciously exploits the Internet's aggregating power to silence others and its disaggregative power to escape social responsibility for the group's actions.

Citron argues that civil rights law should apply in this context:

Online assaults motivated by race discrimination that interfere with an individual's ability to make a living can support civil and criminal actions. Title 42 U.S.C. § 1981 guarantees members of racial minorities "the same right in every State . . . to make and enforce contracts . . . as is enjoyed by white citizens . . . ." A plaintiff must show that the defendant intended to discriminate on the basis of race and that the discrimination concerned the "making and enforcing" of contracts. Courts have upheld § 1981 damages in cases where masked mob members used tactics of intimidation to prevent members of racial minorities from "making a living" in their chosen field. Section 1981 remedies "purely private" acts of racial discrimination and thus does not require state action.

Similarly, 18 U.S.C. § 245(b)(2)(C), a provision of the Civil Rights Act of 1968, criminalizes "force or threat[s] of force" designed to intimidate or interfere with a person's private employment due to that person's race, religion, or national origin. . . .

Gender discrimination that interferes with a person's ability to make a living can be pursued under Title VII of the Civil Rights Act of 1964, which sanctions those who intimidate, threaten, or coerce, or attempt to intimidate, threaten, or coerce someone with the purpose of interfering with employment opportunities due to their gender. The Attorney General can file civil suits for injunctive relief. . . .

Because the Internet fuses our public and private lives and is a workplace for many, online attacks on vulnerable individuals often interfere with their equal right to pursue work. For instance, women who stop blogging in the face of an online mob's attack lose advertising revenue and opportunities for advancement. . . .

Online mob attacks also implicate state laws penalizing those who harass or stalk another by communicating words, images, or language through electronic mail or the Internet, directed to a specific person, which would cause a reasonable person substantial emotional distress or fear of bodily harm. Some states explicitly criminalize posting messages with the intent to urge or incite others to harass a particular individual.[61]

Is the "sole purpose" of those who engage in online attacks of others to silence them? How can we draw the line between harassment triggering civil rights laws and mere crude speech, which is common online? To what extent should individuals be responsible for the actions of the mob? Suppose each

---

[61] Danielle Keats Citron, *Cyber Civil Rights,* 89 B.U. L. Rev. 61, 92-93, 97-98 (2009); *see also* Danielle Keats Citron, *Law's Expressive Value in Combating Cyber Gender Harassment,* 108 Mich. L. Rev. 373 (2009).

individual said one or two nasty things, but collectively, the impact was severe. How should the law handle such an instance? Should the First Amendment look not just to the extent to which the law is restricting speech but also to the extent to which the law's restrictions are promoting speech?

7. *The Value of Gossip.* Diane Zimmerman questions the very existence of the public disclosure tort. She argues that the tort should be "scuttled" as inconsistent with the First Amendment. According to Zimmerman, the "idle gossip" Warren and Brandeis complained about is highly valuable speech, entitled to no less protection than any other form of speech:

> . . . [F]rom the perspective of the anthropologist and sociologist, gossip is a basic form of information exchange that teaches about other lifestyles and attitudes, and through which community values are changed or reinforced. This description is a far cry from that of Warren and Brandeis, which characterized gossip as a trivializing influence that destroys "robustness of thought and delicacy of feeling" and serves the interests primarily of the "prurient" and the "indolent."
>
> Gossip thus appears to be a normal and necessary part of life for all but the rare hermit among us. Perceived in this way, gossip contributes directly to the first amendment "marketplace of ideas," and the comparative weight assigned to an interest in its limitation merits careful consideration.[62]

Do you agree with Zimmerman about the high value of gossip? Does the value of gossip outweigh the harms it causes?

8. *Nonconsensual Pornography.* A growing policy problem is nonconsensual pornography, which refers to the nonconsensual disclosure of a sexually explicit image or video of a person. Other terms used for this kind of behavior include "revenge porn," cyber-stalking, cyber-harassment, or "image-based sexual abuse." For example, an ex-boyfriend may have a nude photo of his ex-girlfriend and post it online to seek revenge by embarrassing her. The behavior in question frequently can involve a repeated course of conduct designed to cause severe emotional distress or fear of physical harm. Some websites now solicit and distribute nonconsensual pornography.

To what extent can victims use the privacy torts and other laws discussed in this chapter to obtain a remedy? Which torts would be most suitable? How strong a case would a plaintiff have under these torts? One practical difficulty is that defendants often lack much money to pay if a plaintiff prevails, and thus lawyers do not want to take these cases on a contingent fee basis.

If victims took the photos or videos themselves, they could bring civil copyright claims against the people who posted them. A person who creates the photo or video has common law copyright in the material, and this branch of intellectual property law provides strong protections.

A movement has begun to criminalize this kind of behavior. Former California Attorney General Kamala Harris brought extortion and identity theft

---

[62] Diane L. Zimmerman, *Requiem for a Heavyweight: A Farewell to Warren and Brandeis's Privacy Tort*, 68 Cornell L. Rev. 291, 333-34, 340 (1983). Katherine Strandburg contends that society does not exalt unfettered gossip and that it is regulated by norms of restraint (which she calls "willpower norms"). Katherine J. Strandburg, *Privacy, Rationality, and Temptation: A Theory of Willpower Norms*, 57 Rutgers L. Rev. 1235 (2005).

charges against Kevin Bolleart, who operated a website called UGotPosted. Bolleart urged users to post revenge porn and then charged a fee to victims to have the material removed. Bolleart was convicted of 27 felonies and sentenced to 18 years in prison. His sentence was later reduced to eight years in prison and ten years of supervised release. The federal cyber stalking statute has been invoked to pursue defendants. *See* 18 U.S.C. § 2261A. For example, in *United States v. Petrovic*, 701 F.3d 849 (8th Cir. 2012), a defendant was convicted of cyber stalking because he posted revenge porn of his ex-wife online and then tried to extort money from her to remove it. In *United States v. Shepard*, 2012 WL 113027 (D. Ariz. Jan. 13, 2012), a defendant was convicted of cyber stalking for posting his ex-girlfriend's nude photos online in porn advertisements. According to Danielle Citron, however, the federal cyber stalking statute has rarely been invoked, with just ten cases from 2010 to 2013.[63] A majority of states have criminalized revenge porn. In 2004, New Jersey adopted the first criminal invasion of privacy statute prohibiting the disclosure of someone's sexually explicit images without that person's consent. *See* N.J. Stat. Ann. § 2C:14-9. Under New Jersey law, a person commits criminal invasion of privacy if, "knowing that he is not licensed or privileged to do so, he discloses any photograph, film, videotape, recording or any other reproduction of the image of another person whose intimate parts are exposed or who is engaged in an act of sexual penetration or sexual contact, unless that person has consented to such disclosure." The crime carries a prison sentence of between three and five years and monetary penalties of up to $30,000.

In 2010, a Rutgers University student, Dahrun Ravi, was charged under the New Jersey statute after he set up a webcam to capture his roommate, Tyler Clementi, having sex with a man. He then streamed it online to watch with several others. When he learned about what happened, Clementi committed suicide. Among other things, Ravi was convicted of two crimes: (1) the nonconsensual observation of Clementi having sex; and (2) the nonconsensual disclosure of the sex video. *See State v. Parsons*, 2011 WL 6089210 (N.J. Super. Ct. App. Div. 2011).

Nonconsensual porn laws in other states vary in their effectiveness and scope. For example, California's law requires that the defendant have the intent to cause the victim substantial emotional distress and does not cover images that victims take of themselves. However, a study revealed that 80 percent of these cases involve images that victims themselves took and then shared with their partners with the understanding that they would be kept private.

Should this kind of behavior be criminalized? Some contend that civil lawsuits are the more appropriate way to address the problem. On the other hand, consider the following argument by Mary Anne Franks, a law professor who has helped states draft revenge porn laws, writing with Citron:

> At a fundamental level, nonconsensual pornography is an extreme invasion of privacy, one that causes serious and often irreversible harm to a person's physical and emotional well-being, damage to their reputations, and can even threaten their financial security. As modern societies, we impose criminal

---

[63] *See* Danielle Keats Citron, *Hate Crimes in Cyberspace* (2014).

punishments for far less. We punish theft, drug possession and destruction of property. So why don't we punish revenge porn?[64]

Do nonconsensual pornography laws violate the First Amendment? Consider Citron's argument:

> Maintaining the confidentiality of someone's sexually explicit images has little impact on a poster's expression of ideas. Revenge porn does not promote civic character or educate us about cultural, religious, or political issues. On the other hand, the nonconsensual disclosure of a person's nude images would assuredly chill private expression. Without any expectation of privacy, victims would not share their naked images. With an expectation of privacy, victims would be more inclined to engage in communications of a sexual nature. Such sharing may enhance intimacy among couples and the willingness to be forthright in other aspects of relationships.[65]

Some have challenged these laws as not being sufficiently narrow and clear and thus raising concerns of overbreadth and vagueness. In defense of these statutes, Citron has argued that they can avoid these problems if they make clear that (1) the "images do not concern matters of public importance"; (2) the defendant shared the revenge porn intentionally; and (3) the defendant knew that sharing the revenge porn would violate the victim's reasonable expectation of privacy or reasonable expectation that the image or video would remain confidential.[66] Would these requirements cure overbreadth and vagueness concerns?

Revenge porn often does not fall into unprotected categories of speech such as obscenity or true threats. Does this mean that it cannot be criminalized? Nonconsensual pornograophy would constitute a violation of one or more of the privacy torts, but should criminalization be treated differently?

Lee Rowland, a lawyer with the ACLU, argues that "revenge porn laws tend to criminalize the sharing of nude images that people lawfully own."[67] Rowland also raises concerns that such laws could potentially criminalize the activities of many teenagers.

Free speech proponents also raise concerns of a slippery slope if revenge porn is a crime. What if all violations of the public disclosure of private facts tort were criminalized?

Citron pushes back against any slippery slope, arguing that "[n]ude photos and sex tapes are amongst the most private and intimate facts; the public has no legitimate interest in seeing someone's nude images without that person's

---

[64] Mary Anne Franks & Danielle Citron, *It's Simple: Criminalize Revenge Porn, or Let Men Punish Women They Don't Like*, The Guardian, Apr. 17, 2014, http://www.theguardian.com/commentisfree/2014/apr/17/revenge-porn-must-be-criminalized-laws.

[65] Citron, *Hate Crimes in Cyberspace, supra*.

[66] Danielle Citron, *How to Make Revenge Porn a Crime* Slate, Nov. 7, 2013, http://www.slate.com/articles/news_and_politics/jurisprudence/2013/11/making_revenge_porn_a_crime_without_trampling_free_speech.html. For more background, see Danielle Keats Citron and Mary Anne Franks, *Criminalizing Revenge Porn*, forthcoming Wake Forest L. Rev.

[67] Liz Halloran, *Race To Stop 'Revenge Porn' Raises Free Speech Worries*, NPR, Mar. 6, 2014, http://www.npr.org/blogs/itsallpolitics/2014/03/06/286388840/race-to-stop-revenge-porn-raises-free-speech-worries.

consent."[68] Are images and videos different from other things? Could merely writing about the private sexual activities of another person be criminalized?

Citron also defends criminalization because a breach of confidentiality is involved, and "confidentiality regulations are less troubling from a First Amendment perspective because they penalize the breach of an assumed or implied duty rather than the injury caused by the publication of words. Instead of prohibiting a certain kind of speech, confidentiality law enforces express or implied promises and shared expectations."[69] Is revenge porn sufficiently distinct to warrant criminal penalties? Are Citron's defenses sufficient to address the slippery slope concerns?

9. ***Contracts, Promises, and the First Amendment.*** Does the enforcement of a contract of confidentiality against a media entity trigger First Amendment scrutiny? In *Cohen v. Cowles Media Co.*, 501 U.S. 663 (1991), a journalist had promised a source confidentiality but nevertheless published the source's name. The source sued and obtained a promissory estoppel damage award. According to the Court, *Florida Star* did not control because "generally applicable laws do not offend the First Amendment simply because their enforcement against the press has incidental effects on its ability to gather and report the news." Why is a suit under contract or promissory estoppel different from a suit under tort, such as public disclosure of private facts?

After *Cohen,* the courts apply two dramatically different rules when it comes to free speech and civil liability. As Daniel Solove and Neil Richards explain:

> For a panoply of torts for harms caused by speech, the well-settled rule is that the First Amendment provides full protection. There are, however, many instances where the Supreme Court applies virtually no First Amendment scrutiny when civil liability implicates speech. In particular, many lawsuits involving the enforcement of contracts or property rights do not trigger any significant First Amendment scrutiny. Thus, there are two radically different ways that the First Amendment addresses civil liability involving speech — either full First Amendment protection or virtually none at all. . . .
>
> Suppose a newspaper obtains the name of a rape victim from a police report and publishes it. The rape victim sues the newspaper under the privacy tort of public disclosure of private facts. Does the First Amendment protect the newspaper? If the story is newsworthy, then the answer is yes. . . .
>
> Now suppose that a rape victim speaks anonymously to a newspaper, which promises not to publish her name. The newspaper publishes a highly newsworthy story about the rape victim, and it decides to break its promise and reveal her identity. She sues for promissory estoppel and breach of implied contract. Does the First Amendment protect the newspaper? The answer is no.
> . . .
> Why do these cases have such different outcomes under the First Amendment? Both involve civil liability, free speech, and newsworthy information.

---

[68] See Franks & Citron, *Criminalizing Revenge Porn, supra.*
[69] *Id.*

Solove and Richards point out that contract and tort are often not distinct categories but bleed into one another. Certain torts, such as the breach of confidentiality tort, are premised on notions of implied contractual duties. They propose a new way to determine which First Amendment rule should apply to certain forms of civil liability:

> We suggest that when government power is used to dictate the terms of civil duties not to speak (what we call the "duty-defining power"), the special dangers of this power warrant application of the First Amendment. In contrast, when private parties create the content of speech-restrictive rules, the First Amendment should not apply.[70]

Should a distinction be made in free speech protection for various forms of civil liability? Does focusing on government power serve as a coherent way to make the distinction? If not, what approach would work better?

BARTNICKI V. VOPPER

532 U.S. 514 (2001)

STEVENS, J. These cases raise an important question concerning what degree of protection, if any, the First Amendment provides to speech that discloses the contents of an illegally intercepted communication. That question is both novel and narrow. Despite the fact that federal law has prohibited such disclosures since 1934, this is the first time that we have confronted such an issue. . . .

During 1992 and most of 1993, the Pennsylvania State Education Association, a union representing the teachers at the Wyoming Valley West High School, engaged in collective-bargaining negotiations with the school board. Petitioner Kane, then the president of the local union, testified that the negotiations were "'contentious'" and received "a lot of media attention." In May 1993, petitioner Bartnicki, who was acting as the union's "chief negotiator," used the cellular phone in her car to call Kane and engage in a lengthy conversation about the status of the negotiations. An unidentified person intercepted and recorded that call.

In their conversation, Kane and Bartnicki discussed the timing of a proposed strike, difficulties created by public comment on the negotiations, and the need for a dramatic response to the board's intransigence. At one point, Kane said: "'If they're not gonna move for three percent, we're gonna have to go to their, their homes. . . . To blow off their front porches, we'll have to do some work on some of those guys. (PAUSES). Really, uh, really and truthfully because this is, you know, this is bad news. (UNDECIPHERABLE).'"

In the early fall of 1993, the parties accepted a non-binding arbitration proposal that was generally favorable to the teachers. In connection with news reports about the settlement, respondent Vopper, a radio commentator who had been critical of the union in the past, played a tape of the intercepted conversation on his public affairs talk show. Another station also broadcast the tape, and local newspapers published its contents. After filing suit against Vopper and other representatives of

---

[70] Daniel J. Solove & Neil M. Richards, *Rethinking Free Speech and Civil Liability,* 109 Colum. L. Rev. 1650, 1651-52, 1686 (2009).

the media, Bartnicki and Kane (hereinafter petitioners) learned through discovery that Vopper had obtained the tape from Jack Yocum, the head of a local taxpayers' organization that had opposed the union's demands throughout the negotiations. Yocum, who was added as a defendant, testified that he had found the tape in his mailbox shortly after the interception and recognized the voices of Bartnicki and Kane. Yocum played the tape for some members of the school board, and later delivered the tape itself to Vopper. . . .

In their amended complaint, petitioners alleged that their telephone conversation had been surreptitiously intercepted by an unknown person using an electronic device, that Yocum had obtained a tape of that conversation, and that he intentionally disclosed it to Vopper, as well as other individuals and media representatives. Thereafter, Vopper and other members of the media repeatedly published the contents of that conversation. The amended complaint alleged that each of the defendants "knew or had reason to know" that the recording of the private telephone conversation had been obtained by means of an illegal interception. Relying on both federal and Pennsylvania statutory provisions, petitioners sought actual damages, statutory damages, punitive damages, and attorney's fees and costs. . . .

[Title 18 U.S.C. § 2511(1)(c) provides that any person who "intentionally discloses, or endeavors to disclose, to any other person the contents of any wire, oral, or electronic communication, knowing or having reason to know that the information was obtained through the interception of a wire, oral, or electronic communication in violation of this subsection; . . . shall be punished. . . ." The Pennsylvania Act contains a similar provision.]

. . . [W]e accept respondents' submission on three factual matters that serve to distinguish most of the cases that have arisen under § 2511. First, respondents played no part in the illegal interception. Rather, they found out about the interception only after it occurred, and in fact never learned the identity of the person or persons who made the interception. Second, their access to the information on the tapes was obtained lawfully, even though the information itself was intercepted unlawfully by someone else. Third, the subject matter of the conversation was a matter of public concern. If the statements about the labor negotiations had been made in a public arena — during a bargaining session, for example — they would have been newsworthy. This would also be true if a third party had inadvertently overheard Bartnicki making the same statements to Kane when the two thought they were alone.

We agree with petitioners that § 2511(1)(c), as well as its Pennsylvania analog, is in fact a content-neutral law of general applicability. . . . In this case, the basic purpose of the statute at issue is to "protec[t] the privacy of wire[, electronic,] and oral communications." S. Rep. No. 1097, 90th Cong., 2d Sess., 66 (1968). The statute does not distinguish based on the content of the intercepted conversations, nor is it justified by reference to the content of those conversations. Rather, the communications at issue are singled out by virtue of the fact that they were illegally intercepted — by virtue of the source, rather than the subject matter.

On the other hand, the naked prohibition against disclosures is fairly characterized as a regulation of pure speech. . . .

As a general matter, "state action to punish the publication of truthful information seldom can satisfy constitutional standards." *Smith v. Daily Mail Publishing Co.*, 443 U.S. 97, 102 (1979). More specifically, this Court has repeatedly held that "if a newspaper lawfully obtains truthful information about a matter of public significance then state officials may not constitutionally punish publication of the information, absent a need . . . of the highest order." *Id.*, at 103; *see also Florida Star v. B.J.F.*; *Landmark Communications, Inc. v. Virginia*. . . .

. . . [T]he issue here is this: "Where the punished publisher of information has obtained the information in question in a manner lawful in itself but from a source who has obtained it unlawfully, may the government punish the ensuing publication of that information based on the defect in a chain?" . . .

The Government identifies two interests served by the statute — first, the interest in removing an incentive for parties to intercept private conversations, and second, the interest in minimizing the harm to persons whose conversations have been illegally intercepted. . . .

The normal method of deterring unlawful conduct is to impose an appropriate punishment on the person who engages in it. If the sanctions that presently attach to a violation of § 2511(1)(a) do not provide sufficient deterrence, perhaps those sanctions should be made more severe. But it would be quite remarkable to hold that speech by a law-abiding possessor of information can be suppressed in order to deter conduct by a non-law-abiding third party. . . .

The Government's second argument, however, is considerably stronger. Privacy of communication is an important interest, and Title III's restrictions are intended to protect that interest, thereby "encouraging the uninhibited exchange of ideas and information among private parties. . . ." Moreover, the fear of public disclosure of private conversations might well have a chilling effect on private speech. . . .

Accordingly, it seems to us that there are important interests to be considered on both sides of the constitutional calculus. . . .

In this case, privacy concerns give way when balanced against the interest in publishing matters of public importance. As Warren and Brandeis stated in their classic law review article: "The right of privacy does not prohibit any publication of matter which is of public or general interest." *The Right to Privacy*, 4 Harv. L. Rev. 193, 214 (1890). One of the costs associated with participation in public affairs is an attendant loss of privacy. . . .

Our opinion in *New York Times Co. v. Sullivan*, 376 U.S. 254 (1964), reviewed many of the decisions that settled the "general proposition that freedom of expression upon public questions is secured by the First Amendment." . . .

We think it clear that parallel reasoning requires the conclusion that a stranger's illegal conduct does not suffice to remove the First Amendment shield from speech about a matter of public concern. The months of negotiations over the proper level of compensation for teachers at the Wyoming Valley West High School were unquestionably a matter of public concern, and respondents were clearly engaged in debate about that concern. . . .

BREYER, J. joined by O'CONNOR, J. concurring. I join the Court's opinion because I agree with its "narrow" holding, limited to the special circumstances present here: (1) the radio broadcasters acted lawfully (up to the time of final public disclosure); and (2) the information publicized involved a matter of unusual public concern, namely a threat of potential physical harm to others. I write separately to explain why, in my view, the Court's holding does not imply a significantly broader constitutional immunity for the media. . . .

As the Court recognizes, the question before us—a question of immunity from statutorily imposed civil liability—implicates competing constitutional concerns. The statutes directly interfere with free expression in that they prevent the media from publishing information. At the same time, they help to protect personal privacy—an interest here that includes not only the "right to be let alone." Given these competing interests "on both sides of the equation, the key question becomes one of proper fit."

I would ask whether the statutes strike a reasonable balance between their speech-restricting and speech-enhancing consequences. Or do they instead impose restrictions on speech that are disproportionate when measured against their corresponding privacy and speech-related benefits, taking into account the kind, the importance, and the extent of these benefits, as well as the need for the restrictions in order to secure those benefits? What this Court has called "strict scrutiny"—with its strong presumption against constitutionality—is normally out of place where, as here, important competing constitutional interests are implicated. The statutory restrictions before us directly enhance private speech. The statutes ensure the privacy of telephone conversations much as a trespass statute ensures privacy within the home. That assurance of privacy helps to overcome our natural reluctance to discuss private matters when we fear that our private conversations may become public. And the statutory restrictions consequently encourage conversations that otherwise might not take place.

At the same time, these statutes restrict public speech directly, deliberately, and of necessity. They include media publication within their scope not simply as a means, say, to deter interception, but also as an end. Media dissemination of an intimate conversation to an entire community will often cause the speakers serious harm over and above the harm caused by an initial disclosure to the person who intercepted the phone call. . . .

As a general matter, despite the statutes' direct restrictions on speech, the Federal Constitution must tolerate laws of this kind because of the importance of these privacy and speech-related objectives. . . . Rather than broadly forbid this kind of legislative enactment, the Constitution demands legislative efforts to tailor the laws in order reasonably to reconcile media freedom with personal, speech-related privacy.

Nonetheless, looked at more specifically, the statutes, as applied in these circumstances, do not reasonably reconcile the competing constitutional objectives. Rather, they disproportionately interfere with media freedom. For one thing, the broadcasters here engaged in no unlawful activity other than the ultimate publication of the information another had previously obtained. They "neither encouraged nor participated directly or indirectly in the interception." No one claims that they ordered, counselled, encouraged, or otherwise aided or abetted the interception, the later delivery of the tape by the interceptor to an intermediary, or the tape's still later delivery by the intermediary to the media. . . .

For another thing, the speakers had little or no *legitimate* interest in maintaining the privacy of the particular conversation. That conversation involved a suggestion about "blow[ing] off . . . front porches" and "do[ing] some work on some of those guys," thereby raising a significant concern for the safety of others. Where publication of private information constitutes a wrongful act, the law recognizes a privilege allowing the reporting of threats to public safety. . . .

Further, the speakers themselves, the president of a teacher's union and the union's chief negotiator, were "limited public figures," for they voluntarily engaged in a public controversy. They thereby subjected themselves to somewhat greater public scrutiny and had a lesser interest in privacy than an individual engaged in purely private affairs. . . .

Here, the speakers' legitimate privacy expectations are unusually low, and the public interest in defeating those expectations is unusually high. Given these circumstances, along with the lawful nature of respondents' behavior, the statutes' enforcement would disproportionately harm media freedom.

REHNQUIST, C.J., joined by SCALIA and THOMAS, JJ., dissenting. Technology now permits millions of important and confidential conversations to occur through a vast system of electronic networks. These advances, however, raise significant privacy concerns. We are placed in the uncomfortable position of not knowing who might have access to our personal and business e-mails, our medical and financial records, or our cordless and cellular telephone conversations. In an attempt to prevent some of the most egregious violations of privacy, the United States, the District of Columbia, and 40 States have enacted laws prohibiting the intentional interception and knowing disclosure of electronic communications. The Court holds that all of these statutes violate the First Amendment insofar as the illegally intercepted conversation touches upon a matter of "public concern," an amorphous concept that the Court does not even attempt to define. But the Court's decision diminishes, rather than enhances, the purposes of the First Amendment: chilling the speech of the millions of Americans who rely upon electronic technology to communicate each day. . . .

The Court correctly observes that these are "content-neutral law[s] of general applicability" which serve recognized interests of the "highest order": "the interest in individual privacy and . . . in fostering private speech." It nonetheless subjects these laws to the strict scrutiny normally reserved for governmental attempts to censor different viewpoints or ideas. There is scant support, either in precedent or in reason, for the Court's tacit application of strict scrutiny.

A content-neutral regulation will be sustained if

> "'it furthers an important or substantial governmental interest; if the governmental interest is unrelated to the suppression of free expression; and if the incidental restriction on alleged First Amendment freedoms is no greater than is essential to the furtherance of that interest.'" *Turner Broadcasting System, Inc. v. FCC*, 512 U.S. 622, 662 (1994). . . .

The Court's attempt to avoid these precedents by reliance upon the *Daily Mail* string of newspaper cases is unpersuasive. In these cases, we held that statutes prohibiting the media from publishing certain truthful information — the name of a rape victim, *Florida Star v. B. J. F.*; *Cox Broadcasting Corp. v. Cohn*, the confidential proceedings before a state judicial review commission, *Landmark Communications, Inc. v. Virginia*, and the name of a juvenile defendant, *Daily Mail*

— violated the First Amendment. In so doing, we stated that "if a newspaper lawfully obtains truthful information about a matter of public significance then state officials may not constitutionally punish publication of the information, absent a need to further a state interest of the highest order." *Daily Mail*. Neither this *Daily Mail* principle nor any other aspect of these cases, however, justifies the Court's imposition of strict scrutiny here. . . .

These laws are content neutral; they only regulate information that was illegally obtained; they do not restrict republication of what is already in the public domain; they impose no special burdens upon the media; they have a scienter requirement to provide fair warning; and they promote the privacy and free speech of those using cellular telephones. It is hard to imagine a more narrowly tailored prohibition of the disclosure of illegally intercepted communications, and it distorts our precedents to review these statutes under the often fatal standard of strict scrutiny. These laws therefore should be upheld if they further a substantial governmental interest unrelated to the suppression of free speech, and they do. . .

The "dry up the market" theory, which posits that it is possible to deter an illegal act that is difficult to police by preventing the wrongdoer from enjoying the fruits of the crime, is neither novel nor implausible. It is a time-tested theory that undergirds numerous laws, such as the prohibition of the knowing possession of stolen goods. We ourselves adopted the exclusionary rule based upon similar reasoning, believing that it would "deter unreasonable searches," by removing an officer's "incentive to disregard [the Fourth Amendment]."

The same logic applies here and demonstrates that the incidental restriction on alleged First Amendment freedoms is no greater than essential to further the interest of protecting the privacy of individual communications. Were there no prohibition on disclosure, an unlawful eavesdropper who wanted to disclose the conversation could anonymously launder the interception through a third party and thereby avoid detection. Indeed, demand for illegally obtained private information would only increase if it could be disclosed without repercussion. The law against interceptions, which the Court agrees is valid, would be utterly ineffectual without these antidisclosure provisions. . . .

These statutes undeniably protect this venerable right of privacy. Concomitantly, they further the First Amendment rights of the parties to the conversation. . . . The chilling effect of the Court's decision upon these private conversations will surely be great. . . .

Although public persons may have forgone the right to live their lives screened from public scrutiny in some areas, it does not and should not follow that they also have abandoned their right to have a private conversation without fear of it being intentionally intercepted and knowingly disclosed. . . .

NOTES & QUESTIONS

1. ***Privacy and Free Speech.*** The concurrence and dissent both recognize that the statutory provisions of federal wiretap law serve to protect, rather than merely infringe, First Amendment values. According to the concurrence, the statutory provisions "directly enhance private speech," and in the words of the dissent, the statutory provisions serve to protect against "chilling the speech of millions

of Americans who rely upon electronic technology to communicate each day." How should the Court analyze statutes that restrict some speech in order to promote more speech? Should such statutes be treated like laws that exclusively restrict speech?

Consider Paul Gewirtz's critique of the majority opinion in *Bartnicki*:

> But there is a more basic problem with Justice Stevens's approach: He looks to the content of the broadcast communication to decide whether the Constitution protects it, rather than to the circumstances under which the conversation took place. . . . [Instead, o]ne could look to whether the original communication takes place within a protected zone. If a zone is deemed a protected private zone — which can be either a place or a kind of situation — then the content of what is communicated within that zone would be irrelevant in deciding whether the First Amendment protects the media in reporting on it. The press could be sanctioned for publishing information about conversations within that zone, regardless of content. In Title III, Congress sought to protect privacy by creating such a protected zone, and made intrusions on that zone illegal. . . . Put another way, speech acts must be understood in terms of audiences as well as content. In our daily narrative transactions, we are always negotiating our relationship to an audience. Privacy is ultimately about our power to choose our audience. When privacy is invaded, we are compelled to have an audience we do not want. The Court in *Bartnicki* says that publishing the intercepted conversation contributed to public debate — but the two people speaking on their cell phones did not wish to contribute to a public debate before a public audience. Their words were taken from them by stealth and put into public debate against their will. If every private statement on a public subject may be forcibly disclosed because it contributes to public debate, then privacy is a dead letter. We cannot have it both ways.[71]

Would this hold true no matter what was said or who was saying it? In *Bartnicki,* it is safe to assume the comment about the bomb was not meant literally. Suppose the conversation was between two terrorists who were really planning to set off a bomb. Or suppose the conversation was the President talking to a chief advisor about covering up major corruption. Should these conversations also be protected because they are within the "protected private zone"?

2. ***The Effect of* Bartnicki *on the Public Disclosure Tort.*** According to Rodney Smolla, "*Bartnicki* accepted the premise that the conflict posed between speech and privacy is a conflict between two rights of constitutional stature. By this important measure, all nine Justices in *Bartnicki* were in agreement." Smolla reads *Bartnicki* to be "inviting the importation into First Amendment jurisprudence of the 'newsworthiness' analysis as it has developed so far in common-law cases."[72] The Court has yet to confront whether the tort of public disclosure is constitutional. As Daniel Solove observes:

> In numerous cases, the Court has articulated a public and private concern distinction, and it has applied the First Amendment to curtail restrictions on

---

[71] Paul Gewirtz, *Privacy and Speech,* 2001 Sup. Ct. Rev. 139, 154-55 (2001).

[72] Rodney A. Smolla, *Information as Contraband: The First Amendment and Liability for Trafficking in Speech,* 96 Nw. U. L. Rev. 1099, 1150, 1153 (2002).

speech of public concern without answering questions about limiting speech of private concern. . . . The Court appears to view the public and private concern distinction as having significance because it has used this distinction to limit the application of heightened scrutiny to restrictions on speech of public concern. Although it has yet to address the private concern side of the distinction, the Court appears to be heading in the direction [of requiring less First Amendment protection to speech of private concern].[73]

Eugene Volokh takes issue with this conclusion:

Though the Court has often said in dictum that political speech or public-issue speech is on the "highest rung" of constitutional protection, it has never held that there's any general exception for speech on matters of "private concern." Political speech, scientific speech, art, entertainment, consumer product reviews, and speech on matters of private concern are thus all doctrinally entitled to the same level of high constitutional protection, restrictable only through laws that pass strict scrutiny.[74]

Does the newsworthiness test adequately deal with the First Amendment concerns of the public disclosure tort?

Consider Neil Richards:

But crafting tort privacy as a remedy for press disclosures of embarrassing information brought privacy directly into tension with the First Amendment. Warren and Brandeis recognized the tension in 1890, but as First Amendment law became more robust over the course of the twentieth century (aided of course by Brandeis), the conflict between the First Amendment and tort privacy's core case against the press only increased. The hallmark of modern American First Amendment jurisprudence is that hurt feelings alone cannot justify the suppression of truthful information or opinion. And under the modern, post-*New York Times v. Sullivan* First Amendment regulation of speech (even by tort) on the grounds that it causes emotional injury is highly disfavored. It should thus be unsurprising that in a series of Supreme Court cases in which psychological privacy harms have been balanced against free press rights, the First Amendment has always prevailed. . . .

In extraordinary cases, perhaps involving sexually-themed disclosures such as sex tapes, tort privacy can survive a direct clash with the First Amendment protections given to the press. A few such cases impose liability for psychological injuries over free press challenges. But such cases are likely to remain outliers, and appropriately so. As Brandeis himself implicitly recognized later in life, a tort-based conception of privacy protecting against purely emotional harm must remain exceptional in a constitutional regime dedicated to speech, publicity, and disclosure.

---

[73] Solove, *Virtues of Knowing Less, supra,* at 987.

[74] Eugene Volokh, *Freedom of Speech and Information Privacy: The Troubling Implications of a Right to Stop People from Speaking About You,* 52 Stan. L. Rev. 1049, 1089, 1092-95 (2000). For other free speech critiques of privacy protections, see Thomas I. Emerson, *The System of Freedom of Expression* (1970); Solveig Singleton, *Privacy Versus the First Amendment: A Skeptical Approach,* 11 Fordham Intell. Prop. Media & Ent. L.J. 97 (2000); Harry Kalven, Jr., *Privacy in Tort Law — Were Warren and Brandeis Wrong?*, 31 Law & Contemp. Probs. 326 (1966); Diane L. Zimmerman, *Requiem for a Heavyweight: A Farewell to Warren and Brandeis's Privacy Tort*, 68 Cornell L. Rev. 291 (1983).

This is not to say that information can never be regulated or that all information nondisclosure rules create constitutional problems. I have argued elsewhere that a wide variety of restrictions can be placed on commercial databases consistent with the First Amendment, a conclusion with which courts have agreed. And in some contexts, the concept of confidentiality has great promise to regulate information disclosure in the context of relationships. But these are not tort privacy rules, as they do not apply to all speakers and they remedy injuries other than emotional injury. As currently understood, tort privacy in the Warren and Brandeis tradition seems too crude an instrument to effectively resolve these problems, particularly because tort remedies based upon emotional harm conflict directly with the post-*New York Times v. Sullivan* First Amendment.[75]

3. ***Protections Against the Disclosure of Leaked Information.*** In *Landmark Communications v. Virginia*, 435 U.S. 829 (1978), a newspaper was indicted for violating a Virginia law making it a misdemeanor to disclose the identity of a state judge whose conduct was being investigated by the Virginia Judicial Inquiry and Review Commission. The law was designed to ensure that judicial disciplinary proceedings would remain confidential (until such proceedings were concluded) to protect judges from the publication of frivolous and unwarranted complaints. The newspaper did not challenge the requirement of confidentiality, only the prohibition of disclosing the identities of judges if the newspaper happened to find out that a judge was the subject of a disciplinary proceeding. The Supreme Court held that such prohibition violated the First Amendment. Although the interest in confidentiality of disciplinary proceedings was legitimate, it was not sufficient to justify the encroachment on the First Amendment because "[t]he operations of the courts and the judicial conduct of judges are matters of utmost public concern." Further, the statutory scheme could remain effective by restricting the improper leaking of such information rather than criminalizing the disclosure of that information by parties that did not participate in the illegal obtaining of such information.

4. ***Interpreting the Scope of* Bartnicki.** In *Boehner v. McDermott*, 484 F.3d 573 (D.C. Cir. 2007), U.S. Representative James McDermott was provided with a tape of a conference call between U.S. Representative John Boehner, then-Speaker of the House Newt Gingrich, and other Republican Party members. Boehner participated via a cell phone, and John and Alice Martin intercepted the call with a police radio scanner. They gave the tape to another member of the U.S. House, and the tape was eventually forwarded on to McDermott, the ranking Democrat on the Ethics Committee. Along with the tape was a letter from the Martins stating that the call was "heard over a scanner" and that they understood that they would be granted immunity. McDermott contacted reporters at the *Atlanta Journal-Constitution* and the *New York Times*. He played the tape to the *New York Times* reporter, who wrote a story about the tape. The Martins were prosecuted for a violation of the Wiretap Act, 18 U.S.C.

---

[75] Neil M. Richards, *The Puzzle of Brandeis, Privacy, and Speech,* 63 Vand. L. Rev. 1295, 1345-47 (2010).

§ 2511(1)(a), prohibiting the interception of wire, oral, or electronic communications. They pled guilty and paid a $500 fine.

Boehner sued McDermott for violating 18 U.S.C. § 2511(1)(c), which prohibits disclosing a communication that one knows or has reason to know is acquired in violation of the Wiretap Act. The D.C. Circuit, en banc, concluded that *Bartnicki* could be distinguished:

> Whatever the *Bartnicki* majority meant by "lawfully obtain," the decision does not stand for the proposition that anyone who has lawfully obtained truthful information of public importance has a First Amendment right to disclose that information. *Bartnicki* avoided laying down such a broad rule of law, and for good reason. There are many federal provisions that forbid individuals from disclosing information they have lawfully obtained. The validity of these provisions has long been assumed. Grand jurors, court reporters, and prosecutors, for instance, may "not disclose a matter occurring before the grand jury." Fed. R. Crim. P. 6(e)(2)(B). The Privacy Act imposes criminal penalties on government employees who disclose agency records containing information about identifiable individuals to unauthorized persons. *See* 5 U.S.C. § 552a(i)(1). The Espionage Act punishes officials who willfully disclose sensitive national defense information to persons not entitled to receive it. *See* 18 U.S.C.   § 793(d). The Intelligence Identities Protection Act prohibits the disclosure of a covert intelligence agent's identity. *See* 50 U.S.C. § 421. Employees of the Internal Revenue Service, among others, may not disclose tax return information. *See* 26 U.S.C. § 6103(a). State motor vehicle department employees may not make public information about an individual's driver's license or registration. *See* 18 U.S.C. § 2721. Employees of the Social Security Administration, as well as other government employees, may not reveal social security numbers or records. *See* 42 U.S.C. § 405(c)(2)(C)(viii)(I), (III). Judicial employees may not reveal confidential information received in the course of their official duties. *See* Code of Conduct for Judicial Employees Canon 3D. And so forth.
>
> In analogous contexts the Supreme Court has sustained restrictions on disclosure of information even though the information was lawfully obtained. The First Amendment did not shield a television station from liability under the common law right of publicity when it filmed a plaintiff's "human cannonball" act and broadcast the film without his permission. *Zacchini v. Scripps-Howard Broad. Co.,* 433 U.S. 562 (1977). When a newspaper divulged the identity of an individual who provided information to it under a promise of confidentiality, the First Amendment did not provide the paper with a defense to a breach of contract claim. *Cohen v. Cowles Media Co.,* 501 U.S. 663 (1991). The First Amendment did not prevent the government from enforcing reasonable confidentiality restrictions on former employees of the CIA. *See Snepp v. United States,* 444 U.S. 507 (1980). Parties to civil litigation did not "have a First Amendment right to disseminate, in advance of trial, information gained through the pretrial discovery process." *Seattle Times Co. v. Rhinehart,* 467 U.S. 20 (1984).
>
> In *United States v. Aguilar,* 515 U.S. 593 (1995), a case closely analogous to this one, the Supreme Court held that the First Amendment did not give a federal judge, who obtained information about an investigative wiretap from another judge, the right to disclose that information to the subject of the wiretap. The judge challenged his conviction for violating 18 U.S.C. § 2232(c), which prohibits the improper disclosure of an investigative wiretap. In rejecting his First Amendment claim, the Court wrote that the judge was not "simply a

member of the general public who happened to lawfully acquire possession of information about the wiretap; he was a Federal District Court Judge who learned of a confidential wiretap application from the judge who had authorized the interception, and who wished to preserve the integrity of the court. Government officials in sensitive confidential positions may have special duties of non-disclosure."

Aguilar stands for the principle that those who accept positions of trust involving a duty not to disclose information they lawfully acquire while performing their responsibilities have no First Amendment right to disclose that information. The question thus becomes whether, in the words of *Aguilar*, Representative McDermott's position on the Ethics Committee imposed a "special" duty on him not to disclose this tape in these circumstances. *Bartnicki* has little to say about that issue. The individuals who disclosed the tape in that case were private citizens who did not occupy positions of trust.

All members of the Ethics Committee, including Representative McDermott, were subject to Committee Rule 9, which stated that "Committee members and staff shall not disclose any evidence relating to an investigation to any person or organization outside the Committee unless authorized by the Committee." . . .

There is no question that the rules themselves are reasonable and raise no First Amendment concerns. . . .

When Representative McDermott became a member of the Ethics Committee, he voluntarily accepted a duty of confidentiality that covered his receipt and handling of the Martins' illegal recording. He therefore had no First Amendment right to disclose the tape to the media.

C. DISSEMINATION OF FALSE INFORMATION

1. DEFAMATION

(a) Introduction

At the most practical level, an understanding of defamation law is essential to understanding some of the aspects and issues related to the privacy torts. While the privacy torts are a relatively recent invention, a remedy for defamation extends far back in history. Since ancient times, one's reputation and character have been viewed as indispensable to one's ability to engage in public life. Accordingly, the importance of permitting people to protect their reputations has given rise to the law of defamation.[76]

Defamation goes way back to pre-Norman times. "Defamation" (*diffamatus*) was a technical term in church law. It signified a reputation bad enough to be put on trial in ecclesiastical court. Money awards for defamation were a way to prevent people from engaging in duels. Defamation law also served as a popular tool of the monarchy to prosecute its critics.[77]

---

[76] For an excellent discussion of the rationales behind defamation law, see Robert C. Post, *The Social Foundations of Defamation Law: Reputation and the Constitution*, 74 Cal. L. Rev. 691 (1986).

[77] *See generally* Theodore F.T. Plucknett, *A Concise History of the Common Law* 484-87 (5th ed. 1956).

According to modern defamation law:

To create liability for defamation there must be:

(a) a false and defamatory statement concerning another;
(b) an unprivileged publication to a third party;
(c) fault amounting at least to negligence on the part of the publisher; and
(d) either actionability of the statement irrespective of special harm or the existence of special harm caused by the publication. Restatement (Second) of Torts § 558.

A "defamatory" statement "tends so to harm the reputation of another as to lower him in the estimation of the community or to deter third persons from associating or dealing with him." Restatement § 559.

A defamatory statement must also be "false." Therefore, a true statement that harms the reputation of another cannot give rise to liability for defamation.

"Publication" means that a defamatory statement is communicated "intentionally or by a negligent act to one other than the person defamed." Restatement § 577. If a person intentionally and unreasonably fails to remove defamatory matter that she knows is under her control, then that person is subject to liability for its continued publication. *See* Restatement § 577. Further "one who repeats or otherwise republishes defamatory matter is subject to liability as if he had originally published it." Restatement § 578.

One who distributes, transmits, or broadcasts on television or radio defamatory material is also liable if she knows or would have reason to know of its defamatory character. *See* Restatement § 581.

Libel vs. Slander. There are two forms of defamation: libel, which consists of written defamatory statements, and slander, which consists of spoken defamatory statements. According to the Restatement:

(1) Libel consists of the publication of defamatory matter by written or printed words, by its embodiment in physical form or by any other form of communication that has the potentially harmful qualities characteristic of written or printed words.

(2) Slander consists of the publication of defamatory matter by spoken words, transitory gestures or by any form of communication other than those stated in Subsection (1). Restatement § 568.

As is demonstrated by the above definitions, the Restatement takes a rather broad view of what constitutes libel.

The classification of certain types of statements as either libel or slander has proven difficult. One example is a statement made over the radio or on television. According to the Restatement, all broadcasting is libel, see Restatement § 568A, but some states take a contrary view.

The distinction between libel and slander is important for the purposes of proving harm. To establish libel, a plaintiff does not need to show "special harm" (i.e., a particular harm or injury); damages are presumed. In contrast, for slander, a plaintiff must show actual pecuniary harm, with the exception of four types of slander known as "slander per se" for which damages are presumed. Slander per se consists of defamatory statements imputing to another (1) a criminal offense;

(2) a loathsome disease; (3) a matter incompatible with one's business, trade, profession, or office; or (4) serious sexual misconduct. *See* Restatement §§ 570-574. The distinction between libel and slander is less important today, since, in the cases you will read below, the Supreme Court curtailed the availability of presumed damages in defamation law.

Why is libel treated more severely than slander? As then Judge Cardozo put it:

> The schism in the law of defamation between the older wrong of slander and the newer one of libel is not the product of mere accident. It has its genesis in evils which the years have not erased. Many things that are defamatory may be said with impunity through the medium of speech. Not so, however, when speech is caught upon the wing and transmuted into print. What gives the sting to writing is its permanence in form. The spoken word dissolves, but the written one abides and perpetuates the scandal. *Ostrowe v. Lee*, 175 N.E. 505, 506 (N.Y. Ct. App. 1931).

Defamation and Privacy. It might strike you that defamation does not have much to do with privacy. After all, defamation involves false information about individuals, whereas privacy seems to be about true information. This, however, is a limited view of privacy. Privacy involves more than finding out true things about individuals. If privacy is understood as an individual's ability to have some control over the self-image she projects to society, then the ability to prevent the spread of false information about oneself is essential for this sort of control. Indeed, one of the cornerstone principles of privacy law is the ability to correct errors in one's records.

(b) Defamation and the Internet

The Internet presents interesting problems for the application of defamation law and the privacy torts because the Internet enables the widespread publication of information by any individual. Typically, it was through the news media that defamatory or private information about individuals was communicated. As a result, it would be viable to sue such entities, since they would be able to pay any judgment a plaintiff might obtain. With the Internet, however, suppose an individual posts defamatory information about another person on her website. Most likely, that individual isn't wealthy enough to be sued. Further, information is sometimes posted anonymously. As a result of this difficulty, plaintiffs have attempted to advance theories upon which Internet Service Providers (ISPs) would be liable.

In defamation law, in addition to the one who makes a libelous statement, other parties who disseminate the libelous statement can also be found liable. Repeating or publishing the libelous statements of others can give rise to "publisher" liability. A newspaper is an example of a publisher because it exercises editorial control over its content. Merely disseminating a libelous statement can give rise to "distributor" liability. In contrast to a publisher, a distributor cannot be found liable unless it is found to be at fault — if it knew or had reason to know about the defamatory statement. Bookstores and libraries are examples of distributors. When a person posts a statement on an ISP's electronic bulletin board or other online forum, is the ISP a "publisher," "distributor," or neither?

The first two courts to reach this issue reached contrary conclusions. In *Cubby, Inc. v. CompuServe, Inc.*, 776 F. Supp. 135 (S.D.N.Y. 1991), CompuServe, an Internet Service Provider, was held not liable for the statements because it didn't have knowledge or reason to know of the statements. The court held that CompuServe was a distributor rather than a publisher: "CompuServe has no more editorial control over such a publication than does a public library, book store, or newsstand, and it would be no more feasible for CompuServe to examine every publication it carries for potentially defamatory statements than it would be for any other distributor to do so."

In *Stratton Oakmont, Inc. v. Prodigy Services Co.*, 23 Media L. Rep. 1794 (N.Y. Sup. 1995), the plaintiff brought a defamation action against Prodigy, the operator of the computer network. An unidentified user posted allegedly defamatory statements on one of Prodigy's electronic bulletin boards. The plaintiffs contended that Prodigy should be considered the "publisher" of the statements. Under Prodigy's stated policy, it was a family-oriented computer network and would screen posts for offensive content. The court concluded that Prodigy was liable as a publisher because "Prodigy held itself out to the public and its members as controlling the content of its computer bulletin boards."

In response to *Stratton Oakmont*, Congress passed § 230 of the Communications Decency Act (CDA) of 1996, which provides in relevant part: "No provider or user of an interactive computer service shall be treated as the publisher or speaker of any information provided by another information content provider." 47 U.S.C. § 230(c)(1). Based on this provision, will ISPs that provide forums where defamatory statements are posted be treated as publishers, distributors, or neither?

ZERAN V. AMERICA ONLINE, INC.

129 F.3d 327 (4th Cir. 1997)

WILKINSON, C.J. . . . On April 25, 1995, an unidentified person posted a message on an [America Online (AOL)] bulletin board advertising "Naughty Oklahoma T-Shirts." The posting described the sale of shirts featuring offensive and tasteless slogans related to the April 19, 1995, bombing of the Alfred P. Murrah Federal Building in Oklahoma City. Those interested in purchasing the shirts were instructed to call "Ken" at [Kenneth] Zeran's home phone number in Seattle, Washington. As a result of this anonymously perpetrated prank, Zeran received a high volume of calls, comprised primarily of angry and derogatory messages, but also including death threats. Zeran could not change his phone number because he relied on its availability to the public in running his business out of his home. Later that day, Zeran called AOL and informed a company representative of his predicament. The employee assured Zeran that the posting would be removed from AOL's bulletin board but explained that as a matter of policy AOL would not post a retraction. The parties dispute the date that AOL removed this original posting from its bulletin board.

On April 26, the next day, an unknown person posted another message advertising additional shirts with new tasteless slogans related to the Oklahoma City bombing. Again, interested buyers were told to call Zeran's phone number, to ask for "Ken," and to "please call back if busy" due to high demand. The angry, threatening phone calls intensified. Over the next four days, an unidentified party continued to post messages on AOL's bulletin board, advertising additional items including bumper stickers and key chains with still more offensive slogans. During this time period, Zeran called AOL repeatedly and was told by company representatives that the individual account from which the messages were posted would soon be closed. Zeran also reported his case to Seattle FBI agents. By April 30, Zeran was receiving an abusive phone call approximately every two minutes.

Meanwhile, an announcer for Oklahoma City radio station KRXO received a copy of the first AOL posting. On May 1, the announcer related the message's contents on the air, attributed them to "Ken" at Zeran's phone number, and urged the listening audience to call the number. After this radio broadcast, Zeran was inundated with death threats and other violent calls from Oklahoma City residents. Over the next few days, Zeran talked to both KRXO and AOL representatives. He also spoke to his local police, who subsequently surveilled his home to protect his safety. By May 14, after an Oklahoma City newspaper published a story exposing the shirt advertisements as a hoax and after KRXO made an on-air apology, the number of calls to Zeran's residence finally subsided to fifteen per day.

Zeran first filed suit on January 4, 1996, against radio station KRXO in the United States District Court for the Western District of Oklahoma. On April 23, 1996, he filed this separate suit against AOL in the same court. Zeran did not bring any action against the party who posted the offensive messages.[78] . . . AOL answered Zeran's complaint and interposed [the Communications Decency Act,] 47 U.S.C. § 230 as an affirmative defense. AOL then moved for judgment on the pleadings pursuant to Fed. R. Civ. P. 12(c). The district court granted AOL's motion, and Zeran filed this appeal.

Because § 230 was successfully advanced by AOL in the district court as a defense to Zeran's claims, we shall briefly examine its operation here. Zeran seeks to hold AOL liable for defamatory speech initiated by a third party. He argued to the district court that once he notified AOL of the unidentified third party's hoax, AOL had a duty to remove the defamatory posting promptly, to notify its subscribers of the message's false nature, and to effectively screen future defamatory material. Section 230 entered this litigation as an affirmative defense pled by AOL. The company claimed that Congress immunized interactive computer service providers from claims based on information posted by a third party.

The relevant portion of § 230 states: "No provider or user of an interactive computer service shall be treated as the publisher or speaker of any information provided by another information content provider." 47 U.S.C. § 230(c)(1). By its plain language, § 230 creates a federal immunity to any cause of action that would make service providers liable for information originating with a third-party user of the service. Specifically, § 230 precludes courts from entertaining claims that would place a computer service provider in a publisher's role. Thus, lawsuits seeking to hold a service provider liable for its exercise of a publisher's traditional

---

[78] Zeran maintains that AOL made it impossible to identify the original party by failing to maintain adequate records of its users. The issue of AOL's recordkeeping practices, however, is not presented by this appeal.

editorial functions — such as deciding whether to publish, withdraw, postpone or alter content — are barred.

The purpose of this statutory immunity is not difficult to discern. Congress recognized the threat that tort-based lawsuits pose to freedom of speech in the new and burgeoning Internet medium. The imposition of tort liability on service providers for the communications of others represented, for Congress, simply another form of intrusive government regulation of speech. . . .

. . . Interactive computer services have millions of users. The amount of information communicated via interactive computer services is therefore staggering. The specter of tort liability in an area of such prolific speech would have an obvious chilling effect. It would be impossible for service providers to screen each of their millions of postings for possible problems. Faced with potential liability for each message republished by their services, interactive computer service providers might choose to severely restrict the number and type of messages posted. Congress considered the weight of the speech interests implicated and chose to immunize service providers to avoid any such restrictive effect.

Another important purpose of § 230 was to encourage service providers to self-regulate the dissemination of offensive material over their services. In this respect, § 230 responded to a New York state court decision, *Stratton Oakmont, Inc. v. Prodigy Servs. Co.* . . .

Congress enacted § 230 to remove the disincentives to self-regulation created by the *Stratton Oakmont* decision. Under that court's holding, computer service providers who regulated the dissemination of offensive material on their services risked subjecting themselves to liability, because such regulation cast the service provider in the role of a publisher. Fearing that the specter of liability would therefore deter service providers from blocking and screening offensive material, Congress enacted § 230's broad immunity "to remove disincentives for the development and utilization of blocking and filtering technologies that empower parents to restrict their children's access to objectionable or inappropriate online material." 47 U.S.C. § 230(b)(4). In line with this purpose, § 230 forbids the imposition of publisher liability on a service provider for the exercise of its editorial and self-regulatory functions.

Zeran argues, however, that the § 230 immunity eliminates only publisher liability, leaving distributor liability intact. Publishers can be held liable for defamatory statements contained in their works even absent proof that they had specific knowledge of the statement's inclusion. According to Zeran, interactive computer service providers like AOL are normally considered instead to be distributors, like traditional news vendors or book sellers. Distributors cannot be held liable for defamatory statements contained in the materials they distribute unless it is proven at a minimum that they have actual knowledge of the defamatory statements upon which liability is predicated. Zeran contends that he provided AOL with sufficient notice of the defamatory statements appearing on the company's bulletin board. This notice is significant, says Zeran, because AOL could be held liable as a distributor only if it acquired knowledge of the defamatory statements' existence.

Because of the difference between these two forms of liability, Zeran contends that the term "distributor" carries a legally distinct meaning from the term "publisher." Accordingly, he asserts that Congress' use of only the term "publisher" in § 230 indicates a purpose to immunize service providers only from publisher liability. He argues that distributors are left unprotected by § 230 and, therefore, his suit should be permitted to proceed against AOL. We disagree. Assuming arguendo that Zeran has satisfied the requirements for imposition of distributor liability, this theory of liability is merely a subset, or a species, of publisher liability, and is therefore also foreclosed by § 230. . . .

AOL falls squarely within this traditional definition of a publisher and, therefore, is clearly protected by § 230's immunity. . . .

Zeran simply attaches too much importance to the presence of the distinct notice element in distributor liability. The simple fact of notice surely cannot transform one from an original publisher to a distributor in the eyes of the law. . . .

If computer service providers were subject to distributor liability, they would face potential liability each time they receive notice of a potentially defamatory statement — from any party, concerning any message. Each notification would require a careful yet rapid investigation of the circumstances surrounding the posted information, a legal judgment concerning the information's defamatory character, and an on-the-spot editorial decision whether to risk liability by allowing the continued publication of that information. Although this might be feasible for the traditional print publisher, the sheer number of postings on interactive computer services would create an impossible burden in the Internet context. Because service providers would be subject to liability only for the publication of information, and not for its removal, they would have a natural incentive simply to remove messages upon notification, whether the contents were defamatory or not. Thus, like strict liability, liability upon notice has a chilling effect on the freedom of Internet speech. . . .

More generally, notice-based liability for interactive computer service providers would provide third parties with a no-cost means to create the basis for future lawsuits. Whenever one was displeased with the speech of another party conducted over an interactive computer service, the offended party could simply "notify" the relevant service provider, claiming the information to be legally defamatory. In light of the vast amount of speech communicated through interactive computer services, these notices could produce an impossible burden for service providers, who would be faced with ceaseless choices of suppressing controversial speech or sustaining prohibitive liability. Because the probable effects of distributor liability on the vigor of Internet speech and on service provider self-regulation are directly contrary to § 230's statutory purposes, we will not assume that Congress intended to leave liability upon notice intact. . . .

NOTES & QUESTIONS

1. *The Applicability of the CDA § 230 to the Privacy Torts.* Is § 230 of the CDA applicable to the privacy torts? In *Barnes v. Yahoo!, Inc.*, 570 F.3d 1096 (9th Cir. 2009), a woman alleged that her former boyfriend created fake profiles under her name on Yahoo. He posted nude photos of her in the profiles and provided contact information for her. She also claimed that he was

impersonating her in chatrooms and directing people to the profiles. She contacted Yahoo and asked them several times to try to put a stop to the boyfriend's misuse of Yahoo's services. She alleged that although Yahoo employees promised they would help her, they failed to stop the boyfriend's conduct. The court held that Yahoo was immune under § 230. However, the court held that Yahoo could be held liable on a promissory estoppel theory because it promised to take down the content.

2. ***Anonymity and Accountability for Harmful Internet Speech.*** Shouldn't plaintiffs sue the people who post defamatory or privacy-invasive statements rather than the ISPs or websites on which the statements appear? Recall in *Zeran* that the anonymous poster of the information could not be identified. Should the website be forced to maintain records of the identities of the individuals who post so that people can sue those individuals? What are the benefits and costs of such a solution?

3. ***Critiques of*** **Zeran.** Consider the following argument against *Zeran* from *Barrett v. Rosenthal*, 5 Cal. Rptr. 3d 416 (Cal. Ct. App. 2003):

> . . . [W]e . . . think it debatable whether notice liability would actually have an unduly chilling effect on cyberspeech. Neither the record before us nor any other information brought to our attention provides an answer to that question. Moreover, the speculative conclusion of the *Zeran* court that exposing Internet intermediaries to knowledge-based liability would significantly chill online speech is disputed by the speculations of other authorities. . . .
>
> It is also asserted that by ignoring how difficult it is for a plaintiff to prevail on a defamation claim or receive significant money damages, the *Zeran* court overstated the danger such claims present to Internet intermediaries, and therefore also exaggerated the danger they would engage in excessive self-censorship.

The California Supreme Court reversed the court of appeals in *Barrett v. Rosenthal*, 146 P.3d 510 (Cal. 2006):

> We agree with the *Zeran* court, and others considering the question, that subjecting Internet service providers and users to defamation liability would tend to chill online speech. . . .
>
> We reject the argument that the difficulty of prevailing on a defamation claim mitigates the deterrent effect of potential liability. Defamation law is complex, requiring consideration of multiple factors. These include whether the statement at issue is true or false, factual or figurative, privileged or unprivileged, whether the matter is of public or private concern, and whether the plaintiff is a public or private figure. Any investigation of a potentially defamatory Internet posting is thus a daunting and expensive challenge. For that reason, we have observed that even when a defamation claim is "clearly nonmeritorious," the threat of liability "ultimately chills the free exercise of expression."
>
> Nor are we convinced by the observation that a "distributor" faces no liability without notice. Distributors are liable not merely upon receiving notice from a third party, but also if they independently "knew or had reason to know" of the defamatory statement. Thus, as the *Zeran* court pointed out, this aspect of distributor liability would discourage active monitoring of Internet postings.

It could also motivate providers to insulate themselves from receiving complaints. Such responses would frustrate the goal of self-regulation.

The third practical implication noted in *Zeran* is no less compelling, and went unaddressed by the Court of Appeal. Notice-based liability for service providers would allow complaining parties to impose substantial burdens on the freedom of Internet speech by lodging complaints whenever they were displeased by an online posting. . . .

Requiring providers, users, and courts to account for the nuances of common law defamation, and all the various ways they might play out in the Internet environment, is a Herculean assignment that we are reluctant to impose. We conclude the *Zeran* court accurately diagnosed the problems that would attend notice-based liability for service providers.

Which opinion has the better argument as to the meaning and purpose of § 230? Consider Daniel Solove:

> Unfortunately, courts are interpreting Section 230 so broadly as to provide too much immunity, eliminating the incentive to foster a balance between speech and privacy. The way courts are using Section 230 exalts free speech to the detriment of privacy and reputation. As a result, a host of websites have arisen that encourage others to post gossip and rumors as well as to engage in online shaming. These websites thrive under Section 230's broad immunity.[79]

Solove contends that a notice and take-down system is preferable to a broader immunity that eliminates distributor liability. What are the benefits and problems of a notice and take-down regime? In copyright law, "one who distributes a device with the object of promoting its use to infringe copyright, as shown by clear expression or other affirmative steps taken to foster infringement, is liable for the resulting acts of infringement by third parties." *MGM Studios, Inc. v. Grokster, Ltd.*, 545 U.S. 913 (2005). Examine the pros and cons of such a rule for defamation or privacy tort liability.

4. *Judicial Interpretive Shift or Amendment?* CDA §230 has been subject to criticism for protecting "bad Samaritans" who engage in nonconsensual pornography, cyber-harassment, and other harmful behavior online. Danielle Citron and Benjamin Wittes argue that numerous bad actors draw on the CDA's protection of Good Samaritans to destructive purposes.[80] In their view, "Extending immunity to Bad Samaritans undermines section 230's purpose by eliminating incentives for better behavior by those in the best position to minimize harm."

How should the law then proceed? In the proposal of Citron and Wittes, change should come from either courts or Congress. One reform path would be for courts to narrow their reading of CDA §230. This interpretative shift would narrow protections to situations that relate to "the congressional goal of incentivizing self-regulation." In particular, Citron and Wittes would not permit CDA immunity to extend "to platforms designed to host illegality or that deliberately host illegal content." If courts do not act in this fashion, however,

---

[79] Daniel J. Solove, *The Future of Reputation: Gossip, Rumor, and Privacy on the Internet* 159 (2007).

[80] Danielle Keats Citron & Benjamin Wittes, *The Internet Will Not Break: Denying Bad Samaritans Section 230 Immunity*, 86 Fordham L. Rev. — (forthcoming 2017).

Congress should revise CDA by adding this language to it: "Nothing in section 230 shall be construed to limit or expand the application of civil or criminal liability for any website or other content host that purposefully encourages cyber stalking, nonconsensual pornography, sex trafficking, child sexual exploitation, or that principally hosts such material."

Do you agree with the need for this change of course for CDA §230? If so, which of the two paths, judicial or congressional, is preferable?

5. ***Who Is the Content Provider?*** In *Batzel v. Smith*, 333 F.3d 1018 (9th Cir. 2003), a handyman (Robert Smith) who worked at Ellen Batzel's home e-mailed Ton Cremers, the director of security at a museum in Amsterdam, who maintained an e-mail listserv about looted art. Smith said that several of Batzel's paintings were stolen from the Jews by the Nazis during World War II. Cremers made a few small changes to the text of Smith's e-mail and sent it out to his listserv. The paintings were not looted art from the Nazis, and Batzel sued both Smith and Cremers. The court concluded that since Cremers was not the originator of the information, he was immune under § 230:

> Obviously, Cremers did not create Smith's e-mail. Smith composed the e-mail entirely on his own. . . . [T]he exclusion of "publisher" liability necessarily precludes liability for exercising the usual prerogative of publishers to choose among proffered material and to edit the material published while retaining its basic form and message.
>
> Because Cremers did no more than select and make minor alterations to Smith's e-mail, Cremers cannot be considered the content provider of Smith's e-mail for purposes of § 230. . . .
>
> We therefore hold that a service provider or user is immune from liability under § 230(c)(1) when a third person or entity that created or developed the information in question furnished it to the provider or user under circumstances in which a reasonable person in the position of the service provider or user would conclude that the information was provided for publication on the Internet or other "interactive computer service."

In dissent, Judge Gould wrote:

> Congress wanted to ensure that excessive government regulation did not slow America's expansion into the exciting new frontier of the Internet. But Congress did not want this new frontier to be like the Old West: a lawless zone governed by retribution and mob justice. The CDA does not license anarchy. A person's decision to disseminate the rankest rumor or most blatant falsehood should not escape legal redress merely because the person chose to disseminate it through the Internet rather than through some other medium. . . .   In this case, I would hold that Cremers is *not* entitled to CDA immunity because Cremers actively selected Smith's e-mail message for publication.

Batzel demonstrates the difficulties in certain situations of determining whether a person is providing content or is merely disseminating the content of another. If a person is deemed the content provider, then § 230 immunity does not apply, as § 230 is designed to immunize a person from being liable for disseminating the content of others. In *Batzel,* is Cremers the content provider because he decided to forward the e-mail? Or is Smith the content provider because he wrote the e-mail? *Batzel* holds that if a person receives a communication sent by another for the purpose of having the person publish it online, then the person is immune under § 230 for publishing it. Few courts have adopted a rule like that in *Batzel* because few have explored situations where it is unclear who precisely is the content provider.

Suppose Cremers has a blog about stolen art. Smith is interested in spreading the rumor about the stolen art on Cremers's blog. Consider the following situations and examine whether Cremers would have § 230 immunity under the majority's rule and also under Judge Gould's:

(a) Cremers's blog allows anybody to post comments. Smith posts a comment about the rumor on Cremers's blog. Batzel wants Cremers to delete the comment, but Cremers refuses to do so.

(b) Cremers has a comment moderation system on his blog where he must approve comments before they are published on his blog. Smith posts the stolen art comment and Cremers approves it, whereupon it is published on the blog.

(c) Smith e-mails Cremers and tells him about the stolen art rumor. Instead of posting the e-mail itself, Cremers writes a blog post about the rumor in his own words and posts it.

(d) Smith calls Cremers and tells him the rumor about the stolen art. Cremers writes a post about the rumor.

Is there any meaningful difference between the above situations and the way that Cremers disseminated Smith's e-mail to the listserv? As a normative matter, should Cremers's liability be different in any of the above situations? How should the law determine when a person should be deemed the content provider and when a person should be deemed to merely be relaying the content of another?

6. ***Wikipedia.*** Wikipedia is an online encyclopedia that anybody can edit. It has millions of entries and is widely used and cited. What are the legal consequences when a Wikipedia entry is defamatory?

A notable case occurred in 2005 involving John Seigenthaler, a former assistant to Attorney General Bobby Kennedy during the Kennedy Administration. His Wikipedia entry falsely accused him of being involved in President John F. Kennedy's assassination. In an article in *USA Today,* Seigenthaler wrote:

> I have no idea whose sick mind conceived the false, malicious "biography" that appeared under my name for 132 days on Wikipedia, the popular, online, free encyclopedia whose authors are unknown and virtually untraceable.[81]

Eventually, the anonymous person who wrote the defamatory statement was identified, and he apologized. If Seigenthaler sued Wikipedia for defamation, would § 230 provide Wikipedia with immunity? Consider the views of Ken Myers on this topic:

---

[81] John Seigenthaler, *A False Wikipedia "Biography,"* USA Today, Nov. 29, 2005.

Because of the unique relationship between Wikipedia and its user-community, the question of whether an individual user-poster is a separate "information content provider," as opposed to somehow being a representative of Wikipedia, is unclear. If Wikipedia is determined to be the relevant "information content provider" then there is no immunity under § 230(c)(1), as Wikipedia itself will be held responsible for the defamatory content. Thus, the definition of "information content provider" raises an important threshold question in this case: what counts as the "person or entity" whose actions the court should analyze in determining whether Wikipedia is the "information content provider" under the third prong? . . .

The Wikipedia community is self-consciously inclusive, designating all of its contributors as "Wikipedians." Presumably, this inclusiveness fosters the cooperative atmosphere critical to Wikipedia's success. However, if *all* members of the Wikipedia community — that is, all contributors — are considered part of the Wikipedia "entity," then it would, by definition and by operation of the third prong, not be eligible for § 230(c)(1) immunity because Wikipedia would be the site's only contributor — there could be no "[]other information content provider." . . .

Wikipedia would argue that, for purposes of § 230(f)(3), only employees of the Wikimedia Foundation should be considered as part of the Wikipedia "entity." However, "the fact that work is performed gratuitously does not relieve a principal of liability."[82]

To the extent that websites like Wikipedia create hierarchies of users, with some having greater editorial powers, does this alter immunity for the actions of the users at the top of the hierarchy?

(c) First Amendment Limitations

NEW YORK TIMES CO. V. SULLIVAN

376 U.S. 254 (1964)

[L.B. Sullivan, one of the three elected Commissioners of Montgomery, Alabama, sued four African-American clergymen and the *New York Times* for libel. Sullivan claimed that a full-page advertisement in the *New York Times* on March 29, 1960, entitled "Heed Their Rising Voices" defamed him. The advertisement discussed the civil rights movement and the wave of terror against the nonviolent protest. It was signed by various clergymen in Southern cities, including the four clergymen named in the lawsuit.

Two paragraphs of the ten in the advertisement were the basis of Sullivan's libel claim.

. . . In Montgomery, Alabama, after students sang "My Country, 'Tis of Thee" on the State Capitol steps, their leaders were expelled from school, and truckloads of police armed with shotguns and tear-gas ringed the Alabama State College Campus. When the entire student body protested to state authorities by refusing

---

[82] Ken S. Myers, *Wikimmunity: Fitting the Communications Decency Act to Wikipedia,* 20 Harv. J.L. & Tech. 163, 188-90 (2006).

to re-register, their dining hall was padlocked in an attempt to starve them into submission. . . .

Again and again the Southern violators have answered Dr. King's peaceful protests with intimidation and violence. They have bombed his home almost killing his wife and child. They have assaulted his person. They have arrested him seven times — for "speeding," "loitering" and similar "offenses." And now they have charged him with "perjury" — a felony under which they could imprison him for ten years. . . .

Although Sullivan was never mentioned by name, he claimed that the word "police" implicated him because he supervised the police department. Although Sullivan made no effort to prove he suffered actual pecuniary loss as a result of the alleged libel, a Montgomery County jury awarded Sullivan damages of $500,000, the full amount claimed against all the petitioners, and the Supreme Court of Alabama affirmed.]

BRENNAN, J. . . . Under Alabama law as applied in this case, a publication is "libelous per se" if the words "tend to injure a person . . . in his reputation" or to "bring (him) into public contempt"; the trial court stated that the standard was met if the words are such as to "injure him in his public office, or impute misconduct to him in his office, or want of official integrity, or want of fidelity to a public trust. . . ." The jury must find that the words were published "of and concerning" the plaintiff, but where the plaintiff is a public official his place in the governmental hierarchy is sufficient evidence to support a finding that his reputation has been affected by statements that reflect upon the agency of which he is in charge. Once "libel per se" has been established, the defendant has no defense as to stated facts unless he can persuade the jury that they were true in all their particulars. His privilege of "fair comment" for expressions of opinion depends on the truth of the facts upon which the comment is based. Unless he can discharge the burden of proving truth, general damages are presumed, and may be awarded without proof of pecuniary injury. A showing of actual malice is apparently a prerequisite to recovery of punitive damages, and the defendant may in any event forestall a punitive award by a retraction meeting the statutory requirements. Good motives and belief in truth do not negate an inference of malice, but are relevant only in mitigation of punitive damages if the jury chooses to accord them weight.

The question before us is whether this rule of liability, as applied to an action brought by a public official against critics of his official conduct, abridges the freedom of speech and of the press that is guaranteed by the First and Fourteenth Amendments.

Respondent relies heavily, as did the Alabama courts, on statements of this Court to the effect that the Constitution does not protect libelous publications. . . . Like insurrection, contempt, advocacy of unlawful acts, breach of the peace, obscenity, solicitation of legal business, and the various other formulae for the repression of expression that have been challenged in this Court, libel can claim no talismanic immunity from constitutional limitations. It must be measured by standards that satisfy the First Amendment.

The general proposition that freedom of expression upon public questions is secured by the First Amendment has long been settled by our decisions. . . .

. . . [W]e consider this case against the background of a profound national commitment to the principle that debate on public issues should be uninhibited, robust, and wide-open, and that it may well include vehement, caustic, and sometimes unpleasantly sharp attacks on government and public officials. The present advertisement, as an expression of grievance and protest on one of the major public issues of our time, would seem clearly to qualify for the constitutional protection. The question is whether it forfeits that protection by the falsity of some of its factual statements and by its alleged defamation of respondent.

Authoritative interpretations of the First Amendment guarantees have consistently refused to recognize an exception for any test of truth — whether administered by judges, juries, or administrative officials — and especially one that puts the burden of proving truth on the speaker. The constitutional protection does not turn upon "the truth, popularity, or social utility of the ideas and beliefs which are offered." . . .

That erroneous statement is inevitable in free debate, and that it must be protected if the freedoms of expression are to have the "breathing space" that they "need to survive." . . .

A rule compelling the critic of official conduct to guarantee the truth of all his factual assertions — and to do so on pain of libel judgments virtually unlimited in amount — leads to a comparable "self-censorship." . . . Under such a rule, would-be critics of official conduct may be deterred from voicing their criticism, even though it is believed to be true and even though it is in fact true, because of doubt whether it can be proved in court or fear of the expense of having to do so. They tend to make only statements which "steer far wider of the unlawful zone." The rule thus dampens the vigor and limits the variety of public debate. It is inconsistent with the First and Fourteenth Amendments.

The constitutional guarantees require, we think, a federal rule that prohibits a public official from recovering damages for a defamatory falsehood relating to his official conduct unless he proves that the statement was made with "actual malice" — that is, with knowledge that it was false or with reckless disregard of whether it was false or not. . . .

We hold today that the Constitution delimits a State's power to award damages for libel in actions brought by public officials against critics of their official conduct. Since this is such an action, the rule requiring proof of actual malice is applicable. While Alabama law apparently requires proof of actual malice for an award of punitive damages, where general damages are concerned malice is "presumed." Such a presumption is inconsistent with the federal rule. Since the trial judge did not instruct the jury to differentiate between general and punitive damages, it may be that the verdict was wholly an award of one or the other. But it is impossible to know, in view of the general verdict returned. Because of this uncertainty, the judgment must be reversed and the case remanded. . . .

NOTES & QUESTIONS

1. ***Should Defamation Have Survived?*** Justices Black, Douglas, and Goldberg would have gone further, eliminating all defamation liability for public officials. In other words, public officials could not sue for defamation even if

the defamatory statement were made with actual malice. As Justice Goldberg explained, the right to criticize public officials is unconditional and "should not depend upon a probing by the jury of the motivation of the citizen or press." Does Justice Brennan's logic lead to this result? Why not just bar all libel actions by public officials? Consider Justice Holmes's dissent in *Abrams v. United States*, 250 U.S. 616, 630 (1919):

> But when men have realized that time has upset many fighting faiths, they may come to believe even more than they believe the very foundations of their own conduct that the ultimate good desired is better reached by free trade in ideas — that the best test of truth is the power of the thought to get itself accepted in the competition of the market, and that truth is the only ground upon which their wishes safely can be carried out. That at any rate is the theory of our Constitution.

If Holmes is right, and the marketplace of ideas will result in the truth eventually winning out, then is defamation law even necessary?[83]

2. ***Actual Malice.*** The actual malice standard is a subjective one. As Randall Bezanson describes it:

> The actual malice inquiry is avowedly focused on the subjective state of mind of the publisher at the time of publication. It asks only whether falsity was calculated or whether the publisher's decision was sufficiently indifferent to likely falsity that the publication decision should not be respected under the First Amendment. Actual malice, in short, reveals a frame of mind, an animating intention for the publication, that belies any significant publisher concern for the audience or for the function being performed in the selection and presentation of information, or news. . . .

In practice, actual malice is very difficult for plaintiffs to establish. Bezanson observes:

> In making actual malice determinations, state courts attempt to determine the speaker's subjective state of mind by two primary means. First, courts examine the speaker's observable conduct at the time of the speech act, viewing such outward manifestations as a potential insight into the speaker's state of mind. . . . The second means by which courts attempt to determine the speaker's state of mind is through the personal testimony of the speaker. State courts grant considerable weight to the speaker's own reflective statements concerning his or her belief as to the truth of the speech at the time the speech judgment was made.[84]

3. ***Public Figures.*** Subsequently, the Court extended the approach in *New York Times* to persons who were not public officials but who were " 'public figures' and involved in issues in which the public has a justified and important interest." *Curtis Publishing Co. v. Butts*, 388 U.S. 130 (1967).

---

[83] For more background about *New York Times v. Sullivan*, see Anthony Lewis, *Make No Law: The Sullivan Case and the First Amendment* (1991).

[84] Randall P. Bezanson, *The Developing Law of Editorial Judgment,* 78 Neb. L. Rev. 754, 774-75, 763-64 (1999).

In *Gertz v. Robert Welch, Inc.*, 418 U.S. 323 (1974), which is excerpted below, the Court turned to the issue of whether the *New York Times* approach should be extended to private figures.

GERTZ V. ROBERT WELCH, INC.

418 U.S. 323 (1974)

[In 1968, Nuccio, a Chicago policeman, shot and killed Nelson, a youth. Nuccio was prosecuted and convicted for murder in the second degree. The Nelson family retained petitioner Elmer Gertz, a reputable attorney, to represent them in civil litigation against Nuccio. Robert Welch, Inc. published *American Opinion*, a monthly magazine representing the views of the John Birch Society. The magazine had been warning of a national conspiracy to discredit local police forces and create a national police force as a step toward establishing a Communist dictatorship. In 1969, the magazine published an article about the murder trial of Officer Nuccio, alleging that he was framed as part of the Communist campaign against the police. Among other things, the article portrayed Gertz as the mastermind of the frame-up. It stated that Gertz was a "Leninist" and a "Communist-fronter," that Gertz belonged to Marxist and Socialist organizations, and that Gertz had a criminal record. All of these statements were false. The managing editor made no effort to verify the charges; in fact, he wrote an editorial introduction stating that the author had conducted extensive research. Gertz sued for libel and won a jury verdict of $50,000. The district court, however, decided that the *New York Times* standard should apply and entered judgment for Robert Welch, Inc.]

POWELL, J. . . . The principal issue in this case is whether a newspaper or broadcaster that publishes defamatory falsehoods about an individual who is neither a public official nor a public figure may claim a constitutional privilege against liability for the injury inflicted by those statements. . . .

The legitimate state interest underlying the law of libel is the compensation of individuals for the harm inflicted on them by defamatory falsehood. We would not lightly require the State to abandon this purpose, for, as Mr. Justice Stewart has reminded us, the individual's right to the protection of his own good name

> reflects no more than our basic concept of the essential dignity and worth of every human being — a concept at the root of any decent system of ordered liberty. The protection of private personality, like the protection of life itself, is left primarily to the individual States under the Ninth and Tenth Amendments. But this does not mean that the right is entitled to any less recognition by this Court as a basic of our constitutional system. *Rosenblatt v. Baer*, 383 U.S. 75, 92 (1966) (concurring opinion). . . .

. . . [W]e have no difficulty in distinguishing among defamation plaintiffs. The first remedy of any victim of defamation is self-help — using available opportunities to contradict the lie or correct the error and thereby to minimize its adverse impact on reputation. Public officials and public figures usually enjoy significantly greater access to the channels of effective communication and hence have a more realistic opportunity to counteract false statements then private individuals normally enjoy. Private individuals are therefore more vulnerable to injury, and the state interest in protecting them is correspondingly greater.

More important than the likelihood that private individuals will lack effective opportunities for rebuttal, there is a compelling normative consideration underlying the distinction between public and private defamation plaintiffs. An individual who decides to seek governmental office must accept certain necessary consequences of that involvement in public affairs. He runs the risk of closer public scrutiny than might otherwise be the case. And society's interest in the officers of government is not strictly limited to the formal discharge of official duties. As the Court pointed out in *Garrison v. Louisiana*, the public's interest extends to "anything which might touch on an official's fitness for office. . . . Few personal attributes are more germane to fitness for office than dishonesty, malfeasance, or improper motivation, even though these characteristics may also affect the official's private character."

Those classed as public figures stand in a similar position. Hypothetically, it may be possible for someone to become a public figure through no purposeful action of his own, but the instances of truly involuntary public figures must be exceedingly rare. For the most part those who attain this status have assumed roles of especial prominence in the affairs of society. Some occupy positions of such persuasive power and influence that they are deemed public figures for all purposes. More commonly, those classed as public figures have thrust themselves to the forefront of particular public controversies in order to influence the resolution of the issues involved. In either event, they invite attention and comment.

Even if the foregoing generalities do not obtain in every instance, the communications media are entitled to act on the assumption that public officials and public figures have voluntarily exposed themselves to increased risk of injury from defamatory falsehood concerning them. No such assumption is justified with respect to a private individual. He has not accepted public office or assumed an "influential role in ordering society." He has relinquished no part of his interest in the protection of his own good name, and consequently he has a more compelling call on the courts for redress of injury inflicted by defamatory falsehood. Thus, private individuals are not only more vulnerable to injury than public officials and public figures; they are also more deserving of recovery.

For these reasons we conclude that the States should retain substantial latitude in their efforts to enforce a legal remedy for defamatory falsehood injurious to the reputation of a private individual. The extension of the *New York Times* test . . . would abridge this legitimate state interest to a degree that we find unacceptable. And it would occasion the additional difficulty of forcing state and federal judges to decide on an ad hoc basis which publications address issues of "general or public interest" and which do not — to determine, in the words of Mr. Justice Marshall, "what information is relevant to self-government." We doubt the wisdom of committing this task to the conscience of judges. . . .

We hold that, so long as they do not impose liability without fault, the States may define for themselves the appropriate standard of liability for a publisher or broadcaster of defamatory falsehood injurious to a private individual. . . .

. . . Under the traditional rules pertaining to actions for libel, the existence of injury is presumed from the fact of publication. Juries may award substantial sums as compensation for supposed damage to reputation without any proof that such harm actually occurred. The largely uncontrolled discretion of juries to award damages where there is no loss unnecessarily compounds the potential of any system of liability for defamatory falsehood to inhibit the vigorous exercise of First Amendment freedoms. Additionally, the doctrine of presumed damages invites juries to punish unpopular opinion rather than to compensate individuals for injury sustained by the publication of a false fact. More to the point, the States have no substantial interest in securing for plaintiffs such as this petitioner gratuitous awards of money damages far in excess of any actual injury. . . .

. . . It is necessary to restrict defamation plaintiffs who do not prove knowledge of falsity or reckless disregard for the truth to compensation for actual injury. . . . Suffice it to say that actual injury is not limited to out-of-pocket loss. Indeed, the more customary types of actual harm inflicted by defamatory falsehood include impairment of reputation and standing in the community, personal humiliation, and mental anguish and suffering. . . .

We also find no justification for allowing awards of punitive damages against publishers and broadcasters held liable under state-defined standards of liability for defamation. In most jurisdictions jury discretion over the amounts awarded is limited only by the gentle rule that they not be excessive. Consequently, juries assess punitive damages in wholly unpredictable amounts bearing no necessary relation to the actual harm caused. And they remain free to use their discretion selectively to punish expressions of unpopular views. Like the doctrine of presumed damages, jury discretion to award punitive damages unnecessarily exacerbates the danger of media self-censorship, but, unlike the former rule, punitive damages are wholly irrelevant to the state interest that justifies a negligence standard for private defamation actions. They are not compensation for injury. Instead, they are private fines levied by civil juries to punish reprehensible conduct and to deter its future occurrence. In short, the private defamation plaintiff who establishes liability under a less demanding standard than that stated by *New York Times* may recover only such damages as are sufficient to compensate him for actual injury.

Notwithstanding our refusal to extend the *New York Times* privilege to defamation of private individuals, respondent contends that we should affirm the judgment below on the ground that petitioner is either a public official or a public figure. . . .

. . . In some instances an individual may achieve such pervasive fame or notoriety that he becomes a public figure for all purposes and in all contexts. More commonly, an individual voluntarily injects himself or is drawn into a particular public controversy and thereby becomes a public figure for a limited range of issues. In either case such persons assume special prominence in the resolution of public questions.

Petitioner has long been active in community and professional affairs. He has served as an officer of local civic groups and of various professional organizations, and he has published several books and articles on legal subjects. Although petitioner was consequently well known in some circles, he had achieved no general fame or notoriety in the community. None of the prospective jurors called at the trial had ever heard of petitioner prior to this litigation, and respondent offered no proof that this response was atypical of the local population. We would not lightly assume that a citizen's participation in community and professional affairs rendered him a public figure for all purposes. Absent clear evidence of general fame or notoriety in the community, and pervasive involvement in the affairs of society, an individual should not be deemed a public personality for all aspects of his life. It is preferable to reduce the public-figure question to a more meaningful context by looking to the nature and extent of an individual's participation in the particular controversy giving rise to the defamation.

In this context it is plain that petitioner was not a public figure. He played a minimal role at the coroner's inquest, and his participation related solely to his representation of a private client. He took no part in the criminal prosecution of Officer Nuccio. Moreover, he never discussed either the criminal or civil litigation with the press and was never quoted as having done so. He plainly did not thrust himself into the vortex of this public issue, nor did he engage the public's attention in an attempt to influence its outcome. We are persuaded that the trial court did not err in refusing to characterize petitioner as a public figure for the purpose of this litigation. . . .

WHITE, J. dissenting. . . . The press today is vigorous and robust. To me, it is quite incredible to suggest that threats of libel suits from private citizens are causing the press to refrain from publishing the truth. I know of no hard facts to support that proposition, and the Court furnishes none.

The communications industry has increasingly become concentrated in a few powerful hands operating very lucrative businesses reaching across the Nation and into almost every home. Neither the industry as a whole nor its individual components are easily intimidated, and we are fortunate that they are not. Requiring them to pay for the occasional damage they do to private reputation will play no substantial part in their future performance or their existence. . . .

NOTES & QUESTIONS

1. ***Public vs. Private Figures.*** What distinguishes a public from a private figure? In *Time, Inc. v. Firestone*, 424 U.S. 448 (1976), Mary Alice Firestone and her husband had a messy divorce. The court issued a judgment granting the divorce, stating that according to the testimony of the husband, the wife's "extramarital escapades . . . were bizarre and of an amatory nature which would have made Dr. Freud's hair curl. Other testimony . . . would indicate that [the husband] was guilty of bounding from one bedpartner to another with the erotic zest of a satyr. The court is inclined to discount much of this testimony as unreliable." *Time* magazine published the following article in its "Milestones" section the following week:

> DIVORCED. By Russell A. Firestone Jr., 41, heir to the tire fortune: Mary Alice Sullivan Firestone, 32, his third wife; a onetime Palm Beach schoolteacher; on grounds of extreme cruelty and adultery; after six years of marriage, one son; in West Palm Beach, Fla. The 17-month intermittent trial produced enough

testimony of extramarital adventures on both sides, said the judge, "to make Dr. Freud's hair curl."

Mary Firestone sued for libel. When the case ended up in the U.S. Supreme Court, the issue was whether Firestone was a public or private figure. According to the Court:

> Petitioner contends that because the Firestone divorce was characterized by the Florida Supreme Court as a "cause celebre," it must have been a public controversy and respondent must be considered a public figure. But in so doing petitioner seeks to equate "public controversy" with all controversies of interest to the public. . . .
>
> Dissolution of a marriage through judicial proceedings is not the sort of "public controversy" referred to in *Gertz*, even though the marital difficulties of extremely wealthy individuals may be of interest to some portion of the reading public. Nor did respondent freely choose to publicize issues as to the propriety of her married life. She was compelled to go to court by the State in order to obtain legal release from the bonds of matrimony. We have said that in such an instance "(r)esort to the judicial process . . . is no more voluntary in a realistic sense than that of the defendant called upon to defend his interests in court." . . . She assumed no "special prominence in the resolution of public questions." *Gertz*, 418 U.S., at 351. We hold respondent was not a "public figure" for the purpose of determining the constitutional protection afforded petitioner's report of the factual and legal basis for her divorce.

In *Wolston v. Readers Digest Ass'n, Inc.*, 443 U.S. 157 (1979), the plaintiff was summoned to appear before a grand jury in connection with an investigation into his aunt and uncle's spying for the Soviet Union in 1958. Due to mental depression, the plaintiff failed to appear before the grand jury and was held in contempt. In 1984, a book about Soviet agents stated that the plaintiff had been indicted for being such an agent. The district court and court of appeals held that the plaintiff was a limited-purpose public figure (regarding Soviet espionage) — those who, under the language of *Gertz*, "thrust themselves to the forefront of particular public controversies in order to influence the resolution of the issues involved." The Supreme Court disagreed:

> . . . [T]he undisputed facts do not justify the conclusion of the District Court and Court of Appeals that petitioner "voluntarily thrust" or "injected" himself into the forefront of the public controversy surrounding the investigation of Soviet espionage in the United States. It would be more accurate to say that petitioner was dragged unwillingly into the controversy. The Government pursued him in its investigation. Petitioner did fail to respond to a grand jury subpoena, and this failure, as well as his subsequent citation for contempt, did attract media attention. But the mere fact that petitioner voluntarily chose not to appear before the grand jury, knowing that his action might be attended by publicity, is not decisive on the question of public-figure status. . . . It is clear that petitioner played only a minor role in whatever public controversy there may have been concerning the investigation of Soviet espionage. We decline to hold that his mere citation for contempt rendered him a public figure for purposes of comment on the investigation of Soviet espionage.
>
> Petitioner's failure to appear before the grand jury and citation for contempt no doubt were "newsworthy," but the simple fact that these events attracted

media attention also is not conclusive of the public-figure issue. A private individual is not automatically transformed into a public figure just by becoming involved in or associated with a matter that attracts public attention. . . . A libel defendant must show more than mere newsworthiness to justify application of the demanding burden of *New York Times*. . . .

If being involved in newsworthy events is not the appropriate test for whether a person is a public figure, then what are the dispositive factors?

Consider *Atlanta Journal-Constitution v. Jewell,* 555 S.E.2d 175 (Ga. Ct. App. 2001). Richard Jewell, a security guard in Olympic Park during the 1996 Olympics in Atlanta, spotted a suspicious unattended package and helped to evacuate the area. The package contained a bomb, and Jewell was initially recognized as a hero for helping prevent the terrorist attack. The FBI, however, believed that Jewell might have planted the bomb to make himself into a hero, and the FBI's suspicions of Jewell were leaked to the press. The *Atlanta Journal-Constitution* published an article entitled "FBI Suspects 'Hero' Guard May Have Planted Bomb." The FBI investigation eventually cleared Jewell. However, during the interim, Jewell's life was turned upside down, and he could not seek employment or even go out in public without being mobbed by reporters. Jewell sued the *Journal-Constitution* for defamation. The trial court held that Jewell was a "voluntary limited-purpose public figure." Jewell appealed, arguing that "he is not [such a public figure] because he did not assume a role of special prominence in the controversy over the safety of Olympic Park, he did not voluntarily thrust himself to the forefront of the controversy of the safety of Olympic Park, and he did not intentionally seek to influence the resolution or outcome of any public controversy surrounding the safety of Olympic Park." The court concluded that the trial court's designation of Jewell as a voluntary limited-purpose public figure was correct:

> In *Silvester v. American Broadcasting Cos.,* 839 F.2d 1491 (11th Cir. 1988), the Eleventh Circuit adopted a three-prong test to determine whether a person is a limited-purpose public figure. Under this test, the court must isolate the public controversy, examine the plaintiff's involvement in the controversy, and determine whether the alleged defamation was germane to the plaintiff's participation in the controversy. Whether a person is a public figure, general or limited, is a question of law for the court to resolve. . . .
>
> While we can envision situations in which news coverage alone would be insufficient to convert Jewell from private citizen to public figure, we agree with the trial court that Jewell's actions show that he voluntarily assumed a position of influence in the controversy. Jewell granted ten interviews and one photo shoot in the three days between the bombing and the reopening of the park, mostly to prominent members of the national press. While no magical number of media appearances is required to render a citizen a public figure, Jewell's participation in the public discussion of the bombing exceeds what has been deemed sufficient to render other citizens public figures. . . .
>
> Furthermore, the United States Supreme Court has held the actual malice rule is applicable whenever "an individual voluntarily injects himself *or is drawn into* a particular public controversy." The evidence in this case, at the very least, supports a finding that Jewell was initially drawn into the controversy unwillingly and thereafter assumed a prominent position as to its outcome. Jewell did not reject any role in the public controversy debate, was a

prominent figure in the coverage of the controversy, and, whatever his reticence regarding his media appearances, encountered them voluntarily. . . .

The third prong of the *Silvester* test requires the court to ascertain whether the allegedly defamatory statements were germane to Jewell's participation in the controversy. Anything which might touch on the controversy is relevant. Misstatements wholly unrelated to the controversy do not require a showing of actual malice to be actionable. . . .

Certainly, the information reported regarding Jewell's character was germane to Jewell's participation in the controversy over the Olympic Park's safety. A public figure's talents, education, experience, and motives are relevant to the public's decision to listen to him. The articles and the challenged statements within them dealt with Jewell's status as a suspect in the bombing and his law enforcement background. . . .

Whether he liked it or not, Jewell became a central figure in the specific public controversy with respect to which he was allegedly defamed: the controversy over park safety. . . .

2. *Are Corporate CEOs Public Figures?* Patricia Sánchez Abril argues that the traditional way courts distinguish between public and private figures unfairly deems many business leaders to be public figures:

> Because contemporary business requires a public face, courts should give businesspeople certain latitude in their public dealings before branding them as public figures. Small-scale promotion, advertising campaigns, and lobbying and networking efforts should be considered part of modern business reality. Even some print and electronic media involvement is commonplace and should not be an automatic marker of larger-scale notoriety.[85]

Although CEOs may be less well known than celebrities, they may have a larger social impact because of the activities of their companies. Perhaps CEOs should be more likely to be deemed public figures than celebrities because of the power and influence they wield. What should entitle the press to have wider latitude in speaking about people? Their fame? Their power? Another factor?

3. *Matters of Private Concern: The* **Dun & Bradstreet** *Case.* Subsequent to *Gertz*, a plurality of the Court examined whether the *Gertz* rule would apply when, in contrast to the situation in *Gertz*, the alleged defamatory statements did not involve a matter of public concern. In *Dun & Bradstreet, Inc. v. Greenmoss Builders, Inc.*, 472 U.S. 749 (1985), Dun & Bradstreet, a credit reporting agency, provided an erroneous report about the financial condition of Greenmoss Builders. Upon learning of the defamatory report, the president of Greenmoss called Dun & Bradstreet and asked for a correction and a list of all those to whom Dun & Bradstreet had sent the report. Dun & Bradstreet corrected the report but did not inform Greenmoss of the list of recipients of the report. Greenmoss sued for defamation, winning $50,000 in compensatory or presumed damages and $300,000 in punitive damages. The Court held that this did not involve a matter of public concern and that therefore the *Gertz* rule should not apply:

---

[85] Patricia Sánchez Abril, The Evolution of Business Celebrity in American Law and Society, 48 Am. Bus. L.J. 177, 223 (2011).

The First Amendment interest . . . is less important than the one weighed in Gertz. We have long recognized that not all speech is of equal First Amendment importance. It is speech on "'matters of public concern'" that is "at the heart of the First Amendment's protection." . . .

In contrast, speech on matters of purely private concern is of less First Amendment concern. As a number of state courts, including the court below, have recognized, the role of the Constitution in regulating state libel law is far more limited when the concerns that activated *New York Times* and *Gertz* are absent. . . .

While such speech is not totally unprotected by the First Amendment, its protections are less stringent. In *Gertz*, we found that the state interest in awarding presumed and punitive damages was not "substantial" in view of their effect on speech at the core of First Amendment concern. . . . In light of the reduced constitutional value of speech involving no matters of public concern, we hold that the state interest adequately supports awards of presumed and punitive damages — even absent a showing of "actual malice." . . .

2. FALSE LIGHT

(a) Introduction

PUBLICITY PLACING PERSON IN FALSE LIGHT
Restatement (Second) of Torts § 652E

One who gives publicity to a matter concerning another that places the other before the public in a false light is subject to liability to the other for invasion of his privacy, if

(a) the false light in which the other was placed would be highly offensive to a reasonable person, and

(b) the actor had knowledge of or acted in reckless disregard as to the falsity of the publicized matter and the false light in which the other would be placed.

NOTES & QUESTIONS

1. *False Light vs. Defamation.* False light is similar in many respects to defamation. Both torts protect against material false statements. However, defamation requires some form of reputational injury (although, once shown, one can collect for emotional distress). False light, on the other hand, can compensate exclusively for emotional distress. According to the Restatement: "It is enough that he is given unreasonable and highly objectionable publicity that attributes to him characteristics, conduct or beliefs that are false, and so is placed before the public in a false position. When this is the case and the matter attributed to the plaintiff is not defamatory, the rule here stated affords a different remedy, not available in an action for defamation." Comment (b). Since false light does not require reputational harm, a plaintiff can recover for

false light that even improves her reputation.[86] While defamation concerns one's status in the community, false light concerns one's peace of mind. As Bryan Lasswell explains, the "false light tort, to the extent distinct from the tort of defamation . . . rests on an awareness that people who are made to seem pathetic or ridiculous may be shunned, and not just people who are thought to be dishonest or incompetent or immoral."[87]

Another difference between false light and defamation is that false light requires a wider communication of the information. False light requires "publicity," which must be made to the public at large. Defamation requires "publication," which means that the communication merely requires communication to another person.

2. Damages for False Light and Defamation. In *Braun v. Flynt*, 726 F.2d 245 (5th Cir. 1984), Jeannie Braun worked at an amusement park and performed a routine with "Ralph the Diving Pig." The pig dove into the pool and was fed by Braun from a milk bottle. One of Larry Flynt's publications, *Chic*, a pornographic magazine, obtained a photograph of Braun's act. The picture appeared in a section of the magazine called "Chic Thrills," implying that something kinky was going on. When Braun saw the photograph, she was mortified. She could not return to work and suffered from depression. She sued Flynt for defamation and false light. A jury awarded her actual and punitive damages for both causes of action. Flynt appealed, arguing among other things that liability was barred by the First Amendment. The court, applying the *Gertz* rule, concluded that Braun was not a public figure and that the First Amendment did not bar her recovery. However, the court concluded that she could not recover damages for both false light and defamation. Accordingly, the case was remanded for a new trial on damages.

3. Critics of the False Light Tort. Diane Zimmerman argues: "Most injuries from untruths will, and should, be handled as defamation actions; of those that cannot be, many will either be too trivial to remedy or will not be actionable because the 'falsity' complained of will be constitutionally-protected opinion or ideas."[88] A number of courts agree. Recall *Lake v. Wal-Mart* from   Chapter 1. There, the court recognized three of the four Warren and Brandeis privacy torts, declining to recognize false light: "We are concerned that claims under false light are similar to claims of defamation, and to the extent that false light is more expansive than defamation, tension between this tort and the First Amendment is increased." *See also Renwick v. News and Observer Publishing Co.*, 312 S.E.2d 405 (N.C. 1984) (declining to recognize false light tort). Does the false light tort serve a viable purpose?

---

[86] *See, e.g.*, Nathan E. Ray, *Let There Be False Light: Resisting the Growing Trend Against an Important Tort*, 84 Minn. L. Rev. 713, 735 (2000).

[87] Bryan R. Lasswell, *In Defense of False Light: Why False Light Must Remain a Viable Cause of Action*, 34 S. Tex. L. Rev. 149, 176 (1993).

[88] Diane Leehneer Zimmerman, *False Light Invasion of Privacy: The Light That Failed*, 64 N.Y.U. L. Rev. 364, 452 (1989). For a defense of the false light tort, see Ray, *Let There Be False Light, supra*; Lasswell, *In Defense of False Light, supra*; Gary T. Schwartz, *Explaining and Justifying a Limited Tort of False Light Invasion of Privacy*, 41 Case W. Res. L. Rev. 885 (1991).

4. ***Forms of False Light.*** An illustration of the type of misleading statement that can give rise to a false light action is when a mostly true story is somewhat embellished. *See Varnish v. Best Medium Publishing Co.*, 405 F.2d 608 (2d Cir. 1968) (viable false light action for false facts about the relationship between husband and wife who killed herself and their three children). Another example of a false light claim is when one's photograph is used out of context. *See, e.g., Thompson v. Close-up, Inc.*, 98 N.Y.S.2d 300 (1950) (article on drug dealing using the plaintiff's photo); *Holmes v. Curtis Publishing Co.*, 303 F. Supp. 522 (D.S.C. 1969) (use of plaintiff's photo with caption that plaintiff was a high-stakes gambler); *Morrell v. Forbes, Inc.*, 603 F. Supp. 1305 (D. Mass. 1985) (photo used in connection with article about organized crime). In *Wood v. Hustler Magazine*, 736 F.2d 1084 (5th Cir. 1984), a photograph of LaJuan Wood was stolen by another person, who sent it into *Hustler*, a pornographic magazine, along with a forged consent form. *Hustler* sent a mailgram to the address given on the forged consent form asking the sender to call *Hustler*. The sender did, and again lied that there was consent. *Hustler* published LaJuan's photo in its magazine stating: "LaJuan Wood is a 22-year old housewife and mother from Bryan, Texas, whose hobby is collecting arrowheads. Her fantasy is 'to be screwed by two bikers.'" LaJuan sued *Hustler*, and the court held that *Hustler* could be liable for false light because of the "publication of the false and highly offensive fantasy." The court reasoned that the magazine was negligent in making sure that the consent form was valid.

5. ***Obvious Fictions.*** Suppose a story is deliberately designed to be fictional and is so preposterous that a reasonable person could not possibly believe it to be true. Would there be a viable claim for false light? The answer is no, although it must be clear that the story is pure fiction. In *People's Bank and Trust Co. v. Globe International Publishing, Inc.*, 978 F.2d 1065 (8th Cir. 1992), a tabloid ran a story about a 97-year-old woman who became pregnant. The story used the name of a real person, who sued. The tabloid contended that no reader could reasonably believe that the story was true. The court rejected the contention because the publisher of the tabloid "holds out the publication as factual and true," and it "mingles factual, fictional, and hybrid stories without overtly identifying one from the other."

(b) First Amendment Limitations

TIME, INC. V. HILL

385 U.S. 374 (1967)

[In 1952, the Hill family was held prisoner in their home for 19 hours by three escaped convicts. The family escaped unharmed and were treated courteously by the convicts. The convicts were later killed by police during their apprehension. The story made the front page news. The Hill family tried hard to remain out of the spotlight. Nevertheless, the Hill family's experience was written about in a novel by Joseph Hayes called *The Desperate Hours*. In contrast to the actual events, the book depicted the convicts beating the father and son and making a verbal sexual insult to the daughter. A Broadway play and a movie were made based on the book. In 1955, *Life* magazine published an article entitled "True Crime Inspires Tense Play." The article stated that "Americans all over the country read about the desperate ordeal of the James Hill family" and "read about it in Joseph Hayes's novel, *The Desperate Hours*, inspired by the family's experience." The article then stated: "Now they can see the story re-enacted in Hayes's Broadway play based on the book." Pictures accompanying the article displayed scenes from the play depicting the son being beaten and the daughter biting the hand of a convict. The *Life* magazine photographs were taken in the Hills' former home, where they had been held hostage. The Hills sued under §§ 50-51 of the New York Civil Rights Law, contending that the *Life* article gave the false impression that the play accurately depicted the Hills' experience. A jury awarded the Hills $50,000 compensatory and $25,000 punitive damages.]

BRENNAN, J. . . . The question in this case is whether appellant, publisher of Life Magazine, was denied constitutional protections of speech and press by the application by the New York courts of §§ 50-51 of the New York Civil Rights Law to award appellee damages on allegations that Life falsely reported that a new play portrayed an experience suffered by appellee and his family.

. . . In *New York Times Co. v. Sullivan*, we held that the Constitution delimits a State's power to award damages for libel in actions brought by public officials against critics of their official conduct. Factual error, content defamatory of official reputation, or both, are insufficient for an award of damages for false statements unless actual malice — knowledge that the statements are false or in reckless disregard of the truth — is alleged and proved. . . .

. . . We hold that the constitutional protections for speech and press preclude the application of the New York statute to redress false reports of matters of public interest in the absence of proof that the defendant published the report with knowledge of its falsity or in reckless disregard of the truth.

The guarantees for speech and press are not the preserve of political expression or comment upon public affairs, essential as those are to healthy government. One need only pick up any newspaper or magazine to comprehend the vast range of published matter which exposes persons to public view, both private citizens and public officials. Exposure of the self to others in varying degrees is a concomitant of life in a civilized community. The risk of this exposure is an essential incident of life in a society which places a primary value on freedom of speech and of press. "Freedom of discussion, if it would fulfill its historic function in this nation, must embrace all issues about which information is needed or appropriate to enable the members of society to cope with the exigencies of their period." . . . We have no doubt that the subject of the Life article, the opening of a new play linked to an actual incident, is a matter of public interest. "The line between the informing and the entertaining is too elusive for the protection of . . . (freedom of the press)." Erroneous statement is no less inevitable in such a case than in the case of comment upon public affairs, and in both, if innocent or merely negligent, ". . . it must be protected if the freedoms of expression are to have the 'breathing space' that they 'need . . . to survive' . . . ." *New York Times Co. v. Sullivan*. . . . We create a grave risk of serious impairment of the indispensable service of a free press in a free society if we saddle the press with the impossible burden of verifying to a certainty the facts associated in news articles with a person's name, picture or portrait, particularly as related to nondefamatory matter. Even negligence would be a most elusive standard, especially when the content of the speech itself affords no warning of prospective harm to another through falsity. A negligence test would place on the press the intolerable burden of guessing how a jury might assess the reasonableness of steps taken by it to verify the accuracy of every reference to a name, picture or portrait.

In this context, sanctions against either innocent or negligent misstatement would present a grave hazard of discouraging the press from exercising the constitutional guarantees. Those guarantees are not for the benefit of the press so much as for the benefit of all of us. A broadly defined freedom of the press assures the maintenance of our political system and an open society. Fear of large verdicts in damage suits for innocent or merely negligent misstatement, even fear of the expense involved in their defense, must inevitably cause publishers to "steer . . . wider of the unlawful zone," *New York Times Co. v. Sullivan*, and thus "create the danger that the legitimate utterance will be penalized."

But the constitutional guarantees can tolerate sanctions against calculated falsehood without significant impairment of their essential function. We held in *New York Times* that calculated falsehood enjoyed no immunity in the case of alleged defamation of a public official concerning his official conduct. Similarly, calculated falsehood should enjoy no immunity in the situation here presented us. . . .

Turning to the facts of the present case, the proofs reasonably would support either a jury finding of innocent or merely negligent misstatement by Life, or a finding that Life portrayed the play as a reenactment of the Hill family's experience reckless of the truth or with actual knowledge that the portrayal was false. . . . [The jury instructions were thus defective because they did not instruct the jury that liability could only be found against *Life* if *Life* acted in reckless disregard for the truth or with actual knowledge that the play was false.]

The judgment of the Court of Appeals is set aside and the case is remanded for further proceedings not inconsistent with this opinion. . . .

FORTAS. J. JOINED BY WARREN, C.J. AND CLARK, J. DISSENTING. The Court's holding here is exceedingly narrow. It declines to hold that the New York "Right of Privacy" statute is unconstitutional. I agree. The Court concludes, however, that the instructions to the jury in this case were fatally defective because they failed to advise the jury that a verdict for the plaintiffs could be predicated only on a finding of knowing or reckless falsity in the publication of the Life article. . . .

I fully agree with the views of my Brethren who have stressed the need for a generous construction of the First Amendment. I, too, believe that freedom of the press, of speech, assembly, and religion, and the freedom to petition are of the essence of our liberty, and fundamental to our values. . . . There are great and important values in our society, none of which is greater than those reflected in the First Amendment, but which are also fundamental and entitled to this Court's careful respect and protection. Among these is the right to privacy, which has been eloquently extolled by scholars and members of this Court. . . .

Privacy, then, is a basic right. The States may, by appropriate legislation and within proper bounds, enact laws to vindicate that right. ... I have no hesitancy to say, for example, that, where political personalities or issues are involved or where the event as to which the alleged invasion of privacy occurred is, in itself, a matter of current public interest, First Amendment values are supreme, and are entitled to at least the types of protection that this Court extended in *New York Times Co. v. Sullivan*. But I certainly concur with the Court that the greatest solicitude for the First Amendment does not compel us to deny to a State the right to provide a remedy for reckless falsity in writing and publishing an article which irresponsibly and injuriously invades the privacy of a quiet family for no purpose except dramatic interest and commercial appeal.

NOTES & QUESTIONS

1. ***An Inside Look at* Time, Inc. v. Hill.** In *Newsworthy*, a valuable history of *Time v. Hill*, Samantha Barbas provides insights into the impact of media attention on the Hills as well as the Supreme Court's path to its opinion. Regarding the incident itself, Babas concisely sums it up: "The family was trapped for nineteen hours by three fugitives who treated them politely, made gracious chitchat with them, took their clothes and car, and left them unharmed."[89]

   The impact of the media attention that followed was different. As Barbas writes regarding the effect of the Life magazine article on the Hill children, "The sudden reappearance of the hostage incident in their lives traumatized them by forcing them to relive it, remember it, and think about it." In his professional life, James Hill, the father, "became an object of spectacle and curiosity." As for Elizabeth, the publicity following the incident had already caused her to become depressed, but after the Life magazine article, her "mental state plummeted." Elizabeth Hill committed suicide in August 1971.

   Originally, the Court voted 6-3 in favor of the Hills, with Chief Justice Earl Warren assigning the majority opinion to Justice Abe Fortas. But after an initial and then a revised draft of Fortas opinion were circulated among the Justices, Justice Hugo Black was able to have a rehearing of the arguments scheduled for the next term. Before the Court heard the case again, Black circulated a pro-press memorandum. He was able to convince a majority of the Court to join him in finding for Time. In Barbas' analysis, this case represented "a lost opportunity." In her view, "Despite being handed an ideal set of facts—an innocent, All-American family victimized by one of the nation's most powerful media empires—the Court missed a change to seriously contemplate the privacy rights of privacy citizens against the press."

2. ***Nixon at the Supreme Court.*** Before the Supreme Court, the Hills were represented by Richard Nixon, the future President, then in private practice. In a memoir, Leonard Garment, a long-time Nixon advisor and his co-counsel on *Time v. Hill*, writes: "Nixon's main effort [as the Hills' attorney] was to

---

[89] Samantha Barbas, *Newsworthy: The Supreme Court Battle Over Privacy and Press Freedom* 2 (2017).

demonstrate that the magazine had consciously presented the fictionalized play as a 're-enacted' account of the Hill incident."[90] This depiction was, however, "a deliberate falsification," a gimmick "to justify the use of the former Hill home as a 'True Crime' site for the magazine's review of the play." Garment also observes that Nixon, in his first argument in any appellate court, "sounded like a polished professional of the bar — his footing confident, his language lawyer-like, his organization clear."

3. ***The Time Line of Leading Constitutional Law Cases.*** *Time, Inc. v. Hill* was decided after *New York Times v. Sullivan* but before *Gertz*. Do false light actions involving private figures also have to prove actual malice under *New York Times*? Although the Court never explicitly applied the *Gertz* rule to a false light case, courts are split in cases involving private figures as to whether *Gertz* applies to false light or whether all false light claims must satisfy the more stringent *New York Times* standard. *See, e.g., Braun v. Flynt*, 726 F.2d 245 (5th Cir. 1984) (applying *Gertz*); *Dietz v. Wometco West Michigan TV*, 407 N.W.2d 649 (Mich. App. 1987) (applying *Gertz*); *Dodrill v. Arkansas Democrat*, 590 S.W.2d 840 (Ark. 1979) (applying *New York Times*); *Schifano v. Greene County Greyhound Park, Inc.*, 624 So. 2d 178 (Ala. 1993) (applying *New York Times*). Consider Restatement (Second) of Torts § 652E comment d:

> If *Time v. Hill* is modified along the lines of *Gertz v. Robert Welch*, then the reckless-disregard rule would apparently apply if the plaintiff is a public official or public figure and the negligence rule will apply to other plaintiffs.

3. INFLICTION OF EMOTIONAL DISTRESS

Another tort remedy for the dissemination of false or misleading information is the tort of infliction of emotional distress. This tort may also serve as a remedy to the disclosure of true information. As defined by the Restatement (Second) of Torts § 46, the tort requires:

> One who by extreme and outrageous conduct intentionally or recklessly causes severe emotional distress to another is subject to liability for such emotional distress, and if bodily harm to the other results from it, for such bodily harm.

The tort has some significant limitations as a remedy for privacy infringements. First, it requires "extreme and outrageous conduct," which is conduct significantly outside the bounds of propriety. This is quite a high bar for a plaintiff to leap over. Second, it requires "severe emotional distress," and many privacy violations may not be viewed by courts as causing such a high level of psychological turmoil. For example, in *DeGregario v. CBS*, 473 N.Y.S.2d 922 (N.Y. Sup. Ct. 1984), a news segment called "Couples in New York" included video of two construction workers, a male and a female, holding hands. Each was married or engaged to another person. After the video was shot, the workers asked the television crew not to include them in the segment, but they were included anyway. The court rejected their infliction of emotional distress claim because

---

[90] Leonard Garment, *Crazy Rhythm: From Brooklyn and Jazz to Nixon's White House, Watergate, and Beyond* (1997).

"broadcasting a film depicting unnamed couples engaging in romantic conduct on a public street . . . in a news report about romance cannot be said to be unusual conduct transcending the norms tolerated by a decent society."

In a similar fashion to the privacy torts, the tort of infliction of emotional distress is subject to First Amendment restrictions. Consider the following case:

HUSTLER MAGAZINE V. FALWELL

485 U.S. 46 (1988)

[A 1983 issue of *Hustler* magazine featured a parody using nationally known minister Jerry Falwell's name and photo. The parody, entitled "Jerry Falwell Talks About His First Time," was patterned after a series of ads for a brand of liquor which interviewed celebrities about their "first times" trying the liquor (but playing on the sexual double meaning). In a similar layout, *Hustler*'s parody interview with Falwell had him drunk and engaging in incest with his mother. In small print, the parody contained the disclaimer, "ad parody — not to be taken seriously." Falwell sued for, among other things, intentional infliction of emotional distress. This issue made it to the U.S. Supreme Court, where the Court confronted the task of defining whether the First Amendment limitations that applied to defamation and false light should also be applied to intentional infliction of emotional distress.]

REHNQUIST, C.J. . . . "Freedoms of expression require 'breathing space.'" This breathing space is provided by a constitutional rule that allows public figures to recover for libel or defamation only when they can prove *both* that the statement was false and that the statement was made with the requisite level of culpability.

Respondent argues, however, that a different standard should apply in this case because here the State seeks to prevent not reputational damage, but the severe emotional distress suffered by the person who is the subject of an offensive publication. *Cf. Zacchini v. Scripps-Howard Broadcasting Co.*, 433 U.S. 562 (ruling that the "actual malice" standard does not apply to the tort of appropriation of a right of publicity). In respondent's view, and in the view of the Court of Appeals, so long as the utterance was intended to inflict emotional distress, was outrageous, and did in fact inflict serious emotional distress, it is of no constitutional import whether the statement was a fact or an opinion, or whether it was true or false. It is the intent to cause injury that is the gravamen of the tort, and the State's interest in preventing emotional harm simply outweighs whatever interest a speaker may have in speech of this type.

Generally speaking the law does not regard the intent to inflict emotional distress as one which should receive much solicitude, and it is quite understandable that most if not all jurisdictions have chosen to make it civilly culpable where the conduct in question is sufficiently "outrageous." But in the world of debate about public affairs, many things done with motives that are less than admirable are protected by the First Amendment. . . .

Thus while such a bad motive may be deemed controlling for purposes of tort liability in other areas of the law, we think the First Amendment prohibits such a result in the area of public debate about public figures.

Were we to hold otherwise, there can be little doubt that political cartoonists and satirists would be subjected to damages awards without any showing that their work falsely defamed its subject. Webster's defines a caricature as "the deliberately distorted picturing or imitating of a person, literary style, etc. by exaggerating features or mannerisms for satirical effect." Webster's New Unabridged Twentieth Century Dictionary of the English Language 275 (2d ed. 1979). The appeal of the political cartoon or caricature is often based on exploitation of unfortunate physical traits or politically embarrassing events — an exploitation often calculated to injure the feelings of the subject of the portrayal. The art of the cartoonist is often not reasoned or evenhanded, but slashing and one-sided. . . .

Several famous examples of this type of intentionally injurious speech were drawn by Thomas Nast, probably the greatest American cartoonist to date, who was associated for many years during the post-Civil War era with Harper's Weekly. In the pages of that publication Nast conducted a graphic vendetta against William M. "Boss" Tweed and his corrupt associates in New York City's "Tweed Ring." . . .

Despite their sometimes caustic nature, from the early cartoon portraying George Washington as an ass down to the present day, graphic depictions and satirical cartoons have played a prominent role in public and political debate. Nast's castigation of the Tweed Ring, Walt McDougall's characterization of Presidential candidate James G. Blaine's banquet with the millionaires at Delmonico's as "The Royal Feast of Belshazzar," and numerous other efforts have undoubtedly had an effect on the course and outcome of contemporaneous debate. Lincoln's tall, gangling posture, Teddy Roosevelt's glasses and teeth, and Franklin D. Roosevelt's jutting jaw and cigarette holder have been memorialized by political cartoons with an effect that could not have been obtained by the photographer or the portrait artist. From the viewpoint of history it is clear that our political discourse would have been considerably poorer without them. Respondent contends, however, that the caricature in question here was so "outrageous" as to distinguish it from more traditional political cartoons. There is no doubt that the caricature of respondent and his mother published in Hustler is at best a distant cousin of the political cartoons described above, and a rather poor relation at that. If it were possible by laying down a principled standard to separate the one from the other, public discourse would probably suffer little or no harm. But we doubt that there is any such standard, and we are quite sure that the pejorative description "outrageous" does not supply one. "Outrageousness" in the area of political and social discourse has an inherent subjectiveness about it which would allow a jury to impose liability on the basis of the jurors' tastes or views, or perhaps on the basis of their dislike of a particular expression. An "outrageousness" standard thus runs afoul of our longstanding refusal to allow damages to be awarded because the speech in question may have an adverse emotional impact on the audience. . . .

We conclude that public figures and public officials may not recover for the tort of intentional infliction of emotional distress by reason of publications such as the one here at issue without showing in addition that the publication contains a false statement of fact which was made with "actual malice," *i.e.*, with knowledge that the statement was false or with reckless disregard as to whether or not it was true. This is not merely a "blind application" of the *New York Times* standard, see *Time, Inc. v. Hill*, 385 U.S. 374 (1967), it reflects our considered judgment that such a standard is necessary to give adequate "breathing space" to the freedoms protected by the First Amendment.

Here it is clear that respondent Falwell is a "public figure" for purposes of First Amendment law. The jury found against respondent on his libel claim when it decided that the Hustler ad parody could not "reasonably be understood as describing actual facts about [respondent] or actual events in which [he] participated." The Court of Appeals interpreted the jury's finding to be that the ad parody "was not reasonably believable," and in accordance with our custom we accept this finding. Respondent is thus relegated to his claim for damages awarded by the jury for the intentional infliction of emotional distress by "outrageous" conduct. But for reasons heretofore stated this claim cannot, consistently with the First Amendment, form a basis for the award of damages when the conduct in question is the publication of a caricature such as the ad parody involved here. . . .

NOTES & QUESTIONS

1. ***Private Figures and the Intentional Infliction of Emotional Distress Tort.*** The *Hustler* Court focused on public figures and public officials, imposing the *New York Times* standard requiring proof of actual malice. What should the standard be for private figures? The standard in *Gertz*? Under the First Amendment, should the intentional infliction of emotional distress tort be treated the same as the defamation torts? Or differently?

2. ***Is the Intentional Infliction of Emotional Distress Tort Too Subjective?*** The Court states:

   > "Outrageousness" in the area of political and social discourse has an inherent subjectiveness about it which would allow a jury to impose liability on the basis of the jurors' tastes or views, or perhaps on the basis of their dislike of a particular expression.

   If this is true, does this make the intentional infliction of emotional distress tort too easy a way for juries to penalize speech they find distasteful?

SNYDER V. PHELPS

131 S. Ct. 1207 (2011)

ROBERTS, C.J. A jury held members of the Westboro Baptist Church liable for millions of dollars in damages for picketing near a soldier's funeral service. The picket signs reflected the church's view that the United States is overly tolerant of sin and that God kills American soldiers as punishment. The question presented is whether the First Amendment shields the church members from tort liability for their speech in this case.

Fred Phelps founded the Westboro Baptist Church in Topeka, Kansas, in 1955. The church's congregation believes that God hates and punishes the United States for its tolerance of homosexuality, particularly in America's military. The church frequently communicates its views by picketing, often at military funerals. In the more than 20 years that the members of Westboro Baptist have publicized their message, they have picketed nearly 600 funerals.

Marine Lance Corporal Matthew Snyder was killed in Iraq in the line of duty. Lance Corporal Snyder's father selected the Catholic church in the Snyders' hometown of Westminster, Maryland, as the site for his son's funeral. Local newspapers provided notice of the time and location of the service.

Phelps became aware of Matthew Snyder's funeral and decided to travel to Maryland with six other Westboro Baptist parishioners (two of his daughters and four of his grandchildren) to picket. On the day of the memorial service, the Westboro congregation members picketed on public land adjacent to public streets near the Maryland State House, the United States Naval Academy, and Matthew Snyder's funeral. The Westboro picketers carried signs that were largely the same at all three locations. They stated, for instance: "God Hates the USA/Thank God for 9/11," "America is Doomed," "Don't Pray for the USA," "Thank God for IEDs," "Thank God for Dead Soldiers," "Pope in Hell," "Priests Rape Boys," "God Hates Fags," "You're Going to Hell," and "God Hates You."

The church had notified the authorities in advance of its intent to picket at the time of the funeral, and the picketers complied with police instructions in staging their demonstration. The picketing took place within a 10- by 25-foot plot of public land adjacent to a public street, behind a temporary fence. That plot was approximately 1,000 feet from the church where the funeral was held. Several buildings separated the picket site from the church. The Westboro picketers displayed their signs for about 30 minutes before the funeral began and sang hymns and recited Bible verses. None of the picketers entered church property or went to the cemetery. They did not yell or use profanity, and there was no violence associated with the picketing.

The funeral procession passed within 200 to 300 feet of the picket site. Although Snyder testified that he could see the tops of the picket signs as he drove to the funeral, he did not see what was written on the signs until later that night, while watching a news broadcast covering the event.[91]

Snyder filed suit against Phelps, Phelps's daughters, and the Westboro Baptist Church (collectively Westboro or the church) in the United States District Court for the District of Maryland under that court's diversity jurisdiction. Snyder alleged five state tort law claims: defamation, publicity given to private life, intentional infliction of emotional distress, intrusion upon seclusion, and civil conspiracy. Westboro moved for summary judgment contending, in part, that the church's speech was insulated from liability by the First Amendment.

The District Court awarded Westboro summary judgment on Snyder's claims for defamation and publicity given to private life, concluding that Snyder could not prove the necessary elements of those torts. A trial was held on the remaining claims. . . .

---

[91] A few weeks after the funeral, one of the picketers posted a message on Westboro's Web site discussing the picketing and containing religiously oriented denunciations of the Snyders, interspersed among lengthy Bible quotations. Snyder discovered the posting, referred to by the parties as the "epic," during an Internet search for his son's name. The epic is not properly before us and does not factor in our analysis. Although the epic was submitted to the jury and discussed in the courts below, Snyder never mentioned it in his petition for certiorari. . . .

A jury found for Snyder on the intentional infliction of emotional distress, intrusion upon seclusion, and civil conspiracy claims, and held Westboro liable for $2.9 million in compensatory damages and $8 million in punitive damages. Westboro filed several post-trial motions, including a motion contending that the jury verdict was grossly excessive and a motion seeking judgment as a matter of law on all claims on First Amendment grounds. The District Court remitted the punitive damages award to $2.1 million, but left the jury verdict otherwise intact. . . .

To succeed on a claim for intentional infliction of emotional distress in Maryland, a plaintiff must demonstrate that the defendant intentionally or recklessly engaged in extreme and outrageous conduct that caused the plaintiff to suffer severe emotional distress. . . .

Whether the First Amendment prohibits holding Westboro liable for its speech in this case turns largely on whether that speech is of public or private concern, as determined by all the circumstances of the case. "[S]peech on 'matters of public concern' . . . is 'at the heart of the First Amendment's protection.'" . . . .

" '[N]ot all speech is of equal First Amendment importance,' " however, and where matters of purely private significance are at issue, First Amendment protections are often less rigorous. That is because restricting speech on purely private matters does not implicate the same constitutional concerns as limiting speech on matters of public interest: "[T]here is no threat to the free and robust debate of public issues; there is no potential interference with a meaningful dialogue of ideas"; and the "threat of liability" does not pose the risk of "a reaction of self-censorship" on matters of public import. *Dun & Bradstreet*. . . .

Speech deals with matters of public concern when it can "be fairly considered as relating to any matter of political, social, or other concern to the community," or when it "is a subject of legitimate news interest; that is, a subject of general interest and of value and concern to the public." The arguably "inappropriate or controversial character of a statement is irrelevant to the question whether it deals with a matter of public concern."

Our opinion in *Dun & Bradstreet,* on the other hand, provides an example of speech of only private concern. In that case we held, as a general matter, that information about a particular individual's credit report "concerns no public issue." The content of the report, we explained, "was speech solely in the individual interest of the speaker and its specific business audience." . . .

The "content" of Westboro's signs plainly relates to broad issues of interest to society at large, rather than matters of "purely private concern." . . . While these messages may fall short of refined social or political commentary, the issues they highlight — the political and moral conduct of the United States and its citizens, the fate of our Nation, homosexuality in the military, and scandals involving the Catholic clergy — are matters of public import. The signs certainly convey Westboro's position on those issues, in a manner designed, unlike the private speech in *Dun & Bradstreet,* to reach as broad a public audience as possible. And even if a few of the signs — such as "You're Going to Hell" and "God Hates You" — were viewed as containing messages related to Matthew Snyder or the Snyders specifically, that would not change the fact that the overall thrust and dominant theme of Westboro's demonstration spoke to broader public issues. . . .

Given that Westboro's speech was at a public place on a matter of public concern, that speech is entitled to "special protection" under the First Amendment. Such speech cannot be restricted simply because it is upsetting or arouses contempt. . . .

The jury here was instructed that it could hold Westboro liable for intentional infliction of emotional distress based on a finding that Westboro's picketing was "outrageous." "Outrageousness," however, is a highly malleable standard with "an inherent subjectiveness about it which would allow a jury to impose liability on the basis of the jurors' tastes or views, or perhaps on the basis of their dislike of a particular expression." . . .

For all these reasons, the jury verdict imposing tort liability on Westboro for intentional infliction of emotional distress must be set aside. . . .

The jury also found Westboro liable for the state law torts of intrusion upon seclusion and civil conspiracy. . . .

Snyder argues that even assuming Westboro's speech is entitled to First Amendment protection generally, the church is not immunized from liability for intrusion upon seclusion because Snyder was a member of a captive audience at his son's funeral. We do not agree. In most circumstances, "the Constitution does not permit the government to decide which types of otherwise protected speech are sufficiently offensive to require protection for the unwilling listener or viewer. Rather, . . . the burden normally falls upon the viewer to avoid further bombardment of [his] sensibilities simply by averting [his] eyes." . . .

As a general matter, we have applied the captive audience doctrine only sparingly to protect unwilling listeners from protected speech. . . .

Here, Westboro stayed well away from the memorial service. Snyder could see no more than the tops of the signs when driving to the funeral. And there is no indication that the picketing in any way interfered with the funeral service itself. We decline to expand the captive audience doctrine to the circumstances presented here. . . .

ALITO, J. dissenting. . . . Respondents and other members of their church have strong opinions on certain moral, religious, and political issues, and the First Amendment ensures that they have almost limitless opportunities to express their views. They may write and distribute books, articles, and other texts; they may create and disseminate video and audio recordings; they may circulate petitions; they may speak to individuals and groups in public forums and in any private venue that wishes to accommodate them; they may picket peacefully in countless locations; they may appear on television and speak on the radio; they may post messages on the Internet and send out e-mails. And they may express their views in terms that are "uninhibited," "vehement," and "caustic."

It does not follow, however, that they may intentionally inflict severe emotional injury on private persons at a time of intense emotional sensitivity by launching vicious verbal attacks that make no contribution to public debate. To protect against such injury, "most if not all jurisdictions" permit recovery in tort for the intentional infliction of emotional distress (or IIED).

This is a very narrow tort with requirements that "are rigorous, and difficult to satisfy." . . .

In this case, respondents brutally attacked Matthew Snyder, and this attack, which was almost certain to inflict injury, was central to respondents' well-practiced strategy for attracting public attention. . . .

After the funeral, the Westboro picketers reaffirmed the meaning of their protest. They posted an online account entitled "The Burden of Marine Lance Cpl. Matthew A. Snyder. The Visit of Westboro Baptist Church to Help the Inhabitants of Maryland Connect the Dots!" Belying any suggestion that they had simply made general comments about homosexuality, the Catholic Church, and the United States military, the "epic" addressed the Snyder family directly:

> "God blessed you, Mr. and Mrs. Snyder, with a resource and his name was Matthew. He was an arrow in your quiver! In thanks to God for the comfort the child could bring you, you had a DUTY to prepare that child to serve the LORD his GOD — PERIOD! You did JUST THE OPPOSITE — you raised him for the devil. . . .
> "Albert and Julie RIPPED that body apart and taught Matthew to defy his Creator, to divorce, and to commit adultery. They taught him how to support the largest pedophile machine in the history of the entire world, the Roman Catholic monstrosity. Every dime they gave the Roman Catholic monster they condemned their own souls. They also, in supporting satanic Catholicism, taught Matthew to be an idolater. . . ."

While commentary on the Catholic Church or the United States military constitutes speech on matters of public concern, speech regarding Matthew Snyder's purely private conduct does not. . . .

The Court concludes that respondents' speech was protected by the First Amendment for essentially three reasons, but none is sound.

First — and most important — the Court finds that "the overall thrust and dominant theme of [their] demonstration spoke to" broad public issues. As I have attempted to show, this portrayal is quite inaccurate; respondents' attack on Matthew was of central importance. But in any event, I fail to see why actionable speech should be immunized simply because it is interspersed with speech that is protected. The First Amendment allows recovery for defamatory statements that are interspersed with nondefamatory statements on matters of public concern, and there is no good reason why respondents' attack on Matthew Snyder and his family should be treated differently.

Second, the Court suggests that respondents' personal attack on Matthew Snyder is entitled to First Amendment protection because it was not motivated by a private grudge, but I see no basis for the strange distinction that the Court appears to draw. Respondents' motivation — "to increase publicity for its views," — did not transform their statements attacking the character of a private figure into statements that made a contribution to debate on matters of public concern. . . .

Third, the Court finds it significant that respondents' protest occurred on a public street, but this fact alone should not be enough to preclude IIED liability.

NOTES & QUESTIONS

1. *Intrusion upon Seclusion.* On what basis could the jury have found that the defendants were liable for intrusion upon seclusion? Should the claim have

been dismissed before it even reached the jury?

2. *Is Actual Malice the Appropriate Standard?* Consider Jeffrey Shulman:

> There is no justification for applying the actual malice standard to emotional distress claims outside the public arena (and little enough inside). The literal application of the actual malice standard offers no protection to the plaintiff claiming emotional injury from rhetorically hyperbolic speech. The victim of a libel can show that the statement was false. The victim of rhetorical hyperbole can prove or disprove nothing that will bring judicial redress. This may be the cost of doing business in the public arena, but why should the private plaintiff be left defenseless against emotionally injurious speech that serves no valid communicative purpose?[92]

If the actual malice standard is not appropriate for public figures or matters of public concern, what should the standard be? Consider Shulman's view:

> The *Hustler* Court was concerned that " '[o]utrageousness' in the area of political and social discourse has an inherent subjectiveness about it which would allow a jury to impose liability on the basis of the jurors' tastes or views, or perhaps on the basis of their dislike of a particular expression." Perhaps so, but in the funeral of a private individual we might find "a principled standard" by which to circumscribe emotional distress claims within a safe constitutional perimeter. Where discourse is not, in fact, of public concern, where it is targeted to a private audience unwilling to receive it but unable to avoid it, where its purpose is to injure, then its restriction is little threat to free speech values; where public concern is a mask for mere personal abuse, private individuals should have full legal recourse to secure their right to be let alone.

Was Westboro Baptist Church's speech directed at specific people? Set aside the online speech, quoted in Justice Alito's dissent, as the Court did not consider it in its analysis. The picketers used the occasion of the funeral to draw attention to their message, but was Snyder at the center of their message? Was their speech of public concern? Was it "targeted to a private audience unwilling to receive it but unable to avoid it"?

Should the First Amendment condone using a private person as fodder for one's speech when that message could have readily been made without any connection to the private person?

---

[92] Jeffrey Shulman, *Free Speech at What Cost?* Snyder v. Phelps *and Speech-Based Tort Liability*, 2010 Cardozo L. Rev. De Novo 312, 315.

D. APPROPRIATION OF NAME OR LIKENESS

1. INTRODUCTION

APPROPRIATION OF NAME OR LIKENESS
Restatement (Second) of Torts § 652C

One who appropriates to his own use or benefit the name or likeness of another is subject to liability to the other for invasion of his privacy.

NOTES & QUESTIONS

1. ***The Development of the Appropriation Tort.*** The tort of appropriation protects "the interest of the individual in the exclusive use of his own identity, in so far as it is represented by his name or likeness, and in so far as the use may be of benefit to him or to others." Restatement § 652C, comment (a). To be liable for appropriation, "the defendant must have appropriated to his own use or benefit the reputation, prestige, social or commercial standing, public interest or other values of the plaintiff's name or likeness." *Id.*, comment (c).

   Recall from section A that two of the first cases to address the creation of new causes of action in response to the Warren and Brandeis article — *Roberson* and *Pavesich* — both involved appropriation claims.

   One of the most widely discussed state appropriation tort formulations is that of New York. New York's statute, passed in response to *Roberson*, which refused to recognize the tort in the common law, provides criminal and civil remedies for appropriation. Pursuant to New York Civil Rights Law § 50:

   > A person, firm or corporation that uses for advertising purposes, or for the purposes of trade, the name, portrait or picture of any living person without having first obtained the written consent of such person, or if a minor of his or her parent or guardian, is guilty of a misdemeanor.

   New York Civil Rights Law § 51 provides a civil remedy:

   > Any person whose name, portrait, picture or voice is used within this state for advertising purposes or for the purposes of trade without the written consent first obtained . . . may maintain an equitable action in the supreme court of this state against the person, firm or corporation so using his name, portrait, picture or voice, to prevent and restrain the use thereof; and may also sue and recover damages for any injuries sustained by reason of such use. . . .

   California has a similar statute, which provides: "Any person who knowingly uses another's name, photograph or likeness, in any manner, for purposes of advertising . . . or for purposes of solicitation of purchases of products . . . without . . . prior consent . . . shall be liable for any damages." Cal. Civ. Code § 3344. In many states, the tort of appropriation is recognized through the common law and is not statutory in nature.

2. ***Appropriation and the "Right of Publicity."*** The original rationale for the tort of appropriation was privacy-based, as a protection of one's dignity against the

exploitation of her identity. However, another rationale for the tort has emerged, one that is property-based. Many courts and commentators refer to this alternative rationale as the "right of publicity."[93] The "right of publicity" was first referred to as such in *Haelan Laboratories v. Topps Chewing Gum, Inc.*, 202 F.2d 866 (2d Cir. 1953), where Judge Jerome Frank held that New York recognized a common law tort of "publicity" distinct from §§ 50-51's remedy for appropriation:

> We think that, in addition to and independent of that right of privacy (which in New York derives from statute), a man has a right in the publicity value of his photograph, i.e., the right to grant the exclusive privilege of publishing his picture, and that such a grant may validly be made "in gross," i.e., without an accompanying transfer of a business or of anything else. Whether it be labeled a "property" right is immaterial; for here, as often elsewhere, the tag "property" simply symbolizes the fact that courts enforce a claim which has pecuniary worth.
>
> This right might be called a "right of publicity." For it is common knowledge that many prominent persons (especially actors and ball-players), far from having their feelings bruised through public exposure of their likenesses, would feel sorely deprived if they no longer received money for authorizing advertisements, popularizing their countenances, displayed in newspapers, magazines, busses, trains and subways.

Subsequently, courts held that the publicity tort was subsumed under § 51 and was not a common law cause of action. *See Welch v. Group W Productions, Inc.*, 525 N.Y.S.2d 466, 468 n.1 (N.Y. Sup. Ct. 1987) ("In New York State the so-called 'right of publicity' is merely an aspect of the right of privacy and is not an independent common-law right.").

How is the "right of publicity" distinct from the privacy interests involved in appropriation? As one court describes the distinction:

> The privacy-based action is designed for individuals who have not placed themselves in the public eye. It shields such people from the embarrassment of having their faces plastered on billboards and cereal boxes without their permission. The interests protected are dignity and peace of mind, and damages are measured in terms of emotional distress. By contrast, a right of publicity action is designed for individuals who have placed themselves in the public eye. It secures for them the exclusive right to exploit the commercial value that attaches to their identities by virtue of their celebrity. The right to publicity protects that value as property, and its infringement is a commercial, rather than a personal tort. Damages stem not from embarrassment but from the unauthorized use of the plaintiffs' property. *Jim Henson Productions, Inc. v. John T. Brady & Associates, Inc.*, 687 F. Supp. 185, 188-89 (S.D.N.Y. 1994).

Thomas McCarthy articulates the distinction most succinctly: "Simplistically put, while the appropriation branch of the right of privacy is invaded by

---

[93] J. Thomas McCarthy, *The Rights of Publicity and Privacy* (2d ed. 2011); Melville B. Nimmer, *The Right of Publicity*, 19 Law & Contemp. Probs. 203 (1954); Sheldon Halpern, *The Right of Publicity: Maturation of an Independent Right Protecting the Associative Value of Personality*, 46 Hastings L.J. 853 (1995); Oliver R. Goodenough, *Go Fish: Evaluating the Restatement's Formulation of the Law of Publicity*, 47 S.C. L. Rev. 709 (1996).

an injury to the psyche, the right of publicity is infringed by an injury to the pocket book."[94]

The Restatement (Third) of the Law of Unfair Competition § 46 provides for a distinct tort of "publicity":

> *Appropriation of the Commercial Value of a Person's Identity: The Right of Publicity.* One who appropriates the commercial value of a person's identity by using without consent the person's name, likeness, or other indicia of identity for purposes of trade is subject to liability for [monetary and injunctive] relief.

The commentary to the Restatement § 46 contrasts the "publicity" right in § 46 with the "appropriation tort" in the Restatement of Torts: "The 'appropriation' tort as described by Prosser and the Restatement, Second, of Torts, subsumes harm to both personal and commercial interests caused by an unauthorized exploitation of the plaintiff's identity." Restatement (Third) of the Law of Unfair Competition § 46, comment (b). A number of jurisdictions recognize a distinct tort of "publicity."

Although there is now a separate "right of publicity" to protect property interests, the tort of appropriation has shifted towards being a property protection similar to the right of publicity. William Prosser, in his 1960 article describing the torts spawned by Warren and Brandeis's article, did not recognize a distinct tort of publicity; it was merely a part of the appropriation tort. Likewise, the Restatement (Second) of Torts did not recognize a distinct tort of publicity. However, according to the Restatement, it appears that the central interest protected by appropriation is property rather than privacy: "Although the protection of [a person's] personal feelings against mental distress is an important factor leading to a recognition of the [appropriation tort], the right created by it is in the nature of a property right. . . ." Restatement (Second) of Torts § 652C, comment (a). A number of jurisdictions follow this approach. *See Ainsworth v. Century Supply Co.*, 693 N.E.2d 510 (Ill. App. 1998); *Candlebat v. Flanagan*, 487 So. 2d 207 (Miss. 1986). According to Jonathan Kahn:

> While publicity is grounded in property rights, appropriation of identity involves the personal right to privacy. Publicity rights implicate monetary interests. In contrast, privacy rights protect and vindicate less tangible personal interests in dignity and integrity of the self. However, both rights are clearly linked and find their common origin in American law around the turn of this century. Yet over the years, the privacy-based tort of appropriation has receded into the background as its flashier cousin, publicity, has risen to prominence. Such is perhaps to be expected in a world where seemingly everything has been turned into a saleable commodity.[95]

Is privacy or property the central interest of appropriation? Or does the tort adequately redress both interests?

---

[94] J. Thomas McCarthy, *The Rights of Publicity and Privacy* § 5:63 (2d ed. 2011).

[95] Jonathan Kahn, *Bringing Dignity Back to Light: Publicity Rights and the Eclipse of the Tort of Appropriation of Identity,* 17 Cardozo Arts & Ent. L.J. 213, 213-14 (1999); *see also* Jonathan Kahn, *What's in a Name? Law's Identity Under the Tort of Appropriation,* 74 Temp. L. Rev. 263 (2001).

2. NAME OR LIKENESS

CARSON V. HERE'S JOHNNY PORTABLE TOILETS, INC.

698 F.2d 831 (6th Cir. 1983)

BROWN, J. . . . Appellant, John W. Carson (Carson), is the host and star of "The Tonight Show," a well-known television program broadcast five nights a week by the National Broadcasting Company. . . . From the time he began hosting "The Tonight Show" in 1962, he has been introduced [by Ed McMahon] on the show each night with the phrase "Here's Johnny." . . . The phrase "Here's Johnny" is generally associated with Carson by a substantial segment of the television viewing public. In 1967, Carson first authorized use of this phrase by an outside business venture, permitting it to be used by a chain of restaurants called "Here's Johnny Restaurants." . . .

. . . The phrase "Here's Johnny" has never been registered by appellants as a trademark or service mark.

Appellee, Here's Johnny Portable Toilets, Inc., is a Michigan corporation engaged in the business of renting and selling "Here's Johnny" portable toilets. Appellee's founder was aware at the time he formed the corporation that "Here's Johnny" was the introductory slogan for Carson on "The Tonight Show." He indicated that he coupled the phrase with a second one, "The World's Foremost Commodian," to make "a good play on a phrase."

[Carson brought an action for, among other things, invasion of privacy and the right to publicity.] . . .

We do not believe that Carson's claim that his right of privacy has been invaded is supported by the law or the facts. Apparently, the gist of this claim is that Carson is embarrassed by and considers it odious to be associated with the appellee's product. Clearly, the association does not appeal to Carson's sense of humor. But the facts here presented do not, it appears to us, amount to an invasion of any of the interests protected by the right of privacy. . . .

The right of publicity has developed to protect the commercial interest of celebrities in their identities. The theory of the right is that a celebrity's identity can be valuable in the promotion of products, and the celebrity has an interest that may be protected from the unauthorized commercial exploitation of that identity. . . .

The district court dismissed appellants' claim based on the right of publicity because appellee does not use Carson's name or likeness. . . . We believe that, on the contrary, the district court's conception of the right of publicity is too narrow. The right of publicity, as we have stated, is that a celebrity has a protected pecuniary interest in the commercial exploitation of his identity. If the celebrity's identity is commercially exploited, there has been an invasion of his right whether or not his "name or likeness" is used. Carson's identity may be exploited even if his name, John W. Carson, or his picture is not used. . . .

In this case, Earl Braxton, president and owner of Here's Johnny Portable Toilets, Inc., admitted that he knew that the phrase "Here's Johnny" had been used for years to introduce Carson. Moreover, in the opening statement in the district court, appellee's counsel stated:

Now, we've stipulated in this case that the public tends to associate the words "Johnny Carson," the words "Here's Johnny" with plaintiff, John Carson and, Mr. Braxton, in his deposition, admitted that he knew that and probably absent that identification, he would not have chosen it.

That the "Here's Johnny" name was selected by Braxton because of its identification with Carson was the clear inference from Braxton's testimony irrespective of such admission in the opening statement.

We therefore conclude that, applying the correct legal standards, appellants are entitled to judgment. The proof showed without question that appellee had appropriated Carson's identity in connection with its corporate name and its product. . . .

. . . It is not fatal to appellant's claim that appellee did not use his "name." Indeed, there would have been no violation of his right of publicity even if appellee had used his name, such as "J. William Carson Portable Toilet" or the "John William Carson Portable Toilet" or the "J. W. Carson Portable Toilet." The reason is that, though literally using appellant's "name," the appellee would not have appropriated Carson's identity as a celebrity. Here there was an appropriation of Carson's identity without using his "name.". . .

KENNEDY, J. dissenting. . . . The majority's extension of the right of publicity to include phrases or other things which are merely associated with the individual permits a popular entertainer or public figure, by associating himself or herself with a common phrase, to remove those words from the public domain. . . .

. . . [T]he majority is awarding Johnny Carson a windfall, rather than vindicating his economic interests, by protecting the phrase "Here's Johnny" which is merely associated with him. In *Zacchini*, the Supreme Court stated that a mechanism to vindicate an individual's economic rights is indicated where the appropriated thing is "the product of . . . [the individual's] own talents and energy, the end result of much time, effort and expense." There is nothing in the record to suggest that "Here's Johnny" has any nexus to Johnny Carson other than being the introduction to his personal appearances. The phrase is not part of an identity that he created. In its content "Here's Johnny" is a very simple and common introduction. The content of the phrase neither originated with Johnny Carson nor is it confined to the world of entertainment. The phrase is not said by Johnny Carson, but said of him. Its association with him is derived, in large part, by the context in which it is said — generally by Ed McMahon in a drawn out and distinctive voice after the theme music to "The Tonight Show" is played, and immediately prior to Johnny Carson's own entrance. Appellee's use of the content "Here's Johnny," in light of its value as a double entendre, written on its product and corporate name, and therefore outside of the context in which it is associated with Johnny Carson, does little to rob Johnny Carson of something which is unique to him or a product of his own efforts. . . .

Protection under the right of publicity confers a monopoly on the protected individual that is potentially broader, offers fewer protections and potentially competes with federal statutory monopolies. As an essential part of three federal monopoly rights, copyright, trademark and patents, notice to the public is required in the form of filing with the appropriate governmental office and use of an appropriate mark. This apprises members of the public of the nature and extent of what is being removed from the public domain and subject to claims of infringement. The right of publicity provides limited notice to the public of the extent of the monopoly right to be asserted, if one is to be asserted at all. As the right of privacy is expanded beyond protections of name, likeness and actual performances, which provide relatively objective notice to the public of the extent of an individual's rights, to more subjective attributes such as achievements and identifying characteristics, the public's ability to be on notice of a common law monopoly right, if one is even asserted by a given famous individual, is severely diminished. Protecting phrases and other things merely associated with an individual provides virtually no notice to the public at all of what is claimed to be protected. By ensuring the invocation of the adjudicative process whenever the commercial use of a phrase or other associated thing is considered to have been wrongfully appropriated, the public is left to act at their peril. The result is a chilling effect on commercial innovation and opportunity.

Also unlike the federal statutory monopolies, this common law monopoly right offers no protections against the monopoly existing for an indefinite time or even in perpetuity. . . .

NOTES & QUESTIONS

1. ***Privacy or Property?*** In *Carson*, Johnny Carson made two claims. First, he contended that a privacy interest was violated because his identity was being associated with toilets, which he found quite unflattering. The court appears to reject this claim. Carson's other claim is that a property interest was violated by his valuable identity being stolen and used for the commercial purposes of another. What do you think was the real reason Carson brought this suit? To vindicate his privacy interest, his property interest, or both? Suppose Carson were not famous and his name had little value. Would he be likely to succeed under the reasoning of the court?

2. ***No Sense of Humor?*** In 2013, Carson's attorney published a memoir about his late boss. Henry Buskin was critical of the decision to pursue the litigation:

   > It even got to the point where it seemed like he couldn't recognize a joke. Somehow we learned of an Ohio company called Here's Johnny Portable Toilets, which advertised its product with the slogan "The World's Foremost Commodian." Carson didn't think that was funny and ordered me to sue the company to make them stop. Ultimately we spent about $500,000 to win less than $40,000 in damages. . . . To me, it didn't matter that we won. I thought it made him look mean and small.[96]

3. ***Post-Mortem Publicity Rights.*** Despite losing the case before the Sixth Circuit in 1987, Earl Braxton, the defendant in the *Carson* case, did not give up his dream. Johnny Carson died in 2005, and in 2006 Braxton sought to trademark the phrase "Here's Johnny." A trademark is a form of intellectual property that identifies the source of a product or service. The Trademark and Trial Appeal

---

[96] Henry Bushkin, *Johnny Carson* 223 (2013).

Board held that the relevant states in question recognized post-mortem rights of publicity and that these rights had passed to Carson's estate.[97] Thus, the *Carson* decision still prevents Braxton from use of the phrase, "Here's Johnny."

Concerning post-mortem rights, the overwhelming majority of states in the United States have also recognized a postmortem dimension to the publicity right. The publicity right can be inherited, sold in whole or in part, and otherwise licensed after the subject's death. The question of whether or not these interests were exploited during a party's life is irrelevant. A survey of the duration of the postmortem right in the United States found periods ranging from a potentially unlimited period to 100 years to 20 years.[98]

In California, the legislature has even extended the applicable statute *backward* in time to protect the interests of those who died as long as 70 years before the state first legislatively acknowledged this right. Publicity rights are also a routine subject in negotiations with prominent individuals and, in the case of deceased celebrities, with their estates.

4. ***First Amendment and Related Limits on Publicity Rights***. Carson won his case against use of the phrase "Here's Johnny" against a toilet company. He did not, however, sue the Beach Boys for their 1977 song, "Johnny Carson," which used the same phrase in a lyric: "Johnny Carson/Ed McMahon comes on and says 'Here's Johnny'/Every night at 11:30 he's so funny." The use of Johnny Carson's celebrity identity and the famous phrase in a song clearly implicates a wide range of different issues, including the freedom of expression.

In a case involving commercial use of a charcoal drawing of the Three Stooges, *Comedy III Productions, Inc. v. Gary Saderup, Inc.*, 25 Cal. 4th 387 (2001), the California Supreme Court found that use of the image on a t-shirt implicated the First Amendment: "First Amendment doctrine does not disfavor nontraditional media of expression." The *Comedy III* court identified a need to balance the right of publicity against the First Amendment. Its key test was whether a work represented a "transformative" use of the celebrity's identity. According to the California Supreme Court, one way to identify a transformative use of a celebrity image was whether the work is "primarily the defendant's own expression rather than the celebrity's likeness." Another inquiry was whether "the marketability and economic value of the challenged work derive primarily from the fame of the celebrity depicted."

Two years after its *Comedy III* decision, the California Supreme Court found that a comic book with characters that resembled two blues musicians, Johnny and Edgar Winter, was "transformative." *Winter v. DC Comics*, 30 Cal. 4th 881(2003). The comic book featured brothers Johnny and Edgar Autumn, who were evil half-worm, half-human creatures. The California Supreme Court found that there was no triable issue of fact and upheld the trial court's summary judgment decision dismissing the case. There could be no right of publicity claim by the Winter brothers because the comic book's use of their persona was protected by the First Amendment. The court stated:

---

[97] *The John W. Carson Foundation v. Toilets.com, Inc.*, Opposition No. 91181092 (T.T.A.B. Mar. 25, 2009).

[98] J. Thomas McCarthy, 2 *The Rights of Publicity and Privacy* 435-37, 445-46 (2009).

> Although the fictional characters Johnny and Edgar Autumn are less-than-subtle evocations of Johnny and Edgar Winter, the books do not depict the plaintiff's literally. Instead, the plaintiffs are merely part of the raw materials from which the comic books were synthesized. To the extent the drawings of the Autumn brothers resembled the plaintiffs at all, they are distorted for the purposes of lampoon, parody, or caricature ... in a larger story, which is itself quite expressive.

The *Winter* court also noted that the comic book would not detract from any interest that the brothers had in their image as it would be "unsatisfactory as a substitute for conventional depictions." Does *Winter* rest on an underlying idea that the overall work did not free-ride, or otherwise unfairly exploit, the Winters' celebrity persona because it added its own "expressive" concepts?

5. ***What Constitutes "Name or Likeness"?*** The appropriation tort has been extended far beyond a person's actual name and likeness. Courts have held that the use of well-known nicknames can give rise to an appropriation action. In *Hirsch v. S.C. Johnson & Son, Inc.*, 280 N.W.2d 129 (Wis. 1979), the Supreme Court of Wisconsin found that an unauthorized commercial use of Elroy Hirsch's (a famous football player) nickname "Crazylegs" raised triable issues regarding violation of the appropriation tort. S.C. Johnson had used "Crazylegs" as the product name for a shaving gel for women. The court rejected the argument that an appropriation claim by Hirsch was not possible because Crazylegs was his nickname, not his actual name. It stated that to overcome the lower court's rejection of the cause of action, "[a]ll that is required is that the name clearly identify the wronged person." It also declared that "[t]he question whether Crazylegs identifies Elroy Hirsch, however, is one of fact to be determined by the jury on remand. . . ."

Courts have also held that certain drawings depicting one's profession but otherwise with no distinctive facial characteristics can still give rise to an appropriation claim. In *Ali v. Playgirl, Inc.*, 447 F. Supp. 723 (S.D.N.Y. 1978), Muhammad Ali, former heavyweight boxing champion, sued *Playgirl* magazine for appropriation when the magazine published a drawing of a nude African-American male sitting on a stool in a corner of a boxing ring with hands taped. The drawing did not mention Ali's name and was entitled "Mystery Man," but accompanying text identified the man in the drawing as "The Greatest." Because "The Greatest" was Ali's nickname, the picture was sufficiently identifiable as Ali to constitute his likeness. The court emphasized the offensive nature of the full frontal nude of Ali; the fact that the portrait was clearly one of Ali; and that the publication was for "purposes of trade" within New York Civil Rights Law § 51. It stated, "the picture is a dramatization, an illustration falling somewhere between representational art and cartoon, and is accompanied by a plainly fictional and allegedly libelous bit of doggerel."

Appropriation has even been extended to identifying characteristics. In *Motschenbacher v. R.J. Reynolds Tobacco Co.*, 498 F.2d 821 (9th Cir. 1974), a famous race car driver alleged that a photograph of his distinctive racing car, which did not include a likeness of himself or use his name, was nevertheless an appropriation of his name or likeness. The court agreed. The photograph did use a "likeness" of the plaintiff because the "distinctive decorations" on his car "were not only peculiar to the plaintiff's cars but they caused some persons to think the car in question was plaintiff's and to infer that the person driving the car was the plaintiff."

Further, appropriation can also extend to use of a look-alike model. In *Onassis v. Christian Dior*, 472 N.Y.S. 2d 254 (N.Y. Supp. 1984), Jacqueline Kennedy Onassis won an injunction against use of a look-alike model in an advertisement. The *Onassis* court found a cause of action under the New York Civil Rights Law § 51, so long as the advertisement created an illusion that the plaintiff herself had appeared in the advertisement.

Courts have also recognized appropriation liability for the imitation of one's voice. In *Midler v. Ford Motor Co.*, 849 F.2d 460 (9th Cir. 1988), the Ninth Circuit held that singer Bette Midler had a viable cause of action for appropriation for the use of a singer to imitate her voice in a commercial. When a voice is a sufficient indication of the celebrity's identity, appropriation protects against a company hiring someone to imitate it for commercial purposes without the celebrity's consent.

In a later sound-alike case, the Ninth Circuit found for Tom Waits, a singer with a distinctive sound. *Waits v. Frito Lay*, 978 F. 2d 1093 (9th Cir. 1992). The court noted that Waits had "a distinctive gravelly singing voice, described by one fan as 'like how you'd sound if you drank a quart of bourbon, smoked a pack of cigarettes and swallowed a pack of razor blades. . . . Late at night. After not sleeping for three days.' " The *Waits* court upheld a jury verdict that found the celebrity plaintiff had a voice that was distinctive, widely known, and deliberately imitated by a defendant for a commercial purpose. The Ninth Circuit added that even if Tom Waits was not as well known as Bette Midler, "'[w]ell-known' is a relative term, and differences in the extent of celebrity are adequately reflected in the amount of damages recoverable."

6. ***Property Rights and Creativity.*** Consider the following argument against the propertization of identity by Judge Kozinski dissenting from the denial of a petition for rehearing en banc in *White v. Samsung Electronics America, Inc.*, 989 F.2d 1512 (9th Cir. 1993):

> . . . Saddam Hussein wants to keep advertisers from using his picture in unflattering contexts. Clint Eastwood doesn't want tabloids to write about him. Rudolf Valentino's heirs want to control his film biography. The Girl Scouts don't want their image soiled by association with certain activities. . . . And scads of copyright holders see purple when their creations are made fun of.
>
> Something very dangerous is going on here. . . .
>
> . . . Overprotecting intellectual property is as harmful as underprotecting it. Creativity is impossible without a rich public domain. . . .
>
> . . . Intellectual property rights aren't free. They're imposed at the expense of future creators and of the public at large. Where would we be if Charles Lindbergh had an exclusive right in the concept of a heroic solo aviator? If Arthur Conan Doyle had gotten a copyright in the idea of the detective story, or Albert Einstein had patented the theory of relativity? If every author and celebrity had been given the right to keep people from mocking them or their work? Surely this would have made the world poorer, not richer, culturally as well as economically. . . .

7. ***Property Rights and the Manufacturing of Identity.*** One of the predominant rationales for the right of publicity is that the celebrity, through her labor, creates her persona. But, with regard to celebrities, does this rationale always hold true? According to Michael Madow, the identity of a celebrity is "the product of a complex social process in which the 'labor' of the celebrity is but one ingredient, and not always the main one."[99] In a similar argument, Rosemary Coombe observes: "Star images are authored by studios, the mass media, public relations agencies, fan clubs, gossip columnists, photographers, hairdressers, body-building coaches, athletic trainers, teachers, screenwriters, ghostwriters, directors, lawyers, and doctors."[100] Why should we afford celebrities property rights in their names and likenesses when frequently a celebrity's persona is manufactured by others?

Madow also argues that individuals and groups participating actively in the process of generating and circulating meanings that constitute "culture." Thus, "against-the-grain readings" of mainstream cultural products are possible. As an example, Madow points to the example of a card showing "John Wayne, wearing cowboy hat and bright red lipstick, above the caption, 'It's such a bitch being butch.' " Wayne's children, among others, objected to the card. Madow comments:

> Against-the-grain readings of John Wayne are also possible. For instance, in a course on how to survive as a prisoner of war, the U.S. Navy uses the term "John Wayning it" to mean trying foolishly to hold out against brutal torture. The particular greeting card that Wayne's children and others objected to so strenuously represents an even more subversive inflection of Wayne's image. The card uses his image to interrogate and challenge mainstream conceptions of masculinity and heterosexuality. It recodes Wayne's image so as to make it carry a cultural meaning that presumably works for gay men, among others, but which Wayne's children (and no doubt many of his fans) find deeply offensive.
>
> . . .
>
> What it comes down to, then, is that the power to license is the power to suppress. When the law gives a celebrity a right of publicity, it does more than funnel additional income her way. It gives her (or her assignee) a substantial measure of power over the production and circulation of meaning and identity in our society: power, if she so chooses, to suppress readings or appropriations of her persona that depart from, challenge, or subvert the meaning she prefers; power to deny to others the use of her persona in the construction and communication of alternative or oppositional identities and social relations; power, ultimately, to limit the expressive and communicative opportunities of the rest of us. The result is a potentially significant narrowing of the space available for alternative cultural and dialogic practice. Do you agree that the tort of appropriation and right of publicity threaten popular cultural production? Or will social debate about the meaning of John Wayne, Madonna, or Elvis continue, more or less unaffected, in spite of these legal interests?

---

[99] Michael T. Madow, *Private Ownership of Public Image: Popular Culture and Publicity Rights*, 81 Cal. L. Rev. 127, 195 (1993).

[100] Rosemary J. Coombe, *The Cultural Life of Intellectual Properties: Authorship, Appropriation, and the Law* 94 (1998).

8. *Are Privacy and Property Rights Mutually Exclusive?* According to Robert Post, the right of publicity views one's personality as "commodified," as an object separate from oneself that can be valued by the market. In his view, Warren and Brandeis's right to privacy, in contrast, "attaches personality firmly to the actual identity of a living individual." The right of publicity protects personality as detachable from individuals, as a commodity that can be bought and sold (and can persist after the death of the individual). The right to privacy, in contrast, protects personality as constitutive of the individual. Post suggests that perhaps we need both property rights and privacy rights to protect our personalities: "Personality can so effortlessly be legally embodied by either property or privacy rights precisely because it embraces both these aspects."[101]

3. FOR ONE'S OWN USE OR BENEFIT

The Restatement of Torts recognizes appropriation of another's name or likeness when it is used for the appropriator's "own use or benefit." Consider the Restatement § 652C comment (b):

> The common form of invasion of privacy under the rule here stated is the appropriation and use of the plaintiff's name or likeness to advertise the defendant's business or product, or for some similar commercial purpose. Apart from statute, however, the rule stated is not limited to commercial appropriation. It applies also when the defendant makes use of the plaintiff's name or likeness for his own purposes and benefit, even though the use is not a commercial one, and even though the benefit sought to be obtained is not a pecuniary one. Statutes in some states have, however, limited the liability to commercial uses of the name or likeness.

What does "use or benefit" mean? In many jurisdictions, appropriation occurs only when the use or benefit is commercial in nature — i.e., used to promote or endorse a service or product.

RAYMEN V. UNITED SENIOR ASSOCIATION, INC.

409 F. Supp. 2d 15 (D.D.C. 2006)

WALTON, J. On March 9, 2005, the plaintiffs filed this action seeking to prevent the defendants from further using their images in an advertising campaign which challenged various public policy positions taken by the American Association of Retired Persons ("AARP") regarding Social Security reform and the military. Currently before the Court are the defendants' motions to dismiss, and the plaintiffs' opposition thereto. . . .

On March 3, 2004, the plaintiffs were among 300 citizens of Multnomah County, Oregon who were married pursuant to a newly established right to same-sex marriage in that county. While at City Hall awaiting their opportunity to marry, the plaintiffs, Steve Hansen and Richard Raymen, kissed. A photographer from a

---

[101] Robert C. Post, *Rereading Warren and Brandeis: Privacy, Property, and Appropriation*, 41 Case W. Res. L. Rev. 647 (1991).

Portland, Oregon newspaper, the *Tribune,* captured the kiss in a photograph he took. The photograph was subsequently published in both the *Tribune* newspaper on March 4, 2004, and later on the *Tribune*'s website. At some later point in time, the *Tribune*'s website photograph was used without permission as part of an advertisement created by defendant Mark Montini. The advertising campaign was created for a nonprofit organization, United Senior Association, Inc., which does business under the name USA Next. The advertisement, which features the photograph of the plaintiffs kissing, was part of a campaign by USA Next challenging various public policy positions purportedly taken by the AARP. Specifically, the advertisement contains two pictures. The first is a picture of an American soldier, who presumably is in Iraq, with a red "X" superimposed over it, and the second is the photograph of the plaintiffs with a green checkmark superimposed over it. The caption under the advertisement reads: "The Real AARP Agenda," suggesting that the AARP opposes the United States military efforts abroad and supports the gay lifestyle. This advertisement ran on the website of *The American Spectator* magazine from February 15, 2005, to February 21, 2005.

According to the plaintiffs, the purpose of the advertising campaign was "to incite viewer passions against the AARP because of its alleged support of equal marriage rights for same-sex couples and its alleged lack of support of American troops." Moreover, the plaintiffs opine that the "advertisement also conveys the message that the plaintiffs . . . are against American troops . . . and are unpatriotic." The plaintiffs contend that the advertisement attracted media attention, which then caused an even wider distribution of the advertisement throughout the media. The plaintiffs assert that because of the advertisement, they "have suffered embarrassment, extreme emotional distress, and the invasion of their privacy." In addition, the plaintiffs represent that as a result of the false and misleading inference "communicated by the [a]dvertisement about [the] plaintiffs, their reputations as patriotic American citizens has been severely damaged." . . .

"'One who appropriates to his own use or benefit the name or likeness of another is subject to liability to the other for invasion of his privacy.'" *Martinez v. Democrat-Herald Publ'g Co., Inc.,* 669 P.2d 818, 820 (1983) (quoting Restatement (Second) of Torts § 652C (1976)). Under § 652C of the Restatement, plaintiffs can recover "damages when their names, pictures or other likenesses have been used without their consent to advertise a defendant's product, to accompany an article sold, to add luster to the name of a corporation or for some other business purpose." However, there is no actionable appropriation of a person's likeness claim "when a person's picture is used to illustrate a noncommercial, newsworthy article." . . . Whether a communication is commercial or non-commercial is a question of law. . . .

The photograph of the plaintiffs was used as part of USA Next's advertising campaign, which sought, at least in part, to engender opposition to AARP's policy position on social security reform. Presumably, the advertisement sought to vilify the AARP by conveying a message concerning AARP's alleged views on two hot button policy issues — support of same-sex marriage and opposition to the military. While the advertisement itself lacked any substantive discussion of these issues, it did convey AARP's purported position on both subjects. And someone who viewed the advertisement online could then access the USA Next's webpages which described the organization and its position on Social Security reform.

Clearly the issues of same-sex marriage and support for the military are issues of public concern and both have been widely discussed in the media. In fact, the plaintiffs contend in their complaint that the purpose of the advertisement was to influence Congress.

The plaintiffs' argument that the advertisement is commercial in nature because it sought contributions and promoted USA Next's lobbying services, is unpersuasive. First, nothing in the advertisement itself seeks donations. Rather, only after using the advertisement (by clicking on it) to access the webpages were viewers exposed to the information about USA Next and the solicitation for financial contributions. This Court cannot conclude that this detached solicitation elevates the advertisement itself to a level where it can be deemed commercial in nature. *See, e.g., Martinez,* 669 P.2d at 820 ("The fact that the defendant is engaged in the business of publication, for example of a newspaper, out of which he makes or seeks to make a profit, is not enough to make the incidental publication of a commercial use of the name or likeness.") (quoting Restatement (Second) Torts § 652C, cmt. D (1976)). Moreover, contrary to the plaintiffs' assertion, this case is not analogous to . . . *Beverley v. Choices Women's Med. Ctr. Inc.,* 587 N.E.2d 275 (N.Y. 1991). . . .

In *Beverley,* the Court concluded that a calendar produced by a for-profit hospital was commercial in nature because it had the hospital's "name, logo, address, and telephone number on each page of the calendar," along with "glowing characterizations and endorsements concerning the services" provided by the hospital, and thus left no doubt that the calendar was created to preserve existing patronage and to solicit new patients. Here, the advertisement does not even associate itself with USA Next through the use of its address, telephone number, logo, or in any other manner. Moreover, the calendar in *Beverley* promoted the use of the hospital's services, while the advertisement here discusses public policy issues that are currently the subject of public debate. . . .

NOTES & QUESTIONS

1. ***The Fuzzy Line Between Commercial and Non-Commercial Uses.*** Is using a person's photograph to solicit donations a commercial use? In *Raymen,* the image of the plaintiffs kissing was used not as a positive endorsement but as a way to spark outrage in their readers and spur them to donate. Isn't this using their image for financial gain? On the other hand, the plaintiffs' anger at the use of their photograph stems from their outrage over the defendants' message. The defendant could argue that the image of the plaintiffs was a popular iconic image representing gay marriage. Should the plaintiffs be able to control that image whenever they dislike the viewpoints of those that use it?

2. ***Girls Gone Wild.*** In *Lane v. MRA Holdings, LLC,* 242 F. Supp. 2d 1205 (M.D. Fla. 2002), the plaintiff was approached by a crew who produced the Girls Gone Wild video series, which featured clips of women stripping at various parties and events, such as spring break or Mardi Gras. The plaintiff claimed that the crew promised that the footage would be for their personal use only, but it was used in a Girls Gone Wild video. Among many claims, the plaintiff argued that

the makers of Girls Gone Wild appropriated her likeness. The court, however, rejected her appropriation claim:

> The Defendants first argue that they are not liable under Fla. Stat. § 540.08 because they did not use Lane's image for trade, commercial, or advertising purposes. Under Fla. Stat. § 540.08, the terms "trade", "commercial", or "advertising purpose" mean using a person's name or likeness to directly promote a product or service.
>
> As a matter of law, this Court finds that Lane's image and likeness were not used to directly promote a product or service. In coming to this conclusion, this Court relies upon Section 47 of the Restatement (Third) of Unfair Competition which defines "the purposes of trade" as follows:
>
>> The names, likeness, and other indicia of a person's identity are used "for the purposes of trade" . . . if they are used in advertising the user's goods or services, or are placed on merchandise marketed by the user, or are used in connection with services rendered by the user. However, use "for the purpose of trade" does not ordinarily include the use of a person's identity in news reporting, commentary, entertainment, works of fiction or nonfiction, or in advertising incidental to such uses.
>
> Therefore, under this definition, the "use of another's identity in a novel, play, or motion picture is . . . not ordinarily an infringement . . . [unless] the name or likeness is used solely to attract attention to a work that is not related to the identified person. . . ." *Id.* at comment c.
>
> In this case, it is irrefutable that the *Girls Gone Wild* video is an expressive work created solely for entertainment purposes. Similarly, it is also irrefutable that while Lane's image and likeness were used to sell copies of *Girls Gone Wild,* her image and likeness were never associated with a product or service unrelated to that work. Indeed, in both the video and its commercial advertisements, Lane is never shown endorsing or promoting a product, but rather, as part of an expressive work in which she voluntarily participated. Consequently, in accordance with Section 47 of the Restatement, the use of Lane's image or likeness in *Girls Gone Wild,* and in the marketing of that video cannot give rise to liability. . . .
>
> Upon reviewing Florida case law, it has come to this Court's attention that only one case has applied the provisions of Fla. Stat. § 540.08 to an expressive work. In *Gritzke v. M.R.A. Holding, LLC,* No. 4:01cv495-RH (N.D. Fla. Mar, 15, 2002), Judge Hinkle of the Northern District of Florida determined that the plaintiff stated a valid claim under § 540.08 by alleging that her half naked image was plastered on the front cover of the videotape *Girls Gone Wild* without her authorization. . . . [T]he plaintiff in *Gritzke* was complaining about the use of her image on the outside cover of a videotape package. In this case, Lane has not alleged that her image was plastered on a billboard or box cover advertising *Girls Gone Wild.* Rather, this cause of action arises from the Defendants truthful and accurate depiction of Lane voluntarily exposing her breasts to a camera, just as she did on Labor Day Weekend in Panama City Beach, Florida. Unlike in *Gritzke,* the Plaintiff's image in this case was never doctored. It has always remained in its original video format. Accordingly, the *Gritzke* case offers Lane little assistance. . . .
>
> Lane's lawsuit arose from an expressive work that has no purpose other than to entertain a segment of the general population. . . . [T]he Plaintiff in this case

> is not shown endorsing or promoting a product, but rather as participating in an expressive work. . . . [T]his Court finds that the publication of *Girls Gone Wild* is not actionable simply because it is sold for a profit.

The court's definition of commercial use in this case appears to be a use for "endorsing or promoting a product." Is this too limited a definition of commercial use? Would selling posters of a celebrity constitute a commercial use according to the *Lane* court?

4. CONNECTION TO MATTERS OF PUBLIC INTEREST

Unlike the tort of public disclosure, the lack of newsworthiness is not an element of the appropriation tort. However, appropriation protects against the "commercial" exploitation of one's name or likeness, not the use of one's name or likeness for news, art, literature, parody, satire, history, and biography. Otherwise, a newspaper would have to obtain the consent of every person it wrote about or photographed for use in a story. People could prevent others from writing their biographies or from criticizing them, making a parody of them, or using their names in a work of literature. In New York, for example, one's name or likeness must be used for "advertising purposes or for the uses of trade." N.Y. Civ. Rights L. §§ 50-51. Although not employing the same language, other states adopt a similar approach, requiring that the use of one's name or likeness be for "commercial" purposes. Some courts refer to this as a "First Amendment privilege" to use one's name or likeness in matters of legitimate public concern.

The quintessential instance where the use of one's name or likeness is newsworthy and not "commercial" is in connection with the reporting of the news. In *Time Inc. v. Sand Creek Partners*, 825 F. Supp. 210 (S.D. Ind. 1993), country singer Lyle Lovett and actress Julia Roberts were photographed together at a Lovett concert immediately prior to their marriage. Roberts was in her wedding gown. A photographer for *People* magazine snapped several rolls of film, but they were confiscated by security. The magazine's publisher sued to get the photos back, but Lovett claimed that they were his, because he had a property interest in his name or likeness. The court sided with the magazine:

> Lovett and Roberts are widely known celebrities and in that sense are public figures and, in addition, their appearance on stage before thousands of people on the day of their highly-publicized but theretofore unannounced and private wedding ceremony, with Roberts still wearing her wedding dress, was a newsworthy event of widespread public interest.

Beyond news, uses that are "commercial" or "for advertising or trade purposes" generally do not encompass works of fiction or nonfiction or artistic expression. In *Rosemont Enterprises, Inc. v. Random House, Inc.*, 294 N.Y.S.2d 122 (1968), the defendants published an unauthorized biography of the reclusive Howard Hughes. The court concluded that the biography "falls within those 'reports of newsworthy people or events'" and is therefore not subject to liability for appropriation. A sculpture of supermodel Cheryl Tiegs was not appropriation because "[w]orks of art, including sculptures, convey ideas, just as do literature, movies or theater." *Simeonov v. Tiegs*, 602 N.Y.S.2d 1014 (Civ. Ct. 1993). The use of a person's identity in a work of fiction generally cannot give rise to an appropriation action. *See, e.g., Maritote v. Desilu Productions, Inc.*, 345 F.2d 418 (7th Cir. 1965); *Loft v. Fuller*, 408 So. 2d 619 (Fla. Ct. App. 1981).

However, in New York and other states, the right of the media to use one's name or likeness for news purposes is not absolute. There must exist a "legitimate connection between the use of plaintiff's name and picture and the matter of public interest sought to be portrayed." *Delan by Delan v. CBS, Inc.*, 458 N.Y.S.2d 608 (N.Y. Ct. App. 1983). As another court articulated the test:

> A picture illustrating an article on a matter of public interest is not considered used for the purpose of trade or advertising within the prohibition of the statute unless it has no real relationship to the article, or unless the article is an advertisement in disguise. It makes no difference whether the article appears in a newspaper; a magazine; a newsreel; on television; in a motion picture; or in a book. The test of permissible use is not the currency of the publication in which the picture appears but whether it is illustrative of a matter of public interest. *Dallesandro v. Henry Holt & Co.*, 106 N.Y.S.2d 805 (1957).

This test has become known as the "real relationship" test. *See, e.g., Haskell v. Stauffer Communications, Inc.*, 990 P.2d 163 (Kan. App. 1999); *Lane v. Random House*, 985 F. Supp. 141 (D.D.C. 1995).

FINGER V. OMNI PUBLICATIONS INTERNATIONAL, LTD.

566 N.E.2d 141 (N.Y. Ct. App. 1990)

ALEXANDER, J. Plaintiffs Joseph and Ida Finger commenced this action on behalf of themselves and their six children against defendant Omni Publications International, Ltd. seeking damages for the publication, without their consent, of a photograph of plaintiffs in conjunction with an article in Omni magazine discussing a research project relating to caffeine-aided fertilization. . . .

. . . The June 1988 issue of Omni magazine included in its "Continuum" segment an article entitled "Caffeine and Fast Sperm," in which it was indicated that based on research conducted at the University of Pennsylvania School of Medicine, in vitro fertilization rates may be enhanced by exposing sperm to high concentrations of caffeine.

A photograph of plaintiffs depicting two adults surrounded by six attractive and apparently healthy children accompanied the article. The caption beneath the photograph read "Want a big family? Maybe your sperm needs a cup of Java in the morning. Tests reveal that caffeine-spritzed sperm swim faster, which may increase the chances for in vitro fertilization." Neither the article nor the caption mentioned plaintiffs' names or indicated in any fashion that the adult plaintiffs used caffeine or that the children were produced through in vitro fertilization.

Plaintiffs commenced this action alleging only violations of Civil Rights Law §§ 50 and 51. Defendant moved to dismiss the complaint, arguing that its use of the photograph in conjunction with the article did not violate Civil Rights Law §§ 50 and 51 because the picture was not used for trade or advertising but to illustrate a related news article on fertility. Defendant contended that because fertility is a topic of legitimate public interest, its use of the picture fit within the "newsworthiness exception" to the prohibitions of Civil Rights Law § 50. . . .

Plaintiffs contend that defendant violated Civil Rights Law §§ 50 and 51 by using their photograph without their consent "for advertising purposes or for the purposes of trade." . . .

Although the statute does not define "purposes of trade" or "advertising," courts have consistently refused to construe these terms as encompassing publications concerning newsworthy events or matters of public interest. Additionally, it is also well settled that "'[a] picture illustrating an article on a matter of public interest is not considered used for the purpose of trade or advertising within the prohibition of the statute . . . unless it has no real relationship to the article . . . or unless the article is an advertisement in disguise.'"

Plaintiffs do not contest the existence of this "newsworthiness exception" and concede that the discussion of in vitro fertilization and the use of caffeine to enhance sperm velocity and motility are newsworthy topics. They contend, however, that their photograph bears "no real relationship" to the article, that none of plaintiffs' children were conceived by in vitro fertilization or any other artificial means, and that they never participated in the caffeine-enhanced reproductive research conducted at the University of Pennsylvania.

Consequently, according to plaintiffs, there was no "real relationship" between their photograph and the article, and any relationship that may exist is too tenuous to be considered a relationship at all. They argue that there are no "external and objective" criteria . . . that would indicate that plaintiffs have any real or legitimate connection with the subject of caffeine-enhanced in vitro fertilization. . . .

Plaintiffs misperceive the "newsworthy" theme of the article, which is fertility or increased fertility. Indeed, the article, in its opening sentences, observes that caffeine "can increase a man's fertility by boosting the performance of his sperm" and further indicates that "those who are looking for a fertility tonic shouldn't head for the nearest coffee pot" because the concentrations of caffeine used in the experiment "were so high [as to] be toxic."

The theme of fertility is reasonably reflected both in the caption beneath the picture, "Want a big family?", and the images used — six healthy and attractive children with their parents to whom each child bears a striking resemblance. Clearly then, there is a "real relationship" between the fertility theme of the article and the large family depicted in the photograph. That the article also discusses in vitro fertilization as being enhanced by "caffeine-spritzed sperm" does no more than discuss a specific aspect of fertility and does not detract from the relationship between the photograph and the article.

As we have noted, the "newsworthiness exception" should be liberally applied. . . . [Q]uestions of "newsworthiness" are better left to reasonable editorial judgment and discretion; judicial intervention should occur only in those instances where there is "no real relationship" between a photograph and an article or where the article is an "advertisement in disguise." . . .

NOTES & QUESTIONS

1. *Levels of Generality in Applying the Real Relationship Test.* Do you agree with the court's approach to the relationship between the photograph and the article? Does the court properly view the topic of the article broadly as about fertility in general? The Fingers' argument, however, is not that the picture has

no relation to the subject matter of the article; rather, they contend that they have nothing to do with the article's specific topic. Is this relevant to the court?

2. ***What Injuries Does the Appropriation Tort Redress?*** What type of interest are the Fingers attempting to protect? Why doesn't the appropriation tort protect that interest?

Consider *Arrington v. New York Times*, 434 N.E.2d 1319 (N.Y. Ct. App. 1982), cert. den. 459 U.S. 1146 (1983). The *New York Times Magazine* published an article called "The Black Middle Class: Making It." On the cover of the publication was the photograph of the plaintiff Clarence W. Arrington in a suit. The photograph was taken without Arrington's consent or knowledge as he was walking down the street. Arrington, a young African-American financial analyst, strongly disagreed with the views stated in the article, which criticized how the "expanding black middle/professional class in today's society" was growing more removed from its "less fortunate brethren." Arrington, along with many other readers, found the article to be "insulting, degrading, distorting and disparaging." Others, including his friends and acquaintances, thought that he had shared the ideas in the article because his picture was featured as the exemplar of the "black middle class." Arrington sued the publisher, the freelance photographer who took the picture, and the agency that arranged for the photo to be sold to the *Times* for appropriation and false light. With regard to appropriation, the New York law recognized the importance of protecting free speech values:

> . . . [W]e not too long ago reiterated that "'[a] picture illustrating an article on a matter of public interest is not considered used for the purposes of trade or advertising within the prohibition of the statute . . . unless it has no real relationship to the article . . . or unless the article is an advertisement in disguise.'" And this holds true though the dissemination of news and views is carried on for a profit or that illustrations are added for the very purpose of encouraging sales of the publications.

Arrington contended that his picture had no "real relationship" to the article, but the court disagreed:

> Plaintiff's emphasis . . . is on the fact that, as he reads it, the article depicts the "black middle class" as one peopled by "materialistic, status-conscious and frivolous individuals without any sense of moral obligation to those of their race who are economically less fortunate," a conception of the "class" with which he disclaims any "legitimate connection." While the concededly innocuous title of the article is superimposed over part of the picture (as is the title of another on Christmas pleasures), nothing of the ideas with which he wishes to disassociate himself appear at this point. And, though the article itself gives the names and quotes the statements and opinions of persons whom the author interviewed, as indicated earlier, the plaintiff is neither mentioned, nor are any of the ideas or opinions it expresses attributed to him. The asserted lack of a "real relationship" boils down then, to his conviction that his views are not consonant with those of the author. . . . [However,] it would be unwise for us to assay the dangerous task of passing on value judgments based on the subjective happenstance of whether there is agreement with views expressed on a social issue.

No more persuasive is plaintiff's perfectly understandable preference that his photograph not have been employed in this manner and in this connection. However, other than in the purely commercial setting covered by [New York's appropriation tort], an inability to vindicate a personal predilection for greater privacy may be part of the price every person must be prepared to pay for a society in which information and opinion flow freely.

However, as to the photographer and the agency that sold the photo, the court declared that Arrington's action could proceed because the sale of the photo "commercialized" it, and the other defendants were not protected in the same way by the statute as the publisher. Subsequent to *Arrington*, the New York legislature amended § 51 to protect photographers and agents.

How would you characterize Arrington's injury? Did it involve the commercial use of his photograph? Or did it involve his being associated with an article that he found distasteful? Should a person have legal recourse from having her image associated, without her consent, with views that she disagrees with?

Arrington also raised a false light claim, but the court rejected it because the use of the photo was not "highly offensive." Do you agree?

3. ***The Limits of the Real Relationship Test.*** In *Spahn v. Julian Messner, Inc.,* 233 N.E.2d 840 (N.Y. 1967), the defendants published a book about the famous baseball player, Warren Spahn. The book was largely a work of fiction, with imaginary events and dialogue. The defendants intended to create a fictitious biography, as they did not engage in research or interviews of Spahn or those who knew him. Spahn sued under New York's appropriation law (Civil Rights Law § 51) and won a jury verdict. The verdict was upheld on appeal:

To hold that this research effort entitles the defendants to publish the kind of knowing fictionalization presented here would amount to granting a literary license which is not only unnecessary to the protection of free speech but destructive of an individual's right — albeit a limited one in the case of a public figure — to be free of the commercial exploitation of his name and personality.

In *Messenger v. Gruner + Jahr Printing and Publishing,* 208 F.3d 122 (2d Cir. 2000), photographs of a young woman were used to illustrate a story called "Love Crisis" in a magazine called *Young and Modern (YM)*:

The column began with a letter to Sally Lee, *YM*'s editor-in-chief, from a 14-year-old girl identified only as "Mortified." Mortified writes that she got drunk at a party and then had sex with her 18-year-old boyfriend and two of his friends. Lee responds that Mortified should avoid similar situations in the future, and advises her to be tested for pregnancy and sexually transmitted diseases. Above the column, in bold type, is a pull-out quotation stating, "I got trashed and had sex with three guys." Three full-color photographs of plaintiff illustrate the column — one, for example, shows her hiding her face, with three young men gloating in the background. The captions are keyed to Lee's advice: "Wake up and face the facts: You made a pretty big mistake;" "Don't try to hide — just ditch him and his buds;" and "Afraid you're pregnant? See a doctor."

The court applied the real relationship test: "[W]here a photograph illustrates an article on a matter of public interest, the newsworthiness exception bars recovery unless there is no real relationship between the photograph and the article, or the article is an advertisement in disguise." The defendants cited *Finger* and *Arrington*. The plaintiff relied on *Spahn*. The court concluded that *Finger* and *Arrington* controlled, not *Spahn*. Like the photographs in *Young and Modern,* the photos used in *Finger* and *Arrington* were used to "illustrate newsworthy articles." In contrast, "*Spahn* concerned a strikingly different scenario from the one before us. . . . [D]efendants invented biographies of plaintiffs' lives. The courts concluded that the substantially fictional works at issue were nothing more than attempts to trade on the persona of Warren Spahn." The court also concluded that the tort of false light was not recognized in New York.

In dissent, Judge Bellacosa argued:

> [The holding of this case] justifies a too-facile escape valve from the operation of the [appropriation] statute, one that is also unilaterally within the control of the alleged wrongdoer. The paradigm for editors is a "newsworthy" homily to lovesick adolescents or any other audience; they then just have to use a journalistic conceit of tying the advice to a purported letter to the editor, with an inescapable first person identification of the letter as originating with any adolescent in the photo array. When an aggrieved person like Messenger reaches for the statutory lifeline, the newsworthiness notion dissipates it into a dry mirage. That is not fair or right.

Assess the strength of a potential defamation suit based on *Young and Modern*'s use of the photo.

5. FIRST AMENDMENT LIMITATIONS

Zacchini v. Scripps-Howard Broadcasting Co.

433 U.S. 562 (1977)

White, J. Petitioner, Hugo Zacchini, is an entertainer. He performs a "human cannonball" act in which he is shot from a cannon into a net some 200 feet away. Each performance occupies some 15 seconds. In August and September 1972, petitioner was engaged to perform his act on a regular basis at the Geauga County Fair in Burton, Ohio. He performed in a fenced area, surrounded by grandstands, at the fair grounds. Members of the public attending the fair were not charged a separate admission fee to observe his act.

On August 30, a freelance reporter for Scripps-Howard Broadcasting Co., the operator of a television broadcasting station and respondent in this case, attended the fair. He carried a small movie camera. Petitioner noticed the reporter and asked him not to film the performance. The reporter did not do so on that day; but on the instructions of the producer of respondent's daily newscast, he returned the following day and videotaped the entire act. This film clip approximately 15 seconds in length, was shown on the 11 o'clock news program that night, together with favorable commentary.

Petitioner then brought this action for damages, alleging that he is "engaged in the entertainment business," that the act he performs is one "invented by his father and . . . performed only by his family for the last fifty years," that respondent "showed and commercialized the film of his act without his consent," and that such conduct was an "unlawful appropriation of plaintiff's professional property." Respondent answered and moved for summary judgment, which was granted by the trial court.

[The Ohio Supreme Court held that the broadcast was protected by the First Amendment because the press "must be accorded broad latitude in its choice of how much it presents of each story or incident, and of the emphasis to be given to such presentation." The United States Supreme Court granted certiorari to determine whether the First Amendment immunized the media broadcaster from damages under Ohio's "right of publicity" (appropriation tort).]

. . . The Ohio Supreme Court relied heavily on *Time, Inc. v. Hill*, 385 U.S. 374 (1967), but that case does not mandate a media privilege to televise a performer's entire act without his consent. Involved in *Time, Inc. v. Hill* was a claim under the New York "Right of Privacy" statute that Life Magazine, in the course of reviewing a new play, had connected the play with a long-past incident involving petitioner and his family and had falsely described their experience and conduct at that time. The complaint sought damages for humiliation and suffering flowing from these nondefamatory falsehoods that allegedly invaded Hill's privacy. The Court held, however, that the opening of a new play linked to an actual incident was a matter of public interest and that Hill could not recover without showing that the Life report was knowingly false or was published with reckless disregard for the truth the same rigorous standard that had been applied in *New York Times Co. v. Sullivan*.

Time, Inc. v. Hill, which was hotly contested and decided by a divided Court, involved an entirely different tort from the "right of publicity" recognized by the Ohio Supreme Court. As the opinion reveals in *Time, Inc. v. Hill*, the Court was steeped in the literature of privacy law and was aware of the developing distinctions and nuances in this branch of the law. . . . The Court was aware that it was adjudicating a "false light" privacy case involving a matter of public interest, not a case involving "intrusion," "appropriation" of a name or likeness for the purposes of trade, or "private details" about a non-newsworthy person or event. It is also abundantly clear that *Time, Inc. v. Hill* did not involve a performer, a person with a name having commercial value, or any claim to a "right of publicity." This discrete kind of "appropriation" case was plainly identified in the literature cited by the Court and had been adjudicated in the reported cases.

The differences between these two torts are important. First, the State's interests in providing a cause of action in each instance are different. "The interest protected" in permitting recovery for placing the plaintiff in a false light "is clearly that of reputation, with the same overtones of mental distress as in defamation." By contrast, the State's interest in permitting a "right of publicity" is in protecting the proprietary interest of the individual in his act in part to encourage such entertainment. As we later note, the State's interest is closely analogous to the goals of patent and copyright law, focusing on the right of the individual to reap the reward of his endeavors and having little to do with protecting feelings or reputation. Second, the two torts differ in the degree to which they intrude on dissemination of information to the public. In "false light" cases the only way to protect the interests involved is to attempt to minimize publication of the damaging matter, while in "right of publicity" cases the only question is who gets to do the publishing. An entertainer such as petitioner usually has no objection to the widespread publication of his act as long as he gets the commercial benefit of such publication. Indeed, in the present case petitioner did not seek to enjoin the broadcast of his act; he simply sought compensation for the broadcast in the form of damages. . . .

. . . *Time, Inc. v. Hill*, *New York Times*, *Metromedia*, *Gertz*, and *Firestone* all involved the reporting of events; in none of them was there an attempt to broadcast or publish an entire act for which the performer ordinarily gets paid. It is evident, and there is no claim here to the contrary, that petitioner's state-law right of publicity would not serve to prevent respondent from reporting the newsworthy facts about petitioner's act. Wherever the line in particular situations is to be drawn between media reports that are protected and those that are not, we are quite sure that the First and Fourteenth Amendments do not immunize the media when they broadcast a performer's entire act without his consent. The Constitution no more prevents a State from requiring respondent to compensate petitioner for broadcasting his act on television than it would privilege respondent to film and broadcast a copyrighted dramatic work without liability to the copyright owner, or to film and broadcast a prize fight, or a baseball game, where the promoters or the participants had other plans for publicizing the event. . . .

The broadcast of a film of petitioner's entire act poses a substantial threat to the economic value of that performance. . . . The effect of a public broadcast of the performance is similar to preventing petitioner from charging an admission fee. The rationale for (protecting the right of publicity) is the straightforward one of preventing unjust enrichment by the theft of good will. . . .

There is no doubt that entertainment, as well as news, enjoys First Amendment protection. It is also true that entertainment itself can be important news. But it is important to note that neither the public nor respondent will be deprived of the benefit of petitioner's performance as long as his commercial stake in his act is appropriately recognized. Petitioner does not seek to enjoin the broadcast of his performance; he simply wants to be paid for it. . . .

We conclude that although the State of Ohio may as a matter of its own law privilege the press in the circumstances of this case, the First and Fourteenth Amendments do not require it to do so. . . .

NOTES & QUESTIONS

1. *Different First Amendment Treatment.* Why does the *Zacchini* Court conclude that the First Amendment impacts the torts of appropriation and publicity differently than the other privacy torts? Do you agree with the distinction the Court makes?

2. *Newsworthiness.* Is Zacchini's human cannonball act newsworthy? The media frequently provides news about entertainment, such as sports and movies. If the act is newsworthy, then why shouldn't the First Amendment protect the broadcast of it? If Zacchini suffered an accident while performing his cannonball act, would a broadcast of it be newsworthy? Would this accident justify broadcast of the entire act?

E. PRIVACY PROTECTIONS FOR ANONYMITY AND RECEIPT OF IDEAS

When it comes to the privacy torts, the First Amendment typically has clashed with privacy. But in other contexts, the First Amendment is used as a way to protect privacy. Anonymous speakers have invoked First Amendment rights to protect themselves from being identified. The First Amendment has been used by those who want to explore ideas without being monitored. And the First Amendment is invoked by journalists seeking to protect themselves from being compelled to reveal their anonymous sources.

1. ANONYMITY

One of the most major such contexts is anonymity. Anonymity (or the use of pseudonyms) involves people's ability to conduct activities without being identified. People may want to speak anonymously because their speech might be unpopular or might be disliked by an employer or others who might retaliate against them. People may also want to read or surf the Internet anonymously because they are concerned about negative reactions toward their intellectual interests. Anonymity promotes freedom to speak or read without fear of reprisal or ostracism. However, when people can engage in anonymous activities, they might cause significant harm to other people and escape from being held accountable because their identities are not known. In a paradoxical way, people might use the cloak of anonymity to violate the privacy of others by revealing their private information.

When should the government be able to remove the cloak of anonymity on a person? When should a private party be able to do so? And to what extent can the government restrict anonymity to prevent fraud, crime, or other problems?

(a) Anonymous Speech

TALLEY V. STATE OF CALIFORNIA

362 U.S. 60 (1960)

BLACK, J. The question presented here is whether the provisions of a Los Angeles City ordinance restricting the distribution of handbills "abridge the freedom of speech and of the press secured against state invasion by the Fourteenth Amendment of the Constitution." The ordinance, § 28.06 of the Municipal Code of the City of Los Angeles, provides:

> No person shall distribute any hand-bill in any place under any circumstances, which does not have printed on the cover, or the face thereof, the name and address of the following:
>
> > (a) The person who printed, wrote, compiled or manufactured the same.

(b) The person who caused the same to be distributed; provided, however, that in the case of a fictitious person or club, in addition to such fictitious name, the true names and addresses of the owners, managers or agents of the person sponsoring said hand-bill shall also appear thereon.

The petitioner was arrested and tried in a Los Angeles Municipal Court for violating this ordinance. . . .

Anonymous pamphlets, leaflets, brochures and even books have played an important role in the progress of mankind. Persecuted groups and sects from time to time throughout history have been able to criticize oppressive practices and laws either anonymously or not at all. The obnoxious press licensing law of England, which was also enforced on the Colonies was due in part to the knowledge that exposure of the names of printers, writers and distributors would lessen the circulation of literature critical of the government. The old seditious libel cases in England show the lengths to which government had to go to find out who was responsible for books that were obnoxious to the rulers. John Lilburne was whipped, pilloried and fined for refusing to answer questions designed to get evidence to convict him or someone else for the secret distribution of books in England. Two Puritan Ministers, John Penry and John Udal, were sentenced to death on charges that they were responsible for writing, printing or publishing books. Before the Revolutionary War colonial patriots frequently had to conceal their authorship or distribution of literature that easily could have brought down on them prosecutions by English-controlled courts. Along about that time the Letters of Junius were written and the identity of their author is unknown to this day. Even the Federalist Papers, written in favor of the adoption of our Constitution, were published under fictitious names. It is plain that anonymity has sometimes been assumed for the most constructive purposes.

We have recently had occasion to hold in two cases that there are times and circumstances when States may not compel members of groups engaged in the dissemination of ideas to be publicly identified. *Bates v. City of Little Rock*, 361 U.S. 516; *N.A.A.C.P. v. State of Alabama*, 357 U.S. 449. The reason for those holdings was that identification and fear of reprisal might deter perfectly peaceful discussions of public matters of importance. This broad Los Angeles ordinance is subject to the same infirmity. We hold that it, like the Griffin, Georgia, ordinance, is void on its face. . . .

McIntyre v. Ohio Elections Commission

514 U.S. 334 (1995)

STEVENS, J. . . . On April 27, 1988, Margaret McIntyre distributed leaflets to persons attending a public meeting at the Blendon Middle School in Westerville, Ohio. At this meeting, the superintendent of schools planned to discuss an imminent referendum on a proposed school tax levy. The leaflets expressed Mrs. McIntyre's opposition to the levy. There is no suggestion that the text of her message was false, misleading, or libelous. She had composed and printed it on her home computer and had paid a professional printer to make additional copies. Some of the handbills identified her as the author; others merely purported to express the views of "CONCERNED PARENTS AND TAX PAYERS." Except for the help provided by her son and a friend, who placed some of the leaflets on car windshields in the school parking lot, Mrs. McIntyre acted independently.

While Mrs. McIntyre distributed her handbills, an official of the school district, who supported the tax proposal, advised her that the unsigned leaflets did not conform to the Ohio election laws. Undeterred, Mrs. McIntyre appeared at another meeting on the next evening and handed out more of the handbills.

The proposed school levy was defeated at the next two elections, but it finally passed on its third try in November 1988. Five months later, the same school official filed a complaint with the Ohio Elections Commission charging that Mrs. McIntyre's distribution of unsigned leaflets violated § 3599.09(A) of the Ohio Code [which prohibited the distribution of political literature without the name and address of the person or organization responsible for the distribution]. The commission agreed and imposed a fine of $100. . . .

Mrs. McIntyre passed away during the pendency of this litigation. Even though the amount in controversy is only $100, petitioner, as the executor of her estate, has pursued her claim in this Court. Our grant of certiorari reflects our agreement with his appraisal of the importance of the question presented. . . .

Ohio maintains that the statute under review is a reasonable regulation of the electoral process. . . .

"Anonymous pamphlets, leaflets, brochures and even books have played an important role in the progress of mankind." *Talley v. California.* Great works of literature have frequently been produced by authors writing under assumed names.[102] Despite readers' curiosity and the public's interest in identifying the creator of a work of art, an author generally is free to decide whether or not to disclose his or her true identity. The decision in favor of anonymity may be motivated by fear of economic or official retaliation, by concern about social ostracism, or merely by a desire to preserve as much of one's privacy as possible. Whatever the motivation may be, at least in the field of literary endeavor, the interest in having anonymous works enter the marketplace of ideas unquestionably outweighs any public interest in requiring disclosure as a condition of entry. Accordingly, an author's decision to remain anonymous, like other decisions concerning omissions or additions to the content of a publication, is an aspect of the freedom of speech protected by the First Amendment.

. . . On occasion, quite apart from any threat of persecution, an advocate may believe her ideas will be more persuasive if her readers are unaware of her identity. Anonymity thereby provides a way for a writer who may be personally unpopular to ensure that readers will not prejudge her message simply because they do not like its proponent. Thus, even in the field of political rhetoric, where "the identity of the speaker is an important component of many attempts to persuade," the most effective advocates have sometimes opted for anonymity. The specific holding in *Talley* related to advocacy of an economic boycott, but the Court's reasoning

---

[102] American names such as Mark Twain (Samuel Langhorne Clemens) and O. Henry (William Sydney Porter) come readily to mind. Benjamin Franklin employed numerous different pseudonyms. Distinguished French authors such as Voltaire (François Marie Arouet) and George Sand (Amandine Aurore Lucie Dupin), and British authors such as George Eliot (Mary Ann Evans), Charles Lamb (sometimes wrote as "Elia"), and Charles Dickens (sometimes wrote as "Boz"), also published under assumed names. . . .

embraced a respected tradition of anonymity in the advocacy of political causes.[103] This tradition is perhaps best exemplified by the secret ballot, the hard-won right to vote one's conscience without fear of retaliation. . . .

. . . [Section] 3599.09(A) of the Ohio Code does not control the mechanics of the electoral process. It is a regulation of pure speech. Moreover, even though this provision applies evenhandedly to advocates of differing viewpoints, it is a direct regulation of the content of speech. Every written document covered by the statute must contain "the name and residence or business address of the chairman, treasurer, or secretary of the organization issuing the same, or the person who issues, makes, or is responsible therefor." Furthermore, the category of covered documents is defined by their content — only those publications containing speech designed to influence the voters in an election need bear the required markings. Consequently, we are not faced with an ordinary election restriction; this case "involves a limitation on political expression subject to exacting scrutiny." . . .

When a law burdens core political speech, we apply "exacting scrutiny," and we uphold the restriction only if it is narrowly tailored to serve an overriding state interest. . . .

Nevertheless, the State argues that, even under the strictest standard of review, the disclosure requirement in § 3599.09(A) is justified by two important and legitimate state interests. Ohio judges its interest in preventing fraudulent and libelous statements and its interest in providing the electorate with relevant information to be sufficiently compelling to justify the anonymous speech ban. These two interests necessarily overlap to some extent, but it is useful to discuss them separately.

Insofar as the interest in informing the electorate means nothing more than the provision of additional information that may either buttress or undermine the argument in a document, we think the identity of the speaker is no different from other components of the document's content that the author is free to include or exclude. . . . The simple interest in providing voters with additional relevant information does not justify a state requirement that a writer make statements or disclosures she would otherwise omit. Moreover, in the case of a handbill written by a private citizen who is not known to the recipient, the name and address of the author add little, if anything, to the reader's ability to evaluate the document's message. . . .

Under our Constitution, anonymous pamphleteering is not a pernicious, fraudulent practice, but an honorable tradition of advocacy and of dissent. Anonymity is a shield from the tyranny of the majority. It thus exemplifies the purpose behind the Bill of Rights, and of the First Amendment in particular: to protect unpopular individuals from retaliation — and their ideas from suppression — at the hand of an intolerant society. . . .

SCALIA, J. joined by REHNQUIST, C.J. dissenting. . . . The Court's unprecedented protection for anonymous speech does not even have the virtue of establishing a clear (albeit erroneous) rule of law. . . . It may take decades to work

---

[103] That tradition is most famously embodied in the Federalist Papers, authored by James Madison, Alexander Hamilton, and John Jay, but signed "Publius." Publius' opponents, the Anti-Federalists, also tended to publish under pseudonyms. . . .

out the shape of this newly expanded right-to-speak-incognito, even in the elections field. And in other areas, of course, a whole new boutique of wonderful First Amendment litigation opens its doors. Must a parade permit, for example, be issued to a group that refuses to provide its identity, or that agrees to do so only under assurance that the identity will not be made public? Must a municipally owned theater that is leased for private productions book anonymously sponsored presentations? Must a government periodical that has a "letters to the editor" column disavow the policy that most newspapers have against the publication of anonymous letters? Must a public university that makes its facilities available for a speech by Louis Farrakhan or David Duke refuse to disclose the on-campus or off-campus group that has sponsored or paid for the speech? Must a municipal "public-access" cable channel permit anonymous (and masked) performers? The silliness that follows upon a generalized right to anonymous speech has no end. . .
.

The Court says that the State has not explained "why it can more easily enforce the direct bans on disseminating false documents against anonymous authors and distributors than against wrongdoers who might use false names and addresses in an attempt to avoid detection." I am not sure what this complicated comparison means. I am sure, however, that (1) a person who is required to put his name to a document is much less likely to lie than one who can lie anonymously, and (2) the distributor of a leaflet which is unlawful because it is anonymous runs much more risk of immediate detection and punishment than the distributor of a leaflet which is unlawful because it is false. Thus, people will be more likely to observe a signing requirement than a naked "no falsity" requirement; and, having observed that requirement, will then be significantly less likely to lie in what they have signed. . . .

I do not know where the Court derives its perception that "anonymous pamphleteering is not a pernicious, fraudulent practice, but an honorable tradition of advocacy and of dissent." I can imagine no reason why an anonymous leaflet is any more honorable, as a general matter, than an anonymous phone call or an anonymous letter. It facilitates wrong by eliminating accountability, which is ordinarily the very purpose of the anonymity. . . .

NOTES & QUESTIONS

1. ***Why Is Anonymity in Speaking Protected by the First Amendment?*** *Talley* and *McIntyre* conclude that anonymous speech is protected under the First Amendment but do so based on different rationales. What are those rationales? Which rationale seems most persuasive to you?
2. ***Identification Requirements.*** In *Buckley v. ACLF*, 525 U.S. 182 (1999), the Court struck down part of a Colorado statute requiring individuals handing out petitions to wear name tags. The Court reasoned:

    > [T]he name badge requirement forces circulators to reveal their identities at the same time they deliver their political message, it operates when reaction to the circulator's message is immediate and may be the most intense, emotional, and unreasoned. . . . The injury to speech is heightened for the petition circulator

because the badge requirement compels personal name identification at the precise moment when the circulator's interest in anonymity is the greatest.

In *Watchtower Bible & Tract Society v. Village of Stratton,* 536 U.S. 150 (2002), a local ordinance required all solicitors of private residences to obtain a permit, which required that the individuals supply data about their cause as well as their name, home addresses, and employers or affiliated organizations. The Supreme Court held that the ordinance violated the First Amendment because there was insufficient evidence that door-to-door solicitation significantly increased fraud or crime.

3. *Anonymity of Petitions.* In *Doe v. Reed*, 130 S. Ct. 1886 (2010), the State of Washington passed a law that provided rights to same-sex domestic partners. A group of petitioners, called "Protect Marriage Washington," collected signatures to put a referendum on the ballot to nullify the law. The group collected more than 137,000 signatures, a sufficient amount to put the referendum (R-71) on the ballot. Several groups sought to obtain copies of the petition and the names and addresses of the people who signed it. The groups indicated they planned to post the names online. Protect Marriage Washington and several signers sought to enjoin the release of the petitions as a violation of the First Amendment. The Supreme Court held that because the plaintiffs sought to bar the state from making all referendum petitions available to the public, the plaintiffs were challenging the disclosure facially rather than as applied. The Court held that the plaintiffs' First Amendment interests were implicated but that their facial challenge to the disclosure was outweighed by the state's interest in "preserving the integrity of the electoral process." The state's interest encompassed fraud prevention and "promoting transparency and accountability in the electoral process."

The Court left open whether the plaintiffs would prevail on a separate "as applied" challenge to the disclosure. The plaintiffs' facial challenge involved the disclosure requirement generally, without proof of specific harm to specific plaintiffs. In contrast, an "as applied" challenge would require specific plaintiffs to prove they were chilled in their speech.

4. *Anonymity in Cyberspace and "John Doe" Lawsuits*. E-mail and the Internet enable people to communicate anonymously with ease. People can send e-mail or post messages to electronic bulletin boards under pseudonyms. However, this anonymity is quite fragile, and in some cases illusory. Websites log the IP address of the computers of visitors of the site, and these IP addresses can be traced back to a person. An individual's Internet Service Provider (ISP) has information linking IP addresses to particular account holders. Under federal wiretap law, an ISP must disclose information identifying a particular user to the government pursuant to a subpoena. However, no subpoena is required for private parties. An ISP "may disclose a record or other information pertaining to a subscriber . . . to any person other than a governmental entity." 18 U.S.C. § 2703(c)(1)(A).

In what is known as a "John Doe" lawsuit, plaintiffs can sue to find out the identity of an anonymous or pseudonymous speaker in order to pursue a defamation or privacy action. Plaintiffs bring a lawsuit against anonymous speakers (the John Does) and then seek civil subpoenas or court orders to compel ISPs to reveal the identities of these speakers. Courts must consider the First Amendment rights of the speakers when determining whether plaintiffs are entitled to discover the identities of speakers people allege have defamed them or invaded their privacy.[104] What standard should courts use to make this determination? The case below addresses this issue.

DOE V. CAHILL

884 A.2d 451 (Del. 2005)

STEELE, C.J. . . . On November 2, 2004, the plaintiffs below, Patrick and Julia Cahill, both residents of Smyrna, Delaware, filed suit against four John Doe defendants asserting defamation and invasion of privacy claims. This appeal involves only one of the John Doe defendants, John Doe No. 1 below and "Doe" in this opinion. Using the alias "Proud Citizen," Doe posted two statements on an internet website sponsored by the Delaware State News called the "Smyrna/Clayton Issues Blog" concerning Cahill's performance as a City Councilman of Smyrna. The "Guidelines" at the top of the blog stated "[t]his is your hometown forum for opinions about public issues." The first of Doe's statements, posted on September 18, 2004, said:

> If only Councilman Cahill was able to display the same leadership skills, energy and enthusiasm toward the revitalization and growth of the fine town of Smyrna as Mayor Schaeffer has demonstrated! While Mayor Schaeffer has made great strides toward improving the livelihood of Smyrna's citizens, Cahill has devoted all of his energy to being a divisive impediment to any kind of cooperative movement. *Anyone who has spent any amount of time with Cahill would be keenly aware of such character flaws, not to mention an obvious mental deterioration.* Cahill is a prime example of failed leadership — his eventual ousting is exactly what Smyrna needs in order to move forward and establish a community that is able to thrive on its own economic stability and common pride in its town.

The next day, Doe posted another statement:

> *Gahill* [sic] *is as paranoid* as everyone in the town thinks he is. The mayor needs support from his citizens and protections from unfounded attacks. . . .

Pursuant to Superior Court Rule 30, the Cahills sought and obtained leave of the Superior Court to conduct a pre-service deposition of the owner of the internet blog, Independent Newspapers. After obtaining the IP addresses associated with the blog postings from the blog's owner, the Cahills learned that Comcast Corporation owned Doe's IP address. An IP address is an electronic number that specifically identifies a particular computer using the internet. IP addresses are often owned by internet service providers who then assign them to subscribers when they use the internet. These addresses are unique and assigned to only one ISP subscriber at a time. Thus, if the ISP knows the time and the date that postings were made from a specific IP address, it can determine the identity of its subscriber.

---

[104] Lyrissa Barnett Lidsky, *Silencing John Doe: Defamation and Discourse in Cyberspace*, 49 Duke L.J. 855 (2000).

Armed with Doe's IP address, the Cahills obtained a court order requiring Comcast to disclose Doe's identity. As required by Federal Statute,[105] when Comcast received the discovery request, it notified Doe. On January 4, 2005, Doe filed an "Emergency Motion for a Protective Order" seeking to prevent the Cahills from obtaining his identity from Comcast. . . .

It is clear that speech over the internet is entitled to First Amendment protection. This protection extends to anonymous internet speech. Anonymous internet speech in blogs or chat rooms in some instances can become the modern equivalent of political pamphleteering. . . .

It also is clear that the First Amendment does not protect defamatory speech. . . . Certain classes of speech, including defamatory and libelous speech, are entitled to no Constitutional protection. . . . Accordingly, we must adopt a standard that appropriately balances one person's right to speak anonymously against another person's right to protect his reputation. . . .

In this case, this Court is called upon to adopt a standard for trial courts to apply when faced with a public figure plaintiff's discovery request that seeks to unmask the identity of an anonymous defendant who has posted allegedly defamatory material on the internet. Before this Court is an entire spectrum of "standards" that could be required, ranging (in ascending order) from a good faith basis to assert a claim, to pleading sufficient facts to survive a motion to dismiss, to a showing of *prima facie* evidence sufficient to withstand a motion for summary judgment, and beyond that, hurdles even more stringent. . . . [W]e hold that a defamation plaintiff must satisfy a "summary judgment" standard before obtaining the identity of an anonymous defendant.

We are concerned that setting the standard too low will chill potential posters from exercising their First Amendment right to speak anonymously. The possibility of losing anonymity in a future lawsuit could intimidate anonymous posters into self-censoring their comments or simply not commenting at all. A defamation plaintiff, particularly a public figure, obtains a very important form of relief by unmasking the identity of his anonymous critics. The revelation of identity of an anonymous speaker "may subject [that speaker] to ostracism for expressing unpopular ideas, invite retaliation from those who oppose her ideas or from those whom she criticizes, or simply give unwanted exposure to her mental processes." Plaintiffs can often initially plead sufficient facts to meet the good faith test applied by the Superior Court, even if the defamation claim is not very strong, or worse, if they do not intend to pursue the defamation action to a final decision. After obtaining the identity of an anonymous critic through the compulsory discovery process, a defamation plaintiff who either loses on the merits or fails to pursue a lawsuit is still free to engage in extra-judicial self-help remedies; more bluntly, the plaintiff can simply seek revenge or retribution.

Indeed, there is reason to believe that many defamation plaintiffs bring suit merely to unmask the identities of anonymous critics. As one commentator has noted, "[t]he sudden surge in John Doe suits stems from the fact that many defamation actions are not really about money." "The goals of this new breed of libel action are largely symbolic, the primary goal being to silence John Doe and

---

[105] 47 U.S.C. 551(c)(2) requires a court order to a cable ISP and notice to the ISP subscriber before an ISP can disclose the identity of its subscriber to a third party.

others like him." This "sue first, ask questions later" approach, coupled with a standard only minimally protective of the anonymity of defendants, will discourage debate on important issues of public concern as more and more anonymous posters censor their online statements in response to the likelihood of being unmasked. . . .

Long-settled doctrine governs this Court's review of dismissals under Rule 12(b)(6). Under that doctrine, the threshold for the showing a plaintiff must make to survive a motion to dismiss is low. Delaware is a notice pleading jurisdiction. Thus, for a complaint to survive a motion to dismiss, it need only give "general notice of the claim asserted." A court can dismiss for failure to state a claim on which relief can be granted only if "it appears with reasonable certainty that the plaintiff could not prove any set of facts that would entitle him to relief." On a motion to dismiss, a court's review is limited to the well-pleaded allegations in the complaint. An allegation, "though vague or lacking in detail" can still be well-pleaded so long as it puts the opposing party on notice of the claim brought against it. Finally, in ruling on a motion to dismiss under Rule 12(b)(6), a trial court must draw all reasonable factual inferences in favor of the party opposing the motion. . . .

We conclude that the summary judgment standard is the appropriate test by which to strike the balance between a defamation plaintiff's right to protect his reputation and a defendant's right to exercise free speech anonymously. We accordingly hold that before a defamation plaintiff can obtain the identity of an anonymous defendant through the compulsory discovery process he must support his defamation claim with facts sufficient to defeat a summary judgment motion.

. . . [T]o the extent reasonably practicable under the circumstances, the plaintiff must undertake efforts to notify the anonymous poster that he is the subject of a subpoena or application for order of disclosure. The plaintiff must also withhold action to afford the anonymous defendant a reasonable opportunity to file and serve opposition to the discovery request. Moreover, when a case arises in the internet context, the plaintiff must post a message notifying the anonymous defendant of the plaintiff's discovery request on the same message board where the allegedly defamatory statement was originally posted. . . .

[T]o obtain discovery of an anonymous defendant's identity under the summary judgment standard, a defamation plaintiff "must submit sufficient evidence to establish a *prima facie* case for each essential element of the claim in question." In other words, the defamation plaintiff, as the party bearing the burden of proof at trial, must introduce evidence creating a genuine issue of material fact for all elements of a defamation claim *within the plaintiff's control.*

Under Delaware law, a public figure defamation plaintiff in a libel case must plead and ultimately prove that: 1) the defendant made a defamatory statement; 2) concerning the plaintiff; 3) the statement was published; and 4) a third party would understand the character of the communication as defamatory. In addition, the public figure defamation plaintiff must plead and prove that 5) the statement is false and 6) that the defendant made the statement with actual malice. Finally, "[p]roof of damages proximately caused by a publication deemed libelous need not be shown in order for a defamed plaintiff to recover nominal or compensatory damages." . . .

[W]e are mindful that public figures in a defamation case must prove that the defendant made the statements with actual malice. Without discovery of the defendant's identity, satisfying this element may be difficult, if not impossible. Consequently, we do NOT hold that the public figure defamation plaintiff is required to produce evidence on this element of the claim. We hold only that a public figure plaintiff must plead the first five elements and offer *prima facie* proof on each of the five elements to create a genuine issue of material fact requiring trial. In other words, a public figure defamation plaintiff must only plead and prove facts with regard to elements of the claim that are within his control. . . .

Having adopted a summary judgment standard, we now apply it to the facts of this case. . . .

In deciding whether or not a statement is defamatory we determine, "*first,* whether alleged defamatory statements are expressions of fact or protected expressions of opinion; and [*second*], whether the challenged statements are capable of a defamatory meaning." . . .

Applying a good faith standard, the trial judge concluded, "it is enough to meet the 'good faith' standard that the Cahills articulate a legitimate basis for claiming defamation in the context of their particular circumstances." He continued "[g]iven that Mr. Cahill is a married man, [Doe's] statement referring to him as "Gahill" might reasonably be interpreted as indicating that Mr. Cahill has engaged in an extra-marital same-sex affair. Such a statement may form the basis of an actionable defamation claim." We disagree. Using a "G" instead of a "C" as the first letter of Cahill's name is just as likely to be a typographical error as an intended misguided insult. Under the summary judgment standard, no reasonable person would interpret this statement to indicate that Cahill had an extra-marital same-sex affair. With respect to Doe's other statements, the trial judge noted:

> Again, the context in which the statements were made is probative. [Doe's] statements might give the reader the impression that [Doe] has personal knowledge that Mr. Cahill's mental condition is deteriorating and that he is becoming "paranoid." Given that Mr. Cahill is a member of the Smyrna Town Council, an elected position of public trust, the impression that he is suffering from diminished mental capacity might be deemed capable of causing harm to his reputation, particularly when disseminated over the internet for all of his constituents to read.

We agree that the context in which the statements were made is probative, but reach the opposite conclusion. Given the context, no reasonable person could have interpreted these statements as being anything other than opinion. The guidelines at the top of the blog specifically state that the forum is dedicated to *opinions* about issues in Smyrna. . . .

Accordingly, we hold that as a matter of law a reasonable person would not interpret Doe's statements as stating facts about Cahill. The statements are, therefore, incapable of a defamatory meaning. Because Cahill has failed to plead an essential element of his claim, he *ipso facto* cannot produce *prima facie* proof of that first element of a libel claim, and thus, cannot satisfy the summary judgment standard we announce today. . . .

NOTES & QUESTIONS

1. ***Postscript.*** The anonymous speaker in *Doe v. Cahill* turned out to be Mayor Schaeffer's 25-year-old stepdaughter. Her identity was revealed inadvertently in discovery. The Schaeffers and Cahills were next-door neighbors, and they had feuded since 2003. Until the mayor's stepdaughter was unmasked, he had denied that anybody in his household made the statements against Cahill. Subsequently, Cahill settled his defamation lawsuit against Schaeffer's stepdaughter.

   After the Delaware Supreme Court decision was issued, Patrick and Julia Cahill were arrested following a shouting match with the Schaeffers. The Cahills were charged with terroristic threatening, harassment, and disorderly conduct. They were subsequently acquitted of these charges, but Patrick Cahill was convicted of violating a police order to avoid contacting the Schaeffers. He was fined $100 and sentenced to a year of probation.

2. ***The Standard for Unmasking an Anonymous Speaker.*** Courts have established different standards for a plaintiff to find out the identity of an anonymous speaker. The most common include:

   (a) *The Motion to Dismiss Standard.* The plaintiff must establish that the case would survive a motion to dismiss. *See Columbia Insurance Co. v. Seescandy.com*, 185 F.R.D. 573 (N.D. Cal. 1999).

   (b) *The Prima Facie Case Standard.* The plaintiff must produce evidence showing a prima facie case on all elements and must demonstrate that revealing the identity of the anonymous speaker will not severely harm the speaker's free speech or privacy rights and will be "necessary to enable plaintiff to protect against or remedy serious wrongs." *Highfields Capital Mgmt., LP v. Doe*, 385 F. Supp. 2d 969 (N.D. Cal. 2005); *Dendrite Int'l v. Doe No. 3*, 775 A.2d 756 (N.J. Super. App. Div. 2001).

   (c) *The Summary Judgment Standard.* The plaintiff must prove the case could survive a motion for summary judgment. *See Doe v. Cahill, supra.*

   (d) *The Variable Standard.* This standard varies depending upon the nature of the speech, with commercial speech being protected by a much lower standard than non-commercial speech. *See In re Anonymous Online Speakers*, 611 F.3d 653 (9th Cir. 2010) (known as the "*Quixtar*" case).

   What are the pros and cons of each approach?

3. ***The Identities of Third Parties to the Litigation.*** In *Doe v. 2TheMart.com, Inc.* 140 F. Supp. 2d 1088 (W.D. Wash. 2001), shareholders of 2TheMart.com, Inc. brought a derivative class action against the corporation. The company, in preparing its defense, subpoenaed the identity of 23 anonymous speakers who posted messages on an online message board. These postings were very critical

of 2TheMart. One of the anonymous speakers challenged the subpoena. The court concluded:

> The Court will consider four factors in determining whether the subpoena should issue. These are whether: (1) the subpoena seeking the information was issued in good faith and not for any improper purpose, (2) the information sought relates to a core claim or defense, (3) the identifying information is directly and materially relevant to that claim or defense, and (4) information sufficient to establish or to disprove that claim or defense is unavailable from any other source. . . .
>
> Only when the identifying information is needed to advance core claims or defenses can it be sufficiently material to compromise First Amendment rights. If the information relates only to a secondary claim or to one of numerous affirmative defenses, then the primary substance of the case can go forward without disturbing the First Amendment rights of the anonymous Internet users.
>
> The information sought by TMRT does not relate to a core defense. Here, the information relates to only one of twenty-seven affirmative defenses raised by the defendant, the defense that "no act or omission of any of the Defendants was the cause in fact or the proximate cause of any injury or damage to the plaintiffs." . . .
>
> [Moreover,] TMRT has failed to demonstrate that the identity of the Internet users is directly and materially relevant to a core defense. These Internet users are not parties to the case and have not been named as defendants as to any claim, cross-claim or third-party claim. . . .

Should the standard for unmasking non-parties to the litigation be stricter than that for parties to a case?

4. ***Can Being Anonymous Online Be Criminalized?*** In *ACLU v. Miller,* 977 F. Supp. 1228 (N.D. Ga. 1997), plaintiffs challenged a law that criminalized falsely identifying oneself in online communications. The court held that the law ran afoul of the First Amendment:

> Defendants allege that the statute's purpose is fraud prevention, which the Court agrees is a compelling state interest. However, the statute is not narrowly tailored to achieve that end and instead sweeps innocent, protected speech within its scope. Specifically, by its plain language the criminal prohibition applies regardless of whether a speaker has any intent to deceive or whether deception actually occurs. Therefore, it could apply to a wide range of transmissions which "falsely identify" the sender, but are not "fraudulent" within the specific meaning of the criminal code. . . .

5. ***The WHOIS Database.*** Currently, the Internet Corporation for Assigned Names and Numbers (ICANN) Registrar Accreditation Agreement (RAA) requires that the identity and addresses of domain name holders be publicly disclosed, as well as the identities, addresses, e-mail addresses, and telephone numbers for technical and administrative contacts. Domain names are the names assigned to particular websites (e.g., cnn.com). In other words, an individual who wants to create her own website must publicly disclose personal information and cannot remain anonymous. The registration scheme extends to anyone who owns a domain name, including commercial services and publishers of political newsletters.

Dawn Nunziato observes that the ICANN identification policy was enacted "[a]t the behest of interested intellectual property owners, who were concerned about their ability to police infringing content on the Internet." She argues:

> Because of the important role anonymous speech serves within expressive forums — which in turn are integral to democratic governments — ICANN should, in reevaluating its policies to accord meaningful protection for freedom of expression, revise its policy requiring domain name holders publicly to disclose their names and addresses. While protecting anonymous Internet speech is clearly an important component of free speech within the United States, it is even more important for ICANN to protect the identity of speakers from countries that are more inclined to retaliate against speakers based on the ideas they express.

Nunziato suggests that ICANN should still collect registrants' names and addresses, but only make public their e-mail addresses. Only upon a "heightened showing by a rights holder" should ICANN release a registrant's name and address.[106]

Should registrants of Internet domain names be able to obtain "proxy registrations" that hide their information from the general public? In February 2005, the National Telecommunication and Information Administration of the Department of Commerce decided that registrars, such as Go Daddy, could not offer proxy registrations for the U.S. domain. Does this decision implicate First Amendment interests?

6. *Anonymity vs. Pseudonymity.* Tal Zarsky argues that anonymity "come[s] at a high price to society" because "[i]n an anonymous society where locations, interactions, and transactions are hidden behind a veil of anonymity, the lack of accountability will spread to all areas of conduct, interfering with the formation of business and other relationships and allowing individuals to act without inhibitions." Zarsky contends that "traceable pseudonymity" is preferable because it "allows us to interact with consistent personalities" yet protects our "physical identity" and because it provides "accountability with partial anonymity."[107] What are the relative benefits and costs of traceable pseudonymity versus anonymity?

(b) Reporter's Privilege

Another instance where anonymity plays an important role in promoting First Amendment rights is anonymity of sources who share information with journalists. One of the most famous anonymous sources was Deep Throat, the source that revealed information about the Watergate burglary and cover-up by the Nixon Administration to Bob Woodward and Carl Bernstein, reporters at *The Washington Post*. Their reporting ultimately lead to President Nixon's resig-nation.

---

[106] Dawn C. Nunziato, *Freedom of Expression, Democratic Norms, and Internet Governance*, 52 Emory L.J. 187, 202, 257, 259 (2003).

[107] Tal Z. Zarsky, *Thinking Outside the Box: Considering Transparency, Anonymity, and Pseudonymity as Overall Solutions to the Problems of Information Privacy in the Internet Society*, 58 U. Miami L. Rev. 991, 1028, 1032, 1044 (2004).

In criminal and civil cases, there are often demands on journalists to reveal the identity of an anonymous source. Journalists have sought protection from divulging the information in what is called "reporter's privilege," "journalist privilege," or "journalist-source privilege."

First Amendment and Federal Recognition of Reporter's Privilege. In *Branzburg v. Hayes*, 408 U.S. 665 (1972), the Supreme Court held that there is no First Amendment reporter's privilege against grand jury requests for evidence. However, at the conclusion of the opinion, the Court noted that:

> [N]ews gathering is not without its First Amendment protections, and grand jury investigations if instituted or conducted other than in good faith, would pose wholly different issues for resolution under the First Amendment. . . . Grand juries are subject to judicial control and subpoenas to motions to quash. We do not expect courts will forget that grand juries must operate within the limits of the First Amendment as well as the Fifth.

Justice Powell, the swing vote in the 5-4 majority, wrote a concurrence to note that the "Court does not hold that newsmen, subpoenaed to testify before a grand jury, are without constitutional rights with respect to the gathering of news or in safeguarding their sources. . . . In short, the courts will be available to newsmen under circumstances where legitimate First Amendment interests require protection." Powell wrote that privilege claims should be assessed "by the striking of a proper balance between freedom of the press and the obligation of all citizens to give relevant testimony with respect to criminal conduct. The balance of these vital constitutional and societal interests on a case-by-case basis accords with the tried and traditional way of adjudicating such questions."

Following *Branzburg,* many federal circuit courts have recognized a qualified reporter's privilege. The reporter's privilege has fared much better in civil cases than in criminal ones.

State Recognition of Reporter's Privilege. In the states, the reporter's privilege has been recognized, with sources in state constitutions, state statutes, and common law. Forty-nine states and the District of Columbia have recognized it.[108] In most states, there is a qualified reporter's privilege, which can be overridden if the government establishes that it has no alternative way to obtain the information and that there is a compelling interest to do so. About 13 states have an absolute privilege, which cannot be overridden.

Currently, there is no reporter's privilege recognized under the Federal Rules of Evidence. In calling for such a privilege Geoffrey Stone argues that at "the hands of unrestrained federal prosecutors, journalists have taken a serious battering." He contends:

> A strong and effective journalist-source privilege is essential to a robust and independent press and to a well-functioning democratic society. It is in society's interest to encourage those who possess information of significant public value to

---

[108] Geoffrey R. Stone, *We Need a Federal Journalist-Source Privilege NOW,* Huffington Post (Feb. 21, 2007), http://www.huffingtonpost.com/geoffrey-r-stone/we-need-a-federal-journal_b_41747.html.

convey it to the public, but without a journalist-source privilege, such communication will often be chilled because sources fear retribution, embarrassment or just plain getting "involved."[109]

Do you think that such a privilege should exist? Would sources with important information about companies come forward if they risked potential losing their jobs? Would sources come forward with information about the government if they risked criminal prosecution? On the other hand, if sources remain anonymous, would that allow them to divulge information and escape punishment?

The Valerie Plame Leak. In 2003, when former Ambassador Joseph Wilson disputed White House claims about weapons of mass destruction in Iraq. White House officials leaked to several reporters the fact that his wife, Valerie Plame, was a CIA agent, blowing her cover. Among the journalists receiving the information was the conservative pundit Robert Novak as well as *Time* magazine reporter Matthew Cooper and *New York Times* reporter Judith Miller.

Leaking the identity of a CIA agent is a crime, and a grand jury was convened to investigate. It subpoenaed from the reporters the identities of their sources. Cooper and Miller refused to comply with the subpoenas. District Court Judge Thomas Hogan ordered that the reporters comply or else face jail time for contempt. *Time* magazine announced that against the wishes of Cooper, it would turn over his notes. Should the journalists be required to hand over the notes?

The leak in this case was not by a source desiring to blow the whistle or reveal government corruption. Instead, the leak was done by government officials to retaliate against Wilson. Should leaks for purposes such as this one be denied the protection of reporter's privilege? If so, how would such an exception be defined?

Should the focus be on whether it is a crime to leak? In many instances, leaking is a crime, such as the Pentagon Papers leak as well as the leak by Edward Snowden. Should the focus be on whether the leak is in the public interest? How should the public interest be defined?

2. PRIVACY OF READING AND INTELLECTUAL EXPLORATION

Privacy is also central to the exploration of ideas. Neil Richards contends that the First Amendment protects what he calls "intellectual privacy." According to Richards:

> Intellectual privacy is the ability, whether protected by law or social circumstances, to develop ideas and beliefs away from the unwanted gaze or interference of others. Surveillance or interference can warp the integrity of our freedom of thought and can skew the way we think, with clear repercussions for the content of our subsequent speech or writing.[110]

To what extent does the First Amendment protect a person's right to privacy in reading, Web-surfing, and exploration of ideas?

---

[109] *Id.*

[110] Neil M. Richards, *Intellectual Privacy,* 87 Tex. L. Rev. 387, 389 (2008).

STANLEY V. GEORGIA

394 U.S. 557 (1969)

MARSHALL, J. . . . An investigation of appellant's alleged bookmaking activities led to the issuance of a search warrant for appellant's home. Under authority of this warrant, federal and state agents secured entrance. They found very little evidence of bookmaking activity, but while looking through a desk drawer in an upstairs bedroom, one of the federal agents, accompanied by a state officer, found three reels of eight-millimeter film. Using a projector and screen found in an upstairs living room, they viewed the films. The state officer concluded that they were obscene and seized them. Since a further examination of the bedroom indicated that appellant occupied it, he was charged with possession of obscene matter and placed under arrest. He was later indicted for "knowingly hav(ing) possession of . . . obscene matter" in violation of Georgia law. Appellant was tried before a jury and convicted. . . .

Appellant argues here . . . that the Georgia obscenity statute, insofar as it punishes mere private possession of obscene matter, violates the First Amendment. . . . [W]e agree that the mere private possession of obscene matter cannot constitutionally be made a crime. . . .

It is true that *Roth* does declare, seemingly without qualification, that obscenity is not protected by the First Amendment. That statement has been repeated in various forms in subsequent cases. However, neither *Roth* nor any subsequent decision of this Court dealt with the precise problem involved in the present case. Roth was convicted of mailing obscene circulars and advertising, and an obscene book, in violation of a federal obscenity statute. . . . None of the statements cited by the Court in *Roth* for the proposition that "this Court has always assumed that obscenity is not protected by the freedoms of speech and press" were made in the context of a statute punishing mere private possession of obscene material; the cases cited deal for the most part with use of the mails to distribute objectionable material or with some form of public distribution or dissemination. Moreover, none of this Court's decisions subsequent to *Roth* involved prosecution for private possession of obscene materials. Those cases dealt with the power of the State and Federal Governments to prohibit or regulate certain public actions taken or intended to be taken with respect to obscene matter. . . .

In this context, we do not believe that this case can be decided simply by citing *Roth*. . . .

It is now well established that the Constitution protects the right to receive information and ideas. "This freedom (of speech and press) . . . necessarily protects the right to receive. . . ." This right to receive information and ideas, regardless of their social worth, is fundamental to our free society. Moreover, in the context of this case — a prosecution for mere possession of printed or filmed matter in the privacy of a person's own home — that right takes on an added dimension. . . .

These are the rights that appellant is asserting in the case before us. He is asserting the right to read or observe what he pleases — the right to satisfy his intellectual and emotional needs in the privacy of his own home. He is asserting the right to be free from state inquiry into the contents of his library. Georgia contends that appellant does not have these rights, that there are certain types of materials that the individual may not read or even possess. Georgia justifies this assertion by arguing that the films in the present case are obscene. But we think that mere categorization of these films as "obscene" is insufficient justification for such a drastic invasion of personal liberties guaranteed by the First and Fourteenth Amendments. Whatever may be the justifications for other statutes regulating obscenity, we do not think they reach into the privacy of one's own home. If the First Amendment means anything, it means that a State has no business telling a man, sitting alone in his own house, what books he may read or what films he may watch. Our whole constitutional heritage rebels at the thought of giving government the power to control men's minds. . . .

We hold that the First and Fourteenth Amendments prohibit making mere private possession of obscene material a crime. *Roth* and the cases following that decision are not impaired by today's holding. As we have said, the States retain broad power to regulate obscenity; that power simply does not extend to mere possession by the individual in the privacy of his own home. Accordingly, the judgment of the court below is reversed and the case is remanded for proceedings not inconsistent with this opinion.

NOTES & QUESTIONS

1. *Possession of Obscenity Outside the Home.* Stanley possessed obscene material that Georgia could constitutionally outlaw because the First Amendment does not protect obscenity. According to the Court, states can ban obscene films outside the home. Thus, were Stanley to step outside the door with his films, a police officer could arrest him. Should Stanley's location inside his home make any difference? Suppose Stanley possessed and used illegal narcotics in his home. Does the state have any business telling a person, sitting alone in her home, what substances she may or may not ingest?

2. *The Limits of* **Stanley.** In *Osborne v. Ohio,* 495 U.S. 103 (1990), the Court held that the rule in *Stanley* does not apply to the possession of child pornography in the home:

   > In *Stanley,* Georgia primarily sought to proscribe the private possession of obscenity because it was concerned that obscenity would poison the minds of its viewers. We responded that "[w]hatever the power of the state to control public dissemination of ideas inimical to the public morality, it cannot constitutionally premise legislation on the desirability of controlling a person's private thoughts." The difference here is obvious: The State does not rely on a paternalistic interest in regulating Osborne's mind. Rather, Ohio has enacted § 2907.323(A)(3) in order to protect the victims of child pornography; it hopes to destroy a market for the exploitative use of children.

3. *The First Amendment and Postal Mail.* In *Lamont v. Postmaster General of the United States,* 381 U.S. 301 (1965), a 1962 federal statute required that all mail (except sealed letters) that originates or is prepared in a foreign country and is determined by the Secretary of the Treasury to be "communist political propaganda" be detained at the post office. The addressee would be notified of the matter, and the mail would be delivered to the addressee only upon her

request. The Court struck down the statute on First Amendment grounds:

> We rest on the narrow ground that the addressee in order to receive his mail must request in writing that it be delivered. This amounts in our judgment to an unconstitutional abridgment of the addressee's First Amendment rights. The addressee carries an affirmative obligation which we do not think the Government may impose on him. This requirement is almost certain to have a deterrent effect, especially as respects those who have sensitive positions. Their livelihood may be dependent on a security clearance. Public officials like schoolteachers who have no tenure, might think they would invite disaster if they read what the Federal Government says contains the seeds of treason. Apart from them, any addressee is likely to feel some inhibition in sending for literature which federal officials have condemned as "communist political propaganda." The regime of this Act is at war with the "uninhibited, robust, and wide-open debate and discussion" that are contemplated by the First Amendment.

4. ***Anonymous Reading and Receiving of Ideas.*** In *Tattered Cover, Inc. v. City of Thornton*, 44 P.3d 1044 (Colo. 2002), law enforcement officials (local City of Thornton police and a federal DEA agent) suspected that a methamphetamine lab was being operated out of a trailer home. On searching through some garbage from the trailer, an officer discovered evidence of drug operations and a mailing envelope from the Tattered Cover bookstore addressed to one of the suspects (Suspect A). There was an invoice and order number corresponding to the books shipped in the envelope, but no evidence about what those books were. Subsequently, a search warrant was obtained for the trailer home. In the bedroom, the police discovered a methamphetamine laboratory and drugs. Although there were a number of suspects, the police believed that Suspect A occupied the bedroom. Among the items seized from the bedroom were two books: *Advanced Techniques of Clandestine Psychedelic and Amphetamine Manufacture*, by Uncle Fester, and *The Construction and Operation of Clandestine Drug Laboratories*, by Jack B. Nimble.

The officers believed that these books were the ones mailed to Suspect A in the mailing envelope from the Tattered Cover found in the trash. The officers served The Tattered Cover with a DEA administrative subpoena, but Tattered Cover refused to comply, citing concern for its customers' privacy and First Amendment rights. The City then obtained a search warrant to search the bookstore's records. The Tattered Cover sued to enjoin the officers from executing the warrant.

The Colorado Supreme Court held that Colorado's First Amendment protects "the right to receive information and ideas." According to the court, "Everyone must be permitted to discover and consider the full range of expression and ideas available in our 'marketplace of ideas.'" The court further reasoned:

> Bookstores are places where a citizen can explore ideas, receive information, and discover myriad perspectives on every topic imaginable. When a person buys a book at a bookstore, he engages in activity protected by the First Amendment because he is exercising his right to read and receive ideas and information. Any governmental action that interferes with the willingness of

customers to purchase books, or booksellers to sell books, thus implicates First Amendment concerns. . . .

The need to protect anonymity in the context of the First Amendment has particular applicability to book-buying activity. . . . The right to engage in expressive activities anonymously, without government intrusion or observation, is critical to the protection of the First Amendment rights of book buyers and sellers, precisely because of the chilling effects of such disclosures. Search warrants directed to bookstores, demanding information about the reading history of customers, intrude upon the First Amendment rights of customers and bookstores because compelled disclosure of book-buying records threatens to destroy the anonymity upon which many customers depend.
. . .

In contrast to the U.S. Supreme Court, which held in *Zurcher v. Stanford Daily*, 436 U.S. 547 (1978) that First Amendment concerns of government searches of expressive material can be satisfied by the government obtaining a search warrant, the Colorado Supreme Court concluded the state's First Amendment "requires a more substantial justification from the government," which must "demonstrate a sufficiently compelling need for the specific customer purchase record sought from the innocent, third-party bookstore."

In applying this standard to the facts of the case, the court noted that the government desired the evidence about the books to link Suspect A to the master bedroom where the lab was located along with the books. The court, however, concluded that physical evidence and witnesses could have been used to establish this fact.

The City also argued that proof that Suspect A purchased the books would link him to the crime. But the court rejected this argument:

> The dangers, both to Suspect A and to the book-buying public, of permitting the government to access the information it seeks, and to use this proof of purchase as evidence of Suspect A's guilt, are grave. Assuming that Suspect A purchased the books in question, he may have done so for any of a number of reasons, many of which are in no way linked to his commission of any crime. He might have bought them for a friend or roommate, unaware that they would subsequently be placed in the vicinity of an illegal drug lab. He might have been curious about the process of making drugs, without having any intention to act on what he read. It may be that none of these scenarios is as likely as that suggested by the City, that Suspect A bought the books intending to use them to help him make an illegal drug. Nonetheless, Colorado's long tradition of protecting expressive freedoms cautions against permitting the City to seize the Tattered Cover's book purchase record. . . .

Do you agree with the decision in *Tattered Cover* that, in addition to the right to speak anonymously, there is also a right to read anonymously? Does such a right follow logically from the Supreme Court's freedom of association and anonymity cases?

Consider the following argument by Julie Cohen:

> For the most part, First Amendment jurisprudence has defined readers' rights only incidentally. Historically, both courts and commentators have been more concerned with protecting speakers than with protecting readers. . . .

When the two readers choose to express their own views, the First Amendment protects both speakers equally. Logically, that zone of protection should encompass the entire series of intellectual transactions through which they formed the opinions they ultimately chose to express. Any less protection would chill inquiry, and as a result, public discourse, concerning politically and socially controversial issues — precisely those areas where vigorous public debate is most needed, and most sacrosanct. . . .

The freedom to read anonymously is just as much a part of our tradition, and the choice of reading materials just as expressive of identity, as the decision to use or withhold one's name.[111]

How far can the rationale of *Tattered Cover* be extended? Suppose the police obtained a search warrant for one's home and sought to seize a person's diary? Would such a seizure be subject to strict scrutiny? What about the search of one's computer, which can reveal anonymous speech as well as one's online reading activities? Isn't the government's questioning of various witnesses to whom a person spoke also likely to interfere with that person's expressive activities? Why are books different (or are they)?

---

[111] Julie E. Cohen, *A Right to Read Anonymously: A Closer Look at "Copyright Management" in Cyberspace*, 28 Conn. L. Rev. 981 (1996); *see also* Marc Jonathan Blitz, *Constitutional Safeguards For Silent Experiments in Living Libraries, the Right to Read, and a First Amendment Theory for an Unaccompanied Right to Receive Information*, 74 U. Mo. Kan. City L. Rev. 799, 881-82 (2006).

CHAPTER 4

PRIVACY AND LAW ENFORCEMENT

CHAPTER OUTLINE

D. DIGITAL SEARCHES AND SEIZURES

1. Searching Computers and Electronic Devices

2. Encryption

3. Video Surveillance

4. E-mail and Online Communications

5. ISP Account Information

6. IP Addresses, URLs, and Internet Searches

One of the central tensions in information privacy law is between privacy and security. Security involves society's interest in protecting its citizens from crimes, including physical and monetary threats. One way that government promotes security is by investigating and punishing crimes. To do this, law enforcement officials must gather information about suspected individuals. Monitoring and information gathering pose substantial threats to privacy. At the same time, however, monitoring and information gathering offer the potential of increasing security. Throughout the twentieth century, technology provided the government significantly greater ability to probe into the private lives of individuals.

The prevailing metaphor for the threat to privacy caused by law enforcement surveillance techniques is George Orwell's novel *Nineteen Eighty-Four*. Written in 1949, the novel depicted an all-powerful and omniscient government called "Big Brother" that monitored and controlled every facet of individuals' lives:

> . . . [T]here seemed to be no colour in anything, except the posters that were plastered everywhere. The black moustachio'd face gazed down from every commanding corner. There was one on the house-front immediately opposite. BIG BROTHER IS WATCHING YOU, the caption said, while the dark eyes looked deep into Winston's own. Down at streetlevel another poster, torn at one corner, flapped fitfully in the wind, alternately covering and uncovering the single word INGSOC. In the far distance a helicopter skimmed down between the roofs, hovered for an instant like a bluebottle, and darted away again with a curving flight. It was the police patrol, snooping into people's windows. The patrols did not matter, however. Only the Thought Police mattered.
>
> Behind Winston's back the voice from the telescreen was still babbling away about pig-iron and the overfulfilment of the Ninth Three-Year Plan. The telescreen received and transmitted simultaneously. Any sound that Winston made, above the level of a very low whisper, would be picked up by it, moreover, so long as he remained within the field of vision which the metal plaque commanded, he could be seen as well as heard. There was of course no way of knowing whether you were being watched at any given moment. How often, or on what system, the Thought Police plugged in on any individual wire was guesswork. It was even conceivable that they watched everybody all the time. But at any rate they could plug in your wire whenever they wanted to. You had to live — did live, from habit that became instinct — in the assumption that every sound you made was overheard, and, except in darkness, every movement scrutinized.[1]

---

[1] George Orwell, *Nineteen Eighty-Four* 3-4 (1949).

Orwell's harrowing portrait of a police state illustrates the importance of limiting the power of the government to monitor its citizens. But consider the reverse as well: Will overly restrictive limitations on the power of the police restrict their ability to protect the public?

Although privacy and security may at times be viewed in conflict, consider the opening words of the Fourth Amendment: "The right of the people to be *secure* in their persons, houses, papers, and effects . . ." (emphasis added). Are the interests in public security and privacy fated to be always at odds? Are there times when the opposition between security and privacy proves a false dichotomy?

In the United States, policing is predominantly carried out by local governments. The Constitution, however, provides a national regulatory regime for police conduct. The Fourth and Fifth Amendments significantly limit the government's power to gather information. The Fourth Amendment regulates the government's activities in searching for information or items as well as the government's seizure of things or people.[2] The Fifth Amendment guarantees that "[n]o person . . . shall be compelled in any criminal case to be a witness against himself. . . ." The Fifth Amendment establishes a "privilege against self-incrimination," and it prohibits the government from compelling individuals to disclose inculpatory information about themselves.

In addition to the U.S. Constitution, federal statutes can regulate law enforcement activity. One of the predominant areas of law enforcement that has been regulated by federal law is electronic surveillance. This chapter will focus extensively on these statutes, as they play an increasingly important role in criminal procedure as more searches involve electronic devices, computers, and the Internet.

At the state level, most state constitutions have provisions similar to the Fourth and Fifth Amendments — sometimes the language is even identical. State courts, however, have sometimes interpreted their state constitutional provisions as being more strict than the way the U.S. Supreme Court has interpreted the Fourth and Fifth Amendments. States have also passed their own statutory regulation of law enforcement, often also in the realm of electronic surveillance. State law enforcement officials will be bound by their state constitutions and laws, as well as by the U.S. Constitution and federal laws. Federal officials are not subject to these state constitutional and statutory restrictions.

---

[2] For a comprehensive historical account of the origins of the Fourth Amendment, see William J. Cuddihy, *The Fourth Amendment: Origins and Original Meaning* 602-1791 (2009).

A. THE FOURTH AMENDMENT AND EMERGING TECHNOLOGY

1. HOW THE FOURTH AMENDMENT WORKS

The Fourth Amendment governs the investigatory power of government officials. The language of the Fourth Amendment reads:

> The right of the people to be secure in their persons, houses, papers, and effects, against unreasonable searches and seizures, shall not be violated, and no warrants shall issue, but upon probable cause, supported by oath or affirmation, and particularly describing the place to be searched, and the persons or things to be seized.

This section explains briefly how the Fourth Amendment works. The first issue is the *applicability of the Fourth Amendment.* Is a particular instance of government information gathering regulated by the Fourth Amendment? There are many instances when the government gathers information about people in a fashion that is not considered to be a search or seizure in the sense of the Fourth Amendment. In those cases, the behavior is considered free from the constraints of the Fourth Amendment. In these instances, however, a federal statute or state constitutional or statutory provision might still limit or otherwise regulate the governmental behavior. If not, then the government information gathering might not be regulated at all.

The second issue is *whether the search or seizure is reasonable.* Generally, a search is reasonable if government officials have obtained a search warrant supported by probable cause. The warrant must be properly circumscribed, and the search must not exceed the scope of the warrant. Only in very rare circumstances will a search within the scope of a valid warrant be deemed unreasonable. There are many instances, however, where a search without a warrant or probable cause will be deemed to be reasonable.

The third issue is *how the Fourth Amendment is enforced.* The primary method of enforcing the Fourth Amendment is by excluding from trial the use of evidence obtained in violation of the Fourth Amendment. People can also bring civil lawsuits for Fourth Amendment violations.

(a) Applicability: Searches and Seizures

The Fourth Amendment applies every time government officials (not just police) conduct a "search" or the "seizure" of an object, document, or person.

Searches. What is a "search" under the Fourth Amendment? This question has proven to be immensely challenging to answer. The cases in this chapter predominantly focus on this question, and the Supreme Court has used different approaches to answering this question. Its current approach is the "reasonable expectation of privacy test," which will be discussed later in this chapter.

Some paradigmatic examples of "searches" include peeking into one's pockets or searching one's person; entering into and looking around one's house, apartment, office, hotel room, or private property; and opening up and examining the contents of one's luggage or parcels. However, when government officials happen to observe something in plain view, then it is not a search.

Seizures. A "seizure" is a taking away of items by the police. A seizure can be of physical things or of persons (arrests).

(b) Reasonable Searches and Seizures

If there is a search or seizure, then the Fourth Amendment applies. It does not bar the search or seizure—it just requires that the search or seizure be "reasonable." What is reasonable and unreasonable under the Fourth Amendment?

Warrants and Probable Cause. Generally, a search or seizure is reasonable if the police have obtained a valid search warrant. To obtain a warrant, the police must go before a judge or magistrate and demonstrate that they have "probable cause" to conduct a search or seizure.

For a search warrant, probable cause requires that government officials have "reasonably trustworthy information" that is sufficient to "warrant a man of reasonable caution in the belief that an offense has been or is being committed" or that evidence will be found in the place to be searched. *Brinegar v. United States*, 338 U.S. 160 (1949). Probable cause is more than "bare suspicion." Probable cause must be measured on a case-by-case basis, via the facts of particular cases. *See Wong Sun v. United States*, 371 U.S. 471 (1963). The purpose of a warrant is to have an independent party (judges) ensure that police really do have probable cause to conduct a search.

A search warrant may be issued if there is probable cause to believe that there is incriminating evidence in the place to be searched. This is not limited to places owned or occupied by the criminal suspect. In certain instances, incriminating documents or things may be possessed by an innocent party.

A search is valid if the warrant is supported by probable cause and the search is within the scope of the warrant.

Unreasonable Searches with Warrants. Even with a warrant, certain searches are unreasonable. For example, in *Winston v. Lee*, 470 U.S. 753 (1985), the removal of a bullet lodged deep in the accused's chest was deemed unreasonable. However, this is one of the very rare circumstances where a search pursuant to a valid warrant will be deemed unreasonable. For example, the taking of blood from a suspect is a reasonable search. *See Schmerber v. California*, 384 U.S. 757 (1966). Barring truly exceptional circumstances, most searches undertaken with a valid warrant will be reasonable.

The Scope of Search Warrants. Search warrants do not authorize an unfettered search. The search must be circumscribed to the evidence being searched for and any other limits the court establishes in the warrant. In *Horton v. California,* 496 U.S. 128 (1990), the Supreme Court held that "[i]f the scope of the search exceeds that permitted by the terms of a validly issued warrant or the character of the relevant exception from the warrant requirement, the subsequent seizure is unconstitutional without more."

Warrants not only limit the search but also who is permitted to enter a person's home if it is being searched. In *Wilson v. Layne*, 526 U.S. 603 (1999), the police obtained a warrant to search the home of Charles and Geraldine Wilson because they were seeking to find their son who had violated his probation. The police entered the Wilsons's home in the early morning hours, accompanied by a reporter and a photographer from the *Washington Post*. After the search came up empty, the officers left. The Supreme Court held that the officers were not entitled to bring along reporters because they "were not present for any reason related to the justification for the police entry into the home."

Exceptions to the Warrant and Probable Cause Requirements. Under a number of circumstances, a search can be reasonable even when government officials do not have a warrant or probable cause to conduct a search or seizure. Some of these exceptions require government officials to have probable cause, but there are other exceptions where neither a warrant nor probable cause is required. For example, one exception is when exigent circumstances make obtaining a warrant impractical. Another exceptions is when a person consents to a search.

The Fourth Amendment applies not just to law enforcement officials but to all government officials. In some instances, however, searches by officials in certain places may fall under the "special needs" exception. Under this doctrine, searches and seizures are reasonable without a warrant or probable cause if "special needs, beyond the normal need for law enforcement, make the warrant and probable-cause requirement impracticable." *Griffin v. Wisconsin*, 483 U.S. 868 (1987). "The validity of a search is judged by the standard of 'reasonableness . . . under all the circumstances.'" *O'Connor v. Ortega*, 480 U.S. 709 (1987).

Searches that may fall under the "special needs" exception include searches by government employers, public school officials, and public hospital officials. As an example, the Supreme Court has upheld random drug tests for high school students participating in any competitive extracurricular activities, including academic extracurricular activities. *Board of Education v. Earls*, 536 U.S. 822 (2002). The special needs doctrine applies only when a search is not for a law enforcement purpose. Thus, in *New Jersey v. T.L.O.*, the Court upheld a search of a student's purse by school officials and noted that the search was "carried out by school authorities acting alone and on their own authority" as opposed to searches that might be conducted "in conjunction with or at the behest of law enforcement officials." *New Jersey v. T.L.O*, 469 U.S. 337 (1985).

Another exception to the warrant and probable cause requirement is a *Terry* stop. In *Terry v. Ohio,* 392 U.S. 1 (1968), the Court held that a police officer can "stop" an individual if the officer has "reasonable suspicion" that criminal activity is afoot. "Reasonable suspicion" is a standard that is lower than probable cause. A stop must be brief or temporary. If it lasts too long, it becomes a seizure, which requires probable cause. During the stop, the officer may "frisk" an individual for weapons if the officer has reasonable suspicion that the person is armed and dangerous. A frisk is not a full search. The officer cannot search the person for other items — only weapons. If, in the course of searching a person for weapons, the officer finds evidence of a crime, it will still be admissible if it was found within the scope of a valid frisk. For example, in *Minnesota v. Dickerson,* 508 U.S. 366 (1993), a police officer was searching a suspect for weapons and felt an object in the suspect's pocket. The officer did not believe it to be a weapon, but continued to inspect it. The Court concluded that this behavior was an invalid search that extended beyond the limited confines of a frisk.

In addition to *Terry* stops, government officials can engage in certain checkpoint stops and information-seeking stops. For example, fixed sobriety checkpoints are constitutional. *See Michigan Dep't of State Police v. Sitz*, 496 U.S. 444 (1990). Such a checkpoint search does not require "particularized suspicion." On the other hand, in *Delaware v. Prouse*, 440 U.S. 648 (1979), the Court held that the police cannot randomly stop cars to check license and registration. In *Indianapolis v. Edmond*, 531 U.S. 32 (2000), the Court held that checkpoints established to investigate possible drug violations were indistinguishable from a general purpose crime control search and were therefore unconstitutional:

> We have never approved a checkpoint program whose primary purpose was to detect evidence of ordinary criminal wrongdoing. Rather, our checkpoint cases have recognized only limited exceptions to the general rule that a seizure must be accompanied by some measure of individualized suspicion. We suggested in *Prouse* that we would not credit the "general interest in crime control" as justification for a regime of suspicionless stops. Consistent with this suggestion, each of the checkpoint programs that we have approved was designed primarily to serve purposes closely related to the problems of policing the border or the necessity of ensuring roadway safety. Because the primary purpose of the Indianapolis narcotics checkpoint program is to uncover evidence of ordinary criminal wrongdoing, the program contravenes the Fourth Amendment.

The Supreme Court in *Illinois v. Lidster*, 540 U.S. 419 (2004), upheld the constitutionality of so-called "information-seeking highway stops." Following a hit-and-run accident that killed a 70-year-old bicyclist, the police in Lombard, Illinois set up a checkpoint at the approximate scene of the accident. The police stopped vehicles, asked the occupants of the car whether they had seen anything the previous weekend, and gave each driver a flyer that described the fatal accident and asked for assistance in identifying the vehicle and driver in the accident. The Court held that the stop was reasonable. The "relevant public concern was grave," the stops were appropriately tailored to the investigatory need, and the stops were minimal because "each stop required only a brief wait," "[c]ontact with the police lasted only a few seconds," and the "contact provided little reason for anxiety or alarm."

(c) Enforcement: The Exclusionary Rule and Civil Remedies

When law enforcement officials violate an individual's Fourth Amendment rights, the individual can seek at least two forms of redress. First, if the individual is a defendant in a criminal trial, she can move to have the evidence obtained in violation of the Fourth Amendment suppressed. This is known as the "exclusionary rule." In *Weeks v. United States*, 232 U.S. 383 (1914), the Court established the exclusionary rule as the way to enforce the Fourth Amendment on federal officials. Later, in *Mapp v. Ohio*, 367 U.S. 643 (1961), the Court held that the exclusionary rule applies to all government searches, whether state or federal. The purpose of the exclusionary rule is to deter law enforcement officials from violating the Constitution.

If the police illegally search or seize evidence in violation of the Constitution, not only is that evidence suppressed but all other evidence derived from the illegally obtained evidence is also suppressed. This is known as the "fruit of the poisonous tree" doctrine. For example, suppose the police illegally search a person's luggage and find evidence that the person is a drug trafficker. Armed with that evidence, the police obtain a warrant to search the person's home, where they uncover new evidence of drug trafficking along with a weapon used in a murder. The person is charged with drug trafficking and murder. Under the Fourth Amendment, the evidence found in the person's luggage will be suppressed. Additionally, since the search warrant could not have been obtained but for the evidence turned up in the illegal search, the evidence found at the house, including the additional drug trafficking evidence as well as the murder evidence, will be suppressed. However, if the police obtained a warrant or located evidence by an "independent source," then the fruit of the poisonous tree doctrine does not apply. *See Silverthorne Lumber Co. v. United States*, 251 U.S. 385 (1920). Returning to the example above, if the police had evidence supplied from the person's cohort that the person was engaged in drug trafficking out of his home and had murdered somebody, this evidence may suffice to give the police probable cause to have a warrant issued to search the person's house. This evidence is independent from the illegal search, and it is admissible.[3]

The second form of redress for a violation of the Fourth Amendment is a civil remedy. A person, whether a criminal defendant or anybody else, can obtain civil damages for a Fourth Amendment violation by way of 42 U.S.C. § 1983.

(d) Subpoenas and Court Orders

A common means for the government to gather information is through a court order or subpoena. Court orders are specified by statutes or regulations as a protection against unfettered government information gathering. Court orders often have different standards than warrants, which require probable cause. When Fourth Amendment applies to the information gathering, it provides the baseline of protection. If the Fourth Amendment requires a warrant before the government can engage in the specific behavior, the government cannot conduct a search or gather the information under a lesser standard. In instances where the Fourth Amendment does not apply, the standards set forth in a court order (if required by a law) will govern. These standards vary considerably depending upon the particular law that defines them. In many cases, the standards are less stringent than probable cause.

A subpoena is an order to obtain testimony or documents. Numerous statutes authorize federal agencies to issue subpoenas. In *Doe v. Ashcroft,* 334 F. Supp. 2d 471 (S.D.N.Y. 2004), the court explained:

---

[3] The exclusionary rule has received significant scholarly attention. A number of scholars question its efficacy and advocate that the Fourth Amendment be enforced through other mechanisms such as civil sanctions. *See* Akhil Reed Amar, *The Constitution and Criminal Procedure* 28 (1997); Christopher Slobogin, *Why Liberals Should Chuck the Exclusionary Rule*, 1999 U. Ill. L. Rev. 363, 400-01 (1999). Other commentators contend that civil sanctions will be ineffective. *See* Arnold H. Loewy, *The Fourth Amendment as a Device for Protecting the Innocent*, 81 Mich. L. Rev. 1229, 1266 (1983); Tracey Maclin, *When the Cure for the Fourth Amendment Is Worse Than the Disease*, 68 S. Cal. L. Rev. 1, 62 (1994).

For example, the Internal Revenue Service (IRS) may issue subpoenas to investigate possible violations of the tax code, and the Securities Exchange Commission (SEC) may issue subpoenas to investigate possible violations of the securities laws. More obscure examples include the Secretary of Agriculture's power to issue subpoenas in investigating and enforcing laws related to honey research, and the Secretary of Commerce's power to issue subpoenas in investigating and enforcing halibut fishing laws. . . .

Where an agency seeks a court order to enforce a subpoena against a resisting subpoena recipient, courts will enforce the subpoena as long as: (1) the agency's investigation is being conducted pursuant to a legitimate purpose, (2) the inquiry is relevant to that purpose, (3) the information is not already within the agency's possession, and (4) the proper procedures have been followed. The Second Circuit has described these standards as "minimal." Even if an administrative subpoena meets these initial criteria to be enforceable, its recipient may nevertheless affirmatively challenge the subpoena on other grounds, such as an allegation that it was issued with an improper purpose or that the information sought is privileged.

In contrast to an administrative subpoena, an ordinary subpoena may be issued in civil or criminal cases. For criminal cases, the government may obtain a subpoena from the clerk of court. Subpoenas are not issued directly by judges. Instead, "[t]he clerk must issue a blank subpoena — signed and sealed — to the party requesting it, and that party must fill in the blanks before the subpoena is served." Fed. R. Crim. P. 17(a). Failure to comply with a subpoena can lead to contempt of court sanctions. A subpoena can broadly compel the production of various documents and items:

A subpoena may order the witness to produce any books, papers, documents, data, or other objects the subpoena designates. The court may direct the witness to produce the designated items in court before trial or before they are to be offered in evidence. When the items arrive, the court may permit the parties and their attorneys to inspect all or part of them. Fed. R. Crim. P. 17(c)(1).

If the party served with the subpoena has an objection, she may bring a motion to quash or modify the subpoena. "[T]he court may quash or modify the subpoena if compliance would be unreasonable or oppressive." Fed. R. Crim. P. 17(c)(2). As *Doe v. Ashcroft,* 334 F. Supp. 2d 471 (S.D.N.Y. 2004) explains:

The reasonableness of a subpoena depends on the context. For example, to survive a motion to quash, a subpoena issued in connection with a criminal trial "must make a reasonably specific request for information that would be both relevant and admissible at trial." By contrast, a grand jury subpoena is generally enforced as long as there is a "reasonable possibility that the category of materials the Government seeks will produce information relevant to the general subject of the grand jury's investigation." Considering the grand jury's broad investigatory power and minimal court supervision, it is accurate to observe, as the Second Circuit did long ago, that "[b]asically the grand jury is a law enforcement agency."

When do subpoenas violate the Fourth or Fifth Amendments? Subpoenas can compel people to produce documents with incriminating information. One of the early cases addressing this issue was *Boyd v. United States*, 116 U.S. 616 (1886). The government issued a subpoena to compel Boyd, a merchant, to produce invoices on cases of imported glass for use in a civil forfeiture proceeding. The Court held that the subpoena violated the Fourth and Fifth Amendments:

> . . . [B]y the proceeding now under consideration, the court attempts to extort from the party his private books and papers to make him liable for a penalty or to forfeit his property. . . .
>
> . . . It is not the breaking of his doors, and the rummaging of his drawers, that constitutes the essence of the offence; but it is the invasion of his indefeasible right to personal security, personal liberty and private property, where the right has never been forfeited by his conviction of some public offence. . . . Breaking into a house and opening boxes and drawers are circumstances of aggravation; but any forcible and compulsory extortion of a man's own testimony or of his private papers to be used as evidence to convict him of crime or to forfeit his goods, is within the condemnation of that judgment. In this regard the Fourth and Fifth Amendments run almost into each other.

In *Gouled v. United States*, 255 U.S. 298 (1921), the Court held that law enforcement officials could not use search warrants to search a person's "house or office or papers" to obtain evidence to use against her in a criminal proceeding. The holdings of *Boyd* and *Gouled* became known as the "mere evidence" rule — the government could only seize papers if they were instrumentalities of a crime, fruits of a crime, or illegal contraband. This idea was based on a property-based approach to the Fourth Amendment.

The holding in *Boyd* has been significantly cut back. In *Warden v. Hayden*, 387 U.S. 294 (1967), the Court abolished the mere evidence rule. As the Court currently interprets the Fifth Amendment, the government can require a person to produce papers and records. *See Shapiro v. United States*, 335 U.S. 1 (1948). The Fifth Amendment also does not protect against subpoenas for a person's records and papers held by third parties. In *Couch v. United States*, 409 U.S. 322 (1973), the Court upheld a subpoena to a person's accountant for documents because "the Fifth Amendment privilege is a personal privilege: it adheres basically to the person, not to information that may incriminate him." The Fifth Amendment, the Court reasoned, only prevents "[i]nquisitorial pressure or coercion against a potentially accused person, compelling her, against her will, to utter self-condemning words or produce incriminating documents." Similarly, in *Fisher v. United States*, 425 U.S. 391 (1976), the Court upheld a subpoena to a person's attorney for documents pertaining to that person. The Fifth Amendment is not a "general protector of privacy" but protects against the "compelled self-incrimination."

Cases expanding the government's ability to use subpoenas to gather information used to maintain a distinction between corporate records (which could be obtained via subpoena) and personal papers (which could not). Christopher Slobogin observes that the Court gradually abandoned this distinction.[4]

In *United States v. Dionisio*, 410 U.S. 1 (1973), the Court held that the Fourth Amendment does not restrict a grand jury subpoena to produce documents (subpoena duces tecum) or to testify:

---

[4] For an excellent history of the Supreme Court's jurisprudence regarding subpoenas, see Christopher Slobogin, *Subpoenas and Privacy,* 53 DePaul L. Rev. 805 (2005).

It is clear that a subpoena to appear before a grand jury is not a 'seizure' in the Fourth Amendment sense, even though that summons may be inconvenient or burdensome. . . .

The compulsion exerted by a grand jury subpoena differs from the seizure effected by an arrest or even an investigative 'stop' in more than civic obligation. For, as Judge Friendly wrote for the Court of Appeals for the Second Circuit: "The latter is abrupt, is effected with force or the threat of it and often in demeaning circumstances, and, in the case of arrest, results in a record involving social stigma. A subpoena is served in the same manner as other legal process; it involves no stigma whatever; if the time for appearance is inconvenient, this can generally be altered; and it remains at all times under the control and supervision of a court."

Thus the Court of Appeals for the Seventh Circuit correctly recognized in a case subsequent to the one now before us, that a 'grand jury subpoena to testify is not that kind of governmental intrusion on privacy against which the Fourth Amendment affords protection once the Fifth Amendment is satisfied.'

The Court was not quite ready to conclude that subpoenas fall entirely outside the Fourth Amendment, stating that "[t]he Fourth Amendment provides protection against a grand jury subpoena duces tecum too sweeping in its terms 'to be regarded as reasonable.'"

2. WIRETAPPING, BUGGING, AND BEYOND

At common law, eavesdropping was considered a nuisance. "Eavesdropping," as William Blackstone defined it, meant to "listen under walls or window, or the eaves of a house, to hearken after discourse, and thereupon to frame slanderous and mischievous tales."[5] Before the advent of electronic communication, people could easily avoid eavesdroppers by ensuring that nobody else was around during their conversations.

The invention of the telegraph in 1844 followed by the telephone in 1876 substantially altered the way people communicated with each other. Today, the telephone has become an essential part of everyday communications. The advent of electronic communications was soon followed by the invention of recording and transmitting devices that enabled new and more sophisticated forms of eavesdropping than overhearing a conversation with the naked ear. One feature of electronic surveillance is that unlike the unsealing of letters, the interception of communications is undetectable. Some of the current forms of electronic surveillance technology include wiretaps, bugs, and parabolic microphones. New legal questions are raised by modern technology such as a cell phone, which can provide information about the physical location of the person using it.

A "wiretap" is a device used to intercept telephone (or telegraph) communications. Wiretapping began before the invention of the telephone. Wiretapping was used to intercept telegraph communications during the Civil War and became very prevalent after the invention of the telephone. The first police wiretap occurred in the early 1890s. In the first half of the twentieth century, wiretaps proliferated due to law enforcement attempts to monitor protests over bad

---

[5] 4 Blackstone, *Commentaries* 168 (1769).

industrial working conditions, social unrest caused by World War I, and the smuggling of alcohol during the Prohibition Years.[6]

A "bug" is a device, often quite miniature in size, that can be hidden on a person or in a place that can transmit conversations in a room to a remote receiving device, where the conversation can be listened to.

A "parabolic microphone" can pick up a conversation from a distance. Typically, a small dish behind the microphone enables the amplification of sound far away from the microphone itself.

Electronic surveillance devices were not in existence at the time that the Fourth Amendment was drafted. How, then, should the Fourth Amendment regulate these devices? In 1928, the Supreme Court attempted to answer this question in *Olmstead v. United States*, the first electronic surveillance case to come before the Court.

OLMSTEAD V. UNITED STATES

277 U.S. 438 (1928)

TAFT, C.J. The petitioners were convicted in the District Court for the Western District of Washington of a conspiracy to violate the National Prohibition Act by unlawfully possessing, transporting and importing intoxicating liquors and maintaining nuisances, and by selling intoxicating liquors. Seventy-two others, in addition to the petitioners, were indicted. Some were not apprehended, some were acquitted, and others pleaded guilty. . . .

The information which led to the discovery of the conspiracy and its nature and extent was largely obtained by intercepting messages on the telephones of the conspirators by four federal prohibition officers. Small wires were inserted along the ordinary telephone wires from the residences of four of the petitioners and those leading from the chief office. The insertions were made without trespass upon any property of the defendants. They were made in the basement of the large office building. The taps from house lines were made in the streets near the houses. . . .

The well-known historical purpose of the Fourth Amendment, directed against general warrants and writs of assistance, was to prevent the use of governmental force to search a man's house, his person, his papers, and his effects, and to prevent their seizure against his will. This phase of the misuse of governmental power of compulsion is the emphasis of the opinion of the court in the *Boyd* Case. . . .

. . . The Fourth Amendment may have proper application to a sealed letter in the mail, because of the constitutional provision for the Post Office Department and the relations between the government and those who pay to secure protection of their sealed letters. . . . It is plainly within the words of the amendment to say that the unlawful rifling by a government agent of a sealed letter is a search and

---

[6] For more background on the history of wiretapping, see generally Robert Ellis Smith, *Ben Franklin's Web Site: Privacy and Curiosity from Plymouth Rock to the Internet* (2000); Priscilla M. Regan, *Legislating Privacy: Technology, Social Values, and Public Policy* (1995); James G. Carr, *The Law of Electronic Surveillance* (1994); Whitfield Diffie & Susan Landau, *Privacy on the Line: The Politics of Wiretapping and Encryption* (1998).

seizure of the sender's papers or effects. The letter is a paper, an effect, and in the custody of a government that forbids carriage, except under its protection.

The United States takes no such care of telegraph or telephone messages as of mailed sealed letters. The amendment does not forbid what was done here. There was no searching. There was no seizure. The evidence was secured by the use of the sense of hearing and that only. There was no entry of the houses or offices of the defendants. . . .

The language of the amendment cannot be extended and expanded to include telephone wires, reaching to the whole world from the defendant's house or office. The intervening wires are not part of his house or office, any more than are the highways along which they are stretched. . . .

Congress may, of course, protect the secrecy of telephone messages by making them, when intercepted, inadmissible in evidence in federal criminal trials, by direct legislation, and thus depart from the common law of evidence. But the courts may not adopt such a policy by attributing an enlarged and unusual meaning to the Fourth Amendment. The reasonable view is that one who installs in his house a telephone instrument with connecting wires intends to project his voice to those quite outside, and that the wires beyond his house, and messages while passing over them, are not within the protection of the Fourth Amendment. Here those who intercepted the projected voices were not in the house of either party to the conversation. . . .

BRANDEIS, J. dissenting. The government makes no attempt to defend the methods employed by its officers. Indeed, it concedes that, if wire tapping can be deemed a search and seizure within the Fourth Amendment, such wire tapping as was practiced in the case at bar was an unreasonable search and seizure, and that the evidence thus obtained was inadmissible. But it relies on the language of the amendment, and it claims that the protection given thereby cannot properly be held to include a telephone conversation.

"We must never forget," said Mr. Chief Justice Marshall in *McCulloch v. Maryland*, "that it is a Constitution we are expounding." Since then this court has repeatedly sustained the exercise of power by Congress, under various clauses of that instrument, over objects of which the fathers could not have dreamed. We have likewise held that general limitations on the powers of government, like those embodied in the due process clauses of the Fifth and Fourteenth Amendments, do not forbid the United States or the states from meeting modern conditions by regulations which "a century ago, or even half a century ago, probably would have been rejected as arbitrary and oppressive." Clauses guaranteeing to the individual protection against specific abuses of power, must have a similar capacity of adaptation to a changing world. It was with reference to such a clause that this court said in *Weems v. United States*, 217 U.S. 349, 373:

> Legislation, both statutory and constitutional, is enacted, it is true, from an experience of evils, but its general language should not, therefore, be necessarily confined to the form that evil had theretofore taken. Time works changes, brings into existence new conditions and purposes. Therefore a principle to be vital must be capable of wider application than the mischief which gave it birth. This is peculiarly true of Constitutions. They are not ephemeral enactments, designed to meet passing occasions. They are, to use the words of Chief Justice Marshall,

"designed to approach immortality as nearly as human institutions can approach it." The future is their care and provision for events of good and bad tendencies of which no prophecy can be made. In the application of a Constitution, therefore, our contemplation cannot be only of what has been but of what may be. Under any other rule a Constitution would indeed be as easy of application as it would be deficient in efficacy and power. Its general principles would have little value and be converted by precedent into impotent and lifeless formulas. Rights declared in words might be lost in reality.

When the Fourth and Fifth Amendments were adopted, "the form that evil had theretofore taken" had been necessarily simple. Force and violence were then the only means known to man by which a government could directly effect self-incrimination. It could compel the individual to testify — a compulsion effected, if need be, by torture. It could secure possession of his papers and other articles incident to his private life — a seizure effected, if need be, by breaking and entry. Protection against such invasion of "the sanctities of a man's home and the privacies of life" was provided in the Fourth and Fifth Amendments by specific language. *Boyd v. United States*, 116 U.S. 616 (1886). But "time works changes, brings into existence new conditions and purposes." Subtler and more far-reaching means of invading privacy have become available to the government. Discovery and invention have made it possible for the government, by means far more effective than stretching upon the rack, to obtain disclosure in court of what is whispered in the closet.

Moreover, "in the application of a Constitution, our contemplation cannot be only of what has been, but of what may be." The progress of science in furnishing the government with means of espionage is not likely to stop with wire tapping. Ways may some day be developed by which the government, without removing papers from secret drawers, can reproduce them in court, and by which it will be enabled to expose to a jury the most intimate occurrences of the home. Advances in the psychic and related sciences may bring means of exploring unexpressed beliefs, thoughts and emotions. "That places the liberty of every man in the hands of every petty officer" was said by James Otis of much lesser intrusions than these. To Lord Camden a far slighter intrusion seemed "subversive of all the comforts of society." Can it be that the Constitution affords no protection against such invasions of individual security?

A sufficient answer is found in *Boyd v. United States*, 116 U.S. 616 (1886), a case that will be remembered as long as civil liberty lives in the United States. This court there reviewed the history that lay behind the Fourth and Fifth Amendments. We said with reference to Lord Camden's judgment in *Entick v. Carrington*, 19 Howell's State Trials, 1030:

> The principles laid down in this opinion affect the very essence of constitutional liberty and security. They reach farther than the concrete form of the case there before the court, with its adventitious circumstances; they apply to all invasions on the part of the government and its employees of the sanctities of a man's home and the privacies of life. It is not the breaking of his doors, and the rummaging of his drawers, that constitutes the essence of the offense; but it is the invasion of his indefeasible right of personal security, personal liberty and private property, where that right has never been forfeited by his conviction of some public offense — it is the invasion of this sacred right which

underlies and constitutes the essence of Lord Camden's judgment. Breaking into a house and opening boxes and drawers are circumstances of aggravation; but any forcible and compulsory extortion of a man's own testimony or of his private papers to be used as evidence of a crime or to forfeit his goods, is within the condemnation of that judgment. In this regard the Fourth and Fifth Amendments run almost into each other.

In *Ex parte Jackson*, 96 U.S. 727 (1877), it was held that a sealed letter entrusted to the mail is protected by the amendments. The mail is a public service furnished by the government. The telephone is a public service furnished by its authority. There is, in essence, no difference between the sealed letter and the private telephone message. . . .

The evil incident to invasion of the privacy of the telephone is far greater than that involved in tampering with the mails. Whenever a telephone line is tapped, the privacy of the persons at both ends of the line is invaded, and all conversations between them upon any subject, and although proper, confidential, and privileged, may be overheard. Moreover, the tapping of one man's telephone line involves the tapping of the telephone of every other person whom he may call, or who may call him. As a means of espionage, writs of assistance and general warrants are but puny instruments of tyranny and oppression when compared with wire tapping.

Time and again this court, in giving effect to the principle underlying the Fourth Amendment, has refused to place an unduly literal construction upon it. . .

The protection guaranteed by the amendments is much broader in scope. The makers of our Constitution undertook to secure conditions favorable to the pursuit of happiness. They recognized the significance of man's spiritual nature, of his feelings and of his intellect. They knew that only a part of the pain, pleasure and satisfactions of life are to be found in material things. They sought to protect Americans in their beliefs, their thoughts, their emotions and their sensations. They conferred, as against the government, the right to be let alone — the most comprehensive of rights and the right most valued by civilized men. To protect that right, every unjustifiable intrusion by the government upon the privacy of the individual, whatever the means employed, must be deemed a violation of the Fourth Amendment. And the use, as evidence in a criminal proceeding, of facts ascertained by such intrusion must be deemed a violation of the Fifth.

Applying to the Fourth and Fifth Amendments the established rule of construction, the defendants' objections to the evidence obtained by wire tapping must, in my opinion, be sustained. It is, of course, immaterial where the physical connection with the telephone wires leading into the defendants' premises was made. And it is also immaterial that the intrusion was in aid of law enforcement. Experience should teach us to be most on our guard to protect liberty when the government's purposes are beneficent. Men born to freedom are naturally alert to repel invasion of their liberty by evil-minded rulers. The greatest dangers to liberty lurk in insidious encroachment by men of zeal, well-meaning but without understanding. . . .

NOTES & QUESTIONS

1. ***Background and Epilogue.*** Roy Olmstead was known as the "King of Bootleggers" as well as "the good bootlegger." The latter reflected his

abhorrence of violence, his refusal to traffic in drugs or become involved in prostitution, and his philosophy of not diluting his wares. Olmstead ran a gigantic illegal alcohol distribution operation on the Pacific Coast during Prohibition. Formerly a police officer, Olmstead had long avoided trouble with state police by bribing them, but federal officials soon caught up with him. The federal investigators, led by Roy Lyle, Director of Prohibition, were wiretapping all of the telephones in Olmstead's communication headquarters for around five months. The case was widely followed in the press, and it was dubbed "the case of the whispering wires."

Olmstead was careful not to leave evidence in his very large home; when the agents searched it, they turned up no evidence. Most of the evidence in the case came from the wiretaps. Olmstead knew he was being wiretapped; in his account, the government's freelance wiretapper tried, at one point, to sell him the wiretap transcripts for ten thousand dollars. But Olmstead believed that because wiretapping was illegal in the state of Washington, the wiretap evidence could not be used against him at trial. He was wrong.

At trial, Olmstead was convicted and sentenced to four years in prison. After Olmstead served his full sentence, President Roosevelt in 1935 pardoned him, which restored his full rights as a citizen. In an ironic twist, while Olmstead was in prison, Roy Lyle was arrested for conspiring with rumrunners. Olmstead testified against Lyle at Lyle's trial. While in prison, Olmstead became a Christian Scientist and stopped drinking alcohol. After his release, he even repudiated alcohol as one of the ills of society.[7]

2. ***The Physical Trespass Doctrine, Detectaphones, and "Spike Mikes."*** In *Olmstead,* the Supreme Court concluded that Fourth Amendment protections are triggered only when there is a physical trespass. The Court followed this approach for nearly 40 years. In *Goldman v. United States*, 316 U.S. 129 (1942), the police placed a device called a "detectaphone" next to a wall adjacent to a person's office. The device enabled the police to listen in on conversations inside the office. The Court concluded that since there was no trespass, there was no Fourth Amendment violation.

In *Silverman v. United States*, 365 U.S. 505 (1961), the police used a device called a "spike mike" to listen in from a vacant row house to conversations in an adjoining row house. The device consisted of a microphone with a spike of about a foot in length attached to it. The spike was inserted into a baseboard of the vacant row house on the wall adjoining the row house next door. The spike hit the heating duct serving the next-door row house, which transformed the heating system into a sound conductor. The Court held that the use of the "spike mike" violated the Fourth Amendment because it constituted an "unauthorized physical encroachment" into the adjoining row house. The Court distinguished *Olmstead* and *Goldman* because those cases did not

[7] Karen Abbott, *The Bootlegger, the Wiretap, and the Beginning of Privacy*, New Yorker (July 5, 2017); Samuel Dash, *The Intruders: Unreasonable Searches and Seizures from King John to John Ashcroft* 74-78 (2004); Robert C. Post, *Federalism, Positive Law, and the Emergence of the American Administrative State: Prohibition in the Taft Court Era*, 48 Wm. & Mary L. Rev. 1, 139-50 (2006).

involve any "physical invasion" or "trespass" onto the defendant's property, whereas the "spike mike" "usurp[ed] part of the [defendant's] house or office." Do you agree with the Court's distinction between *Goldman/Olmstead* and *Silverman* — between surveillance involving physical intrusion (however slight) and surveillance not involving any trespassing on the premises?

3. ***Brandeis's Dissent and the Warren and Brandeis Article.*** Justice Brandeis's dissent is one of the most famous dissents in Supreme Court history. Note the similarities between Brandeis's 1890 article, *The Right to Privacy*, and his dissent nearly 40 years later in *Olmstead*. What themes are repeated? Recall that *The Right to Privacy* concerned locating common law roots for privacy protection. What is Brandeis saying about the roots of constitutional protection of privacy?

4. ***Changing Technology and the Constitution.*** Brandeis contends that the Constitution should keep pace with changing technology. But given the rapid pace of technological change and the fact that the Constitution must serve as the stable foundation for our society, can the Constitution keep pace? How adaptable should the Constitution be?

5. ***Wiretapping vs. Mail Tampering.*** Brandeis contends that wiretapping is more insidious than tampering with the mail. Why? How would you compare wiretapping with intercepting e-mail or instant messages?

6. ***State Wiretapping Law.*** In the state of Washington, where the wiretapping in *Olmstead* took place, wiretapping was a criminal act, and the officers had thus violated the law. In a separate dissenting opinion, Justice Holmes noted that:

> . . . [A]part from the Constitution the government ought not to use evidence obtained and only obtainable by a criminal act. . . . It is desirable that criminals should be detected, and to that end that all available evidence should be used. It also is desirable that the government should not itself foster and pay for other crimes, when they are the means by which the evidence is to be obtained. If it pays its officers for having got evidence by crime I do not see why it may not as well pay them for getting it in the same way, and I can attach no importance to protestations of disapproval if it knowingly accepts and pays and announces that in future it will pay for the fruits. We have to choose, and for my part I think it a less evil that some criminals should escape than that the government should play an ignoble part.

Should it matter in Fourth Amendment analysis whether particular federal law enforcement surveillance tactics are illegal under state law?

7. ***The Birth of Federal Electronic Surveillance Law.*** The *Olmstead* decision was not well received by the public. In 1934, Congress responded to *Olmstead* by enacting § 605 of the Federal Communications Act, making wiretapping a federal crime. This statute will be discussed later in the part on electronic surveillance law.

8. ***Secret Agents and Misplaced Trust.*** In *Hoffa v. United States*, 385 U.S. 293 (1966), an undercover informant, Edward Partin, befriended James Hoffa and elicited statements from him about his plans to bribe jurors in a criminal trial in which Hoffa was a defendant. According to the Court:

In the present case . . . it is evident that no interest legitimately protected by the Fourth Amendment is involved. It is obvious that the petitioner was not relying on the security of his hotel suite when he made the incriminating statements to Partin or in Partin's presence. Partin did not enter the suite by force or by stealth. He was not a surreptitious eavesdropper. Partin was in the suite by invitation, and every conversation which he heard was either directed to him or knowingly carried on in his presence. The petitioner, in a word, was not relying on the security of the hotel room; he was relying upon his misplaced confidence that Partin would not reveal his wrongdoing.

Likewise, in *Lewis v. United States*, 385 U.S. 206 (1966), the defendant sold drugs to an undercover agent in his house. The Court held:

In the instant case . . . the petitioner invited the undercover agent to his home for the specific purpose of executing a felonious sale of narcotics. Petitioner's only concern was whether the agent was a willing purchaser who could pay the agreed price. . . . During neither of his visits to petitioner's home did the agent see, hear, or take anything that was not contemplated, and in fact intended, by petitioner as a necessary part of his illegal business. Were we to hold the deceptions of the agent in this case constitutionally prohibited, we would come near to a rule that the use of undercover agents in any manner is virtually unconstitutional per se. Such a rule would, for example, severely hamper the Government in ferreting out those organized criminal activities that are characterized by covert dealings with victims who either cannot or do not protest. A prime example is provided by the narcotics traffic. . . .

Hoffa and *Lewis* establish that a person does not have a privacy interest in the loyalty of her friends. The government may deceive a person by sending in secret agents to befriend her. Is it problematic that government is permitted to use spies and deception as a law enforcement technique? Consider the following observation by Anthony Amsterdam:

I can see no significant difference between police spies . . . and electronic surveillance, either in their uses or abuses. Both have long been asserted by law enforcement officers to be indispensable tools in investigating crime, particularly victimless and political crime, precisely because they both search out privacies that government could not otherwise invade. Both tend to repress crime in the same way, by making people distrustful and unwilling to talk to one another. The only difference is that under electronic surveillance you are afraid to talk to anybody in your office or over the phone, while under a spy system you are afraid to talk to anybody at all.[8]

9. ***Bugs, Transmitters, and Recording Devices.*** In *On Lee v. United States*, 343 U.S. 747 (1952), Chin Poy, a government informant with a concealed transmitter, engaged On Lee in conversation for the purpose of eliciting that On Lee was a drug dealer. The conversation was transmitted to a law enforcement agent, who later testified at trial about the content of the conversation. The Court held that the Fourth Amendment did not apply:

---

[8] Anthony G. Amsterdam, *Perspectives on the Fourth Amendment*, 58 Minn. L. Rev. 349, 407 (1974). For a detailed analysis of undercover agents, see Gary T. Marx, *Under Cover: Police Surveillance in America* (1988).

Petitioner was talking confidentially and indiscreetly with one he trusted, and he was overheard. This was due to aid from a transmitter and receiver, to be sure, but with the same effect on his privacy as if agent Lee had been eavesdropping outside an open window. The use of bifocals, field glasses or the telescope to magnify the object of a witness' vision is not a forbidden search or seizure, even if they focus without his knowledge or consent upon what one supposes to be private indiscretions. It would be a dubious service to the genuine liberties protected by the Fourth Amendment to make them bedfellows with spurious liberties improvised by farfetched analogies which would liken eavesdropping on a conversation, with the connivance of one of the parties, to an unreasonable search or seizure. We find no violation of the Fourth Amendment here.

Does the use of electronic devices distinguish *On Lee* from *Hoffa* and *Lewis* in a material way?

LOPEZ V. UNITED STATES

373 U.S. 427 (1963)

[The petitioner, German S. Lopez, was tried in a federal court on a four-count indictment charging him with attempted bribery of an Internal Revenue agent, Roger S. Davis. The evidence against him had been obtained by a series of meetings between him and Davis. The last meeting was recorded by Davis with a pocket wire recorder. Prior to trial, Lopez moved to suppress the recorded conversation.]

HARLAN, J. . . . [Petitioner's] argument is primarily addressed to the recording of the conversation, which he claims was obtained in violation of his rights under the Fourth Amendment. Recognizing the weakness of this position if Davis was properly permitted to testify about the same conversation, petitioner now challenges that testimony as well, although he failed to do so at the trial. . . .

Once it is plain that Davis could properly testify about his conversation with Lopez, the constitutional claim relating to the recording of that conversation emerges in proper perspective. The Court has in the past sustained instances of "electronic eavesdropping" against constitutional challenge, when devices have been used to enable government agents to overhear conversations which would have been beyond the reach of the human ear. *See, e.g., Olmstead v. United States.* It has been insisted only that the electronic device not be planted by an unlawful physical invasion of a constitutionally protected area. . . . Indeed this case involves no "eavesdropping" whatever in any proper sense of that term. The Government did not use an electronic device to listen in on conversations it could not otherwise have heard. Instead, the device was used only to obtain the most reliable evidence possible of a conversation in which the Government's own agent was a participant and which that agent was fully entitled to disclose. And the device was not planted by means of an unlawful physical invasion of petitioner's premises under circumstances which would violate the Fourth Amendment. It was carried in and out by an agent who was there with petitioner's assent, and it neither saw nor heard more than the agent himself. . . .

Stripped to its essentials, petitioner's argument amounts to saying that he has a constitutional right to rely on possible flaws in the agent's memory, or to challenge the agent's credibility without being beset by corroborating evidence that is not susceptible of impeachment. For no other argument can justify excluding an accurate version of a conversation that the agent could testify to from memory. We think the risk that petitioner took in offering a bribe to Davis fairly included the risk that the offer would be accurately reproduced in court, whether by faultless memory or mechanical recording. . . .

WARREN, C.J. concurring. I also share the opinion of Mr. Justice Brennan that the fantastic advances in the field of electronic communication constitute a great danger to the privacy of the individual; that indiscriminate use of such devices in law enforcement raises grave constitutional questions under the Fourth and Fifth Amendments; and that these considerations impose a heavier responsibility on this Court in its supervision of the fairness of procedures in the federal court system. However, I do not believe that, as a result, all uses of such devices should be proscribed either as unconstitutional or as unfair law enforcement methods. One of the lines I would draw would be between this case and *On Lee*. . . .

The use and purpose of the transmitter in *On Lee* was substantially different from the use of the recorder here. Its advantage was not to corroborate the testimony of Chin Poy, but rather, to obviate the need to put him on the stand. The Court in *On Lee* itself stated:

> We can only speculate on the reasons why Chin Poy was not called. It seems a not unlikely assumption that the very defects of character and blemishes of record which made On Lee trust him with confidences would make a jury distrust his testimony. Chin Poy was close enough to the underworld to serve as bait, near enough the criminal design so that petitioner would embrace him as a confidante, but too close to it for the Government to vouch for him as a witness. Instead, the Government called agent Lee.

However, there were further advantages in not using Chin Poy. Had Chin Poy been available for cross-examination, counsel for On Lee could have explored the nature of Chin Poy's friendship with On Lee, the possibility of other unmonitored conversations and appeals to friendship, the possibility of entrapments, police pressure brought to bear to persuade Chin Poy to turn informer, and Chin Poy's own recollection of the contents of the conversation. . . .

Thus while I join the Court in permitting the use of electronic devices to corroborate an agent under the particular facts of this case, I cannot sanction by implication the use of these same devices to radically shift the pattern of presentation of evidence in the criminal trial, a shift that may be used to conceal substantial factual and legal issues concerning the rights of the accused and the administration of criminal justice.

BRENNAN, J. joined by DOUGLAS and GOLDBERG, JJ. dissenting. . . . [T]he Government's argument is that Lopez surrendered his right of privacy when he communicated his "secret thoughts" to Agent Davis. The assumption, manifestly untenable, is that the Fourth Amendment is only designed to protect secrecy. If a person commits his secret thoughts to paper, that is no license for the police to seize the paper; if a person communicates his secret thoughts verbally to another, that is no license for the police to record the words. *On Lee* certainly rested on no such theory of waiver. The right of privacy would mean little if it were limited to a person's solitary thoughts, and so fostered secretiveness. It must embrace a concept of the liberty of one's communications, and historically it has. "The common law secures to each individual the right of determining, ordinarily, to what extent his thoughts, sentiments, and emotions shall be communicated to others . . . and even if he has chosen to give them expression, he generally retains the power to fix the limits of the publicity which shall be given them." Warren and Brandeis, *The Right to Privacy*, 4 Harv. L. Rev. 193, 198 (1890).

That is not to say that all communications are privileged. On Lee assumed the risk that his acquaintance would divulge their conversation; Lopez assumed the same risk vis-à-vis Davis. The risk inheres in all communications which are not in the sight of the law privileged. It is not an undue risk to ask persons to assume, for it does no more than compel them to use discretion in choosing their auditors, to make damaging disclosures only to persons whose character and motives may be trusted. But the risk which both *On Lee* and today's decision impose is of a different order. It is the risk that third parties, whether mechanical auditors like the Minifon or human transcribers of mechanical transmissions as in *On Lee* — third parties who cannot be shut out of a conversation as conventional eavesdroppers can be, merely by a lowering of voices, or withdrawing to a private place — may give independent evidence of any conversation. There is only one way to guard against such a risk, and that is to keep one's mouth shut on all occasions. . . .

The risk of being overheard by an eavesdropper or betrayed by an informer or deceived as to the identity of one with whom one deals is probably inherent in the conditions of human society. It is the kind of risk we necessarily assume whenever we speak. But as soon as electronic surveillance comes into play, the risk changes crucially. There is no security from that kind of eavesdropping, no way of mitigating the risk, and so not even a residuum of true privacy. . . .

NOTES & QUESTIONS

1. *Is Electronic Surveillance Different?* Should electronic surveillance be treated similarly or differently than regular eavesdropping? Is it consistent to agree that Davis could testify as to what Lopez said via his memory but cannot introduce a recording of what Lopez said?

KATZ V. UNITED STATES

389 U.S. 347 (1967)

STEWART, J. The petitioner was convicted in the District Court for the Southern District of California under an eight-count indictment charging him with transmitting wagering information by telephone from Los Angeles to Miami and

Boston in violation of a federal statute. At trial the Government was permitted, over the petitioner's objection, to introduce evidence of the petitioner's end of telephone conversations, overheard by FBI agents who had attached an electronic listening and recording device to the outside of the public telephone booth from which he had placed his calls. In affirming his conviction, the Court of Appeals rejected the contention that the recordings had been obtained in violation of the Fourth Amendment, because "[t]here was no physical entrance into the area occupied by, (the petitioner)." We granted certiorari in order to consider the constitutional questions thus presented.

The petitioner had phrased those questions as follows:

A. Whether a public telephone booth is a constitutionally protected area so that evidence obtained by attaching an electronic listening recording device to the top of such a booth is obtained in violation of the right to privacy of the user of the booth.

B. Whether physical penetration of a constitutionally protected area is necessary before a search and seizure can be said to be violative of the Fourth Amendment to the United States Constitution.

We decline to adopt this formulation of the issues. In the first place the correct solution of Fourth Amendment problems is not necessarily promoted by incantation of the phrase "constitutionally protected area." Secondly, the Fourth Amendment cannot be translated into a general constitutional "right to privacy." That Amendment protects individual privacy against certain kinds of governmental intrusion, but its protections go further, and often have nothing to do with privacy at all. Other provisions of the Constitution protect personal privacy from other forms of governmental invasion. But the protection of a person's general right to privacy — his right to be let alone by other people — is, like the protection of his property and of his very life, left largely to the law of the individual States.

Because of the misleading way the issues have been formulated, the parties have attached great significance to the characterization of the telephone booth from which the petitioner placed his calls. The petitioner has strenuously argued that the booth was a "constitutionally protected area." The Government has maintained with equal vigor that it was not. But this effort to decide whether or not a given "area," viewed in the abstract, is "constitutionally protected" deflects attention from the problem presented by this case. For the Fourth Amendment protects people, not places. What a person knowingly exposes to the public, even in his own home or office, is not a subject of Fourth Amendment protection. But what he seeks to preserve as private, even in an area accessible to the public, may be constitutionally protected.

The Government stresses the fact that the telephone booth from which the petitioner made his calls was constructed partly of glass, so that he was as visible after he entered it as he would have been if he had remained outside. But what he sought to exclude when he entered the booth was not the intruding eye — it was the uninvited ear. He did not shed his right to do so simply because he made his calls from a place where he might be seen. No less than an individual in a business office, in a friend's apartment, or in a taxicab, a person in a telephone booth may rely upon the protection of the Fourth Amendment. One who occupies it, shuts the door behind him, and pays the toll that permits him to place a call is surely entitled to assume that the words he utters into the mouthpiece will not be broadcast to the world. To read the Constitution more narrowly is to ignore the vital role that the public telephone has come to play in private communication.

The Government contends, however, that the activities of its agents in this case should not be tested by Fourth Amendment requirements, for the surveillance technique they employed involved no physical penetration of the telephone booth from which the petitioner placed his calls. It is true that the absence of such penetration was at one time thought to foreclose further Fourth Amendment inquiry, *Olmstead v. United States*, *Goldman v. United States*, for that Amendment was thought to limit only searches and seizures of tangible property. But "[t]he premise that property interests control the right of the Government to search and seize has been discredited." . . . [O]nce this much is acknowledged, and once it is recognized that the Fourth Amendment protects people — and not simply "areas" — against unreasonable searches and seizures it becomes clear that the reach of that Amendment cannot turn upon the presence or absence of a physical intrusion into any given enclosure.

We conclude that the underpinnings of *Olmstead* and *Goldman* have been so eroded by our subsequent decisions that the "trespass" doctrine there enunciated can no longer be regarded as controlling. . . .

The question remaining for decision, then, is whether the search and seizure conducted in this case complied with constitutional standards. In that regard, the Government's position is that its agents acted in an entirely defensible manner: They did not begin their electronic surveillance until investigation of the petitioner's activities had established a strong probability that he was using the telephone in question to transmit gambling information to persons in other States, in violation of federal law. Moreover, the surveillance was limited, both in scope and in duration, to the specific purpose of establishing the contents of the petitioner's unlawful telephonic communications. The agents confined their surveillance to the brief periods during which he used the telephone booth, and they took great care to overhear only the conversations of the petitioner himself. . . .

. . . It is apparent that the agents in this case acted with restraint. Yet the inescapable fact is that this restraint was imposed by the agents themselves, not by a judicial officer. They were not required, before commencing the search, to present their estimate of probable cause for detached scrutiny by a neutral magistrate. They were not compelled, during the conduct of the search itself, to observe precise limits established in advance by a specific court order. Nor were they directed, after the search had been completed, to notify the authorizing magistrate in detail of all that had been seized. In the absence of such safeguards, this Court has never sustained a search upon the sole ground that officers reasonably expected to find evidence of a particular crime and voluntarily confined their activities to the least intrusive means consistent with that end. Searches conducted without warrants have been held unlawful "notwithstanding facts unquestionably showing probable cause." . . . "Over and again this Court has emphasized that the mandate of the [Fourth] Amendment requires adherence to judicial processes," and that searches conducted outside the judicial process, without prior approval by judge or magistrate, are per se unreasonable under the

Fourth Amendment — subject only to a few specifically established and well-delineated exceptions. . . .

HARLAN, J. concurring. . . . As the Court's opinion states, "the Fourth Amendment protects people, not places." The question, however, is what protection it affords to those people. Generally, as here, the answer to that question requires reference to a "place." My understanding of the rule that has emerged from prior decisions is that there is a twofold requirement, first that a person have exhibited an actual (subjective) expectation of privacy and, second, that the expectation be one that society is prepared to recognize as "reasonable." Thus a man's home is, for most purposes, a place where he expects privacy, but objects, activities, or statements that he exposes to the "plain view" of outsiders are not "protected" because no intention to keep them to himself has been exhibited. On the other hand, conversations in the open would not be protected against being overheard, for the expectation of privacy under the circumstances would be unreasonable.

The critical fact in this case is that "(o)ne who occupies it, (a telephone booth) shuts the door behind him, and pays the toll that permits him to place a call is surely entitled to assume" that his conversation is not being intercepted. The point is not that the booth is "accessible to the public" at other times, but that it is a temporarily private place whose momentary occupants' expectations of freedom from intrusion are recognized as reasonable.

BLACK, J. dissenting. . . . My basic objection is twofold: (1) I do not believe that the words of the Amendment will bear the meaning given them by today's decision, and (2) I do not believe that it is the proper role of this Court to rewrite the Amendment in order "to bring it into harmony with the times" and thus reach a result that many people believe to be desirable.

While I realize that an argument based on the meaning of words lacks the scope, and no doubt the appeal, of broad policy discussions and philosophical discourses on such nebulous subjects as privacy, for me the language of the Amendment is the crucial place to look in construing a written document such as our Constitution. The Fourth Amendment says that

> The right of the people to be secure in their persons, houses, papers, and effects, against unreasonable searches and seizures, shall not be violated, and no Warrants shall issue, but upon probable cause, supported by Oath or affirmation, and particularly describing the place to be searched, and the persons or things to be seized.

The first clause protects "persons, houses, papers, and effects, against unreasonable searches and seizures. . . ." These words connote the idea of tangible things with size, form, and weight, things capable of being searched, seized, or both. The second clause of the Amendment still further establishes its Framers' purpose to limit its protection to tangible things by providing that no warrants shall issue but those "particularly describing the place to be searched, and the persons or things to be seized." A conversation overheard by eavesdropping, whether by plain snooping or wiretapping, is not tangible and, under the normally accepted meanings of the words, can neither be searched nor seized. . . .

NOTES & QUESTIONS

1. *Who Was Charlie Katz?* David Sklansky describes the background to *Katz*:

> Charlie Katz was a Damon Runyon character plopped into 1960s Los Angeles. Katz was a professional bettor . . . Katz wagered on sports events, sometimes for himself and sometimes on commission for others. He specialized in basketball games, and he had his own, elaborate system for ranking teams and predicting outcomes. In February 1965, he was living in a poolside hotel room on the Sunset Strip.[9]

Sklanksy describes how the FBI would observe Katz leaving his hotel to place his bets from the telephone booth. An agent stationed outside would radio the news to another agent near the booth. This second agent would turn on a tape recorder placed on top of the telephone booth, observe Katz making his calls, and once Katz was finished and left the telephone booth, turn the recorder off and take it down from the top of the booth.

2. *The Reasonable Expectation of Privacy Test.* The *Katz* decision established a widely cited test for whether the Fourth Amendment is applicable in a given situation. That test was articulated not in the majority opinion but in the concurring opinion by Justice Harlan. The rule as articulated in Justice Harlan's concurrence has become known as the "reasonable expectation of privacy test." Under the test, (1) a person must exhibit an "actual (subjective) expectation of privacy" and (2) "the expectation [must] be one that society is prepared to recognize as 'reasonable.' "

According to Christopher Slobogin and Joseph Schumacher:

> For the most part, the Court has been content with fleshing out the meaning of the phrase[] "reasonable expectations of privacy" . . . through [its] application to specific cases. But the Court has also provided two significant guidelines as to how [this phrase] should be interpreted. The first guideline came in *Rakas v. Illinois*, where the majority opinion, by then-Associate Justice Rehnquist, stated that "legitimation of expectations of privacy by law must have a source outside of the Fourth Amendment, either by reference to concepts of real or personal property law or to understandings that are recognized and permitted by society." Most important for present purposes is the last clause of this excerpt, which indicates the Court's willingness to rely on societal understandings in defining "reasonable expectations of privacy." Although this language appeared in a footnote, and was directed solely toward defining the standing concept, it has since been relied upon in the text of several other cases involving the "search" issue, often rephrased in terms of expectations of privacy "society is prepared to recognize as 'reasonable.'"
>
> The second guideline came from the same footnote in *Rakas*. According to the Court, the use of the word "legitimate" or "reasonable" before "expectations of privacy" is meant to convey "more than a subjective expectation of not being discovered." As the Court explained,

> > [a] burglar plying his trade in a summer cabin during the off season may have a thoroughly justified subjective expectation of privacy, but it is not one which the

---

[9] David A. Sklansky, *Katz v. United States*, in *Criminal Procedure Stories* (Carol S. Steiker ed., 2006).

law recognizes as "legitimate." His presence . . . is "wrongful"; his expectation is not "one that society is prepared to recognize as 'reasonable.'"

In short, the Fourth Amendment does not protect expectations of privacy that only a criminal would have.[10]

3. *Variations on* **Katz.** What if the door to the telephone booth in *Katz* had been open? Would the Court still have concluded that the Fourth Amendment applied? What if the cop stood outside the booth, and Katz spoke loud enough for the cop to hear? Suppose the police placed a sound recording device outside the phone booth, and the device could pick up Katz's voice, which would be inaudible to the naked ear outside the phone booth. Would this be a violation of the Fourth Amendment?

4. *"Conditioned" Expectations of Privacy.* Before *Katz*, police sometimes tapped phones. How would this behavior affect a person's expectations of privacy when speaking on the phone? Consider the following observation by the Court in *Smith v. Maryland*, 442 U.S. 735, 741 n.5 (1979):

> Situations can be imagined, of course, in which Katz' two-pronged inquiry would provide an inadequate index of Fourth Amendment protection. For example, if the Government were suddenly to announce on nationwide television that all homes henceforth would be subject to warrantless entry, individuals thereafter might not in fact entertain any actual expectation or privacy regarding their homes, papers, and effects. Similarly, if a refugee from a totalitarian country, unaware of this Nation's traditions, erroneously assumed that police were continuously monitoring his telephone conversations, a subjective expectation of privacy regarding the contents of his calls might be lacking as well. In such circumstances, where an individual's subjective expectations had been "conditioned" by influences alien to well-recognized Fourth Amendment freedoms, those subjective expectations obviously could play no meaningful role in ascertaining what the scope of Fourth Amendment protection was. In determining whether a "legitimate expectation of privacy" existed in such cases, a normative inquiry would be proper.

5. **Berger v. New York.** *Berger v. New York*, 388 U.S. 41 (1967), is an important Fourth Amendment case decided after the Supreme Court agreed to hear *Katz* but before it heard oral arguments in that case. In *Berger*, the Court struck down portions of New York's eavesdropping statute as violating the Fourth Amendment. The New York law authorized the installation of electronic surveillance devices for 60 days, and it allowed the surveillance to be extended beyond the 60 days without a showing of present probable cause to continue the eavesdrop. The Court held:

> . . . The Fourth Amendment commands that a warrant issue not only upon probable cause supported by oath or affirmation, but also "particularly describing the place to be searched, and the persons or things to be seized." New York's statute lacks this particularization. It merely says that a warrant may

---

[10] Christopher Slobogin & Joseph E. Schumacher, *Reasonable Expectations of Privacy and Autonomy in Fourth Amendment Cases: An Empirical Look at "Understandings Recognized and Permitted by Society,"* 42 Duke L.J. 727, 731-32 (1993).

issue on reasonable ground to believe that evidence of crime may be obtained by the eavesdrop. It lays down no requirement for particularity in the warrant as to what specific crime has been or is being committed, nor "the place to be searched," or "the persons or things to be seized" as specifically required by the Fourth Amendment. The need for particularity and evidence of reliability in the showing required when judicial authorization of a search is sought is especially great in the case of eavesdropping. By its very nature eavesdropping involves an intrusion on privacy that is broad in scope. . . .

. . . New York's statute . . . lays down no . . . "precise and discriminate" requirements. . . . New York's broadside authorization rather than being "carefully circumscribed" so as to prevent unauthorized invasions of privacy actually permits general searches by electronic devices, the truly offensive character of which was first condemned in *Entick v. Carrington*, 19 How. St. Tr. 1029, and which were then known as "general warrants." The use of the latter was a motivating factor behind the Declaration of Independence. In view of the many cases commenting on the practice it is sufficient here to point out that under these "general warrants" customs officials were given blanket authority to conduct general searches for goods imported to the Colonies in violation of the tax laws of the Crown. The Fourth Amendment's requirement that a warrant "particularly describ(e) the place to be searched, and the persons or things to be seized," repudiated these general warrants and "makes general searches . . . impossible and prevents the seizure of one thing under a warrant describing another. As to what is to be taken, nothing is left to the discretion of the officer executing the warrant."

We believe the statute here is equally offensive. First, as we have mentioned, eavesdropping is authorized without requiring belief that any particular offense has been or is being committed; nor that the "property" sought, the conversations, be particularly described. The purpose of the probable cause requirement of the Fourth Amendment, to keep the state out of constitutionally protected areas until it has reason to believe that a specific crime has been or is being committed, is thereby wholly aborted. Likewise the statute's failure to describe with particularity the conversations sought gives the officer a roving commission to "seize" any and all conversations. . . . As with general warrants this leaves too much to the discretion of the officer executing the order. Secondly, authorization of eavesdropping for a two-month period is the equivalent of a series of intrusions, searches, and seizures pursuant to a single showing of probable cause. Prompt execution is also avoided. During such a long and continuous (24 hours a day) period the conversations of any and all persons coming into the area covered by the device will be seized indiscriminately and without regard to their connection with the crime under investigation. Moreover, the statute permits, and there were authorized here, extensions of the original two-month period — presumably for two months each — on a mere showing that such extension is "in the public interest." Apparently the original grounds on which the eavesdrop order was initially issued also form the basis of the renewal. This we believe insufficient without a showing of present probable cause for the continuance of the eavesdrop. Third, the statute places no termination date on the eavesdrop once the conversation sought is seized. This is left entirely in the discretion of the officer. Finally, the statute's procedure, necessarily because its success depends on secrecy, has no requirement for notice as do conventional warrants, nor does it overcome this defect by requiring some showing of special facts. On the contrary, it permits uncontested entry without any showing of exigent circumstances. . . . In short, the statute's blanket grant of permission to eavesdrop is without adequate judicial supervision or protective procedures. . . .

As Sklansky points out, the effect of *Berger* combined with two other cases decided immediately before *Katz* — *Warden v. Hayden*, 387 U.S. 294 (1967) and *Camara v. Municipal Court*, 387 U.S. 523 (1967) — was to underscore the "centrality of the warrant requirement to the Fourth Amendment."[11]

UNITED STATES V. WHITE

401 U.S. 745 (1971)

WHITE, J. In 1966, respondent James A. White was tried and convicted under two consolidated indictments charging various illegal transactions in narcotics. . . . He was fined and sentenced as a second offender to 25-year concurrent sentences. The issue before us is whether the Fourth Amendment bars from evidence the testimony of governmental agents who related certain conversations which had occurred between defendant White and a government informant, Harvey Jackson, and which the agents overheard by monitoring the frequency of a radio transmitter carried by Jackson and concealed on his person. On four occasions the conversations took place in Jackson's home; each of these conversations was overheard by an agent concealed in a kitchen closet with Jackson's consent and by a second agent outside the house using a radio receiver. Four other conversations — one in respondent's home, one in a restaurant, and two in Jackson's car — were overheard by the use of radio equipment. The prosecution was unable to locate and produce Jackson at the trial and the trial court overruled objections to the testimony of the agents who conducted the electronic surveillance. The jury returned a guilty verdict and defendant appealed. . . .

Concededly a police agent who conceals his police connections may write down for official use his conversations with a defendant and testify concerning them, without a warrant authorizing his encounters with the defendant and without otherwise violating the latter's Fourth Amendment rights. For constitutional purposes, no different result is required if the agent instead of immediately reporting and transcribing his conversations with defendant, either (1) simultaneously records them with electronic equipment which he is carrying on his person, *Lopez v. United States*; (2) or carries radio equipment which simultaneously transmits the conversations either to recording equipment located elsewhere or to other agents monitoring the transmitting frequency. *On Lee v. United States*. If the conduct and revelations of an agent operating without electronic equipment do not invade the defendant's constitutionally justifiable expectations of privacy, neither does a simultaneous recording of the same conversations made by the agent or by others from transmissions received from the agent to whom the defendant is talking and whose trustworthiness the defendant necessarily risks.

Our problem is not what the privacy expectations of particular defendants in particular situations may be or the extent to which they may in fact have relied on

---

[11] Sklansky, *supra*.

the discretion of their companions. Very probably, individual defendants neither know nor suspect that their colleagues have gone or will go to the police or are carrying recorders or transmitters. Otherwise, conversation would cease and our problem with these encounters would be nonexistent or far different from those now before us. Our problem, in terms of the principles announced in *Katz*, is what expectations of privacy are constitutionally "justifiable" — what expectations the Fourth Amendment will protect in the absence of a warrant. So far, the law permits the frustration of actual expectations of privacy by permitting authorities to use the testimony of those associates who for one reason or another have determined to turn to the police, as well as by authorizing the use of informants in the manner exemplified by *Hoffa* and *Lewis*. If the law gives no protection to the wrongdoer whose trusted accomplice is or becomes a police agent, neither should it protect him when that same agent has recorded or transmitted the conversations which are later offered in evidence to prove the State's case.

Inescapably, one contemplating illegal activities must realize and risk that his companions may be reporting to the police. If he sufficiently doubts their trustworthiness, the association will very probably end or never materialize. But if he has no doubts, or allays them, or risks what doubt he has, the risk is his. In terms of what his course will be, what he will or will not do or say, we are unpersuaded that he would distinguish between probably informers on the one hand and probable informers with transmitters on the other. . . .

Nor should we be too ready to erect constitutional barriers to relevant and probative evidence which is also accurate and reliable. An electronic recording will many times produce a more reliable rendition of what a defendant has said than will the unaided memory of a police agent. It may also be that with the recording in existence it is less likely that the informant will change his mind, less chance that threat or injury will suppress unfavorable evidence and less chance that cross-examination will confound the testimony. Considerations like these obviously do not favor the defendant, but we are not prepared to hold that a defendant who has no constitutional right to exclude the informer's unaided testimony nevertheless has a Fourth Amendment privilege against a more accurate version of the events in question. . . .

HARLAN, J. dissenting. . . . Since it is the task of the law to form and project, as well as mirror and reflect, we should not, as judges, merely recite the expectations and risks without examining the desirability of saddling them upon society. The critical question, therefore, is whether under our system of government, as reflected in the Constitution, we should impose on our citizens the risks of the electronic listener or observer without at least the protection of a warrant requirement.

This question must, in my view, be answered by assessing the nature of a particular practice and the likely extent of its impact on the individual's sense of security balanced against the utility of the conduct as a technique of law enforcement. For those more extensive intrusions that significantly jeopardize the sense of security which is the paramount concern of Fourth Amendment liberties, I am of the view that more than self-restraint by law enforcement officials is required and at the least warrants should be necessary. The impact of the practice of third-party bugging, must, I think, be considered such as to undermine that confidence and sense of security in dealing with one another that is characteristic of individual relationships between citizens in a free society. It goes beyond the impact on privacy occasioned by the ordinary type of "informer" investigation upheld in *Lewis* and *Hoffa*. The argument of the plurality opinion, to the effect that it is irrelevant whether secrets are revealed by the mere tattletale or the transistor, ignores the differences occasioned by third-party monitoring and recording which insures full and accurate disclosure of all that is said, free of the possibility of error and oversight that inheres in human reporting.

Authority is hardly required to support the proposition that words would be measured a good deal more carefully and communication inhibited if one suspected his conversations were being transmitted and transcribed. Were third-party bugging a prevalent practice, it might well smother that spontaneity — reflected in frivolous, impetuous, sacrilegious, and defiant discourse — that liberates daily life. Much offhand exchange is easily forgotten and one may count on the obscurity of his remarks, protected by the very fact of a limited audience, and the likelihood that the listener will either overlook or forget what is said, as well as the listener's inability to reformulate a conversation without having to contend with a documented record. All these values are sacrificed by a rule of law that permits official monitoring of private discourse limited only by the need to locate a willing assistant. . . .

Interposition of a warrant requirement is designed not to shield "wrongdoers," but to secure a measure of privacy and a sense of personal security throughout our society. The Fourth Amendment does, of course, leave room for the employment of modern technology in criminal law enforcement, but in the stream of current developments in Fourth Amendment law I think it must be held that third-party electronic monitoring, subject only to the self-restraint of law enforcement officials, has no place in our society.

DOUGLAS, J. dissenting. . . . *On Lee* and *Lopez* are of a vintage opposed to *Berger* and *Katz*. However they may be explained, they are products of the old common-law notions of trespass. *Katz*, on the other hand, emphasized that with few exceptions "searches conducted outside the judicial process, without prior approval by judge or magistrate, are per se unreasonable under the Fourth Amendment.". . .

Monitoring, if prevalent, certainly kills free discourse and spontaneous utterances. Free discourse — a First Amendment value — may be frivolous or serious, humble or defiant, reactionary or revolutionary, profane or in good taste; but it is not free if there is surveillance. . . .

Now that the discredited decisions in *On Lee* and *Lopez* are resuscitated and revived, must everyone live in fear that every word he speaks may be transmitted or recorded and later repeated to the entire world? I can imagine nothing that has a more chilling effect on people speaking their minds and expressing their views on important matters. The advocates of that regime should spend some time in totalitarian countries and learn firsthand the kind of regime they are creating here.
. . .

NOTES & QUESTIONS

1. **White *vs.* Katz.** Is this case more akin to the bugging in *On Lee* and *Lopez* rather than the wiretapping of *Katz*? Does it matter whether the police heard the conversation simultaneously? Suppose the conversation had been recorded by a hidden recorder and then handed over later to the police.

2. ***Covert Agents and the Misplaced Trust Doctrine.*** *White* suggests that the misplaced trust doctrine in *Hoffa, Lewis, Lopez,* and *On Lee* survives after *Katz.* Under the misplaced trust doctrine, people place their trust in others at their own peril and must assume the risk of betrayal. But should the misplaced trust doctrine survive after *Katz*? Do we have a reasonable expectation that our friends aren't government agents in disguise?

   In a comparative study of how the United States and Germany regulate undercover policing, Jacqueline Ross identifies numerous differences in the two legal systems.[12] She argues:

   > Germany's concern with individual dignity is part of the German Constitution's concern with safeguarding the "free development of personality," in direct reaction to the totalitarian oppression and violations of personal dignity under the Nazi regime. Invasions of privacy also have special salience for residents of the five new eastern states who remember the encompassing surveillance practiced more recently in the GDR [German Democratic Republic, also known as East Germany]. Given these concerns, police infiltration is deeply problematic. It interferes with the rights of all persons to control the face they present to the world; it reveals too much about the intimate details of a person's life; and it disrupts personal relationships. Giving constitutional status to these harms means that the government must satisfy certain requirements before inflicting them. Constitutional protection entails a warrant procedure, a showing of need, and statutory limits on the crimes that the government may target in this way.
   >
   > By contrast, the United States legal system does not treat undercover policing as an intrinsic invasion of privacy rights. Undercover policing is not recognized as a search or seizure under the Fourth Amendment. Because they have no Fourth Amendment significance, undercover investigations require no warrant and no showing of probable cause or even reasonable suspicion as a matter of constitutional law.

   What would be the impact on law enforcement if *White* came out the other way after *Katz*? In other words, suppose that *Katz* eliminated the misplaced trust doctrine. How would the Fourth Amendment apply to covert agents or informers? Would this unduly hamper police investigations of drug rings, mafia activity, and terrorist cells?

3. ***Electronic Surveillance and the First Amendment.*** Justice Douglas contends that electronic surveillance impinges upon and chills freedom of expression for all individuals in society. Is electronic surveillance without a warrant consistent

---

[12] Jacqueline E. Ross, *The Place of Covert Surveillance in Democratic Societies: A Comparative Study of the United States and Germany*, 55 Am. J. Comp. L. 493 (2007).

with the First Amendment? What kind of process should be required to make use of the warrant consistent with the First Amendment?

3. THE REASONABLE EXPECTATION OF PRIVACY TEST

(a) The Third Party Doctrine

SMITH V. MARYLAND

442 U.S. 735 (1979)

BLACKMUN, J. This case presents the question whether the installation and use of a pen register[13] constitutes a "search" within the meaning of the Fourth Amendment, made applicable to the States through the Fourteenth Amendment.

On March 5, 1976, in Baltimore, Md., Patricia McDonough was robbed. She gave the police a description of the robber and of a 1975 Monte Carlo automobile she had observed near the scene of the crime. After the robbery, McDonough began receiving threatening and obscene phone calls from a man identifying himself as the robber. On one occasion, the caller asked that she step out on her front porch; she did so, and saw the 1975 Monte Carlo she had earlier described to police moving slowly past her home. On March 16, police spotted a man who met McDonough's description driving a 1975 Monte Carlo in her neighborhood. By tracing the license plate number, police learned that the car was registered in the name of petitioner, Michael Lee Smith.

The next day, the telephone company, at police request, installed a pen register at its central offices to record the numbers dialed from the telephone at petitioner's home. The police did not get a warrant or court order before having the pen register installed. The register revealed that on March 17 a call was placed from petitioner's home to McDonough's phone. On the basis of this and other evidence, the police obtained a warrant to search petitioner's residence. [A search of Smith's home revealed more evidence that Smith was the robber. Smith moved to suppress all evidence obtained from (and derived from) the pen register. The trial court denied his motion, and Smith was convicted and sentenced to six years' imprisonment.] .
. .

The Fourth Amendment guarantees "[t]he right of the people to be secure in their persons, houses, papers, and effects, against unreasonable searches and seizures." In determining whether a particular form of government-initiated electronic surveillance is a "search" within the meaning of the Fourth Amendment,[14] our lodestar is *Katz v. United States*, 389 U.S. 347 (1967). . . .

---

[13] "A pen register is a mechanical device that records the numbers dialed on a telephone by monitoring the electrical impulses caused when the dial on the telephone is released. It does not overhear oral communications and does not indicate whether calls are actually completed." A pen register is "usually installed at a central telephone facility [and] records on a paper tape all numbers dialed from [the] line" to which it is attached.

[14] In this case, the pen register was installed, and the numbers dialed were recorded, by the telephone company. The telephone company, however, acted at police request. In view of this, respondent appears to concede that the company is to be deemed an "agent" of the police for purposes of this case, so as to render the installation and use of the pen register "state action" under the Fourth and Fourteenth Amendments. We may assume that "state action" was present here.

Consistently with *Katz,* this Court uniformly has held that the application of the Fourth Amendment depends on whether the person invoking its protection can claim a "justifiable," a "reasonable," or a "legitimate expectation of privacy" that has been invaded by government action. This inquiry, as Mr. Justice Harlan aptly noted in his *Katz* concurrence, normally embraces two discrete questions. The first is whether the individual, by his conduct, has "exhibited an actual (subjective) expectation of privacy," — whether, in the words of the *Katz* majority, the individual has shown that "he seeks to preserve [something] as private." The second question is whether the individual's subjective expectation of privacy is "one that society is prepared to recognize as 'reasonable,' — whether, in the words of the *Katz* majority, the individual's expectation, viewed objectively, is "justifiable" under the circumstances.[15]

In applying the *Katz* analysis to this case, it is important to begin by specifying precisely the nature of the state activity that is challenged. The activity here took the form of installing and using a pen register. Since the pen register was installed on telephone company property at the telephone company's central offices, petitioner obviously cannot claim that his "property" was invaded or that police intruded into a "constitutionally protected area." Petitioner's claim, rather, is that, notwithstanding the absence of a trespass, the State, as did the Government in *Katz,* infringed a "legitimate expectation of privacy" that petitioner held. Yet a pen register differs significantly from the listening device employed in *Katz,* for pen registers do not acquire the contents of communications. This Court recently noted:

> Indeed, a law enforcement official could not even determine from the use of a pen register whether a communication existed. These devices do not hear sound. They disclose only the telephone numbers that have been dialed — a means of establishing communication. Neither the purport of any communication between the caller and the recipient of the call, their identities, nor whether the call was even completed is disclosed by pen registers. *United States v. New York Tel. Co.,* 434 U.S. 159, 167 (1977).

Given a pen register's limited capabilities, therefore, petitioner's argument that its installation and use constituted a "search" necessarily rests upon a claim that he had a "legitimate expectation of privacy" regarding the numbers he dialed on his phone.

This claim must be rejected. First, we doubt that people in general entertain any actual expectation of privacy in the numbers they dial. All telephone users realize that they must "convey" phone numbers to the telephone company, since it is through telephone company switching equipment that their calls are completed.

---

[15] Situations can be imagined, of course, in which *Katz*'s two-pronged inquiry would provide an inadequate index of Fourth Amendment protection. For example, if the Government were suddenly to announce on nationwide television that all homes henceforth would be subject to warrantless entry, individuals thereafter might not in fact entertain any actual expectation or privacy regarding their homes, papers, and effects. Similarly, if a refugee from a totalitarian country, unaware of this Nation's traditions, erroneously assumed that police were continuously monitoring his telephone conversations, a subjective expectation of privacy regarding the contents of his calls might be lacking as well. In such circumstances, where an individual's subjective expectations had been "conditioned" by influences alien to well-recognized Fourth Amendment freedoms, those subjective expectations obviously could play no meaningful role in ascertaining what the scope of Fourth Amendment protection was. In determining whether a "legitimate expectation of privacy" existed in such cases, a normative inquiry would be proper.

All subscribers realize, moreover, that the phone company has facilities for making permanent records of the numbers they dial, for they see a list of their long-distance (toll) calls on their monthly bills. In fact, pen registers and similar devices are routinely used by telephone companies "for the purposes of checking billing operations, detecting fraud and preventing violations of law." Electronic equipment is used not only to keep billing records of toll calls, but also "to keep a record of all calls dialed from a telephone which is subject to a special rate structure." Pen registers are regularly employed "to determine whether a home phone is being used to conduct a business, to check for a defective dial, or to check for overbilling." Although most people may be oblivious to a pen register's esoteric functions, they presumably have some awareness of one common use: to aid in the identification of persons making annoying or obscene calls. Most phone books tell subscribers, on a page entitled "Consumer Information," that the company "can frequently help in identifying to the authorities the origin of unwelcome and troublesome calls." Telephone users, in sum, typically know that they must convey numerical information to the phone company; that the phone company has facilities for recording this information; and that the phone company does in fact record this information for a variety of legitimate business purposes. Although subjective expectations cannot be scientifically gauged, it is too much to believe that telephone subscribers, under these circumstances, harbor any general expectation that the numbers they dial will remain secret.

Petitioner argues, however, that, whatever the expectations of telephone users in general, he demonstrated an expectation of privacy by his own conduct here, since he "us[ed] the telephone *in his house* to the exclusion of all others." But the site of the call is immaterial for purposes of analysis in this case. Although petitioner's conduct may have been calculated to keep the *contents* of his conversation private, his conduct was not and could not have been calculated to preserve the privacy of the number he dialed. Regardless of his location, petitioner had to convey that number to the telephone company in precisely the same way if he wished to complete his call. The fact that he dialed the number on his home phone rather than on some other phone could make no conceivable difference, nor could any subscriber rationally think that it would. Second, even if petitioner did harbor some subjective expectation that the phone numbers he dialed would remain private, this expectation is not "one that society is prepared to recognize as 'reasonable.' " This Court consistently has held that a person has no legitimate expectation of privacy in information he voluntarily turns over to third parties. In [*United States v.*] *Miller*, for example, the Court held that a bank depositor has no "legitimate 'expectation of privacy' " in financial information "voluntarily conveyed to . . . banks and exposed to their employees in the ordinary course of business." The Court explained:

> The depositor takes the risk, in revealing his affairs to another, that the information will be conveyed by that person to the Government. . . . This Court has held repeatedly that the Fourth Amendment does not prohibit the obtaining of information revealed to a third party and conveyed by him to Government authorities, even if the information is revealed on the assumption that it will be used only for a limited purpose and the confidence placed in the third party will not be betrayed.

Because the depositor "assumed the risk" of disclosure, the Court held that it would be unreasonable for him to expect his financial records to remain private.

This analysis dictates that petitioner can claim no legitimate expectation of privacy here. When he used his phone, petitioner voluntarily conveyed numerical information to the telephone company and "exposed" that information to its equipment in the ordinary course of business. In so doing, petitioner assumed the risk that the company would reveal to police the numbers he dialed. The switching equipment that processed those numbers is merely the modern counterpart of the operator who, in an earlier day, personally completed calls for the subscriber. Petitioner concedes that if he had placed his calls through an operator, he could claim no legitimate expectation of privacy. We are not inclined to hold that a different constitutional result is required because the telephone company has decided to automate.

Petitioner argues, however, that automatic switching equipment differs from a live operator in one pertinent respect. An operator, in theory at least, is capable of remembering every number that is conveyed to him by callers. Electronic equipment, by contrast can "remember" only those numbers it is programmed to record, and telephone companies, in view of their present billing practices, usually do not record local calls. Since petitioner, in calling McDonough, was making a local call, his expectation of privacy as to her number, on this theory, would be "legitimate."

This argument does not withstand scrutiny. The fortuity of whether or not the phone company in fact elects to make a quasi-permanent record of a particular number dialed does not in our view, make any constitutional difference. Regardless of the phone company's election, petitioner voluntarily conveyed to it information that it had facilities for recording and that it was free to record. In these circumstances, petitioner assumed the risk that the information would be divulged to police. . . .

STEWART, J. joined by BRENNAN, J. dissenting. . . . The numbers dialed from a private telephone — although certainly more prosaic than the conversation itself — are not without "content." Most private telephone subscribers may have their own numbers listed in a publicly distributed directory, but I doubt there are any who would be happy to have broadcast to the world a list of the local or long distance numbers they have called. This is not because such a list might in some sense be incriminating, but because it easily could reveal the identities of the persons and the places called, and thus reveal the most intimate details of a person's life.

MARSHALL, J. joined by BRENNAN, J. dissenting. . . . Privacy is not a discrete commodity, possessed absolutely or not at all. Those who disclose certain facts to a bank or phone company for a limited business purpose need not assume that this information will be released to other persons for other purposes.

The crux of the Court's holding, however, is that whatever expectation of privacy petitioner may in fact have entertained regarding his calls, it is not one "society is prepared to recognize as 'reasonable.'" In so ruling, the Court determines that individuals who convey information to third parties have "assumed the risk" of disclosure to the government. This analysis is misconceived in two critical respects.

Implicit in the concept of assumption of risk is some notion of choice. At least in the third-party consensual surveillance cases, which first incorporated risk analysis into Fourth Amendment doctrine, the defendant presumably had exercised some discretion in deciding who should enjoy his confidential communications. By contrast here, unless a person is prepared to forgo use of what for many has become a personal or professional necessity, he cannot help but accept the risk of surveillance. It is idle to speak of "assuming" risks in contexts where, as a practical matter, individuals have no realistic alternative.

More fundamentally, to make risk analysis dispositive in assessing the reasonableness of privacy expectations would allow the government to define the scope of Fourth Amendment protections. For example, law enforcement officials, simply by announcing their intent to monitor the content of random samples of first-class mail or private phone conversations, could put the public on notice of the risks they would thereafter assume in such communications. . . .

In my view, whether privacy expectations are legitimate within the meaning of *Katz* depends not on the risks an individual can be presumed to accept when imparting information to third parties, but on the risks he should be forced to assume in a free and open society. . . .

The use of pen registers, I believe, constitutes such an extensive intrusion. To hold otherwise ignores the vital role telephonic communication plays in our personal and professional relationships, as well as the First and Fourth Amendment interests implicated by unfettered official surveillance. Privacy in placing calls is of value not only to those engaged in criminal activity. The prospect of unregulated governmental monitoring will undoubtedly prove disturbing even to those with nothing illicit to hide. Many individuals, including members of unpopular political organizations or journalists with confidential sources, may legitimately wish to avoid disclosure of their personal contacts. Permitting governmental access to telephone records on less than probable cause may thus impede certain forms of political affiliation and journalistic endeavor that are the hallmark of a truly free society. Particularly given the Government's previous reliance on warrantless telephonic surveillance to trace reporters' sources and monitor protected political activity, I am unwilling to insulate use of pen registers from independent judicial review. . . .

NOTES & QUESTIONS

1. ***Pen Registers and Trap and Trace Devices.*** A pen register records outgoing telephone calls. Another device, known as a trap and trace device, records all incoming calls. In *Smith v. Maryland*, the Supreme Court ruled that a use of pen registers or trap and trace devices was not a form of wiretap (akin to that in *Katz*). What are the critical differences between the pen register and trap and device, on the one hand, and the wiretap, on the other?

2. ***Critiques of the* Smith *Decision.*** Consider the following observation by Laurence Tribe about *Smith*:

The "assumption of risk" — more aptly, "assumption of broadcast" — notion underling the holding in *Smith* . . . reveals alarming tendencies in the Supreme Court's understanding of what privacy means and ought to mean. The Court treats privacy almost as if it were "a discrete commodity, possessed absolutely or not at all" [quoting Justice Marshall's dissent]. Yet what could be more commonplace than the idea that it is up to the *individual* to *measure out information* about herself *selectively* — to whomever she chooses?[16]

Patricia Bellia contends that *Smith* conflicts with *Katz*: "In *Katz,* the phone company necessarily carried the defendant's telephone call, and the phone company no doubt had the technical ability to hear the contents of that call. That technical ability, however, was no impediment to the Court's conclusion that Katz had an expectation of privacy in the conversation."[17] Likewise, Susan Freiwald contends: "The *Smith* court ignored the lesson of *Katz*: We do not lose privacy in communications merely because they may be intercepted." She goes on to argue that the Court in *Smith* "avoided normative analysis and failed to consider how much privacy the law should actually grant to information. If the law treats information as private, then it will not be acceptable to acquire it, even when it possible to do so."[18]

Deirdre Mulligan explains that the Court addressed the discrepancies between *Katz* and *Smith* by discussing in *Smith* "at some length the limited information that can be gleaned from a phone number, contrasting it with what may be revealed from a telephone conversation."[19] Does the holding of *Smith* rest on the fact that the numbers were exposed to a third party or on the fact that the numbers revealed limited information about a person or on both of these factors?

3. ***The Third Party Doctrine and Bank Records*: United States v. Miller.** The Supreme Court has also applied the third party doctrine to bank records. The Bank Secrecy Act of 1970, 31 U.S.C. § 1081, requires the retention of bank records and creation of reports that would be useful in criminal, tax, or regulatory investigations or proceedings. The Act requires that federally insured banks record the identities of account holders as well as copies of each check, draft, or other financial instrument. The Act authorizes the Secretary of the Treasury to promulgate regulations for the reporting of domestic financial transactions, which require that a report be made for every deposit, withdrawal, or other transfer of currency exceeding $10,000. *See* 31 C.F.R. § 103.22. For transactions exceeding $5,000 into or out of the United States, the amount, the date of receipt, the form of financial instrument, and the person who received it must be reported. *See* 31 C.F.R. §§ 103.23, 103.25.

---

[16] Laurence Tribe, *American Constitutional Law* 1391 (2d ed. 1988). For another critique of *Smith v. Maryland*, see Daniel J. Solove, *Digital Dossiers and the Dissipation*, 75 S. Cal. L. Rev. 1083 (2002).

[17] Patricia Bellia, *Surveillance Law Through Cyberlaw's Lens,* 72 Geo. Wash. L. Rev. 1375, 1405 (2004).

[18] Susan Freiwald, *Online Surveillance: Remembering the Lessons of the Wiretap Act,* 56 Ala. L. Rev. 9, 40, 66 (2004).

[19] Deirdre K. Mulligan, *Reasonable Expectations in Electronic Communications: A Critical Perspective on the Electronic Communications Privacy Act*, 72 Geo. Wash. L. Rev. 1557, 1581 (2004).

In *California Bankers Association v. Shultz,* 416 U.S. 21 (1974), a group of bankers as well as depositors challenged the Bank Secrecy Act as a violation of the First, Fourth, and Fifth Amendments. The Court held that the Act did not violate the Fourth Amendment. First, the Court held that the bankers did not possess Fourth Amendment rights in the information because "corporations can claim no equality with individuals in the enjoyment of a right to privacy." Second, as to the constitutional rights of the individual depositors, the Court concluded that they lacked standing to pursue their claims because none alleged that they "were engaged in the type of $10,000 domestic currency transaction which would necessitate that their bank report it to the Government."

In a dissent, Justice Douglas wrote:

> The records of checks — now available to the investigators — are highly useful. In a sense a person is defined by the checks he writes. By examining them the agents get to know his doctors, lawyers, creditors, political allies, social connections, religious affiliation, educational interests, the papers and magazines he reads, and so on ad infinitum. These are all tied to one's social security number; and now that we have the data banks, these other items will enrich that storehouse and make it possible for a bureaucrat — by pushing one button — to get in an instant the names of the 190 million Americans who are subversives or potential and likely candidates.

The privacy of bank records was again before the Court two years later. In *United States v. Miller*, 425 U.S. 435 (1976), agents from the Alcohol, Tobacco, and Firearms Bureau obtained the defendant's records at two banks where he maintained accounts. The banks provided the records to the government without notifying him. The defendant argued that the records were protected by the Fourth Amendment and that the government needed a warrant to obtain them. The Supreme Court concluded that there is no reasonable expectation of privacy in bank records.

> The checks are not confidential communications but negotiable instruments to be used in commercial transactions. All of the documents obtained, including financial statements and deposit slips, contain only information voluntarily conveyed to the banks and exposed to their employees in the ordinary course of business. . . . .
>
> The depositor takes the risk, in revealing his affairs to another, that the information will be conveyed by that person to the Government. This Court has held repeatedly that the Fourth Amendment does not prohibit the obtaining of information revealed to a third party and conveyed by him to Government authorities, even if the information is revealed on the assumption that it will be used only for a limited purpose and the confidence placed in the third party will not be betrayed. . . .

4. ***The Scope of the Third Party Doctrine.*** How broadly does the third party doctrine extend? To any information exposed to a third party? In *Smith v. Maryland,* the phone numbers were deemed not to be as sensitive as the contents of what was communicated during a phone call. But in *Miller,* the Court held there was no reasonable expectation of privacy in bank records without regard for the sensitivity of the information contained in them. What about medical records maintained by a physician? Is there no reasonable

expectation of privacy in a person's health information if maintained by a doctor, hospital, or insurance company? If the Court were to draw a line to cabin the scope of the third party doctrine, is there a principled manner in which such a line could be drawn?

5. ***Federal and State Law.*** Sometimes when the Court fails to identify a privacy interest involving some aspect of the collection of personal information, Congress responds by enacting legislation that provides protection by statutory means. That happened after *Smith* with the Pen Register Act, 18 U.S.C. §§ 3121–3127. This statute requires that the government obtain a court order by certifying that the use of a pen register is "relevant to an ongoing investigation." This standard, however, is significantly less stringent than the probable cause required to obtain a Fourth Amendment warrant.

Two years after *Miller*, in 1978, Congress passed the Right to Financial Privacy Act (RFPA), Pub. L. No. 95-630, which partially filled the void left by *Miller*. The RFPA prevents banks and other financial institutions from disclosing a person's financial information to the government unless the records are disclosed pursuant to subpoena or search warrant. *See* 29 U.S.C. §§ 3401–3422.

Some states have rejected the *Smith* holding under their constitutions. For example, in *State v. Hunt*, 450 A.2d 952 (N.J. 1982), the New Jersey Supreme Court rejected *Smith* and held that under the New Jersey Constitution, there is a reasonable expectation of privacy in telephone records:

> The telephone has become an essential instrument in carrying on our personal affairs. It has become part and parcel of the home. When a telephone call is made, it is as if two people are having a private conversation in the sanctity of their living room. . . .
>
> The telephone caller is . . . entitled to assume that the numbers he dials in the privacy of his home will be recorded solely for the telephone company's business purposes. From the viewpoint of the customer, all the information which he furnishes with respect to a particular call is private. The numbers dialed are private. . . .
>
> It is unrealistic to say that the cloak of privacy has been shed because the telephone company and some of its employees are aware of this information. Telephone calls cannot be made except through the telephone company's property and without payment to it for the service. This disclosure has been necessitated because of the nature of the instrumentality, but more significantly the disclosure has been made for a limited business purpose and not for release to other persons for other reasons. . . .

In an analysis of state constitutional law, Stephen Henderson concludes that 11 states have rejected the third party doctrine. Ten more states have not explicitly rejected the third party doctrine, but have case law suggesting that they might do so in the future.[20]

6. ***Privacy of the Mail.*** People provide letters and parcels to the government to deliver in the mail. Does this implicate the third party doctrine?

---

[20] Stephen E. Henderson, *Learning from All Fifty States: How to Apply the Fourth Amendment and Its State Analogues to Protect Third Party Information from Unreasonable Seizure*, 55 Cath. U. L. Rev. 373, 395 (2006).

In *Ex Parte Jackson,* 96 U.S. 727 (1877), one of its earliest Fourth Amendment cases, decided long before the third party doctrine, the Supreme Court held that the Fourth Amendment required a warrant to search sealed letters sent via the U.S. Postal Service:

> The constitutional guaranty of the right of the people to be secure in their persons against unreasonable searches and seizures extends to their papers, thus closed against inspection, wherever they may be. Whilst in the mail, they can only be opened and examined under like warrant, issued upon similar oath or affirmation, particularly describing the thing to be seized, as is required when papers are subjected to search in one's own household.

Although the Fourth Amendment protects the contents of a sealed letter, it does not protect the outside of letters, where addressing of information is typically located. As the Court noted in *Ex Parte Jackson,* "the outward form and weight" of letters and sealed packages are unprotected by the Fourth Amendment. Modern caselaw follows this distinction.

Today, federal law also restricts the government's ability to search people's mail. Pursuant to 39 U.S.C. §3623(d):

> No letter of such a class of domestic origin shall be opened except under authority of a search warrant authorized by law, or by an officer or employee of the Postal Service for the sole purpose of determining an address at which the letter can be delivered, or pursuant to the authorization of the addressee.

However, the government can search letters sent from abroad. *See United States v. Various Articles of Obscene Merchandise, Schedule No. 1213,* 395 F. Supp. 791 (S.D.N.Y. 1975), *aff'd,* 538 F.2d 317.

7. ***Third Party Doctrine in the Information Age.*** Daniel Solove contends that *Miller* and *Smith* pose a substantial threat to privacy in the modern world given the dramatic extent to which third parties hold personal information:

> In the Information Age, an increasing amount of personal information is contained in records maintained by private sector entities, Internet Service Providers, phone companies, cable companies, merchants, bookstores, websites, hotels, landlords and employers. Many private sector entities are beginning to aggregate the information in these records to create extensive digital dossiers.
>
> The data in these digital dossiers increasingly flows from the private sector to the government, particularly for law enforcement use. . . . Detailed records of an individual's reading materials, purchases, magazines, diseases and ailments, and website activity, enable the government to assemble a profile of an individual's finances, health, psychology, beliefs, politics, interests, and lifestyle. This data can unveil a person's anonymous speech, groups and personal associations.
>
> The increasing amount of personal information flowing to the government poses significant problems with far-reaching social effects. Inadequately constrained government information gathering can lead to at least three types of harms. First, it can result in the slow creep toward a totalitarian state. Second, it can chill democratic activities and interfere with individual self-determination. Third, it can lead to the danger of harms arising in bureaucratic settings. Individuals, especially in times of crisis, are vulnerable to abuse from

government misuse of personal information. Once government entities have collected personal information, there are few regulations in how it can be used and how long it can be kept. The bureaucratic nature of modern law enforcement institutions can enable sweeping searches, the misuse of personal data, improper exercises of discretion, unjustified interrogation, arrests, roundups of disfavored individuals, and discriminatory profiling.[21]

Because of the third party doctrine in *Miller* and *Smith*, the Fourth Amendment fails to limit the government from gathering personal information maintained by businesses. *Miller* and *Smith* were decided in the 1970s. Should they be reconsidered in light of the extensive computerized records maintained today? What would be the consequences of overruling *Miller* and *Smith*?

8. ***Can a Contract or Promise Create a Reasonable Expectation of Privacy?*** In many instances, companies promise people that they will keep their data confidential — either through express or implied contractual terms or through promises that customers might rely upon. Should contracts or promises be sufficient to create a reasonable expectation of privacy? Consider the following argument of Daniel Solove:

> According to the third party doctrine . . . even a written contract isn't enough to give people an expectation of privacy. But promises and contracts are the foundation of modern civil society. If people couldn't reply on them, business and commerce would grind to a halt. Yet when it comes to privacy, the U.S. Supreme Court thinks that promises and contracts don't matter.[22]

9. ***Critiques and Defenses of the Third Party Doctrine.*** Susan Brenner and Leo Clark argue that the third party doctrine is flawed because it assumes that a "disclosure to a trusted, reputable [third party] is the same as indiscriminate disclosure to the public." If we disclose information on a public website, "we have clearly demonstrated our lack of interest in controlling access to the information in question." In contrast, when we share information with third parties, these are "controlled disclosures, in that they represent the limited, focused sharing of information with a [third party] as an integral part of a legitimate transaction."[23]

Taking a different approach, Thomas Crocker contrasts the third party doctrine with the Supreme Court's protection of interpersonal relations in *Lawrence v. Texas,* 539 U.S. 558 (2003), where it invalidated a Texas state statute criminalizing homosexual sodomy. While the *Lawrence* Court protected "conduct important to interpersonal relations," the third party doctrine leads to a view that "privacy protects only what we keep to ourselves."[24]

---

[21] Daniel J. Solove, *Digital Dossiers and the Dissipation of Fourth Amendment Privacy*, 75 S. Cal. L. Rev. 1083, 1084-86 (2002).

[22] Daniel J. Solove, *Nothing to Hide: The False Tradeoff Between Privacy and Security* 13, 108-09 (2011).

[23] Susan W. Brenner & Leo L. Clarke, *Fourth Amendment Protection for Shared Privacy Rights in Stored Transactional Data*, 14 J.L. & Pol'y 211, 258 (2006). For another critique of the third party doctrine, see Stephen E. Henderson, Beyond the (Current) Fourth Amendment: Protecting Third-Party Information, Third Parties, and the Rest of Us Too, 34 Pepp. L. Rev. 975 (2007).

[24] Thomas P. Crocker, *From Privacy to Liberty: The Fourth Amendment After* Lawrence, 57 UCLA L. Rev. 1 (2009).

Orin Kerr defends the third party doctrine. In his view, it "ensures technological neutrality in Fourth Amendment rules." He argues that

> criminals could use third-party agents to fully enshroud their criminal enterprises in Fourth Amendment protection. A criminal could plot and execute his entire crime from home knowing that the police could not send in undercover agents, record the fact of his phone calls, or watch any aspect of his Internet usage without first obtaining a warrant. He could use third parties to create a bubble of Fourth Amendment protection around the entirety of his criminal activity.

Kerr concludes that the "third-party doctrine blocks such efforts, resulting in a rough equivalence in the overall amount of privacy for criminals acting alone and the amount of privacy for those using third parties."[25] Does modern technology make detecting crime more difficult as Kerr contends? It can also make investigating crime easier. How should the Fourth Amendment respond when new technology affects the way crimes are committed and investigated?

10. ***The First Amendment and the Third Party Doctrine.*** Daniel Solove argues that the First Amendment should be understood as a source of criminal procedure and should protect pen register information:

> Although the Supreme Court has focused on the Fourth Amendment, obtaining pen register data without a warrant potentially violates the First Amendment. A log of incoming and outgoing calls can be used to trace channels of communication. It is relatively easy to link a phone number to a person or organization. Pen registers can reveal associational ties, since association in contemporary times often occurs by way of telephone or e-mail. As David Cole argues, modern communications technology has made association possible without physical assembly. For example, if the government scrutinized the phone logs of the main office of the Communist Party, it might discover many of the Party's members. The information would not be equivalent to a membership list, but it would probably include identifying data about countless individuals who would not want the government to discover their connection to the Communist Party. If the government were to examine the phone logs or e-mail headers of a particular individual, it might discover that the individual contacted particular organizations that the individual wants to keep private. The pen register information, therefore, implicates First Amendment values.[26]

Solove contends that government access to pen register information can violate the First Amendment, and he goes on to argue that the First Amendment should require a warrant before the government can obtain such information. Does pen register information implicate the First Amendment? If so, what kind of protections should the First Amendment require?

Neil Richards also contends that the First Amendment protects what he calls "intellectual privacy," which he defines as the ability "to develop ideas and

---

[25] Orin S. Kerr, *The Case for the Third-Party Doctrine*, 107 Mich. L. Rev. 561, 575-76 (2009). For a critique of Kerr's article, see Richard A. Epstein, *Privacy and the Third Hand: Lessons from the Common Law of Reasonable Expectations*, 24 Berkeley Tech. L.J. 1199 (2009); Erin Murphy, *The Case Against the Case for the Third Party Doctrine: A Response to Epstein and Kerr*, 24 Berkeley Tech. L.J. 1239 (2009).

[26] Daniel J. Solove, *The First Amendment as Criminal Procedure*, 82 N.Y.U. L. Rev. 112, 169 (2007).

beliefs away from the unwanted gaze or interference of others." According to Richards, the "ability to freely make up our minds and to develop new ideas thus depends upon a substantial measure of intellectual privacy. In this way, intellectual privacy is a cornerstone of meaningful First Amendment liberties." Richards argues that the government can implicate intellectual privacy when it seeks to "obtain from third parties intellectual records such as book purchases, library records, Web-use histories, and search-engine queries." Doing so "threaten[s] both the freedom of thought and the freedom of intellectual exploration."[27] When intellectual privacy is involved, heightened constitutional protections should be required. How would Richards's notion of intellectual privacy apply to pen registers?

(b) Items Abandoned or Exposed to the Public

CALIFORNIA V. GREENWOOD
486 U.S. 35 (1988)

[Police investigators searched the plastic garbage bags that Greenwood left on the curb in front of his house to be picked up by the trash collector. The officers found indications of drug use from the search of Greenwood's trash and obtained a warrant to search the house, where they uncovered more evidence of drug trafficking. Greenwood was arrested.]

WHITE, J. . . . The warrantless search and seizure of the garbage bags left at the curb outside the Greenwood house would violate the Fourth Amendment only if respondents manifested a subjective expectation of privacy in their garbage that society accepts as objectively reasonable.

. . . [The Greenwoods] assert . . . that they had, and exhibited, an expectation of privacy with respect to the trash that was searched by the police: The trash, which was placed on the street for collection at a fixed time, was contained in opaque plastic bags, which the garbage collector was expected to pick up, mingle with the trash of others, and deposit at the garbage dump. The trash was only temporarily on the street, and there was little likelihood that it would be inspected by anyone.

It may well be that respondents did not expect that the contents of their garbage bags would become known to the police or other members of the public. An expectation of privacy does not give rise to Fourth Amendment protection, however, unless society is prepared to accept that expectation as objectively reasonable.

Here, we conclude that respondents exposed their garbage to the public sufficiently to defeat their claim to Fourth Amendment protection. It is common knowledge that plastic garbage bags left on or at the side of a public street are readily accessible to animals, children, scavengers, snoops, and other members of the public. Moreover, respondents placed their refuse at the curb for the express purpose of conveying it to a third party, the trash collector, who might himself

---

[27] Neil M. Richards, *Intellectual Privacy,* 87 Tex. L. Rev. 387, 389, 439 (2008).

have sorted through respondents' trash or permitted others, such as the police, to do so. Accordingly, having deposited their garbage "in an area particularly suited for public inspection and, in a manner of speaking, public consumption, for the express purpose of having strangers take it," respondents could have had no reasonable expectation of privacy in the inculpatory items that they discarded. . .

BRENNAN, J. joined by MARSHALL, J. dissenting. . . . . Scrutiny of another's trash is contrary to commonly accepted notions of civilized behavior. I suspect, therefore, that members of our society will be shocked to learn that the Court, the ultimate guarantor of liberty, deems unreasonable our expectation that the aspects of our private lives that are concealed safely in a trash bag will not become public.

"A container which can support a reasonable expectation of privacy may not be searched, even on probable cause, without a warrant." *United States v. Jacobsen*, 466 U.S. 109, 120, n.17 (1984) (citations omitted). Thus, as the Court observes, if Greenwood had a reasonable expectation that the contents of the bags that he placed on the curb would remain private, the warrantless search of those bags violated the Fourth Amendment. . . .

Our precedent, therefore, leaves no room to doubt that had respondents been carrying their personal effects in opaque, sealed plastic bags — identical to the ones they placed on the curb — their privacy would have been protected from warrantless police intrusion. . . .

Respondents deserve no less protection just because Greenwood used the bags to discard rather than to transport his personal effects. Their contents are not inherently any less private, and Greenwood's decision to discard them, at least in the manner in which he did, does not diminish his expectation of privacy.

A trash bag, like any of the above-mentioned containers, "is a common repository for one's personal effects" and, even more than many of them, is "therefore . . . inevitably associated with the expectation of privacy." "[A]lmost every human activity ultimately manifests itself in waste products. . . ." *Smith v. State*, 510 P.2d 793, 798 (Alaska 1973). A single bag of trash testifies eloquently to the eating, reading, and recreational habits of the person who produced it. A search of trash, like a search of the bedroom, can relate intimate details about sexual practices, health, and personal hygiene. Like rifling through desk drawers or intercepting phone calls, rummaging through trash can divulge the target's financial and professional status, political affiliations and inclinations, private thoughts, personal relationships, and romantic interests. It cannot be doubted that a sealed trash bag harbors telling evidence of the "intimate activity associated with the 'sanctity of a man's home and the privacies of life,'" which the Fourth Amendment is designed to protect. . . .

. . . Most of us, I believe, would be incensed to discover a meddler — whether a neighbor, a reporter, or a detective — scrutinizing our sealed trash containers to discover some detail of our personal lives. . . .

The mere possibility that unwelcome meddlers might open and rummage through the containers does not negate the expectation of privacy in their contents any more than the possibility of a burglary negates an expectation of privacy in the home; or the possibility of a private intrusion negates an expectation of privacy in an unopened package; or the possibility that an operator will listen in on a telephone conversation negates an expectation of privacy in the words spoken on the telephone. "What a person . . . seeks to preserve as private, even in an area accessible to the public, may be constitutionally protected." *Katz*, 389 U.S. at 351-52. . . .

NOTES & QUESTIONS

1. ***Recycling and Surveillance of Garbage.*** In dissent in *Greenwood*, Justice Brennan states, "Scrutiny of another's trash is contrary to commonly accepted notions of civilized behavior." The Supreme Court decided *Greenwood* in 1988. In the twenty-first century, however, an increasing number of communities have imposed recycling obligations on their citizens. Sanitation departments sometimes oversee the recycling by routinely checking people's trash, and, in the case of noncompliance, imposing fines. Does this development alter the extent of any reasonable expectation of privacy in one's trash vis-à-vis the police?

2. ***Surveillance 24/7.*** In addition to searching through Greenwood's trash, the police were staking out his home, watching who came and went from his house. Does the Fourth Amendment protect against such surveillance? Imagine that for one year, the police were to stake out a person's home and follow the person wherever he or she went throughout the day. The person would be under 24-hour surveillance, seven days a week. Assume that the police would simply observe the person anytime he or she was in public. Is this more invasive to privacy than a one-time search of particular items, such as one's luggage? Does the Fourth Amendment provide any limitation on the police activities described above?

3. ***State Courts and State Constitutions.*** In examining the same issue as *Greenwood*, some state supreme courts have come to a different conclusion in interpreting their state constitutions. For example, the Supreme Court of Vermont declared that "the Vermont Constitution protects persons from warrantless police searches into the contents of secured opaque trash bags left at curbside for garbage collection and disposal." *State of Vermont v. Morris*, 680 A.2d 90 (Vt. 1996). It observed that the California, Hawaii, New Jersey, and Washington state supreme courts had already declined to follow the *Greenwood* analysis. The court argued that "the mere possibility that unwelcome animals or persons might rummage through one's garbage bags does not negate the expectation of privacy in the contents of those bags any more than the possibility of a burglary or break-in negates an expectation of privacy in one's home or car, or the possibility that a cleaning person or house guest will exceed the scope of a visit negates an expectation of privacy in a hotel room or home." Is one or more of these comparisons more convincing than the other?

4. ***"Abandoned" DNA?*** Frequently, the law views the police's collection of discarded DNA as similar to its examination of trash. In *California v. Greenwood*, 486 U.S. 35 (1988), the Supreme Court held that there was no reasonable expectation of privacy in trash set out at the curb for collection. Law

enforcement officials have collected discarded DNA from a smoked cigarette, a recently used coffee cup, and a licked envelope sent through the mail. In a *New York Times* article, Amy Harmon warns: "The police could collect DNA deemed 'abandoned' from targeted individuals and monitor their movements even if they are not suspected of committing a serious crime. Innocent people whose DNA turns up unexpectedly may find themselves identified by a database." Several hundred suspects over the last few years have been implicated by traces of DNA collected from them secretly. In addition, "[m]any more were eliminated from suspicion without ever knowing that their coffee cups, tissue, straws, utensils and cigarette butts were subject to DNA analysis by the police." Harmon also notes that most people fail to realize that there may be no way to avoid shedding DNA in public "short of living in a bubble."[28] Does *Greenwood* foreclose finding a reasonable expectation of privacy in DNA from discarded items? Should DNA in discarded items be treated differently from regular trash?

For Elizabeth Joh, however, instead of thinking of the collection and analysis of such samples as involving "abandoned" DNA, we should view it as "covert involuntary DNA sampling." Joh argues that the law should end its grant of virtually limitless discretion to the police in collecting such DNA. More limits on police procedures are needed in this context because of the vast potential uses of this information, and the rapidity of scientific research in genetics, which makes it difficult to predict the amount of information about an individual that a single genetic sample might reveal. In Joh's view, the police should be required to obtain a warrant whenever they seek covert, involuntary DNA from a target. She also calls for the more modest step of having legislatures clarify "the applicability of DNA database laws, both federal and state, to the collection of abandoned DNA."[29] What standard, if any, should be required in order for law enforcement officials to collect "abandoned" DNA?

5. ***DNA by Deceit.*** In *State v. Athan*, 158 P.3d 27 (Wash. 2007), police wanted to pursue a cold case involving the rape and murder of a young girl. They had suspected John Athan of the crime but lacked evidence. Twenty years later, they wanted to find out whether the crime scene DNA matched Athan's DNA profile. To obtain Athan's DNA, the police sent Athan a letter pretending to be from a law firm. The letter stated that Athan was part of a class action and that he had to send back a form to receive compensation from the litigation proceeds. Athan sent in the form, and the police used his saliva in sealing the letter to obtain his DNA. The police matched Athan's DNA to the crime scene. Athan challenged the police practice under the Fourth Amendment. The Washington Supreme Court held:

> Police may surreptitiously follow a suspect to collect DNA, fingerprints, footprints, or other possibly incriminating evidence, without violating that suspect's privacy. No case has been cited challenging or declaring this type of police practice unreasonable or unconstitutional. People constantly leave

---

[28] Amy Harmon, *Lawyers Fight Gene Material Gained on Sly*, N.Y. Times, Apr. 3, 2008, at A1.
[29] Elizabeth E. Joh, *Reclaiming "Abandoned" DNA*, 100 Nw. U. L. Rev. 857, 860, 881 (2006).

genetic material, fingerprints, footprints, or other evidence of their identity in public places. There is no subjective expectation of privacy in discarded genetic material just as there is no subjective expectation of privacy in fingerprints or footprints left in a public place. Physical characteristics which are exposed to the public are not subject to Fourth Amendment protection. The analysis of DNA obtained without forcible compulsion and analyzed by the government for comparison to evidence found at a crime scene is not a search under the Fourth Amendment.

Regarding the deceitful tactic used by the police, the court concluded:

Public policy allows for a limited amount of deceitful police conduct in order to detect and eliminate criminal activity. . . . The police's use of a ruse to obtain evidence against a suspect is not determinative. We have upheld police ruses designed to gain warrantless entry into a suspect's house for the purpose of buying illegal drugs. . . . Although the police violated a state statute by posing as lawyers, the trial court noted the effect of the conduct on the integrity of the legal system is not as severe as where the ruse was directed at obtaining confidential information. Public policy allows for some deceitful conduct and violation of criminal laws by police officers in order to detect and eliminate criminal activity. The claimed misconduct in this case does not involve actions similar to those cases which found misconduct warranting dismissal. The police did not induce Athan to commit any crime here nor did they attempt to gain any confidential information from the ruse. The conduct here is not so outrageous as to offend a sense of justice or require dismissal of this case.

Should law enforcement officials be allowed to use deceitful tactics such as the one used in *Athan* in order to obtain people's DNA?

6. ***Who Decides What Constitutes a Reasonable Expectation of Privacy?*** Currently, judges decide whether a defendant has a reasonable expectation of privacy in a particular activity. Is this question appropriate for judges to decide? Or should juries decide it? In all of the cases so far, observe the sources that the Court cites to for support that there is no reasonable expectation of privacy. How is a reasonable expectation of privacy to be measured? Is it an empirical question about what most people in society would generally consider to be private? If so, why aren't polls taken? If you're an attorney arguing that there is a reasonable expectation of privacy in something, what do you cite to? How should courts measure what society as a whole thinks is private?

Christopher Slobogin and Joseph Schumacher conducted a survey of individuals, asking them to rate on a scale of 0 to 100 the intrusiveness of certain types of searches or seizures, with 0 being nonintrusive and 100 being extremely intrusive. Several searches that the Court has concluded do not trigger a reasonable expectation of privacy rated in the middle of the scale. The flyover in *Florida v. Riley* rated at 40.32 on this scale; the dog sniff in *United States v. Place* rated at 58.33; the search of garbage in *California v. Greenwood* rated at 44.95; and the use of a beeper to track a car in *United States v. Knotts* rated at 54.46. Certain searches that the Court held do not involve a reasonable expectation of privacy rated highly on the scale, such as examining bank records in *United States v. Miller,* rated at 71.60. In other highly ranked searches, the Court has concluded that the Fourth Amendment applies, such as monitoring a phone for 30 days, rating at 87.67 and a body cavity search at the border, rating at 90.14. The body cavity search was the highest rated search, and a search of foliage in a public park was the lowest rated at 6.48. Slobogin and Schumacher conclude that "the Supreme Court's conclusions about the scope of the Fourth Amendment are often not in tune with commonly held attitudes about police investigative techniques."[30]

To what extent should empirical evidence such as this study be used by courts in determining whether or not there is a reasonable expectation of privacy? If such evidence should be used, at what point in the scale should the line be drawn to establish the existence of a reasonable expectation of privacy?

7. ***Should the Reasonable Expectation of Privacy Test Be Empirical or Normative?*** There is an interesting paradox at the heart of the reasonable expectation of privacy test: Legal protection is triggered by people's expectations of privacy, but those expectations are, to a notable extent, shaped by the extent of the legal protection of privacy. Consider the following argument by Daniel Solove regarding the privacy of the postal letters:

> [I]n America, the privacy of letters was formed in significant part by a legal architecture that protected the confidentiality of letters from other people and government officials. In colonial America, mail was often insecure; it was difficult to seal letters; and the wax often used to keep letters sealed was not very effective. There was widespread suspicion of postal clerks reading letters; and a number of prominent individuals, such as Thomas Jefferson, Alexander Hamilton, and George Washington, decried the lack of privacy in their letters and would sometimes even write in code. . . . Despite these realities, and people's expectation that letters would not be confidential, the law evolved to provide strong protection of the privacy of letters. Benjamin Franklin, who was in charge of the colonial mails, required his employees to swear an oath not to open mail. In the late eighteenth and early nineteenth centuries, Congress passed several laws prohibiting the improper opening of mail. And the Supreme Court held in 1877 that despite the fact that people turned letters over to the government for delivery in the postal system, sealed parcels were protected from inspection by the Fourth Amendment. This example illustrates that privacy is not just found but constructed. By erecting a legal structure to protect the privacy of letters, our society shaped the practices of letter writing and using the postal system. It occurred because of the desire to make privacy an integral part of these practices rather than to preserve the status quo.[31]

Solove argues that societies seek to protect privacy with the law when they do not expect privacy but desire to have it. If Solove is right, then what should courts look to when applying the reasonable expectation of privacy test?

8. ***Critiques of the Reasonable Expectation of Privacy Test.*** Thomas Crocker argues that the Fourth Amendment protects more than privacy — it protects "political liberty." According to Crocker, "the Fourth Amendment fits into a

---

[30] Christopher Slobogin & Joseph E. Schumacher, *Reasonable Expectations of Privacy and Autonomy in Fourth Amendment Cases: An Empirical Look at "Understandings Recognized and Permitted by Society,"* 42 Duke L.J. 727 (1993).

[31] Daniel J. Solove, *Conceptualizing Privacy*, 90 Cal. L. Rev. 1087, 1142-43 (2002); *see also* Shaun Spencer, *Reasonable Expectations and the Erosion of Privacy,* 39 San Diego L. Rev. 843 (2002).

broader political liberty framework, as it has increasingly focused on protecting a narrow conception of privacy and regulating everyday police practice." Instead, it should broadly "enable freedom of movement and social interaction in private and in public, secure from arbitrary search and seizure."[32] Crocker's argument suggests that the Fourth Amendment should protect assembly in public and other activities out in the open. Some might contend that his view of the Fourth Amendment is too broad and vague. Is it? What are the benefits and problems with Crocker's approach?

Daniel Solove argues that the reasonable expectation of privacy test should be abandoned because "current Fourth Amendment coverage often bears little relation to the problems caused by government investigative activities. It also bears little relation to whether it is best to have judicial oversight of law enforcement activity, what that oversight should consist of, how much limitation we want to impose on various government information gathering activities, and how we should guard against abuses of power." He recommends that "the Fourth Amendment should provide protection whenever a problem of reasonable significance can be identified with a particular form of government information gathering."[33] Is this approach workable? What are the benefits and problems with such an approach?

Susan Freiwald makes a similar argument in the context of communications:

> Courts should focus on the normative inquiry into whether users should be entitled to view their communications as private, but in doing so they should shift the inquiry away from users' apparent knowledge about whether their communications were vulnerable to interception. Instead, courts should discharge their responsibility to mediate the tension between law enforcement's interest in obtaining as much information as possible and users' interest in avoiding excessive government intrusion into their lives.[34]

Is looking at people's expectations the wrong inquiry? Freiwald suggests that courts look to four factors to determine whether Fourth Amendment regulation is appropriate — whether the surveillance is hidden, intrusive, indiscriminate, and continuous. Are these factors, as opposed to people's expectations of privacy, a more coherent and workable approach to determining whether the Fourth Amendment should regulate government surveillance activities?

(c) Surveillance and the Use of Sense Enhancement Technologies

The Plain View Doctrine. "[I]t has long been settled that objects falling in the plain view of an officer who has a right to be in the position to have that view are subject to seizure and may be introduced in evidence." *Harris v. United States*, 390 U.S. 234, 236 (1968). This has become known as the "plain view" doctrine. If it is

---

[32] Thomas P. Crocker, *The Political Fourth Amendment*, 88 Wash. U. L. Rev. 303, 310-11 (2010).

[33] Daniel J. Solove, *Fourth Amendment Pragmatism*, 51 B.C. L. Rev. 1511, 1513-14 (2010). For more about these issues, see Daniel J. Solove, *Nothing to Hide: The False Tradeoff Between Privacy and Security* (2011).

[34] Susan Freiwald, *First Principles of Communications Privacy*, 2007 Stan. Tech. L. Rev. 3, 9.

possible for something to be seen or heard from a public vantage point, there can be no reasonable expectation of privacy.

The Open Fields Doctrine. An extension of the plain view rule is the "open fields" doctrine. An individual does not have a reasonable expectation of privacy in the open fields that she owns. In *Oliver v. United States*, 466 U.S. 170 (1984), the defendant placed "No Trespassing" signs throughout his farm and maintained a locked gate around the farm's entrance. The fields could not be seen from any public vantage point. The police trespassed onto the fields and found marijuana. The Court held, however, that there is no reasonable expectation of privacy in open fields, and the defendant's attempt to keep them secluded and shielded from public view was irrelevant.

An exception to the open fields doctrine is the legal treatment of a house's so-called "curtilage." Under the curtilage doctrine, parts of one's property immediately outside one's home do not fall within the open fields rule. This exception does not mean that the curtilage is automatically afforded Fourth Amendment protection; a reasonable expectation of privacy analysis still must be performed. The question of whether an area constitutes a curtilage depends upon "whether the area in question is so intimately tied to the home itself that it should be placed within the home's 'umbrella' of Fourth Amendment protection." *United States v. Dunn*, 480 U.S. 294, 301 (1987).

FLORIDA V. RILEY

488 U.S. 445 (1989)

WHITE, J. . . . Respondent Riley lived in a mobile home located on five acres of rural property. A greenhouse was located 10 to 20 feet behind the mobile home. Two sides of the greenhouse were enclosed. The other two sides were not enclosed but the contents of the greenhouse were obscured from view from surrounding property by trees, shrubs, and the mobile home. The greenhouse was covered by corrugated roofing panels, some translucent and some opaque. At the time relevant to this case, two of the panels, amounting to approximately 10% of the roof area, were missing. A wire fence surrounded the mobile home and the greenhouse, and the property was posted with a "DO NOT ENTER" sign.

This case originated with an anonymous tip to the Pasco County Sheriff's office that marijuana was being grown on respondent's property. When an investigating officer discovered that he could not see the contents of the greenhouse from the road, he circled twice over respondent's property in a helicopter at the height of 400 feet. With his naked eye, he was able to see through the openings in the roof and one or more of the open sides of the greenhouse and to identify what he thought was marijuana growing in the structure. A warrant was obtained based on these observations, and the ensuing search revealed marijuana growing in the greenhouse. Respondent was charged with possession of marijuana under Florida law. . . .

We agree with the State's submission that our decision in *California v. Ciraolo*, 476 U.S. 207 (1986), controls this case. There, acting on a tip, the police inspected the back-yard of a particular house while flying in a fixed-wing aircraft at 1,000 feet. With the naked eye the officers saw what they concluded was marijuana growing in the yard. A search warrant was obtained on the strength of this airborne inspection, and marijuana plants were found. The trial court refused to suppress this evidence, but a state appellate court held that the inspection violated the Fourth and Fourteenth Amendments to the United States Constitution, and that the warrant was therefore invalid. We in turn reversed, holding that the inspection was not a search subject to the Fourth Amendment. We recognized that the yard was within the curtilage of the house, that a fence shielded the yard from observation from the street, and that the occupant had a subjective expectation of privacy. We held, however, that such an expectation was not reasonable and not one "that society is prepared to honor." Our reasoning was that the home and its curtilage are not necessarily protected from inspection that involves no physical invasion. "'What a person knowingly exposes to the public, even in his own home or office, is not a subject of Fourth Amendment protection.'" As a general proposition, the police may see what may be seen "from a public vantage point where [they have] a right to be." Thus the police, like the public, would have been free to inspect the backyard garden from the street if their view had been unobstructed. They were likewise free to inspect the yard from the vantage point of an aircraft flying in the navigable airspace as this plane was. "In an age where private and commercial flight in the public airways is routine, it is unreasonable for respondent to expect that his marijuana plants were constitutionally protected from being observed with the naked eye from an altitude of 1,000 feet. The Fourth Amendment simply does not require the police traveling in the public airways at this altitude to obtain a warrant in order to observe what is visible to the naked eye."

We arrive at the same conclusion in the present case. In this case, as in *Ciraolo*, the property surveyed was within the curtilage of respondent's home. Riley no doubt intended and expected that his greenhouse would not be open to public inspection, and the precautions he took protected against ground-level observation. Because the sides and roof of his greenhouse were left partially open, however, what was growing in the greenhouse was subject to viewing from the air. Under the holding in *Ciraolo*, Riley could not reasonably have expected the contents of his greenhouse to be immune from examination by an officer seated in a fixed-wing aircraft flying in navigable airspace at an altitude of 1,000 feet or, as the Florida Supreme Court seemed to recognize, at an altitude of 500 feet, the lower limit of the navigable airspace for such an aircraft. Here, the inspection was made from a helicopter, but as is the case with fixed-wing planes, "private and commercial flight [by helicopter] in the public airways is routine" in this country, and there is no indication that such flights are unheard of in Pasco County, Florida. Riley could not reasonably have expected that his greenhouse was protected from public or official observation from a helicopter had it been flying within the navigable airspace for fixed-wing aircraft.

Nor on the facts before us, does it make a difference for Fourth Amendment purposes that the helicopter was flying at 400 feet when the officer saw what was growing in the greenhouse through the partially open roof and sides of the structure. We would have a different case if flying at that altitude had been contrary to law or regulation. But helicopters are not bound by the lower limits of the navigable airspace allowed to other aircraft.[35] Any member of the public could legally have been flying over Riley's property in a helicopter at the altitude of 400 feet and could have observed Riley's greenhouse. The police officer did no more. . . . As far as this record reveals, no intimate details connected with the use of the home or curtilage were observed, and there was no undue noise, and no wind, dust, or threat of injury. In these circumstances, there was no violation of the Fourth Amendment.

O'CONNOR, J. concurring in the judgment. Ciraolo's expectation of privacy was unreasonable not because the airplane was operating where it had a "right to be," but because public air travel at 1,000 feet is a sufficiently routine part of modern life that it is unreasonable for persons on the ground to expect that their curtilage will not be observed from the air at that altitude. Although "helicopters are not bound by the lower limits of the navigable airspace allowed to other aircraft," there is no reason to assume that compliance with FAA regulations alone determines "'whether the government's intrusion infringes upon the personal and societal values protected by the Fourth Amendment.'" Because the FAA has decided that helicopters can lawfully operate at virtually any altitude so long as they pose no safety hazard, it does not follow that the expectations of privacy "society is prepared to recognize as 'reasonable'" simply mirror the FAA's safety concerns. . . .

. . . However, if the public can generally be expected to travel over residential backyards at an altitude of 400 feet, Riley cannot reasonably expect his curtilage from such aerial observation. In my view, the defendant must bear the burden of proving that his expectation of privacy was a reasonable one, and thus that a "search" within the meaning of the Fourth Amendment even took place.

Because there is reason to believe that there is considerable public use of airspace at altitudes of 400 feet and above, and because Riley introduced no evidence to the contrary before the Florida courts, I conclude that Riley's expectation that his curtilage was protected from naked-eye aerial observation from that altitude was not a reasonable one. However, public use of altitudes lower than that — particularly public observations from helicopters circling over the curtilage of a home — may be sufficiently rare that public surveillance from such altitudes would violate reasonable expectations of privacy, despite compliance with FAA air safety regulations.

BRENNAN, J. joined by MARSHALL and STEVENS, JJ. dissenting. Under the plurality's exceedingly grudging Fourth Amendment theory, the expectation of privacy is defeated if a single member of the public could conceivably position herself to see into the area in question without doing anything illegal. It is defeated whatever the difficulty a person would have in so positioning herself, and however infrequently anyone would in fact do so. In taking this view the plurality ignores

---

[35] While Federal Aviation Administration regulations permit fixed-wing-aircraft to be operated at an altitude of 1,000 feet while flying over congested areas and at an altitude of 500 feet above the surface in other than congested areas, helicopters may be operated at less than the minimums for fixed-wing-aircraft "if the operation is conducted without hazard to persons or property on the surface. In addition, each person operating a helicopter shall comply with routes or altitudes specifically prescribed for helicopters by the [FAA] Administrator." 14 CFR § 91.79 (1988).

the very essence of *Katz*. The reason why there is no reasonable expectation of privacy in an area that is exposed to the public is that little diminution in "the amount of privacy and freedom remaining to citizens" will result from police surveillance of something that any passerby readily sees. To pretend, as the plurality opinion does, that the same is true when the police use a helicopter to peer over high fences is, at best, disingenuous. . . .

It is a curious notion that the reach of the Fourth Amendment can be so largely defined by administrative regulations issued for purposes of flight safety.[36] It is more curious still that the plurality relies to such an extent on the legality of the officer's act, when we have consistently refused to equate police violation of the law with infringement of the Fourth Amendment.

The police officer positioned 400 feet above Riley's backyard was not, however, standing on a public road. The vantage point he enjoyed was not one any citizen could readily share. His ability to see over Riley's fence depended on his use of a very expensive and sophisticated piece of machinery to which few ordinary citizens have access. In such circumstances it makes no more sense to rely on the legality of the officer's position in the skies than it would to judge the constitutionality of the wiretap in *Katz* by the legality of the officer's position outside the telephone booth. The simple inquiry whether the police officer had the legal right to be in the position from which he made his observations cannot suffice, for we cannot assume that Riley's curtilage was so open to the observations of passersby in the skies that he retained little privacy or personal security to be lost to police surveillance. The question before us must be not whether the police were where they had a right to be, but whether public observation of Riley's curtilage was so commonplace that Riley's expectation of privacy in his backyard could not be considered reasonable. . . .

. . . The Fourth Amendment demands that we temper our efforts to apprehend criminals with a concern for the impact on our fundamental liberties of the methods we use. I hope it will be a matter of concern to my colleagues that the police surveillance methods they would sanction were among those described 40 years ago in George Orwell's dread vision of life in the 1980's:

> The black-mustachio'd face gazed down from every commanding corner. There was one on the house front immediately opposite. BIG BROTHER IS WATCHING YOU, the caption said. . . . In the far distance a helicopter skimmed down between the roofs, hovered for an instant like a bluebottle, and darted away again with a curving flight. It was the Police Patrol, snooping into people's windows.

Who can read this passage without a shudder, and without the instinctive reaction that it depicts life in some country other than ours? I respectfully dissent.

---

[36] The plurality's use of the FAA regulations as a means for determining whether Riley enjoyed a reasonable expectation of privacy produces an incredible result. Fixed-wing aircraft may not be operated below 500 feet (1,000 feet over congested areas), while helicopters may be operated below those levels. Therefore, whether Riley's expectation of privacy is reasonable turns on whether the police officer at 400 feet above his curtilage is seated in an airplane or a helicopter. This cannot be the law.

NOTES & QUESTIONS

1. ***Privacy in Public.*** The court quotes from *Katz v. United States* that "[w]hat a person knowingly exposes to the public . . . is not a subject of Fourth Amendment protection." How far does this principle extend? Can there be situations where a person might have a reasonable expectation of privacy even when exposed in public?

2. ***Drones.*** The future of law enforcement surveillance likely rests not with helicopters, as in *Florida v. Riley*, but with drones, also known as unmanned aircraft vehicles or unmanned UAVs. In the words of the N.Y. Times, "Drones are becoming a darling of law enforcement authorities across the country."[37] Law enforcement authorities seek use of drones to locate bombs, find lost children, and assist rescue workers. As part of the 2012 federal budget, Congress ordered the FAA to establish rules for integrating UAVs into the national airspace. The FAA has already designated drone test sites in six states, Alaska, Nevada, New York, North Dakota, Texas, and Virginia. In 2014, it plans to launch its rulemaking process for UAVs. The FAA has also noted that its mission "does not include developing or enforcing policies to pertaining privacy or civil liberties" although its experience with the drone test sites can help inform the regulatory dialogue concerning these issues.[38] Does *Florida v. Riley* provide useful Fourth Amendment doctrine for the coming age of law enforcement drones?

3. ***Surveillance Cameras.*** The use of surveillance cameras is increasing. Since 1994, in response to terrorist bombings, Britain has been watching city streets through a system of surveillance cameras monitored by closed circuit television (CCTV).[39] In 2002, the National Park Service announced plans to set up a surveillance system at all major monuments on the National Mall in Washington, D.C. Given the frequent use of surveillance cameras, do we still have an expectation of privacy not to be filmed in our day-to-day activities? Consider Marc Blitz:

> People also need privacy and anonymity in many aspects of public life — for example, when they explore controversial films, books, or ideas, have conversations in public places, or seek aid or counsel of a sort they can only find by venturing into the public sphere. Although walls and windows do not shield these public activities from everyone's view, other features of physical and social architecture, distinctive to public space, do shield them. Crowds and the diversity and separateness of the social circles that people move in allow people to find anonymity; the existence of isolated and unmonitored islands of public space allow them to find seclusion. . . . These privacy-enhancing features of public space cannot easily survive in a world of ubiquitous cameras, and the

---

[37] Somini Sengupta, *Rise of Drones in U.S. Drives Efforts to Limit Police Use*, N.Y. Times (Feb. 15, 2013).

[38] FAA, *Integration of Civil Unmanned Aircraft Systems in the National Airspace System* 11 (1st ed. 2013).

[39] For more background about CCTV, see Clive Norris & Gary Armstrong, *The Maximum Surveillance Society: The Rise of CCTV* (1999); Jeffrey Rosen, *A Cautionary Tale for a New Age of Surveillance*, N.Y. Times Mag. (Oct. 7, 2001).

task of preserving them requires courts to do in a sense the opposite of what *Katz* recommends: They must abandon the task of identifying difficult-to-identify expectations of privacy . . . and instead return to the task of preserving the environment that makes privacy possible.[40]

What precisely are the harms of surveillance cameras? Consider Christopher Slobogin:

> Virtually all of us, no matter how innocent, feel somewhat unnerved when a police car pulls up behind us. Imagine now being watched by an officer, at a discreet distance and without any other intrusion, every time you walk through certain streets. Say you want to run (to catch a bus, for a brief bit of exercise or just for the hell of it). Will you? Or assume you want to obscure your face (because of the wind or a desire to avoid being seen by an officious acquaintance)? How about hanging out on the street corner (waiting for friends or because you have nothing else to do)?
>
> In all of these scenarios, you will probably feel and perhaps act differently than when the officer is not there. Perhaps your hesitancy comes from uncertainty as to the officer's likely reaction or simply from a desire to appear completely law-abiding; the important point is that it exists. Government-run cameras are a less tangible presence than the ubiquitous cop, but better at recording your actions. A police officer in Liverpool, England may have said it best: A camera is like having a cop "on duty 24 hours a day, constantly taking notes."[41]

Are there any other harms you can think of? What are the benefits of surveillance cameras? Should they not be permissible as a low-cost way to extend the reach of police? Do the benefits outweigh the harms? Regarding the benefits of surveillance cameras, consider Jeff Rosen:

> In 2000, Britain's violent-crime rates actually increased by 4.3 percent, even though the cameras continued to proliferate. But CCTV cameras have a mysterious knack for justifying themselves regardless of what happens to crime. When crime goes up, the cameras get the credit for detecting it, and when crime goes down, they get the credit for preventing it.[42]

Would it be possible to design an empirical study that would test the effectiveness of surveillance cameras in preventing crime?

4. *Face Recognition Systems.* In Tampa, a computer software program called "FaceIt" linked to 36 cameras attempts to scan the faces of individuals on public streets to match them against mug shots of wanted fugitives. A similar system was used to scan faces at Super Bowl XXXV in January 2001. The Tampa Police Department argues that "FaceIt" is analogous to a police officer standing on a street holding a mug shot. Philip Agre contends that face recognition systems are different:

---

[40] Marc Jonathan Blitz, *Video Surveillance and the Constitution of Public Space: Fitting the Fourth Amendment to a World that Tracks Image and Identity*, 82 Tex. L. Rev. 1349, 1481 (2004).

[41] Christopher Slobogin, *Public Privacy: Camera Surveillance of Public Places and the Right to Anonymity*, 72 Miss. L.J. 213, 247 (2002).

[42] Jeffrey Rosen, *The Naked Crowd: Reclaiming Security and Freedom in an Anxious Age* 49 (2004).

A human being who spots me in the park has the accountability that someone can spot them as well. Cameras are much more anonymous and easy to hide. More important is the question of scale. Most people understand the moral difference between a single chance observation in a park and an investigator who follows you everywhere you go.[43]

Further, contends Agre, the information used and collected by face recognition systems could fall into the wrong hands and be potentially abused by the government to exercise social control. Additionally, such systems can have errors, resulting in the tracking and potential arrest of innocent persons. As a policy matter, do the costs of facial recognition systems outweigh the benefits? Given the information privacy law you have learned so far, assess the legality and constitutionality of facial recognition systems.

The Tampa face recognition system was ultimately scrapped because of high errors and general ineffectiveness.

5. *The First Amendment and Government Surveillance:* **Laird v. Tatum.** In *Florida v. Riley,* the Fourth Amendment failed to limit government surveillance in public places. Does government surveillance implicate First Amendment rights? Christopher Slobogin contends that expressive public conduct and public associations implicate the First Amendment because "such surveillance can chill conduct, even though it takes place in public and is meant to be seen by others."[44]

In *Laird v. Tatum*, 408 U.S. 1 (1972), a group of individuals brought a First Amendment challenge to the Department of the Army's surveillance of civil rights activities in the aftermath of Dr. Martin Luther King, Jr.'s assassination. The Army harvested the information from news reports and from intelligence agents attending public meetings.[45] Although the Supreme Court noted that chilling the exercise of First Amendment rights could constitute a First Amendment violation, the Court concluded that the plaintiffs failed to establish a cognizable First Amendment injury and that their mere allegations of a "subjective 'chill' are not an adequate substitute for a claim of specific present objective harm or a threat of specific future harm." According to the Court, the plantiffs merely articulated "speculative apprehensiveness that the Army may at some future date misuse the information in some way that would cause direct harm to respondents."

Why doesn't surveillance create a cognizable injury under the First Amendment? Being watched inhibits one's ability to be free and candid in one's expression.

How broad is the Supreme Court's holding? Would the plaintiffs have established standing if they produced evidence that the surveillance was deterring their First Amendment activities? Would the case have come out differently had the surveillance involved gatherings in private as opposed to in public?

[43] Philip E. Agre, *Your Face Is Not a Bar Code: Arguments Against Automatic Face Recognition in Public Places* (Sept. 9, 2001), http://dlis.gseis.ucla.edu/people/pagre/bar-code.html.

[44] Christopher Slobogin, *Public Privacy: Camera Surveillance of Public Places and the Right to Anonymity*, 72 Miss. L.J. 213, 253-55 (2002).

[45] *Id.* at 6.

If *Laird* had been decided in the plaintiffs' favor, could individuals challenge wiretapping and other forms of police surveillance as a violation of the First Amendment? Such a holding could have far-reaching implications because many forms of police monitoring and investigation would be subject not only to Fourth Amendment limitations but to First Amendment ones as well. Where should the line be drawn?

In *Philadelphia Yearly Meeting of the Religious Society of Friends v. Tate,* 519 F.3d 1335 (3d Cir. 1975), the police engaged in surveillance of the plaintiffs' public demonstrations and assemblies. The police shared the information with other government agencies as well as leaked it to the media. Distinguishing *Laird v. Tatum,* the court held that the plaintiffs sufficiently established evidence of a chilling effect. The court reasoned that making the information about the plaintiffs available to non-police entities "could interfere with the job opportunities, careers or travel rights of the individual plaintiffs." Additionally, "disclosure on nationwide television that certain named persons or organizations are subjects of police intelligence files has a potential for a substantial adverse impact on such persons and organizations even though tangible evidence of the impact may be difficult, if not impossible, to obtain." Does *Tate* adequately distinguish *Laird*? Is public disclosure always a more injurious privacy violation than government surveillance and information collection?

DOW CHEMICAL CO. V. UNITED STATES
476 U.S. 227 (1986)

BURGER, C.J. . . . Petitioner Dow Chemical Co. operates a 2,000-acre facility manufacturing chemicals at Midland, Michigan. The facility consists of numerous covered buildings, with manufacturing equipment and piping conduits located between the various buildings exposed to visual observation from the air. At all times, Dow has maintained elaborate security around the perimeter of the complex barring ground-level public views of these areas. It also investigates any low-level flights by aircraft over the facility. Dow has not undertaken, however, to conceal all manufacturing equipment within the complex from aerial views. Dow maintains that the cost of covering its exposed equipment would be prohibitive.

In early 1978, enforcement officials of EPA, with Dow's consent, made an on-site inspection of two power plants in this complex. A subsequent EPA request for a second inspection, however, was denied, and EPA did not thereafter seek an administrative search warrant. Instead, EPA employed a commercial aerial photographer, using a standard floor-mounted, precision aerial mapping camera, to take photographs of the facility from altitudes of 12,000, 3,000, and 1,200 feet. At all times the aircraft was lawfully within navigable airspace.

EPA did not inform Dow of this aerial photography, but when Dow became aware of it, Dow brought suit in the District Court alleging that EPA's action violated the Fourth Amendment and was beyond EPA's statutory investigative authority. The District Court granted Dow's motion for summary judgment on the ground that EPA had no authority to take aerial photographs and that doing so was a search violating the Fourth Amendment. EPA was permanently enjoined from taking aerial photographs of Dow's premises and from disseminating, releasing, or copying the photographs already taken. . . .

The photographs at issue in this case are essentially like those commonly used in mapmaking. Any person with an airplane and an aerial camera could readily duplicate them. In common with much else, the technology of photography has changed in this century. These developments have enhanced industrial processes, and indeed all areas of life; they have also enhanced law enforcement techniques. . . .

. . . Dow claims EPA's use of aerial photography was a "search" of an area that, notwithstanding the large size of the plant, was within an "industrial curtilage" rather than an "open field," and that it had a reasonable expectation of privacy from such photography protected by the Fourth Amendment. . . .

. . . Dow concedes that a simple flyover with naked-eye observation, or the taking of a photograph from a nearby hillside overlooking such a facility, would give rise to no Fourth Amendment problem.

In *California v. Ciraolo*, 476 U.S. 207 (1986), decided today, we hold that naked-eye aerial observation from an altitude of 1,000 feet of a backyard within the curtilage of a home does not constitute a search under the Fourth Amendment.

In the instant case, two additional Fourth Amendment claims are presented: whether the common-law "curtilage" doctrine encompasses a large industrial complex such as Dow's, and whether photography employing an aerial mapping camera is permissible in this context. Dow argues that an industrial plant, even one occupying 2,000 acres, does not fall within the "open fields" doctrine of *Oliver v. United States* but rather is an "industrial curtilage" having constitutional protection equivalent to that of the curtilage of a private home. Dow further contends that any aerial photography of this "industrial curtilage" intrudes upon its reasonable expectations of privacy. Plainly a business establishment or an industrial or commercial facility enjoys certain protections under the Fourth Amendment. . . .

. . . The curtilage area immediately surrounding a private house has long been given protection as a place where the occupants have a reasonable and legitimate expectation of privacy that society is prepared to accept. . . .

Dow plainly has a reasonable, legitimate, and objective expectation of privacy within the interior of its covered buildings, and it is equally clear that expectation is one society is prepared to observe. Moreover, it could hardly be expected that Dow would erect a huge cover over a 2,000-acre tract. In contending that its entire enclosed plant complex is an "industrial curtilage," Dow argues that its exposed manufacturing facilities are analogous to the curtilage surrounding a home because it has taken every possible step to bar access from ground level. . . .

. . . The intimate activities associated with family privacy and the home and its curtilage simply do not reach the outdoor areas or spaces between structures and buildings of a manufacturing plant. . . .

It may well be, as the Government concedes, that surveillance of private property by using highly sophisticated surveillance equipment not generally available to the public, such as satellite technology, might be constitutionally proscribed absent a warrant. But the photographs here are not so revealing of intimate details as to raise constitutional concerns. Although they undoubtedly give EPA more detailed information than naked-eye views, they remain limited to an outline of the facility's buildings and equipment. The mere fact that human vision is enhanced somewhat, at least to the degree here, does not give rise to constitutional problems. An electronic device to penetrate walls or windows so as to hear and record confidential discussions of chemical formulae or other trade secrets would raise very different and far more serious questions; other protections such as trade secret laws are available to protect commercial activities from private surveillance by competitors. . . .

We hold that the taking of aerial photographs of an industrial plant complex from navigable airspace is not a search prohibited by the Fourth Amendment. . . .

POWELL, J. joined by BRENNAN, MARSHALL, and BLACKMUN, JJ. concurring in part and dissenting in part. The Fourth Amendment protects private citizens from arbitrary surveillance by their Government. For nearly 20 years, this Court has adhered to a standard that ensured that Fourth Amendment rights would retain their vitality as technology expanded the Government's capacity to commit unsuspected intrusions into private areas and activities. Today, in the context of administrative aerial photography of commercial premises, the Court retreats from that standard. It holds that the photography was not a Fourth Amendment "search" because it was not accompanied by a physical trespass and because the equipment used was not the most highly sophisticated form of technology available to the Government. Under this holding, the existence of an asserted privacy interest apparently will be decided solely by reference to the manner of surveillance used to intrude on that interest. Such an inquiry will not protect Fourth Amendment rights, but rather will permit their gradual decay as technology advances. . . .

NOTES & QUESTIONS

1. *New Surveillance Technologies.* One of the rationales of *Dow Chemical* is that the device could have been acquired by a member of the general public. Does the case turn on this point? Suppose the police used a special camera that was developed exclusively for law enforcement purposes.

   The *Dow Chemical* Court stated: "It may well be, as the Government concedes, that surveillance of private property by using highly sophisticated surveillance equipment not generally available to the public, such as satellite technology, might be constitutionally proscribed absent a warrant." But does this sentence reflect contemporary technological reality? Mark Monmonier describes the rapid increase in the availability of commercial satellite capacities once the Cold War ended and the U.S. government lifted its restrictions in this area. The public now has cheaper and more detailed satellite images available to it than ever before.[46] As an example, look at maps.google.com, where free high-quality satellite imagery is available for most street maps.

   Recall that in *The Right to Privacy*, Warren and Brandeis complained in 1890 of the then new ability to take candid photographs of individuals. Before the invention of the snap camera, people did not expect to be photographed without their consent. Clearly today the ability to take pictures in public is greatly enhanced. There are video cameras, night-vision cameras, powerful

---

[46] Mark Monmonier, *Spying with Maps* (2002).

zoom lenses, and satellite images available for sale. Google Street View has mapped most of the United States at street level. Are these new technologies eroding our reasonable expectation of privacy?[47] How should the law respond?

2. *Flashlights.* The use of a flashlight "to illuminate a darkened area simply does not constitute a search, and thus triggers no Fourth Amendment protection." *Texas v. Brown*, 460 U.S. 730 (1983). If this conclusion seems evident, how is a flashlight different from other devices that enhance human senses? Is any device that enhances the human senses merely an extension of ordinary senses? What factors should be considered in determining which sense enhancement devices trigger a search under the Fourth Amendment and which do not?

3. *Canine Sniffs.* In *United States v. Place*, 462 U.S. 696 (1983), the Court held that a canine sniff by a narcotics detection dog does not infringe upon a reasonable expectation of privacy. It declared:

> A "canine sniff" by a well-trained narcotics detection dog, however, does not require opening the luggage. It does not expose noncontraband items that otherwise would remain hidden from public view, as does, for example, an officer's rummaging through the contents of the luggage. Thus, the manner in which information is obtained through this investigative technique is much less intrusive than a typical search. Moreover, the sniff discloses only the presence or absence of narcotics, a contraband item. Thus, despite the fact that the sniff tells the authorities something about the contents of the luggage, the information obtained is limited. This limited disclosure also ensures that the owner of the property is not subjected to the embarrassment and inconvenience entailed in less discriminate and more intrusive investigative methods.
>
> In these respects, the canine sniff is *sui generis*. We are aware of no other investigative procedure that is so limited both in the manner in which the information is obtained and in the content of the information revealed by the procedure.

The Court revisited the issue of canine sniffs in *Illinois v. Caballes*, 543 U.S. 405 (2005) where it found that the conducting a dog sniff did not change the constitutional character of a "traffic stop that is lawful at its interception and otherwise executed in a reasonable manner." A dog sniff performed on the exterior of a car whose driver was "lawfully seized for a traffic violation" did not rise to the level of a constitutionally cognizable infringement."

Finally, in *Florida v. Harris*, 568 U.S. ___ (2013), the Supreme Court considered when a canine sniff would constitute probable cause for a further search, in this case of the interior of a truck. Aldo, the dog in the *Harris*, alerted on two separate occasions involving the same individual. The search on the first occasion turned up only chemicals that Aldo was not trained to detect; the search on the second revealed nothing of interest to law enforcement.

A unanimous Supreme Court found that a probable cause assessment based on a trained narcotics dog's alert turned on "whether all the facts surrounding a dog's alert, viewed through the lens of common sense, would make a reasonably prudent person think a search would reveal contraband or evidence

---

[47] For an argument that people do have reasonable expectations of privacy in public, see Helen Nissenbaum, *Protecting Privacy in an Information Age: The Problem of Privacy in Public*, 17 Law & Phil. 559 (1998).

of a crime." Writing for the *Harris* Court, Justice Kagan added: "A sniff is up to snuff when it meets that test." One key factor is making this determination is whether "the State has produced proof from controlled settings that a dog performs reliably in detecting drugs." A defendant is able to contest the State's case "by disputing the reliability of the drug overall or of a particular alert."

In an empirical study of the reliability of dog sniffs, dogs trained to detect narcotics or explosives responded to subconscious cuing by their handlers.[48] In dissenting in *Illinois v. Caballes*, Justice Souter took a similar view: "The infallible dog . . . is a creature of legal fiction."

In *Florida v. Jardines* (2013*)*, the Court considered the issue of sniffs by narcotic canines of the front porch of a house. That case is discussed in a note below following *United States v. Jones.*

KYLLO V. UNITED STATES

533 U.S. 27 (2001)

SCALIA, J. In 1991 Agent William Elliott of the United States Department of the Interior came to suspect that marijuana was being grown in the home belonging to petitioner Danny Kyllo, part of a triplex on Rhododendron Drive in Florence, Oregon. Indoor marijuana growth typically requires high-intensity lamps. In order to determine whether an amount of heat was emanating from petitioner's home consistent with the use of such lamps, at 3:20 A.M. on January 16, 1992, Agent Elliott and Dan Haas used an Agema Thermovision 210 thermal imager to scan the triplex. Thermal imagers detect infrared radiation, which virtually all objects emit but which is not visible to the naked eye. The imager converts radiation into images based on relative warmth — black is cool, white is hot, shades of gray connote relative differences; in that respect, it operates somewhat like a video camera showing heat images. The scan of Kyllo's home took only a few minutes and was performed from the passenger seat of Agent Elliott's vehicle across the street from the front of the house and also from the street in back of the house. The scan showed that the roof over the garage and a side wall of petitioner's home were relatively hot compared to the rest of the home and substantially warmer than neighboring homes in the triplex. Agent Elliott concluded that petitioner was using halide lights to grow marijuana in his house, which indeed he was. Based on tips from informants, utility bills, and the thermal imaging, a Federal Magistrate Judge issued a warrant authorizing a search of petitioner's home, and the agents found an indoor growing operation involving more than 100 plants. Petitioner was indicted on one count of manufacturing marijuana, in violation of 21 U.S.C. § 841(a)(1). He unsuccessfully moved to suppress the evidence seized from his home and then entered a conditional guilty plea. . . .

. . . "At the very core" of the Fourth Amendment "stands the right of a man to retreat into his own home and there be free from unreasonable governmental intrusion." With few exceptions, the question whether a warrantless search of a home is reasonable and hence constitutional must be answered no.

---

[48] Lisa Lit et al., *Handler Beliefs Affect Scent Detection Outcomes*, 14 Animal Cognition 387 (2011).

On the other hand, the antecedent question of whether or not a Fourth Amendment "search" has occurred is not so simple under our precedent. The permissibility of ordinary visual surveillance of a home used to be clear because, well into the 20th century, our Fourth Amendment jurisprudence was tied to common-law trespass. Visual surveillance was unquestionably lawful because "the eye cannot by the laws of England be guilty of a trespass." We have since decoupled violation of a person's Fourth Amendment rights from trespassory violation of his property, but the lawfulness of warrantless visual surveillance of a home has still been preserved. As we observed in *California v. Ciraolo*, 476 U.S. 207, (1986), "[t]he Fourth Amendment protection of the home has never been extended to require law enforcement officers to shield their eyes when passing by a home on public thoroughfares." . . .

The present case involves officers on a public street engaged in more than naked-eye surveillance of a home. We have previously reserved judgment as to how much technological enhancement of ordinary perception from such a vantage point, if any, is too much. While we upheld enhanced aerial photography of an industrial complex in *Dow Chemical*, we noted that we found "it important that this is not an area immediately adjacent to a private home, where privacy expectations are most heightened."

It would be foolish to contend that the degree of privacy secured to citizens by the Fourth Amendment has been entirely unaffected by the advance of technology. For example, as the cases discussed above make clear, the technology enabling human flight has exposed to public view (and hence, we have said, to official observation) uncovered portions of the house and its curtilage that once were private. The question we confront today is what limits there are upon this power of technology to shrink the realm of guaranteed privacy. . . .

. . . [I]n the case of the search of the interior of homes — the prototypical and hence most commonly litigated area of protected privacy — there is a ready criterion, with roots deep in the common law, of the minimal expectation of privacy that exists, and that is acknowledged to be reasonable. To withdraw protection of this minimum expectation would be to permit police technology to erode the privacy guaranteed by the Fourth Amendment. We think that obtaining by sense-enhancing technology any information regarding the interior of the home that could not otherwise have been obtained without physical "intrusion into a constitutionally protected area," *Silverman*, 365 U.S., at 512, constitutes a search — at least where (as here) the technology in question is not in general public use. This assures preservation of that degree of privacy against government that existed when the Fourth Amendment was adopted. On the basis of this criterion, the information obtained by the thermal imager in this case was the product of a search.[49]

---

[49] The dissent's repeated assertion that the thermal imaging did not obtain information regarding the interior of the home is simply inaccurate. A thermal imager reveals the relative heat of various rooms in the home. The dissent may not find that information particularly private or important, but there is no basis for saying it is not information regarding the interior of the home. The dissent's comparison of the thermal imaging to various circumstances in which outside observers might be able to perceive, without technology, the heat of the home — for example, by observing snowmelt on the roof — is quite irrelevant. The fact that equivalent information could sometimes be obtained by other means does not make lawful the use of means that violate the Fourth Amendment. The police might, for example, learn how many people are in a particular house by setting up year-round

The Government maintains, however, that the thermal imaging must be upheld because it detected "only heat radiating from the external surface of the house." The dissent makes this its leading point, contending that there is a fundamental difference between what it calls "off-the-wall" observations and "through-the-wall surveillance." But just as a thermal imager captures only heat emanating from a house, so also a powerful directional microphone picks up only sound emanating from a house — and a satellite capable of scanning from many miles away would pick up only visible light emanating from a house. We rejected such a mechanical interpretation of the Fourth Amendment in *Katz*, where the eavesdropping device picked up only sound waves that reached the exterior of the phone booth. Reversing that approach would leave the homeowner at the mercy of advancing technology — including imaging technology that could discern all human activity in the home. While the technology used in the present case was relatively crude, the rule we adopt must take account of more sophisticated systems that are already in use or in development. The dissent's reliance on the distinction between "off-the-wall" and "through-the-wall" observation is entirely incompatible with the dissent's belief, which we discuss below, that thermal-imaging observations of the intimate details of a home are impermissible. The most sophisticated thermal imaging devices continue to measure heat "off-the-wall" rather than "through-the-wall"; the dissent's disapproval of those more sophisticated thermal-imaging devices, is an acknowledgement that there is no substance to this distinction. As for the dissent's extraordinary assertion that anything learned through "an inference" cannot be a search, that would validate even the "through-the-wall" technologies that the dissent purports to disapprove. Surely the dissent does not believe that the through-the-wall radar or ultrasound technology produces an 8-by-10 Kodak glossy that needs no analysis (i.e., the making of inferences). And, of course, the novel proposition that inference insulates a search is blatantly contrary to *United States v. Karo*, 468 U.S. 705 (1984), where the police "inferred" from the activation of a beeper that a certain can of ether was in the home. The police activity was held to be a search, and the search was held unlawful.

The Government also contends that the thermal imaging was constitutional because it did not "detect private activities occurring in private areas." . . . The Fourth Amendment's protection of the home has never been tied to measurement of the quality or quantity of information obtained. In *Silverman*, for example, we made clear that any physical invasion of the structure of the home, "by even a fraction of an inch," was too much, and there is certainly no exception to the warrant requirement for the officer who barely cracks open the front door and sees nothing but the nonintimate rug on the vestibule floor. . . .

Limiting the prohibition of thermal imaging to "intimate details" would not only be wrong in principle; it would be impractical in application. . . . To begin with, there is no necessary connection between the sophistication of the surveillance equipment and the "intimacy" of the details that it observes—which means that one cannot say (and the police cannot be assured) that use of the relatively crude equipment at issue here will always be lawful. The Agema

---

surveillance, but that does not make breaking and entering to find out the same information lawful. In any event, on the night of January 16, 1992, no outside observer could have discerned the relative heat of Kyllo's home without thermal imaging.

Thermovision 210 might disclose, for example, at what hour each night the lady of the house takes her daily sauna and bath—a detail that many would consider "intimate"; and a much more sophisticated system might detect nothing more intimate than the fact that someone left a closet light on. We could not, in other words, develop a rule approving only that through-the-wall surveillance which identifies objects no smaller than 36 by 36 inches, but would have to develop a jurisprudence specifying which home activities are "intimate" and which are not. And even when (if ever) that jurisprudence were fully developed, no police office would be able to know *in advance* whether his through-the-wall surveillance picks up "intimate" details—and thus would be unable to know in advance whether it is constitutional. . . .

We have said that the Fourth Amendment draws "a firm line at the entrance to the house." That line, we think, must be not only firm but also bright — which requires clear specification of those methods of surveillance that require a warrant. While it is certainly possible to conclude from the videotape of the thermal imaging that occurred in this case that no "significant" compromise of the homeowner's privacy has occurred, we must take the long view, from the original meaning of the Fourth Amendment forward. . . .

Where, as here, the Government uses a device that is not in general public use, to explore details of the home that would previously have been unknowable without physical intrusion, the surveillance is a "search" and is presumptively unreasonable without a warrant. . . .

STEVENS, J. joined by REHNQUIST, C.J. and O'CONNOR and KENNEDY, JJ. dissenting. . . . [S]earches and seizures of property in plain view are presumptively reasonable. Whether that property is residential or commercial, the basic principle is the same: "What a person knowingly exposes to the public, even in his own home or office, is not a subject of Fourth Amendment protection." That is the principle implicated here.

While the Court "take[s] the long view" and decides this case based largely on the potential of yet-to-be-developed technology that might allow "through-the-wall surveillance," this case involves nothing more than off-the-wall surveillance by law enforcement officers to gather information exposed to the general public from the outside of petitioner's home. All that the infrared camera did in this case was passively measure heat emitted from the exterior surfaces of petitioner's home; all that those measurements showed were relative differences in emission levels, vaguely indicating that some areas of the roof and outside walls were warmer than others. As still images from the infrared scans show, no details regarding the interior of petitioner's home were revealed. . . .

. . . Heat waves, like aromas that are generated in a kitchen, or in a laboratory or opium den, enter the public domain if and when they leave a building. A subjective expectation that they would remain private is not only implausible but also surely not "one that society is prepared to recognize as 'reasonable.'" . . .

Despite the Court's attempt to draw a line that is "not only firm but also bright," the contours of its new rule are uncertain because its protection apparently dissipates as soon as the relevant technology is "in general public use." Yet how much use is general public use is not even hinted at by the Court's opinion, which makes the somewhat doubtful assumption that the thermal imager used in this case does not satisfy that criterion. In any event, putting aside its lack of clarity, this criterion is somewhat perverse because it seems likely that the threat to privacy will grow, rather than recede, as the use of intrusive equipment becomes more readily available. . . .

Because the new rule applies to information regarding the "interior" of the home, it is too narrow as well as too broad. Clearly, a rule that is designed to protect individuals from the overly intrusive use of sense-enhancing equipment should not be limited to a home. If such equipment did provide its user with the functional equivalent of access to a private place — such as, for example, the telephone booth involved in *Katz*, or an office building — then the rule should apply to such an area as well as to a home. . . .

NOTES & QUESTIONS

1. ***Thermal Imagers vs. Cameras.*** How does the Court distinguish the thermal imager in *Kyllo* from the camera in *Dow Chemical*? Does this distinction make sense?

2. ***Technology in General Public Use.*** The majority based its holding on the fact that a thermal sensor was *"a device not in general public use."* However, a search of eBay reveals different kinds of thermal-imaging devices for sale at a variety of prices. Hence, the thermal sensor device is one that is publicly available. Is this "eBay test" relevant? One can also imagine the "smartphone test." There are now low-cost thermal camera attachments that work with smartphones. How should a court decide when a technology is "in general public use"?

3. ***The Home.*** A key component to the Court's holding is that the thermal sensor was used to glean information about activities in the home. The home has long enjoyed significant protection as a private place. The maxim that the home is one's "castle" appeared as early as 1499.[50] *Semayne's Case,* 77 Eng. Rep. 194, 195 (K.B. 1604), was the first recorded case in which the sanctity of the home was mentioned: "[T]he house of every one is to him as his castle and fortress." According to William Blackstone, the law has "so particular and tender a regard to the immunity of a man's house that it stiles it his castle, and will never suffer it to be violated with impunity."[51] William Pitt once remarked: "The poorest man may in his cottage bid defiance to the Crown. It may be frail — its roof may shake — the wind may enter — the rain may enter — but the King of England cannot enter — all his force dares not cross the threshold of the ruined tenement!"[52]

In the United States, the importance of privacy in the home has long been recognized. The Supreme Court recognized in 1886 the importance of protecting "the sanctity of a man's home" in *Boyd v. United States,* 116 U.S. 616 (1886). As the Court later observed in *Payton v. New York,* 445 U.S. 573

---

[50] See Note, *The Right to Privacy in Nineteenth Century America*, 94 Harv. L. Rev. 1892, 1894 (1981).
[51] 4 William Blackstone, *Commentaries on the Laws of England* 223 (1769).
[52] Charles J. Sykes, *The End of Privacy* 83 (1999).

(1980): "In none is the zone of privacy more clearly defined when bounded by the unambiguous physical dimensions of an individual's home." In a different case, it stated, "At the very core [of the Fourth Amendment] stands the right of a man to retreat into his own home and there be free from unreasonable governmental intrusion." *Silverman v. United States,* 365 U.S. 505 (1961).

The Court has afforded the home the strongest protection under the Fourth Amendment. For example, automobiles can generally be searched without warrants, while homes rarely can be searched without warrants (except under exigent circumstances). Compare *Chambers v. Maroney,* 399 U.S. 42 (1970), with *Mincey v. Arizona,* 437 U.S. 385 (1978).

In *Chapman v. United States,* 365 U.S. 610 (1961), the Court held that the Fourth Amendment protection of the home extends to apartment tenants, even though they do not own the apartment. Further, in *Bumper v. North Carolina,* 391 U.S. 543 (1968), the Court held that a person living in the home of another was entitled to the same Fourth Amendment protection as if it were her own home. Later, in *Minnesota v. Olson,* 495 U.S. 91 (1990), the Court extended the Fourth Amendment protection of the home to overnight guests in another's home or apartment: However, in *Minnesota v. Carter,* 525 U.S. 83 (1998), the Court held that a visitor who was in a friend's apartment for a short duration (not overnight) had no reasonable expectation of privacy in that apartment because that apartment was used to package cocaine and was not being used as a home.

How much does *Kyllo*'s holding rest on the fact that the thermal sensor was used to learn about activities in the home? What if a thermal sensor were used outside the home?

4. ***The Courts vs. Congress.*** Orin Kerr contends that when new technologies are involved, Congress, not the courts, should be the primary rulemaker. In particular, Kerr critiques the generally held view that "the Fourth Amendment should be interpreted broadly in response to technological change." According to Kerr:

> [C]ourts should place a thumb on the scale in favor of judicial caution when technology is in flux, and should consider allowing legislatures to provide the primary rules governing law enforcement investigations involving new technologies. . . . When technology is in flux, Fourth Amendment protections should remain relatively modest until the technology stabilizes.

Kerr justifies his conclusion by making an argument about the attributes of judicial versus legislative rulemaking:

> The first difference is that legislatures typically create generally applicable rules ex ante, while courts tend to create rules ex post in a case-by-case fashion. That is, legislatures enact generalized rules for the future, whereas courts resolve disputes settling the rights of parties arising from a past event. The difference leads to Fourth Amendment rules that tend to lag behind parallel statutory rules and current technologies by at least a decade, resulting in unsettled and then outdated rules that often make little sense given current technological facts. . . .
> A second difference between judicial and legislative rulemaking concerns their operative constraints. . . . Legislatures are up to the task [of adapting to technological change]; courts generally are not. Legislatures can experiment

with different rules and make frequent amendments; they can place restrictions on both public and private actors; and they can even "sunset" rules so that they apply only for a particular period of time. The courts cannot. As a result, Fourth Amendment rules will tend to lack the flexibility that a regulatory response to new technologies may require. . . .

The third important difference between judicial rules and legislative rules relates to the information environment in which rules are generated. Legislative rules tend to be the product of a wide range of inputs, ranging from legislative hearings and poll results to interest group advocacy and backroom compromises. Judicial rules tend to follow from a more formal and predictable presentation of written briefs and oral arguments by two parties. Once again, the difference offers significant advantages to legislative rulemaking. The task of generating balanced and nuanced rules requires a comprehensive understanding of technological facts. Legislatures are well-equipped to develop such understandings; courts generally are not.[53]

Peter Swire responds that Congress's privacy legislation was shaped by judicial decisions concerning the Fourth Amendment:

At least four mutually reinforcing reasons underscore the importance of judicial decisions to how these privacy protections were enacted. First, the Supreme Court decision made the issue more salient, focusing attention on a topic that otherwise would not climb to the top of the legislative agenda. Second, the importance of the decision to the political process was greater because of what social scientists have called the "endowment effect" or "status quo bias." . . . [T]he concept is that individuals experience a loss as more important than a gain of equal size. . . . [T]he perceived "loss" of Fourth Amendment protections . . . would be a spur to legislative action. Third, the opinions of the Supreme Court shaped the legislative debates. Vigorous dissents in each case articulated reasons why privacy protections should be considered important. . . . Fourth, once the issue had moved high enough on the agenda to warrant a vote, there were persuasive public-policy arguments that some privacy protections were appropriate.[54]

Daniel Solove also disagrees with Kerr's conclusions: "Where the courts have left open areas for legislative rules to fill in, Congress has created an uneven fabric of protections that is riddled with holes and that has weak protections in numerous places." Further, Solove contends, legislative ex ante rules are not necessarily preferable to judicial ex post rules:

The problem with ex ante laws is that they cannot anticipate all of the new and changing factual situations that technology brings about. Ex post rules, in contrast, are often much better tailored to specific types of technology, because such rules arise as technology changes, rather than beforehand. . . .

Solove argues that the "historical record suggests that Congress is actually far worse than the courts in reacting to new technologies." In response to Kerr's argument that the legislature is better equipped to understand new technologies than the judiciary, Solove responds that "merely shifting to a statutory regime

---

[53] Orin S. Kerr, *The Fourth Amendment and New Technologies: Constitutional Myths and the Case for Caution*, 102 Mich. L. Rev. 801, 803-05, 868, 871, 875 (2004).

[54] Peter P. Swire, *Katz Is Dead. Long Live Katz,* 102 Mich. L. Rev. 904, 917 (2004).

will not eliminate Kerr's concern with judges misunderstanding technology. In fact, many judicial misunderstandings stem from courts trying to fit new technologies into old statutory regimes built around old technologies."[55]

5. ***Is the Fourth Amendment Primarily Protective of the Individual or Society?*** Consider the following observation by Anthony Amsterdam:

> [Should the Fourth Amendment] be viewed as a collection of protections of atomistic spheres of interest of individual citizens or as a regulation of governmental conduct[?] Does it safeguard *my* person and *your* house and *her* papers and *his* effects against unreasonable searches and seizures; or is it essentially a regulatory canon requiring government to order its law enforcement procedures in a fashion that keeps us collectively secure in our persons, houses, papers, and effects, against unreasonable searches and seizures?[56]

Under what view does the Supreme Court seem to be operating? Which view do you think is the most appropriate?

6. ***Is Government Observation Different from Observation by Others?*** Amsterdam also argues that one's privacy may be violated by being observed by the police but may not be violated by the very same observation from others:

> [I]f you live in a cheap hotel or in a ghetto flat, your neighbors can hear you breathing quietly even in temperate weather when it is possible to keep the windows and doors closed. For the tenement dweller, the difference between observation by neighbors and visitors who ordinarily use the common hallways and observation by policemen who come into hallways to "check up" or "look around" is the difference between all the privacy that his condition allows and none. Is that small difference too unimportant to claim [F]ourth [A]mendment protection?[57]

Do you agree that our expectations of privacy turn on who is watching rather than simply whether we are being watched? Should the "reasonable expectation of privacy" test be changed to the "reasonable expectation of what the police can observe or search" test?

7. ***Beepers and Tracking Devices.*** In *United States v. Knotts*, 460 U.S. 276 (1983), the police placed a beeper in a five-gallon drum of chloroform purchased by the defendants and placed in their car. The beeper transmitted signals that enabled the police to track the location of the defendants' vehicle. The Court held that the Fourth Amendment did not apply to the use of this device because a "person traveling in an automobile on public thoroughfares has no reasonable expectation of privacy in his movements from one place to another." Therefore, "[t]he governmental surveillance conducted by means of the beeper in this case amounted principally to the following of an automobile

---

[55] Daniel J. Solove, *Fourth Amendment Codification and Professor Kerr's Misguided Call for Judicial Deference*, 74 Fordham L. Rev. 747, 761-74 (2005).

[56] Anthony G. Amsterdam, *Perspectives on the Fourth Amendment*, 58 Minn. L. Rev. 349, 367 (1974). For an additional critique of the reasonable expectation of privacy test, see Andrew E. Taslitz, *The Fourth Amendment in the Twenty-First Century: Technology, Privacy, and Human Emotions*, 65 Law & Contemp. Probs. 125 (2002).

[57] Amsterdam, *Fourth Amendment, supra*, at 404.

on public streets and highways." In *United States v. Karo*, 468 U.S. 705 (1984), law enforcement officials planted a beeper in a can of ether that the defendant bought from an informant. The officials tracked the movements of the can of ether through a variety of places, including within a residence. While the movements in *Knotts* were in public, the movements within the residence were not, and this amounted to an impermissible search of the residence:

> The monitoring of an electronic device such as a beeper is, of course, less intrusive than a full-scale search, but it does reveal a critical fact about the interior of the premises that the Government is extremely interested in knowing and that it could not have otherwise obtained without a warrant. The case is thus not like *Knotts*, for there the beeper told the authorities nothing about the interior of Knotts' cabin. The information obtained in *Knotts* was "voluntarily conveyed to anyone who wanted to look. . . ."

UNITED STATES V. JONES

132 S. Ct. 945 (2012)

SCALIA J. We decide whether the attachment of a Global-Positioning-System (GPS) tracking device to an individual's vehicle, and subsequent use of that device to monitor the vehicle's movements on public streets, constitutes a search or seizure within the meaning of the Fourth Amendment. . . .

In 2004 respondent Antoine Jones, owner and operator of a nightclub in the District of Columbia, came under suspicion of trafficking in narcotics and was made the target of an investigation by a joint FBI and Metropolitan Police Department task force. Officers employed various investigative techniques, including visual surveillance of the nightclub, installation of a camera focused on the front door of the club, and a pen register and wiretap covering Jones's cellular phone.

Based in part on information gathered from these sources, in 2005 the Government applied to the United States District Court for the District of Columbia for a warrant authorizing the use of an electronic tracking device on the Jeep Grand Cherokee registered to Jones's wife. A warrant issued, authorizing installation of the device in the District of Columbia and within 10 days.

On the 11th day, and not in the District of Columbia but in Maryland,[58] agents installed a GPS tracking device on the undercarriage of the Jeep while it was parked in a public parking lot. Over the next 28 days, the Government used the device to track the vehicle's movements, and once had to replace the device's battery when the vehicle was parked in a different public lot in Maryland. By means of signals from multiple satellites, the device established the vehicle's location within 50 to 100 feet, and communicated that location by cellular phone to a Government computer. It relayed more than 2,000 pages of data over the 4-week period.

The Government ultimately obtained a multiple-count indictment charging Jones and several alleged co-conspirators with, as relevant here, conspiracy to distribute and

---

[58] In this litigation, the Government has conceded noncompliance with the warrant and has argued only that a warrant was not required.

possess with intent to distribute five kilograms or more of cocaine and 50 grams or more of cocaine base, in violation of 21 U.S.C. §§ 841 and 846 . . . .

In March 2007, a grand jury returned another indictment, charging Jones and others with the same conspiracy. The Government introduced at trial the same GPS-derived locational data admitted in the first trial, which connected Jones to the alleged conspirators' stash house that contained $850,000 in cash, 97 kilograms of cocaine, and 1 kilogram of cocaine base. The jury returned a guilty verdict, and the District Court sentenced Jones to life imprisonment. . . .

The Fourth Amendment provides in relevant part that "[t]he right of the people to be secure in their persons, houses, papers, and effects, against unreasonable searches and seizures, shall not be violated." It is beyond dispute that a vehicle is an "effect" as that term is used in the Amendment. We hold that the Government's installation of a GPS device on a target's vehicle, and its use of that device to monitor the vehicle's movements, constitutes a "search."

It is important to be clear about what occurred in this case: The Government physically occupied private property for the purpose of obtaining information. We have no doubt that such a physical intrusion would have been considered a "search" within the meaning of the Fourth Amendment when it was adopted. . . .

The text of the Fourth Amendment reflects its close connection to property, since otherwise it would have referred simply to "the right of the people to be secure against unreasonable searches and seizures"; the phrase "in their persons, houses, papers, and effects" would have been superfluous.

Consistent with this understanding, our Fourth Amendment jurisprudence was tied to common-law trespass, at least until the latter half of the 20th century. *Kyllo v. United States,* 533 U.S. 27 (2001); Kerr, *The Fourth Amendment and New Technologies: Constitutional Myths and the Case for Caution*, 102 Mich. L. Rev. 801 (2004). Thus, in *Olmstead v. United States,* 277 U.S. 438 (1928), we held that wiretaps attached to telephone wires on the public streets did not constitute a Fourth Amendment search because "[t]here was no entry of the houses or offices of the defendants."

Our later cases, of course, have deviated from that exclusively property-based approach. In *Katz v. United States,* 389 U.S. 347 (1967), we said that "the Fourth Amendment protects people, not places," and found a violation in attachment of an eavesdropping device to a public telephone booth. Our later cases have applied the analysis of Justice Harlan's concurrence in that case, which said that a violation occurs when government officers violate a person's "reasonable expectation of privacy."

The Government contends that the Harlan standard shows that no search occurred here, since Jones had no "reasonable expectation of privacy" in the area of the Jeep accessed by Government agents (its underbody) and in the locations of the Jeep on the public roads, which were visible to all. But we need not address the Government's contentions, because Jones's Fourth Amendment rights do not rise or fall with the *Katz* formulation. At bottom, we must "assur[e] preservation of that degree of privacy against government that existed when the Fourth Amendment was adopted." *Kyllo.* As explained, for most of our history the Fourth Amendment was understood to embody a particular concern for government trespass upon the areas ("persons, houses, papers, and effects") it enumerates.[59] *Katz* did not repudiate that understanding. . . . *Katz* did not narrow the Fourth Amendment's scope.

The Government contends that several of our post-*Katz* cases foreclose the conclusion that what occurred here constituted a search. It relies principally on two cases in which we rejected Fourth Amendment challenges to "beepers," electronic tracking devices that represent another form of electronic monitoring. The first case, *Knotts,* upheld against Fourth Amendment challenge the use of a "beeper" that had been placed in a container of chloroform, allowing law enforcement to monitor the location of the container. We said that there had been no infringement of Knotts' reasonable expectation of privacy since the information obtained—the location of the automobile carrying the container on public roads, and the location of the off-loaded container in open fields near Knotts' cabin—had been voluntarily conveyed to the public. But as we have discussed, the *Katz* reasonable-expectation-of-privacy test has been *added to,* not *substituted for,* the common-law trespassory test. The holding in *Knotts* addressed only the former, since the latter was not at issue. The beeper had been placed in the container before it came into Knotts' possession, with the consent of the then-owner. *Knotts* would be relevant, perhaps, if the Government were making the argument that what would otherwise be an unconstitutional search is not such where it produces only public information. The Government does not make that argument, and we know of no case that would support it.

The second "beeper" case, *United States v. Karo* does not suggest a different conclusion. There we addressed the question left open by *Knotts,* whether the installation of a beeper in a container amounted to a search or seizure. As in *Knotts,* at the time the beeper was installed the container belonged to a third party, and it did not come into possession of the defendant until later. Thus, the specific question we considered was whether the installation "*with the consent of the original owner* constitute[d] a search or seizure . . . when the container is delivered to a buyer having no knowledge of the presence of the beeper" (emphasis added). We held not. The Government, we said, came into physical contact with the container only before it belonged to the defendant Karo; and the transfer of the container with the unmonitored beeper inside did not convey any information and thus did not invade Karo's privacy. That conclusion is perfectly consistent with the one we reach here. Karo accepted the container as it came to him, beeper and all, and was therefore not entitled to object to the beeper's presence, even though it was used to monitor the container's location. . . .

---

[59] Justice ALITO's concurrence (hereinafter concurrence) doubts the wisdom of our approach because "it is almost impossible to think of late–18th-century situations that are analogous to what took place in this case." But in fact it posits a situation that is not far afield—a constable's concealing himself in the target's coach in order to track its movements. There is no doubt that the information gained by that trespassory activity would be the product of an unlawful search—whether that information consisted of the conversations occurring in the coach, or of the destinations to which the coach traveled.

In any case, it is quite irrelevant whether there was an 18th-century analog. Whatever new methods of investigation may be devised, our task, *at a minimum,* is to decide whether the action in question would have constituted a "search" within the original meaning of the Fourth Amendment. Where, as here, the Government obtains information by physically intruding on a constitutionally protected area, such a search has undoubtedly occurred.

The concurrence begins by accusing us of applying "18th-century tort law." That is a distortion. What we apply is an 18th-century guarantee against unreasonable searches, which we believe must provide *at a minimum* the degree of protection it afforded when it was adopted. The concurrence does not share that belief. It would apply *exclusively Katz* 's reasonable-expectation-of-privacy test, even when that eliminates rights that previously existed. . . .

In fact, it is the concurrence's insistence on the exclusivity of the *Katz* test that needlessly leads us into "particularly vexing problems" in the present case. This Court has to date not deviated from the understanding that mere visual observation does not constitute a search. . . . Thus, even assuming that the concurrence is correct to say that "[t]raditional surveillance" of Jones for a 4–week period "would have required a large team of agents, multiple vehicles, and perhaps aerial assistance," our cases suggest that such visual observation is constitutionally permissible. It may be that achieving the same result through electronic means, without an accompanying trespass, is an unconstitutional invasion of privacy, but the present case does not require us to answer that question.

Justice SOTOMAYOR, concurring. I join the Court's opinion because I agree that a search within the meaning of the Fourth Amendment occurs, at a minimum, "[w]here, as here, the Government obtains information by physically intruding on a constitutionally protected area." . . . The Government usurped Jones' property for the purpose of conducting surveillance on him, thereby invading privacy interests long afforded, and undoubtedly entitled to, Fourth Amendment protection.

Of course, the Fourth Amendment is not concerned only with trespassory intrusions on property. As the majority's opinion makes clear, however, *Katz* 's reasonable-expectation-of-privacy test augmented, but did not displace or diminish, the common-law trespassory test that preceded it. . . . Justice Alito's approach, which discounts altogether the constitutional relevance of the Government's physical intrusion on Jones' Jeep, erodes that longstanding protection for privacy expectations inherent in items of property that people possess or control. By contrast, the trespassory test applied in the majority's opinion reflects an irreducible constitutional minimum: When the Government physically invades personal property to gather information, a search occurs. The reaffirmation of that principle suffices to decide this case.

Nonetheless, as Justice Alito notes, physical intrusion is now unnecessary to many forms of surveillance. With increasing regularity, the Government will be capable of duplicating the monitoring undertaken in this case by enlisting factory- or owner-installed vehicle tracking devices or GPS-enabled smartphones. As Justice Alito incisively observes, the same technological advances that have made possible nontrespassory surveillance techniques will also affect the *Katz* test by shaping the evolution of societal privacy expectations. Under that rubric, I agree with Justice Alito that, at the very least, "longer term GPS monitoring in investigations of most offenses impinges on expectations of privacy."

In cases involving even short-term monitoring, some unique attributes of GPS surveillance relevant to the *Katz* analysis will require particular attention. GPS monitoring generates a precise, comprehensive record of a person's public movements that reflects a wealth of detail about her familial, political, professional, religious, and sexual associations. The Government can store such records and efficiently mine them for information years into the future. . . .

Awareness that the Government may be watching chills associational and expressive freedoms. And the Government's unrestrained power to assemble data that reveal private aspects of identity is susceptible to abuse. . . .

I would take these attributes of GPS monitoring into account when considering the existence of a reasonable societal expectation of privacy in the sum of one's public movements. I would ask whether people reasonably expect that their movements will be recorded and aggregated in a manner that enables the Government to ascertain, more or less at will, their political and religious beliefs, sexual habits, and so on. I do not regard as dispositive the fact that the Government might obtain the fruits of GPS monitoring through lawful conventional surveillance techniques. I would also consider the appropriateness of entrusting to the Executive, in the absence of any oversight from a coordinate branch, a tool so amenable to misuse, especially in light of the Fourth Amendment's goal to curb arbitrary exercises of police power to and prevent "a too permeating police surveillance," *United States v. Di Re,* 332 U.S. 581 (1948).

More fundamentally, it may be necessary to reconsider the premise that an individual has no reasonable expectation of privacy in information voluntarily disclosed to third parties. This approach is ill suited to the digital age, in which people reveal a great deal of information about themselves to third parties in the course of carrying out mundane tasks. People disclose the phone numbers that they dial or text to their cellular providers; the URLs that they visit and the e-mail addresses with which they correspond to their Internet service providers; and the books, groceries, and medications they purchase to online retailers. . . . I for one doubt that people would accept without complaint the warrantless disclosure to the Government of a list of every Web site they had visited in the last week, or month, or year. But whatever the societal expectations, they can attain constitutionally protected status only if our Fourth Amendment jurisprudence ceases to treat secrecy as a prerequisite for privacy. I would not assume that all information voluntarily disclosed to some member of the public for a limited purpose is, for that reason alone, disentitled to Fourth Amendment protection. Resolution of these difficult questions in this case is unnecessary, however, because the Government's physical intrusion on Jones' Jeep supplies a narrower basis for decision. I therefore join the majority's opinion.

Justice ALITO, with whom Justice GINSBURG, Justice BREYER, and Justice KAGAN join, concurring in the judgment. This case requires us to apply the Fourth Amendment's prohibition of unreasonable searches and seizures to a 21st-century surveillance technique, the use of a Global Positioning System (GPS) device to monitor a vehicle's movements for an extended period of time. Ironically, the Court has chosen to decide this case based on 18th-century tort law. By attaching a small GPS device[60] to the underside of the vehicle that respondent drove, the law enforcement officers in this case engaged in conduct that might have provided

---

[60] Although the record does not reveal the size or weight of the device used in this case, there is now a device in use that weighs two ounces and is the size of a credit card. Tr. of Oral Arg. 27.

grounds in 1791 for a suit for trespass to chattels.[61] And for this reason, the Court concludes, the installation and use of the GPS device constituted a search.

This holding, in my judgment, is unwise. It strains the language of the Fourth Amendment; it has little if any support in current Fourth Amendment case law; and it is highly artificial.

I would analyze the question presented in this case by asking whether respondent's reasonable expectations of privacy were violated by the long-term monitoring of the movements of the vehicle he drove. . . .

The Fourth Amendment prohibits "unreasonable searches and seizures," and the Court makes very little effort to explain how the attachment or use of the GPS device fits within these terms. . . .

The Court does claim that the installation and use of the GPS constituted a search, but this conclusion is dependent on the questionable proposition that these two procedures cannot be separated for purposes of Fourth Amendment analysis. If these two procedures are analyzed separately, it is not at all clear from the Court's opinion why either should be regarded as a search. It is clear that the attachment of the GPS device was not itself a search; if the device had not functioned or if the officers had not used it, no information would have been obtained. And the Court does not contend that the use of the device constituted a search either. On the contrary, the Court accepts the holding in *United States v. Knotts* that the use of a surreptitiously planted electronic device to monitor a vehicle's movements on public roads did not amount to a search.

The Court argues—and I agree—that "we must 'assur[e] preservation of that degree of privacy against government that existed when the Fourth Amendment was adopted.'" But it is almost impossible to think of late–18th-century situations that are analogous to what took place in this case. (Is it possible to imagine a case in which a constable secreted himself somewhere in a coach and remained there for a period of time in order to monitor the movements of the coach's owner?[62]) The Court's theory seems to be that the concept of a search, as originally understood, comprehended any technical trespass that led to the gathering of evidence, but we know that this is incorrect. At common law, any unauthorized intrusion on private property was actionable, see Prosser & Keeton 75, but a trespass on open fields, as opposed to the "curtilage" of a home, does not fall within the scope of the Fourth Amendment because private property outside the curtilage is not part of a "hous[e]" within the meaning of the Fourth Amendment. See *Oliver v. United States*, 466 U.S. 170 (1984).

The Court's reasoning in this case is very similar to that in the Court's early decisions involving wiretapping and electronic eavesdropping, namely, that a technical trespass followed by the gathering of evidence constitutes a search. . . .

---

[61] At common law, a suit for trespass to chattels could be maintained if there was a violation of "the dignitary interest in the inviolability of chattels," but today there must be "some actual damage to the chattel before the action can be maintained." W. Keeton, D. Dobbs, R. Keeton, & D. Owen, Prosser & Keeton on Law of Torts 87 (5th ed.1984) (hereinafter Prosser & Keeton). Here, there was no actual damage to the vehicle to which the GPS device was attached.

[62] The Court suggests that something like this might have occurred in 1791, but this would have required either a gigantic coach, a very tiny constable, or both—not to mention a constable with incredible fortitude and patience.

By contrast, in cases in which there was no trespass, it was held that there was no search. Thus, in *Olmstead v. United States* (1928), the Court found that the Fourth Amendment did not apply because "[t]he taps from house lines were made in the streets near the houses." . . .

Katz v. United States (1967) finally did away with the old approach, holding that a trespass was not required for a Fourth Amendment violation. . . . What mattered, the Court now held, was whether the conduct at issue "violated the privacy upon which [the defendant] justifiably relied while using the telephone booth.". . .

Under this approach, as the Court later put it when addressing the relevance of a technical trespass, "an actual trespass is neither necessary *nor sufficient* to establish a constitutional violation." *United States v. Karo,* 468 U.S. 705 (1984) (emphasis added). . . .

Disharmony with a substantial body of existing case law is only one of the problems with the Court's approach in this case.

I will briefly note four others. First, the Court's reasoning largely disregards what is really important (the *use* of a GPS for the purpose of long-term tracking) and instead attaches great significance to something that most would view as relatively minor (attaching to the bottom of a car a small, light object that does not interfere in any way with the car's operation). . . .

Second, the Court's approach leads to incongruous results. If the police attach a GPS device to a car and use the device to follow the car for even a brief time, under the Court's theory, the Fourth Amendment applies. But if the police follow the same car for a much longer period using unmarked cars and aerial assistance, this tracking is not subject to any Fourth Amendment constraints. . . .

Third, under the Court's theory, the coverage of the Fourth Amendment may vary from State to State. If the events at issue here had occurred in a community property State or a State that has adopted the Uniform Marital Property Act, respondent would likely be an owner of the vehicle, and it would not matter whether the GPS was installed before or after his wife turned over the keys. In non-community-property States, on the other hand, the registration of the vehicle in the name of respondent's wife would generally be regarded as presumptive evidence that she was the sole owner.

Fourth, the Court's reliance on the law of trespass will present particularly vexing problems in cases involving surveillance that is carried out by making electronic, as opposed to physical, contact with the item to be tracked. For example, suppose that the officers in the present case had followed respondent by surreptitiously activating a stolen vehicle detection system that came with the car when it was purchased. Would the sending of a radio signal to activate this system constitute a trespass to chattels? Trespass to chattels has traditionally required a physical touching of the property. . . .

The *Katz* expectation-of-privacy test avoids the problems and complications noted above, but it is not without its own difficulties. It involves a degree of circularity, and judges are apt to confuse their own expectations of privacy with those of the hypothetical reasonable person to which the *Katz* test looks. In addition, the *Katz* test rests on the assumption that this hypothetical reasonable person has a well-developed and stable set of privacy expectations. But technology can change those expectations. Dramatic technological change may lead to periods in which popular expectations are in flux and may ultimately produce significant changes in popular attitudes. . . .

Recent years have seen the emergence of many new devices that permit the monitoring of a person's movements. In some locales, closed-circuit television video monitoring is becoming ubiquitous. On toll roads, automatic toll collection systems create a precise record of the movements of motorists who choose to make use of that convenience. Many motorists purchase cars that are equipped with devices that permit a central station to ascertain the car's location at any time so that roadside assistance may be provided if needed and the car may be found if it is stolen.

Perhaps most significant, cell phones and other wireless devices now permit wireless carriers to track and record the location of users—and as of June 2011, it has been reported, there were more than 322 million wireless devices in use in the United States. For older phones, the accuracy of the location information depends on the density of the tower network, but new "smart phones," which are equipped with a GPS device, permit more precise tracking. For example, when a user activates the GPS on such a phone, a provider is able to monitor the phone's location and speed of movement and can then report back real-time traffic conditions after combining ("crowdsourcing") the speed of all such phones on any particular road. Similarly, phone-location-tracking services are offered as "social" tools, allowing consumers to find (or to avoid) others who enroll in these services. The availability and use of these and other new devices will continue to shape the average person's expectations about the privacy of his or her daily movements. . .

A legislative body is well situated to gauge changing public attitudes, to draw detailed lines, and to balance privacy and public safety in a comprehensive way.

To date, however, Congress and most States have not enacted statutes regulating the use of GPS tracking technology for law enforcement purposes. The best that we can do in this case is to apply existing Fourth Amendment doctrine and to ask whether the use of GPS tracking in a particular case involved a degree of intrusion that a reasonable person would not have anticipated.

Under this approach, relatively short-term monitoring of a person's movements on public streets accords with expectations of privacy that our society has recognized as reasonable. *See Knotts.* But the use of longer term GPS monitoring in investigations of most offenses impinges on expectations of privacy. For such offenses, society's expectation has been that law enforcement agents and others would not—and indeed, in the main, simply could not—secretly monitor and catalogue every single movement of an individual's car for a very long period. In this case, for four weeks, law enforcement agents tracked every movement that respondent made in the vehicle he was driving. We need not identify with precision the point at which the tracking of this vehicle became a search, for the line was surely crossed before the 4–week mark. Other cases may present more difficult questions. But where uncertainty exists with respect to whether a certain period of GPS surveillance is long enough to constitute a Fourth Amendment search, the police may always seek a warrant. We also need not consider whether prolonged GPS monitoring in the context of investigations involving extraordinary offenses would similarly intrude on a constitutionally protected sphere of privacy. In such cases, long-term tracking might have been mounted using previously available techniques.

NOTES & QUESTIONS

1. *A New Direction?* Both concurring opinions, involving five justices, embraced a new theory of privacy. In previous cases, the Court has focused extensively on whether something or not was exposed to the public. The concurrences recognize that extensive and aggregated surveillance can violate a reasonable expectation of privacy regardless of whether or not such surveillance occurred in public:

> Under this approach, relatively short-term monitoring of a person's movements on public streets accords with expectations of privacy that our society has recognized as reasonable. *See Knotts.* But the use of longer term GPS monitoring in investigations of most offenses impinges on expectations of privacy. For such offenses, society's expectation has been that law enforcement agents and others would not—and indeed, in the main, simply could not—secretly monitor and catalogue every single movement of an individual's car for a very long period. In this case, for four weeks, law enforcement agents tracked every movement that respondent made in the vehicle he was driving.

> Is this a new direction for the reasonable expectation of privacy test?

2. *Influence on Other Areas of Privacy Law.* Other areas of law often use Fourth Amendment reasonable expectation of privacy determinations as guidance about whether something is a private matter. Will *Jones* affect the privacy torts? Consider *Nader v. General Motors Corp.,* 255 N.E.2d 765 (N.Y. Ct. App. 1970) (excerpted in Chapter 2). There, a court held that "overzealous" surveillance in public could violate privacy and constitute intrusion upon seclusion. To what extent would Justices Alito and Sotomayor agree? Does their approach extend further?

3. *Where Is the Line?* The theory that extensive and aggregated surveillance in public can impinge upon a reasonable expectation of privacy is sometimes referred to as "mosaic theory." Prior to *Jones,* a number of scholars had argued that extensive public surveillance should be viewed as a privacy violation. According to Daniel Solove, "We do many private things in public, such as buy medications and hygiene products in drug stores and browse books and magazines in bookstores. We expect a kind of practical obscurity—to be just another face in the crowd."[63] Helen Nissenbaum notes that "while isolated bits of information (as generated, for example, by merely walking around in public spaces and not taking active steps to avoid notice) are not especially revealing, assemblages are capable of exposing people quite profoundly."[64] In his concurrence, Justice Alito distinguished between short-term monitoring and extensive surveillance, but he did not indicate where the line would be drawn:

---

[63] Daniel J. Solove, *Nothing to Hide: The False Tradeoff Between Privacy and Security* 178 (2011).

[64] Helen Nissenbaum, *Protecting Privacy in the Information Age: The Problem of Privacy in Public,* 17 Law & Phil. 559 (1998).

We need not identify with precision the point at which the tracking of this vehicle became a search, for the line was surely crossed before the 4-week mark. Other cases may present more difficult questions. But where uncertainty exists with respect to whether a certain period of GPS surveillance is long enough to constitute a Fourth Amendment search, the police may always seek a warrant.

Orin Kerr contends that the mosaic theory raises too many questions and is too vague to serve as useful guidance for law enforcement surveillance activities:

> [I]mplementing the mosaic theory would require courts to answer an extensive list of difficult and novel questions. . . . For example, what is the standard for the mosaic? How should courts aggregate conduct to know when a sufficient mosaic has been created? Which techniques should fall within the mosaic approach? Should mosaic searches require a warrant? If so, how can mosaic warrants satisfy the particularity requirement? Should the exclusionary rule apply to violations of the mosaic search doctrine? Who has standing to challenge mosaic searches? Adopting a mosaic theory will require courts to answer all of these questions and more.

Moreover, Kerr notes:

> [T]he amount of private information collected by the surveillance will vary greatly from suspect to suspect. For example, imagine the police know that one suspect rarely uses his car while a second suspect drives several hours a day. The police install GPS devices on both cars for one week, revealing very little about the first suspect and a great deal about the habits of the second. Does the mosaic amount to a search earlier for the second suspect than the first?[65]

4. ***Dogs, the Home, and Property-Based Protection of Privacy.*** Continuing the trend of strong protection of the home (as in *Kyllo*), and reliance on a trespass theory (as in *Jones*), the Supreme Court found that the use of a drug-sniffing dog on a homeowner's porch to investigate the contents of the home was a "search" within the meaning of the Fourth Amendment. Writing for the majority in *Florida v. Jardines*, 133 S.Ct. 1409 (2013), Justice Scalia began by stating that the area immediately surrounding the home, such as the front porch of a house, was part of its curtilage. This area was protected by the Fourth Amendment and the use of drug-sniffing dog by the police exceeded the "implicit license" that homeowner's grant to visitors, including "the Nation's Girl Scouts and trick-or-treaters" as well as law enforcement officers who wish to knock on the front door of the house. According to Justice Scalia, however, "the background social norms that invite a visitor to the front door do not invite him there to conduct a search." Referring to *Jones*, he repeated that the *Katz* reasonable expectation test was added to "the traditional property-based understanding of the Fourth Amendment."

Concurring in the opinion, Justice Kagan, joined by Justices Ginsburg and Sotomayor, found that the use of the drug-sniffing dog implicated *Kyllo*. In her

---

[65] Orin S. Kerr, *The Mosaic Theory of the Fourth Amendment*, 110 Mich. L. Rev. 311 (2012).

view, the trained drug-detection dog was similar to the thermal imaging device in that earlier case, namely a device not in general public use that was being use to explore details of the home that would not otherwise be discovered without entering inside the premises.

In dissent, Justice Alito, joined by Chief Justice Roberts, and Justices Kennedy and Breyer, scoffed at the notion of a violation of any implied license or property interest. The officer in the case simply walked up to the front door, stayed no longer than a minute or two, and used a dog, an animal whose "keen sense of smell has been used in law enforcement for centuries." Moreover, a dog was not a new form of technology or device unlike the thermal imaging device in *Kyllo*.

Is *Florida v. Jardines* best understood as building on *Jones* to re-invigorate property-based theories of privacy? Or does it stand for the narrower proposition that privacy cases involving trespass can gain a slender majority from the current membership of the Supreme Court?

B. INFORMATION GATHERING ABOUT FIRST AMENDMENT ACTIVITIES

In a number of instances, government searches and surveillance implicate First Amendment activities. For example, as Daniel Solove argues:

> First Amendment activities are implicated by a wide array of law enforcement data-gathering activities. Government information gathering about computer and Internet use, for example, can intrude on a significant amount of First Amendment activity. Searching or seizing a computer can reveal personal and political writings. Obtaining e-mail can provide extensive information about correspondence and associations. Similarly, ISP records often contain information about speech, as they can link people to their anonymous communications. AOL, for example, receives about a thousand requests per month for use of its customer records in criminal cases.[66]

Neil Richards contends that government surveillance is particularly dangerous for two reasons:

> First, surveillance is harmful because it can chill the exercise of our civil liberties. With respect to civil liberties, consider surveillance of people when they are thinking, reading, and communicating with others in order to make up their minds about political and social issues. Such intellectual surveillance is especially dangerous because it can cause people not to experiment with new, controversial, or deviant ideas. To protect our intellectual freedom to think without state oversight or interference, we need what I have elsewhere called "intellectual privacy." A second special harm that surveillance poses is its effect on the power dynamic between the watcher and the watched. This disparity creates the risk of a variety of harms, such as discrimination, coercion, and the threat of selective

---

[66] Daniel J. Solove, *The First Amendment as Criminal Procedure*, 82 N.Y.U. L. Rev. 112, 114-15 (2007).

enforcement, where critics of the government can be prosecuted or blackmailed for wrongdoing unrelated to the purpose of the surveillance.[67]

Government information gathering involving First Amendment activities not only involves Fourth Amendment protections, but also First Amendment protections and sometimes special statutory protections.

The Fourth Amendment was heavily influenced by government information gathering about First Amendment activities. The Framers of the Constitution forged the Fourth Amendment in part due to their strong dislike of general warrants, especially in seditious libel cases. A general warrant authorized sweeping searches for all personal papers related to a particular offense. In English common law, speech criticizing the government could be deemed "seditious libel" — a criminal offense. The American colonists were subject to general warrants, and the Framers particularly detested them as an overbearing form of government power.

In the years preceding the American Revolution, there were several high-profile seditious libel cases in England that generated significant attention in the colonies. These cases involved interests that are now protected by both the First and Fourth Amendments. In *Wilkes v. Wood,* 19 Howell's State Trials 982, 982 (C.P. 1763), a publication called *The North Briton* printed anonymous criticism of the King, but it was commonly known that the author was John Wilkes, a member of Parliament. Pursuant to a general warrant authorizing searches for anything connected with *The North Briton*, the government began raiding the homes of various authors and publishers (including Wilkes) to search and seize their personal documents. Wilkes was arrested. Wilkes brought a civil trespass lawsuit to challenge the general warrant. Wilkes prevailed in a jury trial. The Wilkes case was widely celebrated in the American colonies.[68]

Two years later, John Entick challenged a general warrant in a seditious libel investigation. In *Entick v.* Carrington, 19 Howell's State Trials 1029 (C.P. 1765). Lord Camden found for Entick, criticizing general warrants: "[A person's] house is rifled; his most valuable secrets are taken out of his possession, before the paper for which he is charged is found to be criminal by any competent jurisdiction, and before he is convicted either of writing publishing or being concerned in the paper." The *Entick* case was also widely praised in the colonies, and even towns were named after Wilkes and Lord Camden.

The *Wilkes* and *Entick* cases strongly shaped the Framers' intent behind the Fourth Amendment, as well as subsequent interpretations of the Fourth Amendment.

---

[67] Neil M. Richards, *The Dangers of Surveillance*, 126 Harv. L. Rev. 1934, 1935 (2013).

[68] William J. Cuddihy, *The Fourth Amendment: Origins and Original Meaning 602-1781* (2009).

STANFORD V. TEXAS

379 U.S. 476 (1965)

STEWART, J. . . . . On December 27, 1963, several Texas law-enforcement officers presented themselves at the petitioner's San Antonio home for the purpose of searching it under authority of a warrant issued by a local magistrate. By the time they had finished, five hours later, they had seized some 2,000 of the petitioner's books, pamphlets, and papers. The question presented by this case is whether the search and seizure were constitutionally valid.

The warrant was issued under s 9 of Art. 6889-3A of the Revised Civil Statutes of Texas. The Article, enacted in 1955 and known as the Suppression Act, is a sweeping and many-faceted law which, among other things, outlaws the Communist Party and creates various individual criminal offenses, each punishable by imprisonment for up to 20 years. Section 9 authorizes the issuance of a warrant "for the purpose of searching for and seizing any books, records, pamphlets, cards, receipts, lists, memoranda, pictures, recordings, or any written instruments showing that a person or organization is violating or has violated any provision of this Act." The section sets forth various procedural requirements, among them that "if the premises to be searched constitute a private residence, such application for a search warrant shall be accompanied by the affidavits of two credible citizens." . . .

The district judge issued a warrant which specifically described the premises to be searched, recited the allegations of the applicant's and affiants' belief that the premises were "a place where books, records, pamphlets, cards, receipts, lists, memoranda, pictures, recordings and other written instruments concerning the Communist Party of Texas, and the operations of the Communist Party in Texas are unlawfully possessed and used in violation of Article 6889-3 and Article 6889-3A, Revised Civil Statutes of the State of Texas," and ordered the executing officers "to enter immediately and search the above described premises for such items listed above unlawfully possessed in violation of Article 6889--3 and Article 6889-3A, Revised Civil Statutes, State of Texas, and to take possession of same."

The warrant was executed by the two Assistant Attorneys General who had signed the affidavit, accompanied by a number of county officers. They went to the place described in the warrant, which was where the petitioner resided and carried on a mail order book business under the trade name "All Points of View." The petitioner was not at home when the officers arrived, but his wife was, and she let the officers in after one of them had read the warrant to her. . . .

Under the general supervision of one of the Assistant Attorneys General the officers spent more than four hours in gathering up about half the books they found in the house. Most of the material they took came from the stock in trade of the petitioner's business, but they took a number of books from his personal library as well. The books and pamphlets taken comprised approximately 300 separate titles, in addition to numerous issues of several different periodicals. Among the books taken were works by such diverse writers as Karl Marx, Jean Paul Sartre, Theodore Draper, Fidel Castro, Earl Browder, Pope John XXIII, and MR. JUSTICE HUGO L. BLACK. The officers also took possession of many of the petitioner's private documents and papers, including his marriage certificate, his insurance policies, his household bills and receipts, and files of his personal correspondence. All this material was packed into 14 cartons and hauled off to an investigator's office in the county courthouse. The officers did not find any "records of the Communist Party" or any "party lists and dues payments." . . .

. . . [W]e think it is clear that this warrant was of a kind which it was the purpose of the Fourth Amendment to forbid—a general warrant. Therefore, even accepting the premise that some or even all of the substantive provisions of Articles 6889-3 and 6889-3A of the Revised Civil Statutes of Texas are constitutional and have not been pre-empted by federal law, even accepting the premise that the warrant sufficiently specified the offense believed to have been committed and was issued upon probable cause, the magistrate's order denying the motion to annul the warrant and return the property must nonetheless be set aside. . . .

The Fourth Amendment provides that "no Warrants shall issue, but upon probable cause, supported by Oath or affirmation, and particularly describing the place to be searched, and the persons or things to be seized."

These words are precise and clear. They reflect the determination of those who wrote the Bill of Rights that the people of this new Nation should forever "be secure in their persons, houses, papers, and effects" from intrusion and seizure by officers acting under the unbridled authority of a general warrant. Vivid in the memory of the newly independent Americans were those general warrants known as writs of assistance under which officers of the Crown had so bedeviled the colonists. The hated writs of assistance had given customs officials blanket authority to search where they pleased for goods imported in violation of the British tax laws. They were denounced by James Otis as "the worst instrument of arbitrary power, the most destructive of English liberty, and the fundamental principles of law, that ever was found in an English law book," because they placed "the liberty of every man in the hands of every petty officer." . . .

But while the Fourth Amendment was most immediately the product of contemporary revulsion against a regime of writs of assistance, its roots go far deeper. Its adoption in the Constitution of this new Nation reflected the culmination in England a few years earlier of a struggle against oppression which had endured for centuries. The story of that struggle has been fully chronicled in the pages of this Court's reports, and it would be a needless exercise in pedantry to review again the detailed history of the use of general warrants as instruments of oppression from the time of the Tudors, through the Star Chamber, the Long Parliament, the Restoration, and beyond.

What is significant to note is that this history is largely a history of conflict between the Crown and the press. It was in enforcing the laws licensing the publication of literature and, later, in prosecutions for seditious libel that general warrants were systematically used in the sixteenth, seventeenth, and eighteenth centuries. In Tudor England officers of the Crown were given roving commissions to search where they pleased in order to suppress and destroy the literature of dissent, both Catholic and Puritan. In later years warrants were sometimes more specific in content, but they typically authorized of all persons connected of the premises of all persons connected with the publication of a particular libel, or the arrest and seizure of all the papers of a named person thought to be connected with a libel.

It was in the context of the latter kinds of general warrants that the battle for individual liberty and privacy was finally won—in the landmark cases of *Wilkes v. Wood* and *Entick v. Carrington*. The *Wilkes* case arose out of the Crown's attempt to stifle a publication called The North Briton, anonymously published by John Wilkes, then a member of Parliament—particularly issue No. 45 of that journal. Lord Halifax, as Secretary of State, issued a warrant ordering four of the King's messengers "to make strict and diligent search for the authors, printers, and publishers of a seditious and treasonable paper, entitled, The North Briton, No. 45, . . . and them, or any of them, having found, to apprehend and seize, together with their papers." "Armed with their roving commission, they set forth in quest of unknown offenders; and unable to take evidence, listened to rumors, idle tales, and curious guesses. They held in their hands the liberty of every man whom they were pleased to suspect." Holding that this was "a ridiculous warrant against the whole English nation," the Court of Common Pleas awarded Wilkes damages against the Secretary of State.

John Entick was the author of a publication called Monitor or British Freeholder. A warrant was issued specifically naming him and that publication, and authorizing his arrest for seditious libel and the seizure of his "books and papers." The King's messengers executing the warrant ransacked Entick's home for four hours and carted away quantities of his books and papers. In an opinion which this Court has characterized as a wellspring of the rights now protected by the Fourth Amendment, Lord Camden declared the warrant to be unlawful. "This power," he said, "so assumed by the secretary of state is an execution upon all the party's papers, in the first instance. His house is rifled; his most valuable secrets are taken out of his possession, before the paper for which he is charged is found to be criminal by any competent jurisdiction, and before he is convicted either of writing, publishing, or being concerned in the paper." Thereafter, the House of Commons passed two resolutions condemning general warrants, the first limiting its condemnation to their use in cases of libel, and the second condemning their use generally. . . .

In short, what this history indispensably teaches is that the constitutional requirement that warrants must particularly describe the 'things to be seized' is to be accorded the most scrupulous exactitude when the "things" are books, and the basis for their seizure is the ideas which they contain. No less a standard could be faithful to First Amendment freedoms. The constitutional impossibility of leaving the protection of those freedoms to the whim of the officers charged with executing the warrant is dramatically underscored by what the officers saw fit to seize under the warrant in this case.

Two centuries have passed since the historic decision in *Entick v. Carrington*, almost to the very day. The world has greatly changed, and the voice of nonconformity now sometimes speaks a tongue which Lord Camden might find hard to understand. But the Fourth and Fourteenth Amendments guarantee to John Stanford that no official of the State shall ransack his home and seize his books and papers under the unbridled authority of a general warrant—no less than the law 200 years ago shielded John Entick from the messengers of the King.

NOTES & QUESTIONS

1. ***Are Fourth Amendment Warrants Sufficient to Protect First Amendment Activities?*** In *Zurcher v. the Stanford Daily,* 436 U.S. 547 (1978), the police searched the offices of a college newspaper, *The Stanford Daily,* to gather evidence relating to a demonstration that had turned violent. The newspaper was not involved in the demonstration and nobody at the newspaper was suspected of criminal activity. The reason for the search was that the journalists had taken photographs of the demonstration and the police wanted these photos for evidence. The newspaper argued that searches of its offices "will seriously threaten the ability of the press to gather, analyze, and disseminate news." The Court, however, concluded that the Fourth Amendment did not prohibit state authorities from searching the premises if the authorities had a warrant supported by probable cause. The Court recognized that First Amendment activities were implicated by the search but noted that "[w]here the materials sought to be seized may be protected by the First Amendment, the requirements of the Fourth Amendment must be applied with 'scrupulous exactitude.'" The Court then concluded that "the prior cases do no more than insist that the courts apply the warrant requirements with particular exactitude when First Amendment interests would be endangered by the search." Accordingly, First Amendment interests are sufficiently protected by "the preconditions for a warrant." In later cases, the Court clarified that the First Amendment does not require a "higher standard" than a warrant supported by probable cause for seizures of books or films.

2. ***The Privacy Protection Act.*** In 1980, Congress responded to *Zurcher* by passing the Privacy Protection Act (PPA), 42 U.S.C. § 2000aa. The PPA prohibits government officials from searching or seizing work product materials or documents "possessed by a person reasonably believed to have a purpose to disseminate to the public a newspaper, book, broadcast, or other similar form of public communication, in or affecting interstate or foreign commerce." However, if "there is probable cause to believe that the person possessing such materials has committed or is committing the criminal offense to which the materials relate," then such materials may be searched or seized. The "criminal offense" cannot consist of the mere receipt, possession, or communication of the materials (except if it involves national defense data, classified information, or child pornography). § 2000aa(a)(1). The materials may be searched or seized if "there is reason to believe that the immediate seizure of such materials is necessary to prevent the death of, or serious bodily injury to, a human being."

   The effect of the PPA is to require law enforcement officials to obtain a subpoena in order to obtain such information. Unlike search warrants, subpoenas permit the party subject to them to challenge them in court before having to comply. Further, instead of law enforcement officials searching through offices or records, the persons served with the subpoena must produce the documents themselves.

3. *Government Information Gathering About Group Membership.* In *NAACP v. Alabama*, 357 U.S. 449 (1958), the Supreme Court held that the NAACP could not be compelled to publicly disclose the names and addresses of its members. According to the Court, there is a "vital relationship between freedom to associate and privacy in one's associations." Exposing members would subject them "to economic reprisal, loss of employment, threat of physical coercion, and other manifestations of public hostility."

The Court reached a similar conclusion in *Bates v. City of Little Rock,* 361 U.S. 516 (1960)*,* and *Gibson v. Florida Legislative Investigation Commission*, 372 U.S. 539 (1963), cases also involving the compulsory public disclosure of NAACP membership lists.

In *Barenblatt v. United States*, 360 U.S. 109 (1959), a Subcommittee of the House Un-American Activities Committee summoned Lloyd Barenblatt, a 31-year-old teacher of psychology at Vassar College, to testify. The House Un-American Activities Committee was a long-standing Committee that investigated Communist activities by forcing suspected Communist Party members to disclose that they were Party members and reveal the names of other members. Before Barenblatt appeared, his contract with Vassar expired and was not renewed. The Committee wanted to question Barenblatt because another witness had stated that when Barenblatt was a graduate student, he had been associated with a small group of Communists. When called before the Committee, Barenblatt refused to answer questions pertaining to his current and past membership in the Communist Party. He was found in contempt, tried in federal district court, and sentenced to six months in prison. Barenblatt challenged his being compelled to disclose his political associations as a violation of his First Amendment rights. The Supreme Court, however, concluded that Congress's interests in investigating the Communist Party outweighed Barenblatt's rights. Justices Black, Warren, and Douglas dissented:

> The First Amendment says in no equivocal language that Congress shall pass no law abridging freedom of speech, press, assembly or petition. The activities of this Committee, authorized by Congress, do precisely that, through exposure, obloquy and public scorn. . . .
>
> [The majority] balances the right of the Government to preserve itself, against Barenblatt's right to refrain from revealing Communist affiliations. Such a balance, however, mistakes the factors to be weighed. In the first place, it completely leaves out the real interest in Barenblatt's silence, the interest of the people as a whole in being able to join organizations, advocate causes and make political "mistakes" without later being subjected to governmental penalties for having dared to think for themselves. . . .

In *Shelton v. Tucker*, 364 U.S. 479 (1960), the Court struck down a law requiring teachers to list the organizations they belonged or contributed to within the past five years. The Court held that "the statute's comprehensive interference with associational freedom goes far beyond what might be justified in the exercise of the State's legitimate inquiry into the fitness and competency of its teachers":

> The scope of the inquiry required by [the statute] is completely unlimited. The statute requires a teacher to reveal the church to which he belongs, or to which he has given financial support. It requires him to disclose his political party, and every political organization to which he may have contributed over a five-year period. It requires him to list, without number, every conceivable kind of associational tie — social, professional, political, vocational, or religious. Many such relationships could have no possible bearing upon the teacher's occupational competence or fitness.

Can you reconcile the Court's decision in *Barenblatt* with *Shelton v. Tucker* and *NAACP v. Alabama*?

A number of Supreme Court cases involved challenges to questions about Communist Party membership asked by state bar committees. In *Konigsberg v. State Bar of California*, 366 U.S. 36 (1961), an applicant for membership in the California Bar refused to answer questions about his membership in the Communist Party. The committee refused to certify him. The Court held that the applicant's First Amendment rights were not violated because "[t]here is here no likelihood that deterrence of association may result from foreseeable private action, for bar committee interrogations such as this are conducted in private."

In *Baird v. State Bar*, 401 U.S. 1 (1971), an applicant before the Arizona Bar Committee refused to answer whether she was a member of the Communist Party or any organization "that advocates overthrow of the United States Government by force or violence." As a result, the applicant was denied admission to the bar. The Court held that the questioning was improper because the government cannot attempt to conduct "[b]road and sweeping state inquiries" into people's political views or group associations. "In effect this young lady was asked by the State to make a guess as to whether any organization to which she ever belonged 'advocates overthrow of the United States Government by force or violence.' " The Court reasoned:

> The First Amendment's protection of association prohibits a State from excluding a person from a profession or punishing him solely because he is a member of a particular political organization or because he holds certain beliefs. Similarly, when a State attempts to make inquiries about a person's beliefs or associations, its power is limited by the First Amendment. Broad and sweeping state inquiries into these protected areas, as Arizona has engaged in here, discourage citizens from exercising rights protected by the Constitution.
>
> When a State seeks to inquire about an individual's beliefs and associations a heavy burden lies upon it to show that the inquiry is necessary to protect a legitimate state interest. Of course Arizona has a legitimate interest in determining whether petitioner has the qualities of character and the professional competence requisite to the practice of law. But here petitioner has already supplied the Committee with extensive personal and professional information to assist its determination. By her answers to questions other than No. 25, and her listing of former employers, law school professors, and other references, she has made available to the Committee the information relevant to her fitness to practice law. And whatever justification may be offered, a State may not inquire about a man's views or associations solely for the purpose of withholding a right or benefit because of what he believes.

Can you distinguish *Baird* from *Barenblatt*, *Konigsberg*, and the other Communist Party membership cases?

4. *Intellectual Privacy.* Neil Richards argues that surveillance is particularly threatening to what he calls "intellectual privacy," which he defines as "the protection from surveillance or unwanted interference by others when we are engaged in the processes of generating ideas and forming beliefs—when we're thinking, reading, and speaking with confidantes before our ideas are ready for public consumption."[69] Richards argues that intellectual privacy is a necessary protection for intellectual freedom and free speech:

> New ideas—political, scientific, artistic, or otherwise . . . depend on access to the ideas of others and the ability to engage with them. And to do this, we need to be able to read freely and then think privately about what we've read in our own time. . . .
>
> Even access to knowledge isn't by itself enough. We need places and spaces (real and virtual) in which to read, to think, to explore. The process of idea generation is one of trial and error. Very often, what seems like a good idea at the time turns out to be a terrible one after testing or further reflection. But to test or examine ideas, we again turn to other people—our friends and confidantes, our family and colleagues. We rely on these people for their frank and confidential assessments of whether we're on to something, or whether we're crazy. . . .
>
> These activities and expectations allow us to discuss, test, and reevaluate our ideas before they are ready for public exposure. . . .
>
> If we're interested in the creation of new ideas, we should want people to experiment with controversial ideas. . . .

Richards goes on to argue that First Amendment law and theory should focus more on how ideas and beliefs area formed:

> First Amendment cases and scholarship are full of explanations about *why* we allow the expression of large amounts of often offensive and harmful speech—for instance, because lots of speech enhances the search for truth, the processes of democratic self-government, or individual autonomy. By contrast, discussions of free speech have only rarely addressed the question of *how* we ensure new and interesting ideas get generated.
>
> This is a curious omission, because if we care about free speech, we should care about speakers having something interesting to say. Many of today's most cherished ideas were once highly controversial. Consider the notion that governments should be elected by the people, or the separation of church and state, or the idea of the equality of all people under law regardless of race, sex, or religion. At various times, believing or promoting each of these ideas was to be done at your peril. Think of the thousands of people killed in early modern Europe for believing differently in matters of faith, or the violent persecution of American civil rights activists who believed in racial equality. Ideas matter because they can be destabilizing, which explains why those in power have resorted to extreme measures—burnings at the stake, lynchings, Selma Bridge—to keep those destabilizing ideas in check.[70]

---

[69] Neil M. Richards, *Intellectual Privacy* 98-99 (2015).

[70] *Id.*

Is Richards correct? Should the law be concerned with belief formation? Is this too broad an extension of the First Amendment?

5. ***The First Amendment as Criminal Procedure.*** Daniel Solove contends that the First Amendment should be employed to protect against many forms of government searches and surveillance: "The First Amendment is usually taught separately from the Fourth and Fifth Amendments, and judicial decisions on criminal procedure only occasionally mention the First Amendment. [However,] the First Amendment must be considered alongside the Fourth and Fifth Amendments as a source of criminal procedure."

Solove contends that there is a doctrinal foundation for First Amendment protection against government information gathering. If the First Amendment were to apply to certain government law enforcement activities, what level of protections would it provide? Solove argues:

> Even if an instance of government information gathering triggers First Amendment protection, collection of the data will not necessarily be prohibited. Rather, the First Amendment will require the government to demonstrate (1) a significant interest in gathering the information and (2) that the manner of collection is narrowly tailored to achieving that interest. . . . [T]he use of a warrant supported by probable cause will, in most cases, suffice to satisfy the narrow tailoring requirement. In other words, in cases where the First Amendment applies, it often will require procedures similar to those required by the Fourth Amendment.[71]

Solove also posits that the First Amendment would be enforced by way of an exclusionary rule. To what extent does the First Amendment apply to government law enforcement activities? Should the First Amendment require similar protections to those of the Fourth Amendment?

GONZALES V. GOOGLE

234 F.R.D. 674 (N.D. Cal. 2006)

[The government sought information for its use in *ACLU v. Gonzales*, No. 98-CV-5591, pending in the Eastern District of Pennsylvania. That case involved a challenge by the ACLU to the Children's Online Privacy Protection Act (COPPA). Google was not a party to that case, but the government subpoenaed from Google: (1) URL samples: "[a]ll URL's that are available to be located to a query on your company's search engine as of July 31, 2005" and (2) search queries: "[a]ll queries that have been entered on your company's search engine between June 1, 2005 and July 31, 2005 inclusive." Subsequently, the government narrowed its URL sample demand to 50,000 URLs and it narrowed its search query demand to all queries during a one-week period rather than the two-month period mentioned above. Google still raised a challenge, and the government again narrowed its search query request for only 5,000 entries from Google's query log. It continued to seek a sample of 50,000 URLs from Google's search index. Under Federal Rule of Civil

---

[71] Daniel J. Solove, *The First Amendment as Criminal Procedure*, 82 N.Y.U. L. Rev. 112, 114-15, 159 (2007).

Procedure 26, a subpoena sought must be "reasonably calculated to lead to admissible evidence." It may be quashed if the "burden or expense of the proposed discovery outweighs its likely benefit."]

WARE, J. . . . As narrowed by negotiations with Google and through the course of this Miscellaneous Action, the Government now seeks a sample of 50,000 URLs from Google's search index. In determining whether the information sought is reasonably calculated to lead to admissible evidence, the party seeking the information must first provide the Court with its plans for the requested information. The Government's disclosure of its plans for the sample of URLs is incomplete. The actual methodology disclosed in the Government's papers as to the search index sample is, in its entirety, as follows: "A human being will browse a random sample of 5,000-10,000 URLs from Google's index and categorize those sites by content" and from this information, the Government intends to "estimate . . . the aggregate properties of the websites that search engines have indexed." The Government's disclosure only describes its methodology for a study to categorize the URLs in Google's search index, and does not disclose a study regarding the effectiveness of filtering software. Absent any explanation of how the "aggregate properties" of material on the Internet is germane to the underlying litigation, the Government's disclosure as to its planned categorization study is not particularly helpful in determining whether the sample of Google's search index sought is reasonably calculated to lead to admissible evidence in the underlying litigation.

Based on the Government's statement that this information is to act as a "test set for the study" and a general statement that the purpose of the study is to "evaluate the effectiveness of content filtering software," the Court is able to envision a study whereby a sample of 50,000 URLs from the Google search index may be reasonably calculated to lead to admissible evidence on measuring the effectiveness of filtering software. In such a study, the Court imagines, the URLs would be categorized, run through the filtering software, and the effectiveness of the filtering software ascertained as to the various categories of URLs. The Government does not even provide this rudimentary level of general detail as to what it intends to do with the sample of URLs to evaluate the effectiveness of filtering software, and at the hearing neither confirmed nor denied the Court's speculations about the study. In fact, the Government seems to indicate that such a study is not what it has in mind: "[t]he government seeks this information *only* to perform a study, in the aggregate, of trends on the Internet" (emphasis added), with no explanation of how an aggregate study of Internet trends would be reasonably calculated to lead to admissible evidence in the underlying suit where the efficacy of filtering software is at issue. . . .

Given the broad definition of relevance in Rule 26, and the current narrow scope of the subpoena, despite the vagueness with which the Government has disclosed its study, the Court gives the Government the benefit of the doubt. The Court finds that 50,000 URLs randomly selected from Google's data base for use in a scientific study of the effectiveness of filters is relevant to the issues in the case of *ACLU v. Gonzales*.[72]

---

[72] To the extent that the Government is gathering this information for some other purpose than to run the sample of Google's search index through various filters to determine the efficacy of those

In its original subpoena the Government sought a listing of the text of all search queries entered by Google users over a two month period. As defined in the Government's subpoena, "queries" include only the text of the search string entered by a user, and not "any additional information that may be associated with such a text string that would identify the person who entered the text string into the search engine, or the computer from which the text string was entered." The Government has narrowed its request so that it now seeks only a sample of 5,000 such queries from Google's query log. The Government discloses its plans for the query log information as follows: "A random sample of approximately 1,000 Google queries from a one-week period will be run through the Google search engine. A human being will browse the top URLs returned by each search and categorize the sites by content." . . .

Google also argues that it will be unduly burdened by loss of user trust if forced to produce its users' queries to the Government. Google claims that its success is attributed in large part to the volume of its users and these users may be attracted to its search engine because of the privacy and anonymity of the service. According to Google, even a perception that Google is acquiescing to the Government's demands to release its query log would harm Google's business by deterring some searches by some users.

Google's own privacy statement indicates that Google users could not reasonably expect Google to guard the query log from disclosure to the Government. . . . Google's privacy policy does not represent to users that it keeps confidential any information other than "personal information." Neither Google's URLs nor the text of search strings with "personal information" redacted, are reasonably "personal information" under Google's stated privacy policy. Google's privacy policy indicates that it has not suggested to its users that non-"personal information" such as that sought by the Government is kept confidential.

However, even if an expectation by Google users that Google would prevent disclosure to the Government of its users' search queries is not entirely reasonable, the statistic cited by Dr. Stark that over a quarter of all Internet searches are for pornography indicates that at least some of Google's users expect some sort of privacy in their searches. The expectation of privacy by some Google users may not be reasonable, but may nonetheless have an appreciable impact on the way in which Google is perceived, and consequently the frequency with which users use Google. Such an expectation does not rise to the level of an absolute privilege, but does indicate that there is a potential burden as to Google's loss of goodwill if Google is forced to disclose search queries to the Government.

Rule 45(c)(3)(B) provides additional protections where a subpoena seeks trade secret or confidential commercial information from a nonparty. . . . Because Google still continues to claim information about its entire search index and entire query log as confidential, the Court will presume that the requested information, as a small sample of proprietary information, may be somewhat commercially sensitive, albeit not independently commercially sensitive. Successive disclosures, whether in this lawsuit or pursuant to subsequent civil subpoenas, in the aggregate

---

filters, the Court would take a different view of the relevance of the information. For example, the Court would not find the information relevant if it is being sought just to characterize the nature of the URL's in Google's database.

could yield confidential commercial information about Google's search index or query log. . . .

What the Government has not demonstrated, however, is a substantial need for *both* the information contained in the sample of URLs and sample of search query text. Furthermore, even if the information requested is not a trade secret, a district court may in its discretion limit discovery on a finding that "the discovery sought is unreasonably cumulative or duplicative, or is obtainable from some other source that is more convenient, less burdensome, or less expensive." Rule 26(b)(2)(i).

Faced with duplicative discovery, and with the Government not expressing a preference as to which source of the test set of URLs it prefers, this Court exercises its discretion pursuant to Rule 26(b)(2) and determines that the marginal burden of loss of trust by Google's users based on Google's disclosure of its users' search queries to the Government outweighs the duplicative disclosure's likely benefit to the Government's study. Accordingly, the Court grants the Government's motion to compel only as to the sample of 50,000 URLs from Google's search index.

The Court raises, sua sponte, its concerns about the privacy of Google's users apart from Google's business goodwill argument. . . .

Although the Government has only requested the text strings entered, basic identifiable information may be found in the text strings when users search for personal information such as their social security numbers or credit card numbers through Google in order to determine whether such information is available on the Internet. The Court is also aware of so-called "vanity searches," where a user queries his or her own name perhaps with other information. . . . This concern, combined with the prevalence of Internet searches for sexually explicit material — generally not information that anyone wishes to reveal publicly — gives this Court pause as to whether the search queries themselves may constitute potentially sensitive information.

The Court also recognizes that there may a difference between a private litigant receiving potentially sensitive information and having this information be produced to the Government pursuant to civil subpoena. . . . Even though counsel for the Government assured the Court that the information received will only be used for the present litigation, it is conceivable that the Government may have an obligation to pursue information received for unrelated litigation purposes under certain circumstances regardless of the restrictiveness of a protective order. The Court expressed this concern at oral argument as to queries such as "bomb placement white house," but queries such as "communist berkeley parade route protest war" may also raise similar concerns. In the end, the Court need not express an opinion on this issue because the Government's motion is granted only as to the sample of URLs and not as to the log of search queries.

The Court also refrains from expressing an opinion on the applicability of the Electronic Communications Privacy Act. . . . The Court only notes that the ECPA does not bar the Government's request for sample of 50,000 URLs from Google's index though civil subpoena.

NOTES & QUESTIONS

1. *URL Samples vs. Search Queries.* The sought-after subpoena in *Gonzales v. Google* concerned information about both URL samples and search queries. What decision did the district court reach for each type of data? Are there different privacy implications for governmental access to the two kinds of information?

2. *Can People Be Identified from Anonymous Search Data?* An incident involving AOL proved that individuals can be identified based on their search queries. In August 2006, AOL revealed that it had released to researchers about 20 million search queries made by over 650,000 users of its search engine. Although AOL had substituted numerical IDs for the subscribers' actual user names, the personal identity of the user could be found based on the search queries. The *New York Times* demonstrated as much by tracking down AOL user No. 4417749; it linked this person's data trail to a 62-year old widow who lived in Lilburn, Georgia, and admitted to the reporter, "Those are my searches."[73]

C. FEDERAL ELECTRONIC SURVEILLANCE LAW

1. SECTION 605 OF THE FEDERAL COMMUNICATIONS ACT

Recall that in 1928, the Court in *Olmstead* declared that wiretapping did not constitute a Fourth Amendment violation. By the time *Olmstead* was decided, more than 25 states had made wiretapping a crime.

Six years later, responding to significant criticism of the *Olmstead* decision, Congress enacted the Federal Communications Act (FCA) of 1934. Section 605 of the Act provided that "no person not being authorized by the sender shall intercept any communication and divulge or publish the existence, contents, substance, purport, effect, or meaning of such intercepted communications to any person." Although § 605 did not expressly provide for an exclusionary rule, the Court in *Nardone v. United States*, 302 U.S. 379 (1937), held that federal officers could not introduce evidence obtained by illegal wiretapping in federal court.

Section 605 had significant limitations. States could still use evidence in violation of § 605 in state prosecutions. Further, § 605 only applied to wire communications and wiretapping, not to eavesdropping on nonwire communications. Thus, bugging was not covered.

In the words of Attorney General Nicholas Katzenback, § 605 was the "worst of all possible solutions." It prevented law enforcement from using information gleaned from wiretaps in court — even if pursuant to a warrant supported by probable cause. And it did little to restrict government wiretapping since it was interpreted not to prohibit such activity so long as the evidence was not used in court.

---

[73] Michael Barbaro & Tom Zeller, Jr., *A Face is Exposed for AOL Searcher No. 4417749*, N.Y. Times, Aug. 9, 2006.

With the absence of Fourth Amendment protections and the limited protections of § 605, the federal government engaged in extensive wiretapping. During World War II, J. Edgar Hoover, the director of the FBI, successfully urged President Franklin Roosevelt to allow FBI wiretapping to investigate subversive activities and threats to national security. During the Truman Administration, the justification for electronic surveillance expanded to include domestic security as well. In the 1950s, the FBI then expanded its electronic surveillance due to national concern about Communism and communist infiltration of government. During the Cold War Era and beyond, Hoover ordered wiretapping of hundreds of people, including political enemies, dissidents, Supreme Court Justices, professors, celebrities, writers, and others. Among Hoover's files were dossiers on John Steinbeck, Ernest Hemingway, Charlie Chaplin, Marlon Brando, Muhammad Ali, Albert Einstein, John Lennon, and numerous presidents and members of Congress.[74]

The FBI also placed Martin Luther King Jr. under extensive surveillance. Hoover believed King was a Communist (which he was not), and disliked him personally. When the FBI's electronic surveillance of King revealed King's extramarital affairs, the FBI sent copies of the tapes to King along with a letter insinuating that he should commit suicide or else the tapes would be leaked to the public. The FBI also sent the tapes to King's wife and played them to President Lyndon Johnson.[75] In reflecting on the FBI's campaign against King, Frederick Schwarz and Aziz Huq note that an important role was played by Hoover's "personal animus against King, and his profound distaste for the social changes pressed by the civil rights movement." Schwarz and Huq also observe: "But without an institutional underpinning, Hoover's bias would not have taken the form of a massive, multiyear surveillance and harassment campaign. The war against King highlights what happens when checks and balances are abandoned."[76]

During this time, state police also conducted wiretapping. To the extent that this wiretapping was regulated, this regulation was purely that of the individual states. Section 605 only applied at the federal level. In an influential study, Samuel Dash, Richard Schwartz, and Robert Knowlton revealed that regulation of wiretapping by the states was often ineffective. There were numerous unauthorized wiretaps and few checks against abuses.[77]

2. TITLE III

In 1968, in response to *Katz v. United States* and *Berger v. New York*, Congress enacted Title III of the Omnibus Crime Control and Safe Streets Act of 1968, Pub. L. No. 90-351, codified at 18 U.S.C. §§ 2510–2520. This Act is commonly referred to as "Title III" or, subsequent to its amendment in 1986, as the "Wiretap Act."

---

[74] Daniel J. Solove, *Reconstructing Electronic Surveillance Law,* 72 Geo. Wash. L. Rev. 1264, 1273-74 (2004).

[75] David J. Garrow, *The FBI and Martin Luther King, Jr.* (1980).

[76] Frederick A.O. Schwarz, Jr. & Aziz Z. Huq, *Unchecked and Unbalanced: Presidential Power in a Time of Terror* 23 (2007).

[77] *See* Samuel Dash, Richard Schwartz & Robert Knowlton, *The Eavesdroppers* (1959).

Title III extended far beyond § 605; it applied to wiretaps by federal and state officials as well as by private parties. Title III required federal agents to apply for a warrant before wiretapping. The Act criminalized private wiretaps. However, if any party to the conversation consented to the tapping, then there was no violation of Title III.

Title III authorized the Attorney General to apply to a federal judge for an order authorizing the interception of a "wire or oral communication." A judge could not issue a court order unless there was probable cause. Many other procedural safeguards were established.

Title III excluded wiretaps for national security purposes from any restrictions at all. President Nixon frequently used the national security exception to place internal dissidents and radicals under surveillance. However, in *United States v. United States District Court* (the *Keith* case), 407 U.S. 297 (1972), the Court unanimously rejected Nixon's approach, stating that Title III's national security exception does not apply to internal threats but only to foreign threats.

3. THE ELECTRONIC COMMUNICATIONS PRIVACY ACT

In 1986, Congress modernized federal wiretap law by passing the Electronic Communications Privacy Act (ECPA).[78] The ECPA amended Title III (the Wiretap Act), and it also included two new acts in response to developments in computer technology and communication networks. Hence, federal electronic surveillance law on the domestic side contains three parts: (1) the Wiretap Act (the updated version of Title III, which ECPA shifted to its first Title); (2) the Stored Communications Act (SCA); and (3) the Pen Register Act.

Many of the provisions of federal electronic surveillance law apply not only to government officials, but to private individuals and entities as well. In particular, cases involving the violation of federal electronic surveillance law by private parties often occur in the employment context when employers desire to use forms of electronic surveillance on their employees.

Electronic surveillance law operates independently of the Fourth Amendment. Even if a search is reasonable under the Fourth Amendment, electronic surveillance law may bar the evidence. Even if a search is authorized by a judge under federal electronic surveillance law, the Fourth Amendment could still prohibit the wiretap.

Moreover, procedures for obtaining a court order under the Wiretap Act are more stringent than those for obtaining a search warrant under the Fourth Amendment. As an example of how the Wiretap Act is stricter, under the Fourth Amendment, any law enforcement official can apply for a warrant. Under the Wiretap Act, in contrast, only certain officials (prosecuting attorneys) can apply.

---

[78] For more background on electronic surveillance law, see Patricia L. Bellia, *Surveillance Law Through Cyberlaw's Lens*, 72 Geo. Wash. L. Rev. 1375 (2004); Deirdre K. Mulligan, *Reasonable Expectations in Electronic Communications: A Critical Perspective on the Electronic Communications Privacy Act*, 72 Geo. Wash. L. Rev. 1557 (2004); Paul K. Ohm, *Parallel-Effect Statutes and E-mail "Warrants": Reframing the Internet Surveillance Debate*, 72 Geo. Wash. L. Rev. 1599 (2004); Susan Freiwald, *Online Surveillance: Remembering the Lessons of the Wiretap Act*, 56 Ala. L. Rev. 9 (2004). *See generally* Symposium, *The Future of Internet Surveillance Law*, 72 Geo. Wash. L. Rev. 1139-1617 (2004).

In at least one significant way, federal electronic surveillance law is broader than the Fourth Amendment. Under the Fourth Amendment, search warrants generally authorize a single entry and prompt search. Warrants must be narrowly circumscribed. They are not a license for unlimited and continued investigation. Under the Wiretap Act, however, courts can authorize continuing surveillance — 24 hours a day for a 30-day period. This period can also be extended.

In order to comprehend how each of the three acts comprising ECPA works, it is important to know that ECPA classifies all communications into three types: (1) "wire communications"; (2) "oral communications"; and (3) "electronic communications." Each type of communication is protected differently. As a general matter, wire communications receive the most protection and electronic communications receive the least.

Wire Communications. A "wire communication," defined in § 2510(1), involves all "aural transfers" that travel through a wire or a similar medium:

> (1) "wire communication" means any aural transfer made in whole or in part through the use of facilities for the transmission of communications by the aid of wire, cable, or other like connection between the point of origin and the point of reception (including the use of such connection in a switching station) furnished or operated by any person engaged in providing or operating such facilities for the transmission of interstate or foreign communications or communications affecting interstate or foreign commerce.

An "aural transfer" is a communication containing the human voice at any point. § 2510(18). The human voice need only be a minor part of the communication. Further, the human voice need not always be present throughout the journey of the communication. Therefore, a communication that once consisted of the human voice that has been translated into code or tones still qualifies as an "aural transfer."

The aural transfer must travel through wire (i.e., telephone wires or cable wires) or a similar medium. The entire journey from origin to destination need not take place through wire, as many communications travel through a host of different mediums — wire, radio, satellite, and so on. Only part of the communication's journey must be through a wire.

Oral Communications. The second type of communication under federal wiretap law is "oral communications." Pursuant to § 2510(2), an "oral communication" is a communication "uttered by a person exhibiting an expectation that such communication is not subject to interception under circumstances justifying such expectation." Oral communications are typically intercepted through bugs and other recording or transmitting devices.

Electronic Communications. The final type of communication is an "electronic communication." Under § 2510(12), an electronic communication consists of all non-wire and non-oral communications:

> (12) "electronic communication" means any transfer of signs, signals, writing, images, sounds, data, or intelligence of any nature transmitted in whole or in part

by a wire, radio, electromagnetic, photoelectronic or photooptical system that affects interstate or foreign commerce, but does not include —

(A) any wire or oral communication. . . .

In other words, an electronic communication consists of all communications that do not constitute wire or oral communications. An example of an electronic communication is an e-mail — at least as long as it does not contain the human voice.

Although electronic communications are protected under the Stored Communications Act as well as the Wiretap Act, they are treated differently than wire and oral communications. The most notable difference is that the exclusionary rule in the Wiretap Act does not apply to electronic communications. Therefore, wire or oral communications that fall within the Wiretap Act are protected by the exclusionary rule, but not when they fall within the Stored Communications Act (which has no exclusionary rule). Electronic communications are not protected by the exclusionary rule in the Wiretap Act or the Stored Communications Act.

(a) The Wiretap Act

Interceptions. The Wiretap Act, which is codified at Title I of ECPA, 18 U.S.C. §§ 2510–2522, governs the interception of communications. In particular, § 2511 provides that:

(1) Except as otherwise specifically provided in this chapter any person who —

(a) intentionally intercepts, endeavors to intercept, or procures any other person to intercept or endeavor to intercept, any wire, oral, or electronic communication;

(b) intentionally uses, endeavors to use, or procures any other person to use or endeavor to use any electronic, mechanical, or other device to intercept any oral communication when —

(i) such device is affixed to, or otherwise transmits a signal through, a wire, cable, or other like connection used in wire communication; or

(ii) such device transmits communications by radio, or interferes with the transmission of such communication; or

(iii) such person knows, or has reason to know, that such device or any component thereof has been sent through the mail or transported in interstate or foreign commerce. . . .

(c) intentionally discloses, or endeavors to disclose, to any other person the contents of any wire, oral, or electronic communication, knowing or having reason to know that the information was obtained through the interception of a wire, oral, or electronic communication in violation of this subsection;

(d) intentionally uses, or endeavors to use, the contents of any wire, oral, or electronic communication, knowing or having reason to know that the information was obtained through the interception of a wire, oral, or electronic communication in violation of this subsection. . . .

As this provision indicates, the Wiretap Act applies to the intentional interception of a communication. To "intercept" a communication means to acquire its contents through the use of any "electronic, mechanical, or other device." § 2510(4). The classic example of an activity covered by the Act is the wiretapping of a phone conversation — a device is being used to listen to a conversation as it is occurring, as the words are moving through the wires. The Wiretap Act applies when communications are intercepted contemporaneously with their transmission. Once the communication is completed and stored, then the Wiretap Act no longer applies.

In *Bartnicki v. Vopper*, 532 U.S. 514 (2001), which is excerpted in Chapter 3 of this casebook, the Supreme Court held that § 2511(1)(c) could not be applied when an illegally obtained communication concerned a matter of public concern and the person publicizing the communication was not involved in the illegality. As the Court stated, "[A] stranger's illegal conduct does not suffice to remove the First Amendment shield from speech about a matter of public concern."

Exclusionary Rule. Under the Wiretap Act, "any aggrieved person . . . may move to suppress the contents of any wire or oral communication intercepted pursuant to this chapter, or evidence derived therefrom." § 2518 (10)(a).

Penalties. Violations of the Wiretap Act can result in fines of a minimum of $10,000 per violation as well as up to five years' imprisonment. *See* §§ 2511(4)(a); 2520(c)(2)(B).

Court Orders. Pursuant to § 2518, an application for a court wiretapping or electronic surveillance order must be made under oath and contain a variety of information, including details to justify the agent's belief that a crime has been, is being, or will be committed; specific description of place where communications will be intercepted; description of the type of communication; and period of time of interception. The judge may require the applicant to furnish additional testimony or documentary evidence in support of the application. The judge must find probable cause and that the particular communications concerning that offense will be obtained through the interception. Further, the court must find that alternatives to wiretapping were attempted and failed, or reasonably appear to be unlikely to succeed or to be too dangerous. The order can last for up to 30 days and can be renewed.

Under the Wiretap Act, only certain government officials are able to apply to a court for a wiretapping order — for federal law enforcement agencies, the relevant party is the attorney general, or a deputy or assistant attorney general; for state officials, the relevant party is the principal prosecuting attorney of a state or a local government, or any government attorney. In other words, the police themselves cannot obtain a wiretap order alone. The Wiretap Act also provides an exclusive list of crimes for which a wiretap order can be issued. The list is broad and includes most felonies. A wiretap order cannot be obtained, however, to investigate a misdemeanor.

Minimization. The Wiretap Act requires that interception must be minimized to avoid sweeping in communications beyond the purpose for which the order was sought. Pursuant to § 2518(6): "Every order and extension thereof shall contain a provision that the authorization to intercept shall be executed as soon as practicable, shall be conducted in such a way as to minimize the interception of communications not otherwise subject to interception under this chapter, and must terminate upon attainment of the authorized objective." For example, if law enforcement officials are wiretapping the home phone line of a person suspected of running an illegal gambling operation and the person's daughter is talking on the line to a friend about going to the movies, the officials should stop listening to the conversation.

Notice. After the surveillance is over, copies of the recorded conversations must be turned over to the court issuing the order. The court must notify the party that surveillance was undertaken within 90 days after the denial of a surveillance order or after the completion of the surveillance authorized by a granted surveillance order. § 2518(8)(d).

Exceptions. There are two notable exceptions under the Wiretap Act. First, the Act does not apply if one of the parties to the communication consents. § 2511(2)(c). For example, a person can secretly tap and record a communication to which that person is a party. Thus, secretly recording one's own phone conversations is not illegal under federal wiretap law. If they participate in the conversation, government agents and informants can record others without their knowledge. An exception to the consent exception is when an interception is carried out for the purpose of committing any criminal or tortious act. In that case, even when a party has consented, interception is illegal. § 2511(2)(d).

Second, a communications service provider is permitted "to intercept, disclose, or use that communication in the normal course of his employment while engaged in any activity which is a necessary incident to the rendition of his service or to the protection of the rights or property of the provider of that service." § 2511(2)(a). Also, a service provider may intentionally disclose intercepted communications to the proper authorities when criminal activity is afoot; with the consent of the originator, addressee, or intended recipient; or to any intermediary provider. § 2511(3).

(b) The Stored Communications Act

Stored Communications. Whereas communications in transmission are covered by the Wiretap Act, communications in storage are protected by the Stored Communications Act (SCA), codified at 18 U.S.C. §§ 2701–2711.[79] With many forms of modern communication, such as Internet service, communications and subscriber records are often maintained in storage by the electronic communications service provider. Section 2701 states:

(a) Offense. — Except as provided in subsection (c) of this section whoever —

(1) intentionally accesses without authorization a facility through which an electronic communication service is provided; or

---

[79] For more background about the SCA, see Orin S. Kerr, *A User's Guide to the Stored Communications Act, and a Legislator's Guide to Amending It,* 72 Geo. Wash. L. Rev. 1208 (2004).

(2) intentionally exceeds an authorization to access that facility; and thereby obtains, alters, or prevents authorized access to a wire or electronic communication while it is in electronic storage in such system shall be punished as provided in subsection (b) of this section.

The definition of "electronic storage" in the Wiretap Act also applies to the term as used in the SCA. "Electronic storage" means:

(A) any temporary, intermediate storage of a wire or electronic communication incidental to the electronic transmission thereof; and
(B) any storage of such communication by an electronic communications service for purposes of backup protection of such communication. § 2510(17).

Section 2701(a) does not apply to "the person or entity providing a wire or electronic communications service" (such as Internet Service Providers) or to "a user of that service with respect to a communication of or intended for that user." § 2701(c).

The SCA also forbids the disclosure of the contents of stored communications by communications service providers. *See* § 2702(a). There are a number of exceptions, including disclosures to the intended recipient of the communication, disclosures with the consent of the creator or recipient of the communication, disclosures that are "necessarily incident to the rendition of the service or to the protection of the rights or property of the provider of that service," and disclosures to a law enforcement agency under certain circumstances. *See* § 2702(b).

Penalties. The SCA has less severe criminal penalties and civil liability than Title I. Under § 2701(b), violations can result in fines of a minimum of $1,000 per violation and up to six months imprisonment. If the wiretap is done for commercial advantage or gain, then a violation can result in up to one year of imprisonment.

Exclusionary Rule. The SCA does not provide for an exclusionary rule.

Judicial Authority for Obtaining Stored Communications. Under the SCA, the judicial process required for obtaining permission to access stored communications held by electronic communications service providers is much less rigorous than under the Wiretap Act. If the government seeks access to the contents of a communication that has been in storage for 180 days or less, then it must first obtain a warrant supported by probable cause. § 2703(a). If the government wants to access a communication that has been in storage for more than 180 days, the government must provide prior notice to the subscriber and obtain an administrative subpoena, a grand jury subpoena, a trial subpoena, or a court order. § 2703(b). The court order does not require probable cause, only "specific and articulable facts showing that there are reasonable grounds" to believe communications are relevant to the criminal investigation. 18 U.S.C. § 2703(d). However, if the government seeks to access a communication that has been in storage for more than 180 days and does not want to provide prior notice to the subscriber, it must obtain a warrant. § 2703(b). Notice to the subscriber that the government obtained her communications can be delayed for up to 90 days. § 2705.

Court Orders to Obtain Subscriber Records. According to § 2703(c)(1)(B), communication service providers must disclose subscriber information (i.e., identifying information, address, phone number, etc.) to the government under certain circumstances:

> (B) A provider of electronic communication service or remote computing service shall disclose a record or other information pertaining to a subscriber to or customer of such service (not including the contents of communications covered by subsection (a) or (b) of this section) to a governmental entity only when the governmental entity —
>
>> (i) obtains a warrant issued under the Federal Rules of Criminal Procedure or equivalent State warrant;
>> (ii) obtains a court order for such disclosure under subsection (d) of this section;
>> (iii) has the consent of the subscriber or customer to such disclosure

Communications service providers who disclose stored communications in accordance with any of the above orders or subpoenas cannot be held liable for that disclosure. *See* § 2703(e).

Exceptions. Similar to the Wiretap Act, the SCA also has a consent exception, see § 2702(b), and a service provider exception, see § 2701(c)(1). Unlike the service provider exception for the Wiretap Act, which allows interceptions on a limited basis (those necessary to provide the communications service), the SCA's exception is broader, entirely exempting "the person or entity providing a wire or electronic communications service." § 2701(c)(1).

(c) The Pen Register Act

The Pen Register Act, codified at 18 U.S.C. §§ 3121–3127, governs pen registers and trap and trace devices — and their modern analogues. Recall *Smith v. Maryland,* earlier in this chapter, where the Court held that the Fourth Amendment did not extend to pen register information. The Pen Register Act provides some limited protection for such information. Subject to certain exceptions, "no person may install or use a pen register or a trap and trace device without first obtaining a court order." § 3121(a). Traditionally, a pen register was a device that records the telephone numbers dialled from a particular telephone line (phone numbers of outgoing calls). A trap and trace device is the reverse of a pen register — it records the telephone numbers where incoming calls originate.

Definition of "Pen Register." The Pen Register Act defines pen registers more broadly than phone number information:

> [T]he term "pen register" means a device or process which records or decodes dialing, routing, addressing, or signaling information transmitted by an instrument or facility from which a wire or electronic communication is transmitted, provided, however, that such information shall not include the contents of any communication . . . 18 U.S.C. § 3127(3)

Court Orders. If the government certifies that "the information likely to be obtained by such installation and use is relevant to an ongoing investigation," § 3123(a), then courts "shall authorize the installation and use of a pen register or a trap and trace device for a period not to exceed sixty days." § 3123(c). This standard is a low threshold. As Susan Freiwald contends: "[T]he language of the [pen register] court order requirement raises doubt as to its efficacy as a guard against fishing expeditions. . . . The relevance standard in the transaction records provision allows law enforcement to obtain records of people who may be tangentially involved in a crime, even as innocent victims."[80]

Enforcement. There is no exclusionary rule for violations of the Pen Register Act. Rather than a suppression remedy, the Pen Register Act provides: "Whoever knowingly violates subsection (a) shall be fined under this title or imprisoned not more than one year, or both." § 3121(d).

4. THE COMMUNICATIONS ASSISTANCE FOR LAW ENFORCEMENT ACT

In *United States v. New York Telephone*, 434 U.S. 159 (1977), the Supreme Court held that 18 U.S.C. § 2518(4) required telecommunications providers to furnish "any assistance necessary to accomplish an electronic interception." However, the issue of whether a provider had to create and design its technology to facilitate authorized electronic surveillance remained an open question.

In the 1980s, new communications technology was developed to enable more wireless communications — cellular telephones, microwave, and satellite communications. As a result of fears that these new technologies would be harder to monitor, the law enforcement community successfully convinced Congress to force telecommunications providers to ensure that the government could continue to monitor electronic communications.[81]

The Communications Assistance for Law Enforcement Act (CALEA) of 1994, Pub. L. No. 103-414, (also known as the "Digital Telephony Act") requires telecommunication providers to help facilitate the government in executing legally authorized surveillance. Congress appropriated federal funding of $500 million to telephone companies to make the proposed changes.

Requirements. CALEA requires all telecommunications providers to be able to isolate and intercept electronic communications and be able to deliver them to law enforcement personnel. If carriers provide an encryption service to users, then they must decrypt the communications. CALEA permits the telecommunications industry to develop the technology. Under a "safe harbor" provision, carriers that comply with accepted industry standards are in compliance with CALEA. 47 U.S.C. § 1006(a)(2).

---

[80] Susan Freiwald, *Uncertain Privacy: Communications Attributes After the Digital Telephony Act,* 69 S. Cal. L. Rev. 949, 1005-06 (1996).

[81] For a detailed analysis of CALEA, see Susan Freiwald, *Uncertain Privacy: Communication Attributes After the Digital Telephony Act,* 69 S. Cal. L. Rev. 949 (1996).

Limits. CALEA contains some important limits. Carriers must "facilitat[e] authorized communications interceptions and access to call-identifying information . . . in a manner that protects . . . the privacy and security of communications and call-identifying information not authorized to be intercepted." § 1002(a)(4)(A). Further, CALEA is designed to provide "law enforcement no more and no less access to information than it had in the past." H.R. Rep. No. 103-827, pt. 1, at 22. Additionally, CALEA does not apply to "information services," such as e-mail and Internet access. §§ 1001(8)(C)(i), 1002(b)(2)(A).

Voice over Internet Protocol (VoIP). A new way to make telephone calls is to use a broadband Internet connection to transmit the call. This technique, VoIP, converts a voice signal into a digital signal that travels over the Internet and connects to a phone number. On August 4, 2004, the FCC unanimously adopted a Notice of Proposed Rulemaking and Declaratory Ruling regarding VoIP and CALEA. *In the Matter of Communications Assistance for Law Enforcement Act and Broadband Access and Services*, FCC 04-187 (Aug. 4, 2004). It tentatively declared that CALEA applies to any facilities-based providers of any type of broadband Internet access service — including wireline, cable modem, satellite, wireless, and powerline — and to managed or mediated VoIP services. This conclusion was based on an FCC judgment that these services fall under CALEA statutory language as "a replacement for a substantial portion of the local telephone service." 47 U.S.C. § 1001(8)B)(ii).

Susan Landau and Whitfield Diffie argue that inserting wiretap requirements into Internet protocols will make the Internet less secure. A system that permits "legally authorized security breaches" (such as a wiretap by law enforcement officers) is also more open to unauthorized security breaches (such as hacking and other kinds of unlawful intrusions). They argue that "[o]n balance we are better off with a secure computer infrastructure than with one that builds surveillance into the network fabric."[82]

5. THE USA PATRIOT ACT

On the morning of September 11, 2001, terrorists hijacked four planes and crashed three of them into the World Trade Center and the Pentagon, killing thousands of people. The nation was awakened into a world filled with new frightening dangers. Shortly after the September 11 attacks, a still unknown person or persons sent letters laced with the deadly bacteria anthrax through the mail to several prominent individuals in the news media and in politics. Acting with great haste, Congress passed a sweeping new law expanding the government's electronic surveillance powers in many significant ways.[83] Called the "Uniting and Strengthening America By Providing Appropriate Tools Required To Intercept and Obstruct Terrorism Act" (USA PATRIOT Act), the Act made a number of substantial changes to several statutes, including the federal electronic surveillance statutes.

---

[82] Susan Landau & Whitfield Diffie, *Privacy on the Line* 331, 328 (2d ed. 2007).

[83] For background about the passage of the USA PATRIOT Act, see Beryl A. Howell, *Seven Weeks: The Making of the USA Patriot Act,* 72 Geo. Wash. L. Rev. 1145 (2004).

Definition of Terrorism. Section 802 of the USA PATRIOT Act added to 18 U.S.C. § 2331 a new definition of "domestic terrorism." According to the Act, domestic terrorism involves "acts dangerous to human life that are a violation of the criminal laws of the United States or of any State" that "appear to be intended: (i) to intimidate or coerce a civilian population; (ii) to influence the policy of a government by intimidation or coercion; or (iii) to affect the conduct of a government by mass destruction, assassination, or kidnapping; and . . . occur primarily within the territorial jurisdiction of the United States." According to many proponents of civil liberties, this definition is very broad and could potentially encompass many forms of civil disobedience, which, although consisting of criminal conduct (minor violence, threats, property damage), includes conduct that has historically been present in many political protests and has never been considered to be terrorism.

Delayed Notice of Search Warrants. Under the Fourth Amendment, the government must obtain a warrant and provide notice to a person before conducting a search or seizure. Case law provided for certain limited exceptions. Section 213 of the USA PATRIOT Act adds a provision to 18 U.S.C. § 3103a, enabling the government to delay notice if the court concludes that there is "reasonable cause" that immediate notice will create an "adverse result" such as physical danger, the destruction of evidence, delayed trial, flight from prosecution, and other circumstances. § 3103a(b). Warrants enabling a covert search with delayed notice are often referred to as "sneak and peek" warrants. Civil libertarians consider "sneak and peek" warrants dangerous because they authorize covert searches, thus preventing individuals from safeguarding their rights during the search. Moreover, there is little supervision of the government's carrying out of the search. Law enforcement officials argue that covert searches are necessary to avoid tipping off suspects that there is an investigation under way.

New Definition of Pen Registers and Trap and Trace Devices. Under the Pen Register Act of the ECPA, §§ 3121 *et seq.*, the definitions of pen registers and trap and trace devices focused primarily on telephone numbers. A pen register was defined under 18 U.S.C. § 3127(3) as

> a device which records or decodes electronic or other impulses which identify the numbers dialed or otherwise transmitted on the telephone line to which such device is attached. . . .

Section 216 of the USA PATRIOT Act changed the definition to read:

> a device *or process* which records or decodes *dialing, routing, addressing, or signaling information transmitted by an instrument or facility from which a wire or electronic communication is transmitted, provided, however, that such information shall not include the contents of any communication* is attached . . . (changes emphasized).

These changes altered the definition of a pen register from applying not only to telephone numbers but also to Internet addresses, e-mail addressing information (the "to" and "from" lines on e-mail), and the routing information of a wide spectrum of communications. The inclusion of "or process" after "device" enlarges the means by which such routing information can be intercepted beyond the use of a physical device. The definition of a trap and trace device was changed in a similar way. Recall that under the Pen Register Act, a court order to obtain such information does not require probable cause, but merely certification that "the information likely to be obtained by such installation and use is relevant to an ongoing criminal investigation." 18 U.S.C. § 3123. The person whose communications are subject to this order need not even be a criminal suspect; all that the government needs to certify is relevance to an investigation.

Recall *Smith v. Maryland* earlier in this chapter, where the Court held that pen registers were not protected under the Fourth Amendment. Does the new definition of pen register and trap and trace device under the USA PATRIOT Act go beyond *Smith v. Maryland*? Are Internet addresses and e-mail addressing information analogous to pen registers?

Private Right of Action for Government Disclosures. The USA PATRIOT Act adds a provision to the Stored Communications Act that provides for civil actions against the United States for any "willful" violations. 18 U.S.C. § 2712. The court may assess actual damages or $10,000 (whichever is greater) and litigation costs. Such an action must first be presented before the "appropriate department or agency under the procedures of the Federal Tort Claims Act."

6. STATE ELECTRONIC SURVEILLANCE LAW

A number of states have enacted their own versions of electronic surveillance law, some of which are more protective than federal electronic surveillance law. For example, several states require the consent of all parties to a conversation. Unless all parties consent, these states require a warrant for a wiretap. In contrast, federal wiretap law allows law enforcement to listen in to a conversation if any party to it consents to the surveillance.

One prominent example of a more protective state law was the indictment on July 30, 1999, of Linda Tripp on two counts of violating Maryland's wiretapping law. At the request of the Office of the Independent Counsel, Linda Tripp had secretly taped a phone conversation she had with Monica Lewinsky about Lewinsky's affair with President Clinton. Tripp then disclosed the contents of that conversation to a news magazine. Possible penalties under Maryland law included up to ten years' imprisonment and a $20,000 fine. Maryland's wiretapping law, in contrast to federal wiretap law, requires the consent of the other party to a communication. Tripp was indicted by a Maryland grand jury. Although Tripp was protected by a federal grant of immunity from prosecution, Maryland was not part of the immunity agreement and could prosecute Tripp. After a judicial ruling suppressing certain evidence, the case against Tripp was dropped.

Massachusetts also has an all-party-consent electronic surveillance law. Consider *Commonwealth v. Hyde,* 750 N.E.2d 963 (Mass. 2001). The defendant Michael Hyde was stopped by the police for a routine auto stop. The police searched the defendant, his passenger, and his car. No traffic citation was issued. Hyde filed a complaint at the police station about the stop, and he provided a hidden audio recording he had made of the encounter. The police subsequently charged Hyde with illegal electronic surveillance in violation of state law, G.L. c.

272, § 99, which provides that "any person who willfully commits an interception, attempts to commit an interception, or procures any other person to commit an interception or to attempt to commit an interception of any wire or oral communication shall be fined not more than ten thousand dollars, or imprisoned in the state prison for not more than five years, or imprisoned in a jail or house of correction for not more than two and one half years, or both so fined and given one such imprisonment." Hyde was convicted and sentenced to six months probation and a $500 fine.

The *Hyde* court concluded:

> We conclude that the Legislature intended G.L. c. 272, § 99, strictly to prohibit all secret recordings by members of the public, including recordings of police officers or other public officials interacting with members of the public, when made without their permission or knowledge. . . .
>
> We reject the defendant's argument that the statute is not applicable because the police officers were performing their public duties, and, therefore, had no reasonable expectation of privacy in their words. The statute's preamble expresses the Legislature's general concern that "the uncontrolled development and unrestricted use of modern electronic surveillance devices pose[d] grave dangers to the privacy of all citizens of the commonwealth" and this concern was relied on to justify the ban on the public's clandestine use of such devices. While we recognize that G.L. c. 272, § 99, was designed to prohibit the use of electronic surveillance devices by private individuals because of the serious threat they pose to the "privacy of all citizens," the plain language of the statute, which is the best indication of the Legislature's ultimate intent, contains nothing that would protect, on the basis of privacy rights, the recording that occurred here. In *Commonwealth v. Jackson, supra* at 506, 349 N.E.2d 337, this court rejected the argument that, because a kidnapper has no legitimate privacy interest in telephone calls made for ransom purposes, the secret electronic recording of that conversation by the victim's brother would not be prohibited under G.L. c. 272, § 99: "[W]e would render meaningless the Legislature's careful choice of words if we were to interpret 'secretly' as encompassing only those situations where an individual has a reasonable expectation of privacy." . . .
>
> Further, if the tape recording here is deemed proper on the ground that public officials are involved, then the door is opened even wider to electronic "bugging" or secret audio tape recording (both are prohibited by the statute and both are indistinguishable in the injury they inflict) of virtually every encounter or meeting between a person and a public official, whether the meeting or encounter is one that is stressful (like the one in this case or, perhaps, a session with a tax auditor) or nonstressful (like a routine meeting between a parent and a teacher in a public school to discuss a good student's progress). The door once opened would be hard to close, and the result would contravene the statute's broad purpose and the Legislature's clear prohibition of *all* secret interceptions and recordings by private citizens.

In dissent, Chief Justice Marshall wrote:

> The purpose of G.L. c. 272, § 99, is not to shield public officials from exposure of their wrongdoings. I have too great a respect for the Legislature to read any such meaning into a statute whose purpose is plain, and points in another direction entirely. Where the legislative intent is explicit, it violates a fundamental rule of statutory construction to reach a result that is plainly contrary to that

objective. To hold that the Legislature intended to allow police officers to conceal possible misconduct behind a cloak of privacy requires a more affirmative showing than this statute allows.

In our Republic the actions of public officials taken in their public capacities are not protected from exposure. Citizens have a particularly important role to play when the official conduct at issue is that of the police. Their role cannot be performed if citizens must fear criminal reprisals when they seek to hold government officials responsible by recording — secretly recording on occasion — an interaction between a citizen and a police officer. . . .

The court's ruling today also threatens the ability of the press — print and electronic — to perform its constitutional role of watchdog. As the court construes the Massachusetts wiretapping statute, there is no principled distinction to explain why members of the media would not be held to the same standard as all other citizens.

A few years later, Hyde was convicted again of secretly recording a police officer who had pulled him over in a traffic stop. Are all-party electronic surveillance laws too broad? What kinds of exceptions, if any, should be made?

Note as well that these all-party-consent statutes will also regulate surveillance by private sector entities. In *Kearney v. Salomon Smith Barney*, 137 P.2d 914 (Cal. 2006), two California clients sued a financial institution because their telephone calls to brokers in the institution's Georgia office were recorded without their consent. A California statute prohibited recording a telephone conversation without consent of all parties to it. In contrast, a Georgia statute permitted recording a telephone conversation if consent of one party had been granted. The California Supreme Court concluded that "comparative impairment analysis supports the application of California law in this context." It reached this conclusion by assessing the relative harm suffered to each state due to this conflict of law:

> [I]n light of the substantial number of businesses operating in California that maintain out-of-state offices or telephone operators, a resolution of this conflict permitting all such businesses to regularly and routinely record telephone conversations made to or from California clients or consumers without the clients' or consumers' knowledge or consent would significantly impair the privacy policy guaranteed by California law, and potentially would place local California businesses (that would continue to be subject to California's protective privacy law) at an unfair competitive disadvantage vis-à-vis their out-of-state counterparts. At the same time, application of California law will not have a significant detrimental effect on Georgia's interests as embodied in the applicable Georgia law, because applying California law (1) will not adversely affect any privacy interest protected by Georgia law, (2) will affect only those business telephone calls in Georgia that are made to or are received from California clients, and (3) with respect to such calls, will not prevent a business located in Georgia from implementing or maintaining a practice of recording *all* such calls, but will require only that the business *inform* its clients or customers, at the outset of the call, of the company's policy of recording such calls. (. . . if a business informs a client or customer at the outset of a telephone call that the call is being recorded, the recording would not violate the applicable California statute.)

When state government officials are engaging in electronic surveillance, they are often subject to much less public scrutiny than their federal counterparts.

Charles Kennedy and Peter Swire have concluded that there are likely to be significant differences between federal and state electronic surveillance because of differences in the respective "[i]nstitutions, procedures and training" of law enforcement personnel:

> Because state procedures are watched less systematically by the press and civil liberties organizations, abuses at the state level, whether deliberate or the result of inexperience, may not be detected. The under-reporting of state wiretaps . . . is both a symptom of and a contributing factor to this relative lack of oversight. The simple fact is that half of the states have wiretap powers, yet reported no wiretaps in 2001. The utter failure to file the annual wiretap report would be unthinkable at the federal level. In addition, the under-reporting of state wiretaps keeps the use and possible misuse of state wiretaps less visible.[84]

As noted above, moreover, wiretap orders over the last decade have increasingly become a phenomenon of state rather than federal courts. Yet, as Kennedy and Swire observe, we know far less about how state law enforcement agencies make use of their wiretap powers than federal ones. As for the lack of state wiretap reports from many states, the obligation to file a report with the Administrative Office of the U.S. Courts extends only to instances when the states actually make use of these powers. In other words, the Administrative Office does not require reports to be filed if no interception activity took place in the state during a given year.[85] As a simple, initial step at ending the ambiguity about the possible under-reporting of state wiretap orders, should states be required to file a report even if no surveillance activity takes place in it during a particular year?

D. DIGITAL SEARCHES AND SEIZURES

1. SEARCHING COMPUTERS AND ELECTRONIC DEVICES

The Scope of Warrants to Search Computers. In *United States v. Lacy,* 119 F.3d 742 (9th Cir. 1997), the defendant challenged a search warrant authorizing the seizure of his computer hard drive and disks. The defendant contended that the warrant was too general because it applied to his entire computer system. The court upheld the warrant because "this type of generic classification is acceptable when a more precise description is not possible." Several other courts have followed a similar approach as in *Lacy*, upholding generic warrants. In *United States v. Upham*, 168 F.3d 532 (1st Cir. 1999), the court reasoned: "A sufficient chance of finding some needles in the computer haystack was established by the probable-cause showing in the warrant application; and a search of a computer and co-located disks is not inherently more intrusive than the physical search of an entire house for a weapon or drugs." *See also United States v. Hay*, 231 F.3d 630 (9th

---

[84] Charles H. Kennedy & Peter P. Swire, *State Wiretaps and Electronic Surveillance After September 11,* 54 Hastings L.J. 971 (2003).

[85] Paul Schwartz, *German and U.S. Telecommunications Privacy Law*, 54 Hastings L.J. 751, 760 (2003).

Cir. 2000) (following *Lacy* and upholding a "generic" warrant application).[86]

However, there are limits to the scope of a search of a computer. In *United States v. Carey*, 172 F.3d 1268 (10th Cir. 1999), an officer obtained a warrant to search a computer for records about illegal drug distribution. When the officer stumbled upon a pornographic file, he began to search for similar files. The court concluded that these actions amounted to an expansion of the scope of the search and would require the obtaining of a second warrant.

In *United States v. Campos*, 221 F.3d 1143 (10th Cir. 2000), the defendant e-mailed two images of child pornography to a person he talked to in a chat room. The person informed the FBI, and the FBI obtained a warrant to search the defendant's home and computer. The agents seized the defendant's computer, and a search revealed the two images of child pornography as well as six other images of child pornography. The defendant challenged the search as beyond the scope of the warrant because the agents "had grounds to search only for the two images that had been sent." However, the court rejected the defendant's contention, quoting from the FBI's explanation why it is not feasible to search only for particular computer files in one's home:

> . . . Computer storage devices . . . can store the equivalent of thousands of pages of information. Especially when the user wants to conceal criminal evidence, he often stores it in random order with deceptive file names. This requires searching authorities to examine all the stored data to determine whether it is included in the warrant. This sorting process can take weeks or months, depending on the volume of data stored, and it would be impractical to attempt this kind of data search on site. . . .
>
> Searching computer systems for criminal evidence is a highly technical process requiring expert skill and a properly controlled environment. The wide variety of computer hardware and software available requires even computer experts to specialize in some systems and applications, so it is difficult to know before a search which expert should analyze the system and its data. . . . Since computer evidence is extremely vulnerable to tampering or destruction (both from external sources or from destructive code embedded into the system as "booby trap"), the controlled environment of a laboratory is essential to its complete analysis. . . .

Computer Searches and Seizures. Searches and seizures for digital information in computers present some unique conceptual puzzles for existing Fourth Amendment doctrine. Thomas Clancy contends:

> [C]omputers are containers. . . . They . . . contain electronic evidence, that is, a series of digitally stored 0s and 1s that, when combined with a computer program, yield such items as images, words, and spreadsheets. Accordingly, the traditional standards of the Fourth Amendment regulate obtaining the evidence in containers that happen to be computers.[87]

But is a computer a single container or is each computer file its own container? Orin Kerr argues:

---

[86] For more about computer searches, see Raphael Winnick, *Searches and Seizures of Computers and Computer Data*, 88 Harv. J.L. & Tech. 75 (1994).

[87] Thomas K. Clancy, *The Fourth Amendment Aspects of Computer Searches and Seizures: A Perspective and a Primer*, 75 Miss. L.J. 193, 196 (2005).

A single physical storage device can store the private files of thousands of different users. It would be quite odd if looking at one file on a server meant that the entire server had been searched, and that the police could then analyze everything on the server, perhaps belonging to thousands of different people, without any restriction.[88]

Is copying a computer file or other digital information a seizure under the Fourth Amendment? In *United States v. Gorshkov*, 2001 WL 1024026 (W.D. Wash. 2001), the FBI remotely copied the contents of the defendant's computer in Russia. The court held: "The agents' act of copying the data on the Russian computers was not a seizure under the Fourth Amendment because it did not interfere with Defendant's or anyone else's possessory interest in the data." However, as Susan Brenner and Barbara Frederiksen contend:

> [T]he information contained in computer files clearly belongs to the owner of the files. The ownership of information is similar to the contents of a private conversation in which the information belongs to the parties to the conversation. Copying computer data is analogous to recording a conversation. . . . Therefore, copying computer files should be treated as a seizure.[89]

Password-Protected Files. In *Trulock v. Freeh*, 275 F.3d 391 (4th Cir. 2001), Notra Trulock and Linda Conrad shared a computer but maintained separate files protected by passwords. They did not know each other's password and could not access each other's files. When FBI officials, without a warrant, asked to search and seize the computer, Conrad consented. The court held that the FBI could not search Trulock's files since Trulock had not consented:

> Consent to search in the absence of a warrant may, in some circumstances, be given by a person other than the target of the search. Two criteria must be met in order for third party consent to be effective. First, the third party must have authority to consent to the search. Second, the third party's consent must be voluntary. . . .
> We conclude that, based on the facts in the complaint, Conrad lacked authority to consent to the search of Trulock's files. Conrad and Trulock both used a computer located in Conrad's bedroom and each had joint access to the hard drive. Conrad and Trulock, however, protected their personal files with passwords; Conrad did not have access to Trulock's passwords. Although Conrad had authority to consent to a general search of the computer, her authority did not extend to Trulock's password-protected files.

UNITED STATES V. ANDRUS

483 F.3d 711 (10th Cir. 2007)

[Federal authorities believed that Ray Andrus was downloading child pornography to his home computer. Ray Andrus resided at his parents' house. Federal officials obtained the consent of Dr. Andrus (Andrus's father) to search the home. He also

---

[88] Orin S. Kerr, *Searches and Seizures in a Digital World*, 119 Harv. L. Rev. 531, 556 (2005).

[89] Susan W. Brenner & Barbara A. Frederiksen, *Computer Searches and Seizures: Some Unresolved Issues*, 8 Mich. Telecomm. & Tech. L. Rev. 39, 111-12 (2002).

consented to their searching any computers in the home. The officials went into Ray Andrus's bedroom and a forensic expert examined the contents of the computer's hard drive with forensic software. The software enabled direct access to the computer, bypassing any password protection the user put on it. The officials discovered child pornography on the computer. Later, the officials learned that Ray Andrus had protected his computer with a password and that his father did not know the password. Is the father's consent to search the computer valid since he did not know the password?]

MURPHY, J. . . . Subject to limited exceptions, the Fourth Amendment prohibits warrantless searches of an individual's home or possessions. Voluntary consent to a police search, given by the individual under investigation or by a third party with authority over the subject property, is a well-established exception to the warrant requirement. Valid third party consent can arise either through the third party's actual authority or the third party's apparent authority. A third party has actual authority to consent to a search "if that third party has either (1) mutual use of the property by virtue of joint access, or (2) control for most purposes." Even where actual authority is lacking, however, a third party has apparent authority to consent to a search when an officer reasonably, even if erroneously, believes the third party possesses authority to consent. *See Georgia v. Randolph,* 547 U.S. 103 (2006).

Whether apparent authority exists is an objective, totality-of-the-circumstances inquiry into whether the facts available to the officers at the time they commenced the search would lead a reasonable officer to believe the third party had authority to consent to the search. When the property to be searched is an object or container, the relevant inquiry must address the third party's relationship to the object. In *Randolph,* the Court explained, "The constant element in assessing Fourth Amendment reasonableness in consent cases . . . is the great significance given to widely shared social expectations." For example, the Court said, "[W]hen it comes to searching through bureau drawers, there will be instances in which even a person clearly belonging on the premises as an occupant may lack any perceived authority to consent." . . .

It may be unreasonable for law enforcement to believe a third party has authority to consent to the search of an object typically associated with a high expectation of privacy, especially when the officers know or should know the owner has indicated the intent to exclude the third party from using or exerting control over the object.

Courts considering the issue have attempted to analogize computers to other items more commonly seen in Fourth Amendment jurisprudence. Individuals' expectations of privacy in computers have been likened to their expectations of privacy in "a suitcase or briefcase." Password-protected files have been compared to a "locked footlocker inside the bedroom." *Trulock v. Freeh,* 275 F.3d 391, 403 (4th Cir. 2001).

Given the pervasiveness of computers in American homes, this court must reach some, at least tentative, conclusion about the category into which personal computers fall. A personal computer is often a repository for private information the computer's owner does not intend to share with others. . . .

The inquiry into whether the owner of a highly personal object has indicated a subjective expectation of privacy traditionally focuses on whether the subject suitcase, footlocker, or other container is physically locked. Determining whether a computer is "locked," or whether a reasonable officer should know a computer may be locked, presents a challenge distinct from that associated with other types of closed containers. Unlike footlockers or suitcases, where the presence of a locking device is generally apparent by looking at the item, a "lock" on the data within a computer is not apparent from a visual inspection of the outside of the computer, especially when the computer is in the "off" position prior to the search. Data on an entire computer may be protected by a password, with the password functioning as a lock, or there may be multiple users of a computer, each of whom has an individual and personalized password-protected "user profile." . . .

Courts addressing the issue of third party consent in the context of computers, therefore, have examined officers' knowledge about password protection as an indication of whether a computer is "locked" in the way a footlocker would be. For example, in *Trulock,* the Fourth Circuit held a live-in girlfriend lacked actual authority to consent to a search of her boyfriend's computer files where the girlfriend told police she and her boyfriend shared the household computer but had separate password-protected files that were inaccessible to the other. The court in that case explained, "Although Conrad had authority to consent to a general search of the computer, her authority did not extend to Trulock's password-protected files." . . .

In addition to password protection, courts also consider the location of the computer within the house and other indicia of household members' access to the computer in assessing third party authority. Third party apparent authority to consent to a search has generally been upheld when the computer is located in a common area of the home that is accessible to other family members under circumstances indicating the other family members were not excluded from using the computer. In contrast, where the third party has affirmatively disclaimed access to or control over the computer or a portion of the computer's files, even when the computer is located in a common area of the house, courts have been unwilling to find third party authority.

Andrus' case presents facts that differ somewhat from those in other cases. Andrus' computer was located in a bedroom occupied by the homeowner's fifty-one year old son rather than in a true common area. Dr. Andrus, however, had unlimited access to the room. Law enforcement officers did not ask specific questions about Dr. Andrus' use of the computer, but Dr. Andrus said nothing indicating the need for such questions. *Cf. Trulock,* 275 F.3d at 398 (when law enforcement questioned third party girlfriend about computer, she indicated she and boyfriend had separate password-protected files). The resolution of this appeal turns on whether the officers' belief in Dr. Andrus' authority was reasonable, despite the lack of any affirmative assertion by Dr. Andrus that he used the computer and despite the existence of a user profile indicating Ray Andrus' intent to exclude other household members from using the computer. For the reasons articulated below, this court concludes the officers' belief in Dr. Andrus' authority was reasonable. . . .

First, the officers knew Dr. Andrus owned the house and lived there with family members. Second, the officers knew Dr. Andrus' house had internet access and that Dr. Andrus paid the Time Warner internet and cable bill. Third, the officers knew the email address bandrus@kc.rr.com had been activated and used to register on a website that provided access to child pornography. Fourth, although the officers knew Ray Andrus lived in the center bedroom, they also knew that Dr. Andrus had access to the room at will. Fifth, the officers saw the computer in plain view on the desk in Andrus' room and it appeared available for use by other household members. Furthermore, the record indicates Dr. Andrus did not say or do anything to indicate his lack of ownership or control over the computer when Cheatham asked for his consent to conduct a computer search. It is uncontested that Dr. Andrus led the officers to the bedroom in which the computer was located, and, even after he saw Kanatzar begin to work on the computer, Dr. Andrus remained silent about any lack of authority he had over the computer. Even if Ray Andrus' computer was protected with a user name and password, there is no indication in the record that the officers knew or had reason to believe such protections were in place.

Andrus argues his computer's password protection indicated his computer was "locked" to third parties, a fact the officers would have known had they asked questions of Dr. Andrus prior to searching the computer. Under our case law, however, officers are not obligated to ask questions unless the circumstances are ambiguous. In essence, by suggesting the onus was on the officers to ask about password protection prior to searching the computer, despite the absence of any indication that Dr. Andrus' access to the computer was limited by a password, Andrus necessarily submits there is inherent ambiguity whenever police want to search a household computer and a third party has not affirmatively provided information about his own use of the computer or about password protection. Andrus' argument presupposes, however, that password protection of home computers is so common that a reasonable officer ought to know password protection is likely. Andrus has neither made this argument directly nor proffered any evidence to demonstrate a high incidence of password protection among home computer users. . . .

Viewed under the requisite totality-of-the-circumstances analysis, the facts known to the officers at the time the computer search commenced created an objectively reasonable perception that Dr. Andrus was, at least, *one* user of the computer. That objectively reasonable belief would have been enough to give Dr. Andrus apparent authority to consent to a search. Even if Dr. Andrus had no actual ability to use the computer and the computer was password protected, these mistakes of fact do not negate a determination of Dr. Andrus' apparent authority. In this case, the district court found Agent Cheatham properly halted the search when further conversation with Dr. Andrus revealed he did not use the computer and that Andrus' computer was the only computer in the house. These later revelations, however, have no bearing on the reasonableness of the officers' belief in Dr. Andrus' authority at the outset of the computer search.

MCKAY, J., dissenting. This case concerns the reasonable expectation of privacy associated with password-protected computers. In examining the contours of a third party's apparent authority to consent to the search of a home computer, the majority correctly indicates that the extent to which law enforcement knows or should reasonably suspect that password protection is enabled is critical. . . . I take issue with the majority's implicit holding that law enforcement may use software deliberately designed to automatically bypass computer password protection based on third-party consent without the need to make a reasonable inquiry regarding the presence of password protection and the third party's access to that password.

The presence of security on Defendant's computer is undisputed. Yet, the majority curiously argues that Defendant's use of password protection is inconsequential because Defendant failed to argue that computer password protection is "commonplace." Of course, the decision provides no guidance on what would constitute sufficient proof of the prevalence of password protection, nor does it explain why the court could not take judicial notice that password protection is a standard feature of operating systems. Despite recognizing the "pervasiveness of computers in American homes," and the fact that the "personal computer is often a repository for private information the computer's owner does not intend to share with others," the majority requires the invocation of magical language in order to give effect to Defendant's subjective intent to exclude others from accessing the computer. . . .

The unconstrained ability of law enforcement to use forensic software such as the EnCase program to bypass password protection without first determining whether such passwords have been enabled does not "exacerbate[]" this difficulty; rather, it avoids it altogether, simultaneously and dangerously sidestepping the Fourth Amendment in the process. Indeed, the majority concedes that if such protection were "shown to be commonplace, law enforcement's use of forensic software like EnCase . . . may well be subject to question." But the fact that a computer password "lock" may not be *immediately* visible does not render it unlocked. I appreciate that unlike the locked file cabinet, computers have no handle to pull. But, like the padlocked footlocker, computers do exhibit outward signs of password protection: they display boot password screens, username/password log-in screens, and/or screen-saver reactivation passwords.

The fact remains that EnCase's ability to bypass security measures is well known to law enforcement. Here, ICE's forensic computer specialist found Defendant's computer turned off. Without turning it on, he hooked his laptop directly to the hard drive of Defendant's computer and ran the EnCase program. The agents made no effort to ascertain whether such security was enabled prior to initiating the search. . . .

The majority points out that law enforcement "did not ask specific questions" about Dr. Andrus' use of the computer or knowledge of Ray Andrus' use of password protection, but twice criticizes Dr. Andrus' failure to affirmatively disclaim ownership of, control over, or knowledge regarding the computer. Of course, the computer was located in Ray Andrus' very tiny bedroom, but the majority makes no effort to explain how this does not create an ambiguous situation as to ownership.

The burden on law enforcement to identify ownership of the computer was minimal. A simple question or two would have sufficed. Prior to the computer search, the agents questioned Dr. Andrus about Ray Andrus' status as a renter and Dr. Andrus' ability to enter his 51-year-old son's bedroom in order to determine Dr. Andrus' ability to consent to a search of the room, but the agents did not inquire whether Dr. Andrus used the computer, and if so, whether he had access to his son's password. At the suppression hearing, the agents testified that they were not immediately aware that Defendant's computer was the only one in the house, and they began to doubt Dr. Andrus' authority to consent when they learned this fact.

The record reveals that, upon questioning, Dr. Andrus indicated that there was a computer in the house and led the agents to Defendant's room. The forensic specialist was then summoned. It took him approximately fifteen to twenty minutes to set up his equipment, yet, bizarrely, at no point during this period did the agents inquire about the presence of any other computers. . . .

Accordingly, in my view, given the case law indicating the importance of computer password protection, the common knowledge about the prevalence of password usage, and the design of EnCase or similar password bypass mechanisms, the Fourth Amendment and the reasonable inquiry rule, mandate that in consent-based, warrantless computer searches, law enforcement personnel inquire or otherwise check for the presence of password protection and, if a password is present, inquire about the consenter's knowledge of that password and joint access to the computer. . . .

NOTES & QUESTIONS

1. *A Question of Perspective?* Orin Kerr contends:

> From a virtual user's perspective, the child pornography was hidden to the father; it was behind a password-protected gate. Under these facts, the father couldn't consent to a search because he would lack common authority over it. From a physical perspective, however, the file was present on the hard drive just like all the other information. Under these facts, the father could consent to the search because he had access rights to the machine generally. . . .
>
> Viewed from the physical perspective, the investigators reasonably did not know about the user profile and reasonably believed that the father had rights to consent to that part of the hard drive.[90]

2. *Checking for Password Protection.* Was the investigators' belief about the father's authority over the computer reasonable? Should the investigators have asked the father more questions about his use of the computer first? Should they have turned on the machine to see if it was password-protected before hooking up the forensic software? What kinds of incentives does this decision engender for officers doing an investigation?

3. *The Right to Delete.* Paul Ohm contends that the Fourth Amendment should be read to encompass a right to delete: "The text of the Fourth Amendment seems broad enough to protect this 'right to destroy' or, in the computer context, 'right to delete' by its terms through its prohibition on unreasonable seizure."[91] If the government has engaged in an unreasonable search of a computer under the Fourth Amendment, the typical remedy is that the data is excluded from trial. Does it follow that people should also have the right to demand that the data seized by the government be deleted?

4. *Computer Searches at the Border—and Beyond.* Under the border search

---

[90] Orin Kerr, *Virtual Analogies, Physical Searches, and the Fourth Amendment,* Volokh Conspiracy, Apr. 26, 2007, http://www.volokh.com/posts/1177562355.shtml.

[91] Paul Ohm, *The Fourth Amendment Right to Delete,* 119 Harv. L. Rev. F. 10 (2005). For an extensive normative argument for the right to delete, see Viktor Mayer-Schönberger, *Delete: The Virtues of Forgetting in the Digital Age* (2009).

doctrine, the government need not obtain a warrant or even demonstrate reasonable suspicion to justify a search of persons or property at the international border. According to the Supreme Court, "It is axiomatic that the United States, as sovereign, has the inherent authority to protect, and a paramount interest in protecting, its territorial integrity." *United States v. Flores-Montano*, 541 U.S. 149 (2004). The Court has recognized only a few limits on the government's power to engage in searches at the border without any particularized suspicion, such as "invasive searches of the person." *Id.*

In *United States v. Arnold*, 533 F.3d 1003 (9th Cir. 2008), the Ninth Circuit considered whether this doctrine applied to computers and electronic devices at the border. The defendant argued that computers should be treated differently from regular property:

> Arnold argues that "laptop computers are fundamentally different from traditional closed containers," and analogizes them to "homes" and the "human mind." Arnold's analogy of a laptop to a home is based on his conclusion that a laptop's capacity allows for the storage of personal documents in an amount equivalent to that stored in one's home. He argues that a laptop is like the "human mind" because of its ability to record ideas, e-mail, internet chats and web-surfing habits.

The court rejected this argument:

> With respect to these searches, the Supreme Court has refused to draw distinctions between containers of information and contraband with respect to their quality or nature for purposes of determining the appropriate level of Fourth Amendment protection. Arnold's analogy to a search of a home based on a laptop's storage capacity is without merit. The Supreme Court has expressly rejected applying the Fourth Amendment protections afforded to homes to property which is "*capable of functioning as a home*" simply due to its size, or, distinguishing between "'worthy' and 'unworthy' containers."

In *United States v. Cotterman*, 637 F.3d 1068 (9th Cir. 2011), the Ninth Circuit upheld a search of a laptop computer that began at the nation's border and ended two days later in a governmental forensic computer laboratory that was 170 miles away from the border. The court stated, "So long as property has not been officially cleared for entry into the United States and remains in the control of the Government, any further search is simply a continuation of the original border search—the entirety of which is justified by the Government's border search power." According to the court, the defendant never regained his normal expectation of privacy in his computer, the 40-hour detention was reasonably related in scope to the circumstances justifying the initial detention at the border, and requiring forensic computer laboratories at all ports of entry throughout the United States would place an unreasonable burden on the government.

In dissent, Judge Betty Fletcher worried that "the scope of the search will be determined by the Government's desire to be thorough, and the length of seizure by the Government's convenience."

5. ***Government Access to Data Stored in Other Countries.*** In *Microsoft Corp. v.*

United States (Microsoft Ireland), 829 F.3d 197 (2d Cir. July 14, 2016), the government used a warrant under the Stored Communications Act (SCA) to search and seize data about a Microsoft customer whose data was located on a Microsoft server in Ireland. Microsoft refused to comply and produce the data because it argued that the SCA does not apply to data stored outside the United States. Microsoft contended that providing the data under the SCA would violate the law of Ireland and that the government should instead seek the information under the Mutual Legal Assistance Treaty (MLAT). MLATs are treaties countries enter into for law enforcement cooperation.

The government argued that Microsoft still retained control of the data and that government access to the data should not turn on where Microsoft chose to store it. If the data is in Microsoft's custody and control, the government argued, Microsoft should be compelled to provide it to the government. In *Microsoft Ireland*, the government also noted that Microsoft had the technical ability to access the information, although it was stored in Dublin, from its Redmond, Washington headquarters. The government further contended that preventing SCA warrants from reaching to data stored abroad would "seriously impede" law enforcement investigations.

The Second Circuit sided with Microsoft: "Neither explicitly nor implicitly does the statute envision the application of its warrant provisions overseas." The court noted that its holding "serves the interests of comity that, as the MLAT process reflects, ordinarily govern the conduct of cross-boundary criminal investigations." The court further stated that the foreign sovereign's interests are implicated when "a United States judge issues an order requiring a service provider to 'collect' from servers located overseas and 'import' into the United States data, possibly belonging to a foreign citizen, simply because the service provider has a base of operations within the United States."

Suppose a foreign government sought to obtain data from a company doing business in that country but with data located on a server in the U.S. Suppose that this foreign government lacked sufficient privacy protections and its law allowed access to the data with a minimal standard or oversight. Should the foreign government be able to access the data stored in the U.S. with a standard that is not sufficient under U.S. law? Examining this issue, Jennifer Daskal writes: "Data localization mandates are likely to result in foreign governments being able to compel the production of data — including of Americans — based on a much lower standard than what would apply if the data were sought by the United States."

Daskal argues that the positions of both sides of the case are undesirable. She notes that it is arbitrary for "government access to one's data [to] depend upon where the data happens to be stored — particularly if the user does not know and has no role in choosing that location."[92]

In assessing the Second Circuit's judgment in this case, Paul Schwartz makes two recommendations for the future.[93] The first is for heightened

---

[92] Jennifer Daskal, *Law Enforcement Access to Data Across Borders: The Evolving Security and Rights Issues*, 8 J. Nat'l Security L. & Pol'y 473 (2016).

[93] Paul M. Schwartz, *Microsoft Ireland and a Level Playing Field for U.S. Cloud Companies*, 15 PVLR 1549 (Aug. 1, 2016).

awareness among courts in distinctions among cloud computing types. He writes, "The differences among cloud services matter because they bear on the issue of whether the retrieval of the information will be made outside the U.S." In addition, this issue matters because of the extent to which retrieval of information might violate a foreign country's law, including its information privacy protections.

Second, Schwartz calls for clarification of questions regarding the "international reach of a variety of legal authorities and processes." In his view, the need is to balance policy goals including the battle against international terrorism, assisting in domestic litigation, protecting individual privacy, and respecting the law of foreign nations." As part of this process of policy clarification, Schwartz also calls for U.S. lawmakers to "keep a level playing field for U.S. tech companies." He warns against different rules being established for "international data requests based on the home country of the cloud service provider." Such an approach would simply encourage the use of foreign cloud services and disadvantage U.S. companies with no policy benefits.

How should access requests to clouds be evaluated by U.S. courts? For example, should it matter whether the cloud provider for data stored in Ireland is a U.S. corporation, or not? Should the U.S. court consider where networked cloud information is retrieved by the company in responding to a law enforcement request, or where it is stored?

RILEY V. CALIFORNIA

134 S.Ct. 2473 (2014)

ROBERTS, C.J.: These two cases raise a common question: whether the police may, without a warrant, search digital information on a cell phone seized from an individual who has been arrested.

[In the first case, a police officer searched David Riley incident to arrest and found items associated with a street gang. The officer also seized a smart phone from Riley's pants pocket and accessed some information on it. At the station approximately two hours later, a detective specializing in gangs further went through the phone looking for evidence of other crimes. He found a photo of Riley by a car suspected of being involved in a shooting a few weeks earlier. Eventually Riley was also charged with firing at an occupied vehicle, assault with a semiautomatic firearm, and attempted murder in connection with that earlier shooting. He moved to suppress the evidence derived from the search of his cell phone, arguing that the searches violated the Fourth Amendment because they were performed without a warrant and were not otherwise justified by any exceptions to the warrant requirement. Riley was convicted and sentenced to 15 years to life.

In the second case, police officers observed respondent Brima Wurie make an apparent drug sale from a car and subsequently arrested him. After taking him to the station, they seized two cell phones from him, with the one at issue here being a flip phone, which generally has fewer features than a smart phone. The officers noticed that this phone was repeatedly receiving calls from a source labeled as "my house" on the phone's external screen. They opened the phone, accessed the phone's call log, and found the number associated with the "my house" label. After tracing the number to an apartment building, the officers obtained and executed a search warrant for the location, and found and seized 215 grams of crack cocaine, marijuana, drug paraphernalia, a firearm and ammunition, and cash. After being charged with distributing crack cocaine, possessing crack cocaine with intent to distribute, and being a felon in possession of a firearm and ammunition, Wurie moved to suppress the evidence found at the apartment as being the fruit of a warrantless search of his cell phone in violation of the Fourth Amendment. The district court denied the motion and Wurie was convicted and sentenced to 262 months in prison.]

"[T]he ultimate touchstone of the Fourth Amendment is 'reasonableness.' " *Brigham City v. Stuart,* 547 U.S. 398, 403 (2006). Our cases have determined that "[w]here a search is undertaken by law enforcement officials to discover evidence of criminal wrongdoing, . . . reasonableness generally requires the obtaining of a judicial warrant." *Vernonia School Dist. 47J v. Acton,* 515 U.S. 646, 653 (1995). In the absence of a warrant, a search is reasonable only if it falls within a specific exception to the warrant requirement. See *Kentucky v. King,* 131 S. Ct. 1849 (2011).

The two cases before us concern the reasonableness of a warrantless search incident to a lawful arrest . . . . Three related precedents set forth the rules governing such searches: The first, *Chimel v. California,* 395 U.S. 752 (1969), laid the groundwork for most of the existing search incident to arrest doctrine. Police officers in that case arrested Chimel inside his home and proceeded to search his entire three-bedroom house, including the attic and garage. . . . The Court crafted the following rule for assessing the reasonableness of a search incident to arrest.

"When an arrest is made, it is reasonable for the arresting officer to search the person arrested in order to remove any weapons that the latter might seek to use in order to resist arrest or effect his escape . . . . In addition, it is entirely reasonable for the arresting officer to search for and seize any evidence on the arrestee's person in order to prevent its concealment or destruction. . . ."

Four years later, in *United States v. Robinson,* 414 U.S. 218 (1973), the Court applied the *Chimel* analysis in the context of a search of the arrestee's person. A police officer had arrested Robinson for driving with a revoked license. The officer conducted a patdown search and felt an object that he could not identify in Robinson's coat pocket. He removed the object, which turned out to be a crumpled cigarette package, and opened it. Inside were 14 capsules of heroin. . . .

This Court . . . reject[ed] the notion that "case-by-case adjudication" was required . . . [and] explained, "[t]he authority to search the person incident to a lawful custodial arrest, while based upon the need to disarm and to discover evidence, does not depend on what a court may later decide was the probability in a particular arrest situation that weapons or evidence would in fact be found upon the person of the suspect." *Id.* Instead, a "custodial arrest of a suspect based on probable cause is a reasonable intrusion under the Fourth Amendment; that intrusion being lawful, a search incident to the arrest requires no additional justification." *Id.* A few years later, the Court clarified that this exception was limited to "personal property . . . immediately associated with the person of the arrestee." *United States v. Chadwick,* 433 U.S. 1 (1977).

The search incident to arrest trilogy concludes with [*Arizona v. Gant*, 556 U.S. 332 (2009)], which analyzed searches of an arrestee's vehicle. *Gant,* like *Robinson,* recognized that the *Chimel* concerns for officer safety and evidence preservation underlie the search incident to arrest exception. *Gant* added, however, an independent exception for a warrantless search of a vehicle's passenger compartment "when it is 'reasonable to believe evidence relevant to the crime of arrest might be found in the vehicle.' ". . . .

These cases require us to decide how the search incident to arrest doctrine applies to modern cell phones . . . . We first consider each *Chimel* concern in turn. In doing so, [r]ather than requiring the "case-by-case adjudication" that *Robinson* rejected, we ask instead whether application of the search incident to arrest doctrine to this particular category of effects would "untether the rule from the justifications underlying the *Chimel* exception."

Digital data stored on a cell phone cannot itself be used as a weapon to harm an arresting officer or to effectuate the arrestee's escape. Once an officer has secured a phone and eliminated any potential physical threats . . . data on the phone can endanger no one.

The United States and California focus primarily on the second *Chimel* rationale: preventing the destruction of evidence.

Both Riley and Wurie concede that officers could have seized and secured their cell phones to prevent destruction of evidence while seeking a warrant . . . . And once law enforcement officers have secured a cell phone, there is no longer any risk that the arrestee himself will be able to delete incriminating data from the phone.

The United States and California argue that information on a cell phone may nevertheless be vulnerable to two types of evidence destruction unique to digital data—remote wiping and data encryption. Remote wiping occurs when a phone, connected to a wireless network, receives a signal that erases stored data. . . . Encryption is a security feature that some modern cell phones use in addition to password protection. When such phones lock, data becomes protected by sophisticated encryption that renders a phone all but "unbreakable" unless police know the password . . . .

With respect to remote wiping, the Government's primary concern turns on the actions of third parties who are not present at the scene of arrest. And data encryption is even further afield . . . . Moreover, in situations in which an arrest might trigger a remote-wipe attempt or an officer discovers an unlocked phone, it is not clear that the ability to conduct a warrantless search would make much of a difference. The need to effect the arrest, secure the scene, and tend to other pressing matters means that law enforcement officers may well not be able to turn their attention to a cell phone right away. . . . Cell phone data would be vulnerable to remote wiping from the time an individual anticipates arrest to the time any eventual search of the phone is completed . . . .

The search incident to arrest exception rests not only on the heightened government interests at stake in a volatile arrest situation, but also on an arrestee's reduced privacy interests upon being taken into police custody. . . .

The fact that an arrestee has diminished privacy interests does not mean that the Fourth Amendment falls out of the picture entirely. Not every search "is acceptable solely because a person is in custody." To the contrary, when "privacy-related concerns are weighty enough" a "search may require a warrant, notwithstanding the diminished expectations of privacy of the arrestee." One such example, of course, is *Chimel*. . . . Because a search of the arrestee's entire house was a substantial invasion beyond the arrest itself, the Court concluded that a warrant was required. . . .

Cell phones differ in both a quantitative and a qualitative sense from other objects that might be kept on an arrestee's person. The term "cell phone" is itself misleading shorthand; many of these devices are in fact minicomputers that also happen to have the capacity to be used as a telephone. They could just as easily be called cameras, video players, rolodexes, calendars, tape recorders, libraries, diaries, albums, televisions, maps, or newspapers.

One of the most notable distinguishing features of modern cell phones is their immense storage capacity. Before cell phones, a search of a person was limited by physical realities and tended as a general matter to constitute only a narrow intrusion on privacy. See Kerr, *Foreword: Accounting for Technological Change*, 36 Harv. J.L. & Pub. Pol'y 403, 404-405 (2013). Most people cannot lug around every piece of mail they have received for the past several months, every picture they have taken, or every book or article they have read . . . . But the possible intrusion on privacy is not physically limited in the same way when it comes to cell phones. The current top-selling smart phone has a standard capacity of 16 gigabytes (and is available with up to 64 gigabytes). Sixteen gigabytes translates to millions of pages of text, thousands of pictures, or hundreds of videos . . . .

The storage capacity of cell phones has several interrelated consequences for privacy. First, a cell phone collects in one place many distinct types of information—an address, a note, a prescription, a bank statement, a video—that reveal much more in combination than any isolated record. Second, a cell phone's capacity allows even just one type of information to convey far more than previously possible. The sum of an individual's private life can be reconstructed through a thousand photographs labeled with dates, locations, and descriptions; the same cannot be said of a photograph or two of loved ones tucked into a wallet. Third, the data on a phone can date back to the purchase of the phone, or even earlier. A person might carry in his pocket a slip of paper reminding him to call Mr. Jones; he would not carry a record of all his communications with Mr. Jones for the past several months, as would routinely be kept on a phone.

Finally, there is an element of pervasiveness that characterizes cell phones but not physical records. Prior to the digital age, people did not typically carry a cache of sensitive personal information with them as they went about their day. . . . A decade ago police officers searching an arrestee might have occasionally stumbled across a highly personal item such as a diary. But those discoveries were likely to be few and far between. Today, by contrast, it is no exaggeration to say that many of the more than 90% of American adults who own a cell phone keep on their person a digital record of nearly every aspect of their lives—from the mundane to the intimate. . . .

Although the data stored on a cell phone is distinguished from physical records by quantity alone, certain types of data are also qualitatively different. An Internet search and browsing history, for example, can be found on an Internet-enabled phone and could reveal an individual's private interests or concerns . . . . Historic location information is a standard feature on many smart phones and can reconstruct someone's specific movements down to the minute, not only around town but also within a particular building. See *United States v. Jones*, 132 S. Ct. 945, 955 (2012) (SOTOMAYOR, J., concurring) ("GPS monitoring generates a precise, comprehensive record of a person's public movements that reflects a wealth of detail about her familial, political, professional, religious, and sexual associations.") . . . . Mobile application software on a cell phone, or "apps," offer a range of tools for managing detailed information about all aspects of a person's life. . . . The average smart phone user has installed 33 apps, which together can form a revealing montage of the user's life. . . In 1926, Learned Hand observed (in an opinion later quoted in *Chimel*) that it is "a totally different thing to search a man's pockets and use against him what they contain, from ransacking his house for everything which may incriminate him." *United States v. Kirschenblatt,* 16 F.2d 202, 203 (C.A.2). If his pockets contain a cell phone, however, that is no longer true. Indeed, a cell phone search would typically expose to the government far *more* than the most exhaustive search of a house: A phone not only contains in digital form many sensitive records previously found in the home; it also contains a broad array of private information never found in a home in any form—unless the phone is. . . .

We . . . reject the United States' final suggestion that officers should always be able to search a phone's call log, as they did in Wurie's case. The Government relies on *Smith v. Maryland,* 442 U.S. 735 (1979), which held that no warrant was required to use a pen register at telephone company premises to identify numbers dialed by a particular caller. The Court in that case, however, concluded that the use of a pen register was not a "search" at all under the Fourth Amendment. There is no dispute here that the officers engaged in a search of Wurie's cell phone. Moreover, call logs typically contain more than just phone numbers; they include any identifying information that an individual might add, such as the label "my house" in Wurie's case.

Finally, at oral argument California suggested a different limiting principle, under which officers could search cell phone data if they could have obtained the same information from a pre-digital counterpart. . . . But the fact that a search in the pre-digital era could have turned up a photograph or two in a wallet does not justify a search of thousands of photos in a digital gallery . . . . And to make matters worse, such an analogue test would allow law enforcement to search a range of items contained on a phone, even though people would be unlikely to carry such a variety of information in physical form. In Riley's case, for example, it is implausible that he would have strolled around with video tapes, photo albums, and an address book all crammed into his pockets. But because each of those items has a pre-digital analogue, police under California's proposal would be able to search a phone for all of those items—a significant diminution of privacy . . . .

We cannot deny that our decision today will have an impact on the ability of law enforcement to combat crime. Cell phones have become important tools in facilitating coordination and communication among members of criminal enterprises, and can provide valuable incriminating information about dangerous criminals. Privacy comes at a cost.

Our holding, of course, is not that the information on a cell phone is immune from search; it is instead that a warrant is generally required before such a search, even when a cell phone is seized incident to arrest. Our cases have historically recognized that the warrant requirement is "an important working part of our machinery of government," not merely "an inconvenience to be somehow 'weighed' against the claims of police efficiency." *Coolidge v. New Hampshire,* 403 U.S. 443 (1971) . . . . Moreover, even though the search incident to arrest exception does not apply to cell phones, other case-specific exceptions may still justify a warrantless search of a particular phone. "One well-recognized exception applies when the exigencies of the situation make the needs of law enforcement so compelling that [a] warrantless search is objectively reasonable under the Fourth Amendment." . . . . Our cases have recognized that the Fourth Amendment was the founding generation's response to the reviled "general warrants" and "writs of assistance" of the colonial era, which allowed British officers to rummage through homes in an unrestrained search for evidence of criminal activity. Opposition to such searches was in fact one of the driving forces behind the Revolution itself. In 1761, the patriot James Otis delivered a speech in Boston denouncing the use of writs of assistance. A young John Adams was there, and he would later write that "[e]very man of a crowded audience appeared to me to go away, as I did, ready to take arms against writs of assistance." 10 Works of John Adams 247–248 (C. Adams ed. 1856). According to Adams, Otis's speech was "the first scene of the first act of opposition to the arbitrary claims of Great Britain. Then and there the child Independence was born." *Id.,* at 248. . . .

Modern cell phones are not just another technological convenience. With all they contain and all they may reveal, they hold for many Americans "the privacies of life." The fact that technology now allows an individual to carry such information in his hand does not make the information any less worthy of the protection for which the Founders fought. Our answer to the question of what police must do before searching a cell phone seized incident to an arrest is accordingly simple—get a warrant.

NOTES & QUESTIONS

1. *A Quantitative Difference?* The Supreme Court focused on the quantity of information that people store in a cell phone and noted that this was different than carrying a few photos or other items. Likewise, in *Jones,* the Court focused on the quantity of information gathered by GPS. What is the operative test that separates a search of a cell phone or via GPS from other searches?

2. *Implications for* **Smith v. Maryland.** Recall the third party doctrine in *Smith v. Maryland,* where the Court held that a person lacks an expectation of privacy in the numbers a person dials on the phone. The government in *Riley* invoked *Smith v. Maryland* to argue that "officers should always be able to search a phone's call log." The Court, however, rejected this argument because "call logs typically contain more than just phone numbers; they include any identifying information that an individual might add, such as the label 'my house' in Wurie's case." Today, it is quite easy to link phone numbers to identifiable people. Should the fact that phone numbers are already identified in the phone's call log matter if the police can readily identify the phone numbers in a pen register by looking them up online? Does the reasoning of *Smith v. Maryland* still hold up today in light of *Riley*?

3. *Implications for the Third Party Doctrine.* The third party doctrine in *Smith v. Maryland* and *United States v. Miller* was crafted in the 1970s when only certain forms of data were maintained by third parties. Now, much of our activity involves information that is stored with third parties. As Daniel Solove notes: "The Court's reasoning in *Riley* suggests that perhaps the Court is finally recognizing that old physical considerations — location, size, etc. — are no longer as relevant in light of modern technology. What matters is the data involved and how much it reveals about a person's private life. If this is the larger principle the Court is recognizing today, then it strongly undermines some of the reasoning behind the third party doctrine."[94] Do you agree with this assessment? Is there a way that the third party doctrine can be made consistent with the reasoning in *Riley*?

2. ENCRYPTION

Encryption includes the ability to keep communications secure by concealing the contents of a message. With encryption, even if a communication is intercepted, it still remains secure. Encryption works by translating a message into a code of letters or numbers called "cypher text." The parties to the communication hold a *key*, which consists of the information necessary to translate the code back to the original message, or "plain text." Since ancient times, code-makers have devised cryptographic systems to encode messages. But along with the code-makers arose code-breakers, who were able to figure out the keys to cryptographic systems by, for example, examining the patterns in the encoded messages and comparing them to patterns in a particular language and the frequency of use of certain letters in that language. Today, computers have vastly increased the complexity of encryption.

Encryption presents a difficult trade-off between privacy and surveillance. It is an essential technique to protect the privacy of electronic communications in an age when such communications can so easily be intercepted and monitored. On the other hand, it enables individuals to disguise their communications from detection by law enforcement officials.[95] As Whitfield Diffie and Susan Landau observe:

> The explosion in cryptography and the US government's attempts to control it have given rise to a debate between those who hail the new technology's contribution to privacy, business, and security and those who fear both its interference with the work of police and its adverse effect on the collection of

---

[94] Daniel J. Solove, Does the U.S. Supreme Court's Decision on the 4th Amendment and Cell Phones Signal Future Changes to the Third Party Doctrine? LinkedIn, June 25, 2014, https://www.linkedin.com/today/post/article/20140625172659-2259773-does-the-u-s-supreme-court-s-decision-on-the-4th-amendment-and-cell-phones-signal-future-changes-to-the-third-party-doctrine.

[95] For more background on encryption, see Simon Singh, *The Code: The Evolution of Secrecy from Mary, Queen of Scots to Quantum Cryptography* (1999); Steven Levy, *Crypto: How the Code Rebels Beat the Government — Saving Privacy in the Digital Age* (2002); A. Michael Froomkin, *The Metaphor Is the Key: Cryptography, the Clipper Chip, and the Constitution*, 143 U. Pa. L. Rev. 709 (1995); Robert C. Post, *Encryption Source Code and the First Amendment*, 15 Berkeley Tech. L.J. 713 (2000); A. Michael Froomkin, *The Constitution and Encryption Regulation: Do We Need a "New Privacy"?*, 3 N.Y.U. J. Legis. & Pub. Pol'y 25 (1999).

intelligence. Positions have often been extreme. The advocates for unfettered cryptography maintain that a free society depends on privacy to protect freedom of association, artistic creativity, and political discussion. The advocates of control hold that there will be no freedom at all unless we can protect ourselves from criminals, terrorists, and foreign threats. Many have tried to present themselves as seeking to maintain or restore the status quo. For the police, the status quo is the continued ability to wiretap. For civil libertarians, it is the ready availability of conversational privacy that prevailed at the time of the country's founding.[96]

The Clipper Chip. The U.S. government has become increasingly concerned that the growing sophistication of encryption would make it virtually impossible for the government to decrypt. In 1994, the government proposed implementing the "Clipper Chip," a federal encryption standard in which the government would retain a copy of the key in a system called "key escrow." By holding a "spare key," the government could readily decrypt encrypted communications if it desired. The Clipper Chip was strongly criticized, and the government's encryption standard has not been widely used.

Encryption and the First Amendment. In *Junger v. Daley*, 209 F.3d 481 (6th Cir. 2000), the Sixth Circuit concluded that encryption was protected speech under the First Amendment:

> Much like a mathematical or scientific formula, one can describe the function and design of encryption software by a prose explanation; however, for individuals fluent in a computer programming language, source code is the most efficient and precise means by which to communicate ideas about cryptography.

Junger relied on the reasoning of *Bernstein v. United States Dep't of Justice,* 176 F.3d 1132 (9th Cir. 1999) (opinion withdrawn), where the Ninth Circuit struck down a licensing scheme on encryption source code as a violation of the First Amendment:

> Bernstein has submitted numerous declarations from cryptographers and computer programmers explaining that cryptographic ideas and algorithms are conveniently expressed in source code. . . . [T]he chief task for cryptographers is the development of secure methods of encryption. While the articulation of such a system in layman's English or in general mathematical terms may be useful, the devil is, at least for cryptographers, often in the algorithmic details. By utilizing source code, a cryptographer can express algorithmic ideas with precision and methodological rigor that is otherwise difficult to achieve. . . .
>
> Thus, cryptographers use source code to express their scientific ideas in much the same way that mathematicians use equations or economists use graphs. . . .
>
> In light of these considerations, we conclude that encryption software, in its source code form and as employed by those in the field of cryptography, must be viewed as expressive for First Amendment purposes. . . .

Orin Kerr takes issue with *Junger*'s holding: "the court viewed source code using the close-up paradigm of what the code looked like, rather than the deeper

---

[96] Whitfield Diffie & Susan Landau, *Privacy on the Line: The Politics of Wiretapping and Encryption* (1998).

functional perspective of what the code was actually supposed to do. . . . Just as viewing a Seurat painting from inches away reveals only dots, the *Junger* court's myopic view of source code revealed only communications that looked like speech in form, but lacked the deeper significance required to establish constitutional expression."[97]

In the view of Robert Post, the question of First Amendment coverage turns on a "constitutional sociology."[98] The relevant discussion for Post is "between encryption source code that is itself part of public dialogue and encryption source code that is meant merely to be used." He adds, moreover, that "even if encryption source code in not itself a subject of public discussion, its regulation might nevertheless affect public discussion in ways that ought to trigger First Amendment coverage." As an example, a licensing scheme for encryption code that engaged in viewpoint discrimination would be flawed. Even beyond viewpoint discrimination, a viewpoint neutral scheme of regulating encryption software would be flawed if it had a sufficient constitutional impact on "the various First Amendment media that employ" such software.

Consider *Karn v. United States Dep't of State*, 925 F. Supp. 1 (D.D.C. 1996), where the court came to the contrary conclusion from *Junger*:

> . . . The government regulation at issue here is clearly content-neutral. . . . The defendants are not regulating the export of the diskette because of the expressive content of the comments and or source code, but instead are regulating because of the belief that the combination of encryption source code on machine readable media will make it easier for foreign intelligence sources to encode their communications. . . .
>
> . . . [A] content-neutral regulation is justified . . . if it is within the constitutional power of the government, it "furthers an important or substantial governmental interest," and "the incidental restriction on alleged First Amendment freedoms is no greater than is essential to the furtherance of that interest." . . .
>
> . . . By placing cryptographic products on the ITAR, the President has determined that the proliferation of cryptographic products will harm the United States. . . .
>
> . . . [T]he plaintiff has not advanced any argument that the regulation is "substantially broader than necessary" to prevent the proliferation of cryptographic products. Nor has the plaintiff articulated any present barrier to the spreading of information on cryptography "by any other means" other than those containing encryption source code on machine-readable media. Therefore, the Court holds that the regulation of the plaintiff's diskette is narrowly tailored to the goal of limiting the proliferation of cryptographic products and that the regulation is justified. . . .

Encryption and the Fourth Amendment. Suppose law enforcement officials legally obtain an encrypted communication. Does the Fourth Amendment require a warrant before the government can decrypt an encrypted communication? Consider the following argument by Orin Kerr:

---

[97] Orin S. Kerr, *Are We Overprotecting Code? Thoughts on First-Generation Internet Law*, 57 Wash. & Lee L. Rev. 1287, 1292-93 (2000).

[98] Robert Post, *Encryption Source Code and the First Amendment*, 15 Berkeley Tech. L.J. 713 (2000).

Encryption is often explained as a lock-and-key system, in which a "key" is used to "lock" plaintext by turning it into ciphertext, and then a "key" is used to "unlock" the ciphertext by turning it into plaintext. We know that locking a container is a common way to create a reasonable expectation of privacy in its contents: the government ordinarily cannot break the lock and search a closed container without a warrant. . . .

When we use a "lock" and "unlock" in the metaphorical sense to denote understanding, however, a lock cannot trigger the rights-based Fourth Amendment. If I tell you a riddle, I do not have a right to stop you from figuring it out. Although figuring out the secret of an inscrutable communication may "unlock" its meaning, the Fourth Amendment cannot regulate such a cognitive discovery. . . .[99]

Encryption and the Fifth Amendment. Can the government compel the production of a private key if it is stored on a personal computer? What if the key is known only to the individual and not stored or recorded?

3. VIDEO SURVEILLANCE

Prior to the enactment of the ECPA, video surveillance was not encompassed within the language of Title III. When it amended federal electronic surveillance law in 1986 by enacting the ECPA, Congress again failed to address video surveillance. Of course, if the government intercepts a *communication* consisting of video images (such as a transmission of a webcam image or an e-mail containing a video clip), then the Wiretap Act applies. If the government accesses an individual's stored video clip, then the SCA applies. However, being watched by video *surveillance* (such as a surveillance camera) does not involve an interception or an accessing of stored images. The video surveillance must be silent video surveillance, or else it could be an "oral" communication subject to the Wiretap Act. In sum, silent video surveillance is not covered under federal electronic surveillance law. *See, e.g., United States v. Biasuci*, 786 F.2d 504 (2d Cir. 1986); *United States v. Koyomejian*, 970 F.2d 536 (9th Cir. 1992); *United States v. Falls*, 34 F.3d 674 (8th Cir. 1994).

In *United States v. Mesa-Rincon*, 911 F.2d 1433 (10th Cir. 1990), the court observed that although federal electronic surveillance law did not apply to video surveillance, the Fourth Amendment did:

Unfortunately, Congress has not yet specifically defined the constitutional requirements for video surveillance. Nevertheless, the general fourth amendment requirements are still applicable to video surveillance; and suppression is required when the government fails to follow these requirements.

Title III establishes elaborate warrant requirements for wiretapping and bugging. Unfortunately, Title III does not discuss television surveillance in any way. Thus, its requirements are not binding on this court in the context of video surveillance. However, the fact that Title III does not discuss television surveillance is no authority for the proposition that Congress meant to outlaw the practice.

---

[99] Orin S. Kerr, *The Fourth Amendment in Cyberspace: Can Encryption Create a "Reasonable Expectation of Privacy?,"* 33 Conn. L. Rev. 503, 520-21, 522 (2001).

4. E-MAIL AND ONLINE COMMUNICATIONS

STEVE JACKSON GAMES, INC. V. UNITED STATES SECRET SERVICE
36 F.3d 457 (5th Cir. 1994)

BARKSDALE, J. Appellant Steve Jackson Games, Incorporated (SJG), publishes books, magazines, role-playing games, and related products. Starting in the mid-1980s, SJG operated an electronic bulletin board system, called "Illuminati" (BBS), from one of its computers. SJG used the BBS to post public information about its business, games, publications, and the role-playing hobby; to facilitate play-testing of games being developed; and to communicate with its customers and free-lance writers by electronic mail (E-mail).

Central to the issue before us, the BBS also offered customers the ability to send and receive private E-mail. Private E-mail was stored on the BBS computer's hard disk drive temporarily, until the addressees "called" the BBS (using their computers and modems) and read their mail. After reading their E-mail, the recipients could choose to either store it on the BBS computer's hard drive or delete it. In February 1990, there were 365 BBS users. Among other uses, appellants Steve Jackson, Elizabeth McCoy, William Milliken, and Steffan O'Sullivan used the BBS for communication by private E-mail. . . . [In addition, Lloyd Blankenship, an employee of Steve Jackson Games, operated a computer bulletin board system (BBS).] Blankenship had the ability to review, and perhaps delete any data on the BBS.

On February 28, 1990, [Secret Service] Agent Foley applied for a warrant to search SJG's premises and Blankenship's residence for evidence of violations of 18 U.S.C. §§ 1030 (proscribes interstate transportation of computer access information) and 2314 (proscribes interstate transportation of stolen property). A search warrant for SJG was issued that same day, authorizing the seizure of [computer hardware, software, and computer data.]

The next day, March 1, the warrant was executed by the Secret Service, including Agents Foley and Golden. Among the items seized was the computer which operated the BBS. At the time of the seizure, 162 items of unread, private E-mail were stored on the BBS, including items addressed to the individual appellants. . . .

Appellants filed suit in May 1991 against, among others, the Secret Service and the United States, claiming [among other things, a violation of] the Federal Wiretap Act, as amended by Title I of the Electronic Communications Privacy Act (ECPA), 18 U.S.C. §§ 2510-2521; and Title II of the ECPA, 18 U.S.C. §§ 2701-2711. . . .

As stated, the sole issue is a very narrow one: whether the seizure of a computer on which is stored private E-mail that has been sent to an electronic bulletin board, but not yet read (retrieved) by the recipients, constitutes an "intercept" proscribed by 18 U.S.C. § 2511(1)(a).

Section 2511 was enacted in 1968 as part of Title III of the Omnibus Crime Control and Safe Streets Act of 1968, often referred to as the Federal Wiretap Act. Prior to the 1986 amendment by Title I of the ECPA, it covered only wire and oral communications. Title I of the ECPA extended that coverage to electronic communications. In relevant part, § 2511(1)(a) proscribes "intentionally intercept[ing] . . . any wire, oral, or electronic communication," unless the intercept is authorized by court order or by other exceptions not relevant here. Section 2520 authorizes, *inter alia*, persons whose electronic communications are intercepted in violation of § 2511 to bring a civil action against the interceptor for actual damages, or for statutory damages of $10,000 per violation or $100 per day of the violation, whichever is greater. 18 U.S.C. § 2520.

The Act defines "intercept" as "the aural or other acquisition of the contents of any wire, electronic, or oral communication through the use of any electronic, mechanical, or other device." 18 U.S.C. § 2510(4). . . .

Webster's Third New International Dictionary (1986) defines "aural" as "of or relating to the ear" or "of or relating to the sense of hearing." And, the Act defines "aural transfer" as "a transfer containing the human voice at any point between and including the point of origin and the point of reception." 18 U.S.C. § 2510(18). This definition is extremely important for purposes of understanding the definition of a "wire communication," which is defined by the Act as

> any aural transfer made in whole or in part through the use of facilities for the transmission of communications by the aid of wire, cable, or other like connection between the point of origin and the point of reception (including the use of such connection in a switching station) . . . *and such term includes any electronic storage of such communication.*

18 U.S.C. § 2510(1) (emphasis added). In contrast, as noted, an "electronic communication" is defined as "any *transfer* of signs, signals, writing, images, sounds, data, or intelligence of any nature transmitted in whole or in part by a wire, radio, electromagnetic, photoelectric or photooptical system . . . but does not include . . . any wire or oral communication. . . ." 18 U.S.C. § 2510(12) (emphasis added).

Critical to the issue before us is the fact that, unlike the definition of "wire communication," *the definition of "electronic communication" does not include electronic storage of such communications. See* 18 U.S.C. § 2510(12). "Electronic storage" is defined as

> (A) any *temporary*, intermediate *storage* of a wire or *electronic communication incidental to the electronic transmission thereof;* and
> (B) any storage of such communication by an electronic communication service for purposes of backup protection of such communication. . . .

18 U.S.C. § 2510(17) (emphasis added). The E-mail in issue was in "electronic storage." Congress' use of the word "transfer" in the definition of "electronic communication," and its omission in that definition of the phrase "any electronic storage of such communication" (part of the definition of "wire communication") reflects that Congress did not intend for "intercept" to apply to "electronic communications" when those communications are in "electronic storage." . . .

Title II generally proscribes unauthorized access to stored wire or electronic communications. Section 2701(a) provides:

> Except as provided in subsection (c) of this section whoever —

(1) intentionally accesses without authorization a facility through which an electronic communication service is provided; or

(2) intentionally exceeds an authorization to access that facility; and thereby obtains, alters, or prevents authorized access to a wire or electronic communication *while it is in electronic storage in such system* shall be punished. . . .

18 U.S.C. § 2701(a) (emphasis added).

As stated, the district court found that the Secret Service violated § 2701 when it

intentionally accesse[d] without authorization a facility [the computer] through which an electronic communication service [the BBS] is provided . . . and thereby obtain[ed] [and] prevent[ed] authorized access [by appellants] to a[n] . . . electronic communication while it is in electronic storage in such system.

18 U.S.C. § 2701(a). The Secret Service does not challenge this ruling. We find no indication in either the Act or its legislative history that Congress intended for conduct that is clearly prohibited by Title II to furnish the basis for a civil remedy under Title I as well. . . .

NOTES & QUESTIONS

1. ***Interception vs. Electronic Storage.*** Is unread e-mail in storage because it is sitting on a hard drive at the ISP? Or is it in transmission because the recipient hasn't read it yet? Is the court applying an overly formalistic and strict reading of "interception"?

2. ***The Fourth Amendment and E-mail: A Question of Perspective?*** Suppose the police sought to obtain a person's unread e-mail messages that were stored with her ISP waiting to be downloaded. *Steve Jackson Games* demonstrates how ECPA would apply — the weaker provisions of the Stored Communications Act rather than the stronger protections of the Wiretap Act apply to e-mail temporarily stored with a person's ISP. *Steve Jackson Games* is a civil case. In the criminal law context, the Stored Communications Act requires a warrant to obtain e-mails stored at the ISP for 180 days or less. If the e-mails have been stored over 180 days, then the government can obtain them with a mere subpoena.

Would the Fourth Amendment apply? Orin Kerr argues that the answer depends upon the perspective by which one views the Internet. In the "internal perspective," the Internet is viewed as a virtual world, analogous to real space. From the "external perspective," we view the Internet as a network and do not analogize to real space. Kerr provides the following example:

Does the Fourth Amendment require [the police] to obtain a search warrant [to obtain an e-mail]? . . . The answer depends largely upon whether they apply an internal or external perspective of the Internet.

Imagine that the first officer applies an internal perspective of the Internet. To him, e-mail is the cyberspace equivalent of old-fashioned postal mail. His computer announces, "You've got mail!" when an e-mail message arrives and shows him a closed envelope. When he clicks on the envelope, it opens, revealing the message. From his internal perspective, the officer is likely to conclude that the Fourth Amendment places the same restriction on government access to e-mail that it places on government access to ordinary postal mail. He will then look in a Fourth Amendment treatise for the black letter rule on accessing postal mail. That treatise will tell him that accessing a suspect's mail ordinarily violates the suspect's "reasonable expectation of privacy," and that therefore the officer must first obtain a warrant. Because e-mail is the equivalent of postal mail, the officer will conclude that the Fourth Amendment requires him to obtain a warrant before he can access the e-mail.

Imagine that the second police office approaches the same problem from an external perspective. To him, the facts look quite different. Looking at how the Internet actually works, the second police officer sees that when A sent the e-mail to B, A was instructing his computer to send a message to his Internet Service Provider (ISP) directing the ISP to forward a text message to B's ISP. To simplify matters, let's say that A's ISP is EarthLink, and B's ISP is America Online (AOL). . . .

What process does the Fourth Amendment require? The second officer will reason that A sent a copy of the e-mail communication to a third party (the EarthLink computer), disclosing the communication to the third party and instructing it to send the communication to yet another third party (AOL). The officer will ask, what process does the Fourth Amendment require to obtain information that has been disclosed to a third party and is in the third party's possession? The officer will look in a Fourth Amendment treatise and locate to the black letter rule that the Fourth Amendment permits the government to obtain information disclosed to a third party using a mere subpoena. The officer can simply subpoena the system administrator to compel him to produce the e-mails. No search warrant is required.

Who is right? The first officer or the second? The answer depends on whether you approach the Internet from an internal or external perspective. From an internal perspective, the officers need a search warrant; from the external perspective, they do not.[100]

3. ***Previously Read E-mail Stored at an ISP.*** The e-mail stored on the ISP server in *Steve Jackson Games* had not yet been downloaded and read by the recipients. Many people continue to store their e-mail messages with their ISP even after having read them. Does the Stored Communications Act protect them in the same way? The answer to this question is currently in dispute. Daniel Solove observes:

> Because these messages are now stored indefinitely, according to the DOJ's interpretation . . . the e-mail is no longer in temporary storage and is "simply a remotely stored file." Therefore, under this view, it falls outside of much of the Act's protections. Since many people store their e-mail messages after reading them and the e-mail they send out, this enables the government to access their communications with very minimal limitations.[101]

---

[100] Orin S. Kerr, *The Problem of Perspective in Internet Law,* 91 Geo. L.J. 357, 361-62, 365-67 (2003).

[101] Daniel J. Solove, *Reconstructing Electronic Surveillance Law,* 72 Geo. Wash. L. Rev. 1264 (2004).

In *Theofel v. Farey-Jones,* 359 F.3d 1066 (9th Cir. 2004), the court concluded that

[t]he [Stored Communications] Act defines "electronic storage" as "(A) any temporary, intermediate storage of a wire or electronic communication incidental to the electronic transmission thereof; and (B) any storage of such communication by an electronic communication service for purposes of backup protection of such communication." Id. § 2510(17), incorporated by id. § 2711(1). Several courts have held that subsection (A) covers e-mail messages stored on an ISP's server pending delivery to the recipient. Because subsection (A) applies only to messages in "temporary, intermediate storage," however, these courts have limited that subsection's coverage to messages not yet delivered to their intended recipient.

Defendants point to these cases and argue that messages remaining on an ISP's server after delivery no longer fall within the Act's coverage. But, even if such messages are not within the purview of subsection (A), they do fit comfortably within subsection (B). . . .

An obvious purpose for storing a message on an ISP's server after delivery is to provide a second copy of the message in the event that the user needs to download it again — if, for example, the message is accidentally erased from the user's own computer. The ISP copy of the message functions as a "backup" for the user. Notably, nothing in the Act requires that the backup protection be for the benefit of the ISP rather than the user. Storage under these circumstances thus literally falls within the statutory definition.

See also Fraser v. Nationwide Mutual Insurance Co., 352 F.3d 108 (3d Cir. 2003) (suggesting that such e-mail messages were in backup storage under the definition of electronic storage).

4. ***What Constitutes an Interception?*** In *United States v. Councilman,* 373 F.3d 197 (1st Cir. 2004), an Internet bookseller, Interloc, Inc., provided e-mail service for its customers, who were book dealers. Councilman, the vice president of Interloc, directed Interloc employees to draft a computer program to intercept all incoming communications from Amazon.com to the book dealers and make copies of them. Councilman and other Interloc employees then read the e-mails in order to gain a commercial advantage. Councilman was charged with criminal violations of the Wiretap Act. Councilman argued that he did not violate the Wiretap Act because the e-mails were in electronic storage, albeit very briefly, when they were copied. The court followed *Steve Jackson Games* and concluded that the e-mail was in temporary storage and therefore subject to the Stored Communications Act, not the Wiretap Act. However, unlike *Steve Jackson Games,* Interloc accessed the e-mails "as they were being transmitted and in real time."

The *Councilman* case received significant criticism by academic commentators and experts in electronic surveillance law for misunderstanding the fundamental distinction between the interception of a communication and the accessing of a stored communication. An interception occurs contemporaneously — as the communication is being transmitted. Accessing a stored communication occurs later, as the communication sits on a computer. This distinction has practical consequences, since interceptions are protected by the much more protective Wiretap Act rather than the Stored Communications Act. Does such a distinction still make sense? Is the contemporaneous interception of communications more troublesome than the accessing of the communications in *Steve Jackson Games*?

The case was reheard en banc, and the en banc court reversed the panel. *See United States v. Councilman*, 418 F.3d 67 (1st Cir. 2005) (en banc). The court concluded that "the term 'electronic communication' includes transient electronic storage that is intrinsic to the communication process, and hence that interception of an e-mail message in such storage is an offense under the Wiretap Act." The court declined to further elaborate on what constitutes an "interception."

5. *Carnivore.* Beginning in 1998, the FBI began using a hardware and software mechanism called "Carnivore" to intercept people's e-mail and instant messaging information from their Internet Service Providers (ISPs). After obtaining judicial authorization, the FBI would install Carnivore by connecting a computer directly to the ISP's server and initiating the program. Carnivore was designed to locate the e-mails of a suspect at the ISP when the ISP did not have the capacity to do so.

Carnivore was capable of analyzing the entire e-mail traffic of an ISP, although the FBI maintained it was only used to search for the e-mails of a suspect. The program filtered out the e-mail messages of ISP subscribers who are not the subject of the investigation; but to do so, it had to scan the e-mail headers that identify the senders and recipients. The FBI likened e-mail headers to the information captured by a pen register, a device that registers the phone numbers a person dials.

However, Carnivore could be programmed to search through the entire text of all e-mails, to capture e-mails with certain key words. In this way, Carnivore resembles a wiretap. Recall that under federal wiretap law, judicial approval for obtaining pen register information only requires a certification that "the information likely to be obtained by such installation and use is relevant to an ongoing investigation." 18 U.S.C. § 3123. In contrast, judicial approval of a wiretap requires a full panoply of requirements under Title I, including a showing of probable cause.

To eliminate the negative associations with the term "Carnivore," the device was renamed "DCS1000." Many members of Congress viewed Carnivore with great suspicion. Congress held hearings over the summer of 2000 pertaining to Carnivore, and several bills were proposed to halt or limit the use of Carnivore.

The anti-Carnivore sentiment abruptly ended after the September 11, 2001, World Trade Center and Pentagon terrorist attacks. Section 216 of the USA PATRIOT Act of 2001, in anticipation of the use of Carnivore, required reports on the use of Carnivore to be filed with a court. These reports, filed under seal, require (1) the names of the officers using the device; (2) when the device was installed, used, and removed; (3) the configuration of the device; and (4) the information collected by the device. 18 U.S.C. § 3133(a)(3).

The FBI discontinued use of Carnivore because ISPs can readily produce the information the FBI desires without the assistance of the Carnivore device and because commercially available software has similar functionality.

UNITED STATES V. WARSHAK

631 F.3d 266 (6th Cir. 2010)

[Steven Warshak ran several small businesses that sold products and advertisements, including a popular herbal supplement called "Enzyte," which was touted as increasing a man's potency. This supplement was made by Warshak's company, Berkeley Premium Nutraceuticals, Inc., which had 1,500 employees and sales of $250 million per year. A key component of Berkeley's business was the ability to process credit card payments. To do so, it had banks provide a line of credit. In 2002, one of the banks — the Bank of Kentucky — terminated its relationship with Berkeley because of too many "chargebacks" — when customers dispute a charge. In future applications to banks for similar lines of credit, Warshak filed false applications, including lying that he never had an account terminated. To prevent future problems with excessive chargebacks, Berkeley found ways to falsify the figures.

Warshak (along with his mother, Harriet Warshak, who was involved in the scheme) was eventually indicted for various crimes, including mail, wire, and bank fraud, making false statements to banks, and money laundering. He sought to exclude from evidence about 27,000 of his private e-mails seized from his ISP (NuVox). The trial court denied his motion, and he was convicted, sentenced to 25 years in prison, and ordered to forfeit nearly $500 million worth of proceeds.]

BOGGS, J. Warshak argues that the government's warrantless, *ex parte* seizure of approximately 27,000 of his private emails constituted a violation of the Fourth Amendment's prohibition on unreasonable searches and seizures. The government counters that, even if government agents violated the Fourth Amendment in obtaining the emails, they relied in good faith on the Stored Communications Act ("SCA"), 18 U.S.C. §§ 2701 *et seq.*, a statute that allows the government to obtain certain electronic communications without procuring a warrant. The government also argues that any hypothetical Fourth Amendment violation was harmless. We find that the government *did* violate Warshak's Fourth Amendment rights by compelling his Internet Service Provider ("ISP") to turn over the contents of his emails. However, we agree that agents relied on the SCA in good faith, and therefore hold that reversal is unwarranted. . . .

The Stored Communications Act ("SCA"), 18 U.S.C. §§ 2701 *et seq.*, "permits a 'governmental entity' to compel a service provider to disclose the contents of [electronic] communications in certain circumstances." *Warshak II,* 532 F.3d at 523. As this court explained in *Warshak II:*

> . . . The compelled-disclosure provisions give different levels of privacy protection based on whether the e-mail is held with an electronic communication service or a remote computing service and based on how long the e-mail has been in electronic storage. The government may obtain the contents of e-mails that are "in electronic storage" with an electronic communication service for 180 days or less "only pursuant to a warrant." 18 U.S.C. § 2703(a). The government has three options for obtaining communications stored with a remote computing service and communications that have been in electronic storage with an electronic service

provider for more than 180 days: (1) obtain a warrant; (2) use an administrative subpoena; or (3) obtain a court order under § 2703(d). *Id.* § 2703(a), (b). . . .

The Fourth Amendment provides that "[t]he right of the people to be secure in their persons, houses, papers, and effects, against unreasonable searches and seizures, shall not be violated, and no Warrants shall issue, but upon probable cause. . . ." U.S. Const. amend. IV. . . .

A "search" occurs when the government infringes upon "an expectation of privacy that society is prepared to consider reasonable." This standard breaks down into two discrete inquiries: "first, has the [target of the investigation] manifested a subjective expectation of privacy in the object of the challenged search? Second, is society willing to recognize that expectation as reasonable?"

Turning first to the subjective component of the test, we find that Warshak plainly manifested an expectation that his emails would be shielded from outside scrutiny. As he notes in his brief, his "entire business and personal life was contained within the . . . emails seized." Given the often sensitive and sometimes damning substance of his emails, we think it highly unlikely that Warshak expected them to be made public, for people seldom unfurl their dirty laundry in plain view. Therefore, we conclude that Warshak had a subjective expectation of privacy in the contents of his emails.

The next question is whether society is prepared to recognize that expectation as reasonable. This question is one of grave import and enduring consequence, given the prominent role that email has assumed in modern communication. Since the advent of email, the telephone call and the letter have waned in importance, and an explosion of Internet-based communication has taken place. People are now able to send sensitive and intimate information, instantaneously, to friends, family, and colleagues half a world away. Lovers exchange sweet nothings, and businessmen swap ambitious plans, all with the click of a mouse button. Commerce has also taken hold in email. Online purchases are often documented in email accounts, and email is frequently used to remind patients and clients of imminent appointments. In short, "account" is an apt word for the conglomeration of stored messages that comprises an email account, as it provides an account of its owner's life. By obtaining access to someone's email, government agents gain the ability to peer deeply into his activities. Much hinges, therefore, on whether the government is permitted to request that a commercial ISP turn over the contents of a subscriber's emails without triggering the machinery of the Fourth Amendment.

In confronting this question, we take note of two bedrock principles. First, the very fact that information is being passed through a communications network is a paramount Fourth Amendment consideration. Second, the Fourth Amendment must keep pace with the inexorable march of technological progress, or its guarantees will wither and perish.

With those principles in mind, we begin our analysis by considering the manner in which the Fourth Amendment protects traditional forms of communication. In *Katz,* the Supreme Court was asked to determine how the Fourth Amendment applied in the context of the telephone. There, government agents had affixed an electronic listening device to the exterior of a public phone booth, and had used the device to intercept and record several phone conversations.

The Supreme Court held that this constituted a search under the Fourth Amendment, notwithstanding the fact that the telephone company had the capacity to monitor and record the calls. . . .

Letters receive similar protection. While a letter is in the mail, the police may not intercept it and examine its contents unless they first obtain a warrant based on probable cause. This is true despite the fact that sealed letters are handed over to perhaps dozens of mail carriers, any one of whom could tear open the thin paper envelopes that separate the private words from the world outside. Put another way, trusting a letter to an intermediary does not necessarily defeat a reasonable expectation that the letter will remain private.

Given the fundamental similarities between email and traditional forms of communication, it would defy common sense to afford emails lesser Fourth Amendment protection. It follows that email requires strong protection under the Fourth Amendment; otherwise, the Fourth Amendment would prove an ineffective guardian of private communication, an essential purpose it has long been recognized to serve.

If we accept that an email is analogous to a letter or a phone call, it is manifest that agents of the government cannot compel a commercial ISP to turn over the contents of an email without triggering the Fourth Amendment. An ISP is the intermediary that makes email communication possible. Emails must pass through an ISP's servers to reach their intended recipient. Thus, the ISP is the functional equivalent of a post office or a telephone company. As we have discussed above, the police may not storm the post office and intercept a letter, and they are likewise forbidden from using the phone system to make a clandestine recording of a telephone call—unless they get a warrant, that is. It only stands to reason that, if government agents compel an ISP to surrender the contents of a subscriber's emails, those agents have thereby conducted a Fourth Amendment search, which necessitates compliance with the warrant requirement absent some exception. . . .

[Earlier in the litigation of this case,] the government argued that this conclusion was improper, pointing to the fact that NuVox contractually reserved the right to access Warshak's emails for certain purposes. While we acknowledge that a subscriber agreement might, in some cases, be sweeping enough to defeat a reasonable expectation of privacy in the contents of an email account, we doubt that will be the case in most situations, and it is certainly not the case here.

As an initial matter, it must be observed that the mere *ability* of a third-party intermediary to access the contents of a communication cannot be sufficient to extinguish a reasonable expectation of privacy. In *Katz,* the Supreme Court found it reasonable to expect privacy during a telephone call despite the ability of an operator to listen in. Similarly, the ability of a rogue mail handler to rip open a letter does not make it unreasonable to assume that sealed mail will remain private on its journey across the country. Therefore, the threat or possibility of access is not decisive when it comes to the reasonableness of an expectation of privacy. . . .

Our conclusion finds additional support in the application of Fourth Amendment doctrine to rented space. Hotel guests, for example, have a reasonable expectation of privacy in their rooms. *See United States v. Allen,* 106 F.3d 695, 699 (6th Cir. 1997). This is so even though maids routinely enter hotel rooms to replace the towels and tidy the furniture. Similarly, tenants have a legitimate expectation of privacy in their apartments. *See United States v. Washington,* 573

F.3d 279, 284 (6th Cir. 2009). That expectation persists, regardless of the incursions of handymen to fix leaky faucets. Consequently, we are convinced that some degree of routine access is hardly dispositive with respect to the privacy question.

Again, however, we are unwilling to hold that a subscriber agreement will *never* be broad enough to snuff out a reasonable expectation of privacy. As the panel noted in *Warshak I* [an earlier case in this litigation], if the ISP expresses an intention to "audit, inspect, and monitor" its subscriber's emails, that might be enough to render an expectation of privacy unreasonable. But where, as here, there is no such statement, the ISP's "control over the [emails] and ability to access them under certain limited circumstances will not be enough to overcome an expectation of privacy."

We recognize that our conclusion may be attacked in light of the Supreme Court's decision in *United States v. Miller,* 425 U.S. 435 (1976). In *Miller,* the Supreme Court held that a bank depositor does not have a reasonable expectation of privacy in the contents of bank records, checks, and deposit slips. The Court's holding in *Miller* was based on the fact that bank documents, "including financial statements and deposit slips, contain only information voluntarily conveyed to the banks and exposed to their employees in the ordinary course of business."

But *Miller* is distinguishable. First, *Miller* involved simple business records, as opposed to the potentially unlimited variety of "confidential communications" at issue here. Second, the bank depositor in *Miller* conveyed information to the bank so that the bank could put the information to use "in the ordinary course of business." By contrast, Warshak received his emails through NuVox. NuVox was an *intermediary,* not the intended recipient of the emails. Thus, *Miller* is not controlling.

Accordingly, we hold that a subscriber enjoys a reasonable expectation of privacy in the contents of emails "that are stored with, or sent or received through, a commercial ISP." The government may not compel a commercial ISP to turn over the contents of a subscriber's emails without first obtaining a warrant based on probable cause. Therefore, because they did not obtain a warrant, the government agents violated the Fourth Amendment when they obtained the contents of Warshak's emails. Moreover, to the extent that the SCA purports to permit the government to obtain such emails warrantlessly, the SCA is unconstitutional. . . .

Even though the government's search of Warshak's emails violated the Fourth Amendment, the emails are not subject to the exclusionary remedy if the officers relied in good faith on the SCA to obtain them. In [*Illinois v. Krull,* 480 U.S. 340 (1987),] the Supreme Court noted that the exclusionary rule's purpose of deterring law enforcement officers from engaging in unconstitutional conduct would not be furthered by holding officers accountable for mistakes of the legislature. Thus, even if a statute is later found to be unconstitutional, an officer "cannot be expected to question the judgment of the legislature." However, an officer cannot "be said to have acted in good-faith reliance upon a statute if its provisions are such that a reasonable officer should have known that the statute was unconstitutional."

Naturally, Warshak argues that the provisions of the SCA at issue in this case were plainly unconstitutional. He argues that any reasonable law enforcement officer would have understood that a warrant based on probable cause would be required to compel the production of private emails. . . .

However, we disagree that the SCA is so conspicuously unconstitutional as to preclude good-faith reliance. As we noted in *Warshak II,* "[t]he Stored Communications Act has been in existence since 1986 and to our knowledge has not been the subject of any successful Fourth Amendment challenges, in any context, whether to § 2703(d) or to any other provision." Furthermore, given the complicated thicket of issues that we were required to navigate when passing on the constitutionality of the SCA, it was not plain or obvious that the SCA was unconstitutional, and it was therefore reasonable for the government to rely upon the SCA in seeking to obtain the contents of Warshak's emails.

But the good-faith reliance inquiry does not end with the facial validity of the statute at issue. In *Krull,* the Supreme Court hinted that the good-faith exception does not apply if the government acted "outside the scope of the statute" on which it purported to rely. . . . Once the officer steps outside the scope of an unconstitutional statute, the mistake is no longer the legislature's, but the officer's. . . .

Warshak argues that the government violated several provisions of the SCA and should therefore be precluded from arguing good-faith reliance. First, Warshak argues that the government violated the SCA's notice provisions. Under § 2703(b)(1)(B), the government must provide notice to an account holder if it seeks to compel the disclosure of his emails through either a § 2703(b) subpoena or a § 2703(d) order. However, § 2705 permits the government to delay notification in certain situations. The initial period of delay is 90 days, but the government may seek to extend that period in 90-day increments. In this case, the government issued both a § 2703(b) subpoena and a § 2703(d) order to NuVox, seeking disclosure of Warshak's emails. At the time, the government made the requisite showing that notice should be delayed. However, the government did not seek to renew the period of delay. In all, the government failed to inform Warshak of either the subpoena or the order for over a year.

Conceding that it violated the notice provisions, the government argues that such violations are irrelevant to the issue of whether it reasonably relied on the SCA in *obtaining* the contents of Warshak's emails. We agree. As the government notes, the violations occurred *after* the emails had been obtained. Thus, the mistakes at issue had no bearing on the constitutional violations. Because the exclusionary rule was designed to deter constitutional violations, we decline to invoke it in this situation.

But Warshak does not hang his hat exclusively on the government's violations of the SCA's notice provisions. He also argues that the government exceeded its authority under another SCA provision — § 2703(f) — by request-ing NuVox to engage in *prospective* preservation of his future emails. Under § 2703(f), "[a] provider of wire or electronic communication services or a remote computing service, upon the request of a governmental entity, shall take all necessary steps to *preserve* records and other evidence *in its possession* pending the issuance of a court order or other process." 18 U.S.C. § 2703(f) (emphasis added). Warshak argues that this statute permits only *retrospective* preservation — in other words, preservation of emails already in existence. . . .

~~Ultimately, however, this statutory violation,~~ whether it occurred or not, is irrelevant to the issue of good-faith reliance. The question here is whether the government relied in good faith on § 2703(b) and § 2703(d) to *obtain* copies of Warshak's emails. True, the government might not have been able to gain access to the emails without the prospective preservation request, as it was NuVox's practice to delete all emails once they were downloaded to the account holder's computer. Thus, in a sense, the government's use of § 2703(f) was a but-for cause of the constitutional violation. But the actual violation at issue was obtaining the emails, and the government did not rely on § 2703(f) specifically to do that. Instead, the government relied on § 2703(b) and § 2703(d). The proper inquiry, therefore, is whether the government violated either of *those* provisions, and the preservation request is of no consequence to that inquiry. . . .

NOTES & QUESTIONS

1. ***E-mail and the Third Party Doctrine.*** Does the court convincingly distinguish e-mail maintained by an ISP from the third party doctrine cases (*Smith v. Maryland* and *United States v. Miller*)?

2. ***The SCA and E-mail.*** Do the SCA's different levels of protection of e-mail make sense? Consider Patricia Bellia and Susan Freiwald:

   > [W]arrant-level protection for stored e-mail should persist whether or not an e-mail has been opened, accessed, or downloaded. It is hard to imagine why the act of reading or preparing to read an e-mail, which is the entire point of communicating by e-mail, should somehow deprive a user of his reasonable expectation of privacy in the electronic communication. As discussed, the government's distinctions on this basis derive from a strained reading of out-of-date statutory provisions, and neither reflect nor should impact the Fourth Amendment status of stored e-mail.[102]

3. ***Keystroke Logging Systems.*** In *United States v. Scarfo*, 180 F. Supp. 2d 572 (D.N.J. 2001), the FBI wanted to search Nicodemo S. Scarfo's computer for evidence of illegal gambling activities. They obtained a warrant to search his office and computer, but they were unable to access an encrypted file called "Factors." FBI officials obtained additional search warrants to install a key logging system (KLS) on Scarfo's computer to record his keystrokes. The KLS was designed to work only when Scarfo was offline and not using his model to connect to his America Online account.

   Scarfo challenged the use of the KLS device under the Wiretap Act, under which a mere search warrant would be insufficient and a special court order would be required. The court, however, concluded:

   > Recognizing that Scarfo's computer had a modem and thus was capable of transmitting electronic communications via the modem, the F.B.I. configured the KLS to avoid intercepting electronic communications typed on the keyboard and simultaneously transmitted in real time via the communication ports. . . . Hence, when the modem was operating, the KLS did not record keystrokes. It

---

[102] Patricia L. Bellia & Susan Freiwald, *Fourth Amendment Protection for Stored E-Mail,* 2008 U. Chi. Legal F. 121, 135 (2008).

was designed to prohibit the capture of keyboard keystrokes whenever the modem operated. Since Scarfo's computer possessed no other means of communicating with another computer save for the modem, the KLS did not intercept any wire communications.

Suppose the court concluded that the FBI violated the Wiretap Act. Would Scarfo be able to suppress the evidence?

Note that the FBI designed the KLS to avoid triggering the Wiretap Act. Some might argue that this is an unfortunate game of technological cat-and-mouse because the privacy invasion was just as significant regardless of whether Scarfo's modem was on or off. Consider the following argument by Raymond Ku:

> . . . By monitoring what an individual enters into her computer as she enters it, the government has the ability to monitor thought itself. Keystroke-recording devices allow the government to record formless thoughts and ideas an individual never intended to share with anyone, never intended to save on the hard drive and never intended to preserve for future reference in any form. The devices also allow the government to record thoughts and ideas the individual may have rejected the moment they were typed.[103]

Today, ironically, technology would likely forestall the use of the KLS because dial-up modems are increasingly being replaced by always-connected Internet service. This change might expand the coverage of the Wiretap Act. But it raises a broader question: Should interceptions of communications in transmission be protected more stringently than accessing communications that are not in transmission?

5. ISP ACCOUNT INFORMATION

UNITED STATES V. HAMBRICK

55 F. Supp. 2d 504 (W.D. Va. 1999)

MICHAEL, J. Defendant Scott M. Hambrick seeks the suppression of all evidence obtained from his Internet Service Provider ("ISP"), MindSpring, and seeks the suppression of all evidence seized from his home pursuant to a warrant issued by this court. For the reasons discussed below, the court denies the defendant's motion.

On March 14, 1998, J. L. McLaughlin, a police officer with the Keene, New Hampshire Police Department, connected to the Internet and entered a chat room called "Gay dads 4 sex." McLaughlin's screen name was "Rory14." In this chat room, Detective McLaughlin encountered someone using the screen name "Blowuinva." Based on a series of online conversations between "Rory14" (Det. McLaughlin) and "Blowuinva," McLaughlin concluded that "Blowuinva" sought to entice a fourteen-year-old boy to leave New Hampshire and live with "Blowuinva." Because of the anonymity of the Internet, Detective McLaughlin did not know the true identity of the person with whom he was communicating nor did

---

[103] Raymond Ku, *Think Twice Before You Type*, 163 N.J. L.J. 747 (Feb. 19, 2001).

he know where "Blowuinva" lived. "Blowuinva" had only identified himself as "Brad."

To determine Blowuinva's identity and location, McLaughlin obtained a New Hampshire state subpoena that he served on Blowuinva's Internet Service Provider, MindSpring, located in Atlanta, Georgia. The New Hampshire state subpoena requested that MindSpring produce "any records pertaining to the billing and/or user records documenting the subject using your services on March 14th, 1998 at 1210HRS (EST) using Internet Protocol Number 207.69.169.92." MindSpring complied with the subpoena. On March 20, 1998, MindSpring supplied McLaughlin with defendant's name, address, credit card number, e-mail address, home and work telephone numbers, fax number, and the fact that the Defendant's account was connected to the Internet at the Internet Protocol (IP) address.

A justice of the peace, Richard R. Richards, signed the New Hampshire state subpoena. Mr. Richards is not only a New Hampshire justice of the peace, but he is also a detective in the Keene Police Department, Investigation Division. Mr. Richards did not issue the subpoena pursuant to a matter pending before himself, any other judicial officer, or a grand jury. At the hearing on the defendant's motion, the government conceded the invalidity of the warrant. The question before this court, therefore, is whether the court must suppress the information obtained from MindSpring, and all that flowed from it, because the government failed to obtain a proper subpoena. . . .

. . . [Under *Katz v. United States*,] the Fourth Amendment applies only where: (1) the citizen has manifested a subjective expectation of privacy, and (2) the expectation is one that society accepts as "objectively reasonable." . . . Applying the first part of the *Katz* analysis, Mr. Hambrick asserts that he had a subjective expectation of privacy in the information that MindSpring gave to the government. However, resolution of this matter hinges on whether Mr. Hambrick's expectation is one that society accepts as "objectively reasonable."

The objective reasonableness prong of the privacy test is ultimately a value judgment and a determination of how much privacy we should have as a society. In making this constitutional determination, this court must employ a sort of risk analysis, asking whether the individual affected should have expected the material at issue to remain private. The defendant asserts that the Electronic Communications Privacy Act ("ECPA") "legislatively resolves" this question. . . .

The information obtained through the use of the government's invalid subpoena consisted of the defendant's name, address, social security number, credit card number, and certification that the defendant was connected to the Internet on March 14, 1998. Thus, this information falls within the provisions of Title II of the ECPA.

The government may require that an ISP provide stored communications and transactional records only if (1) it obtains a warrant issued under the Federal Rules of Criminal Procedure or state equivalent, or (2) it gives prior notice to the online subscriber and then issues a subpoena or receives a court order authorizing disclosure of the information in question. *See* 18 U.S.C. § 2703(a)-(c)(1)(B). When an ISP discloses stored communications or transactional records to a government entity without the requisite authority, the aggrieved customer's sole remedy is damages.

Although Congress is willing to recognize that individuals have some degree of privacy in the stored data and transactional records that their ISPs retain, the ECPA is hardly a legislative determination that this expectation of privacy is one that rises to the level of "reasonably objective" for Fourth Amendment purposes. Despite its concern for privacy, Congress did not provide for suppression where a party obtains stored data or transactional records in violation of the Act. Additionally, the ECPA's concern for privacy extends only to government invasions of privacy. ISPs are free to turn stored data and transactional records over to nongovernmental entities. *See* 18 U.S.C. § 2703(c)(1)(A) ("[A] provider of electronic communication service or remote computing service may disclose a record or other information pertaining to a subscriber to or customer of such service . . . to any person other than a governmental entity."). For Fourth Amendment purposes, this court does not find that the ECPA has legislatively determined that an individual has a reasonable expectation of privacy in his name, address, social security number, credit card number, and proof of Internet connection. The fact that the ECPA does not proscribe turning over such information to private entities buttresses the conclusion that the ECPA does not create a reasonable expectation of privacy in that information. This, however, does not end the court's inquiry. This court must determine, within the constitutional framework that the Supreme Court has established, whether Mr. Hambrick's subjective expectation of privacy is one that society is willing to recognize.

To have any interest in privacy, there must be some exclusion of others. To have a reasonable expectation of privacy under the Supreme Court's risk-analysis approach to the Fourth Amendment, two conditions must be met: (1) the data must not be knowingly exposed to others, and (2) the Internet service provider's ability to access the data must not constitute a disclosure. In *Katz*, the Supreme Court expressly held that "what a person knowingly exposes to the public, even in his home or office, is not a subject of Fourth Amendment protection." Further, the Court "consistently has held that a person has no legitimate expectation of privacy in information he voluntarily turns over to third parties." *Smith v. Maryland*, 442 U.S. 735, 743-44 (1979). . . .

When Scott Hambrick surfed the Internet using the screen name "Blowuinva," he was not a completely anonymous actor. It is true that an average member of the public could not easily determine the true identity of "Blowuinva." Nevertheless, when Mr. Hambrick entered into an agreement to obtain Internet access from MindSpring, he knowingly revealed his name, address, credit card number, and telephone number to MindSpring and its employees. Mr. Hambrick also selected the screen name "Blowuinva." When the defendant selected his screen name it became tied to his true identity in all MindSpring records. MindSpring employees had ready access to these records in the normal course of MindSpring's business, for example, in the keeping of its records for billing purposes, and nothing prevented MindSpring from revealing this information to nongovernmental actors.[104] Also, there is nothing in the record to suggest that there was a restrictive agreement between the defendant and MindSpring that would limit the right of

---

[104] It is apparently common for ISPs to provide certain information that Mr. Hambrick alleges to be private to marketing firms and other organizations interested in soliciting business from Internet users.

MindSpring to reveal the defendant's personal information to nongovernmental entities. Where such dissemination of information to nongovernment entities is not prohibited, there can be no reasonable expectation of privacy in that information.

Although not dispositive to the outcome of this motion, it is important to note that the court's decision does not leave members of cybersociety without privacy protection. Under the ECPA, Internet Service Providers are civilly liable when they reveal subscriber information or the contents of stored communications to the government without first requiring a warrant, court order, or subpoena. Here, nothing suggests that MindSpring had any knowledge that the facially valid subpoena submitted to it was in fact an invalid subpoena. Had MindSpring revealed the information at issue in this case to the government without first requiring a subpoena, apparently valid on its face, Mr. Hambrick could have sued MindSpring. This is a powerful deterrent protecting privacy in the online world and should not be taken lightly. . . .

NOTES & QUESTIONS

1. *Is There a Reasonable Expectation of Privacy in ISP Records?* The court in *Hambrick* concludes that there is no reasonable expectation of privacy in ISP records based on the third party doctrine in *Smith v. Maryland.* In *United States v. Kennedy,* 81 F. Supp. 2d 1103 (D. Kan. 2000), the court reached a similar conclusion:

   > Defendant has not demonstrated an objectively reasonable legitimate expectation of privacy in his subscriber information. . . . "[A] person has no legitimate expectation of privacy in information he voluntarily turns over to third parties." *Smith v. Maryland,* 442 U.S. 735 (1979). When defendant entered into an agreement with [his ISP], he knowingly revealed all information connected to [his IP address]. He cannot now claim to have a Fourth Amendment privacy interest in his subscriber information.

   Is *Smith v. Maryland* controlling on this issue? Is there a way to distinguish *Smith*?

2. *Statutes as a Basis for a Reasonable Expectation of Privacy?* Hambrick was not seeking relief directly under the Stored Communications Act of ECPA. Why not? Instead, Hambrick asserted he had Fourth Amendment protection in his subscriber records. He argued that under the *Katz* reasonable expectation of privacy test, the ECPA "legislatively resolves" that there is a reasonable expectation of privacy in information that Mindspring gave to the government. Should statutes that protect privacy serve as an indication of a societal recognition of a reasonable expectation of privacy? What are the consequences of using statutes such as ECPA to conclude that the Fourth Amendment applies?

3. *Is There a Remedy?* Mindspring couldn't release information to the government without a warrant or subpoena or else it would face civil liability. However, in this case, the government presented Mindspring with a subpoena that Mindspring had no knowledge was invalid. Therefore, it is unlikely that Mindspring would be liable. If the court is correct in its conclusion that 18

U.S.C. § 2703(a)-(c)(1)(B) of the ECPA only applies to the conduct of Internet Service Providers, then is there any remedy against Officer Richards's blatantly false subpoena? Could a police officer obtain a person's Internet subscriber information by falsifying a subpoena and escape without any civil liability or exclusionary rule?

In *McVeigh v. Cohen,* 983 F. Supp. 215 (D.D.C. 1998), Timothy McVeigh (a different person from the Oklahoma City bomber) was an enlisted Navy serviceman who had served in the Navy for 17 years. A Navy volunteer coordinated a toy drive for the crew members of the submarine that McVeigh was serving on, and she received an email reply from an America Online (AOL) account with the screen name "boysrch" but signed by a "tim." The volunteer searched through AOL's profile directory and found that "boysrch" was a subscriber named Tim who lived in Honolulu, Hawaii, worked in the military, and who listed his marital status as "gay." The volunteer forwarded the email to her husband, an officer aboard the submarine. The email eventually was forwarded to the ship's captain, who called in Lieutenant Karin Morean, the ship's legal advisor, to investigate. They suspected that Tim might be Timothy McVeigh. Lieutenant Morean requested that a paralegal on her staff contact AOL to find out if the "boysrch" profile could be connected to Timothy McVeigh. The paralegal called AOL and stated he had received a fax from "boysrch" and wanted to confirm who it belonged to. The AOL representative informed him that it was indeed Timothy McVeigh.

The Navy initiated proceedings under the "Don't Ask, Don't Tell, Don't Pursue" policy of the U.S. Military. Under this policy, adopted in 1993, the military cannot investigate sexual orientation unless there is "credible information" that a gay serviceman or servicewoman has the "propensity or intent to engage in homosexual acts." The Navy sought to discharge McVeigh under this policy for "homosexual conduct."

McVeigh sued in federal court to prevent his discharge. He argued that he did not "tell" under the policy but was instead "pursued." The court agreed with McVeigh:

> All that the Navy had was an email message and user profile that it suspected was authored by Plaintiff. Under the military regulation, that information alone should not have triggered any sort of investigation. When the Navy affirmatively took steps to confirm the identity of the email respondent, it violated the very essence of "Don't Ask, Don't Pursue" by launching a search and destroy mission. Even if the Navy had a factual basis to believe that the email message and profile were written by Plaintiff, it was unreasonable to infer that they were necessarily intended to convey a propensity or intent to engage in homosexual conduct. . . .

The court then examined how the Navy's contacting AOL to identify "boysrch" violated ECPA:

> The subsequent steps taken by the Navy in its "pursuit" of the Plaintiff were not only unauthorized under its policy, but likely illegal under the Electronic Communications Privacy Act of 1986 ("ECPA"). The ECPA, enacted by Congress to address privacy concerns on the Internet, allows the government to obtain information from an online service provider — as the Navy did in this

instance from AOL — but only if a) it obtains a warrant issued under the Federal Rules of Criminal Procedure or state equivalent; or b) it gives prior notice to the online subscriber and then issues a subpoena or receives a court order authorizing disclosure of the information in question. See 18 U.S.C. § 2703(b)(1)(A)-(B), (c)(1)(B).

In soliciting and obtaining over the phone personal information about the Plaintiff from AOL, his private on-line service provider, the government in this case invoked neither of these provisions and thus failed to comply with the ECPA. From the record, it is undisputed that the Navy directly solicited by phone information from AOL. Lieutenant Karin S. Morean, the ship's principal legal counsel and a member of the JAG corps, personally requested Legalman Kaiser to contact AOL and obtain the identity of the subscriber. Without this information, Plaintiff credibly contends that the Navy could not have made the necessary connection between him and the user profile which was the sole basis on which to commence discharge proceedings.

The government, in its defense, contends that the Plaintiff cannot succeed on his ECPA claim. It argues that the substantive provision of the statute that Plaintiff cites, 18 U.S.C. § 2703(c)(1)(B), puts the obligation on the online service provider to withhold information from the government, and not vice versa. In support of its position, Defendants cite to the Fourth Circuit opinion in *Tucker v. Waddell*, 83 F.3d 688 (4th Cir. 1996), which held that § 2703(c)(1)(B) only prohibits the actions of online providers, not the government. Accordingly, Defendants allege that Plaintiff has no cause of action against the government on the basis of the ECPA. . . .

. . . [However,] Section 2703(c)(1)(B) must be read in the context of the statute as a whole. In comparison, § 2703(a) and (b) imposes on the government a reciprocal obligation to obtain a warrant or the like before requiring disclosure. It appears from the face of the statute that all of the subsections of § 2703 were intended to work in tandem to protect consumer privacy. Even if, however, the government ultimately proves to be right in its assessment of § 2703(c)(1)(B), the Plaintiff has plead § 2703(a) and (b) as alternative grounds for relief. In his claim that the government, at the least, solicited a violation of the ECPA by AOL, the Court finds that there is likely success on the merits with regard to this issue. The government knew, or should have known, that by turning over the information without a warrant, AOL was breaking the law. Yet the Navy, in this case, directly solicited the information anyway. What is most telling is that the Naval investigator did not identify himself when he made his request. While the government makes much of the fact that § 2703(c)(1)(B) does not provide a cause of action against the government, it is elementary that information obtained improperly can be suppressed where an individual's rights have been violated. In these days of "big brother," where through technology and otherwise the privacy interests of individuals from all walks of life are being ignored or marginalized, it is imperative that statutes explicitly protecting these rights be strictly observed. . . .

The Stored Communications Act does not have a suppression remedy; the court is creating an exclusionary rule for the Stored Communications Act. Is this appropriate? Without a suppression remedy for the conduct of the government in this case, what would deter the government from violating the Stored Communications Act?

Subsequent to *McVeigh v. Cohen,* Congress amended §§ 2703(a)-(c) to make it clear that these provisions applied not just to ISPs but also to government conduct. However, an exclusionary rule was not added.

4. ***Cell Site Location Information.*** Recall *United States v. Jones* from earlier in this chapter, where the U.S. Supreme Court held that the Fourth Amendment required a warrant before using a GPS tracking device on a car to track movement and location in public. There is another way to obtain data about a person's movements or location — via records maintained by telecommunications service providers. Providers of cell phone or smartphone service have data about the location of that phone, which most often is the location of the user too. In *United State v. Quartavious*, 754 F.3d 1205 (11th Cir. 2014), the government obtained the defendant's cell site location information under the Stored Communications Act (SCA). Under the SCA, the government need only establish "specific and articulable facts showing that there are reasonable grounds to believe that the information sought is relevant and material to an ongoing criminal investigation." The court held that in light of *Jones,* the Fourth Amendment required a warrant supported by probable cause:

> In light of the confluence of the three opinions in the Supreme Court's decision in Jones, we accept the proposition that the privacy theory is not only alive and well, but available to govern electronic information of search and seizure in the absence of trespass. . . .
>
> *Jones,* as we noted, involved the movements of the defendant's automobile on the public streets and highways. Indeed, the district court allowed the defendant's motion to suppress information obtained when the automobile was not in public places. The circuit opinion and the separate opinions in the Supreme Court concluded that a reasonable expectation of privacy had been established by the aggregation of the points of data, not by the obtaining of individual points. Such a mosaic theory is not necessary to establish the invasion of privacy in the case of cell site location data.
>
> One's car, when it is not garaged in a private place, is visible to the public, and it is only the aggregation of many instances of the public seeing it that make it particularly invasive of privacy to secure GPS evidence of its location. As the circuit and some justices reasoned, the car owner can reasonably expect that although his individual movements may be observed, there will not be a "tiny constable" hiding in his vehicle to maintain a log of his movements. In contrast, even on a person's first visit to a gynecologist, a psychiatrist, a bookie, or a priest, one may assume that the visit is private if it was not conducted in a public way. One's cell phone, unlike an automobile, can accompany its owner anywhere. Thus, the exposure of the cell site location information can convert what would otherwise be a private event into a public one. When one's whereabouts are not public, then one may have a reasonable expectation of privacy in those whereabouts. Therefore, while it may be the case that even in light of the *Jones* opinion, GPS location information on an automobile would be protected only in the case of aggregated data, even one point of cell site location data can be within a reasonable expectation of privacy. In that sense, cell site data is more like communications data than it is like GPS information. That is, it is private in nature rather than being public data that warrants privacy

protection only when its collection creates a sufficient mosaic to expose that which would otherwise be private.

The court rejected the government's argument that the third party doctrine applied to location information because, quoting the court in *In re Application of U.S. for an Order Directing a Provider of Elec. Communication Service to Disclose Records to Gov't*, 620 F.3d 304 (3d Cir.2010): "[W]hen a cell phone user makes a call, the only information that is voluntarily and knowingly conveyed to the phone company is the number that is dialed, and there is no indication to the user that making that call will also locate the caller."

The Fifth Circuit in *In re Application of the United State for Historical Cell Site Data*, 724 F.3d 600 (5th Cir. 2013), reached a contrary conclusion:

> The third party can store data disclosed to it at its discretion. And once an individual exposes his information to a third party, it can be used for any purpose. . . .
>
> Cell phone users . . . understand that their service providers record their location information when they use their phones at least to the same extent that the landline users in *Smith* understood that the phone company recorded the numbers they dialed. . . .
>
> Their use of their phones, moreover, is entirely voluntary. The Government does not require a member of the public to own or carry a phone. As the days of monopoly phone companies are past, the Government does not require him to obtain his cell phone service from a particular service provider that keeps historical cell site records for its subscribers, either. And it does not require him to make a call, let alone to make a call at a specific location. . . .
>
> Because a cell phone user makes a choice to get a phone, to select a particular service provider, and to make a call, and because he knows that the call conveys cell site information, the provider retains this information, and the provider will turn it over to the police if they have a court order, he voluntarily conveys his cell site data each time he makes a call.

Susan Freiwald concludes that the Fourth Amendment requires a warrant to obtain cell site location data:

> Because government compulsion of disclosure of location data constitutes a search under the Fourth Amendment, the judicial oversight inherent in the probable cause warrant requirement is required. The power and intrusiveness of the method, and its susceptibility to abuse, mean that anything less would violate Fourth Amendment rights. While the probable cause standard will not necessarily be that much more demanding than the showing needed for a ["specific and articulable" facts] order [under the SCA], the need to provide notice to the target, after the fact judicial review, and meaningful remedies should make a significant difference. A warrant must be required for location data acquisition as a matter of law, and no Supreme Court precedents pertaining to bumper-beepers, bank records, or telephone numbers counsel a different result.[105]

5. *Historical vs. Real-Time Location Data.* Is there a difference between

---

[105] Susan Freiwald, *Cell Phone Location Data and the Fourth Amendment: A Question of Law, Not Fact*, 70 Md. L. Rev. 677, 742-43 (2011).

historical versus real-time location data? Some courts have concluded that real-time location data requires a warrant whereas historical data does not. One rationale for the distinction is that historical data is stored in records and falls under the third party doctrine. According to Susan Freiwald, the distinction is spurious:

> [H]istorical location data may be at least as informative to law enforcement agents as prospective location data. Historical data may indicate with whom, where, and for how long targets have met. It may put a target at the scene of a crime at the time the crime was committed and thereby refute the target's alibi. Magistrate Judge Lenihan appropriately found that "the privacy and associational interests implicated [by acquisition of location data] are not meaningfully diminished by a delay in disclosure." Other courts have also recognized that law enforcement acquisition of records of historical location data, by virtue of creating a target's complete digital profile, should receive the same Fourth Amendment protection as acquisition of location data in real-time or prospectively.[106]

6. IP ADDRESSES, URLS, AND INTERNET SEARCHES

UNITED STATES V. FORRESTER

512 F.3d 500 (9th Cir. 2008)

FISHER, J. . . . Defendants-appellants Mark Stephen Forrester and Dennis Louis Alba were charged with various offenses relating to the operation of a large Ecstasy-manufacturing laboratory, and were convicted on all counts following a jury trial. They now appeal their convictions and sentences. . . .

During its investigation of Forrester and Alba's Ecstasy-manufacturing operation, the government employed various computer surveillance techniques to monitor Alba's e-mail and Internet activity. The surveillance began in May 2001 after the government applied for and received court permission to install a pen register analogue known as a "mirror port" on Alba's account with PacBell Internet. The mirror port was installed at PacBell's connection facility in San Diego, and enabled the government to learn the to/from addresses of Alba's e-mail messages, the IP addresses of the websites that Alba visited and the total volume of information sent to or from his account. Later, the government obtained a warrant authorizing it to employ imaging and keystroke monitoring techniques, but Alba does not challenge on appeal those techniques' legality or the government's application to use them.

Forrester and Alba were tried by jury. At trial, the government introduced extensive evidence showing that they and their associates built and operated a major Ecstasy laboratory. . . .

Alba contends that the government's surveillance of his e-mail and Internet activity violated the Fourth Amendment and fell outside the scope of the then-applicable federal pen register statute. We hold that the surveillance did not constitute a Fourth Amendment search and thus was not unconstitutional. We also

---

[106] *Id.* at 734.

hold that whether or not the computer surveillance was covered by the then-applicable pen register statute — an issue that we do not decide — Alba is not entitled to the suppression of any evidence (let alone the reversal of his convictions) as a consequence.

The Supreme Court held in *Smith v. Maryland* that the use of a pen register (a device that records numbers dialed from a phone line) does not constitute a search for Fourth Amendment purposes. According to the Court, people do not have a subjective expectation of privacy in numbers that they dial because they "realize that they must 'convey' phone numbers to the telephone company, since it is through telephone company switching equipment that their calls are completed." Even if there were such a subjective expectation, it would not be one that society is prepared to recognize as reasonable because "a person has no legitimate expectation of privacy in information he voluntarily turns over to third parties." Therefore the use of a pen register is not a Fourth Amendment search. Importantly, the Court distinguished pen registers from more intrusive surveillance techniques on the ground that "pen registers do not acquire the *contents* of communications" but rather obtain only the addressing information associated with phone calls.

Neither this nor any other circuit has spoken to the constitutionality of computer surveillance techniques that reveal the to/from addresses of e-mail messages, the IP addresses of websites visited and the total amount of data transmitted to or from an account. We conclude that the surveillance techniques the government employed here are constitutionally indistinguishable from the use of a pen register that the Court approved in *Smith*. First, e-mail and Internet users, like the telephone users in *Smith*, rely on third-party equipment in order to engage in communication. *Smith* based its holding that telephone users have no expectation of privacy in the numbers they dial on the users' imputed knowledge that their calls are completed through telephone company switching equipment. Analogously, e-mail and Internet users have no expectation of privacy in the to/from addresses of their messages or the IP addresses of the websites they visit because they should know that this information is provided to and used by Internet service providers for the specific purpose of directing the routing of information. Like telephone numbers, which provide instructions to the "switching equipment that processed those numbers," e-mail to/from addresses and IP addresses are not merely passively conveyed through third party equipment, but rather are voluntarily turned over in order to direct the third party's servers.

Second, e-mail to/from addresses and IP addresses constitute addressing information and do not necessarily reveal any more about the underlying contents of communication than do phone numbers. When the government obtains the to/from addresses of a person's e-mails or the IP addresses of websites visited, it does not find out the contents of the messages or know the particular pages on the websites the person viewed. At best, the government may make educated guesses about what was said in the messages or viewed on the websites based on its knowledge of the e-mail to/from addresses and IP addresses — but this is no different from speculation about the contents of a phone conversation on the basis of the identity of the person or entity that was dialed. Like IP addresses, certain phone numbers may strongly indicate the underlying contents of the communication; for example, the government would know that a person who dialed the phone number of a chemicals company or a gun shop was likely seeking information about chemicals or firearms. Further, when an individual dials a pre-recorded information or subject-specific line, such as sports scores, lottery results or phone sex lines, the phone number may even show that the caller had access to specific content information. Nonetheless, the Court in *Smith* and *Katz* drew a clear line between unprotected addressing information and protected content information that the government did not cross here.[107]

The government's surveillance of e-mail addresses also may be technologically sophisticated, but it is conceptually indistinguishable from government surveillance of physical mail. In a line of cases dating back to the nineteenth century, the Supreme Court has held that the government cannot engage in a warrantless search of the contents of sealed mail, but can observe whatever information people put on the outside of mail, because that information is voluntarily transmitted to third parties. E-mail, like physical mail, has an outside address "visible" to the third-party carriers that transmit it to its intended location, and also a package of content that the sender presumes will be read only by the intended recipient. The privacy interests in these two forms of communication are identical. The contents may deserve Fourth Amendment protection, but the address and size of the package do not. . . .

We therefore hold that the computer surveillance techniques that Alba challenges are not Fourth Amendment searches. However, our holding extends only to these particular techniques and does not imply that more intrusive techniques or techniques that reveal more content information are also constitutionally identical to the use of a pen register. . . .

Alba claims that the government's computer surveillance was not only unconstitutional but also beyond the scope of the then-applicable pen register statute, 18 U.S.C. § 3121-27 (amended October 2001). Under both the old and new versions of 18 U.S.C. § 3122, the government must apply for and obtain a court order before it can install and use a pen register. When the surveillance at issue here took place in May-July 2001, the applicable statute defined a pen register as a "device which records or decodes electronic or other impulses which identify the numbers dialed or otherwise transmitted on the telephone line to which such device is attached." 18 U.S.C. § 3127(3). Notwithstanding the government's invocation of this provision and application for and receipt of a court order, Alba maintains that the computer surveillance at issue here did not come within the statutory definition of a "pen register."

Even assuming that Alba is correct in this contention, he would not be entitled to the suppression of the evidence obtained through the computer surveillance. As both the Supreme Court and this court have emphasized, suppression is a disfavored remedy, imposed only where its deterrence benefits outweigh its substantial social costs or (outside the constitutional context) where it is clearly contemplated by the relevant statute. . . . Alba does not point to any statutory

---

[107] Surveillance techniques that enable the government to determine not only the IP addresses that a person accesses but also the uniform resource locators ("URL") of the pages visited might be more constitutionally problematic. A URL, unlike an IP address, identifies the particular document within a website that a person views and thus reveals much more information about the person's Internet activity. For instance, a surveillance technique that captures IP addresses would show only that a person visited the New York Times' website at http://www.nytimes.com, whereas a technique that captures URLs would also divulge the particular articles the person viewed.

language requiring suppression when computer surveillance that is similar but not technically equivalent to a pen register is carried out. Indeed, he does not even identify what law or regulation the government may have violated if its surveillance did not come within the scope of the then-applicable pen register statute. The suppression of evidence under these circumstances is plainly inappropriate.

Our conclusion is bolstered by the fact that suppression still would not be appropriate even if the computer surveillance was covered by the pen register statute. Assuming the surveillance violated the statute, there is no mention of suppression of evidence in the statutory text. Instead, the only penalty specified is that "[w]hoever knowingly violates subsection (a)" by installing or using a pen register without first obtaining a court order "shall be fined under this title or imprisoned not more than one year, or both." 18 U.S.C. § 3121(d).

NOTES & QUESTIONS

1. ***IP Addresses vs. URLs.*** The *Forrester* court concludes that e-mail headers and IP addresses are akin to pen registers and that the controlling case is *Smith v. Maryland.* Does *Smith* control because IP address and e-mail header information are not revealing of the contents of the communications or because this information is conveyed to a third party? Recall that in a footnote, the court observes that URLs "might be more constitutionally problematic" because a "URL, unlike an IP address, identifies the particular document within a website that a person views and thus reveals much more information about the person's Internet activity." However, although IP addresses do not reveal specific parts of a websites that a person visits, they do reveal the various websites that a person visits. Why isn't this revealing enough to trigger constitutional protections?

2. ***Content vs. Envelope Information.*** A key distinction under ECPA, as well as Fourth Amendment law, is between "content" and "envelope" information. Orin Kerr explains the distinction:

   . . . [E]very communications network features two types of information: the contents of communications, and the addressing and routing information that the networks use to deliver the contents of communications. The former is "content information," and the latter is "envelope information."

   The essential distinction between content and envelope information remains constant across different technologies, from postal mail to email. With postal mail, the content information is the letter itself, stored safely inside its envelope. The envelope information is the information derived from the outside of the envelope, including the mailing and return addresses, the stamp and postmark, and the size and weight of the envelope when sealed.

   Similar distinctions exist for telephone conversations. The content information for a telephone call is the actual conversation between participants that can be captured by an audio recording of the call. The envelope information includes the number the caller dials, the number from which the caller dials, the time of the call, and its duration.[108]

Under ECPA, content information is generally given strong protection (e.g., the Wiretap Act), whereas envelope information is not (e.g., the Pen Register Act). But is such a distinction viable?

Daniel Solove contends that the distinction breaks down:

> When applied to IP addresses and URLs, the envelope/content distinction becomes even more fuzzy. An IP address is a unique number that is assigned to each computer connected to the Internet. Each website, therefore, has an IP address. On the surface, a list of IP addresses is simply a list of numbers; but it is actually much more. With a complete listing of IP addresses, the government can learn quite a lot about a person because it can trace how that person surfs the Internet. The government can learn the names of stores at which a person shops, the political organizations a person finds interesting, a person's sexual fetishes and fantasies, her health concerns, and so on.
>
> Perhaps even more revealing are URLs. A URL is a pointer — it points to the location of particular information on the Internet. In other words, it indicates where something is located. When we cite to something on the Web, we are citing to its URL. . . . URLs can reveal the specific information that people are viewing on the Web. URLs can also contain search terms. . . .
>
> [Therefore,] the content/envelope distinction is not always clear. In many circumstances, to adapt Marshall McLuhan, the "envelope" *is* the "content." Envelope information can reveal a lot about a person's private activities, sometimes as much (and even more) than can content information.[109]

Orin Kerr disagrees:

> Professor Solove appears to doubt the wisdom of offering lower privacy protection for non-content information. He suggests that the acquisition of non-content information should require a full search warrant based on probable cause. . . .
>
> Despite this, Solove's suggestion that the law should not offer lesser privacy protection for non-content information is unpersuasive. The main reason is that it is quite rare for non-content information to yield the equivalent of content information. It happens in very particular circumstances, but it remains quite rare, and usually in circumstances that are difficult to predict ex ante. In the Internet context, for example, non-content surveillance typically consists of collecting Internet packets; the packets disclose that a packet was sent from one IP address to another IP address at a particular time. This isn't very private information, at least in most cases. Indeed, it is usually impossible to know who asked for the packet, or what the packet was about, or what the person who asked for the packet wanted to do, or even if it was a person (as opposed to the computer) who sent for the packet in the first place. Solove focuses on the compelling example of Internet search terms as an example of non-content information that can be the privacy equivalent of content information. This is a misleading example, however, as Internet search terms very well may be contents. . . . Thus, despite the fact that non-content information can yield private information, in the great majority of

---

[108] Orin S. Kerr, Internet *Surveillance Law After the USA PATRIOT Act: The Big Brother That Isn't,* 97 Nw. U. L. Rev. 607, 611 (2003).
[109] Solove, *Surveillance Law, supra,* at 1287-88.

cases contents of communications implicate privacy concerns on a higher order of magnitude than non-content information, and it makes sense to give greater privacy protections for the former and lesser to the latter.[110]

Solove replies:

> Kerr assumes that a compilation of envelope information is generally less revealing than content information. However, a person may care more about protecting the identities of people with whom she communicates than the content of those communications. Indeed, the identities of the people one communicates with implicates freedom of association under the First Amendment. The difficulty is that the distinction between content and envelope information does not correlate well to the distinction between sensitive and innocuous information. Envelope information can be quite sensitive; content information can be quite innocuous. Admittedly, in many cases, people do not care very much about maintaining privacy over the identities of their friends and associates. But it is also true that in many cases, the contents of communications are not very revealing as well. Many e-mails are short messages which do not reveal any deep secrets, and even Kerr would agree that this should not lessen their protection under the law. This is because content information has the potential to be quite sensitive — but this is also the case with envelope information.[111]

3. ***The Scope of the Pen Register Act.*** The version of the Pen Register Act in effect when the search took place in *Forrester* was the pre-USA PATRIOT Act version, which defined pen registers more narrowly as "numbers dialed." The USA PATRIOT Act expanded the definition of pen register to include "dialing, routing, addressing, or signaling information . . . provided, however, that such information shall not include the contents of any communication." Prior to the USA PATRIOT Act changes, it was an open question as to whether the Pen Register Act applied to e-mail headers, IP addresses, and URLs. The USA PATRIOT Act changes aimed to clarify that the Pen Register Act did apply beyond telephone numbers. E-mail headers seem to fit readily into the new Pen Register Act definition. But what about IP addresses and URLs? They involve "routing" and "addressing" information, but they may also include "the contents" of communications. Do they involve "contents" or are they merely "envelope" information?

4. ***ECPA and the Exclusionary Rule.*** The *Forrester* court concludes that even if the acquisition of information violated the Pen Register Act, the exclusionary rule is not a remedy under the Act. As discussed earlier in this chapter, many provisions of electronic surveillance law lack an exclusionary rule. In the Wiretap Act, wire and oral communications are protected with an exclusionary rule, but electronic communications are not. Solove argues that "[s]ince e-mail has become a central mode of communication, this discrepancy is baseless."[112]

---

[110] Orin S. Kerr, *A User's Guide to the Stored Communications Act — and a Legislator's Guide to Amending It,* 72 Geo. Wash. L. Rev. 1208, 1229 n.142 (2004).

[111] Solove, *Surveillance Law, supra,* at 1288. Susan Freiwald contends that "the current categories of the ECPA do not cover web traffic data. At least one other category of protection is needed. Search terms entered, web-pages visited, and items viewed are neither message contents nor their to/from information." Freiwald, *Online Surveillance, supra,* at 71.

[112] Solove, *Surveillance Law, supra,* at 1282.

Is it? Can you think of a reason why e-mail should receive lesser protection than a phone conversation, which would be protected by the exclusionary rule under the Wiretap Act? Additionally, the Stored Communications Act and Pen Register Act have no exclusionary remedies for any type of communication.

Orin Kerr argues the absence of an exclusionary rule in many of ECPA's provisions leads to inadequate judicial attention to ECPA. Without an exclusionary rule, Kerr contends, "criminal defendants have little incentive to raise challenges to the government's Internet surveillance practices." Therefore, many challenges to Internet surveillance practices "tend to be in civil cases between private parties that raise issues far removed from those that animated Congress to pass the statutes." Adding an exclusionary remedy, Kerr argues, would "benefit both civil libertarian and law enforcement interests alike." He writes:

> On the civil libertarian side, a suppression remedy would considerably increase judicial scrutiny of the government's Internet surveillance practices in criminal cases. The resulting judicial opinions would clarify the rules that the government must follow, serving the public interest of greater transparency. Less obviously, the change could also benefit law enforcement by altering the type and nature of the disputes over the Internet surveillance laws that courts encounter. Prosecutors would have greater control over the types of cases the courts decided, enjoy more sympathetic facts, and have a better opportunity to explain and defend law enforcement interests before the courts. The statutory law of Internet surveillance would become more like the Fourth Amendment law: a source of vital and enforceable rights that every criminal defendant can invoke, governed by relatively clear standards that by and large respect law enforcement needs and attempt to strike a balance between those needs and privacy interests.[113]

5. ***The Internet vs. the Telephone.*** Susan Freiwald contends that while the 1968 Wiretap Act (Title III) provided powerful and effective protection for telephone communications, ECPA in 1986 did not do the same for online communications:

> . . . [O]nline surveillance is even more susceptible to law enforcement abuse and even more threatening to privacy. Therefore, one might expect regulation of online surveillance to be more privacy-protective than traditional wiretapping law. That could not be further from the truth. The law provides dramatically less privacy protection for online activities than for traditional telephone calls and videotapings. Additionally, what makes the Wiretap Act complex makes online surveillance law chaotic. Almost all of the techniques designed to rein in law enforcement have been abandoned in the online context. And, while Congress resolved much of its ambivalence towards wiretapping in 1968, current law suggests the outright hostility of all branches of government to online privacy.[114]

---

[113] Orin S. Kerr, *Lifting the "Fog" of Internet Surveillance: How a Suppression Remedy Would Change Computer Crime Law*, 54 Hastings L.J. 805, 824, 807-08 (2003).

[114] Susan Freiwald, *Online Surveillance: Remembering the Lessons of the Wiretap Act*, 56 Ala. L. Rev. 9, 14 (2004).

In what ways does federal electronic surveillance law protect Internet communication differently from telephone communication? Should the privacy protections differ in these areas?

CHAPTER 5

NATIONAL SECURITY AND FOREIGN INTELLIGENCE

CHAPTER OUTLINE

Should the law treat investigations involving national security differently than other criminal investigations? This question has long been one that the law has struggled with. Additionally, there are times when government intelligence agencies want to gather foreign intelligence within the United States. One example is when there might be a foreign spy within the United States. Another example is when intelligence agencies just want to spy on a foreign individual who is in the United States to see what can be learned about the activities of foreign nations. These instances might not involve a criminal investigation or even an immediate national security threat — they merely involve gathering useful foreign intelligence.

The difficulty is in delineating between these activities. For example, suppose intelligence agencies are monitoring the activities of individuals with connections to a foreign terrorist organization. There will certainly be an interest in gathering foreign intelligence. National security will likely be implicated. And the case may very likely result in a criminal prosecution if evidence is obtained that the individuals are plotting a terrorist act.

The previous chapter provided an introduction to the Fourth Amendment and to electronic surveillance law, with a focus on the Electronic Communications Privacy Act (ECPA). Ordinarily, government information gathering activities would fall under the Fourth Amendment rules discussed in the previous chapter on law enforcement, and government electronic surveillance would be regulated by ECPA. However, with national security and foreign intelligence gathering, the Fourth Amendment rules are different, and ECPA often does not apply. Instead, other statutes and regulations apply.

A. THE INTELLIGENCE COMMUNITY

The United States intelligence community consists of a number of agencies that gather information about threats domestic and foreign. The three most prominent intelligence agencies are the FBI, CIA, and NSA.

Federal Bureau of Investigation (FBI). The FBI was originally created in 1908 and called the "Bureau of Investigation." It was not until 1935 when the FBI received its current name. The focus of the FBI is on domestic criminal investigations involving federal crimes. However, the FBI also has intelligence, counterintelligence, and counterterrorism functions.

Central Intelligence Agency (CIA). Before the creation of the CIA, its functions were handled by the Office of Strategic Services (OSS), which was created in 1942 by President Franklin D. Roosevelt. The OSS was eliminated at the end of World War II. President Harry Truman created the CIA with the National Security Act of 1947.

National Security Agency (NSA). Located within the Department of Defense, the NSA was created by President Truman in 1952 to engage in cryptology—deciphering encryption codes used in foreign communications. Subsequently the size and activities of the NSA have increased, and the agency is now engaged in large-scale information gathering activities.

Other Intelligence Agencies. There are many other intelligence agencies beyond the FBI, CIA, and NSA. These agencies are located within the Department of Defense, Department of Homeland Security, Department of State, and Department of the Treasury, among others. Some of these entities include the Defense Intelligence Agency (DIA), the State Department's Bureau of Intelligence and Research (INR), and the Treasury Department's Office of Terrorism and Financial Intelligence.

B. THE FOURTH AMENDMENT FRAMEWORK

Does the Fourth Amendment apply differently to national security and foreign intelligence gathering than it does for domestic criminal investigations? These questions long remained unresolved, and are still not fully resolved to this day.

In a footnote to *Katz v. United States,* 389 U.S. 347 (1967), the Court stated that perhaps a warrant might not be required in situations involving national security:

> Whether safeguards other than prior authorization by a magistrate would satisfy the Fourth Amendment in a situation involving the national security is a question not presented by this case.

Justice White, in a concurring opinion, declared:

> In joining the Court's opinion, I note the Court's acknowledgment that there are circumstance in which it is reasonable to search without a warrant. In this connection . . . the Court points out that today's decision does not reach national security cases. Wiretapping to protect the security of the Nation has been authorized by successive Presidents. The present Administration would apparently save national security cases from restrictions against wiretapping. We should not require the warrant procedure and the magistrate's judgment if the President of the United States or his chief legal officer, the Attorney General, has considered the requirements of national security and authorized electronic surveillance as reasonable.

Justices Douglas and Brennan, in another concurring opinion, took issue with Justice White:

> . . . Neither the President nor the Attorney General is a magistrate. In matters where they believe national security may be involved they are not detached, disinterested, and neutral as a court or magistrate must be. . . .
>
> There is, so far as I understand constitutional history, no distinction under the Fourth Amendment between types of crimes. Article III, § 3, gives "treason" a very narrow definition and puts restrictions on its proof. But the Fourth Amendment draws no lines between various substantive offenses. The arrests on cases of "hot pursuit" and the arrests on visible or other evidence of probable cause cut across the board and are not peculiar to any kind of crime.
>
> I would respect the present lines of distinction and not improvise because a particular crime seems particularly heinous. When the Framers took that step, as they did with treason, the worst crime of all, they made their purpose manifest.

The Supreme Court finally confronted these issues more squarely in a case decided in 1972, *United States v. United States District Court,* which has become known as the *Keith* case, named after District Court Judge Damon Keith.

The *Keith* case began when three founding members of a group called "the White Panthers" bombed a CIA office located in Michigan. The group was not a racist group and in fact was supportive of the Black Panthers. The White Panther agenda was to abolish money. According to the group's manifesto: "We demand total freedom for everybody! And we will not be stopped until we get it. . . . Rock and Roll music is the spearhead of our attack because it is so effective and so much fun."[1]

When it investigated the bombing, the government wiretapped the phone calls of one of the bombers. This was done without a warrant. Recall from the previous chapter that in 1967 the Supreme Court in *United States v. Katz,* 389 U.S. 347 (1967), held that the Fourth Amendment required a warrant in order for the government to wiretap a phone call. Also recall that in 1968 Congress required special court orders for the government to engage in wiretapping when it passed Title III of the Omnibus Crime Control and Safe Streets Act (which now is the Wiretap Act portion of the Electronic Communications Privacy Act (ECPA)).

The Nixon Administration contended that because this case involved a matter of national security, he was able to conduct surveillance without a Fourth Amendment warrant or Title III court order. The Supreme Court, however, in the *Keith* decision below did not agree.

UNITED STATES V. UNITED STATES DISTRICT COURT
(THE *KEITH* CASE)

407 U.S. 297 (1972)

POWELL, J. . . . The issue before us is an important one for the people of our country and their Government. It involves the delicate question of the President's power, acting through the Attorney General, to authorize electronic surveillance in internal security matters without prior judicial approval. Successive Presidents for more than one-quarter of a century have authorized such surveillance in varying degrees, without guidance from the Congress or a definitive decision of this Court. This case brings the issue here for the first time. Its resolution is a matter of national concern, requiring sensitivity both to the Government's right to protect itself from unlawful subversion and attack and to the citizen's right to be secure in his privacy against unreasonable Government intrusion.

This case arises from a criminal proceeding in the United States District Court for the Eastern District of Michigan, in which the United States charged three defendants with conspiracy to destroy Government property. . . . One of the defendants, Plamondon, was charged with the dynamite bombing of an office of the Central Intelligence Agency in Ann Arbor, Michigan.

Title III of the Omnibus Crime Control and Safe Streets Act, 18 U.S.C. §§ 2510-2520, authorizes the use of electronic surveillance for classes of crimes carefully specified in 18 U.S.C. § 2516. Such surveillance is subject to prior court order. Section 2518 sets forth the detailed and particularized application necessary to obtain such an order as well as carefully circumscribed conditions for its use. The Act represents a comprehensive attempt by Congress to promote more effective control of crime while protecting the privacy of individual thought and expression. Much of Title III was drawn to meet the constitutional requirements

---

[1] Trevor W. Morrison, *The Story of United States v. U.S. District Court (Keith): The Surveillance Power, in Presidential Power Stories* 287 (Christopher Schroeder & Curtis Bradley eds., 2008).

for electronic surveillance enunciated by this Court in *Berger v. New York,* and *Katz v. United States.*

The Government relies on § 2511(3). It argues that "in excepting national security surveillances from the Act's warrant requirement Congress recognized the President's authority to conduct such surveillances without prior judicial approval." The section thus is viewed as a recognition or affirmance of a constitutional authority in the President to conduct warrantless domestic security surveillance such as that involved in this case.

We think the language of § 2511(3), as well as the legislative history of the statute, refutes this interpretation. The relevant language is that: "Nothing contained in this chapter . . . shall limit the constitutional power of the President to take such measures as he deems necessary to protect . . . ." against the dangers specified. At most, this is an implicit recognition that the President does have certain powers in the specified areas. Few would doubt this, as the section refers — among other things — to protection "against actual or potential attack or other hostile acts of a foreign power." But so far as the use of the President's electronic surveillance power is concerned, the language is essentially neutral.

Section 2511(3) certainly confers no power, as the language is wholly inappropriate for such a purpose. It merely provides that the Act shall not be interpreted to limit or disturb such power as the President may have under the Constitution. In short, Congress simply left presidential powers where it found them.

Our present inquiry, though important, is . . . a narrow one. It addresses a question left open by *Katz*:

> Whether safeguards other than prior authorization by a magistrate would satisfy the Fourth Amendment in a situation involving the national security. . . .

We begin the inquiry by noting that the President of the United States has the fundamental duty, under Art. II, § 1, of the Constitution, to "preserve, protect and defend the Constitution of the United States." Implicit in that duty is the power to protect our Government against those who would subvert or overthrow it by unlawful means. In the discharge of this duty, the President — through the Attorney General — may find it necessary to employ electronic surveillance to obtain intelligence information on the plans of those who plot unlawful acts against the Government. The use of such surveillance in internal security cases has been sanctioned more or less continuously by various Presidents and Attorneys General since July 1946.

Though the Government and respondents debate their seriousness and magnitude, threats and acts of sabotage against the Government exist in sufficient number to justify investigative powers with respect to them.[2] The covertness and complexity of potential unlawful conduct against the Government and the necessary dependency of many conspirators upon the telephone make electronic surveillance an effective investigatory instrument in certain circumstances. The

---

[2] The Government asserts that there were 1,562 bombing incidents in the United States from January 1, 1971, to July 1, 1971, most of which involved Government related facilities. Respondents dispute these statistics as incorporating many frivolous incidents as well as bombings against nongovernmental facilities. The precise level of this activity, however, is not relevant to the disposition of this case.

marked acceleration in technological developments and sophistication in their use have resulted in new techniques for the planning, commission, and concealment of criminal activities. It would be contrary to the public interest for Government to deny to itself the prudent and lawful employment of those very techniques which are employed against the Government and its lawabiding citizens. . . .

But a recognition of these elementary truths does not make the employment by Government of electronic surveillance a welcome development — even when employed with restraint and under judicial supervision. There is, understandably, a deep-seated uneasiness and apprehension that this capability will be used to intrude upon cherished privacy of law-abiding citizens. We look to the Bill of Rights to safeguard this privacy. Though physical entry of the home is the chief evil against which the wording of the Fourth Amendment is directed, its broader spirit now shields private speech from unreasonable surveillance. Our decision in *Katz* refused to lock the Fourth Amendment into instances of actual physical trespass.

. . . [N]ational security cases, moreover, often reflect a convergence of First and Fourth Amendment values not present in cases of "ordinary" crime. Though the investigative duty of the executive may be stronger in such cases, so also is there greater jeopardy to constitutionally protected speech. . . . The danger to political dissent is acute where the Government attempts to act under so vague a concept as the power to protect "domestic security." Given the difficulty of defining the domestic security interest, the danger of abuse in acting to protect that interest becomes apparent.

The price of lawful public dissent must not be a dread of subjection to an unchecked surveillance power. Nor must the fear of unauthorized official eavesdropping deter vigorous citizen dissent and discussion of Government action in private conversation. For private dissent, no less than open public discourse, is essential to our free society.

As the Fourth Amendment is not absolute in its terms, our task is to examine and balance the basic values at stake in this case: the duty of Government to protect the domestic security, and the potential danger posed by unreasonable surveillance to individual privacy and free expression. If the legitimate need of Government to safeguard domestic security requires the use of electronic surveillance, the question is whether the needs of citizens for privacy and the free expression may not be better protected by requiring a warrant before such surveillance is undertaken. We must also ask whether a warrant requirement would unduly frustrate the efforts of Government to protect itself from acts of subversion and overthrow directed against it. . . .

[C]ontentions in behalf of a complete exemption from the warrant requirement, when urged on behalf of the President and the national security in its domestic implications, merit the most careful consideration. We certainly do not reject them lightly, especially at a time of worldwide ferment and when civil disorders in this country are more prevalent than in the less turbulent periods of our history. There is, no doubt, pragmatic force to the Government's position.

[W]e do not think a case has been made for the requested departure from Fourth Amendment standards. The circumstances described do not justify complete exemption of domestic security surveillance from prior judicial scrutiny. Official surveillance, whether its purpose be criminal investigation or ongoing intelligence gathering, risks infringement of constitutionally protected privacy of speech. Security surveillances are especially sensitive because of the inherent vagueness of the domestic security concept, the necessarily broad and continuing nature of intelligence gathering, and the temptation to utilize such surveillances to oversee political dissent. We recognize, as we have before, the constitutional basis of the President's domestic security role, but we think it must be exercised in a manner compatible with the Fourth Amendment. In this case we hold that this requires an appropriate prior warrant procedure.

We cannot accept the Government's argument that internal security matters are too subtle and complex for judicial evaluation. Courts regularly deal with the most difficult issues of our society. There is no reason to believe that federal judges will be insensitive to or uncomprehending of the issues involved in domestic security cases. . . . If the threat is too subtle or complex for our senior law enforcement officers to convey its significance to a court, one may question whether there is probable cause for surveillance.

Nor do we believe prior judicial approval will fracture the secrecy essential to official intelligence gathering. The investigation of criminal activity has long involved imparting sensitive information to judicial officers who have respected the confidentialities involved. Judges may be counted upon to be especially conscious of security requirements in national security cases. Title III of the Omnibus Crime Control and Safe Streets Act already has imposed this responsibility on the judiciary in connection with such crimes as espionage, sabotage, and treason, §§ 2516(1)(a) and (c), each of which may involve domestic as well as foreign security threats. Moreover, a warrant application involves no public or adversary proceedings: it is an ex parte request before a magistrate or judge. Whatever security dangers clerical and secretarial personnel may pose can be minimized by proper administrative measures, possibly to the point of allowing the Government itself to provide the necessary clerical assistance. . . .

We emphasize, before concluding this opinion, the scope of our decision. As stated at the outset, this case involves only the domestic aspects of national security. We have not addressed and express no opinion as to, the issues which may be involved with respect to activities of foreign powers or their agents. . . .

Moreover, we do not hold that the same type of standards and procedures prescribed by Title III are necessarily applicable to this case. We recognize that domestic security surveillance may involve different policy and practical considerations from the surveillance of "ordinary crime." The gathering of security intelligence is often long range and involves the interrelation of various sources and types of information. The exact targets of such surveillance may be more difficult to identify than in surveillance operations against many types of crime specified in Title III. Often, too, the emphasis of domestic intelligence gathering is on the prevention of unlawful activity or the enhancement of the Government's preparedness for some possible future crisis or emergency. Thus, the focus of domestic surveillance may be less precise than that directed against more conventional types of crime.

Given those potential distinctions between Title III criminal surveillances and those involving the domestic security, Congress may wish to consider protective standards for the latter which differ from those already prescribed for specified crimes in Title III. Different standards may be compatible with the Fourth

Amendment if they are reasonable both in relation to the legitimate need of Government for intelligence information and the protected rights of our citizens. For the warrant application may vary according to the governmental interest to be enforced and the nature of citizen rights deserving protection. . . .

DOUGLAS, J. concurring. While I join in the opinion of the Court, I add these words in support of it. . . .

If the Warrant Clause were held inapplicable here, then the federal intelligence machine would literally enjoy unchecked discretion. Here, federal agents wish to rummage for months on end through every conversation, no matter how intimate or personal, carried over selected telephone lines, simply to seize those few utterances which may add to their sense of the pulse of a domestic underground. . . .

That "domestic security" is said to be involved here does not draw this case outside the mainstream of Fourth Amendment law. Rather, the recurring desire of reigning officials to employ dragnet techniques to intimidate their critics lies at the core of that prohibition. For it was such excesses as the use of general warrants and the writs of assistance that led to the ratification of the Fourth Amendment. . . .

[W]e are currently in the throes of another national seizure of paranoia, resembling the hysteria which surrounded the Alien and Sedition Acts, the Palmer Raids, and the McCarthy era. Those who register dissent or who petition their governments for redress are subjected to scrutiny by grand juries, by the FBI, or even by the military. Their associates are interrogated. Their homes are bugged and their telephones are wiretapped. They are befriended by secret government informers. Their patriotism and loyalty are questioned. . . .

We have as much or more to fear from the erosion of our sense of privacy and independence by the omnipresent electronic ear of the Government as we do from the likelihood that fomenters of domestic upheaval will modify our form of governing.

NOTES & QUESTIONS

1. *The Fourth Amendment Framework in* **Keith.** The *Keith* Court draws a distinction between electronic surveillance in (1) criminal investigations, regulated under Title III (now ECPA); (2) domestic national security investigations; and (3) foreign intelligence gathering, including investigations involving "activities of foreign powers and their agents."

   (1) Ordinary Criminal Investigations. Regarding ordinary criminal investigations, the *Keith* Court stated that there was no debate regarding "the necessity of obtaining a warrant in the surveillance of crimes unrelated to the national security interest."

   (2) Domestic National Security Investigations. Regarding domestic national security investigations, the focus of the *Keith* Court's opinion, its holding was that the Fourth Amendment required the issuing of a warrant in domestic security investigations. It also held that the precise

requirements for issuing a requirement to investigate domestic security need not be the same as for Title III criminal surveillance.

(3) Foreign Intelligence Gathering. Finally, the *Keith* Court stated that it did not address issues involving foreign powers and their agents.

Does this tripartite distinction seem useful as a policy matter? How does one distinguish between security surveillance (category two) and surveillance for ordinary crime (category one)?

Daniel Solove argues that such a distinction ought not to be made: "'National security' has often been abused as a justification not only for surveillance but also for maintaining the secrecy of government records as well as violating the civil liberties of citizens." He further contends that "the line between national security and regular criminal activities is very blurry, especially in an age of terrorism."[3] In his book, *Nothing to Hide,* Solove further argues:

> It is difficult to distinguish national-security matters from ordinary crime, especially when U.S. citizens are involved. National security threats *are* a form of crime. They are severe crimes. But the rules for investigating ordinary crime are designed to regulate government information gathering no matter how grave the particular crime might be. These rules aren't rigid, and they make allowances for emergencies and unusual circumstances.[4]

On the other hand, Richard Posner contends that the word "unreasonable" in the Fourth Amendment "invites a wide-ranging comparison between the benefits and costs of a search or seizure." He proposes a "sliding scale" standard where "the level of suspicion require to justify the search or seizure should fall . . . as the magnitude of the crime under investigation rises."[5] Paul Rosenzweig argues: "In this time of terror, some adjustment of the balance between liberty and security is both necessary and appropriate. . . . [T]he very text of the Fourth Amendment — with its prohibition only of 'unreasonable' searches and seizures — explicitly recognizes the need to balance the harm averted against the extent of governmental intrusion."[6]

2. ***The Church Committee Report.*** In 1976, a congressional committee led by Senator Frank Church (called the "Church Committee") engaged in an extensive investigation of government national security surveillance. It found extensive abuses, which it chronicled in its famous report known as the Church Committee Report:

> Too many people have been spied upon by too many Government agencies and too much information has been collected. The Government has often undertaken the secret surveillance of citizens on the basis of their political beliefs, even when those beliefs posed no threat of violence or illegal acts on behalf of a hostile foreign power. The Government, operating primarily through

---

[3] Solove, *Surveillance Law,* 72 Geo. Wash. L. Rev. 1264, 1301-02 (2004).

[4] Daniel J. Solove, *Nothing to Hide: The False Tradeoff Between Privacy and Security* 66 (2011).

[5] Richard Posner, *Law, Pragmatism, and Democracy* 303 (2003); *see also* Akhil Reed Amar, *The Constitution and Criminal Procedure* 31 (1997) ("The core of the Fourth Amendment . . . is neither a warrant nor probable cause but reasonableness.").

[6] Paul Rosenzweig, *Civil Liberty and the Response to Terrorism,* 42 Duq. L. Rev. 663 (2004).

secret informants, but also using other intrusive techniques such as wiretaps, microphone "bugs," surreptitious mail opening, and break-ins, has swept in vast amounts of information about the personal lives, views, and associations of American citizens. . . . Groups and individuals have been harassed and disrupted because of their political views and their lifestyles. Investigations have been based upon vague standards whose breadth made excessive collection inevitable. . . .

The FBI's COINTELPRO — counterintelligence program — was designed to "disrupt" groups and "neutralize" individuals deemed to be threats to domestic security. The FBI resorted to counterintelligence tactics in part because its chief officials believed that existing law could not control the activities of certain dissident groups, and that court decisions had tied the hands of the intelligence community. Whatever opinion one holds about the policies of the targeted groups, many of the tactics employed by the FBI were indisputably degrading to a free society. . . .

Since the early 1930's, intelligence agencies have frequently wiretapped and bugged American citizens without the benefit of judicial warrant. . . .

There has been, in short, a clear and sustained failure by those responsible to control the intelligence community and to ensure its accountability.[7]

The Church Committee Report was influential in the creation of FISA as well as the Attorney General Guidelines.

3. *National Security vs. Civil Liberties.* Eric Posner and Adrian Vermeule argue that the legislature and judiciary should defer to the executive in times of emergency and that it is justified to curtail civil liberties when national security is threatened:

The essential feature of the emergency is that national security is threatened; because the executive is the only organ of government with the resources, power, and flexibility to respond to threats to national security, it is natural, inevitable, and desirable for power to flow to this branch of government. Congress rationally acquiesces; courts rationally defer. . . .

During emergencies, when new threats appear, the balance shifts; government should and will reduce civil liberties in order to enhance security in those domains where the two must be traded off. . . .

In emergencies . . . judges are at sea, even more so than are executive officials. The novelty of the threats and of the necessary responses makes judicial routines and evolved legal rules seem inapposite, even obstructive. There is a premium on the executive's capacities for swift, vigorous, and secretive action.[8]

4. *The Fourth Amendment and Foreign Intelligence Surveillance. Keith* did not address how the Fourth Amendment would govern foreign intelligence surveillance (category three). Circuit courts examining the issue have concluded that at a minimum, no warrant is required by the Fourth Amendment

---

[7] *Intelligence Activities and the Rights of Americans* (Vol. 2), Final Report of the Select Committee to Study Government Operations with Respect to Intelligence Activities 5, 10, 15 (Apr. 26, 1976).

[8] Eric A. Posner & Adrian Vermeule, *Terror in the Balance: Security, Liberty, and the Courts* 4, 5, 18 (2006). For another defense of the curtailment of civil liberties for national security, see Richard A. Posner, *Not a Suicide Pact: The Constitution in a Time of National Emergency* (2006).

for foreign intelligence surveillance. In *United States v. Butenko*, 494 F.2d 593 (3d Cir. 1974) (en banc), the court justified this conclusion by reasoning that "foreign intelligence gathering is a clandestine and highly unstructured activity, and the need for electronic surveillance often cannot be anticipated in advance." Reaching a similar conclusion in *United States v. Truong Dinh Hung*, 629 F.2d 908 (4th Cir. 1980), the court reasoned: "[T]he needs of the executive are so compelling in the area of foreign intelligence, unlike the area of domestic security, that a uniform warrant requirement would, following *Keith,* 'unduly frustrate' the President in carrying out his foreign affairs responsibilities."

C. FOREIGN INTELLIGENCE GATHERING

1. THE FOREIGN INTELLIGENCE SURVEILLANCE ACT

In the *Keith* case, the Court explicitly refused to address whether the Fourth Amendment would require a warrant for surveillance of agents of foreign powers.

The Foreign Intelligence Surveillance Act (FISA) of 1978, Pub. L. No. 95-511, codified at 50 U.S.C. §§ 1801–1811, establishes standards and procedures for use of electronic surveillance to collect "foreign intelligence" within the United States. § 1804(a)(7)(B). FISA creates a different regime than ECPA, the legal regime that governs electronic surveillance for law enforcement purposes. The regime created by FISA is designed primarily for intelligence gathering agencies to regulate how they gain general intelligence about foreign powers and agents of foreign powers within the borders of the United States. In contrast, the regime of ECPA is designed for domestic law enforcement to govern the gathering of information for criminal investigations involving people in United States.

Applicability of FISA. When does FISA govern rather than ECPA? FISA generally applies when foreign intelligence gathering is "a significant purpose" of the investigation. 50 U.S.C. § 1804(a)(7)(B) and § 1823(a)(7)(B). The language of "a significant purpose" comes from the USA PATRIOT Act of 2001. Prior to the USA PATRIOT Act, FISA as interpreted by the courts required that the collection of foreign intelligence be the primary purpose for surveillance. After the USA PATRIOT Act, foreign intelligence gathering need no longer be the primary purpose. A further expansion of the FISA occurred in 2008 with amendments to that law, which we discuss below.

The Foreign Intelligence Surveillance Court (FISC). Requests for FISA orders are reviewed by a special court of federal district court judges. The USA PATRIOT Act increased the number of judges on the FISC from 7 to 11. 50 U.S.C. § 1803(a). The proceedings are ex parte, with the Department of Justice (DOJ) making the applications to the court on behalf of the CIA and other agencies. The Court meets in secret, and its proceedings are generally not revealed to the public or to the targets of the surveillance.

In 2007, the FISC declined an ACLU request to access its documents relating to alleged unauthorized surveillance. *In re Motion for Release of Court Records,*

526 F. Supp. 2d (2007). This case was an exception to the usual procedure of *ex parte* only hearings before the FISC. The court found that it had jurisdiction to entertain motions for release of its documents, and then denied the request. It stated:

> The FISC is a unique court. Its entire docket relates to the collection of foreign intelligence by the federal government. The applications submitted to it by the government are classified, as are the overwhelming majority of the FISC's orders. Court sessions are held behind closed doors in a secure facility, and every proceeding in its history prior to this one has been ex parte, with the government the only party. . . . Other courts operate primarily in public with secrecy the exception; the FISC operates primarily in secret, with public access the exception.

Perhaps most importantly, the court noted that "the proper functioning of the FISA process would be adversely affected if submitting sensitive information to the FISC could subject the Executive Branch's classification to a heightened form of judicial review."

Court Orders. The legal test for surveillance under FISA is not whether probable cause exists that the party to be monitored is involved in criminal activity. Rather, the court must find probable cause that the party to be monitored is a "foreign power" or "an agent of a foreign power." § 1801. Therefore, unlike ECPA or the Fourth Amendment, FISA surveillance is not tied to any required showing of a connection to criminal activity. However, if the monitored party is a "United States person" (a citizen or permanent resident alien), the government must establish probable cause that the party's activities "may" or "are about to" involve a criminal violation. § 1801(b)(2)(A).

Surveillance Without Court Orders. In certain circumstances, FISA authorizes surveillance without having to first obtain a court order. § 1802. In particular, the surveillance must be "solely directed at" obtaining intelligence exclusively from "foreign powers." § 1802(a). There must be "no substantial likelihood that the surveillance will acquire the contents of any communications to which a United States person is a party." § 1802(a)(1)(B). Electronic surveillance without a court order requires the authorization of the President, through the Attorney General, in writing under oath. § 1802(a)(1).

Video Surveillance. Unlike ECPA, FISA explicitly regulates video surveillance. In order to have court approval for video surveillance, the FISA requires the government to submit, among other things, "a detailed description of the nature of the information sought and the type of communications or activities to be subjected to the surveillance," § 1804(a)(6); "a certification . . . that such information cannot reasonably be obtained by normal investigative techniques," § 1804(a)(7); and "a statement of the period of time for which the electronic surveillance is required to be maintained," § 1804(a)(10). Video surveillance orders can last for 90 days.

The FISA Amendments Act. In 2008, Congress enacted significant amendments to FISA. The FISA Amendments Act (FAA) was passed in response to the revelation in 2005 that since 9/11 the National Security Agency (NSA) was engaging in an extensive program of warrantless wiretapping of international phone calls. Subsequently, several lawsuits were brought against the telecommunications companies that participated in the surveillance for violating FISA and ECPA. One of the most controversial aspects of the FAA was a grant of retroactive immunity to these companies. The NSA surveillance program and the ensuing litigation will be discussed later in this chapter.

In its other aspects, the FAA both expanded the government's surveillance abilities and added new privacy protections. The FAA explicitly permits collection of information from U.S. telecommunications facilities where it is not possible in advance to know whether a communication is purely international (that is, all parties to it are located outside of the United States) or whether the communication involves a foreign power or its agents. David Kris explains, "With the advent of web-based communication and other developments, the government cannot always determine — consistently, reliably, and in real time — the location of parties to an e-mail message."[9] It is also possible to collect information and then examine it (through data mining) to look for links with a foreign power or its agents. The perceived need, Kris states, was for a kind of "vacuum-cleaner" capacity that would enable the government to sift through large amounts of information without meeting FISA's traditional warrant requirements.

FAA amends FISA to permit "targeting of persons reasonably believed to be located outside the United States to acquire foreign intelligence information." § 702(a). The person targeted must be a non-U.S. person, or certain more restrictive measures apply. §§ 703–04. The critical substantive requirements are that the "target" of the surveillance be someone overseas and that a "significant purpose" of the surveillance be to acquire "foreign intelligence information," which is broadly defined.

The collection of this information must be carried out in accordance with certain "targeting procedures" to ensure that the collection is directed at persons located outside the United States. § 702(c)(1)(A). The acquisition must also involve new minimization procedures, which the Attorney General is to adopt. § 702(e). The Justice Department and the Director of National Intelligence must certify in advance of the surveillance activity that targeting and minimization procedures meet the statutory standards and that "a significant purpose" of the surveillance is to acquire foreign intelligence information. § 702(g)(2). The FAA also states that the government may not engage in a kind of "reverse-targeting" — the government cannot target "a person reasonably believed to be outside the United States if the purpose of such acquisition is to target a particular, known person reasonably believed to be in the United States." § 702(b)(2).

The FISC is to review certifications and the targeting and minimization procedures adopted. If a certification does not "contain all the required elements" or the procedures "are not consistent with the requirements" of the FAA or the

---

[9] David Kris, *A Guide to the New FISA Bill, Part I*, Balkanization (June 21, 2008), at http://balkin.blogspot.com/2008/06/guide-to-new-fisa-bill-part-i.html. Kris is co-author of the leading treatise, J. Douglas Wilson & David Kris, *National Security Investigations and Prosecutions* (2007).

Fourth Amendment to the U.S. Constitution, the FISC is to issue an order directing the government to correct any deficiencies. § 702(i)(3).

As for its expansion of privacy protections, the FAA requires that the FISC approve surveillance of a U.S. citizen abroad based on a showing that includes a finding that the person is "an agent of a foreign power, or an officer or employee of a foreign power." Previously, FISA did not regulate surveillance of targets, whether U.S. citizens or not, when located outside the United States. The FAA also contains new mechanisms for congressional oversight and crafts new audit functions for the Inspector Generals of the Department Justice.

GLOBAL RELIEF FOUNDATION, INC. V. O'NEIL
207 F. Supp. 779 (N.D. Ill. 2002)

. . . [A]gents of the FBI arrived at the corporate headquarters of Global Relief [a U.S.-based Islamic humanitarian relief organization] and the home of its executive director on December 14, 2001 and seized a considerable amount of material they felt was relevant to their investigation of Global Relief's activities. As the defendants have conceded in their briefs, no warrant had been obtained before the FBI arrived either at Global Relief's headquarters or the executive director's residence. Nevertheless, FISA includes a provision which states that, when the Attorney General declares that "an emergency situation exists with respect to the execution of a search to obtain foreign intelligence information" prior to the Foreign Intelligence Surveillance Court acting on the application, a warrantless search is authorized. 50 U.S.C. § 1824(e)(1)(B)(i). When such an emergency situation arises, the government must submit a warrant application to the Foreign Intelligence Surveillance Court within 72 hours of the warrantless search for approval. *See* 50 U.S.C. § 1824(e). In this case, the failure of the FBI agents to present a FISA warrant on December 14 was caused by the Assistant Attorney General's declaration that an emergency situation existed with respect to the targeted documents and material. The defendants did submit a warrant application to the Foreign Intelligence Surveillance Court on December 15, as required by 50 U.S.C. § 1824(e). We have reviewed the warrant that issued and the submissions to the Foreign Intelligence Surveillance Court in support of that warrant.

We conclude that the FISA application established probable cause to believe that Global Relief and the executive director were agents of a foreign power, as that term is defined for FISA purposes, at the time the search was conducted and the application was granted. . . . Given the sensitive nature of the information upon which we have relied in making this determination and the Attorney General's sworn assertion that disclosure of the underlying information would harm national security, it would be improper for us to elaborate further on this subject.

This Court has concluded that disclosure of the information we have reviewed could substantially undermine ongoing investigations required to apprehend the conspirators behind the September 11 murders and undermine the ability of law enforcement agencies to reduce the possibility of terrorist crimes in the future. Furthermore, this Court is persuaded that the search and seizure made by the FBI on December 14 were authorized by FISA. Accordingly, we decline plaintiff's request that we declare the search invalid and order the immediate return of all items seized.

NOTES & QUESTIONS

1. ***Probable Cause.*** Searches under the Wiretap Act require a "super warrant," including a showing of probable cause that an individual has committed or is about to commit an enumerated offense. 18 U.S.C. § 2518(3). What is the required showing of probable cause for a FISA search? FISA requires a judicial finding, as the *O'Neill* case indicates, that probable cause exists to believe that the target is an agent of a foreign power. It also states that no U.S. person can be considered an agent of a foreign power based solely on First Amendment activities.

2. ***Defendants' Rights?*** In *Global Relief Foundation*, the court finds that disclosure of the information that it reviewed in deciding on the validity of the search was not to be revealed to the defendant because it "could substantially undermine ongoing investigations required to apprehend the conspirators behind the September 11 murders and undermine the ability of law enforcement agencies to reduce the possibility of terrorist crimes in the future." However, FISA requires that defendants receive notice about "any information obtained or derived from an electronic surveillance of that aggrieved person" pursuant to FISA when the government seeks to use information at trial or other official proceedings. 50 U.S.C. § 1806(c).

3. ***The Three* Keith *Categories.*** Recall the *Keith* Court's distinction between electronic surveillance in (1) criminal investigations; (2) domestic security investigations; and (3) investigations involving "activities of foreign powers and their agents." Today, ECPA regulates electronic surveillance in criminal investigations (category one above). The Foreign Intelligence Surveillance Act (FISA), as enacted in 1978, regulates electronic and other kinds of surveillance in cases involving foreign powers and their agents (category three).

   What then of the *Keith* category of "domestic security investigations" (category two)? Recall that the defendants in the underlying criminal proceeding were charged with a conspiracy to destroy government property. One of the defendants, for example, was charged with "the dynamite bombing" of a CIA office in Michigan. *Keith* makes it clear that it would be consistent with the Fourth Amendment for Congress to create different statutory requirements for issuing warrants for surveillance in cases involving domestic security. But Congress has not enacted such rules, and, as a consequence, law enforcement is required to carry out surveillance of criminal activities similar to those in *Keith* under the requirements of Title III and other parts of ECPA.

4. ***The Lone Wolf Amendment.*** The *Keith* categories and related rules remain unaltered by the "lone wolf" amendment to FISA in 2004. That year, Congress amended FISA to include any non-U.S. person who "engages in international terrorism or activities in preparation therefor" in the definition of "agent of a foreign power." The change means that the "lone wolf" terrorist need not be tied to a foreign power, but must be a non-U.S. person engaged in or plotting

"international terrorism." FISA defines "international terrorism" as involving, among other things, activities that "[o]ccur totally outside the U.S., or transcend national boundaries in terms of the means by which they accomplished, the persons they appear intended to coerce or intimidate, or the locale in which their perpetrators operate or seek asylum." 50 U.S.C. § 1801(c). As an illustration of the coverage of the "Lone Wolf" amendment, it would not cover Timothy McVeigh, the Oklahoma City bomber.

5. *A New Agency for Domestic Intelligence?* Francesca Bignami notes that in European countries, one governmental agency typically gathers intelligence on threats abroad posed by foreign governments, and another agency "is charged with gathering intelligence at home, on activities sponsored by foreign powers (counter-intelligence) as well as on home-grown security threats."[10] Both of these agencies are generally overseen not by judiciary, but by legislative and executive branches. Both intelligence agencies generally carry out surveillance under a more permissive set of legal rules than the domestic police. In contrast, in the United States, the FBI is charged with both domestic intelligence investigations and criminal investigations of violations of federal law.

Judge Richard Posner has emerged as the leading critic of the assignment of this double function to the FBI. He contends that the combination of criminal investigation and domestic intelligence at the FBI has not been successful: "If the incompatibility between the law enforcement and intelligence cultures is conceded, then it follows that an agency 100 percent dedicated to domestic intelligence would be likely to do a better job than the FBI, which is at most 20 percent intelligence and thus at least 80 percent criminal investigation and in consequence dominated by the criminal investigations."[11] Posner calls for creation of a "pure" domestic intelligence agency, one without any law enforcement responsibilities and located outside of the FBI. For Posner, the new U.S. Security Intelligence Surveillance can be modeled on the United Kingdom's MI5 or the Canadian Security Intelligence Service. What should the rules be for such a domestic intelligence agency concerning tele-communications surveillance? Should the FISA rules be applied to it?

UNITED STATES V. ISA

923 F.2d 1300 (8th Cir. 1991)

[The FBI obtained an order pursuant to FISA to bug the home of Zein Hassan Isa and his wife, Maria Matias. The FBI suspected Isa, a naturalized U.S. citizen, of being an agent of the Palestine Liberation Organization (PLO). One evening, the FBI's recording tapes of the bugged home captured Zein and Maria's murder of their 16-year-old daughter, Tina. Zein and Maria became angry at Tina's general rebelliousness and her defiance of their order not to date a particular young man. On the tape, Zein said to Tina: "Here, listen, my dear daughter, do you know that this is the last day? Tonight, you're going to die!" Tina responded in disbelief:

[10] Francesca Bignami, *European versus American Liberty*, 48 B.C. L. Rev. 609, 621 (2007).
[11] Richard A. Posner, *Uncertain Shield* 101-02 (2006).

"Huh?" Maria held Tina down while Zein stabbed her six times in the chest. While Tina screamed, Zein said: "Quiet, little one! Die my daughter, die!" The FBI turned the tapes over to the State of Missouri, where the Isas resided, where they were used to convict the Isas of murder. The Isas were sentenced to death.[12] Zein Isa argued that the recording should be suppressed because it captured events that had no relevance to the FBI's foreign intelligence gathering.]

GIBSON, J. . . . [A]ppellant argues that his fourth amendment rights were violated because the government failed to comply with the minimization procedures defined in 50 U.S.C. § 1801(h). Specifically, he contends that the tapes turned over to the State of Missouri record a "private domestic matter," which is not relevant material under the Foreign Intelligence Surveillance Act and must therefore be destroyed. In support of this argument, he cites isolated sentences regarding required minimization procedures from the legislative history of the Foreign Intelligence Surveillance Act:

> Minimization procedures might also include restrictions on the use of surveillance to times when foreign intelligence information is likely to be obtained, ... [Furthermore, a target's] communications which are clearly not relevant to his clandestine intelligence activities should be destroyed. S. Rep. No. 95-701, 95th Cong., 2d Sess. 4.

Notwithstanding the minimization procedures required by [FISA], the Act specifically authorizes the retention of information that is "evidence of a crime," 50 U.S.C. § 1801(h)(3), and provides procedures for the retention and dissemination of such information. 50 U.S.C. § 1806(b)-(f). There is no requirement that the "crime" be related to foreign intelligence. . . .

Thus, we conclude that the tapes are "evidence of crime" and that the district court correctly denied appellant's motion to suppress. 50 U.S.C. § 1801(h)(3).

NOTES & QUESTIONS

1. *Use of Information Obtained Through FISA Orders.* As the *Isa* court notes, information obtained via FISA can be used in criminal trials. However, the standard to obtain a FISA order does not require probable cause. Is it appropriate to allow the use of evidence that would ordinarily required a warrant with probable cause to obtain? On the other hand, the FISA order in *Isa* was properly obtained, and the agents unexpectedly obtained evidence of a murder. If the order is obtained properly in good faith, and evidence of a crime is unexpectedly gathered, why should it be excluded from use in a criminal prosecution?

2. *Minimization Procedures and Information Screening "Walls."* As illustrated by *Isa,* FISA allows the use of information properly obtained under FISA to be used in a criminal prosecution. What prevents the government from using the often more lax standards of FISA to gather evidence in a criminal investigation?

---

[12] The Eighth Circuit opinion contains a very meager account of the facts on this case. The facts contained in this book are taken from *Terror and Death at Home Are Caught in F.B.I. Tape,* N.Y. Times, Oct. 28, 1991, at A14.

The standards of FISA are often much less stringent than those of ECPA. Government officials would merely need to say that they are conducting "intelligence gathering" and obtain a FISA order rather than an order under ECPA — and then, if they uncover evidence of a crime, they could use it to prosecute. FISA has some built-in protections against this. For example, it requires that "the purpose" of the surveillance be foreign intelligence gathering. This language was interpreted by courts as the "primary" purpose.

FISA requires that procedures be implemented to minimize the collection, retention, and dissemination of information about U.S. persons. § 1801(h)(1). Minimization procedures are designed to prevent the broad power of "foreign intelligence gathering" from being used for routine criminal investigations. In a number of instances, however, there are overlaps between foreign intelligence gathering and criminal investigations.

One common minimization procedure is what is known as an "information screening wall." With the "wall," an official not involved in the criminal investigation must review the raw materials gathered by FISA surveillance and only pass on information that might be relevant evidence. The wall is designed to prevent criminal justice personnel from initiating or directing the FISA surveillance. The wall does not prevent the sharing of information; rather, it prevents criminal prosecutors from becoming involved in the front end of the investigation rather than on the back end.

How should terrorism investigations, which involve both intelligence gathering and the collection of evidence for criminal prosecution, fit into this scheme?

2. THE USA PATRIOT ACT

THE 9/11 COMMISSION REPORT

Excerpt from pp. 254-75 (2004)

"The System Was Blinking Red"

As 2001 began, counterterrorism officials were receiving frequent but fragmentary reports about threats. Indeed, there appeared to be possible threats almost everywhere the United States had interests — including at home. . . .

Threat reports surged in June and July, reaching an even higher peak of urgency. The summer threats seemed to be focused on Saudi Arabia, Israel, Bahrain, Kuwait, Yemen, and possibly Rome, but the danger could be anywhere — including a possible attack on the G-8 summit in Genoa. . . .

A terrorist threat advisory distributed in late June indicated a high probability of near-term "spectacular" terrorist attacks resulting in numerous casualties. Other reports' titles warned, "Bin Ladin Attacks May Be Imminent" and "Bin Ladin and Associates Making Near-Term Threats." . . .

Most of the intelligence community recognized in the summer of 2001 that the number and severity of threat reports were unprecedented. Many officials told us that they knew something terrible was planned, and they were desperate to stop it.

Despite their large number, the threats received contained few specifics regarding time, place, method, or target. . . .

["Jane," an FBI analyst assigned to the FBI's investigation of the terrorist attack on the USS *Cole*] began drafting what is known as a lead for the FBI's New York Field Office. A lead relays information from one part of the FBI to another and requests that a particular action be taken. . . . [H]er draft lead was not sent until August 28. Her email told the New York agent that she wanted him to get started as soon as possible, but she labeled the lead as "Routine" — a designation that informs the receiving office that it has 30 days to respond.

The agent who received the lead forwarded it to his squad supervisor. That same day, the supervisor forwarded the lead to an intelligence agent to open an intelligence case — an agent who thus was behind "the wall" keeping FBI intelligence information from being shared with criminal prosecutors. He also sent it to the *Cole* case agents and an agent who had spent significant time in Malaysia searching for another Khalid: Khalid Sheikh Mohammad.

The suggested goal of the investigation was to locate Mihdhar, [a member of al Qaeda and a 9/11 hijacker] determine his contacts and reasons for being in the United States, and possibly conduct an interview. Before sending the lead, "Jane" had discussed it with "John," the CIA official on detail to the FBI. . . . The discussion seems to have been limited to whether the search should be classified as an intelligence investigation or as a criminal one. It appears that no one informed higher levels of management in either the FBI or CIA about the case. . . .

One of the *Cole* case agents read the lead with interest, and contacted "Jane" to obtain more information. "Jane" argued, however, that because the agent was designated a "criminal" FBI agent, not an intelligence FBI agent, the wall kept him from participating in any search for Mihdhar. In fact, she felt he had to destroy his copy of the lead because it contained NSA information from reports that included caveats ordering that the information not be shared without OIPR's permission. The agent asked "Jane" to get an opinion from the FBI's National Security Law Unit (NSLU) on whether he could open a criminal case on Mihdhar.

"Jane" sent an email to the *Cole* case agent explaining that according to the NSLU, the case could be opened only as an intelligence matter, and that if Mihdhar was found, only designated intelligence agents could conduct or even be present at any interview. She appears to have misunderstood the complex rules that could apply to this situation.

The FBI agent angrily responded:

> Whatever has happened to this — someday someone will die — and the wall or not — the public will not understand why we were not more effective at throwing every resource we had at certain "problems." . . .

"Jane" replied that she was not making up the rules; she claimed that they were in the relevant manual and "ordered by the [FISA] Court and every office of the FBI is required to follow them including FBI NY."

It is now clear that everyone involved was confused about the rules governing the sharing and use of information gathered in intelligence channels. Because Mihdhar was being sought for his possible connection to or knowledge of the *Cole* bombing, he could be investigated or tracked under the existing *Cole* criminal case. No new criminal case was need for the criminal agent to begin searching for

Mihdhar. And as NSA had approved the passage of its information to the criminal agent, he could have conducted a search using all available information. As a result of this confusion, the criminal agents who were knowledgeable about al Qaeda and experienced with criminal investigative techniques, including finding suspects and possible criminal charges, were thus excluded from the search. . . .

We believe that if more resources had been applied and a significantly different approach taken, Mihdhar and Hazmi might have been found. They had used their true names in the United States. Still, the investigators would have needed luck as well as skill to find them prior to September 11 even if such searches had begun as early as August 23, when the lead was first drafted.

Many FBI witnesses have suggested that even if Mihdhar had been found, there was nothing the agents could have done except follow him onto the planes. We believe this is incorrect. Both Hazmi and Mihdhar could have been held for immigration violations or as material witnesses in the *Cole* bombing case. Investigation or interrogation of them, and investigation of their travel and financial activities, could have yielded evidence of connections to other participants in the 9/11 plot. The simple fact of their detention could have derailed the plan. In any case, the opportunity did not arise. . . .

On August 15, 2001, the Minneapolis FBI Field Office initiated an intelligence investigation on Zacarias Moussaoui. . . . [H]e had entered the United States in February 2001, and had begun flight lessons at Airman Flight School in Norman, Oklahoma. He resumed his training at the Pan Am International Flight Academy in Eagan, Minnesota, starting on August 13. He had none of the usual qualifications for light training on Pan Am's Boeing 747 flight simulators. He said he did not intend to become a commercial pilot but wanted the training as an "ego boosting thing." Moussaoui stood out because with little knowledge of flying, he wanted to learn to "take off and land" a Boeing 747.

The agent in Minneapolis quickly learned that Moussaoui possessed jihadist beliefs. Moreover, Moussaoui had $32,000 in a bank account but did not provide a plausible explanation for this sum of money. He traveled to Pakistan but became agitated when asked if he had traveled to nearby countries while in Pakistan. He planned to receive martial arts training, and intended to purchase a global positioning receiver. The agent also noted that Moussaoui became extremely agitated whenever he was questioned regarding his religious beliefs. The agent concluded that Moussaoui was "an Islamic extremist preparing for some future act in furtherance of radical fundamentalist goals." He also believed Moussaoui's plan was related to his flight training.

Moussaoui can be seen as an al Qaeda mistake and a missed opportunity. An apparently unreliable operative, he had fallen into the hands of the FBI. . . . If Moussaoui had been connected to al Qaeda, questions should instantly have arisen about a possible al Qaeda plot that involved piloting airliners, a possibility that had never been seriously analyzed by the intelligence community. . . .

As a French national who had overstayed his visa, Moussaoui could be detained immediately. The INS arrested Moussaoui on the immigration violation. A deportation order was signed on August 17, 2001.

The agents in Minnesota were concerned that the U.S. Attorney's office in Minneapolis would find insufficient probable cause of a crime to obtain a criminal warrant to search Moussaoui's laptop computer. Agents at FBI headquarters believed there was insufficient probable cause. Minneapolis therefore sought a special warrant under the Foreign Intelligence Surveillance Act. . . .

To do so, however, the FBI needed to demonstrate probable cause that Moussaoui was an agent of a foreign power, a demonstration that was not required to obtain a criminal warrant but was a statutory requirement for a FISA warrant. The agent did not have sufficient information to connect Moussaoui to a "foreign power," so he reached out for help, in the United States and overseas. . .

[Based on information supplied by the French government, Moussaoui was linked to a rebel leader in Chechnya.] This set off a spirited debate between the Minneapolis Field Office, FBI headquarters, and the CIA as to whether Chechen rebels . . . were sufficiently associated with a terrorist organization to constitute a "foreign power" for purposes of the FISA statute. FBI headquarters did not believe this was good enough, and its National Security Law Unit declined to submit a FISA application. . . .

Although the Minneapolis agents wanted to tell the FAA from the beginning about Moussaoui, FBI headquarters instructed Minneapolis that it could not share the more complete report the case agent had prepared for the FAA. . . .

NOTES & QUESTIONS

1. *Confusion About the Law Before 9/11.* The 9/11 Commission Report excerpted above indicated that many law enforcement officials were confused about what FISA required and how information could be shared. The 9/11 Commission Report stated that the FBI headquarters concluded that Moussaoui's association with Chechen rebels was not adequate to justify a FISA order because Chechen rebels were not "sufficiently associated with a terrorist organization to constitute a 'foreign power' for purposes of the FISA statute." Does FISA require that a foreign power involve a terrorist organization? Consider the following excerpt from a Senate Report discussing the problems with the Moussaoui investigation:

> *First,* key FBI personnel responsible for protecting our country against terrorism did not understand the law. The SSA at FBI Headquarters responsible for assembling the facts in support of the Moussaoui FISA application testified before the Committee in a closed hearing that he did not know that "probable cause" was the applicable legal standard for obtaining a FISA warrant. In addition, he did not have a clear understanding of what the probable cause standard meant. . . . In addition to not understanding the probable cause standard, the SSA's supervisor (the Unit Chief) responsible for reviewing FISA applications did not have a proper understanding of the legal definition of the "agent of a foreign power" requirement.[13]

A footnote in the report explained that the FBI agent "was under the incorrect impression that the statute required a link to an already identified or 'recognized' terrorist organization, an interpretation that the FBI and the supervisor himself admitted was incorrect."

---

[13] Senate Report No. 108-040.

According to Senator Arlen Specter (R-PA), the consequences of this misunderstanding of law were grave:

> The failure to obtain a warrant under the Foreign Intelligence Surveillance Act for Zacarias Moussaoui was a matter of enormous importance, and it is my view that if we had gotten into Zacarias Moussaoui's computer, a treasure trove of connections to Al-Qeada, in combination with the FBI report from Phoenix where the young man with Osama bin Laden's picture seeking flight training, added to [the fact that] the CIA knew about two men who turned out to be terrorist pilots on 9/11 . . . there was a veritable blueprint and 9/11 might well have been prevented. . . .
>
> [I]n a way which was really incredulous, the FBI agents didn't know the standard. They didn't know it when they were dealing with the Moussaoui case, and they didn't know it almost a year later when we had the closed-door hearing.[14]

Does this indication regarding law enforcement confusion point to a need for changes in the law, changes in FBI training, or some other action?

2. ***What Did the FISA "Wall" Require?*** Since information validly obtained pursuant to a FISA court order can be used for criminal prosecution, the FISA "wall" prevented criminal enforcement officials from directing the implementation of FISA orders. Consider the following remarks by Jamie Gorelick, who was part of the 9/11 Commission:

> At last week's hearing, Attorney General John Ashcroft, facing criticism, asserted that "the single greatest structural cause for September 11 was the wall that segregated criminal investigations and intelligence agents" and that I built that wall through a March 1995 memo. This simply is not true.
>
> First, I did not invent the "wall," which is not a wall but a set of procedures implementing a 1978 statute (the Foreign Intelligence Surveillance Act, or FISA) and federal court decisions interpreting it. In a nutshell, that law, as the courts read it, said intelligence investigators could conduct electronic surveillance in the United States against foreign targets under a more lenient standard than is required in ordinary criminal cases, but only if the "primary purpose" of the surveillance were foreign intelligence rather than a criminal prosecution.
>
> Second, according to the FISA Court of Review, it was the justice departments under Presidents Ronald Reagan and George H.W. Bush in the 1980s that began to read the statute as limiting the department's ability to obtain FISA orders if it intended to bring a criminal prosecution. . . .
>
> [N]othing in the 1995 guidelines prevented the sharing of information between criminal and intelligence investigators. Indeed, the guidelines require that FBI foreign intelligence agents share information with criminal investigators and prosecutors whenever they uncover facts suggesting that a crime has been or may be committed. . . .[15]

According to Gorelick, why was the "wall" in place? What function did it serve? What precisely did it require?

---

[14] *The USA Patriot Act in Practice: Shedding Light on the FISA Process,* S. Hearing 107-947 (Sept. 10, 2002).

[15] Jamie S. Gorelick, *The Truth About "the Wall,"* Wash. Post, Apr. 18, 2004, at B7.

3. *FISA and the USA PATRIOT Act.* Prior to the USA PATRIOT Act, FISA applied when foreign intelligence gathering was "the purpose" of the investigation. Courts interpreted "the purpose" to mean that the primary purpose of the investigation had to be foreign intelligence gathering. Criminal enforcement could be a secondary purpose, but not the primary one. The USA PATRIOT Act, § 204, changed this language to make FISA applicable when foreign intelligence gathering is "a significant purpose" of the investigation. 50 U.S.C. §§ 1804(a)(7)(B) and 1823(a)(7)(B). Why do you think that this change was made in the USA PATRIOT Act?

IN RE SEALED CASE

310 F.3d 717 (FIS Ct. Rev. 2002)

[In 2002, Attorney General John Ashcroft submitted to the FISA court new procedures for minimization, which significantly curtailed the screening walls. The procedures were reviewed by the FISA court in *In re All Matters Submitted to the Foreign Intelligence Surveillance Court* (May 17, 2002). The court expressed concern over the new procedures in light of the fact that in September 2000, the government had confessed error in about 75 FISA applications, including false statements that the targets of FISA surveillance were not under criminal investigations, that intelligence and criminal investigations were separate, and that information was not shared with FBI criminal investigators and assistant U.S. attorneys. The FISA court rejected the proposed procedures because they would allow criminal prosecutors to advise on FISA information gathering activities. The government appealed to the Foreign Intelligence Surveillance (FIS) Court of Review, which is composed of three judges on the D.C. Circuit. In 2002, the FIS Court of Review published its first and, thus far, only opinion.]

PER CURIAM. This is the first appeal from the Foreign Intelligence Surveillance Court to the Court of Review since the passage of the Foreign Intelligence Surveillance Act (FISA) in 1978. The appeal is brought by the United States from a FISA court surveillance order which imposed certain restrictions on the government. . . .

The court's decision from which the government appeals imposed certain requirements and limitations accompanying an order authorizing electronic surveillance of an "agent of a foreign power" as defined in FISA. There is no disagreement between the government and the FISA court as to the propriety of the electronic surveillance; the court found that the government had shown probable cause to believe that the target is an agent of a foreign power and otherwise met the basic requirements of FISA. . . . The FISA court authorized the surveillance, but imposed certain restrictions, which the government contends are neither mandated nor authorized by FISA. Particularly, the court ordered that law enforcement officials shall not make recommendations to intelligence officials concerning the initiation, operation, continuation or expansion of FISA searches or surveillances. Additionally, the FBI and the Criminal Division [of the Department of Justice] shall ensure that law enforcement officials do not direct or control the use of the FISA procedures to enhance criminal prosecution, and that advice intended to preserve the option of a criminal prosecution does not inadvertently result in the Criminal Division's directing or controlling the investigation using FISA searches and surveillances toward law enforcement objectives.

To ensure the Justice Department followed these strictures the court also fashioned what the government refers to as a "chaperone requirement"; that a unit of the Justice Department, the Office of Intelligence Policy and Review (OIPR) (composed of 31 lawyers and 25 support staff), "be invited" to all meetings between the FBI and the Criminal Division involving consultations for the purpose of coordinating efforts "to investigate or protect against foreign attack or other grave hostile acts, sabotage, international terrorism, or clandestine intelligence activities by foreign powers or their agents." . . .

[The FISA court opinion below] appears to proceed from the assumption that FISA constructed a barrier between counterintelligence/intelligence officials and law enforcement officers in the Executive Branch — indeed, it uses the word "wall" popularized by certain commentators (and journalists) to describe that supposed barrier.

The "wall" emerges from the court's implicit interpretation of FISA. The court apparently believes it can approve applications for electronic surveillance only if the government's objective is *not* primarily directed toward criminal prosecution of the foreign agents for their foreign intelligence activity. But the court neither refers to any FISA language supporting that view, nor does it reference the Patriot Act amendments, which the government contends specifically altered FISA to make clear that an application could be obtained even if criminal prosecution is the primary counter mechanism.

Instead the court relied for its imposition of the disputed restrictions on its statutory authority to approve "minimization procedures" designed to prevent the acquisition, retention, and dissemination within the government of material gathered in an electronic surveillance that is unnecessary to the government's need for foreign intelligence information. 50 U.S.C. § 1801(h). . . .

. . . [I]t is quite puzzling that the Justice Department, at some point during the 1980s, began to read the statute as limiting the Department's ability to obtain FISA orders if it intended to prosecute the targeted agents — even for foreign intelligence crimes. To be sure, section 1804, which sets forth the elements of an application for an order, required a national security official in the Executive Branch — typically the Director of the FBI — to certify that "the purpose" of the surveillance is to obtain foreign intelligence information (amended by the Patriot Act to read "a significant purpose"). But as the government now argues, the definition of foreign intelligence information includes evidence of crimes such as espionage, sabotage or terrorism. Indeed, it is virtually impossible to read the 1978 FISA to exclude from its purpose the prosecution of foreign intelligence crimes, most importantly because, as we have noted, the definition of an agent of a foreign power — if he or she is a U.S. person — is grounded on criminal conduct. . . .

. . . In October 2001, Congress amended FISA to change "the purpose" language in § 1804(a)(7)(B) to "a significant purpose." It also added a provision allowing "Federal officers who conduct electronic surveillance to acquire foreign intelligence information" to "consult with Federal law enforcement officers to coordinate efforts to investigate or protect against" attack or other grave hostile acts, sabotage or international terrorism, or clandestine intelligence activities, by foreign powers or their agents. 50 U.S.C. § 1806(k)(1). . . . Although the Patriot Act amendments to FISA expressly sanctioned consultation and coordination between intelligence and law enforcement officials, in response to the first applications filed by OIPR under those amendments, in November 2001, the FISA court for the first time adopted the 1995 Procedures, as augmented by the January 2000 and August 2001 Procedures, as "minimization procedures" to apply in all cases before the court.

The Attorney General interpreted the Patriot Act quite differently. On March 6, 2002, the Attorney General approved new "Intelligence Sharing Procedures" to implement the Act's amendments to FISA. The 2002 Procedures supersede prior procedures and were designed to permit the complete exchange of information and advice between intelligence and law enforcement officials. They eliminated the "direction and control" test and allowed the exchange of advice between the FBI, OIPR, and the Criminal Division regarding "the initiation, operation, continuation, or expansion of FISA searches or surveillance." . . .

Unpersuaded by the Attorney General's interpretation of the Patriot Act, the court ordered that the 2002 Procedures be adopted, *with modifications,* as minimization procedures to apply in all cases. . . .

. . . [W]hen Congress explicitly authorizes consultation and coordination between different offices in the government, without even suggesting a limitation on who is to direct and control, it necessarily implies that either could be taking the lead. . . .

That leaves us with something of an analytic conundrum. On the one hand, Congress did not amend the definition of foreign intelligence information which, we have explained, includes evidence of foreign intelligence crimes. On the other hand, Congress accepted the dichotomy between foreign intelligence and law enforcement by adopting the significant purpose test. Nevertheless, it is our task to do our best to read the statute to honor congressional intent. The better reading, it seems to us, excludes from the purpose of gaining foreign intelligence information a sole objective of criminal prosecution. We therefore reject the government's argument to the contrary. Yet this may not make much practical difference. Because, as the government points out, when it commences an electronic surveillance of a foreign agent, typically it will not have decided whether to prosecute the agent (whatever may be the subjective intent of the investigators or lawyers who initiate an investigation). So long as the government entertains a realistic option of dealing with the agent other than through criminal prosecution, it satisfies the significant purpose test.

The important point is — and here we agree with the government — the Patriot Act amendment, by using the word "significant," eliminated any justification for the FISA court to balance the relative weight the government places on criminal prosecution as compared to other counterintelligence responses. If the certification of the application's purpose articulates a broader objective than criminal prosecution — such as stopping an ongoing conspiracy — and includes other potential non-prosecutorial responses, the government meets the statutory test. Of course, if the court concluded that the government's sole objective was merely to gain evidence of past criminal conduct — even foreign intelligence crimes — to punish the agent rather than halt ongoing espionage or terrorist activity, the application should be denied. . . .

It can be argued, however, that by providing that an application is to be granted if the government has only a "significant purpose" of gaining foreign intelligence information, the Patriot Act allows the government to have a primary objective of prosecuting an agent for a non-foreign intelligence crime. Yet we think that would be an anomalous reading of the amendment. . . . That is not to deny that ordinary crimes might be inextricably intertwined with foreign intelligence crimes. For example, if a group of international terrorists were to engage in bank robberies in order to finance the manufacture of a bomb, evidence of the bank robbery should be treated just as evidence of the terrorist act itself. But the FISA process cannot be used as a device to investigate wholly unrelated ordinary crimes.

Having determined that FISA, as amended, does not oblige the government to demonstrate to the FISA court that its primary purpose in conducting electronic surveillance is *not* criminal prosecution, we are obliged to consider whether the statute as amended is consistent with the Fourth Amendment. . . . [I]n asking whether FISA procedures can be regarded as reasonable under the Fourth Amendment, we think it is instructive to compare those procedures and requirements with their Title III counterparts. Obviously, the closer those   FISA procedures are to Title III procedures, the lesser are our constitutional concerns. . . .

With limited exceptions not at issue here, both Title III and FISA require prior judicial scrutiny of an application for an order authorizing electronic surveillance. 50 U.S.C. § 1805; 18 U.S.C. § 2518. And there is no dispute that a FISA judge satisfies the Fourth Amendment's requirement of a "neutral and detached magistrate."

The statutes differ to some extent in their probable cause showings. Title III allows a court to enter an *ex parte* order authorizing electronic surveillance if it determines on the basis of the facts submitted in the government's application that "there is probable cause for belief that an individual is committing, has committed, or is about to commit" a specified predicate offense. 18 U.S.C.   § 2518(3)(a). FISA by contrast requires a showing of probable cause that the target is a foreign power or an agent of a foreign power. 50 U.S.C. § 1805(a)(3). We have noted, however, that where a U.S. person is involved, an "agent of a foreign power" is defined in terms of criminal activity. . . . FISA surveillance would not be authorized against a target engaged in purely domestic terrorism because the government would not be able to show that the target is acting for or on behalf of a foreign power. . . .

FISA's general programmatic purpose, to protect the nation against terrorists and espionage threats directed by foreign powers, has from its outset been distinguishable from "ordinary crime control." After the events of September 11, 2001, though, it is hard to imagine greater emergencies facing Americans than those experienced on that date.

We acknowledge, however, that the constitutional question presented by this case — whether Congress' disapproval of the primary purpose test is consistent with the Fourth Amendment — has no definitive jurisprudential answer.

. . . Our case may well involve the most serious threat our country faces. Even without taking into account the President's inherent constitutional authority to conduct warrantless foreign intelligence surveillance, we think the procedures and government showings required under FISA, if they do not meet the minimum Fourth Amendment warrant standards, certainly come close.

NOTES & QUESTIONS

1. *Assessing the Benefits and Problems of the "Wall."* Paul Rosenzweig argues: "Prior to the Patriot Act, a very real wall existed. . . . While information could be 'thrown over the wall' from intelligence officials to prosecutors, the decision to do so always rested with national security personnel — even though law-enforcement agents are in a better position to determine what evidence is pertinent to their case."[16]

   Consider Peter Swire:

   > The principal argument [in favor of the wall] is that criminal prosecutions should be based on the normal rules of criminal procedure, not on evidence gathered in a secret court system. The norm should be the usual constitutional protections rather than the exceptional circumstances that arise in foreign intelligence investigations. . . .

   > "[T]he wall" serves essential purposes. . . . [R]emoval of "the wall" may violate the Constitution for investigations that are primarily not for foreign intelligence purposes. At some point an investigation is so thoroughly domestic and criminal that the usual Fourth Amendment and other protections apply. . . . Second, "the wall" may be important in preventing the spread of the secret FISA system over time. As of 2002, seventy-one percent of the federal electronic surveillance orders were FISA orders rather than Title III orders. The Patriot Act reduction of safeguards in the FISA system means that this figure may climb in the future. . . .

   > . . . [E]arly in an investigation, it may be difficult or impossible for investigators to know whether the evidence will eventually be used for intelligence purposes or in an actual prosecution. For instance, imagine that a FISA wiretap is sought for a group of foreign agents who are planning a bomb attack. On these facts, there would be a strong foreign intelligence purpose, to frustrate the foreign attack. In addition, there would be a strong law enforcement basis for surveillance, to create evidence that would prove conspiracy beyond a reasonable doubt. On these facts, it would be difficult for officials to certify honestly that "the primary purpose" of the surveillance was for foreign intelligence rather than law enforcement. The honest official might say that the surveillance has a dual use — both to create actionable foreign intelligence information and to create evidence for later prosecution.

   > Faced with this possibility of dual use, the Patriot Act amendment was to require only that "a significant purpose" of the surveillance be for foreign intelligence. Under the new standard, an official could honestly affirm both a significant purpose for foreign intelligence and a likely use for law enforcement.

   Swire is troubled by the USA PATRIOT Act's changing FISA's requirement that "the purpose" of the investigation be foreign intelligence gathering to a looser requirement that "a significant purpose" of the investigation constituting foreign intelligence gathering:

---

[16] Paul Rosenzweig, *Civil Liberty and the Response to Terrorism,* 42 Duq. L. Rev. 663 (2004).

The problem with the "significant purpose" standard, however, is that it allows too much use of secret FISA surveillance for ordinary crimes. The FISCR interpreted the new statute in a broad way: "So long as the government entertains a realistic option of dealing with the agent other than through criminal prosecution, it satisfies the significant purpose test." The range of "realistic options" would seem to be so broad, however, that FISA orders could issue for an enormous range of investigations that ordinarily would be handled in the criminal system. . . . The Patriot Act amendment, as interpreted by the FISCR, thus allows the slippery slope to occur. A potentially immense range of law enforcement surveillance could shift into the secret FISA system.[17]

In lieu of the standard that "a significant purpose" of the investigation consists of foreign intelligence gathering, Swire recommends that FISA orders should be granted only if the surveillance is "sufficiently important for foreign intelligence purposes." Will Swire's proposed standard ("sufficiently important for foreign intelligence purposes") make a material difference from that of "a significant purpose"?

2. *The Constitutionality of FISA and the Protect America Act.* At the end of *In re Sealed Case,* the court concludes: "[W]e think the procedures and government showings required under FISA, if they do not meet the minimum Fourth Amendment warrant standards, certainly come close." Is coming close to meeting minimum warrant standards adequate enough to be constitutional?

Prior to the USA PATRIOT Act amendments, a few courts considered the constitutionality of FISA, with all concluding that the statute passed constitutional muster. For example, in *United States v. Duggan,* 743 F.2d 59 (2d Cir. 1984), the Second Circuit concluded that FISA did not violate the Fourth Amendment because

[p]rior to the enactment of FISA, virtually every court that had addressed the issue had concluded that the President had the inherent power to conduct warrantless electronic surveillance to collect foreign intelligence information, and that such surveillances constituted an exception to the warrant requirement of the Fourth Amendment. The Supreme Court specifically declined to address this issue in *United States v. United States District Court,* but it had made clear that the requirements of the Fourth Amendment may change when differing governmental interests are at stake, and it observed . . . that the governmental interests presented in national security investigations differ substantially from those presented in traditional criminal investigations. . . .

Against this background, Congress passed FISA to settle what it believed to be the unresolved question of the applicability of the Fourth Amendment warrant requirement to electronic surveillance for foreign intelligence purposes, and to "remove any doubt as to the lawfulness of such surveillance." . . .

We regard the procedures fashioned in FISA as a constitutionally adequate balancing of the individual's Fourth Amendment rights against the nation's need to obtain foreign intelligence information. . . .

---

[17] Peter Swire, *The System of Foreign Intelligence Surveillance Law,* 72 Geo. Wash. L. Rev. 1306, 1342, 1360-65 (2004).

In 2008, the Foreign Intelligence Surveillance Court of Review (FISCR) upheld the constitutionality of the Protect America Act (PAA) of 2007, a stopgap law enacted before the FISA Amendment Act of 2008. *In re Directives [redacted text]*, 551 F.3d 1004 (FISCR 2008). The FISCR found that the PAA, applied through the relevant directives, satisfied the Fourth Amendment's reasonableness requirements. It observed, "The more important the government's interest, the greater the intrusion that may be constitutionally tolerated under the Fourth Amendment." Moreover, the PAA and accompanying directives provide safeguards, including "targeting procedures, minimization procedures, [and] a procedure to ensure that a significant purpose of a surveillance is to obtain foreign intelligence information." It concluded that "our decision recognizes that where the government has instituted several layers of serviceable safeguards to protect individuals against unwarranted harms and to minimize incidental intrusions, its effort to protect national security should not be frustrated by the courts."

Why should different Fourth Amendment requirements exist for foreign intelligence purposes as opposed to regular domestic law enforcement? Is the distinction between foreign intelligence and domestic law enforcement tenable in light of international terrorism, where investigations often have both a foreign intelligence and domestic law enforcement purpose? Do the USA PATRIOT Act amendments affect FISA's constitutionality?

3. *After-the-Fact Reasonableness Review?* In a critique of the FISA warrant-procedure as amended by the PATRIOT Act, a Note in the *Yale Law Journal* proposes that FISA be repealed and that the United States return to use of warrantless foreign intelligence surveillance in which "targets could challenge the reasonableness of the surveillance in an adversary proceeding in an Article III court after the surveillance was complete."[18]

Do you think that the foreign intelligence context is well suited to the proposed warrantless regime? For the Note, "the possibility of after-the-fact reasonableness review of the merits of their decisions in Article III courts (in camera or note) would help guarantee careful and calm DOJ decisionmaking." Is reasonableness a sufficiently strict standard of review? Furthermore, one of the hallmarks of the Fourth Amendment's warrant procedure is before-the-fact review; law enforcement officials must seek judicial authorization *before* they conduct their search. Would after-the-fact review result in hindsight bias? Another consideration is the extent to which warrantless surveillance would allow the government to "bootstrap" an investigation — the government could undertake broad, unregulated surveillance knowing that it could lead to evidence that may be admissible in court.

4. *Stare Decisis.* Many FISA court opinions remain secret; only some opinions are released. Jack Boeglin and Julius Taranto argue that the FISA courts "should publish any opinion that they consider binding precedent."[19] This action is needed because stare decisis is inconsistent with secret opinions. They

---

[18] Nola K. Breglio, Note, *Leaving FISA Behind: The Need to Return to Warrantless Foreign Intelligence Surveillance*, 113 Yale L.J. 179, 203-04, 209, 212 (2003).

[19] Jack Boeglin & Julius Taranto, Comment, *Stare Decisis and Secret Law: On Precedent and Publication in the Foreign Intelligence Surveillance Court*, 124 Yale L.J. 2189 (2015).

argue that "Granting stare decisis value to secret opinions threatens to entrench legal precedent that has not been subject to the many direct and indirect benefits of public scrutiny." In their view, "Secrecy deprives FISA court judges of helpful external feedback from scholars, the public, and Congress." On the other hand, would the publication of all FISA court opinions harm national security by exposing sensitive security information?

5. ***The USA PATRIOT Act § 215***. Section 215 of the USA PATRIOT Act adds a new § 501 to the Foreign Intelligence Surveillance Act (FISA):

> (a)(1) The Director of the Federal Bureau of Investigation or a designee of the Director (whose rank shall be no lower than Assistant Special Agent in Charge) may make an application for an order requiring the production of any tangible things (including books, records, papers, documents, and other items) for an investigation to protect against international terrorism or clandestine intelligence activities, provided that such investigation of a United States person is not conducted solely upon the basis of activities protected by the first amendment to the Constitution.
>
> (2) An investigation conducted under this section shall —
> (A) be conducted under guidelines approved by the Attorney General under Executive Order 12333 (or a successor order); and
> (B) not be conducted of a United States person solely upon the basis of activities protected by the first amendment to the Constitution of the United States.

Applications for court orders shall be made to a judge and "shall specify that the records are sought for an authorized investigation" and "to protect against international terrorism or clandestine intelligence activities." § 501(b). This section also has a gag order:

> (d) No person shall disclose to any other person (other than those persons necessary to produce the tangible things under this section) that the Federal Bureau of Investigation has sought or obtained tangible things under this section. § 501(d).

The American Library Association (ALA) led a spirited campaign against § 215. It issued a resolution stating, in part, that

> the American Library Association encourages all librarians, library administrators, library governing bodies, and library advocates to educate their users, staff, and communities about the process for compliance with the USA PATRIOT Act and other related measures and about the dangers to individual privacy and the confidentiality of library records resulting from those measures.

In 2003, Attorney General John Ashcroft stated that § 215 had never been used to access library records. He further stated: "The fact is, with just 11,000 FBI agents and over a billion visitors to America's libraries each year, the Department of Justice has neither the staffing, the time nor the inclination to monitor the reading habits of Americans. . . . No offense to the American Library Association, but we just don't care." In 2005, the ALA revealed the results of a survey of librarians indicating a minimum of 137 formal law enforcement inquiries to library officials since 9/11, 49 of which were by federal officials and the remainder by state and local officials. The study did not indicate whether any of these were pursuant to § 215.

The National Security Agency relied on § 215 of the USA PATRIOT Act as authorization for its collection of bulk telephone metadata. The existence of this secret program was first revealed through unauthorized disclosures of classified documents by Edward Snowden, a contractor for the NSA, in June 2013. This chapter addresses the NSA's telephone records program below.

3. NATIONAL SECURITY LETTERS

Provisions in several laws permit the FBI to obtain personal information from third parties merely by making a written request in cases involving national security. No court order is required. These requests are called "National Security Letters" (NSLs).

The Stored Communications Act. ECPA's Stored Communications Act contains an NSL provision, 18 U.S.C. § 2709. This provision allows the FBI to compel communications companies (ISPs, telephone companies) to release customer records when the FBI makes a particular certification. Before the USA PATRIOT Act, the FBI had to certify that the records were "relevant to an authorized foreign counterintelligence investigation" and that "there are specific and articulable facts giving reason to believe that the person or entity to whom the information sought pertains is a foreign power or an agent of a foreign power as defined in section 101 of the Foreign Intelligence Surveillance Act of 1978 (50 U.S.C. 1801)."

Section 505 of the USA PATRIOT Act amended the National Security Letters provision of ECPA by altering what must be certified. The existing requirements regarding counterintelligence and specific and articulable facts that the target was an agent of a foreign power were deleted. The FBI now needs to certify that the records are "relevant to an authorized investigation to protect against terrorism or clandestine intelligence activities, provided that such an investigation of a United States person is not conducted solely on the basis of activities protected by the first amendment to the Constitution of the United States." 18 U.S.C. § 2709.

This provision also has a gag order:

> No wire or electronic communication service provider, or officer, employee, or agent thereof, shall disclose to any person that the Federal Bureau of Investigation has sought or obtained access to information or records under this section. § 2709(c).

Unlike § 215, Ashcroft made no statement about § 505.[20]

The Right to Financial Privacy Act. The Right to Financial Privacy Act (RFPA) also contains an NSL provision. As amended by the Patriot Act, this provision states that the FBI can obtain an individual's financial records if it "certifies in writing to the financial institution that such records are sought for

---

[20] Mark Sidel, *More Secure, Less Free?: Antiterrorism Policy and Civil Liberties After September 11*, at 14 (2004).

foreign counter intelligence purposes to protect against international terrorism or clandestine intelligence activities, provided that such an investigation of a United States person is not conducted solely upon the basis of activities protected by the first amendment to the Constitution of the United States." 12 U.S.C. § 3414(a)(5)(A). As with the Stored Communications Act NSL provision, the RFPA NSL provision contains a "gag" rule prohibiting the financial institution from disclosing the fact it received the NSL. § 3414(a)(5)(D).

The Fair Credit Reporting Act. Likewise, the Fair Credit Reporting Act provides for NSLs. Pursuant to a written FBI request, consumer reporting agencies "shall furnish to the Federal Bureau of Investigation the names and addresses of all financial institutions . . . at which a customer maintains or has maintained an account." 15 U.S.C. § 1681u(a). Consumer reporting agencies must also furnish "identifying information respecting a consumer, limited to name, address, former addresses, places of employment, or former places of employment." 15 U.S.C. § 1681u(b). To obtain a full consumer report, however, the FBI must obtain a court order ex parte. 15 U.S.C. § 1681u(c). Like the other NSL provisions, the FCRA NSL provisions restrict NSLs for investigations based "solely" upon First Amendment activities. The FCRA NSL also has a "gag" rule. 15 U.S.C. § 1681u(d).

The USA PATRIOT Reauthorization Act. In the USA PATRIOT Reauthorization Act of 2005, Congress made several amendments that affected NSLs. It explicitly provided for judicial review of NSLs. It also required a detailed examination by the DOJ's Inspector General "of the effectiveness and use, including any improper or illegal use" of NSLs. This kind of audit proved its value in March 2006 when the Inspector General issued its review of the FBI's use of NSLs. First, the Inspector General found a dramatic underreporting of NSLs. Indeed, the total number of NSL requests between 2003 and 2005 totaled at least 143,074. Of these NSLs requests, as the Inspector General found, "[t]he overwhelming majority . . . sought telephone toll billing records information, subscriber information (telephone or e-mail) or electronic communication transaction records under the ECPA NSL statute."[21]

The Inspector General also carried out a limited audit of investigative case files, and found that 22 percent of them contained at least one violation of investigative guidelines or procedures that was not reported to any of the relevant internal authorities at the FBI. Finally, the Inspector General also found over 700 instances in which the FBI obtained telephone records and subscriber information from telephone companies based on the use of a so-called "exigent letter" authority. This authority, absent from the statute, was invented by the FBI's Counterterrorism Division. Having devised this new power, the FBI did not set limits on its use, or track how it was employed. Witnesses told the Inspector General that many of these letters "were not issued in exigent circumstances, and the FBI was unable to determine which letters were sent in emergency circumstances due to inadequate recordkeeping." Indeed, "in most instances, there

---

[21] Office of the Inspector General, *A Review of the Federal Bureau of Investigations Use of National Security Letters* x-xiv (Mar. 2007).

was no documentation associating the requests with pending national security investigations."[22]

NSL Litigation. In *Doe v. Ashcroft*, 334 F. Supp. 2d 471 (S.D.N.Y. 2004), a federal district court invalidated 18 U.S.C. § 2709 (*Doe I*). It found that § 2709 violated the Fourth Amendment because, at least as applied, it barred or at least substantially deterred a judicial challenge to an NSL request. It did so by prohibiting an NSL recipient from revealing the existence of an NSL inquiry. The court also found that the "all inclusive sweep" of § 2709 violated the First Amendment as a prior-restraint and content-based restriction on sweep that was subject to strict scrutiny review. Additionally, the court found that in some instances the use of an NSL might infringe upon people's First Amendment rights. For example, suppose that the FBI uses an NSL to find out the identity of an anonymous speaker on the Internet. Does the First Amendment limit using an NSL in this manner? Does the First Amendment restriction on the NSL provisions, which prohibits NSLs for investigations based "solely" upon First Amendment activities, adequately address these potential First Amendment problems?

Shortly after *Doe I,* another district court invalidated 18 U.S.C. § 2709(c), which prevented a recipient of an NSL to disclose information about the government's action. *Doe v. Gonzales*, 386 F. Supp. 2d 66, 82 (D. Conn. 2005) (*Doe II*).

While appeals in *Doe I* and *Doe II* were pending, Congress enacted the USA PATRIOT Reauthorization Act of 2005, which made several changes to § 2709 and added several provisions concerning judicial review of NSLs, which were codified at 18 U.S.C. § 3511. Following enactment of these provisions, plaintiffs challenged the amended nondisclosure provisions of §§ 2709(c) and 3511. The same district court that issued the *Doe I* opinion then found §§ 2709(c) and 3511(b) to be facially unconstitutional. *Doe v. Gonzales*, 500 F. Supp. 2d 379 (S.D.N.Y. 2007) (*Doe III*).

The newly enacted § 3511 provided for judicial review of NSLs. As a result, the *Doe III* plaintiffs did not challenge it on Fourth Amendment grounds as in *Doe I*. Instead, they argued, and the court agreed, that the nondisclosure provisions of § 2709(c) remained an unconstitutional prior restraint and content-based restriction on speech. The court also concluded that § 3511(b) was unconstitutional under the First Amendment and the doctrine of separation of powers. Among its conclusions, the court noted that Congress in amending § 2709(c) allowed the FBI to certify on a case-by-case basis whether nondisclosure was necessary. Yet, this narrowing of the statute to reduce the possibility of unnecessary limitation of speech also means that the FBI could conceivably engage in viewpoint discrimination. As a consequence, the amended statute was a content-based restriction as well as a prior restraint on speech and, therefore, subject to strict scrutiny.

The Second Circuit modified the district court's opinion. In *Doe v. Mukasey*, 549 F.3d 861 (2008), the court found that the challenged statutes did not comply with the First Amendment, although not to the extent that the district court found. It also concluded that the lower court's ordered relief was too broad. The Second

---

[22] *Id.* at xxxviii, xxxiv.

Circuit began by construing § 2709(c) to permit a nondisclosure requirement only when senior FBI officials certify that disclosure may result in an enumerated harm that is related to "an authorized investigation to protect against international terrorism or clandestine intelligence activities." It also interpreted § 3511(b)(2) and (b)(3) as placing the burden on the Government "to show that a good reason exists to expect that disclosure of receipt of an NSL will risk an enumerated harm." Additionally, it held the relevant subsections unconstitutional to the extent that they would impose a nondisclosure requirement without placing the burden on the government to initiate judicial review of that obligation, and to the extent that judicial review would treat "a government official's certification that disclosure may endanger the national security of the United States or interfere with diplomatic relations . . . as conclusive."

More recently, the Northern District of California declared NSLs to be unconstitutional due to the statute's nondisclosure and judicial review provisions. *In re: National Security Letter*, 930 F.Supp.2d 1064 (N.D. Cali 2013) found that the nondisclosure provisions represented a significant infringement on speech regarding controversial government powers that violated the First Amendment. The restrictions on judicial review violated the First Amendment as well as separation of powers principles. Given the significant constitutional and national security issues at stake, the district court judge stayed enforcement of the court's order. This decision is now on appeal to the Ninth Circuit as *In re: National Security Letter, Under Seal v. Holder*. Although the litigation is proceeding as a sealed matter, the Ninth Circuit has ordered various litigation documents to be made public and created a website devoted to the case due to the high level of interest in it.[23]

4. INTERNAL OVERSIGHT

Judicial oversight is not the only mechanism that regulates intelligence agencies. There are also several guidelines, internal governance structures and processes, privacy officials, and oversight boards that regulate the activities of various intelligence agencies.

(a) The Attorney General's FBI Guidelines

Unlike many government agencies, the FBI was not created by Congress through a statute. In 1907, Attorney General Charles Bonaparte requested that Congress authorize him to create a national detective force in the Department of Justice (DOJ). The DOJ had been using investigators from the Secret Service, but Bonaparte wanted a permanent force. Congress rejected his request due to concerns over this small group developing into a secret police system. Nevertheless, Bonaparte went ahead with his plans and formed a new subdivision of the DOJ, called the "Bureau of Investigation." President Theodore Roosevelt later authorized the subdivision through an executive order in 1908. J. Edgar

---

[23] *In re: National Security Letter, Under Seal v. Holder (Sealed)*, at http://www.ca9.uscourts.gov/content/view.php?pk_id=0000000715.

Hoover began running the Bureau, which was renamed the Federal Bureau of Investigation in 1935.[24]

The FBI grew at a great pace. In 1933, the FBI had 353 agents and 422 support staff; in 1945, it had 4,380 agents and 7,422 support staff.[25] Today, the FBI has 11,000 agents and 16,000 support staff, as well as 56 field offices, 400 satellite offices, and 40 foreign liaison posts.[26]

FBI surveillance activities are regulated through the U.S. Constitution and electronic surveillance laws, as well as by guidelines promulgated by the Attorney General. In 1976, responding to Hoover's abuses of power, Attorney General Edward Levi established guidelines to control FBI surveillance activities.[27] As William Banks and M.E. Bowman observe:

> The most pertinent Levi Guidelines focused on freedom of speech and freedom of the press. First, investigations based solely on unpopular speech, where there is no threat of violence, were prohibited. Second, techniques designed to disrupt organizations engaged in protected First Amendment activity, or to discredit individuals would not be used in any circumstance.
>
> At the same time, Attorney General Levi emphasized that the Guidelines were intended to permit domestic security investigations where the activities under investigation "involve or will involve the use of force or violence and the violation of criminal law." . . .
>
> On March 7, 1983, Attorney General William French Smith revised the Guidelines regarding domestic security investigations. . . .
>
> The Smith Guidelines were intended to increase the investigative avenues available to the FBI in domestic terrorism cases. Where the Levi/Civiletti Guidelines had established a predicate investigative standard of "specific and articulable facts," the Smith version lowered the threshold to require only a "reasonable indication" as the legal standard for opening a "full" investigation. . . . The "reasonable indication" standard is significantly lower than the Fourth Amendment standard of probable cause required in law enforcement. To balance the lowered threshold for opening an investigation, Attorney General Smith emphasized that investigations would be regulated and would "not be based solely on activities protected by the First Amendment or the lawful exercise of other rights secured by the Constitution."
>
> Nonetheless, the Smith Guidelines authorized FBI Headquarters to approve the use of informants to infiltrate a group "in a manner that may influence the exercise of rights protected by the First Amendment." The Smith Guidelines also stated: "In the absence of any information indicating planned violence by a group or enterprise, mere speculation that force or violence might occur during the course of an otherwise peaceable demonstration is not sufficient grounds for initiation of an investigation." . . .
>
> According to the criminal guidelines, a full investigation may be opened where there is "reasonable indication" that two or more persons are engaged in an enterprise for the purpose of furthering political or social goals wholly or in part

---

[24] Curt Gentry, *J. Edgar Hoover: The Man and the* Secrets 111-13 (1991).

[25] Ronald Kessler, *The Bureau: The Secret History of the FBI* 57 (2002).

[26] Federal Bureau of Investigation, Frequently Asked Questions, http://www.fbi.gov/aboutus/faqs/faqsone.html (Dec. 4, 2003).

[27] *See* United States Attorney General Guidelines on Domestic Security Investigation (1976).

through activities that involve force or violence and are a violation of the criminal laws of the United States. . . .

In order to determine whether an investigation should be opened, the FBI must also take into consideration the magnitude of the threat, the likelihood that the threat will come to fruition, and the immediacy of the jeopardy. In addition to physical danger, the FBI must consider the danger to privacy and free expression posed by an investigation. For example, unless there is a reasonable indication that force or violence might occur during the course of a demonstration, initiation of an investigation is not appropriate. . . .[28]

In 2002, Attorney General John Ashcroft issued revised FBI guidelines. Whereas under the preexisting guidelines, the FBI could engage in surveillance of public political activity and search the Internet when "facts or circumstances reasonably indicate that a federal crime has been, is being, or will be committed,"[29] Ashcroft's guidelines eliminate this requirement. The FBI is permitted to gather "publicly available information, whether obtained directly or through services or resources (whether nonprofit or commercial) that compile or analyze such information; and information voluntarily provided by private entities." The FBI can also "carry out general topical research, including conducting online searches and accessing online sites and forums."[30]

Daniel Solove argues that Congress should pass a legislative charter to regulate the FBI:

> . . . [E]xecutive orders and guidelines can all be changed by executive fiat, as demonstrated by Ashcroft's substantial revision to the guidelines in 2002. Moreover, the Attorney General Guidelines are not judicially enforceable. The problem with the current system is that it relies extensively on self-regulation by the executive branch. Much of this regulation has been effective, but it can too readily be changed in times of crisis without debate or discussion. Codifying the internal executive regulations of the FBI would also allow for public input into the process. The FBI is a very powerful arm of the executive branch, and if we believe in separation of powers, then it is imperative that the legislative branch, not the executive alone, become involved in the regulation of the FBI. The guidelines should be judicially enforceable to ensure that they are strictly followed.[31]

Should other government security agencies have more oversight? Does Solove overlook the FBI's internal administrative processes that serve to limit its power?

(b) The Homeland Security Act

In 2002, Congress passed the Homeland Security Act, 6 U.S.C. § 222, which consolidated 22 federal agencies into the Department of Homeland Security (DHS). Agencies and other major components at the DHS include the

---

[28] William C. Banks & M.E. Bowman, *Executive Authority for National Security Surveillance,* 50 Am. U. L. Rev. 1, 69-74 (2000).

[29] The Attorney General's Guidelines on General Crimes, Racketeering Enterprise and Domestic Security/Terrorism Investigations § II.C.1 (Mar. 21, 1989).

[30] The Attorney General's Guidelines on General Crimes, Racketeering Enterprise and Terrorism Enterprise Investigations § VI (May 30, 2002).

[31] Daniel J. Solove, *Reconstructing Electronic Surveillance Law,* 72 Geo. Wash. L. Rev. 1264, 1304 (2004).

Transportation Security Administration, Customs and Border Protection, Federal Emergency Management Agency, U.S. Citizenship and Immigration Services, U.S. Coast Guard, and U.S. Secret Service. The Office of the Secretary of DHS includes the Office of the Chief Privacy Officer, the Office of Civil Rights and Civil Liberties, the Office of Counter Narcotics, and the Office of State and Local Government Coordination.

Among other things, the Act creates a Privacy Office. 6 U.S.C. § 222. The Secretary must "appoint a senior official to assume primary responsibility for privacy policy." The privacy official's responsibilities include ensuring compliance with the Privacy Act of 1974; evaluating "legislative and regulatory proposals involving the collection, use, and disclosure of personal information by the Federal Government"; and preparing an annual report to Congress.

(c) The Intelligence Reform and Terrorism Prevention Act

Information Sharing and Institutional Culture. The 9/11 Commission found that in addition to the legal restrictions on sharing of foreign intelligence information, limitations in the FBI's institutional culture as well as technology had also prevented the circulation of data. In its final report, the 9/11 Commission stated: "The importance of integrated, all-source analysis cannot be overstated. Without it, it is not possible to 'connect the dots.' "[32] The 9/11 Commission called for a restructuring of the United States Intelligence Community (USIC) through creation of a National Intelligence Director to oversee this process.

In an Executive Order of August 27, 2004, President Bush required executive branch agencies to establish an environment to facilitate sharing of terrorism information.[33] Responding to the 9/11 Commission Report, Congress passed the Intelligence Reform and Terrorism Prevention Act of 2004 (IRPTA), codifying the requirements in Bush's Executive Order. The Act mandates that intelligence be "provided in its most shareable form" that the heads of intelligence agencies and federal departments "promote a culture of information sharing."

The Long and Winding Road: The Creation of the Privacy and Civil Liberties Oversight Board. The IRTPA seeks to establish protection of privacy and civil liberties by setting up a five-member Privacy and Civil Liberties Oversight Board (PCLOB). The Board gives advice to the President and agencies of the executive branch and provides an annual report of activities to Congress. Among its oversight activities, the Board is to review whether "the information sharing practices of the departments, agencies, and elements of the executive branch . . . appropriately protect privacy and civil liberties." The Board is also to "ensure that privacy and civil liberties are appropriately considered in the development and implementation of . . . regulations and executive branch policies." Regarding FISA surveillance, IRTPA mandates that the Attorney General provide more detailed reporting to Congress on governmental surveillance practices and the government's legal interpretations of FISA.

---

[32] The 9/11 Commission Report 408 (2004).

[33] Exec. Order No. 13356, 69 Fed. Reg. 53,599, 53,600-01 (Sept. 1, 2004).

The Privacy and Civil Liberties Board has been the subject of controversy. A year after its creation, in February 2006, the Board still had not met a single time. When the Board issued its first annual report in May 2007, it led to the resignation of Lanny Davis, the Board's only Democratic member. The Bush Administration made more than 200 revisions to the report. The White House defending the actions as "standard operating procedure," and stated that it was appropriate because the board was legally under the President's supervision. In his resignation letter, Davis contested "the extensive redlining of the board's report to Congress by administration officials and the majority of the Board's willingness to accept most [of the edits.]"

Later that year, Congress enacted legislation to strengthen the independence and authority of the Board. It is now an "independent agency" located within the executive branch. No more than three members of the same political party can be appointed to the Board, and the Senate is to confirm all appointments to it. As before, however, the Board cannot issue subpoenas itself. Rather, a majority of Board members have the power to ask the Attorney General to issue a subpoena.[34]

Finally, in August 2012, the Senate confirmed the Board's four part-time members. The Senate confirmed David Medine, the Board's chairman and its only full-time member, in late May 2013. The timing was auspicious as it was five days before news stories began to appear based on Edward Snowden's leaked NSA documents. PCLOB has now issued semi-annual reports to Congress summarizing its initial activities as well as detailed studies of the NSA's telephone records program conduction under Section 214 of the PATRIOT Act and the NSA's surveillance program under Section 702 of the Foreign Intelligence Surveillance Act.[35] We discuss both NSA programs and the PCLOB reports below.

D. NSA SURVEILLANCE

In December 2005, a front page article in the *New York Times* first revealed that the National Security Agency (NSA) was intercepting communications where one party was located outside the United States and another party inside the United States.[36] The Bush Administration named this surveillance program the "Terrorist Surveillance Program" (TSP).

Created in 1952, the NSA collects and analyzes foreign communications. As Frederick Schwarz and Aziz Huq explain, "The NSA collects signals intelligence from telegrams, telephones, faxes, e-mails, and other electronic communications, and then disseminates this information among other agencies of the executive

---

[34] Ronald D. Lee & Paul M. Schwartz, *Beyond the "War on Terrorism": Towards the New Intelligence Network*, 103 Mich. L. Rev. 1446 (2005).

[35] PCLOB, *Report on the Surveillance Program Operated Pursuant to Section 702 of the Foreign Intelligence Surveillance Act* (July 2, 2014); PCLOB, *Report on the Telephone Records Program Conducted under Section 215 of the USA PATRIOT Act and on the Operations of the Foreign Intelligence Surveillance Court* (Jan. 23, 2014).

[36] James Risen & Eric Lichtblau, *Bush Lets U.S. Spy on Callers Without Courts*, N.Y. Times, Dec. 16. 2005, at A1.

branch."[37] Schwarz and Huq also point out that the Church Committee investigation in 1975-76 found that "the NSA had not exercised its vast power with restraint or due regard for the Constitution." In the past, the NSA had engaged in activities such as collecting every international telegram sent from the United States and maintaining watch lists of U.S. citizens involved in political protests.

After 9/11, the NSA again began secret surveillance activities within the United States. Although the Bush Administration has discussed aspects of the NSA surveillance of telecommunications, the complete dimensions of the NSA activities remain unknown. And while the Department of Justice has issued a white paper justifying these activities,[38] the legal opinions said to declare the program lawful are secret.

Several lawsuits ensued, challenging the legality of the NSA surveillance. Some of these cases were brought against telecommunications companies that cooperated with the NSA in conducting the surveillance. Plaintiffs alleged that these companies violated FISA and ECPA.

Early in 2007, a secret FISC decision denied permission for certain NSA surveillance activities. The FISC judgment was said to concern a NSA request for a so-called "basket warrant," under which warrants are issued not on a case-by-case basis for specific suspects, but more generally for surveillance activity involving multiple targets. One anonymous official was quoted as saying that the FISC ruling concerned cases "where one end is foreign and you don't know where the other is."[39] The Administration leaked information about this ruling and argued that it impeded the government's ability to investigate threats of imminent terrorist attacks.

In the summer of 2007, Congress enacted the Protect America Act to authorize the NSA surveillance program.[40] This statute was subject to sunset in 120 days, and it expired without Congress enacting a new law or renewing it.[41] At that point, without the Protect America Act's amendments, the original FISA once again took effect, until Congress enacted FAA in July 2008.

A major roadblock to amending FISA had been the subject of immunity for the telecommunications companies that participated or participate in TSP or similar programs. President Bush stated that telecommunications immunity was needed to provide "meaningful liability protection to those who are alleged to have assisted our nation following the attacks of September 11, 2001." FISA already did contain immunity provisions, and this language was in effect at the time that the TSP began. *See* 18 U.S.C. § 2511(2)(a)(ii). The cooperation of the

---

[37] Frederick A.O. Schwarz Jr. & Aziz Z. Huq, *Unchecked and Unbalanced: Presidential Power in a Time of Terror* 127 (2007).

[38] United States Department of Justice, *Legal Authorities Supporting the Activities of the National Security Agency Described by the President* (Jan. 19, 2006).

[39] Greg Miller, *Court Puts Limits on Surveillance Abroad*, L.A. Times, Aug. 2, 2007.

[40] The Protect America Act created an exception to FISA's requirements. The exception was found in the statute's § 105A. This part of the law exempted all communications "directed at" people outside of the United States from FISA's definition of "electronic surveillance." Once a communication fell within § 105A, the government could carry it out subject to § 105B and its requirements — rather than FISA and its obligation to seek a warrant from the FISC.

[41] As discussed above, the Foreign Intelligence Surveillance Court of Review upheld the constitutionality of the PAA. *In re Directives [redacted text]*, 551 F.3d 1004 (FISCR 2008).

telecommunication companies with the NSA must have been outside the existing safe harbor language.

The FAA of 2008, discussed earlier in this chapter, establishes new rules for at least some of this NSA behavior. Title II of the FAA raises a new challenge to the litigation against the NSA behavior prior to its enactments — it provides statutory defenses for the telecommunications companies that assisted the NSA. Specifically, the FAA prohibits "a civil action" against anyone "for providing assistance to an element of the intelligence community" in connection "with an intelligence activity involving communications" following a specific kind of certification by the Attorney General. § 802. The certification in question requires a determination that the assistance was (1) authorized by the President during the period beginning on September 11, 2001 and ending on January 17, 2007; (2) designed to detect or prevent a terrorist attack; and (3) the subject of a written request from the Attorney General or the head of the intelligence community. A court presented with such a certificate is to review it for the support of "substantial evidence."

As noted above, the FAA of 2008 added a new provision, Section 702, to FISA, which permits the Attorney General and the Director of National Intelligence to jointly authorize surveillance conducted within the U.S. but targeting only non-U.S. persons reasonably believed to be located outside of the U.S. In *Clapper v. Amnesty International USA*, the Supreme Court deciding a standing issue that determined whether a challenge against Section 702 could be brought by "attorneys and human rights, labor, legal, and media organizations whose work allegedly requires them to engage in sensitive and sometimes privileged telephone and e-mail communications with colleagues, clients, sources, and other individuals located abroad."

1. STANDING

CLAPPER V. AMNESTY INTERNATIONAL USA
133 S. Ct. 1138 (2013)

ALITO, J. . . . Section 702 of the Foreign Intelligence Surveillance Act of 1978, 50 U.S.C. § 1881a, allows the Attorney General and the Director of National Intelligence to acquire foreign intelligence information by jointly authorizing the surveillance of individuals who are not "United States persons"[42] and are reasonably believed to be located outside the United States. Before doing so, the Attorney General and the Director of National Intelligence normally must obtain the Foreign Intelligence Surveillance Court's approval. Respondents are United States persons whose work, they allege, requires them to engage in sensitive international communications with individuals who they believe are likely targets of surveillance under § 1881a. Respondents seek a declaration that § 1881a is unconstitutional, as well as an injunction against §1881a-authorized surveillance.

---

42 The term "United States person" includes citizens of the United States, aliens admitted for permanent residence, and certain associations and corporations. 50 U.S.C. § 1801(i); see § 1881(a).

The question before us is whether respondents have Article III standing to seek this prospective relief.

Respondents assert that they can establish injury in fact because there is an objectively reasonable likelihood that their communications will be acquired under § 1881a at some point in the future. But respondents' theory of *future* injury is too speculative to satisfy the well-established requirement that threatened injury must be "certainly impending." And even if respondents could demonstrate that the threatened injury is certainly impending, they still would not be able to establish that this injury is fairly traceable to § 1881a. As an alternative argument, respondents contend that they are suffering *present* injury because the risk of § 1881a-authorized surveillance already has forced them to take costly and burdensome measures to protect the confidentiality of their international communications. But respondents cannot manufacture standing by choosing to make expenditures based on hypothetical future harm that is not certainly impending. We therefore hold that respondents lack Article III standing.. . .

In 1978, after years of debate, Congress enacted the Foreign Intelligence Surveillance Act (FISA) to authorize and regulate certain governmental electronic surveillance of communications for foreign intelligence purposes. In enacting FISA, Congress legislated against the backdrop of our decision in *United States v. United States Dist. Court for Eastern Dist. of Mich.,* 407 U.S. 297 (1972) (*Keith*), in which we explained that the standards and procedures that law enforcement officials must follow when conducting "surveillance of 'ordinary crime' " might not be required in the context of surveillance conducted for domestic national-security purposes.

When Congress enacted the FISA Amendments Act of 2008 (FISA Amendments Act), it left much of FISA intact, but it "established a new and independent source of intelligence collection authority, beyond that granted in traditional FISA." As relevant here, § 702 of FISA, 50 U.S.C. § 1881a, which was enacted as part of the FISA Amendments Act, supplements pre-existing FISA authority by creating a new framework under which the Government may seek the FISC's authorization of certain foreign intelligence surveillance targeting the communications of non-U.S. persons located abroad. Unlike traditional FISA surveillance, § 1881a does not require the Government to demonstrate probable cause that the target of the electronic surveillance is a foreign power or agent of a foreign power. And, unlike traditional FISA, § 1881a does not require the Government to specify the nature and location of each of the particular facilities or places at which the electronic surveillance will occur.

The present case involves a constitutional challenge to § 1881a. . . .

Respondents are attorneys and human rights, labor, legal, and media organizations whose work allegedly requires them to engage in sensitive and sometimes privileged telephone and e-mail communications with colleagues, clients, sources, and other individuals located abroad. Respondents believe that some of the people with whom they exchange foreign intelligence information are likely targets of surveillance under § 1881a. Specifically, respondents claim that they communicate by telephone and e-mail with people the Government "believes or believed to be associated with terrorist organizations," "people located in geographic areas that are a special focus" of the Government's counterterrorism or

~~diplomatic efforts, and activists who oppose~~ governments that are supported by the United States Government.

Respondents claim that § 1881a compromises their ability to locate witnesses, cultivate sources, obtain information, and communicate confidential information to their clients. Respondents also assert that they "have ceased engaging" in certain telephone and e-mail conversations. According to respondents, the threat of surveillance will compel them to travel abroad in order to have in-person conversations. In addition, respondents declare that they have undertaken "costly and burdensome measures" to protect the confidentiality of sensitive communications. . . .

Article III of the Constitution limits federal courts' jurisdiction to certain "Cases" and "Controversies." As we have explained, "[n]o principle is more fundamental to the judiciary's proper role in our system of government than the constitutional limitation of federal-court jurisdiction to actual cases or controversies." *DaimlerChrysler Corp. v. Cuno,* 547 U.S. 332 (2006) (internal quotation marks omitted). "One element of the case-or-controversy requirement" is that plaintiffs "must establish that they have standing to sue."

The law of Article III standing, which is built on separation-of-powers principles, serves to prevent the judicial process from being used to usurp the powers of the political branches. . . .

To establish Article III standing, an injury must be "concrete, particularized, and actual or imminent; fairly traceable to the challenged action; and redressable by a favorable ruling." *Monsanto Co. v. Geertson Seed Farms,* 561 U.S. 139 (2010). . . . Thus, we have repeatedly reiterated that "threatened injury must be *certainly impending* to constitute injury in fact," and that "[a]llegations of *possible* future injury" are not sufficient. . . .

Respondents assert that they can establish injury in fact that is fairly traceable to § 1881a because there is an objectively reasonable likelihood that their communications with their foreign contacts will be intercepted under § 1881a at some point in the future. This argument fails. [R]espondents' argument rests on their highly speculative fear that: (1) the Government will decide to target the communications of non-U.S. persons with whom they communicate; (2) in doing so, the Government will choose to invoke its authority under § 1881a rather than utilizing another method of surveillance; (3) the Article III judges who serve on the Foreign Intelligence Surveillance Court will conclude that the Government's proposed surveillance procedures satisfy § 1881a's many safeguards and are consistent with the Fourth Amendment; (4) the Government will succeed in intercepting the communications of respondents' contacts; and (5) respondents will be parties to the particular communications that the Government intercepts.

First, it is speculative whether the Government will imminently target communications to which respondents are parties. Section 1881a expressly provides that respondents, who are U.S. persons, cannot be targeted for surveillance under § 1881a. See § 1881a(b)(1)–(3). Accordingly, it is no surprise that respondents fail to offer any evidence that their communications have been monitored under § 1881a, a failure that substantially undermines their standing theory. Indeed, respondents do not even allege that the Government has sought the FISC's approval for surveillance of their communications. Accordingly, respondents' theory necessarily rests on their assertion that the Government will target *other individuals*—namely, their foreign contacts.

Yet respondents have no actual knowledge of the Government's §1881a targeting practices. Instead, respondents merely speculate and make assumptions about whether their communications with their foreign contacts will be acquired under §1881a. . . . Moreover, because §1881a at most *authorizes*—but does not *mandate* or *direct*—the surveillance that respondents fear, respondents' allegations are necessarily conjectural. Simply put, respondents can only speculate as to how the Attorney General and the Director of National Intelligence will exercise their discretion in determining which communications to target.

Second, even if respondents could demonstrate that the targeting of their foreign contacts is imminent, respondents can only speculate as to whether the Government will seek to use §1881a-authorized surveillance (rather than other methods) to do so. The Government has numerous other methods of conducting surveillance, none of which is challenged here. . . .

Third, even if respondents could show that the Government will seek the Foreign Intelligence Surveillance Court's authorization to acquire the communications of respondents' foreign contacts under § 1881a, respondents can only speculate as to whether that court will authorize such surveillance. . . .

Fourth, even if the Government were to obtain the Foreign Intelligence Surveillance Court's approval to target respondents' foreign contacts under § 1881a, it is unclear whether the Government would succeed in acquiring the communications of respondents' foreign contacts. And fifth, even if the Government were to conduct surveillance of respondents' foreign contacts, respondents can only speculate as to whether *their own communications* with their foreign contacts would be incidentally acquired.

In sum, respondents' speculative chain of possibilities does not establish that injury based on potential future surveillance is certainly impending or is fairly traceable to §1881a. . . .

Respondents' alternative argument—namely, that they can establish standing based on the measures that they have undertaken to avoid § 1881a-authorized surveillance—fares no better. Respondents assert that they are suffering ongoing injuries that are fairly traceable to § 1881a because the risk of surveillance under § 1881a requires them to take costly and burdensome measures to protect the confidentiality of their communications. Respondents claim, for instance, that the threat of surveillance sometimes compels them to avoid certain e-mail and phone conversations, to "tal[k] in generalities rather than specifics," or to travel so that they can have in-person conversations. . . .

Respondents' contention that they have standing because they incurred certain costs as a reasonable reaction to a risk of harm is unavailing—because the harm respondents seek to avoid is not certainly impending. In other words, respondents cannot manufacture standing merely by inflicting harm on themselves based on their fears of hypothetical future harm that is not certainly impending. . . .

Respondents also suggest that they should be held to have standing because otherwise the constitutionality of § 1881a could not be challenged.

. . .[O]ur holding today by no means insulates § 1881a from judicial review. As described above, Congress created a comprehensive scheme in which the Foreign Intelligence Surveillance Court evaluates the Government's certifications, targeting procedures, and minimization procedures—including assessing whether the targeting and minimization procedures comport with the Fourth Amendment. § 1881a(a), (c)(1), (i)(2), (i)(3). Any dissatisfaction that respondents may have about the Foreign Intelligence Surveillance Court's rulings—or the congressional delineation of that court's role—is irrelevant to our standing analysis.

Additionally, if the Government intends to use or disclose information obtained or derived from a § 1881a acquisition in judicial or administrative proceedings, it must provide advance notice of its intent, and the affected person may challenge the lawfulness of the acquisition. §§ 1806(c), 1806(e), 1881e(a). . . .

Finally, any electronic communications service provider that the Government directs to assist in § 1881a surveillance may challenge the lawfulness of that directive before the FISC. § 1881a(h)(4), (6).

We hold that respondents lack Article III standing because they cannot demonstrate that the future injury they purportedly fear is certainly impending and because they cannot manufacture standing by incurring costs in anticipation of non-imminent harm. We therefore reverse the judgment of the Second Circuit and remand the case for further proceedings consistent with this opinion.

BREYER, J. joined by GINSBURG, SOTOMAYOR, and KAGAN, JJ. dissenting. The plaintiffs' standing depends upon the likelihood that the Government, acting under the authority of 50 U.S.C. § 1881a will harm them by intercepting at least some of their private, foreign, telephone, or e-mail conversations. In my view, this harm is not "speculative." Indeed it is as likely to take place as are most future events that commonsense inference and ordinary knowledge of human nature tell us will happen. This Court has often found the occurrence of similar future events sufficiently certain to support standing. I dissent from the Court's contrary conclusion. . . .

. . . No one here denies that the Government's interception of a private telephone or e-mail conversation amounts to an injury that is "concrete and particularized." Moreover, the plaintiffs, respondents here, seek as relief a judgment declaring unconstitutional (and enjoining enforcement of) a statutory provision authorizing those interceptions; and, such a judgment would redress the injury by preventing it. Thus, the basic question is whether the injury, *i.e.,* the interception, is "actual or imminent."

Since the plaintiffs fear interceptions of a kind authorized by § 1881a, it is important to understand just what kind of surveillance that section authorizes. Congress enacted § 1881a in 2008, as an amendment to the pre-existing Foreign Intelligence Surveillance Act of 1978, 50 U.S.C. § 1801 *et seq.* Before the amendment, the Act authorized the Government (acting within the United States) to monitor private electronic communications between the United States and a foreign country if (1) the Government's purpose was, in significant part, to obtain foreign intelligence information (which includes information concerning a "foreign power" or "territory" related to our "national defense" or "security" or the "conduct of ... foreign affairs"), (2) the Government's surveillance target was "a foreign power or an agent of a foreign power," and (3) the Government used surveillance procedures designed to "minimize the acquisition and retention, and prohibit the dissemination, of" any private information acquired about Americans. §§ 1801(e), (h), 1804(a).

In addition the Government had to obtain the approval of the Foreign Intelligence Surveillance Court. To do so, it had to submit an application describing (1) each "specific target," (2) the "nature of the information sought," and (3) the "type of communications or activities to be subjected to the surveillance." § 1804(a). It had to certify that, in significant part, it sought to obtain foreign intelligence information. *Ibid.* It had to demonstrate probable cause to believe that each specific target was "a foreign power or an agent of a foreign power." §§ 1804(a), 1805(a). It also had to describe instance-specific procedures to be used to minimize intrusions upon Americans' privacy (compliance with which the court subsequently could assess). §§ 1804(a), 1805(d)(3).

The addition of § 1881a in 2008 changed this prior law in three important ways. First, it eliminated the requirement that the Government describe to the court each specific target and identify each facility at which its surveillance would be directed, thus permitting surveillance on a programmatic, not necessarily individualized, basis. § 1881a(g). Second, it eliminated the requirement that a target be a "foreign power or an agent of a foreign power." *Ibid.* Third, it diminished the court's authority to insist upon, and eliminated its authority to supervise, instance-specific privacy-intrusion minimization procedures (though the Government still must use court-approved general minimization procedures). § 1881a(e). Thus, using the authority of § 1881a, the Government can obtain court approval for its surveillance of electronic communications between places within the United States and targets in foreign territories by showing the court (1) that "a significant purpose of the acquisition is to obtain foreign intelligence information," and (2) that it will use general targeting and privacy-intrusion minimization procedures of a kind that the court had previously approved. § 1881a(g).

Several considerations, based upon the record along with commonsense inferences, convince me that there is a very high likelihood that Government, *acting under the authority of § 1881a,* will intercept at least some of the communications just described. First, the plaintiffs have engaged, and continue to engage, in electronic communications of a kind that the 2008 amendment, but not the prior Act, authorizes the Government to intercept. These communications include discussions with family members of those detained at Guantanamo, friends and acquaintances of those persons, and investigators, experts and others with knowledge of circumstances related to terrorist activities. These persons are foreigners located outside the United States. They are not "foreign power[s]" or "agent[s] of ... foreign power [s]." And the plaintiffs state that they exchange with these persons "foreign intelligence information," defined to include information that "relates to" "international terrorism" and "the national defense or the security of the United States." See 50 U.S.C. § 1801.

Second, the plaintiffs have a strong *motive* to engage in, and the Government has a strong *motive* to listen to, conversations of the kind described. A lawyer representing a client normally seeks to learn the circumstances surrounding the crime (or the civil wrong) of which the client is accused. . . . .Journalists and human rights workers have strong similar motives to conduct conversations of this kind.

At the same time, the Government has a strong motive to conduct surveillance of conversations that contain material of this kind. The Government, after all, seeks to learn as much as it can reasonably learn about suspected terrorists (such as those detained at Guantanamo), as well as about their contacts and activities, along with those of friends and family members. And the Government is motivated to do so, not simply by the desire to help convict those whom the Government believes guilty, but also by the critical, overriding need to protect America from terrorism.

Third, the Government's *past behavior* shows that it has sought, and hence will in all likelihood continue to seek, information about alleged terrorists and detainees through means that include surveillance of electronic communications. As just pointed out, plaintiff Scott McKay states that the Government (under the authority of the pre-2008 law) "intercepted some 10,000 telephone calls and 20,000 email communications involving [his client] Mr. Al-Hussayen."

Fourth, the Government has the *capacity* to conduct electronic surveillance of the kind at issue. To some degree this capacity rests upon technology available to the Government. See 1 D. Kris & J. Wilson, National Security Investigations & Prosecutions § 16:6, p. 562 (2d ed. 2012) ("NSA's technological abilities are legendary"); *id.,* § 16:12, at 572-577 (describing the National Security Agency's capacity to monitor "*very* broad facilities" such as international switches). . . .

Of course, to exercise this capacity the Government must have intelligence court authorization. But the Government rarely files requests that fail to meet the statutory criteria. As the intelligence court itself has stated, its review under § 1881a is "narrowly circumscribed." In re Proceedings Required by § 702(i) of the FISA Amendments Act of 2008, No. Misc. 08-01 (Aug. 17, 2008). There is no reason to believe that the communications described would all fail to meet the conditions necessary for approval. Moreover, compared with prior law, § 1881a simplifies and thus expedites the approval process, making it more likely that the Government will use § 1881a to obtain the necessary approval.

The upshot is that (1) similarity of content, (2) strong motives, (3) prior behavior, and (4) capacity all point to a very strong likelihood that the Government will intercept at least some of the plaintiffs' communications, including some that the 2008 amendment, § 1881a, but not the pre–2008 Act, authorizes the Government to intercept.

At the same time, nothing suggests the presence of some special factor here that might support a contrary conclusion. . . . One can, of course, always imagine some special circumstance that negates a virtual likelihood, no matter how strong. But the same is true about most, if not all, ordinary inferences about future events. Perhaps, despite pouring rain, the streets will remain dry (due to the presence of a special chemical). But ordinarily a party that seeks to defeat a strong natural inference must bear the burden of showing that some such special circumstance exists. And no one has suggested any such special circumstance here. . . .

The majority more plausibly says that the plaintiffs have failed to show that the threatened harm is "*certainly impending*." But . . . certainty is not, and never has been, the touchstone of standing. The future is inherently uncertain. Yet federal courts frequently entertain actions for injunctions and for declaratory relief aimed at preventing future activities that are reasonably likely or highly likely, but not absolutely certain, to take place. And that degree of certainty is all that is needed to support standing here.

The Court's use of the term "certainly impending" is not to the contrary. Sometimes the Court has used the phrase "certainly impending" as if the phrase described a *sufficient,* rather than a *necessary,* condition for jurisdiction. See *Pennsylvania v. West Virginia,* 262 U.S. 553 (1923) ("If the injury is certainly

D. NSA SURVEILLANCE | **453**

impending that is enough"). . . . Taken together the case law uses the word "certainly" as if it emphasizes, rather than literally defines, the immediately following term "impending." . . .

In some standing cases, the Court has found that a reasonable probability of *future* injury comes accompanied with *present* injury that takes the form of reasonable efforts to mitigate the threatened effects of the future injury or to prevent it from occurring. Thus, in *Monsanto Co.*, plaintiffs, a group of conventional alfalfa growers, challenged an agency decision to deregulate genetically engineered alfalfa. Without expressing views about that probability, we found standing because the plaintiffs would suffer present harm by trying to combat the threat. *Ibid.* The plaintiffs, for example, "would have to conduct testing to find out whether and to what extent their crops have been contaminated." And they would have to take "measures to minimize the likelihood of potential contamination and to ensure an adequate supply of non-genetically-engineered alfalfa." *Ibid.* We held that these "harms, which [the plaintiffs] will suffer even if their crops are not actually infected with" the genetically modified gene, "are sufficiently concrete to satisfy the injury-in-fact prong of the constitutional standing analysis."

Virtually identical circumstances are present here. Plaintiff McKay, for example, points out that, when he communicates abroad about, or in the interests of, a client (*e.g.,* a client accused of terrorism), he must "make an assessment" whether his "client's interests would be compromised" should the Government "acquire the communications." If so, he must either forgo the communication or travel abroad. ("I have had to take measures to protect the confidentiality of information that I believe is particularly sensitive," including "travel that is both time-consuming and expensive").

Since travel is expensive, since forgoing communication can compromise the client's interests, since McKay's assessment itself takes time and effort, this case does not differ significantly from *Monsanto*. And that is so whether we consider the plaintiffs' present necessary expenditure of time and effort as a separate concrete, particularized, imminent harm, or consider it as additional evidence that the future harm (an interception) is likely to occur. . . .

While I express no view on the merits of the plaintiffs' constitutional claims, I do believe that at least some of the plaintiffs have standing to make those claims. I dissent, with respect, from the majority's contrary conclusion.

NOTES & QUESTIONS

1. ***The Holding in* Clapper.** By a 5-4 vote, the Clapper Court found a lack of standing. For the majority, the claimants were unable to demonstrate a future injury in fact that was "certainly impending" by allegations regarding likely government surveillance pursuant to Section 702. Writing in dissent, Justice Breyer argued that it was constitutionally justifiable to rely on "ordinary inferences about future events." He notes: "Perhaps, despite pouring rain, the streets will remain dry (due to the presence of a special chemical)." Indeed, at some point, a party that seeks to defeat a strong natural inference bears the burden of defeating it. In the national security context, how would you assess

~~the merit of requiring certainly impeding future harm,~~ as the *Clapper* majority does, versus relying on certain "ordinary inferences," as Breyer would do?

2. ***The FISA Amendment Act and TSP.*** In *Hepting v. AT&T Corp.*, 439 F. Supp. 974 (N.D. Cal 2006), the plaintiffs alleged that AT&T was collaborating with the NSA in a massive warrantless surveillance program, namely, the TSP. As customers of AT&T, the plaintiffs alleged that they suffered injury from this surveillance.

The *Hepting* court found that the existence of the TSP was itself not subject to the state secret privilege. This common law evidentiary privilege protects information from discovery when disclosure of it would harm national security. The *Hepting* court found that (1) the Bush Administration had disclosed "the general contours" of the TSP, which (2) "requires the assistance of a telecommunications provider," and (3) AT&T helps the government in classified matters when asked.

This litigation ended, however, due to *In re NSA Telecommunications Records Litigation*, 633 F. Supp. 2d 949 (N.D. Cal. 2008). In that case, the district court found that the FISA Amendment Act had provided retroactive immunity for the defendants and dismissed the action. The court found that Congress in enacting the statute "manifested an unequivocal intention to create an immunity that will shield the telecommunications company defendants from liability in these actions."

At the time of the debates around this law, Congress also considered laws that would have capped the possible liability exposure of the telecommunications companies at fairly modest amounts, but allow the litigation against them to proceed. Do you think that this approach would have been superior to the FISA Amendment Act's outright grant of immunity?

3. ***The End of FISA?*** William Banks argues: "At a minimum, the unraveling of FISA and emergence of the TSP call into question the virtual disappearance of effective oversight of our national security surveillance. The Congress and federal courts have become observers of the system, not even participants, much less overseers."[43] He proposes: "If FISA is to have any meaningful role for the next thirty years, its central terms will have to be restored, one way or another."

In contrast, John Yoo argues that such surveillance should be permitted where there is a reasonable chance that terrorists will appear, or communicate, even if we do not know their specific identities. A law professor, Yoo was in government service at the time of the TSP and wrote the government memorandums at the Department of Justice's Office of Legal Counsel that approved the program.[44] Subsequently, he has proposed that in cases where there is a likelihood, perhaps "a 50 percent chance" that terrorists would use a certain kind of avenue for reaching each other, "[a] FISA-based approach

---

[43] William C. Banks, *The Death of FISA*, 91 Minn. L. Rev. 1209, 1297 (2007).

[44] For a discussion of Yoo's role, see *In re: National Security Telecommunications Records Litigation*, 2010 U.S. Dist. LEXIS 136156, *38-*40 (N.D. Cal. 2010)

would prevent computers from searching through that channel for keywords or names that might suggest terrorist communications."[45]

A third approach is proposed by Orin Kerr, who would update FISA beyond its current approach, which depends "on the identity and location of who is being monitored."[46] In contrast to this "person-focused" approach, Kerr would add "a complementary set of data-focused authorities" to the statute. Under this second approach, "Surveillance practices should be authorized when the government establishes a likelihood that surveillance would yield what I call 'terrorist intelligence information' — information relevant to terrorism investigations. . . ." Kerr is unwilling to state, however, whether the data-focused approach ("used when identities and/or location are unknown") should or should not require any kind of warrant.

2. THE SNOWDEN REVELATIONS

In June 2013, government contractor Edward Snowden began to leak classified National Security Agency (NSA) materials. This material appeared in the *Guardian* in the United Kingdom, the *Washington Post*, and other periodicals. Snowden revealed widespread NSA wiretapping and data collection previously unknown to the public. Senator Diane Feinstein called Snowden's action an "act of treason." A warrant was to be issued for his arrest. In contrast, Daniel Ellsberg, who leaked the Pentagon Papers, said, "there has not been in American history a more important leak" than Snowden's and praised his "civil courage." John Cassidy in the *New Yorker* called Snowden "a hero."[47] In that same periodical, Jeffrey Toobin called him "a grandiose narcissist who deserves to be in prison."[48]

The leaks have affected international relations through the disclosures of NSA spying in foreign nations. Snowden's actions have affected the ongoing development of the Proposed Data Protection Regulation at the European Union, led European Union officials to demand reforms to the Safe Harbor Agreement with the United States, and harmed U.S. technology companies seeking international business. Brazil's president called off a state dinner with President Obama, and Germany cancelled a Cold War surveillance cooperation agreement in reaction to revelations of NSA spying in their country. Germany's Chancellor, Angela Merkel, had a "strongly worded" conversation with President Obama about NSA surveillance of her cell phone.[49] At a European Summit in Brussels, Merkel said, "Spying between friends, that's just not done." She added: "Now trust has to be rebuilt."

What are the chief Snowden revelations in a nutshell? We can break the flood of information about the NSA into categories concerning (1) targeting of non-U.S. persons outside the United States through surveillance occurring in the United States (pursuant to Section 702 of FISA); (2) collecting telephone metadata

---

[45] John Yoo, *War By Other Means: An Insider's Accounts of the War on Terror* 112 (2006).

[46] Orin Kerr, *Updating the Foreign Intelligence Surveillance Act*, 75 U. Chi. L. Rev. 238 (2008).

[47] John Cassidy, *Why Edward Snowden is a Hero*, New Yorker (June 10, 2013).

[48] Jeffrey Toobin, *Edward Snowden is No Hero*, New Yorker (June 10, 2013).

[49] *Embassy Espionage: The NSA's Secret Hub in Berlin*, Der Spiegel (Oct. 13, 2013).

(pursuant to Section 215 of the Patriot Act); (3) spying on foreign countries and their leadership; and (4) acting to weaken encryption standards.

Surveillance of Non-U.S. Persons Outside the United States Conducted Within the United States (Section 702). As the President's Civil Liberties Oversight Board (PCLOB) notes, "Section 702 has its roots in the President's Surveillance Program developed in the immediate aftermath of the September 11th attacks."[50] Following the press disclosures about the Terrorist Surveillance Program in December 2005, the FISA Amendment Acts of 2008 added Section 702 to create a statutory framework for this collection program. Drawing on this section, the NSA then carried out a wide range of surveillance. In particular, and as PCLOB has explained, the NSA has drawn on Section 702 to carry out surveillance under its PRISM program and collection of so-called "upstream communications."

PRISM targets Internet communications and stored data of "non-US persons" outside the United States.[51] In PRISM collection, the government sends a "selector," such as an e-mail address, to a U.S.-based electronic service provider, such as an ISP, and the provider shares communications delivered to that "selector" with the government. PRISM collection does not include telephone calls. Susan Landau notes: "The PRISM documents mention 'direct access' to Microsoft, Yahoo, Google, Facebook, and other U.S. technology companies, but that might be a casual claim rather than a precise statement. Several of the companies involved clarified that this occurs only under legal process—and not through direct access at company servers."[52]

Under "upstream collection," acquisition occurs through the compelled assistance of providers that control the telecommunications backbone. "Upstream collection" also includes telephone calls as well as Internet communications.[53]

Telephone Metadata Collection (Section 215). Leaks by Snowden detailed the bulk collection of domestic telephony metadata. Section 215 of the PATRIOT Act allowed for the collection of individual suspects' "business records." The NSA broadened the scope of Section 215 to include all call detail records generated by certain telephone companies in the United States.[54] Although technically requiring FISC warrants, telephone companies generally complied voluntarily until news media reported on the practice in 2006.[55] Snowden's disclosures also revealed the existence of FISC orders authorizing this practice. Unlike a wiretap, metadata does not describe the content of a phone call, but rather the caller's location, call times

---

[50] PCLOB, *Report on the Surveillance Program Operated Pursuant to Section 702 of the Foreign Intelligence Surveillance Act* 5 (July 2, 2014).

[51] Susan Landau, *Making Sense from Snowden: What's Significant in the NSA Surveillance Revelations*, 11:4 IEEE Security & Privacy 54, 54 (July/Aug. 2013).

[52] *Id.* at 58.

[53] PCLOB, *Report on the 702 Surveillance Program*, 7.

[54] For a clear description of the program and its history, see PCLOB, *Report on the Telephone Records Program Conducted Under Section 215* (Jan. 23, 2014).

[55] Landau, *Making Sense from Snowden, Part II*, IEE Security & Privacy Web Extra v (Jan./Feb. 2014). For a discussion of the Section 215 program, see Joseph D. Mornin, *NSA Metadata Collection and the Fourth Amendment*, 29 BTLJ 985 (2014).

and lengths, and which phone numbers the phone contacted. The NSA used metadata to understand webs of relations by "contact chaining" that compares groups of three "hops" from any "seed." In other words, government analysts would retrieve numbers not only directly in contact with the seed number (the "first hop'), but also numbers in contact with all first hop numbers (the "second hop") and all numbers in contact with all second hop numbers (the "third hop").[56]

Spying on China, G20 leaders, Brazil, Germany, and Other Countries. Snowden claimed that the NSA compromised Chinese telecommunications networks. With the help of the British GCHQ, the UK's NSA-equivalent, the NSA spied on G20 leaders during a 2009 summit in London. The NSA is also said to have spied on Petrobas, Brazil's largest oil and gas company. In Germany, the NSA targeted Chancellor's Merkel's cell phone and ran major listening operations from within the U.S. embassy in Berlin and U.S. military bases throughout the company. In France, initial reports of widespread NSA-spying in that country were followed by reports in *Le Monde* that the activity had been carried out with the cooperation of French intelligence agencies.

Weakening of Encryption Standards. Leaked documents from Snowden showed that the NSA worked to insert vulnerabilities into commercial encryption standards. It did so to make these systems "exploitable" by it. As part of this effort, the NSA covertly influenced the standard-setting process at the National Institute of Standards and Technology. As Susan Landau states, "It appears that NSA […] viewed corrupting cryptography standards as a goal."[57]

In the two cases that follow, *Klayman v. Obama* and *In re FBI*, a district court and the FISC respectively evaluated the legal sufficiency of Section 215.

KLAYMAN V. OBAMA
957 F. Supp. 2d 1 (D.D.C. 2013)

LEON, J. On June 6, 2013, plaintiffs brought the first of two related lawsuits challenging the constitutionality and statutory authorization of certain intelligence-gathering practices by the United States government relating to the wholesale collection of the phone record metadata of all U.S. citizens. These related cases are two of several lawsuits arising from public revelations over the past six months that the federal government, through the National Security Agency ("NSA"), and with the participation of certain telecommunications and internet companies, has conducted surveillance and intelligence-gathering programs that collect certain data about the telephone and internet activity of American citizens within the United States.

On June 5, 2013, the British newspaper *The Guardian* reported the first of several "leaks" of classified material from Edward Snowden, a former NSA contract employee, which have revealed — and continue to reveal — multiple U.S.

---

[56] PCLOB, *Telephone Records Program, supra*, 9.

[57] *Id.* at vii.

government intelligence collection and surveillance programs. *See* Glenn Greenwald, *NSA collecting phone records of millions of Verizon customers daily,* GUARDIAN (London), June 5, 2013. That initial media report disclosed a FISC order dated April 25, 2013, compelling Verizon Business Network Services to produce to the NSA on "an ongoing daily basis ... all call detail records or 'telephony metadata' created by Verizon for communications (i) between the United States and abroad; or (ii) wholly within the United States, including local telephone calls." Secondary Order, *In re Application of the [FBI] for an Order Requiring the Production of Tangible Things from Verizon Business Network Services, Inc. on Behalf of MCI Communication Services, Inc. d/b/a Verizon Business Services, No. BR 13–80* at 2 (FISC Apr. 25, 2013). According to the news article, this order "show[ed] . . . that under the Obama administration the communication records of millions of US citizens are being collected indiscriminately and in bulk—regardless of whether they are suspected of any wrongdoing." Greenwald, *supra.* In response to this disclosure, the Government confirmed the authenticity of the April 25, 2013 FISC Order, and, in this litigation and in certain public statements, acknowledged the existence of a "program" under which "the FBI obtains orders from the FISC pursuant to Section 215 [of the USA PATRIOT Act] directing certain telecommunications service providers to produce to the NSA on a daily basis electronic copies of 'call detail records.'" Follow-on media reports revealed other Government surveillance programs, including the Government's collection of internet data pursuant to a program called "PRISM." *See* Glenn Greenwald & Ewen MacAskill, *NSA Prism program taps in to user data of Apple, Google and others,* GUARDIAN (London), June 6, 2013. . . .

FISA created a procedure for the Government to obtain ex parte judicial orders authorizing domestic electronic surveillance upon a showing that, *inter alia,* the target of the surveillance was a foreign power or an agent of a foreign power. 50 U.S.C. §§ 1804(a)(3), 1805(a)(2). In enacting FISA, Congress also created two new Article III courts—the Foreign Intelligence Surveillance Court ("FISC"), composed of eleven U.S. district judges, "which shall have jurisdiction to hear applications for and grant orders approving" such surveillance, § 1803(a)(1), and the FISC Court of Review, composed of three U.S. district or court of appeals judges, "which shall have jurisdiction to review the denial of any application made under [FISA]," § 1803(b).

Following the September 11, 2001 terrorist attacks, Congress passed the USA PATRIOT Act, which made changes to FISA and several other laws. Pub. L. No. 107–56, 115 Stat. 272 (2001). Section 215 of the PATRIOT Act replaced FISA's business-records provision with a more expansive "tangible things" provision. Codified at 50 U.S.C. § 1861, it authorizes the FBI to apply "for an order requiring the production of any tangible things (including books, records, papers, documents, and other items) for an investigation to obtain foreign intelligence information not concerning a United States person or to protect against international terrorism or clandestine intelligence activities." § 1861(a)(1). While this provision originally required that the FBI's application "shall specify that the records concerned are sought for" such an investigation, § 1861(b)(2), Congress amended the statute in 2006 to provide that the FBI's application must include "a statement of facts showing that there are reasonable grounds to believe that the tangible things sought are relevant to an authorized investigation ... to obtain foreign intelligence information not concerning a United States person or to protect against international terrorism or clandestine intelligence activities." § 1861(b)(2)(A); *see* USA PATRIOT Improvement and Reauthorization Act of 2005, Pub. L. No. 109–177, § 106(b), 120 Stat. 192 ("USA PATRIOT Improvement and Reauthorization Act").

Section 1861 also imposes other requirements on the FBI when seeking to use this authority. For example, the investigation pursuant to which the request is made must be authorized and conducted under guidelines approved by the Attorney General under Executive Order No. 12,333 (or a successor thereto). 50 U.S.C. § 1861(a)(2)(A), (b)(2)(A). And the FBI's application must "enumerat[e] . . . minimization procedures adopted by the Attorney General . . . that are applicable to the retention and dissemination by the [FBI] of any tangible things to be made available to the [FBI] based on the order requested." § 1861(b)(2)(B). . . .

While the recipient of a production order must keep it secret, Section 1861 does provide the recipient — but only the recipient — a right of judicial review of the order before the FISC pursuant to specific procedures. Prior to 2006, recipients of Section 1861 production orders had no express right to judicial review of those orders, but Congress added such a provision when it reauthorized the PATRIOT Act that year.

To say the least, plaintiffs and the Government have portrayed the scope of the Government's surveillance activities very differently. For purposes of resolving these preliminary injunction motions, however, as will be made clear in the discussion below, it will suffice to accept the Government's description of the phone metadata collection and querying program.

In broad overview, the Government has developed a "counterterrorism program" under Section 1861 in which it collect, compiles, retains, and analyzes certain telephone records, which it characterizes as "business records" created by certain telecommunications companies (the "Bulk Telephony Metadata Program"). The records collected under this program consist of "metadata," such as information about what phone numbers were used to make and receive calls, when the calls took place, and how long the calls lasted. According to the representations made by the Government, the metadata records collected under the program do *not* include *any* information about the content of those calls, or the names, addresses, or financial information of any party to the calls. Through targeted computerized searches of those metadata records, the NSA tries to discern connections between terrorist organizations and previously unknown terrorist operatives located in the United States.

The Government has conducted the Bulk Telephony Metadata Program for more than seven years. Beginning in May 2006 and continuing through the present,[58] the FBI has obtained production orders from the FISC under Section 1861 directing certain telecommunications companies to produce, on an ongoing daily basis, these telephony metadata records, which the companies create and maintain as part of their business of providing telecommunications services to customers. The NSA then consolidates the metadata records provided by different

---

[58] The most recent FISC order authorizing the Bulk Telephony Metadata Program that the Government has disclosed (in redacted form, directed to an unknown recipient) expires on January 3, 2014. *See* Oct. 11, 2013 Primary Order at 17.

telecommunications companies into one database, and under the FISC's orders, the NSA may retain the records for up to five years. According to Government officials, this aggregation of records into a single database creates "an historical repository that permits retrospective analysis," enabling NSA analysts to draw connections, across telecommunications service providers, between numbers reasonably suspected to be associated with terrorist activity and with other, unknown numbers.

The FISC orders governing the Bulk Telephony Metadata Program specifically provide that the metadata records may be accessed only for counterterrorism purposes (and technical database maintenance). Specifically, NSA intelligence analysts, *without seeking the approval of a judicial officer,* may access the records to obtain foreign intelligence information only through "queries" of the records performed using "identifiers," such as telephone numbers, associated with terrorist activity. An "identifier" (i.e., selection term, or search term) used to start a query of the database is called a "seed," and "seeds" must be approved by one of twenty-two designated officials in the NSA's Homeland Security Analysis Center or other parts of the NSA's Signals Intelligence Directorate. Such approval may be given only upon a determination by one of those designated officials that there exist facts giving rise to a "reasonable, articulable suspicion" ("RAS") that the selection term to be queried is associated with one or more of the specified foreign terrorist organizations approved for targeting by the FISC. In 2012, for example, fewer than 300 unique identifiers met this RAS standard and were used as "seeds" to query the metadata, but "the number of unique identifiers has varied over the years."

When an NSA intelligence analyst runs a query using a "seed," the minimization procedures provide that query results are limited to records of communications within three "hops" from the seed. The query results thus will include only identifiers and their associated metadata having a direct contact with the seed (the first "hop"), identifiers and associated metadata having a direct contact with first "hop" identifiers (the second "hop"), and identifiers and associated metadata having a direct contact with second "hop" identifiers (the third "hop"). In plain English, this means that if a search starts with telephone number (123) 456–7890 as the "seed," the first hop will include all the phone numbers that (123) 456–7890 has called or received calls from in the last five years (say, 100 numbers), the second hop will include all the phone numbers that each of *those* 100 numbers has called or received calls from in the last five years (say, 100 numbers for each one of the 100 "first hop" numbers, or 10,000 total), and the third hop will include all the phone numbers that each of *those* 10,000 numbers has called or received calls from in the last five years (say, 100 numbers for each one of the 10,000 "second hop" numbers, or 1,000,000 total). The actual number of telephone numbers and their associated metadata captured in any given query varies, of course, but in the absence of any specific representations from the Government about typical query results, it is likely that the quantity of phone numbers captured in any given query would be very large.

Once a query is conducted and it returns a universe of responsive records (i.e., a universe limited to records of communications within three hops from the seed), trained NSA analysts may then perform new searches and otherwise perform intelligence analysis *within* that universe of data without using RAS-approved search terms. According to the Government, following the "chains of communication" — which, for chains that cross different communications networks, is only possible if the metadata is aggregated—allows the analyst to discover information that may not be readily ascertainable through other, targeted intelligence-gathering techniques. For example, the query might reveal that a seed telephone number has been in contact with a previously unknown U.S. telephone number — i.e., on the first hop. And from there, "contact-chaining" out to the second and third hops to examine the contacts made by that telephone number may reveal a contact with other telephone numbers already known to the Government to be associated with a foreign terrorist organization. In short, the Bulk Telephony Metadata Program is meant to detect: (1) domestic U.S. phone numbers calling *outside* of the U.S. to foreign phone numbers associated with terrorist groups; (2) foreign phone numbers associated with terrorist groups calling *into* the U.S. to U.S. phone numbers; and (3) "possible terrorist-related communications" between U.S. phone numbers *inside* the U.S. . . . .

When ruling on a motion for preliminary injunction, a court must consider "whether (1) the plaintiff has a substantial likelihood of success on the merits; (2) the plaintiff would suffer irreparable injury were an injunction not granted; (3) an injunction would substantially injure other interested parties; and (4) the grant of an injunction would further the public interest." *Sottera, Inc. v. Food & Drug Admin.,* 627 F.3d 891, 893 (D.C. Cir. 2010) (internal quotation marks omitted). I will address each of these factors in turn.

In addressing plaintiffs' likelihood of success on the merits of their constitutional claims, I will focus on their Fourth Amendment arguments, which I find to be the most likely to succeed. First, however, I must address plaintiffs' standing to challenge the various aspects of the Bulk Telephony Metadata Program.

"To establish Article III standing, an injury must be concrete, particularized, and actual or imminent; fairly traceable to the challenged action; and redressable by a favorable ruling." *Clapper v. Amnesty Int'l USA,* 133 S. Ct. 1138 (2013) (internal quotation marks omitted). In *Clapper,* the Supreme Court held that plaintiffs lacked standing to challenge NSA surveillance under FISA because their "highly speculative fear" that they would be targeted by surveillance relied on a "speculative chain of possibilities" insufficient to demonstrate a "certainly impending" injury. Moreover, the *Clapper* plaintiffs' "self-inflicted injuries" (i.e., the costs and burdens of avoiding the feared surveillance) could not be traced to any provable government activity.[59] That is not the case here.

The NSA's Bulk Telephony Metadata Program involves two potential searches: (1) the bulk collection of metadata and (2) the analysis of that data

---

[59] I note in passing one significant difference between the metadata collection at issue in this case and the electronic surveillance at issue in *Clapper.* As the Court noted in *Clapper,* "if the Government intends to use or disclose information obtained or derived from a [50 U.S.C.] § 1881a acquisition in judicial or administrative proceedings, it must provide advance notice of its intent, and the affected person may challenge the lawfulness of the acquisition." 133 S. Ct. at 1154 (citing 50 U.S.C. §§ 1806(c), 1806(e), 1881e(a)). Sections 1806(c) and (e) and 1881e(a), however, apply only to "information obtained or derived from an electronic surveillance" authorized by specific statutes; they do *not* apply to business records collected under Section 1861. Nor does it appear that any other statute requires the Government to notify a criminal defendant if it intends to use evidence derived from an analysis of the bulk telephony metadata collection.

through the NSA's querying process. For the following reasons, I have concluded that the plaintiffs have standing to challenge both. First, as to the collection, the Supreme Court decided *Clapper* just months *before* the June 2013 news reports revealed the existence and scope of certain NSA surveillance activities. Thus, whereas the plaintiffs in *Clapper* could only speculate as to whether they would be surveilled at all, plaintiffs in this case can point to strong evidence that, as Verizon customers, their telephony metadata has been collected for the last seven years (and stored for the last five) and will continue to be collected barring judicial or legislative intervention. In addition, the Government has declassified and authenticated an April 25, 2013 FISC Order signed by Judge Vinson, which confirms that the NSA has indeed collected telephony metadata from Verizon.

. . . [I]n one footnote, the Government asks me to find that plaintiffs lack standing based on the theoretical possibility that the NSA has collected a universe of metadata so incomplete that the program could not possibly serve its putative function.[60] Candor of this type defies common sense and does not exactly inspire confidence!

Likewise, I find that plaintiffs also have standing to challenge the NSA's querying procedures. . . . When the NSA runs such a query, its system must necessarily analyze metadata for *every* phone number in the database by comparing the foreign target number against *all* of the stored call records to determine which U.S. phones, if any, have interacted with the target number. Moreover, unlike a DNA or fingerprint database — which contains only a single "snapshot" record of each person therein — the NSA's database is updated every single day with new information about each phone number. And the NSA can access its database whenever it wants, repeatedly querying any seed approved in the last 180 days (for terms believed to be used by U.S. persons) or year (for all other terms).

The threshold issue that I must address . . . is whether plaintiffs have a reasonable expectation of privacy that is violated when the Government indiscriminately collects their telephony metadata along with the metadata of hundreds of millions of other citizens without any particularized suspicion of wrongdoing, retains all of that metadata for five years, and then queries, analyzes, and investigates that data without prior judicial approval of the investigative targets. If they do — and a Fourth Amendment search has thus occurred — then the next step of the analysis will be to determine whether such a search is "reasonable."

The analysis of this threshold issue of the expectation of privacy must start with the Supreme Court's landmark opinion in *Smith v. Maryland,* 442 U.S. 735 (1979), which the FISC has said "squarely control[s]" when it comes to "[t]he production of telephone service provider metadata." Am. Mem. Op., *In re Application of the [FBI] for an Order Requiring the Production of Tangible Things from [REDACTED],* No. BR 13–109 at 6–9 (FISC Aug. 29, 2013).

The question before me is *not* the same question that the Supreme Court confronted in *Smith.* To say the least, "whether the installation and use of a pen

---

[60] To draw an analogy, if the NSA's program operates the way the Government suggests it does, then omitting Verizon Wireless, AT & T, and Sprint from the collection would be like omitting John, Paul, and George from a historical analysis of the Beatles. A Ringo-only database doesn't make any sense, and I cannot believe the Government would create, maintain, and so ardently defend such a system.

register constitutes a 'search' within the meaning of the Fourth Amendment," *id.* at 736, under the circumstances addressed and contemplated in that case — is a far cry from the issue in this case.

Indeed, the question in this case can more properly be styled as follows: When do present-day circumstances — the evolutions in the Government's surveillance capabilities, citizens' phone habits, and the relationship between the NSA and telecom companies — become so thoroughly unlike those considered by the Supreme Court thirty-four years ago that a precedent like *Smith* simply does not apply? The answer, unfortunately for the Government, is now.

In *United States v. Jones* (2012), five justices found that law enforcement's use of a GPS device to track a vehicle's movements for nearly a month violated Jones's reasonable expectation of privacy. Significantly, the justices did so *without* questioning the validity of the Court's earlier decision in *United States v. Knotts,* 460 U.S. 276 (1983), that use of a tracking beeper does not constitute a search because "[a] person travelling in an automobile on public thoroughfares has no reasonable expectation of privacy in his movements from one place to another." Instead, they emphasized the many significant ways in which the short-range, short-term tracking device used in *Knotts* differed from the constant month-long surveillance achieved with the GPS device attached to Jones's car.

Just as the Court in *Knotts* did not address the kind of surveillance used to track Jones, the Court in *Smith* was not confronted with the NSA's Bulk Telephony Metadata Program.[61] Nor could the Court in 1979 have ever imagined how the citizens of 2013 would interact with their phones. For the many reasons discussed below, I am convinced that the surveillance program now before me is so different from a simple pen register that *Smith* is of little value in assessing whether the Bulk Telephony Metadata Program constitutes a Fourth Amendment search. To the contrary, for the following reasons, I believe that bulk telephony metadata collection and analysis almost certainly does violate a reasonable expectation of privacy.

First, the pen register in *Smith* was operational for only a matter of days between March 6, 1976 and March 19, 1976, and there is no indication from the Court's opinion that it expected the Government to retain those limited phone records once the case was over. . . . The NSA telephony metadata program, on the other hand, involves the creation and maintenance of a historical database containing *five years'* worth of data. And I might add, there is the very real prospect that the program will go on for as long as America is combatting terrorism, which realistically could be forever!

Second, the relationship between the police and the phone company in *Smith* is *nothing* compared to the relationship that has apparently evolved over the last seven years between the Government and telecom companies. . . . It's one thing to say that people expect phone companies to occasionally provide information to law enforcement; it is quite another to suggest that our citizens expect all phone companies to operate what is effectively a joint intelligence-gathering operation

---

[61] . . . The Supreme Court itself has recognized that prior Fourth Amendment precedents and doctrines do not always control in cases involving unique factual circumstances created by evolving technology. *See, e.g., Kyllo,* 533 U.S. at 34 ("To withdraw protection of this minimum expectation [of privacy in the home] would be to permit police technology to erode the privacy guaranteed by the Fourth Amendment."). If this isn't such a case, then what is?

with the Government. *Cf. U.S. Dep't of Justice v. Reporters Comm. for Freedom of the Press,* 489 U.S. 749 (1989) ("Plainly there is a vast difference between the public records that might be found after a diligent search of [various third parties' records] and a computerized summary located in a single clearinghouse of information.").

Third, the almost-Orwellian technology that enables the Government to store and analyze the phone metadata of every telephone user in the United States is unlike anything that could have been conceived in 1979. In *Smith,* the Supreme Court was actually considering whether local police could collect one person's phone records for calls made after the pen register was installed and for the limited purpose of a small-scale investigation of harassing phone calls. *See Smith,* 442 U.S. at 737. The notion that the Government could collect similar data on hundreds of millions of people and retain that data for a five-year period, updating it with new data every day in perpetuity, was at best, in 1979, the stuff of science fiction.

Finally, *and most importantly,* not only is the Government's ability to collect, store, and analyze phone data greater now than it was in 1979, but the nature and quantity of the information contained in people's telephony metadata is much greater, as well. . . . In fact, some undoubtedly will be reading this opinion *on their cellphones.* Cell phones have also morphed into multi-purpose devices. They are now maps and music players. They are cameras. They are even lighters that people hold up at rock concerts. They are ubiquitous as well. Count the phones at the bus stop, in a restaurant, or around the table at a work meeting or any given occasion. Thirty-four years ago, *none* of those phones would have been there. Thirty-four years ago, city streets were lined with pay phones. Thirty-four years ago, when people wanted to send "text messages," they wrote letters and attached postage stamps.

Admittedly, what metadata *is* has not changed over time. As in *Smith,* the *types* of information at issue in this case are relatively limited: phone numbers dialed, date, time, and the like.[62] But the ubiquity of phones has dramatically altered the *quantity* of information that is now available and, *more importantly,* what that information can tell the Government about people's lives. Put simply, people in 2013 have an entirely different relationship with phones than they did thirty-four years ago. As a result, people make calls and send text messages now that they would not (really, *could not*) have made or sent back when *Smith* was decided — for example, every phone call today between two people trying to locate one another in a public place. This rapid and monumental shift towards a cell phone-centric culture means that the metadata from each person's phone "reflects a wealth of detail about her familial, political, professional, religious, and sexual

---

[62] There are, however, a few noteworthy distinctions between the data at issue in *Smith* and the metadata that exists nowadays. For instance, the pen register in *Smith* did not tell the government whether calls were completed or the duration of any calls, *see Smith,* 442 U.S. at 741, whereas that information is captured in the NSA's metadata collection. A much more significant difference is that telephony metadata can reveal the user's location, which in 1979 would have been entirely unnecessary given that landline phones are tethered to buildings. . . . That said, not all FISC orders have been made public, and I have no idea how location data has been handled in the past. . . Recent news reports, though not confirmed by the Government, cause me to wonder whether the Government's briefs are entirely forthcoming about the full scope of the Bulk Telephony Metadata Program. *See, e.g.,* Barton Gellman & Ashkan Soltani, *NSA maps targets by their phones,* WASH. POST, Dec. 5, 2013, at A01.

associations," *Jones,* 132 S.Ct. at 955 (Sotomayor, J., concurring), that could not have been gleaned from a data collection in 1979. Records that once would have revealed a few scattered tiles of information about a person now reveal an entire mosaic — a vibrant and constantly updating picture of the person's life.

In sum, the *Smith* pen register and the ongoing NSA Bulk Telephony Metadata Program have so many significant distinctions between them that I cannot possibly navigate these uncharted Fourth Amendment waters using as my North Star a case that predates the rise of cell phones. . . .

[The *Klayman* court next examined the totality of the circumstances to determine whether the search is reasonable within the meaning of the Fourth Amendment. In the absence of individualized suspicion of wrongdoing, the search could only be upheld through the "special needs" caselaw of the Supreme Court.]

The factors I must consider include: (1) "the nature of the privacy interest allegedly compromised" by the search, (2) "the character of the intrusion imposed" by the government, and (3) "the nature and immediacy of the government's concerns and the efficacy of the [search] in meeting them." *Bd. of Educ. v. Earls,* 536 U.S. 822 (2002).

"Special needs" cases, not surprisingly, form something of a patchwork quilt. . . . To my knowledge, however, no court has ever recognized a special need sufficient to justify continuous, daily searches of virtually every American citizen without any particularized suspicion. In effect, the Government urges me to be the first non-FISC judge to sanction such a dragnet.

For reasons I have already discussed at length, I find that plaintiffs have a very significant expectation of privacy in an aggregated collection of their telephony metadata covering the last five years, and the NSA's Bulk Telephony Metadata Program significantly intrudes on that expectation. Whether the program violates the Fourth Amendment will therefore turn on "the nature and immediacy of the government's concerns and the efficacy of the [search] in meeting them." *Earls,* 536 U.S. at 834.

The Government asserts that the Bulk Telephony Metadata Program serves the "programmatic purpose" of "identifying unknown terrorist operatives and preventing terrorist attacks." . . . Yet, turning to the efficacy prong, the Government does *not* cite a single instance in which analysis of the NSA's bulk metadata collection actually stopped an imminent attack, or otherwise aided the Government in achieving any objective that was time-sensitive in nature. In fact, none of the three "recent episodes" cited by the Government that supposedly "illustrate the role that telephony metadata analysis can play in preventing and protecting against terrorist attack" involved any apparent urgency. . . . Given the limited record before me at this point in the litigation—most notably, the utter lack of evidence that a terrorist attack has ever been prevented because searching the NSA database was faster than other investigative tactics—I have serious doubts about the efficacy of the metadata collection program as a means of conducting time-sensitive investigations in cases involving imminent threats of terrorism.

I realize, of course, that such a holding might appear to conflict with other trial courts. . . . Nevertheless, in reaching this decision, I find comfort in the statement in the Supreme Court's recent majority opinion in *Jones* that "[a]t bottom, we must 'assur[e] preservation of that degree of privacy against government that existed when the Fourth Amendment was adopted.'" (quoting *Kyllo*). . . . Indeed, I have little doubt that the author of our Constitution, James Madison, who cautioned us to beware "the abridgement of freedom of the people by gradual and silent encroachments by those in power," would be aghast. . . .

Plaintiffs in this case have also shown a strong likelihood of success on the merits of a Fourth Amendment claim. As such, they too have adequately demonstrated irreparable injury.

. . . [The public interest] looms large in this case, given the significant privacy interests at stake and the unprecedented scope of the NSA's collection and querying efforts, which likely violate the Fourth Amendment. Thus, the public interest weighs heavily in favor of granting an injunction.

. . . [I]n light of the significant national security interests at stake in this case and the novelty of the constitutional issues, I will stay my order pending appeal. In doing so, I hereby give the Government fair notice that should my ruling be upheld, this order will go into effect forthwith.

IN RE FBI

2013 WL 5307991 (FISC 2013)

EAGAN, J. On July 18, 2013, a verified Final "Application for Certain Tangible Things for Investigations to Protect Against International Terrorism" (Application) was submitted to the Court by the Federal Bureau of Investigation (FBI) for an order pursuant to the Foreign Intelligence Surveillance Act of 1978 (FISA or the Act), Title 50, United States Code (U.S.C.), § 1861, as amended (also known as Section 215 of the USA PATRIOT Act), requiring the ongoing daily production to the National Security Agency (NSA) of certain call detail records or "telephony metadata" in bulk. . . .

In conducting its review of the government's application, the Court considered whether the Fourth Amendment to the U.S. Constitution imposed any impediment to the government's proposed collection. Having found none in accord with U.S. Supreme Court precedent, the Court turned to Section 215 to determine if the proposed collection was lawful and that Orders requested from this Court should issue. The Court found that under the terms of Section 215 and under operation of the canons of statutory construction such Orders were lawful and required, and the requested Orders were therefore issued.

Specifically, the government requested Orders from this Court to obtain certain business records of specified telephone service providers. Those telephone company business records consist of a very large volume of each company's call detail records or telephony metadata, but expressly exclude the contents of any communication; the name, address, or financial information of any subscriber or customer; or any cell site location information (CSLI). The government requested production of this data on a daily basis for a period of 90 days. The sole purpose of this production is to obtain foreign intelligence information in support of [TEXT REDACTED] individual authorized investigations to protect against international terrorism and concerning various international terrorist organizations. In granting the government's request, the Court has prohibited the government from accessing the data for any other intelligence or investigative purpose.

By the terms of this Court's Primary Order, access to the data is restricted through technical means, through limits on trained personnel with authorized access, and through a query process that requires a reasonable, articulable suspicion (RAS), as determined by a limited set of personnel, that the selection term (e.g., a telephone number) that will be used to search the data is associated with one of the identified international terrorist organizations. Moreover, the government may not make the RAS determination for selection terms reasonably believed to be used by U.S. persons solely based on activities protected by the First Amendment. To ensure adherence to its Orders, this Court has the authority to oversee compliance, see 50 U.S.C. § 1803(h), and requires the government to notify the Court in writing immediately concerning any instance of non-compliance, see FISC Rule 13(b). According to the government, in the prior authorization period there have been no compliance incidents.[63]

Finally, although not required by statute, the government has demonstrated through its written submissions and oral testimony that this production has been and remains valuable for obtaining foreign intelligence information regarding international terrorist organizations. . . .

The production of telephone service provider metadata is squarely controlled by the U.S. Supreme Court decision in *Smith v. Maryland*, 442 U.S. 735 (1979). The Smith decision and its progeny have governed Fourth Amendment jurisprudence with regard to telephony and communications metadata for more than 30 years. Specifically, the *Smith* case involved a Fourth Amendment challenge to the use of a pen register on telephone company equipment to capture information concerning telephone calls, but not the content or the identities of the parties to a conversation. The same type of information is at issue here.[64]

The Supreme Court in *Smith* recognized that telephone companies maintain call detail records in the normal course of business for a variety of purposes. Furthermore, the Supreme Court found that once a person has transmitted this information to a third party (in this case, a telephone company), the person "has no legitimate expectation of privacy in [the] information...." The telephone user, having conveyed this information to a telephone company that retains the information in the ordinary course of business, assumes the risk that the company will provide that information to the government. Thus, the Supreme Court concluded that a person does not have a legitimate expectation of privacy in telephone numbers dialed and, therefore, when the government obtained that dialing information, it "was not a 'search,' and no warrant was required" under the Fourth Amendment.

In *Smith*, the government was obtaining the telephone company's metadata of one person suspected of a crime. Here, the government is requesting daily

---

[63] The Court is aware that in prior years there have been incidents of non-compliance with respect to NSA's handling of produced information. Through oversight by this Court over a period of months, those issues were resolved.

[64] The Court is aware that additional call detail data is obtained via this production than was acquired through the pen register acquisition at issue in Smith. Other courts have had the opportunity to review whether there is a *Fourth Amendment* expectation of privacy in call detail records similar to the data sought in this matter and have found that there is none. *See United States v. Reed*, 575 F.3d 900, 914 (9th Cir. 2009) (finding that because "data about the 'call origination, length, and time of call' . . . is nothing more than pen register and trap and trace data, there is no *Fourth Amendment* 'expectation of privacy.' "

production of certain telephony metadata in bulk belonging to companies without specifying the particular number of an individual. This Court had reason to analyze this distinction in a similar context in [TEXT REDACTED]. In that case, this Court found that "regarding the breadth of the proposed surveillance, it is noteworthy that the application of the Fourth Amendment depends on the government's intruding into some individual's reasonable expectation of privacy." The Court noted that Fourth Amendment rights are personal and individual, and that "[s]o long as no individual has a reasonable expectation of privacy in meta data, the large number of persons whose communications will be subjected to the . . . surveillance is irrelevant to the issue of whether a Fourth Amendment search or seizure will occur." Put another way, where one individual does not have a Fourth Amendment interest, grouping together a large number of similarly-situated individuals cannot result in a Fourth Amendment interest springing into existence ex nihilo.

In sum, because the Application at issue here concerns only the production of call detail records or "telephony metadata" belonging to a telephone company, and not the contents of communications, *Smith v. Maryland* compels the conclusion that there is no Fourth Amendment impediment to the collection. Furthermore, for the reasons stated in [TEXT REDACTED] and discussed above, this Court finds that the volume of records being acquired does not alter this conclusion. Indeed, there is no legal basis for this Court to find otherwise. . . .

Section 215 of the USA PATRIOT Act created a statutory framework, the various parts of which are designed to ensure not only that the government has access to the information it needs for authorized investigations, but also that there are protections and prohibitions in place to safeguard U.S. person information. . .

This Court must verify that each statutory provision is satisfied before issuing the requested Orders.

Because known and unknown international terrorist operatives are using telephone communications, and because it is necessary to obtain the bulk collection of a telephone company's metadata to determine those connections between known and unknown international terrorist operatives as part of authorized investigations, the production of the information sought meets the standard for relevance under Section 215.

As an initial matter and as a point of clarification, the government's burden under Section 215 is not to prove that the records sought are, in fact, relevant to an authorized investigation. The explicit terms of the statute require "a statement of facts showing that there are *reasonable grounds to believe* that the tangible things sought are relevant. . . ." 50 U.S.C. § 1861(b)(2)(A) (emphasis added). In establishing this standard, Congress chose to leave the term "relevant" undefined. This Court recognizes that the concept of relevance here is in fact broad and amounts to a relatively low standard. Where there is no requirement for specific and articulable facts or materiality, the government may meet the standard under Section 215 if it can demonstrate reasonable grounds to believe that the information sought to be produced has some bearing on its investigations of the identified international terrorist organizations.

This Court has previously examined the issue of relevance for bulk collections. *See* [TEXT REDACTED]. While those matters involved different collections from the one at issue here, the relevance standard was similar. See 50 U.S.C. § 1842(c)(2) ("[R]elevant to an ongoing investigation to protect against international terrorism. . . ."). In both cases, there were facts demonstrating that information concerning known and unknown affiliates of international terrorist organizations was contained within the non-content metadata the government sought to obtain. As this Court noted in 2010, the "finding of relevance most crucially depended on the conclusion that bulk collection is *necessary* for NSA to employ tools that are likely to generate useful investigative leads to help identify and track terrorist operatives." [TEXT REDACTED] Indeed, in [TEXT REDACTED] this Court noted that bulk collections such as these are "necessary to identify the much smaller number of [international terrorist] communications." [TEXT REDACTED] As a result, it is this showing of necessity that led the Court to find that "the entire mass of collected metadata is relevant to investigating [international terrorist groups] and affiliated persons." [TEXT REDACTED]

This case is no different. The government stated, and this Court is well aware, that individuals associated with international terrorist organizations use telephonic systems to communicate with one another around the world, including within the United States. The government argues that the broad collection of telephone company metadata "is necessary to create a historical repository of metadata that enables NSA to find or identify known *and unknown* operatives . . . , some of whom may be in the United States or in communication with U.S. persons." The government would use such information, in part, "to detect and prevent terrorist acts against the United States and U.S. interests." The government posits that bulk telephonic metadata is necessary to its investigations because it is impossible to know where in the data the connections to international terrorist organizations will be found. The government notes also that "[a]nalysts know that the terrorists' communications are located somewhere" in the metadata produced under this authority, but cannot know where until the data is aggregated and then accessed by their analytic tools under limited and controlled queries. As the government stated in its 2006 Memorandum of Law, "[a]ll of the metadata collected is thus relevant, because the success of this investigative tool depends on bulk collection."

The government depends on this bulk collection because if production of the information were to wait until the specific identifier connected to an international terrorist group were determined, most of the historical connections (the entire purpose of this authorization) would be lost. The analysis of past connections is only possible "if the Government has collected and archived a broad set of metadata that contains within it the subset of communications that can later be identified as terrorist-related." Because the subset of terrorist communications is ultimately contained within the whole of the metadata produced, but can only be found after the production is aggregated and then queried using identifiers determined to be associated with identified international terrorist organizations, the whole production is relevant to the ongoing investigation out of necessity.

As the U.S. Supreme Court has stated, "Congress is presumed to be aware of an administrative or judicial interpretation of a statute and to adopt that interpretation when it re-enacts a statute without change." *Lorillard v. Pons*, 434 U.S. 575 (1978). This doctrine of legislative re-enactment, also known as the doctrine of ratification, is applicable here because Congress re-authorized Section 215 of the PATRIOT Act without change in 2011. The record before this Court . .

. demonstrates that the factual basis for applying the re-enactment doctrine and presuming that in 2011 Congress intended to ratify Section 215 as applied by this Court is well supported. Members were informed that this Court's "orders generally require production of the business records (as described above) relating to substantially all of the telephone calls handled by the companies, including both calls made between the United States and a foreign country and calls made entirely within the United States." When Congress subsequently re-authorized Section 215 without change, except as to expiration date, that re-authorization carried with it this Court's interpretation of the statute, which permits the bulk collection of telephony metadata under the restrictions that are in place. Therefore, the passage of the PATRIOT Sunsets Extension Act provides a persuasive reason for this Court to adhere to its prior interpretations of Section 215. . . .

This Court is mindful that this matter comes before it at a time when unprecedented disclosures have been made about this and other highly-sensitive programs designed to obtain foreign intelligence information and carry out counter-terrorism investigations. According to NSA Director Gen. Keith Alexander, the disclosures have caused "significant and irreversible damage to our nation." In the wake of these disclosures, whether and to what extent the government seeks to continue the program discussed in this Memorandum Opinion is a matter for the political branches of government to decide.

As discussed above, because there is no cognizable Fourth Amendment interest in a telephone company's metadata that it holds in the course of its business, the Court finds that there is no Constitutional impediment to the requested production. Finding no Constitutional issue, the Court directs its attention to the statute. The Court concludes that there are facts showing reasonable grounds to believe that the records sought are relevant to authorized investigations. This conclusion is supported not only by the plain text and structure of Section 215, but also by the statutory modifications and framework instituted by Congress. Furthermore, the Court finds that this result is strongly supported, if not required, by the doctrine of legislative re-enactment or ratification.

For these reasons, for the reasons stated in the Primary Order appended hereto, and pursuant to 50 U.S.C. § 1861(c)(1), the Court has GRANTED the Orders requested by the government.

Because of the public interest in this matter, pursuant to FISC Rule 62(a), the undersigned FISC Judge requests that this Memorandum Opinion and the Primary Order of July 19, 2013, appended herein, be published.

NOTES & QUESTIONS

1. *Two Different Results:* **Klayman *and* In re FBI.** The *Klayman* court found that the time had come to reject *Smith v. Maryland* as valid precedent. In contrast, the FISC in *In re FBI* declared it to be still valid. How do these courts approach the issue of the precedential value of this Supreme Court decision? Which arguments do you find most and least convincing?

2. *PCLOB on Section 215.* In its in-depth study of bulk collection of telephone metadata, the Privacy and Civil Liberties Oversight Board (PCLOB) reached highly negative conclusions. In its view, Section 215 "has shown minimal value

in safeguarding the nation from terrorism."[65] Moreover, the program's "implications for privacy and civil liberties" were serious. The Section 215 surveillance involved the government's ongoing collection of "virtually all telephone records of every American."

The time had come to end this program. PCLOB concluded: "Any government program that entails such costs requires a strong showing of efficacy. We do not believe that the NSA"s telephone records program conducted under Section 215 meets that standard." Short of its ultimate recommendation to end this surveillance, the PCLOB also called for immediate changes to the program, including reducing the retention period for bulk telephone records from five years to three and restricting the number of "hops" used in contact chaining from three to two. It also called for Congress to enact legislation permitting the FISC to hear from a panel of outside lawyers who would service as Special Advocates before the FISC.

In separate statements, Board Members Rachel Brand and Elisebeth Collins Cook disagreed with some of the Report. While joining in the Board's recommendation for certain immediate modifications to the program, including removing the "third hop," Brand argued that the program should continue. Brand felt that "the Report gives insufficient weight to the need for a proactive approach to combating terrorism."

Like Brand, Board Member Cook noted that she had "a different view from the Board as to the efficacy and utility of the Section 215 program." She thought that "a tool that allows investigators to more fully understand our adversaries in a relatively nimble way, allows investigators to verify and reinforce intelligence gathered from other programs or tools, and provides 'peace of mind,' has value."

3. ***PCLOB on Section 702.*** In contrast to its call for shutting down the Section 215 program, PCLOB had a largely positive reaction to the NSA's surveillance carried out pursuant to Section 702. It stated: "The program has proven valuable in the government's efforts to combat terrorism as well in other areas of foreign intelligence."[66] Perhaps most crucially, "the program has led the government to identify previously unknown individuals who are involved in international terrorism, and it has played a key role in discovering and disrupting specific terrorist plots aimed at the United States and other countries."

PCLOB also offered specific recommendations regarding this program. It found that the government was unable to assess the precise scope of the incidental collection under the program of information about U.S. persons. As a result, the Board recommended several measures to help provide information about the extent to which the NSA was acquiring and using communications involving U.S. persons or people located in the United States. It also recommended measures to improve accountability and transparency, including the release of declassified versions of the minimization procedures used by the NSA and other government agencies under Section 702.

---

[65] PCLOB, *Telephone Records Program, supra*, 11.

[66] PCLOB, *Section 702 Surveillance Program, supra*, 10.

4. President's Review Board. Following the Snowden leaks, President Obama created a Review Group on Intelligence and Communications Technologies. The members of the ad hoc committee were Richard A. Clarke, Michael J. Morell, Geoffrey R. Stone, Cass R. Sunstein, and Peter Swire. The announcement of the Review Group took place on August 27, 2013, and on December 12 of that year, the Group released its report, *Liberty and Security in a Changing World*. There were 46 recommendations in this report; of these, several concerned Section 215 and Section 720 oversight.

The Group offered numerous recommendations based on the central principles of protecting both national security and personal privacy as well as fulfilling the central task of risk management. With regard to Section 215 of FISA, it called for an end to the government's storage of bulk telephone metadata and the transition to a system in which such metadata is held privately by telephone companies. The government would then query this information when necessary for national security purposes. As a broad principle for the future, the Group noted: "without senior policy review, the government should not be permitted to collect and store mass, undigested, non-public personal information about US persons for the purpose of enabling future queries and data mining for foreign intelligence purposes."[67]

Regarding Section 702, the President's Review Group recommended that if the government legally intercepts a communication under this authority that "either includes a United States person as a participant or reveals information about a United States person[,]" it should purge any information about that United States person "unless it either has foreign intelligence value or is necessary to prevent serious harm to others." It also recommended that in implementing Section 702, the U.S. government should reaffirm that such surveillance "must be directed *exclusively* at the national security of the United States or our allies" and "must *not* be directed at illicit or illegitimate ends, such as the theft of trade secrets or obtaining commercial gain for domestic industries."[68]

5. *Bulk Metadata: Private Sector or Governmental Control?* Regarding the issue of leaving the bulk metadata of the Section 215 program with the private sector, the PCLOB's Rachel Brand took a different view from the President's Review Group's recommendation that it remain with telephone companies. It is worthwhile to contrast the two differing approaches. In her separate statement to the PCLOB's Report on the Telephone Records Program, Brand stated, "I doubt I could support a solution that transfers responsibility for the data to telephone service providers."[69] Legislation would be needed to create a data retention mandate, but this law might also "increase privacy concerns by making the data available for a wide range of purposes other than national security." Indeed, such legislation "would raise a host of questions about the

---

[67] President's Review Group on Intelligence and Communication Technologies, *Liberty and Security in a Changing World* 17 (2013).

[68] *Id.* at 29-30 (emphasis in original).

[69] PCLOB, *Telephone Records Program, supra*, 6 (Separate Statement by Board Member Rachel Brand).

legal status and handling of the data and the role and liabilities of the providers holding it." Brand concludes: "In my view, it would be wiser to leave the program as it is with the NSA than to transfer it to a third party."

6. ***Caselaw on Section 702.*** The FISC has heard multiple cases involving the Section 702 program. In particular, it was troubled by the upstream collection program. In *Redacted*, 2012 WL 9189263 (FISC Sept. 25, 2012), the FISC helpfully summarized its 2011 ruling that "the NSA was annually acquiring tens of thousands of Internet transactions containing at least one wholly domestic communication; that many of these wholly domestic communications were not to, from, or about a targeted facility; and that NSA was also likely acquiring tens of thousands of additional Internet transactions containing one or more targeted communications to and from U.S. persons in the United States."

In its *Redacted* opinion, the FISC decided that the remedial steps taken by the government since October 2011 reduced the risks of past upstream acquisitions under Section 702. For example, the NSA had purged data collected before October 31, 2011 and the utilization of new minimization procedures, which the FISC approved on November 30, 2011. The FISC declared "the outstanding issues raised by NSA's upstream collection of Internet transactions" to be "resolved, subject to the discussion of changes to the minimization procedures that appears below." The subsequent part of the opinion was, however, entirely redacted. Susan Landau argues, "Ultimately, the rules of data minimization should be subject to a public discussion, especially when they directly affect the public." What kind of information do you feel is needed about the Section 702 program to evaluate its policy implications?

In *United States v. Mohamud*, 2014 WL 2866749 (D. Or. 2014), the district court upheld Section 702 against constitutional and other legal challenges. It found that this provision in FISA did not violate the separation of powers doctrine as safeguarded by the Fourth Amendment. FISC review of Section 702 surveillance submissions "provides prior review by a neutral and detached magistrate." The result? This review "strengthens, not undermines, Fourth Amendment rights." The section was also found more generally to comport with the Fourth Amendment. The district court found that Section 702 fell within the exception in the *Keith* case for foreign intelligence. Following a FISC opinion, [Caption Redacted], 2011 WL 10945618 (FISC 2011), the *Mohamud* court decided that the collection under Section 702 was still as a whole directed at national security even if the NSA also acquired communications concerning U.S. persons inside the United States. The court also decided that the governmental action was also reasonable under the Fourth Amendment due to the numerous safeguards, such as targeting and minimization procedures, built into Section 702.

7. ***Lack of Investigative Capacity.*** Judge Reggie Walton, the chief judge of the FISC, has told the *Washington Post* that the court lacks tools to provide oversight of the government's surveillance programs. He stated, "The FISC is forced to rely upon the accuracy of the information that is provided to the Court. The FISC does not have the capacity to investigate issues of noncompliance,

and in that respect the FISC is in the same position as any other court when it comes to enforcing [government] compliance with its orders."[70] Judge Walton's comments came after the *Post* obtained an NSA classified internal NSA report on its failures to follow certain of the agency's privacy rules and other legal restrictions. Should the FISC's oversight be strengthened, or is such a role best played by the Executive Branch, Congress, or through an internal NSA audit function?

8. ***The USA FREEDOM Act.*** In 2015, the USA Freedom Act, H.R. 2048, S. 1123, banned the bulk collection of Americans' Internet metadata and telephone records under the Patriot Act Section 215. The government must now identify a person, account, address, or personal device when requesting records, limiting the scope of tangible things sought "to the greatest extent reasonably possible." However, the bill permits authorities to collect phone records two degrees (or "hops") of separation from targeted individuals.

---

[70] Carol D. Leonnig, *Court: Ability to Police U.S. Spying Program Limited,* Washington Post (Aug. 15, 2013).

CHAPTER **6**

HEALTH PRIVACY

CHAPTER OUTLINE

Health information is considered by many to be among the most private of information. People desire to keep matters about their health confidential because certain diseases have long been associated with great stigma (e.g., leprosy); other diseases are correlated in other people's minds with certain lifestyles and behaviors (e.g., sexually transmitted diseases), and certain debilitating or fatal illnesses might alter people's perception of the sufferer's capabilities and potentialities. Further, people want to keep illnesses private because they want to prevent others from viewing them differently. Knowledge of a person's health can result in being turned down for a job, being fired, being discriminated against, being rejected for a loan, and so on.

Today's health care system is vast and complex. Medical data is frequently disclosed to doctors and is widely circulated among hospitals, insurers, employers, and government agencies. At hospitals, dozens of nurses and staff have access to a patient's records.

The increasing transformation of medical records into digital format brings great benefits, as it can enhance the accuracy of people's medical histories as well as the ease with which doctors can learn about important aspects of their patient's health. However, the increasing flow of health information raises substantial privacy concerns. A widening audience of outsiders now collects patient medical information in order to monitor and shape how health care is administered.[1]

Health privacy in the United States is governed by a myriad of different laws and regulations. States have traditionally been the primary source for health privacy law. The privacy torts can provide remedies for intrusions into areas where one is receiving health care or public disclosures of private medical information. Tort law also regulates the confidentiality of the relationship between patients and their physicians or other health caregivers. Additionally, many states have passed a variety of statutes to regulate health privacy. The level of protection, however, varies widely from state to state.

At the federal level, health privacy was unregulated until the last years of the twentieth century. Pursuant to its authority under the Health Insurance Portability and Accountability Act (HIPAA), enacted in 1996, the Department of Health and Human Services promulgated regulations under HIPAA. The ensuing framework, which became effective in the early 2000s, provides a minimum level of protection for all states. State regulations more protective of privacy still remain in effect. Health privacy is also protected by the constitutional right to privacy, but this protection applies only to data maintained by government officials and entities. This limitation flows from the requirement in the U.S. Constitution that there be "state action" before most constitutional rights apply.

---

[1] Paul M. Schwartz, *Privacy and the Economics of Health Care Information*, 76 Tex. L. Rev. 1 (1997).

A. CONFIDENTIALITY OF MEDICAL INFORMATION

1. PROFESSIONAL ETHICS AND EVIDENTIARY PRIVILEGES

(a) Ethical Rules

OATH AND LAW OF HIPPOCRATES

(circa 400 B.C.)

Whatever, in connection with my professional service, or not in connection with it, I see or hear, in the life of men, which ought not to be spoken of abroad, I will not divulge, as reckoning that all such should be kept secret.

CURRENT OPINIONS OF THE JUDICIAL COUNCIL OF THE AMERICAN MEDICAL ASSOCIATION CANON 5.05

. . . [T]he information disclosed to a physician during the course of the relationship between physician and patient is confidential to the greatest possible degree. . . . The physician should not reveal confidential communications or information without the express consent of the patient, unless required to do so by law.

(b) Evidentiary Privileges

An evidentiary privilege confers on an individual the right to refuse to testify or reveal facts about certain matters or the right to prevent another from doing so. Evidentiary privileges apply to almost all governmental proceedings, particularly judicial proceedings. Privileges permit the suppression of truthful and relevant evidence. For example, a client may tell her attorney certain confidential inculpatory information. The attorney-client privilege protects the confidentiality of that communication; generally, an attorney cannot be forced to testify as to that information.

There are a number of recognized privileges — and certain exceptions to them. The central privilege is the attorney-client privilege. In *Upjohn Co. v. United States*, 449 U.S. 383 (1981), the Supreme Court explained the rationale behind this privilege:

> The attorney-client privilege is the oldest of the privileges for confidential communications known to the common law. Its purpose is to encourage full and frank communication between attorneys and their clients and thereby promote broader public interests in the observance of law and administration of justice. The privilege recognizes that sound legal advice or advocacy serves public ends and that such advice or advocacy depends upon the lawyer's being fully informed by the client. As we stated last Term in *Trammel v. United States*, "The lawyer-client privilege rests on the need for the advocate and counselor to know all that relates to the client's reasons for seeking representation if the professional mission is to be carried out." And in *Fisher v. United States*, we recognized the purpose

~~of the privilege to be~~ "to encourage clients to make full disclosure to their attorneys."

In *Upjohn*, the Court found that the attorney-client privilege extended to in-house counsel at corporations. It also held communications between Upjohn's general counsel and lower level employees to be privileged. These communications were made "within the scope of the employees' corporate duties, and the employees themselves were sufficiently aware that they were being questioned in order that the corporation could obtain legal advice." The Court observed, "Consistent with the underlying purposes of the attorney-client privilege, these communications must be protected against compelled disclosure."

Evidentiary privileges protect only certain confidential relationships. Some recognized privileges include the (1) spousal privilege whereby a person can refuse to testify against his or her spouse in a criminal case; (2) spousal privilege in preventing one's spouse or former spouse from disclosing marital communications in criminal or civil cases; (3) accountant-client privilege; (4) priest-penitent privilege, whereby a person can prevent the disclosure of confidential communications made when seeking spiritual advice from his or her clergy member; (5) physician-patient privilege; (6) voter privilege, whereby a person can refuse to testify as to how he or she voted in any political election; (7) journalist privilege, where journalists can refuse to divulge information sources; and (8) executive privilege, permitting the President of the United States from divulging secrets necessary to the carrying out of his or her constitutional functions. Not all of these privileges are recognized in every state or in the federal courts. Further, the precise contours of each privilege sometimes vary from state to state.

Not all confidential relationships are protected by privileges. Although spousal privileges are widely recognized, the vast majority of jurisdictions do not recognize a parent-child privilege.

Privileges protect communications by both parties to a confidential relationship. Thus, with regard to the physician-patient privilege, statements made by the holder of the privilege (the patient) as well as by the physician to the patient are privileged.

The holder of the privilege may waive the privilege, but the professional remains bound by the privilege and is not permitted to waive it without the holder's consent. It is well settled that a voluntary knowing disclosure waives a privilege. *See Gray v. Bicknell,* 86 F.3d 1472 (8th Cir. 1996). However, courts are split as to whether inadvertent disclosures waive the privilege. *See, e.g., Georgetown Manor, Inc. v. Ethan Allen, Inc.,* 753 F. Supp. 936 (S.D. Fla. 1991) (inadvertent disclosure does not waive the privilege); *In re Sealed Case,* 877 F.2d 976 (D.C. Cir. 1989) (inadvertent disclosure waives the privilege); *Gray v. Bicknell,* 86 F.3d 1472 (8th Cir. 1996) (inadvertent disclosure sometimes waives the privilege based on application of a five-factor test).

In certain circumstances the privilege does not apply. For example, if a patient sues a physician or a client sues an attorney, the physician or attorney can testify as to confidential matters at issue in the lawsuit. Another limitation is the crime-fraud exception, which provides that if the communication is made in furtherance of a crime, fraud, or other misconduct then it is not privileged. *See United States v. Zolin,* 491 U.S. 554 (1989).

Unlike certain other privileges, such as the attorney-client privilege and priest-penitent privilege, the common law did not recognize the physician-patient privilege. In contrast, a majority of states have established a physician-patient privilege.[2] States make exceptions in the physician-patient privilege for the reporting of certain diseases or injuries that implicate public health and safety.

JAFFEE V. REDMOND

518 U.S. 1 (1996)

STEVENS, J. . . . Petitioner is the administrator of the estate of Ricky Allen. Respondents are Mary Lu Redmond, a former police officer, and the Village of Hoffman Estates, Illinois, her employer during the time that she served on the police force. Petitioner commenced this action against respondents after Redmond shot and killed Allen while on patrol duty.

On June 27, 1991, Redmond was the first officer to respond to a "fight in progress" call at an apartment complex. As she arrived at the scene, two of Allen's sisters ran toward her squad car, waving their arms and shouting that there had been a stabbing in one of the apartments. Redmond testified at trial that she relayed this information to her dispatcher and requested an ambulance. She then exited her car and walked toward the apartment building. Before Redmond reached the building, several men ran out, one waving a pipe. When the men ignored her order to get on the ground, Redmond drew her service revolver. Two other men then burst out of the building, one, Ricky Allen, chasing the other. According to Redmond, Allen was brandishing a butcher knife and disregarded her repeated commands to drop the weapon. Redmond shot Allen when she believed he was about to stab the man he was chasing. Allen died at the scene. Redmond testified that before other officers arrived to provide support, "people came pouring out of the buildings," and a threatening confrontation between her and the crowd ensued.

Petitioner filed suit in Federal District Court alleging that Redmond had violated Allen's constitutional rights by using excessive force during the encounter at the apartment complex. The complaint sought damages under Rev. Stat. § 1979, 42 U.S.C. § 1983, and the Illinois wrongful-death statute. At trial, petitioner presented testimony from members of Allen's family that conflicted with Redmond's version of the incident in several important respects. They testified, for example, that Redmond drew her gun before exiting her squad car and that Allen was unarmed when he emerged from the apartment building.

During pretrial discovery petitioner learned that after the shooting Redmond had participated in about 50 counseling sessions with Karen Beyer, a clinical social worker licensed by the State of Illinois and employed at that time by the Village of Hoffman Estates. Petitioner sought access to Beyer's notes concerning the sessions for use in cross-examining Redmond. Respondents vigorously resisted the discovery. They asserted that the contents of the conversations between Beyer and Redmond were protected against involuntary disclosure by a psychotherapist-patient privilege. The district judge rejected this argument. Neither Beyer nor Redmond, however, complied with his order to disclose the contents of Beyer's

---

[2] *See* Glen Weissenberger, *Federal Evidence* § 501.8 (1996).

notes. At depositions and on the witness stand both either refused to answer certain questions or professed an inability to recall details of their conversations.

In his instructions at the end of the trial, the judge advised the jury that the refusal to turn over Beyer's notes had no "legal justification" and that the jury could therefore presume that the contents of the notes would have been unfavorable to respondents. The jury awarded petitioner $45,000 on the federal claim and $500,000 on her state-law claim. . . .

Rule 501 of the Federal Rules of Evidence authorizes federal courts to define new privileges by interpreting "common law principles . . . in the light of reason and experience." . . . The Senate Report accompanying the 1975 adoption of the Rules indicates that Rule 501 "should be understood as reflecting the view that the recognition of a privilege based on a confidential relationship . . . should be determined on a case-by-case basis." The Rule thus did not freeze the law governing the privileges of witnesses in federal trials at a particular point in our history, but rather directed federal courts to "continue the evolutionary development of testimonial privileges."

The common-law principles underlying the recognition of testimonial privileges can be stated simply. "For more than three centuries it has now been recognized as a fundamental maxim that the public . . . has a right to every man's evidence. When we come to examine the various claims of exemption, we start with the primary assumption that there is a general duty to give what testimony one is capable of giving, and that any exemptions which may exist are distinctly exceptional, being so many derogations from a positive general rule." Exceptions from the general rule disfavoring testimonial privileges may be justified, however, by a "public good transcending the normally predominant principle of utilizing all rational means for ascertaining truth."

Guided by these principles, the question we address today is whether a privilege protecting confidential communications between a psychotherapist and her patient "promotes sufficiently important interests to outweigh the need for probative evidence. . . ." Both "reason and experience" persuade us that it does. . . .

Like the spousal and attorney-client privileges, the psychotherapist-patient privilege is "rooted in the imperative need for confidence and trust." Treatment by a physician for physical ailments can often proceed successfully on the basis of a physical examination, objective information supplied by the patient, and the results of diagnostic tests. Effective psychotherapy, by contrast, depends upon an atmosphere of confidence and trust in which the patient is willing to make a frank and complete disclosure of facts, emotions, memories, and fears. Because of the sensitive nature of the problems for which individuals consult psychotherapists, disclosure of confidential communications made during counseling sessions may cause embarrassment or disgrace. For this reason, the mere possibility of disclosure may impede development of the confidential relationship necessary for successful treatment. . . .

The psychotherapist privilege serves the public interest by facilitating the provision of appropriate treatment for individuals suffering the effects of a mental or emotional problem. The mental health of our citizenry, no less than its physical health, is a public good of transcendent importance.

In contrast to the significant public and private interests supporting recognition of the privilege, the likely evidentiary benefit that would result from the denial of the privilege is modest. If the privilege were rejected, confidential conversations between psychotherapists and their patients would surely be chilled, particularly when it is obvious that the circumstances that give rise to the need for treatment will probably result in litigation. Without a privilege, much of the desirable evidence to which litigants such as petitioner seek access — for example, admissions against interest by a party — is unlikely to come into being. This unspoken "evidence" will therefore serve no greater truth-seeking function than if it had been spoken and privileged.

That it is appropriate for the federal courts to recognize a psychotherapist privilege under Rule 501 is confirmed by the fact that all 50 States and the District of Columbia have enacted into law some form of psychotherapist privilege. . . .

. . . [W]e hold that confidential communications between a licensed psychotherapist and her patients in the course of diagnosis or treatment are protected from compelled disclosure under Rule 501 of the Federal Rules of Evidence. . . .

. . . The reasons for recognizing a privilege for treatment by psychiatrists and psychologists apply with equal force to treatment by a clinical social worker such as Karen Beyer. Today, social workers provide a significant amount of mental health treatment. Their clients often include the poor and those of modest means who could not afford the assistance of a psychiatrist or psychologist, but whose counseling sessions serve the same public goals. . . .

SCALIA, J. joined by REHNQUIST, C.J. dissenting. . . . The Court has discussed at some length the benefit that will be purchased by creation of the evidentiary privilege in this case: the encouragement of psychoanalytic counseling. It has not mentioned the purchase price: occasional injustice. That is the cost of every rule which excludes reliable and probative evidence — or at least every one categorical enough to achieve its announced policy objective. . . . For the rule proposed here, the victim is more likely to be some individual who is prevented from proving a valid claim — or (worse still) prevented from establishing a valid defense. The latter is particularly unpalatable for those who love justice, because it causes the courts of law not merely to let stand a wrong, but to become themselves the instruments of wrong. . . .

When is it, one must wonder, that the psychotherapist came to play such an indispensable role in the maintenance of the citizenry's mental health? For most of history, men and women have worked out their difficulties by talking to, *inter alios*, parents, siblings, best friends, and bartenders — none of whom was awarded a privilege against testifying in court. Ask the average citizen: Would your mental health be more significantly impaired by preventing you from seeing a psychotherapist, or by preventing you from getting advice from your mom? I have little doubt what the answer would be. Yet there is no mother-child privilege. . . .

Even where it is certain that absence of the psychotherapist privilege will inhibit disclosure of the information, it is not clear to me that that is an unacceptable state of affairs. Let us assume the very worst in the circumstances of the present case: that to be truthful about what was troubling her, the police officer who sought counseling would have to confess that she shot without reason, and wounded an innocent man. . . . [There is no] reason why she should be enabled to deny her guilt in the criminal trial — or in a civil trial for negligence — while yet obtaining the benefits of psychotherapy by confessing guilt to a social worker who cannot testify. It seems to me entirely fair to say that if she wishes the benefits of telling the truth she must also accept the adverse consequences. . . .

NOTES & QUESTIONS

1. *Mental Health as a Public Good? Privacy as a Public Good?* Justice Stevens's opinion for the Court speaks of mental health for the citizenry as providing "a public good of transcendent importance." The protection of confidential communications between a psychotherapist and her patient from involuntary disclosure serves this important public interest. More generally, Paul Schwartz has argued that privacy is such a public good. He writes: "A public good benefits all of society and is generally viewed as something that cannot be created through an unregulated market."[3] Schwartz also proposes that "information privacy can be seen as a commons that requires some degree of social and legal control to construct and then maintain." Will people decline to engage in a given social interaction (e.g., seeking psychotherapy) without the evidentiary privilege that *Jaffee* recognizes? Most people are unaware of evidence law when speaking with their therapist or doctor. Are privileges necessary to encourage frank disclosures by patients to therapists?

2. *Is There a Dangerous Patient Exception to the Privilege?* Are there any limits to the privilege? In a footnote the Court indicated that there might be certain limits:

> Although it would be premature to speculate about most future developments in the federal psychotherapist privilege, we do not doubt that there are situations in which the privilege must give way, for example, if a serious threat of harm to the patient or to others can be averted only by means of a disclosure by the therapist.

Following *Jaffee*, three federal appellate courts considered whether there was in fact a "dangerous patient exception" to the privilege as suggested by the footnote above. In *United States v. Glass*, 113 F.3d 1356 (10th Cir. 1998), the court acknowledged that there may be "situations in which the privilege must give way." In contrast, the court in *United States v. Hayes*, 227 F.3d 578 (6th Cir. 2000), concluded that there is no "'dangerous patient' exception to the federal psychotherapist/patient testimonial privilege." In *United States v. Chase*, 340 F.3d 978 (9th Cir. 2003) (en banc), the Ninth Circuit agreed with *Hayes*:

> A dangerous-patient exception to the federal psychotherapist-patient testimonial privilege would significantly injure the interests justifying the existence of the privilege; would have little practical advantage; would encroach significantly on the policy prerogatives of the states; and would go against the experience of all but one of the states in our circuit, as well as the persuasive

---

[3] Paul M. Schwartz, *Property, Privacy, and Personal Data*, 117 Harv. L. Rev. 2055, 2087-88 (2004).

Proposed Rules. We therefore decline to recognize a dangerous-patient exception to the federal psychotherapist-patient privilege.

2. TORT LIABILITY FOR DISCLOSURE OF PATIENT INFORMATION

McCORMICK V. ENGLAND

494 S.E.2d 431 (S.C. Ct. App. 1997)

ANDERSON, J. . . . Dr. England was the family physician for McCormick, her former husband, and their children. McCormick and her husband became involved in a divorce action in which custody of the children was at issue. In support of his Motion for Emergency Relief and a Restraining Order, McCormick's husband submitted . . . letters to the family court regarding McCormick's emotional status. . . . [One] letter was prepared by Dr. England and was addressed "To Whom It May Concern." In his letter, Dr. England diagnosed McCormick as suffering from "major depression and alcoholism, acute and chronic." Further, Dr. England stated the children had experienced school difficulties due to the family discord caused by McCormick's drinking. He stated it was his medical opinion that McCormick was "a danger to herself and to her family with her substance abuse and major depressive symptoms," and concluded that she required hospitalization. There is no indication in the record that the letter was prepared under court order. [Among other things, McCormick sued for public disclosure of private facts and breach of confidentiality. The trial court dismissed her breach of confidentiality claim, stating that "It is well known that South Carolina does not recognize the physician-patient privilege at common law." McCormick appeals.] . . .

Whether a separate tort action for a physician's breach of a duty of confidentiality exists under the common law is a novel issue in this state. Dr. England contends South Carolina courts have previously ruled that no duty of confidentiality exists between a physician and patient; therefore, there can be no action for its breach. . . .

"At common law neither the patient nor the physician has the privilege to refuse to *disclose in court* a communication of one to the other, nor does either have a privilege that the communication not be disclosed to a third person." Although many states have statutorily created a "physician-patient testimonial privilege," South Carolina has not enacted a similar statute and does not recognize the physician-patient privilege. However, the absence of a testimonial privilege prohibiting certain in-court disclosures is not determinative of our issue because this evidentiary privilege is distinguishable from a duty of confidentiality. As our Supreme Court recently observed in *South Carolina State Board of Medical Examiners v. Hedgepath,* 480 S.E.2d 724 (S.C. 1997): "The terms 'privilege' and 'confidences' are not synonymous, and a professional's duty to maintain his client's confidences is independent of the issue whether he can be legally compelled to reveal some or all of those confidences, that is, whether those communications are privileged." . . .

A person who lacks medical training usually must disclose much information to his or her physician which may have a bearing upon diagnosis and treatment.

Such disclosures are not totally voluntary; therefore, in order to obtain cooperation, it is expected that the physician will keep such information confidential. "Being a fiduciary relationship, mutual trust and confidence are essential."

The belief that physicians should respect the confidences revealed by their patients in the course of treatment is a concept that has its genesis in the Hippocratic Oath, which states in pertinent part: "Whatever, in connection with my professional practice, or not in connection with it, I see or hear, in the life of men, which ought not to be spoken of abroad, I will not divulge as reckoning that all such should be kept secret."

The modern trend recognizes that the confidentiality of the physician-patient relationship is an interest worth protecting. A majority of the jurisdictions faced with the issue have recognized a cause of action against a physician for the unauthorized disclosure of confidential information unless the disclosure is compelled by law or is in the patient's interest or the public interest.

In the absence of express legislation, courts have found the basis for a right of action for wrongful disclosure in four main sources: (1) state physician licensing statutes, (2) evidentiary rules and privileged communication statutes which prohibit a physician from testifying in judicial proceedings, (3) common law principles of trust, and (4) the Hippocratic Oath and principles of medical ethics which proscribe the revelation of patient confidences. The jurisdictions that recognize the duty of confidentiality have relied on various theories for the cause of action, including invasion of privacy, breach of implied contract, medical malpractice, and breach of a fiduciary duty or a duty of confidentiality. . . .

We find the reasoning of the cases from other jurisdictions persuasive on this issue and today we join the majority and hold that an actionable tort lies for a physician's breach of the duty to maintain the confidences of his or her patient in the absence of a compelling public interest or other justification for the disclosure. . . .

[Breach of confidentiality is a distinct tort from the tort of public disclosure of private facts.] Invasion of privacy consists of the public disclosure of private facts about the plaintiff, and the gravamen of the tort is publicity as opposed to mere publication. The defendant must intentionally reveal facts which are of no legitimate public interest, as there is no right of privacy in public matters. In addition, the disclosure must be such as would be highly offensive and likely to cause serious mental injury to a person of ordinary sensibilities.

Thus, an invasion of privacy claim narrowly proscribes the conduct to that which is "highly offensive" and "likely to cause serious mental injury." This standard is not consistent with the duty attaching to a confidential relationship because it focuses on the *content,* rather than the *source* of the information. The unauthorized revelation of confidential medical information should be protected without regard to the degree of its offensiveness. The privacy standard would not protect information that happens to be very distressing to a particular patient, even though the individual would likely not have revealed it without the expectation of confidentiality.

Further, the requirement of "publicity" is a limitation which would preclude many cases involving a breach of confidentiality. Publicity involves disclosure to the public, not just an individual or a small group. However, where the information disclosed is received in confidence, "one can imagine many cases where the greatest injury results from disclosure to a single person, such as a spouse, or to a small group, such as an insurance company resisting a claim. A confidential relationship is breached if unauthorized disclosure is made to only one person not a party to the confidence, but the right of privacy does not cover such a case." . . .

HAMMONDS V. AETNA CASUALTY & SURETY CO.

243 F. Supp. 793 (D. Ohio 1965)

CONNELL, C.J. Plaintiff has complained that the defendant insurance company, without just cause, had persuaded the plaintiff's treating physician to discontinue that relationship, and, further, that the defendant induced the doctor to divulge confidential information gained through the physician-patient relationship. In particular, it is alleged that the defendant, at the behest of a prominent defense attorney, persuaded Dr. Alexander Ling, the plaintiff's treating physician, to surrender certain undisclosed confidential information for use in pending litigation against the plaintiff on the false pretext that the plaintiff was contemplating a malpractice suit against Dr. Ling. . . .

In all medical jurisprudence there are few problems which have deserved and received more concentrated attention than the protection of the personal information which a patient remits to his physician. This relationship "is one of trust and confidence. It is submitted that the best interest of the patient is served in trusting his welfare to the skill and industry of his physician." To foster the best interest of the patient and to insure a climate most favorable to a complete recovery, men of medicine have urged that patients be totally frank in their discussions with their physicians. To encourage the desired candor, men of law have formulated a strong policy of confidentiality to assure patients that only they themselves may unlock the doctor's silence in regard to those private disclosures. . . .

. . . We conclude, therefore, that ordinarily a physician receives information relating to a patient's health in a confidential capacity and should not disclose such information without the patient's consent, except where the public interest or the private interest of the patient so demands. . . .

Any time a doctor undertakes the treatment of a patient, and the consensual relationship of physician and patient is established, two jural obligations (of significance here) are simultaneously assumed by the doctor. Doctor and patient enter into a simple contract, the patient hoping that he will be cured and the doctor optimistically assuming that he will be compensated. As an implied condition of that contract, this Court is of the opinion that the doctor warrants that any confidential information gained through the relationship will not be released without the patient's permission. Almost every member of the public is aware of the promise of discretion contained in the Hippocratic Oath, and every patient has a right to rely upon this warranty of silence. The promise of secrecy is as much an express warranty as the advertisement of a commercial entrepreneur. Consequently, when a doctor breaches his duty of secrecy, he is in violation of part of his obligations under the contract.

When a patient seeks out a doctor and retains him, he must admit him to the most private part of the material domain of man. Nothing material is more important or more intimate to man than the health of his mind and body. Since the layman is unfamiliar with the road to recovery, he cannot sift the circumstances of his life and habits to determine what is information pertinent to his health. As a consequence, he must disclose all information in his consultations with his doctor — even that which is embarrassing, disgraceful or incriminating. To promote full disclosure, the medical profession extends the promise of secrecy referred to above. The candor which this promise elicits is necessary to the effective pursuit of health; there can be no reticence, no reservation, no reluctance when patients discuss their problems with their doctors. But the disclosure is certainly intended to be private. If a doctor should reveal any of these confidences, he surely effects an invasion of the privacy of his patient. We are of the opinion that the preservation of the patient's privacy is no mere ethical duty upon the part of the doctor; there is a legal duty as well. The unauthorized revelation of medical secrets, or any confidential communication given in the course of treatment, is tortious conduct which may be the basis for an action in damages. . . .

However, we are not critically concerned here solely with an alleged disclosure by a doctor since the complaint accuses Dr. Ling only of a misfeasance predicated upon misinformation and directs its plea for redress not against the doctor but against the defendant insurance company which allegedly supplied this inaccurate information. . . . As we have noted above, the patient necessarily reposes a great deal of trust not only in the skill of the physician but in his discretion as well. The introduction into the relationship of this aura of trust, and the expectation of confidentiality which results therefrom, imposes the fiduciary obligations upon the doctor. As a consequence, all reported cases dealing with this point hold that the relationship of physician and patient is a fiduciary one. . . .

By its very definition, the term "fiduciary relationship" imports the notion that "if a wrong arises, the same remedy exists against the wrongdoer on behalf of the principal as would exist against a trustee on behalf of the cestui que trust." Therefore it is readily apparent that the legal obligations of a trustee are imposed upon any person operating in a fiduciary capacity and the same principles of law participation in breaches of trust must applicable to all fiduciaries.

It also follows that the same principles of law governing third party participation in breaches of trust must also apply to one who participates in or induces the breach of any fiduciary duty. The law is settled in Ohio and elsewhere participation in breaches of trust must also apply to one who participates in or induces the breach of any fiduciary duty. The law is settled in Ohio and elsewhere that a third party who induces a breach of a trustee's duty of loyalty, or participates in such a breach, or knowingly accepts any benefit from such a breach, becomes directly liable to the aggrieved party. . . . [W]hen one induces a doctor to divulge confidential information in violation of that doctor's legal responsibility to his patient, the third party may also be held liable in damages to the patient.

NOTES & QUESTIONS

1. ***The Breach of Confidentiality Tort.*** The "clear modern consensus of the case law" is to recognize the breach of confidentiality tort.[4] The tort creates liability when a duty of confidentiality exists and is breached. In *McCormick,* the court found the existence of a duty of confidentiality in various licensing statutes, evidentiary rules, ethical rules, and the common law principles of trust (fiduciary relationships). Courts have also found duties of confidentiality based on implied contracts of confidentiality.

One of the sources of a duty of confidentiality is the existence of a fiduciary relationship. "A fiduciary relationship is one founded on trust or confidence reposed by one person in the integrity and fidelity of another. Out of such a relation, the laws raise the rule that neither party may exert influence or pressure upon the other, take selfish advantage of his trust[,] or deal with the subject matter of the trust in such a way as to benefit himself or prejudice the other except in the exercise of utmost good faith." *Mobile Oil Corp. v. Rubenfeld,* 339 N.Y.S.2d 623, 632 (1972). According to the Restatement: "[O]ne standing in a fiduciary relation with another is subject to liability to the other for harm resulting from a breach of duty imposed by the relation." Restatement (Second) of Torts § 874. There are no fixed sets of relationships that are fiduciary ones, and courts "have carefully refrained from defining instances of fiduciary relations in such a manner that other and perhaps new cases might be excluded." *Swerhun v. General Motors Corp.,* 812 F. Supp. 1218 (M.D. Fla. 1993). Courts look to the following factors in defining a fiduciary relationship: "[T]he degree of kinship of the parties; the disparity in age, health, and mental condition; education and business experience between the parties; and the extent to which the allegedly subservient party entrusted the handling of . . . business affairs to the other and reposed faith and confidence in [that person or entity]." *Pottinger v. Pottinger,* 605 N.E.2d 1130 (Ill. App. 1992).[5]

The breach of confidentiality tort is not just limited to disclosures by physicians. For example, it has been applied to bankers and other professionals and entities. *See, e.g., Peterson v. Idaho First Nat'l Bank,* 367 P.2d 284 (Idaho 1961) (bankers); *Rich v. New York C. & H. R. R. Co.,* 87 N.Y. 382, 390 (N.Y. 1882) (attorneys); *Wagenheim v. Alexander Grant & Co.,* 482 N.E.2d 955, 961 (Ohio Ct. App. 1983) (accountants). The tort applies whenever a duty of confidentiality exists.

As Neil Richards and Daniel Solove explain:

> Slighted by Warren and Brandeis and virtually ignored by Prosser, confidentiality had a stunted development in the United States during the twentieth century, and it still has not fully penetrated into the culture of American privacy law. In the United States, the breach of confidentiality tort

---

[4] David A. Elder, *Privacy Torts* § 5:2 (2002).

[5] For more background about the breach of confidentiality tort, see Alan B. Vickery, Note, *Breach of Confidence: An Emerging Tort,* 82 Colum. L. Rev. 1426, 1426 (1982); G. Michael Harvey, Comment, *Confidentiality: A Measured Response to the Failure of Privacy,* 140 U. Pa. L. Rev. 2385, 2396 (1992); Susan M. Gilles, *Promises Betrayed: Breach of Confidence as a Remedy for Invasions of Privacy,* 43 Buff. L. Rev. 1, 20-25 (1995).

has grown up in the shadow of the Warren and Brandeis torts. Not only did Prosser overlook breach of confidentiality, but also in many privacy cases, breach of confidentiality could have been an option but often was not explored. Breach of confidentiality remained ignored and underdeveloped while the Warren and Brandeis torts enjoyed the spotlight. Although the tort of breach of confidence has seen some development in recent decades, it remains in a relatively obscure and frequently overlooked corner of American tort law. . . .

The American breach of confidentiality tort has yet to come close to reaching its fullest potential. The tort still applies only to a limited set of relationships, with most cases involving the patient-physician relationship. . . . Having only recently gained momentum, the breach of confidentiality tort often has not been raised in many cases where it might have relevance.

In England, the courts have rejected the Warren and Brandeis privacy torts, but have developed a robust tort of breach of confidence:

The law of confidentiality in England also has attributes that the American privacy torts lack. In America, the prevailing belief is that people assume the risk of betrayal when they share secrets with each other. But in England, spouses, ex-spouses, friends, and nearly anyone else can be liable for divulging confidences. As one English court noted, "when people kiss and later one of them tells, that second person is almost certainly breaking a confidential arrangement." Confidentiality thus recognizes that nondisclosure expectations emerge not only from norms of individual dignity, but also from norms of relationships, trust, and reliance on promises. American privacy law has never fully embraced privacy within relationships; it typically views information exposed to others as no longer private. Although a tort remedying breach of confidence would emerge later on in American law, it developed slowly in comparison to the Warren and Brandeis privacy torts.[6]

One important exception to the tort is that physicians will not be liable for disclosing confidential medical information when it is necessary to protect others from danger or when it is required by law. For example, the court in *Simonsen v. Swenson,* 177 N.W. 831 (Neb. 1920), concluded that a doctor was not liable for disclosing the fact that a patient had syphilis, which at the time was believed to be highly contagious without sexual contact.[7]

2. ***Inducing Breaches of Confidentiality.*** Recall the following statement in the court's opinion: "The law is settled in Ohio and elsewhere that a third party who induces a breach of a trustee's duty of loyalty, or participates in such a breach, or knowingly accepts any benefit from such a breach, becomes directly liable to the aggrieved party." The Restatement provides: "A person who knowingly assists a fiduciary in committing a breach of trust is himself guilty of tortious conduct." Restatement (Second) of Torts § 874 comment (c).

3. ***Holding a Hospital Liable for Breach of Confidentiality.*** In *Biddle v. Warren General Hospital,* 715 N.E.2d 518 (Ohio 1999), a law firm decided to earn extra

---

[6] Neil M. Richards & Daniel J. Solove, *Privacy's Other Path: Recovering the Law of Confidentiality,* 96 Geo. L.J. 123, 156-58, 126 (2007).

[7] For more on this issue, see Lawrence O. Gostin & James G. Hodge, Jr., *Piercing the Veil of Secrecy in HIV/AIDS and Other Sexually Transmitted Diseases: Theories of Privacy and Disclosure in Partner Notification,* 5 Duke J. Gender L. & Pol'y 9, 16-23 (1998).

money by making a deal to assist a hospital in determining whether unpaid patient bills could be submitted to the Social Security Administration (SSA) for payment. Under the plan, the hospital released its patient registration forms to the law firm, which would evaluate which patients could qualify for Social Security benefits and then contact those patients and urge them to apply for benefits. In this way, the hospital would be paid by the SSA for these patients. However, the hospital released the patient data to the firm without obtaining the consent of the patients. The patients brought a class action against the hospital and the firm. The court held that not only was there a viable breach of confidentiality claim against the hospital, but also the firm could be liable for inducing such a breach:

> We hold that a third party can be held liable for inducing the unauthorized, unprivileged disclosure of nonpublic medical information that a physician or hospital has learned within a physician-patient relationship. To establish liability the plaintiff must prove that: (1) the defendant knew or reasonably should have known of the existence of the physician-patient relationship; (2) the defendant intended to induce the physician to disclose information about the patient or the defendant reasonably should have anticipated that his actions would induce the physician to disclose such information; and (3) the defendant did not reasonably believe that the physician could disclose that information to the defendant without violating the duty of confidentiality that the physician owed the patient.

Suppose a person's physician were to disclose, without the patient's consent, the patient's medical file to a journalist. The journalist, knowing that the medical file was disclosed in breach of the doctor's fiduciary duty to the patient, accepted it anyway and published details about the patient's medical condition in the newspaper. Would the patient have a cause of action against the journalist in addition to the doctor? Would your conclusion be different in light of *Bartnicki v. Vopper* (Chapter 2)?

4. ***The Breach of Confidentiality Tort in the Modern Health Care System.*** Consider Lawrence Gostin:

> The rule of confidentiality is widely respected in law and medicine, and rightfully so. Indeed, in the past, confidentiality has worked reasonably well in safeguarding privacy. Much, if not all, of the intimate knowledge of the patient was generated within the physician-patient relationship, which was often meaningful and enduring. The patient's health record contained information primarily obtained during sessions between the physician and patient, so that the entire record was regarded as confidential. The record keepers, moreover, were the physicians themselves who took primary responsibility for the security of medical records.
>
> The rule of confidentiality does not work nearly as well in a modern information society. Health data today, in an era of electronic information gathering, is based only in small part on the physician-patient relationship. Many therapeutic encounters in a managed care context are not with a primary care physician. Patients may see many different physicians, nonphysician specialists, nurse practitioners and other ancillary health care professionals within and outside of the health care plan. The information obtained in these

encounters has uncertain protection under traditional rules of confidentiality. Focusing legal protection on a single therapeutic relationship within this information environment is an anachronistic vestige of an earlier and simpler time in medicine. The health record, moreover, contains a substantial amount of information gathered from numerous primary and secondary sources: laboratories, pharmacies, schools, public health officials, researchers, insurers, and other individuals and institutions. The health records of patients are kept not only in the office of a private physician or in a health plan, but also may be kept by government agencies, regional health database organizations, or information brokers. Databases maintained in each of these settings will be collected and transmitted electronically, reconfigured, and linked.

Rules enforcing informational privacy in health care place a duty on the entity that possesses the information. Thus, the keeper of the record — whether it is in a private physician's office, a hospital, or an HMO — holds the primary duty to maintain the confidentiality of the data. The development of electronic health care networks permitting standardized patient-based information to flow nationwide, and perhaps worldwide, means that the current privacy protection system, which focuses on requiring the institution to protect its records, needs to be reconsidered. Our past thinking assumed a paper or automated record created and protected by the provider. We must now envision a patient-based record that anyone in the system can call up on a screen. Because location has less meaning in an electronic world, protecting privacy requires attaching protection to the health record itself, rather than to the institution that generates it. . . . [8]

In contrast, Peter Winn argues that the breach of confidentiality tort might be strengthened with the new HIPAA regulations and may prove to be quite effective in providing a remedy against privacy invasions:

[A]lthough the HIPAA Privacy Rules create no federal cause of action, an analysis of the case law suggests that the Rules may well be adopted by common law courts to establish a national minimum standard for liability for breach of confidentiality under state law. . . .

With respect to the second perceived weakness of the Rules, because the breach of confidentiality tort traditionally requires that the patient be in a professional or contractual relationship with the person responsible for the wrongful disclosure, and because many harmful disclosures take place by entities such as Business Associates who are not in such a relationship, the breach of confidentiality tort has been viewed as unable to address the problems caused by the widespread dissemination of electronic health information among "downstream" users not in a relationship of confidentiality with the injured person. . . . [U]nder the developing case law, such federally required agreements with Business Associates, while ostensibly creating no liability other than between the contracting parties, are likely to facilitate the establishment of claims for breach of confidentiality against Business Associates by patients for misuse of their personal information in spite of the lack of a professional or contractual relationship. [9]

---

[8] Lawrence O. Gostin, *Health Information Privacy*, 80 Cornell L. Rev. 451 (1995).

[9] Peter A. Winn, *Confidentiality in Cyberspace: The HIPAA Privacy Rules and the Common Law*, 33 Rutgers L.J. 617 (2002).

5. *The Breach of Confidentiality Tort and the First Amendment.* Does the breach of confidentiality tort implicate the First Amendment? Recall that the tort does not include a newsworthiness test. When it comes to civil liability, the Supreme Court applies two very different rules. For certain tort actions, such as defamation and public disclosure of private facts, the First Amendment provides strong protections. *See New York Times Co. v. Sullivan,* 376 U.S. 254 (1964). But for contract actions, the First Amendment provides virtually no protection. *See Cohen v. Cowles Media,* 501 U.S. 663 (1991). Courts have not been strict when it comes to the tort/contract categories, concluding that certain tort actions should be treated under the *Cohen* rule and certain contract actions should be treated under the *Sullivan* rule. As Daniel Solove and Neil Richards argue, "First Amendment law's handling of civil liability is incoherent." They contend that this problem is particularly evident when it comes to the breach of confidentiality tort, which straddles tort and contract:

> Suppose the personal physician to the CEO of a major corporation discloses to the public that the CEO has dementia and that it will compromise the CEO's ability to perform his duties. The company plays a major role in the U.S. economy, and thus the information is highly newsworthy. Hundreds of thousands of jobs are at stake, as are the fortunes of millions of investors. The doctor is about to retire, so she is not concerned with any professional consequences for breaching physician ethics. After the doctor discloses the information, the CEO sues for breach of an implied contract of confidentiality and for violating the breach of confidentiality tort. The doctor claims that the First Amendment bars liability. Should a court restrict liability for the implied contract action? The breach of confidentiality tort action? This hypothetical demonstrates the similarity between certain contract and tort actions. The breach of confidentiality tort is a private cause of action that has both tort-like and contract-like elements. Duties of confidentiality can be created by express contracts or implied as a matter of law from the circumstances of a relationship. In many instances, the breach of confidentiality tort remedies a harm akin to those protected by contract law or promissory estoppel. One party voluntarily assumes a duty, either through an express or implied contract or promise. Breach of confidentiality differs from other torts such as defamation and public disclosure of private facts because the duty of confidentiality is understood as arising from a consensual relationship. Beyond a formalistic distinction between tort and contract, why should such different First Amendment consequences follow from the CEO's breach of confidentiality tort and implied contract actions? For the purposes of the First Amendment, the nature of the information involved is the same regardless of whether contract or tort liability is involved. Moreover, the basic theory upon which liability is premised is also largely the same—an express or implied assumption of a duty of confidentiality.[10]

Solove and Richards develop an approach for determining when civil liability should trigger First Amendment protections, an approach they base on the nature of the exercise of government power. In their view, the government,

---

[10] Daniel J. Solove & Neil M. Richards, *Rethinking Free Speech and Civil Liability,* 109 Colum. L. Rev. 1650 (2009).

by allowing recovery for the breach of confidentiality tort, is not defining what a speaker can or cannot say. Additionally, they invoke the concept of unjust enrichment, arguing that the doctor has information about the CEO because of the confidential nature of the relationship. Without confidentiality, the doctor would not have known the information. The doctor's speech only becomes possible because of the duty of confidentiality, and the tort is not restricting speech that otherwise would have existed without that duty.

Do you agree that the breach of confidentiality tort should be governed by the *Cohen* rule rather than the *Sullivan* rule? Does this tort pose a significant threat to free speech?

3. TORT LIABILITY FOR FAILURE TO DISCLOSE PATIENT INFORMATION

TARASOFF V. REGENTS OF UNIVERSITY OF CALIFORNIA

551 P.2d 334 (Cal. 1976)

TOBRINER, J. On October 27, 1969, Prosenjit Poddar killed Tatiana Tarasoff. Plaintiffs, Tatiana's parents, allege that two months earlier Poddar confided his intention to kill Tatiana to Dr. Lawrence Moore, a psychologist employed by the Cowell Memorial Hospital at the University of California at Berkeley. They allege that on Moore's request, the campus police briefly detained Poddar, but released him when he appeared rational. They further claim that Dr. Harvey Powelson, Moore's superior, then directed that no further action be taken to detain Poddar. No one warned plaintiffs of Tatiana's peril.

Plaintiffs' complaints predicate liability on . . . defendants' failure to warn plaintiffs of the impending danger. . . . Defendants, in turn, assert that they owed no duty of reasonable care to Tatiana. . . .

We shall explain that defendant therapists cannot escape liability merely because Tatiana herself was not their patient. When a therapist determines, or pursuant to the standards of his profession should determine, that his patient presents a serious danger of violence to another, he incurs an obligation to use reasonable care to protect the intended victim against such danger. The discharge of this duty may require the therapist to take one or more of various steps, depending upon the nature of the case. Thus it may call for him to warn the intended victim or others likely to apprise the victim of the danger, to notify the police, or to take whatever other steps are reasonably necessary under the circumstances. . . .

. . . [O]n August 20, 1969, Poddar was a voluntary outpatient receiving therapy at Cowell Memorial Hospital. Poddar informed Moore, his therapist, that he was going to kill an unnamed girl, readily identifiable as Tatiana, when she returned home from spending the summer in Brazil. Moore, with the concurrence of Dr. Gold, who had initially examined Poddar, and Dr. Yandell, Assistant to the director of the department of psychiatry, decided that Poddar should be committed for observation in a mental hospital. Moore orally notified Officers Atkinson and Teel of the campus police that he would request commitment. He then sent a letter to

Police Chief William Beall requesting the assistance of the police department in securing Poddar's confinement.

Officers Atkinson, Brownrigg, and Halleran took Poddar into custody, but, satisfied that Poddar was rational, released him on his promise to stay away from Tatiana. Powelson, director of the department of psychiatry at Cowell Memorial Hospital, then asked the police to return Moore's letter, directed that all copies of the letter and notes that Moore had taken as therapist be destroyed, and "ordered no action to place Prosenjit Poddar in 72-hour treatment and evaluation   facility."
. . .

. . . Poddar persuaded Tatiana's brother to share an apartment with him near Tatiana's residence; shortly after her return from Brazil, Poddar went to her residence and killed her.

Plaintiffs contend that [the defendants were negligent in not notifying them of Poddar's intent to kill Tatiana]. Defendants, however, contend that in the circumstances of the present case they owed no duty of care to Tatiana or her parents and that, in the absence of such duty, they were free to act in careless disregard of Tatiana's life and safety. . . .

. . . As a general principle, a "defendant owes a duty of care to all persons who are foreseeably endangered by his conduct, with respect to all risks which make the conduct unreasonably dangerous." As we shall explain, however, when the avoidance of foreseeable harm requires a defendant to control the conduct of another person, or to warn of such conduct, the common law has traditionally imposed liability only if the defendant bears some special relationship to the dangerous person or to the potential victim. Since the relationship between a therapist and his patient satisfies this requirement, we need not here decide whether foreseeability alone is sufficient to create a duty to exercise reasonable care to protect a potential victim of another's conduct.

Although, as we have stated above, under the common law, as a general rule, one person owed no duty to control the conduct of another, nor to warn those endangered by such conduct, the courts have carved out an exception to this rule in cases in which the defendant stands in some special relationship to either the person whose conduct needs to be controlled or in a relationship to the foreseeable victim of that conduct. Applying this exception to the present case, we note that a relationship of defendant therapists to either Tatiana or Poddar will suffice to establish a duty of care; as explained in section 315 of the Restatement Second of Torts, a duty of care may arise from either "(a) a special relation . . . between the actor and the third person which imposes a duty upon the actor to control the third person's conduct, or (b) a special relation . . . between the actor and the other which gives to the other a right of protection."

Although plaintiffs' pleadings assert no special relation between Tatiana and defendant therapists, they establish as between Poddar and defendant therapists the special relation that arises between a patient and his doctor or psychotherapist. Such a relationship may support affirmative duties for the benefit of third persons. Thus, for example, a hospital must exercise reasonable care to control the behavior of a patient which may endanger other persons. A doctor must also warn a patient if the patient's condition or medication renders certain conduct, such as driving a car, dangerous to others. . . .

. . . Decisions of other jurisdictions hold that the single relationship of a doctor to his patient is sufficient to support the duty to exercise reasonable care to protect others against dangers emanating from the patient's illness. The courts hold that a doctor is liable to persons infected by his patient if he negligently fails to diagnose a contagious disease or, having diagnosed the illness, fails to warn members of the patient's family. . . .

". . . [T]here now seems to be sufficient authority to support the conclusion that by entering into a doctor-patient relationship the therapist becomes sufficiently involved to assume some responsibility for the safety, not only of the patient himself, but also of any third person whom the doctor knows to be threatened by the patient." (Fleming & Maximov, The Patient or His Victim: The Therapist's Dilemma (1974) 62 Cal. L. Rev. 1025, 1030.)

Defendants contend, however, that imposition of a duty to exercise reasonable care to protect third persons is unworkable because therapists cannot accurately predict whether or not a patient will resort to violence. In support of this argument amicus representing the American Psychiatric Association and other professional societies cites numerous articles which indicate that therapists, in the present state of the art, are unable reliably to predict violent acts; their forecasts, amicus claims, tend consistently to overpredict violence, and indeed are more often wrong than right. Since predictions of violence are often erroneous, amicus concludes, the courts should not render rulings that predicate the liability of therapists upon the validity of such predictions.

The role of the psychiatrist, who is indeed a practitioner of medicine, and that of the psychologist who performs an allied function, are like that of the physician who must conform to the standards of the profession and who must often make diagnoses and predictions based upon such evaluations. Thus the judgment of the therapist in diagnosing emotional disorders and in predicting whether a patient presents a serious danger of violence is comparable to the judgment which doctors and professionals must regularly render under accepted rules of responsibility.

We recognize the difficulty that a therapist encounters in attempting to forecast whether a patient presents a serious danger of violence. Obviously we do not require that the therapist, in making that determination, render a perfect performance; the therapist need only exercise "that reasonable degree of skill, knowledge, and care ordinarily possessed and exercised by members of (that professional specialty) under similar circumstances." Within the broad range of reasonable practice and treatment in which professional opinion and judgment may differ, the therapist is free to exercise his or her own best judgment without liability; proof, aided by hindsight, that he or she judged wrongly is insufficient to establish negligence.

In the instant case, however, the pleadings do not raise any question as to failure of defendant therapists to predict that Poddar presented a serious danger of violence. On the contrary, the present complaints allege that defendant therapists did in fact predict that Poddar would kill, but were negligent in failing to warn. . .

The risk that unnecessary warnings may be given is a reasonable price to pay for the lives of possible victims that may be saved. We would hesitate to hold that the therapist who is aware that his patient expects to attempt to assassinate the President of the United States would not be obligated to warn the authorities because the therapist cannot predict with accuracy that his patient will commit the crime. . . .

We realize that the open and confidential character of psychotherapeutic dialogue encourages patients to express threats of violence, few of which are ever executed. Certainly a therapist should not be encouraged routinely to reveal such threats; such disclosures could seriously disrupt the patient's relationship with his therapist and with the persons threatened. To the contrary, the therapist's obligations to his patient require that he not disclose a confidence unless such disclosure is necessary to avert danger to others, and even then that he do so discreetly, and in a fashion that would preserve the privacy of his patient to the fullest extent compatible with the prevention of the threatened danger.

The revelation of a communication under the above circumstances is not a breach of trust or a violation of professional ethics; as stated in the Principles of Medical Ethics of the American Medical Association (1957), section 9: "A physician may not reveal the confidence entrusted to him in the course of medical attendance . . . unless he is required to do so by law or unless it becomes necessary in order to protect the welfare of the individual or of the community." We conclude that the public policy favoring protection of the confidential character of patient-psychotherapist communications must yield to the extent to which disclosure is essential to avert danger to others. The protective privilege ends where the public peril begins. . . .

CLARK, J. dissenting. . . . Overwhelming policy considerations weigh against imposing a duty on psychotherapists to warn a potential victim against harm. While offering virtually no benefit to society, such a duty will frustrate psychiatric treatment, invade fundamental patient rights and increase violence.

The importance of psychiatric treatment and its need for confidentiality have been recognized by this court. "It is clearly recognized that the very practice of psychiatry vitally depends upon the reputation in the community that the psychiatrist will not tell."

Assurance of confidentiality is important for three reasons.

First, without substantial assurance of confidentiality, those requiring treatment will be deterred from seeking assistance. It remains an unfortunate fact in our society that people seeking psychiatric guidance tend to become stigmatized. Apprehension of such stigma — apparently increased by the propensity of people considering treatment to see themselves in the worst possible light — creates a well-recognized reluctance to seek aid. This reluctance is alleviated by the psychiatrist's assurance of confidentiality.

Second, the guarantee of confidentiality is essential in eliciting the full disclosure necessary for effective treatment. The psychiatric patient approaches treatment with conscious and unconscious inhibitions against revealing his innermost thoughts. "Every person, however well-motivated, has to overcome resistances to therapeutic exploration. These resistances seek support from every possible source and the possibility of disclosure would easily be employed in the service of resistance." Until a patient can trust his psychiatrist not to violate their confidential relationship, "the unconscious psychological control mechanism of repression will prevent the recall of past experiences."

Third, even if the patient fully discloses his thoughts, assurance that the confidential relationship will not be breached is necessary to maintain his trust in his psychiatrist — the very means by which treatment is effected. "(T)he essence of much psychotherapy is the contribution of trust in the external world and ultimately in the self, modeled upon the trusting relationship established during therapy." Patients will be helped only if they can form a trusting relationship with the psychiatrist. All authorities appear to agree that if the trust relationship cannot be developed because of collusive communication between the psychiatrist and others, treatment will be frustrated. . . .

Both the legal and psychiatric communities recognize that the process of determining potential violence in a patient is far from exact, being fraught with complexity and uncertainty. In fact precision has not even been attained in predicting who of those having already committed violent acts will again become violent, a task recognized to be of much simpler proportions.

This predictive uncertainty means that the number of disclosures will necessarily be large. As noted above, psychiatric patients are encouraged to discuss all thoughts of violence, and they often express such thoughts. However, unlike this court, the psychiatrist does not enjoy the benefit of overwhelming hindsight in seeing which few, if any, of his patients will ultimately become violent. Now, confronted by the majority's new duty, the psychiatrist must instantaneously calculate potential violence from each patient on each visit. The difficulties researchers have encountered in accurately predicting violence will be heightened for the practicing psychiatrist dealing for brief periods in his office with heretofore nonviolent patients. And, given the decision not to warn or commit must always be made at the psychiatrist's civil peril, one can expect most doubts will be resolved in favor of the psychiatrist protecting himself.

Neither alternative open to the psychiatrist seeking to protect himself is in the public interest. The warning itself is an impairment of the psychiatrist's ability to treat, depriving many patients of adequate treatment. It is to be expected that after disclosing their threats, a significant number of patients, who would not become violent if treated according to existing practices, will engage in violent conduct as a result of unsuccessful treatment. In short, the majority's duty to warn will not only impair treatment of many who would never become violent but worse, will result in a net increase in violence.

The second alternative open to the psychiatrist is to commit his patient rather than to warn. Even in the absence of threat of civil liability, the doubts of psychiatrists as to the seriousness of patient threats have led psychiatrists to overcommit to mental institutions. This overcommitment has been authoritatively documented in both legal and psychiatric studies. This practice is so prevalent that it has been estimated that "as many as twenty harmless persons are incarcerated for every one who will commit a violent act." . . .

NOTES & QUESTIONS

1. ***Background and Postscript.*** Peter Schuck and Daniel Givelber have discovered a strange background fact about the case: Alex Tarasoff, Tatiana's

brother, shared an apartment with Poddar for about three months before the tragic killing:

> Alex had once answered the phone at the Tarasoff home when Poddar was calling for Tatiana; although Alex warned Poddar to "lay off," Poddar — undaunted — asked to meet him. Alex agreed and met Tanya and Poddar at the gas station where Alex worked. . . . The two men had some technical interests in common and became close friends and then roommates . . . . Although Alex later testified that he did not believe that Poddar meant to kill his sister, Poddar's friendship with Alex enabled Poddar to learn when he would find Tatiana alone at her family's home on October 27, 1969, the day of her death.

Schuck and Givelber also examined the intertwining of the California Supreme Court's decision in the criminal case, *People v. Poddar*, 518 P.2d 342 (Cal. 1974), with the tort case excerpted above. In the criminal case, the California Supreme Court had ordered a retrial because the trial court did not instruct the jury about how diminished capacity might affect the specific interest necessary for a verdict of second-degree murder. Poddar was not, however, subjected to another trial; the prosecutors allowed him to return to India. Schuck and Givelber propose that "the California Supreme Court, unable to condemn the therapists' passivity in the criminal case, did so indirectly in the tort case by creating the Tarasoff duty and allowing the jury to apply that duty to the university clinicians. The Court in effect lifted some of the burden of criminal responsibility from Poddar's shoulders while imposing a burden of civil responsibility on the clinicians."[11]

2. ***Warning Patients of a Duty to Disclose.*** Today, a majority of jurisdictions have adopted the *Tarasoff* rule. Given the *Tarasoff* rule, should psychotherapists have an ethical duty to warn patients that they may have to disclose to others when a patient makes a threat? In a study after *Tarasoff*, only 26 percent of psychotherapists informed patients of the possibility of disclosure at the outset of therapy; 51 percent informed patients when the patient threatened violence.[12]

3. ***Too Much Disclosure?*** In a footnote in his dissent, Justice Clark argues:

> However compassionate, the psychiatrist hearing the threat remains faced with potential crushing civil liability for a mistaken evaluation of his patient and will be forced to resolve even the slightest doubt in favor of disclosure or commitment.

Will the result in *Tarasoff* lead to too many disclosures by psychotherapists?

4. ***How Broadly Could the* Tarasoff *Rule Apply?*** *Tarasoff*, although it involved a psychotherapist, would seemingly apply to physicians, nurses, and social workers. Could it apply even more broadly — to marriage counselors or any professional having knowledge of a person's dangerous propensities?

---

[11] Peter H. Schuck & Daniel J. Givelber, Tarasoff v. Regents of the University of California, *in* Torts Stories 99 (Robert L. Rabin & Stephen D. Sugarman, 2003).

[12] *See* D.L. Rosenhan, Terri Wolff Teitelbaum, Kathi Weiss Teitelbaum & Martin Davidson, *Warning Third Parties: The Ripple Effects of* Tarasoff, 24 Pac. L.J. 1165, 1208 (1993).

5. ***Ethical vs. Legal Duties to Disclose.*** The psychiatric community was highly critical of *Tarasoff.* Ironically, however, even before *Tarasoff*, almost 80 percent of therapists believed they had an ethical duty to warn under circumstances akin to those in *Tarasoff*. In a 1987 study, almost all therapists had warned a potential victim, and most believed their duty to warn was based on an ethical obligation regardless of the law.[13] Does it matter whether this is a legal duty or merely an ethical one? What if the option to disclose were simply left to the conscience of medical professionals?

6. **Tarasoff *and the Attorney-Client Privilege.*** Under the ABA Model Rule 1.6(b)(1), an attorney *may* reveal a client's intention to commit future crimes that are likely to cause imminent death or substantial bodily harm. This rule differs among the states, although the majority agrees with this rule. About one-fifth of the states provide that an attorney *must* disclose under such circumstances. Suppose an attorney were in a similar position to the therapist in *Tarasoff*. Although the ethical obligations of each state suggest that the attorney may disclose, the attorney does not. Would the attorney be liable under a *Tarasoff* theory?

7. **Tarasoff *and the Psychotherapist-Patient Privilege.*** In *Menendez v. Superior Court*, 834 P.2d 786 (Cal. 1992), law enforcement officials sought audiotape recordings and written notes of psychotherapy sessions of Erik and Lyle Menendez, two brothers who had murdered their parents. The case of the Menendezes garnered great publicity. Their psychotherapist was Dr. Leon Oziel, and the tapes contained information related to the killings. The tapes also involved threats made by Erik and Lyle to Dr. Oziel. The threats were aimed at him alone, but Dr. Oziel believed that his wife (Laurel Oziel) as well as his lover (Judalon Smyth) could also be endangered, so he warned them. Neither Lyle nor Erik attempted any harm to Dr. Oziel, Laurel, or Smyth. Both Laurel Oziel and Smyth were employed in Dr. Oziel's psychotherapy practice. The police served a search warrant on Dr. Oziel for the recordings and/or notes for three therapy sessions.

   The Menendezes claimed psychotherapist-patient privilege. The government argued that under Evidence Code § 1024 no privilege exists if "the psychotherapist has reasonable cause to believe that the patient is in such mental or emotional condition as to be dangerous to himself or to the person or property of another and that disclosure of the communication is necessary to prevent the threatened danger." The Supreme Court of California concluded that one of the sessions was not privileged, but that the other two were. First, the court held that even though the Menendezes' communications were publicly disclosed to Smyth, the Menendezes did not lose their privilege. "[T]he privilege can cover a communication that has lost its 'confidential' status." Second, the court held that all of the sessions should not be considered one communication; each therapy session should be treated separately. Third, the court concluded that if the conditions for a valid *Tarasoff* warning exist, a communication is not

---

[13] *See* Fillmore Buckner & Marvin Firestone, *"Where the Public Peril Begins": 25 Years After Tarasoff*, 21 J. Legal Med. 187, 219 (2000).

privileged, regardless of whether the therapist actually gave a Tarasoff warning or not. The exception to the privilege is "not keyed to . . . disclosure or warning, but to the existence of the specified factual predicate, viz., reasonable cause for belief in the dangerousness of the patient and the necessity of disclosure." Thus, the one session where the Menendezes made the threat to Dr. Oziel, which gave him reason to believe his wife and lover could be in danger, was not privileged.

McIntosh v. Milano

403 A.2d 500 (N.J. Super. 1979)

PETRELLA, J. Defendant [Michael Milano, M.D., a board-certified psychiatrist] first met Lee Morgenstein, then age 15, and began his treatment on May 5, 1973, after the latter's school psychologist had given Morgenstein's parents defendant's name and that of certain other therapists, partially because of Morgenstein's involvement with drugs. His treatment was on a weekly basis for what was initially diagnosed as "an adjustment reaction of adolescence." Initially it also included family therapy. During the course of therapy over the approximate two-year period, Morgenstein related many "fantasies" to defendant on various subjects, including fantasies of fear of other people, being a hero or an important villain, and using a knife to threaten people who might intimidate or frighten him.

Morgenstein also related certain alleged experiences and emotional involvements with decedent, who in 1973 was about 20 years old and at that time lived with her parents next door to the Morgensteins. Decedent's father was a doctor who from time to time had treated Lee Morgenstein for minor ailments. Defendant considered all such "fantasies" referred to above as just that, but he came to accept, after initial reservations, that the experiences related to him by Morgenstein as to his eventual victim represented truth and not fantasy. Dr. Milano stated he was somewhat "nonplussed" initially about the revelations of Morgenstein concerning Miss [Kimberly] McIntosh and alleged sexual experiences because of the five-year age difference. However, he said that he came to believe it because the way Morgenstein responded emotionally fit with what he told him, and Milano claimed he never had any reason to doubt Morgenstein. The doctor testified at Morgenstein's criminal trial that "(h)e (Morgenstein) didn't spend a lot of time describing in detail what he and Kim did, but that also sort of fit, if anything, his character in that he thought that nobody would believe him." Defendant did indicate in his deposition that he advised Morgenstein to break off the relationship.

Morgenstein had possessive feelings towards Kimberly, according to the doctor, and was "overwhelmed" by the relationship. Although Morgenstein is said to have repeatedly expressed anxiety to defendant over his relationship with Miss McIntosh, defendant asserts she was not the dominant theme of the therapy.

It is undisputed, and Dr. Milano admits, that Morgenstein had confided that he had fired a B.B. gun at what he recalled to be a car (Miss McIntosh's or her boyfriend's) on one occasion when he was upset because she was going on a date with her boyfriend. There is evidence proffered by plaintiff that other windows in the McIntosh house and another vehicle had been shot at and damaged by a B.B.

or some other gun, and a factfinder might infer that these were actions of Morgenstein. It is also undisputed that Dr. Milano had been told by Morgenstein that he had purchased and carried a knife to show to people to scare them away if they should attempt to frighten or intimidate him, and brought it to a therapy session to show the doctor.

Although Dr. Milano said that Morgenstein wished Miss McIntosh would "suffer" as he did and had expressed jealousy and a very possessive attitude towards her, was jealous of other men and hateful towards her boyfriends, had difficulty convincing himself that fights or things were really over or finished, he denied that Morgenstein ever indicated or exhibited any feelings of violence toward decedent or said that he intended to kill her or inflict bodily harm. Morgenstein was also very angry that he had not been able to obtain Miss McIntosh's phone number when she moved from the family home. He may not even have known where she lived in 1975. Plaintiff proffered testimony that Miss McIntosh had told her family of Morgenstein's drug problems, felt sorry for him, and hoped he could get help.

Following an incident in which Morgenstein fell off a bicycle and injured his face the day before the July 8, 1975 therapy session, and after an incident during the course of that day's therapy (apparently when Dr. Milano briefly left the room), he stole a prescription form from the doctor's desk. Later that day he attempted to obtain 30 Seconal tablets from a pharmacist with the stolen form. The pharmacist apparently became suspicious and called Dr. Milano, who instructed him to retain the unauthorized prescription form, not to fill it, and to send Morgenstein home. He later tried to reach Morgenstein at home, but between then and the early evening hours Morgenstein was involved in the tragedy which took Miss McIntosh's life. Whatever exactly transpired thereafter, it would appear that Morgenstein left the pharmacy upset and at some point either late that afternoon or early evening obtained a pistol which he had kept hidden at his home, and knowing Miss McIntosh was expected to visit her parents, waited for her and either got her to go with him, wittingly or unwittingly, to a local park area where he fatally shot her in the back.

Dr. Milano had indicated in his testimony at the criminal trial that sometimes he inquired further when he felt that a patient was in some ways endangering himself or someone else, and in those instances he would contact his patient's parents, school, or people like that. In his deposition in this civil case Dr. Milano said he had spoken to Morgenstein's parents about a problem with a car accident and this resulted in their withholding certain privileges from their son. He also indicated he spoke to a school teacher about one of Morgenstein's problems. Apparently this was usually with Morgenstein's consent. Dr. Milano had said he would "look into it" if he felt the patient was endangering himself or someone else. He apparently talked to Morgenstein's parents in some fashion about the relationship between their son and Miss McIntosh a number of times in late 1974 and in 1975, but never attempted to contact decedent or her parents. Despite Morgenstein's fantasies and the incidents previously recited, and wishes for her suffering, he felt that Morgenstein had never expressed a desire for retaliation or "fantasies" of retaliation. Dr. Milano had said at the criminal trial that Morgenstein had fantasies of magical power and violence, which meant that if somebody said he was a scrawny little runt and wouldn't dare fight back, that he would be able to pull out a gun and shoot them. But he denied that Morgenstein ever had fantasies of pulling out a gun, and claimed that his fantasies apparently related to pulling out a knife and scaring people off. Morgenstein, nevertheless, was quoted as saying that if he had a gun, that would scare men and then nobody would dare threaten him. . . .

Plaintiff [McIntosh's mother] instituted this wrongful death action based in large part on the trial testimony of Dr. Milano. She relies also on a report of a psychiatrist retained as an expert witness expressing the opinion that defendant had a duty to warn Kimberly McIntosh, her parents or appropriate authorities that Morgenstein posed a physical threat or danger to decedent. Plaintiff asserts defendant breached that duty. . . .

The argument in this case is whether principles analogous to those expressed in *Tarasoff* apply or should be applied in New Jersey.

Plaintiff in the instant case asserts that a duty of a therapist towards third parties or potential victims is appropriate under the law of this State and forms a basis for a claim of actionable negligence analogous to that in *Tarasoff.* Defendant asserts such a duty is unworkable. . . .

It may be true that there cannot be 100% accurate prediction of dangerousness in all cases. However, a therapist does have a basis for giving an opinion and a prognosis based on the history of the patient and the course of treatment. Where reasonable men might differ and a fact issue exists, the therapist is only held to the standard for a therapist in the particular field in the particular community. Unless therapists clearly state when called upon to treat patients or to testify that they have no ability to predict or even determine whether their treatment will be efficacious or may even be necessary with any degree of certainty, there is no basis for a legal conclusion negating any and all duty with respect to a particular class of professionals. This is not to say that isolated or vague threats will of necessity give rise in all circumstances and cases to a duty. . . .

The *Tarasoff* duty has received criticism from some, but not all authors, mostly those in the medical professions. However, the concept of legal duties for the medical profession is not new. A doctor-patient relationship in some circumstances admittedly places a duty to warn others of contagious diseases. New Jersey recognizes the general rule that a person who negligently exposes another to a contagious disease, which the other contracts, is liable in damages. Specifically, a physician has the duty to warn third persons against possible exposure to contagious or infectious diseases, e.g., tuberculosis, venereal diseases, and so forth. That duty extends to instances where the physician should have known of the infectious disease.

Physicians also must report tuberculosis, venereal disease, and various other contagious diseases, see, e.g., N.J.S.A. 26:4-15, as well as certain other conditions. There is, to be sure, a relative certainty and uniformity present in a diagnosis of most physical illnesses, conditions and injuries as opposed to a psychiatric prediction of dangerousness based on symptoms and historical performance. Nevertheless, psychiatrists diagnose, treat and give opinions based on medical probabilities, particularly relying on a patient's history, without any clear indication of an inability to predict that is here asserted.

As a further illustration of types of duties imposed by statutes, N.J.S.A. 2A:97-2 provides that any person who has knowledge of actual commission of high misdemeanors and certain other crimes, but fails to report or disclose same, is himself guilty of a misdemeanor. No exception is set forth therein for a physician. To threaten to take the life of another person is also a crime. . . . Disclosure is, therefore, required in numerous situations. . . . [E]ven the Principles of Medical Ethics recognize that confidentiality gives way where "it becomes necessary in order to protect the welfare of the individual or of the community." . . .

. . . [T]his court holds that a psychiatrist or therapist may have a duty to take whatever steps are reasonably necessary to protect an intended or potential victim of his patient when he determines, or should determine, in the appropriate factual setting and in accordance with the standards of his profession established at trial, that the patient is or may present a probability of danger to that person. The relationship giving rise to that duty may be found either in that existing between the therapist and the patient, as was alluded to in *Tarasoff*, or in the more broadly based obligation a practitioner may have to protect the welfare of the community, which is analogous to the obligation a physician has to warn third persons of infectious or contagious disease. . . .

NOTES & QUESTIONS

1. ***Liability for Nondisclosure, Liability for Disclosure.*** Does it seem foresee-able for Dr. Milano to know that Morgenstein would harm McIntosh? Even if Dr. Milano prevails in court, there still is a strong incentive for him to disclose — to avoid a very costly litigation. Does the fear of a long court battle make therapists more likely to err on the side of disclosure? If Dr. Milano did disclose, would Morgenstein have a tort action for breach of confidentiality?

2. ***The Legal Duty: Sources and Scope.*** *McIntosh* recognizes a broader source for the legal duty to disclose than does *Tarasoff*. Consider the following passage at the conclusion of *McIntosh*:

   > The relationship giving rise to that duty may be found either in that existing between the therapist and the patient, as was alluded to in *Tarasoff*, or in the more broadly based obligation a practitioner may have to protect the welfare of the community, which is analogous to the obligation a physician has to warn third persons of infectious or contagious disease.

   If the duty arises in this "more broadly based obligation" to protect the public welfare, does this suggest that the duty itself may be broader than that in *Tarasoff*? Do therapists and medical personnel have a duty to warn the public at large if they believe a patient is generally dangerous and the patient has not made any threats to specific individuals?

3. ***The Duty to Warn About Relatives' Genetic Conditions.*** In *Pate v. Threlkel*, 661 So. 2d 278 (Fla. 1995), plaintiff Heidi Pate's mother received treatment for medullary thyroid carcinoma, a disorder believed to have a genetic component. When Pate learned that she also had the disease, she sued the doctors who treated her mother, alleging that the doctors were under a duty to warn Pate's mother that her children should be tested for the disease. Pate alleged that had she been tested, she would have taken preventive action that might have made

her condition curable. The physicians argued that they lacked a duty of care to Pate. The court held that Pate had a valid claim:

> . . . [T]o whom does the alleged duty to warn [the patient] of the nature of her disease run? The duty obviously runs to the patient who is in privity with the physician. In the past, courts have held that in order to maintain a cause of action against a physician, privity must exist between the plaintiff and the physician. In other professional relationships, however, we have recognized the rights of identified third party beneficiaries to recover from a professional because that party was the intended beneficiary of the prevailing standard of care. . . .
>
> Here, the alleged prevailing standard of care was obviously developed for the benefit of the patient's children as well as the patient. We conclude that when the prevailing standard of care creates a duty that is obviously for the benefit of certain identified third parties and the physician knows of the existence of those third parties, then the physician's duty runs to those third parties. . . .
>
> . . . If there is a duty to warn, to whom must the physician convey the warning? Our holding should not be read to require the physician to warn the patient's children of the disease. In most instances the physician is prohibited from disclosing the patient's medical condition to others except with the patient's permission. Moreover, the patient ordinarily can be expected to pass on the warning. To require the physician to seek out and warn various members of the patient's family would often be difficult or impractical and would place too heavy a burden upon the physician. Thus, we emphasize that in any circumstances in which the physician has a duty to warn of a genetically transferable disease, that duty will be satisfied by warning the patient. . . .

Compare *Pate* to *Safer v. Estate of Pack*, 677 A.2d 1188 (N.J. Super. 1996). The plaintiff, Donna Safer, sued the estate of the deceased physician (Dr. Pack) who treated her father for colon cancer and multiple polyposis. After seven years of treatment, Safer's father died of cancer. Safer was ten years old at the time. About 25 years later, when Safer was 36 years old and newly married, she was diagnosed with colon cancer and multiple polyposis. She had a complete colectomy and one of her ovaries had to be removed. Safer contended that multiple polyposis is a hereditary condition that if untreated leads to colorectal cancer. Since the hereditary nature of the disease was known at the time Dr. Pack was treating Safer's father, Dr. Pack had a duty to warn Safer's father, and perhaps Safer herself. The court agreed with Safer:

> . . . We see no impediment, legal or otherwise, to recognizing a physician's duty to warn those known to be at risk of avoidable harm from a genetically transmissible condition. In terms of foreseeability especially, there is no essential difference between the type of genetic threat at issue here and the menace of infection, contagion or a threat of physical harm. *See generally, e.g., McIntosh v. Milano*; *Tarasoff v. Regents of Univ. of Cal.* . . . The individual or group at risk is easily identified, and substantial future harm may be averted or minimized by a timely and effective warning. . . .
>
> We need not decide, in the present posture of this case, how, precisely, that duty is to be discharged, especially with respect to young children who may be at risk, except to require that reasonable steps be taken to assure that the information reaches those likely to be affected or is made available for their benefit. . . .

We decline to hold as the Florida Supreme Court did in *Pate v. Threlkel,* that, in all circumstances, the duty to warn will be satisfied by informing the patient. It may be necessary, at some stage, to resolve a conflict between the physician's broader duty to warn and his fidelity to an expressed preference of the patient that nothing be said to family members about the details of the disease. . . .

How does the holding in *Pate* differ from that in *Safer*? Are these holdings a logical extension of *Tarasoff* and *McIntosh*? What are the potential privacy risks created by these holdings? Do the potential benefits of the rules established in *Pate* and *Safer* outweigh these privacy risks?

4. STATUTORY REPORTING REQUIREMENTS

HIV Notification Statutes. New York, along with many other states, has enacted a partner notification law when people are diagnosed with HIV. According to N.Y. Pub. Health L. § 2130, an HIV-positive diagnosis shall be reported to public health officials. The report "shall include information identifying the protected individual as well as the names, if available, of any contacts of the protected individual . . . known to the physician or provided to the physician by the infected person."

After the information is collected, any "contacts" of the individual may be notified by public health officials. *See* § 2133. A "contact" means "an identified spouse or sex partner of the protected individual, a person identified as having shared hypodermic needles or syringes with the protected individual or a person who the protected individual may have exposed to HIV under circumstances that present a risk of transmission of HIV, as determined by the commissioner." § 2180(10). The identity of the patient shall not be revealed to the contact. § 2133. "No criminal or civil liability shall arise against any protected individual solely due to his or her failure to cooperate in contact tracing conducted pursuant to section twenty-one hundred thirty-three of this title." § 2136(3).

Thirty-three states have partner notification laws. Thirty-one states collect HIV names. An argument in support of the laws is the difficulty many infected people have telling others of infection. In one study, 40 percent didn't disclose their HIV status to their partners. According to the Centers for Disease Control, 70 percent of partners are not informed. The argument against such disclosure laws is that they might deter people from getting tested. Further, HIV-positive women sometimes experience violence when their partners find out they have HIV. Almost half fear violence. Twenty-five percent were actually assaulted. Finally, it remains unclear whether such notification laws are effective.[14]

Consider Robert Gellman's conclusion about the preferability of legislation rather than existing case law and ethical principles to define the responsibilities of physicians with respect to patient privacy:

> Existing legal and ethical principles that guide physicians with respect to their
> obligations to protect the confidentiality of medical records are generally out of

---

[14] *See* Sonia Bhatnager, Note, *HIV Name Reporting and Partner Notification in New York State,* 26 Fordham Urb. L.J. 1457, 1458 (1999).

date and are not comprehensive. Physicians faced with requests or demands for patient information will find little in law or ethics to define their responsibilities with any precision. Yet the physician frequently is the only one who is in a position to take action to protect the confidentiality of his records and the privacy of his patients. . . .

. . . [A]s demand for medical records increases, the physician is being called upon to play a more central role in the protection of confidentiality. But the role that a physician should play is undefined because the physician's responsibilities are unclear. The result may be increased litigation over medical confidentiality issues and the obligations of physicians.

. . . [B]ecause of the magnitude and complexity of privacy issues today, the courts cannot be expected to develop appropriate solutions in a timely fashion. . .

Therefore, the only practical way to develop suitable guidance defining the responsibilities of physicians, the right of patients, and the proper protection for medical information is through legislation.[15]

Consider the following argument by Richard Turkington about HIV notification:

Are cases involving notification of HIV-related information sufficiently different from infectious disease notification cases and *Tarasoff* to consider adopting policies other than mandatory notification? There is a strong case for treating notification of HIV status differently. Disclosure without consent constitutes a serious invasion of privacy and involves risks of adverse consequences to the patient, such as discrimination or violence, through further publication by the sexual partner. Mandatory disclosure may also exacerbate psychiatric disorders caused by infection. Unless the patient is informed by the professional that HIV status would be disclosed to known current contacts at risk, disclosure threatens the trust necessary for free communication and the integrity of the professional-patient relationship. If the patient is informed of contact notification, he or she may be deterred from being tested. Third-party notification might save some lives in the short run but, in the long run, if it damages the trust between professional and client, and deters persons from voluntary testing, more transmission and deaths may result.

Also, unlike the *Tarasoff* situation, the health professional is not the only potential source of notification to the third party. The infected person and the health department are both in the position to notify third parties, and the infected person is arguably in a better position to do so. Only the subject knows who is at risk. The physician may only know that a spouse is at risk. Imposing a duty upon the physician to discover those that may be sexually involved with the patient requires the physician to undertake a police-type activity that many are reluctant to perform and that ought not to be imposed. . . .

The possibility of significant tort damage awards for disclosure under breach of confidentiality theories and the lack of clarity in the existing law on the duty to disclose to contacts leave the health care professional between a rock and a hard place. . . .[16]

---

[15] Robert M. Gellman, *Prescribing Privacy: The Uncertain Role of the Physician in the Protection of Patient Privacy*, 62 N.C. L. Rev. 255 (1984).

[16] Richard C. Turkington, *Confidentiality Policy for HIV-Related Information: An Analytical Framework for Sorting Out Hard and Easy Cases*, 34 Vill. L. Rev. 871 (1989); *see also* Lawrence O. Gostin & James G. Hodge, Jr., *Piercing the Veil of Secrecy in HIV/AIDS and Other Sexually*

Other Disclosure Requirements. Many states have statutory requirements for physicians to disclose health information for certain types of diseases or injuries. Recall from earlier in this chapter the New York statute upheld in *Whalen v. Roe,* which required the disclosure to the state of information about patients using certain prescription medications. Similar to the statute in *Whalen,* many state statutes require the collection of medical data for state registries. For example, New Jersey maintains a registry of birth defects, see N.J. Stat. 26:8-40.21; blindness, see N.J. Stat. 30:6-1.2; and cancer, see N.J. Stat. 26:2-106.

Other statutes require the reporting of certain conditions to various state agencies and officials. Ohio mandates the disclosure to appropriate government officials of occupational diseases (R.C. 3701.25 and 4123.71); diseases that are infectious, contagious, or dangerous to public health (R.C. 3701.24, 3701.52, 3707.06); health injuries indicative of child abuse or neglect (R.C. 2151.421); and injuries indicative of criminal conduct (R.C. 2921.22). Other states have similar reporting requirements. As discussed above, some states require, or provide for, disclosure of a person's medical condition to other individuals, such as partners and spouses.

A number of states place statutory bars on liability for the disclosure of certain conditions. For example, South Carolina has eliminated the "[t]he privileged quality of [patient-physician] communication" regarding the abuse or neglect of children. *See* S.C. Code Ann. § 20-7-550. Further, in South Carolina, "[a] physician or state agency identifying and notifying a spouse or known contact of a person having . . . (HIV) infection or . . . (AIDS) is not liable for damages resulting from the disclosure." S.C. Code Ann. § 44-29-146.

5. STATE LAW PRIVACY PROTECTIONS FOR MEDICAL INFORMATION

Until the Health Insurance Portability and Accountability Act (HIPAA) of 1996, which mandated federal privacy regulation for medical information, health privacy was a concern of the states. As we have seen, the constitutional right to information privacy and the Fourth Amendment provide some protection for personal health care information, but of a limited nature. While state regulation can be more extensive, it is also uneven in its protection. The Health Privacy Project at Georgetown University has prepared a comprehensive overview and analysis of every state's health privacy statutes and regulations.[17]

Privacy Torts. The Warren and Brandeis privacy torts protect medical information. Recall *Shulman v. Group W Productions, Inc.* from Chapter 2, where the court found that a TV show that taped the plaintiff as she was being rescued from a car accident and transported to the hospital via helicopter could give rise to a cause of action for intrusion upon seclusion (but not for public disclosure of

---

Transmitted Diseases: Theories of Privacy and Disclosure in Partner Notification, 5 Duke J. Gender & Pol'y 9 (1998).

[17] *See* Joy Pritts, Janlori Goldman, Zoe Hudson, Aimee Berenson & Elizabeth Hadley, *The State of Health Privacy: An Uneven Terrain (A Comprehensive Survey of State Health Privacy Statutes),* at http://www.healthprivacy.org.

private facts). In *Estate of Berthiaume v. Pratt,* 365 A.2d 792 (Me. 1976), a doctor attempted to take photographs of his patient, who was dying of cancer of the larynx. The patient raised a clenched fist and tried to remove his head from the camera's range. The patient died later that day. The court held that the patient had a claim for intrusion upon seclusion because the doctor did not have the right, against the patient's wishes, to complete his photographic record by taking pictures of the patient in his dying hours.

Many courts have found that the disclosure of medical information can give rise to a claim for public disclosure of private facts. In *Urbaniak v. Newton,* 277 Cal. Rptr. 354 (Cal. App. 1991), the court held that the disclosure of a patient's HIV status was "clearly a 'private fact' of which the disclosure may 'be offensive and objectionable to a reasonable [person] of ordinary sensibilities.' " *See also Susan S. v. Israels,* 67 Cal. Rptr. 2d 42 (Cal. App. 1997) (public disclosure action for disclosure of mental health records). In *Doe v. Mills,* 536 N.W.2d 824 (Mich. App. 1995), a group of abortion protestors held up large signs displaying the names of the plaintiffs outside the abortion clinic where they were getting abortions. The court held that the plaintiffs could bring a claim for public disclosure:

> . . . [A]bortion concerns matters of sexual relations and medical treatment, both of which are regarded as private matters. Furthermore, even though the abortion issue may be regarded as a matter of public interest, the plaintiffs' identities in this case were not matters of legitimate public concern, nor a matter of public record, but, instead, were purely private matters.

Likewise, in *Y.G. & L.G. v. Jewish Hospital of St. Louis,* 795 S.W.2d 488 (Mo. App. 1990), the court held that the plaintiffs had a viable public disclosure claim against a television station that broadcast the plaintiffs' involvement in a hospital's in vitro fertilization plan: "The in vitro program and its success may well have been matters of public interest, but the identity of the plaintiffs participating in the program was, we conclude, a private matter."

Tort Law Regulation of Patient-Physician Confidentiality. In addition to the privacy torts, a number of states recognize tort liability for instances where physicians disclose a patient's medical information. In certain circumstances, physicians can be liable for failing to disclose medical data about a patient.

Mandatory Reporting Laws. Many states require that medical personnel or institutions report certain health information to state agencies or to others. Depending on the state, the reporting requirements can extend to knife and gunshot wounds, sexually transmitted diseases, including HIV infection, and communicable diseases, such as tuberculosis. Reports are also required in many jurisdictions about injuries occurring to children and to elderly injuries, which are of the type that might indicate abuse.

Research Disclosure Laws. A number of states regulate the use of medical data for research purposes. For example, California generally prohibits nonconsensual disclosure of alcohol and drug abuse data, but permits such nonconsensual disclosure for the purpose of conducting research provided that the individual cannot be identified. *See* Cal. Health & Safety Code § 11977.

Medical Confidentiality Laws. Many states have specific statutes providing civil and criminal protection against the disclosure of medical information. Some laws restrict disclosure of medical data by particular entities: government agencies, HMOs, insurance companies, employers, pharmacists, and health data clearinghouses.

Other laws prohibit the disclosure by any entity of particular types of medical data, such as AIDS/HIV, alcohol or drug abuse, mental health, and genetic information. *See, e.g.,* Cal. Health & Safety Code § 199.21 (prohibiting disclosure of HIV test results); N.Y. Pub. Health L. § 17 (prohibiting the nonconsensual disclosure of medical records of minors relating to sexually transmitted diseases and abortion; even the disclosure to parents is prohibited without consent); Pa. Cons. Stat. § 1690.108 (prohibiting the disclosure of all records prepared during alcohol or drug abuse treatment).

Patient Access Laws. The vast majority of states (44) have statutes providing patients with a right to access certain medical records. A few states grant wide access to medical records held by all types of entities. On the other end of the spectrum, some states have no right of access, and others only have a limited right to access mental health records. The remaining states fall somewhere in between, permitting access to records from certain health care providers but not others (e.g., from some but not all of the following entities: hospitals, HMOs, insurers, and pharmacists).[18]

Comprehensive Health Privacy Laws. Most states do not have a comprehensive law governing medical privacy. According to the Health Privacy Project Report, only three states have a comprehensive law: Hawaii, Rhode Island, and Wisconsin. As the Report notes, most states regulate specific entities handling health data:

> The end result of this legislating by entity is that state laws — with a few notable exceptions — do not extend *comprehensive* protections to people's medical records. Thus, a state statute may impose privacy rules on hospitals but not dentists. The state may restrict the use and disclosure of information derived from a genetic test but not information obtained in a routine physical.[19]

As an example of a state law, California's Confidentiality of Medical Information Act (CMIA) applies to health care providers, health care service plans, and individuals. Cal. Civil Code §§ 56-56.37. It also extends to the contractors of these entities that have access to medical information. The CMIA creates a wide-reaching obligation to protect the confidentiality of medical information. Unless there is a specific statutory exception, the law requires patients to provide written authorization before anyone can use her health information.

Failure to obtain patient authorization or to maintain the confidentiality of information can lead to significant penalties. Even absent a showing of actual harm, the CMIA permits nominal damages up to $1,000. It also allows administrative fines and civil penalties. Both the California Department of Justice

---

[18] *See id.*
[19] *See id.*

and the California Office of Health Information Integrity have important enforcement roles.

The private right of action under the CMIA has led to litigation and large settlements. For example, in 2014, Stanford Hospitals & Clinics and two of its vendors settled a CMIA class action lawsuit for $4.1 million.[20] The lawsuit followed from one of its business associates outsourcing the creation of a graphic analyzing information regarding 20,000 patients. The second vendor wound up being posting this information on a publicly accessible website for over a year until a Stanford patient discovered it. Federal and state investigations of the incident concluded that the hospital was without fault. A class action lawsuit, however, led to the multi-million dollar settlement after over two years of litigation. Stanford denied wrongdoing, but state that it wished to settle to avoid ongoing costs of litigation. Its vendors paid $3.3 million of the settlement.

A 2013 amendment to the statute, A.B. 658, made it clear that the CMIA regulates certain mobile health care apps. The coverage extends to mobile apps, software, and hardware "designed to maintain medical information . . . to make the information available to an individual or a provider of health care at [his or her] request . . . for the purposes of allowing the individual to manager his or her information, or for the diagnosis, treatment, or management of a medical condition of the individual." This language does not necessarily extend to popular mobile apps used in monitoring sport performance or daily life; the key question is whether protected health or medical information will be collected by the mobile app.

6. THE HEALTH INSURANCE PORTABILITY AND ACCOUNTABILITY ACT

The Health Insurance Portability and Accountability Act (HIPAA) regulations are the primary federal regulation of health privacy in the United States. HIPAA has a broad scope and provides a baseline of privacy protection — states can still provide more protection.

(a) A Brief History of HIPAA

The Passage of HIPAA and the Initial Regulation. Congress enacted HIPAA in 1996. HIPAA's primary purpose was focused around insurance, which is why HIPAA does not include the word "privacy" in its title, and the "P" stands for portability of insurance. The goal of HIPAA was to permit employees to change jobs without having their new health plans exclude preexisting conditions.

Congress also mandated a uniform set of transaction codes to process insurance claims more easily. Given the greater ease of data sharing and transmission that uniform codes would enable, Congress was concerned about the privacy and security of medical data. However, Congress did not legislate privacy rules within HIPAA itself. Rather, Congress established a deadline of August 21, 1999, for it to return to this topic and enact comprehensive legislation to provide for privacy

---

[20] Jason Green, *$4.1M settlement possible in Stanford medical information breach*, San Jose Mercury News (Mar. 22, 2014).

of medical information. The Act also provided that if Congress failed to act by that date, then the Department of Health and Human Services (HHS) was to promulgate regulations with regard to health privacy.

No congressional majority could coalesce around a particular statutory solution, and the deadline passed without congressional action. Accordingly, HHS issued regulations, initially in the form of proposed regulations subject to revision. These were published at 64 Fed. Reg. 59,917 (Nov. 3, 1999). HHS received more than 50,000 comment letters on the proposed rule.

The Birth of the HIPAA Privacy Rule. The final version of the regulations — referred to as the "Privacy Rule" — was issued in December 2000 at the end of the Clinton Administration. Due to a procedural error, implementation of the regulations was delayed, and the Bush Administration initially criticized the regulations and vowed to delay and possibly to reconsider them. Later, the Administration changed course and announced that the Privacy Rule would go into effect. However, in 2002, the Bush Administration made significant changes in the regulations. *See* 67 Fed. Reg. 53,182 (Aug. 14, 2002). The Privacy Rule finally became effective in 2003. In a nutshell, and as HHS states, "The Privacy Rule, or *Standards for Privacy of Individually Identifiable Health Information*, establishes national standards for the protection of certain health information."[21]

The Birth of the HIPAA Security Rule. In addition to the Privacy Rule, the HIPAA regulations also contain what is known as the "Security Rule." The Security Rule was published in 2003 and became effective in 2005. HHS sums it up in this fashion: "The Security Rule operationalizes the protections contained in the Privacy Rule by addressing the technical and non-technical safeguards that organizations called "covered entities" must put in place to secure individuals' "electronic protected health information" (e-PHI)."[22]

The HITECH Act. In 2009, Congress passed the Health Information Technology for Economic and Clinical Health (HITECH) Act. The HITECH Act was part of the American Recovery and Reinvestment Act (ARRA). The purpose of the HITECH Act was to facilitate the move to electronic health records, but part of that Act mandated a number of changes to strengthen the HIPAA regulations. In particular, the HITECH Act mandated much higher penalties for violations, made many more organizations directly subject to HHS enforcement, and required HHS to conduct audits of HIPAA compliance. It also contains the first federal data breach notification requirement. It requires notification of affected individuals "without reasonable delay" and not later than 60 days after discovery of the breach.

In 2013, HHS issued a regulation to implement the changes mandated by the HITECH Act. This regulation is commonly called the "Omnibus Final Rule." It amends the Privacy and Security Rule to reflect the HITECH Act's mandates.

---

[21] Dept. of Health & Human Services, *Health Care Privacy, Understanding HIPAA Privacy*, at http://www.hhs.gov/ocr/privacy/hipaa/understanding/srsummary.html.

[22] *Id.*

(b) Scope and Applicability of HIPAA

Covered Entities. Many people mistakenly assume that the HIPAA regulations apply to all people or entities that have access to an individual's health information. Instead, the HIPAA regulations apply "to health plans, health care clearinghouses, and health care providers." 45 C.F.R. § 160.102. Health care plans, clearinghouses, and providers that are covered by the regulation are called "covered entities."

A "health care provider" is a "provider of medical or health services . . . and any other person or organization who furnishes, bills, or is paid for health care in the normal course of business." 45 C.F.R. § 160.103. Examples of health care providers are physicians, hospitals, and pharmacists.

A "health plan" is "an individual or group plan that provides, or pays the cost of, medical care." 45 C.F.R. § 160.103. This definition encompasses health insurers and HMOs.

A "health care clearinghouse" is a public or private entity that processes health information into various formats — either into a standard format or into specialized formats for the needs of specific entities. 45 C.F.R. § 160.103.

Protected Health Information. The data protected by HIPAA is called "protected health information" (PHI), which is defined as "any information, whether oral or recorded in any form or medium, that "is created or received by a health care provider, health plan, public health authority, employer, life insurer, school or university, or health care clearinghouse" and "relates to the past, present, or future physical or mental health or condition of any individual, the provision of health care to an individual, or the past, present, or future payment for the provision of health care to an individual." PHI must be information that "identifies the individual" or creates a "reasonable basis to believe the information can be used to identify the individual." 45 C.F.R. §160.103.

Business Associates. A "business associate" (BA) is any person or entity that, on behalf of a covered entity, "creates, receives, maintains, or transmits protected health information for a function or activity regulated by this subchapter, including claims processing or administration, data analysis, processing or administration, utilization review, quality assurance, patient safety activities listed at 42 CFR 3.20, billing, benefit management, practice management, and repricing."

In order for a covered entity to share PHI with a business associate, the parties must enter into a "business associate agreement" (BAA). HIPAA has a set of provisions that all BAAs must have.

Previously, business associates were regulated by contractual requirements by the covered entity in the BAA. The HITECH Act makes business associates directly liable for compliance with certain aspects of the HIPAA Privacy and Security Rules and makes these entities subject to HIPAA and HHS enforcement. This change is a highly significant one because it widely broadened the direct reach of HIPAA.

Additionally, subcontractors are now considered BAs and are subject to the same direct HHS enforcement. The Omnibus Rule includes within the definition of a BA any "subcontractor that creates, receives, maintains, or transmits protected health information on behalf of the business associate."

Electronic Processing. There is one other important consideration for determining the applicability of the HIPAA regulations — whether the person or entity processes and transmits health information electronically in a "standard" format as described in the HIPAA statute. The HIPAA statute was passed in order to standardize the format of the way health care information is transmitted, and only those entities using that format are covered under the regulations. A few critical definitions establish the jurisdictional scope of the regulations. The Pew Internet and American Life Project explains:

> If a person or an organization is a "health care provider" under the regulation, the next question to ask is whether it engages in the type of "standard transactions" that will bring it within the scope of the privacy rule. Since the intent of the administrative simplification provisions of HIPAA (including the privacy rule) is to simplify the processing of health insurance claims, the privacy rule applies only to providers who conduct insurance related transactions. Some of the electronic transaction that trigger application of HIPAA to a provider include: submitting health claims or equivalent information related to physician-patient interactions; determining eligibility for a health plan; receiving health care payment and remittance advice; and receiving referral certification and authorization. . . .
>
> In a very general sense, the question can be boiled down to: "Does the provider accept health insurance (including Medicaid) or participate in an HMO?"[23]

Hybrid Entities. Many entities provide a variety of products and services, only some of which pertain to health care. These entities are called "hybrid entities." An example of a hybrid entity is an employer that provides health care or a large company that has a division or subsidiary that provides health care or health insurance. Hybrid entities are less stringently regulated than covered entities. With a hybrid entity, the entity as a whole does not have to comply with the regulations — only the component that is actually performing the health care functions must comply. To address the danger that health information will spread beyond the health care component of a hybrid entity, the regulations require that firewalls be erected to protect against improper uses or disclosures within the entity. *See* 45 C.F.R. § 164.504(c)(2).

Under the initial rule, only when the entity's primary mission was not health care related could it be deemed a hybrid rather than a covered entity. Under the revised rule proposed by the Bush Administration, any entity that provides a mixture of health care and other functions can elect to be a hybrid rather than a covered entity.

Type of Information and Records Covered. The Privacy Rule and the Security Rule diverge in the type of information and records they cover. The Privacy Rule covers "individually identifiable health information," which is defined as data that relates to a person's health condition, the provision of health care, or the payment for health care. "Individually identifiable" means that the information either "identifies the individual" or "can be used to identify the individual." 45 C.F.R. §

---

[23] Pew Internet & American Life Project, *Exposed Online: Why the New Federal Health Privacy Regulation Doesn't Offer Much Protection to Internet Users* 13 (Nov. 2001).

160.103. This information can be in either electronic or paper form. Information covered by the Privacy Rule is referred to as "protected health information" (PHI).

The Security Rule only applies to "electronic-protected health information" (e-PHI). This means that unlike the Privacy Rule, the Security Rule only covers digital records and not paper records.

NOTES & QUESTIONS

1. ***Constitutionality of HIPAA.*** In *South Carolina Medical Ass'n v. Thompson,* 327 F.3d 346 (4th Cir. 2003), a group of doctors and doctors' associations challenged the constitutionality of HIPAA. They first argued that HIPAA is an improper delegation of congressional authority because Congress "relinquished its lawmaking function" by allowing an agency to establish privacy regulations rather than directly legislating to protect privacy. The court rejected this argument, contending that "Congress did not abdicate its legislative responsibilities in passing HIPAA, but outlined a broad set of principles to guide HHS action." The plaintiffs also argued that HHS improperly expanded HIPAA's scope beyond electronic health information to all health records maintained by covered entities. The court, however, concluded that "the plain language of HIPAA indicates that HHS could reasonably determine that the regulation of individually identifiable health information should include non-electronic forms of that information."

2. ***Protecting PHI Throughout the Chain of Custody***. Recall that HIPAA applies directly not just to covered entities but to most other entities that receive PHI from a covered entity. Thus, there is direct HHS enforcement against BAs and subcontractors (which are also deemed BAs for the purposes of HIPAA).

   Commentary to the Omnibus Rule provides that "[a]pplying HIPAA privacy and security requirements directly to subcontractors also ensures that the privacy and security protections of the HIPAA Rules extend beyond covered entities to those entities that create or receive protected health information in order for the covered entity to perform its health care functions." According to the commentary: "A subcontractor is then a business associate where that function, activity, or service involves the creation, receipt, maintenance, or transmission of protected health information." The intent, as the regulation commentary explains, is to ensure that HIPAA protections extend "no matter how far 'down the chain' the information flows." BAs are subject to the same civil and criminal penalties under HIPAA as covered entities.

   In contrast, other privacy laws do not permit direct enforcement against entities that receive information from a regulated entity. For example, under the Family Educational Rights and Privacy Act (FERPA), which regulates the privacy of student data at schools, parties receiving student data from schools are not directly regulated by the Department of Education.

   Which approach is preferable?

3. ***The Limits of HIPAA Coverage: Health Websites and Apps.*** Although HIPAA's coverage appears quite broad, it does not apply to all health data. Nor does it apply to all individuals or entities providing medical services. In order

to be covered by HIPAA, a healthcare provider must process and transmits PHI electronically in a standard format under the HIPAA statute. This will happen anytime health insurance is involved, but certain healthcare providers may not take health insurance. These providers may thus not be covered.

Many health websites and apps are not processing and transmitting PHI in the standard HIPAA format. They, too, are not covered entities. As explained in a Pew report:

> Most health-related Web sites engage in a number of different activities, from providing general educational health information to allowing patients to review test results online. Only some of these activities will be protected by the privacy regulations. For example, drugstore.com sells both drugs pursuant to a prescription and over-the-counter products. While information related to the prescription drug will be covered by the privacy regulation, information related to the over-the-counter product will not. The privacy rule covers only identifiable information related to "health care." This term does not include selling or distributing non-prescription health care items. . . .
>
> Many Web sites offer a "health assessment" feature where users may enter all sorts of information from height and weight to drug and alcohol use. . . . For example, HealthStatus.com offers free general health assessments as well as disease specific assessments to determine an individual's risk for some of the leading causes of death. . . . [B]ecause HealthStatus.com does not accept any insurance it will not be covered by the privacy rule.[24]

Should such websites and apps be covered by HIPAA? Should all health data be covered? Many people tend to think of health data as a category of data with a certain level of privacy protections. But HIPAA only protects some health data depending upon who collects and uses it and how the health data is processed and transmitted. This can be confusing for people and can lead to their having incorrect expectations of privacy. However, if all health data is regulated by HIPAA, what about health data that a person tells to a friend? Should the friend be HIPAA regulated? Suppose a person provides health information to a gym instructor or nutritionist. Should these individuals be regulated by HIPAA?

(c) The Privacy Rule

Privacy Officials. Covered entities must designate an individual as the covered entity's privacy official, responsible for the implementation and development of the entity's privacy policies and procedures. A person must be designated as a contact person to receive complaints about privacy and provide information about the matters covered by the entity's notice. The contact person can be the same person as the privacy official.

Responsibilities. HIPAA requires that covered entities and business associates have written policies and procedures. Documentation about HIPAA compliance must be kept for at least six years. HIPAA requires training of all workforce

---

[24] Pew Internet & American Life Project, *The Online Health Care Revolution: How the Web Helps Americans Take Better Care of Themselves* (Nov. 2000).

members. HIPAA requires that covered entities must conduct routine assessments of their privacy practices. An organization must have in place appropriate administrative, technical, and physical safeguards to protect the privacy of protected health information.

Use and Disclosure of PHI. As a general rule, PHI must be kept confidential and cannot be used or disclosed without a person's "authorization."

But there are a number of exceptions when people's authorization is not required. Examples include disclosures to comply with a legal requirement, to report abuse, to avert a serious threat to health or safety, for health oversight activities, for judicial and administrative proceedings, and for "treatment, payment, or healthcare operations" (TPO).

Disclosure to Law Enforcement Officials. Pursuant to 45 C.F.R. § 164.512(f), PHI may be disclosed "for a law enforcement purpose to a law enforcement official" without authorization if in compliance with a "court order or court-ordered warrant, or a subpoena or summons issued by a judicial officer" or a grand jury subpoena; or "an administrative subpoena or summons, a civil or an authorized investigative demand, or similar process authorized under law."

The following requirements must also be met:

(1) The information sought is relevant and material to a legitimate law enforcement inquiry;

(2) The request is specific and limited in scope to the extent reasonably practicable in light of the purpose for which the information is sought; and

(3) De-identified information could not reasonably be used.

Moreover, certain health information may also be disclosed "in response to a law enforcement official's request for such information for the purpose of identifying or locating a suspect, fugitive, material witness, or missing person."

The Minimum Necessary Rule. When using or disclosing protected health information, covered entities must "make reasonable efforts to limit protected health information to the minimum necessary" to accomplish their goal. § 164.502(b)(1). This provision does not apply to disclosures to health care providers for treatment or to disclosures to the individual.

Authorization. A person's authorization must be written and signed. The authorization form must be in plain language and must identify the type of information to be disclosed. It must identify the names or types of entities authorized to make the disclosure as well as those to whom the disclosure will be made. The authorization form must identify the purpose of the disclosure. The authorization must have a time period and an expiration date or event. People have a right to revoke the authorization and must be informed about this right.

Conditioned Authorization. A "covered entity may not condition the provision to an individual of treatment, payment, enrollment in the health plan, or eligibility for benefits on the provision of an authorization." § 164.508(b)(4). There are a number of exceptions to this rule. First, treatment can be conditioned on the provision of research-related disclosure. In other words, a physician or health care facility can make research-related disclosure a quid pro quo for treatment. Second, treatment can be conditioned if authorization is necessary to determine whether the individual is eligible for benefits or enrollment under a health plan, and for underwriting or risk rating determinations (this does not include psychotherapy notes). Third, payment of a claim or benefits can be conditioned upon authorization if the disclosure is necessary to determine a payment and is not for the use or disclosure of psychotherapy notes.

Notice of Privacy Practices. Patients must be given a notice about the privacy practices of a covered entity. This notice is called a Notice of Privacy Practices (NPP). 45 C.F.R. § 164.520

Right of Access. Individuals have a right to access any PHI that is used in whole or in part to make decisions about the individual. People have a right to have a copy of their PHI, including an electronic copy if the PHI is stored in electronic form.

Right of Amendment. People can request that their records be amended. This request can be denied, but people can still place a statement of disagreement in their file.

Right to File a Complaint. People have a right to file a complaint to the covered entity or to HHS alleging a HIPAA violation — without being retaliated against for doing so.

The Right to Request Restrictions. An individual retains the right to request restrictions on the use or disclosure of health information by all covered entities. 45 C.F.R. § 164.502(c). Covered entities must permit individuals to make such requests. 45 C.F.R. § 164.522(a). If an entity agrees to an individual's request, it must adhere to its agreement. However, an entity is not required to agree to a restriction. 45 C.F.R. § 164.522(a).

In emergency treatment situations, an entity can break this agreement, but if it discloses health information to other health care providers, it must request that the provider not further use or disclose the information. 45 C.F.R. § 164.522(a).

Accommodation of Communication Preferences. Under 45 C.F.R. § 164.502(h), individuals have the right to require covered providers to accommodate their requests about how providers communicate with the individual. According to the regulation's commentary,

> [A]n individual who does not want his or her family members to know about a certain treatment may request that the provider communicate with the individual at his or her place of employment, or to send communications to a designated address. Covered providers must accommodate the request unless it is unreasonable.

Marketing. Authorization is required for the use and disclosure of health data for the marketing of items and services. If a covered entity wants to provide a person's health data to a third party who wants to use it to peddle goods or services, it must first obtain that person's authorization. Authorization is required even if the marketing is done by the covered entity or one of its divisions.

Excluded from the definition of "marketing" is the covered entity's own provision of health-related services and products. 45 C.F.R. § 164.501. A covered entity can use an individual's health information without authorization to try to sell to her its own different products, treatments, and services — so long as they are health care related. Since these activities are not defined as "marketing," the individual cannot opt out or remove herself from the mailing list. In the conclusion of one observer, the HIPAA rules permit "marketing . . . to be disguised under operational activities."[25]

Psychotherapy Notes. Authorization is required "for any use or disclosure of psychotherapy notes" even if that use or disclosure is for treatment, payment, and health care operations. 45 C.F.R. § 164.508. According to the regulation commentary, the reason why psychotherapy notes require authorization is because "psychotherapy notes do not include information that covered entities typically need for treatment, payment, or other types of health care operations."

NOTES & QUESTIONS

1. *Compliance and Confusion.* Consider the following from an article by Laura Parker in *USA Today*:

> In thousands of instances, [HIPAA] has been interpreted in extreme — and often incorrect — ways that critics say have been impractical at best and nonsensical at worst. . . .
>
> Thousands of doctors, for example, have stopped sending out appointment-reminder postcards, figuring the cards could be read by someone other than the patient. Some doctors have stopped leaving messages on patients' telephone answering machines, fearing that other family members might listen to them. Wives have been told they could no longer verify dental appointments for their husbands.[26]

Does HIPAA require these measures? HHS provides HIPAA questions and answers on its website:

> Question: *May health care providers use sign-in sheets or call out the names in waiting rooms?*
>
> Answer: Yes. Covered entities, such as physician's offices, may use patient sign-in sheets or call out patient names in waiting rooms, so long as the information disclosed is appropriately limited. . . . For example, the sign-in sheet may not display medical information that is not necessary for the purpose of signing in. . . .

---

[25] June Mary Zekan Makdisi, *Commercial Use of Protected Health Information Under HIPAA's Privacy Rule: Reasonable Disclosure or Disguised Marketing?*, 82 Neb. L. Rev. 741, 781 (2004).

[26] Laura Parker, *Medical Privacy Law Creates Wide Confusion,* USA Today, Oct. 16, 2003.

Question: *May health care providers leave messages at patients' homes or mail reminders to their homes?*

Answer: Yes. . . . [T]he Rule does not prohibit covered entities from leaving messages for patients on their answering machines. However, to reasonably safeguard the individual's privacy, covered entities should take care to limit the amount of information disclosed on the answering machine. . . . The Privacy Rule permits covered entities to disclose limited information to family members, friends, or other persons regarding an individual's care. . . . However, covered entities should use professional judgment to assure that such disclosures are in the best interest of the individual and limit the information disclosed. . . .

In situations where a patient has requested that the covered entity communicate with him in a confidential manner, such as by alternative means or at an alternative location, the covered entity must accommodate that request.

Question: *Can a patient have a friend or family member pick up a prescription for her?*

Answer: Yes. A pharmacist may use professional judgment and experience with common practice to make reasonable inferences of the patient's best interest in allowing a person other than the patient to pick up a prescription.

Question: *May a doctor discuss a patient's health status, treatment, or payment with the patient's family and friends?*

Answer: Yes. The HIPAA Privacy Rule at 45 CFR 164.510(b) specifically permits covered entities to share information that is directly relevant to the involvement of a spouse, family members, friends, or other persons identified by a patient.[27]

2. ***Consent in the Privacy Rule.*** Fred Cate has criticized the requirements of consent in the HIPAA Privacy Rule.[28] For example, subject to certain limitations, the Rule requires the individual's consent prior to the use or disclosure of protected health information to carry out treatment, payment, or health care operations. 45 C.F.R. § 164.506(a). Cate argues that "the focus on choice has done more to undermine — rather than protect — individual privacy, and to diminish — rather than maximize — human welfare."

According to Cate, this result follows for two reasons. First, choice in practice does not work well. Cate notes, "All of the available evidence suggests that notices are widely ignored by individuals and are written in overly broad or overly detailed language. Second, individual choice is not the same thing as personal privacy. As a result, protecting individual decision-making does not necessarily enhance privacy." Indeed, Cate observes, "the preoccupation with choice effectively shifts the burden for protecting privacy from the data user to the data subject."

In response to this situation, Cate makes a number of suggestions, including a shift "to a more proportional, risk-based concept of consent." Under it, "explicit, written consent is only necessary where serious harm is threatened; other uses of personal data might be permitted with oral consent or even opt-

---

[27] http://www.hhs.gov/ocr/hipaa/.

[28] Fred Cate, *Protecting Privacy in Health Research: The Limits of Individual Choice*, 98 Cal. L. Rev. 176 (2010).

out consent." Do you think this approach would lead to a better model of patient consent?

3. ***Law Enforcement Access and the Fourth Amendment.*** Section 164.512(f) has come under significant criticism by commentators who argue that it too broadly allows law enforcement officials to have access to health information.

The Fourth Amendment generally requires a warrant supported by probable cause in order to search a person's documents. However, in what has become known as the "third party doctrine," the Court has held that there is no reasonable expectation of privacy (and hence, no Fourth Amendment protection) when a person's records are maintained by another party. For example, the Court has concluded that people lack a reasonable expectation of privacy in the records of the phone numbers they dial because these records are maintained by the phone company. *See Smith v. Maryland,* 442 U.S. 735 (1979) (excerpted in Chapter 4 of this casebook). Likewise, bank records are not private because the bank, a third party, maintains control over them. *See United States v. Miller,* 425 U.S. 435 (1976) (Chapter 7).

Suppose the government obtains a person's medical records under §
164.512(f). The person raises a Fourth Amendment challenge, contending that the government needed a search warrant to obtain the records. Would the person prevail? These records are maintained by third parties (doctors, hospitals, insurers). But these parties have statutory, common law, and ethical duties to maintain the confidentiality of health information. Does the third party doctrine extend to medical records?

Other federal privacy statues generally provide stronger protection for third-party records than does the HIPAA rule. For example, the privacy subscriber provision in the Cable Communications Policy Act requires (1) "clear and convincing evidence that the subject of the information is reasonably suspected of engaging in criminal activity and that the information sought would be material evidence in the case"; and (2) "the subject of the information is afforded the opportunity to appear and contest such entity's claim." 47 U.S.C. § 551(h). Should cable subscriber records receive greater privacy protection than medical records? What factors might explain this outcome?

4. ***Subpoenas for PHI.*** Consider *New York City Health & Hospitals Corp. v. Morgenthau,* 779 N.E.2d 773 (N.Y. Ct. App. 2002). A district attorney subpoenaed 23 hospitals to obtain emergency room data to investigate a homicide in which the suspect was thought to have been bleeding when he fled the crime scene. The subpoena sought records of those treated for stab wounds. A group of four hospitals refused to turn over the records, citing to Civil Practice Law and Rule § 4504(a), which provided:

> Unless the patient waives the privilege, a person authorized to practice medicine, registered professional nursing [or] licensed practical nursing . . . shall not be allowed to disclose any information which he acquired in attending a patient in a professional capacity, and which was necessary to enable him to act in that capacity. The relationship of a physician and patient shall exist between a medical corporation . . . and the patients to whom [it] . . . render[s] professional medical services.

The court quashed the subpoena:

> We conclude, however, that [*Matter of Grand Jury Investigation of Onondaga County,* 450 N.E.2d 678 (N.Y. 1983)] controls this appeal and directs that the challenged subpoenas be quashed. In *Onondaga County,* as in the instant case, the victim was stabbed to death under circumstances that led investigators to conclude that the assailant may have left the scene bleeding. Endeavoring to identify the assailant, the District Attorney of Onondaga County issued a grand jury subpoena on a hospital, seeking "all medical records pertaining to treatment of any person with stab wounds or other wounds caused by a knife." In quashing the subpoena, the Court held that compliance might have "require[d] the hospital to which it is addressed to divulge information protected by the physician-patient privilege." The Court concluded that under those circumstances, it was "not . . . possible to comply with a demand for names and addresses of all persons treated for a knife wound without disclosing privileged information concerning diagnosis and treatment."
>
> We perceive no difference of any actual substance between the subpoena quashed in *Onondaga County* and the ones challenged here. The records potentially responsive to the HHC subpoenas are precisely the same as those sought in *Onondaga County.* Though the District Attorney crafted the instant subpoenas with *Onondaga County* in mind by broadening their scope (to include most bleeding wounds rather than only knife wounds) and narrowing their reach (to include only wounds "plainly observable to a lay person"), the subpoenas still run afoul of *Onondaga County.* . . .

In light of this court's reasoning, consider HIPAA, § 164.512(f). Is there a conflict? If so, and if a subpoena pursuant to § 164.512(f) were issued in that case, would HIPAA or the New York statute control?

NORTHWESTERN MEMORIAL HOSPITAL V. ASHCROFT

362 F.3d 923 (7th Cir. 2004)

POSNER, J. The government appeals from an order by the district court quashing a subpoena commanding Northwestern Memorial Hospital in Chicago to produce the medical records of certain patients on whom Dr. Cassing Hammond had performed late-term abortions at the hospital using the controversial method known [as partial birth abortion]. . . .

The subpoenaed records, apparently some 45 in number, are sought for use in the forthcoming trial in the Southern District of New York of a suit challenging the constitutionality of the Partial-Birth Abortion Ban Act of 2003, 18 U.S.C. § 1531. Dr. Hammond is one of the plaintiffs in that suit and will also be testifying as an expert witness. The district court held that the production of the records is barred by regulations issued under the Health Insurance Portability and Accountability Act of 1996 (HIPAA), Pub. L. 104-191, 110 Stat. 1936, and let us begin there.

[HIPAA provides that its regulations] "shall not supercede a contrary provision of State law, if the provision of State law imposes requirements, standards, or implementation specifications that are more stringent than the requirements, standards, or implementation specifications imposed under the regulation." See also 45 C.F.R. § 160.203(b). A standard is "more stringent" if it "provides greater privacy protection for the individual who is the subject of the individually identifiable health information" than the standard in the regulation.

The particular focus of the appeal is an HHS regulation . . . which authorizes a "covered entity" (such as Northwestern Memorial Hospital) to disclose private health information in judicial or administrative proceedings "in response to an order of a court." § 164.512(e)(1)(i). . . .

The district court in our case ruled that the Illinois law, because it sets a "more stringent" standard for disclosure than the HIPAA regulation, trumps that regulation by virtue of HIPAA's supersession provision. So he quashed the subpoena, precipitating this appeal.

Although the issue is not free from doubt, we agree with the government that the HIPAA regulations do not impose state evidentiary privileges on suits to enforce federal law. Illinois is free to enforce its more stringent medical records privilege (there is no comparable federal privilege) in suits in state court to enforce state law and, by virtue of an express provision in Fed. R. Evid. 501, in suits in federal court (mainly diversity suits) as well in which state law supplies the rule of decision. But the Illinois privilege does not govern in federal-question suits. . . .

All that 45 C.F.R. § 164.512(e) should be understood to do, therefore, is to create a procedure for obtaining authority to use medical records in litigation. Whether the records are actually admissible in evidence will depend among other things on whether they are privileged. And the evidentiary privileges that are applicable to federal-question suits are given not by state law but by federal law, Fed. R. Evid. 501, which does not recognize a physician-patient (or hospital-patient) privilege. . . .

The district court did not reach a further ground urged by Northwestern Memorial Hospital for quashing the government's subpoena, which is simply that the burden of compliance with it would exceed the benefit of production of the material sought by it. Fed. R. Civ. P. 45(c)(3)(A)(iv). . . .

The hospital had urged both the lack of probative value of the records and the loss of privacy by the patients. The government had responded in generalities, arguing that redaction would eliminate any privacy concern and that since Dr. Hammond had "made assertions of fact about his experience and his patients that plaintiffs are using to support their claim that, without a health exception, the Act is unconstitutional," the government should be permitted to test those assertions; but the government had not indicated what assertions these were or how the records might bear on them. Although on appeal the hospital repeated at length its reasons for believing that the records sought by the government would have little or no probative value, the government's response in both its opening brief and its reply brief remained vague to the point of being evasive.

At the oral argument we pressed the government's lawyer repeatedly and hard for indications of what he hoped to learn from the hospital records, and drew a blank. . . .

Like the district judge, we think the balance weighs in favor of quashing the subpoena. The government does not deny that the hospital is an appropriate representative of the privacy interests of its patients. But it argues that since it is seeking only a limited number of records and they would be produced to it minus the information that would enable the identity of the patient to be determined, there is no hardship to either the hospital or the patients of compliance. The argument is unrealistic and incomplete. What is true is that the *administrative* hardship of compliance would be modest. But it is not the only or the main hardship. The natural sensitivity that people feel about the disclosure of their medical records — the sensitivity that lies behind HIPAA — is amplified when the records are of a procedure that Congress has now declared to be a crime. Even if all the women whose records the government seeks know what "redacted" means, they are bound to be skeptical that redaction will conceal their identity from the world. This is hardly a typical case in which medical records get drawn into a lawsuit. Reflecting the fierce emotions that the long-running controversy over the morality and legality of abortion has made combustible, the Partial-Birth Abortion Ban Act and the litigation challenging its constitutionality — and even more so the rash of suits around the country in which the Department of Justice has been seeking the hospital records of abortion patients — have generated enormous publicity. These women must know that, and doubtless they are also aware that hostility to abortion has at times erupted into violence, including criminal obstruction of entry into abortion clinics, the firebombing of clinics, and the assassination of physicians who perform abortions.

Some of these women will be afraid that when their redacted records are made a part of the trial record in New York, persons of their acquaintance, or skillful "Googlers," sifting the information contained in the medical records concerning each patient's medical and sex history, will put two and two together, "out" the 45 women, and thereby expose them to threats, humiliation, and obloquy. As the court pointed out in *Parkson v. Central DuPage Hospital,* "whether the patients' identities would remain confidential by the exclusion of their names and identifying numbers is questionable at best. The patients' admit and discharge summaries arguably contain histories of the patients' prior and present medical conditions, information that in the cumulative can make the possibility of recognition very high." In its opening brief, as throughout the district court proceeding, the government expressly reserved the right, at a later date, to seek the identity of the patients whose records are produced. Pressed at argument, the government's lawyer abandoned the reservation; but we do not know what would prevent reconsideration should the government, the subpoena having been enforced, discover that particular medical records that it had obtained were incomplete, opaque, or ambiguous.

Even if there were no possibility that a patient's identity might be learned from a redacted medical record, there would be an invasion of privacy. Imagine if nude pictures of a woman, uploaded to the Internet without her consent though without identifying her by name, were downloaded in a foreign country by people who will never meet her. She would still feel that her privacy had been invaded. The revelation of the intimate details contained in the record of a late-term abortion may inflict a similar wound.

If Northwestern Memorial Hospital cannot shield its abortion patients' records from disclosure in judicial proceedings, moreover, the hospital will lose the confidence of its patients, and persons with sensitive medical conditions may be inclined to turn elsewhere for medical treatment. . . .

[Therefore, the subpoena is quashed] on the basis of relative hardship under Fed. R. Civ. P. 45(c).

MANION, J. concurring in part, dissenting in part. . . . This court should enforce the subpoena. I therefore concur in part and dissent in part. . . .

In this case, the government seeks only redacted medical records and agrees that all identifying information may be removed before Northwestern makes the records available for its review. Because the records will be redacted, they will not identify the individual. Nor is there a reasonable basis to believe that the information can be used to identify the individual. . . .

. . . [T]he relevance [of the subpoenaed records] cannot be overstated: Congress made explicit findings that a partial-birth abortion is never medically necessary to protect a women's health. Yet, Dr. Hammond claims Congress is wrong. . . . Dr. Hammond seeks to testify accordingly, and it is therefore imperative that the government be able to determine the veracity of his testimony. There is no better way than by determining if Dr. Hammond's actual practice supports his testimony. And this is not a question only of impeachment, but rather concerns the heart of this case. . . .

NOTES & QUESTIONS

1. *Postscript.* Not all courts facing the issue agreed with the Seventh Circuit. The judge in New York ordered that hospitals there turn over the records. *National Abortion Federation v. Ashcroft*, 2004 WL 555701 (S.D.N.Y. 2004) (not reported in F. Supp. 2d). Partially in response to considerable criticism, however, the DOJ abandoned its request for the records in that case.

2. *De-Identified Records.* The Seventh Circuit in *Northwestern Memorial Hospital* concluded that even though the patients' identities were not disclosed along with the records, the records should still be protected. Part of the court's holding appears to rest on the fact that the patients' identities could not be protected with the complete assurance that they would not be revealed down the road. However, another part of the court's holding suggests that even in a system where the patients' identities would be completely protected, the release of the records would still interfere with the patient-physician relationship. Is the court giving too much protection to the records here? Assuming that the records can be properly de-identified, is there any valid reason to withhold their disclosure in discovery if they bear some relevance to the case?

3. *The Privacy Rule and De-Identification of Personal Information.* Under the Privacy Rule, de-identified personal health information is "not individually identifiable health information," and is free from the requirements of the Rule. 45 C.F.R. § 164.502(d)(2). The Privacy Rule presents two paths for information to be deemed de-identified. First, health information is considered de-identified if entities with "appropriate knowledge of and experience with generally accepted statistical and scientific principles" determine "that there is a very low probability of identifying individuals with such information." 45 C.F.R. § 164.502(b)(1). Second, de-identification is considered achieved through the removal of 18 enumerated data elements. These include name, contact information, most geographic subdivisions smaller than a state, all date elements other than year, and any biometric identifiers. 45 C.F.R.

§ 164.502(b)(2).

Fred Cate criticizes the de-identification requirements regarding suppression of identifiers as "useless for most medical research because researchers require access to information about the patient's medical history, the time and date drugs were administered, or other data prohibited under the de-identification standard."[29] Raising a different objection to the Privacy Rule, Paul Ohm characterizes it as "the high-water mark for use of PII to balance privacy risks against valuable uses of information."[30] The flaw is that its static list of identifiers to be removed is "frozen in amber." Ohm argues that other information that might be contained in a health record can, in fact, be used to identify.

In contrast, Jane Yakowitz is more sanguine about the benefits of de-identification under the Privacy Rule.[31] She points to a study of Office of the National Coordinator for Health Information Technology (ONC), which is located at the Department of Health and Human Services. Yakowitz terms the study the only one in the last decade that replicated "what a real adversary would face" in trying to use readily available outside data to re-identify patient. As she summarizes, "The team determined that it was able to accurately re-identify two of the fifteen thousand individuals, for a match rate of 0.013%. In other words, the risk, even after extraordinary effort, was very small." Paul Schwartz and Daniel Solove propose a new standard for defining PII, one based upon the risk of re-identification. Because the ability to re-identify data changes with new technology and as new public information about individuals becomes available, Schwartz and Solove contend that de-identification ought to be defined more flexibly as a standard rather than as a rule.[32]

(d) The Security Rule

Purpose. The Security Rule requires covered entities to "protect against reasonably anticipated threats or hazards to the security and integrity of [e-PHI.]" 45 C.F.R. § 164.306(a). The Security Rule sets forth a number of administrative, physical, and technical safeguards for e-PHI.

e-PHI. The Security Rule has a different scope than the Privacy Rule. The Privacy Rule applies to all PHI, but the Security Rule only applies to electronic PHI (e-PHI). However, the Privacy Rule requires administrative, physical, and technical safeguards to all PHI.

---

[29] Fred H. Cate, *Protecting Privacy in Health Research: The Limits of Individual Choice,* 98 Cal. L. Rev. 1765, 1789 (2010).

[30] Paul Ohm, *Broken Promises of Privacy,* 57 UCLA L. Rev. 1701, 1737 (2009).

[31] Jane Yakowitz, *Tragedy of the Data Commons,* 25 Harv. J.L. & Tech. 1 (2011).

[32] Paul M. Schwartz & Daniel J. Solove, *The PII Problem: Privacy and a New Concept of Personally Identifiable Information,* 86 N.Y.U. L. Rev. 1814 (2011).

Required vs. Addressable Security Standards. The Security Rule's safeguards are either required or "addressable." An addressable safeguard does not mean that it is optional; it means that an alternative can be chosen if justified by an explanation.

Administrative, Physical, and Technical Safeguards. The Security Rule requires administrative, physical, and technical safeguards for e-PHI. Administrative safeguards include risk analysis and management, access authorization, security awareness and training, and procedures for dealing with security incidents, among other things.

Physical safeguards include a facility security plan, access limitations to records, a process for the safe disposal of records and for data backup and storage.

Technical safeguards include login authentication, encryption, and audit controls.

(e) The Breach Notification Rule

The HITECH Act also created a Breach Notification Rule. This rule requires individuals to be notified if their PHI is involved in a data security breach — the first such requirement in federal law.

Definition of a "Breach." A breach "means the acquisition, access, use, or disclosure of protected health information in a manner not permitted . . . which compromises the security or privacy of the protected health information." 45 C.F.R. § 164.402. The definition of a breach only applies to "unsecured PHI." Being "unsecured" basically means being unencrypted.

Notification. Affected individuals must be notified "without reasonable delay" — and no later than 60 days after discovering the breach. Larger breaches (500 people or more) require notice to the media and to HHS.

(f) HIPAA Enforcement and Preemption

Enforcement Entities. The HIPAA regulations provide for civil and criminal penalties. Civil violations of HIPAA are enforced by the HHS's Office for Civil Rights (OCR). Criminal HIPAA violations are enforced by the DOJ. Additionally, state attorneys general may enforce HIPAA.

Civil Fines. HIPAA fines range between $50,000 up to $1.5 million per provision of HIPAA violated. In any one incident, a number of provisions of HIPAA may be violated.

Criminal Penalties. If people violate HIPAA with a malicious motive, HIPAA authorizes personal fines up to $250,000 and up to ten years in jail.

No Private Right of Action. The HIPAA regulations do not grant a private cause of action. Enforcement of the statute is solely through the Secretary of Health and Human Services.

Preemption. HIPAA provides a baseline of protections but still allows states to pass more stringent requirements. § 160.203(b).

PARKVIEW HEALTH SYSTEM, INC. RESOLUTION AGREEMENT AND CORRECTIVE ACTION PLAN

(June 23, 2014)

RESOLUTION AGREEMENT

I. Recitals

1. *Parties.* The Parties to this Resolution Agreement (Agreement) are the United States Department of Health and Human Services, Office for Civil Rights (HHS) and Parkview Health System, Inc. d/b/a Parkview Physicians Group, f/k/a Parkview Medical Group, a nonprofit Indiana corporation, which shall be referred to as "Parkview" or "Covered Entity". Parkview and HHS shall together be referred to as the "Parties."

2. *Factual Background and Covered Conduct*

a. Authority of HHS

HHS enforces the Federal standards that govern the Privacy of Individually Identifiable Health Information (the Privacy Rule), the Security Standards for the Protection of Electronic Protected Health Information (the Security Rule), and the Notification in the Case of Breach of Unsecured Protected Health Information (the Breach Notification Rule). . . .

Parkview is a covered entity as defined in 45 C.F.R. § 160.103. Thus, Parkview is required to comply with the HIPAA Rules.

Parkview is an affiliated covered entity pursuant to 45 C.F.R. § 164.105(b).

b. Covered Conduct

On June 10, 2009, Dr. Christine Hamilton filed a complaint with HHS against Parkview, Complaint Number 09-99157 ("the Complaint"), alleging that Parkview had violated the Privacy Rule. On May 16, 2011, HHS began investigating the allegations in the Complaint alleging that the Covered Entity is in violation of the Privacy Rule.

HHS's investigation indicates that the following conduct occurred ("Covered Conduct"):

1. In September 2008, Parkview received and took custody and control of medical records pertaining to approximately 5,000 to 8,000 of Dr. Hamilton's patients, all of which contained protected health information (PHI) in non-electronic form. Parkview was assisting Dr. Hamilton to transition the patients to new providers, and was considering the possibility of purchasing some of the records from Dr. Hamilton, who was retiring and closing her practice.

2. Parkview was required by 45 C.F.R. §164.530(c) to appropriately and reasonably safeguard the PHI throughout the time the PHI was in Parkview's possession and was maintained by Parkview until the PHI was permissibly transferred in accordance with 45 C.F.R. §164.502 or rendered unreadable, unusable or indecipherable to unauthorized persons.

3. On June 4, 2009, Parkview failed to appropriately and reasonably safeguard the PHI, when Parkview employees, with notice that Dr. Hamilton had refused delivery and was not at home, delivered and left 71 cardboard boxes of these medical records unattended and accessible to unauthorized persons on the driveway of Dr. Hamilton's home, within 20 feet of the public road and a short distance away (four doors down) from a heavily trafficked public shopping venue.

3. *No Admission.* This Agreement is not an admission of liability by Parkview.

4. *No Concession.* This Agreement is not a concession by HHS that Parkview is not in violation of the Privacy Rule and not liable for civil money penalties.

5. *Intention of Parties to Effect Resolution.* This Agreement is intended to resolve Complaint No. 09-99157 regarding possible violations of the Privacy Rule promulgated by HHS pursuant to the administrative simplification provisions of [HIPAA]. In consideration of the Parties' interest in avoiding the uncertainty, burden and expense of further investigation and formal proceedings, the Parties agree to resolve this matter according to the Terms and Conditions below.

II. Terms and Conditions

6. *Payment.* Parkview agrees to pay HHS the amount of $800,000 ("Resolution Amount"). Parkview agrees to pay the Resolution Amount on the Effective Date of this Agreement as defined in paragraph II.14 by automated clearing house transaction pursuant to written instructions to be provided by HHS.

7. *Corrective Action Plan.* Parkview has entered into and agrees to comply with the Corrective Action Plan (CAP), attached as Appendix A, which is incorporated into this Agreement by reference. If Parkview breaches the CAP, and fails to cure the breach as set forth in the CAP, then Parkview will be in breach of this Agreement and HHS will not be subject to the Release set forth in paragraph II.8 of this Agreement.

8. *Release by HHS.* In consideration and conditioned upon Parkview's performance of its obligations under this Agreement, HHS releases Parkview from any actions it may have against Parkview under the Privacy Rule for the Covered Conduct identified in paragraph I.2. HHS does not release Parkview from, nor waive any rights, obligations, or causes of action other than those specifically referred to in this paragraph. This release does not extend to actions that may be brought under section 1177 of the Social Security Act, 42 U.S.C. § 1320d-6. . . .

III. Effective Date and Term of CAP

The Effective Date for this CAP shall be calculated in accordance with paragraph 14 of the Agreement (Effective Date). The period of compliance obligations assumed by Parkview under this CAP shall expire on the one (1) year anniversary of HHS's approval of Parkview's training materials, pursuant to section V.E.2 of this CAP. In addition, Parkview shall be obligated to submit the Final Report, as set forth in section VI, and comply with the document retention requirement set forth in section VII, both of which extend beyond the compliance period for all other corrective action obligations. . . .

V. CORRECTIVE ACTION OBLIGATIONS

Parkview agrees to the following:

A. Policies and Procedures

1. Parkview shall develop, maintain, and revise, as necessary, written policies and procedures ("Policies and Procedures") for its workforce that: (a) address the requirements stated in section V.C. . . .

2. Parkview shall provide such Policies and Procedures, consistent with subparagraph 1 above, to HHS within thirty (30) days of the Effective Date for HHS's review and either approval or disapproval. . . . Upon receiving any required changes to such Policies and Procedures from HHS, Parkview shall have thirty (30) days in which to revise its Policies and Procedures accordingly, and then submit the revised Policies and Procedures to HHS for review and approval. This process shall continue until HHS approves the Policies and Procedures. . . .

C. Minimum Content of the Policies and Procedures

The Policies and Procedures referenced herein shall, at minimum, provide for administrative, physical and technical safeguards ("safeguards") to protect the privacy of non-electronic PHI to ensure that such PHI is appropriately and reasonably safeguarded from any intentional, unintentional or incidental use or disclosure that is in violation of the Privacy Rule.

D. Reportable Events

If Parkview determines that a workforce member has violated the Policies and Procedures required by section V.A.1., Parkview shall notify HHS in writing within thirty (30) days. Such violations shall be known as "Reportable Events." The report to HHS shall include a complete description of the event, including the relevant facts, the persons involved, and the provisions of the Policies and Procedures implicated; and a description of Parkview's actions taken to mitigate any harm and further steps Parkview plans to take to address the matter and prevent it from recurring.

E. Training

1. Parkview shall provide general safeguards training to all workforce members who have access to PHI, as required by the Privacy Rule. . . .

VI. FINAL REPORT

The one-year period after the date upon which HHS gives final approval to Parkview's training materials, as required by section V.E.2, shall be referred to as the "Compliance Period." Within 60 days after the expiration of the Compliance Period, Parkview shall submit a Final Report to HHS regarding Parkview's compliance with this CAP. . . .

NOTES & QUESTIONS

1. ***Fines Without Harm?*** In *Parkview Health System,* the PHI was left in boxes unattended in a driveway to a house. But there were no allegations that any unauthorized individual accessed the PHI or took the records. There were no allegations that any PHI was lost. Should this be a case of "no harm, no foul"? Was the fine appropriate?

2. ***Just a Mistake by Employees?*** This incident seems to have been caused by the carelessness of Parkview employees. It is not clear from the facts alleged that Parkview failed to have appropriate policies or training. Should the organization be fined $800,000 merely because some of its employees did not act properly? Should organizations that have appropriate policies and training yet whose employees nevertheless violate HIPAA be treated differently from organizations that lack appropriate policies and training?

3. ***The Corrective Action Plan (CAP).*** What parts of the CAP are different from what HIPAA already requires? The CAP lasts 1 year; in contrast, many FTC consent agreements with companies that commit privacy or data security violations have a 20-year duration. What should the appropriate length of the CAP be?

UNIVERSITY OF CALIFORNIA AT LOS ANGELES HEALTH SYSTEM RESOLUTION AGREEMENT AND CORRECTIVE ACTION PLAN

(July 6, 2011)

. . . . On June 5, 2009 and June 30, 2009, HHS began investigations of two separate complaints alleging that the Covered Entity was in violation of the Privacy and/or Security Rules. The investigations indicated that the following conduct occurred ("Covered Conduct"):

(i) During the period from August 31, 2005 to November 16, 2005, numerous Covered Entity workforce members repeatedly and without a permissible reason examined the electronic protected health information of Covered Entity patients, and during the period from January 31, 2008 to February 2, 2008, numerous Covered Entity workforce members repeatedly and without a permissible reason examined the electronic protected health information of a Covered Entity patient.

(ii) During the period 2005-2008, a workforce member of Covered Entity employed in the office of the Director of Nursing repeatedly and without a permissible reason examined the electronic protected health information of many patients.

(iii) During the period 2005-2008, Covered Entity did not provide and/or did not document the provision of necessary and appropriate Privacy and/or Security Rule training for all members of its workforce to carry out their function within the Covered Entity.

(iv) During the period 2005-2008, Covered Entity failed to apply appropriate sanctions and/or document sanctions on workforce members who impermissibly examined electronic protected health information.

(v) During the period from 2005-2009, Covered Entity failed to implement security measures sufficient to reduce the risks of impermissible access to electronic protected health information by unauthorized users to a reasonable and appropriate level. . . .

This Agreement is intended to resolve Complaint Nos. 08-82727 and 08-83510 regarding possible violations related to the Covered Conduct of the Privacy and Security Rules promulgated by HHS pursuant to the administrative simplification provisions of the Health Insurance Portability and Accountability Act of 1996 (HIPAA), Pub. L. 104-191, 110 Stat. 1936. In consideration of the Parties' interest in avoiding the uncertainty, burden, and expense of further investigation and formal proceedings, the Parties agree to resolve these matters according to the terms and conditions below. II. Terms and Conditions 6. Payment. Covered Entity agrees to pay HHS the amount of $865,500.00 ("Resolution Amount"). . . .

[The Corrective Action Plan required revised policies and procedures and workforce training, among other things.]

NEW YORK PRESBYTERIAN HOSPITAL
RESOLUTION AGREEMENT AND CORRECTIVE ACTION PLAN

(April 21, 2016)

. . . . On January 27, 2013, the HHS Office for Civil Rights received a complaint against [New York Presbyterian Hospital (NYP)] alleging that on April 28, 2011, NYP impermissibly disclosed protected health information (PHI) to a film crew and other staff of "NY Med," a television program being filmed in the hospital. On May 29, 2013, HHS notified NYP of HHS' investigation regarding NYP's compliance with the Privacy Rule promulgated by HHS pursuant to the administrative simplification provisions of the Health Insurance Portability and Accountability Act of 1996 (HIPAA), Pub.L. 104-191, 110 Stat. 1936.

HHS' investigation indicated that the following conduct occurred ("Covered Conduct"):

a. NYP impermissibly disclosed the PHI of two identified patients to the film crew and other staff of "NY Med" (See 45 C.F.R. § 164.502(a)).

b. NYP failed to appropriately and reasonably safeguard its patients' PHI from disclosure during the filming of "NY Med" on its premises. NYP also failed to implement policies, procedures and practices to protect the privacy of its 1 patients' PHI during the filming of aforementioned television show (See 45 C.F.R. § 164.530(c)). . . .

HHS has agreed to accept, and NYP has agreed to pay HHS, the amount of $2,200,000 ("Resolution Amount"). . . .

[The Corrective Action Plan required revised policies and procedures and workforce training, among other things.]

NORTH MEMORIAL HEALTH CARE
RESOLUTION AGREEMENT AND CORRECTIVE ACTION PLAN

(Mar. 16, 2016)

. . . . On September 27, 2011, North Memorial reported to the HHS Office for Civil Rights that, on July 25, 2011, an unencrypted laptop that contained the electronic protected health information of approximately 2,800 individuals (later amended to include an additional 6,697 individuals) who received care from North Memorial was stolen from an Accretive Health ("Accretive") workforce member's locked vehicle. In its report, North Memorial noted that Accretive was its business associate.

HHS' investigation indicated that the following conduct appears to have occurred ("Covered Conduct"):

A. North Memorial provided Accretive, a business associate, with access to North Memorial's protected health information (PHI) without obtaining satisfactory assurances from Accretive, in the form of a written business associate agreement, that Accretive would appropriately safeguard the PHI. North Memorial began providing Accretive with access to North Memorial's PHI on March 21, 2011, and did not enter into a written business associate agreement with Accretive until October 14, 2011. See 45 C.F.R. § 164.308(b) and 45 C.F.R § 164.502(e).

B. From March 21, 2011 to October 14, 2011, North Memorial impermissibly disclosed the PHI of at least 289,904 individuals to Accretive when North Memorial provided Accretive with access to PHI without obtaining Accretive's 2 satisfactory assurances, in the form of a written business associate agreement, that Accretive would appropriately safeguard the PHI. See 45 C.F.R. § 164.502(a). C. North Memorial failed to conduct an accurate and thorough risk analysis that incorporated all of North Memorial's information technology equipment, applications, and data systems using electronic PHI. See 45 C.F.R. § 164.308(a)(1)(ii)(A). . . .

North Memorial agrees to pay HHS the amount of $1,550,000 ("Resolution Amount").

[The Corrective Action Plan required NYP to revise its policies and procedures with regard to business associate agreements, modify its risk analysis process, develop and implement a risk management plan, and implement workforce training, among other things.]

NOTES & QUESTIONS

1. *HIPAA Complaints.* In the decade after HIPAA became effective in April 2003, HHS received about 97,000 HIPAA complaints. The most investigated complaints have been for issues involving:

   1. Impermissible uses and disclosures of protected health information;

   2. Lack of safeguards of protected health information;

   3. Lack of patient access to their protected health information;

   4. Uses or disclosures of more than the minimum necessary protected health information; and

   5. Lack of administrative safeguards of electronic protected health information.[33]

2. *A Change in the Approach to HIPAA Enforcement.* In the first two years the HIPAA Privacy Rule was enforced, despite more than 13,000 privacy complaints, OCR did not bring any civil enforcement actions. By 2008, more than 33,000 complaints had been filed with OCR. Only about 8,400 were investigated, about 5,600 of which led to entities taking corrective action. No fines had yet been issued.[34] The reason for the lack of fines through 2008 is that HHS had a cooperative enforcement philosophy — it saw its role as helping covered entities understand HIPAA.

   One purpose of the HITECH Act was to give HIPAA enforcement more sting. Following the passage of the HITECH Act in 2009, OCR shifted its enforcement approach to a more penal one. OCR reached a number of settlements with significant monetary penalties. For example, in 2009 ,OCR settled with CVS Caremark for $2.25 million. In 2012, HHS settled with the Alaska Department of Health and Social Services for $1.7 million. Also in 2012, OCR settled with Phoenix Cardiac Surgery, a small physician group, for $100,000. And in 2011, OCR fined Cignet Health Center $4.35 million.

   Is this penal shift in HIPAA enforcement justified? Is it preferable to the more cooperative approach prior to the HITECH Act?

3. *HHS Enforcement Post-HITECH.* In the years following HITECH, OCR began negotiating a number of settlement agreements with financial sanctions. Under the Breach Notification Rule, data breaches involving 500 or more persons are posted on what is known as the HHS "wall of shame."[35] In the past 5 years, about 1,000 such breaches have been posted. Is the number of settlement agreements with financial sanctions too low?

4. *HIPAA Enforcement vs. FTC Enforcement.* FTC enforcement under Section 5 of the FTC Act focuses only on entities engaged in commercial activity. Non-

---

[33] HHS, *Enforcement Highlights*, http://www.hhs.gov/ocr/privacy/hipaa/enforcement/highlights/index.html.

[34] *Enforcement of Privacy Rule Stresses Voluntary Compliance, HHS Official Says*, 7 Privacy & Sec. L. 479 (Mar. 31, 2008).

[35] HHS, *Breaches Affecting 500 or More Individuals*, http://www.hhs.gov/ocr/privacy/hipaa/administrative/breachnotificationrule/breachtool.html.

profits and governmental entities are not subject to FTC enforcement. In contrast, HIPAA enforcement does not have these limitations. HHS has brought actions against Columbia University, Skagit County, Washington, UCLA Health System, and the Alaska Department of Health and Social Services, among others.

Another difference is that the HHS can issue fines for HIPAA violations whereas the FTC is much more limited in its ability to issue fines. Nevertheless, FTC cases have settled for larger sums than HHS cases.

Finally, another key difference is the length of the settlement's corrective action plan. FTC consent decrees do not speak in terms of a "corrective action plan" but contain the functional equivalent — a set of required steps that a company must take to remedy the situation and auditing by the FTC. This remedial period lasts for 20 years in many FTC settlements. In contrast, HHS corrective action plans last for one year.

5. *Incidents, HIPAA Violations, and HHS Enforcement.* Many of the FTC resolution agreements involving monetary settlements and fines began with an incident. Some of these incidents were caused by one employee or a small group of employees. For example, a breach of ePHI that occurred on a shared data network between New York Presbyterian Hospital and Columbia University was caused by a physician who had developed an application for the network. The HIPAA violation extended beyond the particular incident to other broader problems. For example, HHS alleged that New York Presbyterian failed to have processes to monitor its network, lacked adequate security measures, and failed to have appropriate procedures for authorizing access to its patient databases. New York Presbyterian agreed to pay HHS $3.3 million.[36] Columbia University was also involved in the incident, and HHS found that it failed to conduct a proper risk analysis.[37] Columbia agreed to pay $1.5 million to settle the case.

Note the contrast between the alleged failures of New York Presbyterian and Columbia and the failures of Parkview Health Services. The former institutions lacked policies, risk analysis, and access controls. Parkview was one of the rare cases where the incident was not traced back to failures in governance and control.

An incident can spark an investigation by HHS, and this investigation can uncover more than just the particular violation that led to the incident. For example, in *QCA Health Plan, Inc.*, an unencrypted laptop computer containing the ePHI of 148 individuals was stolen from a workforce member's car. In addition to finding that the loss of this ePHI was a HIPAA violation, OCR also found other violations including failure to implement policies and procedures, conduct risk assessments, failure to implement physical safeguards for workstations, and failure to restrict access to only authorized users.[38] QCA

---

[36] New York Presbyterian Resolution Agreement (May 7, 2014), http://www.hhs.gov/ocr/privacy/hipaa/enforcement/examples/ny-and-presbyterian-hospital-settlement-agreement.pdf.

[37] Columbia University Resolution Agreement (May 7, 2014), http://www.hhs.gov/ocr/privacy/hipaa/enforcement/examples/columbia-university-resolution-agreement.pdf

[38] QCA Health Plan, Inc. Resolution Agreement (Apr. 14, 2014), http://www.hhs.gov/ocr/privacy/hipaa/enforcement/examples/qca_agreement.pdf

settled for $250,000. In *Adult & Pediatric Dermatology,* the incident was a stolen thumb drive, and OCR found a lack of policies and inadequate training in addition to the improper loss of patient data on the thumb drive.[39]

6. ***Filming in the Hospital.*** In *Shulman v. Group W*, excepted in this casebook's Chapter 3, a reality show had filmed an accident victim with the cooperation of medical personnel. That litigation tested various tort theories for the ensuing privacy violations. In 2016, in *New York Presbyterian Hospital Resolution Agreement*, a New York hospital agreed to pay a $2.2 million penalty to HHS for allowing television crews to film two patients without their permission. One patient was dying, the other was in significant distress.[40]

At the time of the settlement in *New York Presbyterian Hospital*, the Office of Civil Rights of HHS released a FAQ concerning HIPAA and media access to treatment facilities.[41] It found that health care providers could not permit media personnel into treatment or other areas of facilities where PHI would be accessible without prior authorization. Covered PHI was in "written, electronic, oral, or other visual audio form." The FAQ stated, "It is not sufficient for a health care provider to request or require media personnel to mask the identities of patients (using techniques such as blurring, pixilation or voice alternation software) for whom an authorization was not obtained because the HIPAA Privacy Rule does not allow media access to the patients' PHI, absent an authorization, in the first place."

7. ***"More Stringent State Law."*** HIPAA and its regulations preempt state law unless that state law relates to the privacy of individually identifiable health information and is "more stringent" than HIPAA's requirements. In *Law v. Zuckerman*, 307 F. Supp. 2d 705 (D. Md. 2004), a plaintiff was suing her surgeon for malpractice. The surgeon's lawyers attempted to engage in ex parte communications with another physician of hers, who had carried out an elective procedure on her. The defendant in the malpractice lawsuit thought that the plaintiff's damages were caused by that other procedure, and not by his allegedly negligent care. The plaintiff was not notified that the defendant's attorneys would be communicating with her physician, and she contended that such communication is a violation of HIPAA. The court concluded that in a lawsuit based on diversity of citizenship in federal court, Maryland substantive law was to be applied where it did not conflict with controlling federal law. Whether or not this conflict existed turned on whether Maryland law was more stringent than HIPAA. According to the court:

> The key component in analyzing HIPAA's "more stringent" requirement is the ability of the patient to withhold permission and to effectively block disclosure.

[39] Adult & Pediatric Dermatology Resolution Agreement (Dec. 24, 2013), http://www.hhs.gov/ocr/privacy/hipaa/enforcement/examples/apderm-resolution-agreement.pdf

[40] For background on the incidents, see Charles Orenstein, *New York Hospital to Pay $2.2 Million Over Unauthorized Filming of 2 Incidents*, N.Y. Times A24 (April 21, 2016); Charles Ornstein, *Dying in the E.R., and on TV*, N.Y. Times MB1 (Jan. 2, 2015).

[41] HHS, Can health care providers invite or arrange for members of the media, including film crews, to enter treatment areas of their facilities without prior written authorization? (content last reviewed on April 18, 2016), at https://www.hhs.gov/hipaa/for-professionals/faq/2023/film-and-media/index.html.

HIPAA's permissive disclosure requirements give each patient more control over the dissemination of their medical records than [the Maryland Confidentiality of Medical Records Act (MCMRA), which] sacrifices the patient's control of their private health information in order to expedite medical litigation. If state law can force disclosure without a court order, or the patient's consent, it is not "more stringent" than the HIPAA regulation. MCMRA is designed to give adverse counsel access to a patient's medical records without consent.

Under the circumstances of the case, therefore, ex parte communications were to be conducted in accordance with HIPAA procedures.

8. ***What Constitutes a Data Breach?*** The HITECH Act defines data breach as "the unauthorized acquisition, access, use, or disclosure of protected health information which compromises the security or privacy of such information, except where an unauthorized person to whom such information is disclosed would not reasonably have been able to retain such information." 42 U.S.C.A. § 17921.

The HIPAA Breach Notification Rule, 45 CFR §§ 164.400-414, makes clear that "an acquisition, access, use, or disclosure of protected health information in a manner not permitted under ... [the Privacy Rule] is presumed to be a breach unless the covered entity or business associate, as applicable, demonstrates that there is a low probability that the protected health information has been compromised based on a risk assessment." The Breach Notification Rule also introduces a list of four non-exclusive factors to be weighed in determining whether such a "low probability" of compromised information:

> (i) The nature and extent of the protected health information involved, including the types of identifiers and the likelihood of re-identification;
> (ii) The unauthorized person who used the protected health information or to whom the disclosure was made;
> (iii) Whether the protected health information was actually acquired or viewed; and
> (iv) The extent to which the risk to the protected health information has been mitigated.

Chapter 10 of this casebook considers state data breach notification laws. Compared to these laws, the HIPAA Breach Notification Law can be said to be pro-disclosure in orientation.

9. ***Criminal Enforcement, the Richard Gibson Case, and the OLC Opinion.*** The HIPAA statute, 42 U.S.C. § 1320d-6(a), contains civil and criminal penalties for when:

> A person who knowingly and in violation of this part —
>
> > (1) uses or causes to be used a unique health identifier;
> > (2) obtains individually identifiable health information relating to an individual; or
> > (3) discloses individually identifiable health information to another person.

The statute further provides: "A person described in subsection (a) shall . . . be fined not more than $50,000, imprisoned not more than 1 year, or both."

During the first two years after the HIPAA Privacy Rule became effective, there was only one criminal action:

> In 2004 the U.S. attorney in Seattle announced that Richard Gibson was being indicted for violating the HIPAA privacy law. Gibson was a phlebotomist — a lab assistant — in a hospital. While at work he accessed the medical records of a person with a terminal cancer condition. Gibson then got credit cards in the patient's name and ran up over $9,000 in charges, notably for video game purchases. In a statement to the court, the patient said he "lost a year of life both mentally and physically dealing with the stress" of dealing with collection agencies and other results of Gibson's actions. Gibson signed a plea agreement and was sentenced to 16 months in jail.[42]

On June 1, 2005, the Office of Legal Counsel (OLC) issued a controversial opinion on the criminal enforcement of the HIPAA:

> We conclude that health plans, health care clearinghouses, those health care providers specified in the statute, and Medicare prescription drug card sponsors may be prosecuted for violations of section 1320d-6. In addition, depending on the facts of a given case, certain directors, officers, and employees of these entities may be liable directly under section 1320d-6, in accordance with general principles of corporate criminal liability, as these principles are developed in the course of particular prosecutions. Other persons may not be liable directly under this provision.[43]

According to Swire, based on this opinion, "Gibson could no longer be prosecuted under HIPAA." Swire criticized the OLC opinion:

> When Congress targeted these information crimes, and called for jail time, it created a criminal provision that is different from the civil provision. The OLC opinion essentially assumes that the scope of the civil and criminal provisions is the same. The OLC opinion tries to suppress the clear text of the criminal provision about "person," "false pretenses," "obtaining" and other terms. A fairer and more neutral reading of the statute would be to recognize the different scope that follows from the different language and different goals of the civil and criminal provisions.[44]

Since this controversy in 2005, however, additional criminal prosecutions have occurred for HIPAA violations — in all of these cases, moreover, an employee, rather than a covered entity, was prosecuted. How was the prosecution possible in light of the OLC opinion?

As Assistant U.S. Attorney Peter Winn points out, 18 U.S.C. § 2(b) "provides a path for prosecutions of employees and business associates of

---

[42] Peter P. Swire, *Justice Department Opinion Undermines Protection of Medical Privacy* (Jun 7, 2005), at http://www.americanprogress.org/site/pp.asp?c 5 biJRJ8OVF&b 5 743281.

[43] *Scope of Criminal Enforcement Under 42 U.S.C. § 1320d-6*, Memorandum Opinion for the General Counsel Department of HHS and the Senior Counsel to the Deputy Attorney General, at http://www.usdoj.gov/olc/hipaa_final.htm.

[44] Swire, Justice Department Opinion, *supra*.

HIPAA covered-entities."[45] This statute states: "Whoever wilfully causes an act to be done which if directly performed by him or another would be an offense against the United States, is punishable as a principal." Winn observes that U.S.C. § 2(b) codifies the common law maxim: "He who acts through another, acts himself." It permits an employee to be punished as a principal as if the covered entity, itself, had performed the act. In sum, the necessary connection is that the employee commit "an act that would be an offense *if committed directly by the covered entity*."

The "Winn theory" has proved highly influential. As a 2007 article in the United States Attorneys' Bulletin by Ian DeWaal stated: "The bottom line is that [Assistant United States Attorneys] should be increasingly comfortable investigating and prosecuting HIPAA medical privacy criminal violations by individuals who do not fall within the enumerated classes of covered entities."[46] Thus, despite the OLC opinion, it is possible to hold an employee criminally liable in HIPAA enforcement cases — even when an employer is not prosecuted.[47]

In 2009, Congress responded to the OLC opinion by amending 42 U.S.C. § 1320d-6, to make it clear that the persons subject to the criminal privacy offense were individuals (including employees or other individuals) who obtained or disclosed information in violation of the HIPPA privacy regulation without authorization. See American Recovery and Reinvestment Act, P.L. 111-5, §13409 (2009), codified at 42 U.S.C. § 1320d–6. The new version of Section 1320d-6 states:

> (a) Offense. A person who knowingly and in violation of this part—
> (1) uses or causes to be used a unique health identifier;
> (2) obtains individually identifiable health information relating to an individual; or
> (3) discloses individually identifiable health information to another person,
> shall be punished as provided in subsection (b) of this section. For purposes of the previous sentence, a person (including an employee or other individual) shall be considered to have obtained or disclosed individually identifiable health information in violation of this part if the information is maintained by a covered entity . . .and the individual obtained or disclosed such information without authorization.

This amendment to the statute eliminated the ambiguity that allowed the narrow reading of the statute by the OLC. Nonetheless, prosecutors charging a violation of 42 U.S.C. § 1320d-6 continue to combine it with a violation of 18 U.S.C. § 2 in the indictment in order to ensure that no other possible gaps in the statute might be left open.

---

[45] Peter A. Winn, *Criminal Prosecutions Under HIPAA*, 53 U.S. Att'ys Bull. 21 (Sept. 2005). *See* Peter A. Winn, *Who Is Subject to Criminal Prosecutions Under HIPAA?*, A.B.A. (Nov. 1, 2005), at http://www.abanet.org/health/01_interest_groups/01_media/WinnABA2005-11.pdf.

[46] Ian C. Smith DeWaal, *Successfully Prosecuting Health Insurance Portability and Accountability Act Medical Privacy Violations Against Noncovered Entities*, 55 U.S. Att'ys Bull., 10, 15, (July 2007).

[47] Cicely N. Tingle, *Developments in HIPAA and Health Information Technology*, 3 I/S 677, 686 (2008).

UNITED STATES V. ZHOU

678 F.3d 1110 (9th Cir. 2012)

SMITH, J. Defendant–Appellant Huping Zhou, a former research assistant at the University of California at Los Angeles Health System (UHS), accessed patient records without authorization after his employment was terminated. . . .

Zhou was hired as a research assistant in rheumatology at UHS on February 2, 2003. On October 29, 2003, UHS issued Zhou a notice of intent to dismiss due to "continued serious job deficiencies and poor judgment." On November 12, 2003, after a formal internal grievance hearing, Zhou received a dismissal letter effective November 14, 2003.

After his termination on November 14, 2003, there were at least four instances, on November 17 and 19, in which Zhou accessed patient records without authorization. The information charged Zhou with crimes only for accessing patients' medical information after he was terminated and no longer treating patients at the hospital.

HIPAA provides that: "[a] person who knowingly and in violation of this part—(1) uses or causes to be used a unique health identifier; (2) obtains individually identifiable health information relating to an individual; or (3) discloses individually identifiable health information to another person, shall be punished as provided in subsection (b)." 42 U.S.C. § 1320d–6(a).

On November 17, 2008, Zhou was charged by information under subsection 2 of that HIPAA provision. The four misdemeanor counts in the information stated that Zhou "knowingly and for reasons other than permitted by Title 42 United States Code Chapter 7, Subchapter XI, Part C, obtained and caused to be obtained individually identifiable health information relating to an individual...." Each count alleged access to a patient record after Zhou's termination.

On October 19, 2009, Zhou moved to dismiss the information, arguing that the information did not allege that he knew that it was illegal to obtain the health information. On November 12, 2009, the magistrate judge denied the motion in a ruling from the bench. . . .

On January 8, 2010, Zhou entered a conditional guilty plea, reserving his right to appeal the court's denial of his motion to dismiss the information. Zhou was sentenced to four months in prison, followed by a year of supervised release, a $2,000 fine, and a $100 special assessment. Zhou filed a timely notice of appeal. . . .

Under Zhou's interpretation of the statute, a defendant is guilty only if he knew that obtaining the personal healthcare information was illegal.

We reject Zhou's argument because it contradicts the plain language of HIPAA. The statute's misdemeanor criminal penalty applies to an individual who "knowingly and in violation of this part.... obtains individually identifiable health information relating to an individual." 42 U.S.C. § 1320d–6(a)(2) (emphasis added). The word "and" unambiguously indicates that there are two elements of a Section 1320d–6(a)(2) violation: 1) knowingly obtaining individually identifiable health information relating to an individual; and 2) obtaining that information in violation of Title 42 United States Code Chapter 7, Subchapter XI, Part C. Thus, the term "knowingly" applies only to the act of obtaining the health information.

If the statute did not contain "and," then Zhou's argument might be more persuasive. However, we cannot ignore "and" because its presence often dramatically alters the meaning of a phrase. Without "and," the Second Amendment would guarantee "the right of the people to keep bear arms," Leo Tolstoy would have published "War Peace," and James Taylor would have confusingly crooned about "Fire Rain." To overlook "and" would be to violate "an important rule of statutory construction—that every word and clause in a statute be given effect." . . .

Moreover, our conclusion is supported by Congress's decision not to require willfulness as an element of the crime. Section 1320d–6(a)(2) uses only the term "knowingly," but other criminal statutes require the crime be committed both "knowingly" and "willfully." . . .

In sum, we hold that 42 U.S.C. § 1320d–6(a)(2) is not limited to defendants who knew that their actions were illegal. Rather, the defendant need only know that he obtained individually identifiable health information relating to an individual.

NOTES & QUESTIONS

1. ***Is HIPAA Criminal Liability Too Broad?*** The only mens rea that a person must have for a criminal violation of HIPAA is to know that the data is individually identifiable health information relating to an individual. If a person then accesses it, uses it, or discloses it in violation of HIPAA, it will be a crime. In most situations, employees at covered entities will have knowledge that data is individually identifiable health information. They may not know, however, that certain uses and disclosures may violate HIPAA.

   Suppose a celebrity is rushed into a hospital and operated upon. A nurse not involved in the celebrity's treatment is curious about what is going on, and she accesses the celebrity's medical file. Could she be subject to criminal liability?

BYRNE V. AVERY CENTER FOR OBSTETRICS AND GYNECOLOGY

102 A.3d 32 (Conn. 2014)

NORCOTT, J. [The plaintiff, Emily Byrne, received gynecological and obstetrical care and treatment at the Avery Center for Obstetrics and Gynecology (defendant). After she ended her relationship with Andro Mendoza, she instructed the defendant not to provide her medical records to Mendoza. Mendoza filed paternity actions against the plaintiff in two states. Mendoza served a subpoena on Avery Center requesting plaintiff's medical records. Without informing the plaintiff or moving to quash the subpoena, Avery Center mailed the plaintiff's medical records to Mendoza.

The plaintiff sued Avery Center for a number of causes of action including negligence and negligent infliction of emotional distress for failing to follow HIPAA. Specifically, the plaintiff alleged that Avery Center failed to provide her with notice of the request for her records, failed to follow her "request for additional privacy protection of her protected health information from production to the party requesting it," and failed to provide only the minimum necessary data. More broadly, the plaintiff claimed that a subpoena was "not a valid authorization to produce the records."

The defendant argued that the plaintiff's negligence and negligent infliction of emotional distress claims that were based on HIPAA were preempted because HIPAA lacks a private cause of action.]

A state law is "contrary" to HIPAA if "(1) A covered entity would find it impossible to comply with both the [s]tate and [f]ederal requirements; or (2) [t]he provision of [s]tate law stands as an obstacle to the accomplishment and execution of the full purposes and objectives of part C of title XI of [HIPPA]." . . . .

As relevant to this appeal, state laws exempted from preemption include those that "[relate] to the privacy of individually identifiable health information and [are] more stringent than a standard, requirement, or implementation specification.". . .

This statutory and regulatory background brings us to the question in the present appeal, namely, whether HIPAA preempts a state law claim sounding in negligence arising from a health care provider's alleged breach of physician-patient confidentiality in the course of complying with a subpoena. It is by now well settled that the "statutory structure of HIPAA . . . precludes implication of a private right of action. . . ."

Nevertheless, it is similarly well established that, "[o]rdinarily, state causes of action are not [preempted] solely because they impose liability over and above that authorized by federal law." . . . .

Consistent with these principles, the regulatory history of the HIPAA demonstrates that neither HIPAA nor its implementing regulations were intended to preempt tort actions under state law arising out of the unauthorized release of a plaintiff's medical records. . . . In its administrative commentary to the final rule as promulgated in the Federal Register, the department responded to this question by stating, inter alia, that "the fact that a state law allows an individual to file [a civil action] to protect privacy does not conflict with the HIPAA penalty provisions," namely, fines and imprisonment. This agency commentary on final rules in the Federal Register is significant evidence of regulatory intent. . . .

Consistent with this regulatory history, the parties' briefs and our independent research disclose a number of cases from the federal and sister state courts holding that HIPAA, and particularly its implementation through the Privacy Rule regulations, does not preempt causes of action, when they exist as a matter of state common or statutory law, arising from health care providers' breaches of patient confidentiality in a variety of contexts; indeed, several have determined that HIPAA may inform the relevant standard of care in such actions. . . .

[W]e conclude that, if Connecticut's common law recognizes claims arising from a health care provider's alleged breach of its duty of confidentiality in the course of complying with a subpoena, HIPAA and its implementing regulations do not preempt such claims. We further conclude that, to the extent it has become the common practice for Connecticut health care providers to follow the procedures required under HIPAA in rendering services to their patients, HIPAA and its implementing regulations may be utilized to inform the standard of care applicable to such claims arising from allegations of negligence in the disclosure of patients' medical records pursuant to a subpoena. The availability of such private rights of action in state courts, to the extent that they exist as a matter of state law, do not preclude, conflict with, or complicate health care providers' compliance with HIPAA. On the contrary, negligence claims in state courts support "at least one of HIPAA's goals by establishing another disincentive to wrongfully disclose a patient's health care record."

NOTES & QUESTIONS

1. *An End-Run Around HIPAA's Method of Enforcement?* HIPAA explicitly relies on enforcement by HHS and state attorneys general and omits a private right of action. Does *Byrne* upend this enforcement method by effectively adding a private right of action for HIPAA violations? If HIPAA can serve as the standard of care for common law actions such as negligence, breach of confidentiality, or negligent infliction of emotional distress, then through these torts, plaintiffs can sue for many HIPAA violations. Courts addressing this issue have ruled consistently with *Byrne*. For example, in *Bonney v. Stephens Memorial Hosp. et al.*, 17 A.3d 123 (Maine 2011), the court held: "Although . . . HIPAA standards, like state laws and professional codes of conduct, may be admissible to establish the standard of care associated with a state tort claim, [HIPAA] itself does not authorize a private action." *See also Yath v. Fairview Clinics, N.P.*, 767 N.W.2d 34 (Minn. App. 2009).

   In R.K. v. St. Mary's Medical Center, 735 S.E.2d 715 (W.Va. 2012), R.K was admitted to St. Mary's as a psychiatric patient while in divorce proceedings with his estranged wife. While a patient, an employee of the hospital inappropriately accessed his files and shared confidential information with his wife. R.K. sued claiming negligence, among other causes of action. The defendant argued that many of R.K.'s claims were pre-empted by HIPAA. The West Virginia Supreme Court of Appeals held that not only did HIPAA fail to preempt state law, but HIPAA may provide the standard of care for tort claims including negligence per se.

2. *The Implications of* **Byrne.** Daniel Solove points out the powerful implications of *Byrne:* "Other privacy and data security laws can serve as sources of common law duties and standards of care, regardless of whether they have a private cause of action." Such laws include the Children's Online Privacy Protection Act (COPPA), the Family Educational Rights and Privacy Act (FERPA), the Gramm-Leach-Bliley Act (GLBA), and the FTC Act — all laws lacking a private right of action. Further, Solove notes, ethical rules and professional codes of conduct can serve as standards of care for common law torts:

   > For privacy and data security, there are a number of industry codes such as the Payment Card Industry's Data Security Standard (PCI-DSS). Perhaps this could be used to establish common law duties and standard of care.
   >
   > So could other codes, such as advertising industry codes regarding privacy and data security (NAI, DMA, etc.). So could the widely-articulated and adopted Fair Information Practice Principles (FIPPs).

   Recall *McCormick v. England*, 494 S.E.2d 431 (S.C. Ct. App. 1997), where the court recognized a duty of confidentiality for physicians based on, among other things, the Hippocratic Oath and medical ethics rules. Solove writes: "Nearly anything can be used as evidence of a common law duty or standard of care . . . even an oath from antiquity."

B. CONSTITUTIONAL PROTECTION OF MEDICAL INFORMATION

1. THE CONSTITUTIONAL RIGHT TO PRIVACY

Although the U.S. Constitution does not explicitly mention privacy, in a line of cases commonly referred to as "substantive due process," the Supreme Court has held that there exists a "right to privacy" in the U.S. Constitution.

As early as 1891, in *Union Pacific Railway v. Botsford*, 141 U.S. 250 (1891), the Court articulated some of the basic reasoning that would later develop into the "right to privacy" as it exists today. There, in holding that a court could not compel a plaintiff in a civil action to submit to a surgical examination, the Court declared:

> No right is held more sacred, or is more carefully guarded by the common law, than the right of every individual to the possession and control of his own person, free from all restraint or interference of others, unless by clear and unquestionable authority of law. As well said by Judge Cooley: "The right to one's person may be said to be a right of complete immunity; to be let alone." . . . The inviolability of the person is as much invaded by a compulsory stripping and exposure as by a blow. To compel any one, and especially a woman, to lay bare the body, or to submit it to the touch of a stranger, without lawful authority, is an indignity, an assault, and a trespass.

Later, in *Pierce v. Society of Sisters*, 268 U.S. 510 (1925), the Court held that parents cannot be compelled to have their children attend public schools because of the "liberty of parents and guardians to direct the upbringing and education of children under their control." In *Meyer v. Nebraska*, 262 U.S. 390 (1923) the Court declared:

> Fourteenth Amendment due process "denotes not merely freedom from bodily restraint but also the right of the individual to contract, to engage in any of the common occupations of life, to acquire useful knowledge, to marry, establish a home and bring up children, to worship God according to the dictates of his own conscience, and generally to enjoy those privileges long recognized at common law as essential to the orderly pursuit of happiness by free men."

The watershed case for substantive due process privacy was *Griswold v. Connecticut*, 381 U.S. 479 (1965).

GRISWOLD V. CONNECTICUT

381 U.S. 479 (1965)

DOUGLAS, J. [The directors of Planned Parenthood Association challenged a Connecticut law criminalizing contraceptives and counselling about contraceptives to married couples.]

Coming to the merits, we are met with a wide range of questions that implicate the Due Process Clause of the Fourteenth Amendment. Overtones of some arguments suggest that *Lochner v. State of New York*, 198 U.S. 45, should be our guide. But we decline that invitation. . . . We do not sit as a super-legislature to determine the wisdom, need, and propriety of laws that touch economic problems, business affairs, or social conditions. This law, however, operates directly on an intimate relation of husband and wife and their physician's role in one aspect of that relation.

The association of people is not mentioned in the Constitution nor in the Bill of Rights. The right to educate a child in a school of the parents' choice — whether public or private or parochial — is also not mentioned. Nor is the right to study any particular subject or any foreign language. Yet the First Amendment has been construed to include certain of those rights.

By *Pierce v. Society of Sisters*, the right to educate one's children as one chooses is made applicable to the States by the force of the First and Fourteenth Amendments. By *Meyer v. State of Nebraska*, the same dignity is given the right to study the German language in a private school. In other words, the State may not, consistently with the spirit of the First Amendment, contract the spectrum of available knowledge. The right of freedom of speech and press includes not only the right to utter or to print, but the right to distribute, the right to receive, the right to read and freedom of inquiry, freedom of thought, and freedom to teach — indeed the freedom of the entire university community. Without those peripheral rights the specific rights would be less secure. And so we reaffirm the principle of the *Pierce* and the *Meyer* cases.

In *NAACP v. State of Alabama*, 357 U.S. 449, we protected the "freedom to associate and privacy in one's associations," noting that freedom of association was a peripheral First Amendment right. Disclosure of membership lists of a constitutionally valid association, we held, was invalid "as entailing the likelihood of a substantial restraint upon the exercise by petitioner's members of their right to freedom of association." Ibid. In other words, the First Amendment has a penumbra where privacy is protected from governmental intrusion. In like context, we have protected forms of "association" that are not political in the customary sense but pertain to the social, legal, and economic benefit of the members. . . .

Those cases involved more than the "right of assembly" — a right that extends to all irrespective of their race or ideology. The right of "association," like the right of belief (*West Virginia State Board of Education v. Barnette*, 319 U.S. 624), is more than the right to attend a meeting; it includes the right to express one's attitudes or philosophies by membership in a group or by affiliation with it or by other lawful means. Association in that context is a form of expression of opinion; and while it is not expressly included in the First Amendment its existence is necessary in making the express guarantees fully meaningful.

The foregoing cases suggest that specific guarantees in the Bill of Rights have penumbras, formed by emanations from those guarantees that help give them life and substance. Various guarantees create zones of privacy. The right of association contained in the penumbra of the First Amendment is one, as we have seen. The Third Amendment in its prohibition against the quartering of soldiers "in any house" in time of peace without the consent of the owner is another facet of that privacy. The Fourth Amendment explicitly affirms the "right of the people to be secure in their persons, houses, papers, and effects, against unreasonable searches and seizures." The Fifth Amendment in its Self-Incrimination Clause enables the citizen to create a zone of privacy which government may not force him to surrender to his detriment. The Ninth Amendment provides: "The enumeration in the Constitution, of certain rights, shall not be construed to deny or disparage others retained by the people."

The Fourth and Fifth Amendments were described in *Boyd v. United States*, 116 U.S. 616, as protection against all governmental invasions "of the sanctity of a man's home and the privacies of life." We recently referred in *Mapp v. Ohio*, 367 U.S. 643, to the Fourth Amendment as creating a "right to privacy, no less important than any other right carefully and particularly reserved to the people."

We have had many controversies over these penumbral rights of "privacy and repose." These cases bear witness that the right of privacy which presses for recognition here is a legitimate one.

The present case, then, concerns a relationship lying within the zone of privacy created by several fundamental constitutional guarantees. And it concerns a law which, in forbidding the use of contraceptives rather than regulating their manufacture or sale, seeks to achieve its goals by means having a maximum destructive impact upon that relationship. Such a law cannot stand in light of the familiar principle, so often applied by this Court, that a "governmental purpose to control or prevent activities constitutionally subject to state regulation may not be achieved by means which sweep unnecessarily broadly and thereby invade the area of protected freedoms." Would we allow the police to search the sacred precincts of marital bedrooms for telltale signs of the use of contraceptives? The very idea is repulsive to the notions of privacy surrounding the marriage relationship.

We deal with a right of privacy older than the Bill of Rights — older than our political parties, older than our school system. Marriage is a coming together for better or for worse, hopefully enduring, and intimate to the degree of being sacred. It is an association that promotes a way of life, not causes; a harmony in living, not political faiths; a bilateral loyalty, not commercial or social projects. Yet it is an association for as noble a purpose as any involved in our prior decisions.

BLACK and STEWART, JJ. dissenting. . . . The Court talks about a constitutional "right of privacy" as though there is some constitutional provision or provisions forbidding any law ever to be passed which might abridge the "privacy" of individuals. But there is not. There are, of course, guarantees in certain specific constitutional provisions which are designed in part to protect privacy at certain times and places with respect to certain activities. Such, for example, is the Fourth Amendment's guarantee against "unreasonable searches and seizures." . . .

One of the most effective ways of diluting or expanding a constitutionally guaranteed right is to substitute for the crucial word or words of a constitutional guarantee another word or words, more or less flexible and more or less restricted in meaning. This fact is well illustrated by the use of the term "right of privacy" as a comprehensive substitute for the Fourth Amendment's guarantee against "unreasonable searches and seizures." "Privacy" is a broad, abstract and ambiguous concept which can easily be shrunken in meaning but which can also, on the other hand, easily be interpreted as a constitutional ban against many things other than searches and seizures. I have expressed the view many times that First Amendment freedoms, for example, have suffered from a failure of the courts to stick to the simple language of the First Amendment in construing it, instead of invoking multitudes of words substituted for those the Framers used. For these reasons I get nowhere in this case by talk about a constitutional "right or privacy" as an emanation from one or more constitutional provisions. I like my privacy as well as the next one, but I am nevertheless compelled to admit that government has a right to invade it unless prohibited by some specific constitutional provision. For these reasons I cannot agree with the Court's judgment and the reasons it gives for holding this Connecticut law unconstitutional. . . .

NOTES & QUESTIONS

1. *Finding "Privacy" in the Constitution.* There is no explicit "right to privacy" mentioned in the Constitution. Does the Court make a persuasive case that (a) rights need not be explicitly mentioned to be constitutionally protected; and (b) that the right to privacy can be inferred from the penumbras of several other rights?

   Recall Warren and Brandeis's article, *The Right to Privacy* (Chapter 1). They located the "right to be let alone" as an overarching principle in the common law based on examining specific common law rights. The *Griswold* Court applies a similar logic to its interpretation of the Constitution. Warren and Brandies claimed that they were not legislating; rather, they located the "right to be let alone" by interpreting the common law. Can the *Griswold* Court make the same claim?

   Consider Robert Bork:

   > Justice Douglas called the amendments and their penumbras "zones of privacy," though of course they are not that at all. They protect both private and public behavior and so would more properly be labeled "zones of freedom." If we follow Justice Douglas in his next step, these zones would then add up to an independent right of freedom, which is to say, a general constitutional right to be free of legal coercion, a manifest impossibility in any imaginable society. . .
   > .
   >
   > *Griswold*, then, is an unprincipled decision, both in the way in which it derives a new constitutional right and in the way it defines that right, or rather fails to define it. We are left with no idea of the sweep of the right of privacy and hence no notion of the cases to which it may or may not be applied in the future.[48]

---

[48] Robert H. Bork, *Neutral Principles and Some First Amendment Problems*, 47 Ind. L.J. 1, 8-9 (1971).

2. *Is* Griswold *a Decisional or Informational Privacy Case?* Consider Neil Richards:

> Many commentators see *Griswold* as the first of the line of constitutional cases culminating in *Roe v. Wade* and its progeny protecting the right to make intimate decisions including the right to abortion. Understandings of the privacy right recognized in *Griswold* as being related to informational meanings of the word are generally considered by scholars to be beside the point. . . . For example, although he notes the peculiarity of the label "privacy," Louis Henkin asserts that *Griswold* was about autonomy in marital relationships and not about information.
>
> Nevertheless, *Griswold* can, and perhaps should, be read as an information privacy case as well. . . .
>
> . . . [A] fear of government intrusion into private zones (both physical and social) in pursuit of information was a large part of the rationale behind the conclusion that the Constitution protects a right of privacy. The Court was not recognizing a fundamental individual right to contraception, but rather invalidating the government's power to regulate commercial products where such regulation requires intrusion into private spaces and confidential relationships. . . .
>
> In marshaling precedent for his holding that the Constitution protected the right of marital privacy, Douglas relied extensively upon several lines of cases now commonly considered as falling on the information privacy side of the informational/decisional binary by information privacy scholars. Thus, he relied heavily upon the "associational privacy" cases of *NAACP v. Alabama* and *NAACP v. Button*; Fourth Amendment privacy cases such as *Boyd v. United States* and *Mapp v. Ohio*, and scholarship dealing with the privacy aspects of Fourth Amendment search and seizure; and Fifth Amendment self-incrimination law. . . .
>
> When viewed against this larger intellectual context, an information privacy reading of *Griswold* begins to take shape. According to Douglas, the First Amendment created a zone of privacy, not only in a person's home but also in the various intimate associations into which he might enter. The "free society" envisioned by the framers of the Constitution and embodied in the text of the First Amendment placed a substantive bar upon the state when it sought to probe or investigate those intimate associations. . . . The focus of the analysis was on the state's ability to monitor, and the individual right was conceived not in terms of individual autonomy but in freedom from intrusion and scrutiny — the classic "right to be let alone" of Warren and Brandeis's article and Brandeis's *Olmstead* dissent.[49]

The constitutional right to privacy cases are often referred to as "decisional privacy" because they involve certain decisions people make regarding their family life, health, body, reproduction, and child rearing. Is *Griswold* about decisional privacy? Information privacy? Or both?

3. *The Privacy Rights of Non-Married Couples.* Subsequent to *Griswold*, the Court elaborated upon the right to privacy in *Eisenstadt v. Baird*, 405 U.S. 438 (1972). *Eisenstadt* involved a statute that permitted the use of contraceptives only to married couples. Although *Griswold* rested upon the sanctity of the

---

[49] Neil M. Richards, *The Information Privacy Law Project*, 94 Geo. L.J. 1087, 1107-12 (2006); *see also* Daniel J. Solove, *A Taxonomy of Privacy*, 154 U. Pa. L. Rev. 477, 557-62 (2006).

marital bedroom, the Court held that this law was also unconstitutional because right of privacy "is the right of the individual, married or single, to be free from unwarranted government intrusion into matters so fundamentally affecting a person as the decision whether to bear or beget a child."

4. ***The Right to Marry.*** In *Loving v. Virginia,* 388 U.S. 1 (1967), the Supreme Court struck down a statute that banned interracial marriage: "The freedom to marry has long been recognized as one of the vital personal rights essential to the orderly pursuit of happiness by free men." As the Court declared later in *Cleveland Board of Education v. LaFleur,* 414 U.S. 642 (1974): "This Court has long recognized that freedom of personal choice in matters of marriage and family life is one of the liberties protected by the Due Process Clause of the Fourteenth Amendment."

5. **Roe v. Wade.** A year after *Eisenstadt,* the Court decided *Roe v. Wade,* 410 U.S. 113 (1973), one of the most controversial cases. There, the Court concluded that a Texas statute criminalizing abortion was unconstitutional as "violative of the Due Process Clause of the Fourteenth Amendment." As the Court explained:

> The Constitution does not explicitly mention any right of privacy. In a line of decisions, however, going back perhaps as far as *Union Pacific R.R. Co. v. Botsford*, the Court has recognized that a right of personal privacy, or a guarantee of certain areas or zones of privacy, does exist under the Constitution. In varying contexts, the Court or individual Justices have, indeed, found at least the roots of that right in the First Amendment; in the Fourth and Fifth Amendments; in the penumbras of the Bill of Rights; or in the concept of liberty guaranteed by the first section of the Fourteenth Amendment. These decisions make it clear that only personal rights that can be deemed "fundamental" or "implicit in the concept of ordered liberty" are included in this guarantee of personal privacy. They also make it clear that the right has some extension to activities relating to marriage; procreation; contraception; family relationships; and child rearing and education.
>
> This right of privacy, whether it be founded in the Fourteenth Amendment's concept of personal liberty and restrictions upon state action, as we feel it is, or, as the District Court determined, in the Ninth Amendment's reservation of rights to the people, is broad enough to encompass a woman's decision whether or not to terminate her pregnancy. The detriment that the State would impose upon the pregnant woman by denying this choice altogether is apparent. Specific and direct harm medically diagnosable even in early pregnancy may be involved. Maternity, or additional offspring, may force upon the woman a distressful life and future. Psychological harm may be imminent. Mental and physical health may be taxed by child care. There is also the distress, for all concerned, associated with the unwanted child, and there is the problem of bringing a child into a family already unable, psychologically and otherwise, to care for it. In other cases, as in this one, the additional difficulties and continuing stigma of unwed motherhood may be involved. All these are factors the woman and her responsible physician necessarily will consider in consultation.

John Ely contends that *Roe* does not follow logically from *Griswold*:

[The regulation of contraceptives in *Griswold*] *would have been virtually impossible without* the most outrageous sort of governmental prying into the privacy of the home. [No] such rationalization is [possible in *Roe v. Wade*], for whatever else may be involved, it is not a case about governmental snooping.[50]

Is *Griswold* a "case about governmental snooping"? Should only laws where enforcement would require extensive governmental snooping be restricted under the constitutional right to privacy?

6. *What Should the Constitutional Right to Privacy Protect?* Consider Louis Henkin:

[What] is it that makes my right to use contraceptives a right of Privacy, and fundamental, but my right to contract to work 16 hours a day or to pay more for milk than the law fixes, not a right of Privacy and not fundamental? Is it, as some suspect, that the game is being played backwards: that the private right which intuitively commends itself as valuable in our society in our time, or at least to a majority of our Justices at this time, is called fundamental, and if it cannot fit comfortably into specific constitutional provisions it is included in Privacy?[51]

What kinds of activities and decisions fall within the protection of the constitutional right to privacy? They generally involve matters of family, health, and body. Recall Robert Bork's criticism that *Griswold* provided "no idea of the sweep of the right of privacy." Is this correct?

David Meyer notes that the Supreme Court "has never seriously attempted to offer a comprehensive theory which might explain why some intimate conduct or relationships, but not others, are entitled to special constitutional solicitude."[52]

Jed Rubenfeld argues that the laws that the right to privacy restricts are ones that go to the heart of one's existence: "These laws do not simply proscribe one act or remove one liberty; they inform the totality of a person's life. . . . It is the fundamental freedom not to have one's life too totally determined by a progressively more normalizing state."[53] In this way, laws that restrict contraception and abortion are different from laws that restrict contract or that regulate behavior.

One way of defining the scope of the right to privacy is to use John Stuart Mill's formulation in *On Liberty*:

The only part of the conduct of anyone, for which he is amenable to society, is that which concerns others. In the part which merely concerns himself, his independence is, of right, absolute. Over himself, over his own body and mind, the individual is sovereign.[54]

---

[50] John H. Ely, *The Wages of Crying Wolf: A Comment on* Roe v. Wade, 82 Yale L.J. 920, 930 (1973).

[51] Louis Henkin, *Privacy and Autonomy*, 74 Colum. L. Rev. 1410, 1427 (1974).

[52] David D. Meyer, *The Paradox of Family Privacy*, 53 Vand. L .Rev. 527, 532 (2000).

[53] Jed Rubenfeld, *The Right to Privacy*, 102 Harv. L. Rev. 737, 784 (1989).

[54] John Stuart Mill, *On Liberty* (1859).

Is this a workable principle? Do marriage, contraception, and abortion merely concern the individuals involved, or do they concern others?

PLANNED PARENTHOOD OF SOUTHEASTERN PENNSYLVANIA V. CASEY
505 U.S. 833 (1992)

O'CONNOR, KENNEDY, and SOUTER, JJ. . . . Liberty finds no refuge in a jurisprudence of doubt. Yet 19 years after our holding that the Constitution protects a woman's right to terminate her pregnancy in its early stages, *Roe v. Wade,* 410 U.S. 113 (1973), that definition of liberty is still questioned. . . .

At issue in these cases are five provisions of the Pennsylvania Abortion Control Act of 1982, as amended in 1988 and 1989. 18 Pa. Cons. Stat. §§ 3203-3220 (1990). The Act requires that a woman seeking an abortion give her informed consent prior to the abortion procedure, and specifies that she be provided with certain information at least 24 hours before the abortion is performed. For a minor to obtain an abortion, the Act requires the informed consent of one of her parents, but provides for a judicial bypass option if the minor does not wish to or cannot obtain a parent's consent. Another provision of the Act requires that, unless certain exceptions apply, a married woman seeking an abortion must sign a statement indicating that she has notified her husband of her intended abortion. The Act exempts compliance with these three requirements in the event of a "medical emergency." . . .

Before any of these provisions took effect, the petitioners, who are five abortion clinics and one physician representing himself as well as a class of physicians who provide abortion services, brought this suit seeking declaratory and injunctive relief. Each provision was challenged as unconstitutional on its face. . .

Constitutional protection of the woman's decision to terminate her pregnancy derives from the Due Process Clause of the Fourteenth Amendment. It declares that no State shall "deprive any person of life, liberty, or property, without due process of law." The controlling word in the cases before us is "liberty." Although a literal reading of the Clause might suggest that it governs only the procedures by which a State may deprive persons of liberty, for at least 105 years, . . . the Clause has been understood to contain a substantive component as well, one "barring certain government actions regardless of the fairness of the procedures used to implement them." . . .

Our law affords constitutional protection to personal decisions relating to marriage, procreation, contraception, family relationships, child rearing, and education. Our cases recognize "the right of the *individual,* married or single, to be free from unwarranted governmental intrusion into matters so fundamentally affecting a person as the decision whether to bear or beget a child." *Eisenstadt v. Baird.* Our precedents "have respected the private realm of family life which the state cannot enter." *Prince v. Massachusetts,* 321 U.S. 158 (1944). These matters, involving the most intimate and personal choices a person may make in a lifetime, choices central to personal dignity and autonomy, are central to the liberty protected by the Fourteenth Amendment. At the heart of liberty is the right to define one's own concept of existence, of meaning, of the universe, and of the mystery of human life. Beliefs about these matters could not define the attributes of personhood were they formed under compulsion of the State.

These considerations begin our analysis of the woman's interest in terminating her pregnancy but cannot end it, for this reason: though the abortion decision may originate within the zone of conscience and belief, it is more than a philosophic exercise. Abortion is a unique act. It is an act fraught with consequences for others: for the woman who must live with the implications of her decision; for the persons who perform and assist in the procedure; for the spouse, family, and society which must confront the knowledge that these procedures exist, procedures some deem nothing short of an act of violence against innocent human life; and, depending on one's beliefs, for the life or potential life that is aborted. Though abortion is conduct, it does not follow that the State is entitled to proscribe it in all instances. That is because the liberty of the woman is at stake in a sense unique to the human condition and so unique to the law. The mother who carries a child to full term is subject to anxieties, to physical constraints, to pain that only she must bear. That these sacrifices have from the beginning of the human race been endured by woman with a pride that ennobles her in the eyes of others and gives to the infant a bond of love cannot alone be grounds for the State to insist she make the sacrifice. Her suffering is too intimate and personal for the State to insist, without more, upon its own vision of the woman's role, however dominant that vision has been in the course of our history and our culture. The destiny of the woman must be shaped to a large extent on her own conception of her spiritual imperatives and her place in society.

It should be recognized, moreover, that in some critical respects the abortion decision is of the same character as the decision to use contraception, to which *Griswold v. Connecticut, Eisenstadt v. Baird,* and *Carey v. Population Services International* afford constitutional protection. We have no doubt as to the correctness of those decisions. They support the reasoning in *Roe* relating to the woman's liberty because they involve personal decisions concerning not only the meaning of procreation but also human responsibility and respect for it. . . .

Section 3209 of Pennsylvania's abortion law provides, except in cases of medical emergency, that no physician shall perform an abortion on a married woman without receiving a signed statement from the woman that she has notified her spouse that she is about to undergo an abortion. The woman has the option of providing an alternative signed statement certifying that her husband is not the man who impregnated her; that her husband could not be located; that the pregnancy is the result of spousal sexual assault which she has reported; or that the woman believes that notifying her husband will cause him or someone else to inflict bodily injury upon her. A physician who performs an abortion on a married woman without receiving the appropriate signed statement will have his or her license revoked, and is liable to the husband for damages. . . .

In well-functioning marriages, spouses discuss important intimate decisions such as whether to bear a child. But there are millions of women in this country who are the victims of regular physical and psychological abuse at the hands of their husbands. Should these women become pregnant, they may have very good reasons for not wishing to inform their husbands of their decision to obtain an abortion. Many may have justifiable fears of physical abuse, but may be no less fearful of the consequences of reporting prior abuse to the Commonwealth of

Pennsylvania. Many may have a reasonable fear that notifying their husbands will provoke further instances of child abuse; these women are not exempt from § 3209's notification requirement. Many may fear devastating forms of psychological abuse from their husbands, including verbal harassment, threats of future violence, the destruction of possessions, physical confinement to the home, the withdrawal of financial support, or the disclosure of the abortion to family and friends. These methods of psychological abuse may act as even more of a deterrent to notification than the possibility of physical violence, but women who are the victims of the abuse are not exempt from § 3209's notification requirement. And many women who are pregnant as a result of sexual assaults by their husbands will be unable to avail themselves of the exception for spousal sexual assault, § 3209(b)(3), because the exception requires that the woman have notified law enforcement authorities within 90 days of the assault, and her husband will be notified of her report once an investigation begins, § 3128(c). If anything in this field is certain, it is that victims of spousal sexual assault are extremely reluctant to report the abuse to the government; hence, a great many spousal rape victims will not be exempt from the notification requirement imposed by § 3209.

The spousal notification requirement is thus likely to prevent a significant number of women from obtaining an abortion. It does not merely make abortions a little more difficult or expensive to obtain; for many women, it will impose a substantial obstacle. We must not blind ourselves to the fact that the significant number of women who fear for their safety and the safety of their children are likely to be deterred from procuring an abortion as surely as if the Commonwealth had outlawed abortion in all cases. . . .

This conclusion is in no way inconsistent with our decisions upholding parental notification or consent requirements. Those enactments, and our judgment that they are constitutional, are based on the quite reasonable assumption that minors will benefit from consultation with their parents and that children will often not realize that their parents have their best interests at heart. We cannot adopt a parallel assumption about adult women.

We recognize that a husband has a "deep and proper concern and interest . . . in his wife's pregnancy and in the growth and development of the fetus she is carrying." With regard to the children he has fathered and raised, the Court has recognized his "cognizable and substantial" interest in their custody. . . .

Before birth, however, the issue takes on a very different cast. It is an inescapable biological fact that state regulation with respect to the child a woman is carrying will have a far greater impact on the mother's liberty than on the father's. . . .

The husband's interest in the life of the child his wife is carrying does not permit the State to empower him with this troubling degree of authority over his wife. The contrary view leads to consequences reminiscent of the common law. A husband has no enforceable right to require a wife to advise him before she exercises her personal choices. If a husband's interest in the potential life of the child outweighs a wife's liberty, the State could require a married woman to notify her husband before she uses a postfertilization contraceptive. Perhaps next in line would be a statute requiring pregnant married women to notify their husbands before engaging in conduct causing risks to the fetus. After all, if the husband's interest in the fetus' safety is a sufficient predicate for state regulation, the State could reasonably conclude that pregnant wives should notify their husbands before drinking alcohol or smoking. Perhaps married women should notify their husbands before using contraceptives or before undergoing any type of surgery that may have complications affecting the husband's interest in his wife's reproductive organs. . . . A State may not give to a man the kind of dominion over his wife that parents exercise over their children.

Women do not lose their constitutionally protected liberty when they marry. The Constitution protects all individuals, male or female, married or unmarried, from the abuse of governmental power, even where that power is employed for the supposed benefit of a member of the individual's family. These considerations confirm our conclusion that § 3209 is invalid. . . .

SCALIA, REHNQUIST, WHITE, and THOMAS, JJ. concurring in part and dissenting in part. . . . The States may, if they wish, permit abortion on demand, but the Constitution does not require them to do so. The permissibility of abortion, and the limitations upon it, are to be resolved like most important questions in our democracy: by citizens trying to persuade one another and then voting. . . . A State's choice between two positions on which reasonable people can disagree is constitutional even when (as is often the case) it intrudes upon a "liberty" in the absolute sense. Laws against bigamy, for example — with which entire societies of reasonable people disagree — intrude upon men and women's liberty to marry and live with one another. But bigamy happens not to be a liberty specially "protected" by the Constitution.

That is, quite simply, the issue in these cases: not whether the power of a woman to abort her unborn child is a "liberty" in the absolute sense; or even whether it is a liberty of great importance to many women. Of course it is both. The issue is whether it is a liberty protected by the Constitution of the United States. I am sure it is not. I reach that conclusion not because of anything so exalted as my views concerning the "concept of existence, of meaning, of the universe, and of the mystery of human life." *Ibid.* Rather, I reach it for the same reason I reach the conclusion that bigamy is not constitutionally protected — because of two simple facts: (1) the Constitution says absolutely nothing about it, and (2) the longstanding traditions of American society have permitted it to be legally proscribed. . . .

The Imperial Judiciary lives. It is instructive to compare this Nietzschean vision of us unelected, life-tenured judges — leading a Volk who will be "tested by following," and whose very "belief in themselves" is mystically bound up in their "understanding" of a Court that "speak[s] before all others for their constitutional ideals" — with the somewhat more modest role envisioned for these lawyers by the Founders. . . .

We should get out of this area, where we have no right to be, and where we do neither ourselves nor the country any good by remaining.

NOTES & QUESTIONS

1. *The Most Intimate and Personal Choices.* Recall the following passage in *Casey*:

> These matters, involving the most intimate and personal choices a person may make in a lifetime, choices central to personal dignity and autonomy, are central to the liberty protected by the Fourteenth Amendment. At the heart of liberty is the right to define one's own concept of existence, of meaning, of the universe, and of the mystery of human life. Beliefs about these matters could not define the attributes of personhood were they formed under compulsion of the State.

   In what ways does the rationale for protecting substantive due process differ in *Griswold* and *Casey*? What choices are "central to personal dignity and autonomy"?

2. *The "Undue Burden" Standard.* Although affirming *Roe,* the plurality opinion sets forth a new standard to evaluate whether regulations on abortion pass constitutional muster:

> The very notion that the State has a substantial interest in potential life leads to the conclusion that not all regulations must be deemed unwarranted. Not all burdens on the right to decide whether to terminate a pregnancy will be undue. In our view, the undue burden standard is the appropriate means of reconciling the State's interest with the woman's constitutionally protected liberty. . . .
>
> A finding of an undue burden is a shorthand for the conclusion that a state regulation has the purpose or effect of placing a substantial obstacle in the path of a woman seeking an abortion of a nonviable fetus. . . .

   Justice Scalia criticizes the "undue burden" standard, contending that it was "inherently manipulable and will prove hopelessly unworkable in practice."

   The "undue burden" test, endorsed only by a plurality in *Casey,* became the standard of the Court in *Stenberg v. Carhart,* 530 U.S. 914 (2000), when the Court struck down a statute restricting partial-birth abortions.

3. *Spousal Notification.* The spousal notification provision the Court struck down in *Casey* only required that the woman notify her husband if she was going to have an abortion. Should this be something a husband is entitled to know? Note that the notification provision is not directed toward the biological father — it is the husband who must be notified. Does this notification, as the Court notes, give the husband a "troubling degree of authority over his wife"? Suppose a statute required that the biological father be notified. Does he have a right to learn that the fetus is being aborted?

4. *Partial Birth Abortion.* In *Gonzales v. Carhart*, 550 U.S. 124 (2007), the Supreme Court upheld the Partial-Birth Abortion Act, which prohibited abortions in which a living fetus is partially delivered through the vagina and is killed. The Act makes an exception to save the mother's life but does not make an exception to protect the woman's health.

5. *The Right to Refuse Medical Treatment.* In *Cruzan v. Director, Missouri Dep't of Health,* 497 U.S. 261 (1990), the Court held that a competent person has a liberty interest in refusing unwanted medical treatment, but that the state could

require proof of "clear and convincing" evidence that an incompetent person would have wanted to discontinue medical treatment.

6. ***The Right to Die.*** The Court refused to extend the right to privacy to the so-called right to die. *Washington v. Glucksberg*, 521 U.S. 702 (1997). The plaintiffs challenged a state's ban on assisted suicide. The Court reasoned:

> First, Washington has an "unqualified interest in the preservation of human life." The State's prohibition on assisted suicide, like all homicide laws, both reflects and advances its commitment to this interest. . . . This interest is symbolic and aspirational as well as practical. . . .
>
> Those who attempt suicide — terminally ill or not — often suffer from depression or other medical disorders. . . . Research indicates, however, that many people who request physician-assisted suicide withdraw that request if their depression and pain are treated.
>
> The State also has an interest in protecting the integrity and ethics of the medical profession. . . . And physician-assisted suicide could, it is argued, undermine the trust that is essential to the doctor-patient relationship by blurring the time-honored line between healing and harming.

7. ***Homosexual Sodomy.*** In *Bowers v. Hardwick*, 478 U.S. 186 (1986), the Court upheld a Georgia statute criminalizing sodomy because the Constitution does not confer "a fundamental right upon homosexuals to engage in sodomy." The Court rejected a reading of *Pierce, Meyer, Griswold, Roe,* and *Eisenstadt* as protecting acts homosexual sodomy in the home:

> [W]e think it evident that none of the rights announced in those cases bears any resemblance to the claimed constitutional right of homosexuals to engage in acts of sodomy that is asserted in this case. No connection between family, marriage, or procreation on the one hand and homosexual activity on the other has been demonstrated, either by the Court of Appeals or by respondent. Moreover, any claim that these cases nevertheless stand for the proposition that any kind of private sexual conduct between consenting adults is constitutionally insulated from state proscription is unsupportable. . . .
>
> Precedent aside, however, respondent would have us announce, as the Court of Appeals did, a fundamental right to engage in homosexual sodomy. This we are quite unwilling to do.

Frank Easterbrook considers *Roe* and *Bowers* to be "irreconcilable."[55] Do you agree?

---

[55] Frank Easterbrook, *Abstraction and Authority*, 59 U. Chi. L. Rev. 349 (1992).

LAWRENCE V. TEXAS

539 U.S. 558 (2003)

KENNEDY, J. Liberty protects the person from unwarranted government intrusions into a dwelling or other private places. In our tradition the State is not omnipresent in the home. And there are other spheres of our lives and existence, outside the home, where the State should not be a dominant presence. Freedom extends beyond spatial bounds. Liberty presumes an autonomy of self that includes freedom of thought, belief, expression, and certain intimate conduct. The instant case involves liberty of the person both in its spatial and more transcendent dimensions.

The question before the Court is the validity of a Texas statute making it a crime for two persons of the same sex to engage in certain intimate sexual conduct.

In Houston, Texas, officers of the Harris County Police Department were dispatched to a private residence in response to a reported weapons disturbance. They entered an apartment where one of the petitioners, John Geddes Lawrence, resided. The right of the police to enter does not seem to have been questioned. The officers observed Lawrence and another man, Tyron Garner, engaging in a sexual act. The two petitioners were arrested, held in custody over night, and charged and convicted before a Justice of the Peace.

The complaints described their crime as "deviate sexual intercourse, namely anal sex, with a member of the same sex (man)." The applicable state law is Tex. Penal Code Ann. § 21.06(a) (2003). It provides: "A person commits an offense if he engages in deviate sexual intercourse with another individual of the same sex." The statute defines "[d]eviate sexual intercourse" as follows:

(A) any contact between any part of the genitals of one person and the mouth or anus of another person; or

(B) the penetration of the genitals or the anus of another person with an object. § 21.01(1). . . .

[The men were convicted, and they challenged their conviction as violative of substantive due process. Their challenge was rejected by Texas courts based on *Bowers v. Hardwick,* 478 U.S. 186 (1986).]

We conclude the case should be resolved by determining whether the petitioners were free as adults to engage in the private conduct in the exercise of their liberty under the Due Process Clause of the Fourteenth Amendment to the Constitution. For this inquiry we deem it necessary to reconsider the Court's holding in *Bowers. . . .*

The Court began its substantive discussion in *Bowers* as follows: "The issue presented is whether the Federal Constitution confers a fundamental right upon homosexuals to engage in sodomy and hence invalidates the laws of the many States that still make such conduct illegal and have done so for a very long time." That statement, we now conclude, discloses the Court's own failure to appreciate the extent of the liberty at stake. To say that the issue in *Bowers* was simply the right to engage in certain sexual conduct demeans the claim the individual put forward, just as it would demean a married couple were it to be said marriage is simply about the right to have sexual intercourse. The laws involved in *Bowers* and here are, to be sure, statutes that purport to do no more than prohibit a particular sexual act. Their penalties and purposes, though, have more far-reaching consequences, touching upon the most private human conduct, sexual behavior, and in the most private of places, the home. The statutes do seek to control a personal relationship that, whether or not entitled to formal recognition in the law, is within the liberty of persons to choose without being punished as criminals.

This, as a general rule, should counsel against attempts by the State, or a court, to define the meaning of the relationship or to set its boundaries absent injury to a person or abuse of an institution the law protects. It suffices for us to acknowledge that adults may choose to enter upon this relationship in the confines of their homes and their own private lives and still retain their dignity as free persons. When sexuality finds overt expression in intimate conduct with another person, the conduct can be but one element in a personal bond that is more enduring. The liberty protected by the Constitution allows homosexual persons the right to make this choice. . . .

Equality of treatment and the due process right to demand respect for conduct protected by the substantive guarantee of liberty are linked in important respects, and a decision on the latter point advances both interests. If protected conduct is made criminal and the law which does so remains unexamined for its substantive validity, its stigma might remain even if it were not enforceable as drawn for equal protection reasons. When homosexual conduct is made criminal by the law of the State, that declaration in and of itself is an invitation to subject homosexual persons to discrimination both in the public and in the private spheres. . . .

Bowers was not correct when it was decided, and it is not correct today. It ought not to remain binding precedent. *Bowers v. Hardwick* should be and now is overruled. . . .

The case does involve two adults who, with full and mutual consent from each other, engaged in sexual practices common to a homosexual lifestyle. The petitioners are entitled to respect for their private lives. The State cannot demean their existence or control their destiny by making their private sexual conduct a crime. . . .

SCALIA, REHNQUIST, and THOMAS, JJ. dissenting. . . . State laws against bigamy, same-sex marriage, adult incest, prostitution, masturbation, adultery, fornication, bestiality, and obscenity are . . . sustainable only in light of *Bowers'* validation of laws based on moral choices. Every single one of these laws is called into question by today's decision; the Court makes no effort to cabin the scope of its decision to exclude them from its holding. The impossibility of distinguishing homosexuality from other traditional "morals" offenses is precisely why *Bowers* rejected the rational-basis challenge. . . .

Texas Penal Code Ann. § 21.06(a) (2003) undoubtedly imposes constraints on liberty. So do laws prohibiting prostitution, recreational use of heroin, and, for that matter, working more than 60 hours per week in a bakery. But there is no right to "liberty" under the Due Process Clause, though today's opinion repeatedly makes that claim. . . .

Let me be clear that I have nothing against homosexuals, or any other group, promoting their agenda through normal democratic means. Social perceptions of sexual and other morality change over time, and every group has the right to persuade its fellow citizens that its view of such matters is the best. That homosexuals have achieved some success in that enterprise is attested to by the fact that Texas is one of the few remaining States that criminalize private, consensual homosexual acts. But persuading one's fellow citizens is one thing, and imposing one's views in absence of democratic majority will is something else. I would no more *require* a State to criminalize homosexual acts — or, for that matter, display *any* moral disapprobation of them — than I would *forbid* it to do so. What Texas has chosen to do is well within the range of traditional democratic action, and its hand should not be stayed through the invention of a brand-new "constitutional right" by a Court that is impatient of democratic change. . . .

NOTES & QUESTIONS

1. ***Decisional vs. Informational Privacy.*** Recall Neil Richards's argument that *Griswold* can be read as an informational privacy case. Can *Lawrence*?

   Lior Strahilevitz notes four possible interpretations of the primary rationale of *Lawrence*:

   > Perhaps *Lawrence* is about keeping Texas police officers from coming into a bedroom and arresting him on the basis of what they see. Perhaps *Lawrence* is about permitting gay couples to make decisions about how to live their lives without the state's interference. Perhaps *Lawrence* is about respecting intimacy established within homosexual relationships. Or perhaps *Lawrence* is about protecting the dignity of homosexuals and rejecting Texas's efforts to make second-class citizens out of them because anti-sodomy laws stigmatized and triggered further discrimination against gays and lesbians.[56]

2. ***The Victorian Compromise.*** The Court notes that "[l]aws prohibiting sodomy do not seem to have been enforced against consenting adults acting in private." This conclusion is an example of what Lawrence Friedman calls the "Victorian compromise":

   > The first two-thirds or so of the nineteenth century is the heyday of what I have called the Victorian compromise. This compromise comes out most clearly in laws about sex and morality. These laws lost some of their absolute all-or-nothing quality. It is as if society — or most of society, at any rate — was aware that vice, crime, and sexual misconduct were never going to go away. Vice at least was tolerable, although only in small amounts and only if discreet and under a good deal of control. . . .
   >
   > Law and norms performed this function by making a sharp distinction between the surface of the law and its dark underbelly. It was important to maintain purity and high ideals in the external, visible sphere, the *public* and official sphere. What went on underneath was another story. The dark underbelly was meant to be kept invisible. Its secrets should never be leached out into daylight — and should never be granted legitimacy. . . .

---

[56] Lior Jacob Strahilevitz, *Consent, Aesthetics, and the Boundaries of Sexual Privacy after Lawrence v. Texas*, 54 DePaul L. Rev. 671, 678 n.35 (2005).

~~Sex was strictly a private affair. Decent people never talked about it. Sex~~ was meant for the privacy of the home.[57]

Friedman notes that the laws and norms regulating sex (sodomy, prostitution, adultery, etc.) were selectively enforced and focused primarily on keeping deviant sex in the shadows.

3. *Blackmail.* The Court notes that the Model Penal Code recommended against criminalizing sodomy to prevent the crime of blackmail. Blackmail involves threatening to disclose a secret in return for "hush money." Consider Angus McLaren:

> Modern blackmail first emerged when criminals in the eighteenth century recognized that the laws against sodomy provided them with the means by which they could extort money from those whom they could entrap. . . .
>
> In the eighteenth century English men were so alarmed by the thought of criminals extorting money by threatening to accuse innocent victims of sodomy — which at the time was a capital offense — that the government made the leveling of such charges a felony. In the nineteenth century men began to fear that even their heterosexual peccadilloes could put them at the mercy of a blackmailer. With the increasing centrality of family life, an unsullied sexual reputation increased in importance. . . .
>
> The courts for the most part did not want to know if the blackmailers made up their stories or if the victims actually had engaged in homosexual practices. . . . Victims who appeared to have engaged in same-sex activities put the courts in a potentially awkward position. On the one hand the law stated that the truth of the blackmailer's accusation in no way mitigated the offence. On the other hand the courts did not want to be seen as defending immoralists. The way out for the prosecution and judge was to assert that there was no truth to the charge.[58]

Why is blackmail a crime? Why should courts prohibit contracts to keep secrets? Consider James Lindgren:

> In blackmail, the heart of the problem is that two separate acts, each of which is a moral and legal right, can combine to make a moral and legal wrong. For example, if I threaten to expose a criminal act unless I am paid money, I have committed blackmail. Or if I threaten to expose a sexual affair unless I am given a job, once again I have committed blackmail. I have a legal right to expose or threaten to expose the crime or affair, and I have a legal right to seek a job or money, but if I combine these rights it is blackmail. If both a person's ends — seeking a job or money — and his means — threatening to expose — are otherwise legal, why is it illegal to combine them? Therein lies what has been called the "paradox of blackmail."[59]

4. *The "Culture War."* In his dissent, Justice Scalia declares that "the Court has taken sides in the culture war, departing from its role of . . . [serving as a] neutral observer." Robert Post contends that the Supreme Court must "take sides" in a

---

[57] Lawrence M. Friedman, *Guarding Life's Dark Dark Secrets: Legal and Social Controls over Reputation, Propriety, and Privacy* 66-68 (2007).

[58] Angus McLaren, *Sexual Blackmail: A Modern History* 3, 6, 21 (2002).

[59] James Lindgren, *Unravelling the Paradox of Blackmail*, 84 Colum. L. Rev. 670, 670-71 (1984).

"culture war" and cannot remain neutral: "Instead of pursuing the chimerical objective of neutrality, the Court would do better to analyze the conditions under which courts should properly make cultural judgments."[60] Can the Court be neutral? Should it be?

The Court discusses and cites foreign authorities in its decision. Some have criticized the Court for doing so. Is the Court's use of foreign authorities appropriate?[61]

5. ***Invalidating DOMA.*** In *United States v. Windsor*, 133 S. Ct. 2675 (2013), a 5-4 majority of the Court found that the Defense of Marriage Act (DOMA) violated the Fifth Amendment. For purposes of federal law, DOMA defined "marriage" only as a legal union between a man and a woman and "spouse" only as a person of the opposite sex was a husband or wife. For federal law, it prevented New York State from recognizing the marriage of New York residents Edith Windsor and Thea Speyer, who had wed in Ontario, Canada, in 2007.

For the majority, Justice Kennedy declared, "Under DOMA, same-sex married couples have their lives burdened by reason of government decree in visible and public ways. By its great reach, DOMA touches many aspects of married and family life, from the mundane to the profound." The statute violated the Fifth Amendment "for no legitimate purpose overcomes the purpose and effect to disparage and to injure those whom the State, by its marriage laws, sought to protect in personhood and dignity."

In dissent, Justice Scalia returned to his dissent in *Lawrence v. Texas* and re-iterated his belief that "the Constitution does not forbid the government to enforce traditional normal and sexual norms." He added: "I will not swell the U.S. Reports with restatements of that point. It is enough to say that the Constitution neither requires nor forbids our society to approve of same-sex marriage, much as it neither requires nor forbids us to approve of no-fault divorce, polygamy, or the consumption of alcohol." He also warned: "The only thing that will 'confine' the Court's holding is its sense of what it can get away with."

---

[60] Robert C. Post, *Foreword: Fashioning the Legal Constitution: Culture, Courts and Law*, 117 Harv. L. Rev. 4 (2003).

[61] For an excellent discussion of the issue, see Rex D. Glensy. *Which Countries Count?: Lawrence v. Texas and the Selection of Foreign Persuasive Authority*, 45 Va. J. Int'l L. 347 (2005).

2. THE CONSTITUTIONAL RIGHT TO INFORMATION PRIVACY

WHALEN V. ROE

429 U.S. 589 (1977)

STEVENS, J. . . . Many drugs have both legitimate and illegitimate uses. In response to a concern that such drugs were being diverted into unlawful channels, in 1970 the New York Legislature created a special commission to evaluate the State's drug-control laws. The commission found the existing laws deficient in several respects. There was no effective way to prevent the use of stolen or revised prescriptions, to prevent unscrupulous pharmacists from repeatedly refilling prescriptions, to prevent users from obtaining prescriptions from more than one doctor, or to prevent doctors from over-prescribing, either by authorizing an excessive amount in one prescription or by giving one patient multiple prescriptions. . . .

The new New York statute classified potentially harmful drugs in five schedules. Drugs, such as heroin, which are highly abused and have no recognized medical use, are in Schedule I; they cannot be prescribed. Schedules II through V include drugs which have a progressively lower potential for abuse but also have a recognized medical use. Our concern is limited to Schedule II which includes the most dangerous of the legitimate drugs.[62]

With an exception for emergencies, the Act requires that all prescriptions for Schedule II drugs be prepared by the physician in triplicate on an official form. The completed form identifies the prescribing physician; the dispensing pharmacy; the drug and dosage; and the name, address, and age of the patient. One copy of the form is retained by the physician, the second by the pharmacist, and the third is forwarded to the New York State Department of Health in Albany. A prescription made on an official form may not exceed a 30-day supply, and may not be refilled.

The District Court found that about 100,000 Schedule II prescription forms are delivered to a receiving room at the Department of Health in Albany each month. They are sorted, coded, and logged and then taken to another room where the data on the forms is recorded on magnetic tapes for processing by a computer. Thereafter, the forms are returned to the receiving room to be retained in a vault for a five-year period and then destroyed as required by the statute.[63] The receiving room is surrounded by a locked wire fence and protected by an alarm system. The computer tapes containing the prescription data are kept in a locked cabinet. When the tapes are used, the computer is run "off-line," which means that no terminal outside of the computer room can read or record any information. Public disclosure of the identity of patients is expressly prohibited by the statute and by a Department

---

[62] These include opium and opium derivatives, cocaine, methadone, amphetamines, and methaqualone. Pub. Health Law § 3306. These drugs have accepted uses in the amelioration of pain and in the treatment of epilepsy, narcolepsy, hyperkinesia, schizo-affective disorders, and migraine headaches.

[63] Pub. Health Law § 3370(3), 1974 N.Y.Laws, c. 965, § 16. The physician and the pharmacist are required to retain their copies for five years also, but they are not required to destroy them.

of Health regulation. Willful violation of these prohibitions is a crime punishable by up to one year in prison and a $2,000 fine. At the time of trial there were 17 Department of Health employees with access to the files; in addition, there were 24 investigators with authority to investigate cases of overdispensing which might be identified by the computer. Twenty months after the effective date of the Act, the computerized data had only been used in two investigations involving alleged overuse by specific patients.

A few days before the Act became effective, this litigation was commenced by a group of patients regularly receiving prescriptions for Schedule II drugs, by doctors who prescribe such drugs, and by two associations of physicians. After various preliminary proceedings, a three-judge District Court conducted a one-day trial. Appellees offered evidence tending to prove that persons in need of treatment with Schedule II drugs will from time to time decline such treatment because of their fear that the misuse of the computerized data will cause them to be stigmatized as "drug addicts."[64]

Appellees contend that the statute invades a constitutionally protected "zone of privacy." The cases sometimes characterized as protecting "privacy" have in fact involved at least two different kinds of interests. One is the individual interest in avoiding disclosure of personal matters, and another is the interest in independence in making certain kinds of important decisions. Appellees argue that both of these interests are impaired by this statute. The mere existence in readily available form of the information about patients' use of Schedule II drugs creates a genuine concern that the information will become publicly known and that it will adversely affect their reputations. This concern makes some patients reluctant to use, and some doctors reluctant to prescribe, such drugs even when their use is medically indicated. It follows, they argue, that the making of decisions about matters vital to the care of their health is inevitably affected by the statute. Thus, the statute threatens to impair both their interest in the nondisclosure of private information and also their interest in making important decisions independently.

We are persuaded, however, that the New York program does not, on its face, pose a sufficiently grievous threat to either interest to establish a constitutional violation.

Public disclosure of patient information can come about in three ways. Health Department employees may violate the statute by failing, either deliberately or negligently, to maintain proper security. A patient or a doctor may be accused of a violation and the stored data may be offered in evidence in a judicial proceeding.

---

[64] Two parents testified that they were concerned that their children would be stigmatized by the State's central filing system. One child had been taken off his Schedule II medication because of this concern. Three adult patients testified that they feared disclosure of their names would result from central filing of patient identifications. One of them now obtains his drugs in another State. The other two continue to receive Schedule II prescriptions in New York, but continue to fear disclosure and stigmatization. Four physicians testified that the prescription system entrenches on patients' privacy, and that each had observed a reaction of shock, fear, and concern on the part of their patients whom they had informed of the plan. One doctor refuses to prescribe Schedule II drugs for his patients. On the other hand, over 100,000 patients per month have been receiving Schedule II drug prescriptions without their objections, if any, to central filing having come to the attention of the District Court. The record shows that the provisions of the Act were brought to the attention of the section on psychiatry of the New York State Medical Society, but that body apparently declined to support this suit.

Or, thirdly, a doctor, a pharmacist, or the patient may voluntarily reveal information on a prescription form.

The third possibility existed under the prior law and is entirely unrelated to the existence of the computerized data bank. Neither of the other two possibilities provides a proper ground for attacking the statute as invalid on its face. There is no support in the record, or in the experience of the two States that New York has emulated, for an assumption that the security provisions of the statute will be administered improperly. And the remote possibility that judicial supervision of the evidentiary use of particular items of stored information will provide inadequate protection against unwarranted disclosures is surely not a sufficient reason for invalidating the entire patient-identification program.

Even without public disclosure, it is, of course, true that private information must be disclosed to the authorized employees of the New York Department of Health. Such disclosures, however, are not significantly different from those that were required under the prior law. Nor are they meaningfully distinguishable from a host of other unpleasant invasions of privacy that are associated with many facets of health care. Unquestionably, some individuals' concern for their own privacy may lead them to avoid or to postpone needed medical attention. Nevertheless, disclosures of private medical information to doctors, to hospital personnel, to insurance companies, and to public health agencies are often an essential part of modern medical practice even when the disclosure may reflect unfavorably on the character of the patient. Requiring such disclosures to representatives of the State having responsibility for the health of the community, does not automatically amount to an impermissible invasion of privacy.

Appellees also argue, however, that even if unwarranted disclosures do not actually occur, the knowledge that the information is readily available in a computerized file creates a genuine concern that causes some persons to decline needed medication. The record supports the conclusion that some use of Schedule II drugs has been discouraged by that concern; it also is clear, however, that about 100,000 prescriptions for such drugs were being filled each month prior to the entry of the District Court's injunction. Clearly, therefore, the statute did not deprive the public of access to the drugs. . . .

We hold that neither the immediate nor the threatened impact of the patient-identification requirements in the New York State Controlled Substances Act of 1972 on either the reputation or the independence of patients for whom Schedule II drugs are medically indicated is sufficient to constitute an invasion of any right or liberty protected by the Fourteenth Amendment. . . .

A final word about issues we have not decided. We are not unaware of the threat to privacy implicit in the accumulation of vast amounts of personal information in computerized data banks or other massive government files. The collection of taxes, the distribution of welfare and social security benefits, the supervision of public health, the direction of our Armed Forces, and the enforcement of the criminal laws all require the orderly preservation of great quantities of information, much of which is personal in character and potentially embarrassing or harmful if disclosed. The right to collect and use such data for public purposes is typically accompanied by a concomitant statutory or regulatory duty to avoid unwarranted disclosures. Recognizing that in some circumstances that duty arguably has its roots in the Constitution, nevertheless New York's statutory scheme, and its implementing administrative procedures, evidence a proper concern with, and protection of, the individual's interest in privacy. We therefore need not, and do not, decide any question which might be presented by the unwarranted disclosure of accumulated private data whether intentional or unintentional or by a system that did not contain comparable security provisions. We simply hold that this record does not establish an invasion of any right or liberty protected by the Fourteenth Amendment. . . .

BRENNAN, J. concurring. . . . The information disclosed by the physician under this program is made available only to a small number of public health officials with a legitimate interest in the information. As the record makes clear, New York has long required doctors to make this information available to its officials on request, and that practice is not challenged here. Such limited reporting requirements in the medical field are familiar and are not generally regarded as an invasion of privacy. Broad dissemination by state officials of such information, however, would clearly implicate constitutionally protected privacy rights, and would presumably be justified only by compelling state interests.

What is more troubling about this scheme, however, is the central computer storage of the data thus collected. Obviously, as the State argues, collection and storage of data by the State that is in itself legitimate is not rendered unconstitutional simply because new technology makes the State's operations more efficient. However, as the example of the Fourth Amendment shows the Constitution puts limits not only on the type of information the State may gather, but also on the means it may use to gather it. The central storage and easy accessibility of computerized data vastly increase the potential for abuse of that information, and I am not prepared to say that future developments will not demonstrate the necessity of some curb on such technology. . . .

NOTES & QUESTIONS

1. ***The Constitutional Right to Information Privacy.*** The *Whalen* Court characterizes the line of substantive due process cases protecting the right to privacy as involving two "different kinds of interests" — (1) "the individual interest in avoiding disclosure of personal matters" and (2) "the interest in independence in making certain kinds of important decisions." In one reading, the latter interest can be referred to as decisional privacy because it involves the extent to which the state can become involved with the decisions an individual makes with regard to her body and family. The former interest involves the privacy implications of the collection, use, and disclosure of personal information. This former interest is often referred to as the "constitutional right to information privacy." What is the Court's implicit conception of privacy as manifested by this interest?

In a different reading of *Whalen*, the Court identified a bifurcated information privacy interest. In other words, both *Whalen* interests serve to protect informational privacy. Regarding the second *Whalen* interest, for example, Paul Schwartz argues that the Court "extends the constitutional protection offered important activities or decisions to *information* that reports activities or decisions."[65] Schwartz notes, however, that lower courts "have been reluctant to use the second *Whalen* interest as a bar to the state's information gathering practices." In this reading of the case, one open question is whether the second *Whalen* interest should be restricted only to information about fundamental interests, such as those typically protected by substantive due process cases, or extended more generally to situations in which the government's collection and processing of information will chill decision making. Moreover, Schwartz calls for use of this second interest in judicial exploration of "the means of processing, the types of data bases to be linked, and the purposes for which the processing information will be utilized." How practical is this constitutional standard?

2. **Nixon v. Administrator of General Services.** After *Whalen*, the Court affirmed this notion of constitutional protection for information privacy in *Nixon v. Administrator of General Services*, 433 U.S. 425 (1977), concluding that President Nixon had a constitutional privacy interest in records of his private communications with his family but not in records involving his official duties. Although ex-President Nixon had a legitimate expectation of privacy in private communications with his family, doctor, and minister, it was outweighed by the public interest in Nixon's papers.

3. *The Constitutional Right to Information Privacy After* **Whalen** *and* **Nixon.** Subsequent to *Whalen* and *Nixon*, the Court did little to develop the right of information privacy. As one court observed, the right "has been infrequently examined; as a result, its contours remain less than clear." *Davis v. Bucher*, 853 F.2d 718, 720 (9th Cir. 1988). Most federal circuit courts have recognized the right. *See, e.g., Barry v. City of New York*, 712 F.2d 1554, 1559 (2d Cir. 1983); *United States v. Westinghouse Electric Corp.*, 638 F.2d 570, 577-80 (3d Cir. 1980); *Walls v. City of Petersburg*, 895 F.2d 188, 192 (4th Cir. 1990); *Plante v. Gonzalez*, 575 F.2d 1119, 1132, 1134 (5th Cir.1978); *Kimberlin v. United States Dep't of Justice*, 788 F.2d 434 (7th Cir. 1986); *In re Crawford*, 194 F.3d 954, 959 (9th Cir. 1999).

In contrast to other circuits, the Sixth Circuit has adopted the constitutional right to information privacy in a very narrow manner. In *J.P. v. DeSanti*, 653 F.2d 1080, 1090 (6th Cir. 1981), the Sixth Circuit concluded that "[a]bsent a clear indication from the Supreme Court we will not construe isolated statements in *Whalen* and *Nixon* more broadly than their context allows to recognize a general constitutional right to have disclosure of private information measured against the need for disclosure." *Id.* at 1089; *see also Bloch v. Ribar*, 156 F.3d 673, 684 (6th Cir. 1998) ("[T]he right to informational privacy will be triggered only when the interest at stake relates to those personal rights that can be deemed 'fundamental' or 'implicit in the concept of ordered liberty.' ") (quoting *J.P. v. DeSanti*, 653 F.2d 1080, 1090 (6th Cir. 1981)).

At least one other circuit court has expressed doubts as to whether the constitutional right to information privacy exists at all. In *American Federation*

---

[65] Paul M. Schwartz, *Privacy and Participation: Personal Information and Public Sector Regulation in the United States*, 80 Iowa L. Rev. 553, 581-82 (1995).

of Government Employees, AFL-CIO v. Department of Housing & Urban Development, 118 F.3d 786 (D.C. Cir. 1997), the court observed:

> We begin our analysis by expressing our grave doubts as to the existence of a constitutional right of privacy in the nondisclosure of personal information. Were we the first to confront the issue we would conclude with little difficulty that such a right does not exist, but we do not, of course, write on a blank slate. The Supreme Court [in *Whalen v. Roe*] has addressed the issue in recurring dicta without, we believe, resolving it. . . .
>
> The Court was equally Delphic in *Nixon v. Administrator of General Services.* . . .

Based upon your reading of *Whalen*, do you conclude (1) there is a broad constitutional right to information privacy that pertains to a variety of kinds of personal information; (2) there is a narrow constitutional right to information privacy that only pertains to personal information relating to one's health, family, children, and other interests protected by the Court's substantive due process right to privacy decisions; or (3) there is no constitutional right to information privacy, and the passage in *Whalen* was mere dicta?

In 2011, the Supreme Court finally decided another case involving the constitutional right to information privacy. The case, *National Aeronautics and Space Administration v. Nelson,* 131 S. Ct. 746 (2011), involved government employees who argued that background questionnaires unduly pried into their personal life and were an invasion of their constitutional right to information privacy. The Court declined to consider the viability of this right, stating: "We assume, without deciding, that the Constitution protects a privacy right of the sort mentioned in *Whalen* and *Nixon*. We hold, however, that the challenged portions of the Government's background check do not violate this right in the present case."

In a concurrence joined by Justice Thomas, Justice Scalia flatly stated, "A federal constitutional right to 'information privacy' does not exist." Justice Scalia objected to the majority's choosing to "assume, without deciding." He noted that the "Court decides that the Government did not violate the right to information privacy, and without even deciding whether there *is* a right to information privacy, and without even describing what hypothetical standard should be used to assess whether the hypothetical right has been violated."

4. ***The* Westinghouse *Test.*** Since the constitutional right to information privacy has yet to develop a distinctive identity, courts applying the right often draw from other types of privacy law. At least one court has observed that the constitutional right to information privacy "closely resembles — and may be identical to — the interest protected by the common law prohibition against unreasonable publicity given to one's private life." *Smith v. City of Artesia,* 772 P.2d 373, 376 (N.M. App. 1989). One court has looked to the "reasonable expectations of privacy" test to determine whether information is entitled to protection under the constitutional right to information privacy. *See Fraternal Order of Police, Lodge No. 5, Philadelphia* 812 F.2d 105, 112 (3d Cir. 1987).

The Third Circuit has developed the most well-known test for deciding constitutional right to information privacy cases. In *United States v. Westinghouse Electric Corp.*, 638 F.2d 570, 578 (3d Cir. 1980), the court articulated seven factors that "should be considered in deciding whether an intrusion into an individual's privacy is justified": (1) "the type of record requested"; (2) "the information it does or might contain"; (3) "the potential for harm in any subsequent nonconsensual disclosure"; (4) "the injury from disclosure to the relationship in which the record was generated"; (5) "the adequacy of safeguards to prevent unauthorized disclosure"; (6) "the degree of need for access"; and (7) "whether there is an express statutory mandate, articulated public policy, or other recognizable public interest militating toward access."

In addition to the Third Circuit, the *Westinghouse* test is used by some other circuit courts. For example, the Ninth Circuit has simplified the language in the test and kept five of the seven factors. *Tucson Woman's Clinic v. Eden*, 379 F.3d 531, 551 (9th Cir. 2004); *Planned Parenthood of Southern Arizona v. Lawall*, 307 F.3d 783, 789-90 (9th Cir. 2002). In *Tucson Woman's Clinic v. Eden*, the Ninth Circuit invalidated certain aspects of an Arizona statutory and regulatory scheme that regulated abortion providers. Based on its reading of *Whalen*, the court struck down the state requirement that unredacted medical reports be given to the Arizona Department of Health Services. It found that there was "little, if any need for much of this information, such as the names and addresses of patients." It also invalidated the Arizona requirement that ultrasound prints of pregnant women be shared with patient identifying information on them to a private contractor.

5. ***The Constitutionality of Disclosure and Reporting Requirements.*** Consider *Greenville Women's Clinic v. Commissioner*, 317 F.3d 357 (4th Cir. 2002). A state regulation required that abortion clinics disclose to state officials patients' names and records. The abortion clinics argued that this regulation ran afoul of *Whalen v. Roe*. The state argued that it needed "the information to monitor abortions and to assure complaints with the health-care standards . . . aimed at preserving maternal health." The court concluded that the regulation did not violate the constitutional right to information privacy because the regulation "explicitly requires [that the state maintain the] confidentiality of patients' records." Judge King dissented, arguing that the state does not adequately safeguard patient confidentiality because the state statutes mandating confidentiality "contain gaping holes in the protections they afford against public disclosures" and because "despite the State's assurances of confidentiality, private medical information has been leaked to the public." This case, argued King, presents more severe privacy threats than in *Whalen* because the plaintiffs in *Whalen* feared the stigma of disclosure, whereas "women seeking abortions in South Carolina have a great deal more to fear than stigma. The protests designed to harass and intimidate women entering abortion clinics, and the violence inflicted on abortion providers, provide women with ample reason to fear for their physical safety."

In *Planned Parenthood of Central Missouri v. Danforth*, 428 U.S. 52 (1976), Missouri required that physicians report abortions to the state, which would keep the data confidential, except that the data can "be inspected and health data acquired by local, state, or national public health officers." The records must also be retained for seven years in the permanent files of the health facility where the abortion was performed. The reporting requirements were challenged "on the ground that they . . . impose an extra layer and burden of regulation" on a woman's right to seek an abortion. The Court held that the regulations were constitutional: "Recordkeeping and reporting requirements that are reasonably directed to the preservation of maternal health and that properly respect a patient's confidentiality and privacy are permissible."

42 U.S.C. § 1983 AND "CONSTITUTIONAL TORTS"

Most cases involving the constitutional right to information privacy are litigated by way of 42 U.S.C. § 1983. This statute was part of the Civil Rights Act of 1871 and was designed to facilitate the enforcement of civil rights protected by the Constitution and federal law. This famous civil rights statute provides:

> Every person who, under color of any statute, ordinance, regulation, custom, or usage, of any state or territory, subjects, or causes to be subjected, any citizen of the United States or other person within the jurisdiction thereof to the deprivation of any rights, privileges, or immunities secured by the Constitution and laws, shall be liable to the party injured in an action at law, suit at equity, or other proper proceeding for redress.

Section 1983 provides a way to remedy constitutional violations in the civil law (as opposed to criminal) context. Section 1983 creates a cause of action against those who, acting under state governmental authority, violate federal law and the federal Constitution. Section 1983 transforms constitutional violations into tort actions and enables plaintiffs to collect damages and obtain injunctive relief.

Section 1983 requires that the wrongful conduct be "under color of state law, custom, or usage." This is often referred to as the "state action" requirement.

The word "person" in § 1983 includes government entities and officials. However, state governments are not "persons," and the Eleventh Amendment immunizes states against suits by private citizens. The Eleventh Amendment provides:

> The Judicial power of the United States shall not be construed to extend to any suit in law or equity, commenced or prosecuted against one of the United States by Citizens of another State, or by Citizens or Subjects of any Foreign State.

The Supreme Court has interpreted the Eleventh Amendment not just to bar a citizen of one state from suing another state, but also to bar a citizen from suing his or her own state. *See Hans v. Louisiana*, 134 U.S. 1 (1890). Therefore, instead of suing states directly, plaintiffs sue state officials.

Although states cannot be sued directly, municipalities and local governments can. In *Monell v. New York City Dep't of Social Services*, 436 U.S. 658 (1978), the Court held that municipalities can be sued as "persons" under § 1983. However, municipalities cannot be sued for the acts of their employees. In other words, municipalities are not liable under § 1983 on the basis of the *respondeat superior* doctrine. Municipalities are liable "when execution of a government's policy or custom, whether made by its lawmakers or by those whose edicts or acts may fairly represent official policy, inflicts the injury." Of course, *Monell* does not bar a suit against a local official directly.

In short, any state or local official can be sued directly under § 1983. State governments cannot be sued. Local governments can be sued, but only when their policy or custom inflicts the injury, not merely because they employ the officials who caused the injury.

What about federal officials? Section 1983 does not authorize suits against federal officials. However, the Supreme Court held that federal officials can be sued for violating constitutional rights. *See Bivens v. Six Unknown Named Agents of Federal Bureau of Narcotics*, 403 U.S. 388 (1971). *Bivens* claims are addressed in a similar way as § 1983 claims.

When sued, government officials (both state and local) can raise certain defenses known as "immunities." Certain officials are absolutely immune from liability under § 1983 — they cannot be liable at all if they are acting in their capacities as officials. Such officials include legislators and judges. Executive officials such as police officers only receive a limited immunity defense known as "qualified immunity." They are immune if "their conduct does not violate *clearly established* statutory or constitutional rights of which a reasonable person would have known." *Harlow v. Fitzgerald*, 457 U.S. 800 (1982). Immunities are generally the same for federal officials, with at least one notable exception. Although state governors only receive qualified immunity, see *Scheuer v. Rhodes*, 416 U.S. 232 (1974), the President of the United States receives absolute immunity, see *Nixon v. Fitzgerald*, 457 U.S. 731 (1982).

This introduction is by no means a comprehensive background into § 1983. It is important, however, to understand the basic structure of § 1983 because constitutional right to information privacy cases are often litigated by way of   § 1983.

CARTER V. BROADLAWNS MEDICAL CENTER

667 F. Supp. 1269 (S.D. Iowa 1987)

[The Broadlawns Medical Center (BMC), a public county hospital located in Des Moines, Iowa, decided to employ a full-time chaplain. Its previous reliance on volunteer chaplains proved to be inadequate because it was difficult for volunteer chaplains to visit patients regularly. The Board of Trustees for BMC hired Maggie Alenzo Rogers, a female who was not an ordained minister. Rogers graduated from the University of Dubuque Theological Seminary in 1984 and was "endorsed" by the United Church of Christ. Her job description stated that she would "provide consistent pastoral care throughout the Medical Center, adding spiritual support and counseling to the ongoing healing effort." BMC had a policy of allowing Rogers to have open access to patient medical records. A group of plaintiffs challenged this policy as a violation of the constitutional right to information privacy.]

O'BRIEN, C.J. . . . The Court also concludes that the policy of chaplains having open access to patient medical records is constitutionally infirm under the Fourteenth Amendment. Patients at BMC have a right of privacy founded on the

Fourteenth Amendment's concept of personal liberty. *Whalen v. Roe*, 429 U.S. 589 (1977). One facet of the right of privacy "is the right of an individual not to have his private affairs made public by the government." In *Planned Parenthood v. Danforth*, 428 U.S. 52 (1976), the Supreme Court refused to strike down record-keeping and reporting requirements regarding abortions that were (1) reasonably directed to the preservation of maternal health and which (2) properly respect a patient's confidentiality and privacy. In allowing chaplains free access to medical records, BMC is not properly respecting a patient's confidentiality and privacy. The Court concludes that patient medical records can only be accessed by a chaplain upon prior express approval of the individual patient or his guardian. This will not be so broad as to bar doctors, medical and psychiatric professionals and nurses to provide to the chaplain basic information, not privileged, which would enable the chaplain to understand what the patient's basic problem was, e.g., a suicide attempt. The Court shall enter injunctive relief regarding this violation. . .

DOE V. BOROUGH OF BARRINGTON

729 F. Supp. 376 (D.N.J. 1990)

BROTMAN, J. . . . On March 25, 1987, Jane Doe, her husband, and their friend James Tarvis were traveling in the Doe's pickup truck through the Borough of Barrington ("Barrington"). At approximately 9:00 A.M., a Barrington police officer stopped the truck and questioned the occupants. As a result of the vehicle stop, Barrington officers arrested Jane Doe's husband and impounded the pickup truck. Barrington officers escorted Jane Doe, her husband, and James Tarvis to the Barrington Police Station.

When he was initially arrested, Jane Doe's husband told the police officers that he had tested HIV positive and that the officers should be careful in searching him because he had "weeping lesions.". . . Barrington police released Jane Doe and James Tarvis from custody, but detained Jane Doe's husband on charges of unlawful possession of a hypodermic needle and a burglary detainer entered by Essex County.

Sometime in the late afternoon of the same day, Jane Doe and James Tarvis drove Tarvis's car to the Doe residence in the Borough of Runnemede ("Runnemede"). The car engine was left running, and the car apparently slipped into gear, rolling down the driveway into a neighbor's fence. The neighbors owning the fence are Michael DiAngelo and defendant Rita DiAngelo. Rita DiAngelo is an employee in the school district in Runnemede.

Two Runnemede police officers, Steven Van Camp and defendant Russell Smith, responded to the radio call about the incident. While they were at the scene, Detective Preen of the Barrington police arrived and, in a private conversation with Van Camp, revealed that Jane Doe's husband had been arrested earlier in the day and had told Barrington police officers that he had AIDS. Van Camp then told defendant Smith.

After Jane Doe and Tarvis left the immediate vicinity, defendant Smith told the DiAngelos that Jane Doe's husband had AIDS and that, to protect herself, Rita DiAngelo should wash with disinfectant. . . . Defendant Rita DiAngelo became upset upon hearing this information. Knowing that the four Doe children attended the Downing School in Runnemede, the school that her own daughter attended, DiAngelo contacted other parents with children in the school. She also contacted the media. The next day, eleven parents removed nineteen children from the Downing School due to a panic over the Doe children's attending the school. The media was present, and the story was covered in the local newspapers and on television. At least one of the reports mentioned the name of the Doe family. Plaintiffs allege that as a result of the disclosure, they have suffered harassment, discrimination, and humiliation. They allege they have been shunned by the community.

Plaintiffs brought this civil rights action against the police officer Smith and the municipalities of Barrington and Runnemede for violations of their federal constitutional rights pursuant to 42 U.S.C. § 1983. The federal constitutional right is their right to privacy under the fourteenth amendment. . . .

AIDS is a viral disease that weakens or destroys the body's immune system. The disease is caused by the presence of the Human Immunodeficiency Virus ("HIV"), which attacks the body's T-lymphocyte cells that are a critical part of the body's immune system. As a result, the body is unable to withstand infections it would normally suppress. These resulting infections, known as "opportunistic diseases," eventually cause permanent disability and death. . . .

HIV is transmitted through contact with contaminated blood, semen, or vaginal fluids. The virus is transmitted through activities such as sexual intercourse, anal sex, use of nonsterile hypodermic needles, and transfusions of contaminated blood or blood products. Additionally, women infected with HIV can transmit the virus to their children before or during birth. Although HIV has been detected in other bodily fluids such as saliva and urine, the virus is much less concentrated, and there are no known cases of transmission of the virus by such means. The Centers for Disease Control ("CDC") terms the risk of infection from such fluids as "extremely low or nonexistent."

In 1986, the Surgeon General announced that HIV is not transmitted through casual contact with an infected person, such as shaking hands, kissing, or contacting an object used by an infected person. . . .

This court finds that the Constitution protects plaintiffs from governmental disclosure of their husband's and father's infection with the AIDS virus. The United States Supreme Court has recognized that the fourteenth amendment protects two types of privacy interests. "One is the individual interest in avoiding disclosure of personal matters, and another is the interest in independence in making certain kinds of important decisions." *Whalen v. Roe*, 429 U.S. 589, 599-600 (1977). Disclosure of a family member's medical condition, especially exposure to or infection with the AIDS virus, is a disclosure of a "personal matter."

The Third Circuit recognizes a privacy right in medical records and medical information. *United States v. Westinghouse*, 638 F.2d 570 (3d Cir. 1980). . . .

Lower courts have held that, once the government has confidential information, it has the obligation to avoid disclosure of the information. In *Carter v. Broadlawns Medical Center*, the court held that a public hospital had violated plaintiffs' constitutional rights by giving chaplains open access to patient medical records without patient authorization. The court noted that, in permitting free access to medical records, the hospital did not properly respect a patient's confidentiality and privacy as recognized in *Whalen v. Roe*. . . . The case demonstrates that, not only is the government restricted from collecting personal medical information, it may be restricted from disclosing such private information it lawfully receives. . . .

The sensitive nature of medical information about AIDS makes a compelling argument for keeping this information confidential. Society's moral judgments about the high-risk activities associated with the disease, including sexual relations and drug use, make the information of the most personal kind. Also, the privacy interest in one's exposure to the AIDS virus is even greater than one's privacy interest in ordinary medical records because of the stigma that attaches with the disease.

The hysteria surrounding AIDS extends beyond those who have the disease. The stigma attaches not only to the AIDS victim, but to those in contact with AIDS patients. Revealing that one's family or household member has AIDS causes the entire family to be ostracized. The right to privacy in this information extends to members of the AIDS patient's immediate family. Those sharing a household with an infected person suffer from disclosure just as the victim does. Family members, therefore, have a substantial interest in keeping this information confidential. Disclosures about AIDS cause a violation of the family's privacy much greater than simply revealing any other aspect of their family medical history.

An individual's privacy interest in medical information and records is not absolute. The court must determine whether the societal interest in disclosure outweighs the privacy interest involved. To avoid a constitutional violation, the government must show a compelling state interest in breaching that privacy.

The government's interest in disclosure here does not outweigh the substantial privacy interest involved. The government has not shown a compelling state interest in breaching the Does' privacy. The government contends that Officer Smith advised the DiAngelos to wash with disinfectant because of his concern for the prevention and avoidance of AIDS, an incurable and contagious disease. While prevention of this deadly disease is clearly an appropriate state objective, this objective was not served by Smith's statement that the DiAngelos should wash with disinfectant. Disclosure of the Does' confidential information did not advance a compelling governmental interest in preventing the spread of the disease because there was no risk that Mr. or Mrs. DiAngelo might be exposed to the HIV virus through casual contact with Jane Doe. The state of medical knowledge at the time of this incident established that AIDS is not transmitted by casual contact. Smith's statement could not prevent the transmission of AIDS because there was no threat of transmission present.

This court concludes that the Does have a constitutional right of privacy in the information disclosed by Smith and the state had no compelling interest in revealing that information. As such, the disclosure violated the Does' constitutional rights. . . .

. . . [Defendant Smith] argues that plaintiffs have no standing to bring this action because Smith's statement violated only the privacy rights of Jane Doe's husband. . . .

Plaintiffs here do not assert the constitutional rights of Jane Doe's husband. Jane Doe sues as guardian for her minor children for the violation of their own rights to privacy. The children have standing to sue for the violation of their right to privacy from governmental disclosure of their father's infection with AIDS. Likewise, Jane Doe individually asserts a violation of her constitutional right to privacy. That the officer did not reveal information about the children's own medical condition is immaterial. A family member's diagnosis with AIDS is a personal matter, as defined in *Whalen v. Roe*, that falls within the protection of the Constitution.

This court rejects the standing argument because Smith's statement communicated private, confidential information about Jane Doe and her children. The stigma of AIDS extends to all family members, whether or not they actually have the disease. Smith's statement also implicitly suggested that Jane Doe herself might somehow transmit the disease to the DiAngelos. Jane Doe clearly has standing to assert a violation of her right to privacy. . . .

. . . [Next, the Defendant] asserts that, because Jane Doe's husband told police that he had AIDS, the husband "published" the information, giving up any right to privacy in the information. . . .

Clearly, an arrestee's disclosure to police that he or she has AIDS is preferable to nondisclosure. Police can take whatever precautions are necessary to prevent transmission of the disease. Police have more than "casual contact" with arrestee, increasing the likelihood that the disease can be transmitted. For example, by frisking an arrested person, police may come into contact with hypodermic needles. Thus, disclosure should be encouraged to protect police officers. Common sense demands that persons with AIDS be able to make such disclosures without fear that police will inform neighbors, employers, or the media. Smith's publication argument, therefore, is rejected as contrary to public policy. . . .

NOTES & QUESTIONS

1. ***Private Parties.*** Suppose only private parties had disclosed that Mr. Doe had AIDS. Would there be a cause of action?
2. ***Does It Matter Who Is Being Informed?*** Suppose Mrs. Doe didn't know that her husband had HIV. Would the police violate Mr. Doe's constitutional right to information privacy by telling her?
3. ***Public Health Concerns.*** What if the disease were highly contagious with casual contact? Does that matter for the application of the constitutional right to information privacy? The facts of this case occurred early on in the AIDS epidemic, when information about AIDS was just beginning to dispel some of the myths and hysteria surrounding AIDS. What effect should this have on the liability of the police?

DOE V. SOUTHEASTERN PENNSYLVANIA TRANSPORTATION AUTHORITY

72 F.3d 1133 (3d Cir. 1995)

ROSENN, J. This appeal requires that we probe the depth and breadth of an employee's conditional right to privacy in his prescription drug records. John Doe, an employee of the Southeastern Pennsylvania Transportation Authority (SEPTA), initiated this action under 42 U.S.C. § 1983 against his self-insured employer, alleging that the defendants violated his right to privacy. Plaintiff claims that, in monitoring the prescription drug program put in place by SEPTA for fraud, drug abuse and excessive costs, the Chief Administrative Officer, Judith Pierce, and the Director of Benefits, Jacob Aufschauer, learned that John Doe had contracted Acquired Immunodeficiency Syndrome (AIDS). This, he alleges, invaded his right to privacy.

A jury found for the plaintiff and awarded him $125,000 in compensatory damages for his emotional distress. . . .

We set forth the facts as the jury could have found them in support of its verdict. Accordingly, all evidence and inferences therefrom must be taken in the light most favorable to the verdict winner. In 1990, Judith Pierce became the Chief Administrative Officer for SEPTA. Her responsibilities included containing the costs of SEPTA's self-insured health program. In 1992, a bargaining agreement with Local Union 234 required SEPTA to provide, inter alia, prescription drugs for the employees. SEPTA entered into a contract with Rite-Aid Drug Store to be the sole provider for all of SEPTA's prescription drug programs. As part of this contract, Rite-Aid provided SEPTA with an estimate of the yearly costs of this program. If, at the end of the year, the actual cost to Rite-Aid amounted to over 115% of that estimate, SEPTA would have to pay substantial penalties; however, if the actual cost was 90% or less of that estimate, SEPTA would be entitled to rebates. Pierce was responsible for monitoring those costs.

John Doe is a SEPTA employee. At all times relevant to this appeal, Doe was HIV-positive, and had contracted AIDS by the time of trial. In 1991, Doe began to take Retrovir for his condition. Retrovir is a prescription drug used solely to treat HIV. Before filling his prescription, Doe asked Dr. Richard Press, the head of SEPTA's Medical Department and Doe's direct supervisor, if he or anyone else reviewed employee names in association with the drugs the employees were taking. Doe wished to keep his condition a secret from his co-workers. Dr. Press assured Doe that he had only been asked to review names on prescriptions in cases of suspected narcotics abuse and knew of no other review that included names. After receiving this information, Doe filled his prescription through the employer's health insurance. He continued to do so after SEPTA switched to Rite-Aid; he was never informed that this change might alter his confidentiality status.

In November of 1992, Pierce requested and received utilization reports from Rite-Aid. These reports were part of the contract between Rite-Aid and SEPTA. Pierce did not request the names of SEPTA employees in the reports, and Rite-Aid sent the reports in their standard format. . . . [One report] listed employees who were filling prescriptions at a cost of $100 or more per employee in the past month. Each line of the report included the name of an employee or dependent, a code to identify the prescribing doctor, the dispense date of the prescription, the name of the drug, the number of days supplied, and the total cost. Pierce called Aufschauer into her office, and the two of them reviewed the report. It was immediately apparent to Pierce that the reports would reveal employees' medications; however, she reviewed them in the format as submitted. . . .

Pierce stated that her purpose in reviewing the reports with Aufschauer was several-fold. First, she wanted to look for signs of fraud and drug abuse. . . . Second, Pierce wanted to determine if Rite-Aid was fulfilling its promise to use generic rather than brand name drugs whenever possible. Third, although they were both covered in the Rite-Aid contract, Pierce wanted to determine the cost to SEPTA of fertility drugs and medications to help employees stop smoking, such as nicotine patches. Finally, Pierce wanted to determine whether the reports were in a summary form and whether they would permit an audit. Her review, however, focused almost entirely on the current report, which included employees' names. . . .

Pierce and Aufschauer scanned the reports. When they came across a drug name neither one recognized, they would look it up in a Physician's Desk Reference (PDR) that Pierce had. Pierce then called Dr. Louis Van de Beek, a SEPTA staff physician, and inquired about the drugs not listed in the PDR. She asked the doctor for what Retrovir was used. When Dr. Van de Beek told her it was used in the treatment of AIDS, she inquired whether there was any other use for it. He told her no. She then asked about the three other medications that Doe was taking, and was informed that they were all AIDS medications as well. Pierce discreetly never mentioned Doe by name; however, Dr. Van de Beek was aware of Doe's condition and Doe's medications because Doe himself had disclosed this information to him. Therefore, Dr. Van de Beek deduced that Pierce was asking about Doe. He told her that if she were trying to diagnose employees' conditions through prescriptions, he felt this was improper and possibly illegal. Pierce immediately ended the conversation and told him not to speak of the conversation to anyone.

Pierce then took the report to Dr. Press. She asked him if he would be able to perform an audit using the information in the report. Press noted that Pierce had highlighted certain lines on the report, including employees' names and the drugs that each of those highlighted employees were taking. Press testified that the drugs highlighted were all HIV or AIDS-related. Pierce asked Press if he knew whether any of the people whose names were highlighted were HIV-positive. Press said that he was aware of Doe's condition. He then told Pierce that he was uncomfortable with the presence of the names on the report. . . .

Dr. Van de Beek informed Doe of Pierce's questions. He told Doe that Pierce had likely found out that Doe was HIV-positive. Doe claims he became upset at this news. He avers that he became more upset upon discovering from Dr. Press that Pierce had his name highlighted on a list because he didn't know who had access to or had seen this "AIDS list" and only a few SEPTA employees knew of his HIV-status. He had told Press and Van de Beek, as well as his acting supervisor and the administrative assistant of his department that he had AIDS. . . .

After these incidents, Doe remained at SEPTA in his current position. He makes no claim of personal discrimination or of any economic deprivation. He later received a salary upgrade and promotion. However, he testified that he felt as though he were being treated differently. A proposal he had made for an in house employee assistance program met with scant interest; he felt that this was because of his HIV condition. In addition, an administrator who reported to Pierce did not call on Doe to assist in the same way that he had called on Doe earlier. Doe testified that he felt as though there was less social chitchat, co-workers ate less of the baked goods he brought to the office to share, and that his work space seemed more lonely than before. He also became fearful of Pierce, who never told Doe that she knew of his illness. Doe alleges that he became depressed and requested a prescription for Zoloft, an antidepressant, from his physician. Later, another antidepressant called Elavil was added to the medications Doe was taking. . . .

As a preliminary matter, this court must decide if a person's medical prescription record is within the ambit of information protected by the Constitution. If there is no right to privacy, our inquiry stops. A § 1983 action cannot be maintained unless the underlying act violates a plaintiff's Constitutional rights. . . .

. . . The Supreme Court, in *Whalen v. Roe*, noted that the right to privacy encompasses two separate spheres. One of these is an individual's interest in independence in making certain decisions. The other is an interest in avoiding disclosure of personal information. Medical records fall within the second category. Therefore, the Court held that individuals do have a limited right to privacy in their medical records. . . .

An individual using prescription drugs has a right to expect that such information will customarily remain private. The district court, therefore, committed no error in its holding that there is a constitutional right to privacy in one's prescription records. . . .

As with many individual rights, the right of privacy in one's prescription drug records must be balanced against important competing interests.

Before we can perform this balancing test, we must first assess whether, and to what extent, Pierce disclosed Doe's prescription drug information. . . .

Both Pierce and Aufschauer learned of Doe's illness through the Rite-Aid report. Pierce's initial discovery of the names on the report was inadvertent. . . . However, Pierce then spent some time and effort researching the report with the names on it. She highlighted, for her research purposes, those names on the report whose medications she was unfamiliar with and which were expensive, including Doe's, and called two SEPTA staff physicians to ask about medications she did not recognize. It was through this inquiry that Pierce learned about Doe's condition. She did not know the uses of Retrovir before she did this research.

Aufschauer learned of Doe's condition through his work as Director of Benefits and Pierce's subordinate. Pierce disclosed the information to him in the course of their work. SEPTA argues that this disclosure was necessary, as Aufschauer also had reasons for needing this information. Aufschauer's legitimate need for this information may affect whether the disclosure is an actionable one. It does not alter the existence of disclosure.

Nor can Pierce and Aufschauer be considered as a single unit for the purpose of determining disclosure. A disclosure occurs in the workplace each time private information is communicated to a new person, regardless of the relationship between the co-workers sharing that information. . . . Therefore, we hold that each person who learned of Doe's condition constitutes a separate disclosure for the purposes of Doe's invasion of privacy action.

To hold differently would lead us to a decision that Doe had waived his right to privacy by voluntarily disclosing his medical condition to co-workers at SEPTA. We are not faced with a situation where persons to whom Doe disclosed this information told others. Rather, Pierce and Aufschauer learned his condition completely independently of Doe's disclosures. His decision to give private information to some co-workers does not give carte blanche to other co-workers to invade his privacy.

However, we are not persuaded that the impingement on Doe's privacy by the disclosure to SEPTA's Chief Medical Officer, Dr. Press, amounts to a constitutional violation. Doe himself had already voluntarily informed Dr. Press of his condition. Dr. Press did not learn any new information from Pierce's actions. . . . Van de Beek, like Dr. Press, had already heard of Doe's condition from Doe himself. . . . [These disclosures] did not "amount to an impermissible invasion of privacy," because John Doe had already provided [the doctors] with this information. . . .

As we noted earlier, an individual's privacy interest in his or her prescription records is not an absolute right against disclosure. This interest must be weighed against the interests of the employer in obtaining the information. We apply an intermediate standard of review in making this determination. . . . The intrusion upon Doe's privacy was minimal at worst.

This court has previously enumerated the factors to be weighed in determining whether a given disclosure constitutes an actionable invasion of privacy in *United States v. Westinghouse Electric Corp.*, 638 F.2d 570 (3d Cir. 1980). . . . *Westinghouse* mandates a consideration of seven different factors. They are: (1) the type of record requested; (2) the information it does or might contain; (3) the potential for harm in any subsequent nonconsensual disclosure; (4) the injury from disclosure to the relationship in which the record was generated; (5) the adequacy of safeguards to prevent unauthorized disclosure; (6) the degree of need for access; and (7) whether there is an express statutory mandate, articulated public policy, or other recognizable public interest favoring access. Although some of these factors may be in Doe's favor, overall, we believe the balance weighs on the side of permitting the disclosures present here. There is a strong public interest of the Transportation Authority, and the many thousands of people it serves, in containing its costs and expenses by permitting this sort of research by authorized personnel. This interest outweighs the minimal intrusion, particularly given the lack of any economic loss, discrimination, or harassment actually suffered by plaintiff. . . .

. . . In *Doe v. Borough of Barrington*, a borough police officer, without justification, told the neighbors of a man suffering from AIDS that the entire family had AIDS. The neighbors reacted by organizing a protest, and trying to prevent the man's children from attending public school. In that case, the court quite rightly held such conduct violated the plaintiffs' privacy rights, and there was no competing interest to justify the disclosure.

By contrast, SEPTA had legitimate reasons for obtaining the prescription information from Rite-Aid. Pierce had requested the information in Rite-Aid's standard format; she did not request the names of any employees. She did not disclose the information relating to Doe except to Aufschauer, in connection with their review, and to Dr. Press, for purposes of an audit. Dr. Press, the Chief Medical Officer, already knew of Doe's condition through Doe's voluntary disclosure. Moreover, Pierce destroyed the first report. Under these circumstances, we cannot conclude that Westinghouse factor (3) would impose liability on SEPTA. . . .

Factors six and seven strongly favor the defendants. Pierce had a genuine, legitimate and compelling need for the document she requested. Aufschauer, as Director of Benefits, also had a need for the document. Each had a responsibility and obligation to keep insurance costs down and to detect fraudulent and abusive behavior. The report was intended for that purpose. Employers have a legitimate need for monitoring the costs and uses of their employee benefit programs, especially employers who have fiscal responsibilities, as does SEPTA, to the public. . . .

Employers also have a right to ensure that their health plan is only being used by those who are authorized to be covered. Finally, the employers have a right to contain costs by requiring that employees use generic drugs rather than brand name when an adequate substitute exists. To accomplish these goals, employers must have access to reports from their prescription suppliers, and they must inspect and audit those reports. That is precisely what Pierce and Aufschauer were engaged in, and this was a legitimate function of their positions. They had a legitimate need for access to information from the drug supplier, and they carefully controlled its use. . . .

We hold that a self-insured employer's need for access to employee prescription records under its health insurance plan, when the information disclosed is only for the purpose of monitoring the plans by those with a need to know, outweighs an employee's interest in keeping his prescription drug purchases confidential. Such minimal intrusion, although an impingement on privacy, is insufficient to constitute a constitutional violation. . . .

NOTES & QUESTIONS

1. *Private vs. Public Sector Employers.* What if SEPTA were a private sector employer? Would Doe have a good case under the public disclosure of private facts tort?
2. *Medical Privacy in the Workplace.* Should employers be permitted to ask for or receive health information from their employees? Does it matter whether the employer is providing health insurance? Should parents be permitted to ask their babysitter for health information (such as mental health, HIV, and other diseases) as part of the hiring decision?
3. *Conceptualizing Doe's Privacy Harm.* Daniel Solove argues that the court in *Doe v. SEPTA* misconceptualized Doe's claim that his privacy was invaded:

   > [The court] missed the nature of Doe's complaint. Regardless of whether he was imagining how his co-workers were treating him, he was indeed suffering a real palpable fear. His real injury was the powerlessness of having no idea who else knew he had HIV, what his employer thought of him, or how the information could be used against him. This feeling of unease changed the way he perceived everything at his place of employment. The privacy problem was not merely the fact that Pierce divulged his secret or that Doe himself had lost control over his information, but rather that the information appeared to be entirely out of anyone's control.[66]

   Is this a type of injury that the law should recognize? Had the court recognized the injury in this way, how would its analysis have been different?

---

[66] Daniel J. Solove, *Privacy and Power: Computer Databases and Metaphors for Information Privacy*, 53 Stan. L. Rev. 1393, 1438-39 (2001).

4. *The Storm Lake Case.* In 2002, in Storm Lake, Iowa, a baby's mangled body was found in a trash bin. Law enforcement officials sought and obtained a court order to obtain all of the pregnancy records at medical facilities in the area. In particular, the officials were seeking the names and addresses of women who had positive pregnancy tests. Planned Parenthood of Greater Iowa challenged the order. When the case made it up to the Iowa Supreme Court, the law enforcement officials stated that they would no longer seek the records, and the case was dismissed. Suppose, however, that the officials did not drop their request. Based on the privacy laws you learned thus far, how would you resolve this case?[67]

5. *Subpoenas for Abortion Records.* In *Alpha Medical Clinic v. Anderson,* 128 P.3d 364 (Kan. 2006), Kansas Attorney General Phill Kline subpoenaed the records of 90 females who received abortions at two clinics. Kline sought the subpoenas to investigate whether there were violations of Kansas law. In particular, he sought information about whether abortions were being performed after 22 weeks' gestational age, which K.S.A. § 65-6703 prohibits except to protect the physical health of the woman. Kline also sought information about whether Kansas child abuse statutes were violated. The trial court, Judge Anderson, ordered that the records be produced to the court for an *in camera* review. The clinics brought an action for mandamus. The Supreme Court of Kansas concluded that the clinics had "third-party standing to assert their patients' information privacy rights." The court analyzed whether Kline's subpoenas infringed upon the patients' constitutional right to information privacy. The court concluded:

> The type of information sought by the State here could hardly be more sensitive, or the potential harm to patient privacy posed by disclosure more substantial. Judge Anderson's order does not do all it can to narrow the information gathered or to safeguard that information from unauthorized disclosure once it is in the district court's hands. Although the criminal inquisition statutes do not speak to the need for such narrowing and safeguards, the constitutional dimensions of this case compel them. . . .
>
> Only if Judge Anderson is satisfied that the attorney general is on firm legal ground should he permit the inquisition to continue and some version of the subpoenas to remain in effect. Then he also must enter a protective order that sets forth at least the following safeguards: (1) Petitioners' counsel must redact patient-identifying information from the files before they are delivered to the judge under seal; (2) the documents should be reviewed initially in camera by a lawyer and a physician or physicians appointed by the court, who can then advise the court if further redactions should be made to eliminate information unrelated to the legitimate purposes of the inquisition.

---

[67] For more information about the case, see Poornima L. Ravishankar, Comment, *Planned Parenthood Is Not a Bank: Closing the Clinic Doors to the Fourth Amendment Third Party Doctrine,* 34 Seton Hall L. Rev. 1093 (2004).

3. THE FOURTH AMENDMENT

FERGUSON V. CITY OF CHARLESTON

532 U.S. 67 (2001)

[A Charleston public hospital operated by the Medical University of South Carolina (MUSC) developed a policy of testing pregnant patients suspected of drug use. The drug testing was done by examining urine samples. Patients with positive results were provided with referrals for education and treatment and were sometimes arrested and prosecuted for drug offenses or child neglect. In rejecting a Fourth Amendment challenge to the testing, the Fourth Circuit concluded that the testing was reasonable under the "special needs" doctrine. Under this doctrine, a search without a warrant or probable cause can be reasonable under the Fourth Amendment if special needs make the warrant or probable cause requirements impractical.]

STEVENS, J. . . . Because MUSC is a state hospital, the members of its staff are government actors, subject to the strictures of the Fourth Amendment. Moreover, the urine tests conducted by those staff members were indisputably searches within the meaning of the Fourth Amendment. Neither the District Court nor the Court of Appeals concluded that any of the nine criteria used to identify the women to be searched provided either probable cause to believe that they were using cocaine, or even the basis for a reasonable suspicion of such use. Rather, the District Court and the Court of Appeals viewed the case as one involving MUSC's right to conduct searches without warrants or probable cause. Furthermore, given the posture in which the case comes to us, we must assume for purposes of our decision that the tests were performed without the informed consent of the patients.

Because the hospital seeks to justify its authority to conduct drug tests and to turn the results over to law enforcement agents without the knowledge or consent of the patients, this case differs from the four previous cases in which we have considered whether comparable drug tests "fit within the closely guarded category of constitutionally permissible suspicionless searches." In three of those cases, we sustained drug tests for railway employees involved in train accidents, *Skinner v. Railway Labor Executives' Assn.*, 489 U.S. 602 (1989), for United States Customs Service employees seeking promotion to certain sensitive positions, *Treasury Employees v. Von Raab*, 489 U.S. 656 (1989), and for high school students participating in interscholastic sports, *Vernonia School Dist. v. Acton*, 515 U.S. 646 (1995). In the fourth case, we struck down such testing for candidates for designated state offices as unreasonable. *Chandler v. Miller*, 520 U.S. 305, 513 (1997).

In each of those cases, we employed a balancing test that weighed the intrusion on the individual's interest in privacy against the "special needs" that supported the program. As an initial matter, we note that the invasion of privacy in this case is far more substantial than in those cases. In the previous four cases, there was no misunderstanding about the purpose of the test or the potential use of the test results, and there were protections against the dissemination of the results to third parties. The use of an adverse test result to disqualify one from eligibility for a particular benefit, such as a promotion or an opportunity to participate in an extracurricular activity, involves a less serious intrusion on privacy than the unauthorized dissemination of such results to third parties. The reasonable expectation of privacy enjoyed by the typical patient undergoing diagnostic tests in a hospital is that the results of those tests will not be shared with nonmedical personnel without her consent. . . .

The critical difference between those four drug-testing cases and this one, however, lies in the nature of the "special need" asserted as justification for the warrantless searches. In each of those earlier cases, the "special need" that was advanced as a justification for the absence of a warrant or individualized suspicion was one divorced from the State's general interest in law enforcement. . . . In this case, however, the central and indispensable feature of the policy from its inception was the use of law enforcement to coerce the patients into substance abuse treatment. This fact distinguishes this case from circumstances in which physicians or psychologists, in the course of ordinary medical procedures aimed at helping the patient herself, come across information that under rules of law or ethics is subject to reporting requirements, which no one has challenged here.

Respondents argue in essence that their ultimate purpose — namely, protecting the health of both mother and child — is a beneficent one. . . . In this case, a review of the M-7 policy plainly reveals that the purpose actually served by the MUSC searches "is ultimately indistinguishable from the general interest in crime control." . . .

. . . [T]hroughout the development and application of the policy, the Charleston prosecutors and police were extensively involved in the day-to-day administration of the policy. . . .

While the ultimate goal of the program may well have been to get the women in question into substance abuse treatment and off of drugs, the immediate objective of the searches was to generate evidence *for law enforcement purposes* in order to reach that goal. . . . Given the primary purpose of the Charleston program, which was to use the threat of arrest and prosecution in order to force women into treatment, and given the extensive involvement of law enforcement officials at every stage of the policy, this case simply does not fit within the closely guarded category of "special needs.". . .

As respondents have repeatedly insisted, their motive was benign rather than punitive. Such a motive, however, cannot justify a departure from Fourth Amendment protections, given the pervasive involvement of law enforcement with the development and application of the MUSC policy. . . . The Fourth Amendment's general prohibition against nonconsensual, warrantless, and suspicionless searches necessarily applies to such a policy. . . .

NOTES & QUESTIONS

1. *Mandatory AIDS Testing of Firefighters and Paramedics.* In contrast to *Ferguson*, consider *Anonymous Fireman v. City of Willoughby*, 779 F. Supp. 402 (N.D. Ohio 1991). In *Anonymous Fireman*, firefighters and paramedics challenged a city's mandatory annual testing for the AIDS virus as part of their annual physical examination. They claimed that the testing violated their Fourth Amendment rights. The court found that the "protection of the public from the

contraction and transmission of AIDS by firefighters and paramedics is a compelling governmental interest." It also declared:

> The medical evidence demonstrates that the risk of HIV transmission in the performance of the duties of firefighter paramedic is high. . . .
>
> State and local authorities have compelling interests in ensuring that its firefighters and paramedics are performing their duties free of having AIDS. Reasonable and particularized suspicion is not necessary as a precondition to mandatory AIDS testing of firefighters and paramedics.

Does *Ferguson* affect the reasoning of this case?

2. ***Medical Testing of Accused Sex Offenders.*** In *In re J.G.,* 701 A.2d 1260 (N.J. 1997), New Jersey enacted statutes providing for AIDS testing at the request of the victim of assailants who were charged with sexual assault. Three juveniles charged with sexual assault violations and required to submit to AIDS testing challenged the statutes on Fourth Amendment grounds. Experts testifying on behalf of the juveniles stated that the harms of testing would be outweighed by the benefits:

> In the opinion of Dr. James Oleske, testing sexual assailants for HIV would provide no medical benefit in the diagnosis or treatment of victims because the test would not reveal whether transmission, which does not occur in all cases, had in fact occurred, and because testing the assailant might produce a false-negative result due to the three- to six-month latency period. . . .
>
> The experts offered their opinions about whether there was any "psycho-social benefit" to the victim in knowing the HIV status of the assailant. In Dr. Oleske's view, victims may suffer actual harm from knowing their assailants' status. They may wrongly rely on a false-negative result and discontinue medical care and testing, or they may react to a positive result without considering their actual risk of infection or their own status. He acknowledged, however, that for the victim and the victim's family "[t]he question of peace of mind, . . . in lay terms, may be real." . . .

The court, however, concluded that on balance, the alleged offenders' Fourth Amendment rights were outweighed by the benefits of the testing:

> . . . A court must balance the encroachment on an individual's Fourth Amendment interests against the advancement of legitimate state goals. When a search is conducted in furtherance of a criminal investigation, the balance is most often tipped "in favor of the procedures described by the Warrant Clause of the Fourth Amendment," that is, toward a finding that the search "is not reasonable unless it is accomplished pursuant to a judicial warrant issued upon probable cause."
>
> An exception to the Warrant Clause may apply "when 'special needs, beyond the normal need for law enforcement, make the warrant and probable-cause requirement impracticable.' " . . .
>
> Serological testing of sex offenders . . . is not intended to facilitate the criminal prosecution of those offenders. HIV test results are required to be kept confidential (with certain limited exceptions). Notably, the statute does not authorize disclosure to the prosecutor's office. The State has said that the tests are not intended to be used to gain evidence for criminal prosecutions and do not place offenders at risk of a new conviction or longer sentence. We agree,

and hold that the results of HIV tests . . . may not be used against an accused sex offender in a criminal prosecution.

Moreover, both the warrant and individualized suspicion requirements are impractical in this context. . . . "HIV infected sexual offenders often have no outward manifestations of infection," which means that probable cause or individualized suspicion that an assailant is infected with the AIDS virus could not be found without testing. Requiring probable cause or individualized suspicion before testing could be conducted would create the proverbial Catch-22 and would "frustrate the governmental purpose behind the search." . . .

Unquestionably, the state has a compelling interest in making information available when it directly affects the physical and mental well-being of survivors of sexual assault. . . .

. . . Survivors of sexual assault, and those close to them, face significant psychological as well as physical trauma. [The statutes] respond to these significant concerns by requiring the testing of offenders at the victim's request, and by establishing counseling, testing, and other support services for victims. . . .

The dissemination of test results . . . is carefully restricted. It is, therefore, reasonable to require assailants to submit to this intrusion upon their privacy. . . .

. . . [However, only if] . . . a demonstration of a risk that the AIDS virus may have been transmitted from the offender to the victim . . . is made will the interests of the state in enacting the testing statutes outweigh the privacy interests of the offender. . . .

C. GENETIC INFORMATION

1. GENETIC PRIVACY

Deoxyribonucleic acid, otherwise known as DNA, is present in all cellular organisms and contains the information an organism needs to live and to transfer genetic material. The DNA molecule's structure consists of two strands coiled around one another forming a double helix. Each strand of DNA is comprised of different sequences of four chemical compounds. The chemical compounds are adenine, guanine, thymine, and cytosine, denoted with A, G, T, and C, respectively. A "nucleotide" is a subunit of a DNA strand that contains one of these four chemical compounds. Nucleotides, each containing A, G, T, or C, are arranged in sequences along each strand of DNA. The nucleotides in one strand of DNA are paired with the nucleotides in the other DNA strand. Each pair of nucleotides is known as a base pair. The base pairs are joined to each other by chemical bonds called "hydrogen bonds." There are about 3 billion base pairs in the human genome.

DNA contains the recipe for the creation of proteins. A protein consists of smaller molecules known as amino acids. The structure of each protein is determined by the sequence of its amino acids. The sequence of base pairs of nucleotides in DNA determines the sequence of amino acids.

A "gene" is a sequence of nucleotides that codes for the production of a particular protein. Genes are responsible for transmitting inherited traits. Genes are located inside chromosomes, which are contained in the nucleus of each cell.[68] Humans have 23 pairs of chromosomes. It had been previously estimated that there are about 100,000 genes in the 23 chromosomes, but recent research suggests that the number is between 20,000 and 25,000.

Every cell in the human body, which is comprised of about 100 trillion cells, contains DNA (except red blood cells). DNA can be isolated from white blood cells, sperm cells, cells in saliva, nasal secretions, sweat, and the cells surrounding the roots of hair.

An individual's complete genetic makeup is known as a "genome." With the exception of identical twins, no two humans have an identical genome. However, only a small portion of DNA differs among individuals. About 99 percent of the 3 billion base pairs of nucleotides are the same in all humans. The 1 percent that is different enables DNA forensic analysis.

The Human Genome Project, the first draft of which was completed in 2000, has mapped out all of the genes in the human chromosomes. With further study, the Human Genome Project will enable the identification of the particular genes that cause certain diseases.

Along with these developments comes a new threat to privacy. Once genes and gene mutations are better understood, and are linked to particular diseases and traits, one's genetic information can reveal one's medical history and even the future of one's health. Further, one's genetic information can reveal information about one's family members. As Anita Allen explains:

> According to legal doctrine, to appropriate a person's name or likeness is a way of invading his or her privacy. Privacy, it appears, has something to do with controlling one's identity. . . .
>
> The question whether our genes comprise our identities is a difficult one. Proprietary genetic privacy is suggested by the idea that the human DNA is a repository of valuable human personality. Proprietary genetic privacy is further suggested by the related notion that human DNA is owned by the persons from whom it is taken, as a species of private property.
>
> If DNA is the human essence — that is, the thing that makes individuals special and perhaps unique — it arguably ought to belong to the individual from whom it was ultimately derived. If DNA "belongs" to individual sources, it might belong to them exclusively and inalienably. Or DNA could qualify as alienable property that others can acquire both lawfully through voluntary private transactions and wrongfully through nonconsensual appropriation. . . .[69]

---

[68] Some cells, such as red blood cells, do not contain a nucleus and do not have nuclear DNA (but they may have mitochondrial DNA).

[69] Anita L. Allen, Genetic *Privacy: Emerging Concepts and Values, in Genetic Secrets: Protecting Privacy and Confidentiality in the Genetic Era* (Mark A. Rothstein ed., 1997).

2. PROPERTY RIGHTS IN BODY PARTS AND DNA

MOORE V. REGENTS OF THE UNIVERSITY OF CALIFORNIA
793 P.2d 479 (Cal. 1990)

PANELLI, J. . . . The plaintiff is John Moore (Moore), who underwent treatment for hairy-cell leukemia at the Medical Center of the University of California at Los Angeles (UCLA Medical Center). The five defendants are: (1) Dr. David W. Golde (Golde), a physician who attended Moore at UCLA Medical Center; (2) the Regents of the University of California (Regents), who own and operate the university; (3) Shirley G. Quan, a researcher employed by the Regents; (4) Genetics Institute, Inc. (Genetics Institute); and (5) Sandoz Pharmaceuticals Corporation and related entities (collectively Sandoz).

Moore first visited UCLA Medical Center on October 5, 1976, shortly after he learned that he had hairy-cell leukemia. After hospitalizing Moore and "withdr[awing] extensive amounts of blood, bone marrow aspirate, and other bodily substances," Golde confirmed that diagnosis. At this time all defendants, including Golde, were aware that "certain blood products and blood components were of great value in a number of commercial and scientific efforts" and that access to a patient whose blood contained these substances would provide "competitive, commercial, and scientific advantages."

On October 8, 1976, Golde recommended that Moore's spleen be removed. Golde informed Moore "that he had reason to fear for his life, and that the proposed splenectomy operation . . . was necessary to slow down the progress of his disease." Based upon Golde's representations, Moore signed a written consent form authorizing the splenectomy.

Before the operation, Golde and Quan "formed the intent and made arrangements to obtain portions of [Moore's] spleen following its removal" and to take them to a separate research unit. Golde gave written instructions to this effect on October 18 and 19, 1976. These research activities "were not intended to have . . . any relation to [Moore's] medical . . . care." However, neither Golde nor Quan informed Moore of their plans to conduct this research or requested his permission. Surgeons at UCLA Medical Center, whom the complaint does not name as defendants, removed Moore's spleen on October 20, 1976.

Moore returned to the UCLA Medical Center several times between November 1976 and September 1983. He did so at Golde's direction and based upon representations "that such visits were necessary and required for his health and well-being, and based upon the trust inherent in and by virtue of the physician-patient relationship. . . ." On each of these visits Golde withdrew additional samples of "blood, blood serum, skin, bone marrow aspirate, and sperm." On each occasion Moore traveled to the UCLA Medical Center from his home in Seattle because he had been told that the procedures were to be performed only there and only under Golde's direction.

"In fact, [however,] throughout the period of time that [Moore] was under [Golde's] care and treatment, . . . the defendants were actively involved in a number of activities which they concealed from [Moore]. . . ." Specifically, defendants were conducting research on Moore's cells and planned to "benefit financially and competitively . . . [by exploiting the cells] and [their] exclusive access to [the cells] by virtue of [Golde's] on-going physician-patient relationship. . . ."

Sometime before August 1979, Golde established a cell line from Moore's T-lymphocytes.[70] [In 1984, the Regents had the cell line patented. The potential market value for products derived from the cell line was estimated to be in the billions of dollars.] . . .

Moore attempted to state 13 causes of action, [which included among them a cause of action for conversion, for breach of fiduciary duty, and for lack of informed consent]. . . .

A. *Breach of Fiduciary Duty and Lack of Informed Consent.* Moore repeatedly alleges that Golde failed to disclose the extent of his research and economic interests in Moore's cells before obtaining consent to the medical procedures by which the cells were extracted. These allegations, in our view, state a cause of action against Golde for invading a legally protected interest of his patient. This cause of action can properly be characterized either as the breach of a fiduciary duty to disclose facts material to the patient's consent or, alternatively, as the performance of medical procedures without first having obtained the patient's informed consent.

Our analysis begins with three well-established principles. First, "a person of adult years and in sound mind has the right, in the exercise of control over his own body, to determine whether or not to submit to lawful medical treatment." Second, "the patient's consent to treatment, to be effective, must be an informed consent." Third, in soliciting the patient's consent, a physician has a fiduciary duty to disclose all information material to the patient's decision.

These principles lead to the following conclusions: (1) a physician must disclose personal interests unrelated to the patient's health, whether research or economic, that may affect the physician's professional judgment; and (2) a physician's failure to disclose such interests may give rise to a cause of action for performing medical procedures without informed consent or breach of fiduciary duty.

To be sure, questions about the validity of a patient's consent to a procedure typically arise when the patient alleges that the physician failed to disclose medical risks, as in malpractice cases, and not when the patient alleges that the physician had a personal interest, as in this case. The concept of informed consent, however, is broad enough to encompass the latter. "The scope of the physician's communication to the patient . . . must be measured by the patient's need, and that need is whatever information is material to the decision."

Indeed, the law already recognizes that a reasonable patient would want to know whether a physician has an economic interest that might affect the

---

[70] A T-lymphocyte is a type of white blood cell. T-lymphocytes produce lymphokines, or proteins that regulate the immune system. Some lymphokines have potential therapeutic value. If the genetic material responsible for producing a particular lymphokine can be identified, it can sometimes be used to manufacture large quantities of the lymphokine through the techniques of recombinant DNA. . . . While the genetic code for lymphokines does not vary from individual to individual, it can nevertheless be quite difficult to locate the gene responsible for a particular lymphokine. Because T-lymphocytes produce many different lymphokines, the relevant gene is often like a needle in a haystack. Moore's T-lymphocytes were interesting to the defendants because they overproduced certain lymphokines, thus making the corresponding genetic material easier to identify.

physician's professional judgment. As the Court of Appeal has said, "[c]ertainly a sick patient deserves to be free of any reasonable suspicion that his doctor's judgment is influenced by a profit motive." . . .

A physician who adds his own research interests to this balance may be tempted to order a scientifically useful procedure or test that offers marginal, or no, benefits to the patient. The possibility that an interest extraneous to the patient's health has affected the physician's judgment is something that a reasonable patient would want to know in deciding whether to consent to a proposed course of treatment. It is material to the patient's decision and, thus, a prerequisite to informed consent. . . .

B. *Conversion.* Moore also attempts to characterize the invasion of his rights as a conversion — a tort that protects against interference with possessory and ownership interests in personal property. He theorizes that he continued to own his cells following their removal from his body, at least for the purpose of directing their use, and that he never consented to their use in potentially lucrative medical research. Thus, to complete Moore's argument, defendants' unauthorized use of his cells constitutes a conversion. As a result of the alleged conversion, Moore claims a proprietary interest in each of the products that any of the defendants might ever create from his cells or the patented cell line. . . .

1. *Moore's Claim Under Existing Law.* "To establish a conversion, plaintiff must establish an actual interference with his ownership or right of possession. . . . Where plaintiff neither has title to the property alleged to have been converted, nor possession thereof, he cannot maintain an action for conversion."

Since Moore clearly did not expect to retain possession of his cells following their removal, to sue for their conversion he must have retained an ownership interest in them. But there are several reasons to doubt that he did retain any such interest. First, no reported judicial decision supports Moore's claim, either directly or by close analogy. Second, California statutory law drastically limits any continuing interest of a patient in excised cells. Third, the subject matters of the Regents' patent — the patented cell line and the products derived from it — cannot be Moore's property. . . .

Lacking direct authority for importing the law of conversion into this context, Moore relies, as did the Court of Appeal, primarily on decisions addressing privacy rights. One line of cases involves unwanted publicity. These opinions hold that every person has a proprietary interest in his own likeness and that unauthorized, business use of a likeness is redressible as a tort. But in neither opinion did the authoring court expressly base its holding on property law. Each court stated, following Prosser, that it was "pointless" to debate the proper characterization of the proprietary interest in a likeness. For purposes of determining whether the tort of conversion lies, however, the characterization of the right in question is far from pointless. Only property can be converted.

Not only are the wrongful-publicity cases irrelevant to the issue of conversion, but the analogy to them seriously misconceives the nature of the genetic materials and research involved in this case. Moore, adopting the analogy originally advanced by the Court of Appeal, argues that "[i]f the courts have found a sufficient proprietary interest in one's persona, how could one not have a right in one's own genetic material, something far more profoundly the essence of one's human uniqueness than a name or a face?" However, as the defendants' patent makes clear — and the complaint, too, if read with an understanding of the scientific terms which it has borrowed from the patent — the goal and result of defendants' efforts has been to manufacture lymphokines. Lymphokines, unlike a name or a face, have the same molecular structure in every human being and the same, important functions in every human being's immune system. Moreover, the particular genetic material which is responsible for the natural production of lymphokines, and which defendants use to manufacture lymphokines in the laboratory, is also the same in every person; it is no more unique to Moore than the number of vertebrae in the spine or the chemical formula of hemoglobin.[71]

Another privacy case offered by analogy to support Moore's claim establishes only that patients have a right to refuse medical treatment. In this context the court in *Bouvia* wrote that " '[e]very human being of adult years and sound mind has a right to determine what shall be done with his own body. . . .' " Relying on this language to support the proposition that a patient has a continuing right to control the use of excised cells, the Court of Appeal in this case concluded that "[a] patient must have the ultimate power to control what becomes of his or her tissues. To hold otherwise would open the door to a massive invasion of human privacy and dignity in the name of medical progress." Yet one may earnestly wish to protect privacy and dignity without accepting the extremely problematic conclusion that interference with those interests amounts to a conversion of personal property. Nor is it necessary to force the round pegs of "privacy" and "dignity" into the square hole of "property" in order to protect the patient, since the fiduciary-duty and informed-consent theories protect these interests directly by requiring full disclosure.

The next consideration that makes Moore's claim of ownership problematic is California statutory law, which drastically limits a patient's control over excised cells. Pursuant to Health and Safety Code section 7054.4, "[n]otwithstanding any other provision of law, recognizable anatomical parts, human tissues, anatomical human remains, or infectious waste following conclusion of scientific use shall be disposed of by interment, incineration, or any other method determined by the state department [of health services] to protect the public health and safety." Clearly the Legislature did not specifically intend this statute to resolve the question of whether a patient is entitled to compensation for the nonconsensual use of excised cells. A primary object of the statute is to ensure the safe handling of potentially hazardous biological waste materials. Yet one cannot escape the conclusion that the statute's practical effect is to limit, drastically, a patient's control over excised cells. By restricting how excised cells may be used and requiring their eventual destruction, the statute eliminates so many of the rights ordinarily attached to

---

[71] By definition, a gene responsible for producing a protein found in more than one individual will be the same in each. It is precisely because everyone needs the same basic proteins that proteins produced by one person's cells may have therapeutic value for another person. (See generally OTA Rep., supra, at pp. 38-40.) Thus, the proteins that defendants hope to manufacture — lymphokines such as interferon — are in no way a "likeness" of Moore. Because all normal persons possess the genes responsible for production of lymphokines, it is sometimes possible to make normal cells into overproducers. According to a research paper to which defendants contributed, Moore's cells overproduced lymphokines because they were infected by a virus, HTLV-II (human T-cell leukemia virus type II). The same virus has been shown to transform normal T-lymphocytes into overproducers like Moore's.

property that one cannot simply assume that what is left amounts to "property" or "ownership" for purposes of conversion law. . . .

Finally, the subject matter of the Regents' patent—the patented cell line and the products derived from it—cannot be Moore's property. This is because the patented cell line is both factually and legally distinct from the cells taken from Moore's body. Federal law permits the patenting of organisms that represent the product of "human ingenuity," but not naturally occurring organisms. Human cell lines are patentable because "[l]ong-term adaptation and growth of human tissues and cells in culture is difficult — often considered an art . . . ," and the probability of success is low. It is this inventive effort that patent law rewards, not the discovery of naturally occurring raw materials. . . .

2. Should Conversion Liability Be Extended? As we have discussed, Moore's novel claim to own the biological materials at issue in this case is problematic, at best. Accordingly, his attempt to apply the theory of conversion within this context must frankly be recognized as a request to extend that theory. . . .

There are three reasons why it is inappropriate to impose liability for conversion based upon the allegations of Moore's complaint. First, a fair balancing of the relevant policy considerations counsels against extending the tort. Second, problems in this area are better suited to legislative resolution. Third, the tort of conversion is not necessary to protect patients' rights. For these reasons, we conclude that the use of excised human cells in medical research does not amount to a conversion.

Of the relevant policy considerations, two are of overriding importance. The first is protection of a competent patient's right to make autonomous medical decisions. That right, as already discussed, is grounded in well-recognized and long-standing principles of fiduciary duty and informed consent. This policy weighs in favor of providing a remedy to patients when physicians act with undisclosed motives that may affect their professional judgment. The second important policy consideration is that we not threaten with disabling civil liability innocent parties who are engaged in socially useful activities, such as researchers who have no reason to believe that their use of a particular cell sample is, or may be, against a donor's wishes. . . .

Liability based upon existing disclosure obligations, rather than an unprecedented extension of the conversion theory, protects patients' rights of privacy and autonomy without unnecessarily hindering research. . . .

Research on human cells plays a critical role in medical research. This is so because researchers are increasingly able to isolate naturally occurring, medically useful biological substances and to produce useful quantities of such substances through genetic engineering. . . .

The extension of conversion law into this area will hinder research by restricting access to the necessary raw materials. . . . At present, human cell lines are routinely copied and distributed to other researchers for experimental purposes, usually free of charge. This exchange of scientific materials, which still is relatively free and efficient, will surely be compromised if each cell sample becomes the potential subject matter of a lawsuit. . . .

. . . [T]he theory of liability that Moore urges us to endorse threatens to destroy the economic incentive to conduct important medical research. If the use of cells in research is a conversion, then with every cell sample a researcher purchases a ticket in a litigation lottery. Because liability for conversion is predicated on a continuing ownership interest, "companies are unlikely to invest heavily in developing, manufacturing, or marketing a product when uncertainty about clear title exists." . . .

BROUSSARD, J. concurring and dissenting. [Justice Broussard concurred in the majority's holding that the complaint states a cause of action for breach of fiduciary duty.]

With respect to the conversion cause of action, I dissent from the majority's conclusion that the facts alleged in this case do not state a cause of action for conversion. . . .

Because plaintiff alleges that defendants wrongfully interfered with his right to determine, prior to the removal of his body parts, how those parts would be used after removal, I conclude that the complaint states a cause of action under traditional, common law conversion principles. . . .

Although the majority opinion, at several points, appears to suggest that a removed body part, by its nature, may never constitute "property" for purposes of a conversion action, there is no reason to think that the majority opinion actually intends to embrace such a broad or dubious proposition. If, for example, another medical center or drug company had stolen all of the cells in question from the UCLA Medical Center laboratory and had used them for its own benefit, there would be no question but that a cause of action for conversion would properly lie against the thief, and the majority opinion does not suggest otherwise. Thus, the majority's analysis cannot rest on the broad proposition that a removed body part is not property, but rather rests on the proposition that a patient retains no ownership interest in a body part once the body part has been removed from his or her body.

The majority opinion fails to recognize, however, that, in light of the allegations of the present complaint, the pertinent inquiry is not whether a patient generally retains an ownership interest in a body part after its removal from his body, but rather whether a patient has a right to determine, before a body part is removed, the use to which the part will be put after removal. Although the majority opinion suggests that there are "reasons to doubt" that a patient retains "any" ownership interest in his organs or cells after removal, the opinion fails to identify any statutory provision or common law authority that indicates that a patient does not generally have the right, before a body part is removed, to choose among the permissible uses to which the part may be put after removal. On the contrary, the most closely related statutory scheme — the Uniform Anatomical Gift Act (Health & Saf. Code, § 7150 et seq.) — makes it quite clear that a patient does have this right.

The Uniform Anatomical Gift Act is a comprehensive statutory scheme that was initially adopted in California in 1970 and most recently revised in 1988. . . . [T]he act clearly recognizes that it is the donor of the body part, rather than the hospital or physician who receives the part, who has the authority to designate, within the parameters of the statutorily authorized uses, the particular use to which the part may be put.

Although, as noted, the Uniform Anatomical Gift Act applies only to anatomical gifts that take effect on or after the death of the donor, the general principle of "donor control" which the act embodies is clearly not limited to that setting. In the transplantation context, for example, it is common for a living donor to designate the specific donee — often a relative — who is to receive a donated organ. If a hospital, after removing an organ from such a donor, decided on its own to give the organ to a different donee, no one would deny that the hospital had violated the legal right of the donor by its unauthorized use of the donated organ. Accordingly, it is clear under California law that a patient has the right, prior to the removal of an organ, to control the use to which the organ will be put after removal.

It is also clear, under traditional common law principles, that this right of a patient to control the future use of his organ is protected by the law of conversion. As a general matter, the tort of conversion protects an individual not only against improper interference with the right of possession of his property but also against unauthorized use of his property or improper interference with his right to control the use of his property. . . . California cases have also long recognized that "unauthorized use" of property can give rise to a conversion action.

The application of these principles to the present case is evident. If defendants had informed plaintiff, prior to removal, of the possible uses to which his body part could be put and plaintiff had authorized one particular use, it is clear under the foregoing authorities that defendants would be liable for conversion if they disregarded plaintiff's decision and used the body part in an unauthorized manner for their own economic benefit. Although in this case defendants did not disregard a specific directive from plaintiff with regard to the future use of his body part, the complaint alleges that, before the body part was removed, defendants intentionally withheld material information that they were under an obligation to disclose to plaintiff and that was necessary for his exercise of control over the body part; the complaint also alleges that defendants withheld such information in order to appropriate the control over the future use of such body part for their own economic benefit. If these allegations are true, defendants clearly improperly interfered with plaintiff's right in his body part at a time when he had the authority to determine the future use of such part, thereby misappropriating plaintiff's right of control for their own advantage. Under these circumstances, the complaint fully satisfies the established requirements of a conversion cause of action. . . .

Finally, the majority maintains that plaintiff's conversion action is not viable because "the subject matter of the Regents' patent — the patented cell line and the products derived from it — cannot be Moore's property." Even if this is an accurate statement of federal patent law, it does not explain why plaintiff may not maintain a conversion action for defendants' unauthorized use of his own body parts, blood, blood serum, bone marrow, and sperm. Although the damages which plaintiff may recover in a conversion action may not include the value of the patent and the derivative products, the fact that plaintiff may not be entitled to all of the damages which his complaint seeks does not justify denying his right to maintain any conversion action at all. . . .

MOSK, J. dissenting. . . . The majority claim that a conversion cause of action threatens to "destroy the economic incentive" to conduct the type of research here in issue. . . .

In any event, in my view whatever merit the majority's single policy consideration may have is outweighed by two contrary considerations, i.e., policies that are promoted by recognizing that every individual has a legally protectible property interest in his own body and its products. First, our society acknowledges a profound ethical imperative to respect the human body as the physical and temporal expression of the unique human persona. One manifestation of that respect is our prohibition against direct abuse of the body by torture or other forms of cruel or unusual punishment. Another is our prohibition against indirect abuse of the body by its economic exploitation for the sole benefit of another person. The most abhorrent form of such exploitation, of course, was the institution of slavery. Lesser forms, such as indentured servitude or even debtor's prison, have also disappeared. Yet their specter haunts the laboratories and boardrooms of today's biotechnological research-industrial complex. It arises wherever scientists or industrialists claim, as defendants claim here, the right to appropriate and exploit a patient's tissue for their sole economic benefit — the right, in other words, to freely mine or harvest valuable physical properties of the patient's body: "Research with human cells that results in significant economic gain for the researcher and no gain for the patient offends the traditional mores of our society in a manner impossible to quantify. Such research tends to treat the human body as a commodity — a means to a profitable end. The dignity and sanctity with which we regard the human whole, body as well as mind and soul, are absent when we allow researchers to further their own interests without the patient's participation by using a patient's cells as the basis for a marketable product." (Danforth, *supra*.) . . . .

The majority's final reason for refusing to recognize a conversion cause of action on these facts is that "there is no pressing need" to do so because the complaint also states another cause of action that is assuredly adequate to the task; that cause of action is "the breach of a fiduciary duty to disclose facts material to the patient's consent or, alternatively, . . . the performance of medical procedures without first having obtained the patient's informed consent" . . . I disagree . . . with the majority's further conclusion that in the present context a nondisclosure cause of action is an adequate — in fact, a superior — substitute for a conversion cause of action. . . .

The remedy is largely illusory. . . . There are two barriers to recovery. First, "the patient must show that if he or she had been informed of all pertinent information, he or she would have declined to consent to the procedure in question." . . .

The second barrier to recovery is still higher, and is erected on the first: it is not even enough for the plaintiff to prove that he personally would have refused consent to the proposed treatment if he had been fully informed; he must also prove that in the same circumstances no reasonably prudent person would have given such consent. . . .

. . . [I]t may be difficult for a plaintiff to prove that no reasonably prudent person would have consented to the proposed treatment if the doctor had disclosed the particular risk of physical harm that ultimately caused the injury. This is because in many cases the potential benefits of the treatment to the plaintiff clearly outweigh the undisclosed risk of harm. . . . Few if any judges or juries are likely to believe that disclosure of such a possibility of research or development would dissuade a reasonably prudent person from consenting to the treatment. For example, in the case at bar no trier of fact is likely to believe that if defendants had disclosed their plans for using Moore's cells, no reasonably prudent person in Moore's position — i.e., a leukemia patient suffering from a grossly enlarged spleen — would have consented to the routine operation that saved or at least prolonged his life. . . .

The second reason why the nondisclosure cause of action is inadequate for the task that the majority assign to it is that it fails to solve half the problem before us: it gives the patient only the right to refuse consent, i.e., the right to prohibit the commercialization of his tissue; it does not give him the right to grant consent to that commercialization on the condition that he share in its proceeds. "Even though good reasons exist to support informed consent with tissue commercialization, a disclosure requirement is only the first step toward full recognition of a patient's right to participate fully. Informed consent to commercialization, absent a right to share in the profits from such commercial development, would only give patients a veto over their own exploitation. But recognition that the patient[s] [have] an ownership interest in their own tissues would give patients an affirmative right of participation. Then patients would be able to assume the role of equal partners with their physicians in commercial biotechnology research." . . .

Third, the nondisclosure cause of action fails to reach a major class of potential defendants: all those who are outside the strict physician-patient relationship with the plaintiff. . . . [T]he nondisclosure cause of action will thus be inadequate to reach a number of parties to the commercial exploitation of his tissue. Such parties include, for example, any physician-researcher who is not personally treating the patient, any other researcher who is not a physician, any employer of the foregoing (or even of the treating physician), and any person or corporation thereafter participating in the commercial exploitation of the tissue. Yet some or all of those parties may well have participated more in, and profited more from, such exploitation than the particular physician with whom the plaintiff happened to have a formal doctor-patient relationship at the time. . . .

NOTES & QUESTIONS

1. *A Right to Own or Control Genetic Information?* The *Moore* case asks us to examine whether we can own our body parts (specifically, a spleen) once they are removed from our bodies. This suggests a broader question: Do we own our genetic information? To what extent can we control this information? Moore certainly had a property right in his spleen when it was in his body. Why does he lose that right when the spleen is removed?

2. *Fiduciary Duties.* The majority concludes that the interests of privacy and dignity can adequately be protected with a fiduciary duty; therefore, it is unnecessary to resort to property rights. Is a fiduciary duty sufficient to protect Moore's privacy interest?

3. *Property or Privacy?* Compare Broussard's view of Moore's claim of harm to that of the majority. Is the real harm to Moore, as Broussard argues, that he lost control over his body parts rather than, as the majority characterizes Moore's claim, that his property was taken? Is Broussard's view not one of property but of privacy? Is ownership of the spleen the same as control over it?

Suppose Moore had a privacy interest in his cells — a right to control future use. Moore would be entitled to damages for his loss of privacy (i.e., for the emotional harm of knowing his cells were used without his consent). Are these damages likely to deter the doctors considering the billions of dollars that the cell line was worth?

4. ***What Is the Privacy Interest in Genetic Information?*** If Moore has a privacy interest in his genetic information, how would you characterize it? According to James Boyle, it is difficult to view genetic information alone as implicating privacy. Only when genetic information is deciphered (to reveal certain traits or diseases) will it yield the type of information we consider to be private:

> [O]ur intuitive notions of privacy are constructed around the notion of preventing disclosure of intimate, embarrassing, or simply "personal" *socially constructed facts* about ourselves to others like ourselves. I could stare at my genetic code all day and not even know it was mine. . . .
>
> The difficulty with Moore's case is, first, that no one would think worse of him for having a genetic make-up that could be mined for a socially valuable drug and, second, that specialized knowledge would be necessary to make the connection between the "facts revealed" and the "inner life." . . .
>
> If Moore's claim is not to the protection of his "privacy" . . . but rather to the protection of his ability to commodify the genetic information derived from his cells, then the inquiry shifts from privacy to [property], from the home and the secret to the market and the commodity. . . .[72]

5. ***Methods of Protecting Genetic Privacy.*** How should genetic privacy be protected? With a property right that gives people complete ownership of their genetic information? With a fiduciary duty that remedies duplicitous actions to take one's genetic information or the unlawful disclosure of one's genetic information? With tort damages for the loss of a privacy right in one's genetic information (i.e., for the loss of control over one's genetic information)? With a limited right to control one's genetic information short of complete ownership? Or with a rule that genetic information is in the public domain and belongs to society as a whole?

6. ***Is Genetic Information Property?*** Consider Radhika Rao:

> [P]roperty traditionally implies alienability — the power to transfer rights to others. Although many categories of inalienable property exist, alienability is the norm for property. The law views limits upon alienability as exceptions, justifiable only in response to market failure or other externalities. Consequently, inalienable property is an inherently unstable and precarious category, destined to be the target of sustained assault.
>
> Privacy, on the other hand, does not carry the same connotations. Personal privacy encompasses the right to possess one's own body and the right to exclude others, but does not embrace the power to give, sell, or otherwise transfer body rights to other individuals. And relational privacy safeguards intimate and consensual relationships, but affords little shelter to commercial transactions. Accordingly, we should adopt the language of privacy rather than

---

[72] James Boyle, *Shamans, Software, and Spleens: Law and the Construction of the Information Society* 105-06 (1996).

that of property when we seek to protect self-ownership without suggesting that rights in the human body can be conveyed to others and when we wish to distinguish gifts of the body to family members from sales to strangers.

The principal feature of bodily property may be this power to transfer rights to others, whether by sale, gift, or disposition after death. By contrast, the right of personal privacy can be curtailed or relinquished altogether, but it cannot be conveyed to another. . . .

As a result, the lines that courts draw in many of these decisions precisely track the parameters of privacy jurisprudence. Common law cadaver cases, for example, grant the right to control disposition of a dead body to decedents and their close relatives, but repeatedly deny the right to treat the corpse as an article of commerce. Similarly, *Moore v. Regents of the University of California* affirms the patient's autonomy over his own body but rejects his claim to receive a share of the profits reaped from the valuable cell line derived from his spleen cells. In addition, *Hecht v. Superior Court* ultimately held that a man may bestow his sperm upon a lover, but the recipient may not trade the sperm to others. These decisions differentiate between self-ownership and sale of the body to others, while separating the rights of intimate relatives from the interests of strangers. Although such subtle distinctions are alien to property law, they are entirely consistent with the right of privacy.[73]

Also consider the following argument by Sonia Suter:

As property rights increasingly dominate the world of genetics, it seems only natural to use property rights to protect an individual's interest in his or her own genetic information. . . . [However,] the property model is deeply problematic as a tool to protect our interests in genetic information. . . . At heart, the term "property" connotes control within the marketplace and therefore protects economic interests in genetic information. "Privacy," in contrast, connotes a different kind of control — control over access to the self as well as things close to, intimately connected to, and about the self. It therefore has the potential to protect us against the many ways in which we and our relationships are made vulnerable by improper uses of genetic information. . . .

[When viewed as property,] [g]enetic information is seen as a commodity, disaggregated from the self, rather than something in which we have a dignitary and personhood interest. In addition, even when the property model successfully protects some of the interests we have in our genetic information, the property model undermines the relationships in which we share this information, pushing them toward arms-length transactions as opposed to relationships of trust. Using property rights in this context, in other words, harms the individual and the relationships around which genetic information is disclosed in a way that privacy does not.[74]

7. ***State Genetic Privacy Statutes.*** At least 18 states have passed statutes protecting the privacy of genetic information.[75] In 1996, New Jersey passed the Genetic Privacy Act, N.J.S.A. §§ 10:5-43 *et seq.,* one of the broadest state

---

[73] Radhika Rao, *Property, Privacy, and the Human Body*, 80 B.U. L. Rev. 359 (2000).

[74] Sonia M. Suter, *Disentangling Privacy from Property: Toward a Deeper Understanding of Genetic Privacy,* 72 Geo. Wash. L. Rev. 737, 739-40, 746-47 (2004).

[75] *See* Joy Pritts, Janlori Goldman, Zoe Hudson, Aimee Berenson & Elizabeth Hadley, *The State of Health Privacy: An Uneven Terrain (A Comprehensive Survey of State Health Privacy Statutes)* (1999), available at http://www.georgetown.edu/research/ihcrp/privacy/statereport.pdf.

protections of genetic privacy. The Act prohibits discrimination based on genetic information. The Act further limits the collection, retention, or disclosure of genetic information about an individual without first obtaining the individual's informed consent. Exceptions include the use of genetic information by law enforcement for the purposes of establishing the identity of a person in the course of a criminal investigation, to determine paternity, to determine the identity of deceased individuals, and a number of other exceptions. Section 7 declares: "An individual's genetic information is the property of the individual." Among exceptions to the retention restriction, Section 7 provides for retention if it "is for anonymous research where the identity of the subject will not be released." Section 8 provides, subject to certain exceptions, that "[r]egardless of the manner of receipt or the source of genetic information, including information received from an individual, a person may not disclose or be compelled, by subpoena or other means, to disclose the identity of an individual upon whom a genetic test has been performed or to disclose genetic information about the individual in a manner that permits identification of the individual."

How does the Act deal with the trade-off in *Moore* between property rights and research? How does the Act affect the case of *Safer v. Estate of Pack,* where the court held that a duty of care may require a doctor to disclose genetic information about a parent to a child?

8. ***The "Future Diary" Metaphor.*** Consider George Annas, who contends that genetic information constitutes a "future diary" about individuals:

> First, let us examine the nature of privacy and why genetic information is private. The first thing that must be understood is that all your genetic information is contained in the nucleus of each of your cells. All that a geneticist needs is one cell from you to read your genetic code. It could be a blood cell — most genetic testing is done with blood cells. It could also be hair cells or even saliva. Once someone has a drop of your blood, or, perhaps, hair or saliva, they have your DNA from which your genetic code can be extracted.
>
> Therefore, we have to think of one drop of blood as a medical record. It is in code, it is a code that has not been broken yet, and it will require sophisticated codebreakers to break it. But the fact remains that it is a complete record of your DNA. You do not have to agree with many boosters of the Genome Project who think it is the Book of Life, that your DNA is going to tell the story of your life. I would not get that carried away, but it does contain an enormous amount of information about you and your probable medical future.[76]

Pauline Kim argues that "[t]he metaphor of genes as a 'blueprint' or 'future diary' is misleading. It suggests that our genetic material determines our future in some fixed, unalterable way."[77] Consider Judge Douglas Ginsburg's critique of the "future diary" metaphor:

> I believe it was Dr. Annas who coined the term "future diary" to describe the information in our genes. The metaphor derives its power from the jealousy

[76] George J. Annas, *Genetic Privacy: There Ought to Be a Law,* 4 Tex. Rev. L. & Pol. 9 (1999).
[77] Pauline T. Kim, *Genetic Discrimination, Genetic Privacy: Rethinking Employee Protections for a Brave New Workplace*, 96 Nw. U. L. Rev. 1497, 1536-37 (2002).

with which people guard the secrets in their written diaries and therefore implicitly supports genetic exceptionalism. Upon analysis, however, the metaphor breaks down. First, our future diaries are much less diverse than our written ones: "while a child is 99.95 percent the same as its genetic mother at the level of the DNA molecule, it is also 99.90 percent the same as any randomly chosen person on the planet earth." Second, unlike the past thoughts and actions contained in our written diaries, the secrets that our future diaries are supposed to hold, like our family histories, speak only to probabilities. . . .

The sober, unexciting realization that genetic information is but the latest iteration of our evolving medical knowledge yields one final suggestion: areas in which changes in degree are endemic are not well suited to statutory solutions. Courts, following in the common law tradition, can address the issues that genetic information raises as the extension of an existing phenomenon. Recognizing that genetic information is not qualitatively different from other types of medical information allows courts to draw upon past experience and to adapt that experience to meet new challenges. Engrafting a unique statutory solution for genetic information onto this common law landscape will simply create two divergent legal regimes for what is essentially a single problem.[78]

Which of these views of genetic information do you find most convincing? Which metaphor is likely to help shape the best legal approach?

3. GENETIC TESTING AND DISCRIMINATION

Information About Genetic Disorders. A genetic disorder occurs as a result of a particular genetic mutation. Sometimes, a mutation of a single gene alone can cause the disorder. Sometimes, disorders are caused by many mutated genes and environmental factors. Genetic testing can give people the opportunity to find out if they have a high risk of contracting certain genetic disorders — such as cystic fibrosis, muscular dystrophy, Huntington's disease, and some rare forms of breast and colon cancer. Often, genetic testing does not predict with 100 percent accuracy whether a person will come down with a particular disorder. But it can predict that the risks will be very high for contracting certain disorders.

The information that a person has a high risk to contract a disorder that is disabling or fatal is not merely of use to that person, but also is of great interest to one's spouse, fiancée, or partner. Additionally, such information is useful to one's health or life insurer, since having the disorder dramatically affects the potential risk the insurer expects as well as the level of insurance payments it demands. It may be of interest to one's creditors, who might not want to risk lending money to a borrower who is at high risk of contracting a fatal disorder. Further, it may be of interest to one's employer, who may not want to spend the time, resources, and money training a worker who may have to retire earlier than expected. Employers that self-insure may also be interested in the information, as the potential employee will affect the employer's financial condition.

Genetic Testing by Employers. Currently, most companies do not require genetic testing, but 20 percent require data about the medical history of employees'

---

[78] Douglas H. Ginsburg, *Genetics and Privacy,* 4 Tex. Rev. L. & Pol. 17 (1999).

families, which can serve as a source for genetic information.[79] In 2001, Burlington Northern Santa Fe Railroad secretly tested employees suffering from carpal tunnel syndrome to see if they were genetically predisposed to coming down with the condition. When the testing came to light, and the company was sued by the EEOC and a workers' union, the company settled, agreeing to halt the testing. Thirty states have statutes restricting employers from gathering, using, and/or disclosing employee genetic data.[80]

The Genetic Information Nondiscrimination Act. In 2008, Congress enacted the Genetic Information Nondiscrimination Act (GINA). This statute prevents insurance companies and employers from using genetic tests to deny individuals health coverage or employment. In enacting the statute, Congress found, "Federal law addressing genetic discrimination in health insurance and employment is incomplete in both the scope and depth and its protections." The findings to the statute also noted that state laws "vary widely with respect to their approach, application, and level of protection."

In its Title I, GINA prohibits genetic discrimination in health insurance. It does so by forbidding insurers, whether in the group or individual market, from adjusting "premium or contribution amounts" on the basis of genetic information. In its Title II, it prohibits employment discrimination on the basis of genetic information. It is an unfair employment practice for an employer "to fail, or refuse to hire, or to discharge, any employee, or otherwise to discriminate against any employee" because of genetic information. GINA also prohibits an employee from requesting, requiring, or purchasing genetic information about any employee, subject, however, to some exception.

The Equal Employment Opportunity Commission is to enforce the statute. GINA does not, however, cover the use of genetic testing results in life insurance, or long term care and disability insurance. Before enactment of this statute, Richard Epstein and Paul Schwartz considered the merits of such legislation. Epstein was against such a law; Schwartz was in favor.

RICHARD A. EPSTEIN, *THE LEGAL REGULATION OF GENETIC DISCRIMINATION: OLD RESPONSES TO NEW TECHNOLOGY*

74 B.U. L. Rev. 1 (1994)

. . . Must the person disclose the information [learned from a genetic test] to other parties? I think that in the case of Huntington's disease it is immoral for a person to marry (or even take a job) and conceal the condition from the potential spouse or employer. This conclusion is valid in commercial settings as well as in marital ones so long as the concealment results in selective knowledge to one side that is denied to the other. When an individual has knowledge that he is at risk of incapacitation, perhaps from family history, then full disclosure should be the

---

[79] *See* Health Privacy Project, *Report: Genetics and Privacy: A Patchwork of Protections* 19 (2002).

[80] National Conference of State Legislatures, http://www.ncsl.org/programs/health/genetics/ndiscrim.htm.

norm. When the individual knows to a certainty that he is a carrier of the trait, from a reliable genetic test, the same is true. The principle does not change; all that changes is the information that must be disclosed. . . .

At this point it is critical to note that the plea for privacy is often a plea for the right to misrepresent one's self to the rest of the world. In and of itself that may not be a bad thing. We are certainly not obligated to disclose all of our embarrassing past to persons in ordinary social conversations; and it is certainly acceptable to use long sleeves to cover an ugly scar. White lies are part of the glue that makes human interaction possible without shame and loss of face. Strictly speaking, people may be deceived, but they are rarely hurt, and they may even be relieved to be spared an awkward encounter. However, when a major change in personal or financial status is contemplated by another party, the white lies that make human interaction possible turn into frauds of a somewhat deeper dye. In order to see why this is the case, recall that the traditional tort of misrepresentation stressed the usual five fingers: a false statement, known to be false, material to the listener, and relied on, to the listener's detriment. There is little question, whether we deal with marriage or with business, that concealment of relevant genetic information satisfies each element. The only question, therefore, is whether one can justify what is a prima facie wrong.

I am hard pressed to see what that justification might be. No doubt the individual who engages in this type of deception has much to gain. But equally there can be no doubt that this gain exists in all garden variety cases of fraud as well. To show the advantage of the fraud to the party who commits it is hardly to excuse or to justify it, for the same can be said of all cases of successful wrongs. On the other side of the transaction, there is a pronounced loss from not knowing the information when key decisions have to be made. . . .

False statements about or deliberate concealment of genetic information is as much a fraud as false statements about or concealment of any other issue. The only possible justification for concealment, therefore, would be that it is unfair for the person with the pending disorder to deal alone with the suffering and financial loss. Yet, that loss is not sustained because of the wrong of another. Could the victim of a natural catastrophe keep it secret, and single out one other person to bear some substantial fraction of the loss? If not, then why give that same privilege to the victim of a genetic defect? Today, it is easy to find strong support for socializing losses. But why should a person laboring under a genetic defect be entitled to pick the person or group that has to pay the subsidy? . . .

PAUL M. SCHWARTZ, *PRIVACY AND THE ECONOMICS OF HEALTH CARE INFORMATION*
76 Tex. L. Rev. 1 (1997)

. . . Most people who receive health benefits in this country obtain it at their place of employment. In the United States approximately 140 million people, or nearly two-thirds of the population under sixty-five, receive medical benefits through their job. Because these benefits are an increasingly costly part of the overall package of compensation, employers have a great incentive to weed out workers with expensive health care needs. Despite any amount of soothing statements about the rationality of employers, the actual use of genetic information and health records in employment decisions is far from efficient. . . .

The argument against [Richard Epstein's] position is greatly strengthened by the generally poor societal record in this area; a considerable historical pattern exists of misapplication of [genetic] information. This story begins with the eugenics movement, whose misunderstanding and deformation of genetic science encouraged public policies that included the sterilization of "inferior" members of society. As for the recent era of modern genetics, the United States has far from a perfect record. Genetic discrimination already takes place in the United States. Studies by scientists at Stanford and Harvard have documented numerous instances of genetic discrimination in the public and private sectors. Another study found a high rate of discrimination in obtaining insurance and employment for people who have a genetic condition or for their family members. Many of these individuals will never suffer from any genetic illness; yet, the testing process itself creates a category of individuals now deemed to be genetically unfit. . . .

Like genetic information, health care data are also being used to make employment decisions. According to one empirical study of privacy in the workplace, over one-third of Fortune 500 companies surveyed in 1995 admitted to using the medical records of their personnel in employment-related decisions. In previous years, this survey found that as many as one-half of these companies admitted to engaging in such behavior. Evidence also indicates that some of this reliance on employees' health data is leading to economically inefficient employment decisions. According to a recent nationwide survey, for example, cancer patients currently lose their jobs at over five times the rate of those who do not have the disease. Considerable ignorance has also been found regarding the workplace implications of this disease; another survey found common overestimation by supervisors of the actual experience of cancer patients regarding fatigue, infections, and nausea during treatment. To consider another socially charged illness, one can point to evidence that greater insurance discrimination is faced by those who are HIV-positive than individuals who suffer from equally serious illnesses with similar costs. Discrimination between employees with different health conditions can be based on social stigma and misunderstandings rather than the relative costs of different workers' medical conditions. . . .

. . . The individual to whom these data refer faces a high price when attempting to explain the significance or insignificance of the information, and these explanatory costs can exceed the value of unrestricted disclosure to society. Indeed, many parties, including employers, believe that they are not ignorant about the full dimensions or implications of certain personal data, and will continue to (mis)apply genetic personal information based simply on their popular beliefs. Thus, achieving economic efficiency necessitates placing certain kinds of limits on access to personal information because of the excessive social costs of placing such data in the proper context under a policy of unrestricted access. . . .

An excessive disclosure norm for certain kinds of information will distort or eliminate the kinds of personal information that health care consumers share in future transactions with physicians. . . . Inadequate safeguards for protecting medical data will make the encounters that take place between physicians and patients less effective because of the likelihood that patients will withhold important information. . . .

Open access to health care or genetic information has a final negative effect on individual behavior. It ties individuals to current jobs out of the fear that they will be denied new employment or health insurance. . . . These workers were afraid that their health history or that of family members would lead a new insurer to reject or limit their coverage. As this Article has indicated, such fears are far from baseless. The resulting phenomenon, which has been termed "job lock," introduces significant distortions in the labor market. As health care economist Victor Fuchs notes, "[L]abor market efficiency suffers" when health insurance considerations affect workers' choices of jobs and decisions about job change. . . .

To summarize our argument thus far, employers are not making purely rational use of medical and genetic data. Rather, this information provides an excuse for the exercise of social stigma and misunderstandings of science. Open access to these data also distorts individual behavior by encouraging patients to share incomplete data with physicians and by causing employees to be locked in jobs that they would otherwise leave. Moreover, open disclosure permits certain workers to be cast off into an increasingly strained public insurance market. This process has contributed to an increase in aggregate health care costs. . . .

NOTES & QUESTIONS

1. *Executive Order 13145.* On February 8, 2000, President Clinton issued Executive Order 13145: To Prohibit Discrimination in Federal Employment Based on Genetic Information. It applies to all Executive departments and agencies with regard to all employees covered by § 717 of Title VII of the Civil Rights Act of 1964. The Order protects "protected genetic information," which is defined as "information about an individual's genetic tests," "information about the genetic tests of an individual's family members," or "information about the occurrence of a disease, or medical condition or disorder in family members of the individual." Pursuant to the Order:

> (a) The employing department or agency shall not discharge, fail or refuse to hire, or otherwise discriminate against any employee with respect to the compensation, terms, conditions, or privileges of employment of that employee, because of protected genetic information with respect to the employee, or because of information about a request for or the receipt of genetic services by such employee.
>
> (b) The employing department or agency shall not limit, segregate, or classify employees in any way that would deprive or tend to deprive any employee of employment opportunities or otherwise adversely affect that employee's status, because of protected genetic information with respect to the employee or because of information about a request for or the receipt of genetic services by such employee.
>
> (c) The employing department or agency shall not request, require, collect, or purchase protected genetic information with respect to an employee, or information about a request for or the receipt of genetic services by such employee.

2. *State Law, Genetic Discrimination, and Preemption Under GINA.* As of 2002, 30 states have laws prohibiting employment discrimination based on

genetic information.[81] Thirty-four states have statutes barring the use of genetic data by insurers for risk classification.[82] GINA states that it does not "limit the rights or protections of an individual under any other Federal or State statute that provides equal or greater protection to an individual than the rights or protections provided for under this title." § 209(a). GINA therefore sets a federal preemptive "floor" and not a "ceiling." State laws may exceed its protection, but GINA supplants weaker state laws, or adds protections for those states that lack a law prohibiting employment discrimination based on genetic data.

3. ***Is Genetic Information Different?*** Recall from Chapter 1 Judge Posner's view that privacy is a desire to misrepresent oneself, a type of fraud. How does this compare to Epstein's view of privacy? Suppose a person has diabetes, heart disease, or cancer. In an application for health or life insurance, that person would have to disclose all preexisting conditions. Otherwise, the individual would be committing a fraud if she deliberately left out health conditions that she was aware of. Why not view the knowledge of genetic predisposition the same way? What is the difference between the nondisclosure of regular medical information versus genetic information?

4. ***Combating Genetic Discrimination: Discrimination Law vs. Privacy Law.*** What is the best way to combat genetic discrimination? Consider the following argument by Pauline Kim:

> [T]he analogy between genetic discrimination, and race and sex discrimination, is fundamentally flawed. . . . For example, the societal consensus condemning race discrimination emerged in reaction to a history of systematic social disadvantage imposed on identifiable groups of people because of their race. By contrast, the threat of genetic discrimination is entirely prospective; advocates fear new technologies will be misused to reveal hidden information that will disadvantage certain individuals. In the employment context, race and sex discrimination are believed to be wrong because those characteristics are irrelevant to a worker's ability to perform the job. However, genetic technologies offer the potential to provide information that is arguably relevant to an employee's future job performance.

Kim suggests that the law of privacy is more suited to redressing the harms of genetic discrimination than discrimination law:

> As a practical matter, then, prohibiting employer reliance on genetic traits presents a different challenge than prohibiting discrimination based on an easily observed characteristic such as race or sex. Because employer knowledge of an employee's race or sex is nearly always unavoidable, preventing race discrimination requires direct prohibition of a discriminatory motive. By contrast, employers cannot detect genetic anomalies by casual observation. The issue of genetic privacy, then, is prior to that of discrimination. If employers have access to workers' genetic information, divining when they have used that information improperly will be extremely difficult. If, however, that

---

[81] National Conference of State Legislatures, http://www.ncsl.org/programs/health/genetics/ndiscrim.htm.

[82] *Id.*

information is unavailable, discrimination on the basis of genetic traits becomes impossible. Those concerned about preventing genetic discrimination, then, ought to be concerned first and foremost with protecting the privacy of workers' genetic information.[83]

---

[83] Pauline T. Kim, *Genetic Discrimination, Genetic Privacy: Rethinking Employee Protections for a Brave New Workplace*, 96 Nw. U. L. Rev. 1497, 1500, 1537 (2002).

CHAPTER 7

GOVERNMENT RECORDS

CHAPTER OUTLINE

In the United States, government began to use records widely about citizens after the rise of the administrative state in the early part of the twentieth century. The administrative state's extensive and complex systems of regulation, licensing, and entitlements demanded the collection of a significant amount of personal information. For example, the Social Security system, created in 1935, required that records be kept about every employed individual's earnings. To ensure that each record was correctly identified, the Social Security Administration assigned each individual a unique nine-digit number known as a Social Security number (SSN).

Technology has also been developed that helps government create detailed databases of personal information. Indeed, one of the greatest catalysts for the creation of government records has been technology — namely, the computer. The invention of the mainframe computer in 1946 sparked a revolution in recordkeeping. By the 1960s, computers provided a fast, efficient, and inexpensive way to store, analyze, and transfer information. Federal and state agencies began to computerize their records, often using SSNs as identifiers for these records.[1]

Today, federal agencies maintain thousands of databases. States also keep a panoply of public records, pertaining to births, marriages, divorces, property ownership, licensing, voter registration, and the identity and location of sex offenders. State public records will be covered later in this chapter.

The vast stores of personal information spread throughout government databases have given rise to significant fears that one day this information might be combined to create a file on each citizen. In his influential book on privacy from 1971, Arthur Miller warned of the "possibility of constructing a sophisticated data center capable of generating a comprehensive womb-to-tomb dossier on every individual and transmitting it to a wide range of data users over a national network."[2]

A. PUBLIC ACCESS TO GOVERNMENT RECORDS

1. PUBLIC RECORDS AND COURT RECORDS

As noted above, states maintain a panoply of records about individuals, many available to the public. These records contain varying kinds of information. Birth records often disclose one's name, date of birth, place of birth, the names and ages of one's parents, and one's mother's maiden name. States also maintain driver's license records, as well as accident reports. Voting records, which can disclose one's political party affiliation, date of birth, e-mail address, home address, and telephone number, are publicly available in many states. Several types of professions require state licensing, such as doctors, attorneys, engineers, nurses, police, and teachers. Property ownership records contain a physical description of

---

[1] *See* Alan F. Westin & Michael A. Baker, *Databanks in a Free Society: Computers, Record-Keeping and Privacy* 229 (1972); Priscilla Regan, *Legislating Privacy* 69 (1995); Daniel J. Solove, *Privacy and Power: Computer Databases and Metaphors for Information Privacy*, 53 Stan. L. Rev. 1393, 1400-03 (2001).

[2] Arthur Miller, *Assault on Privacy* 39 (1971).

one's property, including the number and size of rooms as well as the value of the property. Police records, such as records of arrests, are also frequently made publicly available.

Court records are public in all states, though settlements in civil actions are sometimes sealed. A significant amount of personal data can find its way into court records. In a civil case, for example, medical and financial information often is entered into evidence. The names, addresses, and occupations of jurors become part of the court record, as well as the jurors' answers to voir dire questions. In some states, family court proceedings are public.

For information in court records, privacy is protected by way of protective orders, which are issued at the discretion of trial court judges. Courts also have the discretion to seal certain court proceedings or portions of court proceedings from the public, as well as to permit parties to proceed anonymously under special circumstances.

Privacy in records maintained by state agencies is protected under each state's freedom of information law. Most states have some form of exemption for privacy, often patterned after the federal Freedom of Information Act's (FOIA) privacy exemptions. Not all states interpret their privacy exemptions as broadly as the Supreme Court has interpreted FOIA's. Further, certain state FOIAs do not have privacy exemptions.

Until recently, public and court records were difficult to access. These documents were only available in local offices. The Internet revolution has now made it possible to access records from anywhere. Furthermore, private sector entities have consolidated these records into gigantic new databases.

DOE V. SHAKUR

164 F.R.D. 359 (S.D.N.Y. 1996)

CHIN, J. This diversity action raises the difficult question of whether the victim of a sexual assault may prosecute a civil suit for damages under a pseudonym. Plaintiff has brought this action charging that defendants Tupac A. Shakur and Charles L. Fuller sexually assaulted her on November 18, 1993. On December 1, 1994, a jury trial in Supreme Court, New York County, found Shakur and Fuller guilty of sexual abuse and not guilty of sodomy, attempted sodomy and weapons violations. They were sentenced on February 7, 1995 and an appeal is pending.

This civil suit was filed approximately two weeks after Shakur and Fuller were sentenced. The complaint seeks $10 million in compensatory damages and $50 million in punitive damages. Before filing her complaint, plaintiff obtained an order *ex parte* from Judge Sprizzo, sitting as Part I judge, sealing the complaint and permitting plaintiff to file a substitute complaint using a pseudonym in place of her real name. Neither defendant filed a timely answer and thus the Clerk of the Court entered a default.

Shakur has moved to vacate the entry of default. In his motion papers, which have not yet been filed with the Clerk of the Court but which have been served on plaintiff, Shakur identifies plaintiff by her real name. Shakur justifies his use of plaintiff's name by noting that Judge Sprizzo's order allowing plaintiff to file her complaint using a pseudonym was signed after an *ex parte* appearance and merely sealed the complaint. That order did not provide that this entire proceeding was to be conducted under seal. In response, plaintiff claims that Judge Sprizzo's order requires all papers filed with the Court to use plaintiff's pseudonym. In the alternative, plaintiff requests that I issue such an order now.

As a threshold matter, it is plain from the face of Judge Sprizzo's order that he did not decide the issue now before me. Judge Sprizzo's order merely allowed plaintiff to file the *complaint* under seal. Judge Sprizzo did not order that all documents filed in this case be sealed. Nor did Judge Sprizzo hold that plaintiff could prosecute the entire lawsuit under a pseudonym. Nor do I believe that Judge Sprizzo, sitting as Part I judge on the basis of an *ex parte* application, intended to foreclose defendants from being heard on the issue.

Rule 10(a) of the Federal Rules of Civil Procedure provides that a complaint shall state the names of all the parties. The intention of this rule is to apprise parties of who their opponents are and to protect the public's legitimate interest in knowing the facts at issue in court proceedings. Nevertheless, in some circumstances a party may commence a suit using a fictitious name.

It is within a court's discretion to allow a plaintiff to proceed anonymously. *Doe v. Bell Atlantic Business Sys. Servs., Inc.,* 162 F.R.D. 418, 420 (D. Mass. 1995). In exercising its discretion, a court should consider certain factors in determining whether plaintiffs may proceed anonymously. These factors include (1) whether the plaintiff is challenging governmental activity; (2) whether the plaintiff would be required to disclose information of the utmost intimacy; (3) whether the plaintiff would be compelled to admit his or her intention to engage in illegal conduct, thereby risking criminal prosecution; (4) whether the plaintiff would risk suffering injury if identified; and (5) whether the party defending against a suit brought under a pseudonym would be prejudiced.

In considering these and other factors, a court must engage in a balancing process. As the Eleventh Circuit has held,

> The ultimate test for permitting a plaintiff to proceed anonymously is whether the plaintiff has a substantial privacy right which outweighs the "customary and constitutionally-embedded presumption of openness in judicial proceedings." It is the exceptional case in which a plaintiff may proceed under a fictitious name.

Frank, 951 F.2d at 323 (*citing Doe v. Stegall,* 653 F.2d 180, 186 (5th Cir. 1981)).

The present case is a difficult one. If the allegations of the complaint are true, plaintiff was the victim of a brutal sexual assault. Quite understandably, she does not want to be publicly identified and she has very legitimate privacy concerns. On balance, however, these concerns are outweighed by the following considerations.

First, plaintiff has chosen to bring this lawsuit. She has made serious charges and has put her credibility in issue. Fairness requires that she be prepared to stand behind her charges publicly.

Second, this is a civil suit for damages, where plaintiff is seeking to vindicate primarily her own interests. This is not a criminal case where rape shield laws might provide some anonymity to encourage victims to testify to vindicate the public's interest in enforcement of our laws. *See id.* (rape shield laws "apply to situations where the government chooses to prosecute a case, and offer[ ] anonymity to a victim who does not have a choice in or control over the prosecution"). Indeed, the public's interest in bringing defendants to justice for breaking the law — assuming that they did — is being vindicated in the criminal proceedings.

Third, Shakur has been publicly accused. If plaintiff were permitted to prosecute this case anonymously, Shakur would be placed at a serious disadvantage, for he would be required to defend himself publicly while plaintiff could make her accusations from behind a cloak of anonymity.

Finally, the public has a right of access to the courts. Indeed, "lawsuits are public events and the public has a legitimate interest in knowing the facts involved in them. Among those facts is the identity of the parties." . . .

Plaintiff argues that Shakur's notoriety will likely cause this case to attract significant media attention, and she contends that disclosure of her name will cause her to be "publicly humiliated and embarrassed." Such claims of public humiliation and embarrassment, however, are not sufficient grounds for allowing a plaintiff in a civil suit to proceed anonymously, as the cases cited above demonstrate. Moreover, plaintiff has conceded that the press has known her name for some time. Indeed, plaintiff makes it clear that the press has been aware of both her residence and her place of employment. Hence, her identity is not unknown.

Plaintiff's allegation that she has been subjected to death threats would provide a legitimate basis for allowing her to proceed anonymously. Plaintiff has not, however, provided any details, nor has she explained how or why the use of her real name in court papers would lead to harm, since those who presumably would have any animosity toward her already know her true identity. Thus, plaintiff simply has not shown that she is entitled to proceed under a pseudonym in this action.

It may be, as plaintiff suggests, that victims of sexual assault will be deterred from seeking relief through civil suits if they are not permitted to proceed under a pseudonym. That would be an unfortunate result. For the reasons discussed above, however, plaintiff and others like her must seek vindication of their rights publicly.

NOTES & QUESTIONS

1. *Pseudonymous Litigation. Doe v. Shakur* involved a party's request to proceed under a pseudonym. The court refused this request. The standard for allowing a party to proceed with a fictitious name gives significant room for judicial discretion. Consider *Doe v. Blue Cross & Blue Shield United of Wisconsin*, 112 F.3d 869 (7th Cir. 1997):

> The plaintiff is proceeding under a fictitious name because of fear that the litigation might result in the disclosure of his psychiatric records. The motion to proceed in this way was not opposed, and the district judge granted it without comment. The judge's action was entirely understandable given the absence of objection and the sensitivity of psychiatric records, but we would be remiss if we failed to point out that the privilege of suing or defending under a fictitious name should not be granted automatically even if the opposing party does not object. The use of fictitious names is disfavored, and the judge has an independent duty to determine whether exceptional circumstances justify such a departure from the normal method of proceeding in federal courts. *See United States v. Microsoft Corp.,* 56 F.3d 1448, 1463-64 (D.C. Cir. 1995) (per curiam), and cases cited there, and our recent dictum in *K.F.P. v. Dane County,* 110 F.3d

516, 518-19 (7th Cir. 1997). Rule 10(a) of the Federal Rules of Civil Procedure, in providing that the complaint shall give the names of all the parties to the suit (and our plaintiff's name is *not* "John Doe"), instantiates the principle that judicial proceedings, civil as well as criminal, are to be conducted in public. Identifying the parties to the proceeding is an important dimension of publicness. The people have a right to know who is using their courts.

There are exceptions. Records or parts of records are sometimes sealed for good reasons, including the protection of state secrets, trade secrets, and informers; and fictitious names are allowed when necessary to protect the privacy of children, rape victims, and other particularly vulnerable parties or witnesses. But the fact that a case involves a medical issue is not a sufficient reason for allowing the use of a fictitious name, even though many people are understandably secretive about their medical problems. "John Doe" suffers, or at least from 1989 to 1991 suffered, from a psychiatric disorder — obsessive-compulsive syndrome. This is a common enough disorder — some would say that most lawyers and judges suffer from it to a degree — and not such a badge of infamy or humiliation in the modern world that its presence should be an automatic ground for concealing the identity of a party to a federal suit. To make it such would be to propagate the view that mental illness is shameful. Should "John Doe"'s psychiatric records contain material that would be highly embarrassing to the average person yet somehow pertinent to this suit and so an appropriate part of the judicial record, the judge could require that this material be placed under seal.

Also consider *Doe No. 2 v. Kolko*, 242 F.R.D. 193 (2006). An adult plaintiff alleged that he was sexually abused as a child by a rabbi at a private Jewish school. The court allowed the plaintiff to proceed anonymously by looking to several factors, including: the public's strong interest in protecting sexual abuse victims; the opinion of the plaintiff's psychologist that the alleged abuse had caused the plaintiff severe psychological and emotional injuries; plaintiff's assertion that he feared retaliation and ostracism if his name was disclosed; a lack of showing that knowledge of plaintiff's identity was widespread; any additional prejudice to defendant's reputation due to pursuit of legal action under pseudonym was minimal due to two similar lawsuits against the rabbi by named plaintiffs; and, finally, a lack of showing that defendants' ability to conduct discovery or impeach plaintiff's credibility would be impaired by allowing plaintiff to proceed anonymously. On the final point, the court noted that defendants would need to make redactions and take measures not to disclose plaintiff's identity, but would otherwise not be hampered by plaintiff's mere anonymity in court papers. These restrictions could also be reconsidered before the case went to trial.

When is it appropriate for a judge to allow a party to proceed under a pseudonym? Does the test give too much discretion to judges to make this determination? If so, how would you draft a rule that limits judicial discretion in approaching this issue?

Lior Strahilevitz proposes that pseudonymity be used as a tool to have parties raise their grievances in the appropriate forums — either formally through litigation or informally via other dispute resolution mechanisms. Strahilevitz argues that pseudonymity should be granted in cases where we want parties to use litigation to resolve their disputes. The issue of whether a party can litigate pseudonymously should be resolved at the conclusion of the litigation rather than at the beginning:

> There is no reason why the issue of pseudonymity needs to be resolved at the outset of the litigation. A court is free to keep the identity of a party or both parties under seal until a final judgment is entered and all appeals are exhausted. It would be straightforward to unseal the parties' identities at that later date, via an amended opinion. At that point, a court can more reliably answer questions about whether the plaintiff raised novel legal issues, whether her injuries were serious enough to warrant judicial intervention, and whether alternatives to litigation might have ameliorated the controversy more efficiently.[3]

As an alternative, Strahilevitz proposes that parties should be able to obtain pseudonymity if they prevail in the litigation. However, will the uncertainty associated with any determination of pseudonymity deter plaintiffs from pursuing their claims in court? Are there other benefits and costs of pseudonymous litigation for which Strahilevitz's theory does not account?

2. ***Protective Orders.*** Federal Rule of Civil Procedure 26(c) provides that judges may, "for good cause shown," issue protective orders where disclosure of information gleaned in discovery might cause a party "annoyance, embarrassment, oppression, or undue burden or expense." In other words, a protective order serves to place limits on the process of discovery. Most states have protective order provisions similar to the federal one. There is a presumption in favor of access to information through discovery, and the party seeking the protective order must overcome this presumption. Courts will issue a protective order when a party's interest in privacy outweighs the public interest in disclosure.[4] Although the standard for obtaining a protective order is easier to satisfy than the standard for proceeding under a pseudonym, the thumb on the scale is on the side of public access. Consider the "good cause shown" standard of Federal Rule of Civil Procedure 26(c). Does it grant too much discretion to a court in granting protective orders?

3. ***Personal Information in Court Records.*** Under some court practices, certain information is categorically excluded from court records. As Natalie Gomez-Velez notes:

> The list of data elements categorically excluded from case records varies from state to state, depending to some extent on the degree to which case records are being made available and the extent to which a particular state precludes public access to certain categories of cases and information. . . .
>
> To a great extent, the federal courts, New York, Indiana, and courts in other states that exclude whole classes of sensitive cases like matrimonial, adoption,

---

[3] Lior Jacob Strahilevitz, *Pseudonymous Litigation*, 77 U. Chi. L. Rev. 1239 (2010).

[4] For more information about court records, see Gregory M. Silverman, *Rise of the Machines: Justice Information Systems and the Question of Public Access to Court Records Over the Internet*, 79 Wash. L. Rev. 175 (2004).

~~juvenile, and family law cases from public access,~~ have fewer problems to solve than courts that permit public access to these kinds of cases.[5]

2. THE FREEDOM OF INFORMATION ACT

Until the second half of the twentieth century, only a few states had created a statutory right of public access to government records. The federal government had no such statute until the passage in 1966 of the Freedom of Information Act (FOIA). President Lyndon Johnson, in signing FOIA into law, stated:

> This legislation springs from one of our most essential principles: A democracy works best when the people have all the information that the security of the Nation permits. No one should be able to pull curtains of secrecy around decisions which can be revealed without injury to the public interest.[6]

Significant amendments to FOIA in 1974 strengthened the Act. *See* Pub. L. No. 93-502. Key provisions established administrative deadlines, reduced fees, imposed sanctions for arbitrary and capricious withholding of agency records, and provided for attorneys' fees and costs.

Right to Access. FOIA grants all persons the right to inspect and copy records and documents maintained by any federal agency, federal corporation, or federal department. Certain documents must be disclosed automatically — without anybody explicitly requesting them. FOIA requires disclosure in the Federal Register of descriptions of agency functions, procedures, rules, and policies. 5 U.S.C. § 552(a)(1). FOIA also requires that opinions, orders, administrative staff manuals, and other materials be automatically released into the public domain. § 552(a)(2).

To obtain a document under FOIA, a requester must invoke FOIA in the request and follow the "published rules stating the time, place, fees (if any), and procedures to be followed." § 552(a)(3)(A). The agency must make "reasonable efforts" to answer any request that "reasonably describe[s]" the information sought. §§ 552(a)(3)(A)-(C). A requester can submit a request by mail or through an online form. The agency receiving the request is required to respond to the request within 20 business days unless the agency requests extra time based on "unusual circumstances." § 552(a)(6)(A). A requester may ask for expedited processing upon a showing of "compelling need." § 552(a)(6)(E)(i)(I).

There is an administrative appeals process to challenge any agency denial of a request that an agency must detail in its denial letter. § 552(a)(6)(A). The requester has 20 business days to invoke the process. After exhausting any administrative appeals or if any agency fails to adhere to statutory time limits, a requester may also file a complaint against the agency in federal court. § 552(a)(4)(B).

Exemptions. FOIA contains nine enumerated exemptions to disclosure. Pursuant to § 552(b):

---

[5] Natalie Gomez-Velez, *Internet Access to Court Records — Balancing Public Access and Privacy*, 51 Loy. L. Rev. 365, 434-35 (2005).

[6] 2 *Public Papers of the Presidents of the United States: Lyndon B. Johnson* 699 (1967), quoted in H.R. Rep. 104-795 (104th Cong. 2d Sess.), at 8 (1996).

(b) This section does not apply to matters that are —

(1)(A) specifically authorized under criteria established by an Executive order to be kept secret in the interest of national defense or foreign policy and (B) are in fact properly classified pursuant to such Executive order;

(2) related solely to the internal personnel rules and practices of an agency;

(3) specifically exempted from disclosure by statute (other than section 552b of this title), provided that such statute (A) requires that the matters be withheld from the public in such a manner as to leave no discretion on the issue, or (B) establishes particular criteria for withholding or refers to particular types of matters to be withheld;

(4) trade secrets and commercial or financial information obtained from a person and privileged or confidential;

(5) inter-agency or intra-agency memorandums or letters which would not be available by law to a party other than an agency in litigation with the agency;

(6) personnel and medical files and similar files the disclosure of which would constitute a clearly unwarranted invasion of personal privacy;

(7) records or information compiled for law enforcement purposes, but only to the extent that the production of such law enforcement records or information (A) could reasonably be expected to interfere with enforcement proceedings, (B) would deprive a person of a right to a fair trial or an impartial adjudication, (C) could reasonably be expected to constitute an unwarranted invasion of personal privacy, (D) could reasonably be expected to disclose the identity of a confidential source, including a State, local, or foreign agency or authority or any private institution which furnished information on a confidential basis, and, in the case of a record or information compiled by a criminal law enforcement authority in the course of a criminal investigation or by an agency conducting a lawful national security intelligence investigation, information furnished by a confidential source, (E) would disclose techniques and procedures for law enforcement investigations or prosecutions, or would disclose guidelines for law enforcement investigations or prosecutions if such disclosure could reasonably be expected to risk circumvention of the law, or (F) could reasonably be expected to endanger the life or physical safety of any individual;

(8) contained in or related to examination, operating, or condition reports prepared by, on behalf of, or for the use of an agency responsible for the regulation or supervision of financial institutions; or

(9) geological and geophysical information and data, including maps, concerning wells.

Redaction. If a portion of a document that falls under an exemption can be redacted (blacked out), then the remainder of the document must be provided to the requester:

Any reasonably segregable portion of a record shall be provided to any person requesting such record after deletion of the portions which are exempt under this subsection. § 552(b).

The Privacy Exemptions. Two of the exemptions involve privacy concerns.

Exemption (6) exempts from disclosure "personnel and medical files and similar files the disclosure of which would constitute a clearly unwarranted invasion of personal privacy." § 552(b)(6). Exemption (7)(C) exempts from disclosure "records or information compiled for law enforcement purposes . . . which could reasonably be expected to constitute an unwarranted invasion of personal privacy." § 552(b)(7)(C). Further, FOIA provides that "[t]o the extent required to prevent a clearly unwarranted invasion of personal privacy, an agency may delete identifying details when it makes available or publishes an opinion, statement of policy, interpretation, or staff manual or instruction." § 552(a)(2). Consider the textual differences between Exemptions (6) and 7(c). Which exemption is more protective of privacy interests?

The exemptions are permissive; that is, agencies are not required to apply the exemptions. Only the government agency can raise Exemptions 6 and 7(C). The individual to whom the information pertains has no right to litigate the issue if the agency does not choose to; nor does the individual have a right to be given notice that her personal information falls within a FOIA request.[7]

The Law Enforcement Exemption. Exemption § 552(b)(7) depends upon the agency demonstrating "that the files were generated during legitimate law enforcement activity." *Freeman v. United States Dep't of Justice,* 723 F. Supp. 1115 (D. Md. 1988). "Exemption 7(E) may not be used to withhold information regarding investigative techniques that are illegal or of questionable legality." *Wilkinson v. FBI,* 633 F. Supp. 336, 349-50 (C.D. Cal. 1986). However, even if people become "an object of investigation because their names were obtained from an unlawful search," FOIA does not "require that documents generated in the investigation . . . be turned over." *Becker v. Internal Revenue Service,* 34 F.2d 398 (7th Cir. 1994).

State FOIAs. Every state has an open records law, most of which are patterned after the federal FOIA. These statutes are often referred to as "freedom of information," "open access," "right to know," or "sunshine" laws.

---

[7] For more background about FOIA's privacy exemptions, see James T. O'Reilly, *Expanding the Purpose of Federal Records Access: New Private Entitlement or New Threat to Privacy?,* 50 Admin. L. Rev. 371 (1998); Patricia M. Wald, *The Freedom of Information Act: A Short Case Study in the Perils and Paybacks of Legislating Democratic Values,* 33 Emory L.J. 649 (1984); Anthony T. Kronman, *The Privacy Exemption to the Freedom of Information Act,* 9 J. Legal Stud. 727 (1980).

United States Department of Justice v. Reporters Committee for Freedom of the Press

489 U.S. 749 (1989)

STEVENS, J. The Federal Bureau of Investigation (FBI) has accumulated and maintains criminal identification records, sometimes referred to as "rap sheets," on over 24 million persons. The question presented by this case is whether the disclosure of the contents of such a file to a third party "could reasonably be expected to constitute an unwarranted invasion of personal privacy" within the meaning of the Freedom of Information Act (FOIA), 5 U.S.C. § 552(b)(7)(C). . . .

In 1924 Congress appropriated funds to enable the Department of Justice (Department) to establish a program to collect and preserve fingerprints and other criminal identification records. That statute authorized the Department to exchange such information with "officials of States, cities and other institutions." Six years later Congress created the FBI's identification division, and gave it responsibility for "acquiring, collecting, classifying, and preserving criminal identification and other crime records and the exchanging of said criminal identification records with the duly authorized officials of governmental agencies, of States, cities, and penal institutions." Rap sheets compiled pursuant to such authority contain certain descriptive information, such as date of birth and physical characteristics, as well as a history of arrests, charges, convictions, and incarcerations of the subject. Normally a rap sheet is preserved until its subject attains age 80. . . .

. . . As a matter of executive policy, the Department has generally treated rap sheets as confidential and, with certain exceptions, has restricted their use to governmental purposes. . . .

Although much rapsheet information is a matter of public record, the availability and dissemination of the actual rap sheet to the public is limited. Arrests, indictments, convictions, and sentences are public events that are usually documented in court records. In addition, if a person's entire criminal history transpired in a single jurisdiction, all of the contents of his or her rap sheet may be available upon request in that jurisdiction. That possibility, however, is present in only three States. All of the other 47 States place substantial restrictions on the availability of criminal-history summaries even though individual events in those summaries are matters of public record. Moreover, even in Florida, Wisconsin, and Oklahoma, the publicly available summaries may not include information about out-of-state arrests or convictions. . . .

The statute known as FOIA is actually a part of the Administrative Procedure Act (APA). Section 3 of the APA as enacted in 1946 gave agencies broad discretion concerning the publication of governmental records. In 1966 Congress amended that section to implement " 'a general philosophy of full agency disclosure.' " . . . The amendment . . . requires every agency "upon any request for records which . . . reasonably describes such records" to make such records "promptly available to any person." If an agency improperly withholds any documents, the district court has jurisdiction to order their production. Unlike the review of other agency action that must be upheld if supported by substantial evidence and not arbitrary or capricious, FOIA expressly places the burden "on the agency to sustain its action" and directs the district courts to "determine the matter de novo."

Congress exempted nine categories of documents from FOIA's broad disclosure requirements. Three of those exemptions are arguably relevant to this case. Exemption 3 applies to documents that are specifically exempted from disclosure by another statute. § 552(b)(3). Exemption 6 protects "personnel and medical files and similar files the disclosure of which would constitute a clearly unwarranted invasion of personal privacy." § 552(b)(6). Exemption 7(C) excludes records or information compiled for law enforcement purposes, "but only to the extent that the production of such [materials] . . . could reasonably be expected to constitute an unwarranted invasion of personal privacy." § 552(b)(7)(C). . . .

This case arises out of requests made by a CBS news correspondent and the Reporters Committee for Freedom of the Press (respondents) for information concerning the criminal records of four members of the Medico family. The Pennsylvania Crime Commission had identified the family's company, Medico Industries, as a legitimate business dominated by organized crime figures. Moreover, the company allegedly had obtained a number of defense contracts as a result of an improper arrangement with a corrupt Congressman.

FOIA requests sought disclosure of any arrests, indictments, acquittals, convictions, and sentences of any of the four Medicos. Although the FBI originally denied the requests, it provided the requested data concerning three of the Medicos after their deaths. In their complaint in the District Court, respondents sought the rap sheet for the fourth, Charles Medico (Medico), insofar as it contained "matters of public record." . . .

Exemption 7(C) requires us to balance the privacy interest in maintaining, as the Government puts it, the "practical obscurity" of the rap sheets against the public interest in their release.

The preliminary question is whether Medico's interest in the nondisclosure of any rap sheet the FBI might have on him is the sort of "personal privacy" interest that Congress intended Exemption 7(C) to protect.[8] . . . Because events summarized in a rap sheet have been previously disclosed to the public, respondents contend that Medico's privacy interest in avoiding disclosure of a federal compilation of these events approaches zero. We reject respondents' cramped notion of personal privacy.

To begin with, both the common law and the literal understandings of privacy encompass the individual's control of information concerning his or her person. In an organized society, there are few facts that are not at one time or another divulged to another. Thus the extent of the protection accorded a privacy right at common law rested in part on the degree of dissemination of the allegedly private fact and the extent to which the passage of time rendered it private. According to Webster's initial definition, information may be classified as "private" if it is "intended for or restricted to the use of a particular person or group or class of persons: not freely available to the public." Recognition of this attribute of a privacy interest supports

---

[8] The question of the statutory meaning of privacy under the FOIA is, of course, not the same as the question whether a tort action might lie for invasion of privacy or the question whether an individual's interest in privacy is protected by the Constitution. *See, e.g., Cox Broadcasting Corp. v. Cohn,* 420 U.S. 469 (1975) (Constitution prohibits State from penalizing publication of name of deceased rape victim obtained from public records). . . .

the distinction, in terms of personal privacy, between scattered disclosure of the bits of information contained in a rap sheet and revelation of the rap sheet as a whole. The very fact that federal funds have been spent to prepare, index, and maintain these criminal-history files demonstrates that the individual items of information in the summaries would not otherwise be "freely available" either to the officials who have access to the underlying files or to the general public. Indeed, if the summaries were "freely available," there would be no reason to invoke the FOIA to obtain access to the information they contain. Granted, in many contexts the fact that information is not freely available is no reason to exempt that information from a statute generally requiring its dissemination. But the issue here is whether the compilation of otherwise hard-to-obtain information alters the privacy interest implicated by disclosure of that information. Plainly there is a vast difference between the public records that might be found after a diligent search of courthouse files, county archives, and local police stations throughout the country and a computerized summary located in a single clearinghouse of information. . . .

We have also recognized the privacy interest in keeping personal facts away from the public eye. In *Whalen v. Roe*, 429 U.S. 589 (1977), we held that "the State of New York may record, in a centralized computer file, the names and addresses of all persons who have obtained, pursuant to a doctor's prescription, certain drugs for which there is both a lawful and an unlawful market." In holding only that the Federal Constitution does not prohibit such a compilation, we recognized that such a centralized computer file posed a "threat to privacy":

> We are not unaware of the threat to privacy implicit in the accumulation of vast amounts of personal information in computerized data banks or other massive government files. The collection of taxes, the distribution of welfare and social security benefits, the supervision of public health, the direction of our Armed Forces, and the enforcement of the criminal laws all require the orderly preservation of great quantities of information, much of which is personal in character and potentially embarrassing or harmful if disclosed. The right to collect and use such data for public purposes is typically accompanied by a concomitant statutory or regulatory duty to avoid unwarranted disclosures. Recognizing that in some circumstances that duty arguably has its roots in the Constitution, nevertheless New York's statutory scheme, and its implementing administrative procedures, evidence a proper concern with, and protection of, the individual's interest in privacy.

In sum, the fact that "an event is not wholly 'private' does not mean that an individual has no interest in limiting disclosure or dissemination of the information." The privacy interest in a rap sheet is substantial. The substantial character of that interest is affected by the fact that in today's society the computer can accumulate and store information that would otherwise have surely been forgotten long before a person attains age 80, when the FBI's rap sheets are discarded. . . .

Exemption 7(C), by its terms, permits an agency to withhold a document only when revelation "could reasonably be expected to constitute an unwarranted invasion of personal privacy." We must next address what factors might warrant an invasion of the interest described [above].

Our previous decisions establish that whether an invasion of privacy is warranted cannot turn on the purposes for which the request for information is made. Except for cases in which the objection to disclosure is based on a claim of privilege and the person requesting disclosure is the party protected by the privilege, the identity of the requesting party has no bearing on the merits of his or her FOIA request. . . . As we have repeatedly stated, Congress "clearly intended" the FOIA "to give any member of the public as much right to disclosure as one with a special interest [in a particular document]."

Thus whether disclosure of a private document under Exemption 7(C) is warranted must turn on the nature of the requested document and its relationship to "the basic purpose of the Freedom of Information Act 'to open agency action to the light of public scrutiny,'" rather than on the particular purpose for which the document is being requested. In our leading case on FOIA, we declared that the Act was designed to create a broad right of access to "official information." *EPA v. Mink,* 410 U.S. 73, 80, (1973). In his dissent in that case, Justice Douglas characterized the philosophy of the statute by quoting this comment by Henry Steele Commager:

> " 'The generation that made the nation thought secrecy in government one of the instruments of Old World tyranny and committed itself to the principle that a democracy cannot function unless the people are permitted to know *what their government is up to.*' " (quoting from *The New York Review of Books*, Oct. 5, 1972, p. 7) (emphasis added).

. . . This basic policy of "'full agency disclosure unless information is exempted under clearly delineated statutory language,'" indeed focuses on the citizens' right to be informed about "what their government is up to." Official information that sheds light on an agency's performance of its statutory duties falls squarely within that statutory purpose. That purpose, however, is not fostered by disclosure of information about private citizens that is accumulated in various governmental files but that reveals little or nothing about an agency's own conduct. In this case — and presumably in the typical case in which one private citizen is seeking information about another — the requester does not intend to discover anything about the conduct of the agency that has possession of the requested records. Indeed, response to this request would not shed any light on the conduct of any Government agency or official. . . .

Respondents argue that there is a two-fold public interest in learning about Medico's past arrests or convictions: He allegedly had improper dealings with a corrupt Congressman, and he is an officer of a corporation with defense contracts. But if Medico has, in fact, been arrested or convicted of certain crimes, that information would neither aggravate nor mitigate his allegedly improper relationship with the Congressman; more specifically, it would tell us nothing directly about the character of the Congressman's behavior. Nor would it tell us anything about the conduct of the Department of Defense (DOD) in awarding one or more contracts to the Medico Company. . . . Conceivably Medico's rap sheet would provide details to include in a news story, but, in itself, this is not the kind of public interest for which Congress enacted the FOIA. In other words, although there is undoubtedly some public interest in anyone's criminal history, especially if the history is in some way related to the subject's dealing with a public official or agency, the FOIA's central purpose is to ensure that the Government's activities be opened to the sharp eye of public scrutiny, not that information about private citizens that happens to be in the warehouse of the Government be so disclosed. . . .

. . . The privacy interest in maintaining the practical obscurity of rap-sheet information will always be high. When the subject of such a rap sheet is a private citizen and when the information is in the Government's control as a compilation, rather than as a record of "what the Government is up to," the privacy interest protected by Exemption 7(C) is in fact at its apex while the FOIA-based public interest in disclosure is at its nadir. Such a disparity on the scales of justice holds for a class of cases without regard to individual circumstances; the standard virtues of bright-line rules are thus present, and the difficulties attendant to ad hoc adjudication may be avoided. Accordingly, we hold as a categorical matter that a third party's request for law enforcement records or information about a private citizen can reasonably be expected to invade that citizen's privacy, and that when the request seeks no "official information" about a Government agency, but merely records that the Government happens to be storing, the invasion of privacy is "unwarranted." . . .

BLACKMUN J., joined by BRENNAN, J. concurring in the judgment: I concur in the result the Court reaches in this case, but I cannot follow the route the Court takes to reach that result. In other words, the Court's use of "categorical balancing" under Exemption 7(C), I think, is not basically sound. Such a bright-line rule obviously has its appeal, but I wonder whether it would not run aground on occasion, such as in a situation where a rap sheet discloses a congressional candidate's conviction of tax fraud five years before. Surely, the FBI's disclosure of that information could not "reasonably be expected" to constitute an invasion of personal privacy, much less an unwarranted invasion, inasmuch as the candidate relinquished any interest in preventing the dissemination of this information when he chose to run for Congress. In short, I do not believe that Exemption 7(C)'s language and its legislative history, or the case law, support interpreting that provision as exempting all rap-sheet information from the FOIA's disclosure requirements.

NOTES & QUESTIONS

1. ***The Privacy Interest and "Practical Obscurity."*** Many courts, including the Supreme Court in other contexts, have held that once information is exposed to the public, it can no longer be considered private. In *Reporters Committee,* however, the Court recognizes a privacy interest in the rap sheets despite the fact that they are compiled from information in public records. The Court concludes that "there is a vast difference between the public records that might be found after a diligent search of courthouse files, county archives, and local police stations throughout the country and a computerized summary located in a single clearinghouse of information." Is the Court stretching privacy too far by claiming it can be violated by altering "practical obscurity"?

Daniel Solove argues in support of the Court's conception of privacy: "Privacy involves an expectation of a certain degree of accessibility of information. . . . Privacy can be violated by altering levels of accessibility, by taking obscure facts and making them widely accessible."[9] Is such a conception of privacy feasible?

2. ***The Interest in Public Access.*** The Court also denies access to the rap sheets because "this [FOIA] request would not shed any light on the conduct of any Government agency or official." What kind of use of government records is being sought in *Reporters Committee*? Does this use contribute to the public interest? Does the use comport with the purpose of FOIA?

3. ***The Court's Rationale Beyond the FOIA Context.*** In a footnote, the Court stated that the reasoning of this case is confined to the FOIA context. As a hypothetical case, imagine that there were no privacy exemptions to FOIA, and the FBI disclosed the rap sheets. The Medicos sue, claiming a violation of their constitutional right to information privacy. What would the result likely be? Can the Court coherently claim that people have a privacy interest in their rap sheet information under FOIA but not in the context of the constitutional right to information privacy?

4. ***Exemption 6.*** The *Reporters Committee* case concerned Exemption 7(C). Exemption 6 provides that FOIA's disclosure provisions do not apply to "*personnel and medical files and similar files* the disclosure of which would constitute a clearly unwarranted invasion of personal privacy." § 552(b)(6) (emphasis added). Does Exemption 6 only apply to "personnel and medical files"? What does "similar files" mean?

The Supreme Court answered these questions in *United States Dep't of State v. Washington Post Co.*, 456 U.S. 595 (1982). There, the *Washington Post* requested documents indicating whether two Iranian nationals were holding valid United States passports. According to the Department of State, the two individuals were prominent figures in Iran's Revolutionary Government; several Iranian revolutionary leaders had been strongly criticized in Iran for ties to the United States; and the two could be subject to violence if United States ties, such as passports, were disclosed. The *Washington Post* contended that the language of Exemption 6 simply did not cover these types of documents. The Court disagreed:

> The language of Exemption 6 sheds little light on what Congress meant by "similar files." Fortunately, the legislative history is somewhat more illuminating. The House and Senate Reports, although not defining the phrase "similar files," suggest that Congress' primary purpose in enacting Exemption 6 was to protect individuals from the injury and embarrassment that can result from the unnecessary disclosure of personal information. . . .
>
> . . . Congress' statements that it was creating a "general exemption" for information contained in "great quantities of files," suggest that the phrase "similar files" was to have a broad, rather than a narrow, meaning. This impression is confirmed by the frequent characterization of the "clearly

---

[9] Daniel J. Solove, *Access and Aggregation: Public Records, Privacy, and the Constitution*, 86 Minn. L. Rev. 1137, 1176-78 (2002).

unwarranted invasion of personal privacy" language as a "limitation" which holds Exemption 6 "within bounds." Had the words "similar files" been intended to be only a narrow addition to "personnel and medical files," there would seem to be no reason for concern about the exemption's being "held within bounds," and there surely would be clear suggestions in the legislative history that such a narrow meaning was intended. We have found none.

A proper analysis of the exemption must also take into account the fact that "personnel and medical files," the two benchmarks for measuring the term "similar files," are likely to contain much information about a particular individual that is not intimate. Information such as place of birth, date of birth, date of marriage, employment history, and comparable data is not normally regarded as highly personal, and yet respondent does not disagree that such information, if contained in a "personnel" or "medical" file, would be exempt from any disclosure that would constitute a clearly unwarranted invasion of personal privacy. . . .

. . . "[T]he protection of an individual's right of privacy" which Congress sought to achieve by preventing "the disclosure of [information] which might harm the individual," surely was not intended to turn upon the label of the file which contains the damaging information. . . .

In sum, we do not think that Congress meant to limit Exemption 6 to a narrow class of files containing only a discrete kind of personal information. Rather, "[t]he exemption [was] intended to cover detailed Government records on an individual which can be identified as applying to that individual." When disclosure of information which applies to a particular individual is sought from Government records, courts must determine whether release of the information would constitute a clearly unwarranted invasion of that person's privacy. . . .

5. *Definition of Agency.* FOIA requires only that "agencies" respond to requesters. Congress is not a federal agency and is therefore not subject to the Act. Nor is the President or his advisors, whose "sole function" is to "advise and assist" the President. For similar reasons, the National Security Council is not an agency. *Armstrong v. Executive Office of the President*, 90 F.3d 556 (D.C. Cir. 1996).

NATIONAL ARCHIVES AND RECORDS ADMINISTRATION V. FAVISH

541 U.S. 157 (2004)

KENNEDY, J. This is case requires us to interpret the Freedom of Information Act (FOIA), 5 U.S.C. § 552. FOIA does not apply if the requested data fall within one or more exemptions. Exemption 7(C) excuses from disclosure "records or information compiled for law enforcement purposes" if their production "could reasonably be expected to constitute an unwarranted invasion of personal privacy." § 552(b)(7)(C).

In *Department of Justice v. Reporters Comm. for Freedom of Press,* 489 U.S. 749 (1989), we considered the scope of Exemption 7(C) and held that release of the document at issue would be a prohibited invasion of the personal privacy of the person to whom the document referred. The principal document involved was the criminal record, or rap sheet, of the person who himself objected to the disclosure. Here, the information pertains to an official investigation into the circumstances surrounding an apparent suicide. The initial question is whether the exemption extends to the decedent's family when the family objects to the release of photographs showing the condition of the body at the scene of death. If we find the decedent's family does have a personal privacy interest recognized by the statute, we must then consider whether that privacy claim is outweighed by the public interest in disclosure.

Vincent Foster, Jr., deputy counsel to President Clinton, was found dead in Fort Marcy Park, located just outside Washington, D.C. The United States Park Police conducted the initial investigation and took color photographs of the death scene, including 10 pictures of Foster's body. The investigation concluded that Foster committed suicide by shooting himself with a revolver. Subsequent investigations by the Federal Bureau of Investigation, committees of the Senate and the House of Representatives, and independent counsels Robert Fiske and Kenneth Starr reached the same conclusion. Despite the unanimous finding of these five investigations, a citizen interested in the matter, Allan Favish, remained skeptical. Favish is now a respondent in this proceeding. . . .

It is common ground among the parties that the death-scene photographs in [the Office of Independent Counsel's, or] OIC's possession are "records or information compiled for law enforcement purposes" as that phrase is used in Exemption 7(C). This leads to the question whether disclosure of the four photographs "could reasonably be expected to constitute an unwarranted invasion of personal privacy." Favish contends the family has no personal privacy interest covered by Exemption 7(C). . . .

We disagree. The right to personal privacy is not confined, as Favish argues, to the "right to control information about oneself.". . . To say that the concept of personal privacy must "encompass" the individual's control of information about himself does not mean it cannot encompass other personal privacy interests as well. *Reporters Committee* had no occasion to consider whether individuals whose personal data are not contained in the requested materials also have a recognized privacy interest under Exemption 7(C). *Reporters Committee* explained, however, that the concept of personal privacy under Exemption 7(C) is not some limited or "cramped notion" of that idea. 489 U.S. at 763. Records or information are not to be released under the Act if disclosure "could reasonably be expected to constitute an unwarranted invasion of personal privacy." 5 U.S.C. § 552(b)(7). This provision is in marked contrast to the language in Exemption 6, pertaining to "personnel and medical files," where withholding is required only if disclosure "would constitute a clearly unwarranted invasion of personal privacy." § 552(b)(6). The adverb "clearly," found in Exemption 6, is not used in Exemption 7(C). In addition, "whereas Exemption 6 refers to disclosures that 'would constitute' an invasion of privacy, Exemption 7(C) encompasses any disclosure that 'could reasonably be expected to constitute' such an invasion." *Reporters Committee,* 489 U.S., at 756. . . .

Law enforcement documents obtained by Government investigators often contain information about persons interviewed as witnesses or initial suspects but whose link to the official inquiry may be the result of mere happenstance. There is special reason, therefore, to give protection to this intimate personal data, to which the public does not have a general right of access in the ordinary course. In this class of cases where the subject of the documents "is a private citizen," "the privacy interest . . . is at its apex."

. . . Foster's relatives . . . invoke their own right and interest to personal privacy. They seek to be shielded by the exemption to secure their own refuge from a sensation-seeking culture for their own peace of mind and tranquility, not for the sake of the deceased. . . .

. . . We have little difficulty . . . in finding in our case law and traditions the right of family members to direct and control disposition of the body of the deceased and to limit attempts to exploit pictures of the deceased family member's remains for public purposes.

Burial rites or their counterparts have been respected in almost all civilizations from time immemorial. See generally 26 *Encyclopaedia Britannica* 851 (15th ed. 1985) (noting that "[t]he ritual burial of the dead" has been practiced "from the very dawn of human culture and . . . in most parts of the world"); 5 *Encyclopedia of Religion* 450 (1987) ("[F]uneral rites . . . are the conscious cultural forms of one of our most ancient, universal, and unconscious impulses"). They are a sign of the respect a society shows for the deceased and for the surviving family members. The power of Sophocles' story in Antigone maintains its hold to this day because of the universal acceptance of the heroine's right to insist on respect for the body of her brother. *See* Antigone of Sophocles, 8 *Harvard Classics: Nine Greek Dramas* 255 (C. Eliot ed. 1909). The outrage at seeing the bodies of American soldiers mutilated and dragged through the streets is but a modern instance of the same understanding of the interests decent people have for those whom they have lost. Family members have a personal stake in honoring and mourning their dead and objecting to unwarranted public exploitation that, by intruding upon their own grief, tends to degrade the rites and respect they seek to accord to the deceased person who was once their own.

In addition this well-established cultural tradition acknowledging a family's control over the body and death images of the deceased has long been recognized at common law. Indeed, this right to privacy has much deeper roots in the common law than the rap sheets held to be protected from disclosure in *Reporters Committee.* An early decision by the New York Court of Appeals is typical:

> It is the right of privacy of the living which it is sought to enforce here. That right may in some cases be itself violated by improperly interfering with the character or memory of a deceased relative, but it is the right of the living, and not that of the dead, which is recognized. A privilege may be given the surviving relatives of a deceased person to protect his memory, but the privilege exists for the benefit of the living, to protect their feelings, and to prevent a violation of their own rights in the character and memory of the deceased. *Schuyler v. Curtis,* 147 N.Y. 434 (1895). . . .

We can assume Congress legislated against this background of law, scholarship, and history when it enacted FOIA and when it amended Exemption 7(C) to extend its terms. . . .

We have observed that the statutory privacy right protected by Exemption 7(C) goes beyond the common law and the Constitution. See *Reporters Committee,* 489 U.S., at 762, n.13 (contrasting the scope of the privacy protection under FOIA with the analogous protection under the common law and the Constitution). . . . It would be anomalous to hold in the instant case that the statute provides even less protection than does the common law.

The statutory scheme must be understood, moreover, in light of the consequences that would follow were we to adopt Favish's position. As a general rule, withholding information under FOIA cannot be predicated on the identity of the requester. See *Reporters Committee, supra,* at 771. We are advised by the Government that child molesters, rapists, murderers, and other violent criminals often make FOIA requests for autopsies, photographs, and records of their deceased victims. Our holding ensures that the privacy interests of surviving family members would allow the Government to deny these gruesome requests in appropriate cases. We find it inconceivable that Congress could have intended a definition of "personal privacy" so narrow that it would allow convicted felons to obtain these materials without limitations at the expense of surviving family members' personal privacy.

. . . [W]e hold that FOIA recognizes surviving family members' right to personal privacy with respect to their close relative's death-scene images. Our holding is consistent with the unanimous view of the Courts of Appeals and other lower courts that have addressed the question. . . .

Our ruling that the personal privacy protected by Exemption 7(C) extends to family members who object to the disclosure of graphic details surrounding their relative's death does not end the case. Although this privacy interest is within the terms of the exemption, the statute directs nondisclosure only where the information "could reasonably be expected to constitute an unwarranted invasion" of the family's personal privacy. The term "unwarranted" requires us to balance the family's privacy interest against the public interest in disclosure. . . .

FOIA is often explained as a means for citizens to know "what the Government is up to." This phrase should not be dismissed as a convenient formalism. It defines a structural necessity in a real democracy. The statement confirms that, as a general rule, when documents are within FOIA's disclosure provisions, citizens should not be required to explain why they seek the information. A person requesting the information needs no preconceived idea of the uses the data might serve. The information belongs to citizens to do with as they choose. Furthermore, as we have noted, the disclosure does not depend on the identity of the requester. As a general rule, if the information is subject to disclosure, it belongs to all.

When disclosure touches upon certain areas defined in the exemptions, however, the statute recognizes limitations that compete with the general interest in disclosure, and that, in appropriate cases, can overcome it. In the case of Exemption 7(C), the statute requires us to protect, in the proper degree, the personal privacy of citizens against the uncontrolled release of information compiled through the power of the state. The statutory direction that the information not be released if the invasion of personal privacy could reasonably be expected to be unwarranted requires the courts to balance the competing interests in privacy and disclosure. To effect this balance and to give practical meaning to the exemption, the usual rule that the citizen need not offer a reason for requesting the information must be inapplicable.

Where the privacy concerns addressed by Exemption 7(C) are present, the exemption requires the person requesting the information to establish a sufficient reason for the disclosure. First, the citizen must show that the public interest sought to be advanced is a significant one, an interest more specific than having the information for its own sake. Second, the citizen must show the information is likely to advance that interest. Otherwise, the invasion of privacy is unwarranted.

. . . In the case of photographic images and other data pertaining to an individual who died under mysterious circumstances, the justification most likely to satisfy Exemption 7(C)'s public interest requirement is that the information is necessary to show the investigative agency or other responsible officials acted negligently or otherwise improperly in the performance of their duties. . . .

We hold that, where there is a privacy interest protected by Exemption 7(C) and the public interest being asserted is to show that responsible officials acted negligently or otherwise improperly in the performance of their duties, the requester must establish more than a bare suspicion in order to obtain disclosure. Rather, the requester must produce evidence that would warrant a belief by a reasonable person that the alleged Government impropriety might have occurred. In *Department of State v. Ray,* 502 U.S. 164 (1991), we held there is a presumption of legitimacy accorded to the Government's official conduct. The presumption perhaps is less a rule of evidence than a general working principle. However the rule is characterized, where the presumption is applicable, clear evidence is usually required to displace it. . . . Given FOIA's prodisclosure purpose, however, the less stringent standard we adopt today is more faithful to the statutory scheme. Only when the FOIA requester has produced evidence sufficient to satisfy this standard will there exist a counterweight on the FOIA scale for the court to balance against the cognizable privacy interests in the requested records. . . . It would be quite extraordinary to say we must ignore the fact that five different inquiries into the Foster matter reached the same conclusion. . . . Favish has not produced any evidence that would warrant a belief by a reasonable person that the alleged Government impropriety might have occurred to put the balance into play. . . .

NOTES & QUESTIONS

1. *Characterizing the Public Interest in Disclosure.* Consider Lior Strahilevitz:

> [T]he *Favish* Court's conclusion that the [death-scene] photographs were made less newsworthy as a result of the previous investigations is unsatisfying. Favish requested the photographs because he believed that there was a conspiracy to cover up Foster's murder, and the Court noted that multiple separate investigations had debunked that murder theory. But suppose Favish had sought the release of the photographs to suggest different wrongdoing by the government—not its murder of a high government official, but its wasteful expenditure of resources on multiple investigations of what was obviously an open-and-shut case of suicide. Under the reasoning of the *Favish* opinion, a person seeking the disclosure of the autopsy photographs under such a theory ought to be able to prevail under the Court's balancing approach. If we take the reasoning of the opinion seriously, you or I should be able to obtain the Foster autopsy photos if we just recharacterize the government's misconduct.[10]

---

[10] Lior Jacob Strahilevitz, *Reunifying Privacy Law,* 98 Cal. L. Rev. 2007, 2024 (2010).

Had the Court characterized the public interest in disclosure as Strahilevitz suggests, should that tip the balance to disclosure? Conspiracy theorists might question the validity of any government investigation, no matter how thorough or convincing. Should the Court make qualitative judgments about when curiosity about a matter is legitimate as opposed to unjustified or paranoid?

2. ***The Implications of Post-Mortem Privacy.*** Apart from the narrow context of FOIA, how will post-mortem privacy interests function in other areas of law? Are there other privacy interests that should or should not exist after one's death?

3. ***Corporations and Exemption 7(C).*** In *Federal Communications Commission v. AT&T*, 131 S. Ct. 1177 (2011), the Supreme Court, in a unanimous opinion, found that corporations did not have "personal privacy" for the purposes of FOIA's Exemption 7(C). As a result, corporations cannot claim that this exemption shields corporate documents from release. Part of the Court's argument was linguistic; part turned on the specific context of FOIA. Regarding FOIA's language, the Court declared, "in ordinary usage, a noun and its adjective form may have meanings as disparate as any two unrelated words." Thus, while FOIA defined "person" to include corporations, this definition was not dispositive for the word "personal" in Exemption 7(C). The Court noted that, "we often use the word 'personal' to mean precisely the *opposite* of business-related: We speak of personal expenses and business expenses, personal life and work life, personal opinion and a company's view."

As far as FOIA was concerned, the Court noted that Exemption 7(C) used language that traced Exemption 6, which concerns "personnel and medical files" as well any "similar" file and not the language in Exemption 4, which pertains to "trade secrets and commercial or financial information." Exemption 4 clearly pertains to corporations, and Congress did not follow the language that "plainly covered" corporations.[11]

4. ***National Security and Critical Infrastructure Information.*** Post 9/11, the federal government has taken a new restrictive approach to FOIA. First, as part of the Homeland Security Act, the Bush Administration oversaw enactment of a new exemption to FOIA in the Critical Infrastructure Information Act of 2002 (CIIA). The CIIA exempts from FOIA disclosure any information that a private party voluntarily provides to the Department of Homeland Security (DHS) if the information relates to the security of vital infrastructure.

"Critical infrastructure information" is "information not customarily in the public domain and related to the security of critical infrastructure or protected [computer] systems." 6 U.S.C. § 131. In a report prepared for Rep. Henry A. Waxman (Waxman Report), the Minority Staff, Special Investigation Division, Committee on Government Reform, stated:

> Communications from the private sector to government agencies are routinely released under FOIA (apart from confidential business information). This is an

---

[11] In closing his opinion for the Court in *Federal Communications v. AT&T*, Chief Justice Roberts concludes with a great closing quip: "The protection in FOIA against disclosure of law enforcement information on the ground that it would constitute an unwarranted invasion of personal privacy does not extend to corporation. We trust that AT&T will not take it personally."

important check against capture of governmental agencies by special interests. But under the critical infrastructure information exemption even routine communications can be withheld from disclosure.[12]

In an op-ed in the *Washington Post*, Mark Tapscott of the Heritage Foundation asked for clarification of "what constitutes vulnerabilities" of infrastructure in order to prevent the CIIA from being "manipulated by clever corporate and government operators to hide endless varieties of potentially embarrassing and/or criminal information from public view."

The Waxman Report also noted that CIIA exempts from FOIA all information that is marked critical infrastructure information. As a consequence, the CIIA may not permit the redaction that is otherwise normally carried out under FOIA. As the Report states, "None of the information in a submission marked as critical infrastructure information is likely to be disclosed, even when portions of the information do not themselves constitute critical infrastructure information."[13]

Second, beyond the enactment of CIIA, a further move toward a restrictive approach to FOIA was made through the Executive Branch's introduction of the concept of "sensitive but unclassified information." On March 19, 2002, Andrew Card, White House Chief of Staff, issued an important memorandum that instructs federal agencies to deny disclosure of "sensitive but unclassified information."[14] The Card Memorandum urged agencies to safeguard records regarding weapons of mass destruction and "other information that could be misused to harm the security of our Nation and the safety of our people." The Card Memorandum urged agencies to apply FOIA's Exemption 2 or Exemption 4 in withholding such records. Please reread these exemptions reprinted earlier in this section. How do you think they are being extended to apply to "sensitive but unclassified information"?

Consider the following argument by Mary-Rose Papandrea:

> FOIA is riddled with large, undefined exceptions. When information arguably involves national security, courts are too timid to force the executive branch to provide a thorough explanation for continued secrecy. . . .
>
> The "right to know" has encountered additional and more disturbing problems since the terrorist attacks of September 11. Not only has the courts' tendency to defer to the Executive's national security risk assessment become exaggerated, but courts now appear overtly hostile to the very existence of a right of access during a time of crisis. Instead, they suggest that an enforceable right to know is unnecessary because the political process is adequate to force government disclosure.[15]

---

[12] U.S. House of Representatives, *Committee on Government Reform, Minority Staff, Special Investigations Division, Secrecy in the Bush Administration* 9 (Sept. 14, 2004).

[13] *Id.* at 10.

[14] Andrew H. Card, Jr., Assistant to the President and Chief of Staff, *Memorandum for the Heads of Executive Departments and Agencies; Subject: Action to Safeguard Information Regarding Weapons of Mass Destruction and Other Sensitive Documents Relating to Homeland Security* (Mar. 19, 2002), at http://www.usdoj.gov/oip/foiapost/2002foiapost10.htm.

[15] Mary-Rose Papandrea, *Under Attack: The Public's Right to Know and the War on Terror*, 25 B.C. Third World L.J. 35, 79-80 (2005).

David Vladek has offered a similar negative view of FOIA.[16] He faults the slow process of "drafting and submitting FOIA requests and waiting for the agency's response." Vladek also argues that it has been "subject to political manipulation by administrations that are intent on limiting public access to government held information" and undercut by judicial interpretation of its provisions.

Finally, Seth Kreimer provides a positive analysis of the impact of FOIA.[17] In his judgment, it "must be understood as functioning within a broader ecology of transparency." Moreover, "[a]s part of that system, it has done underappreciated service in the past half-decade and partakes of virtues of resiliency and efficacy that should be acknowledged and preserved." Kreimer identifies a number of successful FOIA actions that have taken place in the context of the "Global War on Terror." He finds, "It has been predominately the availability of well-financed NGOs, combined with the possibility of assistance from the private bar, that has made FOIA a force to be reckoned with in this arena."

How should open government be reconciled with national security concerns?

5. ***Desired and Undesired Privacy.*** In *Associated Press v. Department of Defense,* 554 F.3d 274 (2d Cir. 2009), the Associated Press requested from the Department of Defense (DOD) identifying information about detainees alleging abuse at the Guantanamo Bay detention facility as well as identifying information about the detainee's family members. The DOD asserted that disclosure would violate the detainees' privacy interests and that the FOIA privacy Exemptions 6 and 7(C) applied. Regarding the detainees, the court held that Exemption 7(C) barred disclosure of their identities. The court first concluded that the detainees had a right to privacy:

> We first consider the detainees who allegedly have been abused by military personnel or other detainees. Certainly they have an interest in both keeping the personal facts of their abuse from the public eye and in avoiding disclosure of their identities in order to prevent embarrassment. As victims of abuse, they are entitled to some protection of personal information that would be revealed if their names were associated with the incidents of abuse. The disclosure of their names could certainly subject them to embarrassment and humiliation. . . .

Turning to the public interest in the disclosure of the detainee identities, the court held:

> AP's first argument appears to suggest that the alleged government impropriety in handling these allegations of various abuses may be tied to the nationalities or religions of the detainees involved. In essence, AP implies that DOD may have responded differently to allegations of abuse depending on the nationalities or religions of the abused detainees. Without that underlying assumption, knowing the detainees' nationalities or religions would not serve the public interest because it would shed no light on what the government is up

---

[16] David C. Vladek, *Information Access: Surveying the Current Legal Landscape of Federal Right-to-Know Laws*, 86 Tex. L. Rev. 1787 (2008).

[17] Seth F. Kreimer, *The Freedom of Information Act and the Ecology of Transparency*, 10 U. Pa. J. Const. L. 101 (2008).

to. AP's argument in this regard is squarely foreclosed by *Favish,* in which the Supreme Court held:

> [W]here there is a privacy interest protected by Exemption 7(C) and the public interest being asserted is to show that responsible officials acted negligently or otherwise improperly in the performance of their duties, the requester must establish more than a bare suspicion in order to obtain disclosure. Rather, the requester must produce evidence that would warrant a belief by a reasonable person that the alleged Government impropriety might have occurred.
>
> . . . AP has produced no evidence that DOD responded differently to allegations of abuse depending on the nationalities or religions of the detainees involved. Because there is no evidence of government impropriety in that regard, we cannot find that the public interest would be furthered based on a rationale grounded in disclosure of an individual's religion or nationality.
>
> AP's second argument, that the names and identifying information would allow the public to track these detainees' treatment in other aspects of DOD actions, including transfer and release decisions, deserves more attention. . . . [I]f the identities of the detainees involved in the abuse allegations were known, it might be possible to see whether those allegations affected the government's decision to transfer, release, or continue to detain them. Although under this rationale the public interest might be further served, the speculative nature of the result is insufficient to outweigh the detainees' privacy interest in nondisclosure.
>
> AP's third argument, that the information will allow the public to seek out the detainees' side of the story, calls upon a "derivative use" theory. That theory posits that the public interest can be read more broadly to include the ability to use redacted information to obtain additional as yet undiscovered information outside the government files. . . . [T]he Supreme Court [has] reasoned that "[m]ere speculation about hypothetical public benefits cannot outweigh a demonstrably significant invasion of privacy."

Lior Strahilevitz argues that some of the detainees would have welcomed the disclosure of their identities. In a footnote to the opinion, the court reasoned that it was not analyzing the privacy interests of the prisoners categorically or individually, but Strahilevitz counters that the logical implication of the court's ruling was to choose the categorical approach. As Strahilevitz explains:

> A categorical approach necessarily would result in complete disclosure or non-disclosure, whereas an individuated approach — constructive partition of the list of detainees — necessarily would result in partial disclosure. By ruling in favor of complete non-disclosure, the court had to embrace a categorical basis for deciding the issue, its protests to the contrary notwithstanding.
>
> As the court saw it, the fact that some detainees wanted their identities disclosed was irrelevant. Moreover, under the court's holding, and its categorical-though-ostensibly-not-categorical approach, the objections of one privacy seeking detainee would trump the desires of scores of other publicity-seeking detainees.[18]

---

[18] Lior Jacob Strahilevitz, *Collective Privacy*, in *The Offensive Internet: Privacy, Speech, and Reputation* 219, 226–27 (Saul Levmore & Martha C. Nussbaum eds. 2010).

Should the court have examined the desires of the detainees individually? Was the government using "privacy" as a tool to make it harder for the press to investigate the alleged abuse?

3. CONSTITUTIONAL REQUIREMENTS OF PUBLIC ACCESS

The Common Law Right to Access Public Records. As the Supreme Court held in *Nixon v. Warner Communications, Inc.,* 435 U.S. 589 (1978): "It is clear that the courts of this country recognize a general right to inspect and copy public records and documents, including judicial records and documents." The right to access public records is justified by "the citizen's desire to keep a watchful eye on the workings of public agencies, and in a newspaper publisher's intention to publish information concerning the operation of government." Thus, under the common law, the Court concluded, there is a general right to access public records and court records. The Court noted that the right to access is not absolute.

Court Records. Courts have a long tradition of allowing open access to court records. In *Nixon v. Warner Communications, Inc.,* 435 U.S. 589 (1978), the Supreme Court stated: "Every court has supervisory power over its own records and files, and access has been denied where court files might have become a vehicle for improper purposes." Access to court records is "best left to the sound discretion of the trial court, a discretion to be exercised in light of the relevant facts and circumstances of the particular case." In *Seattle Times Co. v. Rhinehart,* 467 U.S. 20, 33 (1984), the Court held that "pretrial depositions and interrogatories are not public components of a civil trial. Such proceedings were not open to the public at common law, and, in general, they are conducted in private as a matter of modern practice."

The First Amendment Right to Access. The First Amendment requires that certain judicial proceedings be open to the public. In *Globe Newspaper v. Superior Court,* 457 U.S. 596 (1982), the Supreme Court articulated a test to determine whether the First Amendment requires public access to a proceeding: (1) whether the proceeding "historically has been open to the press and general public" and (2) whether access "plays a particularly significant role in the functioning of the judicial process and the government as a whole." The court in *Globe* concluded that the First Amendment requires public access to criminal trials, and the government can deny access only if "the denial is necessitated by a compelling governmental interest and is narrowly tailored to serve that interest." According to the Court, the First Amendment right to access extends to voir dire in a capital murder trial. *Press-Enterprise Co. v. Superior Court* ("*Press-Enterprise I*"), 464 U.S. 501 (1984). It also extends to pre-trial proceedings. *Press-Enterprise Co. v. Superior Court* ("*Press-Enterprise II*"), 478 U.S. 1 (1986).

Privacy of Litigants and Jurors. A court can permit plaintiffs to proceed under a pseudonym, although "it is the exceptional case in which a plaintiff may proceed under a fictitious name." *Doe v. Frank,* 951 F.2d 320, 323 (11th Cir. 1992). Courts can also provide for jurors to remain anonymous. Is such anonymity appropriate?

Consider the case of Juror Number Four. In a well-publicized criminal trial against Tyco International executive L. Dennis Kozlowski, during the jury's 12 days of deliberating, newspapers identified Juror Number Four by name because she appeared to gesture an "O.K." sign to the defense table. The articles stated that she lived on the Upper East Side of Manhattan and that the apartment building staff found her to be cold and stingy. The newspapers reported that friends described her as opinionated and stubborn. Extensive coverage of the juror continued. As a result of the coverage, the juror received a threatening note, and the judge declared a mistrial. On the one hand, the media was reporting on possible juror misconduct. On the other hand, the media coverage interfered with the trial. Suppose on retrial, the judge were to order that the identities of all the jurors shall not be disclosed. Would such an order be constitutional?

Consider *United States v. Blagojevich,* 612 F.3d 558 (7th Cir. 2010), where the court held that jurors' names in the highly publicized case of former Illinois Governor Rod Blagojevich must be released to the public. The court based its decision on the common law right to access public records. Dissenting from a denial to rehear the case en banc, Judge Posner wrote:

> Whatever the situation in England, there is no *general* federal common-law right of public access to information relating to federal litigation. Such a right would create a presumption of access to jury deliberations, appellate judicial deliberations, depositions whether or not used at trial, terms of settlement, grand jury proceedings, judges' discussions with their law clerks, and so on. No one thinks that the media can demand access to any of these phases of the litigation process, or that if they do the judge must hold a hearing to consider their demand; why should the media have a presumptive right to the names of the jurors before a trial ends?
>
> The panel cites *Nixon v. Warner Communications, Inc.,* 435 U.S. 589 (1978), which created a "presumption . . . in favor of public access to judicial records" to enable the public to "monitor the functioning of our courts, thereby insuring quality, honesty and respect for our legal system." But jurors' *names*—as distinct from evidence, materials attached to dispositive motions, and judicial rulings—are not judicial records. "The courts have not extended [the common law right of access] beyond materials on which a court relies in determining the litigants' substantive rights." *Anderson v. Cryovac, Inc.,* 805 F.2d 1, 13 (1st Cir. 1986).

In some jurisdictions, the court records of divorce cases are made public. Is such a policy advisable? This issue is best illustrated by what happened in June 2004, when at the request of the *Chicago Tribune* and a TV station, a judge ordered the unsealing of the divorce records of Illinois Republican Senate candidate Jack Ryan and his wife, actress Jeri Ryan. Both Jack and Jeri had vigorously objected to the unsealing of the records, which they contended would cause harm to them as well as their nine-year-old child. The records revealed Jeri's accusations that Jack had taken her to sex clubs and asked her to perform sex acts that made her uncomfortable. A few days after the release of the records, Jack abandoned his quest for the Senate. Was the release of the records appropriate in this case? Jack was a political candidate, and Jeri was a well-known actress. Does their public figure status affect the analysis? Should it? To what extent should the effect of the release of the information on a couple's children be a factor in the analysis?

LOS ANGELES POLICE DEPARTMENT V. UNITED REPORTING
PUBLISHING CORP.

528 U.S. 32 (1999)

REHNQUIST, C.J. California Government Code § 6254(f)(3) places two conditions on public access to arrestees' addresses — that the person requesting an address declare that the request is being made for one of five prescribed purposes, and that the requestor also declare that the address will not be used directly or indirectly to sell a product or service.

The District Court permanently enjoined enforcement of the statute, and the Court of Appeals affirmed, holding that the statute was facially invalid because it unduly burdens commercial speech. We hold that the statutory section in question was not subject to a "facial" challenge.

Petitioner, the Los Angeles Police Department, maintains records relating to arrestees. Respondent, United Reporting Publishing Corporation, is a private publishing service that provides the names and addresses of recently arrested individuals to its customers, who include attorneys, insurance companies, drug and alcohol counselors, and driving schools.

Before July 1, 1996, respondent received arrestees' names and addresses under the old version of § 6254, which generally required state and local law enforcement agencies to make public the name, address, and occupation of every individual arrested by the agency. Cal. Govt. Code § 6254(f). Effective July 1, 1996, the state legislature amended § 6254(f) to limit the public's access to arrestees' and victims' current addresses. The amended statute provides that state and local law enforcement agencies shall make public:

> [T]he current address of every individual arrested by the agency and the current address of the victim of a crime, where the requester declares under penalty of perjury that the request is made for a scholarly, journalistic, political, or governmental purpose, or that the request is made for investigation purposes by a licensed private investigator . . . except that the address of the victim of [certain crimes] shall remain confidential. Address information obtained pursuant to this paragraph shall not be used directly or indirectly to sell a product or service to any individual or group of individuals, and the requester shall execute a declaration to that effect under penalty of perjury. Cal. Govt. Code § 6254(f)(3).

Sections 6254(f)(1) and (2) require that state and local law enforcement agencies make public, inter alia, the name, occupation, and physical description, including date of birth, of every individual arrested by the agency, as well as the circumstances of the arrest. Thus, amended § 6254(f) limits access only to the arrestees' addresses.

Before the effective date of the amendment, respondent sought declaratory and injunctive relief pursuant to 42 U.S.C. § 1983 to hold the amendment unconstitutional under the First and Fourteenth Amendments to the United States Constitution. On the effective date of the statute, petitioner and other law enforcement agencies denied respondent access to the address information because, according to respondent, "[respondent's] employees could not sign section 6254(f)(3) declarations." Respondent did not allege, and nothing in the record before this Court indicates, that it ever "declar[ed] under penalty of perjury" that it was requesting information for one of the prescribed purposes and that it would not use the address information to "directly or indirectly . . . sell a product or service," as would have been required by the statute. *See* § 6254(f)(3).

Respondent then amended its complaint and sought a temporary restraining order. The District Court issued a temporary restraining order, and, a few days later, issued a preliminary injunction. Respondent then filed a motion for summary judgment, which was granted. In granting the motion, the District Court construed respondent's claim as presenting a facial challenge to amended § 6254(f). The court held that the statute was facially invalid under the First Amendment.

The Court of Appeals affirmed the District Court's facial invalidation. The court concluded that the statute restricted commercial speech, and, as such, was entitled to "'a limited measure of protection, commensurate with its subordinate position in the scale of First Amendment values.'" The court applied the test set out in *Central Hudson Gas & Elec. Corp. v. Public Serv. Comm'n of N.Y.*, 447 U.S. 557 (1980), and found that the asserted governmental interest in protecting arrestees' privacy was substantial. But, the court held that "the numerous exceptions to § 6254(f)(3) for journalistic, scholarly, political, governmental, and investigative purposes render the statute unconstitutional under the First Amendment." The court noted that "[h]aving one's name, crime, and address printed in the local paper is a far greater affront to privacy than receiving a letter from an attorney, substance abuse counselor, or driving school eager to help one overcome his present difficulties (for a fee, naturally)," and thus that the exceptions "undermine and counteract" the asserted governmental interest in preserving arrestees' privacy. Thus, the Court of Appeals affirmed the District Court's grant of summary judgment in favor of respondent and upheld the injunction against enforcement of § 6254(f)(3). We granted certiorari.

We hold that respondent was not, under our cases, entitled to prevail on a "facial attack" on § 6254(f)(3).

Respondent's primary argument in the District Court and the Court of Appeals was that § 6254(f)(3) was invalid on its face, and respondent maintains that position here. But we believe that our cases hold otherwise.

The traditional rule is that "a person to whom a statute may constitutionally be applied may not challenge that statute on the ground that it may conceivably be applied unconstitutionally to others in situations not before the Court."

Prototypical exceptions to this traditional rule are First Amendment challenges to statutes based on First Amendment overbreadth. "At least when statutes regulate or proscribe speech . . . the transcendent value to all society of constitutionally protected expression is deemed to justify allowing 'attacks on overly broad statutes with no requirement that the person making the attack demonstrate that his own conduct could not be regulated by a statute drawn with the requisite narrow specificity.'" "This is deemed necessary because persons whose expression is constitutionally protected may well refrain from exercising their right for fear of criminal sanctions provided by a statute susceptible of application to protected expression." . . .

Even though the challenge be based on the First Amendment, the overbreadth doctrine is not casually employed. "Because of the wide-reaching effects of striking down a statute on its face at the request of one whose own conduct may be punished despite the First Amendment, we have recognized that the overbreadth doctrine is 'strong medicine' and have employed it with hesitation, and then 'only as a last resort.'" . . .

The Court of Appeals held that § 6254(f)(3) was facially invalid under the First Amendment. Petitioner contends that the section in question is not an abridgment of anyone's right to engage in speech, be it commercial or otherwise, but simply a law regulating access to information in the hands of the police department.

We believe that, at least for purposes of facial invalidation, petitioner's view is correct. This is not a case in which the government is prohibiting a speaker from conveying information that the speaker already possesses. The California statute in question merely requires that if respondent wishes to obtain the addresses of arrestees it must qualify under the statute to do so. Respondent did not attempt to qualify and was therefore denied access to the addresses. For purposes of assessing the propriety of a facial invalidation, what we have before us is nothing more than a governmental denial of access to information in its possession. California could decide not to give out arrestee information at all without violating the First Amendment.

To the extent that respondent's "facial challenge" seeks to rely on the effect of the statute on parties not before the Court — its potential customers, for example — its claim does not fit within the case law allowing courts to entertain facial challenges. No threat of prosecution, for example, or cutoff of funds hangs over their heads. They may seek access under the statute on their own just as respondent did, without incurring any burden other than the prospect that their request will be denied. Resort to a facial challenge here is not warranted because there is "no possibility that protected speech will be muted." . . .

GINSBURG, J. joined by O'CONNOR, SOUTER, and BREYER, JJ. concurring. I join the Court's opinion, which recognizes that California Government Code § 6254(f)(3) is properly analyzed as a restriction on access to government information, not as a restriction on protected speech. That is sufficient reason to reverse the Ninth Circuit's judgment.

As the Court observes, the statute at issue does not restrict speakers from conveying information they already possess. Anyone who comes upon arrestee address information in the public domain is free to use that information as she sees fit. It is true, as Justice Scalia suggests, that the information could be provided to and published by journalists, and § 6254(f)(3) would indeed be a speech restriction if it then prohibited people from using that published information to speak to or about arrestees. But the statute contains no such prohibition. Once address information is in the public domain, the statute does not restrict its use in any way.

California could, as the Court notes, constitutionally decide not to give out arrestee address information at all. It does not appear that the selective disclosure of address information that California has chosen instead impermissibly burdens speech. To be sure, the provision of address information is a kind of subsidy to people who wish to speak to or about arrestees, and once a State decides to make such a benefit available to the public, there are no doubt limits to its freedom to decide how that benefit will be distributed. California could not, for example, release address information only to those whose political views were in line with the party in power. But if the award of the subsidy is not based on an illegitimate criterion such as viewpoint, California is free to support some speech without supporting other speech.

Throughout its argument, respondent assumes that § 6254(f)(3)'s regime of selective disclosure burdens speech in the sense of reducing the total flow of information. Whether that is correct is far from clear and depends on the point of comparison. If California were to publish the names and addresses of arrestees for everyone to use freely, it would indeed be easier to speak to and about arrestees than it is under the present system. But if States were required to choose between keeping proprietary information to themselves and making it available without limits, States might well choose the former option. In that event, disallowing selective disclosure would lead not to more speech overall but to more secrecy and less speech. As noted above, this consideration could not justify limited disclosures that discriminated on the basis of viewpoint or some other proscribed criterion. But it does suggest that society's interest in the free flow of information might argue for upholding laws like the one at issue in this case rather than imposing an all-or-nothing regime under which "nothing" could be a State's easiest response.

STEVENS, J. joined by KENNEDY, J. dissenting. . . . To determine whether the Amendment is valid as applied to respondent, it is similarly not necessary to invoke the overbreadth doctrine. That doctrine is only relevant if the challenger needs to rely on the possibility of invalid applications to third parties. In this case, it is the application of the Amendment to respondent itself that is at issue. Nor, in my opinion, is it necessary to do the four-step *Central Hudson* dance, because I agree with the majority that the Amendment is really a restriction on access to government information rather than a direct restriction on protected speech. For this reason, the majority is surely correct in observing that "California could decide not to give out arrestee information at all without violating the First Amendment." Moreover, I think it equally clear that California could release the information on a selective basis to a limited group of users who have a special, and legitimate, need for the information.

A different, and more difficult, question is presented when the State makes information generally available, but denies access to a small disfavored class. In this case, the State is making the information available to scholars, news media, politicians, and others, while denying access to a narrow category of persons solely because they intend to use the information for a constitutionally protected purpose. As Justice Ginsburg points out, if the State identified the disfavored persons based on their viewpoint, or political affiliation, for example, the discrimination would clearly be invalid.

What the State did here, in my opinion, is comparable to that obviously unconstitutional discrimination. In this case, the denial of access is based on the fact that respondent plans to publish the information to others who, in turn, intend to use it for a commercial speech purpose that the State finds objectionable. Respondent's proposed publication of the information is indisputably lawful — petitioner concedes that if respondent independently acquires the data, the First Amendment protects its right to communicate it to others. Similarly, the First Amendment supports the third parties' use of it for commercial speech purposes. Thus, because the State's discrimination is based on its desire to prevent the information from being used for constitutionally protected purposes, I think it must assume the burden of justifying its conduct.

The only justification advanced by the State is an asserted interest in protecting the privacy of victims and arrestees. Although that interest would explain a total ban on access, or a statute narrowly limiting access, it is insufficient when the data can be published in the news media and obtained by private investigators or others who meet the Amendment's vague criteria. . . . By allowing such widespread access to the information, the State has eviscerated any rational basis for believing that the Amendment will truly protect the privacy of these persons.

That the State might simply withhold the information from all persons does not insulate its actions from constitutional scrutiny. For even though government may withhold a particular benefit entirely, it "may not deny a benefit to a person on a basis that infringes his constitutionally protected interests — especially his interest in freedom of speech." A contrary view would impermissibly allow the government to "'produce a result which [it] could not command directly.'" It is perfectly clear that California could not directly censor the use of this information or the resulting speech. It follows, I believe, that the State's discriminatory ban on access to information — in an attempt to prohibit persons from exercising their constitutional rights to publish it in a truthful and accurate manner — is equally invalid.

Accordingly, I respectfully dissent.

NOTES & QUESTIONS

1. ***Reconciling Privacy and Transparency.*** Consider the following argument by Daniel Solove:

> How can the tension between transparency and privacy be reconciled? Must access to public records be sacrificed at the altar of privacy? Or must privacy be compromised as the price for a government disinfected by sunlight?
>
> It is my thesis that both transparency and privacy can be balanced through limitations on the access and use of personal information in public records. . . . We can make information accessible for certain purposes only. When government discloses information, it can limit how it discloses that information by preventing it from being amassed by companies for commercial purposes, to be sold to others, or to be combined with other information and sold back to the government. . . .
>
> . . . [B]y making access conditional on accepting certain responsibilities when using data — such as using it for specific purposes, not disclosing it to others, and so on, certain functions of transparency can be preserved at the same time privacy is protected.[19]

However, does this approach, as Justice Stevens contends in his dissent, impermissibly single out certain types of speakers? What if the California statute limited disclosure of the information to anybody who would use a form of mass communication or widespread publicity to disclose that information? In other words, what if it excluded journalists and the media from access?

---

[19] Daniel J. Solove, *Access and Aggregation: Public Records, Privacy, and the Constitution*, 86 Minn. L. Rev. 1137 (2002).

2. **Florida Star v. B.J.F.** In *Florida Star v. B.J.F.,* 491 U.S. 524 (1989), the Supreme Court struck down a Florida law that prohibited the press from publishing a rape victim's name that inadvertently appeared in a public record. The Court held: "[W]here a newspaper publishes truthful information which it has lawfully obtained, punishment may lawfully be imposed, if at all, only when narrowly tailored to a state interest of the highest order." Daniel Solove notes:

> Governments can make a public record available *on the condition that* certain information is not disclosed or used in a certain manner. However, governments cannot establish post-access restrictions on the disclosure or use of information that is publicly available. Once the information is made available to the public, the *Florida Star* cases prohibit a state from restricting use.[20]

Is *United Reporting* consistent with *Florida Star*? Suppose Florida passed a law that in order for the press to access its police reports about sexual assaults, journalists would have to agree to not disclose rape victims' names from the reports. Would this law be constitutional?

3. ***Disclosure of Social Security Numbers in Public Records.*** In *Ostergren v. Cuccinelli,* 615 F.3d 263 (4th Cir. 2010), privacy activist Betty Ostergren obtained real estate records for politicians and disclosed them online with unredacted Social Security numbers (SSNs) to demonstrate the problems of the availability of SSNs in public records. Ostergren challenged a law criminalizing the intentional communication of another person's SSN to the general public. The court held:

> Virginia argues that the unredacted SSNs on Ostergren's website should not be protected under the First Amendment because they facilitate identity theft and are no essential part of any exposition of ideas. Although these observations might be true under certain circumstances, we cannot agree with Virginia's argument here. The unredacted SSNs on Virginia land records that Ostergren has posted online are integral to her message. Indeed, they *are* her message. Displaying them proves Virginia's failure to safeguard private information and powerfully demonstrates why Virginia citizens should be concerned. . . . Thus, although we do not foreclose the possibility that communicating SSNs might be found unprotected in other situations, we conclude, on these facts, that the First Amendment does reach Ostergren's publication of Virginia land records containing unredacted SSNs.

After concluding that Ostergren's posting of the records was protected by the First Amendment, the Fourth Circuit proceeded to analyze whether the state law survived strict scrutiny. The court concluded that protecting people's SSNs from disclosure was an interest of the highest order. The law, however, was not narrowly tailored to achieve this goal:

> We cannot conclude that prohibiting Ostergren from posting public records online would be narrowly tailored to protecting individual privacy when Virginia currently makes those same records available through secure remote access without having redacted SSNs. The record reflects that 15 clerks of court

---

[20] *Id.*

have not finished redacting SSNs from their land records, which are nonetheless available online. Under *Cox Broadcasting* and its progeny, the First Amendment does not allow Virginia to punish Ostergren for posting its land records online without redacting SSNs when numerous clerks are doing precisely that. *Cf. Florida Star,* 491 U.S. at 535 ("[W]here the government has made certain information publicly available, it is highly anomalous to sanction persons other than the source of its release."). Virginia could curtail SSNs' public disclosure much more narrowly by directing clerks not to make land records available through secure remote access until after SSNs have been redacted.

4. CONSTITUTIONAL LIMITATIONS ON PUBLIC ACCESS

(a) Public Records

Like the federal FOIA, many states have privacy exemptions in their freedom of information laws. But not all states balance privacy and transparency equally. Are there limitations on what information governments can release to the public? Consider the cases below:

KALLSTROM V. CITY OF COLUMBUS

136 F.3d 1055 (6th Cir. 1998)

MOORE, J. . . . The three plaintiffs, Melissa Kallstrom, Thomas Coelho, and Gary Householder, are undercover officers employed by the Columbus Police Department. All three were actively involved in the drug conspiracy investigation of the Short North Posse, a violent gang in the Short North area of Columbus, Ohio. In *United States v. Derrick Russell, et al.,* No. CR-2 95-044, (S.D. Ohio), forty-one members of the Short North Posse were prosecuted on drug conspiracy charges. Plaintiffs testified at the trial of eight of the *Russell* defendants.

During the *Russell* criminal trial, defense counsel requested and obtained from the City Kallstrom's personnel and pre-employment file, which defense counsel appears to have passed on to several of the *Russell* defendants. Officers Coelho and Householder also suspect that copies of their personnel and pre-employment files were obtained by the same defense attorney. The City additionally released Officer Coelho's file to the Police Officers for Equal Rights organization following its request for the file in the fall of 1995 in order to investigate possible discriminatory hiring and promotion practices by the City. The officers' personnel files include the officers' addresses and phone numbers; the names, addresses, and phone numbers of immediate family members; the names and addresses of personal references; the officers' banking institutions and corresponding account information, including account balances; their social security numbers; responses to questions regarding their personal life asked during the course of polygraph examinations; and copies of their drivers' licenses, including pictures and home addresses. The district court found that in light of the Short North Posse's propensity for violence and intimidation, the release of these personnel files created a serious risk to the personal safety of the plaintiffs and those relatives named in the files.

Prior to accepting employment with the City, the plaintiffs were assured by the City that personal information contained in their files would be held in strict confidence. Despite its earlier promise of confidentiality, however, the City believed Ohio's Public Records Act, Ohio Rev. Code Ann. § 149.43, required it to release the officers' files upon request from any member of the public.

The officers brought suit under 42 U.S.C. §§ 1983 and 1988 against the City, claiming that the dissemination of personal information contained in their personnel files violates their right to privacy as guaranteed by the Due Process Clause of the Fourteenth Amendment. . . . In addition to seeking compensatory damages, the officers request an injunction restraining the City from releasing personal information regarding them. . . .

Section 1983 imposes civil liability on a person acting under color of state law who deprives another of the "rights, privileges, or immunities secured by the Constitution and laws." 42 U.S.C. § 1983. The threshold question, therefore, is whether the City deprived the officers of a right "secured by the Constitution and laws." . . .

In *Whalen v. Roe,* the Supreme Court declared that the constitutional right to privacy grounded in the Fourteenth Amendment respects not only individual autonomy in intimate matters, but also the individual's interest in avoiding divulgence of highly personal information. The court echoed these sentiments in *Nixon v. Administrator of Gen. Servs.,* 433 U.S. 425 (1977), acknowledging that "[o]ne element of privacy has been characterized as 'the individual interest in avoiding disclosure of personal matters.'" Although *Whalen* and *Nixon* appear to recognize constitutional protection for an individual's interest in safeguarding personal matters from public view, in both cases the Court found that public interests outweighed the individuals' privacy interests.

This circuit has read *Whalen* and *Nixon* narrowly, and will only balance an individual's interest in nondisclosure of informational privacy against the public's interest in and need for the invasion of privacy where the individual privacy interest is of constitutional dimension. . . . We hold that the officers' privacy interests do indeed implicate a fundamental liberty interest, specifically their interest in preserving their lives and the lives of their family members, as well as preserving their personal security and bodily integrity. . . .

In light of the Short North Posse's propensity for violence and intimidation, the district court found that the City's release of the plaintiffs-appellants' addresses, phone numbers, and driver's licenses to defense counsel in the *Russell* case, as well as their family members' names, addresses, and phone numbers, created a serious risk to the personal safety of the plaintiffs and those relatives named in the files. We see no reason to doubt that where disclosure of this personal information may fall into the hands of persons likely to seek revenge upon the officers for their involvement in the *Russell* case, the City created a very real threat to the officers' and their family members' personal security and bodily integrity, and possibly their lives. Accordingly, we hold that the City's disclosure of this private information about the officers to defense counsel in the *Russell* case rises to constitutional dimensions, thereby requiring us . . . to balance the officers' interests against those of the City.

The district court found that although there was no indication that the Police Officers for Equal Rights organization posed any threat to the officers and their family members, disclosure even to that group of the officers' phone numbers, addresses, and driver's licenses, and their family members' names, addresses and phone numbers "increases the risk that the information will fall into the wrong hands." . . . Since the district court did not indicate its view of the severity of risks inherent in disclosure of information to the Police Officers for Equal Rights organization, we remand to the district court for reconsideration in light of this opinion of issues regarding disclosure of personal information to that organization.

In finding that the City's release of private information concerning the officers to defense counsel in the *Russell* case rises to constitutional dimensions by threatening the personal security and bodily integrity of the officers and their family members, we do not mean to imply that every governmental act which intrudes upon or threatens to intrude upon an individual's body invokes the Fourteenth Amendment. But where the release of private information places an individual at substantial risk of serious bodily harm, possibly even death, from a perceived likely threat, the "magnitude of the liberty deprivation . . . strips the very essence of personhood." . . .

Where state action infringes upon a fundamental right, such action will be upheld under the substantive due process component of the Fourteenth Amendment only where the governmental action furthers a compelling state interest, and is narrowly drawn to further that state interest. Having found that the officers have a fundamental constitutional interest in preventing the release of personal information contained in their personnel files where such disclosure creates a substantial risk of serious bodily harm, we must now turn to whether the City's actions narrowly serve a compelling public purpose.

The City believed Ohio's Public Records Act, Ohio Rev. Code Ann. § 149.43, required it to disclose the personal information contained in the officers' records. Ohio's Public Records Act requires the state to make available all public records to any person, unless the record falls within one of the statute's enumerated exceptions. The State mandates release of state agency records in order to shed light on the state government's performance, thereby enabling Ohio citizens to understand better the operations of their government. In the judicial setting, courts have long recognized the importance of permitting public access to judicial records so that citizens may understand and exercise oversight over the judicial system. We see no reason why public access to government agency records should be considered any less important. For purposes of this case, we assume that the interests served by allowing public access to agency records rises to the level of a compelling state interest. Nevertheless, the City's release to the criminal defense counsel of the officers' and their family members' home addresses and phone numbers, as well as the family members' names and the officers' driver's licenses, does not narrowly serve these interests.

While there may be situations in which the release of the this type of personal information might further the public's understanding of the workings of its law enforcement agencies, the facts as presented here do not support such a conclusion. The City released the information at issue to defense counsel in a large drug conspiracy case, who is asserted to have passed the information onto his clients. We simply fail to see how placing this personal information into the hands of the *Russell* defendants in any way increases public understanding of the City's law enforcement agency where the *Russell* defendants and their attorney make no claim that they sought this personal information about the officers in order to shed light on the internal workings of the Columbus Police Department. We therefore cannot conclude that the disclosure narrowly serves the state's interest in ensuring accountable governance. Accordingly, we hold that the City's actions in automatically disclosing this information to any member of the public requesting it are not narrowly tailored to serve this important public interest. . . .

Injunctive relief involving matters subject to state regulation may be no broader than necessary to remedy the constitutional violation. . . . [T]he constitutional violation arises when the release of private information about the officers places their personal security, and that of their families, at substantial risk without narrowly serving a compelling state interest. Thus, the officers are entitled to notice and an opportunity to be heard prior to the release of private information contained in their personnel files only where the disclosure of the requested information could potentially threaten the officers' and their families' personal security. As discussed above, release of the officers' addresses, phone numbers, and driver's licenses, as well as their family members' names, addresses, and phone numbers, is likely to result in a substantial risk to their personal security. On remand, the district court should consider whether release of other private information contained in the officers' personnel files also poses the same risk. . . . [B]ecause the City's decision to continue releasing this information potentially places the officers and their families at risk of irreparable harm that cannot be adequately remedied at law, the officers are entitled to injunctive relief prohibiting the City from again disclosing this information without first providing the officers meaningful notice.

NOTES & QUESTIONS

1. *How Broad Is the* Kallstrom *Decision?* In his reading of *Kallstrom*, Paul Schwartz argues that the case showed that "[o]nly the threat of life-threatening harm to officers and their families and the City of Columbus' plan for automatic disclosure of this information" allowed an interest in nondisclosure to triumph.[21] Schwartz also notes that the Sixth Circuit granted merely a limited injunction to the undercover officers that allowed them a chance to object when someone requested their personal data.

   In *Kallstrom v. City of Columbus* [*Kallstrom II*], 165 F. Supp. 2d 686 (S.D. Ohio 2001), when the case was back in district court after the Sixth Circuit ruling, a group of media entities intervened in the case to "inspect or copy the requested information from plaintiffs' personnel files." The request of the intervenors "specifically excludes information identifying the Officers' banking institutions and financial account numbers; personal credit card numbers; social security numbers; information about any psychological conditions the Officers may have; responses to polygraph examinations; and, 'medical records' or any other recorded information exempt from mandatory disclosure under Ohio Revised Code § 149.43." The district held that the "plaintiffs do not have a constitutional privacy interest in the information

---

[21] Paul M. Schwartz, *Internet Privacy and the State*, 32 Conn. L. Rev. 815, 828-29 (2000).

requested by intervenors." The court reasoned that plaintiffs failed to prove that the release of the information would place them at any "risk of serious bodily harm." Nor did they establish a "perceived likely threat."

The court further reasoned that the disciplinary records could be revealed because "the Constitution does not provide a shield against disclosure of potentially embarrassing or even improper activities by public servants." Regarding home addresses, the court determined that they are "part of the public domain" because "[a]nyone with an individual's name and either Internet access or the initiative to visit a local government office can scan county property records, court records, or voter registration records for such information as an individual's address, the exact location of his or her residence, and even a floor plan of the home." Moreover, the court reasoned that even if the plaintiffs had a constitutional interest in the data in their files, "the City's disclosure of public records, including police officer personnel files, is narrowly tailored to achieve this compelling state interest." The court noted that there was a difference between disclosing the data to criminal defendants versus the press: "The full disclosure of these personnel files is necessary to enable the press to do its job. As nothing less than full disclosure will ensure transparency in government, the Court finds full disclosure is narrowly tailored to meet the state's compelling interest."

What is left of the Sixth Circuit's opinion after *Kallstrom II*? Under what basis did the district court in *Kallstrom II* decide that the information should be released to the press?

In *Barber v. Overton*, 496 F.3d 449 (6th Cir. 2007), the Sixth Circuit revisited the *Kallstrom I* and found that this decision was not implicated by a (mistaken) release of Social Security numbers and birth dates of prison officers to prisoners: "*Kallstrom* created a narrowly tailored right, limited to circumstances where the information was particularly sensitive and the persons to whom it was disclosed were particularly dangerous *vis-à-vis the plaintiffs*" (emphasis in original). In sum, the *Barber* court stated that the release of the information "was not sensitive enough nor the threat of retaliation apparent enough to warrant constitution protection here."

2. ***Statutory vs. Constitutional Privacy Exemptions.*** Contrast the operation of statutory privacy exemptions to FOIA and exceptions based on the constitutional right to information privacy, as in *Kallstrom I*. How does the presence of the Ohio Public Records Act affect the analysis in *Kallstrom II*?

3. ***The Scope of Privacy Exemptions.*** In *Moak v. Philadelphia Newspapers, Inc.*, 336 A.2d 920 (Pa. 1975), the court held that the employee records of a police department, which contained the name, gender, date of birth, salary, and other personal information about the employees, did not fall within the privacy exemption to Pennsylvania's Right to Know Law because the records would not "operate to the prejudice or impairment of a person's reputation or personal security." Should the privacy of personal information turn on whether it will harm a person's reputation or security?

4. ***Public Records in a Digital World.*** Public records are increasingly being stored in electronic format. The paper records of the past were difficult to access. Now, they can be collected in databases and searched en masse. To what extent

should the increased accessibility of records created by the digital age affect open record laws?

In 2001, the Judicial Conference Committee on Court Administration and Case Management issued a report with policies regarding public access to electronic case files. As Peter Winn describes it:

> Before the Judicial Conference Committee on Court Administration and Case Management (Committee) issued the Report, a study of the problem was prepared by the staff of the Administrative Office of the United States Courts. The staff white paper described two general approaches to the problem. One approach was to treat electronic judicial records as governed by exactly the same rules as paper records — what the white paper calls the "public is public" approach. The second approach advocated treating electronic and paper files differently in order to respect the practical obscurity of paper case files, urging that the rules regulating electronic court records reflect the fact that unrestricted online access to court records would undoubtedly, as a practical matter, compromise privacy, as well as increase the risk of personal harm to litigants and third parties whose private information appeared in case files. The white paper suggested that different levels of privileges could be created to govern electronic access to court records. Under this approach, judges and court staff would generally have broad, although not unlimited, remote access to all electronic case files, as would other key participants in the judicial process, such as the U.S. Attorney, the U.S. Trustee, and bankruptcy case trustees. Litigants and their attorneys would have unrestricted access to the files relevant to their own cases. The general public would have remote access to a subset of the full case file, including, in most cases, pleadings, briefs, orders, and opinions. Under this approach, the entire electronic case file could still be viewed at the clerk's office, just as the paper file is available now for inspection, but would not generally be made available on the Internet.
>
> Unfortunately, at least with respect to civil cases and bankruptcy cases, few, if any, of the suggestions contained in the staff white paper were ultimately adopted in the Report. Instead, the Committee adopted the "public is public" approach to the problem, rejecting the view that courts have a responsibility to adopt rules governing the use of their computer systems to try to recreate in cyberspace the practical balance that existed in the world of paper judicial records. In supporting this decision, the Committee took the position that attempting to recreate the "practical obscurity" of the brick and mortar world was simply too complicated an exercise for the courts to undertake.[22]

In March 2004, the Judicial Conference issued a report recommending that, with certain exceptions, all criminal records be placed online accessible to the public.[23]

5. ***911 Calls.*** In many states, the recordings of 911 calls are disclosed to the public. Is such a practice a violation of the constitutional right to information privacy? When these calls involve celebrities, gossip sites on the Internet, such as TMZ or Radaronline, will post the audio of the call on their sites. One example is the 911 call made from Michael Jackson's house on June 25, 2009, as he was dying.

---

[22] Peter A. Winn, *Online Court Records: Balancing Judicial Accountability and Privacy in an Age of Electronic Information*, 79 Wash. L. Rev. 307, 322-25 (2004).

[23] http://www.privacy.uscourts.gov/crimimpl.htm.

As this example shows, many 911 calls involve matters about people's physical health and times of extreme stress. Matters of mental health can also be discussed in 911 calls.

Doctors and nurses are under a duty of confidentiality, so why not 911 call centers, especially when people are revealing medical information? On the other hand, proponents of making 911 calls available to the public might contend that publicly disclosing the calls is necessary for the public to vet how well the 911 operators respond to calls, and to provide background on subsequent police or medical action. What interests should be predominate in the balance?

6. ***Public Disclosure of Political Campaign Contributions.*** When people make contributions to political campaigns, records are kept of their contributions. The Federal Election Campaign Act (FECA) of 1971 mandates that information about these political contributions is disclosed to the public. Today, it is possible to find online the political contributions that a person has made. Should people's political contributions be publicly accessible?

In *Buckley v. Valeo*, 424 U.S. 1 (1976), the Court applied "exacting scrutiny" to disclosure requirements for certain campaign contributions and expenditures under FECA. Although ultimately upholding the law, the Court noted that "[i]t is undoubtedly true that public disclosure of contributions to candidates and political parties will deter some individuals who otherwise might contribute."

Pursuant to FECA, the personal information of people making contributions to candidates over a certain amount ($100 at the time *Buckley* was decided, and $200 today) is disclosed publicly. The revealed information includes one's name, employer, and occupation. In *Buckley v. Valeo,* 424 U.S. 1 (1976), one of the issues the Court considered was whether mandatory political campaign disclosures pursuant to the FECA violated the First Amendment. The Court recognized that such disclosures implicate First Amendment rights:

> We long have recognized that significant encroachments on First Amendment rights of the sort that compelled disclosure imposes cannot be justified by a mere showing of some legitimate governmental interest. Since *NAACP v. Alabama* we have required that the subordinating interests of the State must survive exacting scrutiny. . . .
>
> The strict test established by *NAACP v. Alabama* is necessary because compelled disclosure has the potential for substantially infringing the exercise of First Amendment rights.

The Court concluded, however, that the disclosure requirements were the least restrictive means for achieving compelling government interests:

> First, disclosure provides the electorate with information "as to where political campaign money comes from and how it is spent by the candidate" in order to aid the voters in evaluating those who seek federal office. . . . The sources of a candidate's financial support also alert the voter to the interests to which a candidate is most likely to be responsive and thus facilitate predictions of future performance in office.

Second, disclosure requirements deter actual corruption and avoid the appearance of corruption by exposing large contributions and expenditures to the light of publicity. . . .

Third, and not least significant, recordkeeping, reporting, and disclosure requirements are an essential means of gathering the data necessary to detect violations of the contribution limitations described above.

The challengers of the law argued that the disclosure rules should not apply to minor parties and independent candidates because their views are less likely to be mainstream, heightening the potential chilling effects of disclosure. Despite this claim, the Court concluded:

> We are not unmindful that the damage done by disclosure to the associational interests of the minor parties and their members and to supporters of independents could be significant. These movements are less likely to have a sound financial base and thus are more vulnerable to falloffs in contributions. In some instances fears of reprisal may deter contributions to the point where the movement cannot survive. The public interest also suffers if that result comes to pass, for there is a consequent reduction in the free circulation of ideas both within and without the political arena.

In *Citizens United v. Federal Election Commission*, 558 U.S. 310 (2010), the Supreme Court upheld disclosure provisions of the Bipartisan Campaign Reform Act (BCRA) of 2002, relying on the reasoning in *Buckley v. Valeo* that "disclosure can be justified by a governmental interest in providing "the electorate with information" about election-related spending sources."

William McGeveran contends that *Buckley*'s holding on disclosure requirements should be revisited. He notes that modern technology has made political contribution records significantly more accessible, as organizations are now creating searchable online databases of such records. McGeveran argues that people might be chilled from making political contributions because of negative professional consequences or the stigma of being associated with unpopular non-mainstream candidates: "Political contributions label us, and disclosure displays that label to others without our consent. Forced revelations are intrusions into a sphere of personal liberty." He contends:

> [D]isclosure is more likely to deter contributions aligned with certain ideological positions — more controversial ones — a correlation that threatens both the First Amendment protection of contributions and the open debate we strive for in elections. Those with mainstream views who choose to sacrifice privacy may contribute an amount above the threshold while others, whose views are more likely to be unorthodox, are chilled from doing so.

Regarding *Buckley*'s stated compelling government interests, they often fail "to justify disclosure of modest-sized contributions." Most small contributions are too insignificant to have a corrupting influence. Moreover, "very few voters actually give much consideration to the nature of candidates' donors when choosing whether to support them."[24]

---

[24] William McGeveran, *McIntyre's Checkbook: Privacy Costs of Political Contribution Disclosure*, 6 U. Pa. J. Const. L. 1, 19, 30, 38 (2003).

(b) Police Records

In *Paul v. Davis*, 424 U.S. 693 (1976), a police department circulated flyers to about 800 merchants with the names and mug shots of people under the heading "ACTIVE SHOPLIFTERS." The plaintiff's name and photo appeared on the flyer. The plaintiff had been arrested on a shoplifting charge, but the charge was later dismissed. The inclusion of the plaintiff on the flyer came to the attention of his supervisor, and the plaintiff had to explain his situation. Ultimately, the plaintiff was not fired but instead warned that he "had best not find himself in a similar situation" in the future. The plaintiff brought a § 1983 action claiming his constitutional rights had been violated.

The U.S. Supreme Court, however, rejected the plaintiff's claim:

> Respondent's complaint also alleged a violation of a "right to privacy guaranteed by the First, Fourth, Fifth, Ninth, and Fourteenth Amendments." . . .
>
> While there is no "right of privacy" found in any specific guarantee of the Constitution, the Court has recognized that "zones of privacy" may be created by more specific constitutional guarantees and thereby impose limits upon government power. *See Roe v. Wade*, 410 U.S. 113 (1973). Respondent's case, however, comes within none of these areas. He does not seek to suppress evidence seized in the course of an unreasonable search. *See Katz v. United States*, 389 U.S. 347 (1967). And our other "right of privacy" cases, while defying categorical description, deal generally with substantive aspects of the Fourteenth Amendment. In *Roe* the Court pointed out that the personal rights found in this guarantee of personal privacy must be limited to those which are "fundamental" or "implicit in the concept of ordered liberty" as described in *Palko v. Connecticut*, 302 U.S. 319 (1937). The activities detailed as being within this definition were ones very different from that for which respondent claims constitutional protection matters relating to marriage, procreation, contraception, family relationships, and child rearing and education. In these areas it has been held that there are limitations on the States' power to substantively regulate conduct.
>
> Respondent's claim is far afield from this line of decisions. He claims constitutional protection against the disclosure of the fact of his arrest on a shoplifting charge. His claim is based, not upon any challenge to the State's ability to restrict his freedom of action in a sphere contended to be "private," but instead on a claim that the State may not publicize a record of an official act such as an arrest. None of our substantive privacy decisions hold this or anything like this, and we decline to enlarge them in this manner. . .

Paul v. Davis was decided one year prior to *Whalen v. Roe,* 429 U.S. 589 (1977), where the Supreme Court recognized that the constitutional right to privacy involves "the individual interest in avoiding disclosure of personal matters." How does *Paul* square with *Whalen*? Does *Whalen* implicitly overrule *Paul* by recognizing a constitutional right to avoid disclosure of certain information? How can these cases be reconciled?

CLINE V. ROGERS

87 F.3d 176 (6th Cir. 1996)

BATCHELDER, J. . . . The plaintiff-appellant, Jackie Ray Cline ("Cline"), alleges that in 1992, a private citizen contacted the Sheriff's Department of McMinn County, Tennessee ("the County"), and asked Sheriff George Rogers to check Cline's arrest record. According to Cline, Rogers searched state and local records and requested a computer search of National Crime Information Center ("NCIC") records of the Federal Bureau of Investigation ("FBI"). Cline alleges that Rogers disclosed to the private citizen the information Rogers obtained regarding Cline's criminal history, in violation of both Tennessee and federal law.

Cline filed this lawsuit against Rogers, individually and in his official capacity as sheriff. Cline also named the County as a defendant, alleging that improper searches of criminal records is "a routine and customary practice in McMinn County," that the County "lacks adequate controls to ensure that access to criminal records is for authorized purposes only," that the County did not have in place an adequate system to detect misuse of criminal records, that the County had provided inadequate training to prevent such abuse, and that the County had "been indifferent to the civil rights of private citizens by allowing such abuses to continue."

Cline's complaint sought damages under 42 U.S.C. § 1983 for violation of his federal civil rights. . . . [The district court dismissed Cline's complaint, and Cline appealed.]

There is no violation of the United States Constitution in this case because there is no constitutional right to privacy in one's criminal record. Nondisclosure of one's criminal record is not one of those personal rights that is "fundamental" or "implicit in the concept of ordered liberty." *See Whalen v. Roe.* In *Whalen*, the Supreme Court distinguished fundamental privacy interests in "matters relating to marriage, procreation, contraception, family relationships, and child rearing and education" and "individual interest in avoiding disclosure of personal matters."

Moreover, one's criminal history is arguably not a private "personal matter" at all, since arrest and conviction information are matters of public record. *See Paul v. Davis* (rejecting a similar claim based on facts more egregious than those alleged here). Although there may be a dispute among the circuit courts regarding the existence and extent of an individual privacy right to nondisclosure of "personal matters," see *Slayton v. Willingham*, 726 F.2d 631 (10th Cir. 1984); *Fadjo v. Coon*, 633 F.2d 1172, 1176 (5th Cir. Unit B 1981) (both opining that *Paul* has been at least partially overruled by the Supreme Court's decisions in *Whalen* and *Nixon*), this circuit does not recognize a constitutional privacy interest in avoiding disclosure of, e.g., one's criminal record. See *DeSanti*, 653 F.2d at 1090 (regarding disclosure of juvenile delinquents' "social histories"); see also *Doe v. Wigginton*, 21 F.3d 733 (6th Cir. 1994) (disclosure of inmate's HIV infection did not violate constitutional right of privacy).

Because there is no privacy interest in one's criminal record that is protected by the United States Constitution, Cline could prove no set of facts that would entitle him to relief; therefore, the district court correctly dismissed this claim. . .

Scheetz v. The Morning Call, Inc.

946 F.2d 202 (3d Cir. 1991)

NYGAARD, J. . . . . Kenneth Scheetz is a police officer in the City of Allentown. Rosann Scheetz is his wife. In the course of an argument between them in their home in January of 1988, Kenneth struck Rosann. Rosann left the house, but returned approximately a half an hour later. The argument resumed, and Kenneth again struck Rosann.

Rosann called the Allentown police. Two officers responded and prepared a standard "offense/incident" report, consisting of a face sheet and supplemental reports. The "face sheet" of this report[25] stated that Rosann Scheetz had reported a domestic disturbance, that two police cars had responded, and that Rosann had left the home.

In the meantime, Rosann had driven to the Allentown police station, apparently with the intention of filing a Pennsylvania Protection From Abuse Petition. The officers who interviewed Rosann prepared two "supplemental reports" and made them part of the file. They reveal that Rosann stated that her husband had beaten her before and had refused counseling. The police gave Rosann three options: file criminal charges, request a protection from abuse order, or initiate department disciplinary action against Kenneth. These supplements also note that Rosann had visible physical injuries, that Rosann did not want to return home and that she was permitted to spend the night in the shift commander's office.

Chief Wayne Stephens filed a third supplement to the report. He had spoken to Kenneth about the incident, and the third supplement memorialized this fact, as well as Kenneth's statement to the Chief that he and his wife were scheduled to speak with a marriage counselor. None of the supplements indicated that the Chief took any disciplinary action against Kenneth.

Shortly after the incident, Kenneth Scheetz was named "Officer of the Year" by Chief Stephens. Several months later, as part of "Respect for Law Week," press releases and photos of Kenneth were released. A dinner and official ceremony were held in Kenneth's honor. The Morning Call ("The Call"), a local newspaper, published a story and photo on this honor.

Terry Mutchler, a reporter for The Call, became interested in investigating the prior incident involving Kenneth and Rosann. Another reporter from the paper had tried to get the police report from the police, who refused to release it. Mutchler's request for a copy of the report from the department was also formally refused. Mutchler nonetheless managed to get a copy of the report.

Mutchler then interviewed Chief Stephens about the incident. Chief Stephens initially denied the incident, but when confronted with Mutchler's information, he claimed that the report was stolen and refused further comment. Chief Stephens did, however, offer his insights into the subject of spousal abuse, stating "people fake it" and "women . . . tear their dresses and rip up their bras and say they were raped." Mutchler also interviewed Deputy Chief Monaghan, who offered assorted

---

[25] The "face sheet" is a public document similar to a police blotter. The parties agree that this document is a public record. The parties dispute whether the "supplemental reports" are public records available under Pennsylvania's Right to Know Law. There is some evidence that these reports were generally available, subject to the approval of a police supervisor.

rationalizations for why no follow-up had been done on the Scheetz incident. The Scheetzes refused comment on the incident.

The Call published an article by Mutchler titled "Police didn't investigate assault complaint against officer." Eight paragraphs of the article were comprised of quotes from the police report of the beating incident which detailed the injuries Rosann received. The bulk of the article, however, focused on the lack of investigation and follow-up by the police department. Chief Stephens was quoted as saying that the incident had not been investigated. The article also quoted the comments Chief Stephens had made to Mutchler about domestic abuse, as well as Deputy Chief Monaghan's explanations for why no charges were pressed. The last two columns of the article consisted of quotes from Kenneth's superiors praising his work. . . .

. . . Kenneth and Rosann then sued Mutchler, The Call, and "John or Jane Doe." The complaint alleged that Mutchler and The Call had conspired with an unknown state actor (the Doe defendant) to deprive the Scheetzes of their constitutional right to privacy in violation of 42 U.S.C. § 1983. The complaint also raised several pendent state law claims. . . .

The district court granted the defendants' motion for summary judgment in part, denied it in part, granted judgment to the defendants on the § 1983 claim, dismissed the pendent state claims, dismissed the Doe defendant and dismissed all remaining motions as moot. The Scheetzes appeal. . . .

. . . Because we conclude that the Scheetzes have not alleged a violation of a constitutionally protected privacy interest, we will affirm.

The defendants rely on dicta in *Paul v. Davis* to support their argument that "garden variety" invasion of privacy claims are not actionable under section 1983. . . . The Supreme Court rejected the proposition that reputation alone was a liberty or property interest within the meaning of the due process clause. In dicta, the Court went on to consider the alternative argument that the police chiefs' action constituted a violation of the plaintiff's right to privacy. After first noting that privacy decisions had been limited in the past to family and procreative matters, the Court concluded that publication by the state of an official act such as an arrest could not constitute invasion of the constitutional right to privacy.

The very next year, however, the Court held in *Whalen v. Roe*, that the right to privacy extends to both "the individual interest in avoiding disclosure of personal matters, and . . . the interest in independence in making certain kinds of important decisions." *Whalen* recognized that the information contained in medical records is constitutionally protected under the confidentiality branch of the privacy right.

Thus, some confidential information is protected under the confidentiality branch of the right to privacy, the dicta in *Paul* notwithstanding.[26] Accordingly, the Scheetzes in this case contend that the information contained in the police incident report is similarly protected by the federal right.

Although cases exploring the autonomy branch of the right of privacy are legion, the contours of the confidentiality branch are murky. We have recognized that some confidential information, such as medical records, is constitutionally protected under the confidentiality branch of the federal privacy right. Other courts

---

[26] *Paul* can be reconciled with *Whalen* since the information at issue in *Paul* (the fact of plaintiff's arrest for shoplifting) is not the kind of information entitled to constitutional protection.

have similarly recognized that § 1983 may be used to redress violations of a constitutional confidentiality right.

Concluding that violations of the confidentiality right of privacy may be actionable under § 1983 does not, however, end our inquiry. Although defendants are wrong in arguing that *Paul* prohibits any privacy § 1983 action, we conclude that they correctly argue that the Scheetzes did not have a constitutionally protected privacy interest in the information they divulged in a police report. . . .

Although the outlines of the confidentiality right are not definite, the information that has been protected in other cases was information that the disclosing person reasonably expected to remain private. In reporting this potential crime to the police, Rosann Scheetz could not reasonably expect the information to remain secret. The police could have brought charges without her concurrence, at which point all the information would have wound up on the public record, where it would have been non-confidential. *See Cox Broadcasting Corp. v. Cohn*, 420 U.S. 469 (1975) (privacy interest fades when information is in the public record). This information is not like medical or financial records (which have been accorded some constitutional protection by this court) where there is a reasonable expectation that privacy will be preserved. When police are called, a private disturbance loses much of its private character. We conclude that the information Rosann Scheetz disclosed in the police reports is not constitutionally protected. . . .

.

MANSMANN, J. dissenting. . . . I agree that some of the information contained in the police report, specifically that information contained in the "Offense/Incident Report," is not protected under a constitutional privacy interest. Because the "Offense/Incident Report" is classified as a public document under the police department's policy, that information was not treated as confidential. . .

.

Some of the information reported by The Call, however, was contained only in confidential portions of the police report entitled "Investigative Supplements" and was not discernable from the public portion of the report. That information detailed the private facts of the Scheetzes' marital counseling and precise details of their marital disturbance, including a description of Rosann's injuries and her statements. Since this information is clearly confidential, I would then examine the nature of the Scheetzes' privacy interest in keeping it confidential. . . .

. . . The majority suggests that because the information could have been publicly disclosed, the Scheetzes had no privacy interest. While it is true that criminal charges could have been brought without Rosann's concurrence, it does not necessarily follow that in spite of the fact that she declined to press charges or take alternative legal action, and no legal action ensued, Rosann Scheetz could have reasonably expected public disclosure of the confidential information that had remained quietly dormant in confidential police department reports.

This is especially true where the public disclosure occurred 16 months after the incident. *See, e.g., Briscoe v. Reader's Digest Ass'n*, 483 P.2d 34 (Cal. 1971) (common law right to privacy infringed by publication of truck hijacking conviction of 11 years ago); *Melvin v. Reid*, 297 P. 91 (Cal. 1931) (liability for common law invasion of privacy imposed upon producers of movie that revealed prior life of prostitution and crime of woman who had long since taken a new name and established a respectable life). . . .

. . . Because this confidential information had lain undisclosed in the confidential police department files for over a year and Rosann Scheetz had not pursued any legal action, the Scheetzes could reasonably have expected that the confidential information would never be publicly disclosed. In light of this delay, I cannot agree with the majority's otherwise appropriate assertion that "[w]hen police are called, a private disturbance loses much of its private character." Information that has remained confidential over a period of time, absent any legal action, can reasonably be expected to recede from public notice. . . .

NOTES & QUESTIONS

1. ***Privacy as a Way to Conceal a Scandal.*** The information about the police department's treatment of Ken Scheetz's abuse of his wife is highly newsworthy. The information reveals a police department that praised rather than disciplined Ken Scheetz and virtually ignored his wife's complaints of abuse. Is privacy being used to cover up the scandalous way the police department reacted to Rosann Scheetz's complaint?

2. ***Deterring Reporting of Spousal Abuse.*** Would routine disclosure of complaints of spousal abuse inhibit victims such as Rosann Scheetz from coming forward? Keep in mind that it is Rosann Scheetz, in addition to her husband, who is suing for a violation of her privacy.

3. ***Limits on Police Reports.*** The court concluded that Rosann Scheetz lacked an expectation of privacy in the information because it was included in a police report: "In reporting this potential crime to the police, Rosann Scheetz could not reasonably expect the information to remain secret. The police could have brought charges without her concurrence, at which point all the information would have wound up on the public record, where it would have been non-confidential." Are there limits to what information the police should include in a police report?

4. ***Police Threats to Disclose.*** Consider *Sterling v. Borough of Minersville*, 232 F.3d 190 (3d Cir. 2000). Marcus Wayman, 18 years old, was in a parked car along with a 17-year-old male friend. The car was parked in a lot adjacent to a beer distributor. F. Scott Wilinsky, a police officer, observed the vehicle and became suspicious that the youths might be attempting to burglarize the beer distributor. Wilinsky called for backup. After investigating, the officers determined that a break-in had not occurred at the beer distributor, but that the youths had been drinking. Wilinsky searched the vehicle and discovered two condoms and asked about the boys' sexual orientation. The boys said that they were gay, and that they were in the lot to engage in consensual sex. The boys were arrested for underage drinking and taken to the police station, where Wilinsky lectured them that homosexual activity was contrary to the dictates of the Bible. Wilinsky then told Wayman that he must inform his grandfather about his homosexuality or else Wilinsky himself would inform Wayman's grandfather. When he was released from custody, Wayman committed suicide.

Wayman's mother filed a § 1983 suit against the Borough of Minersville, Wilinksy, and other officers and officials alleging, among other things, a violation of the constitutional right to information privacy. The court reasoned:

> We first ask whether Wayman had a protected privacy right concerning Wilinsky's threat to disclose his suspected sexual orientation. . . .
>
> It is difficult to imagine a more private matter than one's sexuality and a less likely probability that the government would have a legitimate interest in disclosure of sexual identity.
>
> We can, therefore, readily conclude that Wayman's sexual orientation was an intimate aspect of his personality entitled to privacy protection under *Whalen*. . . .
>
> Before we can definitely conclude that a constitutional tort has occurred, however, we must further ask whether Wilinsky's threat of disclosure, rather than actual disclosure, constituted a violation of Wayman's right to privacy. . .
>
> The threat to breach some confidential aspect of one's life . . . is tantamount to a violation of the privacy right because the security of one's privacy has been compromised by the threat of disclosure. Thus, Wilinsky's threat to disclose Wayman's suspected homosexuality suffices as a violation of Wayman's constitutionally protected privacy interest. . . .

(c) Megan's Laws

In 1994, in New Jersey, a seven-year-old girl, Megan Kanka, was brutally raped and murdered by her neighbor, Jesse Timmendequas, who had two earlier sexual assault convictions. Nobody in Megan's family knew about Timmendequas's prior criminal record. Seventeen days after Megan's death, New Jersey Assembly Speaker Chuck Haytaian declared a legislative emergency. A law was proposed, called "Megan's Law," to establish a system for people to learn of the whereabouts of sexual offenders who were released from prison. The statute passed without committee hearings and without supportive research. Within three months of Megan's death, the law was signed by Governor Christie Whitman and became law. Similar laws appeared in other states. These laws, commonly called "Megan's Laws," set up databases of personal information about sexual offenders so that people can learn their identities and where they live.

In 1996, Congress passed a federal Megan's Law restricting states from receiving federal anti-crime funds unless they agreed to "release relevant information that is necessary to protect the public" from released sex offenders. *See* Pub. L. No. 104-145, codified at 42 U.S.C. § 14071(d)(2). Today, all 50 states have passed a version of Megan's Law. Sex offender registries under Megan's Law often contain information such as the sex offender's Social Security number, photograph, address, prior convictions, and places of employment.

States differ in how they disseminate sexual offender information. In California, booths are set up at county fairs so that individuals can browse through the registry. Some states have 1-800 or 1-900 numbers where people can call in and ask if particular people are sex offenders. At least 16 states have made their registries available on the Internet.

PAUL P. V. VERNIERO

170 F.3d 396 (3d Cir. 1999)

SLOVITER, J. Plaintiff Paul P. sues on his behalf and on behalf of a class of persons who, having been convicted of specified sex crimes, are required to comply with N.J. Stat. Ann. § 2c:7-1 et seq., known as "Megan's Law," which provides for a system of registration and community notification. . . .

In a related action, *E.B. v. Verniero*, 119 F.3d 1077 (3d Cir. 1997), this court rejected the claims of comparably situated persons that the community notification requirements violate the Double Jeopardy Clause or the Ex Post Facto Clause of the United States Constitution. That holding of *E.B.* was predicated on the conclusion that the notification required by Megan's Law does not constitute punishment. . . .

In this case, plaintiffs raise a challenge to Megan's Law that they claim is different from that considered in *E.B.* They argue that the statutory requirement that the class members provide extensive information to local law enforcement personnel, including each registrant's current biographical data, physical description, home address, place of employment, schooling, and a description and license plate number of the registrant's vehicle, and the subsequent community notification is a violation of their constitutionally protected right to privacy.

The statutory scheme is described in detail in *E.B.*, and we refer only briefly to the salient details. We explained the registration requirements as follows:

The registrant must provide the following information to the chief law enforcement officer of the municipality in which he resides: name, social security number, age, race, sex, date of birth, height, weight, hair and eye color, address of legal residence, address of any current temporary legal residence, and date and place of employment. N.J.S.A. 2C:7-4b(1). He must confirm his address every ninety days, notify the municipal law enforcement agency if he moves, and re-register with the law enforcement agency of any new municipality. N.J.S.A. 2C:7-2d to e.

The information provided by the registrant is put into a central registry, open to other law enforcement personnel but not to public inspection. Law enforcement officials then use the data provided to apply a "Risk Assessment Scale," a numerical scoring system, to determine the registrant's "risk of offense" and the tier in which the registrant should be classified. In the case of Tier 1 registrants, notification is given only to law enforcement agents "likely to encounter" the registrant. Tier 2, or "moderate risk," notification is given to law enforcement agents, schools, and community organizations "likely to encounter" the registrant. Tier 3, or "high risk," notification goes to all members of the public "likely to encounter" the registrant. Notifications generally contain a warning that the information is confidential and should not be disseminated to others, as well as an admonition that actions taken against the registrant, such as assaults, are illegal.

The prosecutor must provide the registrant with notice of the proposed notification. A pre-notification judicial review process is available for any registrant who wishes to challenge his or her classification.

The plaintiffs are Tier 2 and Tier 3 registrants who have been certified as a class and whose offenses were committed after the enactment of Megan's Law. . .

The legal foundation for plaintiffs' claim is the Supreme Court's recognition that there is "a right of personal privacy, or a guarantee of certain areas or zones of privacy," protected by the United States Constitution. *Roe v. Wade*, 410 U.S. 113, 152 (1973). This "guarantee of personal privacy" covers "only personal rights that can be deemed 'fundamental' or 'implicit in the concept of ordered liberty.'" This privacy right "has some extension to activities relating to marriage, procreation, contraception, family relationships, and child rearing and education."

Plaintiffs argue that Megan's Law infringes upon their constitutionally protected privacy interests in two ways. One is by the dissemination of information about them, most particularly by disseminating both their home addresses and a "compilation of information which would otherwise remain 'scattered' or 'wholly forgotten.'" Their other claim is that the community notification infringes upon their "privacy interests in their most intimate relationships — those with their spouses, children, parents, and other family members."

Plaintiffs thus seek to invoke the two categories of privacy interests identified by the Supreme Court in *Whalen v. Roe*. . . .

The parties dispute the extent to which our decision in *E.B.* is dispositive of the privacy issue before us in this case. Plaintiffs contend that no privacy issue was raised, briefed, or argued in *E.B.* and that the discussion in *E.B.* relating to cases on which they rely is dictum. The State defendants, on the other hand, regard "[t]he portions of the *E.B.* decision holding that community notification does not implicate a fundamental privacy interest and the finding of a compelling state interest in protecting the public from recidivist sex offenders," as "control[ling] the decision in this case." We thus turn to examine the *E.B.* decision.

The privacy issue arose in *E.B.* during our analysis of whether community notification mandated by Megan's Law constitutes punishment for purposes of the Ex Post Facto and Double Jeopardy Clauses. In that context, we stated that the "primary sting from Megan's law notification comes by way of injury to what is denoted . . . as reputational interests. This includes . . . the myriad of . . . ways in which one is treated differently by virtue of being known as a potentially dangerous sex offender." *E.B.*, 119 F.3d at 1102. We then referred to the Supreme Court's holding in *Paul v. Davis*, stating:

> Just as Davis sought constitutional protection from the consequences of state disclosure of the fact of his shoplifting arrest and law enforcement's assessment that he was a continuing risk, so registrants seek protection from what may follow disclosure of facts related to their sex offense convictions and the resulting judgment of the state that they are a continuing risk. It follows that, just as the officers' publication of the official act of Davis' arrest did not violate any fundamental privacy right of Davis', neither does New Jersey's publication (through notification) of registrants' convictions and findings of dangerousness implicate any interest of fundamental constitutional magnitude.

We rejected the contention that dissemination of information about criminal activity beyond law enforcement personnel is analogous to historical punishments, such as the stocks, cages, and scarlet letters. We found instead that the dissemination is more like the dissemination of "rap sheet" information to regulatory agencies, bar associations, prospective employers, and interested members of the public that public indictment, public trial, and public imposition of sentence necessarily entail. We noted that although the Supreme Court later recognized in *United States Department of Justice v. Reporters Committee for Freedom of the Press*, 489 U.S. 749 (1989), that the dissemination of "rap sheets" implicates a privacy interest, the Court there was determining whether a "rap sheet" fell under the "privacy interest" protected by an exemption to the Freedom of Information Act ("FOIA"), not that protected by the Constitution. We pointed out that the Supreme Court itself made the distinction between the two types of privacy interest, and we quoted its statement in *Reporters Committee*, that "[t]he question of the statutory meaning of privacy under the FOIA is, of course, not the same as the question . . . whether an individual's interest in privacy is protected by the Constitution." . . .

. . . Finally, we concluded in *E.B.* that even if a "fundamental right" were implicated, "the state's interest here would suffice to justify the deprivation." . . .

The District Court here concluded that there was no privacy interest in the plaintiffs' home addresses, stating that "[b]ecause such information is public, plaintiffs' privacy interests are not implicated." As to the argument based on the "compilation" of various information, the court held that "[i]t is of little consequence whether this public information is disclosed piecemeal or whether it is disclosed in compilation."

To the extent that plaintiffs' alleged injury stems from the disclosure of their sex offender status, alone or in conjunction with other information, the District Court's opinion is in line with other cases in this court and elsewhere holding specifically that arrest records and related information are not protected by a right to privacy. See *Fraternal Order of Police*, 812 F.2d at 117 (holding that "arrest records are not entitled to privacy protection" because they are public); *Cline v. Rogers*, 87 F.3d 176, 179 (6th Cir.) (holding that "there is no constitutional right to privacy in one's criminal record" because "arrest and conviction information are matters of public record"). . . .

We are not insensitive to the argument that notification implicates plaintiffs' privacy interest by disclosing their home addresses. The compilation of home addresses in widely available telephone directories might suggest a consensus that these addresses are not considered private were it not for the fact that a significant number of persons, ranging from public officials and performers to just ordinary folk, choose to list their telephones privately, because they regard their home addresses to be private information. Indeed, their view is supported by decisions holding that home addresses are entitled to privacy under FOIA, which exempts from disclosure personal files "the disclosure of which would constitute a clearly unwarranted invasion of personal privacy." 5 U.S.C. § 552(b)(6). . . .

Although these cases are not dispositive, they reflect the general understanding that home addresses are entitled to some privacy protection, whether or not so required by a statute. We are therefore unwilling to hold that absent a statute, a person's home address is never entitled to privacy protection. . . .

Accepting therefore the claim by the plaintiffs that there is some nontrivial interest in one's home address by persons who do not wish it disclosed, we must engage in the balancing inquiry repeatedly held appropriate in privacy cases. . . .

The nature and significance of the state interest served by Megan's Law was considered in *E.B.* There, we stated that the state interest, which we characterized as compelling, "would suffice to justify the deprivation even if a fundamental right of the registrant's were implicated." We find no reason to disagree. The public interest in knowing where prior sex offenders live so that susceptible individuals can be appropriately cautioned does not differ whether the issue is the registrant's claim under the Double Jeopardy or Ex Post Facto Clauses, or is the registrant's claim to privacy. . . .

The other argument raised by plaintiffs as part of their privacy claim is that community notification infringes upon their fundamental interest in family relationships. . . . In *E.B.*, we recognized that Megan's Law "impose[s] no restrictions on a registrant's ability to live and work in a community," but that plaintiffs complain of the law's "indirect effects: Actions that members of the community may take as a result of learning of the registrant's past, his potential danger, and his presence in the community." Even if we concede, as the District Court did, that "being subject to Megan's Law community notification places a constitutionally cognizable strain upon familial relationships," these indirect effects which follow from plaintiffs' commission of a crime are too substantially different from the government actions at issue in the prior cases to fall within the penumbra of constitutional privacy protection. Megan's Law does not restrict plaintiffs' freedom of action with respect to their families and therefore does not intrude upon the aspect of the right to privacy that protects an individual's independence in making certain types of important decisions. . . .

During the pendency of this appeal, appellants filed a series of motions under seal, six in all, seeking to supplement the record with evidence of recent incidents which have caused serious adverse consequences to them and their families. . . .

. . . [T]his court has previously held that "[t]he fact that protected information must be disclosed to a party who has a particular need for it . . . does not strip the information of its protection against disclosure to those who have no similar need," and we have required the government to implement adequate safeguards against unnecessary disclosure. Because these motions were filed in this court in the first instance, the District Court has not had the opportunity to consider the information contained therein and to determine whether any action is appropriate in light of our precedent.

[We] will remand this matter so that the District Court can consider whether plaintiffs' interest in assuring that information is disclosed only to those who have a particular need for it has been accorded adequate protection in light of the information set forth in the motions. . . .

NOTES & QUESTIONS

1. *The Privacy Interest.* In *Russell v. Gregoire*, 124 F.3d 1079 (9th Cir. 1997), the court considered a similar challenge under the constitutional right to information privacy to Washington's version of Megan's Law, which involved public dissemination of the offender's photo, name, age, birth date, other identifying information, and a summary of his or her crime. It includes the general vicinity of his or her residence, but not the exact address. Wash. Rev.

Code § 9A.44.130(1). The court held that the statute did not run afoul of the constitutional right to information privacy:

> In this case, the collection and dissemination of information is carefully designed and narrowly limited. Even if *Whalen* and *Nixon* had established a broad right to privacy in data compilations, the Act does not unduly disseminate private information about Russell and Stearns.
>
> Moreover, any such right to privacy, to the extent it exists at all, would protect only personal information. The information collected and disseminated by the Washington statute is already fully available to the public and is not constitutionally protected, with the exception of the general vicinity of the offender's residence (which is published) and the offender's employer (which is collected but not released to the public). Neither of these two items are generally considered "private."

Recall that in *Paul P. v. Verniero,* the court held that the reasoning of *United States Department of Justice v. Reporters Committee for Freedom of the Press*, 489 U.S. 749 (1989), was inapplicable to the constitutional right to information privacy. In *Reporters Committee*, the Court concluded that the disclosure of FBI "rap sheets" (compilations of a person's arrests, charges, and convictions) under the Freedom of Information Act (FOIA) implicated a privacy interest:

> In an organized society, there are few facts that are not at one time or another divulged to another. Thus, the extent of the protection accorded a privacy right at common law rested in part on the degree of dissemination of the allegedly private fact and the extent to which the passage of time rendered it private. . . . Recognition of this attribute of a privacy interest supports the distinction, in terms of personal privacy, between scattered disclosure of the bits of information contained in a rap sheet and revelation of the rap sheet as a whole.

The reasoning of this case suggests that sexual offenders have a privacy interest in their prior convictions. Should the reasoning of *Reporters Committee* apply to the constitutional right to information privacy?

Prior to *Paul P.*, the New Jersey Supreme Court had upheld New Jersey's Megan's Law in *Doe v. Poritz*, 662 A.2d 367 (N.J. 1995). There, the court, relying on *Reporters Committee*, recognized a privacy interest in some of the information divulged by New Jersey's Megan's Law:

> . . . We find . . . that considering the totality of the information disclosed to the public, the Notification Law implicates a privacy interest. That the information disseminated under the Notification Law may be available to the public, in some form or other, does not mean that plaintiff has no interest in limiting its dissemination. As the Court recognized in *United States Department of Justice v. Reporters Committee for Freedom of the Press*, 489 U.S. 749 (1989), privacy "encompass[es] the individual's control of information concerning his or her person." . . .
>
> . . . [T]he Court recognized a "distinction . . . between scattered disclosure of the bits of information contained in a rap sheet and revelation of the rap sheet as a whole." . . . The Court noted, furthermore, that there was a "privacy interest inherent in the nondisclosure of certain information even when the information may have been at one time public." . . .

In exposing those various bits of information to the public, the Notification Law links various bits of information — name, appearance, address, and crime — that otherwise might remain unconnected. However public any of those individual pieces of information may be, were it not for the Notification Law, those connections might never be made. We believe a privacy interest is implicated when the government assembles those diverse pieces of information into a single package and disseminates that package to the public, thereby ensuring that a person cannot assume anonymity — in this case, preventing a person's criminal history from fading into obscurity and being wholly forgotten. Those convicted of crime may have no cognizable privacy interest in the fact of their conviction, but the Notification Law, given the compilation and dissemination of information, nonetheless implicates a privacy interest. The interests in privacy may fade when the information is a matter of public record, but they are not non-existent. . . .

The court, however, concluded that the state interest outweighed the sexual offender's privacy interest:

There is an express public policy militating toward disclosure: the danger of recidivism posed by sex offenders. The state interest in protecting the safety of members of the public from sex offenders is clear and compelling. The Legislature has determined that there is a substantial danger of recidivism by sex offenders, and public notification clearly advances the purpose of protecting the public from that danger. . . .

Compare the treatment of *Reporters Committee* in *Paul P.* and *Poritz*. How do the cases differ in the way they deal with the import of *Reporters Committee*?[27]

2. *Postscript to* **Paul P.** In 2000, New Jersey amended its constitution by a referendum that provided that nothing in the New Jersey Constitution shall prohibit the disclosure of Megan's Law information over the Internet. New Jersey subsequently posted its sexual offender data on a website, excluding the offenders' current home addresses.

In *A.A. v. New Jersey,* 341 F.3d 206 (3d Cir. 2003), the Third Circuit upheld New Jersey's Megan's Law against a privacy claim against a public Internet registry posting personal information against convicted sex offenders. The court found that the Internet registry, which contains information about certain high-risk and moderate-risk sex offenders, was permissible due to the state's compelling interest to prevent sex offenses. Although the convicted sex offenders have a "nontrivial" privacy interest in their home addresses, the court concluded that a need exists to access information in a mobile society. The court stated: "Consider parents with young children who want to purchase a new home in New Jersey. Without the Registry, they would not be notified of the presence of convicted sex offenders, even those with a high risk of re-offense, until they had already purchased their new home which may be in the proximity of a Registrant's home. . . . So too a family planning a vacation at the New Jersey shore."

---

[27] *See also Cutshall v. Sundquist,* 193 F.3d 466 (6th Cir. 1999) (rejecting reliance on *Reporters Committee* and concluding that constitutional right to information privacy is not implicated by Megan's Law).

Like New Jersey, many states are placing their Megan's Law information on the Internet. Is such a practice going too far? Or is it necessary to make accessing the information more convenient? Consider Daniel Solove's critique of posting Megan's Law disclosures on the Internet:

> Megan's Law disclosures may be relevant for certain types of relationships, such as child care. Still, what most Megan's Laws lose sight of the use of the information in question. Megan's Law data is beneficial when disclosed for certain purposes, but not necessarily for all purposes. When placed on the Internet for any curious individual around the world to see, Megan's Law information becomes disconnected from its goals.[28]

3. *The Breadth of Megan's Laws.* Megan's Law does not merely involve offenses against children. It encompasses a wide range of sex offenses, which can range from sodomy, prostitution, consensual homosexual acts, masturbation in public places, flashing, and statutory rape. In some states, the disclosure does not indicate what particular sexual offense the offender committed. Is such a general listing appropriate? Is Megan's Law justified under the constitutional right to information privacy for every offense that a state classifies as a sexual offense? Or does the balance weigh in favor of Megan's Law only for specific offenses? If so, how should such offenses be distinguished from ones in which the balance does not weigh in favor of Megan's Law?[29]

4. *Recidivism Rates.* One of the justifications for Megan's Law is that sexual offenders have a high recidivism rate and, hence, pose a threat to the community. But sexual offenders have a lower recidivism rate than those who commit other forms of violent crime, such as robbers. In one study of offenders re-arrested within three years for any crime, previously convicted murderers had approximately a 42 percent re-arrest rate; rapists had a 51.5 percent re-arrest rate; other sexual offenders had a 48 percent re-arrest rate; and robbers had a 66 percent re-arrest rate. However, re-arrest rates, without more information, are misleading. Of the 51.5 percent of rapists who were re-arrested within three years after being released, only 7.7 percent were re-arrested for a sex crime. Further, different types of sexual offenders have different recidivism rates.[30]

5. *Family Stigma.* The majority of sexual offenses against children are committed by family members or close friends of the family (estimated at about 92

---

[28] Daniel J. Solove, *The Virtues of Knowing Less: Justifying Privacy Protections Against Disclosure*, 53 Duke L.J. 967, 1061 (2003).

[29] For more on the privacy implications of Megan's Laws, see Caroline Louise Lewis, *The Jacob Wetterling Crimes Against Children and Sexually Violent Offender Registration Act: An Unconstitutional Deprivation of the Right to Privacy and Substantive Due Process*, 31 Harv. C.R.-C.L. L. Rev. 89 (1996); Symposium, *Critical Perspectives on Megan's Law: Protection vs. Privacy*, 13 N.Y.L. Sch. J. Hum. Rts. 1 (1996).

[30] *See* Jane A. Small, *Who Are the People in Your Neighborhood? Due Process, Public Protection, and Sex Offender Notification Laws*, 74 N.Y.U. L. Rev. 1451 (1999). For a contrary view regarding recidivism rates for sex offenders, see Daniel L. Feldman, *The "Scarlet Letter Laws" of the 1990s: A Response to Critics*, 60 Alb. L. Rev. 1081 (1997).

percent).[31] When a child's parent is released and is listed in the sex offender registry, the child's privacy can also be compromised because the entire family is under the stigma of harboring a sexual offender.

In *Doe v. Quiring,* 686 N.W.2d 918 (S.D. 2004), a young woman, who was the victim of incest by her father, brought suit to have her father's name removed from the sex offender public registry. Among the information that the registry contains is the type of crime that the offender committed. The victim argued that "public access to incest offenders and their crimes through the Registry 'necessarily' involves the 'release of . . . identifying information regarding the victim of the crime.' " Pursuant to South Dakota's Megan's Law: "Nothing in this section allows the release of the name or any identifying information regarding the victim of the crime to any person other than law enforcement agencies, and such victim identifying information is confidential." SDCL 22-22-40. The victim contended that "because the crime of incest involves familial relationships, the very definition of the crime of incest 'so narrows the group of possible victims that identification of the victim is necessarily implicated by the name of the offense.' " The court, however, disagreed:

> [B]ecause the Registry does not reveal the victim's familial relationship, age, physical description, address, or gender, a victim could be any one of a number of less than 21-year-old relatives of the offender. Under these circumstances, we believe that the mere listing of the offender and type of offense is not the disclosure of the "identifying information" that the Legislature intended to prohibit. . . .

In dissent, Justices Meierhenry and Sabers argued:

> Initially, the legislative purpose "of alerting the public in the interest of community safety" is satisfied by identifying the crime as "rape" or "sexual contact." To note the crime specifically as incest only serves to narrow the class of victims to a small number capable of being identified. The size of the class of incest victims is limited to family members. The number of family members under the age of twenty-one is even smaller and, in some cases, may include only a couple of children. Publicly identifying the crime as "incest" significantly increases the risk of providing "identifying information of the victim" and may bring opprobrium on family members who were not victims. It may also have the effect of making victims or family members reluctant to report the crimes knowing the registry will list the crime as incest. Often incest crimes go unreported because of the fear of public exposure and embarrassment created for the family, victim, and perpetrator. Michele L. Earl-Hubbard, *The Child Sex Offender Registration Laws: The Punishment, Liberty Deprivation, and Unintended Results Associated with the Scarlet Letter Laws of the 1990s,* 90 Nw. U. L. Rev. 788, 856 (1996). As one author noted, "Ironically, Megan's Laws may stigmatize the very victims of sex offenses whom they are designed to protect, many of whom are children living in the same house as the sex

---

[31] Michele L. Earl-Hubbard, Comment, *The Child Sex Offender Registration Laws: The Punishment, Liberty Deprivation, and Unintended Results Associated with the Scarlet Letter Laws of the 1990s,* 90 Nw. U. L. Rev. 788, 851-52 (1996).

offender." Daniel J. Solove, *The Virtues of Knowing Less: Justifying Privacy Protections Against Disclosure,* 53 Duke L.J. 967, 1060 (2003).

6. ***Shaming Punishments.*** In colonial America, marking criminals with branding, mutilation, or letter-wearing (such as the scarlet letter) was common. Marks would be burned into the convict's hand or forehead. This was often done because there was no way of imprisoning people. Nathaniel Hawthorne's *The Scarlet Letter* involves a famous example of a shaming punishment where Hester Prynne was made to stitch a red letter "A" to her clothing to punish her for adultery. Does Megan's Law amount to a shaming punishment? Is this form of punishment appropriate?

Amitai Etzioni has praised shaming in the context of Megan's Law. He argues: "[S]haming is particularly communitarian in that it does not occur unless the community approves of the values at stake."[32] In his view, moreover, due to recidivism among sex offenders, a likely alternative to publicizing the presence of the sex offender in the community plus shaming will be "to keep the offender longer in jail" to protect the community. Will antisocial behavior expand in the absence of shaming?

7. ***Is Megan's Law a Punishment?*** In *Smith v. Doe,* 538 U.S. 84 (2003), the Supreme Court examined whether Alaska's Megan's Law violated the constitutional prohibitions on ex post facto laws. An ex post facto law is a law that applies after the fact. In other words, the federal government and the states cannot pass a law that criminalizes past actions. Pursuant to U.S. Constitution art. I, § 9, "No . . . ex post facto Law shall be passed" by the federal government. U.S. Constitution art. I, § 10 provides that "No state shall . . . pass any . . . ex post facto Law."

Alaska's Megan's Law makes public the following information: "name, aliases, address, photograph, physical description, description[,] license [and] identification numbers of motor vehicles, place of employment, date of birth, crime for which convicted, date of conviction, place and court of conviction, length and conditions of sentence, and a statement as to whether the offender or kidnapper is in compliance with [the update] requirements . . . or cannot be located." Alaska Stat. § 18.65.087(b). The Supreme Court noted that if the sex offender registration and notification law is designed to "impose punishment," then it "constitutes retroactive punishment" and is an impermissible ex post facto law. The Court concluded that "the intent of the Alaska Legislature was to create a civil, nonpunitive regime." Further, the Court concluded that the effect of the law did not "negate Alaska's intention to establish a civil regulatory scheme." In reaching this latter conclusion, the Court dismissed an argument that Megan's Law resembles the "shaming punishments of the colonial period."

> Any initial resemblance to early punishments is, however, misleading. Punishments such as whipping, pillory, and branding inflicted physical pain and staged a direct confrontation between the offender and the public. Even

---

[32] Amitai Etzioni, The *Limits of Privacy* 60-61 (1999).

punishments that lacked the corporal component, such as public shaming, humiliation, and banishment, involved more than the dissemination of information. They either held the person up before his fellow citizens for face-to-face shaming or expelled him from the community. By contrast, the stigma of Alaska's Megan's Law results not from public display for ridicule and shaming but from the dissemination of accurate information about a criminal record, most of which is already public. Our system does not treat dissemination of truthful information in furtherance of a legitimate governmental objective as punishment. On the contrary, our criminal law tradition insists on public indictment, public trial, and public imposition of sentence. Transparency is essential to maintaining public respect for the criminal justice system, ensuring its integrity, and protecting the rights of the accused. The publicity may cause adverse consequences for the convicted defendant, running from mild personal embarrassment to social ostracism. In contrast to the colonial shaming punishments, however, the State does not make the publicity and the resulting stigma an integral part of the objective of the regulatory scheme.

The Court reasoned that although the "reach of the Internet is greater than anything which could have been designed in colonial times," the goal of the notification is "to inform the public for its own safety, not to humiliate the offender. . . . The Internet makes the document search more efficient, cost effective, and convenient for Alaska's citizenry."

Justices Stevens, Ginsburg, and Breyer dissented. In Justices Ginsburg and Breyer's dissent, they observed:

And meriting heaviest weight in my judgment, the Act makes no provision whatever for the possibility of rehabilitation: Offenders cannot shorten their registration or notification period, even on the clearest demonstration of rehabilitation or conclusive proof of physical incapacitation. However plain it may be that a former sex offender currently poses no threat of recidivism, he will remain subject to long-term monitoring and inescapable humiliation.

John Doe I, for example, pleaded *nolo contendere* to a charge of sexual abuse of a minor nine years before the Alaska Act was enacted. He successfully completed a treatment program, and gained early release on supervised probation in part because of his compliance with the program's requirements and his apparent low risk of re-offense. He subsequently remarried, established a business, and was reunited with his family. He was also granted custody of a minor daughter, based on a court's determination that he had been successfully rehabilitated. The court's determination rested in part on psychiatric evaluations concluding that Doe had "a very low risk of re-offending" and is "not a pedophile." Notwithstanding this strong evidence of rehabilitation, the Alaska Act requires Doe to report personal information to the State four times per year, and permits the State publicly to label him a "Registered Sex Offender" for the rest of his life.

8. ***Megan's Law Disclosures for All Crimes?*** A growing number of states are furnishing online databases of all of their current inmates and parolees. Do these databases serve the statutory purpose of protecting the community? Should registries of felons stop at sexual offenders? Why not all people convicted of a crime?

9. ***How Far Can Disclosure Go?*** In May 2001, Judge J. Manuel Banales of Texas ordered 21 convicted sex offenders to post signs in their front yards stating: "Danger! Registered Sex Offender Lives Here." Additionally, the offenders must place bumper stickers on their cars stating: "Danger! Registered Sex Offender in Vehicle." Other offenders were ordered to send letters to all the people who lived within three blocks of their homes. Compliance is monitored by the probation department. "The whole idea is that everybody is looking at you," Judge Banales said to the offenders. "You have no one else to blame but yourself." Under the reasoning of either *Russell* or *Paul P.*, is this court order a violation of the constitutional right to information privacy?

10. ***A Prison-Privacy Trade-off?*** Suppose that instead of enacting Megan's Laws, society just decided to extend the sentences for sexual offenses and lock up sexual offenders for life. Perhaps if states could not enact a Megan's Law, they would resort to more life sentences for sexual offenders. Most likely, many offenders would choose a regime where they would be released from prison and subject to Megan's Law to a regime where they would spend the rest of their lives in prison. What do you think about this potential trade-off?

5. THE DRIVER'S PRIVACY PROTECTION ACT

For decades, many states had been selling to private sector companies their motor vehicle records. Motor vehicle records contain information such as one's name, address, phone number, Social Security number, medical information, height, weight, gender, eye color, photograph, and date of birth. This information was highly desired by marketers, who paid states millions of dollars to obtain these records. In 1994, Congress passed the Driver's Privacy Protection Act (DPPA), 18 U.S.C. §§ 2721–2725, to halt this practice.

Restriction on Disclosure. Pursuant to DPPA:

[A] State department of motor vehicles . . . shall not knowingly disclose or otherwise make available to any person or entity personal information about any individual obtained by the department in connection with a motor vehicle record. 18 U.S.C. § 2721(a).

"Personal information" is defined as data "that identifies an individual, including an individual's photograph, social security number, driver identification number, name, address (but not the 5-digit zip code), telephone number, and medical or disability information." § 2725(3). The definition of "personal information" specifically excludes "information on vehicular accidents, driving violations, and driver's status." § 2725(3).

DPPA applies to state DMVs and their officials and employees. Further, DPPA only applies to motor vehicle records.

Consent. State DMVs can disclose personal information in motor vehicle records if the individual consents. In order to disclose a driver's personal information for marketing or other restricted uses, the driver must affirmatively indicate her consent (opt in). § 2721(b) and (d).

Exceptions. The DPPA contains a number of exceptions. Personal information can be disclosed for purposes of law enforcement, recalls, legal proceedings, and insurance claims investigations. § 2721(b). Additionally, DPPA permits disclosure to licensed private investigative agencies. § 2721(b). Ironically, the event that motivated Congress to pass the DPPA was the murder of actress Rebecca Shaeffer. Her murderer ascertained her address from a private detective, who had received it from the DMV.[33]

Restrictions on Further Dissemination. If private entities obtain motor vehicle record information, they cannot resell or further disseminate that information. 18 U.S.C. § 2721(c). However, if the driver consents to the disclosure of her data, then information may be disseminated for any purpose.

Enforcement. The DPPA establishes criminal fines for any "person" who knowingly obtains or discloses motor vehicle record data in ways prohibited by the DPPA. §§ 2722, 2723(a), 2725(2).

The DPPA, § 2724, provides for a private right to action for violations:

> A person who knowingly obtains, discloses or uses personal information, from a motor vehicle record, for a purpose not permitted under this chapter shall be liable to the individual to whom the information pertains, who may bring a civil action in a United States district court.

Note that this section purportedly applies to any "person who knowingly obtains, discloses or uses personal information, from a motor vehicle record." In other words, it does not just apply to state DMVs but to anybody who uses data from a motor vehicle record. States and state agencies are generally excluded from the DPPA, but the U.S. Attorney General may impose a civil penalty of up to $5,000 per day for state agencies that maintain a "policy or practice of substantial noncompliance" with the DPPA. § 2723(b).

In *Margan v. Niles*, 250 F. Supp. 2d 63 (N.D.N.Y. 2003), the court found that the DPPA provided a cause of action beyond the motor operator whose motor vehicle record was disclosed. The court found that "any individual whose address was obtained from a motor vehicle record is a proper plaintiff." Hence, in *Niles*, the spouse and children of an individual whose address was obtained from a motor vehicle record could "maintain an action under the DPPA where the spouse and children share the same address as that individual." The court also found that a municipality whose agent violated the DPPA could be held vicariously liable under this statute. *See also Luparello v. The Incorporated Village of Garden City,* 290 F. Supp. 2d 341 (E.D.N.Y. 2003).

The Scope of Congressional Power. In *Reno v. Condon*, 528 U.S. 141 (2000), the Supreme Court upheld the DPPA against a constitutional challenge that DPPA violated the Tenth and Eleventh Amendments:

> The United States asserts that the DPPA is a proper exercise of Congress' authority to regulate interstate commerce under the Commerce Clause, U.S.

---

[33] *See* Charles J. Sykes, *The End of Privacy: Personal Rights in the Surveillance Society* 30-31 (1999).

Const., Art. I, § 8, cl. 3. The United States bases its Commerce Clause argument on the fact that the personal, identifying information that the DPPA regulates is a "thin[g] in interstate commerce," and that the sale or release of that information in interstate commerce is therefore a proper subject of congressional regulation. We agree with the United States' contention. The motor vehicle information which the States have historically sold is used by insurers, manufacturers, direct marketers, and others engaged in interstate commerce to contact drivers with customized solicitations. The information is also used in the stream of interstate commerce by various public and private entities for matters related to interstate motoring. Because drivers' information is, in this context, an article of commerce, its sale or release into the interstate stream of business is sufficient to support congressional regulation.

Based on *Reno v. Condon*, what is the extent of Congress's power to regulate information maintained by the states? Suppose Congress amended the Privacy Act to apply not just to federal agencies but to all state and local governments as well. Would such an extension of the Privacy Act be constitutional?

B. GOVERNMENT RECORDS AND USE OF PERSONAL DATA

1. FAIR INFORMATION PRACTICES

In the 1960s, the increasing use of computers gave rise to a significant public debate about privacy. In particular, commentators expressed opposition to the increasing amount of personal information collected by government agencies and stored in computer databases.

In 1973, the Department of Housing, Education, and Welfare (HEW) issued a highly influential report about government records maintained in computer databases. The HEW Report characterized the growing concern over privacy:

> It is no wonder that people have come to distrust computer-based record-keeping operations. Even in non-governmental settings, an individual's control over the personal information that he gives to an organization or that an organization obtains about him, is lessening as the relationship between the giver and receiver of personal data grows more attenuated, impersonal, and diffused. There was a time when information about an individual tended to be elicited in face-to-face contacts involving personal trust and a certain symmetry, or balance, between giver and receiver. Nowadays, an individual must increasingly give information about himself to large and relatively faceless institutions, for handling and use by strangers — unknown, unseen, and, all too frequently, unresponsive. Sometimes the individual does not even know that an organization maintains a record about him. Often he may not see it, much less contest its accuracy, control its dissemination, or challenge its use by others. . . .
>
> The poet, the novelist, and the social scientist tell us, each in his own way, that the life of a small-town man, woman, or family is an open book compared to the more anonymous existence of urban dwellers. Yet the individual in a small town can retain his confidence because he can be more sure of retaining control. He lives in a face-to-face world, in a social system where irresponsible behavior can

be identified and called to account. By contrast, the impersonal data system, and faceless users of the information it contains, tend to be accountable only in the formal sense of the word. In practice they are for the most part immune to whatever sanctions the individual can invoke.

To remedy these growing concerns over the accumulation and use of personal information by the government, the HEW Report recommended that a Code of Fair Information Practices be established:

- There must be no personal-data record-keeping systems whose very existence is secret.

- There must be a way for an individual to find out what information about him is in a record and how it is used.

- There must be a way for an individual to prevent information about him obtained for one purpose from being used or made available for other purposes without his consent.

- There must be a way for an individual to correct or amend a record of identifiable information about him.

- Any organization creating, maintaining, using, or disseminating records of identifiable personal data must assure the reliability of the data for their intended use and must take reasonable precautions to prevent misuse of the data.[34]

Fair Information Practices can be understood most simply as the rights and responsibilities that are associated with the transfer and use of personal information. Since the intent is to correct information asymmetries that result from the transfer of personal data from an individual to an organization, Fair Information Practices typically assign rights to individuals and responsibilities to organizations.

MARC ROTENBERG, *FAIR INFORMATION PRACTICES AND THE ARCHITECTURE OF PRIVACY (WHAT LARRY DOESN'T GET)*

2001 Stan. Tech. L. Rev. 1

. . . Not only have Fair Information Practices played a significant role in framing privacy laws in the United States, these basic principles have also contributed to the development of privacy laws around the world and even to the development of important international guidelines for privacy protection. The most well known of these international guidelines are the Organization for Economic Cooperation and Development's Recommendations Concerning and Guidelines Governing the Protection of Privacy and Transborder Flows of Personal Data ("OECD Guidelines"). The OECD Guidelines set out eight principles for data protection that are still the benchmark for assessing privacy policy and legislation: Collection Limitation; Data Quality; Purpose Specification; Use Limitation; Security Safeguards; Openness; Individual Participation; and Accountability. The

[34] U.S. Dep't of Health, Educ. & Welfare, Records, *Computers, and the Rights of Citizens: Report of the Secretary's Advisory Comm. on Automated Personal Data Systems* 29-30, 41-42 (1973) ("HEW Report").

principles articulate in only a couple of pages a set of rules that have guided the development of national law and increasingly the design of information systems.

It is generally understood that the challenge of privacy protection in the information age is the application and enforcement of Fair Information Practices and the OECD Guidelines. While some recommendations for improvement have been made, the level of consensus, at least outside of the United States, about the viability of Fair Information Practices as a general solution to the problem of privacy protection is remarkable. As recently as 1998 the OECD reaffirmed support for the 1980 guidelines, and countries that are adopting privacy legislation have generally done so in the tradition of Fair Information Practices.

While some commentators have made recommendations for updating or expanding the principles, there is general agreement that the concept of Fair Information Practices and the specific standards set out in the OECD Guidelines continue to provide a useful and effective framework for privacy protection in information systems.

Commentators have also noted a remarkable convergence of privacy policies. Countries around the world, with very distinct cultural backgrounds and systems of governance, nonetheless have adopted roughly similar approaches to privacy protection. Perhaps this is not so surprising. The original OECD Guidelines were drafted by representatives from North America, Europe, and Asia. The OECD Guidelines reflect a broad consensus about how to safeguard the control and use of personal information in a world where data can flow freely across national borders. Just as it does today on the Internet. . . .

Viewed against this background, the problem of privacy protection in the United States in the early 1990s was fairly well understood. The coverage of U.S. law was uneven: Fair Information Practices were in force in some sectors and not others. There was inadequate enforcement and oversight. Technology continued to outpace the law. And the failure to adopt a comprehensive legal framework to safeguard privacy rights could jeopardize transborder data flows with Europe and other regions. These factors should all have played a significant role in coding a solution to the privacy problem. . . .

2. THE PRIVACY ACT

Influenced by the HEW Report's Fair Information Practices and inspired by the Watergate scandal, Congress enacted the Privacy Act of 1974 four months after President Nixon resigned from office. In passing the Privacy Act, Congress found that "the privacy of an individual is directly affected by the collection, maintenance, use, and dissemination of personal information by Federal agencies" and that "the increasing use of computers and sophisticated information technology, while essential to the efficient operations of the Government, has greatly magnified the harm to individual privacy that can occur from any collection, maintenance, use, or dissemination of personal information."

Purposes of the Privacy Act. The Privacy Act's stated purposes are, among other things, to: (1) "permit an individual to determine what records pertaining to him are collected, maintained, used, or disseminated by [federal] agencies"; (2) "permit an individual to prevent records pertaining to him obtained by such agencies for a particular purpose from being used or made available for another purpose without his consent"; (3) allow an individual to access and correct his personal data maintained by federal agencies; and (4) ensure that information is "current and accurate for its intended use, and that adequate safeguards are provided to prevent misuse of such information."

Applicability and Scope. The Privacy Act applies to federal agencies. It does not apply to businesses or private sector organizations. Moreover, it does not apply to state and local agencies—only federal ones.

In order to establish a violation of the Privacy Act, a plaintiff must prove several things:

First, the plaintiff must prove that the agency violated its obligations under the Act (most often, that the agency improperly disclosed information).

Second, the information disclosed must be a "record" contained within a "system of records." A "record" must be identifiable to an individual (contain her name or other identifying information) and must contain information about the individual. § 552a(a)(4). The record must be kept as part of a "system of records," which is "a group of any records under the control of any agency from which information is retrieved by the name of the individual or by some identifying number, symbol, or other identifying particular assigned to the individual." § 552a(a)(5).

Third, to collect damages, the plaintiff must show that an adverse impact resulted from the Privacy Act violation and that the violation was "willful or intentional."

Limits on Disclosure. Pursuant to the Privacy Act:

> No agency shall disclose any record which is contained in a system of records by any means of communication to any person, or to another agency, except pursuant to a written request by, or with prior written consent of, the individual to whom the record pertains. 5 U.S.C. § 552a(b).

Responsibilities for Recordkeeping. The Privacy Act establishes restrictions and responsibilities for agencies maintaining records about individuals. Agencies shall maintain "only such information about an individual as is relevant and necessary to accomplish a purpose of the agency required to be accomplished by statute or by executive order of the President." § 552a(e)(1). Additionally, agencies shall "collect information to the greatest extent practicable directly from the subject individual when the information may result in adverse determinations about an individual's rights, benefits, and privileges under Federal programs." § 552a(e)(2). Agencies shall inform individuals who make a request about how their personal information will be used. § 552a(e)(3). Agencies must publish in the Federal Register notices about the systems of records they maintain. § 552a(e)(4). Agencies must also "establish appropriate administrative, technical, and physical safeguards to insure the security and confidentiality of records." § 552a(e)(10).

Right to Access and Correct Records. Pursuant to the federal Privacy Act, upon request, individuals can review their records and can ask that the agency correct any inaccuracies in their records. § 552a(d).

Enforcement. If an agency fails to comply with any provision of the Privacy Act, or refuses to comply with an individual's request to obtain access to her records or correct her records, individuals can bring a civil action in federal court. § 552a(g)(1). The court can enjoin the agency from withholding access of records. § 552a(g)(3). In limited circumstances, monetary damages may be awarded:

> (4) In any suit brought under the provisions of subsection (g)(1)(C) or (D) of this section in which the court determines that the agency acted in a manner which was intentional or willful, the United States shall be liable to the individual in an amount equal to the sum of —
>
>> (A) actual damages sustained by the individual as a result of the refusal or failure, but in no case shall a person entitled to recovery receive less than the sum of $1,000; and
>> (B) the costs of the action together with reasonable attorney fees as determined by the court. § 552a(g)(4).

Law Enforcement Exceptions. Pursuant to § 552a(j), the "head of any agency may promulgate rules . . . to exempt any system of records within the agency from any part of [the Privacy Act] if the system of records" is (1) maintained by the CIA or (2) maintained by a law enforcement agency and consists of (A) identifying and criminal history information compiled to identify criminal offenders or (B) "information compiled for the purpose of criminal investigation, including reports of informants and investigators, and associated with an identifiable individual"; or (C) "reports identifiable to an individual compiled at any stage of the process of enforcement of the criminal laws from arrest or indictment through release from supervision." This exception does not apply to § 552a(b), §§ 552a(c)(1) and (2), and certain portions of § 552(e).

Additionally, § 552(k)(2) allows the head of any agency to promulgate rules to exempt "investigatory material compiled for law enforcement purposes" from the Act's accounting and access provisions. However, "if any individual is denied any right, privilege, or benefit that we would otherwise be entitled by Federal law . . . as a result of the maintenance of such material, such material shall be provided to the individual, except to the extent that the disclosure of such material would reveal the identity of a [government informant]."

FOIA Exception. When FOIA requires that information be released, the Privacy Act does not apply. § 552a(b)(3).

Routine Use Exception. The broadest exception under the Privacy Act is that information may be disclosed for any "routine use" if disclosure is "compatible" with the purpose for which the agency collected the information. § 552a(b)(3).

Information Sharing Among Agencies. The Privacy Act permits one agency to disclose information "to another agency or to an instrumentality of any governmental jurisdiction within or under the control of the United States for a civil or criminal law enforcement activity" if the agency or instrumentality's head makes "a written request to the agency which maintains the record." § 552a(b)(7).

Other Exceptions. In all, there are about a dozen exceptions to the Privacy Act. Other exceptions allow disclosure to the Census Bureau, "to a person pursuant to a showing of compelling circumstances affecting the health or safety of an individual"; to Congress; to the Comptroller General, pursuant to a court order, or to a credit reporting agency. § 552a(b).

State Privacy Acts. Although every state has a statute comparable to the federal FOIA, requiring public access to government records, most states do not have a statute comparable to the federal Privacy Act. Only about a third of states have adopted such a statute.

PIPPINGER V. RUBIN

129 F.3d 519 (10th Cir. 1997)

EBEL, C.J. . . . Because of a romantic relationship with a subordinate, Plaintiff–Appellant John Pippinger was temporarily suspended from his job as an Internal Revenue Service ("IRS") branch manager. Several IRS employees were involved in helping the local IRS District Director reach the decision to suspend Pippinger. Eventually, many IRS employees in the district knew why Pippinger was suspended.

Before Pippinger's suspension was carried out, Pippinger's supervisor Patrick Schluck got into trouble with the IRS because he too had a romantic relationship with a subordinate. During the depositions and proceedings pertaining to Schluck's case, Pippinger's case was discussed and the IRS disclosed information from records of Pippinger's case to Schluck and his attorneys.

Pippinger sued the IRS, alleging violations of the Privacy Act of 1974, 5 U.S.C. § 552a (1994). The district court granted summary judgment in favor of the IRS. Pippinger appeals. Because we agree with the district court that Pippinger's rights under the Privacy Act were not violated, we affirm. . . .

Since 1978, Plaintiff–Appellant John Pippinger has been employed by the Internal Revenue Service ("IRS") as a manager. In July 1988, IRS employee Lynn Boak1 began to work under Pippinger's supervision in the IRS's Cheyenne, Wyoming office. Although both Pippinger and Boak were married to other people at the time, they began having an affair in November 1992. . . .

[Based on some anonymous tips, Pippinger and Boak's relationship was brought to the attention of their supervisors. After several investigations, Pippinger was suspended without pay for two days based on his actions in connection with the affair.

One of Pippinger's supervisors, Patrick Schluck, became involved in an affair with a subordinate himself, and was demoted. One reason for the demotion was that Schluck had presided over Pippinger's disciplinary proceedings when he was engaged in similar conduct as Pippinger. Schluck challenged his demotion in a proceeding with the Merit Systems Protection Board ("MSPB"). During discovery, various IRS officials testified in depositions disclosing information from Schluck's records about Pippinger. Schluck's attorney and a court reporter also were present during this testimony.]

Pippinger learned that his case had been discussed, and his and Boak's identities revealed, during discovery in Schluck's MSPB proceeding. At that time, Pippinger also learned that the IRS had been maintaining a computer database known as the "Automated Labor Employee Relations Tracking System" ("ALERTS"). The nationwide ALERTS system was used by the IRS permanently to record all disciplinary action proposed or taken against any IRS employee. [The ALERTS system contained information about Pippinger's misconduct and suspension.]

On January 19, 1995, Pippinger sued the Secretary of the Treasury (also referred to in this opinion as the "IRS"), alleging that the IRS had violated the Privacy Act of 1974, 5 U.S.C. § 552a (1994), by maintaining disciplinary records on Pippinger in the allegedly unlawful ALERTS database and also by allegedly disclosing information from those records on several occasions. . . .

The IRS moved pursuant to Fed.R.Civ.P. 12(b)(6) to dismiss Pippinger's constitutional claims, and moved for summary judgment with respect to Pippinger's Privacy Act claims. . . . [The district court granted summary judgment for the IRS.]

The Privacy Act of 1974 limits the circumstances under which government agencies, including the IRS, may disclose information contained in their records. In general, the Act provides that:

> No agency shall disclose any record which is contained in a system of records by any means of communication to any person, or to another agency, except pursuant to a written request by, or with the prior written consent of, the individual to whom the record pertains

However, the Act goes on to enumerate twelve exceptions to this general prohibition.

Pippinger, who did not consent to any disclosure, claims that the IRS unlawfully disclosed his employment records on three different occasions. In analyzing each of these three claims, we must decide whether a record was "disclosed," and, if so, whether it was disclosed pursuant to an exception enumerated in 5 U.S.C. § 552a(b).

Although "disclosure" is not defined in the text of the Privacy Act, the Office of Personnel Management ("OPM") has defined "disclosure" under the Privacy Act to mean "providing personal review of a record, or a copy thereof, to someone other than the data subject or the data subject's authorized representative...." 5 C.F.R. § 297.102. Although the OPM's definition of "disclosure" would appear to be limited to disclosures of the physical records themselves (or mechanical reproductions thereof), this court and other courts have assumed or held that the Privacy Act more broadly prohibits disclosure of information directly or indirectly derived from an agency system of records, even where the physical records are not disclosed. . . .

[Regarding disclosure about Pippinger's data to IRS staff members,] the district court held that Taylor did not violate the Privacy Act because: (1) Taylor's staff had "a need for the record in the performance of their duties," a condition which allows disclosure to them under 5 U.S.C. § 552a(b)(1), and (2) Taylor did not "act[ ] in a manner which was intentional or willful," a requirement for governmental liability under 5 U.S.C. § 552a(g)(4). . . .

[The staff members'] jobs included helping Taylor decide whether and how to discipline Pippinger. For this reason, the staff members clearly "needed to know" the information contained in Pippinger's files pertaining to Pippinger's relationship with Boak and his subsequent allegedly misleading statements pertaining thereto. In addition, contrary to Pippinger's argument, knowledge of Pippinger's identity allowed Taylor's staff members to put the investigation in context, and might potentially have enabled them to connect the information about Pippinger's alleged misconduct with other data already know to them. . . .

Pippinger also claims that the IRS violated the Privacy Act because most of the people in [the IRS district office] new about Pippinger's two-day suspension and the reasons underlying it. Pippinger claims that this widespread knowledge gives rise to an inference that [his information was improperly disclosed to his co-workers.]

. . . [T]he mere fact that information contained in Pippinger's personnel files was well-known in his workplace does not give rise to an inference that such knowledge was widespread because of a disclosure from Pippinger's personnel files. As the district court correctly noted, the Privacy Act does not prohibit disclosure of information or knowledge obtained from sources other than "records." In particular, it does not prevent federal employees or officials from talking—even gossiping—about anything of which they have non-record-based knowledge.

A number of people in Pippinger's workplace had personally observed Pippinger's relationship with Boak. Several learned the details of Pippinger's suspension from Pippinger himself. Accordingly, in the absence of any evidence suggesting that the IRS actually disclosed information from Pippinger's records, Pippinger's "inferential" evidence of such disclosure cannot withstand summary judgment.

[Regarding the disclosure of the records during the MSPB proceeding, the] district court found that these disclosures did not violate Pippinger's rights under the Privacy Act because they were authorized by either the "need to know" exception of 5 U.S.C. § 552a(b)(1), or the "routine use" exception of 5 U.S.C. § 552a(b)(3). . . .

. . . Pippinger's records, though stored in the ALERTS system, were culled from two systems of records described in the Federal Register: the Appeals, Grievance, and Complaint System; and the General Personnel and Payroll Records System. The routine uses of records in both systems have been defined in the Federal Register to include "provid[ing] records and information to the ... Merit Systems Protection Board . . . for the purpose of properly administering Federal Personnel Systems in accordance with applicable laws, Executive Orders, and regulations."

This language is broad enough to authorize the disclosure of Pippinger 's records to the Merit Systems Protection Board during the course of Schluck 's MSPB proceeding, so long as such disclosure is made "for the purpose of properly administering Federal Personnel Systems." In the case at bar, Pippinger has presented no evidence suggesting that his records were disclosed to the MSPB for any other purpose. Accordingly, the disclosures made by Taylor, Webb, Probasco, Wicks, and Neiser to the MSPB were authorized, "routine uses" of Pippinger's records.

The disclosures to Schluck, Schluck's attorney, and the court reporter were similarly made in conjunction with the MSPB proceeding and, accordingly, fall within the same "routine use" exception. . . .

NOTES & QUESTIONS

1. *The "Routine Use" Exemption: "The Biggest Loophole."* Consider Robert Gellman:

> The act limits use of personal data to those officers and employees of the agency maintaining the data who have a need for the data in the performance their duties. This vague standard is not a significant barrier to the sharing of personal information within agencies. . . . No administrative process exists to control or limit internal agency uses. Suits have been brought by individuals who objected to specific uses, but most uses have been upheld. . . .
>
> The legislation left most decisions about external uses to the agencies, and this created the biggest loophole in the law.
>
> An agency can establish a "routine use" if it determines that a disclosure is compatible with the purpose for which the record was collected. This vague formula has not created much of a substantive barrier to external disclosure of personal information. . . . Later legislation, political pressures, and bureaucratic convenience tended to overwhelm the law's weak limitations. Without any effective restriction on disclosure, the Privacy Act lost much of its vitality and became more procedural and more symbolic.[35]

Other observers have noted the problematic nature of the Privacy Act's "routine use" exemption. According to the Privacy Act's language, a routine use must be "a purpose which is compatible with the purpose for which it was collected." 5 U.S.C. § 552a(7). Paul Schwartz observes:

> Not only is the "routine use" exemption applied in a fashion that ignores relevant statutory language, such agency practice continues despite prolonged and well-placed criticism of it. As early as 1977, the Privacy Protection Study Commission, a blue-ribbon commission created by Congress at the time of the Privacy Act's enactment, noted its disapproval of overbroad applications of the routine use exemption. In 1983, the House Committee on Government Operations issued a condemnation of such agency practice. Three years later, the Congressional Office of Technology Assessment complained that the routine use exemption had become "a catchall exemption." . . . David Flaherty, in a pathbreaking comparative study of data protection law, *Protecting Privacy in Surveillance Societies*, called the American routine use exemption "a huge loophole." Despite these comments, agencies continue to justify almost any use of information as a "routine use" of the data.[36]

Only a few courts have placed substantive limits on an agency's proposed "routine use" of personal information. Justin Franklin and Robert Bouchard

---

[35] Robert Gellman, *Does Privacy Law Work? in Technology and Privacy: The New Landscape* (Philip E. Agre & Marc Rotenberg eds., 1997).

[36] Paul M. Schwartz, *Privacy and Participation*, 80 Iowa L. Rev. 553, 586 (1995).

conclude: "In practice, many of the cases where a 'routine use' defense is raised are resolved in favor of the government."[37]

2. ***What Is an "Agency"?*** The Privacy Act only applies to federal agencies. In *Tripp v. Executive Office of the President,* 200 F.R.D. 140 (D.D.C. 2001), Linda Tripp sued the Executive Office of the President (EOP), the Department of Defense (DOD), and the FBI. Tripp, the friend of Monica Lewinsky who secretly recorded their conversations to assist Kenneth Starr in his investigation of President Clinton, contended that the EOP, DOD, and FBI leaked confidential information about her to the media in retaliation for her role in the Clinton investigation. The EOP moved to dismiss claiming that it was not an "agency" within the meaning of the Privacy Act. The Privacy Act adopts FOIA's definition of "agency," which "includes any executive department . . . or other establishment in the executive branch of the Government (including the Executive Office of the President), or any independent regulatory agency." 5 U.S.C. § 552(f). However, the court concluded:

> The plain language of the Privacy Act directs one to look to the FOIA for the definition of "agency." 5 U.S.C. § 552a(1). While on its face, the FOIA states that the definition of "agency" includes the Executive Office of the President, the U.S. Supreme Court, the D.C. Circuit, and Congress, through the FOIA's legislative history, have all made it abundantly clear this does not include the Office of the President.

Unlike the EOP, the FBI and DOD are agencies under the Privacy Act. In 2003, Tripp settled her Privacy Act suit against the Defense Department for $590,000.

3. ***What Constitutes a "Record" in a "System of Records"?*** The Privacy Act does not apply to all information or records that an agency maintains. Rather, it applies to records contained in a "system of records." A "system of records" is a group of records where data is retrieved by an individual's name or other identifying information. 5 U.S.C. § 552a(a)(4). A "record" is "any item, collection, or grouping of information about an individual . . . that contains his name [or other identifying information]." In *Albright v. United States,* 631 F.2d 915 (D.C. Cir. 1980), the court analyzed whether a videotape of a meeting constituted a "record" under the Privacy Act. The court concluded that it was: "As long as the tape contains a means of identifying an individual by picture or voice, it falls within the definition of 'record' under the Privacy Act."

3. ***Government Privacy and Security Management.*** In addition to the Privacy Act, several other laws and regulations govern how federal agencies manage the privacy and security of personal data. For example, the E-Government Act, 44 U.S.C. § 208, requires federal agencies to conduct a Privacy Impact Assessment (PIA) whenever they develop a new technology involving the collection, use, or disclosure of personal data.

The Federal Information Security Management Act (FISMA), 44 U.S.C. § 3541, provides a comprehensive framework for protecting the security of

---

[37] Justin D. Franklin & Robert E. Bouchard, *Guidebook to the Freedom of Information and Privacy Acts* §2:18 (2007).

federal information systems. Federal agencies must designate a chief information officer (CIO), develop an information security program, and evaluate the effectiveness of information security policies and practices.

OMB Circular A-130 sets policy and provides guidance on information technology management for federal executive agencies. After a massive data breach at the Office of Personnel Management (OPM), the Obama Administration extensively updated Circular A-130 in 2016. The update focused on such areas as cyber-security, information governance, privacy, security, and open data. It requires proactive privacy and security risk analysis.

DOE V. CHAO

540 U.S. 614 (2004)

SOUTER, J. The United States is subject to a cause of action for the benefit of at least some individuals adversely affected by a federal agency's violation of the Privacy Act of 1974. The question before us is whether plaintiffs must prove some actual damages to qualify for a minimum statutory award of $1,000. We hold that they must.

Petitioner Buck Doe filed for benefits under the Black Lung Benefits Act, 83 Stat. 792, 30 U.S.C. § 901 *et seq.,* with the Office of Workers' Compensation Programs, the division of the Department of Labor responsible for adjudicating it. The application form called for a Social Security number, which the agency then used to identify the applicant's claim, as on documents like "multicaptioned" notices of hearing dates, sent to groups of claimants, their employers, and the lawyers involved in their cases. The Government concedes that following this practice led to disclosing Doe's Social Security number beyond the limits set by the Privacy Act. See 5 U.S.C. § 552a(b).

Doe joined with six other black lung claimants to sue the Department of Labor, alleging repeated violations of the Act and seeking certification of a class of "'all claimants for Black Lung Benefits since the passage of the Privacy Act.'" Pet. for Cert. 6a. Early on, the United States stipulated to an order prohibiting future publication of applicants' Social Security numbers on multicaptioned hearing notices, and the parties then filed cross-motions for summary judgment. The District Court denied class certification and entered judgment against all individual plaintiffs except Doe, finding that their submissions had raised no issues of cognizable harm. As to Doe, the court accepted his uncontroverted evidence of distress on learning of the improper disclosure, granted summary judgment, and awarded $1,000 in statutory damages under 5 U.S.C. § 552a(g)(4).

A divided panel of the Fourth Circuit affirmed in part but reversed on Doe's claim, holding the United States entitled to summary judgment across the board. 306 F.3d 170 (2002). The Circuit treated the $1,000 statutory minimum as available only to plaintiffs who suffered actual damages because of the agency's violation, and then found that Doe had not raised a triable issue of fact about actual damages, having submitted no corroboration for his claim of emotional distress, such as evidence of physical symptoms, medical treatment, loss of income, or impact on his behavior. In fact, the only indication of emotional affliction was Doe's conclusory allegations that he was " 'torn . . . all to pieces' " and " 'greatly concerned and worried' " because of the disclosure of his Social Security number and its potentially " 'devastating' " consequences.

Doe petitioned for review of the holding that some actual damages must be proven before a plaintiff may receive the minimum statutory award. . . .

"[I]n order to protect the privacy of individuals identified in information systems maintained by Federal agencies, it is necessary . . . to regulate the collection, maintenance, use, and dissemination of information by such agencies." Privacy Act of 1974. The Act gives agencies detailed instructions for managing their records and provides for various sorts of civil relief to individuals aggrieved by failures on the Government's part to comply with the requirements.

Subsection (g)(1) recognizes a civil action for agency misconduct fitting within any of four categories (the fourth, in issue here, being a catchall), 5 U.S.C. §§ 552a(g)(1)(A)–(D), and then makes separate provision for the redress of each. The first two categories cover deficient management of records: subsection (g)(1)(A) provides for the correction of any inaccurate or otherwise improper material in a record, and subsection (g)(1)(B) provides a right of access against any agency refusing to allow an individual to inspect a record kept on him. . . .

Like the inspection and correction infractions, breaches of the statute with adverse consequences are addressed by specific terms governing relief:

> In any suit brought under the provisions of subsection (g)(1)(C) or (D) of this section in which the court determines that the agency acted in a manner which was intentional or willful, the United States shall be liable to the individual in an amount equal to the sum of —
>
>> (A) actual damages sustained by the individual as a result of the refusal or failure, but in no case shall a person entitled to recovery receive less than the sum of $1,000; and
>> (B) the costs of the action together with reasonable attorney fees as determined by the court. § 552a(g)(4).

Doe argues that subsection (g)(4)(A) entitles any plaintiff adversely affected by an intentional or willful violation to the $1,000 minimum on proof of nothing more than a statutory violation: anyone suffering an adverse consequence of intentional or willful disclosure is entitled to recovery. The Government claims the minimum guarantee goes only to victims who prove some actual damages. We think the Government has the better side of the argument.

To begin with, the Government's position is supported by a straightforward textual analysis. When the statute gets to the point of guaranteeing the $1,000 minimum, it not only has confined any eligibility to victims of adverse effects caused by intentional or willful actions, but has provided expressly for liability to such victims for "actual damages sustained." It has made specific provision, in other words, for what a victim within the limited class may recover. When the very next clause of the sentence containing the explicit provision guarantees $1,000 to a "person entitled to recovery," the simplest reading of that phrase looks back to the immediately preceding provision for recovering actual damages, which is also the Act's sole provision for recovering anything (as distinct from equitable relief). With such an obvious referent for "person entitled to recovery" in the plaintiff who sustains "actual damages," Doe's theory is immediately questionable in ignoring the "actual damages" language so directly at hand and instead looking for "a person entitled to recovery" in a separate part of the statute devoid of any mention either of recovery or of what might be recovered.

Nor is it too strong to say that Doe does ignore statutory language. When Doe reads the statute to mean that the United States shall be liable to any adversely affected subject of an intentional or willful violation, without more, he treats willful action as the last fact necessary to make the Government "liable," and he is thus able to describe anyone to whom it is liable as entitled to the $1,000 guarantee. But this way of reading the statute simply pays no attention to the fact that the statute does not speak of liability (and consequent entitlement   to recovery) in a freestanding, unqualified way, but in a limited way, by reference to enumerated damages.

Doe's manner of reading "entitle[ment] to recovery" as satisfied by adverse effect caused by intentional or willful violation is in tension with more than the text, however. It is at odds with the traditional understanding that tort recovery requires not only wrongful act plus causation reaching to the plaintiff, but proof of some harm for which damages can reasonably be assessed. Doe, instead, identifies a person as entitled to recover without any reference to proof of damages, actual or otherwise. Doe might respond that it makes sense to speak of a privacy tort victim as entitled to recover without reference to damages because analogous common law would not require him to show particular items of injury in order to receive a dollar recovery. Traditionally, the common law has provided such victims with a claim for "general" damages, which for privacy and defamation torts are presumed damages: a monetary award calculated without reference to specific harm. . . .

This [conclusion] . . . is underscored by drafting history showing that Congress cut out the very language in the bill that would have authorized any presumed damages. The Senate bill would have authorized an award of "actual and general damages sustained by any person," with that language followed by the guarantee that "in no case shall a person entitled to recovery receive less   than the sum of $1,000." S. 3418, 93d Cong., 2d Sess., § 303(c)(1) (1974). Although the provision for general damages would have covered presumed damages, this language was trimmed from the final statute, subject to any later revision that might be recommended by the Commission. The deletion of "general damages" from the bill is fairly seen, then, as a deliberate elimination of any possibility of imputing harm and awarding presumed damages. The deletion thus precludes any hope of a sound interpretation of entitlement to recovery without reference to actual damages.

Finally, Doe's reading is open to the objection that no purpose is served by conditioning the guarantee on a person's being entitled to recovery. As Doe treats the text, Congress could have accomplished its object simply by providing that the Government would be liable to the individual for actual damages "but in no case . . . less than the sum of $1,000" plus fees and costs. Doe's reading leaves the reference to entitlement to recovery with no job to do, and it accordingly accomplishes nothing. . . .

Next, Doe also suggests there is something peculiar in offering some guaranteed damages, as a form of presumed damages not requiring proof of amount, only to those plaintiffs who can demonstrate actual damages. But this approach parallels another remedial scheme that the drafters of the Privacy Act would probably have known about. At common law, certain defamation torts were redressed by general damages but only when a plaintiff first proved some "special harm," *i.e.,* "harm of a material and generally of a pecuniary nature." 3 Restatement of Torts § 575, Comments *a* and *b* (1938) (discussing defamation torts that are "not actionable per se"). Plaintiffs claiming such torts could recover presumed damages only if they could demonstrate some actual, quantifiable pecuniary loss. Because the recovery of presumed damages in these cases was supplemental to compensation for specific harm, it was hardly unprecedented for Congress to make a guaranteed minimum contingent upon some showing of actual damages, thereby avoiding giveaways to plaintiffs with nothing more than "abstract injuries." . . .

The "entitle[ment] to recovery" necessary to qualify for the $1,000 minimum is not shown merely by an intentional or willful violation of the Act producing some adverse effect. The statute guarantees $1,000 only to plaintiffs who have suffered some actual damages.

GINSBURG, STEVENS, and BREYER, JJ. dissenting. "It is 'a cardinal principle of statutory construction' that 'a statute ought, upon the whole, to be so construed that, if it can be prevented, no clause, sentence, or word shall be superfluous, void, or insignificant.'" The Court's reading of § 552a(g)(4) is hardly in full harmony with that principle. Under the Court's construction, the words "a person entitled to recovery" have no office, and the liability-determining element "adverse effect" becomes superfluous, swallowed up by the "actual damages" requirement. Further, the Court's interpretation renders the word "recovery" nothing more than a synonym for "actual damages," and it turns the phrase "shall be liable" into "may be liable." . . .

The purpose and legislative history of the Privacy Act, as well as similarly designed statutes, are in harmony with the reading of § 552a(g)(4) most federal judges have found sound. Congress sought to afford recovery for "*any* damages" resulting from the "willful or intentional" violation of "any individual's rights under th[e] Act." § 2(b)(6), 88 Stat. 1896 (emphasis added). Privacy Act violations commonly cause fear, anxiety, or other emotional distress — in the Act's parlance, "adverse effects." Harm of this character must, of course, be proved genuine. In cases like Doe's, emotional distress is generally the only harm the claimant suffers, *e.g.,* the identity theft apprehended never materializes. . . .

The Government, although recognizing that "actual damages" may be slender and easy to generate, fears depletion of the federal fisc were the Court to adopt Doe's reading of § 552a(g)(4). Experience does not support those fears. As the Government candidly acknowledged at oral argument: "[W]e have not had a problem with enormous recoveries against the Government up to this point." No doubt mindful that Congress did not endorse massive recoveries, the District Court in this very case denied class-action certification, and other courts have similarly refused to certify suits seeking damages under § 552a(g)(4) as class actions. Furthermore, courts have disallowed the runaway liability that might ensue were they to count every single wrongful disclosure as a discrete basis for a $1,000 award.

The text of § 552a(g)(4), it is undisputed, accommodates two concerns. Congress sought to give the Privacy Act teeth by deterring violations and providing remedies when violations occur. At the same time, Congress did not want to saddle the Government with disproportionate liability. . . .

Congress has used language similar to § 552a(g)(4) in other privacy statutes. See 18 U.S.C. § 2707(c); 26 U.S.C. § 6110(j)(2); 26 U.S.C. § 7217(c) (1976 ed., Supp. V). These other statutes have been understood to permit recovery of the $1,000 statutory minimum despite the absence of proven actual damages. . . .

Doe has standing to sue, the Court agrees, based on "allegations that he was 'torn . . . all to pieces' and 'greatly concerned and worried' because of the disclosure of his Social Security number and its potentially 'devastating' consequences." Standing to sue, but not to succeed, the Court holds, unless Doe also incurred an easily arranged out-of-pocket expense. In my view, Congress gave Privacy Act suitors like Doe not only standing to sue, but the right to a recovery if the fact trier credits their claims of emotional distress brought on by an agency's intentional or willful violation of the Act. For the reasons stated in this dissenting opinion, which track the reasons expressed by Circuit Judge Michael dissenting in part in the Fourth Circuit, I would reverse the judgment of the Court of Appeals.

NOTES & QUESTIONS

1. ***Postscript.*** In subsequent litigation, the district court concluded that Buck Doe was still entitled to attorneys' fees and costs under the Privacy Act because he established that the government had willfully violated the Act. The court awarded $57,520.97 for attorneys' fees and costs. On appeal, in *Doe v. Chao*, 435 F.3d 492 (4th Cir. 2006), the Fourth Circuit held that attorneys' fees and costs could still be recovered despite failing to show actual damages. However, the court concluded that the district court erred in assessing the amount of the award because it failed to "give primary consideration to the amount of damages awarded as compared to the amount sought." On remand, the district court awarded $15,887.50 in attorneys' fees and costs to Doe's counsel.

2. ***Damages Under the Privacy Act.*** One of the difficulties in privacy cases that involve the leakage of personal information is establishing damages. In most cases, people might be made more vulnerable to harms like identity theft, but they might not yet be victimized. Damages for the violation of many Privacy Act violations will involve emotional distress rather than overt physical or psychological harm. By requiring "actual damages" in order to receive statutory damages, does the Court's holding in *Doe v. Chao* make it nearly impossible to recover for a Privacy Act violation? On the other hand, should any violation of the Privacy Act result in automatic damages for thousands of dollars?

   What constitutes "actual damages" under the Privacy Act? The *Chao* Court did not reach an opinion on the issue, noting in a footnote:

   > The Courts of Appeals are divided on the precise definition of actual damages. Compare *Fitzpatrick v. IRS,* 665 F.2d 327, 331 (11th Cir. 1982) (actual damages are restricted to pecuniary loss), with *Johnson v. Department of Treasury, IRS,* 700 F.2d 971, 972-974 (5th Cir. 1983) (actual damages can cover adequately

demonstrated mental anxiety even without any out-of-pocket loss). That issue is not before us. . . . We assume without deciding that the Fourth Circuit was correct to hold that Doe's complaints in this case did not rise to the level of alleging actual damages. We do not suggest that out-of-pocket expenses are necessary for recovery of the $1,000 minimum; only that they suffice to qualify under any view of actual damages.

3. ***Can Emotional Distress Alone Qualify for "Actual Damages"?*** In *Federal Aviation Administration v. Cooper,* 132 S. Ct. 1441 (2012), the U.S. Supreme Court held that emotional distress alone did not qualify for "actual damages" under the Privacy Act.

The Court began by noting that "ambiguities in the statutory language are to be construed in favor of immunity so that the Government's consent to be sued is never enlarged beyond what a fair reading of the text requires." The Court then reasoned that the term "actual damages" was ambiguous:

> Even as a legal term, however, the meaning of "actual damages" is far from clear. The latest edition of Black's Law Dictionary available when Congress enacted the Privacy Act defined "actual damages" as "[r]eal, substantial and just damages, or the amount awarded to a complainant in compensation for his actual and real loss or injury, as opposed on the one hand to 'nominal' damages, and on the other to 'exemplary' or 'punitive' damages." Black's Law Dictionary 467 (rev. 4th ed.1968). But this general (and notably circular) definition is of little value here because, as the Court of Appeals accurately observed, the precise meaning of the term "changes with the specific statute in which it is found."
>
> The term is sometimes understood to include nonpecuniary harm. . . .
>
> A number of courts have construed "actual" damages in the remedial provisions of both statutes to include compensation for mental and emotional distress.
>
> In other contexts, however, the term has been used or construed more narrowly to authorize damages for only pecuniary harm. . . .

The Court looked to the law of defamation as an analogy:

> This parallel between the Privacy Act and the common-law torts of libel *per quod* and slander suggests the possibility that Congress intended the term "actual damages" in the Act to mean special damages. The basic idea is that Privacy Act victims, like victims of libel *per quod* or slander, are barred from any recovery unless they can first show actual—that is, pecuniary or material— harm. Upon showing some pecuniary harm, no matter how slight, they can recover the statutory minimum of $1,000, presumably for any unproven harm. That Congress would choose to use the term "actual damages" instead of "special damages" was not without precedent. The terms had occasionally been used interchangeably.

In a dissent, Justices Sotomayor, Ginsburg, and Breyer argued that "traditional tools of statutory construction—the statute's text, structure, drafting history, and purpose—provide a clear answer: The term 'actual damages' permits recovery for all injuries established by competent evidence in the record, whether pecuniary or nonpecuniary, and so encompasses damages for mental and emotional distress." The dissenters disputed the majority's claim that the Black's Law Dictionary definition of "actual damages" was "circular." They stated: "The definition is plain enough: 'Actual damages' compensate for actual injury, and thus the term is synonymous with compensatory damages. There is nothing circular about that definition." More broadly, the dissenters contended that the Court's interpretation creates discord between the Privacy Act's protections and its remedies:

> Congress established substantive duties in the Act that are expressly designed to prevent agency conduct resulting in intangible harms to the individual. The Act requires agencies to "establish appropriate administrative, technical, and physical safeguards" to ensure against security breaches that could result in "substantial harm, embarrassment, inconvenience, or unfairness to any individual." 5 U.S.C. § 552a(e)(10). It also requires agencies to "maintain all records" used in making a determination about an individual in a manner that is "reasonably necessary to assure fairness to the individual in the determination." § 552a(e)(5). Thus an agency violates the terms of the Act if it fails, *e.g.,* to maintain safeguards protecting against "embarrassment"; there is no additional requirement that the pocketbook be implicated. An agency's intentional or willful violation of those duties triggers liability for "actual damages" under § 552a(g)(4) in the event of an adverse impact. § 552a(g)(1)(C)–(D), (g)(4).
>
> Adopting a reading of "actual damages" that permits recovery for pecuniary loss alone creates a disconnect between the Act's substantive and remedial provisions. It allows a swath of Government violations to go unremedied: A federal agency could intentionally or willfully forgo establishing safeguards to protect against embarrassment and no successful private action could be taken against it for the harm Congress identified. Only an interpretation of "actual damages" that permits recovery for nonpecuniary harms harmonizes the Act's substantive and remedial provisions. . . .
>
> After today, no matter how debilitating and substantial the resulting mental anguish, an individual harmed by a federal agency's intentional or willful violation of the Privacy Act will be left without a remedy unless he or she is able to prove pecuniary harm. That is not the result Congress intended when it enacted an Act with the express purpose of safeguarding individual privacy against Government invasion. And it is not a result remotely suggested by anything in the text, structure, or history of the Act. For those reasons, I respectfully dissent.

What effect does the majority opinion, in combination with *Doe v. Chao,* have on the Privacy Act? Should the Act be amended to provide for liquidated damages or to allow damages based on emotional distress alone? If so, critics might claim that it would be too easy for plaintiffs to claim emotional distress for a Privacy Act violation. Unlike pecuniary loss or physical injury, emotional distress injuries rely heavily—and sometimes exclusively—on the assertions of the plaintiff. Are there ways to ensure that plaintiffs will not falsely claim emotional distress? Are there ways to make such damages more objective in nature?

4. ***The Linda Tripp Case.*** Recall the Linda Tripp case above in the notes to *Pippinger v. Rubin.* The Department of Defense (DOD) settled the case for $590,000. In light of *Doe v. Chao,* should the DOD have settled?

5. ***Willful vs. Negligent Violations of the Privacy Act.*** In *Andrews v. Veterans Administration,* 838 F.2d 418 (10th Cir. 1988), an employee of the Veterans

Administration (VA) was responding to a FOIA request for proficiency reports of various nurses. The VA employee attempted to redact the identities of nurses from the reports, but failed to do so properly. As a result, several nurses could be identified on their reports. At trial, the district court concluded that the nurses "suffered some degree of anguish, embarrassment, or other mental trauma" from the disclosure and that the VA employee "acted conscientiously, in good faith, though inadvertently negligently, in releasing the proficiency reports in an inadequately sanitized condition." Furthermore, the district court concluded that the VA was grossly negligent in failing to adequately train the employee about the release of personal information. On appeal, the Tenth Circuit concluded that the disclosure of the information was improper. The identities of the nurses were protected under Exemption 6 of FOIA. However, the VA, despite acting with gross negligence, could not be held liable to the nurses:

> . . . [E]ven if the Privacy Act is violated, no punishment may be imposed unless the agency acted in a manner which was intentional or willful. In this case the district court equated "intentional or willful" with gross negligence. . . .
>
> . . . [T]he term "willful or intentional" clearly requires conduct amounting to more than gross negligence. We are persuaded by the District of Columbia Circuit's definitions of willful or intentional that contemplate action "so 'patently egregious and unlawful' that anyone undertaking the conduct should have known it 'unlawful,' " or conduct committed "without grounds for believing it to be lawful" or action "flagrantly disregarding others' rights under the Act," and we adopt those definitions, and add the view . . . that the conduct must amount to, at the very least, reckless behavior. Those, and similar definitions, describe conduct more extreme than gross negligence.
>
> Applying that standard to this case, our review of the record convinces us that the VA's conduct falls far short of a "willful or intentional" violation of the Privacy Act. Indeed, we find that it falls short of even the gross negligence standard applied by the district court to that conduct. . . .

According to Paul Schwartz, "individuals who seek to enforce their rights under the Privacy Act face numerous statutory hurdles, limited damages, and scant chance to affect an agency's overall behavior."[38] The most common form of improper disclosure of records is due to carelessness rather than willful behavior. Does the requirement that disclosure be done "willfully and intentionally" make damages under the Privacy Act virtually impossible to collect? What if the standard for collecting damages were negligence? Would agencies that must handle millions of records and respond to thousands of FOIA requests be exposed to too great a risk of liability?

Consider Robert Gellman:

> The Privacy Act contains civil and criminal penalties for violations, but it is far from clear that the enforcement methods are useful. . . . In more than 20 years, federal prosecutors have brought no more than a handful of criminal cases, and perhaps only one, under the Privacy Act.
>
> The basic method for enforcing the Privacy Act is the individual lawsuit. Aggrieved individuals can sue the government for violations. . . . The former

---

[38] Paul M. Schwartz, *Privacy and Participation*, 80 Iowa L. Rev. 553, 596 (1995).

General Counsel to the Privacy Protection Study Commission testified that the act was "to a large extent, unenforceable by individuals." The main reasons are that it is difficult to recover damages and that limited injunctive relief is available under the law. Individual enforcement does not offer any significant incentive for agencies to comply more carefully with the Privacy Act's provisions.[39]

6. ***The Interaction Between the Privacy Act and FOIA.*** The Privacy Act does not apply to information that must be disclosed pursuant to FOIA. § 552a(k)(1). However, if one of FOIA's privacy exceptions applies, then the Privacy Act would require that the government refrain from disclosing certain information.

United States Dep't of Defense v. Federal Labor Relations Authority, 510 U.S. 487 (1994), clearly illustrates the interaction between these two statutes. There, two local unions requested the names and home addresses of employees in federal agencies. The agencies disclosed the employees' names and work stations to the unions but refused to release their home addresses. The unions filed unfair labor practice charges with the Federal Labor Relations Authority (FLRA), arguing that federal labor law required the agencies to disclose the addresses. Pursuant to the Federal Service Labor-Management Relations Statute, 5 U.S.C. §§ 7101–7135, agencies must, "to the extent not prohibited by law," furnish unions with data necessary for collective-bargaining purposes. § 7114(b)(4). The agencies argued that disclosure of the home addresses was prohibited by the Privacy Act. The Court agreed with the agencies:

> The employee addresses sought by the unions are "records" covered by the broad terms of the Privacy Act. Therefore, unless FOIA would require release of the addresses, their disclosure is "prohibited by law," and the agencies may not reveal them to the unions.
>
> We turn, then, to FOIA. . . . The exemption potentially applicable to employee addresses is Exemption 6, which provides that FOIA's disclosure requirements do not apply to "personnel and medical files and similar files the disclosure of which would constitute a clearly unwarranted invasion of personal privacy." 5 U.S.C. § 552(b)(6).
>
> Thus, although this case requires us to follow a somewhat convoluted path of statutory cross-references, its proper resolution depends upon a discrete inquiry: whether disclosure of the home addresses "would constitute a clearly unwarranted invasion of [the] personal privacy" of bargaining unit employees within the meaning of FOIA. . . .
>
> We must weigh the privacy interest of bargaining unit employees in nondisclosure of their addresses against the only relevant public interest in the FOIA balancing analysis — the extent to which disclosure of the information sought would "she[d] light on an agency's performance of its statutory duties" or otherwise let citizens know "what their government is up to."
>
> The relevant public interest supporting disclosure in this case is negligible, at best. Disclosure of the addresses might allow the unions to communicate more effectively with employees, but it would not appreciably further "the citizens' right to be informed about what their government is up to." Indeed,

---

[39] Robert Gellman, *Does Privacy Law Work?* in *Technology and Privacy: The New Landscape* (Philip E. Agre & Marc Rotenberg eds., 1997).

such disclosure would reveal little or nothing about the employing agencies or their activities. . . .

Against the virtually nonexistent FOIA-related public interest in disclosure, we weigh the interest of bargaining unit employees in nondisclosure of their home addresses. . . .

It is true that home addresses often are publicly available through sources such as telephone directories and voter registration lists, but "[i]n an organized society, there are few facts that are not at one time or another divulged to another." *Reporters Comm.* The privacy interest protected by Exemption 6 "encompass[es] the individual's control of information concerning his or her person." An individual's interest in controlling the dissemination of information regarding personal matters does not dissolve simply because that information may be available to the public in some form. Here, for the most part, the unions seek to obtain the addresses of nonunion employees who have decided not to reveal their addresses to their exclusive representative. . . . Whatever the reason that these employees have chosen not to become members of the union or to provide the union with their addresses, however, it is clear that they have *some* nontrivial privacy interest in nondisclosure, and in avoiding the influx of union-related mail, and, perhaps, union-related telephone calls or visits, that would follow disclosure.

Many people simply do not want to be disturbed at home by work-related matters. . . . Moreover, when we consider that other parties, such as commercial advertisers and solicitors, must have the same access under FOIA as the unions to the employee address lists sought in this case, it is clear that the individual privacy interest that would be protected by nondisclosure is far from insignificant.

Because the privacy interest of bargaining unit employees in nondisclosure of their home addresses substantially outweighs the negligible FOIA-related public interest in disclosure, we conclude that disclosure would constitute a "clearly unwarranted invasion of personal privacy." 5 U.S.C. § 552(b)(6). FOIA, thus, does not require the agencies to divulge the addresses, and the Privacy Act, therefore, prohibits their release to the unions. . . .

Suppose the agencies opted not to litigate and disclosed the addresses of their employees. Would an employee have a cause of action under the Privacy Act for the disclosure of her address? Would that employee likely prevail in such an action? What type of remedy could the employee obtain?

7. ***Government Access to Private Sector Databases.*** The Privacy Act also applies to private companies that contract with the government to administer systems of records. 5 U.S.C. § 552a(m). However, as Christopher Hoofnagle observes, "a database of information that originates at a [commercial data broker] would not trigger the requirements of the Privacy Act." Hoofnagle goes on to observe:

> This limitation to the Privacy Act is critical — it allows [commercial data brokers] to amass huge databases that the government is legally prohibited from creating. Then, when the government needs the information, it can request it from the [commercial data broker].[40]

---

[40] Christopher Jay Hoofnagle, *Big Brother's Little Helpers: How ChoicePoint and Other Commercial Data Brokers Collect and Package Your Data for Law Enforcement*, 29 N.C. J. Int'l L. & Com. Reg. 595, 623 (2004).

8. ***The First Amendment Restriction.*** Pursuant to the Privacy Act, 5 U.S.C. § 552a(e)(7), agencies shall

> maintain no record describing how any individual exercises rights guaranteed by the First Amendment unless expressly authorized by statute or by the individual about whom the record is maintained or unless pertinent to and within the scope of an authorized law enforcement activity.

In *Becker v. Internal Revenue Service,* 34 F.2d 398 (7th Cir. 1994), three brothers, Thomas, Jeffrey, and Steven Becker, sought to have IRS records about them expunged pursuant to the Privacy Act. The files pertained to a criminal investigation of their failure to pay taxes and their activities as "tax protestors." Some of the records in the IRS's files pertained to the brothers' First Amendment rights, such as "a flyer advertising a book and a collection of newspaper articles regarding various IRS actions against certain individuals and groups who are alleged tax protesters or cheats."

The district court concluded that maintaining these materials in the Beckers' records "unquestionably implies that they are associated with the tax protesters and cheats described in the newspaper articles" and thus describes "how the plaintiffs exercise their First Amendment rights of speech and association." However, the district court concluded that the documents are "pertinent to and within the scope of an authorized law enforcement activity." Accordingly, the district court concluded, "the IRS may lawfully maintain these records and may withhold this information from plaintiffs under the Privacy Act pursuant to 5 U.S.C. § 552a(k)(2)." Section 552a(k)(2) allows agencies to exempt certain systems of records from individual access. The IRS claimed that it exempted the records because "to grant access to an investigative file could interfere with investigative and enforcement proceedings . . . and disclose investigative techniques and procedures."

The Seventh Circuit, however, concluded that § 551a(k)(2) does not allow agencies to be exempt from the First Amendment activities exclusion. The court noted that these documents were contained in files closed several years ago, and that the Beckers' ultimate objective was to have the records removed from their files, not just to gain access. The court reasoned:

> We conclude that the IRS has not sufficiently justified the maintenance of the documents in the Beckers' files. The IRS asserts that it may maintain these articles for possible future uses. Under some circumstances, this may be a legitimate justification for maintaining documents in a file for an extended period of time. We have examined the material, and any thought that it could be helpful in future enforcement activity concerning the Beckers is untenable.

The court ordered that the documents be expunged.

Compare *Becker* with *J. Roderick MacArthur Foundation v. Federal Bureau of Investigation*, 102 F.3d 600 (D.C. Cir. 1996). The J. Roderick MacArthur Foundation and its former president Lance Lindblom sought to have the FBI expunge records relating to associational activities. The FBI was maintaining a 23-page file on Lindblom's associations with foreign leaders and political dissidents. According to Lindblom, the Privacy Act forbids maintaining data about First Amendment activities unless it serves a "current law enforcement necessity." The court rejected Lindblom's argument:

> The noun "record" in § (e)(7) is modified in only two ways: the record must be "[1] pertinent to and [2] within the scope of an authorized law enforcement activity." We do not understand this to mean, as Lindblom would in essence require, that the record must be pertinent to an active investigation; "an authorized law enforcement activity" such as foreign counter-intelligence, is a concept far broader than either an active investigation or a "current law enforcement necessity." . . .
>
> Information that was pertinent to an authorized law enforcement activity when collected does not later lose its pertinence to that activity simply because the information is not of current interest (let alone "necessity") to the agency — a point seemingly lost upon our dissenting colleague. . . .
>
> . . . Lindblom's interpretation of the Act would place new and daunting burdens, both substantive and administrative, upon the FBI and other government agencies, with little or no gain to individual privacy. If a law enforcement agency were required to purge its files of information regarding an individual so requesting whenever it had closed a particular investigation, then its ability to accomplish its mission would inevitably suffer. As we have said before, intelligence gathering is "akin to the construction of a mosaic"; to appreciate the full import of a single piece may require the agency to take a broad view of the whole work. Suppose, for example, that a citizen is contacted by a foreign agent but the FBI, after investigation, determines that the contact is innocent. If the same individual is later contacted by another foreign agent and perhaps thereafter by a third, then what had earlier appeared to be innocent when viewed in isolation may, when later viewed as part of a larger whole, acquire a more sinister air. Simply put, information that was once collected as part of a now-closed investigation may yet play a role in a new or reopened investigation. If the earlier record had been purged, however, then the agency's later investigation could not be informed by the earlier event(s).
>
> Furthermore, if federal law enforcement agencies were required upon request to purge all such records, then they would surely be inundated with requests to do so. Responding to each such request could be difficult and time-consuming. . . .

Which court, *Becker* or *MacArthur Foundation,* comes to a more convincing interpretation of the First Amendment restriction? Based on the *MacArthur Foundation* court's interpretation, to what would the First Amendment restriction apply?

3. THE COMPUTER MATCHING AND PRIVACY PROTECTION ACT

In 1977, the federal government initiated Project Match, a program where it compared computer employee records to records of people receiving benefits through Aid to Families with Dependent Children to detect fraud. This was considered by the government to be exempted from the Privacy Act under the "routine use" exception. According to Priscilla Regan:

> . . . The scope of computer matches . . . raises Fourth Amendment questions. Computer matches are generalized electronic searches of millions of records. Under the Fourth Amendment, the Supreme Court has determined that searches must not be overly inclusive; no "fishing expeditions" or "dragnet investigations" are allowed. Yet in computer matches, many people who have not engaged in fraud or are not actually suspected of criminal activity are subject to the computer search. This raises questions about the presumption of innocence, as reflected in Fourth and Fifth Amendment case law. If matches are considered a Fourth Amendment search, then some limitations on the breadth of the match and/or justifications for a match are necessary. For example, a government agency could be required to show that a less intrusive means of carrying out the search was not available and that procedural safeguards limiting the dangers of abuse and agency discretion were applied. Additionally, procedural safeguards are required under due process protections. A final constitutional issue is whether matching conflicts with the equal protection clause because categories of people, not individual suspects, are subject to computer matches. Two groups — federal employees and welfare recipients — are most often the subjects of computer matching.
>
> Despite these arguments about the constitutionality of computer matches, the courts have generally not upheld individual privacy claims in cases challenging computer-matching programs. Moreover, there has been little litigation in this area for two reasons. First, the damage requirements of the Privacy Act are so difficult to prove that they serve as a deterrent to its use. . . . Secondly, in large-scale computer matching, single individuals are rarely sufficiently harmed to litigate claims and most individuals are not even aware of the match. . . . [41]

In 1988, Congress passed the Computer Matching and Privacy Protection Act (CMPPA), Pub. L. No. 100-503, to regulate the practice of computer matching. The CMPPA amends the Privacy Act and provides that in order for agencies to disclose records to engage in computer matching programs, they must establish "a written agreement between the source agency and the recipient agency or non-Federal agency stating" the purpose and legal authority for the program, a justification for the program, a description of the records to be matched, procedures for the accuracy of the information, and prohibitions on redisclosure of the records. § 552a(o)(1). These agreements must be available upon request to the public.

The CMPPA establishes Data Integrity Boards within each agency to oversee matching, requires agencies to perform a cost-benefit analysis of proposed matching endeavors, and requires agencies to notify individuals of the termination of benefits due to computer matching and permit them an opportunity to refute the termination. § 552a(p).

---

[41] Priscilla Regan, *Legislating Privacy* 89-90 (1995).

Is computer matching a violation of the Fourth Amendment? If you believe that matching contravenes the Fourth Amendment, are the due process rights provided by the CMPPA sufficient to cure the constitutional deficiencies?[42]

4. THE USE OF GOVERNMENT RECORDS

(a) Airline Passenger Screening

THE 9/11 COMMISSION REPORT

Excerpts from pp. 1-4, 392-95 (2004)

Boston: American 11 and United 175. [Mohamed] Atta and [Abdul Aziz al] Omari boarded a 6:00 A.M. flight from Portland [Maine] to Boston's Logan International Airport.

When he checked in for his flight to Boston, Atta was selected by a computerized prescreening system known as CAPPS (Computer Assisted Passenger Prescreening System), created to identify passengers who should be subject to special security measures. Under the security rules in place at the time, the only consequence of Atta's selection by CAPPS was that his checked bags were held off the plane until it was confirmed that he boarded the aircraft. This did not hinder Atta's plans. . . .

While Atta had been selected by CAPPS in Portland, three members of his hijacking team — Suqami, Wail al Shehri, and Waleed al Shehri — were selected in Boston. Their selection affected only the handling of their checked bags, not their screening at the checkpoint.

Washington Dulles: American 77. Hundreds of miles southwest of Boston, at Dulles International Airport . . . five more men were preparing to take their early morning flight. At 7:15, a pair of them, Khalid al Mihdhar and Majed Moqed, checked in at the American Airlines ticket counter for Flight 77, bound for Los Angeles. Within the next 20 minutes, they would be followed by Nani Hanjour and two brothers, Nawaf al Hazmi and Salem al Hazmi.

Hani Hanjour, Khalid al Mihdhar, and Majed Moqed were flagged by CAPPS. The Hazmi brothers were also selected for extra scrutiny by the airline's customer service representative at the check-in counter. He did so because one of the brothers did not have photo identification nor could he understand English, and because the agent found both of the passengers to be suspicious. The only consequence of their selection was that their checked bags were held off the plane until it was confirmed that they had boarded the aircraft. . . .

[Overall, on] 9/11, the 19 hijackers were screened by a computer-assisted screening system called CAPPS. More than half were identified for further inspection, which applied only to their checked luggage.

---

[42] For an interesting account of the psychological effects and other harms caused by endeavors such as computer matching on welfare recipients, see John Gilliom, *Overseers of the Poor: Surveillance, Resistance, and the Limits of Privacy* (2001).

Under current practices, air carriers enforce government orders to stop certain known and suspected terrorists from boarding commercial flights and to apply secondary screening procedures to others. The "no-fly" and "automatic selectee" lists include only those individuals who the U.S. government believes pose a direct threat of attacking aviation.

Because air carriers implement the program, concerns about sharing intelligence information with private firms and foreign countries keep the U.S. government from listing all terrorist and terrorist suspects who should be included. The TSA has planned to take over this function when it deploys a new screening system to take the place of CAPPS. The deployment of this system has been delayed because of claims it may violate civil liberties.

Recommendation: Improved use of "no-fly" and "automatic selectee" lists should not be delayed while the argument about a successor to CAPPS continues. This screening function should be performed by the TSA, and it should utilize the larger set of watchlists maintained by the federal government. Air carriers should be required to supply the information needed to test and implement this new system. . . .

NOTES & QUESTIONS

1. *False Positives.* The 9/11 Report mentioned the number of "hits" that the CAPPS system made, flagging more than half of the 19 terrorists. Each day, there are approximately 1.9 million airline passengers. Imagine a false positive rate of just 1 percent, which by current estimates of such rates would be quite a good rate. At a 1 percent error rate, 19,000 people would be flagged as false positives. Merely talking about the "hits" rather than the "misses" paints only a partial picture of the effectiveness of the system.

After 9/11, the airline screening system incorrectly singled out a number of high-profile individuals. For example, Senator Edward Kennedy (D-Mass.) and Rep. Donald E. Young (R-Alaska) were tapped for secondary screening. Cat Stevens, a singer who now goes by the name Yusuf Islam, was placed on the no-fly list. According to *Time* magazine, this incident rested in a spelling mistake: "According to aviation sources with access to the list, there is no Yusuf Islam on the no-fly registry, though there is a 'Youssouf Islam.' " The article goes on, however, to state that the U.S. Transportation Safety Administration "alleges that Islam has links to terrorist groups, which he has denied; British foreign minister Jack Straw said the TSA action 'should never have been taken.' "[43]

Supporters of computerized airline screening argue that even with a significant number of false positives, CAPPS is useful in singling out passengers for extra scrutiny, since the most extensive screening cannot be done on 1.9 million passengers each day.

Some argue that if the government were able to collect more data, the false positives would drop. Is the answer obtaining more data? Are screening systems

---

[43] Sally B. Donnelly, *You Say Yusuf, I Say Youssouf* . . . , Time.com, Sept. 25, 2004, www.time.com/time/nation/article/0,8599,702062,00.html.

like CAPPS effective security measures? Bruce Schneier, a noted security expert, discusses whether a system like CAPPS might in the end be worth the trade-offs:

> System like CAPPS will be likely to single out lone terrorists who meet the profile, or a terrorist group whose entire membership fits the profile, or copycat terrorist groups without the wisdom, time, and resources to probe [the system]. But terrorists are a surprisingly diverse group . . . CAPPS works best combined with random screening.

Schneier also notes two basic problems with CAPPS. First, it can be probed. In other words, "a terrorist organization can probe the system repeatedly and identify which of its people, or which ticket characteristics, are less likely to be searched." Second, a system "that is more likely to select a certain class of passenger is also less likely to select other classes of passengers."[44] As a consequence, terrorists who do not fit a profile may slip by unnoticed.

2. *The Evolution of Airline Passenger Screening.* Since September 11th, the government has been attempting to design an airline passenger screening program. In 2001, the FAA created two lists — a list of people who were barred from flying and a list of people selected for secondary screening. In 2002, the Transportation Security Administration (TSA) was created, and it took over the security functions from the FAA. The Terrorist Screening Center in the FBI maintains the no-fly list as well as the selectee list. The no-fly list, which had only 16 names on it in 2001, now has over 20,000 names. The precise number remains unknown. The names on these lists are kept secret.

In 2003, the federal government announced the creation of CAPPS II, which was to be the successor to CAPPS. CAPPS II would have classified people according to their "threat level" when flying. Passengers would be classified as green, yellow, or red. Green passengers would be screened normally; yellow ones would be given extra scrutiny; and red passengers would not be allowed to fly.

Critics of CAPPS II criticized the lack of transparency in the system. They objected that the data used in the profiling along with the factors that go into the profiles would not be publicly disclosed. What are the costs and benefits of requiring public disclosure of the types of information and the logic used in the profiling?

In July 2004, the government announced that it was abandoning CAPPS II. Shortly thereafter, the Transportation Security Agency proposed a new screening system called "Secure Flight." This system became operational in 2009.

Some argue that the benefit of a computerized airline passenger screening system is that without such a system, more individuals must be subjected to extensive searching. With the system, only those individuals profiled as a risk will be subject to extra scrutiny. Therefore, airline screening systems such as Secure Flight protect privacy by narrowing the number of people who must be intrusively searched. On the other hand, the system has costs in terms of both

---

[44] Bruce Schneier, *Beyond Fear* 164-65 (2003).

privacy and equality. Privacy is affected not just in a search, but in the gathering of data for profiling. Equality is implicated because some passengers, very possibly based on race and nationality, will be treated differently than other passengers. How do you weigh the costs and benefits? What about the people who are banned from flying? What kind of legal challenge should they have?

3. ***PNR Data.*** Airline passenger screening systems rely on passenger name record (PNR) data, which commercial airlines maintain for each passenger. This record includes financial information, such as credit card numbers, as well as itineraries for travel, phone numbers, and any special meal requests. After 9/11, the government requested that airlines turn over their PNR data. Although sharing the information with the government was not authorized in their privacy policies, many airlines willingly complied. Is it problematic for the government to have PNR data? What can be learned about an individual through PNR data?

In 2005, it was revealed that the FBI was keeping 257.5 million PNR records on people who flew between June and September 2001.[45] To what extent does the Privacy Act restrict the FBI from retaining this information?

(b) Government Data Mining

Data mining involves examining personal information in databases to look for patterns or unusual activity, or to identify links between a suspect and other individuals. Computer matching programs are an example of data mining — they seek to detect fraud by making comparisons in personal information residing in different databases.

Total Information Awareness. In 2002, the press reported that the Department of Defense was developing a project called "Total Information Awareness" (TIA), headed by Admiral John Poindexter. TIA would consist of a database of dossiers of people constructed with information about their finances, education, travel, health, and more. The information would be obtained from various private sector companies. The information would then be used to profile people to single out those engaged in terrorist activities. TIA generated a significant public outcry, and the Senate amended its spending bill early in 2003 to bar funding for TIA until the details of the program were explained to Congress.

In its report to Congress on May 20, 2003, the Department of Defense renamed the program "Terrorism Information Awareness" and stated that the program would be protective of privacy. Later in 2003, the Senate voted to deny funding for TIA. According to some media reports, however, the classified part of the federal budget still contains funding for certain aspects of TIA.[46] What laws or constitutional rights would be implicated by TIA or a similar program?

Consider K.A. Taipale:

[I]t is my view that the recent defunding of DARPA's Information Awareness Office ("IAO") and its Terrorism Information Awareness program and related projects will turn out to be a pyrrhic "victory" for civil liberties as the program

---

[45] Leslie Miller, *FBI Keeping Records on Pre-9/11 Travelers*, Associated Press, Jan. 14, 2005.

[46] Ira S. Rubinstein, Ronald D. Lee & Paul M. Schwartz, *Data Mining and Internet Profiling*, 75 U. Chi. L. Rev. 261, 265 (2008).

provided a focused opportunity around which to publicly debate the rules and procedures for the future use of these technologies and, importantly, to oversee the development of the appropriate technical features required to support any concurred upon implementation or oversight policies to protect privacy.[47]

Daniel Solove predicted in 2004 that TIA was far from dead:

> . . . TIA is only one part of the story of government access to personal information and its creation of dossiers on American citizens. In fact, for quite some time, the government has been increasingly contracting with businesses to acquire databases of personal information. Database firms are willing to supply the information and the government is willing to pay for it. Currently, government agencies such as the FBI and IRS are purchasing databases of personal information from private-sector companies. A private company called ChoicePoint, Inc. has amassed a database of 10 billion records and has contracts with at least 35 federal agencies to share the data with them. . . .
>
> Thus, we are increasingly seeing collusion, partly voluntary, partly coerced, between the private sector and the government. While public attention has focused on the Total Information Awareness project, the very same goals and techniques of the program continue to be carried out less systematically by various government agencies and law enforcement officials. We are already closer to Total Information Awareness than we might think.[48]

Pattern-Based vs. Subject-Based Data Mining. There are at least two general types of data mining. "Subject-based" data mining involves searching the data of a specific identified person. It might involve examining whom that person associates and does business with. "Pattern-based" data mining involves starting with a particular profile for terrorist activity and then analyzing databases to see which individuals' patterns of activity match that profile. Do these forms of data mining present different privacy concerns? If so, what are they? How should each type of data mining be regulated?

DATA MINING: FEDERAL EFFORTS COVER A WIDE RANGE OF USES

U.S. General Accountability Office, excerpt from pp. 2-3 (May 2004)

Federal agencies are using data mining for a variety of purposes, ranging from improving service or performance to analyzing and detecting terrorist patterns and activities. Our survey of 128 federal departments and agencies on their use of data mining shows that 52 agencies are using or are planning to use data mining. These departments and agencies reported 199 data mining efforts, of which 68 were planned and 131 were operational. . . .

The Department of Defense reported having the largest number of data mining efforts aimed at improving service or performance and at managing human resources. Defense was also the most frequent user of efforts aimed at analyzing

[47] K.A. Taipale, *Data Mining and Domestic Security: Connecting the Dots to Make Sense of Data*, 5 Colum. Sci. & Tech. L. Rev. 9-12 (2003).

[48] Daniel J. Solove, *The Digital Person: Technology and Privacy in the Information Age* 169, 175 (2004).

intelligence and detecting terrorist activities, followed by the Departments of Homeland Security, Justice, and Education. . . .

Data mining efforts for detecting criminal activities or patterns, however, were spread relatively evenly among the reporting agencies.

In addition, out of all 199 data mining efforts identified, 122 used personal information. For these efforts, the primary purposes were detecting fraud, waste, and abuse; detecting criminal activities or patterns; analyzing intelligence and detecting terrorist activities; and increasing tax compliance.

Agencies also identified efforts to mine data from the private sector and data from other federal agencies, both of which could include personal information. Of 54 efforts to mine data from the private sector (such as credit reports or credit card transactions), 36 involve personal information. Of 77 efforts to mine data from other federal agencies, 46 involve personal information (including student loan application data, bank account numbers, credit card information, and taxpayer identification numbers).

Data mining enables corporations and government agencies to analyze massive volumes of data quickly and relatively inexpensively. The use of this type of information retrieval has been driven by the exponential growth in the volumes and availability of information collected by the public and private sectors, as well as by advances in computing and data storage capabilities. In response to these trends, generic data mining tools are increasingly available for — or built into — major commercial database applications. Today, mining can be performed on many types of data. . . .

MARY DeRosa, Data Mining and Data Analysis for Counterterrorism

Center for Strategic and International Studies (CSIS) 6-8 (2004)

A relatively simple and useful data-analysis tool for counterterrorism is subject-based "link analysis." This technique uses aggregated public records or other large collections of data to find links between a subject — a suspect, an address, or other piece of relevant information — and other people, places, or things. This can provide additional clues for analysts and investigators to follow. Link analysis is a tool that is available now and is used for, among other things, background checks of applicants for sensitive jobs and as an investigatory tool in national security and law enforcement investigations.

A hindsight analysis of the September 11 attacks provides an example of how simple, subject-based link analysis could be used effectively to assist investigations or analysis of terrorist plans. By using government watch list information, airline reservation records, and aggregated public record data, link analysis could have identified all 19 September 11 terrorists — for follow-up investigation — before September 11. The links can be summarized as follows:

Direct Links — Watch List Information

• Khalid Almihdhar and Nawaf Alhazmi, both hijackers of American Airlines (AA) Flight 77, which crashed into the Pentagon, appeared on a U.S.

government terrorist watch list. Both used their real names to reserve their flights. . . .

Link Analysis — One Degree of Separation

- Two other hijackers used the same contact address for their flight reservations that Khalid Almihdhar listed on his reservation. These were Mohamed Atta, who hijacked AA Flight 11, which crashed into the World Trade Center North Tower, and Marwan Al Shehhi, who hijacked UA Flight 175.

- Salem Alhazmi, who hijacked AA Flight 77, used the same contact address on his reservation as Nawaf Alhazmi.

- The frequent flyer number that Khalid Almihdhar used to make his reservation was also used by hijacker Majed Moqed to make his reservation on AA Flight 77.

- Hamza Alghamdi, who hijacked UA Flight 175, used the same contact address on his reservation as Ahmed Alghamdi used on his.

- Hani Hanjour, who hijacked AA Flight 77, lived with both Nawaf Alhazmi and Khalid Almihdhar, a fact that searches of public records could have revealed. . . .

Thus, if the government had started with watch list data and pursued links, it is at least possible that all of the hijackers would have been identified as subjects for further investigation. Of course, this example does not show the false positives — names of people with no connection to the terror attacks that might also have been linked to the watch list subjects.

Pattern-based data analysis also has potential for counterterrorism in the longer term, if research on uses of those techniques continues. . . . [D]ata-mining research must find ways to identify useful patterns that can predict an extremely rare activity — terrorist planning and attacks. It must also identify how to separate the "signal" of pattern from the "noise" of innocent activity in the data. One possible advantage of pattern-based searches — if they can be perfected — would be that they could provide clues to "sleeper" activity by unknown terrorists who have never engaged in activity that would link them to known terrorists. Unlike subject-based queries, pattern-based searches do not require a link to a known suspicious subject.

Types of pattern-based searches that could prove useful include searches for particular combinations of lower-level activity that together are predictive of terrorist activity. For example, a pattern of a "sleeper" terrorist might be a person in the country on a student visa who purchases a bomb-making book and 50 medium-sized loads of fertilizer. Or, if the concern is that terrorists will use large trucks for attacks, automated data analysis might be conducted regularly to identify people who have rented large trucks, used hotels or drop boxes as addresses, and fall within certain age ranges or have other qualities that are part of a known terrorist pattern. Significant patterns in e-mail traffic might be discovered that could reveal terrorist activity and terrorist "ringleaders." Pattern-based searches might also be very useful in response and consequence management. For example, searches of hospital data for reports of certain combinations of symptoms, or of other databases for patterns of behavior, such as pharmaceutical purchases or work absenteeism might provide an early signal of a terrorist attack using a biological weapon. . . .

NOTES & QUESTIONS

1. *The TAPAC Committee Report.* The Technology and Privacy Advisory Committee (TAPAC) was appointed by Secretary of Defense Donald Rumsfeld to examine the privacy implications of data mining. In its report, it noted that TIA was "a flawed effort to achieve worthwhile ends. It was flawed by its perceived insensitivity to critical privacy issues, the manner in which it was presented to the public, and the lack of clarity and consistency with which it was described." The report recommended:

> If the data mining is limited to searches based on particularized suspicion about a specific individual, we believe existing law should govern. Because, by definition, there is enough evidence about such a person to warrant further investigation, and that investigation is clearly subject to the protections of the Fourth Amendment, supplemented by federal statutes, we rely on existing law. We understand this category of data mining to include searches seeking to identify or locate a specific individual (e.g., a suspected terrorist) from airline or cruise ship passenger manifests or other lists of names or other non-sensitive information about U.S. persons. . . .
>
> For all other government data mining that involves personally identifiable information about U.S. persons, we recommend below that the government be required to first establish a predicate demonstrating the need for the data mining to prevent or respond to terrorism, and second, unless exigent circumstances are present, obtain authorization from the Foreign Intelligence Surveillance Court for its data mining activities. As we stress, that authorization may be sought either for programs that include data mining known or likely to include information on U.S. persons, or for specific applications of data mining where the use of personally identifiable information concerning U.S. persons is clearly anticipated. Legislation will be required for the Foreign Intelligence Surveillance Court to fulfill the role we recommend.[49]

The TAPAC Report's central recommendation is for a secret Foreign Intelligence Surveillance Act (FISA) court to approve various data mining projects. Is this a viable way to regulate data mining?

2. *The Markle Foundation Reports.* The Markle Foundation, a private sector philanthropic organization, established a Task Force on National Security in the Information Age that has issued two reports about government data mining. In these reports, the Markle Task Force is enthusiastic about the potential benefits of government data mining and recommends moving ahead with projects that will draw on this technique. The Markle Task Force recommends that government have ready access to private sector databases, but that the databases not be combined into a centralized database like the one envisioned for TIA:

---

[49] Technology and Privacy Advisory Committee (TAPAC), *Safeguarding Privacy in the Fight Against Terrorism*, vii-x, 45-49 (2004).

Attempting to centralize [databases of personal] information is not the answer because it would not link the information to the dispersed analytical capabilities of the network. Centralization could also lead to information becoming obsolete, since a centralized analytical entity would not have the ability to keep up-to-date much of the information collected from dispersed sources. . . .

Our Task Force's fundamental objective, then, is to identify the technological tools and infrastructure, the policies, and the processes necessary to link these different communities so that important information can be shared among the people who need it, and as rapidly as possible. . . .

Today, the private sector is on the frontline of the homeland security effort. Its members are holders of the data that may prove crucial to identifying and locating terrorists or thwarting terrorist attacks. . . . We therefore start from the premise that the government must have access to that information, which is needed to protect our country, and that through a combination of well-crafted guidelines, careful articulation of the types of information needed for identified purposes, and effective oversight using modern information technology, it will be possible to assure that government gets that information in a way that protects our essential liberties.[50]

Is decentralization sufficient to safeguard privacy? While mentioning privacy and civil liberty concerns, the Markle Foundation Task Force does not suggest much in the way of legal controls, but it mentions the possibility of technology to help protect privacy. The report does not, however, explain what concrete limitations should be established to protect privacy.

3. *The CMPPA and Government Data Mining.* To what extent does the Computer Matching and Privacy Protection Act (CMPPA) regulate government data mining? Consider the view of the Markle Foundation:

Based upon past applications of the routine use exception [to the Privacy Act], it seems likely that future government initiatives promoting increased interagency information sharing to protect national security will meet with little resistance. A routine use need only meet [two requirements] to be valid: (1) compatible with the purpose of the information collection and (2) published in the Federal Register. . . .

In today's age of information, data mining has the potential to become one of the government's most powerful tools for analyzing information on terrorism. Congress, however, has restricted the kinds of data mining federal agencies can do. In 1977, the Department of Health, Education, and Welfare initiated Project Match to identify federal employees fraudulently receiving welfare payments. . . . Over the next decade, such computer matching became pervasive. In a 1986 study, the Office of Technology Assessment reported that in 1984, eleven cabinet level departments and four independent agencies conducted 110 separate computer matching programs, consisting of 700 total matches and involving seven billion records. . . .

The widespread disclosure of information across agencies promoted Congress to act in 1988. To address these problems, Congress amended the Privacy Act by passing the Computer Matching Act, which precluded government agencies from treating computer matching as a routine use in most cases. Congress, however, explicitly excluded "matches performed for foreign

---

[50] Markle Foundation Task Force, *Creating a Trusted Information Network for Homeland Security* 14-15 (2003).

counterintelligence purposes or to produce background checks for security clearances of Federal personnel." . . . Thus, so long as an agency lists something like "analyzing information to improve national security or prevent terrorism" as a routine use for the agency's information, a counterterrorism intelligence agency should be able to data mine the agency's records.[51]

4. *The Privacy Act and Government Data Mining.* What, if any, limits would the Privacy Act place on the kinds of government data mining discussed earlier in this section? Do any other laws discussed thus far regulate the practice?

Consider the following observation by Stewart Baker in the Markle Foundation Report regarding the limitations of the Privacy Act:

> [The Privacy Act] requirements are just restrictive enough to make it awkward for the government to take direct access of private databases for data-mining analysis. As a result, one of the emerging solutions being adopted by the government is to encourage or even require industry to keep the databases in private hands, run pattern recognition themselves, and report suspicious results to the government. . . . [T]his approach has been used in the anti-money-laundering context. The Administration has discussed adopting similar approaches with respect to other records that might be of interest in counter-terrorism investigations.[52]

UNITED STATES V. SOKOLOW

490 U.S. 1 (1989)

Respondent Andrew Sokolow was stopped by Drug Enforcement Administration (DEA) agents upon his arrival at Honolulu International Airport. The agents found 1,063 grams of cocaine in his carry-on luggage. When respondent was stopped, the agents knew, *inter alia,* that (1) he paid $2,100 for two airplane tickets from a roll of $20 bills; (2) he traveled under a name that did not match the name under which his telephone number was listed; (3) his original destination was Miami, a source city for illicit drugs; (4) he stayed in Miami for only 48 hours, even though a round-trip flight from Honolulu to Miami takes 20 hours; (5) he appeared nervous during his trip; and (6) he checked none of his luggage. A divided panel of the United States Court of Appeals for the Ninth Circuit held that the DEA agents did not have a reasonable suspicion to stop respondent, as required by the Fourth Amendment. 831 F.2d 1413 (CA9 1987). We take the contrary view.

This case involves a typical attempt to smuggle drugs through one of the Nation's airports. On a Sunday in July 1984, respondent went to the United Airlines ticket counter at Honolulu Airport, where he purchased two round-trip tickets for a flight to Miami leaving later that day. The tickets were purchased in the names of "Andrew Kray" and "Janet Norian" and had open return dates. Respondent paid $2,100 for the tickets from a large roll of $20 bills, which appeared to contain a total of $4,000. He also gave the ticket agent his home

---

[51] Markle Foundation Task Force, *Protecting America's Freedom in the Information Age* 131 (2002).

[52] *Id.*

telephone number. The ticket agent noticed that respondent seemed nervous; he was about 25 years old; he was dressed in a black jumpsuit and wore gold jewelry; and he was accompanied by a woman, who turned out to be Janet Norian. Neither respondent nor his companion checked any of their four pieces of luggage.

After the couple left for their flight, the ticket agent informed Officer John McCarthy of the Honolulu Police Department of respondent's cash purchase of tickets to Miami. Officer McCarthy determined that the telephone number respondent gave to the ticket agent was subscribed to a "Karl Herman," who resided at 348-A Royal Hawaiian Avenue in Honolulu. Unbeknownst to McCarthy (and later to the DEA agents), respondent was Herman's roommate. The ticket agent identified respondent's voice on the answering machine at Herman's number. Officer McCarthy was unable to find any listing under the name "Andrew Kray" in Hawaii. McCarthy subsequently learned that return reservations from Miami to Honolulu had been made in the names of Kray and Norian, with their arrival scheduled for July 25, three days after respondent and his companion had left. He also learned that Kray and Norian were scheduled to make stopovers in Denver and Los Angeles.

On July 25, during the stopover in Los Angeles, DEA agents identified respondent. He "appeared to be very nervous and was looking all around the waiting area." Later that day, at 6:30 p.m., respondent and Norian arrived in Honolulu. As before, they had not checked their luggage. Respondent was still wearing a black jumpsuit and gold jewelry. The couple proceeded directly to the street and tried to hail a cab, where Agent Richard Kempshall and three other DEA agents approached them. Kempshall displayed his credentials, grabbed respondent by the arm, and moved him back onto the sidewalk. Kempshall asked respondent for his airline ticket and identification; respondent said that he had neither. He told the agents that his name was "Sokolow," but that he was traveling under his mother's maiden name, "Kray."

Respondent and Norian were escorted to the DEA office at the airport. There, the couple's luggage was examined by "Donker," a narcotics detector dog, which alerted on respondent's brown shoulder bag. The agents arrested respondent. He was advised of his constitutional rights and declined to make any statements. The agents obtained a warrant to search the shoulder bag. They found no illicit drugs, but the bag did contain several suspicious documents indicating respondent's involvement in drug trafficking. The agents had Donker reexamine the remaining luggage, and this time the dog alerted on a medium-sized Louis Vuitton bag. By now, it was 9:30 p.m., too late for the agents to obtain a second warrant. They allowed respondent to leave for the night, but kept his luggage. The next morning, after a second dog confirmed Donker's alert, the agents obtained a warrant and found 1,063 grams of cocaine inside the bag.

Respondent was indicted for possession with the intent to distribute cocaine in violation of 21 U.S.C. § 841(a)(1). The United States District Court for Hawaii denied his motion to suppress the cocaine and other evidence seized from his luggage, finding that the DEA agents had a reasonable suspicion that he was involved in drug trafficking when they stopped him at the airport. . . .

The United States Court of Appeals for the Ninth Circuit reversed respondent's conviction by a divided vote, holding that the DEA agents did not have a reasonable suspicion to justify the stop. The majority divided the facts bearing on

reasonable suspicion into two categories. In the first category, the majority placed facts describing "ongoing criminal activity," such as the use of an alias or evasive movement through an airport; the majority believed that at least one such factor was always needed to support a finding of reasonable suspicion. In the second category, it placed facts describing "personal characteristics" of drug couriers, such as the cash payment for tickets, a short trip to a major source city for drugs, nervousness, type of attire, and unchecked luggage. The majority believed that such characteristics, "shared by drug couriers and the public at large," were only relevant if there was evidence of ongoing criminal behavior and the Government offered "[e]mpirical documentation" that the combination of facts at issue did not describe the behavior of "significant numbers of innocent persons." Applying this two-part test to the facts of this case, the majority found that there was no evidence of ongoing criminal behavior, and thus that the agents' stop was impermissible. . .
.

Our decision . . . turns on whether the agents had a reasonable suspicion that respondent was engaged in wrongdoing when they encountered him on the sidewalk. In *Terry v. Ohio,* 392 U.S. 1 (1968), we held that the police can stop and briefly detain a person for investigative purposes if the officer has a reasonable suspicion supported by articulable facts that criminal activity "may be afoot," even if the officer lacks probable cause.

The officer, of course, must be able to articulate something more than an "inchoate and unparticularized suspicion or 'hunch.'" The Fourth Amendment requires "some minimal level of objective justification" for making the stop. That level of suspicion is considerably less than proof of wrongdoing by a preponderance of the evidence. We have held that probable cause means "a fair probability that contraband or evidence of a crime will be found," *Illinois v. Gates,* 462 U.S. 213 (1983), and the level of suspicion required for a *Terry* stop is obviously less demanding than that for probable cause. . . .

In evaluating the validity of a stop such as this, we must consider "the totality of the circumstances — the whole picture." . . .

The rule enunciated by the Court of Appeals, in which evidence available to an officer is divided into evidence of "ongoing criminal behavior," on the one hand, and "probabilistic" evidence, on the other, is not in keeping with the quoted statements from our decisions. It also seems to us to draw a sharp line between types of evidence, the probative value of which varies only in degree. The Court of Appeals classified evidence of traveling under an alias, or evidence that the suspect took an evasive or erratic path through an airport, as meeting the test for showing "ongoing criminal activity." But certainly instances are conceivable in which traveling under an alias would not reflect ongoing criminal activity: for example, a person who wished to travel to a hospital or clinic for an operation and wished to conceal that fact. One taking an evasive path through an airport might be seeking to avoid a confrontation with an angry acquaintance or with a creditor. This is not to say that each of these types of evidence is not highly probative, but they do not have the sort of ironclad significance attributed to them by the Court of Appeals.

On the other hand, the factors in this case that the Court of Appeals treated as merely "probabilistic" also have probative significance. Paying $2,100 in cash for two airplane tickets is out of the ordinary, and it is even more out of the ordinary to pay that sum from a roll of $20 bills containing nearly twice that amount of cash. Most business travelers, we feel confident, purchase airline tickets by credit card or check so as to have a record for tax or business purposes, and few vacationers carry with them thousands of dollars in $20 bills. We also think the agents had a reasonable ground to believe that respondent was traveling under an alias; the evidence was by no means conclusive, but it was sufficient to warrant consideration. While a trip from Honolulu to Miami, standing alone, is not a cause for any sort of suspicion, here there was more: surely few residents of Honolulu travel from that city for 20 hours to spend 48 hours in Miami during the month of July.

Any one of these factors is not by itself proof of any illegal conduct and is quite consistent with innocent travel. But we think taken together they amount to reasonable suspicion. Indeed, *Terry* itself involved "a series of acts, each of them perhaps innocent" if viewed separately, "but which taken together warranted further investigation." . . .

We do not agree with respondent that our analysis is somehow changed by the agents' belief that his behavior was consistent with one of the DEA's "drug courier profiles." A court sitting to determine the existence of reasonable suspicion must require the agent to articulate the factors leading to that conclusion, but the fact that these factors may be set forth in a "profile" does not somehow detract from their evidentiary significance as seen by a trained agent. . . .

We hold that the agents had a reasonable basis to suspect that respondent was transporting illegal drugs on these facts. . . .

MARSHALL and BRENNAN, JJ. dissenting. Because the strongest advocates of Fourth Amendment rights are frequently criminals, it is easy to forget that our interpretations of such rights apply to the innocent and the guilty alike. In the present case, the chain of events set in motion when respondent Andrew Sokolow was stopped by Drug Enforcement Administration (DEA) agents at Honolulu International Airport led to the discovery of cocaine and, ultimately, to Sokolow's conviction for drug trafficking. But in sustaining this conviction on the ground that the agents reasonably suspected Sokolow of ongoing criminal activity, the Court diminishes the rights of *all* citizens "to be secure in their persons," U.S. Const., Amdt. 4, as they traverse the Nation's airports. Finding this result constitutionally impermissible, I dissent.

The Fourth Amendment cabins government's authority to intrude on personal privacy and security by requiring that searches and seizures usually be supported by a showing of probable cause. The reasonable-suspicion standard is a derivation of the probable-cause command, applicable only to those brief detentions which fall short of being full-scale searches and seizures and which are necessitated by law enforcement exigencies such as the need to stop ongoing crimes, to prevent imminent crimes, and to protect law enforcement officers in highly charged situations. By requiring reasonable suspicion as a prerequisite to such seizures, the Fourth Amendment protects innocent persons from being subjected to "overbearing or harassing" police conduct carried out solely on the basis of imprecise stereotypes of what criminals look like, or on the basis of irrelevant personal characteristics such as race.

To deter such egregious police behavior, we have held that a suspicion is not reasonable unless officers have based it on "specific and articulable facts." It is not enough to suspect that an individual has committed crimes in the past, harbors unconsummated criminal designs, or has the propensity to commit crimes. On the contrary, before detaining an individual, law enforcement officers must reasonably suspect that he is engaged in, or poised to commit, a criminal act *at that moment.* . . .

Evaluated against this standard, the facts about Andrew Sokolow known to the DEA agents at the time they stopped him fall short of reasonably indicating that he was engaged at the time in criminal activity. It is highly significant that the DEA agents stopped Sokolow because he matched one of the DEA's "profiles" of a paradigmatic drug courier. In my view, a law enforcement officer's mechanistic application of a formula of personal and behavioral traits in deciding whom to detain can only dull the officer's ability and determination to make sensitive and fact-specific inferences "in light of his experience," *Terry, supra,* particularly in ambiguous or borderline cases. Reflexive reliance on a profile of drug courier characteristics runs a far greater risk than does ordinary, case-by-case police work of subjecting innocent individuals to unwarranted police harassment and detention. This risk is enhanced by the profile's "chameleon-like way of adapting to any particular set of observations." *Compare, e.g., United States v. Moore,* 675 F.2d 802 (CA6 1982) (suspect was first to deplane), cert. denied, 460 U.S. 1068 (1983), *with United States v. Mendenhall,* 446 U.S. 544 (1980) (last to deplane), *with United States v. Buenaventura-Ariza,* 615 F.2d 29 (CA2 1980) (deplaned from middle); *United States v. Sullivan,* 625 F.2d 9 (CA4 1980) (one-way tickets), *with United States v. Craemer,* 555 F.2d 594 (CA6 1977) (round-trip tickets), with *United States v. McCaleb,* 552 F.2d 717 (CA6 1977) (nonstop flight), with *United States v. Sokolow,* 808 F.2d 1366, (CA9) (changed planes); *Craemer, supra* (no luggage), *with United States v. Sanford,* 658 F.2d 342 (CA5 1981) (gym bag), with *Sullivan, supra,* at 12 (new suitcases); *United States v. Smith,* 574 F.2d 882 (CA6 1978) (traveling alone), *with United States v. Fry,* 622 F.2d 1218 (CA5 1980) (travelling with companion); *United States v. Andrews,* 600 F.2d 563 (CA6 1979) (acted nervously), *with United States v. Himmelwright,* 551 F.2d 991 (CA5) (acted too calmly). . . . In asserting that it is not "somehow" relevant that the agents who stopped Sokolow did so in reliance on a prefabricated profile of criminal characteristics, the majority thus ducks serious issues relating to a questionable law enforcement practice, to address the validity of which we granted certiorari in this case. . . .

[T]raveler Sokolow gave no indications of evasive activity. On the contrary, the sole behavioral detail about Sokolow noted by the DEA agents was that he was nervous. With news accounts proliferating of plane crashes, near collisions, and air terrorism, there are manifold and good reasons for being agitated while awaiting a flight, reasons that have nothing to do with one's involvement in a criminal endeavor.

The remaining circumstantial facts known about Sokolow, considered either singly or together, are scarcely indicative of criminal activity. . . . [T]he fact that Sokolow took a brief trip to a resort city for which he brought only carry-on luggage also "describe[s] a very large category of presumably innocent travelers." That Sokolow embarked from Miami, "a source city for illicit drugs," is no more suggestive of illegality; thousands of innocent persons travel from "source cities" every day and, judging from the DEA's testimony in past cases, nearly every major city in the country may be characterized as a source or distribution city. That Sokolow had his phone listed in another person's name also does not support the majority's assertion that the DEA agents reasonably believed Sokolow was using an alias; it is commonplace to have one's phone registered in the name of a roommate, which, it later turned out, was precisely what Sokolow had done. That Sokolow was dressed in a black jumpsuit and wore gold jewelry also provides no grounds for suspecting wrongdoing, the majority's repeated and unexplained allusions to Sokolow's style of dress notwithstanding. For law enforcement officers to base a search, even in part, on a "pop" guess that persons dressed in a particular fashion are likely to commit crimes not only stretches the concept of reasonable suspicion beyond recognition, but also is inimical to the self-expression which the choice of wardrobe may provide.

Finally, that Sokolow paid for his tickets in cash indicates no imminent or ongoing criminal activity. The majority "feel[s] confident" that "[m]ost business travelers . . . purchase airline tickets by credit card or check." Why the majority confines its focus only to "business travelers" I do not know, but I would not so lightly infer ongoing crime from the use of legal tender. Making major cash purchases, while surely less common today, may simply reflect the traveler's aversion to, or inability to obtain, plastic money. . . .

NOTES & QUESTIONS

1. *Profiling.* What sorts of criteria would be sufficient to find reasonable suspicion for a *Terry* stop for potential terrorist activity at an airport? Having a one-way ticket? Having only carry-on luggage? One of the difficulties in creating a profile of a terrorist, Anita Ramasastry notes, is that "[t]here is no well-defined and reinforced profile for terrorists. Further, attacks are relatively infrequent, making it harder to reinforce any profiles that do exist."[53]

   Is the use of profiles to detain or search people problematic? Fred Schauer contends that making generalizations is not necessarily problematic, even when doing so leads to some mistakes:

   > Here Justice Marshall [dissenting in *Sokolow*] went right to the heart of the matter. He recognized that the question of the profile is not about profiles as such, but is about *rules*. The issue is whether preexisting and general rules should be employed to determine which people to stop, as the majority was willing to permit, or whether that determination must, as Justice Marshall insisted, be made on a particularistic basis by individual officers using their own best judgment in each case, even if that best judgment can itself be seen as just another version of profiling. Once we understand that the issue is not about whether to use profiles or not but instead about whether to use (or to prefer) formal written profiles or informal unwritten ones, it becomes clear that this is not a question of profiles or not, but a question about discretion. Should individual customs officers have the discretion to create their own profiles, as

---

[53] Anita Ramasastry, *Lost in Translation? Data Mining, National Security, and the "Adverse Inference" Problem*, 22 Santa Clara Computer & High Tech. L.J. 757, 773 (2006).

Justice Marshall preferred, or is it at least permissible, even if not constitutionally mandatory, for formal written profiles to be used as a way of regularizing the process and limiting the discretion of individual officers?

Once we understand the choice as being one between profiles that are constructed in advance and have the potential to be both under- and overinclusive, on the one hand, and profiles that are constructed on a case-by-case basis by law-enforcement officials making, in Justice Marshall's words, "sensitive and fact-specific inferences in light of [their] experience," on the other, we can see that the issue is not about profiling at all, for profiling is inevitable.[54]

Is the use of data mining laudable because it involves a computer searching for written pre-established patterns rather than the ad hoc discretion of airline screening officials at the security checkpoints? Pre-established profiles can eliminate the use of race or other problematic factors that might be used in an official's ad hoc discretion. Then again, even pre-established profiles can employ improper factors.

What factors should be considered to be improper? Should information about a person's associations and group memberships be included? Information about a person's political and expressive activity? Information about a person's religion or race?

Fred Schauer examines the issue of whether race should be a factor in the profile:

Those who commit acts of airplane terrorism, both before and after September 11, 2001, are disproportionately younger Muslim men of Middle Eastern background. . . .

On the evidence we now have, it is more than plausible to suppose that Middle Eastern ethnicity is a significant contributory factor, such that including it in the algorithm will make the algorithm substantially more effective than excluding it.

Because allowing the use of race and ethnicity imposes a cost on those members of the targeted groups who are in the area of overinclusion — Middle Easterners who have done nothing wrong — it might be preferable to distribute the cost more broadly, and in doing so raise the cost without lowering the degree of security. If excluding the relevant factor of Middle Eastern appearance from the algorithm made it necessary to increase the scrutiny of everyone — if excluding ethnicity while still including everything else increased waiting time at airports an average of thirty minutes per passenger — this might still be a price worth paying. . . . Put starkly, the question of racial or ethnic profiling in air travel is not the question of whether racial and ethnic sensitivity must be bought at the price of thousands of lives. Rather, it is most often the question of whether racial and ethnic sensitivity should be bought at the price of arriving thirty minutes earlier at the airport.[55]

Consider the following document obtained by the Electronic Privacy Information Center from NASA regarding airline passenger data:

---

[54] Frederick Schauer, *Profiles, Probabilities, and Stereotypes* 173-74 (2003).
[55] *Id.* at 181-90.

ISLE ran a simple anomaly detection algorithm that it developed as part of this project on a subset of the census database, and it found some interesting anomalies. Many of the anomalies were people from unusual countries. One anomaly was a 22-year-old African American man who was not a college graduate but had over $100,000 in capital gains.

We ran Gritbot on a subset of the census database. It discovered many interesting anomalies, including a woman whose ancestry is Mexican but who speaks Chinese at home, a 16-year-old veteran, and some people who reported their race to be white and their ancestry to be African-American. . . .[56]

Profiles ultimately involve human judgment about what patterns should be singled out as suspicious. One difficulty with data mining is that if the profiles remain secret, how can there be oversight to prevent improper factors from being used? Who decides what factors are appropriate?

2. *An Assessment of Government Data Mining.* Consider the following account of the problems of government data mining by Daniel Solove:

Usually, the government has some form of particularized suspicion, a factual basis to believe that a particular person may be engaged in illegal conduct. Particularized suspicion keeps the government's profound investigative powers in check, preventing widespread surveillance and snooping into the lives and affairs of all citizens. Computer matches . . . investigate everyone, and most people who are investigated are innocent.

With the new information supplied by the private sector, there is an increased potential for more automated investigations, such as searches for all people who purchase books about particular topics or those who visit certain websites, or perhaps even people whose personal interests fit a profile for those likely to engage in certain forms of criminal activity. Profiles work similarly to the way that Amazon.com predicts which products customers will want to buy. They use particular characteristics and patterns of activity to predict how people will behave in the future. Of course, profiles can be mistaken, but they are often accurate enough to tempt people to rely on them. But there are even deeper problems with profiles beyond inaccuracies. Profiles can be based on stereotypes, race, or religion. A profile is only as good as its designer. Profiles are often kept secret, enabling prejudices and faulty assumptions to exist unchecked by the public.[57]

3. *A Hypothetical Data Mining Problem.* Suppose the FBI receives a tip from a credible source that two young males, both naturalized U.S. citizens, who are Muslim and who were originally born in Saudi Arabia, have rented a U-Haul truck and are planning to use it to detonate a bomb at a crowded building or place in Los Angeles, CA within the next week. The source says he met the two males at his mosque, which has over 1,000 worshippers. This is all the information the FBI agents have. The FBI would like to: (1) obtain the records of the people who attend the mosque; (2) obtain the records of U-Haul. The FBI would like to engage in data mining on the records to narrow their search for the two males. Notwithstanding existing law, should the FBI agents be

---

[56] NASA Documents, available at http://www.epic.org/privacy/airtravel/nasa/.

[57] Daniel J. Solove, *The Digital Person: Technology and Privacy in the Information Age* 179-85 (2004).

permitted to obtain the records? If so, what privacy protections should be established?

ARIZONA V. EVANS

514 U.S. 1 (1995)

REHNQUIST, J. This case presents the question whether evidence seized in violation of the Fourth Amendment by an officer who acted in reliance on a police record indicating the existence of an outstanding arrest warrant — a record that is later determined to be erroneous — must be suppressed by virtue of the exclusionary rule regardless of the source of the error. . . .

In January 1991, Phoenix police officer Bryan Sargent observed respondent Isaac Evans driving the wrong way on a one-way street in front of the police station. The officer stopped respondent and asked to see his driver's license. After respondent told him that his license had been suspended, the officer entered respondent's name into a computer data terminal located in his patrol car. The computer inquiry confirmed that respondent's license had been suspended and also indicated that there was an outstanding misdemeanor warrant for his arrest. Based upon the outstanding warrant, Officer Sargent placed respondent under arrest. While being handcuffed, respondent dropped a hand-rolled cigarette that the officers determined smelled of marijuana. Officers proceeded to search his car and discovered a bag of marijuana under the passenger's seat.

The State charged respondent with possession of marijuana. When the police notified the Justice Court that they had arrested him, the Justice Court discovered that the arrest warrant previously had been quashed and so advised the police. Respondent argued that because his arrest was based on a warrant that had been quashed 17 days prior to his arrest, the marijuana seized incident to the arrest should be suppressed as the fruit of an unlawful arrest. Respondent also argued that "[t]he 'good faith' exception to the exclusionary rule [was] inapplicable . . . because it was police error, not judicial error, which caused the invalid arrest." . . .

"The question whether the exclusionary rule's remedy is appropriate in a particular context has long been regarded as an issue separate from the question whether the Fourth Amendment rights of the party seeking to invoke the rule were violated by police conduct." The exclusionary rule operates as a judicially created remedy designed to safeguard against future violations of Fourth Amendment rights through the rule's general deterrent effect. As with any remedial device, the rule's application has been restricted to those instances where its remedial objectives are thought most efficaciously served. Where the exclusionary rule does not result in appreciable deterrence, then, clearly, its use . . . is unwarranted. . . .

If court employees were responsible for the erroneous computer record, the exclusion of evidence at trial would not sufficiently deter future errors so as to warrant such a severe sanction. First, as we noted in [*United States v. Leon,* 468 U.S. 897 (1984)], the exclusionary rule was historically designed as a means of deterring police misconduct, not mistakes by court employees. Second, respondent offers no evidence that court employees are inclined to ignore or subvert the Fourth Amendment or that lawlessness among these actors requires application of the extreme sanction of exclusion. To the contrary, the Chief Clerk of the Justice Court testified at the suppression hearing that this type of error occurred once every three or four years.

Finally, and most important, there is no basis for believing that application of the exclusionary rule in these circumstances will have a significant effect on court employees responsible for informing the police that a warrant has been quashed. Because court clerks are not adjuncts to the law enforcement team engaged in the often competitive enterprise of ferreting out crime, they have no stake in the outcome of particular criminal prosecutions. The threat of exclusion of evidence could not be expected to deter such individuals from failing to inform police officials that a warrant had been quashed. . . .

In fact, once the court clerks discovered the error, they immediately corrected it, and then proceeded to search their files to make sure that no similar mistakes had occurred. There is no indication that the arresting officer was not acting objectively reasonably when he relied upon the police computer record. Application of the *Leon* framework supports a categorical exception to the exclusionary rule for clerical errors of court employees. . . .

O'CONNOR, SOUTER, and BREYER, JJ. concurring. The evidence in this case strongly suggests that it was a court employee's departure from established recordkeeping procedures that caused the record of respondent's arrest warrant to remain in the computer system after the warrant had been quashed. Prudently, then, the Court limits itself to the question whether a court employee's departure from such established procedures is the kind of error to which the exclusionary rule should apply. . . .

In limiting itself to that single question, however, the Court does not hold that the court employee's mistake in this case was necessarily the *only* error that may have occurred and to which the exclusionary rule might apply. While the police were innocent of the court employee's mistake, they may or may not have acted reasonably in their reliance *on the recordkeeping system itself*. Surely it would *not* be reasonable for the police to rely, say, on a recordkeeping system, their own or some other agency's, that has no mechanism to ensure its accuracy over time and that routinely leads to false arrests, even years after the probable cause for any such arrest has ceased to exist (if it ever existed). . . .

In recent years, we have witnessed the advent of powerful, computer-based recordkeeping systems that facilitate arrests in ways that have never before been possible. The police, of course, are entitled to enjoy the substantial advantages this technology confers. They may not, however, rely on it blindly. With the benefits of more efficient law enforcement mechanisms comes the burden of corresponding constitutional responsibilities.

GINSBURG and STEVENS, JJ. dissenting. This case portrays the increasing use of computer technology in law enforcement; it illustrates an evolving problem this Court need not, and in my judgment should not, resolve too hastily. . . .

Widespread reliance on computers to store and convey information generates, along with manifold benefits, new possibilities of error, due to both computer malfunctions and operator mistakes. Most germane to this case, computerization greatly amplifies an error's effect, and correspondingly intensifies the need for prompt correction; for inaccurate data can infect not only one agency, but the many agencies that share access to the database. The computerized data bases of the Federal Bureau of Investigation's National Crime Information Center (NCIC), to take a conspicuous example, contain over 23 million records, identifying, among other things, persons and vehicles sought by law enforcement agencies nationwide. NCIC information is available to approximately 71,000 federal, state, and local agencies. Thus, any mistake entered into the NCIC spreads nationwide in an instant.

Isaac Evans' arrest exemplifies the risks associated with computerization of arrest warrants. Though his arrest was in fact warrantless — the warrant once issued having been quashed over two weeks before the episode in suit — the computer reported otherwise. Evans' case is not idiosyncratic. . . .

In the instant case, the Court features testimony of the Chief Clerk of the Justice Court in East Phoenix to the effect that errors of the kind Evans encountered are reported only "on[c]e every three or four years." But the same witness also recounted that, when the error concerning Evans came to light, an immediate check revealed that three other errors of the very same kind had occurred on "that same day." . . .

In the Court's view, exclusion of evidence, even if capable of deterring police officer errors, cannot deter the carelessness of other governmental actors. Whatever federal precedents may indicate — an issue on which I voice no opinion — the Court's conclusion is not the lesson inevitably to be drawn from logic or experience.

In this electronic age, particularly with respect to recordkeeping, court personnel and police officers are not neatly compartmentalized actors. Instead, they serve together to carry out the State's information-gathering objectives. Whether particular records are maintained by the police or the courts should not be dispositive where a single computer data base can answer all calls. Not only is it artificial to distinguish between court clerk and police clerk slips; in practice, it may be difficult to pinpoint whether one official, *e.g.,* a court employee, or another, *e.g.,* a police officer, caused the error to exist or to persist. Applying an exclusionary rule as the Arizona court did may well supply a powerful incentive to the State to promote the prompt updating of computer records. . . .

NOTES & QUESTIONS

1. *Accuracy.* Pattern-based data mining is often not a highly accurate way of identifying suspects. Daniel Steinbock explores the arguments relating to data mining's accuracy:

   It must be noted at the outset that, in one sense, accuracy is not a particularly high priority in data matching and data mining. To the extent that their results are used for heightened scrutiny or for terrorist profiling, even the staunchest advocates would not pretend that these indicators are foolproof, but would simply respond that they do not need to be. This is especially true for predictive uses; the goal is simply to sort the higher from the lower risks and, perhaps, to see if a certain threshold of risk has been reached. On the other hand, even with predictive uses, errors in the data will produce a larger number of falsely positive results, thereby imposing unnecessary harms. This effectively externalizes the error costs of the computer-generated decision onto its subjects.[58]

Anita Ramasastry notes that data can often be "lost in translation" when it is taken from other contexts and used for government data mining purposes:

> First, data may not be accurate when provided initially by a consumer or may only reflect a partial truth. Second, data may get mistranslated due to human error (e.g. typing in a birth date incorrectly) when placed into a database. Third, when data is used in a new context, it may not be interpreted in the same way as previously used, because the new party using the data may not understand how the data was originally classified. For example, racial or ethnic classifications in one database may be different than in a new database. Fourth, when data from different sources is combined into a larger database, it may be incorrectly integrated. In other words, data from different people who share the same surname might be incorrectly merged, creating a new profile that is incorrect. Thus, there are multiple ways in which data may be erroneous. Where human agents are involved in compiling or aggregating different data, data sources can be mistranslated.[59]

2. *Due Process.* Consider Daniel Steinbock:

> The most striking aspect of virtually all antiterrorist and data mining decisions is the total absence of even the most rudimentary procedures for notice, hearing, or other opportunities for meaningful participation before, or even after, the deprivation is imposed.

Steinbock examines four ways to bring due process to data mining programs:

> One is summary hearings, along the lines of those required in brief school suspensions, prior to denial of access to flights or infringements of other liberty or property rights. A second involves correction opportunities after the initial data matching or data mining consequence, in a fuller process with disclosure and a right to respond. A third means of redress is after-the-fact compensatory damages for false positives in outcome. This solution allows for less process but makes wrongly identified persons whole, at least monetarily. Finally, given the frequent need for secrecy in data matching and data mining decision algorithms and the difficulty of addressing challenges to them in individual hearings, this Article proposes examination of their validity by independent oversight bodies. Evaluating whether a decisional system meets constitutional demands of due process requires attention to all stages of the process.[60]

3. *Transparency.* Consider Daniel Solove:

> The problem with many data mining programs is that they lack adequate transparency. The reason for the secrecy of the programs is that exposing the algorithms and patterns that trigger identification as a possible future terrorist will tip off terrorists about what behaviors to avoid. This is indeed a legitimate concern. Our society, however, is one of open government, public

---

[58] Daniel J. Steinbock, *Data Matching, Data Mining, and Due Process*, 40 Ga. L. Rev. 1, 82-83 (2005).

[59] Anita Ramasastry, *Lost in Translation? Data Mining, National Security, and the "Adverse Inference" Problem*, 22 Santa Clara Computer & High Tech. L.J. 757, 778 (2006).

[60] Steinbock, Data Mining, *supra*, at 57.

accountability, and oversight of government officials — not one of secret blacklists maintained in clandestine bureaucracies. Without public accountability, unelected bureaucrats can administer data mining programs in ways often insulated from any scrutiny at all. For example, the information gathered about people for use in data mining might be collected from sources that do not take sufficient steps to maintain its accuracy. Without oversight, it is unclear what level of accuracy the government requires for the information it gathers and uses. If profiles are based on race, speech, or other factors that society might not find desirable to include, how is this to be aired and discussed? If a person is routinely singled out based on a profile and wants to challenge the profile, there appears no way to do so unless the profile is revealed.

The lack of transparency in data mining programs makes it nearly impossible to balance the liberty and security interests. Given the significant potential privacy issues and other constitutional concerns, combined with speculative and unproven security benefits as well as many other alternative means of promoting security, should data mining still be on the table as a viable policy option?[61]

UNITED STATES V. ELLISON

462 F.3d 557 (6th Cir. 2006)

GIBBONS, J. . . . The central issue in this case is whether the Fourth Amendment is implicated when a police officer investigates an automobile license plate number using a law enforcement computer database. While on routine patrol, Officer Mark Keeley of the Farmington Hills (Michigan) Police Department pulled into a two-lane service drive adjacent to a shopping center. Keeley testified that a white van, with a male driver inside, was idling in the lane closest to the stores, in an area marked with "Fire Lane" and "No Parking" signs. Keeley did not issue the van a citation for being illegally parked, nor did he request that the driver move the van. Rather, he moved into a parking spot to observe the van and entered the vehicle's license plate number into his patrol car's Law Enforcement Information Network ("LEIN") computer. The LEIN search revealed that the vehicle was registered to Curtis Ellison, who had an outstanding felony warrant. Following standard procedure, Keeley radioed for back-up and continued observing the van. After two minutes, another male got into the van, and it drove away. Officer Keeley followed the van until his back-up was nearby, and then activated his lights and stopped the van.

Officer Keeley approached the driver's-side window as his back-up arrived. He advised the driver that he was being stopped for parking in a fire lane and asked for license, registration and proof of insurance. The driver, identified as Edward Coleman, stated that he had only stopped in front of the store to wait for the passenger. At this time the passenger stated that he was the registered owner of the vehicle. Keeley verified the passenger's identity as Curtis Ellison and moved to the passenger side of the van. Keeley notified Ellison that he was being arrested on the outstanding warrant. Ellison stepped out of the van, and during the routine

---

[61] Daniel J. Solove, *Data Mining and the Security-Liberty Debate*, 74 U. Chi. L. Rev. 343 (2008).

safety pat-down, two firearms were found. Coleman was released with a warning about parking in a fire lane.

Ellison was indicted for being a felon in possession of a firearm in violation of 18 U.S.C. § 922(g). Prior to trial, he made a timely motion to suppress the firearm as the fruit of an illegal search. After holding a hearing, the district court made a factual finding that the van was not parked illegally, and thus, the officer did not have probable cause to run the LEIN check of Ellison's license plate. The court issued a Memorandum Opinion and Order granting the motion to suppress under the "fruit of the poisonous tree" doctrine. . . .

The government argues on appeal that Ellison had no reasonable expectation of privacy in the information contained on his license plate, and thus, no probable cause was required for Officer Keeley to run the LEIN check. . . .

Although the district court did not expressly state that Ellison had a reasonable expectation of privacy in the information contained on his license plate, such a conclusion was necessarily implied by the court's ruling that a Fourth Amendment violation occurred. Thus, the district court could only find that the LEIN search violated the Fourth Amendment if it first concluded that Ellison had a "constitutionally protected reasonable expectation of privacy" in his license plate number. . . .

A tenet of constitutional jurisprudence is that the Fourth Amendment protects only what an individual seeks to keep private. *Katz,* 389 U.S. at 351-52. "What a person knowingly exposes to the public . . . is not a subject of Fourth Amendment protection." It is also settled that "objects falling in the plain view of an officer who has a right to be in the position to have that view are subject to seizure." . . .

No argument can be made that a motorist seeks to keep the information on his license plate private. The very purpose of a license plate number, like that of a Vehicle Identification Number, is to provide identifying information to law enforcement officials and others. . . .

The dissent implies that even if an individual has no expectation of privacy in a license plate number, a privacy interest is somehow created by the entry of this information into a law-enforcement computer database. This argument flies in the face of established Fourth Amendment doctrine. First, despite the dissent's concerns over the information available in a LEIN search, Ellison had no privacy interest in the information retrieved by Officer Keely. The obvious purpose of maintaining law enforcement databases is to make information, such as the existence of outstanding warrants, readily available to officers carrying out legitimate law enforcement duties. The dissent fails to state how using a license plate number-in which there is no expectation of privacy-to retrieve other non-private information somehow creates a "search" for the purposes of the Fourth Amendment. . . . This is not a case where the police used a technology not available to the public to discover evidence that could not otherwise be obtained without "intrusion into a constitutionally-protected area." *Kyllo v. United States,* 533 U.S. 27, 34-35 (2001) (holding that the use of thermal-imaging technology to detect heat inside a private home violates the Fourth Amendment). The technology used in this case does not allow officers to access any previously-unobtainable information; it simply allows them to access information more quickly. As the information was obtained without intruding upon a constitutionally-protected area, there was no "search" for Fourth Amendment purposes. . . .

MOORE, J. dissenting. . . . The majority rests its conclusion that the Fourth Amendment was not implicated by the LEIN search on the relatively uncontroversial fact that the operator of a vehicle has no privacy interest in the particular combination of letters and numerals that make up his license-plate number, but pays short shrift to the crucial issue of how the license-plate information is used. . . . This approach misses the crux of the issue before the court: even if there is no privacy interest in the license-plate number per se, can the police, without any measure of heightened suspicion or other constraint on their discretion, conduct a search using the license-plate number to access information about the vehicle and its operator that may not otherwise be public or accessible by the police without heightened suspicion? . . . .

The use of a computer database to acquire information about drivers through their license-plate numbers without any heightened suspicion is in tension with many of the Fourth Amendment concerns expressed in *Delaware v. Prouse,* 440 U.S. 648, 655-63 (1979). In *Prouse,* the Supreme Court held that an officer may not stop a vehicle to check the operator's license and registration without "at least articulable and reasonable suspicion that a motorist is unlicensed or that an automobile is not registered, or that either the vehicle or an occupant is otherwise subject to seizure for violation of law," despite the fact that the state requires drivers to be licensed and vehicles to be registered. The Court stated that the Fourth Amendment aims "to safeguard the privacy and security of individuals against arbitrary invasions. . . . Thus, the permissibility of a particular law enforcement practice is judged by balancing its intrusion on the individual's Fourth Amendment interests against its promotion of legitimate governmental interests." The Court then explained the constitutional concerns that flow from the unbridled discretion associated with permitting random searches of drivers' information:

> To insist neither upon an appropriate factual basis for suspicion directed at a particular automobile nor upon some other substantial and objective standard or rule to govern the exercise of discretion "would invite intrusions upon constitutionally guaranteed rights based on nothing more substantial than inarticulate hunches. . . ." *Terry v. Ohio,* 392 U.S. [1], at 22 [1968]. . . . When there is not probable cause to believe that a driver is violating any one of the multitude of applicable traffic and equipment regulations — or other articulable basis amounting to reasonable suspicion that the driver is unlicensed or his vehicle unregistered — we cannot conceive of any legitimate basis upon which a patrolman could decide that stopping a particular driver for a spot check would be more productive than stopping any other driver. This kind of standardless and unconstrained discretion is the evil the Court has discerned when in previous cases it has insisted that the discretion of the official in the field be circumscribed, at least to some extent. . . .

Although the license-plate search at issue here is arguably less invasive than a license-and-registration check, the constitutional concerns regarding abuse of discretion do not disappear simply because drivers are not stopped to conduct the license-plate search. First, a search can implicate the Fourth Amendment even when the individual does not know that she is being searched. Second, the balancing of Fourth Amendment interests also requires consideration of "psychological intrusion[s] visited upon" the individuals searched in assessing the extent of intrusion that a particular police practice imposes. *See Prouse,* 440 U.S. at 657. The psychological invasion that results from knowing that one's personal information is subject to search by the police, for no reason, at any time one is driving a car is undoubtedly grave.

Because the government incorrectly limits its Fourth Amendment analysis to the plain view of the license plate without exploring the constitutional implications of the subsequent LEIN search, it does not provide any explanation as to the governmental interests promoted by license-plate searches. . . .

In addition, the possibility and the reality of errors in the computer databases accessed by MDT systems lead to great concern regarding the potential for license-plate searches to result in unwarranted intrusions into privacy in the form of stops made purely on the basis of incorrect information. . . .

NOTES & QUESTIONS

1. *The Fourth Amendment and Government Data Mining.* Does the Fourth Amendment provide any limits on government data mining? Lee Tein argues that it does:

> The use of patterns discovered through data mining raises . . . particularity issues. Imagine a database of a million people and a hypothesis that those who meet certain criteria are highly likely to be terrorists. But you don't know whether any of these million people actually do meet these criteria; if you did, you wouldn't need to run the search. The basic problem is lack of particularized suspicion; data about these persons would be "searched" without any reason to believe either that the database contains evidence of terrorist activity or that any person "in" the database is a terrorist. . . .[62]

> When the government engages in data mining, it often analyzes information that it already possesses. Is this a search? If the government has information about a person in its records and analyzes it, does this trigger the Fourth Amendment?

In contrast, Richard Posner argues in favor of data mining: "Computer searches do not invade privacy because search programs are not sentient beings. Only the human search should raise constitutional or other legal issues."[63] Consider the following argument in response to Posner: "[T]here is human intervention in data mining even before the first automated search is run; humans will write the software, shape the database parameters, and decide on the kinds of matches that count. And the task of data mining itself is guided by some degree of human interaction."[64] To the extent there is a human element in data mining, how ought it to be regulated? Do the problems of data mining stem solely from the human element?

---

[62] Lee Tien, Privacy, *Technology and Data Mining*, 30 Ohio N.U. L. Rev. 389, 405 (2004).

[63] Richard Posner, *Privacy, Surveillance, and Law*, 75 U. Chi. L. Rev. 245 (2008).

[64] Ira Rubinstein, Ronald D. Lee & Paul M. Schwartz, *Data Mining and Internet Profiling*, 75 U. Chi. L. Rev. 261 (2008).

(c) DNA Databases

DNA Typing. "DNA fingerprinting" or "DNA typing" involves the comparison of DNA from two samples. At a crime scene, most often with violent crimes, the criminal might have unwittingly deposited genetic material. A pulled-out hair, a drop of blood, a scratched-off skin cell, semen, and so on can enable forensic scientists to extract DNA. The entire genome is not used, only particular portions or fragments of DNA that are known to contain differences among individuals. An early method of analyzing DNA was restriction fragment length polymorphism (RFLP). DNA was extracted from samples using special enzymes and cut into fragments and organized by size. These fragments were then exposed on X-ray film, where they formed a pattern of dark bands, which are unique to each type of DNA. Today, a newer technology called "short tandem repeat" (STR) analysis is the most common method of DNA typing. STR analysis examines length polymorphisms known as "short tandem repeats."[65]

The fact that a suspect's DNA matches the DNA found at a crime scene does not indicate with certainty that the suspect is likely to be the culprit or even is likely to have been at the crime scene. Statistically, a portion of the population will match the DNA found at a crime scene. What DNA evidence can determine with near certainty is that certain individuals do not match the DNA at the scene. In other words, DNA evidence can more accurately exclude individuals as suspects than include them.

CODIS. The FBI maintains a national DNA database known as the "Combined DNA Indexing System" (CODIS).[66] These DNA databases do not contain a person's entire genetic code, just fragments useful for identification.

The Fourth Amendment and DNA Collection. The following case involves a Fourth Amendment challenge to the creation of a DNA database. For the purposes of understanding this case, the Fourth Amendment requires that searches (looking around for evidence) and seizures (taking of items and evidence) be "reasonable" and generally be authorized by a warrant supported by probable cause. The warrant requirement ensures that a neutral judge or magistrate approves of the search and that the police have a good justification for a search. This typically means "individualized suspicion" — that there is a good reason to suspect that a particular individual has engaged in a crime. This requirement prevents searches that are "fishing expeditions." However, there are exceptions to the warrant requirement, as indicated by the case below.

UNITED STATES V. KINCADE

379 F.3d 813 (9th Cir. 2004) (en banc)

O'SCANNLAIN, J. (for the plurality). . . . Pursuant to the DNA Analysis Backlog Elimination Act of 2000 ("DNA Act"), individuals who have been convicted of

---

[65] *See* William C. Thompson, *DNA Testing*, in 2 *Encyclopedia of Crime and Punishment* 537 (David Levinson ed., 2002).

[66] *See id.*

certain federal crimes and who are incarcerated, or on parole, probation, or supervised release must provide federal authorities with "a tissue, fluid, or other bodily sample . . . on which a[n] . . . analysis of the [sample's] deoxyribonucleic acid (DNA) identification information" can be performed. . . .

Once collected by a phlebotomist, qualified federal offenders' blood samples are turned over to the [FBI] for DNA analysis — the identification and recording of an individual's "genetic fingerprint. . . .

. . . [T]he resulting record is loaded into the Bureau's Combined DNA Index System ("CODIS") — a massive centrally-managed database linking DNA profiles culled from federal, state, and territorial DNA collection programs, as well as profiles drawn from crime-scene evidence, unidentified remains, and genetic samples voluntarily provided by relatives of missing persons. . . .

On July 20, 1993, driven by escalating personal and financial troubles, decorated Navy seaman Thomas Cameron Kincade robbed a bank using a firearm. . . . He pleaded guilty . . . and was sentenced to 97 months imprisonment, followed by three years' supervised release. . . .

On March 25, 2002, Kincade's probation officer asked him to submit a blood sample pursuant to the DNA Act. He refused, eventually explaining that his objections were purely a matter of personal preference — in his words, "not a religious conviction." . . . [The court concluded that Kincade's refusal to follow his probation officer's order was a violation of his supervised release. Kincade was sentenced to four months' imprisonment. Kincade challenges the DNA Act under the Fourth Amendment.]

"The touchstone of our analysis under the Fourth Amendment is always 'the reasonableness in all the circumstances of the particular governmental invasion of a citizen's personal security.' " *Pennsylvania v. Mimms,* 434 U.S. 106 (1977) (quoting *Terry v. Ohio,* 392 U.S. 1 (1968)).

Ordinarily, the reasonableness of a search depends on governmental compliance with the Warrant Clause, which requires authorities to demonstrate probable cause to a neutral magistrate and thereby convince him to provide formal authorization to proceed with a search by issuance of a particularized warrant. However, the general rule of the Warrant Clause is not unyielding. . . .

[The court concluded that a warrant or probable cause was not required. Instead, it proceeded to approach the case by conducting a Fourth Amendment "reasonableness" balance between privacy and the governmental interest.]

In evaluating the totality of the circumstances, we must balance the degree to which DNA profiling interferes with the privacy interests of qualified federal offenders against the significance of the public interests served by such profiling.

As we have recognized, compulsory blood tests implicate the individual's interest in bodily integrity — "a cherished value of our society." *Schmerber v. California,* 384 U.S. 757 (1966). Nonetheless, it is firmly established that "the intrusion occasioned by a blood test is not significant, since such 'tests are a commonplace in these days of periodic physical examinations.'" . . .

The concerns raised by amici and by Judge Reinhardt in his dissent are indeed weighty ones, and we do not dismiss them lightly. . . . In our system of government, courts base decisions not on dramatic Hollywood fantasies. . . . If, as Kincade's aligned amici and Judge Reinhardt's dissent insist, and when, some future program permits the parade of horribles the DNA Act's opponents fear . . . we have every confidence that courts will respond appropriately. As currently structured and implemented, however, the DNA Act's compulsory profiling of qualified federal offenders can only be described as minimally invasive — both in terms of the bodily intrusion it occasions, and the information it lawfully produces.

In contrast, the interests furthered by the federal DNA Act are undeniably compelling. By establishing a means of identification that can be used to link conditional releasees to crimes committed while they are at large, compulsory DNA profiling serves society's "'overwhelming interest' in ensuring that a parolee complies with the requirements [of his release] and is returned to prison if he fails to do so." The deterrent effect of such profiling similarly fosters society's enormous interest in reducing recidivism. . . . Finally, by contributing to the solution of past crimes, DNA profiling of qualified federal offenders helps bring closure to countless victims of crime who long have languished in the knowledge that perpetrators remain at large. Together, the weight of these interests is monumental. . . .

. . . [We] conclude that compulsory DNA profiling of qualified federal offenders is reasonable under the totality of the circumstances. . . . [T]he DNA Act satisfies the requirements of the Fourth Amendment. . . .

REINHARDT, PREGERSON, KOZINSKI, and WARDLAW, JJ. dissenting. Today this court approves the latest installment in the federal government's effort to construct a comprehensive national database into which basic information concerning American citizens will be entered and stored for the rest of their lives — although no majority exists with respect to the legal justification for this conclusion. . . . We would be lucky indeed if it were possible to so limit the effect of their opinions. For, under the rationales they espouse, . . . all Americans will be at risk, sooner rather than later, of having our DNA samples permanently placed on file in federal cyberspace, and perhaps even worse, of being subjected to various other governmental programs providing for suspicionless searches conducted for law enforcement purposes.

Neither Supreme Court precedent nor any established rule of Fourth Amendment law supports today's plurality or concurring opinion. Never has the Court approved of a search like the one we confront today: a programmatic search designed to produce and maintain evidence relating to ordinary criminal wrongdoing, yet conducted without any level of individualized suspicion. . . .

The approval of such a program carries with it all of the dangers inherent in allowing the government to collect and store information about its citizens in a centralized place. J. Edgar Hoover terrorized leaders of the civil rights movement by exploiting the information he collected in his files. Our government's surveillance and shameful harassment of suspected communists and alleged communist-sympathizers in the middle of the twentieth century depended largely on the centralization of information collected about countless numbers of non-communist members of our citizenry — often by means that violated the Fourth Amendment. The same was true of the Palmer Raids a few decades earlier and of our roundup of Japanese Americans and their placement in internment camps during World War Two. *See generally* Daniel J. Solove, *Digital Dossiers and the Dissipation of Fourth Amendment Privacy,* 75 S. Cal. L. Rev. 1083 (2002).

Even governments with benign intentions have proven unable to regulate or use wisely vast stores of information they collect regarding their citizens. The problem with allowing the government to collect and maintain private information about the intimate details of our lives is that the bureaucracy most often in charge of the information "is poorly regulated and susceptible to abuse. This [ ] has profound social effects because it alters the balance of power between the government and the people, exposing individuals to a series of harms, increasing their vulnerability and decreasing the degree of power that they exercise over their lives." *Id.* at 1105. To allow such information to be collected through the compulsory extraction of blood from the bodies of non-consenting Americans runs contrary to the values on which this country was founded. . . .

[The totality of the circumstances approach does not apply in this context.]

Indeed, the "totality of the circumstances" test was designed to guide the Court in its probable cause and reasonable suspicion determinations. The test has never been used, however, to justify suspicionless law enforcement searches. To the contrary, in "totality of the circumstances" cases, the presence of *some level* of suspicion has always been a given and a *sine qua non.* Cases involving suspicionless programmatic search regimes are not "general" Fourth Amendment cases. That is why the plurality cannot cite a single case that has applied the totality of the circumstances test to a regime of suspicionless searches. . . .

KOZINSKI, J. dissenting: . . . If collecting DNA fingerprints can be justified on the basis of the plurality's multi-factor, gestalt high-wire act, then it's hard to see how we can keep the database from expanding to include everybody. Of course, anyone who already has to give up bodily fluids for alcohol or drug testing — airline pilots, high school athletes, customs inspectors and people suspected of driving while intoxicated — would be easy prey under the mushy multi-factor test. But, with only a little waggling, we can shoehorn the rest of us in. As the plurality notes, blood is taken from us from the day we are born pretty much till the day we die, and on many days in between. What exactly happens to that blood after it leaves our veins? Most of us don't know or care, presuming (if we consider it at all) that whatever isn't used for testing is discarded. But what if Congress were to require medical labs to submit the excess blood for DNA fingerprinting so it can be included in CODIS? . . .

This isn't an issue we can leave for another day. Later, when further expansions of CODIS are proposed, information from the database will have been credited with solving hundreds or thousands of crimes, and we will have become inured to the idea that the government is entitled to hold large databases of DNA fingerprints. . . . A highly expansive opinion like the plurality's, one that draws no hard lines and revels in the boon that new technology will provide to law enforcement, is an engraved invitation to future expansion. And when that inevitable expansion comes, we will look to the regime we approved today as the new baseline and say, this too must be OK because it's just one small step beyond the last thing we approved. My colleagues in the plurality assure us that, when that day comes, they will stand vigilant and guard the line, but by then the line — never very clear to begin with — will have shifted. The fishbowl will look like home. . . .

NOTES & QUESTIONS

1. ***DNA Databases: Defining the Privacy Injury.*** What is the privacy injury with regard to the use of DNA databases? Is it the physical invasion of the body to remove the blood? Or is it the fact that DNA can include significant information about a person? Currently, DNA identification only involves a small portion of one's DNA. The entire genome is not mapped out. Sequencing is done for certain known sites where particular genes show a significant variability, as much of our DNA is identical. DNA databases do not contain the entire DNA of an individual but only samples of certain genes. Should this fact alleviate any concern over DNA databases? What if one's entire genome were included in the database?

2. ***The Law of DNA Databases.*** Thus far, every other circuit to examine whether DNA databases violate the Fourth Amendment has upheld them. *See, e.g., Jones v. Murray,* 962 F.2d 302 (4th Cir. 1992); *Boling v. Romer,* 101 F.3d 1336 (10th Cir. 1996); *Shaffer v. Saffle,* 148 F.3d 1180 (10th Cir. 1998); *Roe v. Marcotte,* 193 F.3d 72 (2d Cir. 1999).

   Does the existence of the DNA databases mean that for offenders in the database, they will always be investigated (by a search in the database) every time there is a certain type of crime? Is this any different from what is already done through the use of fingerprints and mug shots?

3. ***How Expansive Should DNA Databases Be?*** Although the law appears to be clear that DNA samples can be collected from convicts, can samples also be collected from arrestees? In 2006, Congress authorized the collection of DNA from "individuals who are arrested, facing charges, or convicted." 42 U.S.C. § 14135a(a)(1)(A). Consider the following case:

MARYLAND V. KING

133 S. Ct. 1958 (2013)

KENNEDY, J. . . . In 2003 a man concealing his face and armed with a gun broke into a woman's home in Salisbury, Maryland. He raped her. The police were unable to identify or apprehend the assailant based on any detailed description or other evidence they then had, but they did obtain from the victim a sample of the perpetrator's DNA.

In 2009 Alonzo King was arrested in Wicomico County, Maryland, and charged with first- and second-degree assault for menacing a group of people with a shotgun. As part of a routine booking procedure for serious offenses, his DNA sample was taken by applying a cotton swab or filter paper—known as a buccal swab—to the inside of his cheeks. The DNA was found to match the DNA taken from the Salisbury rape victim. King was tried and convicted for the rape. Additional DNA samples were taken from him and used in the rape trial, but there seems to be no doubt that it was the DNA from the cheek sample taken at the time he was booked in 2009 that led to his first having been linked to the rape and charged with its commission.

The Court of Appeals of Maryland, on review of King's rape conviction, ruled that the DNA taken when King was booked for the 2009 charge was an unlawful seizure because obtaining and using the cheek swab was an unreasonable search of the person. It set the rape conviction aside. This Court granted certiorari and now reverses the judgment of the Maryland court. . . .

All 50 States require the collection of DNA from felony convicts, and respondent does not dispute the validity of that practice. Twenty-eight States and the Federal Government have adopted laws similar to the Maryland Act authorizing the collection of DNA from some or all arrestees. . . .

It can be agreed that using a buccal swab on the inner tissues of a person's cheek in order to obtain DNA samples is a search. Virtually any "intrusio[n] into the human body," *Schmerber v. California*, 384 U.S. 757, 770 (1966), will work an invasion of " 'cherished personal security' that is subject to constitutional scrutiny," *Cupp v. Murphy*, 412 U.S. 291, 295 (1973).

To say that the Fourth Amendment applies here is the beginning point, not the end of the analysis. . . . As the text of the Fourth Amendment indicates, the ultimate measure of the constitutionality of a governmental search is 'reasonableness.' . . .

This application of "traditional standards of reasonableness" requires a court to weigh "the promotion of legitimate governmental interests" against "the degree to which [the search] intrudes upon an individual's privacy." . . .

The legitimate government interest served by the Maryland DNA Collection Act is one that is well established: the need for law enforcement officers in a safe and accurate way to process and identify the persons and possessions they must take into custody. . . .

An individual's identity is more than just his name or Social Security number, and the government's interest in identification goes beyond ensuring that the proper name is typed on the indictment. Identity has never been considered limited to the name on the arrestee's birth certificate. . . . An "arrestee may be carrying a false ID or lie about his identity," and "criminal history records . . . can be inaccurate or incomplete." . . .

The DNA collected from arrestees is an irrefutable identification of the person from whom it was taken. Like a fingerprint, the 13 CODIS loci are not themselves evidence of any particular crime, in the way that a drug test can by itself be evidence of illegal narcotics use. A DNA profile is useful to the police because it gives them a form of identification to search the records already in their valid possession. In this respect the use of DNA for identification is no different than matching an arrestee's face to a wanted poster of a previously unidentified suspect; or matching tattoos to known gang symbols to reveal a criminal affiliation; or matching the arrestee's fingerprints to those recovered from a crime scene. . . .

Second, law enforcement officers bear a responsibility for ensuring that the custody of an arrestee does not create inordinate "risks for facility staff, for the existing detainee population, and for a new detainee." DNA identification can provide untainted information to those charged with detaining suspects and detaining the property of any felon. For these purposes officers must know the type of person whom they are detaining, and DNA allows them to make critical choices about how to proceed. . . .

Third, looking forward to future stages of criminal prosecution, "the Government has a substantial interest in ensuring that persons accused of crimes are available for trials." A person who is arrested for one offense but knows that he has yet to answer for some past crime may be more inclined to flee the instant charges, lest continued contact with the criminal justice system expose one or more other serious offenses. . . .

Fourth, an arrestee's past conduct is essential to an assessment of the danger he poses to the public, and this will inform a court's determination whether the individual should be released on bail. . . .

Finally, in the interests of justice, the identification of an arrestee as the perpetrator of some heinous crime may have the salutary effect of freeing a person wrongfully imprisoned for the same offense. . . .

DNA identification is an advanced technique superior to fingerprinting in many ways, so much so that to insist on fingerprints as the norm would make little sense to either the forensic expert or a layperson. The additional intrusion upon the arrestee's privacy beyond that associated with fingerprinting is not significant, and DNA is a markedly more accurate form of identifying arrestees. . . .

By comparison to this substantial government interest and the unique effectiveness of DNA identification, the intrusion of a cheek swab to obtain a DNA sample is a minimal one. . . .

. . . [T]he CODIS loci come from noncoding parts of the DNA that do not reveal the genetic traits of the arrestee. . . .

And even if non-coding alleles could provide some information, they are not in fact tested for that end. . . .

Finally, the Act provides statutory protections that guard against further invasion of privacy. . . .

Upon these considerations the Court concludes that DNA identification of arrestees is a reasonable search that can be considered part of a routine booking procedure. When officers make an arrest supported by probable cause to hold for a serious offense and they bring the suspect to the station to be detained in custody, taking and analyzing a cheek swab of the arrestee's DNA is, like fingerprinting and photographing, a legitimate police booking procedure that is reasonable under the Fourth Amendment.

SCALIA, J. joined by GINSBURG, SOTOMOMAYOR, AND KAGAN, JJ. dissenting: The Fourth Amendment forbids searching a person for evidence of a crime when there is no basis for believing the person is guilty of the crime or is in possession of incriminating evidence. That prohibition is categorical and without exception; it lies at the very heart of the Fourth Amendment. Whenever this Court has allowed a suspicionless search, it has insisted upon a justifying motive apart from the investigation of crime.

It is obvious that no such noninvestigative motive exists in this case. The Court's assertion that DNA is being taken, not to solve crimes, but to *identify* those in the State's custody, taxes the credulity of the credulous. And the Court's comparison of Maryland's DNA searches to other techniques, such as fingerprinting, can seem apt only to those who know no more than today's opinion has chosen to tell them about how those DNA searches actually work. . . .

The portion of the Court's opinion that explains the identification rationale is strangely silent on the actual workings of the DNA search at issue here. To know those facts is to be instantly disabused of the notion that what happened had anything to do with identifying King.

King was arrested on April 10, 2009, on charges unrelated to the case before us. That same day, April 10, the police searched him and seized the DNA evidence at issue here. What happened next? Reading the Court's opinion, particularly its insistence that the search was necessary to know "who [had] been arrested," one might guess that King's DNA was swiftly processed and his identity thereby confirmed—perhaps against some master database of known DNA profiles, as is done for fingerprints. After all, was not the suspicionless search here crucial to avoid "inordinate risks for facility staff" or to "existing detainee population"? Surely, then—*surely*—the State of Maryland got cracking on those grave risks immediately, by rushing to identify King with his DNA as soon as possible.

Nothing could be further from the truth. Maryland officials did not even begin the process of testing King's DNA that day. Or, actually, the next day. Or the day after that. And that was for a simple reason: Maryland law forbids them to do so. A "DNA sample collected from an individual charged with a crime . . . *may not* be tested or placed in the statewide DNA data base system prior to the first scheduled arraignment date." And King's first appearance in court was not until three days after his arrest. . . .

Does the Court really believe that Maryland did not know whom it was arraigning? . . . The truth, known to Maryland and increasingly to the reader: this search had nothing to do with establishing King's identity. . . .

Today, it can fairly be said that fingerprints really are used to identify people— so well, in fact, that there would be no need for the expense of a separate, wholly redundant DNA confirmation of the same information. What DNA adds—what makes it a valuable weapon in the law-enforcement arsenal—is the ability to solve unsolved crimes, by matching old crime-scene evidence against the profiles of people whose identities are already known. That is what was going on when King's DNA was taken, and we should not disguise the fact. Solving unsolved crimes is a noble objective, but it occupies a lower place in the American pantheon of noble objectives than the protection of our people from suspicionless law-enforcement searches. The Fourth Amendment must prevail. . . .

Today's judgment will, to be sure, have the beneficial effect of solving more crimes; then again, so would the taking of DNA samples from anyone who flies on an airplane (surely the Transportation Security Administration needs to know the "identity" of the flying public), applies for a driver's license, or attends a public school. Perhaps the construction of such a genetic panopticon is wise. But I doubt that the proud men who wrote the charter of our liberties would have been so eager to open their mouths for royal inspection.

NOTES & QUESTIONS

1. *Government Data Mining?* The majority opinion and the dissent clash on the true purpose for the DNA collection, with the dissent claiming that the main interest is the "ability to solve unsolved crimes, by matching old crime-scene evidence against the profiles of people whose identities are already known." If this were the government's interest, why are the dissenters so against it?

Compare the majority opinion's view of the privacy interest with the dissent's. The majority focuses on the physical invasion and the potential for the DNA information to reveal genetic traits. In contrast, the dissent views the privacy interest as the avoidance of creating a "genetic panopticon." To what extent does the dissent see DNA matching as akin to a form of data mining or dragnet search?

2. ***Broadening the Concept of "Identity."*** On its surface, *King v. Maryland* is another Fourth Amendment case involving balancing tests. Erin Murphy explains, however, that "the most radical aspect of *King* is its reimagination of the idea of 'identity' to include criminal history and other information beyond 'name and social security number."[67] For the Supreme Court in *King*, the government had an interest in knowing "whom they are dealing with." Information in identity currently can involve criminal history, a record of violence or mental disorder, and for decisions about bail, factors such as family ties, employment status, character, and mental condition. Murphy notes that "risk assessment tools of questionable reliability" are already used to "help make determinations from bail to sentencing and beyond, including civil commitment of sexual predators." She argues: "Folding a genetic assessment into the profile — so that the offenders report includes both performance on a clinical or actuarial instrument as well as any genetic predispositions that may be of concern — hardly seems incredible." Should the *King* Court have addressed the retention of the full DNA sample in this case? Or is that simply a matter for another day and case?

3. ***DNA Dragnets.*** As Erin Murphy explains, a DNA dragnet involves law enforcement officials investigating an offense by descending on a community and requesting "voluntary submission of DNA samples from the entire eligible population."[68]

For example, in 1987, British authorities collected DNA samples from every male citizen in Leicestershire after two young women were raped. This technique has been dubbed a "DNA dragnet," and this case was explored in depth in Joseph Wambaugh's *The Blooding* (1989). Since 1995, British authorities have been collecting DNA from everybody taken into police custody.

In 2000, in a small rural Australian village, police used a mass DNA screening investigation technique to identify the man who raped a 91-year-old woman. Villagers were free to refuse the DNA test, but critics said that the DNA testing was not really voluntary because a person who refused would appear guilty in the eyes of the rest of the village.

DNA dragnets have also occurred in the United States on many occasions. For example, in February 2008, the Daytona Beach Police responded to a serial killer targeting prostitutes by taking DNA samples from "persons of interest" during traffic stops and announcing plans to take DNA samples from anyone arrested in that locality beginning in the near future.

---

[67] Erin Murphy, *License, Registration, Cheek Swab*, 127 Harv. L. Rev. 161 (2013).

[68] Erin Murphy, *The New Forensics,* 95 Cal. L. Rev. 721 (2007).

Will the scope of DNA "dragnets" spread to involve more and more people? What legal challenges can be raised to DNA dragnets?

4. *A National DNA Database?* What is wrong with the government having a DNA database of convicts and doing searches to identify the perpetrators of crimes? Would your opinion change if the database contained the DNA of everybody, not just those who were convicted of a crime? Would a national DNA database consisting of DNA for every citizen collected through a mandatory collection program be constitutional? Suppose that the DNA were obtained without requiring a physical intrusion into the body. Would this affect your view of the constitutionality of the national DNA database?

C. IDENTIFICATION RECORDS AND REQUIREMENTS

When should the government be able to mandate the identification of people? One common method used in many countries is to require people to carry identification cards or papers. Such an approach has generally been rejected in the United States, though there are a number of identification requirements. Are there Constitutional or other legal limitations on the extent to which people can be made to carry identification or otherwise identify themselves?

The ability to authenticate identity has important social benefits. It enables greater accountability and efficiency in economic transactions. Quickly and accurately linking people to data can also be useful when others need to learn information about them (e.g., when doctors need to obtain a person's medical history). Identification systems can promote security by enabling the better detection of criminals and terrorists. Additionally, requiring identification can prevent fraud.

However, greater identification makes anonymity more difficult, and in many instances, impossible. Further, identification can alter the type of society we are building, curtailing freedom and subjecting people to the ills of bureaucracy. As Roger Clarke observes:

> The need to identify oneself may be intrinsically distasteful to some people. For example, they may regard it as demeaning, or implicit recognition that the organisation with whom they are dealing exercises power over them. Many people accept that, at least in particular contexts, an organisation with which they are dealing needs to have their name. Some, however, feel it is an insult to human dignity to require them to use a number or code instead of a name. Some feel demeaned by demands, as part of the identification process, that they reveal information about themselves or their family, or embarrassed at having to memorize a password or PIN.[69]

---

[69] Roger Clarke, *Human Identification in Information Systems: Management Challenges and Public Policy Issues*, 7 Information Tech. & People 6 (1994), available at http://www.anu.edu.au/people/Roger.Clarke/DV/HumanID.html.

1. IDENTIFICATION AND THE CONSTITUTION

In *Kolender v. Lawson*, 461 U.S. 352 (1983), the Court considered a facial challenge to a law that required any person who "loiters or wanders . . . without apparent reason or business" to "identify himself and to account for his presence when requested by any peace officer to do so." The Court struck down the statute as unconstitutionally vague:

> . . . [The statute] as presently drafted and construed by the state courts, contains no standard for determining what a suspect has to do in order to satisfy the requirement to provide a "credible and reliable" identification. As such, the statute vests virtually complete discretion in the hands of the police to determine whether the suspect has satisfied the statute and must be permitted to go on his way in the absence of probable cause to arrest. An individual, whom police may think is suspicious but do not have probable cause to believe has committed a crime, is entitled to continue to walk the public streets "only at the whim of any police officer" who happens to stop that individual under § 647(e). Our concern here is based upon the potential for arbitrarily suppressing First Amendment liberties. In addition, [the statute] implicates consideration of the constitutional right to freedom of movement.

Justice Brennan concurred, arguing that the statute also violated the Fourth Amendment:

> . . . [U]nder the Fourth Amendment, police officers with reasonable suspicion that an individual has committed or is about to commit a crime may detain that individual, using some force if necessary, for the purpose of asking investigative questions. They may ask their questions in a way calculated to obtain an answer. But they may not compel an answer, and they must allow the person to leave after a reasonably brief period of time unless the information they have acquired during the encounter has given them probable cause sufficient to justify an arrest.

In *Carey v. Nevada Gaming Control Board*, 279 F.3d 873 (9th Cir. 2002), James Carey was detained by an official of the Nevada Gaming Control Board on suspicion of cheating while gambling. When asked to identify himself verbally or through identification documents, Carey refused. Although the official determined that there was no probable cause that Carey violated gaming laws, the official arrested Carey for refusing to identify himself. The official cited two statutes that required individuals detained by officials to identify themselves or else face criminal sanctions. Carey spent the evening in prison. No charges were brought against him. Carey sued under § 1983 alleging a violation of, among other things, his Fourth Amendment rights. The court agreed with Carey:

> [S]uch [identification] statutes violate the Fourth Amendment because as a result of the demand for identification, the statutes bootstrap the authority to arrest on less than probable cause and because the serious intrusion on personal security outweighs the mere possibility that identification might provide a link leading to arrest. . . . [The official] was able to arrest Carey even though there was no probable cause to believe that Carey had violated the gaming laws, and even though Carey's name was not relevant to determining whether Carey had cheated. An arrest under such circumstances is unreasonable. We therefore hold that Carey's arrest violated the Fourth Amendment.

HIIBEL V. SIXTH JUDICIAL DISTRICT COURT

542 U.S. 177 (2004)

KENNEDY, J. The petitioner was arrested and convicted for refusing to identify himself during a stop allowed by *Terry v. Ohio,* 392 U.S. 1 (1968). [Hiibel] challenges his conviction under the Fourth and Fifth Amendments to the United States Constitution. . . .

The sheriff's department in Humboldt County, Nevada, received an afternoon telephone call reporting an assault. The caller reported seeing a man assault a woman in a red and silver GMC truck on Grass Valley Road. Deputy Sheriff Lee Dove was dispatched to investigate. When the officer arrived at the scene, he found the truck parked on the side of the road. A man was standing by the truck, and a young woman was sitting inside it. The officer observed skid marks in the gravel behind the vehicle, leading him to believe it had come to a sudden stop.

The officer approached the man and explained that he was investigating a report of a fight. The man appeared to be intoxicated. The officer asked him if he had "any identification on [him]," which we understand as a request to produce a driver's license or some other form of written identification. The man refused and asked why the officer wanted to see identification. The officer responded that he was conducting an investigation and needed to see some identification. The unidentified man became agitated and insisted he had done nothing wrong. The officer explained that he wanted to find out who the man was and what he was doing there. After continued refusals to comply with the officer's request for identification, the man began to taunt the officer by placing his hands behind his back and telling the officer to arrest him and take him to jail. This routine kept up for several minutes: the officer asked for identification 11 times and was refused each time. After warning the man that he would be arrested if he continued to refuse to comply, the officer placed him under arrest.

We now know that the man arrested on Grass Valley Road is Larry Dudley Hiibel. Hiibel was charged with "willfully resist[ing], delay[ing], or obstruct[ing] a public officer in discharging or attempting to discharge any legal duty of his office" . . . . The government reasoned that Hiibel had obstructed the officer in carrying out his duties under § 171.123, a Nevada statute that defines the legal rights and duties of a police officer in the context of an investigative stop. Section 171.123 provides in relevant part:

> 1. Any peace officer may detain any person whom the officer encounters under circumstances which reasonably indicate that the person has committed, is committing or is about to commit a crime. . . .
>
> 3. The officer may detain the person pursuant to this section only to ascertain his identity and the suspicious circumstances surrounding his presence abroad. Any person so detained shall identify himself, but may not be compelled to answer any other inquiry of any peace officer.

. . . Hiibel was convicted and fined $250. . . .

NRS § 171.123(3) is an enactment sometimes referred to as a "stop and identify" statute. . . .

Stop and identify statutes often combine elements of traditional vagrancy laws with provisions intended to regulate police behavior in the course of investigatory stops. The statutes vary from State to State, but all permit an officer to ask or require a suspect to disclose his identity. . . . In some States, a suspect's refusal to identify himself is a misdemeanor offense or civil violation; in others, it is a factor to be considered in whether the suspect has violated loitering laws. In other States, a suspect may decline to identify himself without penalty.

. . . In *Brown v. Texas,* 443 U.S. 47 (1979), the Court invalidated a conviction for violating a Texas stop and identify statute on Fourth Amendment grounds. The Court ruled that the initial stop was not based on specific, objective facts establishing reasonable suspicion to believe the suspect was involved in criminal activity. Absent that factual basis for detaining the defendant, the Court held, the risk of "arbitrary and abusive police practices" was too great and the stop was impermissible. Four Terms later, the Court invalidated a modified stop and identify statute on vagueness grounds. *See Kolender v. Lawson,* 461 U.S. 352 (1983). The California law in *Kolender* required a suspect to give an officer " 'credible and reliable' " identification when asked to identify himself. The Court held that the statute was void because it provided no standard for determining what a suspect must do to comply with it, resulting in " 'virtually unrestrained power to arrest and charge persons with a violation.' "

The present case begins where our prior cases left off. Here there is no question that the initial stop was based on reasonable suspicion, satisfying the Fourth Amendment requirements noted in *Brown.* Further, the petitioner has not alleged that the statute is unconstitutionally vague, as in *Kolender.* Here the Nevada statute is narrower and more precise. The statute in *Kolender* had been interpreted to require a suspect to give the officer "credible and reliable" identification. In contrast, the Nevada Supreme Court has interpreted NRS   § 171.123(3) to require only that a suspect disclose his name. As we understand it, the statute does not require a suspect to give the officer a driver's license or any other document. Provided that the suspect either states his name or communicates it to the officer by other means — a choice, we assume, that the suspect may make — the statute is satisfied and no violation occurs. . . .

Hiibel argues that his conviction cannot stand because the officer's conduct violated his Fourth Amendment rights. We disagree.

Asking questions is an essential part of police investigations. In the ordinary course a police officer is free to ask a person for identification without implicating the Fourth Amendment. Beginning with *Terry v. Ohio,* 392 U.S. 1 (1968), the Court has recognized that a law enforcement officer's reasonable suspicion that a person may be involved in criminal activity permits the officer to stop the person for a brief time and take additional steps to investigate further. . . .

Obtaining a suspect's name in the course of a *Terry* stop serves important government interests. Knowledge of identity may inform an officer that a suspect is wanted for another offense, or has a record of violence or mental disorder. On the other hand, knowing identity may help clear a suspect and allow the police to concentrate their efforts elsewhere. Identity may prove particularly important in cases such as this, where the police are investigating what appears to be a domestic assault. Officers called to investigate domestic disputes need to know whom they are dealing with in order to assess the situation, the threat to their own safety, and possible danger to the potential victim. . . .

Petitioner further contends that his conviction violates the Fifth Amendment's prohibition on compelled self-incrimination. The Fifth Amendment states that "[n]o person . . . shall be compelled in any criminal case to be a witness against himself." To qualify for the Fifth Amendment privilege, a communication must be testimonial, incriminating, and compelled.

Respondents urge us to hold that the statements NRS § 171.123(3) requires are nontestimonial, and so outside the Clause's scope. We decline to resolve the case on that basis. Even if these required actions are testimonial, . . . petitioner's challenge must fail because in this case disclosure of his name presented no reasonable danger of incrimination. . . .

In this case petitioner's refusal to disclose his name was not based on any articulated real and appreciable fear that his name would be used to incriminate him, or that it "would furnish a link in the chain of evidence needed to prosecute" him. As best we can tell, petitioner refused to identify himself only because he thought his name was none of the officer's business. . . . The narrow scope of the disclosure requirement is also important. One's identity is, by definition, unique; yet it is, in another sense, a universal characteristic. Answering a request to disclose a name is likely to be so insignificant in the scheme of things as to be incriminating only in unusual circumstances. Even witnesses who plan to invoke the Fifth Amendment privilege answer when their names are called to take the stand. Still, a case may arise where there is a substantial allegation that furnishing identity at the time of a stop would have given the police a link in the chain of evidence needed to convict the individual of a separate offense. In that case, the court can then consider whether the privilege applies, and, if the Fifth Amendment has been violated, what remedy must follow. We need not resolve those questions here.

STEVENS, J. dissenting. . . . A person's identity obviously bears informational and incriminating worth, "even if the [name] itself is not inculpatory." A name can provide the key to a broad array of information about the person, particularly in the hands of a police officer with access to a range of law enforcement databases. And that information, in turn, can be tremendously useful in a criminal prosecution. It is therefore quite wrong to suggest that a person's identity provides a link in the chain to incriminating evidence "only in unusual circumstances." . . .

NOTES & QUESTIONS

1. **Hiibel *and* Terry *Stops*.** A *Terry* stop is a special exception to ordinary Fourth Amendment procedures. Ordinarily, if a police officer wants to search a person, she needs a warrant supported by probable cause. If she wants to seize a person (i.e., detain or arrest a person), then she needs probable cause. *Terry* permits limited searches and seizures based on less than probable cause — reasonable suspicion that criminal activity is afoot. Prior to *Hiibel*, the only search permitted under *Terry* was a "frisk" for weapons. *Hiibel* suggests that the state can allow an officer to search in a different way — to compel a person to

identify herself under penalty of law. To what extent can such an expansion be justified under *Terry*?

2. ***The Fifth Amendment and Identification.*** The majority states: "Still, a case may arise where there is a substantial allegation that furnishing identity at the time of a stop would have given the police a link in the chain of evidence needed to convict the individual of a separate offense. In that case, the court can then consider whether the privilege applies, and, if the Fifth Amendment has been violated, what remedy must follow." Is the majority admitting that under certain circumstances, the application of the Nevada statute will violate the Fifth Amendment? How are such violations to be prevented? The opinion suggests that the privilege can be enforced after the fact, in court. Is this post-hoc remedy sufficient to protect people's Fifth Amendment rights?

3. ***The Breadth of* Hiibel.** How broad or narrow is *Hiibel*? Does the opinion imply that the police can request of every citizen an identity document? Several aspects of the opinion suggest it is quite narrow. First, the majority notes that "the statute does not require a suspect to give the officer a driver's license or any other document." The suspect is merely required to state his name. Second, the request for identification must be "reasonably related" to the purpose of a *Terry* stop, which itself requires reasonable suspicion that criminal activity is afoot. The majority states that "an officer may not arrest a suspect for failure to identify himself if the request for identification is not reasonably related to the circumstances justifying the stop."

Under what circumstances may a person who is stopped by the police lawfully withhold their name? For example, could a person with an outstanding warrant invoke a Fifth Amendment right not to reveal her name? How might the police respond in such a situation? Based on *Hiibel,* what other questions can a state demand a person answer?

4. ***Disparate Effects on Class and Race.*** Jamie L. Stulin argues that "history has suggested that when the Court diminishes privacy rights, it is often poor and minority populations who suffer the most."[70] Will *Hiibel* have a disproportionate impact on certain communities and neighborhoods?

5. ***Identification at the Airport.*** In *Gilmore v. Gonzales*, 435 F.3d 1125 (9th Cir. 2006), the court considered whether the requirement to show identification before boarding an airplane constituted a violation of the right to travel and the Fourth Amendment. On July 4, 2002, John Gilmore, a California resident and U.S. citizen, attempted to fly from Oakland International Airport to Baltimore-Washington International Airport. He later attempted to fly to Washington, D.C., from San Francisco International Airport. There, a United Airlines agent explained that a traveler without identification was subject to secondary screening, which involved a more intensive search than that to which most air travelers were subject.

Regarding the right to travel, the Ninth Circuit concluded that a person "does not possess a fundamental right to travel by airplane even though it is the most convenient mode of travel for him." The court stated that "the Constitution does

---

[70] Jamie L. Stulin, *Does* Hiibel *Redefine* Terry?, 54. Am. U. L.Rev. 1449, 1483 (2005).

not guarantee the right to travel by any particular form of transportation." Additionally, the court held that "the identification policy's 'burden' is not unreasonable. The identification policy requires that airline passengers either present identification or be subjected to a more extensive search. The more extensive search is similar to searches that we have determined were reasonable."

As for the Fourth Amendment, the Ninth Circuit concluded that the request for identification was not a seizure. An individual is seized within the meaning of the Fourth Amendment when, in light of all the circumstances, a reasonable person would have believed that she was not free to leave. Since people who fail to present identification are not arrested or otherwise detained, no seizure is involved. As the court noted, "Gilmore twice tried to board a plane without presenting identification and twice left the airport when he was unsuccessful." There was no threatened punishment for his noncompliance with the identification requirement; he was simply not permitted to board the plane.

Finally, the court held that if a passenger were to choose the search option, this would not be an unreasonable search under the Fourth Amendment because the passenger had consented to the search and the search is reasonable in light of its purpose and scope. Moreover, Gilmore has a meaningful choice. As the Ninth Circuit summarized: "He could have presented identification, submitted to a search, or left the airport."

2. SOCIAL SECURITY NUMBERS

The closest thing that the United States has to a national identifier is the Social Security number (SSN). A nine-digit identifier, the SSN was created in 1936 as part of the Social Security System. Because Social Security benefits would not be paid until a worker's retirement or death, a unique number was necessary to identify his or her account. At the time of its introduction, some observers worried that the new system would depersonalize individuals "by treating them as numbers."[71]

Over time, various federal agencies began to use the SSN for other purposes. In 1961, for example, the IRS was authorized by Congress to use SSNs as taxpayer identification numbers. Subsequently, throughout the 1960s and 1970s, the SSN began to be used for military personnel, legally admitted aliens, anyone receiving or applying for federal benefits, food stamps, school lunch program eligibility, draft registration, and federal loans. State and local governments, as well as private sector entities such as schools and banks, began to use SSNs as well — for driver's licenses, birth certificates, blood donation, jury selection, workers' compensation, occupational licenses, and marriage licenses.[72]

In the early 1970s, the early spurt in the growing uses of the SSN raised serious concerns that the SSN would become a de facto universal identifier. In 1973, the

---

[71] James R. Beniger, *The Control Revolution* 409 (1986).

[72] For a chart of the increasing uses of the SSN, see Simson Garfinkel, *Database Nation: The Death of Privacy in the 21st Century* 33-34 (2000). *See also* Social Security Administration, *Social Security: Your Number* (1998), available at http://www.ssa.gov/pubs/10002.html.

Department of Health, Education, and Welfare issued a major report on privacy, criticizing the use of the SSN for identification purposes.[73]

In the Privacy Act of 1974, Congress partially responded to these concerns by prohibiting any governmental agency from denying any right, benefit, or privilege merely because an individual refused to disclose his or her SSN. Pursuant to § 7 of the Privacy Act:

> (a)(1) It shall be unlawful for any federal, state or local government agency to deny to any individual any right, benefit, or privilege provided by law because of such individual's refusal to disclose his Social Security account number.
>
> (2) The provisions of paragraph (1) of this subsection shall not apply with respect to —
>
> (A) Any disclosure which is required by federal statute, or
>
> (B) The disclosure of a social security number to any federal, state, or local agency maintaining a system of records in existence and operating before January 1, 1975, if such disclosure was required under statute or regulation adopted prior to such date to verify the identity of an individual.
>
> (b) Any federal, state, or local government agency which requests an individual to disclose his social security account number shall inform that individual whether that disclosure is mandatory or voluntary, by what statutory or other authority such number is solicited, and what uses will be made of it. 5 U.S.C. § 552a note.

The Privacy Act was passed to "curtail the expanding use of social security numbers by federal and local agencies and, by so doing, to eliminate the threat to individual privacy and confidentiality of information posed by common numerical identifiers." *Doyle v. Wilson*, 529 F. Supp. 1343, 1348 (D. Del. 1982).

Nevertheless, the use of SSNs continued to escalate after the Privacy Act. In 1977, a Privacy Protection Study Commission acknowledged a belief of some individuals "that being labeled with the SSN is dehumanizing." At the same time, it argued against further restrictions on the collection and use of the SSN; in its view, such measures "would be costly and cumbersome in the short run, ineffectual in the long run, and would also distract public attention from the need to formulate general policies on record exchanges."

Today, SSNs continue to be widely used. SSNs are collected by private-sector database firms from a number of public and nonpublic sources, such as court records and credit reports. It is currently legal for private firms to sell or disclose SSNs. As one commentator has observed:

> . . . [W]ith respect to collecting SSNs from individuals (1) federal law does not bar private actors from requesting SSNs or refusing to do business with someone if they refuse; and (2) state laws, although reaching a few private actors, contain no general prohibitions against SSN use or collection. . . . [G]overnmental use of SSNs is forbidden by Section 7 of the Privacy Act unless an exception applies, but . . . over the years Congress has made so many exceptions, that the collection of SSNs in government is quite widespread. This is the case for two reasons: Congress has passed many mandates of SSN use, and where states or private

---

[73] U.S. Department of Health, Education, and Welfare, *Report of the Secretary's Advisory Committee on Automated Personal Data Systems: Records, Computers, and the Rights of Citizens* xxxii (1973).

actors are left to decide whether or not to require the SSN, these entities generally choose to use it. . . .

. . . [T]he fact remains that governmental dissemination of personal identifying numbers is still widespread, and limits on private actors are also virtually nonexistent.[74]

GREIDINGER V. DAVIS

988 F.2d 1344 (4th Cir. 1993)

HAMILTON, J. The Constitution of Virginia requires all citizens otherwise qualified to vote and possessing a [Social Security number (SSN)] (registering after July 1, 1971) to provide their SSN on their Virginia Voter Registration Application (Application) in order to become registered to vote. Va. Const. art. II, § 2. If an individual otherwise qualified to vote does not possess a SSN, a "dummy" number will be provided. The scheme also provides that any registered voter may inspect the voter registration books in the Office of the General Registrar. In practice, these books contain the registration application of a registered voter.

The scheme further provides that Statewide Voter Registration lists containing the SSNs of voters can be obtained by: (a) candidates for election to further their candidacy, (b) political party committees for political purposes only, (c) incumbent office holders to report to their constituents, and (d) nonprofit organizations which promote voter participation and registration for that purpose only.

On July 24, 1991, appellant, Marc Alan Greidinger, filled out an Application, but refused to disclose his SSN. Because of this omission, Greidinger received a Denial of Application for Virginia Voter Registration from the General Registrar of Stafford County. Consequently, the Virginia State Board of Elections (the Board) prevented Greidinger from voting in the November 5, 1991, general election. . . .

Greidinger argues that the "public disclosure" accompanying Virginia's requirement that he provide his SSN on his voter registration application unconstitutionally burdens his right to vote as protected by the First and Fourteenth Amendments. In making this argument, Greidinger attacks two components of Virginia's voter registration scheme. He objects to Virginia's permitting registered voters to obtain another registered voter's SSN via § 24.1-56, which provides that all registration books, containing all of the registration forms, "shall be opened to the inspection of any qualified voter." He also objects to § 24.1-23(8) which allows dissemination of a registered voter's SSN to a candidate for election or political party nomination, political party committee or official, incumbent office holder, and nonprofit organization which promotes voter participation and registration.

Notably, Greidinger does not challenge Virginia's receipt and internal use of his SSN. He challenges only the dissemination of the SSN to the public pursuant to § 24.1-23(8) (candidates, political parties and officials, incumbents, and nonprofit organizations which promote voter participation and voter registration) and § 24.1-56 (general public). In addition, Greidinger does not assert any

---

[74] Flavio L. Komuves, *We've Got Your Number: An Overview of Legislation and Decisions to Control the Use of Social Security Numbers as Personal Identifiers*, 16 J. Marshall J. Computer & Info. L. 529, 569 (1998).

constitutional right to privacy in his SSN. Rather, he argues that the privacy interest in his SSN is sufficiently strong that his right to vote cannot be predicated on the disclosure of his SSN to the public or political entities.

It is axiomatic that "[n]o right is more precious in a free country than that of having a voice in the election of those who make the laws under which, as good citizens, we must live. Other rights, even the most basic, are illusory if the right to vote is undermined." Despite the fundamental nature of the right to vote, states may nevertheless impose certain qualifications on and regulate access to the franchise. . . .

. . . If a substantial burden exists [on the right to vote, the restriction] on the right to vote must serve a compelling state interest and be narrowly tailored to serve that state interest. . . .

Before we begin examining the burden on Greidinger's right to vote, we note that the Virginia statutes at issue, for all practical purposes, condition Greidinger's right to vote on the public disclosure of his SSN. . . .

Because Virginia's voter registration scheme conditions Greidinger's right to vote on the public disclosure of his SSN, we must examine whether this condition imposes a substantial burden. . . .

Since the passage of the Privacy Act, an individual's concern over his SSN's confidentiality and misuse has become significantly more compelling. For example, armed with one's SSN, an unscrupulous individual could obtain a person's welfare benefits or Social Security benefits, order new checks at a new address on that person's checking account, obtain credit cards, or even obtain the person's paycheck. Succinctly stated, the harm that can be inflicted from the disclosure of a SSN to an unscrupulous individual is alarming and potentially financially ruinous. These are just examples, and our review is by no means exhaustive; we highlight a few to elucidate the egregiousness of the harm. . . .

The statutes at issue compel a would-be voter in Virginia to consent to the possibility of a profound invasion of privacy when exercising the fundamental right to vote. As illustrated by the examples of the potential harm that the dissemination of an individual's SSN can inflict, Greidinger's decision not to provide his SSN is eminently reasonable. In other words, Greidinger's fundamental right to vote is substantially burdened to the extent the statutes at issue permit the public disclosure of his SSN.

Having identified that Greidinger's right to vote is substantially burdened by the public disclosure of his SSN, we must next determine whether Virginia has advanced a compelling state interest that justifies the disclosure and dissemination of his SSN. If Virginia advances a compelling state interest, we must determine whether disclosure of the SSN is narrowly tailored to fulfill that state interest.

. . . Unquestionably, Virginia has a compelling state interest in preventing voter fraud and promoting voter participation. However, the inquiry does not end here. We must determine whether the disclosure of the SSN under § 24.1-23(8) and/or § 24.1-56 is narrowly tailored to fulfill that state interest. We conclude that it is not.

Virginia's voter registration form requires a registrant to supply, among other things, his name, address, SSN, age, place of birth, and county of previous registration. Virginia's interest in preventing voter fraud and voter participation could easily be met without the disclosure of the SSN and the attendant possibility of a serious invasion of privacy that would result from that disclosure. . . . Most assuredly, an address or date of birth would sufficiently distinguish among voters that shared a common name. Moreover, the same state interest could be achieved through the use of a voter registration number as opposed to a SSN. . . . Thus, to the extent § 24.1-23(8) and § 24.1-56 allow Virginia's voter registration scheme to "sweep [ ] broader than necessary to advance electoral order," it creates an intolerable burden on Greidinger's fundamental right to vote.

NOTES & QUESTIONS

1. *Is There a Reasonable Expectation of Privacy in SSNs?* Consider *Beacon Journal v. City of Akron*, 70 Ohio St. 3d 605 (Ohio 1994). There, private parties requested that a city provide them with public employees' personnel records containing employees' names, addresses, telephone numbers, birth dates, education, employment status, and SSNs. The city provided the records with the SSNs deleted. The private parties sued to obtain the SSNs. The court concluded that the SSNs were not "public records" for the purposes of Ohio's Public Records Act:

> . . . R.C. 149.43(A) expressly excludes the release of records which would violate state or federal law. Because we find that the disclosure of the SSNs would violate the federal constitutional right to privacy, we find them to be excluded from mandatory disclosure. . . .
>
> We must determine whether the city employees have a legitimate expectation of privacy in their SSNs and then whether their privacy interests outweigh those interests benefited by disclosure of the numbers. . . .
>
> Due to the federal legislative scheme involving the use of SSNs, city employees have a legitimate expectation of privacy in their SSNs. [The court quoted § 7 of the Privacy Act of 1974.] . . .
>
> Congress when enacting the Privacy Act of 1974 was codifying the societal perception that SSNs should not to be available to all. This legislative scheme is sufficient to create an expectation of privacy in the minds of city employees concerning the use and disclosure of their SSNs. . . .
>
> The city's refusal to release its employees' SSNs does not significantly interfere with the public's right to monitor governmental conduct. The numbers by themselves reveal little information about the city's employees. The city provided appellees with enormous amounts of other information about each city employee; only the SSNs numbers were deleted. . . .
>
> While the release of all city employees' SSNs would provide inquirers with little useful information about the organization of their government, the release of the numbers could allow an inquirer to discover the intimate, personal details of each city employee's life, which are completely irrelevant to the operations of government. As the *Greidinger* court warned, a person's SSN is a device which can quickly be used by the unscrupulous to acquire a tremendous amount of information about a person. . . .
>
> Thanks to the abundance of data bases in the private sector that include the SSNs of persons listed in their files, an intruder using an SSN can quietly discover the intimate details of a victim's personal life without the victim ever knowing of the intrusion.

We find today that the high potential for fraud and victimization caused by the unchecked release of city employee SSNs outweighs the minimal information about governmental processes gained through the release of the SSNs. . . .

How does the legal theory in *Beacon* differ from that in *Greidinger*?

2. ***Disclosure of Social Security Numbers and the First Amendment.*** In *City of Kirkland v. Sheehan*, 29 Media L. Rep. 2367 (Wash. Sup. Ct. 2001), a group of law enforcement personnel sued the operators of a website critical of the police that listed their names, addresses, dates of birth, phone numbers, Social Security numbers, and other personal data. Although the court held that the disclosure of most of the personal data was protected under the First Amendment, the disclosure of Social Security numbers was different:

> In this case, as in numerous others, in the absence of a credible specific threat of harm, the publication of lawfully obtained addresses and telephone numbers, while certainly unwelcome to those who had desired a greater degree of anonymity, is traditionally viewed as having the ability to promote political speech. Publication may arguably expose wrongdoers and/or facilitate peaceful picketing of homes or worksites and render other communication possible.
>
> However, Social Security numbers are different from addresses and telephone numbers. The blanket identification of the Social Security numbers of a group of people, without more, does not provide a similar opportunity for or otherwise facilitate or promote substantive communication. It cannot reasonably be disputed that at its core the SSN is simply a government-originated identifying number. It is a key or a tool, created by the government and unique for each individual. Access to an individual's SSN enables a new holder to obtain access to and to control, manipulate or alter other personal information. In effect, access to an SSN allows a person, agency or company to more efficiently and effectively search for and seize information and assets of another, a power originally available only to the government and one which was subject to direct Constitutional restraint. . . .
>
> On its face, the SSN is a tag or an identifier which at best has only a distant possibility of a substantive communicative purpose. Keeping Social Security numbers private is a compelling interest for the government and citizens alike.
> . . .

3. NATIONAL IDENTIFICATION SYSTEMS

A national identification system is a nationwide system for identifying individuals. It consists of linking a database of information about individuals to an identifier, so that individuals can be readily connected to a stream of data about them.

More than 100 countries have some form of national identification card. These countries include most nations in Europe (including Germany, France, Spain, Greece, Finland, and others), Malaysia, Singapore, Thailand, and many others. However, Americans have repeatedly eschewed such systems. Throughout the latter half of the twentieth century, government officials entertained the idea of creating a national identification system on a number of occasions, but each time, the idea was rejected.

Proponents of national identification systems point to greater efficiencies, ease of use, prevention of fraud, and greater capacity to screen for terrorists and criminals. Critics contend that having one single identification card can vastly increase the dangers if the card is lost or stolen. Such a system of national identification could magnify the effects of fraud. To the extent that the card would bring added efficiency in terms of cardholders having to undergo less stringent security checks, the possessors of forged or stolen cards could better avoid such screenings. Cards could impede free movement throughout the country. Errors in the bureaucratic system administering the cards and linking the cardholders to information in a database could have a severe impact on people's lives. Further, national identifiers would be used by the private sector to link together data about individuals.

RICHARD SOBEL, *THE DEGRADATION OF POLITICAL IDENTITY UNDER A NATIONAL IDENTIFICATION SYSTEM*

8 B.U. J. Sci. & Tech. L. 37 (2002)

America is moving toward a system of national identification numbers, databanks, and identity cards that contradicts the constitutional and philosophical bases of democratic government and undermines the moral economy of political and personal identity. Because the kinds of problems that a national identification system ("NIDS") is supposed to solve tend to occur in relatively closed societies, the troubles a NIDS creates as a bureaucratic scheme may soon foreclose options and opportunities central to a free society. . . . The growing impact of NIDS on due process, burden of proof, freedom from search, free expression, freedom of travel, the right to employment, and federalism makes this issue particularly appropriate for contemporary ethical and policy analysis. . . .

The ongoing developments toward a NIDS, as privacy advocate Robert Ellis Smith notes, fundamentally contradict what it means to be an American. In an open democratic society, the government derives its powers from the consent of the governed, constitutions are developed to circumscribe state power, and activities such as work, travel, and medical care are readily available and treated in ways respectful of privacy. In contrast, the government in authoritarian societies bestows, or denies, identities and opportunities through identification numbers or documents, intruding into individuals' lives. In addition, especially because the government has the power to coerce individuals and to control their lives, people confront force when they must follow, or if they disobey, the government's directions. . . .

A formal NIDS would require an identity number, databank, and ID card. The system would begin by assigning each American resident a unique national identity number. Each citizen and identifiable immigrant would be uniquely identified by a numeral. Resident enumeration and data collection would begin at birth, defining each newborn as a data point to be tracked from cradle to grave through a government-issued number. Such a process has already begun with the relatively recent practice of issuing Social Security numbers at birth and requiring them to obtain marriage licenses and tax deductions for one's children of any age. . . .

For the existence and implementation of a NIDS, particularly a national identity card, there must also be a national computer databank organized by ID numbers. An individual would have to be entered into the databank to exist in a legal sense or to have a bureaucratic existence. Receiving an ID card would require meeting the criteria for being registered in the databank. ID numbers would be used for multiple purposes, and computer databanks would collect disparate pieces of information. For reasons of proposed efficiency, such a computer system would centralize and interconnect with educational, employment, social security, tax, and medical information. These data would paint a detailed portrait of each individual's habits and preference even though such collections would not be fully accurate or secure. One would not, moreover, have a political identity or be able to exercise political rights without proper ID. Inclusion in the databank would create a paper, plastic, or electronic person. . . .

Citizens or residents might be required to carry their national ID at all times or produce it when entering school, applying for a job or government benefits, and traveling away from home. . . .

Identity systems and documents have a long history of uses and abuses for social control and discrimination. Through the Civil War, slaves were required to carry passes in order to travel outside of plantations. . . .

A system of identification cards was used to isolate and round up Jews in Germany and other Nazi-occupied territories prior to World War II and in the occupied countries once the war began. All German Jews were required to apply for such cards by December 31, 1938. . . .

Even before the Japanese attack on Pearl Harbor, however, President Franklin Delano Roosevelt . . . ordered the Census Bureau to collect all information on "foreign-born and American-born Japanese" from the Census data lists. Within days, information from the 1930 and 1940 censuses on all Japanese Americans was gathered and distributed to the Federal Bureau of Investigation, the governors, and the top military officials in western states. Its use facilitated the internment of Japanese Americans on the West Coast.

NOTES & QUESTIONS

1. *National Identification Systems: Pro and Con.* As a policy matter, do you agree with Richard Sobel that efforts to collect and combine information should be blocked or perhaps undone? Consider the contrary view of Amitai Etzioni:

   American society incurs high costs — social, economic, and other kinds — because of its inability to identify many hundreds of thousands of violent criminals, white-collar criminals, welfare and credit card cheats, parents who do not pay child support, and illegal immigrants. If individuals could be properly identified, public safety would be significantly enhanced and social and economic costs would be reduced significantly. . . .

   In response to the claim that universal identifiers will cause a police state or totalitarian regime to arise, it should be noted that ID cards are quite common in European democracies and have been in place for quite some time without undermining these democracies. . . .

   If a totalitarian regime were to arise, and no universal identification system was in place, the new secret police would have only to consolidate existing private databases and add existing public ones (those maintained by the IRS, INS, FBI, and SSA, among others) to have a very elaborate description of most Americans. . . .[75]

What are the benefits of a national identification system? What are the costs? What privacy interests could a national identification card in the United States implicate?

2. *Anonymity.* Consider the cases on anonymity. What would be the impact of a national identification system on First Amendment values?

3. *The Intelligence Reform and Terrorism Prevention Act of 2004.* The Intelligence Reform and Terrorism Prevention Act of 2004 requires standardization of birth certificates and driver's licenses for acceptance by federal agencies. § 7212. The law also establishes standards for common machine-readable identity information to be included on each driver's license or personal identification card, including minimum data elements. Identification security standards are required to ensure that driver's licenses and personal identification cards are resistant to tampering, alteration, or counterfeiting. The cards must be capable of accommodating and ensuring the security of a digital photograph or other unique identifier. A state may confiscate a driver's license or personal identification card if any component or security feature of the document is compromised.

4. *The REAL ID Act.* The REAL ID Act of 2005 (Pub. L. No. 109-13) sets minimum document requirements for state driver's licenses or identification cards. Unless these standards are met, a federal agency is not to accept the state document in question for any official purposes.

The Act establishes the kinds of multiple documents that must be shown to verify identity before a license can be issued or renewed. Moreover, it requires states to produce standardized, tamper-resistant licenses that include machine-readable data. It also mandates states to store digital images of "identity source documents" (such as birth certificates) as well as the photographs on driver's licenses. It requires driver's license data to be kept in linked databases available to all states. Finally, undocumented immigrants will not be able to obtain a driver's license as the REAL ID Act requires evidence of lawful status in the United States to obtain a driver's license or ID card.

The REAL ID Act proved controversial from its time of enactment. Proponents of the law say it will help prevent terrorists and illegal immigrants from obtaining ID documents. Opponents of the law argue that it creates a national ID card and a de facto national ID database, and that it will not improve security. As security expert Bruce Schneier contends:

> [T]he main problem with any strong identification system is that it requires the existence of a database. In this case, it would have to be 50 linked databases of private and sensitive information on every American — one widely and instantaneously accessible from airline check-in stations, police cars, schools, and so on.

---

[75] Amitai Etzioni, *The Limits of Privacy* 103-104, 126, 130 (1999).

The security risks of this database are enormous. It would be a kludge of existing databases that are incompatible, full of erroneous data, and unreliable. Computer scientists don't know how to keep a database of this magnitude secure, whether from outside hackers or the thousands of insiders authorized to access it.

But even if we could solve all these problems, and within the putative $11 billion budget, we still wouldn't be getting very much security. A reliance on ID cards is based on a dangerous security myth, that if only we knew who everyone was, we could pick the bad guys out of the crowd.[76]

In contrast, Michael Chertoff, Secretary of the Department of Homeland Security (DHS), declared: "Do you think your privacy is better protected if someone can walk around with phony docs with your name and your social security number, or is your privacy better protected if you have the confidence that the identification relied upon is in fact reliable and uniquely tied to a single individual?"

---

[76] Bruce Schneier, *REAL ID: Costs and Benefits*, Schneier on Security (Jan. 30, 2007), http://www.schneier.com/blog/archives/2007/01/realid_costs_an.html.

CHAPTER 8

FINANCIAL DATA

CHAPTER OUTLINE

A. THE FAIR CREDIT REPORTING ACT

Increasingly, companies in the United States make sales based on credit. Since 1980, almost all homes and most new cars are purchased on credit. Well over half of retail items are purchased on credit as well.[1]

As a result of the centrality of different forms of consumer borrowing, consumer reporting agencies play an increasingly significant role in economic transactions. Consumer reporting agencies prepare credit reports about people's credit history for use by creditors seeking to loan people money. Credit reports contain financial information such as bankruptcy filings, judgments and liens, mortgage foreclosures, and checking account data. Some companies also prepare

---

[1] *See generally* Robert Ellis Smith, *Ben Franklin's Web Site: Privacy and Curiosity from Plymouth Rock to the Internet* 313-25 (2000); Steven L. Nock, *The Costs of Privacy: Surveillance and Reputation in America* (1993).

investigative consumer reports, which supplement the credit report with information about an individual's character and lifestyle. Creditors depend upon credit reports to determine whether or not to offer a person a loan as well as what interest rate to charge that person. Credit reports are also reviewed by some landlords before renting out an apartment.

Credit reports contain a "credit score" that is used to assess a person's credit risk. In many cases, a low score will not necessarily mean the denial of a loan, mortgage, or credit card; rather, it means that a higher rate of interest will be charged. As Evan Hendricks notes:

> According to the Fair Isaac Corporation, a leading developer of credit scoring models, one delinquent account can lower a credit score from 70 to 120 points. A consumer with excellent credit (credit score of 720-850) would pay about 7.85% interest rate for a home equity loan, while a consumer with marginal credit (640-659) would pay 9.2% and one with poor credit (500-559) would pay a 12.1% rate. The rate swings for a new car loan are even greater, with good credit risks paying a 5.2% rate, moderate risks paying 11.4% and poor risks paying 17.2%.[2]

Credit reports are not only used in connection with granting credit. Employers use credit reports to make hiring and promotion decisions. The issuance of professional licenses, such as admittance to the bar, also can require the examination of one's credit report.

There are three major national consumer reporting agencies: Experian, Equifax, and Trans Union. Each of these three companies has information on virtually every adult American citizen, and they routinely prepare credit reports about individuals.

According to Peter Swire, our financial system has been shifting toward more traceable payment transactions: "The shift from cash to checks to credit and debit cards shows an evolution toward creating records, placing the records automatically in databases, and potentially linking the databases to reveal extremely detailed information about an individual's purchasing history."[3] This evolution is generating new problems for the protection of privacy.

In 1970, Congress passed the Fair Credit Reporting Act (FCRA), Pub. L. No. 90-321, to regulate consumer reporting agencies. The Act was inspired by allegations of abuse and lack of responsiveness of credit agencies to consumer complaints. In its statement of purpose, the FCRA states: "There is a need to insure that consumer reporting agencies exercise their grave responsibilities with fairness, impartiality, and a respect for the consumer's right to privacy." 15 U.S.C. § 1681. The FCRA requires credit reporting companies to provide an individual access to her records, establishes procedures for correcting information, and sets limitations on disclosure.

In 2003, Congress passed the Fair and Accurate Credit Transactions Act (FACTA), which amended FCRA. Evan Hendricks explains the impetus for passing the FACTA:

---

[2] Evan Hendricks, *Credit Scores and Credit Reports: How the System Really Works, What You Can Do* 3-4 (2004).

[3] Peter P. Swire, *Financial Privacy and the Theory of High-Tech Government Surveillance*, 77 Wash. U. L.Q. 461 (1999).

[K]ey provisions of the FCRA that preempted State law were set to expire on December 31, 2003. These provisions dealt with issues affecting billions of dollars in commerce: pre-approved credit card offers, duties on creditors (furnishers) to report accurately and to reinvestigate, and the sharing of personal data among corporate affiliates. Industry expressed fears that if legislation was not passed and the preemption expired, state legislatures would begin passing conflicting laws that would raise compliance costs, and worse, interfere with profits.

To consumer and privacy groups, legislation was long overdue because the 1996 FCRA Amendments were not getting the job done. All of the long-standing problems related to privacy and fair information practices persisted: inaccuracy, faulty reinvestigations, reinsertion, non-responsiveness, and lax security. More dramatically, identity theft had been crowned the nation's "fastest growing crime," and the biggest harm from identity theft, everyone knew, was to the privacy of credit reports. . . .

Both sides wanted legislation, but not the same legislation. Industry wanted a simple, straightforward bill that would do nothing more than make FCRA preemption permanent.

Consumer privacy groups called for a detailed reform bill that would set a "floor" of new protections, but which would leave the states free to go further.[4]

FACTA required credit bureaus to disclose credit scores to individuals. The requirement to disclose explanatory information regarding the basis for these credit scores is limited. As Danielle Citron and Frank Pasquale explain, "The law does not require credit scorers to tell individuals how much any given factor mattered to a particular score. . . . The industry remains highly opaque, with scored individuals unable to determine the exact consequences of their decisions" regarding financial matters.[5]

1. FCRA'S SCOPE AND STRUCTURE

Scope. FCRA applies to "any consumer reporting agency" that furnishes a "consumer report." 15 U.S.C. § 1681b. As a consequence, the scope of the FCRA turns on the definitions of "consumer report" and "consumer reporting agencies."

Consumer Report. A "consumer report" is any type of communication by a consumer reporting agency "bearing on a consumer's credit worthiness, credit standing, credit capacity, character, general reputation, personal characteristics, or mode of living." This communication must be used or expected to be used in part to establish a consumer's eligibility for credit, insurance, employment, or other permissible uses of credit reports as defined in FCRA. 15 U.S.C. § 1681a.

Consumer Reporting Agency. A "consumer reporting agency" is defined as "[a]ny person which, for monetary fees, dues, or on a cooperative nonprofit basis, regularly engages in whole or in part in the practice of assembling or evaluating consumer credit information or other information on consumers for the purpose of

[4] Hendricks, *Credit Scores, supra*, at 307-08.
[5] Danielle Keats Citron & Frank Pasquale, *The Scored Society: Due Process for Automated Predictions*, 89 Wash. L. Rev. 1, 17 (2014).

furnishing consumer reports to third parties." § 1681b(f).

Courts have held that "even if a report is used or expected to be used for a non-consumer purpose, it may still fall within the definition of a consumer report if it contains information that was originally collected by a consumer reporting agency with the expectation that it would be used for a consumer purpose." *Ippolito v. WNS, Inc.*, 864 F.2d 440 (7th Cir. 1988); *Bakker v. McKinnon*, 152 F.3d 1007 (8th Cir. 1998).

FTC and CFBP Enforcement. For the first 40 years after the passage of FCRA, the Federal Trade Commission (FTC) was the agency mainly responsible for rulemaking and enforcement under FCRA.

In 2010, the Dodd-Frank Act created a new federal agency called the Consumer Financial Protection Bureau (CFPB) and assigned it primary enforcement and rulemaking authority for FCRA. However, the FTC still retains some FCRA enforcement power and shares this with the CFPB.

In 2012, the FTC and CFPB signed a memorandum of understanding regarding coordinating their enforcement of FCRA.[6]

Private Right of Action. Additionally, people who are harmed by violations of FCRA can sue for negligent or willful failure to comply with FCRA's requirements.

Preemption. FCRA preempts state law relatively broadly and does so by reserving a large number of subjects for federal law. These include the pre-screening of consumer reports, procedures and requirements relating to the duties of a person who takes any adverse action with respect to a consumer, and procedures and requirements regarding the information contained in consumer reports. §§ 1681c-1, 1681t(b)(5). These are examples of subject matter preemption; the federal law occupies the regulatory area.

In 2003, FACTA amended FCRA by adding narrower restrictions targeted to mandated behavior. As an example, FACTA requires consumer reporting agencies to place fraud alerts on consumer credit files under certain circumstances. In so doing, it streamlines an area of industry procedures while, at the same time, permitting states to engage in further regulation regarding the larger subject area, which is identity theft.[7] As an example of "required conduct" preemption, FCRA requires consumer agencies to place fraud alerts on consumer credit files under certain circumstances. At the same time, it permits states to engage in further regulation regarding the larger subject area, which is identity theft.

---

[6] Memorandum of Understanding Between the Consumer Financial Protection Bureau and the Federal Trade Commission (Jan. 20, 2012) http://files.consumerfinance.gov/f/2012/01/FTC.MOUwSig.1.20.pdf

[7] For a discussion, see Paul M. Schwartz, *Preemption and Privacy*, 118 Yale L.J. 902, 943-44 (2009).

UNITED STATES V. SPOKEO, INC.

No. CV12-05001MMM(JHx) (C.D. Cal., June 7, 2012)

COMPLAINT

Plaintiff, the United States of America, acting upon notification and authorization to the Attorney General by the Federal Trade Commission ("FTC" or "Commission"), for its Complaint alleges that:

1. Plaintiff brings this action under sections 5(a), 13(b), and 16(a) of the Federal Trade Commission Act ("FTC Act"), 15 U.S.C. §§ 45(a), 53(b), and 56(a); and section 621(a) of the Fair Credit Reporting Act ("FCRA"), 15 U.S.C. § 1681 s(a), to obtain monetary civil penalties, and injunctive or other relief from Defendant for engaging in violations of the FTC Act. . . .

5. Defendant Spokeo, Inc. ("Spokeo") is a privately-held Delaware C-type corporation doing business in California. . . .

9. Spokeo assembles consumer information from "hundreds of online and offline sources," such as social networking sites, data brokers, and other sources to create consumer profiles, which Defendant promotes as "coherent people profiles" and "powerful intelligence." These consumer profiles identify specific individuals and display such information as the individual's physical address, phone number, marital status, age range, or email address. Spokeo profiles are further organized by descriptive headers denoting, among other things, a person's hobbies, ethnicity, religion, or participation on social networking sites, and may contain photos or other information, such as economic health graphics, that Spokeo attributes to a particular individual. Among other things, Spokeo sells the profiles through paid subscriptions, which provide a set number of searches based on subscription level, as well as through Application Program Interfaces ("API") that provide customized and/or higher volume access.

10. Since at least 2008, Spokeo has provided its consumer profiles to businesses, including entities operating in the human resources ("HR"), background screening, and recruiting industries, to serve as a factor in deciding whether to interview a job candidate or whether to hire a candidate after a job interview. . . .

11. In 2010, Spokeo changed its website Terms of Service to state that it was not a consumer reporting agency and that consumers may not use the company's website or information for FCRA-covered purposes. However, Spokeo failed to revoke access to or otherwise ensure that existing users, including subscribers who may have joined Spokeo through its Spokeo.com/HR page, or those who had previously purchased access to profiles through API user agreements, did not use the company's website or information for FCRA-covered purposes.

12. The consumer profiles Spokeo provides to third parties are "consumer reports" as defined in section 603(d) of the FCRA, 15 U.S.C. § 1681a(d). . . .

Spokeo profiles are consumer reports because they bear on a consumer's character, general reputation, personal characteristics, or mode of living and/or other attributes listed in section 603(d), and are "used or expected to be used ...in whole or in part" as a factor in determining the consumer's eligibility for employment or other purposes specified in section 604.

13. In providing "consumer reports" Spokeo is now and has been a "consumer reporting agency" ("CRA") as that term is defined in section 603(f) of the FCRA, 15 U.S.C. § 1681a(f). . . .

18. Section 607(a) of the FCRA, 15 U.S.C. § 1681e(a), requires that every consumer reporting agency maintain reasonable procedures to limit the furnishing of consumer reports for enumerated "permissible purposes." These reasonable procedures include making reasonable efforts to verify the identity of each prospective user of consumer report information and the uses certified by each prospective user prior to furnishing such user with a consumer report.

19. . . . Spokeo has failed to maintain such reasonable procedures. For example, Spokeo has failed to require that prospective users of the profiles identify themselves, certify the purposes for which the information is sought, and certify that the information will be used for no other purpose.

22. Section 607(b) of the FCRA, 15 U.S.C. § 1681e(b), requires consumer reporting agencies to follow reasonable procedures to assure maximum possible accuracy of the information concerning the individual about whom the report relates.

23. . . . Defendant has failed to use reasonable procedures to assure maximum possible accuracy of consumer report information. . . .

26. Section 607(d) of the FCRA, 15 U.S.C. § 1681e(d), requires that a consumer reporting agency provide, to any person to whom it provides a consumer report ("users"), a User Notice.

27. . . . Defendant has failed to provide User Notices to users and thereby has violated section 607(d) of the FCRA, 15 U.S.C. § 1681e(d). . . .

30. Section 604 of the FCRA, 15 U.S.C. § 1681b prohibits CRAs from furnishing consumer reports to persons that it did not have reason to believe had a permissible purpose to obtain a consumer report.

31. . . . Spokeo has furnished consumer reports to persons that it did not have reason to believe had a permissible purpose to obtain a consumer report. . . .

39. Section 621(a)(2)(A) of the FCRA, 15 U.S.C. § 1681s(a)(2)(A), authorizes the Court to award monetary civil penalties in the event of a knowing violation of the FCRA, which constitutes a pattern or practice. Spokeo's violations of the FCRA, as alleged in this Complaint, have been knowing and have constituted a pattern or practice of violations. As specified by the Federal Civil Penalty Inflation Adjustment Act of 1990, 28 U.S.C. § 2461, as amended by the Debt Collection Improvements Act of 1996, Pub. L. 104-134, § 31001(s)(1), 110 Stat. 1321-373, the Court is authorized to award a penalty of not more than $2,500 per violation for violations occurring before February 10, 2009, and $3,500 per violation for violations occurring on or after that date.

40. Each instance in which Spokeo has failed to comply with the FCRA constitutes a separate violation of the FCRA for the purpose of assessing monetary civil penalties under section 621 of the FCRA, 15 U.S.C. § 1681s. Plaintiff seeks monetary civil penalties for every separate violation of the FCRA.

41. Under section 621(a) of the FCRA, 15 U.S.C. § 1681s(a), and section 13(b) of the FTC Act, 15 U.S.C. § 53(b), this Court is authorized to issue a permanent injunction prohibiting Defendant from violating the FTC Act and the FCRA. . . .

CONSENT DECREE AND ORDER FOR CIVIL PENALTIES,
INJUNCTION AND OTHER RELIEF

. . . The parties have agreed to entry of this Stipulated Final Judgment and Order for Civil Penalties, Permanent Injunction, and Other Equitable Relief ("Order") to resolve all matters in dispute in this action without trial or adjudication of any issue of law or fact herein and without Defendant admitting the truth of, or liability for, any of the matters alleged in the Complaint. Defendant has waived service of the Summons and Complaint.

THEREFORE, IT IS HEREBY ORDERED, ADJUDGED, AND DECREED as follows: . . . .

4. Defendant makes no admissions to the allegations in the Complaint, other than the jurisdictional facts. . . .

IT IS ORDERED that:

1. Judgment in the amount of eight hundred thousand dollars ($800,000) is hereby entered against Defendant, as a civil penalty for violations of the FCRA. . . .

IT IS FURTHER ORDERED that Defendant, and all other persons or entities within the scope of Fed. R. Civ. P. 65, whether acting directly or through any sole proprietorship, partnership, limited liability company, corporation, subsidiary, branch, division, device, or other business entity who receive actual notice of this Order by personal service or otherwise, are hereby permanently restrained and enjoined from violating the Fair Credit Reporting Act, 15 U.S.C. §§1681-1681x. . . .

IT IS FURTHER ORDERED that Defendant make timely submissions to the Commission: . . . .

2. For 20 years following entry of this Order, Defendant must submit a compliance notice, sworn under penalty of perjury, within 14 days of any change in the following: (a) any designated point of contact; or (b) the structure of any entity that Defendant has any ownership interest in or directly or indirectly controls that may affect compliance obligations arising under this Order, including: creation, merger, sale, or dissolution of the entity or any subsidiary, parent, or affiliate that engages in any acts or practices subject to this Order.

IT IS FURTHER ORDERED that Defendant must create certain records for 20 years after entry of the Order, and retain each such record for five (5) years. Specifically, Defendant must maintain the following records [including accounting records, personnel records, training materials, compliance documents, a copy of each advertisement and marketing material, and others.]

IT IS FURTHER ORDERED that, for the purpose of monitoring Defendant's compliance with this Order, including any failure to transfer any assets as required by this Order:

1. Within 14 days of receipt of a written request from a representative of the Commission or Plaintiff, Defendant must: submit additional compliance reports or other requested information, which must be sworn under penalty of perjury; appear for depositions; and produce documents, for inspection and copying. . . .

NOTES & QUESTIONS

1. *Unwittingly Falling Under FCRA.* According to Spokeo's founder, he did not realize Spokeo was regulated under FCRA:

> Six years ago, my Stanford roommates and I built Spokeo to help us keep in touch with friends across a dizzying array of social networks. We are honored today to be at the helm of a principal destination for millions of Americans searching for and looking to connect with others. . . .
>
> A few years ago, we were eager to share our social network search tool with anyone who could find good use for it. Focusing on a prior version of our website, the U.S. Federal Trade Commission (FTC) believes that our targeted marketing (at that time) implicated the Fair Credit Reporting Act (FCRA), which regulates the collection, dissemination and use of consumer information, including credit information provided by consumer reporting agencies. It has never been our intention to act as a consumer reporting agency. We have made changes to our site and our internal business practices in order to ensure we don't infringe upon the FCRA's important consumer protections, and to ensure an honest and transparent service that will continue to be easy for our customers to use. We are a technology company organizing people-related data in innovative ways. We do not create our own content, we do not possess or have access to private financial information, and we do not offer consumer reports.[8]

Is it fair to charge Spokeo with violating FCRA when it did not even realize that it had to follow FCRA? Should small start-up companies be required to know when they trigger FCRA?

2. *The Digital Frontier of Credit Services.* An online frontier of credit services exists beyond traditional consumer reporting agencies, namely, Equifax, Experian, and Transunion (the traditional "Big Three" of the industry). Like Spokeo, a variety of new entities draw on digital information in innovative ways to estimate credit worthiness and offer credit services. This information can then be combined with up-to-date signals about whether a customer is looking for a financial product or service. As Ed Mierzwinski and Jeff Chester note, "A new data market has emerged, selling access to a consumer's intent to be 'in-market' for a product or service."[9] Online data warehouse companies, such as BlueKai, offer online marketers access to such "intent information" gathered from databrokers, such as Acxiom. For Mierzwinski and Chester, the law should view these "online scoring databases" as "equivalent to prescreened lists, which are consumer reports." These authors call on the FTC to determine whether companies that sell this information should fall under the FCRA's restrictions due to their "establishing the consumer's eligibility for personal, family, or household purposes; employment purposes; or any other purpose authorized under section 1681b [citing FCRA, 15 U.S.C. §1681a(d)(1)(A)-(C)]."

---

[8] Harrison Tang, Empowering Spokeo's Users, June 12, 2012, http://blog.spokeo.com/2012/06/empowering-spokeos-users-2.

[9] Ed Mierzwinski & Jeff Chester, *Selling Consumers Not Lists*, 46 Suffolk U. L. Rev. 845, 875 (2013).

3. **Standing to Sue for FRCRA Violations.** In *Spokeo, Inc. v. Robins*, 136 S.Ct. 1540 (2016), the Supreme Court considered a case involving a plaintiff suing Spokeo under FCRA for inaccuracies in his data. The Court remanded the case back to the 9th Circuit in light of its clarification about the nature of standing. The Court stated that "concrete" injury "must actually exist" and must be "real and not abstract." The Court noted that "intangible injuries can nevertheless be concrete." Congress may "elevat[e] to the status of legally cognizable injuries concrete, *de facto* injuries that were previously inadequate in law." Congress can deem even injuries "previously inadequate in law" to be concrete injuries sufficient to confer standing. But the Court also declared that "Article III standing requires a concrete injury even in the context of a statutory violation. For that reason, Robins could not, for example, allege a bare procedural violation, divorced from any concrete harm, and satisfy the injury-in-fact requirement of Article III." This means that despite the fact that FCRA has a cause of action for violations, plaintiffs cannot use that cause of action for violations that do not amount to an injury-in-fact. According to the Court, "not all inaccuracies cause harm or present any material risk of harm. An example that comes readily to mind is an incorrect zip code. It is difficult to imagine how the dissemination of an incorrect zip code, without more, could work any concrete harm." Are inaccuracies such as the example above not likely to lead to any concrete harm?

4. **Big Data and the Frontiers of FCRA.** In a 2016 report on Big Data, the FTC noted that new kinds of data use can trigger the protections of FCRA. It stated, "Some data brokers that compile non-traditional information including social media information, may also be considered [Credit Reporting Agencies] subject to the FCRA."[10] The FTC also presented an interesting case study:

> Suppose a company asks a consumer to provide her zip code and information about her social media and shopping behavior on a credit application, strips the consumer's identifying information, and sends the application to an analytics firm. The firm then analyzes the creditworthiness of people in the same zip code with similar social media and shopping behaviors as the consumer and provides that analysis—be it, for example, in the form of a score, a grade, or a recommendation—to the company, knowing that it is to be used for a credit decision.[11]

In the FTC's assessment, FCRA requirements and protections would apply to the actions of this company. FCRA applies because "the company is using information about the consumer to generate an analysis of a group that shares some characteristics with the consumer and then is using that analysis to make a decision about the consumer."

---

[10] FTC Report, *Big Data: A Tool for Inclusion or Exclusion?* 13 (Jan. 2016).
[11] Id. at 16.

2. PERMISSIBLE USES OF CONSUMER REPORTS

Permissible Uses of Consumer Reports. Pursuant to 15 U.S.C. § 1681b, a consumer reporting agency can furnish a consumer report only under certain circumstances or for certain uses: (1) in response to a court order or grand jury subpoena; (2) to the person to whom the report pertains; (3) to a "person which [the agency] has reason to believe" intends to use the information in connection with (a) the extension of credit to a consumer; (b) employment purposes; (c) insurance underwriting; (d) licensing or the conferral of government benefits; (e) assessment of credit risks associated with an existing credit obligation; (f) "legitimate business need" when engaging in "a business transaction involving the consumer"; (4) to establish a person's capacity to pay child support.

A Private Right of Action and Restrictions on "[A]ny Person." FCRA does not merely place restrictions on consumer reporting agencies. More broadly, it creates a private right of action for "any consumer" regarding "[a]ny person" who under false pretenses gains a consumer report, or who willfully or knowingly fails to comply with certain of its requirements. §1681n(a). It also provides for punitive damages, reasonable attorney's fees, and statutory damages of $1,000 or actual damages. This section provides the basis for the litigation in *Smith v. Bob Smith Chevrolet*, excerpted below.

Consumer Reports for Employment Purposes. When an employer or potential employer seeks a consumer report for employment purposes, she must first disclose in writing to the consumer that a consumer report may be obtained, and the consumer must authorize in writing that the report can be obtained. The person seeking the report from a consumer reporting agency must certify that she obtained the consent of the individual and that she will not use the information in violation of any equal employment opportunity law or regulation. § 1681b(b). If the person who obtained the report takes adverse action based in any way on the report, she must provide the consumer a copy of the report and a description of the consumer's rights under the FCRA. § 1681b(b).

Pursuant to § 1681b(g):

> A consumer reporting agency shall not furnish for employment purposes, or in connection with a credit or insurance transaction or a direct marketing transaction, a consumer report that contains medical information about a consumer, unless the consumer consents to the furnishing of the report.

Law Enforcement Access. Pursuant to FCRA, "a consumer reporting agency may furnish identifying information respecting any customer, limited to his name, address, former addresses, places of employment, or former places of employment, to a governmental agency." § 1681f. The FBI can obtain "the names and addresses of all financial institutions . . . at which a consumer maintains or has maintained an account" by presenting a written request to a consumer reporting agency. § 1681u(a). Additionally, pursuant to a written request by the FBI, a consumer reporting agency must disclose "identifying information respecting a consumer, limited to name, address, former addresses, places of employment, or former places of employment." The FBI, however, must certify that the information is sought in an investigation to protect against "international terrorism or clandestine intelligence activities" and that the investigation "is not conducted solely upon the basis of activities protected by the first amendment to the Constitution of the United States." § 1681u(b). To obtain additional information from a consumer report, the FBI must obtain a court order and meet the same standard as above. § 1681u(c).

Moreover, § 1681v provides a broad release exemption "to a government agency authorized to conduct investigations of, or intelligence or counterintelligence activities or analysis related to, international terrorism." These entities can obtain a consumer report on an individual when the government agency provides "a written certification" to a consumer reporting agency that the information is "necessary" for an agency investigation or other agency activity.

Unauthorized Disclosures of Consumer Reports: Prescreening. A typical American receives a flood of credit cards offers each year. These offers follow due to the practice of "prescreening" consumers for such offers, which FCRA permits. A consumer reporting agency can furnish a consumer report, without the consumer's authorization, if

> (i) the transaction consists of a firm offer of credit or insurance;
> (ii) the consumer reporting agency has complied with subsection (e); and
> (iii) there is not in effect the election by the consumer, made in accordance
> with subsection (e), to have the consumer's name and address excluded from lists
> of names provided by the agency pursuant to this paragraph. § 1681b(c).

Subsection (e) of § 1681b provides the consumer with a right to opt out of such unauthorized disclosures. If the consumer notifies the consumer reporting agency by phone, the opt out shall last for two years and then expire. If the consumer notifies the consumer reporting agency by submitting a signed opt-out form, then the opt out remains effective until the consumer notifies the agency otherwise. § 1681b(e).

Limitations on Information Contained in Consumer Reports. Consumer reporting agencies are excluded from providing certain information in consumer reports, such as bankruptcy proceedings more than ten years old; suits and judgments more than seven years old; paid tax liens more than seven years old; and records of arrest, indictment, or conviction of a crime more than seven years old. § 1681c(a). These limitations do not apply, however, when a company is preparing a consumer report used in connection with a credit transaction more than $150,000; underwriting a life insurance policy more than $150,000; or employing an individual with an annual salary more than $75,000. § 1681c(b).

Investigative Consumer Reports. An "investigative consumer report" is "a consumer report or portion thereof in which information on a consumer's character, general reputation, personal characteristics, or mode of living is obtained through personal interviews, with neighbors, friends, or associates." § 1681a(f). The FCRA provides limitations on investigative consumer reports. These reports cannot be prepared unless "it is clearly and accurately disclosed to the consumer that an investigative consumer report including information as to his character, general reputation, personal characteristics and mode of living, whichever are applicable, may be made." § 1681d(a)(1). The consumer, if she requests, can require disclosure "of the nature and scope of the investigation requested." § 1681d(b). Further, if the report contains any adverse information about a person gleaned from interviews with neighbors, friends, or associates, the agency must take reasonable steps to corroborate that information "from an additional source that has independent and direct knowledge of the information" or ensure that "the person interviewed is the best possible source of the information." § 1681d(d).

SMITH V. BOB SMITH CHEVROLET, INC.

275 F. Supp. 2d 808 (W.D. Ky. 2003)

HEYBURN, J. Christopher Smith ("Plaintiff") alleges that Defendant Bob Smith Chevrolet, Inc. violated the Fair Credit Reporting Act, 15 U.S.C. § 1681 *et seq.,* and invaded his privacy in violation of Kentucky common law. . . . [B]oth parties have moved for summary judgment on the issue of whether Smith Chevrolet lacked a permissible purpose when it accessed Plaintiff's credit report; Smith Chevrolet moved to dismiss the Kentucky invasion of privacy claim. . . .

The underlying facts concern the disputed sale of a 2001 GMC Suburban. Having decided that he wanted to purchase a car, on December 13, 2000, Plaintiff completed a GMAC credit application to determine his eligibility for financing. On December 23, 2000, Plaintiff went to Smith Chevrolet with the intention of purchasing the Suburban to use on a family Christmas vacation.

After arriving at the dealership, Plaintiff met with a company employee to discuss the terms of the sale. Two factors complicated the sale. First, Plaintiff wanted to trade in his 1997 Mercury Villager. Second, as an employee of General Electric — a General Motors ("GM") supplier — he was entitled to a standard discount upon proof of employment. Although Plaintiff did have the 1997 Mercury Villager to trade-in on December 23, 2000, he did not have the proper documentation needed to secure the discount. Notwithstanding this fact, a Smith Chevrolet representative agreed to sell Plaintiff the Suburban at the GM discounted price provided he proved his entitlement to the full discount at a later date. After calculating the Villager's trade-in value and the GM discount, the two sides agreed on a price and set forth the terms of the sale in a handwritten purchase order. . . .

On January 10, 2001, Plaintiff faxed and mailed proof of his eligibility for the GM discount. Shortly thereafter, Plaintiff's bank issued Smith Chevrolet a check in the amount of the balance due.

About a week or ten days later, another dispute arose which gives rise to the current litigation. At that point Smith Chevrolet claims it realized the employee who generated the typewritten Purchase Agreement inadvertently doubled the amount of Plaintiff's discount. Smith Chevrolet contacted Plaintiff, explained the calculation error and told Plaintiff that he owed the dealership more money. Furthermore, Smith Chevrolet told Plaintiff that, until he paid the difference, it refused to transfer the Suburban's title and pay off the outstanding loan attached on the Villager trade-in. These were both actions Smith Chevrolet had promised Plaintiff it would take when Plaintiff left the lot on December 23, 2000.

Following from this dispute, on February 21, 2000, Smith Chevrolet accessed Plaintiff's consumer report. The decision to access Plaintiff's report was made by Drew Smith, Smith Chevrolet's chief executive officer and part-owner. Smith Chevrolet says it accessed Plaintiff's report to determine whether Plaintiff was (1) continuing to make payments on the Villager's loan and (2) maintaining insurance on the Villager. Plaintiff disputes Smith Chevrolet's motivations in this regard and claims that it simply wanted to invade Plaintiff's privacy.

When the parties could not agree on the amount due, Plaintiff sued Smith Chevrolet in Jefferson Circuit Court for breach of the sale contract. He demanded specific performance so that he could receive the Suburban's title and transfer the Villager loan obligations to Smith Chevrolet. About a year later, a state court jury found in Plaintiff's favor. One day earlier, on May 13, 2002, Plaintiff filed this suit in federal court. . . .

The heart of [Plaintiff's] case is the contention that Smith Chevrolet violated the FCRA when it accessed Plaintiff's credit report on February 21, 2001. Specifically, Plaintiff contends Smith Chevrolet is liable for negligently and willfully violating the responsibilities imposed by the FCRA. *See* 15 U.S.C. § 1681o (creating a private cause of action for negligent violations of the FCRA); 15 U.S.C. § 1681n (creating a private cause of action for willful violations). Both sides have filed motions for summary judgment addressing whether Smith Chevrolet had a "permissible purpose" for accessing Plaintiff's credit report. The facts central to this claim are not in dispute. Smith Chevrolet may access Plaintiff's credit report only if, as a matter of law, its actions are consistent with one of the permissible purposes set forth in 15 U.S.C. § 1681b(a)(3).

The FCRA identifies a limited set of "permissible purposes" for obtaining and using a consumer report. *See* 15 U.S.C. § 1681b(a)(3); *see also* 15 U.S.C. § 1681b(f). Those permissible purposes provide that a person may only access a consumer report if he:

> (A) intends to use the information in connection with a credit transaction involving the consumer on whom the information is to be furnished and involving the extension of credit to, or review or collection of an account of, the consumer; or
>
> (B) intends to use the information for employment purposes; or
>
> (C) intends to use the information in connection with the underwriting of insurance involving the consumer; or
>
> (D) intends to use the information in connection with a determination of the consumer's eligibility for a license or other benefit granted by a governmental instrumentality required by law to consider an applicant's financial responsibility or status; or
>
> (E) intends to use the information, as a potential investor or servicer, or current insurer, in connection with a valuation of, or an assessment of the credit or prepayment risks associated with, an existing credit obligation; or
>
> (F) otherwise has a legitimate business need for the information—
>
>> (i) in connection with a business transaction that is initiated by the consumer; or
>>
>> (ii) to review an account to determine whether the consumer continues to meet the terms of the account.

15 U.S.C. § 1681b(a)(3).

In its summary judgment motion, Smith Chevrolet contends it had three bases for accessing Plaintiff's credit report. The Court now addresses each of these arguments.

First and most persuasively, Smith Chevrolet contends its actions complied with § 1681b(a)(3)(f)(i). That section provides that one may obtain a consumer report if it "has a legitimate business need for the information . . . in connection with a business transaction that is initiated by the consumer. . ." Smith Chevrolet argues that because the transaction was in dispute, it needed to ascertain the value of its collateral. If it appeared that Plaintiff was not current on his payments for the Mercury Villager, then his indebtedness would have increased over and above the amount owed Smith Chevrolet.

As a starting point, the Court begins with the FCRA's text. The applicability of this permissible purpose boils down to whether Smith Chevrolet's use of the credit report was "in connection with a transaction initiated by the consumer," as the statute uses those terms. That restriction to the actual statutory usage is important here because, in the abstract, it is true Smith Chevrolet accessed Plaintiff's credit report in connection with a transaction Plaintiff at one point initiated. The Court concludes, however, that the statute uses the terms "in connection with a transaction initiated by the consumer" more restrictively.

Turning to the text at issue, when Congress defined the term "consumer report," it stated:

> The term "consumer report" means any written, oral, or other communication of any information by a consumer reporting agency bearing on a consumer's credit worthiness, credit standing, credit capacity, character, general reputation, personal characteristics, or mode of living which is used or expected to be used or collected in whole or in part for the purpose of serving as a factor in establishing the consumer's eligibility for—
>
> > (A) credit or insurance to be used primarily for personal, family, or household purposes;
> >
> > (B) employment purposes; or
> >
> > (C) any other purpose authorized under section 604 [15 U.S.C. § 1681b].

15 U.S.C. § 1681a(d).

This definition suggests that Congress primarily envisioned consumer reports being disseminated for the purposes of assessing "eligibility." Then, in § 1681b(a)(3), Congress listed additional specific permissible purposes pertaining to the extension of credit, collection of an account, employment purposes, the underwriting of insurance for a consumer, determining a consumer's eligibility for a governmental benefit, and the valuation of a consumer's credit risk. The rule of *ejusdem generis* provides that when general words follow an enumeration of specific terms, the general words are construed to embrace only objects similar in nature to those objects enumerated by the preceding specific words. The definition of "consumer report" therefore includes those reports needed to assess a consumer's eligibility for a benefit, as well as other predictable needs — such as collecting money owed under an agreement and assessing a particular consumer's credit or insurance risk — that arise in the midst of a typical business transaction.

In fact, in every one of these situations, the consumer report is obtained either to provide a benefit to a consumer or to collect a pre-existing debt.

Tellingly, the two permissible purposes stated in § 1681b(a)(3)(F) can also be read to effectuate these same ends. That is, § 1681b(a)(3)(F)(i) suggests the retention of a credit report for the purpose of furthering a business transaction initiated by a consumer and § 1681b(a)(3)(F)(ii) permits the use of a credit report to determine whether a consumer continues to be eligible for a benefit. It is a basic principle of statutory construction that a statute should be read and construed as a whole. Like the definition of "consumer report" and consistent with the other five specific permissible purposes, these two permissible purposes also suggest that Congress intended to allow access to a consumer report either when that access would benefit a consumer or would facilitate the collection of pre-existing debt.

To be precise, Smith Chevrolet's stated reason for accessing the credit report was not in connection with a standard business transaction that Plaintiff initiated. Instead, and quite significantly in this Court's view, Smith Chevrolet accessed the credit report to determine how much additional money it could collect, apart from what the two parties agreed upon in a standard business transaction. Almost certainly, it did not access Plaintiff's credit report for a reason beneficial to the consumer. Nor did it access the credit report to collect on a pre-existing debt. Rather, it accessed the report for its own business purposes and as part of a new event: the recovery of the duplicative discount. Although this is a fine distinction, it may be an important one. Smith Chevrolet's interpretation of the phrase "in connection with" is limitless. Under its reading, so long as any company had a reason to question any part of a transaction, it could access a consumer's credit report "in connection with a business transaction" that at some point was "initiated by the consumer." That is, five weeks, five months, or five years down the line, Smith Chevrolet could access Plaintiff's credit report if some dispute ever arose about the contracted price. In the Court's view, such an interpretation would give commercial entities an unlimited blank check to access and *reaccess* a consumer credit report long after the typical issues of eligibility, price, and financing were determined. Neither the specific language nor the overall scope of the FCRA can be said to support such an interpretation. . . .

Moreover, nearly every federal court addressing this issue has similarly held that the "legitimate business need" permissible purpose should be narrowly construed in the context of the other five enumerated purposes. . . .

The Court concludes, therefore, that when Smith Chevrolet accessed Plaintiff's credit report it was not, as a practical matter, part of the transaction which Plaintiff initiated. That transaction, in so far as Plaintiff's eligibility and debt was concerned, ended when the parties created a contract for the car's price and Plaintiff paid that price in full. Under any conceivable interpretation of the facts in this case, Smith Chevrolet cannot be said to have a "legitimate business need" for Plaintiff's credit report "in connection with a transaction initiated by the consumer." § 604(a)(3)(F)(i).

Smith Chevrolet also argues that its actions were protected both by §§ 1681b(3)(A) and 1681b(a)(1)(F)(ii) which provide that:

> Any consumer reporting agency may furnish a consumer report under the following circumstances and no other: . . .

(A) to a person which it has reason to believe intends to use the information in connection with a credit transaction involving the consumer on whom the information is to be furnished and involving the extension of credit to, or review or collection of an account of the consumer; or . . .

(F) otherwise has a legitimate business need for the information . . . (ii) to review an account to determine whether the consumer continues to meet the terms of the account.

Smith Chevrolet claims that it had a permissible purpose under both of these provisions because, due to its own error, Plaintiff received twice the discount he was entitled to and so a debt remained. Therefore, Smith Chevrolet says that it was reviewing whether Plaintiff owed any additional debt. And, because reviewing the size of the debt Plaintiff owed is synonymous with "collection of an account" and with determining "whether [Chris Smith] continue[d] to meet the terms of the account," Smith Chevrolet contends it therefore clearly had a permissible purpose.

The problem with this argument is that there was no outstanding debt and, consequently, there was no "account" to collect on. To be sure, Smith Chevrolet thought there *should be* an outstanding debt. Thinking there *should be* a debt, Smith Chevrolet contacted Plaintiff and ordered him to pay. At that point, Plaintiff refused to pay. Only then did Smith Chevrolet access Plaintiff's credit report.

Whether a debt or existing account exists simply cannot be a function of whether Smith Chevrolet alleges the existence of a debt. To do so would allow Smith Chevrolet infinite opportunities to access Plaintiff's credit report, so long as he could come up with a reason for thinking the account should continue in existence. As this Court has explained elsewhere, the FCRA intended to strike a balance between protecting the needs of commerce and the consumer's privacy interest. The Court finds that Smith Chevrolet must have a reasonable belief that the debt existed. Here, Smith Chevrolet's decision to investigate Plaintiff's credit report was not based on a reasonable belief that debt was owed; it was based on a belief that the original transaction was mistaken. Plaintiff had no reason to suspect that any new debt would arise after the initial transaction was completed. For all practical purposes that transaction was closed when the vehicle was delivered and Plaintiff made his payment. To find these permissible purposes applicable in this instance would extend the FCRA's language well beyond its intended purpose. . .

Both sides have also moved for summary judgment on Plaintiff's claim of willful non-compliance. Section 1681n provides for civil liability in cases where the defendant willfully fails to comply with FCRA. In such a case, punitive damages may be awarded. 15 U.S.C. § 1681n(a)(2). This Court has recently explained the standard for liability under § 1681n, stating that, "[t]o show willful noncompliance with the FCRA, [the Plaintiff] must show that [defendant] knowingly and intentionally committed an act in conscious disregard for the rights of others, but need not show malice or evil motive."

Questions involving a party's state of mind are generally appropriately resolved by a jury rather than on summary judgment. From what the Court can ascertain at this point, the following facts are undisputed. Carol Hodges, a former Finance and Insurance Manager for Smith Chevrolet, has testified that the company did not have "written polices" regarding the acquisition of credit reports. She said that salespeople could freely access consumer credit reports. Hodges also said that the company had some unwritten rules for accessing customer credit reports, but these rules were not strictly followed. In fact, Smith Chevrolet's practices were "haphazard" and "very sloppy." Hodges had no part in the February 21, 2001, events and has no idea if Smith Chevrolet acted responsibly the day it accessed Plaintiff's credit report.

Based on these disputed facts, the Court cannot enter summary judgment on the issue of Smith Chevrolet's state of mind and will therefore deny the parties cross motions for summary judgment as they pertain to § 1681n.

Last, Smith Chevrolet has moved for summary judgment on Plaintiff's invasion of privacy claim. The Supreme Court of Kentucky adopted the principles for invasion of privacy as enunciated in the Restatement (Second) of Torts (1976) in *McCall v. Courier-Journal and Louisville Times Co.,* 623 S.W.2d 882, 887 (Ky. 1981). . . :

NOTES & QUESTIONS

1. ***Legitimate Business Need.*** A critical element in the court's decision in *Smith Chevrolet* is its finding that the auto dealership must have a "reasonable belief" that the debt existed to access the credit report. But the decision to investigate the credit report was based, in fact, on a belief that the Plaintiff should owe the car dealer more than he did (due to the mistaken double discount). How does the court interpret the FCRA's statutory provision that allows businesses access to consumer credit reports when there is "a legitimate business need for the information"?

2. ***Permissible Uses of Consumer Reports.*** The FCRA contains a provision that provides for civil liability for "obtaining a consumer report under false pretenses or knowingly without a permissible purpose." 15 U.S.C. § 1681n(a)(1)(B). But what, exactly, is a "consumer report"? A consumer report is defined based on the purposes for which it is used. These purposes include credit, insurance, and employment background checks, among others. 15 U.S.C. § 1681b.

    In *Phillips v. Grendahl,* 312 F.3d 357 (8th Cir. 2002), Mary Grendahl became suspicious of her daughter Sarah's fiancé, Lavon Phillips. She believed he was lying about being an attorney as well as his ex-wives and girlfriends. Grendahl contacted Kevin Fitzgerald, a friend who worked for a detective agency. By searching computer databases, Fitzgerald obtained Phillips's Social Security number and previous addresses. He then submitted the data to Econ Control to obtain a report called a "Finder's Report." A Finder's Report includes a person's "address, aliases, birthdate, employer addresses, and the identity of firms with which the consumer had credit accounts and firms that had made inquiries about the consumer."

    When Phillips discovered the investigation, he sued Grendahl, the detective agency Fitzgerald worked for, and Econ Control. The court concluded that the Finder's Report was a "consumer report" under FCRA. It also concluded that the defendants did not have a valid purpose under FCRA for obtaining the report:

The only purpose for obtaining the report was to obtain information on Mary Grendahl's prospective son-in-law. Investigating a person because he wants to marry one's daughter is not a statutory consumer purpose under section 1681b(a). Even if getting married can be characterized as a consumer transaction under section 1681b(a)(3), it was not Mary Grendahl, but her daughter, whom Phillips was engaged to marry. He had no business transaction pending with Mary Grendahl. There was no permissible purpose for obtaining or using a consumer report.

3. CONSUMER RIGHTS AND AGENCY RESPONSIBILITIES

Accuracy. "Whenever a consumer reporting agency prepares a consumer report it shall follow reasonable procedures to assure maximum possible accuracy of the information concerning the individual about whom the report relates." § 1681e(b).

Disclosures to the Consumer. The FCRA requires that consumer reporting agencies, upon request of the consumer, disclose, among other things:

(1) All information in the consumer's file at the time of the request,   except . . . any information concerning credit scores or any other risk scores or predictors relating to the consumer.
(2) The sources of the information. . . .
(3) Identification of each person . . . that procured a consumer report [within two years for employment purposes; within one year for all other purposes] . . . .
(4) The dates, original payees, and amounts of any checks upon which is based any adverse characterization of the consumer, included in the file at the time of disclosure. . . . § 1681g.

Responsiveness to Consumer Complaints. National consumer reporting agencies must provide consumers who request disclosures under the FCRA with a toll-free telephone number at which personnel are accessible to respond to consumer inquiries during normal business hours. § 1681g(c).

Procedures in Case of Disputed Accuracy. Pursuant to § 1681i(a)(1):

If the completeness or accuracy of any item of information contained in a consumer's file at a consumer reporting agency is disputed by the consumer and the consumer notifies the agency directly of such dispute, the agency shall reinvestigate free of charge and record the current status of the disputed information or delete the item from the file. . . .

The consumer reporting agency must provide written notice to a consumer of the results of a reinvestigation within five business days after completing the investigation. § 1681i.

If the information is found to be inaccurate or incomplete or cannot be verified, the consumer reporting agency must promptly delete it from the file.   § 1681i. At the request of the consumer, the consumer reporting agency must furnish notification that the item has been deleted to "any person specifically designated by the consumer who has within two years prior thereto received a consumer report for employment purposes, or within six months prior thereto received a consumer report for any other purpose." § 1681i(d).

"If the reinvestigation does not resolve the dispute, the consumer may file a brief statement setting forth the nature of the dispute." § 1681i(b).

In any subsequent consumer report, the agency must clearly note that the information in question is disputed by the consumer and provide the consumer's statement. § 1681i(c).

While FCRA provides an opportunity to dispute items on their credit history, it does not require credit reporting agencies to reveal how they translated this history to a credit score. As Citron and Pasquale note, "That is a trade secret; a designation offering powerful legal protections to companies that want to keep their business practices a secret."[12]

Public Record Information for Employment Purposes. If a consumer reporting agency furnishes a consumer report for employment purposes containing information obtained in public records that is likely to have an adverse effect on the consumer, it must either notify the consumer of the fact that public record information is being reported along with the name and address of the person to whom the information is being reported or "maintain strict procedures designed to insure that whenever public record information which is likely to have an adverse effect on a consumer's ability to obtain employment is reported it is complete and up to date." § 1681k.

Requirements on Users of Consumer Reports. If a user of a consumer report takes any adverse action on a consumer based in any way on the report, the user shall provide notice of the adverse action to the consumer, information for the consumer to contact the consumer reporting agency that prepared the report, and notice of the consumer's right to obtain a free copy of the report and to dispute the accuracy of the report. § 1681m(a). Whenever credit is denied based on information obtained through sources other than a consumer report, upon the consumer's written request, the person or entity denying credit shall disclose the nature of that information. § 1681m(b).

4. CIVIL LIABILITY AND QUALIFIED IMMUNITY

Civil Liability. As noted above, any person who "willfully fails to comply with any requirement" of the FCRA is liable to the consumer for actual damages or statutory damages between $100 and $1,000, as well as punitive damages and attorneys' fees and costs. § 1681n. Willful means that one intentionally commits an act "in conscious disregard for the rights of others." In *Safeco Insurance Co. v. Burr,* 551 U.S. 47 (2007), the Supreme Court held that acting in "reckless disregard" of a consumer's rights under FCRA was sufficient to establish willfulness.

---

[12] Keats & Pasquale, *supra*, at 17.

Negligent failure to comply with any requirement of the FCRA results in liability to the consumer for actual damages as well as attorneys' fees and costs. § 1681.

Liability for Furnishing Data to a Consumer Reporting Agency. Businesses and financial institutions "furnish" the information about consumers to the consumer reporting agencies. For example, a bank that issues a consumer a credit card will furnish information about the timeliness and consistency of the consumer's payments. This is how consumer reporting agencies learn about a consumer's reliability. What if one of these entities furnishes false data to a consumer reporting agency? The data adversely affects a consumer's credit score and results in harm to the consumer. The consumer can sue not just the consumer reporting agency but also the entity that furnished the false data. However, as discussed below, FCRA's qualified immunity will apply.

Qualified Immunity from State Tort Law. Consumer reporting agencies — as well as those that furnish data to consumer reporting agencies — could potentially face extensive liability under state tort law. Under defamation law, a person or entity can be liable for disseminating false information about a person that injures the person's reputation. Disseminating false information might also give rise to a false light action. And disclosing true information could give rise to liability for public disclosure of private facts.

However, FCRA provides qualified immunity to credit reporting agencies and to the furnishers of information to credit reporting agencies:

> Except as provided in sections 1681n and 1681o of this title, no consumer may bring any action or proceeding in the nature of defamation, invasion of privacy, or negligence with respect to the reporting of information against any consumer reporting agency, or any user of information, or any person who furnishes information to a consumer reporting agency, based on information disclosed pursuant to section 1681g, 1681h, or 1681m of this title, or based on information disclosed by a user of a consumer report to or for a consumer against whom the user has taken adverse action, based in whole or in part on the report except as to false information furnished with malice or willful intent to injure such consumer. § 1681h(e).

Plaintiffs can only state tort actions when "defendants acted with malice or willful intent to injure plaintiff." § 1681h.

In *Lema v. Citibank,* 935 F. Supp. 695 (D. Md. 1996), Citibank issued the plaintiff a credit card. When the plaintiff's account became delinquent, Citibank reported the information to consumer reporting agencies. The plaintiff sued Citibank under FCRA, claiming that the information it supplied to the consumer reporting agencies was inaccurate. The court dismissed the claim:

> The FCRA imposes civil liability only on consumer reporting agencies and users of consumer information. Thus, plaintiff must show that defendants are either of those entities in order to withstand defendants' summary judgment motion. . . .
>
> Plaintiff alleges only that defendants reported to third parties information regarding transactions between defendants and plaintiff. Defendants did not

therefore furnish a consumer report regarding plaintiff, nor did they act as a consumer reporting agency with respect to him.

Statute of Limitations. FCRA's statute of limitation extends to two years after the date when the plaintiff discovers the violation or five years after the date of the violation, whichever occurs earlier.

SARVER V. EXPERIAN INFORMATION SOLUTIONS

390 F.3d 969 (7th Cir. 2004)

EVANS, J. Lloyd Sarver appeals from an order granting summary judgment to Experian Information Solutions, Inc., a credit reporting company, on his claim under the Fair Credit Reporting Act (FCRA), 15 U.S.C. §§ 1681 *et seq.*

Experian reported inaccurate information on Sarver's credit report, which on August 2, 2002, caused the Monogram Bank of Georgia to deny him credit. Monogram cited the Experian credit report and particularly a reference to a bankruptcy which appeared on the report. Both before and after Monogram denied him credit, Sarver asked for a copy of his credit report. He received copies both times and both reports showed that accounts with Cross Country Bank were listed as having been "involved in bankruptcy." No other accounts had that notation, although other accounts had significant problems. A Bank One installment account had a balance past due 180 days, and another company, Providian, had written off $3,099 on a revolving account.

On August 29, 2002, Sarver wrote Experian informing it that the bankruptcy notation was inaccurate and asking that it be removed from his report. Sarver provided his full name and address but no other identifying information. On September 11, Experian sent Sarver a letter requesting further information, including his Social Security number, before it could begin an investigation. Sarver did not provide the information, but instead filed the present lawsuit, which resulted in summary judgment for Experian. It was later confirmed that the notation on the Cross Country Bank account was inaccurate and, as it turned out, another Lloyd Sarver was the culprit on that account.

In this appeal from the judgment dismissing his case, Sarver claims summary judgment was improper because issues of fact exist as to whether Experian violated FCRA, §§ 1681i and 1681e(b). . . .

Section 1681i requires a credit reporting agency to reinvestigate items on a credit report when a consumer disputes the validity of those items. An agency can terminate a reinvestigation if it determines the complaint is frivolous, "including by reason of a failure by a consumer to provide sufficient information to investigate the disputed information." § 1681i(a)(3). We do not need to decide whether Sarver's failure to provide the information Experian requested rendered his complaint frivolous; his claim under § 1681i(a) fails for another reason, a lack of evidence of damages. In order to prevail on his claims, Sarver must show that he suffered damages as a result of the inaccurate information. As we have said in *Crabill v. Trans Union, L.L.C.,* 259 F.3d 662, 664 (7th Cir. 2001):

> Without a causal relation between the violation of the statute and the loss of credit, or some other harm, a plaintiff cannot obtain an award of "actual damages."

On this point, the district court concluded that there were no damages. Our review of the record leads us to agree.

Sarver, however, disagrees and claims that he suffered damages when he was denied credit from Monogram Bank of Georgia on August 2, 2002. This letter cannot be a basis for his damage claim, however, because as of August 2, Experian had no notice of any inaccuracies in the report. Even though Sarver asked for a copy of his report on July 18, he did not notify Experian of a problem until a month and a half later. Experian must be notified of an error before it is required to reinvestigate. As we have made clear, the FCRA is not a strict liability statute. *Henson v. CSC Credit Servs.*, 29 F.3d 280 (7th Cir. 1994).

Sarver also does not show that he suffered pecuniary damages between August 29 (when he notified Experian of the error) and February 20, 2003 (when the Cross Country account was removed from his file). He does not claim that he applied for credit during that time period or that a third party looked at his report. In addition, his claim for emotional distress fails. We have maintained a strict standard for a finding of emotional damage "because they are so easy to manufacture." *Aiello v. Providian Fin. Corp.*, 239 F.3d 876, 880 (7th Cir. 2001). We have required that when "the injured party's own testimony is the only proof of emotional damages, he must explain the circumstances of his injury in reasonable detail; he cannot rely on mere conclusory statements." *Denius v. Dunlap*, 330 F.3d 919, 929 (7th Cir. 2003). Finally, to obtain statutory damages under FCRA § 1681n(a), Sarver must show that Experian willfully violated the Act. There is similarly no evidence of willfulness. Summary judgment was properly granted on this claim.

We turn to Sarver's claim under § 1681e(b), which requires that a credit reporting agency follow "reasonable procedures to assure maximum possible accuracy" when it prepares a credit report. The reasonableness of a reporting agency's procedures is normally a question for trial unless the reasonableness or unreasonableness of the procedures is beyond question. *Crabill*, 259 F.3d at 663. However, to state a claim under the statute,

> a consumer must sufficiently allege "that a credit reporting agency prepared a report containing 'inaccurate' information." However, the credit reporting agency is not automatically liable even if the consumer proves that it prepared an inaccurate credit report because the FCRA "does not make reporting agencies strictly liable for all inaccuracies." A credit reporting agency is not liable under the FCRA if it followed "reasonable procedures to assure maximum possible accuracy," but nonetheless reported inaccurate information in the consumer's credit report.

Henson, 29 F.3d at 284. The Commentary of the Federal Trade Commission to the FCRA, 16 C.F.R. pt. 600, app., section 607 at 3.A, states that the section does not hold a reporting agency responsible where an item of information, received from a source that it reasonably believes is reputable, turns out to be inaccurate unless the agency receives notice of systemic problems with its procedures.

Experian has provided an account of its procedures. The affidavit of David Browne, Experian's compliance manager, explains that the company gathers credit information originated by approximately 40,000 sources. The information is stored in a complex system of national databases, containing approximately 200 million names and addresses and some 2.6 billion trade lines, which include information about consumer accounts, judgments, etc. The company processes over 50 million updates to trade information each day. Lenders report millions of accounts to Experian daily; they provide identifying information, including address, social security number, and date of birth. The identifying information is used to link the credit items to the appropriate consumer. Mr. Browne also notes that Experian's computer system does not store complete credit reports, but rather stores the individual items of credit information linked to identifying information. The credit report is generated at the time an inquiry for it is received.

One can easily see how, even with safeguards in place, mistakes can happen. But given the complexity of the system and the volume of information involved, a mistake does not render the procedures unreasonable. In his attempt to show that Experian's procedures are unreasonable, Sarver argues that someone should have noticed that only the Cross Country accounts were shown to have been involved in bankruptcy. That anomaly should have alerted Experian, Sarver says, to the fact that the report was inaccurate. What Sarver is asking, then, is that each computer-generated report be examined for anomalous information and, if it is found, an investigation be launched. In the absence of notice of prevalent unreliable information from a reporting lender, which would put Experian on notice that problems exist, we cannot find that such a requirement to investigate would be reasonable given the enormous volume of information Experian processes daily.

We found in *Henson* that a consumer reporting agency was not liable, as a matter of law, for reporting information from a judgment docket unless there was prior notice from the consumer that the information might be inaccurate. We said that a

> contrary rule of law would require credit reporting agencies to go beyond the face of numerous court records to determine whether they correctly report the outcome of the underlying action. Such a rule would also require credit reporting agencies to engage in background research which would substantially increase the cost of their services. In turn, they would be forced to pass on the increased costs to their customers and ultimately to the individual consumer.

Henson, 29 F.3d at 285. The same could be said for records from financial institutions. As we said, in his affidavit Mr. Browne proclaims, and there is nothing in the record to make us doubt his statement, that lenders report many millions of accounts to Experian daily. Sarver's report, dated August 26, 2002, contains entries from six different lenders. The increased cost to Experian to examine each of these entries individually would be enormous. We find that as a matter of law there is nothing in this record to show that Experian's procedures are unreasonable.

NOTES & QUESTIONS

1. *A Critical Perspective on* **Sarver.** Consider Elizabeth De Armond:

> In justifying the agency's failure to resolve the anomalies within the records attributed to the plaintiff, the court emphasized the 200 million names and addresses, the 2.6 billion trade lines, and the complexity of the system. This reasoning overlooks that the very complexity of the system reveals the ability of the agency to control the high volume of individuals and records, and that ability should alert the agency to the high risk of misattributing information.

The court ruled that the agency's failure to investigate the inconsistency was not unreasonable because the agency had no notice that the specific lender who had provided information about the impaired accounts was unreliable. However, the question, in order to protect individuals from reckless attribution, should not be whether any single provider is unreliable. The question should have been whether reporting it as the plaintiff's without checking it, given the obvious inconsistency, was reckless. Where the agency was aware of the risk of misattribution from fuzzy matching, and that matching produced a record that was unlike the others, a jury should decide whether the failure to take any steps to verify the anomalous data breached the FCRA's accuracy standard.

The *Sarver* court also reasoned that to require an agency to further investigate the accuracy of a consumer's records when an anomaly appeared would impose "enormous" increased costs. However, the court did not refer to any estimate of the costs or explain why an already complex system capable of making many comparisons among different records could not inexpensively adjust to cross-checking data when reliability was at issue. Furthermore, when an anomaly appears that would work to the consumer's detriment, an agency could simply decline to attribute the negative data should it not want to take the extra effort of verifying it. The decision allows the agency all of the benefits of its database technology with none of the responsibilities.[13]

This criticism raises a baseline issue: who should bear the costs of relative degrees of inaccuracy and accuracy in the credit system? If credit agencies need investigate more kinds of inconsistencies in credit reports, will consumers as a group bear the additional costs?

2. *Is FCRA Too Deferential to Industry Interests?* Consider De Armond on the flaws of FCRA:

[FCRA] inadequately protects individuals from the consequential and emotional damages caused by misattributed acts for several reasons. . . .

The Act's most significant flaw is that it imposes meaningful accuracy requirements only after a false and negative item has been reported, has already been put into the data sea. However, given that digitized data is far more available, accessible, duplicable, and transmittable than old paper records, once a false record has been put into the data sea, it is very hard to ever completely cull it out. . . .

The Act is designed to impose meaningful accuracy standards only after inaccurate information has already been provided by a data provider and reported by a data aggregator. The Act permits the original data provider, called a furnisher under the Act, to furnish nearly any item in a consumer's name without first verifying that it belongs to that consumer. But the Act only prohibits the furnisher from furnishing information that the furnisher either "knows or has reasonable cause to believe" to be inaccurate. A furnisher only has "'reasonable cause to believe that an item of information is inaccurate'" if the furnisher has "specific knowledge, other than solely allegations by the consumer, that would cause a reasonable person to have substantial doubts about the accuracy of the information." . . .

Thus, the agency acquires information that likely has not been subjected to any scrutiny, let alone verified. The agency acquires the information, either

---

[13] Elizabeth D. De Armond, *Frothy Chaos: Modern Data Warehousing and Old-Fashioned Defamation*, 41 Val. U. L. Rev. 1061, 1099-1102, 1108 (2007).

electronically or via magnetic tape from the provider, and stores it electronically, where it sits until needed for a report. Just as the Act imposes a relatively weak accuracy requirement on data providers at the point of initial provision, the Act places only loose limits on aggregators that then report the information. When a subscriber requests a report on a particular consumer, the aggregator, the consumer reporting agency, must only follow "reasonable procedures to assure maximum possible accuracy" of the information that it returns to the subscriber. The provision does not in fact require agencies to ensure the maximum possible accuracy of every item of information, or to do much if anything to match, verify, or cross-check the information. . . .

It is only after an individual has learned that an agency has falsely charged him or her with negative data that the individual can require an aggregator to examine the data. . . .

As *Sarver* also points out, the Experian computer system does not store computer credit reports, but only generates them when an inquiry is received. Individual items of credit information are stored linked to identifying information, which allows their retrieval and compilation into a credit report. Should individual items of information be reviewed for accuracy at the initial time that the credit agency collects them?

3. *Is Negligence the Best Standard?* Jeff Sovern notes that the FCRA's fault standard for liability — negligence — is inadequate to allow many victims to pursue relief because victims "are not normally aware of the procedures a credit bureau uses when issuing an erroneous credit report or what constitutes reasonable procedures." Because each individual consumer's losses will not be very high, consumers may not bring valid cases because of high litigation costs. Therefore, Sovern argues, credit reports should "be made strictly liable for attributing the transactions of identity thieves to innocent customers." Sovern also recommends liquidated damages for identity theft cases in order to reduce litigation costs.[14]

4. *What Constitutes Negligence in Investigating Errors in Consumer Reports?* In *Dennis v. BEH-1, LLC*, 520 F.3d 1066 (9th Cir. 2007), Jason Dennis was sued by his landlord, but the parties agreed to drop the lawsuit after reaching a settlement. The parties filed a "Request for Dismissal" with the court clerk, and the court register properly registered the dismissal. Later on, Experian Information Solutions, Inc. stated on Dennis's credit report that a civil claim judgment had been entered against him for $1,959. Dennis contacted Experian to complain about the error. Experian had Hogan Information Services, a third-party contractor, verify Dennis's claims. Hogan replied that Experian's information was correct and sent along a copy of the stipulation of settlement between Dennis and his landlord. Experian told Dennis that it would not correct his report. Dennis sued under FCRA, contending that Experian failed to maintain "reasonable procedures" under § 1681e(b) to ensure the accuracy of credit reports and that it failed to adequately reinvestigate the disputed

---

[14] Jeff Sovern, *The Jewel of Their Souls: Preventing Identity Theft Through Loss Allocation Rules,* 64 U. Pitt. L. Rev. 343, 393, 406-07 (2003).

information under § 1681i. The district court dismissed Dennis's case on summary judgment. The court of appeals, however, concluded:

> The district court erred insofar as it held that Dennis couldn't make the prima facie showing of inaccurate reporting required by sections 1681e and 1681i. Experian's credit report on Dennis *is* inaccurate. Because the case against Dennis was dismissed, there could have been no "Civil claim judgment" against him: "A dismissal without prejudice . . . has the effect of a final judgment *in favor* of the defendant." Dennis has made the prima facie showing of inaccuracy required by sections 1681e and 1681i.
>
> The district court also seems to have awarded summary judgment to Experian because Dennis didn't offer evidence of "actual damages" as required by section 1681o(a)(1). Here, too, the district court erred. Dennis testified that he hoped to start a business and that he diligently paid his bills on time for years so that he would have a clean credit history when he sought financing for the venture. The only blemish on his credit report in April 2003 was the erroneously reported judgment. According to Dennis, that was enough to cause several lenders to decline his applications for credit, dashing his hopes of starting a new business. Dennis also claims that Experian's error caused his next landlord to demand that Dennis pay a greater security deposit. In addition to those tangible harms, Dennis claims that Experian's inaccurate report caused him emotional distress, which we've held to be "actual damages."

The court of appeals reasoned that Hogan failed to understand the meaning of the Request for Dismissal document and that Experian could readily have detected this mistake:

> Experian could have caught Hogan's error if it had consulted the Civil Register in Dennis's case, which can be viewed free of charge on the Los Angeles Superior Court's excellent website. As described above, the Register clearly indicates that the case against Dennis was dismissed. Experian apparently never looked at the Register.
>
> Experian also could have detected Hogan's mistake by examining the document Hogan retrieved from Dennis's court file. Hogan mistakenly believed that this document proved that judgment had been entered against Dennis; in fact, the document confirms Dennis's account of what happened. The document is a written stipulation between Dennis and his landlord that no judgment would be entered against Dennis so long as Dennis complied with the payment schedule. The parties couldn't have been clearer on this point: "If paid, case dismissed. If not paid, judgment to enter upon [landlord's] declaration of non-payment. . . ."

The court of appeals further concluded that it had no need to remand the case for a jury trial regarding Experian's negligence:

> Even accepting as true everything Experian has claimed, no rational jury could find that the company wasn't negligent. The stipulation Hogan retrieved from Dennis's court file may be unusual, but it's also unambiguous, and Experian was negligent in mis-interpreting it as an entry of judgment. Experian is also responsible for the negligence of Hogan, the investigation service it hired to review Dennis's court file. . . .
>
> When conducting a reinvestigation pursuant to 15 U.S.C. § 1681i, a credit reporting agency must exercise reasonable diligence in examining the court file

to determine whether an adverse judgment has, in fact, been entered against the consumer. A reinvestigation that overlooks documents in the court file expressly stating that *no* adverse judgment was entered falls far short of this standard. On our own motion, therefore, we grant summary judgment to Dennis on his claim that Experian negligently failed to conduct a reasonable reinvestigation in violation of section 1681i. Whether Experian's failure was also willful, in violation of section 1681n, is a question for the jury on remand.

This case illustrates how important it is for Experian, a company that traffics in the reputations of ordinary people, to train its employees to understand the legal significance of the documents they rely on. Because Experian negligently failed to conduct a reasonable reinvestigation, we grant summary judgment to Dennis on this claim. We remand only so that the district court may calculate damages and award attorney's fees. As to all other claims under the Fair Credit Reporting Act, we reverse summary judgment for Experian and remand for trial. Dennis is also entitled to attorney's fees for an entirely successful appeal. 15 U.S.C. § 1681*o*(a)(2). . . .

5. IDENTITY THEFT AND CONSUMER REPORTING

Identity theft is one of the most rapidly growing forms of crime. Identity theft occurs when a criminal obtains an individual's personal information and uses it to open new bank accounts, acquire credit cards, and obtain loans in that individual's name. Consider the following example from journalist Bob Sullivan:

> Starting in August 1998, Anthony Lemar Taylor spent a year successfully pretending to be the golf superstar [Tiger Woods]. Taylor's $50,000 spending spree included a big-screen television, stereo speakers, a living room set, even a U-Haul to move all the stolen goods. Taylor, who looks nothing like the golf legend, simply obtained a driver's license using Tiger's real name, Eldrick Woods; then, he used Wood's Social Security number to get credit in his name.
> . . .
> When Tiger himself testified during the case in 2001, Taylor, a 30-year-old career criminal, didn't stand a chance. Wood's star power helped the state throw the book at Taylor. . . . The firm, swift justice might have made other potential identity thieves think twice, but for this: Precious few identity thefts are even investigated, let alone prosecuted to the full extent of the law. The average victim has enough trouble getting the police to bother filling out an incident report. . . .
> The real world of identity theft . . . is . . . a haunting, paperwork nightmare, one often compared to financial rape, littered with small and large tragedies. . . . Couples can't buy homes because their credit is damaged. Identity theft victims are often denied access to the lowest interest rates and can pay as much as 50 percent more to borrow money. . . . And thousands of people face hundreds of hours of electronic trials against their erroneous credit reports and eventually end with fraudulent debts and endless nightly threatening calls from collection agencies.[15]

According to a 2007 report to the FTC, "approximately 8.3 million U.S. adults discovered that they were victims of some form of ID theft in 2005."[16] According to this report's estimates, the total losses from ID theft in that year were $15.6

---

[15] Bob Sullivan, *Your Evil Twin: Behind the Identity Theft Epidemic* 35-36 (2004).

[16] Synovate, Federal Trade Commission — 2006 Identity Theft Survey Report (Nov. 2007).

billion. Moreover, "victims of all types of ID theft spent hours of their time resolving the various problems that result from ID theft. The median value for the number of hours spent resolving problems by all victims was four. However, 10 percent of all victims spent at least 55 hours resolving their problems."

In an important caveat, however, this report also notes that it may not capture all types of identity theft. In particular, it does not measure "synthetic ID theft." This activity involves a criminal creating a fictitious identity by combining information from one or more consumers. Affected consumers face considerable obstacles in detecting synthetic ID theft; therefore, any survey of identity theft, which depends on consumer self-reporting, is likely to underreport it.

A significant amount of identity theft involves the consumer reporting system. When an identity thief starts creating delinquent debts in a person's name, creditors report the delinquencies to the consumer reporting agencies, and the delinquencies begin to appear on the person's credit report. This can severely affect the person's credit score and make it impossible for the person to secure credit. What are the responsibilities of consumer reporting agencies in ensuring that the data it reports about individuals really pertains to them rather than to the identity thief who impersonated them?

In addition to protections already in FCRA, the FACTA added a few additional measures to address identity theft.

One-Call Fraud Alerts. The FACTA amends FCRA to enable consumers to alert only one consumer reporting agency of potential fraud rather than all of them. That agency must notify the other consumer reporting agencies. 15 U.S.C. § 1681c-1.

Business Transaction Data. The FACTA gives victims of identity theft the right to require certain disclosures from the creditors used by the identity thief; these disclosures concern information about the fraudulent transactions carried out in the victim's name. 15 U.S.C. § 1681g(e)(1). To obtain this information from the creditors, however, the victim must provide one form of identification from a list (that the business gets to pick) as well as proof of the claim of identity theft (police report, affidavit). The victim's request must be in writing and must specify the date of the transaction and other transaction data. Business entities can decline this request if they believe in good faith that there is not "a high degree of confidence in knowing the true identity of the individual requesting the information." § 1681g(e)(2). Further, business entities cannot be sued if they make a disclosure in good faith under these provisions. § 1681g(e)(7). Business entities are not required to alter their record-keeping practices to provide the information required by these provisions. § 1681g(e)(8).

Block of Identity Theft Information. The FACTA amends the FCRA to provide:

> (a) *Block.* Except as otherwise provided in this section, a consumer reporting agency shall block the reporting of any information in the file of a consumer that the consumer identifies as information that resulted from an alleged identity theft, not later than 4 business days after the date of receipt by such agency of —

(1) appropriate proof of the identity of the consumer;

(2) a copy of an identity theft report;

(3) the identification of such information by the consumer; and

(4) a statement by the consumer that the information is not information relating to any transaction by the consumer.

(b) *Notification.* A consumer reporting agency shall promptly notify the furnisher of information identified by the consumer under subsection (a) —

(1) that the information may be a result of identity theft;

(2) that an identity theft report has been filed;

(3) that a block has been requested under this section; and

(4) of the effective dates of the block. § 1681c-2.

Social Security Number Truncation. If a consumer requests it, consumer reporting agencies must not disclose the first five digits of the consumer's Social Security Number. § 1681g(a)(1)(A).

Free Consumer Reports. FACTA requires consumer reporting agencies to provide a free consumer report once a year at the request of a consumer. § 1681j.

Disclosure of Credit Scores. FACTA requires consumer reporting agencies to disclose to a consumer her credit score. Many consumer reporting agencies previously would not divulge a person's credit score. § 1681g.

SLOANE V. EQUIFAX INFORMATION SERVICES, LLC

510 F.3d 495 (4th Cir. 2007)

DIANA GRIBBON MOTZ, J. After Suzanne Sloane discovered that a thief had stolen her identity and ruined her credit, she notified the police and sought to have Equifax Information Services, LLC, a credit reporting service, correct the resulting errors in her credit report. The police promptly arrested and jailed the thief. But twenty-one months later, Equifax still had not corrected the errors in Suzanne's credit report. Accordingly, Suzanne brought this action against Equifax for violations of the Fair Credit Reporting Act (FCRA), 15 U.S.C.A. §§ 1681 *et seq.* A jury found that Equifax had violated the Act in numerous respects and awarded Suzanne $351,000 in actual damages ($106,000 for economic losses and $245,000 for mental anguish, humiliation, and emotional distress). The district court entered judgment in the amount of $351,000. In addition, without permitting Equifax to file a written opposition, the court also awarded Suzanne attorney's fees in the amount of $181,083. On appeal, Equifax challenges the award of damages and attorney's fees. We affirm in part and reverse and remand in part.

On June 25, 2003, Suzanne Sloane entered Prince William Hospital to deliver a baby. She left the hospital not only a new mother, but also the victim of identity theft. A recently hired hospital employee named Shovana Sloan noticed similarity in the women's names and birth dates and, in November and December 2003, began using Suzanne's social security number to obtain credit cards, loans, cash advances, and other goods and services totaling more than $30,000. At the end of

January 2004, Suzanne discovered these fraudulent transactions when Citibank notified her that it had cancelled her credit card and told her to contact Equifax if she had any concerns.

Unable to reach Equifax by telephone on a Friday evening, Suzanne went instead to the Equifax website, where she was able to access her credit report and discovered Shovana Sloan's name and evidence of the financial crimes Shovana had committed. Suzanne promptly notified the police, and contacted Equifax, which assertedly placed a fraud alert on her credit file. Equifax told Suzanne to "roll up her sleeves" and start calling all of her "20-some" creditors to notify them of the identity theft. Suzanne took the next two days off from work to contact each of her creditors, and, at their direction, she submitted numerous notarized forms to correct her credit history.

Suzanne, however, continued to experience problems with Equifax. On March 31, 2004, almost two months after reporting the identity theft to Equifax and despite her efforts to work with individual creditors as Equifax had advised, Suzanne and her husband, Tracey, tried to secure a pre-qualification letter to buy a vacation home, but were turned down. The loan officer told them that Suzanne's credit score was "terrible" — in fact, the "worst" the loan officer had ever seen — and that no loan would be possible until the numerous problems in Suzanne's Equifax credit report had been corrected. The loan officer also told Suzanne not to apply for additional credit in the meantime, because each credit inquiry would appear on her credit report and further lower her score.

Chagrined that Equifax had not yet corrected these errors in her credit report, Suzanne refrained from applying for any type of consumer credit for seven months. But, in October 2004, after the repeated breakdown of their family car, Suzanne and Tracey attempted to rely on Suzanne's credit to purchase a used car at a local dealership. Following a credit check, the car salesman pulled Tracey aside and informed him that it would be impossible to approve the financing so long as Suzanne's name appeared on the loan. Similarly, when the Sloanes returned to the mortgage company to obtain a home loan in January 2005, eight months after their initial visit, they were offered only an adjustable rate loan instead of a less expensive 30-year fixed rate loan in part because of Equifax's still inaccurate credit report.

In frustration, on March 9, 2005, more than thirteen months after first reporting the identity theft to Equifax, Suzanne sent a formal letter to the credit reporting agency, disputing twenty-four specific items in her credit report and requesting their deletion. Equifax agreed to delete the majority of these items, but after assertedly verifying two accounts with Citifinancial, Inc., Equifax notified Suzanne that it would not remove these two items. At trial, Equifax admitted that under its "verified victim policy," it should have automatically removed these Citifinancial items at Suzanne's request, but it failed to do so in violation of its own written procedures.

Two months later, on May 9, 2005, Suzanne again wrote to Equifax, still disputing the two Citifinancial accounts, and now also contesting two Washington Mutual accounts that Equifax had previously deleted but had mistakenly restored to Suzanne's report. When Equifax attempted to correct these mistakes, it exacerbated matters further by generating a second credit file bearing Shovana Sloan's name but containing Suzanne's social security number. Compounding this mistake, on May 23, 2005, Equifax sent a letter to Suzanne's house addressed to Shovana Sloan, warning Shovana that *she* was possibly the victim of identity theft and offering to sell her a service to monitor her credit file. Then, on June 7, 2005, Equifax sent copies of *both* credit reports to Suzanne; notably, both credit reports still contained the disputed Citifinancial accounts.

The stress of these problems weighed on Suzanne and significantly contributed to the deterioration of her marriage to Tracey. . . . In May 2005, the credit situation forced Tracey, a high school teacher, to abandon his plans to take a sabbatical during which he had hoped to develop land for modular homes with his father. The Sloanes frequently fought during the day and slept in separate rooms at night. . . . Also, during this period, Suzanne was frequently unable to sleep at night, and as her insomnia worsened, she found herself nodding off while driving home from work in the evening. Even after the couple took a vacation to reconcile in August 2005, when they returned home, they were greeted with the denial of a line of credit from Wachovia Bank. . . .

On November 4, 2005 — following twenty-one months of struggle to correct her credit report — Suzanne filed this action against Equifax, Trans Union, LLC, Experian Information Solutions, Inc., and Citifinancial, alleging violations of the FCRA. After settling a separate suit against Prince William Hospital and the personnel company that placed Shovana Sloan in the hospital's accounting department, Suzanne settled her claims in this action against Experian, Trans Union, and Citifinancial. Equifax, however, refused to settle. Thus, the case proceeded to trial with Equifax the sole remaining defendant. The jury returned a verdict against Equifax, awarding Suzanne $106,000 for economic loss and $245,000 for mental anguish, humiliation, and emotional distress.

Equifax moved for judgment as a matter of law and for a new trial or remittitur on the jury's award of damages for emotional distress. The district court denied Equifax's post-trial motions and then, without permitting Equifax to submit an opposition to Suzanne's request for attorney's fees, ordered Equifax to pay $181,083 in attorney's fees. This appeal followed. . . .

In this case, the jury specifically found, via a special verdict, that Suzanne proved by a preponderance of the evidence that Equifax violated the FCRA by negligently: (1) failing to follow reasonable procedures designed to assure maximum accuracy on her consumer credit report; (2) failing to conduct a reasonable investigation to determine whether disputed information in her credit report was inaccurate; (3) failing to delete information from the report that it found after reinvestigation to be inaccurate, incomplete, or unverified; and (4) reinserting information into her credit file that it had previously deleted. On appeal, Equifax does not challenge the jury's findings that Suzanne proved that it violated the FCRA in all of these respects.

The FCRA provides a private cause of action for those damaged by violations of the statute. *See* 15 U.S.C.A. §§ 1681n, 1681o. A successful plaintiff can recover both actual and punitive damages for willful violations of the FCRA, *id.* § 1681n(a), and actual damages for negligent violations, *id.* § 1681o(a). Actual damages may include not only economic damages, but also damages for humiliation and mental distress. The statute also provides that a successful plaintiff suing under the FCRA may recover reasonable attorney's fees. 15 U.S.C.A. §§ 1681n(a)(3), 1681o(a)(2). . . .

Equifax first argues that because Suzanne assertedly suffered a single, indivisible injury, she should not recover any damages from Equifax or, alternatively, her recovery should be reduced to take account of her prior settlements with other defendants. According to Equifax, the prior settlements have fully, or almost fully, compensated Suzanne for all of her injuries.

Equifax relies on the "one satisfaction rule" to support its argument. *See Chisholm v. UHP Projects, Inc.,* 205 F.3d 731, 737 (4th Cir. 2000) ("[T]his equitable doctrine operates to reduce a plaintiff's recovery from the nonsettling defendant to prevent the plaintiff from recovering twice from the same assessment of liability."). But, in the case at hand, we cannot find, as a matter of law, that Suzanne has suffered from a "single, indivisible harm" that has already been redressed by other parties. . . .

To the contrary, Suzanne provided credible evidence that her emotional and economic damages resulted from separate acts by separate parties. She did not attempt to hold any of the credit reporting agencies responsible for damages arising from either the identity theft itself or the initial inaccuracies that the theft generated in her credit reports. Moreover, although some of Suzanne's interactions with Equifax overlapped with exchanges with other credit reporting agencies, her encounters with Equifax both predate and postdate these other exchanges. . . .

Further, during the period when Suzanne attempted to correct the mistakes made by all three agencies, each agency produced reports with different inaccuracies, and each agency either corrected or exacerbated these mistakes independently of the others. Thus, even during this period, the inaccuracies in Equifax's credit reports caused Suzanne discrete injuries independent of those caused by the other credit reporting agencies.

For all of these reasons, we reject Equifax's argument that Suzanne has suffered from a single, indivisible injury or has been doubly compensated as a consequence of her prior settlements.

Equifax next argues that the evidence does not support any award for economic losses. Equifax claims that only speculation and conjecture support such an award, and so the district court erred in denying Equifax's motion for judgment as to this award.

We disagree. The evidence at trial in this case clearly demonstrates that on numerous occasions Suzanne attempted to secure lines of credit from a variety of financial institutions, only to be either denied outright or offered credit on less advantageous terms that she might have received absent Equifax's improper conduct. At times, these financial institutions consulted credit reports from other agencies, but at other times these institutions relied exclusively on the erroneous credit information provided by Equifax. Based on these incidents, we find that there is a legally sufficient evidentiary basis for a reasonable jury to have found that Equifax's conduct resulted in economic losses for Suzanne. Therefore, the district court did not err in denying Equifax's motion regarding this award.

Additionally, Equifax asserts that the district court erred in refusing to order remittitur of the mental anguish, humiliation, and emotional distress damages award to no more than $25,000. Equifax contends that the jury's award of $245,000 is inconsistent with awards in similar cases and is disproportionate to any actual injury proved at trial. Suzanne, by contrast, contends that the evidence provides more than adequate support for the jury's award. To resolve this question, we set forth the relevant governing principles, apply these principles to the evidence before the jury, and compare the evidence and emotional distress award in Suzanne's case with the evidence and award in all assertedly relevant cases. . .

We begin with Federal Rule of Civil Procedure 59(a), which provides that if a court concludes that a jury award of compensatory damages is excessive, it may order a new trial nisi remittitur. . . . A district court abuses its discretion only by upholding an award of damages when "the jury's verdict is against the weight of the evidence or based on evidence which is false."

In this case, the district court found that the jury's emotional distress award was "not an unreasonable conclusion from this evidence." The court noted that the jury could base its award on Equifax's specific actions, as distinct from those of the other credit reporting agencies, and that Equifax's actions directly led to the mounting frustration and distress that Suzanne felt for almost two years. As one example of Equifax's specific actions, the court recalled the letter that Equifax sent to Suzanne, many months after she had notified Equifax of the identity theft, bearing the name of the identity thief and warning the thief, not Suzanne, that the thief's personal information was in peril. . . .

Moreover, Equifax does not deny that Suzanne suffered emotional distress. Nor does Equifax contend that Suzanne failed to produce sufficient evidence to sustain some award for this injury. Rather, Equifax simply proposes replacing the jury's number with one of its own invention — offering $25,000 in place of $245,000. Yet when asked at oral argument to explain the basis for the proposed remittitur, Equifax's counsel could offer no legal or factual basis for this amount, conceding that the number had been taken "out of the air." Not only is such an unprincipled approach intrinsically unsound, but it also directly contravenes the Seventh Amendment, which precludes an appellate court from replacing an award of compensatory damages with one of the court's own choosing. In short, the issue before us is neither whether Suzanne offered sufficient evidence at trial to sustain an award for emotional distress nor whether we believe that Equifax's "out of the air" $25,000 represents a fair estimate of those damages, but whether the jury's award is *excessive* in light of evidence presented at trial.

Our previous cases establish the type of evidence required to support an award for emotional damages. We have warned that "[n]ot only is emotional distress fraught with vagueness and speculation, it is easily susceptible to fictitious and trivial claims." *Price v. City of Charlotte,* 93 F.3d 1241, 1250 (4th Cir. 1996). For this reason, although specifically recognizing that a plaintiff's testimony can provide sufficient evidence to support an emotional distress award, we have required a plaintiff to "reasonably and sufficiently explain the circumstances of [the] injury and not resort to mere conclusory statements." Thus, we have distinguished between plaintiff testimony that amounts only to "conclusory statements" and plaintiff testimony that "sufficiently articulate[s]" true "demonstrable emotional distress."

In *Knussman v. Maryland,* 272 F.3d 625 (4th Cir. 2001), we summarized the factors properly considered in determinating the potential excessiveness of an award for emotional distress. They include the factual context in which the emotional distress arose; evidence corroborating the testimony of the plaintiff; the nexus between the conduct of the defendant and the emotional distress; the degree of such mental distress; mitigating circumstances, if any; physical injuries suffered due to the emotional distress; medical attention resulting from the emotional duress; psychiatric or psychological treatment; and the loss of income, if any.

In the present case, Suzanne offered considerable objective verification of her emotional distress, chronic anxiety, and frustration during the twenty-one months that she attempted to correct Equifax's errors. First, her repeated denials of credit and continuous problems with Equifax furnish an objective and inherently reasonable "factual context" for her resulting claims of emotional distress. Suzanne also corroborated her account in two ways. She offered "sufficiently articulated" descriptions of her protracted anxiety through detailed testimony of specific events and the humiliation and anger she experienced as a result of each occurrence. She also provided evidence that the distress was apparent to others, particularly her family; Tracey, for instance, described in detail his wife's ongoing struggles with Equifax and the emotional toll these events took upon her. In addition, substantial trial evidence attested to the direct "nexus" between Equifax's violations of the FCRA and Suzanne's emotional distress. Furthermore, Suzanne's emotional distress manifested itself in terms of physical symptoms, particularly insomnia. . .

.

Reviewing this evidence in light of the appropriate factors already set forth, we conclude that substantial, if not overwhelming, objective evidence supports an emotional distress award. Equifax ignores much of this evidence, however, and insists that an award of $245,000 is "inconsistent with awards in other similar cases." But Equifax relies on cases which are in fact not very "similar" to the case at hand and so provide little assistance in assessing the amount of the emotional distress award here. . . .

As Equifax's authorities indicate, finding helpful precedent for comparison here is not a simple task. The recent emergence of identity theft and the rapid growth of the credit-reporting industry present a unique dilemma without clear precedent. When Congress enacted the FCRA in 1970, it recognized the vital role that credit-reporting agencies had assumed within the burgeoning culture of American consumerism. Since the mid-1980s, the introduction of computerized information technology and data-warehousing has led to the national consolidation of the credit-reporting industry into the "Big Three" — Equifax, Experian, and Trans Union — and rendered credit reporting an integral part of our most ordinary consumer transactions. According to recent data, each of these national credit-reporting agencies has perhaps 1.5 billion credit accounts held by approximately 190 million individuals. Each receives more than two billion items of information every month, and together these three agencies issue approximately two million consumer credit reports each day.

Against this backdrop, identity theft has emerged over the last decade as one of the fastest growing white-collar crimes in the United States. . . . Given the rapid emergence of identity theft in the last decade, it comes as no surprise that past precedent fails to fully reflect the unfortunate current reality. . . .

A survey of the other, more recent FCRA cases that involve requests for remittitur of emotional distress awards suggests that approved awards more typically range between $20,000 and $75,000.

This handful of cases, while helpful, differs from the case at hand. For, unlike the plaintiffs in those cases, Suzanne did not suffer from isolated or accidental reporting errors. Rather, as a victim of identity theft, she suffered the systematic manipulation of her personal information, which, despite her best efforts, Equifax failed to correct over a protracted period of time. Of course, Equifax bore no responsibility for the initial theft, but the FCRA makes the company responsible for taking reasonable steps to correct Suzanne's credit report once she brought the theft to the company's attention; this Equifax utterly failed to do. A reasonable jury could conclude that Equifax's repeated errors engendered more emotional distress than that found in these other FCRA cases.

We also believe that some guidance can be gained from case law concerning defamation. Prior to the enactment of the FCRA, defamation was one of several common-law actions used by plaintiffs in response to the dissemination of inaccurate credit information.[17] These common-law causes of action parallel those offered under the FCRA in that they typically involve a defendant found liable for propagating inaccurate information about the plaintiff, and the effects, while unquestionably harmful, are difficult to translate into monetary terms. . . . [C]ourts frequently sustain emotional distress awards in the range of $250,000 in defamation cases.

We do not believe the evidence presented here permits an award of this magnitude because, after all, this case does not involve actual defamation. Moreover, Suzanne presented almost no evidence at trial to suggest that Equifax's violations of the FCRA resulted in harm to her reputation, and it appears that few people beyond Suzanne's family and potential creditors knew of her disastrous credit file. We therefore believe that the maximum award supported by the evidence here must be significantly less than these defamation awards. But, considering the extensive corroboration offered at trial concerning the many months of emotional distress, mental anguish, and humiliation suffered by Suzanne, we believe that the evidence does support an award in the maximum amount of $150,000. We recognize that even this amount is appreciably more than that awarded for emotional distress in most other FCRA cases. But, as explained earlier, the case at hand differs significantly from those cases. A $150,000 award reflects those differences—the repeated violations of the FCRA found by the jury in its special verdict, the number of errors contained in Equifax's credit reports, and the protracted length of time during which Equifax failed to correct Suzanne's credit file. Accordingly, we reduce the emotional distress award to $150,000 and grant a new trial nisi remittitur at Suzanne's option. . . .

[The court vacated the district court's grant of attorney's fees in the amount of $181,083 because the district court failed to allow Equifax to submit a written opposition to Sloane's motion for attorney's fees. The case was remanded to allow Equifax to file its opposition.]

---

[17] A provision of the FCRA bars consumers from bringing actions "in the nature of defamation, invasion of privacy, or negligence" in certain specified contexts, except as those causes of action arise under sections 1681n and 1681o of the FCRA. 15 U.S.C.A. § 1681h(e).

NOTES & QUESTIONS

1. ***Damages.*** Was the remittitur to $150,000 appropriate? Why should damage awards be limited based on the damage awards in other cases? As the court noted, they involve very different facts than the case at bar.

   Also recall the court's statement that "this case does not involve actual defamation. . . . Suzanne presented almost no evidence at trial to suggest that Equifax's violations of the FCRA resulted in harm to her reputation, and it appears that few people beyond Suzanne's family and potential creditors knew of her disastrous credit file." Why doesn't this case involve "harm to her reputation"? Don't reports on people's creditworthiness affect their financial reputations, that is, their ability to pay back their debts, their trustworthiness, and dependability?

2. ***The Harm of Identity Theft.*** When assessing the damages Sloane suffered from her identity theft ordeal, how much of the harm was caused by Equifax's actions? Purportedly, the entire incident of identity theft caused her marital discord, insomnia, and emotional distress. Yet, the identity theft did involve, after all, not only Equifax, but the identity thief, creditors, and other credit reporting agencies. Are the damages assessed to Equifax proportionate to Equifax's contribution to Sloane's ordeal? Or should Equifax be viewed as the "least cost avoider," the party who can internalize the costs of preventing this harm at the least overall cost?

3. ***Transparency.*** Chris Hoofnagle proposes that policy responses to identity theft are hobbled by a lack of information about the dimensions of the problem.[18] He argues: "We are asking the wrong people about the crime. . . . Victims often do not know how their personal data were stolen or who stole the information." Hoofnagle's solution is to create a reporting requirement on financial institutions, including all lenders and organizations that control access to accounts (such as PayPal and Western Union). There would be three disclosure requirements for these entities: "(1) the number of identity theft incidents suffered or avoided; (2) the forms of identity theft attempted and the financial products targeted (e.g., mortgage loan or credit card); and (3) the amount of loss suffered or avoided."

   Do you think that consumers would respond to such market information and actually switch accounts from one organization to another? Personal information might be stolen from nonfinancial institutions, such as a college, and then used by a criminal for fraud at a bank. How can incentives be provided for nonfinancial institutions to have adequate security?

---

[18] Chris Jay Hoofnagle, *Identity Theft: Making the Known Unknowns Known*, 21 Harv. J. L. & Tech. 97 (2007).

B. THE GRAMM-LEACH-BLILEY ACT

In 1999, Congress passed the Financial Services Modernization Act, more commonly known as the Gramm-Leach-Bliley Act (GLBA), Pub. L. No. 106-102, codified at 15 U.S.C. §§ 6801–6809. The GLBA was designed to restructure the financial services industries, which had long been regulated under the Glass-Steagall Act of 1933. The Glass-Steagall Act, passed in response to the Great Depression, prevented different types of financial institutions (e.g., banks, brokerage houses, insurers) from affiliating with each other. The GLBA enables the creation of financial conglomerates that provide a host of different forms of financial services. The ideas was to create new "financial supermarkets" that would democratize financial opportunities by bringing Wall Street to Main Street.

The law authorizes widespread sharing of personal information by financial institutions such as banks, insurers, and investment companies. The law permits sharing of personal information between companies that are joined together or affiliated with each other as well as sharing of information between unaffiliated companies. To protect privacy, the Act requires a variety of agencies (FTC, Comptroller of Currency, SEC, and a number of others) to establish "appropriate standards for the financial institutions subject to their jurisdiction" to "insure security and confidentiality of customer records and information" and "protect against unauthorized access" to the records. 15 U.S.C. § 6801.

Nonpublic Personal Information. The privacy provisions of the GLBA only apply to "nonpublic personal information" that consists of "personally identifiable financial information." § 6809(4). Thus, the law only protects *financial* information that is *not public*.

Sharing of Information with Affiliated Companies. The GLBA permits financial institutions that are joined together to share the "nonpublic personal information" that each affiliate possesses. The test for affiliation looks to whether there is control by one company of the other, or a situation of "common control." For affiliated companies, widespread sharing is permitted. After all, the policy behind the GLBA was to permit the creation of financial conglomerates to provide a broader palette of services to ordinary Americans. Data sharing within these new entities was seen as helping them target their customers to better meet their needs.

For example, suppose an affiliate has access to a person's medical information. This information could be shared with an affiliate bank that could then turn down a person for a loan. Affiliates must tell customers that they are sharing such information. § 6802(a). The disclosure can be in the form of a general disclosure in a privacy policy. § 6803(a). There is no way for individuals to block this sharing of information.

Sharing of Information with Nonaffiliated Companies. Financial institutions can share personal information with nonaffiliated companies only if they first provide individuals with the ability to opt out of the disclosure. § 6802(b). However, people cannot opt out if the financial institution provides personal data to nonaffiliated third parties "to perform services for or functions on behalf of the financial institution, including marketing of the financial institution's own products and services, or financial products or services offered pursuant to joint agreements between two or more financial institutions." § 6802(b)(2). The financial institution must disclose the information sharing and must have a contract with the third party requiring the third party to maintain the confidentiality of the information. § 6802(b)(2). Third parties receiving personal data from a financial institution cannot reuse that information. § 6802(c). These provisions do not apply to disclosures to credit reporting agencies.

Limits on Disclosure. Financial institutions cannot disclose (other than to credit reporting agencies) account numbers or credit card numbers for use in direct marketing (telemarketing, e-mail, or mail). § 6802(d).

Privacy Notices. The GLBA requires that financial institutions inform customers of their privacy policies. In particular, customers must be informed about policies concerning the disclosure of personal information to affiliates and other companies and categories of information that are disclosed and the security of personal data. § 6803(a).

The Safeguards Rule. The GLBA requires the FTC and other agencies to establish security standards for nonpublic personal information. *See* 15 U.S.C. §§ 6801(b), 6805(b)(2). The FTC issued its final regulations on May 23, 2002. According to the regulations, financial institutions "shall develop, implement, and maintain a comprehensive information security program" that is appropriate to the "size and complexity" of the institution, the "nature and scope" of the institution's activities, and the "sensitivity of any customer information at issue." 16 C.F.R. § 314.3(a). An "information security program" is defined as "the administrative, technical, or physical safeguards [an institution uses] to access, collect, distribute, process, store, use, transmit, dispose of, or otherwise handle customer information." § 314.2(b).

Preemption. The GLBA does not preempt state laws that provide greater protection to privacy. § 6807(b). As will be discussed below, Vermont has made use of this provision and requires opt in, or affirmative consumer consent, before a financial institution can share nonpublic personal financial information pertaining to a consumer to a nonaffiliated third party.

Critics and Supporters. Consider the following critique by Ted Janger and Paul Schwartz:

> The GLB Act has managed to disappoint both industry leaders and privacy advocates alike. Why are so many observers frustrated with the GLB Act? We have already noted the complaint of financial services companies regarding the expense of privacy notices. These organizations also argue that there have been scant pay-off from the costly mailings — and strong evidence backs up this claim. For example, a survey from the American Banker's Association found that 22% of banking customers said that they received a privacy notice but did not read it,

and 41% could not even recall receiving a notice. The survey also found only 0.5% of banking customers had exercised their opt-out rights. . . .

Not only are privacy notices difficult to understand, but they are written in a fashion that makes it hard to exercise the opt-out rights that GLB Act mandates. For example, opt-out provisions are sometimes buried in privacy notices. As the Public Citizen Litigation Group has found, "Explanations of how to opt-out invariably appear at the end of the notices. Thus, before they learn how to opt-out, consumers must trudge through up to ten pages of fine print. . . ." Public Citizen also identified many passages regarding opt-out that "are obviously designed to discourage consumers from exercising their rights under the statute." For example, some financial institutions include an opt-out box only "in a thicket of misleading statements." . . . A final tactic of GLB Act privacy notices is to state that consumers who opt-out may fail to receive "valuable offers." . . .

The GLB Act merely contains an opt-out requirement; as a result, information can be disclosed to non-affiliated entities unless individuals take affirmative action, namely, informing the financial entity that they refuse this sharing of their personal data. By setting its default as an opt-out, the GLB Act fails to create any penalty on the party with superior knowledge, the financial entity, should negotiations fail to occur. In other words, the GLB leaves the burden of bargaining on the less informed party, the individual consumer. These doubts about the efficacy of opt-out are supported, at least indirectly, by the evidence concerning sometimes confusing, sometimes misleading privacy notices. . . . An opt-out default creates incentives for privacy notices that lead to *inaction* by the consumer.[19]

Marcy Peek argues that the GLBA has actually done more to facilitate information sharing than to protect privacy. Enabling greater information uses so long as customers have a right to opt out has resulted in much more information sharing since "the opt-out right is meaningless in practice; the right to opt out of the trafficking of one's personal information is explained in lengthy, legalistic privacy policies that most people throw away as just more junk mail." More broadly, Peek argues, several laws purporting to protect privacy often "represent a façade of protection for consumers, keeping them complacent in the purported knowledge that someone is protecting their privacy interests." In the end, Peek argues, "corporate power drives information privacy law."[20]

In contrast, Peter Swire argues that the GLBA "works surprisingly well as privacy legislation":

Recognizing the criticisms to date, and the limits of the available evidence, I would like to make the case for a decidedly more optimistic view of the effect of the GLB notices. Even in their current flawed form and even if not a single consumer exercised the opt-out right, I contend that a principal effect of the notices has been to require financial institutions to inspect their own practices. In this respect, the detail and complexity of the GLB notices is actually a virtue. In order to draft the notice, many financial institutions undertook an extensive process, often for the first time, to learn just how data is and is not shared between different parts of the organization and with third parties. Based on my extensive

[19] Ted Janger & Paul M. Schwartz, *The Gramm-Leach-Bliley Act, Information Privacy, and the Limits of Default Rules*, 86 Minn. L. Rev. 1219, 1230-32, 1241 (2002).

[20] Marcy E. Peek, Information *Privacy and Corporate Power: Towards a Re-Imagination of Information Privacy Law*, 37 Seton Hall L. Rev. 127, 147-49, 137 (2006).

discussions with people in the industry, I believe that many institutions discovered practices that they decided, upon deliberation, to change. One public example of this was the decision of Bank of America no longer to share its customers' data with third parties, even subject to opt-out. The detailed and complex notice, in short, created a more detailed roadmap for privacy compliance.[21]

The critics of the GLBA and Swire appear to be looking at the statute from two different perspectives. The critics are looking at it from a consumer-centric view; Swire sees the positive effect that the statute has on practices within institutions. Is there a way for a statute to have a positive impact in both areas?

C. FEDERAL AND STATE FINANCIAL PRIVACY LAWS

1. STATE FINANCIAL LAWS

The Vermont Opt-In Approach. In contrast to the GLBA approach, Vermont permits sharing of personal data by financial institutions with nonaffiliated companies only if companies obtain an individual's consent. This requirement of a positive response before information can be shared is termed an "opt in." State of Vermont, Department, Insurance, Securities & Health Care Administration, Banking Division, Regulation B-2001-01, Privacy of Consumer Financial and Health Information Regulation. This regulation also carefully defines the acceptable form of and process for opt-in notice. For example, when consumers want to revoke their opting in to information sharing, financial institutions cannot force "the consumer to write his or her own letter." Financial institutions also cannot make consumers "use a check-off box that was provided with the initial notice but [that] is not included with subsequent notices."

California's SB1. California's Financial Information Privacy Act, known as "SB1," Cal. Fin. Code §§ 4050–4060, was enacted "to afford persons greater privacy protections that those provided in . . . the federal Gramm-Leach-Bliley Act." § 4051. Specifically, the California legislature found that the Gramm-Leach-Bliley Act "increases the likelihood that the personal financial information of California residents will be widely shared among, between, and within companies" and that "the policies intended to protect financial privacy imposed by the Gramm-Leach-Bliley Act are inadequate to meet the privacy concerns of California residents." § 4051.5.

In contrast to the Gramm-Leach-Bliley Act, which provides people with an opt-out right, SB1, like the Vermont regulation, requires opt in:

[A] financial institution shall not sell, share, transfer, or otherwise disclose nonpublic personal information to or with any nonaffiliated third parties without the explicit prior consent of the consumer to whom the nonpublic personal information relates. § 4052.5.

---

[21] Peter P. Swire, *The Surprising Virtues of the New Financial Privacy Law*, 86 Minn. L. Rev. 1263, 1315-16 (2002).

SB1 permits financial institutions to offer incentives or discounts for people to opt in. § 4053.

Financial institutions challenged SB1, arguing that it was preempted by the FCRA. In *American Bankers Ass'n v. Lockyer*, 541 F.3d 1214 (9th Cir. 2008), the Ninth Circuit found that § 4053(b)(1) of SB1 had applications that federal law did not preempt. In particular, it ruled that the affiliate-sharing provisions of SB1 could be narrowed to "exclude the regulation of consumer report infor-mation as defined by the FCRA, 15 U.S.C. 1681a(d)(1)." This ruling means that the opt-in provided for Californian residents by SB1 survives for nonpublic personal information that does not fall within the definition of a "consumer report" in FCRA.

The North Dakota Opt-In Referendum and Other States. In June 2002, North Dakotans overwhelmingly rejected, by a 73 percent vote, a 2001 state law that had established an opt-out rather than opt-in standard for financial institutions in North Dakota. The Privacy Rights Clearinghouse noted: "The referendum in North Dakota was the first time this issue has been taken directly to voters."[22] New Mexico has also provided an opt-in requirement for financial institutions before sharing of personal consumer data is permitted with nonaffiliated companies.

2. LAWS REGULATING GOVERNMENT ACCESS TO FINANCIAL DATA

Access to financial data is a key tool for law enforcement to investigate criminal activity. Although this material is covered in more depth in Chapter 5, this section will briefly describe some of the key laws and cases that regulate government access to financial data.

The Bank Secrecy Act. The Bank Secrecy Act of 1970, 31 U.S.C. § 1081, requires the retention of bank records and creation of reports that would be useful in criminal, tax, or regulatory investigations or proceedings. The Act requires that federally insured banks record the identities of account holders as well as copies of each check, draft, or other financial instrument. Regulations promulgated under the Act by the Secretary of the Treasury require reporting to the government of financial transactions exceeding $10,000 if made within the United States and exceeding $5,000 if into or out of the United States. *See* 31 C.F.R. § 103.

A group of bankers challenged the law as violating the Fourth Amendment, but the U.S. Supreme Court held that the bankers did not possess Fourth Amendment rights in the information because "corporations can claim no equality with individuals in the enjoyment of a right to privacy." *California Bankers Association v. Shultz,* 416 U.S. 21 (1974). Depositors who were also involved in the case lacked standing because they failed to allege that they "were engaged in the type of $10,000 domestic currency transaction which would necessitate that their bank report it to the Government."

---

[22] Privacy Rights Clearinghouse, *North Dakota Votes for "Opt-In" Financial Privacy*, June 21, 2002, at www.privacyrights.org/ar/nd_optin.htm.

The Fourth Amendment. In *United States v. Miller*, 425 U.S. 435 (1976), the U.S. Supreme Court held that people lack a reasonable expectation of privacy in their bank records because they "contain only information voluntarily conveyed to the banks and exposed to their employees in the ordinary course of business." The Court followed the doctrine that has become known as the third party doctrine, which holds that when data is maintained by third parties, there is no reasonable expectation of privacy — and no Fourth Amendment protection.

The Right to Financial Privacy Act. In response to *Miller*, in 1978, Congress passed the Right to Financial Privacy Act (RFPA), Pub. L. No. 95-630. The RFPA prevents banks and other financial institutions from disclosing a person's financial information to the government unless the records are disclosed pursuant to subpoena or search warrant. *See* 29 U.S.C. §§ 3401–3422.

3. IDENTITY THEFT STATUTES

The Identity Theft Assumption and Deterrence Act. Congress responded to the growth of identity theft by passing the Identity Theft and Assumption Deterrence Act in 1998. The Act makes it a federal crime to "knowingly transfer or use, without lawful authority, a means of identification of another person with the intent to commit, or to aid or abet, any unlawful activity that constitutes a violation of Federal law, or that constitutes a felony under any applicable State or local law." 18 U.S.C. § 1028.

State Legislative Responses. The vast majority of states now have statutes concerning identity theft. Before 1998, only three states had enacted statutes dealing explicitly with identity theft.[23] Arizona was one of these states; it punishes identity theft as a low-grade felony, but its statute does not address victims' rights and remedies. Ariz. Rev. Stat. Ann. § 13-2008(D). The passage of the federal Identity Theft Assumption and Deterrence Act in 1998 sparked most states to pass their own identity theft legislation — more than 40 states now have identity theft statutes on the books.[24]

Many identity theft statutes focus on defining criminal penalties for the crime. Penalties are tied to the amount of money the thief steals. For example, in Florida, identity theft is a second-degree felony if it results in an injury of $75,000 or more, Fla. Stat. Ann. § 817.568(2)(b), but is only a first-degree misdemeanor if the individual is harassed without having reached the $75,000 threshold. Fla. Stat. Ann. § 817.568(3). New Jersey likewise penalizes identity thefts resulting in injury over $75,000 as a second-degree crime; injuries between $500 and $75,000 constitute a third-degree crime; injuries between $200 and $500 constitute a fourth-degree crime; and injuries less than $200 constitute a disorderly persons offense. N.J.S.A. §§ 2C:21-17(c)(1)–(2). Pennsylvania punishes identity thefts in a similar manner. *See* Pa. Stat. Ann. tit. 18, § 4120(c)(1).

---

[23] U.S. General Accountability Office, *Report to the Honorable Sam Johnson House of Representatives, Identity Theft: Greater Awareness and Use of Existing Data Are Needed* 7 (June 2002).

[24] *Id.* at 6.

Should penalties be tied to the dollar value of the things the thief wrongfully took or to the mental distress and harm caused to the victims, which might not be correlated to such a dollar value?

California, in contrast to most other states, has some of the most comprehensive and powerful identity theft laws. For example, California permits victims to obtain the fraudulent applications that the identity thief made as well as a record of the thief's transactions in the victim's name. Cal. Penal Code § 530.8; Cal. Civil Code § 1748.95. California also assists victims in stopping debt collectors from continuing to try to collect debts that the thief created. Cal. Civ. Code § 1788.18. The central difference between California's approach and that of other states is that California grants powerful rights to victims to assist them in fixing the damage of an identity theft. California also requires companies to notify consumers of data security breaches where personal information about consumers is compromised. Cal. Civ. Code § 1798.82(a).

Assessing Identity Theft Statutes. Daniel Solove contends that many statutes addressing identity theft focus mainly on enhancing criminal penalties and ignore the real roots of the problem:

> [T]he prevailing approach toward dealing with identity theft — by relying on increasing criminal penalties and by depending upon individuals to take great lengths to try to protect themselves against their vulnerabilities to identity theft — has the wrong focus. . . . The underlying cause of identity theft is an architecture that makes us vulnerable to such crimes and unable to adequately repair the damage. . . .
>
> This architecture is not created by identity thieves; rather, it is exploited by them. It is an architecture of vulnerability, one where personal information is not protected with adequate security, where identity thieves have easy access to data and the ability to use it in detrimental ways. We are increasingly living with what I call "digital dossiers" about our lives, and these dossiers are not controlled by us but by various entities, such as private-sector companies and the government. These dossiers play a profound role in our lives in modern society. The identity thief taps into these dossiers and uses them, manipulates them, and pollutes them. The identity thief's ability to so easily access and use our personal data stems from an architecture that does not provide adequate security to our personal information and that does not afford us with a sufficient degree of participation in the collection, dissemination, and use of that information. Consequently, it is difficult for the victim to figure out what is going on and how she can remedy the situation. . . .
>
> Private sector entities lack adequate ways of controlling access to records and accounts in a person's name, and numerous companies engage in the common practice of using SSNs, mother's maiden names, and addresses for access to account information. Additionally, creditors give out credit and establish new accounts if the applicant supplies a name, SSN, and address.[25]

---

[25] Daniel J. Solove, *Identity Theft, Privacy, and the Architecture of Vulnerability,* 54 Hastings L.J. 1227 (2003). For a response to Solove's proposals for solutions and a defense of his own proposed solution, see Lynn M. LoPucki, *Did Privacy Cause Identity Theft?*, 54 Hastings L.J. 1277 (2003).

Lynn LoPucki and Solove agree that the problem of identity theft is caused by the frequent use of Social Security numbers as identifiers. According to LoPucki:

> The problem is not that thieves have access to personal information, but that creditors and credit-reporting agencies often lack both the means and the incentives to correctly identify the persons who seek credit from them or on whom they report.[26]

LoPucki suggests that the problem is caused by the lack of a reliable means for identification. He proposes a system where the government maintains a database of identification information that people submit, such as biometric data, photographs, and other personal information. Solove argues that more sophisticated identification systems come with other problems, such as an increase in data gathering about people and an inability of people who are the victims of abusive spouses or stalkers to hide. However, both Solove and LoPucki agree that identity theft is, in large part, a problem caused by the system in which credit is granted in the United States.

4. TORT LAW

WOLFE V. MBNA AMERICA BANK

485 F. Supp. 2d 874 (W.D. Tenn. 2007)

DONALD, J. Before the Court is Defendant MBNA America Bank's ("Defendant") Motion to Dismiss Plaintiff's Fourth Amended Complaint made pursuant to Rule 12(b)(6) of the Federal Rules of Civil Procedure. Plaintiff Mark Wolfe ("Plaintiff") filed his Fourth Amended Complaint on September 15, 2006, alleging a claim under the Tennessee Consumer Protection Act of 1977 ("TCPA"), Tenn. Code Ann. § 47-18-104(a)-(b), as well as claims for negligence, gross negligence, and defamation.

Plaintiff, now a twenty-seven year old male, is a resident of the State of Tennessee. In or about April 2000, Defendant received a credit account application in Plaintiff's name from a telemarketing company. The application listed Plaintiff's address as 3557 Frankie Carolyn Drive, Apartment 4, Memphis, Tennessee 38118. Plaintiff did not reside and had never resided at this address.

Upon receipt of the application, Defendant issued a credit card bearing Plaintiff's name to an unknown and unauthorized individual residing at the address listed on the application. Plaintiff alleges that Defendant, prior to issuing the card, did not attempt to verify whether the information contained in the credit account application was authentic and accurate. After receiving the card, the unknown and unauthorized individual charged $864.00 to the credit account, exceeding the account's $500.00 credit limit. When no payments were made on the account, Defendant, without investigating whether the account was obtained using a stolen identity, declared the account delinquent and transferred the account to NCO

---

[26] Lynn M. LoPucki, *Human Identification Theory and the Identity Theft Problem,* 80 Tex. L. Rev. 89, 94 (2001).

Financial Systems, Inc. ("NCO"), a debt collection agency. Defendant also notified various credit reporting agencies that the account was delinquent.

In order to collect the debt on the delinquent account, NCO hired an attorney, who discovered Plaintiff's actual address. The attorney, in a letter dated November 29, 2004, notified Plaintiff of the delinquent account and requested payment. Upon receipt of this letter, Plaintiff contacted the attorney to inquire about the account, but was told that he would receive information about the account in thirty (30) days. Plaintiff never received any further information.

In January 2005, Plaintiff applied for a job with a bank, but Plaintiff was not hired due to his poor credit score. Following this denial, Plaintiff contacted Defendant numerous times to dispute the delinquent account but was unable to obtain any "adequate or real explanation" from Defendant. At some point in time, Defendant mailed a notice of arbitration proceedings to the address listed on the credit account application, which subsequently resulted in an arbitration award against Plaintiff. Despite Plaintiff notifying Defendant that his identity was stolen, Defendant continues to list the credit account bearing Plaintiff's name as delinquent and has not corrected the information provided to credit reporting agencies regarding the account. . . .

A motion to dismiss for failure to state a claim only tests whether the plaintiff has pleaded a cognizable claim. . . .

Plaintiff alleges that Defendant had a *duty to verify* "the accuracy and authenticity of a credit application completed in Plaintiff's name before issuing a credit card." . . . Plaintiff alleges that Defendant failed to comply with [its duty to verify], and thus, is negligent and/or grossly negligent.

In Tennessee, negligence is established if a plaintiff demonstrates: "(1) a duty of care owed by the defendant to the plaintiff; (2) conduct falling below the applicable standard of care amounts to a breach of that duty; (3) an injury or loss; (4) causation in fact; and (5) proximate, or legal cause." To establish gross negligence, a plaintiff "must demonstrate ordinary negligence and must then prove that the defendant acted 'with utter unconcern for the safety of others,   or . . . with such reckless disregard for the rights of others that a conscious indifference to consequences is implied in law' ". . . .

Addressing the first context or duty, Defendant asserts that Plaintiff's negligence and gross negligence claims should be dismissed because Tennessee negligence law does not impose a duty on Defendant to verify the authenticity and accuracy of a credit account application prior to issuing a credit card. Defendant, characterizing Plaintiff's claim as one for the "negligent enablement of identity theft," argues that a duty to verify essentially constitutes a duty to prevent third-party criminal activity. Defendant argues that Tennessee courts have never held that commercial banks have a common law duty to prevent the theft of a non-customer's identity. Defendant further argues that it, like Plaintiff, is a victim of identity theft.

Under Tennessee negligence law, a duty is defined as "the legal obligation a defendant owes to a plaintiff to conform to the reasonable person standard of care in order to protect against unreasonable risks of harm." "Whether a defendant owes a duty to a plaintiff in any given situation is a question of law for the court." The "existence and scope of the duty of the defendant in a particular case rests on all the relevant circumstances, including the foreseeability of harm to the plaintiff and other similarly situated persons." A harm is foreseeable "if a reasonable person could foresee the probability of its occurrence or if the person was on notice that the likelihood of danger to the party to whom is owed a duty is probable."

Because Tennessee courts have not specifically addressed whether Tennessee negligence law imposes a duty to verify on commercial banks, Defendant cites in support of its argument the Supreme Court of South Carolina's decision in *Huggins v. Citibank, N.A.,* 585 S.E.2d 275 (S.C. 2003). In *Huggins,* the plaintiff alleged, among other things, that the defendant bank was negligent for issuing a credit card in the plaintiff's name to an unknown and unauthorized person "without any investigation, verification, or corroboration" of the authenticity and accuracy of the credit account application. The defendant argued that under South Carolina negligence law, it had no duty to verify the accuracy and authenticity of the credit account application because plaintiff was technically a non-customer. The South Carolina Supreme Court, despite finding that "it is foreseeable that injury may arise by the negligent issuance of a credit card," ultimately found that no duty to verify existed because "[t]he relationship, if any, between credit card issuers and potential victims of identity theft is far too attenuated to rise to the level of a duty between them." Noting the similarity between negligence law in Tennessee and South Carolina, Defendant argues that its relationship with Plaintiff, like the parties in *Huggins,* was and is too attenuated to warrant the imposition of a duty to verify.

Upon review, the Court finds the South Carolina Supreme Court's conclusion in *Huggins* to be flawed. In reaching its conclusion, the *Huggins* court relied heavily on the fact that there was no prior business relationship between the parties, that is, the plaintiff was not a customer of the defendant bank. The Court believes that the court's reliance on this fact is misplaced. While the existence of a prior business relationship might have some meaning in the context of a contractual dispute, a prior business relationship has little meaning in the context of negligence law. Instead, to determine whether a duty exists between parties, the Court must examine all relevant circumstances, with emphasis on the foreseeability of the alleged harm. As to the issue of foreseeability, the South Carolina Supreme Court found that "it is foreseeable that injury may arise by the negligent issuance of a credit card" and that such injury "could be prevented if credit card issuers carefully scrutinized credit card applications." The Court agrees with and adopts these findings.

With the alarming increase in identity theft in recent years, commercial banks and credit card issuers have become the first, and often last, line of defense in preventing the devastating damage that identity theft inflicts. Because the injury resulting from the negligent issuance of a credit card is foreseeable and preventable, the Court finds that under Tennessee negligence law, Defendant has a duty to verify the authenticity and accuracy of a credit account application before issuing a credit card. The Court, however, emphasizes that this duty to verify does not impose upon Defendant a duty to prevent all identity theft. The Court recognizes that despite banks utilizing the most reasonable and vigilant verification methods, some criminals will still be able to obtain enough personal information to secure a credit card with a stolen identity. Rather, this duty to verify merely requires Defendant to implement reasonable and cost-effective verification methods that can prevent criminals, in some instances, from obtaining a credit card with a stolen identity. Whether Defendant complied with this duty before issuing a credit card in Plaintiff's name is an issue for the trier of fact. Accordingly, Defendant's motion to dismiss Plaintiff's negligence and gross negligence claims in the first factual context is DENIED.

NOTES & QUESTIONS

1. ***Tort Law to the Rescue?*** In *Wolfe*, the district court located a duty in tort law that required a bank to take steps to verify identity before issuing a credit card in the plaintiff's name to a person. The court operated under a negligence theory: the bank need not prevent all identity theft (strict liability), but merely use reasonable verification methods. What kind of practical steps might a bank take to make sure that the person to whom it issues a credit card is, in fact, the intended person? In light of the LoPucki-Solove debate (excerpted above) about the flawed system for checking and otherwise verifying identity, how successful are any "reasonable" means likely to be?

2. ***The Breach of Confidentiality Tort and Financial Institutions.*** Recall the breach of confidentiality tort from Chapter 6. Under the common law, a doctor can be liable to a patient if she discloses the patient's personal information. A number of jurisdictions extend the tort of breach of confidentiality to disclosures by banks and financial institutions of their customers' financial information. In *Peterson v. Idaho First Nat'l Bank*, 367 P.2d 284 (Idaho 1961), the court held that a bank could be sued for breach of confidentiality for disclosing customer information:

> It is generally stated that the relation between a bank and its general depositor is that of debtor and creditor. . . . But it is also said that in discharging its obligation to a depositor a bank must do so subject to the rules of agency. . . .
>
> All agree that a bank should protect its business records from the prying eyes of the public, moved by curiosity or malice. No one questions its right to protect its fiduciary relationship with its customers, which, in sound banking practice, as a matter of common knowledge, is done everywhere. . . .
>
> To give such information to third persons or to the public at the instance of the customer or depositor is certainly not beyond the scope of banking powers. It is a different matter, however, when such information is sought from the bank without the consent of the depositor or customer of the bank. Indeed, it is an implied term of the contract between the banker and his customer that the banker will not divulge to third persons, without the consent of the customer, express or implied, either the state of the customer's account or any of his transactions with the bank, or any information relating to the customer acquired through the keeping of his account. . . .
>
> It is inconceivable that a bank would at any time consider itself at liberty to disclose the intimate details of its depositors' accounts. Inviolate secrecy is one of the inherent and fundamental precepts of the relationship of the bank and its customers or depositors.

Several other jurisdictions have held likewise. *See, e.g., Barnett Bank of West Florida v. Hooper*, 498 So. 2d 923 (Fla. 1986); *Indiana Nat'l Bank v. Chapman*, 482 N.E.2d 474 (Ind. App. 1985); *Suburban Trust Co. v. Waller*, 408 A.2d 758

(Md. App. 1979); *Richfield Bank & Trust Co. v. Sjogren,* 244 N.W.2d 648 (Minn. 1976); *McGuire v. Shubert,* 722 A.2d 1087 (Pa. Super. 1998).

CHAPTER 9

CONSUMER DATA

CHAPTER OUTLINE

We live in a world where commercial entities collect and maintain extensive databases of personal information about individuals. These businesses amass this information for a myriad of purposes. One of their chief reasons for their interest in personal data is to enhance their ability to market products and services to people.

A burgeoning form of marketing today consists of behavioral marketing— examining the behavior patterns of consumers to target advertisements to them. Today's marketer can draw on a wealth of knowledge and insights about human behavior to maximize the effectiveness of advertising. Interactions on the Internet and with other digital platforms permit the creation of an immense trail of personal data, as almost everything that people do online can be tracked. Individuals can now be followed across different websites or digital media. Advertisements can be tailored to specific individuals.

Consumer data can be used for other purposes too. It can be used to make inferences about a person's trustworthiness or aptitude for a job. It can be used for background checks or to determine whether a person will be an easy or difficult customer to deal with. The government can access consumer data for use in criminal investigations, general profiling, or a broad-scale amassing of data.

This chapter explores how the law regulates the collection and use of consumer data.

A. THE U.S. SYSTEM OF CONSUMER DATA PRIVACY REGULATION

In the United States, myriad types of law, which form a complicated patchwork of regulation, regulate consumer data privacy. In some contexts, the law provides strong protections of privacy. In other contexts, the law provides minimal protections. And in a number of contexts, there is hardly any legal protection.

1. STRUCTURE

The Sectoral Approach. Consumer privacy in the United States is regulated by "sectoral" laws that focus on various sectors of the economy. Different laws regulate different industries. In contrast to the United States, Europe and many other countries have an "omnibus" approach toward regulating privacy. Under an omnibus approach, one overarching statute regulates personal information use irrespective of the entities or industry that wishes to process the information. These general laws are frequently then supplemented in European countries and elsewhere outside of the United States by more targeted, sectoral laws. The "omnibus" law provides a general safety-net in these countries for areas or regulatory issues that a sectoral statute may not address.

The sectoral approach in the United States can sometimes draw even finer distinctions for similar kinds of information. For example, cable TV records are regulated differently from video rental or sale records. There are no industry-specific federal statutes directed towards the personal information contained in records of most merchants (bookstores, supermarkets, clothing stores, electronics stories, etc.).

Self-Regulation. Self-regulation has formed a key foundation for U.S. consumer privacy law. As businesses began offering their products and services on the Internet in the 1990s, they operated in a realm that was largely unregulated. To ease concerns of consumers and to demonstrate that they could regulate themselves, businesses began to post privacy policies on their websites. These policies describe the information that is collected, how it will be used and shared, and how it will be safeguarded. Consumers are sometimes offered a choice to opt-out of some uses of their data.

Although privacy regulation has proliferated, some industries still lack a sectoral law. Privacy regulation also tends to allow businesses great flexibility in how they collect, use, or disclose personal data. Most companies use an approach called "notice and choice." They provide a privacy policy (sometimes called a "privacy notice") that describes the ways in which personal data will be collected, used, or disclosed. Consumers are then considered to have a choice. They can accept these terms and do business with the company, or they can refrain from doing business with the company. Sometimes companies offer choices to consumers regarding specific uses or disclosures of their information. Consumers may be given the ability to "opt in" or "opt out" of certain uses or disclosures. An "opt out" means that a consumer's information will be processed unless she takes action to contact the data processing entity and indicate her contrary wishes.

Since the late 1990s, the Federal Trade Commission (FTC) has deemed violations of privacy policies to be an "unfair or deceptive" practice under the FTC Act. The FTC has the power to enforce the FTC Act. The result of the FTC's involvement has been to create a system of quasi-self-regulation, where companies define the substantive terms of how they will collect, use, and disclose personal data, but they are then held accountable to these terms by the FTC. Over time, however, the FTC has interpreted the FTC Act as requiring more of companies than merely following promises.

The Chief Privacy Officer. Over the last two decades, there has been a significant rise in the number of "privacy professionals." The association for such individuals — the International Association of Privacy Professionals (IAPP) — has grown at rates from 30 percent to 40 percent. Beyond the large membership of this organization, a further indication of the ongoing development and specialization of privacy work is provided by the three certification titles that the IAPP grants. By taking examinations, an applicant can become a Certified Information Privacy Professional (CIPP), a Certified Information Privacy Manager (CIPM), or a Certified Information Privacy Technologist (CIPT).

Many companies have a chief privacy officer (CPO) who, among other things, develops a "privacy program" within an institution.[1] A privacy program typically has both elements involving compliance and strategy. Compliance means

---

[1] For two practitioner-oriented guides to the role of a CPO, see Michelle Finneran Dennedy et al., *The Privacy Engineer's Manifesto* (2014); *Building a Privacy Program* (Kirk M. Herath ed., 2011).

developing safeguards, including training the workface, to make sure that the company follows all privacy and security laws and regulations. Strategy means assessing privacy risks, training the workforce about privacy awareness, helping to shape products and services so that they minimize any potential privacy concerns, and stopping or limiting a company's actions that consumers might find too privacy-invasive. The CPO often helps manage not only the information companies have about consumers but also the data maintained about the workforce.

In some industries, laws or regulations require that companies have a designated employee to handle privacy and security responsibilities. An example would be the FTC's Safeguards Rule, issued pursuant to the Gramm-Leach-Bliley Act, which requires the designation of one employee at the covered entity to manage the company's responsibilities pursuant to the Rule. In other industries, businesses voluntarily have CPOs. In such companies, the rise of the CPO is tied to an increase of privacy and security obligations, whether through statutes, regulations, or contracts. As a consequence, it is efficient for a company to have a specialized employee to do this work. CPOs are now common in most large and medium-sized businesses.

As Kenneth Bamberger and Deirdre Mulligan note, "[C]orporate privacy management in the United States has undergone a profound transformation."[2] Based on a series of interviews with leading CPOs, Bamberger and Mulligan present an account of "privacy on the ground." In their view, these firms, driven by the leadership of CPOs, have adopted a dynamic approach to privacy issues. The approach "stressed the importance of integrating practices into corporate decision-making that would prevent the violation of consumer expectations." The respondent CPOs also emphasized the importance of developing "company law," by which they meant "consistent and coordinated firm-specific global privacy policies intended to ensure that a firm both complies with the requirements of all relevant jurisdictions and acts concordantly when dealing with additional business issues not governed by any particular regulation."

2. TYPES OF LAW

Tort Law. Tort law has been used by plaintiffs in response to various forms of data collection, use, or disclosure. Plaintiffs have attempted to use the Warren and Brandeis privacy torts, which were originally developed to address issues involving privacy and the media, as well as other torts, such as negligence. Later in this chapter we will explore how these attempts have fared.

Contract Law. In many instances, companies have a privacy policy that specifies how that information is to be collected, used, or disclosed. Later in this chapter we will explore whether these policies can be enforced as contracts or via promissory estoppel.

---

[2] Kenneth A. Bamberger & Deirdre K. Mulligan, *Privacy on the Books and on the Ground*, 63 Stan. L. Rev. 247, 251 (2011).

Property Law. Some commentators argue that personal data should be treated akin to property. If businesses want to collect or use it in certain ways, they must buy it from the individual, or otherwise trade for it. Later in this chapter we will explore whether treating personal data this way will result in the appropriate forms of data protection.

FTC Section 5 Enforcement. Since the mid-1990s, the Federal Trade Commission (FTC) has used Section 5 of the FTC Act to regulate consumer privacy. Section 5 prohibits "unfair or deceptive acts or practices in or affecting commerce." 15 U.S.C. § 45. The FTC views violations of privacy policies as a "deceptive" practice. It views a number of other practices as "unfair." The FTC's Section 5 jurisdiction is quite broad and encompasses most industries (except for a few carve outs). As a result, it has become the dominant agency regulating privacy in the United States. We will explore the FTC's enforcement of Section 5 later in this chapter.

Federal Statutory Regulation. There are numerous federal statutes pertaining to consumer privacy. As discussed above, the United States follows a sectoral approach to privacy regulation, so statutes differ in different industries and some industries lack their own law. The federal statutes will be discussed later in this chapter.

State Statutory Regulation. Many states have passed sectoral legislation regulating business records and databases. These state statutes sometimes have stronger protections of privacy than federal statutes. There are thousands of state statutes involving privacy, and because there are so many, this chapter focuses primarily on the federal statutes.

State statutes play a key role in the protection of privacy — even beyond the borders of a particular state. For example, California has passed a series of strong privacy protections, and, as a general matter, California can be said to have the strongest privacy law in the United States.[3] These statutes typically protect the personal data of California residents regardless of where the data processing occurs. Many companies have a segment of their business involving customers from California, which is not surprising because this state would be the world's eighth largest economy if it were a stand-alone country. Thus, these companies must comply with California's privacy laws for their customers based in this economically important state. Some companies carve out different policies and procedures to deal with California law, but others just follow California law for all customers because it is easier to follow just one set of rules, and California's laws are often the strictest.

The list of California privacy laws is extensive. California passed the first data breach notification law in 2002, and 46 states have now followed suit. One of California's more unique consumer privacy protections is its "Shine the Light" law. Passed in 2003, SB27, Cal. Civ. Code § 1798.83, allows consumers to obtain from businesses information about the personal data that the businesses disclosed

---

[3] The California Office of Privacy Protection maintains a comprehensive summary of California's privacy statutes: http://www.privacy.ca.gov/lawenforcement/laws.htm.

to third parties for direct marketing purposes. People can find out the kinds of personal information that a company provided to third parties for direct marketing purposes as well as the "names and addresses of all of the third parties that received personal information from the business." § 1798.83(1). The law applies to businesses with 20 or more employees. § 1798(c)(1). Companies with privacy policies that allow people to opt out of sharing of their data with third parties are exempt. § 1798(c)(2).

Other California privacy laws include an obligation placed on rental car companies to inform customers if they have a "black box" in their vehicles; the Confidentiality of Medical Information Act (CMIA), which is a general health information privacy law for the state; and the Song-Beverly Credit Card Act, discussed below, which limits the kinds of personal information collected by companies that accept credit cards.

NOTES & QUESTIONS

1. ***The Case for Less Privacy Regulation.*** Several commentators argue that self-regulation is preferable to creating more state and federal privacy laws. Fred Cate points out that self-regulation is "more flexible and more sensitive to specific contexts and therefore allow[s] individuals to determine a more tailored balance between information uses and privacy than privacy laws do."[4]
Eric Goldman argues:

> Relatively few consumers have bought privacy management tools, such as software to browse anonymously and manage Internet cookies and e-mail. Many vendors are now migrating away from consumer-centric business models. So, although consumers can take technological control over their own situation, few consumers do.
>
> Plus, as most online marketers know, people will "sell" their personal data incredibly cheaply. As Internet pundit Esther Dyson has said: "You do a survey, and consumers say they are very concerned about their privacy. Then you offer them a discount on a book, and they'll tell you everything." Indeed, a recent Jupiter report said that 82% of respondents would give personal information to new shopping sites to enter a $100 sweepstakes.
>
> Clearly consumers' stated privacy concerns diverge from what consumers do. Two theories might explain the divergence.
>
> First, asking consumers what they care about reveals only whether they value privacy. That's half the equation. Of more interest is how much consumers will pay — in time or money — for the corresponding benefits. For now, the cost-benefit ratio is tilted too high for consumers to spend much time or money on privacy.
>
> Second, consumers don't have uniform interests. Regarding online privacy, consumers can be segmented into two groups: activists, who actively protect their online privacy, and apathetics, who do little or nothing to protect themselves. The activists are very vocal but appear to be a tiny market segment.
>
> Using consumer segmentation, the analytical defect of broad-based online privacy regulations becomes apparent. The activists, by definition, take care of

---

[4] Fred H. Cate, *Privacy in Perspective* 26 (2001); *see also* Fred H. Cate, *Privacy in the Information Age* (1997).

themselves. They demand privacy protections from businesses and, if they don't get it, use technology to protect themselves or take their business elsewhere.

In contrast, mainstream consumers don't change their behavior based on online privacy concerns. If these people won't take even minimal steps to protect themselves, why should government regulation do it for them?

Further, online businesses will invest in privacy when it's profitable. . . . When companies believed that few consumers would change their behavior if they were offered greater privacy, those companies did nothing or put into place privacy policies that disabused consumers of privacy expectations. Of course, if companies later discovered that they were losing business because customers wanted more privacy, they would increase their privacy initiatives.

Consumer behavior will tell companies what level of privacy to provide. Let the market continue unimpeded rather than chase phantom consumer fears through unnecessary regulation.[5]

In contrast, Peter Swire contends that privacy legislation need not be antithetical to business interests. According to Swire, privacy legislation should be viewed as similar to the "trustwrap" that Johnson & Johnson placed around bottles of Tylenol after a scare involving cyanide poisoning of the pain reliever.[6] Swire believes that "privacy legislation targeted at online practices" would provide the kind of safety to allow consumers to engage in cyberspace activities with confidence.

2. Flexible Regulation. Some commentators contend that a middle ground can be found between traditional legal regulation and self-regulation. Dennis Hirsch argues that environmental law suggests ways to regulate privacy that are flexible and that mix legal regulation with self-regulation:

Over the past forty years, environmental law has been at the epicenter of an intense and productive debate about the most effective way to regulate. Initial environmental laws took the form of prescriptive, uniform standards that have come to be known as "command-and-control" regulation. These methods, while effective in some settings, proved costly and controversial. In the decades that followed, governments, academics, environmental and business groups, and others poured tremendous resources into figuring out how to improve upon these methods. This work has produced a "second generation" of environmental regulation. . . .

Second generation initiatives encourage the regulated parties themselves to choose the means by which they will achieve environmental performance goals. That is what defines them and distinguishes them from first generation regulations under which the agency has the primary decision-making power over pollution control methods. This difference tends to make second generation strategies more cost-effective and adaptable than command-and-control rules. The proliferation of second generation strategies has led some to identify the environmental field as having "some of the most innovative regulatory instruments in all of American law."

Privacy regulation today finds itself in a debate similar to the one that the environmental field has been engaged in for years. On the one hand, there is a

[5] Eric Goldman, *The Privacy Hoax,* Forbes (Oct. 14, 2002), available at http://www.ericgoldman.org/Articles/privacyhoax.htm.

[6] Peter P. Swire, *Trustwrap: The Importance of Legal Rules to Electronic Commerce and Internet Privacy*, 54 Hastings L.J. 847 (2003).

growing sense that the digital age is causing unprecedented damage to privacy and that action must be taken immediately to mitigate these injuries. On the other, a chorus of voices warns against the dangers of imposing intrusive and costly regulation on the emerging business sectors of the information economy. Missing thus far from the dialogue is any significant discussion of the more flexible "second generation" regulatory strategies that might be able to bridge this gap. It took environmental law decades to arrive at these alternatives. The privacy field could capitalize on this experience by looking to these environmental policies as models for privacy regulation.[7]

Is the analogy of privacy law to environmental law an apt one? To what extent are the privacy statutes discussed in this book thus far command-and-control rules versus flexible rules? Is Hirsch calling less for self-regulation than for industry input into the form and content of rules?

3. ***Is Privacy Still Possible?*** Is privacy still possible in an Information Age? Scott McNealy, CEO of Sun Microsystems, Inc., once remarked: "You already have zero privacy. Get over it." Should we eulogize the death of privacy and move on? Or is it possible to protect privacy in modern times?

Consider David Brin:

> . . . [I]t is already far too late to prevent the invasion of cameras and databases. The *djinn* cannot be crammed back into its bottle. No matter how many laws are passed, it will prove quite impossible to legislate away the new surveillance tools and databases. They are here to stay.
>
> Light *is* going to shine into nearly every corner of our lives. . . .
>
> If neo-Western civilization has one great trick in its repertoire, a technique more responsible than any other for its success, that trick is *accountability*. Especially the knack — which no other culture ever mastered — of making accountability apply to the mighty. . . .
>
> Kevin Kelly, executive editor of *Wired* magazine, expressed the same idea with the gritty clarity of information-age journalism: "The answer to the whole privacy question is more knowledge. More knowledge about who's watching you. More knowledge about the information that flows between us — particularly the meta-information about who knows what and where it's going."
>
> In other words, we may not be able to eliminate the intrusive glare shining on citizens of the next century, but the glare just might be rendered harmless through the application of more light aimed in the other direction.[8]

Is greater transparency the solution to the increasing threats to privacy?

4. ***Privacy Enhancing Technologies and Privacy by Design.*** As part of the self-governance, technology can assist companies as well as consumers in making privacy choices. Privacy on the Internet can be protected by another form of regulatory mechanism — technology. According to Joel Reidenberg, "law and government regulation are not the only source of rule-making. Technological capabilities and system design choices impose rules on participants."[9]

---

[7] Dennis D. Hirsch, *Protecting the Inner Environment: What Privacy Regulation Can Learn from Environmental Law*, 41 Ga. L. Rev. 1, 8-10 (2006).

[8] David Brin, *The Transparent Society* 8-23 (1998).

[9] Joel Reidenberg, *Lex Informatica: The Formulation of Information Policy Rules Through Technology*, 76 Tex. L. Rev. 553 (1998).

Reidenberg calls such forms of technological governance "Lex Informatica." In *Code*, Lawrence Lessig developed similar ideas, as expressed in his famous adage: code is law.[10] By that he means that a central fashion in which regulation takes place in cyberspace is through technological configurations and system design choice.[11]

In the privacy context, Privacy Enhancing Technologies (PETs) have received much attention from scholars and the privacy policy community. Herbert Burkert describes PETs as "technical and organizational concepts that aim at protecting personal identity. These concepts usually involve encryption in the form digital signatures, blind signature or digital pseudonyms."[12]

Ann Cavoukian, the Information and Privacy Commissioner of Ontario, Canada, has coined the term "privacy by design," a related concept to PETs. According to Cavoukian, "*Privacy by Design* refers to the philosophy and approach of embedding privacy into the design, operation and management of information technologies and systems, across the entire information life cycle."[13]

Ira Rubinstein has developed a useful taxonomy of PETs as either "substitute PETs" or "complementary PETs."[14] In his definition, "[s]ubstitute PETs seek to protect privacy by ensuring that little or no personal data is collected in the first place, thereby making legal protections superfluous." As an example, Rubinstein points to client-centric architecture, such as the Tor network, that prevents or minimizes the collection of personal data by permitting anonymous browsing. He also notes that in "practice, many substitute PETs are more theoretical than practical" with few being widely deployed.

In contrast, complementary PETs are designed to implement legislative privacy principles or related legal requirements. Here, Rubinstein draws a further distinction and identifies two types of complementary PETs. First, there are "privacy-friendly PETs," which give people more control over their personal data through improved notice and consent mechanisms, browser management tools, and dashboard interfaces. Second, "privacy-preserving PETs" resemble substitute PETs in that they rely on technology to limit data collection while also complementing legal requirements. Rubinstein's examples of this final category are privacy-preserving data mining and privacy-preserving targeted advertising. He concludes by arguing that "the market incentives for substitute PETs are feeble" and that "regulatory incentives may still be necessary to overcome the reluctance of private firms to increase their investments in PETs, especially in the face of limited consumer demand, competing business needs, and a weak economy."

---

[10] Larry Lessig, Code and Other Laws of Cyberspace (1999).

[11] For an analysis of Lessig's suggestions for privacy, see Paul M. Schwartz, *Beyond Lessig's Code for Internet Privacy*, 2000 Wisc. L. Rev. 743.

[12] Herbert Burkert, Privacy-Enhancing Technologies: Typology, Critique, Vision, in Technology and Privacy: The New Landscape 123, 125, 128 (Philip E. Agre & Marc Rotenberg, eds., 1997).

[13] Ann Cavoukian, Privacy by Design Resolution (2010), http://www.ipc.on.ca/site_documents/pbd-resolution.pdf.

[14] Ira S. Rubinstein, *Regulating Privacy by Design*, 26 Berkeley Tech. L.J. 1409 (2012).

Additionally, Rubinstein contrasts PETs with privacy by design. Whereas most PETs are "added-on to existing systems, sometimes as an afterthought by designers and sometimes by privacy-sensitive end-users," privacy by design is a systematic approach to developing any product or service "that embeds privacy into the underlying specifications or architecture." Although this approach has great potential, Rubinstein suggests that in order for privacy by design to achieve greater success than PETs, governments will have to clarify what it means for companies to "build in" privacy from the outset rather than "bolt it on" at the end and create regulatory incentives that will spur broader adoption.

3. PERSONALLY IDENTIFIABLE INFORMATION (PII)

PII is one of the most central concepts in privacy regulation. It defines the scope and boundaries of a large range of privacy statutes and regulations. Federal statutes that turn on this distinction include the Children's Online Privacy Protection Act, the Gramm-Leach-Bliley Act, the HITECH Act, and the Video Privacy Protection Act. Moreover, state statutes that rely on PII as a jurisdictional trigger include California's Song-Beverly Credit Card Act and the many data security breach notification laws. These laws all share the same basic assumption—that in the absence of PII, there is no privacy harm. Thus, privacy regulation focuses on the collection, use, and disclosure of PII and leaves non-PII unregulated.

Given PII's importance, it is surprising that information privacy law in the United States lacks a uniform definition of the term. Computer science has also shown that the very concept of PII is far from straightforward. Increasingly, technologists can take information that appears on its face to be non-identifiable and turn it into identifiable data. Instead of defining PII in a coherent and consistent manner, privacy law offers multiple competing definitions, each with some significant problems and limitations.

Approaches to PII. There are three predominant approaches to defining PII in various laws and regulations: (1) the "tautological" approach, (2) the "non-public" approach, and (3) the "specific-types" approach.[15] These approaches are also made either as a rule or standard. A standard is an open-ended decision-making yardstick, and a rule, its counterpart, is a harder-edged decision-making tool.

The tautological approach defines PII as any information that identifies a person. The Video Privacy Protection Act (VPPA) demonstrates this model. The VPPA, which safeguards the privacy of video sales and rentals, simply defines "personally identifiable information" as "information which identifies a person." One problem with this approach is that it simply states that PII is PII without providing guidance about how to identify PII.

---

[15] Paul M. Schwartz & Daniel J. Solove, *The PII Problem: Privacy and a New Concept of Personally Identifiable Information,* 86 N.Y.U. L. Rev. 1815 (2011). For an analysis of concepts of personal information in the European Union, see Paul M. Schwartz & Daniel J. Solove, *Reconciling Personal Information in the U.S. and EU*, 102 Cal. L. Rev. 877 (2014).

A second approach toward defining PII focuses on non-public information. The Gramm-Leach-Bliley Act (GLB Act) epitomizes this approach by defining "personally identifiable financial information" as "nonpublic personal information." The statute fails to define "nonpublic," but presumably this term means information not found within the public domain. The non-public approach, however, does not map onto whether the information is in fact identifiable.

The third approach is to list specific types of data that constitute PII. In the context of the specific-types approach, if the information falls into an enumerated group, it becomes a kind of statutory "per se" PII. The federal Children's Online Privacy Protection Act (COPPA) of 1998 illustrates this approach. COPPA states that personal information is "individually identifiable information about an individual collected online" that includes a number of elements beginning with "first and last name," and continuing through a physical address, Social Security number, telephone number, and e-mail address. Its definition of PII also includes "any other identifier that the [Federal Trade Commission (FTC)] determines permits the physical or online contacting of a specific individual." A limitation with the specific-types approach is that it can fail to respond to new technology, which is capable of transforming the kinds of data that are PII.

State privacy laws also define personal information. One of the most important of these laws is the Song-Beverly Credit Card Act, which prevents business from requesting "personal identification information" during credit card transactions. This statute has been the object of considerable litigation. In *Pineda v. Williams-Sonoma Stores* (2011), the California Supreme Court evaluated whether a ZIP code was protection personal information under the Song-Beverly Act. In *Apple v. Krescent* (2013), the same court considered whether this law's prohibitions extended to online merchants offering products that were downloadable.

PINEDA V. WILLIAMS-SONOMA STORES

246 P.3d 162 (Cal. 2011)

MORENO, J. The Song-Beverly Credit Card Act of 1971 (Credit Card Act) (Civ. Code, § 1747 *et seq.*) is "designed to promote consumer protection." *Florez v. Linens 'N Things, Inc.*, 108 Cal. App. 4th 447, 450, (2003). One of its provisions, section 1747.08, prohibits businesses from requesting that cardholders provide "personal identification information" during credit card transactions, and then recording that information.

Plaintiff sued defendant retailer, asserting a violation of the Credit Card Act. Plaintiff alleges that while she was paying for a purchase with her credit card in one of defendant's stores, the cashier asked plaintiff for her ZIP code. Believing it necessary to complete the transaction, plaintiff provided the requested information and the cashier recorded it. Plaintiff further alleges that defendant subsequently used her name and ZIP code to locate her home address.

We are now asked to resolve whether section 1747.08 is violated when a business requests and records a customer's ZIP code during a credit card transaction. In light of the statute's plain language, protective purpose, and legislative history, we conclude a ZIP code constitutes "personal identification information" as that phrase is used in section 1747.08. Thus, requesting and recording a cardholder's ZIP code, without more, violates the Credit Card Act. We therefore reverse the contrary judgment of the Court of Appeal and remand for further proceedings consistent with our decision. . . .

Plaintiff visited one of [defendant Williams-Sonoma's] California stores and selected an item for purchase. She then went to the cashier to pay for the item with her credit card. The cashier asked plaintiff for her ZIP code and, believing she was required to provide the requested information to complete the transaction, plaintiff provided it. The cashier entered plaintiff's ZIP code into the electronic cash register and then completed the transaction. At the end of the transaction, defendant had plaintiff's credit card number, name, and ZIP code recorded in its database.

Defendant subsequently used customized computer software to perform reverse searches from databases that contain millions of names, e-mail addresses, telephone numbers, and street addresses, and that are indexed in a manner resembling a reverse telephone book. The software matched plaintiff's name and ZIP code with plaintiff's previously undisclosed address, giving defendant the information, which it now maintains in its own database. Defendant uses its database to market products to customers and may also sell the information it has compiled to other businesses. . . .

Section 1747.08, subdivision (a) provides, in pertinent part, "[N]o person, firm, partnership, association, or corporation that accepts credit cards for the transaction of business shall . . . : (2) Request, or require as a condition to accepting the credit card as payment in full or in part for goods or services, the cardholder to provide *personal identification information,* which the person, firm, partnership, association, or corporation accepting the credit card writes, causes to be written, or otherwise records upon the credit card transaction form or otherwise. Subdivision (b) defines personal identification information as "information concerning the cardholder, other than information set forth on the credit card, and including, but not limited to, the cardholder's address and telephone number." Because we must accept as true plaintiff's allegation that defendant requested and then recorded her ZIP code, the outcome of this case hinges on whether a cardholder's ZIP code, without more, constitutes personal identification information within the meaning of section 1747.08. We hold that it does.

Subdivision (b) defines personal identification information as "information *concerning* the cardholder . . . including, but not limited to, the cardholder's address and telephone number" (italics added). "Concerning" is a broad term meaning "pertaining to; regarding; having relation to; [or] respecting. . . ." (Webster's New Internat. Dict. (2d ed. 1941) p. 552.) A cardholder's ZIP code, which refers to the area where a cardholder works or lives is certainly information that pertains to or regards the cardholder.

In nonetheless concluding the Legislature did not intend for a ZIP code, without more, to constitute personal identification information, the Court of Appeal pointed to the enumerated examples of such information in subdivision (b), i.e., "the cardholder's address and telephone number." . . . [T]he Court of Appeal reasoned that an address and telephone number are "specific in nature regarding an individual." By contrast, the court continued, a ZIP code pertains to the *group* of individuals who live within the ZIP code. Thus, the Court of Appeal concluded, a ZIP code, without more, is unlike the other terms specifically identified in subdivision (b).

There are several problems with this reasoning. First, a ZIP code is readily understood to be part of an address; when one addresses a letter to another person, a ZIP code is always included. The question then is whether the Legislature, by providing that "personal identification information" includes "the cardholder's address" intended to include components of the address. The answer must be yes. Otherwise, a business could ask not just for a cardholder's ZIP code, but also for the cardholder's street and city in addition to the ZIP code, so long as it did not also ask for the house number. Such a construction would render the statute's protections hollow. Thus, the word "address" in the statute should be construed as encompassing not only a complete address, but also its components.

Second, the court's conclusion rests upon the assumption that a complete address and telephone number, unlike a ZIP code, are specific to an individual. That this assumption holds true in all, or even most, instances is doubtful. In the case of a cardholder's home address, for example, the information may pertain to a group of individuals living in the same household. Similarly, a home telephone number might well refer to more than one individual. The problem is even more evident in the case of a cardholder's *work* address or telephone number—such information could easily pertain to tens, hundreds, or even thousands of individuals. Of course, section 1747.08 explicitly provides that a cardholder's address and telephone number constitute personal identification information; that such information *might also* pertain to individuals other than the cardholder is immaterial. Similarly, that a cardholder's ZIP code pertains to individuals in addition to the cardholder does not render it dissimilar to an address or telephone number.

More significantly, the Court of Appeal ignores another reasonable interpretation of what the enumerated terms in section 1747.08, subdivision (b) have in common, that is, they both constitute information unnecessary to the sales transaction that, alone or together with other data such as a cardholder's name or credit card number, can be used for the retailer's business purposes. Under this reading, a cardholder's ZIP code is similar to his or her address or telephone number, in that a ZIP code is both unnecessary to the transaction and can be used, together with the cardholder's name, to locate his or her full address. The retailer can then, as plaintiff alleges defendant has done here, use the accumulated information for its own purposes or sell the information to other businesses.

There are several reasons to prefer this latter, broader interpretation over the one adopted by the Court of Appeal. The Court of Appeal's interpretation, by contrast, would permit retailers to obtain indirectly what they are clearly prohibited from obtaining directly, "end-running" the statute's clear purpose. This is so because information that can be permissibly obtained under the Court of Appeal's construction could easily be used to locate the cardholder's complete address or telephone number. Such an interpretation would vitiate the statute's effectiveness.
. . .

[T]he legislative history of section 1747.08 offers additional evidence that plaintiff's construction is the correct one. . . .

Thus, in light of the statutory language, as well as the legislative history and evident purpose of the statute, we hold that personal identification information, as that term is used in section 1747.08, includes a cardholder's ZIP code.

APPLE V. KRESCENT

292 P.3d 883 (Cal. 2013)

LIU, J. The Song-Beverly Credit Card Act of 1971 (Credit Card Act) governs the issuance and use of credit cards. ([Cal.] Civ. Code, § 1747 *et seq.*). One of its provisions, section 1747.08, prohibits retailers from "[r]equest[ing], or requir[ing] as a condition to accepting the credit card as payment . . ., the cardholder to write any personal identification information upon the credit card transaction form or otherwise". . . . It also prohibits retailers from requesting or requiring the cardholder "to provide personal identification information, which the [retailer] . . . writes, causes to be written, or otherwise records upon the credit card transaction form or otherwise," and from "[u]tiliz[ing] . . . a credit card form which contains preprinted spaces specifically designed for filling in any personal identification information of the cardholder." . . . .

We must resolve whether section 1747.08 prohibits an online retailer from requesting or requiring personal identification information from a customer as a condition to accepting a credit card as payment for an electronically downloadable product. Upon careful consideration of the statute's text, structure, and purpose, we hold that section 1747.08 does not apply to online purchases in which the product is downloaded electronically. . . .

Petitioner Apple Inc. (Apple), defendant below, operates an Internet Web site and an online iTunes store through which it sells digital media such as downloadable audio and video files. In June 2011, plaintiff below, David Krescent, sued Apple on behalf of himself and a putative class of similarly situated individuals for alleged violations of section 1747.08. Specifically, Krescent alleged that he purchased media downloads from Apple on various occasions and that, as a condition of receiving these downloads, he was required to provide his telephone number and address in order to complete his credit card purchase. He further alleged that Apple records each customer's personal information, is not contractually or legally obligated to collect a customer's telephone number or address in order to complete the credit card transaction, and does not require a customer's telephone number or address for any special purpose incidental but related to the individual credit card transaction, such as shipping or delivery. Although he alleged that "the credit card transaction would be permitted to proceed" without any personal identification information, Krescent also contended that "even if the credit card processing company or companies required a valid billing address and [credit card identification number], under no circumstance would [plaintiff's] telephone number be required to complete his transaction, that is, under no circumstance does [Apple] need [plaintiff's] phone number in order to complete a [media] download transaction.". . .

We review de novo questions of statutory construction. In doing so, "our fundamental task is to ascertain the intent of the lawmakers so as to effectuate the purpose of the statute." As always, we start with the language of the statute, "giv[ing] the words their usual and ordinary meaning . . . while construing them in light of the statute as a whole and the statute's purpose." *Pineda v. Williams Sonoma,* 246 P.3d 612 (Cal. 2011). . . .

We begin with the text of the statute. Section 1747.08(a) provides: "Except as provided in subdivision (c), no person, firm, partnership, association, or corporation that accepts credit cards for the transaction of business shall do any of the following: (1) Request, or require as a condition to accepting the credit card as payment in full or in part for goods or services, the cardholder to write any personal identification information upon the credit card transaction form or otherwise. (2) Request, or require as a condition to accepting the credit card as payment in full or in part for goods or services, the cardholder to provide personal identification information, which the person, firm, partnership, association, or corporation accepting the credit card writes, causes to be written, or otherwise records upon the credit card transaction form or otherwise. (3) Utilize, in any credit card transaction, a credit card form which contains preprinted spaces specifically designated for filling in any personal identification information of the cardholder." Section 1747.08, subdivision (b) (hereafter section 1747.08(b)) defines "personal identification information" as "information concerning the cardholder, other than information set forth on the credit card, and including, but not limited to, the cardholder's address and telephone number." . . .

Although section 1747.08 does not explicitly reference online transactions, both parties maintain that the Legislature's intent is apparent from the plain meaning of the statute's terms. Krescent contends that the language of section 1747.08(a) "must be read as an all-inclusive prohibition on every businesses [sic] regardless of the form of the transaction." According to Krescent, in directing the statutory prohibition at any "person, firm, partnership, association, or corporation that accepts credit cards for the transaction of business" (§ 1747.08(a)), the Legislature intended to include all retailers without exception. If the Legislature intended to exempt online retailers, he contends, it could have done so.

Apple, on the other hand, argues that the first sentence of section 1747.08(a) must be construed in light of other language in the statute indicating that the Legislature had in mind only in-person business transactions. For example, section 1747.08(a)(1) prohibits a retailer from requesting or requiring a "cardholder to *write* any personal identification information *upon the credit card transaction form* or otherwise." (Italics added.) Section 1747.08(a)(2) prohibits a retailer from requesting or requiring the cardholder to provide such information, which the retailer "*writes, causes to be written, or otherwise records upon the credit card transaction form* or otherwise." (Italics added.) And section 1747.08(a)(3) prohibits the retailer from utilizing "a *credit card form which contains preprinted spaces.*" (Italics added.) Apple says the terms "write" and "forms" imply, by their physicality, that section 1747.08 applies only to in-person transactions. Apple further argues that the definition of "credit card" in section 1747.02—"any card, plate, coupon book, or other single credit device existing for the purpose of being used from time to time *upon presentation* to obtain money, property, labor, or services on credit"—indicates that the Legislature contemplated only those transactions in which the card is physically presented or displayed to the retailer. (§ 1747.02, subd. (a), italics added.)

We think the text of section 1747.08(a) alone is not decisive on the question before us. The statutory language suggests that the Legislature, at the time it enacted former section 1747.8, did not contemplate commercial transactions conducted on the Internet. But it does not seem awkward or improper to describe the act of typing characters into a digital display as "writing" on a computerized "form." In construing statutes that predate their possible applicability to new technology, courts have not relied on wooden construction of their terms. Fidelity to legislative intent does not "make it impossible to apply a legal text to technologies that did not exist when the text was created. . . . Drafters of every era know that technological advances will proceed apace and that the rules they create will one day apply to all sorts of circumstances they could not possibly envision." (Scalia & Garner, *Reading Law: The Interpretation of Legal Texts* (2012). . . .

In this case . . . the plain meaning of the statutes text is not decisive. An examination of the statutory scheme as a whole is necessary to determine whether it is applicable to a transaction made possible by technology that the Legislature did not envision. . . .

We recently considered the history and purpose of the [Song-Beverly Act and determined that] "[t]he statute's overriding purpose was to "protect the personal privacy of consumers who pay for transactions with credit cards." (*Pineda,* 246 P.3d at 636). . . . Specifically, the Legislature "sought to address the misuse of personal identification information for, *inter alia*, marketing purposes, and found that there would be no legitimate need to obtain such information from credit card customers if it was not necessary to the completion of the credit card transaction."
. . .

While it is clear that the Legislature enacted the Credit Card Act to protect consumer privacy, it is also clear that the Legislature did not intend to achieve privacy protection without regard to exposing consumers and retailers to undue risk of fraud. The legislative history shows that the Legislature enacted the statute's prohibitions only after carefully considering and rejecting the possibility that the collection of personal identification information by brick-and-mortar retailers could serve a legitimate purpose such as fraud prevention. In particular, the Senate Judiciary Committee considered the standard procedure followed by brick-and-mortar retailers in the 1990s to verify the identity of credit card users—which included "verify[ing] the identification of the cardholder by comparing the signature on the credit card transaction form with the signature on the back of the card" and "contact [ing] the credit card issuer's authorization center [to] obtain approval" for sales above a specified "floor limit"—and concluded that the collection of personal identification information was not a necessary step in that procedure. (Sen. Judiciary Com., Analysis of Assem. Bill No. 2920 (1989–1990 Reg. Sess.) as amended June 27, 1990, p. 3.) This finding supported the Legislature's judgment that brick-and-mortar retailers in the 1990s had no genuine need to collect personal identification information and would instead use such information primarily for unsolicited marketing. (See *id.* at pp. 3-4 [noting that the "problem" the bill was designed to address was retailers' practice of leading consumers "to mistakenly believe that [personal identification information] is a necessary condition to complete the credit card transaction, when, in fact, it is not" and "acquir[ing] this additional personal information for their own business purposes—for example, to build mailing or telephone lists which they can subsequently use for their own in-house marketing efforts, or sell to direct-mail or tele-marketing specialists, or to others"]; *id.* at pp. 5-7 [explaining that retailers had no genuine need for personal identification information to address problems such as billing errors, lost credit cards, and product problems].) We cannot assume that the Legislature, had it confronted a type of transaction in which the standard mechanisms for verifying a cardholder's identity were not available, would have made the same policy choice as it did with respect to transactions in which it found no tension between privacy protection and fraud prevention. . . .

The safeguards against fraud that are provided in section 1747.08(d) are not available to the online retailer selling an electronically downloadable product. Unlike a brick-and-mortar retailer, an online retailer cannot visually inspect the credit card, the signature on the back of the card, or the customer's photo identification. Thus, section 1747.08(d)—the key antifraud mechanism in the statutory scheme—has no practical application to online transactions involving electronically downloadable products. We cannot conclude that if the Legislature in 1990 had been prescient enough to anticipate online transactions involving electronically downloadable products, it would have intended section 1747.08(a) 's prohibitions to apply to such transactions despite the unavailability of section 1747.08 (d)'s safeguards.

Krescent's complaint reinforces our conclusion insofar as it failed to allege that Apple does not require any personal identification information to verify the identity of the credit card user. His complaint merely alleged that "the credit card transaction would be permitted to proceed without any further information" and that Apple "is not contractually obligated to provide a consumer's telephone number and/or address in order to complete the credit card transaction," thereby rendering inapplicable the exception set forth in section 1747.08(c)(3)(A). Even if credit card transactions may proceed without any personal identification information under the contractual terms that bind retailers and credit card companies, the fact remains that the Legislature saw fit to include section 1747.08(d) 's safeguards against fraud in the statutory scheme. The inclusion of section 1747.08(d), separate and apart from the exception in section 1747.08(c)(3)(A), reflects the Legislature's judgment that consumers and retailers have an interest in combating fraud that is independent of whatever security measures are (or are not) required by contracts between retailers and credit card issuers. Consistent with this legislative judgment, both parties acknowledged at oral argument that retailers often bear the risk of loss from fraudulent credit card charges. . . .

KENNARD, J. DISSENTING. . . . To protect consumer privacy, California statutory law prohibits retail sellers from recording the personal identification information, such as home addresses and telephone numbers, of their credit-card-using customers. Cal. Civ. Code § 1747.08, Subdiv. (a). The statute does not exempt online sales of downloadable products from this prohibition, and on its face the statute applies to sales conducted over the Internet just as it does to sales conducted face-to-face or by mail or telephone. Yet the majority holds that online sales of downloadable products are not covered by the statute, thus leaving Internet retailers free to demand personal identification information from their credit-card-using customers and to resell that information to others. The majority's decision is a major win for these sellers, but a major loss for consumers, who in their online activities already face an ever-increasing encroachment upon their privacy.

Unlike the majority, I conclude that the statute means just what it says and contains no exemption, express or implied, for online sales of downloadable products. The majority's expressed concern that this plain-meaning construction of the statute leaves online sellers with no way to detect and prevent fraudulent purchases is unjustified. . . .

BAXTER, J. DISSENTING. . . . Section 1747.08 of the [Cal.] Civil Code was enacted to prevent any retailer such as defendant Apple Inc. from collecting and exploiting the personal identification information of consumers who use credit cards to make their purchases. Plaintiff's complaint sufficiently states a cause of action under this statute: it alleges that defendant required and recorded plaintiff's address and telephone number as a condition to his online purchases of electronically downloadable products, and that defendant's actions were not otherwise permitted by the statute. In holding to the contrary, the majority relies on speculation and debatable factual assumptions to carve out an expansive exception to section 1747.08 that leaves online retailers free to collect and use the personal identification information of credit card users as they wish. . . .

The majority implicitly agrees that defendant's conduct falls within the plain terms of section 1747.08(a). . . . The majority holds, however, that plaintiff was not entitled to protection of his personal identification information because online credit card purchases of electronically downloadable products are categorically exempt from the statute's application. . . . Although recognizing this is a question of statutory construction, the majority reaches a result that is contrary to the terms, purpose, and legislative history of section 1747.08. . . .

NOTES & QUESTIONS

1. **Pineda *and the "Specific Types" Approach to PII.*** The California Supreme Court reversed the lower courts in *Pineda*, but did so on the narrowest possible grounds. It analyzed the statutory language and legislative history, and found that both supported a legislative intent to include a ZIP code as part of the "cardholder's address." In other words, that statutory category included "not only a complete address, but its components."

In a sense, the California Supreme Court in *Pineda* only tweaked a subcategory within the specific-types approach to defining PII. It did not reach the broader conclusion that the Song-Beverly Act reflected a policy to prevent retailers from collecting "identification" indices that would permit a definitive linkage between a customer and her address. In fact, the law can be read simply as a prohibition on merchants collecting information that is specific enough to allow the unique identification of a person. Although as many as tens of thousands of people might share a ZIP code, it was precisely the piece of information, when added to a person's name, which permitted linkage of the customer to a wealth of PII about her.

2. **Krescent *and Antifraud Considerations.*** Two years after *Pineda*, the California Supreme Court in *Krescent* decided that the overall statutory scheme of the Song-Beverly Act indicated a legislative desire to balance privacy protection and fraud protection. In particular, for electronically downloadable products, merchants faced limitations on their anti-fraud activities, which brick-and-mortar retailers did not. Ultimately, the California Supreme Court found that the legislature did not intend to have the relevant prohibitions in the Act extend to online merchants. How do you think the legislature should respond to this decision? Should online merchants be prevented from collecting telephone numbers and addresses from customers?

3. ***E-mailed Receipts, ZIP Codes, and Deposits.*** The Song-Beverly Act has led to litigation beyond *Pineda* and *Krescent*. For example, a federal court found that Nordstrom violated the act by requesting an e-mail address to mail a customer a receipt and then also using the e-mail to send the customer promotional communications and materials. Capp v. Nordstrom, 2013 WL 5739102 (E.D. Cal. 2013). The court found that an e-mail address was "personal identification information" under the Song-Beverly Act. It declared that a credit cardholder's e-mail address was an even "more specific and personal" reference to the person than the ZIP code at stake in *Pineda*. It stated, "Instead of referring to the general area in which a cardholder lives or works, a cardholder's email address permits direct contact and implicates the privacy interests of a cardholder."

   The Ninth Circuit has also considered whether the Song-Beverly Act prevented Redbox, a self-service kiosk used to rent movies and video games, from collecting ZIP codes. Sinibaldi v. Redbox Automated Retail, 754 F.3d 703 (9th Cir. 2014). The Ninth Circuit noted that the Song-Beverly Act contained a specific exemption where "the credit card is being used as a deposit to secure payment in the event of default, loss, damage, or similar occurrence." Cal. Civ. Code 1747.08(c)(1). While Redbox's request for the ZIP code was one for "personal identification information" under the Song-Beverly Act, it was collecting this information along with the credit card number as a deposit to secure payment should the customer not return the DVD after the first day. Hence, Redbox did not violate the Song-Beverly Act by requesting this personal data.

4. ***Behavioral Marketing and PII.*** The burgeoning practice of behavioral marketing, which is also sometimes termed "targeted marketing," involves examining the behavioral patterns of consumers to target advertisements to them. In this technique, companies generally do not track individuals through use of their names. Instead they utilize software to build personal profiles that exclude this item but that contain a wealth of details about the individual. Typically, these firms associate these personal profiles with a single alphanumerical code placed on an individual's computer. These codes are used to decide which advertisements people see as well as the kinds of products that are offered to them.

   While advertising networks may not know a person's name, identification of individuals is nonetheless possible in many cases. For example, enough pieces of information linked to a single person, even in the absence of a name, Social Security number, or financial information, will permit identification of the individual. Nonetheless, online companies have attempted to short-circuit the discussion of privacy harms and necessary legal reforms by simply asserting that they do not collect PII.

5. ***Ohm on the PII Problem.*** In the view of Paul Ohm, privacy law must abandon its reliance on PII and find a new regulatory paradigm.[16] He argues that the concept of PII is unworkable and unfixable. He points to new re-identification research that has demonstrated that de-identified records can be re-identified "with astonishing ease." This occurs because there is already so much data available about individuals that is linked to their identity. To re-identify records, one can simply try to match the information in the records to other available data about an identified person. For example, Netflix, a popular online movie rental service, made a supposedly de-identified database of ratings publicly available as part of a contest to improve the predictive capabilities of its movie recommending software. Two researchers, Arvind Narayanan and Vitaly Shmatikov, found a way to link this data with the movie ratings that some participating individuals gave to films in the Internet Movie Database (IMDb), a popular website with information and ratings about movies.[17] They did this by matching the data to individuals' public movie ratings on IMDb.[18]

Because data can be so readily linked to a person's identity, Ohm contends that the "list of potential PII will never stop growing until it includes everything." Ohm proposes that regulators abandon PII and instead "prevent privacy harm by squeezing and reducing the flow of information in society, even though in doing so they may need to sacrifice, at least a little, important counter values like innovation, free speech, and security." He would replace the current reliance on PII as a gatekeeper for privacy law with a cost-benefit analysis for *all* data processing and data collection of any kind. Ohm proposes that privacy regulation "should weigh the benefits of unfettered information flow against the cost of privacy harms." He proposes a minimum floor of safe handling of data for every data processor in the United States plus even stricter practices to be imposed on the entities that he terms "large entropy reducers." Ohm writes:

> Large entropy reducers are entities that amass massive databases containing so many links between so many disparate kinds of information that they represent a significant part of the database of ruin, even if they delete from their databases all particularly sensitive and directly linkable information. We can justify treating these entities differently using the language of duty and fault. Because large entropy reducers serve as one-stop shops for adversaries trying to link

---

[16] Paul Ohm, *Broken Promises of Privacy*, 57 UCLA L. Rev. 1701 (2010).

[17] Arvind Narayanan & Vitaly Shmatikov, *Robust De-Anonymization of Large Sparse Datasets,* 2008 IEEE Symp. on Security and Privacy 111 (Feb. 5, 2008), available at http://arxiv.org/PS_cache/cs/pdf/0610/0610105v2.pdf.

[18] Narayanan & Shmatikov concede that the results did not "imply anything about the percentage of IMDb users who can be identified in the Netflix Prize dataset." *Id.* For an insightful technical analysis of the limits of the Netflix study and how it is has been misunderstood, see Jane Yakowitz, *Tragedy of the Data Commons*, 25 Harv. J.L. & Tech. 1 (2011).

people to ruinous facts, they owe their data subjects a heightened duty of care. When a large entropy reducer loses control of its massive database, it causes much more harm than an entity holding much less data.

More specifically, Ohm identifies as "large entropy reducers" companies such as the credit reporting agencies (i.e., Equifax), data brokers (i.e., LexisNexis), and Internet search engines (i.e., Google). Do you think that a specific set of regulations should be devoted to companies such as the ones that Ohm identifies?

6. ***Schwartz and Solove Propose PII 2.0.*** In contrast to Ohm, Paul Schwartz and Daniel Solove contend that information privacy law needs a concept of PII.[19] Without such a concept, information privacy law will be a boundless area—it will grow to regulate all information use. At the same time, Schwartz and Solove also propose that PII must be reconceptualized if privacy law is to remain effective in the future.

In their concept of PII 2.0, they propose three different regulatory categories, each of which would be treated differently. Schwartz and Solove write:

> Rather than a hard "on-off" switch, this approach allows legal safeguards for both identified and identifiable information, ones that permit tailored FIPs built around the different levels of risk to individuals. In our model of PII 2.0, information refers to (1) an identified, (2) identifiable, or (3) non-identifiable person. The continuum runs from actually being identified to no risk of identification, and our three categories divide up this spectrum and provide three different regimes of regulation. Because these categories do not have hard boundaries and are fluid, we define them in terms of standards.
>
> Information refers to an *identified* person when it singles out a specific individual from others. Put differently, a person has been identified when her identity is ascertained. There is general international agreement about the content of this category, albeit not of the implications of being placed in it. For example, in the U.S., the General Accounting Office, Office of Management and Budget, and National Institute of Standards and Technology associate this concept with information that distinguishes or traces a specific individual's identity.[20] In Europe, the Article 29 Group states that a person is identified "when, within a group of persons, he or she is 'distinguished' from all other members of the group."[21]
>
> In the middle of the risk continuum, information refers to an *identifiable* individual when a specific identification, while possible, is not a significantly probable event. In other words, an individual is identifiable when there is some non-remote possibility of future identification. The risk level is moderate to low. This information should be treated differently than an important sub-category of nominally identifiable information, where a linkage to a specific

---

[19] Paul Schwartz & Daniel Solove, *The PII Problem: Privacy and a New Concept of Personally Identifiable Information*, 86 N.Y.U. L. Rev. 1815 (2011).

[20] National Institute of Standards and Technology, *Guide to Protecting the Confidentiality of Personally Identifiable Information* (PII) 2–1 (2010); General Accounting Office, *Privacy: Alternatives Exist for Enhancing Protection of Personally Identifiable Information* (May 2008); Office of Management & Budget, *Memorandum 07-16, Safeguarding Against and Responding to the Breach of Personally Identifiable Information* (2007).

[21] Article 29 Data Protection Working Party, *Opinion 4/2007 on the Concept of Personal Data* 12 (June, 20, 2007).

person has not yet been made, but where such a connection is more likely. . . . [S]uch nominally identifiable data should be treated the same as identified data.

At the other end of the risk continuum, *non-identifiable* information carries only a remote risk of identification. Such data cannot be said to be relatable to a person taking account of the means reasonably likely to be used for identification. In certain kinds of data sets, for example, the original sample is so large that other information will not enable the identification of individuals.

Schwartz and Solove argue that re-identification is a risk rather than a certainty, and the law should be based upon the degree of risk. That risk, however, is changing, because the ability to transform non-PII into identified information depends in part on the amount of personal data about people that is available — the more data, the easier it is to find a match. The risk also depends upon technology, which is changing. How should privacy regulation deal with this evolving landscape? Does PII 2.0 adequately address this problem?

7. ***Risks in De-Identified Data?*** For Jane Yakowitz, the key question is "how much marginal risk does a public research database create in comparison to the background risks we already endure?"[22] Yakowitz assesses this marginal risk from data-sharing involving de-identified data as "trivially small." She reaches this conclusion by arguing that actual "adversaries" who will seek to de-identify are scarce, in part because of "lower hanging fruit," such as consumer databases that can be purchased, compared to anonymized databases. Yakowitz also points out that re-identifying subjects in anonymized databases is far from easy, but requires statistical expertise, and that "large repeat players" who share anonymized databases do not make "rookie mistakes."

A white paper by Ann Cavoukian, the Information and Privacy Commissioner of Ontario, Canada, and Khaled El Emam has argued along similar lines.[23] In their view, despite "a residual risk of re-identification, in the vast majority of cases, de-identification will protect the privacy of individuals, as long as additional safeguards are in place." In their four-step process, the re-identification risk exposure of a data disclosure depends upon: "the re-identification probability; the mitigating controls that are in place; the motives and capacity of the data recipient to re-identify the data; and the extent to which an inappropriate disclosure would be an invasion of privacy."

Data security breach laws also rely on definitions of PII. We examine this area of law in the next chapter.

---

[22] Jane Yakowitz, *Tragedy of the Data Commons*, 25 Harv. J.L. & Tech.1 (2011).

[23] Ann Cavoukian & Khaled El Emam, *Dispelling the Myths Surrounding De-Identification: Anonymization Remains a Strong Tool for Protecting Privacy* (Information and Privacy Commissioner of Ontario, June 2011).

4. INJURY AND STANDING

An overarching issue in privacy cases is whether the privacy violation caused any harm. Suppose a company violates a promise made in its privacy policy not to share data with third parties. The company shares personal data about consumers with a marketing company that uses the data to create more tailored ad profiles and deliver targeted advertisements to consumers. Did the consumers suffer any harm?

Plaintiffs must typically allege a cognizable injury in order to have a viable cause of action. In federal courts, in order to have standing, the plaintiff

> must show that (1) it has suffered an 'injury in fact' that is (a) concrete and particularized and (b) actual or imminent, not conjectural or hypothetical; (2) the injury is fairly traceable to the challenged action of the defendant; and (3) it is likely, as opposed to merely speculative, that the injury will be redressed by a favorable decision. *Friends of the Earth, Inc. v. Laidlaw Envtl. Sys. (TOC), Inc.,* 528 U.S. 167 (2000).

If a plaintiff cannot establish standing, then a plaintiff's lawsuit cannot proceed forward in federal court.

Sometimes, statutes define the elements of a cognizable injury, but in the absence of such a statutorily defined harm, courts will look to general legal principles to determine if an injury occurred. In both data security breach cases and privacy cases, courts have struggled to recognize harm. Daniel Solove argues that courts often look for harms that are "visceral and vested":

> Harms must be *visceral* — they must involve some dimension of palpable physical injury or financial loss. And harms must be *vested* — they must have already occurred.
>
> For harms that involve emotional distress, courts are skeptical because people can too easily say they suffered emotional distress. It can be hard to prove or disprove statements that one suffered emotional distress, and these difficulties make courts very uneasy.
>
> For the future risk of harm, courts generally want to see harm that has actually manifested rather than harm that is incubating. Suppose you're exposed to a virus that silently waits in your bloodstream for 10 years and then suddenly might kill you. Most courts would send you away and tell you to come back after you've dropped dead, because then we would know for sure you're injured. But then, sadly, the statute of limitations will have run out, so it's too late to sue. Tough luck, the courts will say.[24]

Clapper v. Amnesty International USA, 133 S. Ct. (2013) has been a highly-influential standing case for lawsuits involving privacy and security violations. Although *Clapper* involved a constitutional challenge to national security surveillance, the case has had a significant impact on data breach and privacy litigation among private parties. In *Clapper*, a group of attorneys, journalists, and others contended that government surveillance under the Foreign Intelligence Surveillance Act (FISA) violated their constitutional rights. They could not prove that they were definitely under surveillance, but they had reason to fear they were

---

[24] Daniel J. Solove, *Privacy and Data Security Violations: What's the Harm*, LinkedIn (June 25, 2014), https://www.linkedin.com/today/post/article/20140625045136-2259773-privacy-and-data-security-violations-what-s-the-harm.

under surveillance because they represented or spoke to individuals whom the government would likely deem as suspicious.

The Supreme Court held that the plaintiffs could not establish standing. The Court reasoned that "it is speculative whether the Government will imminently target communications to which respondents are parties." The FISA "at most *authorizes*—but does not *mandate* or *direct*—the surveillance that respondents fear, respondents' allegations are necessarily conjectural. Simply put, respondents can only speculate as to how the Attorney General and the Director of National Intelligence will exercise their discretion in determining which communications to target."

The plaintiffs also contended that they were injured because they had to take measures to avoid the risk that they were under surveillance. "Respondents claim, for instance, that the threat of surveillance sometimes compels them to avoid certain e-mail and phone conversations, to 'tal[k] in generalities rather than specifics,' or to travel so that they can have in-person conversations." The Court rejected these costs as a basis for injury because "parties cannot manufacture standing by incurring costs in anticipation of non-imminent harm."

After *Clapper,* many federal courts have used the Supreme Court's decision to deny standing to plaintiffs in data breach cases when plaintiffs claim injury due to a risk of future harm or spending money on protective measures against such harm. There are, however, a number of courts that have distinguished *Clapper* and concluded that plaintiffs have alleged a concrete injury. See the chapter on data security for more about these cases.

SPOKEO, INC. V. ROBINS

136 S.Ct. 1540 (2016)

ALITO, J. This case presents the question whether respondent Robins has standing to maintain an action in federal court against petitioner Spokeo under the Fair Credit Reporting Act of 1970 (FCRA or Act).

Spokeo operates a "people search engine." If an individual visits Spokeo's Web site and inputs a person's name, a phone number, or an e-mail address, Spokeo conducts a computerized search in a wide variety of databases and provides information about the subject of the search. Spokeo performed such a search for information about Robins, and some of the information it gathered and then disseminated was incorrect. When Robins learned of these inaccuracies, he filed a complaint on his own behalf and on behalf of a class of similarly situated individuals.

The District Court dismissed Robins' complaint for lack of standing, but a panel of the Ninth Circuit reversed. . . .

The FCRA seeks to ensure "fair and accurate credit reporting." To achieve this end, the Act regulates the creation and the use of "consumer report[s]" by "consumer reporting agenc[ies]" for certain specified purposes, including credit transactions, insurance, licensing, consumer-initiated business transactions, and employment. Enacted long before the advent of the Internet, the FCRA applies to companies that regularly disseminate information bearing on an individual's "credit worthiness, credit standing, credit capacity, character, general reputation, personal characteristics, or mode of living."

The Act . . . provides that "[a]ny person who willfully fails to comply with any requirement [of the Act] with respect to any [individual[3]] is liable to that [individual]" for, among other things, either "actual damages" or statutory damages of $100 to $1,000 per violation, costs of the action and attorney's fees, and possibly punitive damages. § 1681n(a).

Spokeo is alleged to qualify as a "consumer reporting agency" under the FCRA. It operates a Web site that allows users to search for information about other individuals by name, e-mail address, or phone number. In response to an inquiry submitted online, Spokeo searches a wide spectrum of databases and gathers and provides information such as the individual's address, phone number, marital status, approximate age, occupation, hobbies, finances, shopping habits, and musical preferences. According to Robins, Spokeo markets its services to a variety of users, including not only "employers who want to evaluate prospective employees," but also "those who want to investigate prospective romantic partners or seek other personal information." Persons wishing to perform a Spokeo search need not disclose their identities, and much information is available for free.

At some point in time, someone (Robins' complaint does not specify who) made a Spokeo search request for information about Robins, and Spokeo trawled its sources and generated a profile. By some means not detailed in Robins' complaint, he became aware of the contents of that profile and discovered that it contained inaccurate information. His profile, he asserts, states that he is married, has children, is in his 50's, has a job, is relatively affluent, and holds a graduate degree. According to Robins' complaint, all of this information is incorrect.

Robins filed a class-action complaint in the United States District Court for the Central District of California, claiming, among other things, that Spokeo willfully failed to comply with the FCRA requirements enumerated above. . . .

Although the Constitution does not fully explain what is meant by "[t]he judicial Power of the United States," it does specify that this power extends only to "Cases" and "Controversies," Art. III, § 2. . . .

Standing to sue is a doctrine rooted in the traditional understanding of a case or controversy. The doctrine developed in our case law to ensure that federal courts do not exceed their authority as it has been traditionally understood. The doctrine limits the category of litigants empowered to maintain a lawsuit in federal court to seek redress for a legal wrong.

Our cases have established that the "irreducible constitutional minimum" of standing consists of three elements. [Lujan v. Defenders of Wildlife, 504 U.S. 555 (1992).] The plaintiff must have (1) suffered an injury in fact, (2) that is fairly traceable to the challenged conduct of the defendant, and (3) that is likely to be redressed by a favorable judicial decision. The plaintiff, as the party invoking federal jurisdiction, bears the burden of establishing these elements. . . .

This case primarily concerns injury in fact, the "[f]irst and foremost" of standing's three elements. Injury in fact is a constitutional requirement, and "[i]t is settled that Congress cannot erase Article III's standing requirements by statutorily granting the right to sue to a plaintiff who would not otherwise have standing."

To establish injury in fact, a plaintiff must show that he or she suffered "an invasion of a legally protected interest" that is "concrete and particularized" and "actual or imminent, not conjectural or hypothetical." Lujan, 504 U.S., at 560.

Particularization is necessary to establish injury in fact, but it is not sufficient. An injury in fact must also be "concrete." Under the Ninth Circuit's analysis, however, that independent requirement was elided. As previously noted, the Ninth Circuit concluded that Robins' complaint alleges "concrete, de facto " injuries for essentially two reasons. First, the court noted that Robins "alleges that Spokeo violated his statutory rights, not just the statutory rights of other people." Second, the court wrote that "Robins's personal interests in the handling of his credit information are individualized rather than collective." Both of these observations concern particularization, not concreteness. We have made it clear time and time again that an injury in fact must be both concrete and particularized.

A "concrete" injury must be "de facto"; that is, it must actually exist. . . .

"Concrete" is not, however, necessarily synonymous with "tangible." Although tangible injuries are perhaps easier to recognize, we have confirmed in many of our previous cases that intangible injuries can nevertheless be concrete.

In determining whether an intangible harm constitutes injury in fact, both history and the judgment of Congress play important roles. Because the doctrine of standing derives from the case-or-controversy requirement, and because that requirement in turn is grounded in historical practice, it is instructive to consider whether an alleged intangible harm has a close relationship to a harm that has traditionally been regarded as providing a basis for a lawsuit in English or American courts. In addition, because Congress is well positioned to identify intangible harms that meet minimum Article III requirements, its judgment is also instructive and important. Thus, we said in Lujan that Congress may "elevat[e] to the status of legally cognizable injuries concrete, de facto injuries that were previously inadequate in law."

Congress' role in identifying and elevating intangible harms does not mean that a plaintiff automatically satisfies the injury-in-fact requirement whenever a statute grants a person a statutory right and purports to authorize that person to sue to vindicate that right. Article III standing requires a concrete injury even in the context of a statutory violation. For that reason, Robins could not, for example, allege a bare procedural violation, divorced from any concrete harm, and satisfy the injury-in-fact requirement of Article III.

This does not mean, however, that the risk of real harm cannot satisfy the requirement of concreteness. *See,* e.g., Clapper v. Amnesty Int'l USA, 133 S.Ct. 1138 (2013). For example, the law has long permitted recovery by certain tort victims even if their harms may be difficult to prove or measure. Just as the common law permitted suit in such instances, the violation of a procedural right granted by statute can be sufficient in some circumstances to constitute injury in fact. In other words, a plaintiff in such a case need not allege any additional harm beyond the one Congress has identified.

In the context of this particular case, these general principles tell us two things: On the one hand, Congress plainly sought to curb the dissemination of false information by adopting procedures designed to decrease that risk. On the other hand, Robins cannot satisfy the demands of Article III by alleging a bare procedural violation. A violation of one of the FCRA's procedural requirements may result in no harm. For example, even if a consumer reporting agency fails to provide the required notice to a user of the agency's consumer information, that information regardless may be entirely accurate. In addition, not all inaccuracies cause harm or present any material risk of harm. An example that comes readily to mind is an incorrect zip code. It is difficult to imagine how the dissemination of an incorrect zip code, without more, could work any concrete harm.

Because the Ninth Circuit failed to fully appreciate the distinction between concreteness and particularization, its standing analysis was incomplete. It did not address the question framed by our discussion, namely, whether the particular procedural violations alleged in this case entail a degree of risk sufficient to meet the concreteness requirement. We take no position as to whether the Ninth Circuit's ultimate conclusion—that Robins adequately alleged an injury in fact—was correct.

GINSBURG, J. joined by SOTOMAYOR, J. dissenting. . . . Judged by what we have said about "concreteness," Robins' allegations carry him across the threshold. . . .

Inspection of the Court's decisions suggests that the particularity requirement bars complaints raising generalized grievances, seeking relief that no more benefits the plaintiff than it does the public at large. Robins' claim does not present a question of that character. He seeks redress, not for harm to the citizenry, but for Spokeo's spread of misinformation specifically about him. . . .

Robins would not qualify, the Court observes, if he alleged a "bare" procedural violation, one that results in no harm, for example, "an incorrect zip code." Far from an incorrect zip code, Robins complains of misinformation about his education, family situation, and economic status, inaccurate representations that could affect his fortune in the job market. See Brief for Center for Democracy & Technology et al. as Amici Curiae (Spokeo's inaccuracies bore on Robins' "ability to find employment by creating the erroneous impression that he was overqualified for the work he was seeking, that he might be unwilling to relocate for a job due to family commitments, or that his salary demands would exceed what prospective employers were prepared to offer him."). The FCRA's procedural requirements aimed to prevent such harm. I therefore see no utility in returning this case to the Ninth Circuit to underscore what Robins' complaint already conveys concretely: Spokeo's misinformation "cause[s] actual harm to [his] employment prospects."

NOTES & QUESTIONS

1. *How Tangible Must a "Concrete" Injury Be?* Standing has been a particularly challenging issue in privacy cases, with many such cases being dismissed for lack of standing because of courts concluding that plaintiffs have not suffered harm. The Court states that a "concrete" injury "must actually exist" and must be "real and not abstract." Yet, the court also states that "we have confirmed in many of our previous cases that intangible injuries can nevertheless be concrete." Privacy is often an intangible injury. When is an intangible injury "real and not abstract"?

2. *When Can Congress Define What Is Recognized as a Concrete Injury?* The Court notes that Congress may "elevat[e] to the status of legally cognizable injuries concrete, *de facto* injuries that were previously inadequate in law." Congress can deem even injuries "previously inadequate in law" to be concrete injuries sufficient to confer standing.

However, the Court also states:

> Congress' role in identifying and elevating intangible harms does not mean that a plaintiff automatically satisfies the injury-in-fact requirement whenever a statute grants a person a statutory right and purports to authorize that person to sue to vindicate that right. Article III standing requires a concrete injury even in the context of a statutory violation. For that reason, Robins could not, for example, allege a bare procedural violation, divorced from any concrete harm, and satisfy the injury-in-fact requirement of Article III.

If legislatures are not limited to defining harms in the same way as courts, why should courts override a legislative determination of harm? In the FCRA, Congress determined that certain violations of the statute constituted a harm. Why does the Court not defer to Congress?

What is the implication of *Spokeo* for statutory damages? Legislatures enact statutory damage provisions so that statutes may be enforced even if it is difficult to prove harm. Under *Spokeo*, people's rights under FCRA may be violated, Congress may have given people the right to sue to enforce these rights, but courts could still disallow people to sue. Is this a judicial usurpation of Congress's power as to how it wants its statutes to be enforced?

What is a "bare procedural violation"? The Court states that "the violation of a procedural right granted by statute can be sufficient in some circumstances to constitute injury in fact. In other words, a plaintiff in such a case need not allege any *additional* harm beyond the one Congress has identified." Moreover, the Court states that a "real risk of harm" can "satisfy the requirement of concreteness." Additionally, the Court notes that "the law has long permitted recovery by certain tort victims even if their harms may be difficult to prove or measure." Taking these statements all together, what does the Court mean?

3. *The Nature of the Harm.* The Court notes: "[N]ot all inaccuracies cause harm or present any material risk of harm. An example that comes readily to mind is an incorrect zip code. It is difficult to imagine how the dissemination of an incorrect zip code, without more, could work any concrete harm." Do you agree with this example? Is the dissent correct that Robins did allege a concrete injury?

IN RE GOOGLE, INC. PRIVACY POLICY LITIGATION

2013 WL 6248499 (N.D. Cal. 2013)

GREWAL, MAGISTRATE J. . . . By now, most people know who Google is and what Google does. Google serves billions of online users in this country and around the world. What started as simply a search engine has expanded to many other products such as YouTube and Gmail. Google offers these products and most others without charge. With little or no revenue from its users, Google still manages to turn a healthy profit by selling advertisements within its products that rely in substantial part on users' personal identification information ("PII"). As some before have observed, in this model, the users are the real product.

Before March 1, 2012, Google maintained separate privacy policies for each of its products, each of which confirmed that Google used a user's PII to provide that particular product. These policies also confirmed that Google would not use the PII for any other purpose without the user's explicit consent. As Google put it, "[w]hen you sign up for a particular service that requires registration, we ask you to provide personal information. If we use this information in a manner different than the purpose for which it was collected, then we will ask for your consent prior to such use." . . .

On March 1, 2012, Google announced a new policy. The majority of its separate privacy policies were eliminated in favor of a single, universal privacy policy that spells out that Google may combine a user's PII across multiple Google products. Google explained the basis for the change in policy as follows:

> Our new Privacy Policy makes clear that, if you're signed in, we may combine information that you've provided from one service with information from other services. In short, we'll treat you as a single user across all our products, which will mean simpler, more intuitive Google experience.

In other words, through the new policy, Google is explicit that it may combine PII collected from a user's Gmail or YouTube account, including the content of that account, with PII collected from that user's Google search queries, along with the user's activities on other Google products, such as Picasa, Maps, Docs, and Reader. This PII includes:

- first and last name;
- home or other physical address (including street name and city);
- current, physical location, a user's email address, and other online contact information (such as the identifier or screen name);
- IP address;
- telephone number (both home and mobile numbers);
- list of contacts;
- search history from Google's search engine;
- web surfing history from cookies placed on the computer; and
- posts on Google+.

Plaintiffs contend that Google's new policy violates its prior policies because the new policy no longer allows users to keep information gathered from one Google product separate from information gathered from other Google products. Plaintiffs further contend that Google's new policy violates users' privacy rights by allowing Google to take information from a user's Gmail account, for which users may have one expectation of privacy, for use in a different context, such as to personalize Google search engine results, or to personalize advertisements shown while a user is surfing the internet, products for which a user may have an entirely different expectation of privacy. In addition to commingling Plaintiffs' PII across the various Google products, Plaintiff contend Google has shared Plaintiffs' PII with third-party entities who have partnered with Google in order to develop applications for the Google Play app store to help it place targeted advertisements. . . .

To satisfy Article III, a plaintiff "must show that (1) it has suffered an 'injury in fact' that is (a) concrete and particularized and (b) actual or imminent, not conjectural or hypothetical; (2) the injury is fairly traceable to the challenged action of the defendant; and (3) it is likely, as opposed to merely speculative, that the injury will be redressed by a favorable decision." A suit brought by a plaintiff without Article III standing is not a "case or controversy," and an Article III court therefore lacks subject matter jurisdiction over the suit. In that event, the suit should be dismissed under Fed. R. Civ. Pro. 12(b)(1). The injury required by Article III may exist by virtue of "statutes creating legal rights, the invasion of which creates standing." In such cases, the "standing question . . . is whether the constitutional or standing provision on which the claim rests properly can be understood as granting persons in the plaintiff's position a right to judicial relief." At all times the threshold question of standing "is distinct from the merits of [a] claim" and does not require "analysis of the merits." The Supreme Court also has instructed that the "standing inquiry requires careful judicial examination of a complaint's allegations to ascertain whether the particular plaintiff is entitled to an adjudication of the particular claims asserted."

A complaint must state a "short plain statement of the claim showing that the pleader is entitled to relief." While "detailed factual allegations" are not required, a complaint must include more than an unadorned, the defendant-unlawfully-harmed-me accusation." In other words, a complaint must have sufficient factual allegations to "state a claim to relief that is plausible on its face." A claim is facially plausible "when the pleaded factual content allows the court to draw the reasonable inference that the defendant is liable for the misconduct alleged." Accordingly, under Fed. R. Civ. P. 12(b)(6), which tests the legal sufficiency of the claims alleged in the complaint, "[d]ismissal can be based on the lack of cognizable legal theory or the absence of sufficient facts alleged under a cognizable legal theory."

When evaluating a Rule 12(b)(6) motion, the court must accept all material allegations in the complaint as true and construe them in the light most favorable to the non-moving party. . . .

"Dismissal with prejudice and without leave to amend is not appropriate unless it is clear that the complaint could not be saved by amendment. A dismissal with prejudice, except one for lack of jurisdiction, improper venue, or failure to join a party operates as an adjudication on the merits. . . .

Before considering the standing question, however, the court cannot help but make a few observations. First, despite generating little or no discussion in most other cases, the issue of injury-in-fact has become standard fare in cases involving data privacy. In fact, the court is hard-pressed to find even one recent data privacy case, at least in this district, in which injury-in-fact has not been challenged. Second, in this district's recent case law on data privacy claims, injury-in-fact has proven to be a significant barrier to entry. And so even though injury-in-fact may not generally be Mount Everest, as then-Judge Alito observed, in data privacy cases in the Northern District of California, the doctrine might still reasonably be described as Kilimanjaro. *Danvers Motor Co., Inc. v. Ford Motor Co.*, 432 F.3d 286, 294 (3d Cir. 2005).

1. *Personal Identification Information.* Plaintiffs claim that when Google combined information that Plaintiffs provided to discrete Google products, without Plaintiffs' consent, Google injured them in two different ways. First, Google did not compensate them for the substantial economic value of the combined information. Second, Google's unauthorized comingling of their information, especially their likeness, was a breach of contract. Neither alleged harm, however, is sufficient to establish an injury-in-fact.

. . . [I]njury-in-fact in this context requires more than an allegation that a defendant profited from a plaintiff's personal identification information. Rather, a plaintiff must allege how the defendant's use of the information deprived the plaintiff of the information's economic value. Put another way, a plaintiff must do more than point to the dollars in a defendant's pocket; he must sufficient allege that in the process he lost dollars of his own. Plaintiffs' allegations certainly plead that Google made money using information about them for which they were provided no compensation beyond free access to Google's services. But an allegation that Google profited is not enough equivalent to an allegation that such profiteering deprived Plaintiffs' of economic value from that same information.

As before, the court finds the reasoning in *LaCourt v. Specific Media,* [2011 WL 1661532, at *5 (C.D. Cal. 2011),] instructive. There the plaintiffs alleged that the defendant installed cookies to track users' internet browsing to build behavior profiles to better target advertisements. The court found the tracked users lacked standing because, among other reasons, they did not "explain how they were 'deprived' of the economic value of their personal information simply because their unspecified personal information was purportedly collected by a third party." Other courts have agreed.

Addressing a set of facts similar to the present case, in *In re Google Android User Privacy Litig.,* [No. 11–MD–02264 JSW, 2013 WL 1283236, at *4 (N.D. Cal. Mar. 26, 2013)] the court found no Article III standing where plaintiffs alleged that Google's unauthorized use of PII reduced its value to them because the plaintiffs failed to tie Google's use to their alleged loss, such as being foreclosed from capitalizing on its value. Here, Plaintiffs similarly have not alleged how Google's use of PII in any way deprives them of the ability to profit from the same information. . . .

Finally, although Plaintiffs assert that the breach of contract arising from Google's unauthorized commingling activities offers a separate basis for injury-in-fact, they still fail to articulate a sufficient contract injury. Nominal damages are not available in California for breach of contract, and the amended complaint does not allege any other injury based on the breach. In their opposition, Plaintiffs assert that "one of the most egregious ways in which Google breaches its contracts . . . is by misusing Plaintiffs' information to misappropriate their likeness. But even if this point in opposition were presented in the complaint itself, which it is not, Plaintiffs still cite no case law holding that a contract breach by itself constitutes an injury in fact. This is insufficient.

2. *Direct Economic Injuries.* The court next considers whether Plaintiffs have alleged direct economic injuries sufficient to establish injury-in-fact. As the Supreme Court has noted, "palpable economic injuries have long been recognized

as sufficient to lay the basis for standing." Plaintiffs each allege that they were injured when their Android devices sent their respective names, email addresses, and locations to the developer of each app they purchased or downloaded because they had to pay for the battery and bandwidth consumed by the unauthorized transmissions. Mr. Nisenbaum, representing the Android Device Switch Subclass, claims further injury in that he overpaid for his Android phone in 2010 because he would not have bought the phone had Google disclosed its intention to use his information as alleged in the complaint. Mr. Nisenbaum also claims that he replaced his Android phone with an iPhone in 2012 as a result of Google's policy change, causing him further economic injury.

The Court will consider each of these direct economic injury theories in turn to determine if they articulate "something more" than pure economic harm to support subject-matter jurisdiction under Rule 12(b)(1).

With respect to Plaintiffs' injury claims based on battery and bandwidth consumption, courts have found that the unauthorized use of system resources can suffice to establish a cognizable injury. For example, in *Goodman* [*vs. HTC*, No. C11–1793MJP, 2012 WL 2412070, at *5 (W.D. Wash. Jun. 26, 2012)], the court found standing based upon battery discharge where the application at issue sent fine location data every three hours or whenever the device's screen was refreshed. Similarly, in *In re iPhone Application Litigation* [844 F. Supp. 2d 1040, 1054–56 (N.D. Cal. 2012)], the court found standing where the device systematically collected and transmitted location information. In *In re Google Android User Privacy Litigation* [2013 WL 1283236, at *2, 4 (N.D. Cal. Mar. 26, 2013)], the plaintiffs did not clearly allege how frequently Google collected geolocation data from a phone, but did allege that collecting relocation data was particularly battery intensive, that "their batteries discharged more quickly[,] and that their services were interrupted." This latter allegation was deemed sufficient to establish standing. At the same time, in *Hernandez v. Path, Inc.* [2012 WL 5194120, at *8 (N.D. Cal. Oct. 19, 2012)], the court found that any harm from the use of phone resources in an app's uploading a user's address book a single time upon first running the app was *de minimis* and thus insufficient to establish injury.

Plaintiffs' allegations here are closer to *Goodman, iPhone I* and *Android* than *Hernandez*. Like *Hernandez*, Plaintiffs' alleged unauthorized battery consumption only happened infrequently, when a plaintiff first downloaded an app. But in *Hernandez* the allegedly unauthorized upload only happened once, when a plaintiff downloaded the Path app. Here, it happens each time a user downloads any app. The plaintiff who downloaded the most apps, according to the amended complaint, did so at least 27 times. In addition, like the plaintiffs in *Goodman* and *Android,* Plaintiffs here specifically allege a greater discharge of battery power as a result of unauthorized conduct and as in *iPhone I* the discharge is systemic rather than episodic. This is sufficient to establish more than a *de minimis* injury.

With respect to Mr. Nisenbaum's further allegations of injury, they, too, support standing for purposes of Article III.

First, the allegation that Mr. Nisenbaum bought a new phone after the policy change and that his motivation for choosing an iPhone over the Android device was substantially for privacy reasons, establishes that he was injured by making the purchase. To be sure, users frequently replace old phones for all kinds of reasons beyond privacy. For example, from the complaint, it appears Mr.

Nisenbaum had his Android device for approximately two years, the length of most phone contracts that often include a discount for bundled phones, before purchasing a new phone. But Mr. Nisenbaum specifically alleges that but for the policy switch he would not have otherwise have bought a new phone. The alleged injury is fairly traceable to Google based on Mr. Nisenbaum's allegation that he relied on Google's previous policies in purchasing the Android phone in the first place.

Second, Mr. Nisembaum's allegations regarding overpayment establish injury. In *Pirozzi v. Apple* [913 F. Supp. 2d 840, 846–47 (N.D. Cal. 2012)], the court explained that Article III standing under an overpayment theory may be supported by "allegations [by plaintiffs] that, when they purchased their [ ] devices, they relied upon representations regarding privacy protection, which caused them to pay more than they would have for their devices." Similarly, in *Goodman,* the court found standing for overpayment of a smartphone where plaintiffs alleged they would have "paid less for the phones had [d]efendant's not misrepresented the relevant features." The court held that a "general averment of quality, alleged to be false, was sufficient to constitute an alleged injury in the form of overpayment." The allegations here are equally sufficient.

Google highlights that Mr. Nisenbaum has not alleged that he bought his phone from Google or that Google manufactured the phone. But the complaint is clear that Mr. Nisenbaum's phone ran on Android, Google's open-source operating system, and that in order to access the Google Play marketplace included in Android, Mr. Nisenbaum had to create a Google account. Under such circumstances, the alleged harm of overpayment to a third party is fairly traceable to Google. . . .

NOTES & QUESTIONS

1. ***Postscript.*** The *Goog*le court went on to analyze the various claims, and it found that none of the claims was viable, so the court granted Google's motion to dismiss. Note that in federal court, plaintiffs must establish sufficient injury for standing, and then must still establish sufficient facts to justify a prima facie case on various causes of action.

2. ***Financial Harm.*** Is the *Google* court looking for the appropriate type of harm? Recall that Warren and Brandeis defined privacy as primarily an emotional injury, not a financial one. Should courts be focusing on financial harm? Was there non-financial harm when Google changed its privacy policies? Should courts recognize such harm?

   In *In Re Google, Inc. Cookie Placement Consumer Privacy Litigation*, 988 F. Supp. 2d 434 (D. Del. 2013), plaintiffs alleged that Google "'tricked' their Apple Safari and/or Internet Explorer browsers into accepting cookies, which then allowed defendants to display targeted advertising." The court held that the plaintiffs couldn't prove a harm because they couldn't demonstrate that Google interfered with their ability to "monetize" their personal data:

   > Examining the facts alleged in the light most favorable to plaintiffs, the court concludes that, while plaintiffs have offered some evidence that the online personal information at issue has some modicum of identifiable value to an

individual plaintiff, plaintiffs have not sufficiently alleged that the ability to monetize their PII has been diminished or lost by virtue of Google's previous collection of it.

3. ***The EU Reaction.*** Google's consolidation of its privacy policies also led to a reaction in the European Union. On December 19, 2013, the Spanish Data Protection Authority fined it 900,000 Euros, or approximately $1.2 million, for violating Spanish data protection provisions. The *Agencia Española de Protección de Datos* (AEPD) found that the combination of data by the different Google services widely exceeded the reasonable expectations of the majority of users. It also noted that Google hindered and, in some cases, prevented rights of access, rectification, and cancellation. Finally, the AEPD declared that Google did not obtain valid consent from the concerned individuals.

In France, the French Data Protection authority fined Google 150,000 Euros, or approximately $200,000, which was the maximum fine that French law permitted to be placed on first time violators. The *Commission nationale de l'information et des libertés* (CNIL) also required Google to publish a copy of its order on its website in France. The CNIL found that Google "did not sufficiently inform its users of the conditions in which their personal data are processed, nor of the purposes of this processing." Google also failed to comply with its obligation to obtain user consent and to define retention periods for the data that it processes. As a final matter, Google "permits itself to combine all the data it collects about its users across all its services without any legal basis."[25]

What lessons do you draw from the different reactions in the EU and United States to this same action by Google?

4. ***Possible Future Harm and Mitigation Expenses.*** In privacy cases, plaintiffs have alleged that defendants' activities create risks of possible future harm. Courts have generally not been receptive to this argument. In *Clapper v. Amnesty International*, 133 S. Ct. 1138 (2013), which we excerpted in Chapter 5, the U.S. Supreme Court held that plaintiffs failed to allege a legally cognizable injury when they challenged a provision of the law that permits the government to engage in surveillance of their communications. Although this case does not involve consumer privacy issues, its reasoning has applicability for consumer privacy cases.

The plaintiffs claimed that there was an "objectively reasonable likelihood" that their communications would be monitored, and as a result, they had to take "costly and burdensome measures to protect the confidentiality of their international communications." The Supreme Court concluded that the plaintiffs were speculating and that "allegations of possible future injury are not sufficient" to establish an injury. According to the Court, "fears of hypothetical future harm" cannot justify the countermeasures the plaintiffs

---

[25] CNIL, *Deliberation No. 2013-420 of the Sanctions Committee of CNIL imposing a financial penalty against Google Inc.* (Jan. 3, 2014).

took. "Enterprising" litigants could establish an injury "simply by making an expenditure based on a nonparanoid fear."

In data breach cases, most courts have rejected claims that the breach increased the risk of future identity theft. *See, e.g., Amburgy v. Express Scripts, Inc.,* 671 F. Supp.2d 1046 (E.D. Mo. 2009); *Key v. DSW, Inc.,* 454 F. Supp. 2d 684 (S.D. Ohio 2006). Likewise, courts reject cases when plaintiffs spend money for mitigation expenses — measures to protect themselves against future harm. One case, however, accepted this theory. In *Anderson v. Hannaford Bros. Co.,* 659 F.3d 151 (1st Cir. 2011), the court held:

> Under Maine negligence law, damages must be both reasonably foreseeable, and, even if reasonably foreseeable, of the type which Maine has not barred for policy reasons. Generally, under Maine law, "the fundamental test [for both tort and contract recovery] is one of reasonable foreseeability: if the loss or injury for which damages are claimed was not reasonably foreseeable under the circumstances, there is no liability." But liability in negligence also "ordinarily requires proof of personal injury or property damage." . . . In cases of nonphysical harm, Maine courts limit recovery by considering not only reasonable foreseeability, but also relevant policy considerations such as "societal expectations regarding behavior and individual responsibility in allocating risks and costs." . . .
>
> It is clear that, as a matter of policy, Maine law "encourages plaintiffs to take reasonable steps to minimize losses caused by a defendant's negligence." To recover mitigation damages, plaintiffs need only show that the efforts to mitigate were reasonable, and that those efforts constitute a legal injury, such as actual money lost, rather than time or effort expended.
>
> Maine has interpreted this "reasonableness" requirement for mitigation, judging whether the decision to mitigate was reasonable "at the time it was made." . . .
>
> The Seventh Circuit, for example, has held that under Restatement § 919 incidental costs expended in good faith to mitigate harm are recoverable—even if the costs turn out to exceed the savings. . . .
>
> The Fourth Circuit has noted, applying Restatement § 919, that plaintiffs should not face "a Hobson's choice" between allowing further damage to occur or mitigating the damage at their own expense. Toll Bros., Inc. v. Dryvit Sys., Inc., 432 F.3d 564, 570 (4th Cir.2005) (applying Connecticut law). In Toll, a real estate developer removed and replaced defective stucco from homes that it built, and sued the stucco manufacturer in negligence to recover its costs. The court concluded that, as a matter of policy, a plaintiff may recover the cost of its reasonable attempts to mitigate, even if the injury is "wholly financial" in nature.

However, in the *Hannaford Brothers* case the information was obtained by a ring of identity thieves and some people were already victimized. The court noted that the plaintiffs "were not merely exposed to a hypothetical risk, but to a real risk of misuse." Another case that found standing in a data breach case is *Resnick v. AvMed Inc.* (11th Cir. 2012), which is excerpted in Chapter 10.

B. TORT LAW

DWYER V. AMERICAN EXPRESS CO.

652 N.E.2d 1351 (Ill. App. 1995)

BUCKLEY, J. Plaintiffs, American Express cardholders, appeal the circuit court's dismissal of their claims for invasion of privacy and consumer fraud against defendants, American Express Company, American Express Credit Corporation, and American Express Travel Related Services Company, for their practice of renting information regarding cardholder spending habits.

On May 13, 1992, the New York Attorney General released a press statement describing an agreement it had entered into with defendants. The following day, newspapers reported defendants' actions which gave rise to this agreement. According to the news articles, defendants categorize and rank their cardholders into six tiers based on spending habits and then rent this information to participating merchants as part of a targeted joint-marketing and sales program. For example, a cardholder may be characterized as "Rodeo Drive Chic" or "Value Oriented." In order to characterize its cardholders, defendants analyze where they shop and how much they spend, and also consider behavioral characteristics and spending histories. Defendants then offer to create a list of cardholders who would most likely shop in a particular store and rent that list to the merchant.

Defendants also offer to create lists which target cardholders who purchase specific types of items, such as fine jewelry. The merchants using the defendants' service can also target shoppers in categories such as mail-order apparel buyers, home-improvement shoppers, electronics shoppers, luxury lodgers, card members with children, skiers, frequent business travelers, resort users, Asian/European travelers, luxury European car owners, or recent movers. Finally, defendants offer joint-marketing ventures to merchants who generate substantial sales through the American Express card. Defendants mail special promotions devised by the merchants to its cardholders and share the profits generated by these advertisements. . . .

Plaintiffs have alleged that defendants' practices constitute an invasion of their privacy [in particular, a violation of the intrusion upon seclusion tort]. . . .

. . . [There are] four elements [to intrusion upon seclusion] which must be alleged in order to state a cause of action: (1) an unauthorized intrusion or prying into the plaintiff's seclusion; (2) an intrusion which is offensive or objectionable to a reasonable man; (3) the matter upon which the intrusion occurs is private; and (4) the intrusion causes anguish and suffering. . . .

Plaintiffs' allegations fail to satisfy the first element, an unauthorized intrusion or prying into the plaintiffs' seclusion. The alleged wrongful actions involve the defendants' practice of renting lists that they have compiled from information contained in their own records. By using the American Express card, a cardholder is voluntarily, and necessarily, giving information to defendants that, if analyzed, will reveal a cardholder's spending habits and shopping preferences. . . .

Plaintiffs claim that because defendants rented lists based on this compiled information, this case involves the disclosure of private financial information and most closely resembles cases involving intrusion into private financial dealings, such as bank account transactions. Plaintiffs cite several cases in which courts have recognized the right to privacy surrounding financial transactions.

However, we find that this case more closely resembles the sale of magazine subscription lists, which was at issue in *Shibley v. Time, Inc.* In *Shibley*, the plaintiffs claimed that the defendant's practice of selling and renting magazine subscription lists without the subscribers' prior consent "constitut[ed] an invasion of privacy because it amount[ed] to a sale of individual 'personality profiles,' which subjects the subscribers to solicitations from direct mail advertisers." The plaintiffs also claimed that the lists amounted to a tortious appropriation of their names and "personality profiles." . . .

The *Shibley* court found that an Ohio statute, which permitted the sale of names and addresses of registrants of motor vehicles, indicated that the defendant's activity was not an invasion of privacy. . . .

Defendants rent names and addresses after they create a list of cardholders who have certain shopping tendencies; they are not disclosing financial information about particular cardholders. These lists are being used solely for the purpose of determining what type of advertising should be sent to whom. We also note that the Illinois Vehicle Code authorizes the Secretary of State to sell lists of names and addresses of licensed drivers and registered motor-vehicle owners. Thus, we hold that the alleged actions here do not constitute an unreasonable intrusion into the seclusion of another. We so hold without expressing a view as to the appellate court conflict regarding the recognition of this cause of action.

Considering plaintiffs' appropriation claim, the elements of the tort are: an appropriation, without consent, of one's name or likeness for another's use or benefit. This branch of the privacy doctrine is designed to protect a person from having his name or image used for commercial purposes without consent. According to the Restatement, the purpose of this tort is to protect the "interest of the individual in the exclusive use of his own identity, in so far as it is represented by his name or likeness." Illustrations of this tort provided by the Restatement include the publication of a person's photograph without consent in an advertisement; operating a corporation named after a prominent public figure without the person's consent; impersonating a man to obtain information regarding the affairs of the man's wife; and filing a lawsuit in the name of another without the other's consent.

Plaintiffs claim that defendants appropriate information about cardholders' personalities, including their names and perceived lifestyles, without their consent. Defendants argue that their practice does not adversely affect the interest of a cardholder in the "exclusive use of his own identity," using the language of the Restatement. Defendants also argue that the cardholders' names lack value and that the lists that defendants create are valuable because "they identify a useful aggregate of potential customers to whom offers may be sent." . . .

To counter defendants' argument, plaintiffs point out that the tort of appropriation is not limited to strictly commercial situations.

Nonetheless, we again follow the reasoning in *Shibley* and find that plaintiffs have not stated a claim for tortious appropriation because they have failed to allege the first element. Undeniably, each cardholder's name is valuable to defendants. The more names included on a list, the more that list will be worth. However, a single, random cardholder's name has little or no intrinsic value to defendants (or a merchant). Rather, an individual name has value only when it is associated with one of defendants' lists. Defendants create value by categorizing and aggregating these names. Furthermore, defendants' practices do not deprive any of the cardholders of any value their individual names may possess. . . .

NOTES & QUESTIONS

1. **Shibley v. Time.** In *Shibley v. Time, Inc.,* 341 N.E.2d 337 (Ohio Ct. App. 1975), the plaintiff sued the publishers of a number of magazines for selling subscription lists to direct mail advertising businesses. The plaintiff sued under the public disclosure tort and the appropriation tort. Despite the fact that the purchasers of the lists can learn about the plaintiff's lifestyle from the data, the court dismissed the plaintiff's public disclosure action. The court found that the sale of the lists did not "cause mental suffering, shame or humiliation to a person of ordinary sensibilities." The court also rejected the plaintiff's argument that by selling the lists, the defendants were appropriating his name and likeness because the tort of appropriation is available only in those "situations where the plaintiff's name or likeness is displayed to the public to indicate that the plaintiff indorses the defendant's product or business."

    According to *Shibley* and *Dwyer*, why does the public disclosure tort fail to provide a remedy for the disclosure of personal information to other companies? Why does the tort of intrusion upon seclusion fail? Why does the tort of appropriation fail? More generally, can tort law adequately remedy the privacy problems created by profiling and databases?[26]

2. *A Fair Information Practices Tort?* Sarah Ludington recommends that a new tort should be developed in the common law, one that "would impose on data traders a duty to use Fair Information Practices (based on the principles of notice, choice, access, and security)." Why the common law rather than legislation? Ludington argues:

    > [B]ecause it is now clear that industry lobbying has succeeded while self-regulation has failed, and that legislatures have either failed to act or provided solutions that inadequately address the injuries, individuals must — indeed, should — look to the judiciary to help resolve the misuse of personal information.[27]

    Would the use of the common law to regulate the collection and use of personal data be effective or appropriate? What would be the strengths and weaknesses of such a regulatory approach?

---

[26] For an interesting argument about how the tort of breach of confidentiality might provide a weak but potential solution to the problem, see Jessica Litman, *Information Privacy/Information Property*, 52 Stan. L. Rev. 1283 (2000). For a discussion of the use of the tort of appropriation, see Andrew J. McClurg, *A Thousand Words Are Worth a Picture: A Privacy Tort Response to Consumer Data Profiling*, 98 Nw. U. L. Rev. 63 (2003).

[27] Sarah Ludington, *Reining in the Data Traders: A Tort for the Misuse of Personal Information*, 66 Md. L. Rev. 140, 172-73 (2007).

3. ***Defining the Harm.*** What is the harm of commercial entities collecting and using personal information? One might contend that the kind of information that companies collect about individuals is not very sensitive or intimate. How much is a person harmed by sharing data that she prefers Coke to Pepsi or Puffs to Kleenex? Is there a significant privacy problem in revealing that a person has purchased tennis products, designer sunglasses, orange juice, or other things? One might view the harm as so minimal as to be trivial.

Does information about a person's consumption patterns reveal something about that person's identity? Stan Karas argues that "consumption patterns may identify one as a liberal, moderate Republican, radical feminist or born-again Christian. . . . For some individuals, consumption is no longer a way of expressing identity but is synonymous with identity. . . . [T]he identity of many subcultures is directly related to distinctive patterns of consumption. One need only think of the personal styles of punk rockers, hip-hoppers, or Harley-fetishizing bikers."[28]

According to Jerry Kang, data collection and compiling is a form of surveillance that inhibits individual freedom and choice: "[I]nformation collection in cyberspace is more like surveillance than like casual observation." He notes that "surveillance leads to self-censorship. This is true even when the observable information would not be otherwise misused or disclosed."[29]

Daniel Solove contends that the problem of computer databases does not stem from surveillance. He argues that numerous theorists describe the problem in terms of the metaphor of Big Brother, the ruthless totalitarian government in George Orwell's *1984*, which constantly monitors its citizens. Solove contends that the Big Brother metaphor fails to adequately conceptualize the problem:

> A large portion of our personal information involves facts that we are not embarrassed about: our financial information, race, marital status, hobbies, occupation, and the like. Most people surf the web without wandering into its dark corners. The vast majority of the information collected about us concerns relatively innocuous details. The surveillance model does not explain why the recording of this non-taboo information poses a problem.[30]

In contrast, Solove proposes that data collection and processing is most aptly captured by Franz Kafka's *The Trial*, where the protagonist (Joseph K.) is arrested by officials from a clandestine court system but is not informed of the reason for his arrest. From what little he manages to learn about the court system, which operates largely in secret, Joseph K. discovers that a vast bureaucratic court has examined his life and assembled a dossier on him. His records, however, are "inaccessible," and K.'s life gradually becomes taken over by his frustrating quest for answers:

> *The Trial* captures the sense of helplessness, frustration, and vulnerability one experiences when a large bureaucratic organization has control over a vast dossier of details about one's life. At any time, something could happen to

[28] Stan Karas, *Privacy, Identity, Databases,* 52 Am. U. L. Rev. 393, 438-39 (2002).

[29] Jerry Kang, *Information Privacy in Cyberspace Transactions*, 50 Stan. L. Rev. 1193 (1998).

[30] Daniel J. Solove, *Privacy and Power: Computer Databases and Metaphors for Information Privacy*, 53 Stan. L. Rev. 1393 (2001).

Joseph K.; decisions are made based on his data, and Joseph K. has no say, no knowledge, and no ability to fight back. He is completely at the mercy of the bureaucratic process. . . .

The problem with databases emerges from subjecting personal information to the bureaucratic process with little intelligent control or limitation, resulting in a lack of meaningful participation in decisions about our information. . . .

Under this view, the problem with databases and the practices currently associated with them is that they disempower people. They make people vulnerable by stripping them of control over their personal information. There is no diabolical motive or secret plan for domination; rather, there is a web of thoughtless decisions made by low-level bureaucrats, standardized policies, rigid routines, and a way of relating to individuals and their information that often becomes indifferent to their welfare.[31]

Joel Reidenberg points out that the lack of protection of information privacy will "destroy anonymity" and take away people's "freedom to choose the terms of personal information disclosure."[32] According to Paul Schwartz, the lack of privacy protection can threaten to expose not just information about what people purchase, but also information about their communication and consumption of ideas:

In the absence of strong rules for information privacy, Americans will hesitate to engage in cyberspace activities—including those that are most likely to promote democratic self-rule. . . . Current polls already indicate an aversion on the part of some people to engage even in basic commercial activities on the Internet. Yet, deliberative democracy requires more than shoppers; it demands speakers and listeners. But who will speak or listen when this behavior leaves finely-grained data trails in a fashion that is difficult to understand or anticipate?[33]

4. ***Using Consumers in Ads: Facebook's Sponsored Stories.*** In *Fraley v. Facebook*, 830 F. Supp. 2d 785 (N.D. Cal. 2011), plaintiffs sued Facebook for its "Sponsored Stories" advertising program. A Sponsored Story is a paid ad appearing on a person's Facebook page. It uses the name and photo of a person's friend who "likes" the advertiser:

For example, Plaintiff Angel Fraley, who registered as a member with the name Angel Frolicker, alleges that she visited Rosetta Stone's Facebook profile page and clicked the "Like" button in order to access a free software demonstration. Subsequently, her Facebook user name and profile picture, which bears her likeness, appeared on her Friends' Facebook pages in a "Sponsored Story" advertisement consisting of the Rosetta Stone logo and the sentence, "Angel Frolicker likes Rosetta Stone."

Among the causes of action plaintiffs brought was appropriation of name or likeness under Cal. Civ. Code § 3344. Facebook moved to dismiss. Facebook

---

[31] *Id.*

[32] Joel R. Reidenberg, *Setting Standards for Fair Information Practice in the U.S. Private Sector*, 80 Iowa L. Rev. 497 (1995).

[33] Paul M. Schwartz, *Privacy and Democracy in Cyberspace,* 52 Vand. L. Rev. 1609, 1651 (1999).

argued that the plaintiffs consented to being used in the ads because it had stated in its Terms of Use:

> You can use your privacy settings to limit how your name and profile picture may be associated with commercial, sponsored, or related content (such as a brand you like) served or enhanced by us. You give us permission to use your name and [Facebook] profile picture in connection with that content, subject to the limits you place.

The plaintiffs argued that Sponsored Stories did not exist when they signed up with Facebook and were never informed before they were suddenly used in the ads. The court held that there were factual issues in dispute on the consent issue that prevented dismissal.

Facebook also argued that there was no injury. The court however, concluded that plaintiffs had alleged sufficient facts to establish injury to withstand a motion to dismiss:

> Here, Plaintiffs allege not that they suffered mental anguish as a result of Defendant's actions, but rather that they suffered economic injury because they were not compensated for Facebook's commercial use of their names and likenesses in targeted advertisements to their Facebook Friends. Defendant does not deny that Plaintiffs may assert economic injury, but insists that, because they are not celebrities, they must demonstrate some preexisting commercial value to their names and likenesses, such as allegations that they "previously received remuneration for the use of their name or likeness, or that they have ever sought to obtain such remuneration."
>
> First, the Court finds nothing in the text of the statute or in case law that supports Defendant's interpretation of § 3344 as requiring a plaintiff pleading economic injury to provide proof of *preexisting* commercial value and efforts to capitalize on such value in order to survive a motion to dismiss. The plain text of § 3344 provides simply that "[a]ny person who knowingly uses another's name, voice, signature, photograph, or likeness, in any manner . . . for purposes of advertising or selling . . . without such person's consent . . . shall be liable for any damages sustained by the person or persons injured as a result thereof." The statutory text makes no mention of preexisting value, and in fact can be read to presume that a person whose name, photograph, or likeness is used by another for commercial purposes without their consent is "injured as a result thereof."
>
> Nor does the Court find any reason to impose a higher pleading standard on non-celebrities than on celebrities. California courts have clearly held that "the statutory right of publicity exists for celebrity and non-celebrity plaintiffs alike."
>
> Moreover, . . . the Court finds that Plaintiffs' allegations satisfy the requirements for pleading a claim of economic injury under § 3344. Plaintiffs quote Facebook CEO Mark Zuckerberg stating that "[n]othing influences people more than a recommendation from a trusted friend. A trusted referral influences people more than the best broadcast message. A trusted referral is the Holy Grail of advertising." . . .

In August 2013, the court in this case approved a $20 million settlement with Facebook. As this casebook goes to press, there is an appeal to the settlement that argues that it violates state law in allowing Facebook to use images of minors without parental consent.[34]

<h3 align="center">REMSBURG V. DOCUSEARCH, INC.</h3>

816 A.2d 1001 (N.H. 2003)

DALIANIS, J. . . . [Liam Youens contacted Docusearch and purchased the birth date of Amy Lynn Boyer for a fee. He again contacted Docusearch and placed an order for Boyer's SSN. Docusearch obtained Boyer's SSN from a credit reporting agency and provided it to Youens. Youens then asked for Boyer's employment address. Docusearch hired a subcontractor, Michele Gambino, who obtained it by making a "pretext" phone call to Boyer. Gambino lied about her identity and the purpose of the call, and she obtained the address from Boyer. The address was then given to Youens. Shortly thereafter, Youens went to Boyer's workplace and shot and killed her and then killed himself.]

All persons have a duty to exercise reasonable care not to subject others to an unreasonable risk of harm. Whether a defendant's conduct creates a risk of harm to others sufficiently foreseeable to charge the defendant with a duty to avoid such conduct is a question of law, because "the existence of a duty does not arise solely from the relationship between the parties, but also from the need for protection against reasonably foreseeable harm." Thus, in some cases, a party's actions give rise to a duty. Parties owe a duty to those third parties foreseeably endangered by their conduct with respect to those risks whose likelihood and magnitude make the conduct unreasonably dangerous.

In situations in which the harm is caused by criminal misconduct, however, determining whether a duty exists is complicated by the competing rule "that a private citizen has no general duty to protect others from the criminal attacks of third parties." This rule is grounded in the fundamental unfairness of holding private citizens responsible for the unanticipated criminal acts of third parties, because "[u]nder all ordinary and normal circumstances, in the absence of any reason to expect the contrary, the actor may reasonably proceed upon the assumption that others will obey the law."

In certain limited circumstances, however, we have recognized that there are exceptions to the general rule where a duty to exercise reasonable care will arise. We have held that such a duty may arise because: (1) a special relationship exists; (2) special circumstances exist; or (3) the duty has been voluntarily assumed. The special circumstances exception includes situations where there is "an especial temptation and opportunity for criminal misconduct brought about by the defendant." This exception follows from the rule that a party who realizes or should realize that his conduct has created a condition which involves an unreasonable risk of harm to another has a duty to exercise reasonable care to prevent the risk from occurring. The exact occurrence or precise injuries need not have been foreseeable. Rather, where the defendant's conduct has created an

---

[34] For more on the case and a proposed "holistic economic and non-economic approach to the right of publicity" in online social networks, see Jesse Koehler, Fraley v. Facebook: *The Right of Publicity in Online Social Networks*, 28 Berkeley Tech. L.J. 963 (2013).

unreasonable risk of criminal misconduct, a duty is owed to those foreseeably endangered.

Thus, if a private investigator or information broker's (hereinafter "investigator" collectively) disclosure of information to a client creates a foreseeable risk of criminal misconduct against the third person whose information was disclosed, the investigator owes a duty to exercise reasonable care not to subject the third person to an unreasonable risk of harm. In determining whether the risk of criminal misconduct is foreseeable to an investigator, we examine two risks of information disclosure implicated by this case: stalking and identity theft.

It is undisputed that stalkers, in seeking to locate and track a victim, sometimes use an investigator to obtain personal information about the victims.

Public concern about stalking has compelled all fifty States to pass some form of legislation criminalizing stalking. Approximately one million women and 371,000 men are stalked annually in the United States. Stalking is a crime that causes serious psychological harm to the victims, and often results in the victim experiencing post-traumatic stress disorder, anxiety, sleeplessness, and sometimes, suicidal ideations.

Identity theft, *i.e.*, the use of one person's identity by another, is an increasingly common risk associated with the disclosure of personal information, such as a SSN. A person's SSN has attained the status of a quasi-universal personal identification number. At the same time, however, a person's privacy interest in his or her SSN is recognized by state and federal statutes. . . .

Like the consequences of stalking, the consequences of identity theft can be severe. . . . Victims of identity theft risk the destruction of their good credit histories. This often destroys a victim's ability to obtain credit from any source and may, in some cases, render the victim unemployable or even cause the victim to be incarcerated.

The threats posed by stalking and identity theft lead us to conclude that the risk of criminal misconduct is sufficiently foreseeable so that an investigator has a duty to exercise reasonable care in disclosing a third person's personal information to a client. And we so hold. This is especially true when, as in this case, the investigator does not know the client or the client's purpose in seeking the information. . . .

[The plaintiff also brought an action for intrusion upon seclusion.] A tort action based upon an intrusion upon seclusion must relate to something secret, secluded or private pertaining to the plaintiff. Moreover, liability exists only if the defendant's conduct was such that the defendant should have realized that it would be offensive to persons of ordinary sensibilities.

In addressing whether a person's SSN is something secret, secluded or private, we must determine whether a person has a reasonable expectation of privacy in the number. . . . As noted above, a person's interest in maintaining the privacy of his or her SSN has been recognized by numerous federal and state statutes. As a result, the entities to which this information is disclosed and their employees are bound by legal, and, perhaps, contractual constraints to hold SSNs in confidence to ensure that they remain private. Thus, while a SSN must be disclosed in certain circumstances, a person may reasonably expect that the number will remain private.

Whether the intrusion would be offensive to persons of ordinary sensibilities is ordinarily a question for the fact-finder and only becomes a question of law if reasonable persons can draw only one conclusion from the evidence. The evidence underlying the certified question is insufficient to draw any such conclusion here, and we therefore must leave this question to the fact-finder. In making this determination, the fact-finder should consider "the degree of intrusion, the context, conduct and circumstances surrounding the intrusion as well as the intruder's motives and objectives, the setting into which he intrudes, and the expectations of those whose privacy is invaded." Accordingly, a person whose SSN is obtained by an investigator from a credit reporting agency without the person's knowledge or permission may have a cause of action for intrusion upon seclusion for damages caused by the sale of the SSN, but must prove that the intrusion was such that it would have been offensive to a person of ordinary sensibilities.

We next address whether a person has a cause of action for intrusion upon seclusion where an investigator obtains the person's work address by using a pretextual phone call. We must first establish whether a work address is something secret, secluded or private about the plaintiff.

In most cases, a person works in a public place. "On the public street, or in any other public place, [a person] has no legal right to be alone." . . . Thus, where a person's work address is readily observable by members of the public, the address cannot be private and no intrusion upon seclusion action can be maintained.

[Additionally, the plaintiff brought a cause of action for appropriation.] "One who appropriates to his own use or benefit the name or likeness of another is subject to liability to the other for invasion of his privacy." *Restatement (Second) of Torts* § 652E.

. . . Appropriation is not actionable if the person's name or likeness is published for "purposes other than taking advantage of [the person's] reputation, prestige or other value" associated with the person. Thus, appropriation occurs most often when the person's name or likeness is used to advertise the defendant's product or when the defendant impersonates the person for gain.

An investigator who sells personal information sells the information for the value of the information itself, not to take advantage of the person's reputation or prestige. The investigator does not capitalize upon the goodwill value associated with the information but rather upon the client's willingness to pay for the information. In other words, the benefit derived from the sale in no way relates to the social or commercial standing of the person whose information is sold. Thus, a person whose personal information is sold does not have a cause of action for appropriation against the investigator who sold the information. . . .

NOTES & QUESTIONS

1. *The Scope of the Duty.* The court concludes that Docusearch has a duty to people "foreseeably endangered" by its disclosure of personal information. Is this too broad a duty to impose on those who collect and disseminate personal data? What could Docusearch have done to avoid being negligent in this case? Suppose Jill tells Jack the address of Roe. Jack goes to Roe's house and kills her. Based on *Remsburg*, can Jill be liable?

2. ***Tort Liability and the First Amendment.*** Does liability for Docusearch implicate the First Amendment?

C. CONTRACT LAW

1. PRIVACY POLICIES

Privacy policies are statements made by companies about their practices regarding personal information. Privacy policies are also referred to as "privacy notices." Increasingly, companies on the Internet are posting privacy policies, and statutes such as the Gramm-Leach-Bliley Act require certain types of companies (financial institutions, insurance companies, and brokerage companies) to maintain privacy policies.

One of the common provisions of many privacy policies is an "opt-out" provision. An opt-out provision establishes a default rule that the company can use or disclose personal information in the ways it desires so long as the consumer does not indicate otherwise. The consumer must take affirmative steps, such as checking a box, calling the company, or writing a letter, to express her desire to opt out of a particular information use or disclosure. In contrast, an "opt-in" provision establishes a default rule that the company cannot use or disclose personal information without first obtaining the express consent of the individual.

JEFF SOVERN, *OPTING IN, OPTING OUT, OR NO OPTIONS AT ALL: THE FIGHT FOR CONTROL OF PERSONAL INFORMATION*

74 Wash. L. Rev. 1033 (1999)

. . . [F]ew consumers understand how much of their personal information is for sale, although they may have a general idea that there is a trade in personal data and that the specifics about that trade are kept from them. . . .

. . . [C]onsumers cannot protect their personal information when they are unaware of how it is being used by others. . . .

The second reason consumers have not acted to protect their privacy, notwithstanding surveys that suggest considerable consumer concern with confidentiality, has to do with how difficult it is to opt out. . . .

. . . Even if consumers can obtain the information needed to opt out, the cost in time and money of communicating and negotiating with all the relevant information gatherers may be substantial. . . .

Companies may not be eager to offer opt-outs because they may rationally conclude that they will incur costs when consumers opt out, while receiving few offsetting benefits. When consumers exercise the option of having their names deleted, mailing lists shrink and presumably become less valuable. . . .

Because of these added costs, companies might decide that while they must offer an opt-out plan, they do not want consumers to take advantage of it. . . . [C]ompanies that offer opt-outs have an incentive to increase the transaction costs incurred by consumers who opt out. . . .

Companies can increase consumers' transaction costs in opting out in a number of ways. A brochure titled "Privacy Notice," which my local cable company included with its bill, provides an example. This Privacy Notice discussed, among other things, how cable subscribers could write to the company to ask that the company not sell their names and other information to third parties. There are at least four reasons why this particular notice may not be effective in eliciting a response from consumers troubled by the sale of their names to others.

First, the Privacy Notice may be obscured by other information included in the mailing. . . .

The second reason why consumers may not respond to the Privacy Notice is its length. The brochure is four pages long and contains 17 paragraphs, 36 sentences, and 1062 words. . . .

Some companies have gone in the other direction, providing so little information in such vague terms that consumers are unable to discern what they are being told. . . .

A third reason why the Privacy Notice may not be effective stems from its prose. Notwithstanding the Plain Language Law in my home state, computer analysis of the text found it extremely difficult, requiring more than a college education for comprehension. By comparison, a similar analysis of this Article found that it required a lower reading level than that of the Privacy Notice.

[Sovern suggests that an opt-in system would be more preferable than an opt-out system.]

One benefit of an opt-in system is that it minimizes transaction costs. While some transaction costs are inevitable in any system in which consumers can opt out or opt in, strategic-behavior transaction costs, at least, can be avoided by using a system which discourages parties from generating such costs. The current system encourages businesses to inflate strategic-behavior costs to increase their own gains, albeit at the expense of consumers and the total surplus from exchange. An opt-in system would encourage businesses to reduce strategic-behavior costs without giving consumers an incentive to increase these costs. Instead of an opt-out situation in which merchants are obligated to provide a message they do not wish consumers to receive, an opt-in regime would harness merchants' efforts in providing a message they want the consumer to receive. . . .

An opt-in system thus increases the likelihood that consumers will choose according to their preferences rather than choosing according to the default. . . .

MICHAEL E. STATEN & FRED H. CATE, *THE IMPACT OF OPT-IN PRIVACY RULES ON RETAIL MARKETS: A CASE STUDY OF MBNA*

52 Duke L.J. 745, 750-51, 766, 770-74, 776 (2003)

To illustrate the costs of moving to an opt-in system, we examine MBNA Corporation, a financial institution that offers consumers a variety of loan and insurance products (primarily credit cards), takes deposits, but operates entirely without a branch network. Incorporated in 1981 and publicly traded since 1991, the company has compiled a stunning growth record in just two decades. As of the end of 2000, the company provided credit cards and other loan products to 51 million consumers, had $89 billion of loans outstanding, and serviced 15 percent of all Visa/MasterCard credit card balances outstanding in the United States.

MBNA's ability to access and use information about potential and existing customers is largely responsible for it becoming the second largest credit card issuer in the United States in less than twenty years. . . . MBNA harnessed information technology as the engine for establishing and building customer relationships without ever physically meeting its customers. By using direct mail, telephone and, most recently, Internet contacts, the company has reached out to new prospects throughout the population, regardless of where they live, with offers tailored to their individual interests. . . .

At the core of its marketing and targeting strategies is the proposition that consumers who share a common institutional bond or experience will have an affinity for using a card that lets them demonstrate their affiliation each time they use it to pay for a purchase. . . . Following this "affinity group" marketing strategy, MBNA designs a card product tailored to members of a particular group, negotiates a financial arrangement with the organization for the exclusive rights to market an affinity card to its members, and uses the member list as a source of potential names to contact via direct mail or telemarketing. . . .

Given that MBNA's fundamental business is lending money via an unsecured credit card with a revolving line of credit attached, the company wants to put the card in the hands of customers who will use it, but who will not default on their balances. Consequently, MBNA uses information to screen prospects both before it makes card offers (the targeting process) and after it receives applications (the underwriting process). . . .

How large a drag does an "explicit-consent" system impose on economic efficiency? According to the U.S. Postal Service, 52 percent of unsolicited mail in this country is never read. If that figure translates to opt-in requests, then more than half of all consumers in an opt-in system would lose the benefits or services that could result from the use of personal information because the mandatory request for consent would never receive their attention. Moreover, even if an unsolicited offer is read, experience with company-specific and industry-wide opt-out lists demonstrates that less than 10 percent of the U.S. population ever opts out of a mailing list — often the figure is less than 3 percent. Indeed, the difficulty (and cost) of obtaining a response of any sort from consumers is the primary drawback of an opt-in approach. . . .

MBNA's core product is the affinity card tailored for and marketed to each of more than 4,700 affinity groups. . . . [T]he foundation of MBNA's affinity strategy is access to the member lists of each of its affinity organizations. . . . [A] third-party opt-in regime could effectively end MBNA's unique direct marketing approach by sharply limiting an organization's ability to share its member list. . . .

Like all major credit card issuers, MBNA uses personal information to increase the chance that its credit card offer will reach an interested and qualified customer. This process greatly reduces the number of solicitations that must be sent to achieve a given target volume of new accounts, thereby reducing the cost of account acquisition. It also reduces the volume of junk mail in the form of card offers sent to consumers who are not qualified. Third-party or affiliate opt-in systems would eliminate MBNA's access to a significant portion of the information that it currently uses to identify which individuals on the member lists it receives would be good prospects for a given credit card or other product. A blanket opt-in system applicable to marketing activities would impose similar limits. . . .

NOTES & QUESTIONS

1. ***Opt Out vs. Opt In.*** Do you agree with Sovern that an opt-in policy is more efficient than an opt-out policy? Do you think that an opt-in policy is feasible? Are the views of Staten and Cate convincing on this score? Do you think opt out or opt in should be required by law?

2. ***Internalizing Costs.*** Staten and Cate claim that MBNA's business model will be threatened by opt in. This business model relies in part, however, on sending out 400 million of mostly unwanted solicitations for credit in order to receive a 0.6 percent response rate. In other words, this model views as an externality the added cost of sorting through mail for 99.4 percent of those individuals solicited. Should MBNA be obliged to internalize these costs?

3. ***Does Privacy-Self Management Work?*** Privacy policies form the backbone of what Daniel Solove calls "privacy self-management" where the law seeks to foster people's ability to make choices about their personal data. The privacy policy describes the ways that a business will collect, use, and share personal data, and people can either consent to these practices or not engage in transactions with businesses whose practices they do not find acceptable. Solove finds severe problems with this approach:

> Although privacy self-management is certainly a laudable and necessary component of any regulatory regime, I contend that it is being tasked with doing work beyond its capabilities. Privacy self-management does not provide people with meaningful control over their data. First, empirical and social science research demonstrates that there are severe cognitive problems that undermine privacy self-management. These cognitive problems impair individuals' ability to make informed, rational choices about the costs and benefits of consenting to the collection, use, and disclosure of their personal data.
>
> Second, and more troubling, even well-informed and rational individuals cannot appropriately self-manage their privacy due to several structural problems. There are too many entities collecting and using personal data to make it feasible for people to manage their privacy separately with each entity. Moreover, many privacy harms are the result of an aggregation of pieces of data over a period of time by different entities. It is virtually impossible for people to weigh the costs and benefits of revealing information or permitting its use or transfer without an understanding of the potential downstream uses, further limiting the effectiveness of the privacy self-management framework.[35]

4. ***Visceral Notice.*** Ryan Calo argues that policymakers should explore "innovative new ways to deliver privacy notice." He contends that notice can be made more "visceral" so that people are more aware of it and understand it

---

[35] Daniel J. Solove, *Privacy Self-Management and the Consent Dilemma,* 126 Harv. L. Rev. 1880 (2013).

better. For example, a "regulation might require that a cell phone camera make a shutter sound so people know their photo is being taken."[36] Can you think of ways that privacy notices might be made more visceral? Would visceral notice address the problems that Solove has identified?

As a related approach, there has been a discussion about "just-in-time" notice. A Staff Report from the FTC has noticed that "a disclosure (*e.g.*, "why did I get this ad?") located in close proximity to an advertisement and links to the pertinent section of a privacy policy explaining how data is collected for purposes of delivering targeted advertising, could be an effective way to communicate with consumers."[37] Is "just-in-time" notice a promising approach?

2. CONTRACT AND PROMISSORY ESTOPPEL

A privacy policy can be thought of as a type of contract, though the terms are typically dictated by the company and are non-negotiable. Consider the following advice of Scott Killingsworth to the drafters of website privacy policies:

> Considering enforcement leads to the question: what is the legal effect of a privacy policy? As between the website and the user, a privacy policy bears all of the earmarks of a contract, but perhaps one enforceable only at the option of the user. It is no stretch to regard the policy as an offer to treat information in specified ways, inviting the user's acceptance, evidenced by using the site or submitting the information. The website's promise and the user's use of the site and submission of personal data are each sufficient consideration to support a contractual obligation. Under this analysis, users would have the right to sue and seek all available remedies for breach of the privacy policy, without the need for private rights of action under such regulatory statutes as the FTC Act.[38]

Privacy policies can also be viewed simply as notices that warn consumers about the use of their personal information. Assuming that these notices are subject to change as business practices evolve, how effective are privacy policies as a means to protect privacy?

IN RE NORTHWEST AIRLINES PRIVACY LITIGATION

2004 WL 1278459 (D. Minn. 2004) (not reported in F. Supp. 2d)

MAGNUSON, J. . . . Plaintiffs are customers of Defendant Northwest Airlines, Inc. ("Northwest"). After September 11, 2001, the National Aeronautical and Space Administration ("NASA") requested that Northwest provide NASA with certain passenger information in order to assist NASA in studying ways to increase airline security. Northwest supplied NASA with passenger name records ("PNRs"),

[36] *See* M. Ryan Calo, *Against Notice Skepticism in Privacy (and Elsewhere)*, 87 Notre Dame L. Rev. 1027 (2012).

[37] FTC Staff Report, *Self-Regulatory Principles for Online Behavioral Advertising* 35-36 (Feb. 12, 2009).

[38] Scott Killingsworth, *Minding Your Own Business: Privacy Policies in Principle and in Practice*, 7 J. Intell. Prop. L. 57, 91-92 (1999).

which are electronic records of passenger information. PNRs contain information such as a passenger's name, flight number, credit card data, hotel reservation, car rental, and any traveling companions.

Plaintiffs contend that Northwest's actions constitute violations of the Electronic Communications Privacy Act ("ECPA"), 18 U.S.C. § 2701 *et seq.,* the Fair Credit Reporting Act ("FCRA"), 15 U.S.C. § 1681, and Minnesota's Deceptive Trade Practices Act ("DTPA"), Minn. Stat. § 325D.44, and also constitute invasion of privacy, trespass to property, negligent misrepresentation, breach of contract, and breach of express warranties. The basis for most of Plaintiffs' claims is that Northwest's website contained a privacy policy that stated that Northwest would not share customers' information except as necessary to make customers' travel arrangements. Plaintiffs contend that Northwest's provision of PNRs to NASA violated Northwest's privacy policy, giving rise to the legal claims noted above.

Northwest has now moved to dismiss the Amended Consolidated Class Action Complaint (hereinafter "Amended Complaint"). . . .

The ECPA prohibits a person or entity from

> (1) intentionally access[ing] without authorization a facility through which an electronic communication service is provided; or
> (2) intentionally exceeds an authorization to access that facility; and thereby obtains, alters, or prevents authorized access to a wire or electronic communication while it is in electronic storage in such system shall be punished. 18 U.S.C. § 2701(a).

Plaintiffs argue that Northwest's access to its own electronic communications service is limited by its privacy policy, and that Northwest's provision of PNRs to NASA violated that policy and thus constituted unauthorized access to the "facility through which an electronic communication service is provided" within the meaning of this section. Plaintiffs also allege that Northwest violated § 2702 of the ECPA, which states that "a person or entity providing an electronic communications service to the public shall not knowingly divulge to any person or entity the contents of a communication while in electronic storage by that service." 18 U.S.C. § 2702(a)(1). Northwest argues first that it cannot violate § 2702 because it is not a "person or entity providing an electronic communications service to the public." . . .

Defining electronic communications service to include online merchants or service providers like Northwest stretches the ECPA too far. Northwest is not an internet service provider. . . .

Similarly, Northwest's conduct as outlined in the Amended Complaint does not constitute a violation of § 2701. Plaintiffs' claim is that Northwest improperly disclosed the information in PNRs to NASA. Section 2701 does not prohibit improper disclosure of information. Rather, this section prohibits improper access to an electronic communications service provider or the information contained on that service provider. . . .

Finally, Northwest argues that Plaintiffs' remaining claims fail to state a claim on which relief can be granted. These claims are: trespass to property, intrusion upon seclusion, breach of contract, and breach of express warranties.

To state a claim for trespass to property, Plaintiffs must demonstrate that they owned or possessed property, that Northwest wrongfully took that property, and that Plaintiffs were damaged by the wrongful taking. Plaintiffs contend that the information contained in the PNRs was Plaintiffs' property and that, by providing that information to NASA, Northwest wrongfully took that property.

As a matter of law, the PNRs were not Plaintiffs' property. Plaintiffs voluntarily provided some information that was included in the PNRs. It may be that the information Plaintiffs provided to Northwest was Plaintiffs' property. However, when that information was compiled and combined with other information to form a PNR, the PNR itself became Northwest's property. Northwest cannot wrongfully take its own property. Thus, Plaintiffs' claim for trespass fails. . . .

Intrusion upon seclusion exists when someone "intentionally intrudes, physically or otherwise, upon the solitude or seclusion of another or his private affairs or concerns . . . if the intrusion would be highly offensive to a reasonable person." . . . In this instance, Plaintiffs voluntarily provided their personal information to Northwest. Moreover, although Northwest had a privacy policy for information included on the website, Plaintiffs do not contend that they actually read the privacy policy prior to providing Northwest with their personal information. Thus, Plaintiffs' expectation of privacy was low. Further, the disclosure here was not to the public at large, but rather was to a government agency in the wake of a terrorist attack that called into question the security of the nation's transportation system. Northwest's motives in disclosing the information cannot be questioned. Taking into account all of the factors listed above, the Court finds as a matter of law that the disclosure of Plaintiffs' personal information would not be highly offensive to a reasonable person and that Plaintiffs have failed to state a claim for intrusion upon seclusion. . . .

Northwest contends that the privacy policy on Northwest's website does not, as a matter of law, constitute a unilateral contract, the breach of which entitles Plaintiffs to damages. Northwest also argues that, even if the privacy policy constituted a contract or express warranty, Plaintiffs' contract and warranty claims fail because Plaintiffs have failed to plead any contract damages. . . .

Plaintiffs' rely on the following statement from Northwest's website as the basis for their contract and warranty claims:

> When you reserve or purchase travel services through Northwest Airlines nwa.com Reservations, we provide only the relevant information required by the car rental agency, hotel, or other involved third party to ensure the successful fulfillment of your travel arrangements. . . .

The usual rule in contract cases is that "general statements of policy are not contractual." . . .

The privacy statement on Northwest's website did not constitute a unilateral contract. The language used vests discretion in Northwest to determine when the information is "relevant" and which "third parties" might need that information. Moreover, absent an allegation that Plaintiffs actually read the privacy policy, not merely the general allegation that Plaintiffs "relied on" the policy, Plaintiffs have failed to allege an essential element of a contract claim: that the alleged "offer" was accepted by Plaintiffs. Plaintiffs' contract and warranty claims fail as a matter of law.

Even if the privacy policy was sufficiently definite and Plaintiffs had alleged that they read the policy before giving their information to Northwest, it is likely that Plaintiffs' contract and warranty claims would fail as a matter of law. Defendants point out that Plaintiffs have failed to allege any contractual damages arising out of the alleged breach. . . .

[The case is dismissed.]

NOTES & QUESTIONS

1. **Breach of Contract.** In *Dyer v. Northwest Airlines Corp.,* 334 F. Supp. 2d 1196 (D.N.D. 2004), another action involving Northwest Airlines' disclosure of passenger records to the government, the court reached a similar conclusion on the plaintiffs' breach of contract claim:

> To sustain a breach of contract claim, the Plaintiffs must demonstrate (1) the existence of a contract; (2) breach of the contract; and (3) damages which flow from the breach. . . .
> . . . [T]he Court finds the Plaintiffs' breach of contract claim fails as a matter of law. First, broad statements of company policy do not generally give rise to contract claims. . . . Second, nowhere in the complaint are the Plaintiffs alleged to have ever logged onto Northwest Airlines' website and accessed, read, understood, actually relied upon, or otherwise considered Northwest Airlines' privacy policy. Finally, even if the privacy policy was sufficiently definite and the Plaintiffs had alleged they did read the policy prior to providing personal information to Northwest Airlines, the Plaintiffs have failed to allege any contractual damages arising out of the alleged breach.

2. **Damages.** In *In re Jet Blue Airways Corp. Privacy Litigation*, 379 F. Supp. 2d 299 (E.D.N.Y. 2005), a group of plaintiffs sued Jet Blue Airlines for breach of contract for sharing passenger records with the government. The court granted Jet Blue's motion to dismiss:

> An action for breach of contract under New York law requires proof of four elements: (1) the existence of a contract, (2) performance of the contract by one party, (3) breach by the other party, and (4) damages. . . .
> JetBlue . . . argues that plaintiffs have failed to meet their pleading requirement with respect to damages, citing an absence of any facts in the Amended Complaint to support this element of the claim. Plaintiffs' sole allegation on the element of contract damages consists of the statement that JetBlue's breach of the company privacy policy injured plaintiffs and members of the class and that JetBlue is therefore liable for "actual damages in an amount to be determined at trial." . . . At oral argument, when pressed to identify the "injuries" or damages referred to in the Amended Complaint, counsel for plaintiffs stated that the "contract damage could be the loss of privacy," acknowledging that loss of privacy "may" be a contract damage. It is apparent based on the briefing and oral argument held in this case that the sparseness of the damages allegations is a direct result of plaintiffs' inability to plead or prove any actual contract damages. As plaintiffs' counsel concedes, the only damage that can be read into the present complaint is a loss of privacy. At least one

recent case has specifically held that this is not a damage available in a breach of contract action. *See Trikas v. Universal Card Services Corp.,* 351 F. Supp. 2d 37 (E.D.N.Y. 2005). This holding naturally follows from the well-settled principle that "recovery in contract, unlike recovery in tort, allows only for economic losses flowing directly from the breach."

Plaintiffs allege that in a second amended complaint, they could assert as a contract damage the loss of the economic value of their information, but while that claim sounds in economic loss, the argument ignores the nature of the contract asserted. . . . [T]he "purpose of contract damages is to put a plaintiff in the same economic position he or she would have occupied had the contract been fully performed." Plaintiffs may well have expected that in return for providing their personal information to JetBlue and paying the purchase price, they would obtain a ticket for air travel and the promise that their personal information would be safeguarded consistent with the terms of the privacy policy. They had no reason to expect that they would be compensated for the "value" of their personal information. In addition, there is absolutely no support for the proposition that the personal information of an individual JetBlue passenger had any value for which that passenger could have expected to be compensated. . . . There is likewise no support for the proposition that an individual passenger's personal information has or had any compensable value in the economy at large.

If you were the plaintiffs' attorney, how would you go about establishing the plaintiffs' injury? Is there any cognizable harm when an airline violates its privacy policy by providing passenger information to the government?

3. *Promissory Estoppel.* Under the Restatement (Second) of Contracts § 90:

A promise which the promisor should reasonably expect to induce action or forbearance on the part of the promisee or a third person and which does induce such action or forbearance is binding if injustice can be avoided only by enforcement of the promise. The remedy granted for breach may be limited as justice requires.

If website privacy policies are not deemed to be contracts, can they be enforced under the promissory estoppel doctrine?

4. *Breach of Confidentiality Tort.* Would the plaintiffs have a cause of action based on the breach of confidentiality tort?

5. *Enforcing Privacy Policies as Contracts Against Consumers.* Suppose privacy policies were enforceable as contracts. Would this be beneficial to consumers? It might not be, Allyson Haynes argues:

[T]here is a distinct possibility that as website operators grow savvier with respect to the law, they will respond to the lack of substantive privacy protection (and lack of consumer awareness) by including in privacy policies terms that are not favorable to consumers.

On the flip side of consumers seeking to enforce privacy policies as contracts, companies might also desire to hold customers to be contractually bound to the companies' privacy policies. Would a privacy policy be enforceable as a contract against the customer? Haynes contends:

[P]articularly in cases where consumers are deemed to have assented to privacy policies by virtue of their presence on the site or by giving information without affirmatively clicking acceptance, the consumer has a good argument that he or she did not assent to the privacy policy, preventing the formation of a binding contract, and preventing the website from enforcing any of its terms against the consumer.[39]

6. ***Standing in Misrepresentation Claims.*** In *In re iPhone Application Litigation*, 2013 WL 6212591 (N.D. Cal. Nov. 25, 2013), plaintiffs sued Apple in a class action alleging, among other things, that Apple made misrepresentations about iPhone privacy:

> Plaintiffs claim that they relied upon Apple's representations about privacy and data collection in purchasing their iPhones. In light of Apple's statements about protecting users' privacy, Plaintiffs did not consent to the App developers transmitting Plaintiffs' information to third parties. Plaintiffs assert that as a result of Apple's misrepresentations regarding its privacy and data collection practices, Plaintiffs both overpaid for their iPhones and suffered diminishment to their iPhones' battery, bandwidth, and storage "resources."

Some of the statements Apple made in its privacy policy included:

> Your privacy is important to Apple. So we've developed a Privacy Policy that covers how we collect, use, disclose, transfer, and store your information. . . .

> To make sure your personal information is secure, we communicate our privacy and security guidelines to Apple employees and strictly enforce privacy safeguards within the company. . . .

> Apple takes precautions—including administrative, technical, and physical measures—to safeguard your personal information against loss, theft, and misuse as well as against unauthorized access, disclosure, alteration, and destruction. . . .

The court held:

> While the iDevice Plaintiffs identify numerous purported misrepresentations and argue that they relied on them in purchasing their iPhones the evidentiary record is devoid of "specific facts" to support Plaintiffs' assertions. Critically, *none* of the Plaintiffs presents evidence that he or she even saw, let alone read and relied upon, the alleged misrepresentations contained in the Apple Privacy Policies . . . or App Store Terms and Conditions, either prior to purchasing his or her iPhone, or at any time thereafter.
>
> In their depositions, Plaintiffs either could not recall having read any of these policies (or any other Apple representation) in connection with obtaining their iPhones, or expressly disavowed having read any Apple policy, or anything else about the iPhone, prior to purchasing one.

The court further reasoned:

---

[39] Allyson W. Haynes, *Online Privacy Policies: Contracting Away Control Over Personal Information?*, 111 Penn. St. L. Rev. 587, 612, 618 (2007).

First, Plaintiffs suggest that standing is established as long as a plaintiff "receives" a misrepresentation. The implication of this argument seems to be that a plaintiff can show standing as long as the defendant has disseminated the alleged misrepresentation to her in some fashion, regardless of whether the plaintiff ever actually sees, reads, or hears the defendant's statement. The Court questions how one can act in reliance on a statement one does not see, read, or hear. . . .

Second, Plaintiffs argue that the Court should infer reliance from the fact that Plaintiffs had iTunes accounts and therefore had to, at some point, agree to Apple's Terms and Conditions and Privacy Policy. . . . [B]y virtue of having active iTunes accounts, Plaintiffs would have been asked to agree to Apple's updated Privacy Policy at some point during the class period. . . . Plaintiffs ask the Court to infer that Plaintiffs must have read and relied on misrepresentations contained in Apple's Privacy Policy at some point during the class period.

There are two problems with this theory. Most critically, it has no evidentiary support. No Plaintiff, in either a deposition or declaration, identified an Apple Privacy Policy as the source of his or her "understanding" regarding Apple's policies concerning privacy and data collection. . . .

What is more, the mere fact that Plaintiffs had to scroll through a screen and click on a box stating that they agreed with the Apple Privacy Policy in July 2010 does not establish, standing alone, that Plaintiffs actually read the alleged misrepresentations contained in that Privacy Policy, let alone that these misrepresentations subsequently formed the basis for Plaintiffs' "understanding" regarding Apple's privacy practices. Accordingly, the existence of Plaintiffs' iTunes accounts does not, *by itself,* demonstrate that Plaintiffs actually read and relied on any misrepresentations contained in the updated Privacy Policy from July 2010.

7. ***Promises of Anonymity.*** In *Saffold v. Plain Dealer Publishing Co.,* a state court judge (Shirley Strickland Saffold) sued the *Cleveland Plain Dealer* for stating that comments posted on the newspaper's website under the screen name "lawmiss" originated from a computer used by the judge and her daughter. Some of these comments related to cases before Judge Saffold. Judge Saffold claimed that the newspaper's disclosure of the identity of "lawmiss" violated its website's privacy policy, which stated that "personally identifiable information is protected." Moreover, the user agreement that was part of the registration process to create an account on the website incorporated the privacy policy. The case was settled before any judicial decision was issued. Suppose, however, the litigation had proceeded. Would Judge Saffold have a claim for breach of contract or promissory estoppel?

8. ***Website Communities and Promissory Estoppel.*** Consider Woodrow Hartzog:

> Suppose a person improperly provides others with access to a friend's Facebook profile. Suppose a member of a dating website copies another's dating profile and discloses the information to the general public. Or suppose a member of an online support community for recovering alcoholics reveals the names and other personal information of other members. Should members of an online community be able to expect and legally enforce the confidentiality of their data? . . .

I contend that the law can ensure confidentiality for members of online communities through promissory estoppel. . . .

One of the immediate difficulties with using promissory estoppel is that members of online communities have not made agreements between each other. They have merely agreed to the terms of use of the website and community. Suppose Member A of an online community discloses the private information of Member B. Would Member B be able to sue Member A for promissory estoppel even though Member A never made a direct promise to Member B?

In order to allow all users within the community the ability to rely on promises of confidentiality, I propose application of either the third-party beneficiary doctrine or the concept of dual agency effectuated through a website's terms of use. Although the implementation of promissory estoppel in this context would be challenging, I conclude that the promissory estoppel theory for confidential disclosure could have positive practical effects and advance both privacy and free speech objectives.[40]

What are the pros and cons of Hartzog's proposal? Should members of online communities have any obligations to each other?

9. *Are Website Privacy Settings Part of a Contract?* Woodrow Hartzog contends that website privacy settings and other design features should be considered as part of the contract between the website and the user:

> When courts seek to determine a website user's privacy expectations and the website's promises to that user, they almost invariably look to the terms of use agreement or to the privacy policy. They rarely look to the privacy settings or other elements of a website where users specify their privacy preferences. These settings and elements are typically not considered to be part of any contract or promise to the user. Yet studies have shown that few users actually read or rely upon terms of service or privacy policies. In contrast, users regularly take advantage of and rely upon privacy settings. . . . [T]o the extent website design is incorporated into or consistent with a website's terms of use, or to the extent website design induces reliance, courts should consider these design features as enforceable promises.[41]

Facebook and other social media websites, for example, have privacy settings that allow users to establish how broadly their information will be shared. If Facebook were to expose a person's information more broadly than he set it in his privacy settings, could that be the basis of a contract or promissory estoppel lawsuit? What other design elements might be considered part of a website's contract or promise with a user?

10. *Contract and Morality.* In Canada, Gabrielle Nagy sued her cellphone company, Rogers Communications, for breach of contract when it incorporated her cell phone bill into the family phone bill. The result was that her husband discovered that she was frequently calling another man. Nagy eventually confessed to her husband that she was having an affair, and they divorced. Consider David Hoffman:

---

[40] Woodrow Hartzog, *Promises and Privacy: Promissory Estoppel and Confidential Disclosure in Online Communities*, 82 Temp. L. Rev. 891, 893-96 (2009).

[41] Woodrow Hartzog, *Website Design as Contract*, 60 Am. U. L. Rev. 1635 (2011).

I think the breach of contract lawsuit, if filed in an American court applying fairly ordinary domestic contract principles, would be a loser. . . .

The common law generally dislikes punishing breach with liability or damages when the inevitable consequence of performance is to motivate socially wrongful conduct, and nonperformance to retard it. . . .

What about cases where A and B contract not to disclose some fact X, and the nondisclosure will create harm for innocent third parties. These contracts are often enforced (every confidentiality clause probably shelters some fact with the potential for third party harm). But the degree to which the nonbreaching party can recover ought to turn on what's being kept secret: if the secret is particularly socially harmful (oozing toxic sludge!) we might believe that the hiding, non-breaching, party doesn't get to recover for breach. Thus, you sometimes see cases where fraud-revealing employees are protected from consequences of nondisclosure agreements by (effectively) common law whistleblower doctrines.

Where the third-party harm *relates to marriage*, the law appears to be more categorical. Public policy concerns about contracting and third party harm are strongest in agreements touching on issues of family life and infidelity.[42]

Is Hoffman correct that such a breach of contract case would lose under American law? Should courts choose which contracts to enforce based on morality? If a company breaches a contract and reveals that a person is doing something immoral, should that breach go unremedied?

11. ***Interpreting Promises.*** In *In re iPhone Application Litigation*, 844 F. Supp. 2d 1040 (N.D. Cal. June 12, 2012), plaintiffs sued Apple for the practices of third-party apps. Apple argued that its Privacy Policy and Terms of Use disclaimed liability from third-party conduct. However, the court concluded:

Additionally, to the extent that Apple argues that it has no duty to review or evaluate apps and that it has disclaimed any liability arising from the actions of third parties, this argument both ignores contradictory statements made by Apple itself, and the allegations asserted by Plaintiffs regarding Apple's own conduct with respect to the alleged privacy violations. For one, it is not clear that Apple disclaimed all responsibility for privacy violations because, while Apple claimed not to have any liability or responsibility for any third party materials, websites or services, Apple also made affirmative representations that it takes precautions to protect consumer privacy. Additionally, Plaintiffs' allegations go beyond asserting that Apple had a duty to review or police third party apps. Instead, Plaintiffs allege Apple was responsible for providing user's information to third parties. Plaintiffs allege that Apple is independently liable for any statutory violations that have occurred. At the motion to dismiss stage, then, the Court is not prepared to rule that the Agreement establishes an absolute bar to Plaintiffs' claims.

The court recognized that increased security risks and lessened device resources (storage, battery life, and bandwidth) from third-party apps could constitute concrete injuries.

---

[42] David Hoffman, *Contracts and Privacy,* Concurring Opinions (June 21, 2010), http://www.concurringopinions.com/archives/2010/06/contracts-and-privacy.html.

Should a more general statement that a company protects privacy override more specific statements such as disclaiming responsibility for third-party apps? Or should the more specific statements govern over the more general ones? Suppose a company's founder in an interview states: "We care deeply about our the privacy of our customers and protect it zealously." Could this trump a statement in the privacy policy that allows personal data to be shared with third parties unless people opt out?

12. ***The Cost of "Free".*** Many online services, such as Google and Facebook, are free. Chris Hoofnagle and Jan Whittington argue that these services are not really free:

> [C]onceiving of transactions as free can harm both consumers and competition. These exchanges often carry a hidden charge: the forfeit of one's personal information. The service provider may expect to earn revenues from the personal information collected about consumers who devote their attention to advertising and other services, such as games, from third parties. The more time the consumer spends using the service and revealing information, the more the service can adjust the product to reveal more information about the consumer and tailor its advertising of products to that consumer's personal information.[43]

Hoofnagle and Wittington contend that many "information-intensive companies misuse the term 'free' to promote products and services that incur myriad hidden, nonpecuniary costs." What are the implications of recognizing that consumers are paying a price for sharing their personal data? To what extent does this fact affect contract law analysis when it comes to privacy policies?

D. PROPERTY LAW

A number of commentators propose that privacy can be protected by restructuring the property rights that people have in personal information. For example, according to Richard Murphy, personal information "like all information, is property." He goes on to conclude:

> . . . [I]n many instances, privacy rules are in fact implied contractual terms. To the extent that information is generated through a voluntary transaction, imposing nondisclosure obligations on the recipient of the information may be the best approach for certain categories of information. The value that information has ex post is of secondary importance; the primary question is what is the efficient contractual rule. Common-law courts are increasingly willing to impose an implied contractual rule of nondisclosure for many categories of transactions, including those with attorneys, medical providers, bankers, and accountants. Many statutes can also be seen in this light — that is, as default rules of privacy.

---

[43] Chris Jay Hoofnagle and Jan Whittington, *Free: Accounting for the Costs of the Internet's Most Popular Price*, 61 UCLA L. Rev. 606 (2014).

And an argument can be made for the efficiency of a privacy default rule in the generic transaction between a merchant and a consumer.[44]

Lawrence Lessig also contends that privacy should be protected with property rights. He notes that "[p]rivacy now is protected through liability rules — if you invade someone's privacy, they can sue you and you must then pay." A "liability regime allows a taking, and payment later." In contrast, a property regime gives "control, and power, to the person holding the property right." Lessig argues: "When you have a property right, before someone takes your property they must negotiate with you about how much it is worth."[45]

Jerry Kang proposes a type of fusion between property and contract regulation when he proposes that there be a default rule that individuals retain control over information they surrender during Internet transactions. He contends that this default rule is more efficient than a default rule where companies can use the data as they see fit. The default rule that Kang proposes could be bargained around: "With this default, if the firm valued personal data more than the individual, then the firm would have to buy permission to process the data in functionally unnecessary ways."[46] In essence, Kang is creating a property right in personal data, and people could sell the right to use it to companies.

Other commentators critique the translation of privacy into a form of property right that can be bartered and sold. For example, Katrin Schatz Byford argues that viewing "privacy as an item of trade . . . values privacy only to the extent it is considered to be of personal worth by the individual who claims it." She further contends: "Such a perspective plainly conflicts with the notion that privacy is a collective value and that privacy intrusions at the individual level necessarily have broader social implications because they affect access to social power and stifle public participation."[47]

Consider Pamela Samuelson's argument as to why property rights are inadequate to protect privacy:

> . . . Achieving information privacy goals through a property rights system may be difficult for reasons other than market complexities. Chief among them is the difficulty with alienability of personal information. It is a common, if not ubiquitous, characteristic of property rights systems that when the owner of a property right sells her interest to another person, that buyer can freely transfer to third parties whatever interest the buyer acquired from her initial seller. Free alienability works very well in the market for automobiles and land, but it is far from clear that it will work well for information privacy. . . . Collectors of data may prefer a default rule allowing them to freely transfer personal data to whomever they wish on whatever terms they can negotiate with their future buyers. However, individuals concerned with information privacy will generally want a default rule prohibiting retransfer of the data unless separate permission is

---

[44] Richard S. Murphy, *Property Rights in Personal Information: An Economic Defense of Privacy*, 84 Geo. L.J. 2381, 2416-17 (1996).

[45] Lawrence Lessig, *Code and Other Laws of Cyberspace* (1999).

[46] Jerry Kang, *Information Privacy in Cyberspace Transactions*, 50 Stan. L. Rev. 1193 (1998).

[47] Katrin Schatz Byford, *Privacy in Cyberspace: Constructing a Model of Privacy for the Electronic Communications Environment*, 24 Rutgers Computer & Tech. L.J. 1 (1998). For an argument about the problems of commodifying certain goods and of viewing all human conduct in light of the market metaphor, see Margaret Jane Radin, *Contested Commodities* (1996).

negotiated. They will also want any future recipient to bind itself to the same constraints that the initial purchaser of the data may have agreed to as a condition of sale. Information privacy goals may not be achievable unless the default rule of the new property rights regime limits transferability. . . .

. . . From a civil liberties perspective, propertizing personal information as a way of achieving information privacy goals may seem an anathema. Not only might it be viewed as an unnecessary and possibly dangerous way to achieve information privacy goals, it might be considered morally obnoxious. If information privacy is a civil liberty, it may make no more sense to propertize personal data than to commodify voting rights. . . .[48]

Daniel Solove also counsels against protecting privacy as a form of property right because the "market approach has difficulty assigning the proper value to personal information":

. . . [T]he aggregation problem severely complicates the valuation process. An individual may give out bits of information in different contexts, each transfer appearing innocuous. However, the information can be aggregated and could prove to be invasive of the private life when combined with other information. It is the totality of information about a person and how it is used that poses the greatest threat to privacy. As Julie Cohen notes, "[a] comprehensive collection of data about an individual is vastly more than the sum of its parts." From the standpoint of each particular information transaction, individuals will not have enough facts to make a truly informed decision. The potential future uses of that information are too vast and unknown to enable individuals to make the appropriate valuation. . . .

[Property rights] cannot work effectively in a situation where the power relationship and information distribution between individuals and public and private bureaucracies is so greatly unbalanced. In other words, the problem with market solutions is not merely that it is difficult to commodify information (which it is), but also that a regime of default rules alone (consisting of property rights in information and contractual defaults) will not enable fair and equitable market transactions in personal information. . . .[49]

In contrast to these skeptics, Paul Schwartz develops a model of propertized personal data that would help fashion a market for data trade that would respect individual privacy and help maintain a democratic order. Schwartz calls for "limitations on an individual's right to alienate personal information; default rules that force disclosure of the terms of trade; a right of exit for participants in the market; the establishment of damages to deter market abuses; and institutions to police the personal information market and punish privacy violations." In his judgment, a key element of this model is its approach of "hybrid inalienability" in which a law allows individuals to share their personal information, but also places limitations on future use of the information. Schwartz explains:

This hybrid consists of a use-transferability restriction plus an opt-in default. In practice, it would permit the transfer for an initial category of use of personal data, but only if the customer is granted an opportunity to block further transfer or use

---

[48] Pamela Samuelson, *Privacy as Intellectual Property?*, 52 Stan. L. Rev. 1125, 1137-47 (2000).

[49] Daniel J. Solove, *Privacy and Power: Computer Databases and Metaphors for Information Privacy*, 53 Stan. L. Rev. 1393 (2001).

by unaffiliated entities. Any further use or transfer would require the customer to opt in — that is, it would be prohibited unless the customer affirmatively agrees to it.

As an initial example concerning compensated telemarketing, a successful pitch for Star Trek memorabilia would justify the use of personal data by the telemarketing company and the transfer of it both to process the order and for other related purposes. Any outside use or unrelated transfers of this information would, however, require obtaining further permission from the individual. Note that this restriction limits the alienability of individuals' personal information by preventing them from granting one-stop permission for all use or transfer of their information. A data processor's desire to carry out further transfers thus obligates the processor to supply additional information and provides another chance for the individual to bargain with the data collector. . . .

To ensure that the opt-in default leads to meaningful disclosure of additional information, however, two additional elements are needed. First, the government must have a significant role in regulating the way that notice of privacy practices is provided. As noted above, a critical issue will be the "frame" in which information about data processing is presented. . . .

Second, meaningful disclosure requires addressing what Henry Hansmann and Reinier Kraakman term "verification problems." Their scholarship points to the critical condition that third parties must be able to verify that a given piece of personal information has in fact been propertized and then identify the specific rules that apply to it. As they explain, "[a] verification rule sets out the conditions under which a given right in a given asset will run with the asset." In the context of propertized personal information, the requirement for verification creates a role for nonpersonal metadata, a tag or kind of barcode, to provide necessary background information and notice.[50]

Finally, consider what Warren and Brandeis said about privacy as a property claim:

> The aim of [copyright] statutes is to secure to the author, composer, or artist the entire profits arising from publication. . . .
>
> But where the value of the production is found not in the right to take the profits arising from publication, but in the peace of mind or the relief afforded by the ability to prevent any publication at all, it is difficult to regard the right as one of property, in the common acceptation of that term.[51]

E. FTC SECTION 5 ENFORCEMENT

Beyond private law actions such as contract and promissory estoppel, the promises that companies make regarding their privacy practices can be enforced by the government through public law. Private law actions are initiated on behalf of harmed individuals, who can obtain monetary or other redress for their injuries.

---

[50] Paul M. Schwartz, *Property, Privacy and Personal Data*, 117 Harv. L. Rev. 2055, 2056, 2098-99 (2004). *See also* Vera Bergelson, *It's Personal But Is It Mine? Toward Property Rights in Personal Information*, 37 U.C. Davis L. Rev. 379 (2003) (although a collector may have rights in individuals' personal information, a property approach would correctly subordinate these rights to the rights of the individuals).

[51] Samuel Warren & Louis Brandeis, *The Right to Privacy*, 4 Harv. L. Rev. 193 (1890).

In contrast, public law actions are initiated by government agencies or officials, and they typically involve fines and penalties.

In 1995, Congress and privacy experts first asked the Federal Trade Commission (FTC) to become involved with consumer privacy issues. Since 1998, the FTC has maintained the position that the use or dissemination of personal information in a manner contrary to a posted privacy policy is a deceptive practice under the FTC Act, 15 U.S.C. § 45.

The Act prohibits "unfair or deceptive acts or practices in or affecting commerce." § 45(n).

Deception. A deceptive act or practice is a material "representation, omission or practice that is likely to mislead the consumer acting reasonably in the circumstances, to the consumer's detriment."[52]

Unfairness. The FTC Act classifies a trade practice as unfair if it "causes or is likely to cause substantial injury to consumers which is not reasonably avoidable by consumers themselves and is not outweighed by countervailing benefits to consumers or competition." 15 U.S.C. § 45(n). Actions of a company can be both deceptive and unfair.

The Scope of Section 5. Section 5 provides very broad jurisdiction to the FTC. However, the FTC does not have jurisdiction over all companies. Exempt from the FTC's jurisdiction are many types of financial institutions, airlines, telecommunications carriers, and other types of entities. § 45(a)(2). Additionally, non-profit institutions such as schools are often not covered.

The FTC's Structure. The FTC is headed by five commissioners, who are appointed by the President and confirmed by the Senate. They each serve a seven-year term. The commissioners must be a bipartisan group — no more than three can be members of the same political party. One of the commissioners is designated by the President as chairman.

Enforcement. The FTC can obtain injunctive remedies. § 53. The Act does not provide for private causes of action; only the FTC can enforce the Act. The FTC does not have the ability to issue fines for violations of Section 5, but the FTC can issue fines when companies violate a consent decree previously entered into for a violation of Section 5.

Rulemaking. The FTC lacks practical rulemaking authority under Section 5. The FTC has only Magnuson-Moss rulemaking authority, which is highly burdensome as a procedural matter. According to Beth DeSimone and Amy Mudge:

> Right now, the FTC is constrained in its rulemaking by the so-called "Magnuson-Moss" rules. These rules require the FTC Staff to engage in an industry-wide

---

[52] Letter from James C. Miller III, Chairman, FTC, to Hon. John D. Dingell, Chairman, House Comm. on Energy & Commerce (Oct. 14, 1983).

investigation, prepare draft staff reports, propose a rule, and engage in a series of public hearings, including cross-examination opportunities prior to issuing a final rule in any area. These processes are so burdensome that the FTC has not engaged in a Magnuson-Moss rule-making in 32 years.[53]

The Growing Role of the FTC. Since it began enforcing the FTC Act for breaches of privacy policies in 1998, the FTC has brought a number of actions, most of which have settled. The FTC has brought about 170 privacy and data security actions under Section 5, averaging about 10 per year, though the number per year has increased throughout the years.

According to Daniel Solove and Woodrow Hartzog:

> Despite over fifteen years of FTC enforcement, there are hardly any judicial decisions to show for it. The cases have nearly all resulted in settlement agreements. Nevertheless, companies look to these agreements to guide their decisions regarding privacy practices. Those involved with helping businesses comply with privacy law—from chief privacy officers to inside counsel to outside counsel—parse and analyze the FTC's settlement agreements, reports, and activities as if they were pronouncements by the Chairman of the Federal Reserve. Thus, in practice, FTC privacy jurisprudence has become the broadest and most influential regulating force on information privacy in the United States—more so than nearly any privacy statute or common law tort.[54]

Companies that violate settlement orders are liable for a civil penalty of up to $16,000 for each violation. Injunctive or other equitable relief is also available.

FTC Privacy Enforcement Beyond Section 5. Beyond Section 5, the FTC also enforces the Gramm-Leach-Bliley Act (GLBA) and the Children's Online Privacy Protection Act (COPPA). Additionally, it enforces the US-EU Safe Harbor Arrangement. The FTC used to be the primary enforcer of the Fair Credit Reporting Act (FCRA), but that responsibility has largely been passed to the Consumer Financial Protection Bureau (CFPB). The FTC still retains some limited enforcement power over FCRA that is shared with CFPB. Although the FTC cannot issue fines under Section 5, it has the power to issue fines under the GLBA, COPPA, and FCRA.

IN THE MATTER OF SNAPCHAT, INC.

2014 WL 1993567 (FTC May 8, 2014)

COMPLAINT

The Federal Trade Commission, having reason to believe that Snapchat, Inc. ("respondent") has violated the provisions of the Federal Trade Commission Act,

---

[53] Beth DeSimone & Amy Mudge, *Is Congress Putting the FTC on Steroids?*, Seller Beware Blog, Arnold & Porter (Apr. 26, 2010), http://www.consumeradvertisinglawblog.com/2010/04/is-congress-putting-the-ftc-on-steroids.html.

[54] Daniel J. Solove & Woodrow Hartzog, *The FTC and the New Common Law of Privacy,* 114 Colum. L. Rev. 583, 585-86 (2014).

and it appearing to the Commission that this proceeding is in the public interest, alleges: . . . .

3. Snapchat provides a mobile application that allows consumers to send and receive photo and video messages known as "snaps." Before sending a snap, the application requires the sender to designate a period of time that the recipient will be allowed to view the snap. Snapchat markets the application as an "ephemeral" messaging application, having claimed that once the timer expires, the snap "disappears forever." . . .

6. Snapchat marketed its application as a service for sending "disappearing" photo and video messages, declaring that the message sender "control[s] how long your friends can view your message." Before sending a snap, the application requires the sender to designate a period of time — with the default set to a maximum of 10 seconds — that the recipient will be allowed to view the snap. . .

8. From October 2012 to October 2013, Snapchat disseminated, or caused to be disseminated, to consumers the following statement on the "FAQ" page on its website:

> Is there any way to view an image after the time has expired?

> No, snaps disappear after the timer runs out. . . .

9. Despite these claims, several methods exist by which a recipient can use tools outside of the application to save both photo and video messages, allowing the recipient to access and view the photos or videos indefinitely.

10. For example, when a recipient receives a video message, the application sstores the video file in a location outside of the application's "sandbox" (*i.e.*, the application's private storage area on the device that other applications cannot access). Because the file is stored in this unrestricted area, until October 2013, a recipient could connect his or her mobile device to a computer and use simple file browsing tools to locate and save the video file. This method for saving video files sent through the application was widely publicized as early as December 2012. Snapchat did not mitigate this flaw until October 2013, when it began encrypting video files sent through the application.

11. Furthermore, third-party developers have built applications that can connect to Snapchat's application programming interface ("API"), thereby allowing recipients to log into the Snapchat service without using the official Snapchat application. Because the timer and related "deletion" functionality is dependent on the recipient's use of the official Snapchat application, recipients can instead simply use a third-party application to download and save both photo and video messages. . . .

14. Snapchat claimed that if a recipient took a screenshot of a snap, the sender would be notified. . . .

15. However, recipients can easily circumvent Snapchat's screenshot detection mechanism. For example, on versions of iOS prior to iOS 7, the recipient need only double press the device's Home button in rapid succession to evade the detection mechanism and take a screenshot of any snap without the sender being notified. This method was widely publicized.

16. As described in Paragraphs 6, 7, and 8, Snapchat has represented, expressly or by implication, that when sending a message through its application, the message will disappear forever after the user-set time period expires.

17. In truth and in fact, as described in Paragraph 9-12, when sending a message through its application, the message may not disappear forever after the user-set time period expires. Therefore, the representation set forth in Paragraph 16 is false or misleading.

18. As described in Paragraphs 7 and 14, Snapchat has represented, expressly or by implication, that the sender will be notified if the recipient takes a screenshot of a snap.

19. In truth and in fact, as described in Paragraph 15, the sender may not be notified if the recipient takes a screenshot of a snap. Therefore, the representation set forth in Paragraph 18 is false or misleading. . . .

20. From June 2011 to February 2013, Snapchat disseminated or caused to be disseminated to consumers the following statements in its privacy policy:

> We do not ask for, track, or access any location-specific information from your device at any time while you are using the Snapchat application.

21. In October 2012, Snapchat integrated an analytics tracking service in the Android version of its application that acted as its service provider. While the Android operating system provided notice to consumers that the application may access location information, Snapchat did not disclose that it would, in fact, access location information, and continued to represent that Snapchat did "not ask for, track, or access any location-specific information . . . ."

22. Contrary to the representation in Snapchat's privacy policy, from October 2012 to February 2013, the Snapchat application on Android transmitted Wi-Fi-based and cell-based location information from users' mobile devices to its analytics tracking service provider. . . .

AGREEMENT CONTAINING CONSENT ORDER

The Federal Trade Commission ("Commission") has conducted an investigation of certain acts and practices of Snapchat, Inc. ("Snapchat" or "proposed respondent"). Proposed respondent, having been represented by counsel, is willing to enter into an agreement containing a consent order resolving the allegations contained in the attached draft complaint. Therefore,

IT IS HEREBY AGREED by and between Snapchat, Inc., by its duly authorized officers, and counsel for the Federal Trade Commission that: . . .

2. Proposed respondent neither admits nor denies any of the allegations in the draft complaint, except as specifically stated in this order. Only for purposes of this action, proposed respondent admits the facts necessary to establish jurisdiction. . . .

IT IS ORDERED that respondent and its officers, agents, representatives, and employees, directly or indirectly, shall not misrepresent in any manner, expressly or by implication, in or affecting commerce, the extent to which respondent or its products or services maintain and protect the privacy, security, or confidentiality of any covered information, including but not limited to: (1) the extent to which a message is deleted after being viewed by the recipient; (2) the extent to which respondent or its products or services are capable of detecting or notifying the sender when a recipient has captured a screenshot of, or otherwise saved, a message; (3) the categories of covered information collected; or (4) the steps taken to protect against misuse or unauthorized disclosure of covered information.

IT IS FURTHER ORDERED that respondent, in or affecting commerce, shall, no later than the date of service of this order, establish and implement, and thereafter maintain, a comprehensive privacy program that is reasonably designed to: (1) address privacy risks related to the development and management of new and existing products and services for consumers, and (2) protect the privacy and confidentiality of covered information, whether collected by respondent or input into, stored on, captured with, or accessed through a computer using respondent's products or services. Such program, the content and implementation of which must be fully documented in writing, shall contain privacy controls and procedures appropriate to respondent's size and complexity, the nature and scope of respondent's activities, and the sensitivity of the covered information, including:

A. the designation of an employee or employees to coordinate and be accountable for the privacy program;

B. the identification of reasonably foreseeable, material risks, both internal and external, that could result in the respondent's unauthorized collection, use, or disclosure of covered information, and assessment of the sufficiency of any safeguards in place to control these risks. At a minimum, this privacy risk assessment should include consideration of risks in each area of relevant operation, including, but not limited to: (1) employee training and management, including training on the requirements of this order; and (2) product design, development and research;

C. the design and implementation of reasonable privacy controls and procedures to address the risks identified through the privacy risk assessment, and regular testing or monitoring of the effectiveness of the privacy controls and procedures;

D. the development and use of reasonable steps to select and retain service providers capable of maintaining security practices consistent with this order, and requiring service providers by contract to implement and maintain appropriate safeguards;

E. the evaluation and adjustment of respondent's privacy program in light of the results of the testing and monitoring required by subpart C, any material changes to respondent's operations or business arrangements, or any other circumstances that respondent knows, or has reason to know, may have a material impact on the effectiveness of its privacy program.

IT IS FURTHER ORDERED that, in connection with its compliance with Part II of this order, respondent shall obtain initial and biennial assessments and reports ("Assessments") from a qualified, objective, independent third-party professional, who uses procedures and standards generally accepted in the profession. A person qualified to prepare such Assessments shall have a minimum of three (3) years of experience in the field of privacy and data protection. . . .

This order will terminate twenty (20) years from the date of its issuance. . . .

NOTES & QUESTIONS

1. ***FTC Consent Decrees.*** When FTC cases are settled, the complaint and consent decree are typically issued together. The complaint is not released during the investigation or settlement negotiations.

    FTC consent decrees often contain at least some of the following elements: (1) prohibition on the activities in violation of the FTC Act; (2) steps to remediate the problematic activities, such as software patches or notice to consumers; (3) deletion of wrongfully-obtained consumer data; (4) modifications to privacy policies; (5) establishment of a comprehensive privacy program, including risk assessment, appointment of a person to coordinate the program, and employee training, among other things; (6) biennial assessment reports by independent auditors; (7) recordkeeping to facilitate FTC enforcement of the order; (8) obligation to alert the FTC of any material changes in the company that might affect compliance obligations (such as mergers or bankruptcy filings).

2. ***Types of Section 5 Privacy and Security Violations.*** What are the types of cases the FTC brings? Under the "deception" prong of its authority, the FTC brings cases for broken promises of privacy, general deception, insufficient notice, and unreasonable data security practices. Under the "unfairness" prong, the FTC brings cases for retroactive changes to privacy policies, deceitful data collection, improper use of data, unfair design or unfair default settings, and unfair data security practices.[55]

3. ***Broken Promises and Deception.*** Snapchat represents a classic privacy deception case, where a company is found to be in violation of promises it makes in its privacy policy. Recall the definition of a deceptive practice: it is a material "representation, omission or practice that is likely to mislead the consumer acting reasonably in the circumstances, to the consumers' detriment." Can the FTC bring a deception action for statements that are not made in a company's privacy policy? Suppose the founder of a company states in an interview that her company will never provide consumer data to a third party. This statement contradicts the company's own privacy policy, which correctly indicates that the company does provide consumer to data to certain third parties. Could the founder's statement be the basis of an FTC action for deception?

4. ***FTC Enforcement: A Slap on the Wrist?*** The FTC does not have the power to issue fines under Section 5. The FTC can issue fines if enforcing other statutory regimes that permit such monetary sanctions, such as the GLBA.

    Does the FTC have sufficient enforcement teeth to deter companies from engaging in privacy violations? To what extent does the FTC's settlement with Snapchat require more than complying appropriately with the law in the future?

    Farhad Manjoo, in commenting on Snapchat notes that FTC consent agreements "have become something of a rite of passage for tech companies." He goes on to argue:

---

[55] Solove & Hartzog, *FTC and the New Common Law of Privacy, supra.*

But there is little evidence that these agreements have led to a wholesale shift in how tech companies handle private data. While the F.T.C. deals might push the companies to be more careful about privacy changes, being careful is not the same as being private. It's possible — and seems likely — that agreements with the government serve mainly to add a veneer of legitimacy over whatever moves the companies planned to make anyway.[56]

Manjoo also comments on a case where the FTC found that Google violated a 2011 consent decree that Google made with the FTC. The FTC issued the largest-ever fine against a company. Manjoo writes:

How much was that record-setting fine? $22.5 million. Note that in 2012, Google made a profit of $10.7 billion, most of it through advertising that was based in some way on data it collected from users. If you do the math, the agency's fine represented about 0 percent of Google's income that year.[57]

One aspect of the settlement to note is that the consent order lasts for 20 years. This is quite a long period of time. In comparison, an HHS consent order typically lasts for 1 to 3 years. Is 20 years too long? Or appropriate?

5. *If People Do Not Read Privacy Policies, Why Enforce Them?* Daniel Solove points out that people rarely read privacy policies:

Most people do not read privacy notices on a regular basis. As for other types of notices, such as end-user license agreements and contract boilerplate terms, studies show only a miniscule percentage of people read them. Moreover, few people opt out of the collection, use, or disclosure of their data when presented with the choice to do so. Most people do not even bother to change the default privacy settings on websites.[58]

Why should the FTC enforce privacy policies if people do not read them? Solove points out that privacy policies are often difficult for consumers to understand and there is a tradeoff between making policies understandable and providing sufficient detail to explain the complex ways personal data is used and protected:

The evidence suggests that people are not well informed about privacy. Efforts to improve education are certainly laudable, as are attempts to make privacy notices more understandable. But such efforts fail to address a deeper problem — privacy is quite complicated. This fact leads to a tradeoff between providing a meaningful notice and providing a short and simple one.

Privacy policies not only serve to inform consumers; they also serve to inform privacy advocates and regulators, and they are a way to hold companies

---

[56] Farhad Manjoo, *Another Tech Company Finds the F.T.C. Looking Over Its Shoulder*, N.Y. Times Bits Blog, May 8, 2014, http://bits.blogs.nytimes.com/2014/05/08/will-a-government-settlement-improve-snapchats-privacy-dont-count-on-it/.

[57] *Id.* Editors' Note: the 0 percent estimation may seem surprising. But in 2012, Google reported $10.74 billion in total profits. That year, online advertising accounted for about 95 percent of Google's profits. Ninety-five percent of $10.74 billion is approximately $10.203 billion. A $22.5 million dollar fine represents 0.002205 percent of Google profits. Hence, a 0 percent estimation follows normal rounding conventions.

[58] Daniel J. Solove, *Privacy Self-Management and the Consent Dilemma,* 126 Harv. L. Rev. 1880 (2013).

to their word. But if experts are the audience for privacy policies, then doesn't this conflict with the needs of the consumer audience, for whom simpler is better?

6. ***Why Did the FTC Become the Leading U.S. Privacy Agency?*** In 2000, Steven Hetcher assessed the FTC's behavior in enforcing privacy in these terms:

> By the Agency's lights, its promotion of the fair practice principles should satisfy privacy advocates, as the fair information practice principles are derived from pre-existing norms of the advocacy community. Public interest advocates contend to the contrary, however, that privacy policies ill serve their aspirational privacy norms. They argue that privacy policies are typically not read by website users. They are written in legalese such that even if people read them, they will not understand them. Hence, they do not provide notice and thus cannot lead to consent. In addition, there is evidence that many sites do not adhere to their own policies. The policies are subject to change when companies merge, such that one company's policy is likely to go unheeded. Finally, very few privacy policies guarantee security or enforcement. Thus, the provision of a privacy policy by a website does not automatically promote the fair practice principles.
>
> Despite these problems, the FTC has strongly endorsed privacy policies. This raises a question as to why the Agency should do so, given the severe criticism privacy policies have received. Why, for instance, is the FTC not coming out in support of the creation of a new agency to oversee privacy protection? . . .
>
> There is a public choice answer as to why the Agency has promoted privacy policies, despite their problems (and despite the fact that they do not appear to promote the interests of any industry groups whose favor the FTC might be seeking). It is through privacy policies that the FTC is gaining jurisdiction over the commercial Internet. Jurisdiction is power. In other words, the FTC acts as if it has a plan to migrate its activities to the Internet, and privacy policies have been at the core of this plan. . . .[59]

After the writings by Hetcher, however, the FTC developed an additional role — the agency began to enforce standards of data security. Does this role fit in with Hetcher's analysis ("through privacy policies . . . the FTC is gaining jurisdiction over the commercial Internet")?

7. ***The Scope of the FTC's Power.*** How much power does Section 5 provide to the FTC to regulate the way companies collect, use, and share personal data? In *FTC v. Wyndham Worldwide Corp.*, 10 F.Supp.3d 602 (D.N.J. 2014), Wyndham Hotels challenged the scope of the FTC's power.

The *Wyndham* case arose from a series of data breaches suffered by Wyndham. In its complaint against Wyndham, the FTC alleged a variety of poor data security practices by Wyndham that led to the breaches. Although the case involves data security and is excerpted and discussed in more depth in Chapter 10, the arguments in the case could apply to the FTC's privacy enforcement. One of the arguments made by Wyndham was that because

---

[59] Steven Hetcher, *The FTC as Internet Privacy Norm Entrepreneur*, 53 Vand. L. Rev. 2041 (2000). *See also* Steven Hetcher, *Norms in a Wired World* (2004); Steven Hetcher, *Changing the Social Meaning of Privacy in Cyberspace*, 15 Harv. J.L. & Tech. 149 (2001); Steven A. Hetcher, *Norm Proselytizers Create a Privacy Entitlement in Cyberspace*, 16 Berkeley Tech. L.J. 877 (2001).

Congress enacted targeted data security legislation elsewhere, yet failed to create a statute explicitly authorizing the FTC to regulate data security, the FTC lacked the power to regulate. The court rejected this argument, concluding that the FTC's Section 5 power is very broad and that the context-specific data security statutes simply enhance data security protection in certain contexts. The court concluded that Wyndham "fails to explain how the FTC's unfairness authority over data security would lead to a result that is incompatible with more recent legislation and thus would 'plainly *contradict* congressional policy.' "

As Hartzog and Solove argue: "Congress gave the FTC very broad and general regulatory authority by design to allow for a more nimble and evolutionary approach to the regulation of consumer protection." They contend that normatively the FTC's broad power is justified and that "the FTC not only should have broad data protection enforcement powers, but that it also should be exercising these powers more robustly. The FTC should enforce more expansively, embrace consensus norms more quickly, and take more of a leadership role in the development of privacy norms and standards."[60] Should the FTC take an even greater role and more aggressively try to develop privacy norms?

8. *Are FTC Consent Decrees Similar to Common Law?* Daniel Solove and Woodrow Hartzog argue that the body of FTC consent decrees has some key similarities to common law. "Practitioners look to FTC settlements as though they have precedential weight. The result is that lawyers consult and analyze these settlements in much the same way as they do judicial decisions."

9. *Fair Notice.* Some commentators critique the FTC for failing to articulate its standards clearly enough. In the context of the FTC's data security cases, Gerard Stegmaier and Wendell Bartnick argue:

> The FTC's current practice. . . relies heavily upon the publication of negotiated resolutions that consist of draft complaints coupled with consent agreements, as well as the release of reports and other interpretive guidance that blend best practices with law. The result is that legal requirements are generally shrouded in mystery and uncertain risk of enforcement discretion. Finally, . . . a standard based on "reasonableness" grounded solely in settlements raises its own questions of whether constitutionally adequate fair notice was provided. Such a standard seems unfair and problematic to those tasked with assisting entities in avoiding unfair and deceptive trade practices.[61]

In another case, LabMD challenged the FTC with an argument quite similar to Stegmaier and Bartnick's. Writing for the FTC in denying LabMD's motion to dismiss, Commissioner Wright stated:

> LabMD's due process claim is particularly untenable when viewed against the backdrop of the common law of negligence. Every day, courts and juries subject companies to tort liability for violating uncodified standards of care, and the

---

[60] Woodrow Hartzog & Daniel J. Solove, *The Scope and Potential of FTC Data Protection*, 83 Geo. Wash. L. Rev. 2230 (2015).

[61] Gerard M. Stegmaier & Wendell Bartnick, *Psychics, Russian Roulette, and Data Security: The FTC's Hidden Data-Security Requirements*, 20 Geo. Mason L. Rev. 673 (2013).

contexts in which they make those fact-specific judgments are as varied and fast-changing as the world of commerce and technology itself.

Hartzog and Solove contend:

> In a common law system — or any system where matters are decided case-by-case and there is an attempt at maintaining consistency across decisions, any reasonableness standard will evolve into something more akin to a rule with specifics over time. Indeed, any broad standard will follow this evolutionary trajectory. . . .
>
> While some initial uncertainty might be the present at the outset, the clarity provided by each additional legal action virtually guarantees ever increasing determinism for those already charged with a reasonable adherence to commonly shared industry standards.
>
> The FTC is not exceeding its authority because this developmental pattern is practically inevitable and quite predictable given the clarity offered by incorporation of generally accepted industry practices and the wiggle room provided by requiring reasonable but not strict adherence to those practices.[62]

FTC v. TOYSMART.COM
Civ. Action No. 00-11341-RGS (FTC July 21, 2000),

COMPLAINT

. . . . 4. Defendants Toysmart.com, Inc. and Toysmart.com, LLC (collectively "Toysmart" or "defendant") are Delaware corporations. . . .

6. Since at least January 1999, Toysmart has advertised, promoted, and sold toys on the Internet, located at www.toysmart.com. Toysmart markets its products and services throughout the United States and the world via the Internet.

7. In connection with its Web site, Toysmart collects personal customer information including, but not limited to, consumers' names, addresses, billing information, shopping preferences, and family profile information ("Customer Lists").

8. In September 1999, Toysmart became a licensee of TRUSTe, an organization that certifies the privacy policies of online businesses and allows such businesses to display a TRUSTe trustmark or seal.

9. From September 1999 to the present, the privacy policy posted on the Toysmart.com Web site has stated, *inter alia*, (1) "Personal information voluntarily submitted by visitors to our site, such as name, address, billing information and shopping preferences, is never shared with a third party. All information obtained by toysmart.com is used only to personalize your experience online;" and (2) "When you register with toysmart.com, you can rest assured that your information will never be shared with a third party." A true and correct copy of the Toysmart privacy policy is attached hereto as Exhibit 1.

10. On May 22, 2000, Toysmart announced that, as of midnight on May 19, 2000, it had officially ceased operations. Toysmart also announced that it had retained the services of a Boston-based management consultant, The Recovery

[62] Solove & Hartzog, *Scope and Potential of FTC, supra.*

Group, to locate parties interested in acquiring Toysmart.com's business and assets.

11. On May 22, 2000, Toysmart began soliciting bids for the purchase of its assets. Bids have been sought for the purchase of all of the company's assets or for individual assets. Among the individual assets offered for sale by Toysmart.com are its Customer Lists (on either an exclusive or non-exclusive basis). Other assets available include inventory; warehouse fixtures and equipment; intangible assets including domain name, product databases, and Web site source code; and a B2B business plan. Bids were due to Toysmart by 6:00 p.m. EST on June 19, 2000.

12. On June 9, 2000, Toysmart's creditors filed a petition for involuntary bankruptcy. *See In Re: Toysmart.com, LLC*, No. 00-13995-CJK (Bankr. D. Mass).

13. On June 19, 2000, bidding for Toysmart's assets concluded. Toysmart informed the Federal Trade Commission that its Customer Lists will not be transferred to a third party absent bankruptcy court approval. . . .

17. From at least September 1999 to the present, defendant Toysmart, directly or through its employees and agents, in connection with its collection of personal consumer information, expressly and/or by implication, represented that it would "never" disclose, sell, or offer for sale customers' or registered members' personal information to third parties.

18. In truth and in fact, Toysmart has disclosed, sold, or offered for sale its customer lists and profiles. Therefore, the representation set forth in Paragraph 17 was, and is, a deceptive practice. . . .

STIPULATION AND ORDER ESTABLISHING CONDITIONS ON SALE OF CUSTOMER INFORMATION

This Stipulation is entered into this twentieth day of July, 2000, by and between, Toysmart.com, LLC, debtor and debtor-in-possession ("Debtor" or "Toysmart"), and the Federal Trade Commission ("FTC"). . . .

For the purposes of this Agreement, the following definitions shall apply:

"Qualified Buyer" shall mean an entity that (1) concentrates its business in the family commerce market, involving the areas of education, toys, learning, home and/or instruction, including commerce, content, product and services, and (2) expressly agrees to be Toysmart's successor-in-interest as to the Customer Information, and expressly agrees to the obligations set forth in Paragraphs 2, 3 and 4, below. . . .

The Debtor shall only assign or sell its Customer Information as part of the sale of its Goodwill and only to a Qualified Buyer approved by the Bankruptcy Court. In the process of approving any sale of the Customer Information, the Bankruptcy Court shall require that the Qualified Buyer agree to and comply with the terms of this Stipulation.

The Qualified Buyer shall treat Customer Information in accordance with the terms of the Privacy Statement and shall be responsible for any violation by it following the date of purchase. Among other things, the Qualified Buyer shall use Customer Information only to fulfill customer orders and to personalize customers' experience on the Web site, and shall not disclose, sell or transfer Customer Information to any Third Party.

If the Qualified Buyer materially changes the Privacy Statement, prior notice will be posted on the Web site. Any such material change in policy shall apply only to information collected following the change in policy. The Customer Information shall be governed by the Privacy Statement, unless the consumer provides affirmative consent ("opt-in") to the previously collected information being governed by the new policy.

In the event that an order is not entered on or before July 31, 2001, approving the sale of the Customer Information to a Qualified Buyer or approving a plan of reorganization, the Debtor shall, on or before August 31, 2001, delete or destroy all Customer Information in its possession, custody or control, and provide written confirmation to the FTC, sworn to under penalty of perjury, that all such Customer Information has been deleted or destroyed. Pending approval of any sale of the Customer Information to a Qualified Buyer or of a plan of reorganization, the Debtor shall handle Customer Information in accordance with the Privacy Statement.

This Stipulation and Order, after approval by the Bankruptcy Court, shall be attached to and incorporated in full into the terms of any plan of liquidation or reorganization that is ultimately approved in this bankruptcy case.

STATEMENT OF COMMISSIONER MOZELLE W. THOMPSON

. . . I have voted to approve the settlement in this matter resolving the Commission's charges that Toysmart violated Section 5 of the Federal Trade Commission Act because I believe the terms of the settlement are consistent with Toysmart's privacy policy. More specifically, the settlement permits Toysmart to sell its information only to a "qualified buyer," defined as an entity engaged in the family commerce market who *expressly agrees to be Toysmart's successor-in-interest as to that information.* Accordingly, Toysmart may transfer its data only to someone who specifically "stands" in the shoes of Toysmart.

Despite the consistency between the settlement and Toysmart's privacy policy, my decision to approve the settlement is not without reservation. Like my colleagues Commissioner Anthony and Commissioner Swindle, I think that consumers would benefit from notice and choice before a company transfers their information to a corporate successor. Indeed, many of the consumers who disclosed their families' personal information to Toysmart might not have been willing to turn over the same information to the particular corporate entity that ultimately succeeds Toysmart. This is true even where Toysmart's corporate successor must pursue the same line of business as its predecessor.

I urge any successor to provide Toysmart customers with notice and an opportunity to "opt out" as a matter of good will and good business practice. . . .

STATEMENT OF COMMISSIONER SHEILA F. ANTHONY

The settlements attempt to satisfy both the privacy interests of consumers and the business needs of a failing firm by establishing the conditions on the sale of Toysmart's customer list. Specifically, the order proposed to be filed with the bankruptcy court limits to whom Toysmart may sell its customer list. Toysmart may only sell the customer list in connection with its goodwill, not as a stand-alone asset, and only to a qualified buyer. . . .

To accept the bankruptcy settlement would place business concerns ahead of consumer privacy. Although the proposed settlement's definition of a qualified buyer attempts to ensure that only an entity "similar" to Toysmart is eligible to purchase the list, I do not believe that this limitation is an adequate proxy for consumer privacy interests. In my view, consumer privacy would be better protected by requiring that consumers themselves be given notice and choice before their detailed personal information is shared with or used by another corporate entity — especially where, as here, consumers provided that information pursuant to a promise not to transfer it.

DISSENTING STATEMENT OF COMMISSIONER ORSON SWINDLE

Defendant Toysmart.com, Inc. ("Toysmart") represented that it would never disclose, sell, or offer to sell the personal information of its customers to a third party. When faced with severe financial difficulties, however, Toysmart solicited bids for its customer lists, which include or reflect the personal information of its customers. . . .

I agree that a sale to a third party under the terms of the Bankruptcy Order would be a substantial improvement over the sale that likely would have occurred without Commission action. Nevertheless, I do not think that the Commission should allow the sale. If we really believe that consumers attach great value to the privacy of their personal information and that consumers should be able to limit access to such information through private agreements with businesses, we should compel businesses to honor the promises they make to consumers to gain access to this information. Toysmart promised its customers that their personal information would *never* be sold to a third party, but the Bankruptcy Order in fact would allow a sale to a third party. In my view, such a sale should not be permitted because "never" really means never.

I dissent.

NOTES & QUESTIONS

1. *Postscript.* After the FTC approved the settlement in *Toysmart* by a 3-2 vote by the commissioners, the settlement attracted the support of Toysmart's creditors, since it would allow the sale of the database to certain purchasers, and hence could be used to pay back the creditors. However, in August 2000, Judge Carol Kenner of the U.S. Bankruptcy Court rejected the settlement because there were currently no offers on the table to buy the database, and it would hurt the creditors to restrict the sale to certain types of purchasers without first having a potential buyer. In February 2001, Judge Kenner agreed to let Toysmart sell its customer database to Disney, the primary shareholder, for $50,000. Disney agreed, as part of the deal, to destroy the list.

   The Toysmart bankruptcy also led Amazon.com, the Internet's largest retailer, to change its privacy policy. Prior to the Toysmart case, Amazon's privacy policy provided:

> Amazon.com does not sell, trade, or rent your personal information to others.
> We may choose to do so in the future with trustworthy third parties, but you can
> tell us not to by sending a blank e-mail message to never@amazon.com.

In its new policy, Amazon.com stated:

> Information about our customers is an important part of our business, and we
> are not in the business of selling it to others. We share customer information
> only with the subsidiaries Amazon.com, Inc., controls and as described below.
> . . .
>
> As we continue to develop our business, we might sell or buy stores or assets.
> In such transactions, customer information generally is one of the transferred
> business assets. Also, in the unlikely event that Amazon.com, Inc., or
> substantially all of its assets are acquired, customer information will of course
> be one of the transferred assets. . . .

Amazon.com's new policy was criticized by some privacy organizations.
One of the criticisms was that the policy did not provide an opt-out right.
Suppose Amazon.com went bankrupt and decided to sell all of its customer
data. Can it sell data supplied by consumers under the old policy? Can the new
policy apply retroactively?

2. ***Bankruptcy: Property Rights vs. Contract Rights.*** Edward Janger proposes
that a property rights regime (as opposed to the contractual rights of a privacy
policy) will best protect the privacy of personal data when companies
possessing such data go bankrupt:

> Property rules are viewed as reflecting undivided entitlements. They allocate,
> as Carol Rose puts it, the "whole meatball" to the "owner." Liability rules, by
> contrast are viewed as dividing an entitlement between two parties. One party
> holds the right, but the other party is given the option to take the right and
> compensate the right holder for the deprivation (to breach and pay damages). .
> . .
>
> Propertization has some crucial benefits, but it also has some serious costs.
> Both the bankruptcy and non-bankruptcy treatment of privacy policies turn on
> whether a privacy policy creates a right enforceable only through civil damages,
> or a right with the status of property. If bankruptcy courts treat privacy policies
> solely as contract obligations [the liability rule], the debtor will be free to breach
> (or reject) the contract in bankruptcy. Any damage claim will be treated as a
> prepetition claim, paid, if at all, at a significant discount. Consumer
> expectations (contractual or otherwise) of privacy are likely to be defeated. By
> contrast, if personal information is deemed property subject to an encumbrance,
> then the property interest must be respected, or to use the bankruptcy term,
> "adequately protected."

In other words, Janger contends that giving individuals property rights in
their personal data will provide more protection than giving individuals
contract rights in the event a company goes bankrupt.[63]

---

[63] Edward J. Janger, *Muddy Property: Generating and Protecting Information Privacy Norms
in Bankruptcy*, 44 Wm. & Mary L. Rev. 1801 (2002).

3. ***Customer Databases as Collateral.*** Xuan-Thao Nguyen points out that companies are using their customer databases as collateral for loans, since these databases are one of their most significant assets:

> Whether intentional or unintentional, many Internet companies ignore their own privacy policy statements when the companies pledge their customer database as collateral in secured financing schemes. This practice renders on-line privacy statements misleading because the statements are silent on collateralization of the company's assets. . . .
>
> The secured party can use the consumer database in its business or sell the consumer database to others. The collateralization of the consumer database and its end result may contradict the debtor's consumer privacy statement declaring that the debtor does not sell or lease the consumer information to others. Though there is no direct sale of the consumer database to the secured party, the effect of the collateralization of the consumer database is the same: the consumer database is in the hands of third parties with unfettered control and rights. Essentially, the collateralization of consumer databases violates the privacy policies publicized on debtors' Web sites.[64]

4. ***Retroactive Changes to Privacy Policies.*** In *In the Matter of Gateway, Inc.,* 2004 WL 261847 (FTC Sept. 10, 2004), Gateway Learning Corp. collected personal information from its consumers pursuant to a privacy policy stating that it would not sell, rent, or loan personal information to third parties unless people consented. It also promised that if it changed its privacy policy, it would give consumers the opportunity to "opt out" of having their data shared.

Subsequently, Gateway altered its privacy policy to allow the renting of personal information to third parties without informing customers and obtaining their explicit consent. The FTC filed a complaint alleging that this practice was an unfair practice. The FTC also charged that Gateway's failure to inform consumers of its changes to its privacy policies, despite its promises to do so, constituted a deceptive practice. Gateway settled with the FTC, agreeing that it would "not misrepresent . . . [t]he manner in which [it] will collect, use, or disclose personal information." It also agreed to pay $4,608, which was the amount it earned from renting the information.

Suppose a company puts the following line in its privacy policy: "Please be aware that we may change this policy at any time." Would this allow for the retroactive application of a revised policy? Or is there an argument that even with a statement such as this one, the revised policy could not be applied retroactively?

5. ***Apps with Privacy Policies.*** Increasingly, users of various websites, software, and mobile devices are using applications (called "apps") developed by third parties. These apps add special features and functions and are quite popular. Many app developers are small companies or individuals without the normal cadre of lawyers, privacy officers, and other experts. At the same time, many apps gather a lot of personal information. In 2011, the Future of Privacy Forum (FPF), a privacy think tank, examined the top paid apps for mobile devices (such as the iPhone, Android, and Blackberry). FPF found that 22 out of 30 did

---

[64] Xuan-Thao N. Nguyen, *Collateralizing Privacy,* 78 Tul. L. Rev. 553, 571, 590 (2004).

not have a privacy policy. Without a privacy policy, would the FTC have theories upon which it could enforce privacy protections against the app? Could the FTC require apps to have privacy policies?

IN THE MATTER OF FACEBOOK, INC.

2012 WL 3518628 (FTC July 27, 2012)

COMPLAINT

The Federal Trade Commission, having reason to believe that Facebook, Inc., a corporation ("Respondent") has violated the Federal Trade Commission Act ("FTC Act"), and it appearing to the Commission that this proceeding is in the public interest, alleges: . . . .

3. Since at least 2004, Facebook has operated www.facebook.com, a social networking website. Users of the site create online profiles, which contain content about them such as their name, interest groups they join, the names of other users who are their "friends" on the site, photos albums and videos they upload, and messages and comments they post or receive from their friends. Users also may add content to other users' profiles by sharing photos, sending messages, or posting comments. As of March 2012, Facebook had approximately 900 million users.

4. Since approximately May 2007, Facebook has operated the Facebook Platform ("Platform"), a set of tools and programming interfaces that enables third parties to develop, run, and operate software applications, such as games, that users can interact with online ("Platform Applications"). . . .

6. Facebook has collected extensive "profile information" about its users, including, but not limited to [name, gender, email address, birthday, profile picture, photos, friends, and other personal data]. . . .

9. Facebook has designed its Platform such that Platform Applications can access user profile information in two main instances. First, Platform Applications that a user authorizes can access the user's profile information. Second, if a user's "Friend" authorizes a Platform Application, that application can access certain of the user's profile information, even if the user has not authorized that Application. For example, if a user authorizes a Platform Application that provides reminders about Friends' birthdays, that application could access, among other things, the birthdays of the user's Friends, even if these Friends never authorized the application.

10. Since at least November 2009, Facebook has, in many instances, provided its users with a "Central Privacy Page," the same or similar to the one depicted below. Among other things, this page has contained a "Profile" link, with accompanying text that has stated "[c]ontrol who can see your profile and personal information."

11. When users have clicked on the "Profile" link, Facebook has directed them to a "Profile Privacy Page," the same or similar to the one depicted below, which has stated that users could "[c]ontrol who can see your profile and related information." For each "Profile Privacy Setting," depicted below, users could click on a drop-down menu and restrict access to specified users, *e.g.*, "Only Friends," or "Friends of Friends."

12. Although the precise language has changed over time, Facebook's Central Privacy Page and Profile Privacy Page have, in many instances, stated that the Profile Privacy Settings allow users to "control who can see" their profile information, by specifying who can access it, *e.g.*, "Only Friends" or "Friends of Friends."

13. Similarly, although the precise interface has changed over time, Facebook's Profile Privacy Settings have continued to specify that users can restrict access to their profile information to the audience the user selects, *e.g.*, "Only Friends," "Friends of Friends." . . .

14. None of the pages described in Paragraphs 10-13 have disclosed that a user's choice to restrict profile information to "Only Friends" or "Friends of Friends" would be ineffective as to certain third parties. Despite this fact, in many instances, Facebook has made profile information that a user chose to restrict to "Only Friends" or "Friends of Friends" accessible to any Platform Applications that the user's Friends have used (hereinafter "Friends' Apps"). Information shared with such Friends' Apps has included, among other things, a user's birthday, hometown, activities, interests, status updates, marital status, education (*e.g.*, schools attended), place of employment, photos, and videos. . . .

19. On approximately November 19, 2009, Facebook changed its privacy policy to designate certain user information as "publicly available" ("PAI"). On approximately December 8, 2009, Facebook began implementing the changes referenced in its new policy ("the December Privacy Changes") to make public in new ways certain information that users previously had provided.

20. Before December 8, 2009, users could, and did, use their Friends' App Settings to restrict Platform Applications' access to their PAI. For example, as of November 2009, approximately 586,241 users had used these settings to "block" Platform Applications that their Friends used from accessing any of their profile information, including their Name, Profile Picture, Gender, Friend List, Pages, and Networks. Following the December Privacy Changes, Facebook users no longer could restrict access to their PAI through these Friends' App Settings, and all prior user choices to do so were overridden. . . .

22. Before December 8, 2009, users could, and did, use their Search Privacy Settings (available through the "Search" link on the Privacy Settings Page. . . .Following the December Privacy Changes, Facebook users could no longer restrict the visibility of their Profile Picture and Pages through these settings, and all prior user choices to do so were overridden.

23. To implement the December Privacy Changes, Facebook required each user to click through a multi-page notice, known as the Privacy Wizard. . . .

24. The Privacy Wizard did not disclose adequately that users no longer could restrict access to their newly-designated PAI via their Profile Privacy Settings, Friends' App Settings, or Search Privacy Settings, or that their existing choices to restrict access to such information via these settings would be overridden. . . .

26. Facebook's designation of PAI caused harm to users, including, but not limited to, threats to their health and safety, and unauthorized revelation of their affiliations. Among other things:

a. certain users were subject to the risk of unwelcome contacts from persons who may have been able to infer their locale, based on the locales of their Friends (*e.g.*, their Friends' Current City information) and of the organizations reflected in their Pages;

b. each user's Pages became visible to anyone who viewed the user's profile, thereby exposing potentially controversial political views or other sensitive information to third parties — such as prospective employers, government organizations, or business competitors — who sought to obtain personal information about the user;

c. each user's Friend List became visible to anyone who viewed the user's profile, thereby exposing potentially sensitive affiliations, that could, in turn, reveal a user's political views, sexual orientation, or business relationships, to third parties — such as prospective employers, government organizations, or business competitors — who sought to obtain personal information about the user; and

d. each user's Profile Photo became visible to anyone who viewed the user's profile, thereby revealing potentially embarrassing or political images to third parties whose access users previously had restricted.

27. As described in Paragraph 23, Facebook has represented, expressly, or by implication, that its December Privacy Changes provided users with "more control" over their information, including by allowing them to preserve their "Old Settings," to protect the privacy of their profile information.

28. As described in Paragraph 24-26, Facebook failed to disclose, or failed to disclose adequately, that, following the December Privacy Changes, users could no longer restrict access to their Name, Profile Picture, Gender, Friend List, Pages, or Networks by using privacy settings previously available to them. Facebook also failed to disclose, or failed to disclose adequately, that the December Privacy Changes overrode existing user privacy settings that restricted access to a user's Name, Profile Picture, Gender, Friend List, Pages, or Networks. These facts would be material to consumers. Therefore, Facebook's failure to adequately disclose these facts, in light of the representation made, constitutes a deceptive act or practice.

29. As described in Paragraphs 19-26, by designating certain user profile information publicly available that previously had been subject to privacy settings, Facebook materially changed its promises that users could keep such information private. Facebook retroactively applied these changes to personal information that it had previously collected from users, without their informed consent, in a manner that has caused or has been likely to cause substantial injury to consumers, was not outweighed by countervailing benefits to consumers or to competition, and was not reasonably avoidable by consumers. This practice constitutes an unfair act or practice. . . .

34. Facebook has displayed advertisements ("ads") from third-parties ("Platform Advertisers") on its web site.

35. Facebook has allowed Platform Advertisers to target their ads ("Platform Ads") by requesting that Facebook display them to users whose profile information reflects certain "targeted traits," including, but not limited to [location, age, sex, birthday, relationship status, likes, and interests, among other things]. . . .

36. Facebook has disseminated or caused to be disseminated numerous statements that it does not share information about its users with advertisers, including:

a. Facebook may use information in your profile without identifying you as an individual to third parties. We do this for purposes such as ... personalizing advertisements and promotions so that we can provide you Facebook. We believe this benefits you. You can know more about the world around you and, where there are advertisements, they're more likely to be interesting to you. For example, if you put a favorite movie in your profile, we might serve you an advertisement highlighting a screening of a similar one in your town. But we don't tell the movie company who you are. (Facebook Privacy Policy, November 26, 2008). . . .

d. Still others asked to be opted-out of having their information shared with advertisers. This reflects a common misconception about advertising on Facebook. We don't share your information with advertisers unless you tell us to ([*e.g.,*] to get a sample, hear more, or enter a contest). Any assertion to the contrary is false. Period ... we never provide the advertiser any names or other information about the people who are shown, or even who click on, the ads. (Facebook Blog, http://blog.facebook.com/blog.php, "Responding to Your Feedback," Barry Schnitt, April 5, 2010). . . .

37. Contrary to the statements set forth in Paragraph 36(a)-(d), in many instances, Facebook has shared information about users with Platform Advertisers by identifying to them the users who clicked on their ads and to whom those ads were targeted. . . .

38. As a result of the conduct described in Paragraph 37, Platform Advertisers potentially could take steps to get detailed information about individual users. . . .

50. As described above, Facebook has collected and stored vast quantities of photos and videos that its users upload, including, but not limited to: at least one such photo from approximately ninety-nine percent of its users, and more than 100 million photos and 415,000 videos from its users, collectively, every day.

51. Facebook has stored users' photos and videos such that each one is assigned a Content URL — a uniform resource locator that specifies its location on Facebook's servers. Facebook users and Platform Applications can obtain the Content URL for any photo or video that they view on Facebook's web site by, for example, right-clicking on it. If a user or Application further disseminates this URL, Facebook will "serve" the user's photo or video to anyone who clicks on the URL.

52. Facebook has disseminated or caused to be disseminated statements communicating that a user can restrict access to his or her profile information — including, but not limited to, photos and videos that a user uploads — by deleting or deactivating his or her user account. Such statements include:

a. Deactivating or deleting your account. If you want to stop using your account you may deactivate it or delete it. When you deactivate an account, no user will be able to see it, but it will not be deleted. . . . When you delete an account, it is permanently deleted from Facebook. . . .

Backup copies. Removed and deleted information may persist in backup copies for up to 90 days, but will not be available to others; (Facebook Privacy Policy, November 19, 2009). . . .

53. Contrary to the statements set forth in Paragraph 52, Facebook has continued to display users' photos and videos to anyone who accesses Facebook's

Content URLs for them, even after such users have deleted or deactivated their accounts. . . .

NOTES & QUESTIONS

1. ***Postscript.*** Facebook settled with the FTC, agreeing to refrain from misrepresenting the privacy of consumer personal data, obtain consent before changing consumer privacy preferences, and establish a comprehensive privacy program, among other things.

2. ***Statements Beyond the Privacy Policy.*** In *Facebook,* the FTC cites statements made in blog posts by Facebook employees when listing various false or misleading claims made by Facebook. When should statements by a company's employees count as official statements of the company? Suppose a company allows employees to have blogs hosted by the company and each blog does not contain any language that indicates that employees are speaking for themselves only. Should statements the employees write on these blogs be considered promises made by the company?

   How specific do statements need to be? In an interview, Mark Zuckerberg assured Facebook users that "[p]rivacy is very important to us."[65] Could vague or broad statements like this one be used by the FTC against Facebook?

   Consider Solove and Hartzog:

   > These cases have made it clear that the question of what constitutes a deceptive trade practice is holistic. Not only does the FTC consider representations beyond what exists in a privacy policy, but it considers consumer expectations as well. This raises a number of interesting questions. The first is the extent to which other representations can contradict explicit representations in the privacy policy. While contract law tends to give great weight to the boilerplate terms of a contract, the FTC does not appear to recognize any kind of significant presumption to exculpatory representations buried in dense legalese that run contrary to other representations or consumer expectations. . . .
   >
   > Finally, given the universe of potential privacy-related statements the FTC could have (and has) drawn from to find deception, has there been a shift from explicit, insular representations to larger framing effects that create consumer trust? In other words, it appears that what a company has promised is simply one factor in a larger approach to determining whether a company has been deceptive. The FTC looks at architecture, shared norms, and cultural assumptions likely held by consumers to determine consumer expectations. This framework developed by the FTC logically would also consider any statement made by the company that would materially contribute to the creation of trust on the part of the consumer.[66]

3. ***Website Design Elements.*** Woodrow Hartzog argues that the privacy expectations of many users of websites is formed not by the privacy policy but by the various privacy settings and design elements of the site.[67] Websites such

---

[65] John Paczkowski, *Facebook CEO Mark Zuckerberg in the Privacy Hot Seat*, All Things D (June 2, 2010), http://allthingsd.com/20100602/mark-zuckerberg-session/.

[66] Solove & Hartzog, *FTC and the New Common Law of Privacy, supra.*

[67] Woodrow Hartzog, *Website Design as Contract,* 60 Am. U. L. Rev. 1635 (2011).

as Facebook have multiple privacy settings on a page distinct from the privacy policy or terms of use. More people might interact with the privacy settings page than read the privacy policy page.

Suppose certain forms of data sharing are disclosed in the privacy policy but not on the privacy settings page. These forms of data sharing exist no matter what a person's settings are. A user might argue that she did not expect this data sharing because based on the privacy settings page, it appeared as though all her data would only be shared per the settings she set. On the settings page, the company has the following statement, with a link to the privacy policy page: "Please refer to our privacy policy for information about how we collect, use, and share your data." Is this sufficient?

4. *Is Touting a Service as "Free" a Deceptive Trade Practice?* Recall Chris Hoofnagle and Jan Whittington's argument that many online services that are purportedly "free" actually have a cost because they gather personal data about consumers and sell this data to advertisers.[68] The FTC, however, has allowed free offers that require a purchase. As Hoofnagle and Whittington describe the FTC's approach:

> [T]he FTC will generally consider the use of free offers to be unfair and deceptive unless two conditions are met. First, the conditions and obligations accompanying the free offer must be set forth at the outset, "so as to leave no reasonable probability that the terms of the advertisement or offer might be misunderstood." Second, sellers cannot offset the cost of providing a free product by increasing the ordinary price, quality, or size of the product that must be purchased in order to obtain the free offer.

According to Hoofnagle and Whittington, under the guidance of the 1971 FTC Guide and subsequent decisions, "sites such as Facebook.com [can] continue to use the term 'free' even when offers are contingent on the consumer's performance of certain obligations, so long as Facebook clearly discloses those obligations." Hoofnagle and Whittington suggest that the FTC should change its approach and take measures to help consumers realize the true nature of online services. For example, they suggest that the FTC could mandate "notice at the time the transaction occurs that the consumer's personal information is the basis of the bargain and that such information may be used for tracking or other secondary purposes." Another solution might be to require free services to offer a paid alternative where personal data would not be used.

---

[68] Chris Jay Hoofnagle and Jan Whittington, *Free: Accounting for the Costs of the Internet's Most Popular Price*, 61 UCLA L. Rev. 606 (2014).

IN THE MATTER OF SEARS HOLDINGS MANAGEMENT CORP.

2009 WL 2979770 (FTC Aug. 31, 2009)

COMPLAINT

The Federal Trade Commission, having reason to believe that Sears Holdings Management Corporation, a corporation, has violated the provisions of the Federal Trade Commission Act, and it appearing to the Commission that this proceeding is in the public interest, alleges:

1. Respondent Sears Holdings Management Corporation ("respondent" or "SHMC") is a Delaware corporation with its principal office or place of business at 3333 Beverly Road, Hoffman Estates, Illinois 60179. SHMC, a subsidiary of Sears Holdings Corporation ("SHC") with shares owned by Sears, Roebuck and Co. and Kmart Management Corporation, handles marketing operations for the Sears Roebuck and Kmart retail stores, and operates the sears.com and kmart.com retail Internet websites. . . .

3. From on or about April 2007 through on or about January 2008, SHMC disseminated or caused to be disseminated via the Internet a software application for consumers to download and install onto their computers (the "Application"). The Application was created, developed, and managed for respondent by a third party in connection with SHMC's "My SHC Community" market research program.

4. The Application, when installed, runs in the background at all times on consumers' computers and transmits tracked information, including nearly all of the Internet behavior that occurs on those computers, to servers maintained on behalf of respondent. Information collected and transmitted includes: web browsing, filling shopping baskets, transacting business during secure sessions, completing online application forms, checking online accounts, and, through select header information, use of web-based email and instant messaging services.

5. SHMC, during the relevant time period, presented fifteen out of every hundred visitors to the sears.com and kmart.com websites with a "My SHC Community" pop-up box that said:

> Ever wish you could talk directly to a retailer? Tell them about the products, services and offers that would really be right for you?
>
> If you're interested in becoming part of something new, something different, we'd like to invite you to become a member of My SHC Community. My SHC Community, sponsored by Sears Holdings Corporation, is a dynamic and highly interactive on-line community. It's a place where your voice is heard and your opinion matters, and what you want and need counts!

The pop-up box made no mention of the Application. Likewise, the general "Privacy Policy" statement accessed via the hyperlink in the pop-up box did not mention the Application.

6. The pop-up box message further invited consumers to enter their email address to receive a follow-up email from SHMC with more information. Subsequently, invitation messages were emailed to those consumers who supplied their email address. These emails stated, in pertinent part:

From shopping, current events, social networking, to entertainment and email, it seems that the Internet is playing a bigger and bigger role in our daily lives these days.

If you're interested in becoming part of something new, something different, we'd like to invite you to join a new and exciting online community; My SHC Community, sponsored by Sears Holdings Corporation. *Membership is absolutely free!*

My SHC Community is a dynamic and highly interactive online community. It's a place where your voice is heard and your opinion matters, and what you want and need counts! As a member of My SHC Community, you'll partner directly with the retail industry. You'll participate in exciting, engaging and on-going interactions — always on your terms and always by your choice. My SHC Community gives you the chance to help shape the future by sharing and receiving information about the products, services and offers that would really be right for you.

To become a member of My SHC Community, we simply ask you to complete the registration process which includes providing us with your contact information as well as answering a series of profile questions that will help us get to know you better. You'll also be asked to take a few minutes to download software that is powered by (VoiceFive). This research software will confidentially track your online browsing. This will help us better understand you and your needs, enabling us to create more relevant future offerings for you, other community members, and eventually all shoppers. You can uninstall the software at any time through the Add/Remove program utility on your computer. During the registration process, you'll learn more about this application software and you'll always have the opportunity to ask any and every question you may have.

Once you're a member of My SHC Community, you'll regularly interact with My SHC Community members as well as employees of Sears Holdings Corporation through special online engagements, surveys, chats and other fun and informative online techniques. We'll ask you to journal your shopping and purchasing behavior. Again, this will be when you want and how you want to record it — always on your terms and always by your choice. We'll also collect information on your internet usage. Community engagements are always fun and always voluntary!

The email invitation message then described what consumers would receive in exchange for becoming a member of the My SHC Community, including a $10 payment for joining the "online community," contingent upon the consumer retaining the Application on his or her computer for at least one month. Consumers who wished to proceed further would need to click a button, at the bottom, center portion of the invitation email, that said "Join Today!"

7. Consumers who clicked on the "Join Today!" button in the email invitation were directed to a landing page that restated many of the aforementioned representations about the potential interactions between members and the "community" and about the putative benefits of membership. The landing page did not mention the Application.

8. Consumers who clicked on the "Join Today" button in the landing page were directed to a registration page. To complete registration, consumers needed to enter information, including their name, address, age, and email address. Below the fields for entering information, the registration page presented a "Privacy Statement and User License Agreement" ("PSULA") in a "scroll box" that

displayed ten lines of the multi-page document at a time. A description of the Application's specific functions begins on approximately the 75 line down in the scroll box:

Computer hardware, software, and other configuration information: Our application may collect certain basic hardware, software, computer configuration and application usage information about the computer on which you install our application, including such data as the speed of the computer processor, its memory capacities and Internet connection speed. In addition, our application may report on devices connected to your computer, such as the type of printer or router you may be using.

Internet usage information: Once you install our application, it monitors all of the Internet behavior that occurs on the computer on which you install the application, including both your normal web browsing and the activity that you undertake during secure sessions, such as filling a shopping basket, completing an application form or checking your online accounts, which may include personal financial or health information. We may use the information that we monitor, such as name and address, for the purpose of better understanding your household demographics; however, we make commercially viable efforts to automatically filter confidential personally identifiable information such as UserID, password, credit card numbers, and account numbers. Inadvertently, we may collect such information about our panelists; and when this happens, we make commercially viable efforts to purge our database of such information.

The software application also tracks the pace and style with which you enter information online (for example, whether you click on links, type in webpage names, or use shortcut keys), the usage of cookies, and statistics about your use of online applications (for example, it may observe that during a given period of use of a computer, the computer downloaded X number of bytes of data using a particular Internet enabled gaming application).

Please note: Our application does not examine the text of your instant messages or e-mail messages. We may, however, review select e-mail header information from web-based e-mails as a way to verify your contact information and online usage information.

The PSULA went on to describe how the information the Application would collect was transmitted to respondent's servers, how it might be used, and how it was maintained. It also described how consumers could stop participating in the online community and remove the Application from their computers. Respondent stated in the PSULA that it reserved the right to continue to use information collected prior to a consumer's "resignation."

9. Below the scroll box on the registration page was a link that consumers could click to access a printable version of the PSULA, and a blank checkbox next to the statement: "I am the authorized user of this computer and I have read, agree to, and have obtained the agreement of all computer users to the terms and conditions of the Privacy Statement and User License Agreement." To continue with the registration process, consumers needed to check the box and click the "Next" button at the bottom of the registration page.

10. Consumers who completed the required information, checked the box, and clicked the "Next" button on the registration page, were directed to an installation page that explained the Application download and installation process. Consumers were required to click a "Next" button to begin the download, and then click an

"Install" or "Yes" button in a "security warning" dialog box to install the Application. Nothing on the installation page provided information on the Application.

11. When installed, the Application functioned and transmitted information substantially as described in the PSULA. The Application, when installed, would run in the background at all times on consumers' computers. Although the Application would be listed (as "mySHC Community") in the "All Programs" menu and "Add/Remove" utilities of those computers, and the Application's executable file name ("srhc.exe") would be listed as a running process in Windows Task Manager, the Application would display to users of those computers no visible indication, such as a desktop or system tray icon, that it was running.

12. The Application transmitted, in real time, tracked information to servers maintained on behalf of respondent. The tracked information included not only information about websites consumers visited and links that they clicked, but also the text of secure pages, such as online banking statements, video rental transactions, library borrowing histories, online drug prescription records, and select header fields that could show the sender, recipient, subject, and size of web-based email messages.

13. Through the means described in paragraphs 3-12, respondent has represented, expressly or by implication, that the Application would track consumers' "online browsing." Respondent failed to disclose adequately that the software application, when installed, would: monitor nearly all of the Internet behavior that occurs on consumers' computers, including information exchanged between consumers and websites other than those owned, operated, or affiliated with respondent, information provided in secure sessions when interacting with third-party websites, shopping carts, and online accounts, and headers of web-based email; track certain non-Internet-related activities taking place on those computers; and transmit nearly all of the monitored information (excluding selected categories of filtered information) to respondent's remote computer servers. These facts would be material to consumers in deciding to install the software. Respondent's failure to disclose these facts, in light of the representations made, was, and is, a deceptive practice.

14. The acts and practices of respondent as alleged in this complaint constitute unfair or deceptive acts or practices in or affecting commerce in violation of Section 5(a) of the Federal Trade Commission Act. . . .

NOTES & QUESTIONS

1. *Adequate Notice.* Sears did disclose how the application worked, though it was buried in a lengthy statement. How prominently must something be mentioned for notice to be adequate? One factor in this case involved the highly invasive functions of the application. Perhaps the prominence of notice should be proportionate to the invasiveness to privacy. But who decides? If many people do not read privacy notices at all, does it matter if a statement appears in line 5 or line 75?

2. *From Broken Promises to Broken Expectations?* Solove and Hartzog contend that the FTC has begun to focus away from the explicit promises a company

makes and towards ways in which consumer expectations are being thwarted:

> Although the FTC began enforcing broken *promises* of privacy, its focus seems to have shifted to broken *expectations* of consumer privacy. The shift might seem subtle, but it is dramatic in effect. Instead of the core question being what was promised, which largely focuses on a company's language, the core question has become what was expected, which incorporates the universe of preexisting consumer backgrounds, norms, and dispositions, as well as elements of design, functionality, and other nonlinguistic factors besides privacy-related statements that shape a consumer's expectations.
>
> The FTC could simply look at what a company's polices and design/architecture are and compare that with the company's actions. But it is not doing that. Instead, it seems to be taking consumers as it finds them, full of preexisting expectations, contextual norms, and cognitive limitations, and prohibiting companies from exploiting these assumptions and rational ignorance. . . .
>
> If the FTC takes into account the growing evidence about how consumers form their expectations, then it could increasingly demand that companies engage in practices that will correct mistaken consumer assumptions, or at the very least not exploit such assumptions. Existing forms of notice might not be deemed sufficient because the empirical evidence shows that consumers are not really being notified. [69]

3. ***Constructive Sharing of Personally Identifiable Information.*** *In the Matter of MySpace, LLC* (FTC 2012) involved the "constructive sharing" of non-personally identifiable information (PII) — sharing non-PII with third parties that can be used by third parties to access PII. The FTC alleged that MySpace shared non-PII in this manner without indicating to users that the non-PII could be used by third parties to obtain PII. Hence, MySpace's statement that it does not share PII with third parties was misleading.

4. ***Violating the Privacy Policies of Others.*** Most FTC enforcement actions against companies are for violating their own privacy policies. What if a company violates the privacy policy of another company? In In re Vision I Properties (FTC 2005), Vision I Properties licensed shopping cart software and provided related services to small online retail merchants. The company's software created customizable shopping cart pages for client merchants' websites. The resulting pages resided on websites managed by Vision I Properties, but resembled the other pages on its client merchants' websites. Vision I Properties violated the privacy promises of some of these client merchants as stated in their websites; it rented consumers' personal information collected through its shopping cart software. This personal information was then used by third parties to send direct mail and make telemarketing calls to consumers. For the FTC, it was reasonable for consumers to rely on merchants' privacy policies. Moreover, Vision I Properties did not adequately inform merchants of its information sharing. Vision I settled, agreeing to cease selling the data, to provide better notice and to disgorge $9,101 of profits.

---

[69] Solove & Hartzog, *FTC and the New Common Law of Privacy, supra.*

5. ***Duties When Contracting with Data Service Providers.*** *In the Matter of GMR Transcription Services, Inc.* (FTC 2014) concerned the inadvertent disclosure of medical data by a data service provider hired by GMR, a company that provides medical transcription services. The FTC faulted GMR for its data service provider management practices. According to the FTC complaint, GMR failed to "adequately verify that their service provider, Fedtrans, implemented reasonable and appropriate security measures to protect personal information in audio and transcript files on Fedtrans' network and computers used by Fedtrans' typists."

Moreover, the FTC faulted GMR for failures in contracting with its data service provider. The FTC complaint alleged that GMR failed to "require Fedtrans by contract to adopt and implement appropriate security measures to protect personal information in medical audio and transcript files, such as by requiring that files be securely stored and securely transmitted to typists (e.g., through encryption) and authenticating typists (e.g., through unique user credentials) before granting them access to such files; take adequate measures to monitor and assess whether Fedtrans employed measures to appropriately protect personal information under the circumstances."

The FTC additionally found GMR to be deficient in doing due diligence before hiring its data service provider: "Respondents did not request or review relevant information about Fedtrans' security practices, such as, for example, Fedtrans' written information security program or audits or assessments Fedtrans may have had of its computer network."

Looking broadly at the complaint, there are three things that the FTC requires companies to do when contracting with data service providers: (1) exercise due diligence before hiring these third parties; (2) have appropriate protections of data in their contracts with data service providers; and (3) take steps to verify that the data service providers are adequately protecting data.

6. ***State Deceptive Trade Practices Acts.*** In addition to the FTC Act, which is enforced exclusively by the FTC, every state has some form of deceptive trade practices act of its own. Many of these statutes not only enable a state attorney general to bring actions but also provide a private cause of action to consumers. Several of these laws have provisions for statutory minimum damages, punitive damages, and attorneys' fees. *See, e.g.,* Cal. Civ. Code § 1780(a)(4) (punitive damages); Conn. Gen. Stat. § 42-110g(a) (punitive damages); N.Y. Gen. Bus. Law § 349(h) (minimum damages). In interpreting these state laws, many state courts have been heavily influenced by FTC Act jurisprudence. However, as Jeff Sovern notes, many states "have been more generous to consumers than has the FTC," and "even if the FTC concludes that practices pass muster under the FTC Act, it is still at least theoretically possible for a state to find the practices deceptive under their own legislation." Thus, Sovern concludes, "information practices that are currently in widespread use may indeed violate state little FTC Acts. Marketers should think carefully about whether they wish to alter their practices."[70]

---

[70] Jeff Sovern, *Protecting Privacy with Deceptive Trade Practices Legislation*, 69 Fordham L. Rev. 1305, 1352-53, 1357 (2001).

IN THE MATTER OF NOMI TECHNOLOGIES, INC.

2015 WL 5304114 (FTC Aug. 28, 2015)

COMPLAINT

3. Nomi uses mobile device tracking technology to provide analytics services to brick and mortar retailers through its "Listen" service. . . .

4. Nomi places sensors in its clients' retail locations that detect the media access control ("MAC") address broadcast by a mobile device when it searches for WiFi networks. A MAC address is a 12-digit identifier that is unique to a particular device. Alternatively, in some instances Nomi collects MAC addresses through its clients' existing WiFi access points. . . .

7. Nomi uses the information it collects to provide analytics reports to its clients about aggregate customer traffic patterns. . . .

10. Nomi does not require its clients to post disclosures or otherwise notify consumers that they use the Listen service. Through October 22, 2013, most, if not all, of Nomi's clients did not post any disclosure, or otherwise notify consumers, regarding their use of the Listen service.

11. Nomi provided, and continues to provide, an opt out on its website for consumers who do not want Nomi to store observations of their mobile device. Once a consumer has entered the MAC address of their device into Nomi's website opt out, Nomi adds it to a blacklist of MAC addresses for which information will not be stored. Nomi did not make an opt out available through any other means, including at any of its clients' retail locations.

12. From at least November 2012, until October 22, 2013, Nomi disseminated or caused to be disseminated privacy policies on its website, nomi.com or getnomi.com, which included the following statement:

> Nomi pledges to .... Always allow consumers to opt out of Nomi's service on its website as well as at any retailer using Nomi's technology. (*See* Exhibits A-C).

13. In order to opt out of the Listen service on Nomi's website, consumers were required to provide Nomi with all of their mobile devices' MAC addresses, without knowing whether they would ever shop at a retail location using the Listen service. Consumers who did not opt out on Nomi's website and instead wanted to make the opt out decision at retail locations were unable to do so, despite the explicit promise in Nomi's privacy policies. Consumers were not provided any means to opt out at retail locations and were unaware that the service was even being used.

VIOLATIONS OF THE FTC ACT

14. As described in Paragraph 12, Nomi represented, directly or indirectly, expressly or by implication, that consumers could opt out of Nomi's Listen service at retail locations using this service.

15. In fact, Nomi did not provide an opt-out mechanism at its clients' retail locations. Therefore, the representation set forth in Paragraph 14 is false or misleading.

16. As described in Paragraph 12, Nomi represented, directly or indirectly, expressly or by implication, that consumers would be given notice when a retail location was utilizing Nomi's Listen service.

17. In fact, neither Nomi nor its clients disclosed to consumers that Nomi's Listen service was being used at a retail location. Therefore, the representation set forth in Paragraph 16 is false or misleading.

18. The acts and practices of respondent as alleged in this complaint constitute unfair or deceptive acts or practices in or affecting commerce in violation of Section 5(a) of the Federal Trade Commission Act. . . .

DISSENTING STATEMENT OF COMMISSIONER MAUREEN K. OHLHAUSEN

On April 23, 2015, a divided Commission issued a complaint and accepted a proposed consent order with regard to the practices of Nomi Technologies, Inc., a startup company offering its retail merchant clients the ability to analyze aggregate data about consumer traffic in the merchants' stores. . . .

The record now before the Commission confirms that the FTC should not have adopted this complaint and order because it undermines the Commission's own goals of increased consumer choice and transparency of privacy practices and because the order imposes a penalty far out of proportion to the non-existent consumer harm.

The FTC has long called on companies to implement best practices "giving consumers greater control over the collection and use of their personal data through simplified choices and increased transparency."[4] Consistent with such best practices, Nomi went beyond its legal duty by offering increased transparency and consumer choice through an easy and effective global opt-out. Granted, part of Nomi's privacy policy was inaccurate because the company promised, but failed to implement, an additional privacy choice for consumers. However, by applying a *de facto* strict liability deception standard absent any evidence of consumer harm, the proposed complaint and order inappropriately punishes a company that acted consistently with the FTC's privacy goals by offering more transparency and choice than legally required.

The record demonstrates that this enforcement action may, ironically, undermine the FTC's own established privacy goals. Commenters generally agree that the order will diminish companies' incentives to be transparent about their privacy practices. . . .

I share one commenter's particular concern that "the takeaway for most companies will be: if you do not want the FTC to come after you, do the bare-minimum on privacy." . . . Another pointed out that "[t]he ironic upshot of the majority decision is that Nomi could have avoided the FTC enforcement action altogether by not posting a privacy policy, not describing its practices to consumers, and not offering an opt-out mechanism at all."[1] Indeed, upon learning of the Commission's investigation, Nomi simply eliminated a potential privacy choice from its privacy policy. . . .

I conclude that the comments on the record and the marketplace reaction to the complaint and order provide additional persuasive evidence that the costs of this enforcement action outweigh the benefits. The Commission therefore ought to vacate the proposed complaint and consent order. Because the majority declines to do so, I dissent.

DISSENTING STATEMENT OF COMMISSIONER JOSHUA WRIGHT

Nomi does *not* track individual consumers—that is, Nomi's technology records whether individuals are unique or repeat visitors, but it does not identify them. Nomi provides analytics services based upon data collected from mobile device tracking technology to brick-and-mortar retailers through its "Listen" service. ...

The Commission's complain focuses upon a single statement in Nomi's privacy policy. Specifically, Nomi's privacy policy states that "Nomi pledges to ... Always allow consumers to opt out of Nomi's service on its websites as well as at any retailer using Nomi's technology." ...

The fundamental failure of the Commission's complaint is that the evidence simply does not support the allegation that Nomi's representation about an opportunity to opt out of the Listen service at the retail level – in light of the immediate and easily accessible opt out available on the webpage itself – was material to consumers. This failure alone is fatal. ... Deception causes consumer harm because it influences consumer behavior – that is, the deceptive statement is one that is not merely misleading in the abstract but one that causes consumers to make choices to their detriment that they would not have otherwise made.

STATEMENT OF COMMISSIONER JULIE BRILL

I vote to finalize the Nomi case, for the reasons articulated in the Majority Statement.

In her dissent, Commissioner Ohlhausen expresses concern that our order will deter companies from offering privacy choices in the marketplace. I agree that, in approving our orders, we should always consider whether they provide the appropriate marketplace incentives. I believe this order provides companies with an incentive to periodically review the statements they make to consumers, and make sure their practices line up with those statements. In this case, we took issue with the fact that Nomi offered a deceptive choice to consumers for nearly a year. Our order today makes sure that this doesn't happen again. In addition, the concern that our order will deter companies from offering choices is belied by the fact that, like many of its competitors in retail mobile location tracking, Nomi continues to offer an online choice to consumers to opt-out of retail mobile tracking. However, as a result of our order, the company no longer offers a deceptive choice.

NOTES & QUESTIONS

1. ***Penalized for Providing Privacy Beyond Legal Requirements?*** Commissioner Ohlhausen argues that the FTC action against Nomi penalizes it for offering opt out rights to individuals when it is not forced to do so. She notes that Nomi could simply have not made such a promise to individuals. Commissioner Brill implies that Nomi's decision to offer choices to consumers might be a

competitive business decision. Whom do you think has the better argument? If companies are not held accountable for their promises to provide privacy choices or protections beyond the minimum required, then would people trust such promises? Should it matter whether or not privacy promises are being made by a company to obtain a competitive advantage?

F. STATUTORY REGULATION

Numerous statutes are directly and potentially applicable to the collection, use, and transfer of personal information by commercial entities. Congress's approach is best described as "sectoral," as each statute is narrowly tailored to particular types of businesses and services. The opposite of sectoral in this context is omnibus, and the United States lacks such a comprehensive statute regulating the private sector's collection and use of personal information. Such omnibus statutes are standard in much of the rest of the world. All member nations of the European Union have enacted omnibus information privacy laws.

In the United States, sectoral laws also do not regulate all commercial entities in their collection and use of personal information. Thus far, federal statutes regulate three basic areas: (a) entertainment records (video and cable television); (b) Internet use and electronic communications; and (c) marketing (telemarketing and spam). As you examine the existing statutes, think about the kinds of commercial entities that the law does not currently regulate. Consider whether these entities should be regulated. Also consider whether one omnibus privacy law can adequately apply to all commercial entities. Would the differences between types of commercial entities make a one-size-fits-all privacy law impractical?

The sectoral statutes embody the Fair Information Practices originally developed by HEW and incorporated into the Privacy Act. However, not all statutes embody all of the Fair Information Practices. As you study each statute, examine which of the Fair Information Practices are required by each statute and which are not.

1. ENTERTAINMENT RECORDS

(a) The Video Privacy Protection Act

Incensed when a reporter obtained a list of videos that Supreme Court Justice Nominee Robert Bork and his family had rented from a video store, Congress passed the Video Privacy Protection Act (VPPA) of 1988, Pub. L. No. 100-618. The VPPA is also known as the "Bork Bill."

Scope. The VPPA is written in technology-neutral terms. It defines a "video tape service provider" as "any person engaged in the business, in or affecting interstate or foreign commerce, of rental, sale, or delivery of prerecorded video cassette tapes or similar audio visual materials. . . ." § 2710(a)(4). This statutory language allows the VPPA to extend to DVDs (as opposed to video cassette tapes) and also covers online delivery of movies and other content.

Opt in for Disclosure. The VPPA prohibits videotape service providers from knowingly disclosing personal information, such as titles of videocassettes rented or purchased, without the individual's written consent.

Online providers of video content lobbied Congress, contending that VPPA's opt-in requirement prevented them from integrating into Facebook. They complained that VPPA required consent before each instance where video preferences were shared on social networks. They wanted a single consent to the practice of displaying video "likes" rather than a requirement of consent for each video.

In 2012, Congress passed the Video Privacy Protection Act Amendments Act, which was signed into law in early 2013. These amendments make it easier to obtain consent. Now, consumers can consent via electronic means. Additionally, consent can be obtained in advance for a period of two years. People can later withdraw consent if they choose. A videotape service provider must provide an opportunity "in a clear and conspicuous manner, for the consumer to withdraw on a case-by-case basis or to withdraw from ongoing disclosures, at the consumer's election."

Exceptions Allowing Disclosure Without Consent. The VPPA contains several exceptions, permitting videotape providers to disclose "to any person if the disclosure is incident to the ordinary course of business of the video tape service provider." § 2710(b)(2)(E).

The statute provides that "the subject matter of such materials may be disclosed if the disclosure is for the exclusive use of marketing goods and services directly to the consumer." § 2710(b)(2)(D)(ii). Videotape service providers can disclose the names and addresses of consumers if the consumer has been given the right to opt out, and the disclosure does not identify information about the videos the consumer rents. § 2710(b)(2)(D).

The statute also permits disclosure to the consumer, § 2710(b)(2)(A); disclosure with the informed written consent of the consumer, § 2710(b)(2)(B); disclosure to a law enforcement agency pursuant to a warrant or subpoena, § 2710(b)(2)(C); and disclosure for civil discovery if there is notice and an opportunity to object, § 2710(b)(2).

Destruction of Records. The VPPA requires that records of personal information be destroyed as soon as practicable. § 2710(e).

Preemption. The VPPA does not block states from enacting statutes that are more protective of privacy. § 2710(f).

Enforcement. The VPPA creates a private cause of action when a videotape service provider "knowingly discloses . . . personally identifiable information concerning any consumer of such provider." 18 U.S.C. § 2710(b)(1). The VPPA permits recovery of actual damages and provides for liquidated damages in the amount of $2,500. The Act also authorizes recovery for punitive damages, attorneys' fees, and enables equitable and injunctive relief. § 2710(c). The VPPA also includes a statutory exclusionary rule that prevents the admission into evidence of any information obtained in violation of the statute. § 2710(d).

VPPA damages are only available for unauthorized disclosures, not failure to meet other requirements of the act such as the destruction of records. In *Sterk v. Redbox Automated Retail LLC*, 672 F.3d 535 (2012), the court rejected a plaintiff's lawsuit for failure to destroy plaintiff's records in a timely manner, concluding that "[u]nlawful disclosure is the only misconduct listed in the statute for which an award of damages is an appropriate remedy."

NOTES & QUESTIONS

1. *Netflix and Frictionless Sharing.* William McGeveran criticizes the Video Privacy Protection Act Amendments Act, which permits Netflix and other online video service providers to obtain a broad ongoing consent from consumers to display the videos they like on Facebook and other social media sites. According to McGeveran, the former VPPA requirement that users must provide consent for each and every disclosure of videos they watch created a type of "friction" on sharing information. The change to VPPA makes sharing videos more "frictionless."[71] McGeveran warns that frictionless sharing interfaces can be "badly designed" leading to misdisclosures and a lack of clear notice to consumers. People can readily forget that their actions are being broadcast and might end up disclosing things they did not want to disclose. McGeveran suggests that friction can be a good thing and should not be removed entirely from sharing. He suggests one way that friction could be added:

   > Netflix could simply put a "PLAY AND SHARE" button next to the "PLAY" button that viewers already must click to stream any video. An interface would not satisfy this law of friction if it required more effort for customers to start viewing a movie than to inform all their Facebook friends what they are watching.

   To what extent should the law mandate that friction be included in the design of online sharing technologies?

2. *Private Right of Action vs. Agency Enforcement.* The VPPA is enforced by a private right of action. Other privacy laws are enforced by agencies, such as HIPAA which is enforced by HHS and COPPA which is enforced by the FTC. Should VPPA have been written to not include a private right of action and be enforced by the FTC instead? Is a private right of action a better or worse method of enforcement than agency enforcement? If the answer depends upon specific contexts and types of data, what factors should be considered in evaluating the desirability of having a private right of action?

3. *The Narrow Focus of VPPA.* The VPPA was passed in reaction to an attempt to obtain data on what videos Judge Bork watched. The law has been criticized for being too specifically focused on videos and ignoring other forms of media, such as books, magazines, and music. Should VPPA be expanded to cover such things? What about the Internet sites one visits? Or other merchandise one buys,

---

[71] William McGeveran, *The Law of Friction*, 2013 U. Chi. Legal F. 15, 18.

including food, furniture, cars, etc.? Is there a reasonable limiting principle that would limit such an expanded law's scope?

DANIEL V. CANTELL

375 F.3d 377 (6th Cir. 2004)

CUDAHY, J. The plaintiff, Alden Joe Daniel, Jr. (Daniel) was charged with and eventually pleaded guilty to the sexual molestation of three underage girls. Allegedly, part of his *modus operandi* was showing pornographic movies to the underage girls. . . . Therefore, as part of the criminal investigation into his conduct, law enforcement officials sought and were able to obtain his video rental records. . . .

Daniel brings this suit against (1) various police officers, attorneys, and the parents of one of Daniel's victims, as well as (2) the employees and owners of two video stores where Daniel rented pornographic videos. There is no dispute that the defendants making up this second category are proper parties under the Act. The only question which we must answer is whether the defendants not associated with the video stores are proper parties under the Act. We believe that based on the plain language of the Act, this first group of defendants are *not* proper parties. . . .

Section (b) provides that "[a] *video tape service provider* who knowingly discloses, to any person, personally identifiable information concerning any consumer of such provider shall be liable to the aggrieved person for the relief provided in subsection (d)." 18 U.S.C. § 2710(b)(1) (emphasis added). Therefore, under the plain language of the statute, only a "video tape service provider" (VTSP) can be liable. The term VTSP is defined by the statute to mean "any person, engaged in the business, in or affecting interstate or foreign commerce, of rental, sale, or delivery of prerecorded video cassette tapes or similar audio video materials, or any person or other entity to whom a disclosure is made under subparagraph (D) or (E) of subsection (b)(2), but only with respect to the information contained in the disclosure." *Id.* at § 2710(a)(4). Daniel does not allege that the defendants in question are engaged in the business of rental, sale or delivery of prerecorded video cassette tapes. Therefore, the defendants may only be VTSPs if personal information was disclosed to them under subparagraph (D) or (E) of subsection (b)(2).

Subparagraph (D) applies "if the disclosure is solely the names and addresses of consumers." *Id.* at § 2710(b)(2)(D). Moreover, disclosure under subparagraph (D) must be "for the exclusive use of marketing goods and services directly to the consumer." *Id.* at § 2710(b)(2)(D)(ii). For instance, if a video store provided the names and addresses of its patrons to a movie magazine publisher, the publisher would be considered a VTSP, but only with respect to the information contained in the disclosure. No disclosure in this case was made under subparagraph (D). The information provided was not limited to Daniel's name and address. Instead, the disclosure was of Daniel's history of renting pornographic videotapes and included the specific titles of those videos. Additionally, the disclosure was not for marketing purposes but for purposes of a criminal investigation. Therefore, subparagraph (D) is inapplicable in this case.

Daniel properly does not argue that the disclosure falls within subparagraph (E). . . . Subparagraph (E) applies only to disclosures made "incident to the ordinary course of business" of the VTSP. *Id.* at § 2710(b)(2)(E). The term "ordinary course of business" is "narrowly defined" in the statute to mean "only debt collection activities, order fulfillment, request processing, and the transfer of ownership." *Id.* at § 2710(a)(2) . . . In sum, because Daniel has presented no evidence suggesting that a disclosure was made under subparagraph (D) or (E) in this case, the non-video store defendants are not VTSPs under the Act and therefore, are not proper parties to this litigation.

Daniel argues, however, that any person, not just a VTSP, can be liable under the Act based on *Dirkes v. Borough of Runnemede,* 936 F. Supp. 235 (D.N.J. 1996). *Dirkes* did reach this conclusion but only by misreading the Act. The court in *Dirkes* was focused on language in the Act stating that "[a]ny person aggrieved by any act of *a person* in violation of this section may bring a civil action in the United States district court." 18 U.S.C. § 2710(c)(1) (emphasis added). Because the statute states that a suit can be based upon an act of "a person" rather than an act of "a VTSP," *Dirkes* found that any person can be liable under the Act. *Dirkes*, however, ignored the rest of the sentence. A lawsuit under the Act must be based on an "act of a person *in violation of this section.* . . ." 18 U.S.C. § 2710(c)(1) (emphasis added). The statute makes it clear that only a VTSP can be in violation of section 2710(b). *See* § 2710(b)(1) ("A video tape service provider who knowingly discloses . . . personally identifiable information . . . shall be liable. . . ."). Moreover, if any person could be liable under the Act, there would be no need for the Act to define a VTSP in the first place. More tellingly, if any person could be liable under the Act, there is no reason that the definition of a VTSP would be limited to "any person . . . to whom a disclosure is made under subparagraph (D) or (E) of subsection (b)(2)." *Dirkes* would have us ignore this limitation and find that any person can be liable under the Act whether or not a disclosure was made to him under subparagraph (D) or (E). We avoid interpretations of a statute which would render portions of it superfluous.

The court in *Dirkes* found otherwise because the "clear intent of the Act," as demonstrated by its legislative history, "is to prevent the disclosure of private information." Where the plain language of a statute is clear, however, we do not consult the legislative history. . . . In any case, our interpretation of the statute — that only a VTSP can be liable under § 2710(b) — does not conflict with Congress' purpose in adopting the Act. One can "prevent the disclosure of private information" simply by cutting off disclosure at its source, i.e., the VTSP. Just because Congress' goal was to prevent the disclosure of private information, does not mean that Congress intended the implementation of every conceivable method of preventing disclosures. Printing all personal information in hieroglyphics instead of English would also help prevent the disclosure of such information. However, nothing in the legislative history suggests that Congress was encouraging hieroglyphics and, similarly, nothing suggests that Congress intended that anyone other than VTSPs would be liable under the Act. In sum, the Act is clear that only a VTSP can be liable under § 2710(b). Because the non-video store defendants do not fit within the definition of a VTSP, they are not proper parties.

NOTES & QUESTIONS

1. *To Whom Does VPPA Apply?* The key question in *Dirkes* and *Daniel* is whether the VPPA *only* regulates videotape service providers. The *Daniel* court answered this question affirmatively; the *Dirkes* court would apply the VPPA to additional parties, including law enforcement officers. Which interpretation of the statutory language do you find most convincing? Would policy reasons support a broader or narrower application of the statute?

2. *Facebook, Beacon, Blockbuster, and a VPPA Violation?* In April 2008, Cathryn Elain Harris filed a lawsuit against Blockbuster Video (a video tape service provider) and Facebook claiming violations of the VPPA. The complaint objected to Blockbuster reporting its customers' activities to Facebook through the Beacon program.

   Facebook introduced Beacon in November 2007; under it, partner companies shared information with Facebook about Facebook user activity that took place on their websites. Initially, this information became part of one's Facebook profile unless the user opted out. After consumer protest, Facebook changed its policy to require that a Facebook user would have to opt in to Beacon before information was disclosed on her Facebook page. It is not clear, however, whether opting out of Beacon stops partner companies from sharing information with Facebook.

   The Harris complaint alleges that Blockbuster's website is still reporting a user's activities back to Facebook, whether or not the consumer opts out of having the information associated with her Facebook profile. Does the Blockbuster-Beacon-Facebook behavior, if as alleged, violate the VPPA? If so, what measure of damages should be used?

IN RE HULU PRIVACY LITIGATION

2012 WL 3282960 (N.D. Cal. 2012)

BEELER, MAGISTRATE J. . . . In this putative class action, viewers of Hulu's on-line video content allege that Hulu wrongfully disclosed their video viewing selections and personal identification information to third parties such as online ad networks, metrics companies (meaning, companies that track data), and social networks, in violation of the Video Privacy Protection Act, 18 U.S.C. § 2710. . . .

Defendant Hulu moves to dismiss the claim under Federal Rule of Civil Procedure 12(b)(1). . . .

Hulu operates a website called Hulu.com that provides video content, both previously released and posted and originally developed. . . .

Plaintiffs and Class Members used their Internet-connected computers and browsers to visit hulu.com and view video content. They were renters, purchasers, and/or subscribers of goods and/or services from Hulu and so were consumers as defined in the Video Privacy Protection Act. . . .

Plaintiffs value their privacy while web-browsing; they do not want to be tracked online; their web browsing (including their viewing choices) involves personal information that is private. . . .

Hulu allowed a metrics company called KISSmetrics to place code containing tracking identifiers on Plaintiffs' computers in the browser cache, Adobe Flash local storage, or DOM local storage. This code allegedly "respawned" or "resurrected" previously-deleted cookies. This code was "inescapable" and allowed Plaintiffs' data to be "retained ... so that they could be tracked over long periods of time and across multiple websites, regardless of whether they were registered and logged in." As a result, when Class Members viewed video content on Hulu.com, Hulu transmitted their video viewing choices and personally identifiable information to third parties without obtaining their written consent before the disclosure. The third parties included online ad networks, metrics companies, and social networks such as Scorecard Research ("Scorecard") (an online market research company), Facebook (the online social network), DoubleClick (an online ad network), Google Analytics (an online web analytics company), and QuantCast (an online ad network and web analytics company).

The information transmitted to Scorecard and Facebook included information that identified Plaintiffs and Class Members personally. As to Facebook, Hulu included their Facebook IDs, connecting the video content information to Facebook's personally identifiable user registration information. As to Scorecard, Hulu provided Plaintiffs' "Hulu profile identifiers" linked to their "individual Hulu profile pages that included name, location, preference information designated by the user as private, and Hulu username (which, in the case of many individuals, is the same screen name used in other online environments.)" . . . .

Plaintiffs allege that Hulu "knowingly and without . . . [their] consent disclosed to third parties . . . [their] video viewing selections and personally identifiable information, knowing that such disclosure included the disclosure of [their] personally identifying information . . . and their requests for and/or obtaining of specific video materials and/or services from Hulu," in violation of the Video Privacy Protection Act ("VPPA"), 18 U.S.C. § 2710(b)(1).

The Act prohibits a "video tape service provider" from (1) knowingly disclosing to any person (2) personally identifiable information concerning any consumer of such provider (3) except for certain disclosures—such as to the consumer or law enforcement—allowed under section 2710(b)(2). 18 U.S.C. § 2710. "'Personally identifiable information' includes information which identifies a person as having requested or obtained specific video materials or services." Such disclosures are not prohibited if they are "incident to the ordinary course of business" of the video tape service provider. The VPPA defines "ordinary course of business" as "debt collection activities, order fulfillment, request processing, and the transfer of ownership."

The VPPA defines "video tape service provider" as "any person, engaged in the business, in or affecting interstate or foreign commerce, of rental, sale, or delivery of prerecorded video cassette tapes or similar audio visual materials."18 U.S.C. § 2710(a)(4).

Hulu does not deal in prerecorded video cassette tapes. Thus, whether Hulu is a "video tape service providers" turns on the scope of the phrase "similar audio visual materials."

Citing dictionary definitions, Hulu contends that "materials" are things "composed of physical matter." . . . As drafted, Hulu contends, the VPPA "only regulates businesses that sell or rent physical objects (i.e., 'video cassettes or other similar audio visual materials') . . . and not businesses that transmit digital content over the Internet." . . . Had Congress wanted to regulate businesses dealing in digital content, it would have defined "video tape service provider" to include businesses that "traffic in audio-visual information or data."

To this reader, a plain reading of a statute that covers videotapes and "similar audio visual materials" is about the video content, not about how that content was delivered (e.g. via the Internet or a bricks-and-mortar store). Still, the online streaming mechanism of delivery here did not exist when Congress enacted the statute in 1988. A dictionary definition helps some. The undersigned looked at the third edition of Oxford English Dictionary, which defines "material" both as "relating to substance" and as "Text or images in printed or electronic form; also with distinguishing word, as reading material, etc." . . .

Also, the Senate Report confirms that Congress was concerned with protecting the confidentiality of private information about viewing preferences regardless of the business model or media format involved. . . .

The court concludes that Congress used "similar audio video materials" to ensure that VPAA's protections would retain their force even as technologies evolve. . . .

The court denies Hulu's motion to dismiss.

IN RE HULU PRIVACY LITIGATION

2014 WL 1724344 (N.D. Cal. 2014)

BEELER, MAGISTRATE J. . . . In this putative class action, viewers of Hulu's on-line video content allege that Hulu wrongfully disclosed their video viewing selections and personal identification information to third parties such as metrics companies (meaning, companies that track data) and social networks, in violation of the Video Privacy Protection Act ("VPPA"), 18 U.S.C. § 2710. . . .

The Act prohibits a "video tape service provider" from knowingly disclosing "personally identifiable information of a consumer of the provider" to third parties except under identified exceptions that do not apply here. See 18 U.S.C. § 2710. "The term 'personally identifiable information' includes information that identifies a person as having requested or obtained specific video materials or services from a video tape service provider." Id. § 2710(a)(3).

Hulu argues that it did not violate the VPPA because (I) it disclosed only anonymous user IDs and never linked the user IDs to identifying data such as a person's name or address; (II) it did not disclose the information "knowingly" and thus is not liable. . . .

The issue is whether Hulu's disclosures here (unique numeric identifications tied to video watching) are PII under the VPPA. The statute's plain language prohibits disclosure of information that "identifies a person" as having (in the Hulu context) viewed specific video content. 28 U.S.C. § 2710(a)(3). It does not say "identify by name" and thus plainly encompasses other means of identifying a person. Indeed, PII is not given one definition: "the term . . . includes information which identifies a person." . . .

The plain language of the statute suggests, and the Senate Report confirms, that the statute protects personally identifiable information that identifies a specific person and ties that person to particular videos that the person watched.

The issue then is whether the disclosures here are merely an anonymized ID or whether they are closer to linking identified persons to the videos they watched.

[Hulu made three types of disclosures: (1) video names and Hulu user ID numbers to comScore; (2) a unique ID number for each user created specifically for comScore's use; and (3) user IP addresses and cookies with a user's Facebook ID to Facebook, along with URL web addresses with video names in them.] . . .

Hulu . . . argues that the disclosure has to be the person's actual name. That position paints too bright a line. One could not skirt liability under the VPPA, for example, by disclosing a unique identifier and a correlated look-up table. The statute does not require a name. It defines PII as a term that "includes information which identifies a person." The legislative history shows Congress used the word "includes" when it defined PII to establish a minimum, but not exclusive, definition. It is information that "identifies a particular person as having engaged in a specific transaction with a video tape service provider" by retaining or obtaining specific video materials or services. It does not require identification by a name necessarily. One can be identified in many ways: by a picture, by pointing, by an employee number, by the station or office or cubicle where one works, by telling someone what "that person" rented. In sum, the statute, the legislative history, and the case law do not require a name, instead require the identification of a specific person tied to a specific transaction, and support the conclusion that a unique anonymized ID alone is not PII but context could render it not anonymous and the equivalent of the identification of a specific person. . . .

Hulu's liability here is based on the hypothetical that comScore could use the Hulu ID to access the Hulu user's profile page to obtain the user's name. Hulu characterizes this argument as "reverse engineering" its data. The idea is that comScore could capture the data from the watch page, extract the relevant information (the video name and Hulu User ID), and plug the data into the standard-format URL for the profile page to capture the user's name from that page. There is no evidence that comScore did this. The issue is only that it could. . . .

. . . [The evidence] does not suggest any linking of a specific, identified person and his video habits. The court grants summary judgment in Hulu's favor on this theory. . . .

[Regarding the Facebook disclosures,] Hulu argues that it never sent the "actual" name of any Facebook user. Instead, the name came from the user's web browser and the interaction that Facebook had with its users. . . .

It may be true—as Hulu says—that accessing a remote browser involves sending that browser's cookies. But according to Plaintiffs' expert, it was straightforward to develop a webpage that would not communicate information to Facebook. Put another way, it was not necessary to send the "Facebook user" cookies, and they were sent because Hulu chose to include the Like button on watch pages. . . .

Hulu argues that it needed to send an actual name to be liable and that it sent only cookies. The statute does not require an actual name and requires only something akin to it. If the cookies contained a Facebook ID, they could show the Hulu user's identity on Facebook. . . .

Hulu also argues that there is no evidence that Facebook took any actions with the cookies after receiving them. It also says that there is no evidence that Facebook tied its Facebook user cookies to the URL for the watch page (and the accompanying title). In contrast to comScore, where the user was not tied to the video in one transmission, the transmission to Facebook included the video name and Facebook user cookies. Thus, the link between user and video was more obvious. But Hulu's point is that the information really was not disclosed to Facebook in the sense that the information about Judge Bork's video viewing was disclosed to the Washington Post.

Whether this link was the equivalent of a disclosure under the VPPA depends on the facts. One can think of analogies in a paper world. Throwing Judge Bork's video watch list in the recycle bin is not a disclosure. Throwing it in the bin knowing that the Washington Post searches your bin every evening for intelligence about local luminaries might be. The issue is whether Hulu made a "knowing" disclosure.

The statute requires a "knowing" disclosure "to any person." See 18 U.S.C. § 2710(b)(1). The emphasis is on disclosure, not comprehension by the receiving person. Thus, the Seventh Circuit held that the practice of placing PII on parking tickets in the view of the public was a disclosure that violated the analogous Driver's Privacy Protection Act, regardless of whether anyone viewed the PII. *See Senne v. Village of Palatine Ill.*, 695 F.3d 597 (7th Cir.2012) (en banc). By analogy, if a video store knowingly hands a list of Judge Bork's rented videos to a Washington Post reporter, it arguably violates the VPPA even if the reporter does not look at the list. . . .

. . . [A]rguing that transmitting cookies is just the normal way that webpages and the Like button load is not enough to negate knowledge or show the absence of evidence about knowledge. . . .

The court denies Hulu's summary judgment motion regarding the disclosures to Facebook. . . .

NOTES & QUESTIONS

1. *What Is a "Video Tape Service Provider"?* The court holds that Hulu is a videotape service provider, even though the statutory language refers to videotapes and was written in 1994, long before online streaming video. Should the phrase "rental, sale, or delivery of prerecorded video cassette tapes or similar audio visual materials" be interpreted broadly as the court interprets it?

2. *What Is PII?* The second opinion excerpted above involves what constitutes personally identifiable information (PII) under the VPPA. The court recognizes that the VPPA does not require actual names in order for a disclosure to be of PII — disclosing an ID could be the "equivalent to the identification of a specific person" depending upon the context. However, the court grants summary judgment to Hulu regarding the comScore disclosure because of a lack of evidence comScore was re-identifying the data by linking the ID to a

person's name. Why is sending the cookies to Facebook different? The court writes:

> Hulu also argues that there is no evidence that Facebook took any actions with the cookies after receiving them. It also says that there is no evidence that Facebook tied its Facebook user cookies to the URL for the watch page (and the accompanying title). In contrast to comScore, where the user was not tied to the video in one transmission, the transmission to Facebook included the video name and Facebook user cookies. Thus, the link between user and video was more obvious.

Do you agree with this distinction? In dismissing comScore, the court also focused on the lack of actions comScore took after receiving the ID information. The court noted that "if a video store knowingly hands a list of Judge Bork's rented videos to a Washington Post reporter, it arguably violates the VPPA even if the reporter does not look at the list." Suppose a video store hands a list of rented videos to a *Washington Post* reporter with a unique ID number of the customer on the list. The *Washington Post* reporter can readily look up the unique ID number to figure out who the individual is. Why is the reporter who does not look at the list treated differently from the reporter who does not look up the unique ID number?

(b) The Cable Communications Policy Act

In 1984, Congress passed the Cable Communications Policy Act (CCPA or "Cable Act"), Pub. L. No. 98-549. The Act applies to cable operators and service providers. 47 U.S.C. § 551(a)(1).

Notice and Access. The Cable Act requires cable service providers to notify subscribers (in a written privacy policy) of the nature and uses of personal information collected. § 551(a)(1). Subscribers must have access to their personal data held by cable operators. § 551(d).

Limitations on Data Collection. Cable operators "shall not use the cable system to collect personally identifiable information concerning any subscriber without the prior written or electronic consent of the subscriber concerned." § 551(b)(1).

Limitations on Data Disclosure. Cable operators cannot disclose personally identifiable information about any subscriber without the subscriber's consent:

> [A] cable operator shall not disclose personally identifiable information concerning any subscriber without the prior written or electronic consent of the subscriber concerned and shall take such actions as are necessary to prevent unauthorized access to such information by a person other than the subscriber or cable operator. § 551(c)(1).

However, cable operators can disclose personal data under certain circumstances, such as when necessary for a "legitimate business activity" or pursuant to a court order if the subscriber is notified. Cable operators may disclose subscriber names and addresses if "the cable operator has provided the subscriber the opportunity to prohibit or limit such disclosure." § 551(c)(2).

Data Destruction. Cable operators must destroy personal data if the information is no longer necessary for the purpose for which it was collected. § 551(e).

Government Access to Cable Information. Pursuant to § 551(h):

> A governmental entity may obtain personally identifiable information concerning a cable subscriber pursuant to a court order only if, in the court proceeding relevant to such court order —
>
>> (1) such entity offers clear and convincing evidence that the subject of the information is reasonably suspected of engaging in criminal activity and that the information sought would be material evidence in the case; and
>> (2) the subject of the information is afforded the opportunity to appear and contest such entity's claim.

Note that a court order to obtain cable records requires "clear and convincing evidence," a standard higher than probable cause. There is no exclusionary rule for information obtained in violation of the Cable Act.

Enforcement. The Cable Act provides for a private cause of action and actual damages, with a minimum of $1,000 or $100 for each day of the violation, whichever is higher. The plaintiff can collect any actual damages that are more than the statutory minimum. Further, the Cable Act provides for punitive damages and attorneys' fees. § 551(f).

Cable Internet Service. Section 211 of the USA PATRIOT Act amended the Cable Act, 47 U.S.C. § 551(c)(2)(D), to provide disclosure to a government entity under federal wiretap law when the government seeks information from cable companies except that "such disclosure shall not include records revealing cable subscriber selection of video programming from a cable operator." This provision of the PATRIOT Act will not sunset.

New Cable Services and Products? In March 2011, the *Wall Street Journal* reported on the testing by cable companies of new systems that are designed to show households highly targeted ads.[72] The goal is to "emulate the sophisticated tracking widely used on people's personal computers with new technology that reaches the living room." In one test of Cablevision's technology, for example, the U.S. Army used it to target four different recruitment ads to different categories of viewers. In many of these systems, companies generally seek to remove personal data, including names, before data is sent to third party companies who match ads to households.

In August 2014, the *Washington Post* predicted that the cable industry was about to start serving targeted ads on a large scale. It discussed how a cable-owned service, called NBCU+, was planning to combine cable subscriber information

---

[72] Jessica E. Vascellaro, *TV's Next Wave: Tuning into You*, Wall St. J., Mar. 7, 2011.

with data from other sources, "such as loyalty card purchases, box office sales, and even car registrations."[73] The plan was said likely to involve purchasing data from data brokers, such as Acxiom and Experian.

Does these practices comport with the Cable Act?

2. INTERNET USE AND ELECTRONIC COMMUNICATIONS

(a) The Children's Online Privacy Protection Act

Passed in 1998, the Children's Online Privacy Protection Act (COPPA), Pub. L. No. 106-170, 15 U.S.C. §§ 6501–6506, regulates the collection and use of children's information by Internet websites. In January 2013, the FTC issued an important amendment to its COPPA Rule, which it included in a complete re-issued Final COPPA Rule. 16 C.F.R. Part 312. These Rules took effect in July 2013.

Scope. COPPA applies to "an operator of a website or online service directed to children, or any operator that has actual knowledge that it is collecting personal information from a child." 15 U.S.C. § 6502(a)(1). COPPA only applies to websites that collect personal information from children under age 13. § 6502(1). COPPA does not apply to information collected from adults about children under 13; it only applies to personal data collected *from* children themselves.

Personal Information. In 2013, the FTC clarified that "personal information" under COPPA includes a voice, audio, image file containing a child's voice and/or image; geolocation data that reveals a street name plus city, or equally revealing information; online contact information such as a screen name or user name, persistent identifiers that recognize users across time and sites or services, such as an IP address or device serial number. COPPA Final Rule, 78 Fed. Reg. 3971 (Jan. 17, 2013), 16 C.F.R. § 312.

Collection of Personal Information. The "collection" of personal information is defined broadly. It means "the gathering of any personal information from a child by any means, including but not limited to: (1) Requesting, prompting, or encouraging a child to submit personal information online; (2) Enabling a child to make personal information publicly available in identifiable form." 16 C.F.R. § 312.2.

Notice. Children's websites must post privacy policies, describing "what information is collected from children by the operator, how the operator uses such information, and the operator's disclosure practices for such information." § 6502(b)(1)(A)(i).

---

[73] Brian Fung, *Blogs: The Switch, Targeted Ads Are About to Take Over Your TV*, Wash. Post (Jan. 31, 2014).

Consent. Children's websites must "obtain verifiable parental consent for the collection, use or disclosure of personal information from children." § 6502(b)(1)(A)(ii). Websites cannot condition child's participation in a game or receipt of a prize on the disclosure of more personal information than is necessary to participate in that activity. § 6502(b)(1)(C). When information is not maintained in retrievable form, then consent is not required. § 6502(b)(2).

Right to Restrict Uses of Personal Information. If parent requests it, the operator must provide to the parent a description of the "specific types of personal information collected," the right to "refuse to permit the operator's further use or maintenance in retrievable form, or future online collection, of personal information from that child," and the right to "obtain any personal information collected from the child." § 6502(b)(1)(B).

Liability When Sites Operate in Connection with Third Parties. As of the 2013 rule change, both hosts of sites and third parties operating through sites are subject to enforcement under COPPA. Hosts regulated by COPPA are strictly liable for the activities of third parties operating on their site if the third party is an agent of the regulated service or the primary regulated service receives a benefit from a third party. The third party is liable if it has "actual knowledge" that the host site is directed to children. For example, a website using ads from an ad network is strictly liable for information collected by the ad network. The ad network would be liable if it has actual knowledge that the website is directed to children. *See* COPPA Final Rule, 16 § C.F.R. 312.

Enforcement. Violations of COPPA are "treated as a violation of a rule defining an unfair or deceptive act or practice" under 15 U.S.C. § 57a(a)(1)(B). Thus, the FTC enforces the law and can impose fines up to $16,000 per violation. The amount of the fine depends upon a number of factors including "the egregiousness of the violations, whether the operator has previously violated the Rule, the number of children involved, the amount and type of personal information collected, how the information was used, whether it was shared with third parties, and the size of the company."[74]

There is no private cause of action for violations of COPPA. States can bring civil actions for violations of COPPA in the interests of its citizens to obtain injunctions and damages. § 6504.

Preemption. COPPA preempts state law. § 6502(d).

Safe Harbor. If an operator follows self-regulatory guidelines issued by marketing or online industry groups that are approved by the FTC, then the COPPA requirements will be deemed satisfied. § 6503.

Should COPPA be extended to apply to everyone, not just children? Should there be a private cause of action under COPPA? Note that COPPA only applies

---

[74] FTC, *Complying with COPPA: Frequently Asked Questions* (July 16, 2014), http://www.business.ftc.gov/documents/0493-Complying-with-COPPA-Frequently-Asked-Questions.

when a website has "actual knowledge" that a user is under 13 or operates a website specifically targeted to children. Is this too limiting? Would a rule dispensing with the "actual knowledge" requirement be feasible?[75]

UNITED STATES V. PATH, INC.

2012 WL 7006381 (N.D. Cal. 2012)

COMPLAINT

Plaintiff, the United States of America, acting upon notification and authorization to the Attorney General by the Federal Trade Commission ("FTC" or "Commission"), for its Complaint alleges:

1. Plaintiff brings this action under . . . the Children's Online Privacy Protection Act of 1998 ("COPPA") . . .

7. Defendant Path, Inc. ("Path") . . . develops, markets, distributes, or sells software applications for mobile devices to consumers throughout the U.S. and provides online services to users of its applications. From at least 2010, Defendant has operated a social networking online service that is accessible worldwide on the Internet through a website and mobile applications. . . .

10. Defendant describes its social networking service as "the smart journal that helps you share life with the ones you love," and allows users to keep a journal about "moments" in the user's life and to share that journal with a network of up to 150 persons. Through the Path App, the user can upload, store and share photos, written "thoughts," the user's location, and the names of songs to which the user is listening. On the "About" page of its website, Defendant describes its "Values" and espouses that "Path should be private by default. Forever. You should always be in control of your information and experience."

11. At all times relevant to this Complaint, when a user registers for Defendant's social networking service, the user must provide an email address, a first name, and a last name. The user's email address serves as his or her login identity. At registration, the user is also invited to provide gender, phone number, and date of birth. The Path App for iOS has been downloaded and installed over 2.5 million times. . . .

20. In addition to its Path App for iOS, Defendant's social networking service is also accessible through a Path App for Google, Inc.'s Android operating system, and, until December 2011, through Defendant's website, path.com. The Path App for iOS, the Path App for Android, and the Defendant's website were all intended for a general audience, but also attracted a significant number of children.

21. As discussed in Paragraph 11, when a user registered for the Defendant's social networking service, whether through one of the Path Apps or through Defendant's website, the user was required to provide an email address, a first name, and a last name, and was invited to provide gender, phone number, and date of birth.

---

[75] For more information about COPPA, see Dorothy A. Hertzel, Note, *Don't Talk to Strangers: An Analysis of Government and Industry Efforts to Protect Child's Privacy Online*, 52 Fed. Comm. L.J. 429 (2000).

22. From November 14, 2010, through May 4, 2012, Defendant accepted registrations from users who entered a date of birth indicating that the user was under the age of 13. As a result, Defendant knowingly collected email address, first name, last name, date of birth, and if provided, gender and phone number, from approximately 3,000 children under age 13. Defendant, therefore, was an "operator" as defined in the Rule.

23. From November 29, 2011, through February 8, 2012, Defendant also knowingly collected from these children the following personal information for each contact in the child's mobile device address book, if available: first name, last name, address, phone numbers, email addresses, and date of birth.

24. A child who registered through the Path App or Defendant's website was able to create a journal and upload, store and share photos, written "thoughts," the child's precise location, and the names of songs to which the child was listening. In fact, each time a child uploaded a photo or posted a "thought," the Path App would invite the child to also share his or her location through the application's geo-location tracking feature and the names of any friends that were with the child when the photo was taken or the thought was posted. Likewise, if the child decided to share his or her location through the application's geo-location tracking feature, the Path App would invite the child to also share the names of friends that were with the child at that location, and prompt the child to add a "thought." The child could also comment on the posts of other users in the child's network.

25. Until May 4, 2012, Defendant knowingly collected children's personal information and enabled children to publicly disclose their personal information through the Defendant's social networking service.

26. Defendant's online notice of its information practices did not clearly, completely, or accurately disclose all of Defendant's information collection, use, and disclosure practices for children, as required by the Rule.

27. Defendant did not provide parents with a direct notice of its information practices prior to collecting, using, or disclosing children's personal information.

28. Defendant did not obtain verifiable consent from parents prior to collecting, using, or disclosing children's personal information.

29. In approximately 3,000 instances, Defendant knowingly collected, used, and/or disclosed personal information from children in violation of the Children's Online Privacy Protection Rule. . . .

34. In numerous instances, in connection with operating its Path App for iOS, its Path App for the Android operating system, and its website, path.com, Defendant collected, used, and/or disclosed, with actual knowledge, personal information online from children younger than age 13. Defendant failed to: (1) provide sufficient notice on its website or online services of the information it collects online from children, how it uses such information, and its disclosure practices, among other required content; (2) provide direct notice to parents of the information Defendant collects online from children, how it uses such information, and its disclosure practices for such information, among other required content; and (3) obtain verifiable parental consent before any collection, use, and/or disclosure of personal information from children. . . .

NOTES & QUESTIONS

1. *Settlement.* Path settled with the FTC, agreeing to destroy the data it had collected about children. Path also agreed to pay a civil payment of $800,000.

2. *Inadvertently Triggering COPPA.* Path's online service was not directed at children under 13; rather, it was for all users. It triggered COPPA because it collected birth dates, thus giving it actual knowledge that some users were under 13. Is it fair to punish Path for what might have been an inadvertent triggering of COPPA?

3. *Restricting Use to Users 13 Years or Older.* Some websites seek to avoid triggering COPPA by requiring users to be 13 or older. For example, Facebook states:

   > Facebook requires everyone to be at least 13 years old before they can create an account (in some jurisdictions, this age limit may be higher). Creating an account with false info is a violation of our terms. This includes accounts registered on the behalf of someone under 13

   The result of COPPA thus means fewer sites that allow users under 13. Is this result desirable?

   The reality is, however, that many children under 13 lie about their age in order to sign up for Facebook accounts. In June 2011, Consumer Reports found that "more than one-third of the 20 million minors who actively used Facebook in the past year" were under 13.[76] This meant 7.5 million users of Facebook who were younger than 13. It stated: "Parents of kids 10 and younger on Facebook seem to be largely unconcerned." The magazine also warned, "Ten-year-olds need protection from . . . hazards that might lurk on the Internet, such as links that might infect their computer with malware and invitations from strangers, not to mention bullies."

   To what extent should Facebook have an obligation to make it harder for children under 13 to sign up deceitfully? For all the children who do lie about their age, is Facebook just putting its head in the sand?

   One possible solution is to remove the "actual knowledge" prong of COPPA and only apply the law to websites specifically directed at children. But would that be too limiting of COPPA and allow too much of an end-run around its protections?

4. *FTC Enforcement Actions.* The FTC has engaged in several enforcement actions pursuant to COPPA. These cases have resulted in settlements simultaneously with the filing of complaints. Heavy penalties have been assessed as part of some of the settlements. In 2011, the FTC received its largest civil settlement yet under COPPA. Playdom, an operator of online virtual worlds, agreed to pay $3 million to settle FTC charges that it had violated COPPA. The company was alleged to have illegally collected and disclosed personal information from hundreds of thousands of children under age 13 without their parents' prior consent.

---

[76] *That Facebook Friend Might Be 10 Years Old, and Other Troubling News*, Consumer Reports (June 2011).

In its complaint, the FTC stated that Playdom violated its stated privacy policy by collecting children's personal information and enabling children to publicly disclose this information through their personal profile pages and in community forums at its websites. The company also did not take necessary steps "to provide parents with a direct notice of [its] information practices prior to collecting, using, or disclosing children's personal information" and to collect "verifiable consent from parents." The FTC tallied no fewer than 1.2 million instances of the company's collection, use, and/or disclosure of personal information in violation of COPPA.

As a further example, the FTC announced a settlement in 2006 with Xanga.com, which included a $1 million civil penalty. The complaint charges that Xanga.com, a social networking website, had actual knowledge of its collection of disclosure of children's personal information. The Xanga website stated that children under 13 could not join its social network, but it allowed visitors to create Xanga accounts even if they provided a birth date indicating that they were younger than that age. Moreover, Xanga did not provide parents with access to and control over their children's information, and did not notify the parents of children who joined the site of its information practices. Finally, the FTC found that Xanga had created 1.7 million accounts for users who submitted age information that indicated they were younger than 13 years old.

In 2011, in *United States v. W3 Innovations, LLC,* No. CV-11-03958-PSG (Aug. 12, 2011), the FTC settled an action against a developer of children's gaming apps for the iPhone and iPod. W3 Innovations (doing business as Broken Thumbs Apps) failed to have a privacy policy or to obtain parental consent before collecting and disclosing children's personal data. Under the settlement, W3 was fined $50,000 and ordered to delete all information collected in violation of COPPA.

5. *Is COPPA Too Paternalistic?* Consider the following critique of COPPA by Anita Allen:

> Not all parents welcome the veto power COPPA confers. New power has meant new responsibility. The statute forces parents who would otherwise be content to give their children free rein over their computers to get involved in children's use of Internet sites that are geared toward children and collect personal information. . . .
>
> Prohibiting voluntary disclosures by children lacking parental consent in situations in which they and their parents may be indifferent to privacy losses and resentful of government intervention, COPPA is among the most paternalistic and authoritarian of the federal privacy statutes thus far.[77]

More recently, Allen has wondered whether young adults might also need paternalistic laws.[78] At the same time, she concedes, "Sharing data is the way of the contemporary world. There is no chance the United States government will intervene in a strict censorship mode to curb radical forms of self-disclosure online." On a pessimistic note, Allen also notes:

---

[77] Anita L. Allen, *Minor Distractions: Children, Privacy and E-Commerce*, 38 Hous. L. Rev. 751, 752-53, 768-69, 775-76 (2001).

[78] Anita L. Allen, *Unpopular Privacy* 190-94 (2011).

[COPPA] could be viewed as part of a nation's formative educational project: the young are to be taught the value of privacy by imposing privacy protection rules limiting their choices until they are old enough to choose responsibly. But it will be difficult for children to get the message that privacy is a duty of self-care if they closely observe the actual behavior of teens and young adults. Everyone under the age of forty seems to be freely sharing personal facts, ideas, fantasies, and revealing images of themselves all the time.

Is COPPA doomed by a decline of modesty about self-revelation on the Internet? What role, if any, should the law play in nudging or coercing people to protect their own privacy?

(b) The Electronic Communications Privacy Act

In several cases, plaintiffs have attempted to use the Electronic Communications Privacy Act (ECPA) to prevent certain kinds of information collection, use, and disclosure by commercial entities. Recall from Chapter 3 that EPCA consists of three acts: (1) the Wiretap Act, 18 U.S.C. §§ 2510–2522, which regulates the interception of communications; (2) the Stored Communications Act (SCA), 18 U.S.C. §§ 2701–2711, which regulates communications in storage and ISP subscriber records; and (3) the Pen Register Act, 18 U.S.C. §§ 3121–3127, which regulates the use of pen register and trap and trace devices. The attempts to use ECPA to regulate commercial entities using personal information primarily seek to use the Wiretap Act or the SCA.

IN RE GOOGLE, INC. GMAIL LITIGATION

2013 WL 5423918 (N.D. Cal. 2013)

KOH, J. In this consolidated multi-district litigation, Plaintiffs . . . allege that Defendant Google, Inc., has violated state and federal antiwiretapping laws in its operation of Gmail, an email service. Before the Court is Google's Motion to Dismiss Plaintiffs' Consolidated Complaint. . . .

Plaintiffs challenge Google's operation of Gmail under state and federal anti-wiretapping laws. The Consolidated Complaint seeks damages on behalf of a number of classes of Gmail users and non–Gmail users for Google's interception of emails over a period of several years. . . . Plaintiffs allege . . . that in all iterations of Google's email routing processes since 2008, Google has intercepted, read and acquired the content of emails that were sent or received by Gmail user while the emails were in transit. . . .

Plaintiffs further allege that Google used these . . . data to create user profiles and models. Google then allegedly used the emails, affiliated data, and user profiles to serve their profit interests that were unrelated to providing email services to particular users. . . .

Gmail implicates several different, but related, systems of email delivery, three of which are at issue here. The first is a free service, which allows any user to register for an account with Google to use Gmail. This system is supported by advertisements, though users can opt-out of such advertising or access Gmail accounts in ways that do not generate advertising, such as accessing email on a smartphone.

The second is Google's operation of email on behalf of Internet Service Providers ("ISPs"). Google, through its Google Apps Partner program, enters into contracts with ISPs, such as Cable One, to provide an email service branded by the ISP. The ISP's customers can register for email addresses from their ISP (such as "@mycableone.com"), but their email is nevertheless powered by Google through Gmail.

Third, Google operates Google Apps for Education, through which Google provides email on behalf of educational organizations for students, faculty, staff, and alumni. These users receive "@name.institution.edu" email addresses, but their accounts are also powered by Google using Gmail. *Id.* Universities that are part of Google Apps for Education require their students to use the Gmail–provided service.

Google Apps users, whether through the educational program or the partner program, do not receive content-based ads but can opt in to receiving such advertising. Google processes emails sent and received from all Gmail users, including Google Apps users, in the same way except that emails of users who do not receive advertisements are not processed through Google's advertising infrastructure, which attaches targeted advertisements to emails. . . . [E]mails to and from users who did not receive advertisements are nevertheless intercepted to create user profiles. . . .

The operation of the Gmail service implicates several legal agreements. Gmail users were required to agree to one of two sets of Terms of Service during the class periods. The first Terms of Service was in effect from April 16, 2007, to March 1, 2012, and the second has been in effect since March 1, 2012. The 2007 Terms of Service stated that:

> Google reserves the right (but shall have no obligation) to pre-screen, review, flag, filter, modify, refuse or remove any or all Content from any Service. For some Services, Google may provide tools to filter out explicit sexual content. These tools include the SafeSearch preference settings.... In addition, there are commercially available services and software to limit access to material that you may find objectionable.

A subsequent section of the 2007 Terms of Service provided that "[s]ome of the Services are supported by advertising revenue and may display advertisements and promotions" and that "[t]hese advertisements may be content-based to the content information stored on the Services, queries made through the Service or other information."

The 2012 Terms of Service deleted the above language and stated that users "give Google (and those [Google] work[s] with) a worldwide license to use . . . , create derivative works (such as those resulting from translations, adaptations or other changes we make so that your content works better with our Services), . . . and distribute such content."

Both Terms of Service reference Google's Privacy Policies, which have been amended three times thus far during the putative class periods. These Policies, which were largely similar, stated that Google could collect information that users provided to Google, cookies, log information, user communications to Google, information that users provide to affiliated sites, and the links that a user follows. The Policies listed Google's provision of "services to users, including the display of customized content and advertising" as one of the reasons for the collection of this information.

Google also had in place Legal Notices, which stated . . . that Google "will not use any of [users'] content for any purpose except to provide [users] with the service." . . .

Importantly, Plaintiffs who are not Gmail or Google Apps users are not subject to any of Google's express agreements. Because non-Gmail users exchange emails with Gmail users, however, their communications are nevertheless subject to the alleged interceptions at issue in this case.

Plaintiffs bring these cases alleging that Google, in the operation of its Gmail system, violated federal and state anti-wiretapping laws. . . .

The Wiretap Act, as amended by the ECPA, generally prohibits the interception of "wire, oral, or electronic communications." 18 U.S.C. § 2511(1); More specifically, the Wiretap Act provides a private right of action against any person who "intentionally intercepts, endeavors to intercept, or procures any other person to intercept or endeavor to intercept, any wire, oral, or electronic communication." 18 U.S.C. § 2511(1)(a); *see id.* § 2520 (providing a private right of action for violations of § 2511). The Act further defines "intercept" as "the aural or other acquisition of the contents of any wire, electronic, or oral communication through the use of any electronic, mechanical, or other device."

Plaintiffs contend that Google violated the Wiretap Act in its operation of the Gmail system by intentionally intercepting the content of emails that were in transit to create profiles of Gmail users and to provide targeted advertising. . . .

1. *"Ordinary Course of Business" Exception.* Google first contends that it did not engage in an interception because its reading of users' emails occurred in the ordinary course of its business. . . . The Court finds that the ordinary course of business exception is narrow. The exception offers protection from liability only where an electronic communication service provider's interception facilitates the transmission of the communication at issue or is incidental to the transmission of such communication. Specifically, the exception would apply here only if the alleged interceptions were an instrumental part of the transmission of email. Plaintiffs have alleged, however, that Google's interception is not an instrumental component of Google's operation of a functioning email system. In fact, Google's alleged interception of email content is primarily used to create user profiles and to provide targeted advertising—neither of which is related to the transmission of emails. The Court further finds that Plaintiffs' allegations that Google violated Google's own agreements and internal policies with regard to privacy also preclude application of the ordinary course of business exception. . . .

The narrow construction of "ordinary course of business" is most evident in section 2510(5)(a)(i) cases where an employer has listened in on employees' phone calls in the workplace. These cases suggest that an employer's eavesdropping on an employee's phone call is only permissible where the employer has given notice to the employee. Further, these cases have suggested that an employer may only listen to an employee's phone call for the narrow purpose of determining whether a call is for personal or business purposes. . . .

In light of the statutory text, case law, statutory scheme, and legislative history concerning the ordinary course of business exception, the Court finds that the section 2510(5)(a)(ii) exception is narrow and designed only to protect electronic communication service providers against a finding of liability under the Wiretap Act where the interception facilitated or was incidental to provision of the electronic communication service at issue. Plaintiffs have plausibly alleged that Google's reading of their emails was not within this narrow ordinary course of its business. Specifically, Plaintiffs allege that Google intercepts emails for the purposes of creating user profiles and delivering targeted advertising, which are not instrumental to Google's ability to transmit emails. . . . Plaintiffs support their assertion by suggesting that Google's interceptions of emails for targeting advertising and creating user profiles occurred independently from the rest of the email-delivery system. . . .

Accordingly, the Court denies Google's Motion to Dismiss based on the section 2510(5)(a)(ii) exception.

2. *Consent.* Google's second contention with respect to Plaintiffs' Wiretap Act claim is that all Plaintiffs consented to any interception of emails in question in the instant case. Specifically, Google contends that by agreeing to its Terms of Service and Privacy Policies, all Gmail users have consented to Google reading their emails Google further suggests that even though non–Gmail users have not agreed to Google's Terms of Service or Privacy Policies, all non–Gmail users impliedly consent to Google's interception when non-Gmail users send an email to or receive an email from a Gmail user.

If either party to a communication consents to its interception, then there is no violation of the Wiretap Act. 18 U.S.C. § 2511(2)(d). Consent to an interception can be explicit or implied, but any consent must be actual. Courts have cautioned that implied consent applies only in a narrow set of cases. The critical question with respect to implied consent is whether the parties whose communications were intercepted had adequate notice of the interception. That the person communicating knows that the interceptor has the *capacity* to monitor the communication is insufficient to establish implied consent. Moreover, consent is not an all-or-nothing proposition. Rather, "[a] party may consent to the interception of only part of a communication or to the interception of only a subset of its communications." . . .

In its Motion to Dismiss, Google marshals both explicit and implied theories of consent. Google contends that by agreeing to Google's Terms of Service and Privacy Policies, Plaintiffs who are Gmail users expressly consented to the interception of their emails. Google further contends that because of the way that email operates, even non-Gmail users knew that their emails would be intercepted, and accordingly that non-Gmail users impliedly consented to the interception. Therefore, Google argues that in all communications, both parties—regardless of whether they are Gmail users—have consented to the reading of emails. The Court rejects Google's contentions with respect to both explicit and implied consent. Rather, the Court finds that it cannot conclude that any party—Gmail users or non-Gmail users—has consented to Google's reading of email for the purposes of creating user profiles or providing targeted advertising.

Google points to its Terms of Service and Privacy Policies, to which all Gmail and Google Apps users agreed, to contend that these users explicitly consented to the interceptions at issue. The Court finds, however, that those policies did not explicitly notify Plaintiffs that Google would intercept users' emails for the purposes of creating user profiles or providing targeted advertising.

Section 8 of the Terms of Service that were in effect from April 16, 2007, to March 1, 2012, stated that "Google reserves the right (but shall have no obligation) to pre-screen, review, flag, filter, modify, refuse or remove any or all Content from any Service." This sentence was followed by a description of steps users could take to avoid sexual and objectionable material. Later, section 17 of the Terms of Service stated that "advertisements may be targeted to the content of information stored on the Services, queries made through the Services or other information."

The Court finds that Gmail users' acceptance of these statements does not establish explicit consent. Section 8 of the Terms of Service suggests that content may be intercepted under a different set of circumstances for a different purpose—to exclude objectionable content, such as sexual material. This does not suggest to the user that Google would intercept emails for the purposes of creating user profiles or providing targeted advertising. Therefore, to the extent that section 8 of the Terms of Service establishes consent, it does so only for the purpose of interceptions to eliminate objectionable content. The Consolidated Complaint suggests, however, that Gmail's interceptions for the purposes of targeted advertising and creation of user profiles was separate from screening for any objectionable content. Because the two processes were allegedly separate, consent to one does not equate to consent to the other.

Section 17 of the Terms of Service—which states that Google's "advertisements may be targeted to the content of information stored on the Services, queries made through the Services or other information"—is defective in demonstrating consent for a different reason: it demonstrates only that Google has the *capacity* to intercept communications, not that it will. Moreover, the language suggests only that Google's advertisements were based on information "stored on the Services" or "queries made through the Services"—not information in transit via email. Plaintiffs here allege that Google violates the Wiretap Act, which explicitly protects communications in transit, as distinguished from communications that are stored. Furthermore, providing targeted advertising is only one of the alleged reasons for the interceptions at issue in this case. Plaintiffs also allege that Google intercepted emails for the purposes of creating user profiles. Section 17, to the extent that it suggests interceptions, only does so for the purposes of providing advertising, not creating user profiles. Accordingly, the Court finds that neither section of the Terms of Service establishes consent.

The Privacy Policies explicitly state that Google collects "user communications . . . *to Google.*" This could mislead users into believing that user communications to each other or to nonusers were not intercepted and used to target advertising or create user profiles. As such, these Privacy Policies do not demonstrate explicit consent, and in fact suggest the opposite.

After March 1, 2012, Google modified its Terms of Service and Privacy Policy. The new policies are no clearer than their predecessors in establishing consent. The relevant part of the new Terms of Service state that when users upload content to Google, they "give Google (and those [Google] work[s] with) a worldwide license to use . . . , create derivative works (such as those resulting from translations, adaptations or other changes we make so that your content works better with our Services), . . . and distribute such content."

The Terms of Service cite the new Privacy Policy, in which Google states to users that Google "may collect information about the services that you use and how you use them, like when you visit a website that uses our advertising services or you view and interact with our ads and content. This information include [device information, log information, location information, unique application numbers, local storage, cookies, and anonymous identifiers]. The Privacy Policy further states that Google "use[s] the information [it] collect[s] from all [its] services to provide, maintain, protect and improve them, to develop new ones, and to protect Google and [its] users. [Google] also use[s] this information to offer you tailored content—like giving you more relevant search results and ads." These new policies do not specifically mention the content of users' emails to each other or to or from non-users; these new policies are not broad enough to encompass such interceptions. Furthermore, the policies do not put users on notice that their emails are intercepted to create user profiles. The Court therefore finds that a reasonable Gmail user who read the Privacy Policies would not have necessarily understood that her emails were being intercepted to create user profiles or to provide targeted advertisements. Accordingly, the Court finds that it cannot conclude at this phase that the new policies demonstrate that Gmail user Plaintiffs consented to the interceptions.

Finally, Google contends that non-Gmail users—email users who do not have a Gmail account and who did not accept Gmail's Terms of Service or Privacy Policies—nevertheless impliedly consented to Google's interception of their emails to and from Gmail users, and to Google's use of such emails to create user profiles and to provide targeted advertising. Google's theory is that all email users understand and accept the fact that email is automatically processed. However, the cases Google cites for this far-reaching proposition hold only that the sender of an email consents to the intended recipients' recording of the email—not, as has been alleged here, interception by a third-party service provider. Google has cited no case that stands for the proposition that users who send emails impliedly consent to interceptions and use of their communications by third parties other than the intended recipient of the email. Nor has Google cited anything that suggests that by doing nothing more than receiving emails from a Gmail user, non–Gmail users have consented to the interception of those communications. Accepting Google's theory of implied consent—that by merely sending emails to or receiving emails from a Gmail user, a non–Gmail user has consented to Google's interception of such emails for any purposes—would eviscerate the rule against interception. The Court does not find that non-Gmail users who are not subject to Google's Privacy Policies or Terms of Service have impliedly consented to Google's interception of their emails to Gmail users.

Because Plaintiffs have adequately alleged that they have not explicitly or implicitly consented to Google's interceptions, the Court denies Google's Motion to Dismiss on the basis of consent. . . .

NOTES & QUESTIONS

1. ***Gmail's Business Model.*** Google offers Gmail for free to users and makes money from Gmail through targeted advertising. Google can fix its problems obtaining user consent by providing more explicit notice to Gmail account holders. But how should it deal with non-Gmail users who correspond with Gmail users? Does this problem make the business model unworkable? Is there a way to readily obtain the consent of non-Gmail users?

2. ***The Scope of the Wiretap Act.*** In *Joffe v. Google, Inc.,* 746 F.3d 920 (9th Cir. 2013), plaintiffs sued Google alleging that it violated the Wiretap Act by collecting data from unencrypted Wi-Fi networks. Google argued that data transmitted via Wi-Fi is a "radio communication" that is "readily accessible to the general public" and exempt from the Wiretap Act. The court rejected Google's argument.

3. ***Does ECPA Prohibit Cookies?*** When a person interacts with a website, the site can record certain information about the person, such as what parts of the website the user visited, what the user clicked on, and how long the user spent reading different parts of the website. This information is called "clickstream data."

   Websites use "cookies" to identify particular users.[79] A cookie is a small text file that is downloaded into the user's computer when a user accesses a Web page. The text in a cookie, which is often encoded, usually includes an identification number and several other data elements, such as the website and the expiration date. The cookie lets a website know that a particular user has returned. The website can then access any information it collected about that individual on her previous visits to the website. Cookies can also be used to track users as they visit multiple websites.

   In *In re DoubleClick Inc. Privacy Litigation*, 154 F. Supp. 2d 497 (S.D.N.Y. 2001), a group of plaintiffs challenged DoubleClick's use of cookies under the Stored Communications Act (SCA) and Wiretap Act. In 2001, DoubleClick was the leading company providing online advertising. DoubleClick helps advertisers distribute advertisements to websites based on information about specific web surfers. When a person visits a DoubleClick-affiliated website, DoubleClick places a cookie on that person's computer. As the person visits other sites that use DoubleClick, it builds a profile of that person's Web surfing activity. DoubleClick then can target ads to specific people based on their profile. For example, suppose a news website uses DoubleClick. A person visits the news website. The website checks with DoubleClick to see if DoubleClick recognizes the person. If the person's computer has a DoubleClick cookie, DoubleClick then looks up the profile associated with the cookie and sends the website advertisements tailored to that person's interests. Suppose Person A likes tennis and Person B likes golf. When Person A goes to the news website, a banner ad for tennis might appear. When Person B visits the same site, a banner ad for golf might appear.

---

[79] For a discussion of the *DoubleClick* case, see Tal Zarsky, *Cookie Viewers and the Undermining of Data-Mining: A Critical Review of the DoubleClick Settlement*, 2002 Stan. Tech. L. Rev. 1.

The plaintiffs in the *DoubleClick* case raised an SCA claim and a Wiretap Act claim. Regarding the SCA claim, the Act provides:

> [W]hoever (1) intentionally accesses without authorization a facility through which an electronic information service is provided; or (2) intentionally exceeds an authorization to access that facility; and thereby obtains . . . access to a wire or electronic communication while it is in electronic storage in such system shall be punished. . . . 18 U.S.C. § 2701(a).

Although the court ultimately concluded that the SCA did not apply, its reasoning was very controversial. The court first held that an individual's computer, when connected to the Internet, was a "facility through which an electronic information service is provided." This means that when DoubleClick accessed cookies on people's computers, it was "intentionally access[ing] without authorization a facility through which an electronic information service is provided." However, the consent exception to this provision of the SCA is that "users" may authorize access "with respect to a communication of or intended for that user." § 2701(c). The individuals whose computers were accessed were obviously users, and they did not consent. But the websites that the users visited that used DoubleClick cookies were also "users" in the court's interpretation, and they consented. Only one party needs to consent for the SCA consent exception to apply.

Moreover, the court noted that the SCA only applies to "temporary, intermediate storage of a wire or electronic communication," § 2510(17), and that DoubleClick's cookies were not "temporary" because they exist on people's hard drives for a virtually infinite time period.

Commentators argue that the court's application of the SCA is wrong because a "facility" refers to an Internet Service Provider, not an individual computer. Consider Orin Kerr:

> [T]he Stored Communications Act regulates the privacy of Internet account holders at ISPs and other servers; the law was enacted to create by statute a set of Fourth Amendment-like set of rights in stored records held by ISPs. The theory of the *Doubleclick* plaintiffs turned this framework on its head, as it attempted to apply a law designed to give account holders privacy rights in information held at third-party ISPs to home PCs interacting with websites.[80]

In *In re Pharmatrak Inc. Privacy Litigation*, 220 F. Supp. 2d 4 (D. Mass. 2002), aff'd 392 F.3d 9 (1st Cir. 2003), the court interpreted the SCA as Kerr suggests, holding that an individual's personal computer was not a "facility" under the SCA.

Regarding the Wiretap Act claim, DoubleClick conceded, for the purposes of summary judgment, that it had "intercepted" electronic communications. Orin Kerr also takes issue with this concession:

> [T]he Wiretap Act prohibits a third-party from intercepting in real-time the contents of communications between two parties unless one of the two parties consents. This law had no applicability to Doubleclick's cookies, as the cookies

---

[80] Orin S. Kerr, *Lifting the "Fog" of Internet Surveillance: How a Suppression Remedy Would Change Computer Crime Law*, 54 Hastings L.J. 805, 831 (2003).

did not intercept any contents and did not intercept anything in real-time. The cookies merely registered data sent to it from Doubleclick's servers.[81]

DoubleClick argued that even if it intercepted electronic communications, the consent exception applied, since one party (the websites using DoubleClick) consented. The court agreed. The consent exception, however, does not apply if even with consent the "communication is intercepted for the purpose of committing any criminal or tortious act." 18 U.S.C. § 2511(2)(d). The court concluded: "DoubleClick's purpose has plainly not been to perpetuate torts on millions of Internet users, but to make money by providing a valued service to commercial Web sites."

4. *Web Bugs.* Beyond cookies, another device for collecting people's data is called a "Web bug." As one court describes it, Web bugs (or "action tags") are very tiny pixels on a website that can record how a person navigates around the Internet. Unlike a cookie, which can be accepted or declined by a user, a Web bug is a very small graphic file that is secretly downloaded to the user's computer. Web bugs enable the website to monitor a person's keystrokes and cursor movement. Web bugs can also be placed in e-mail messages that use HTML, or HyperText Markup Language. E-mail using HTML enables users to see graphics in an e-mail. A Web bug in an e-mail message can detect whether the e-mail was read and to whom it was forwarded. According to computer security expert Richard M. Smith, a Web bug can gather the IP address of the computer that fetched the Web bug; the URL of the page that the Web bug is located on; the URL of the Web bug image; the time the Web bug was viewed; the type of browser that fetched the Web bug image; and a previously set cookie value. Is the use of a Web bug a violation of federal electronic surveillance law?

DYER V. NORTHWEST AIRLINES CORP.

334 F. Supp. 2d 1196 (D.N.D. 2004)

HOVLAND, C.J. . . . Following September 11, 2001, the National Aeronautical and Space Administration ("NASA") requested system-wide passenger data from Northwest Airlines for a three-month period in order to conduct research for use in airline security studies. Northwest Airlines complied and, unbeknownst to its customers, provided NASA with the names, addresses, credit card numbers, and travel itineraries of persons who had flown on Northwest Airlines between July and December 2001.

The discovery of Northwest Airlines' disclosure of its customers' personal information triggered a wave of litigation. Eight class actions — seven in Minnesota and one in Tennessee — were filed in federal court prior to March 19, 2004. The seven Minnesota actions were later consolidated into a master file.

[In this case, t]he complaint alleges that Northwest Airlines' unauthorized disclosure of customers' personal information constituted a violation of the Electronic Communications Privacy Act ("ECPA"), 18 U.S.C. §§ 2702(a)(1) and (a)(3). . . .

---

[81] *Id.* at 831.

The Electronic Communications Privacy Act (ECPA) provides in relevant part that, with certain exceptions, a person or entity providing either an electronic communication service or remote computing service to the public shall not:

- knowingly divulge to any person or entity the contents of a communication while in electronic storage by that service (18 U.S.C. § 2702(a)(1)); and

- knowingly divulge a record or other information pertaining to a subscriber to or customer of such service . . . to any governmental entity (18 U.S.C. § 2702(a)(3)).

In its complaint, the Plaintiffs asserted claims under both 18 U.S.C. §§ 2702(a)(1) and (a)(3) of the ECPA. The plaintiffs have conceded no claim exists under 18 U.S.C. § 2702(a)(1). Consequently, the Court's focus will be directed at the Plaintiffs' ability to sustain a claim against Northwest Airlines under 18 U.S.C. § 2702(a)(3). To sustain a claim under 18 U.S.C. § 2702(a)(3), the Plaintiffs must establish that Northwest Airlines provides either electronic communication services or remote computing services. It is clear that Northwest Airlines provides neither.

The ECPA defines "electronic communication service" as "any service which provides the users thereof the ability to send or receive wire or electronic communications." 18 U.S.C. § 2510(15). In construing this definition, courts have distinguished those entities that sell access to the internet from those that sell goods or services on the internet. 18 U.S.C. § 2702(a)(3) prescribes the conduct only of a "provider of a remote computing service or electronic communication service to the public." A provider under the ECPA is commonly referred to as an internet service provider or ISP. There is no factual allegation that Northwest Airlines, an airline that sells airline tickets on its website, provides internet services.

Courts have concluded that "electronic communication service" encompasses internet service providers as well as telecommunications companies whose lines carry internet traffic, but does not encompass businesses selling traditional products or services online. See *In re DoubleClick Inc. Privacy Litig.*, 154 F. Supp. 2d 497 (S.D.N.Y. 2001). . . .

The distinction is critical in this case. Northwest Airlines is not an electronic communications service provider as contemplated by the ECPA. Instead, Northwest Airlines sells its products and services over the internet as opposed to access to the internet itself. The ECPA definition of "electronic communications service" clearly includes internet service providers such as America Online, as well as telecommunications companies whose cables and phone lines carry internet traffic. However, businesses offering their traditional products and services online through a website are not providing an "electronic communication service." As a result, Northwest Airlines falls outside the scope of 18 U.S.C. § 2702 and the ECPA claim fails as a matter of law. The facts as pled do not give rise to liability under the ECPA. 18 U.S.C. § 2702(a) does not prohibit or even address the dissemination of business records of passenger flights and information as described in the complaint. Instead, the focus of 18 U.S.C. § 2702(a) is on "communications" being stored by the communications service provider for the purpose of subsequent transmission or for backup purposes.

[The plaintiffs also raised a claim under the Minnesota Deceptive Trade Practices Act. The court held that the claim was barred by the federal Airline Deregulation Act, which preempts state regulation of "a price, route, or service of an airline carrier." 49 U.S.C. § 4173(b)(1).]

NOTES & QUESTIONS

1. *ISPs vs. Non-ISPs.* In this case, Northwest Airlines violated its privacy policy by disclosing its customer records to the government. Suppose Northwest Airlines had been an ISP like AOL or Earthlink. Would it have been liable under the Stored Communications Act?

2. *Other Remedies.* What other potential remedies might the plaintiffs have in this case? The plaintiffs brought an action for breach of contract, which was discussed earlier in this chapter in the section on privacy policies. Besides breach of contract, can you think of any other causes of action that might be brought?

(c) The Computer Fraud and Abuse Act

The Computer Fraud and Abuse Act (CFAA) of 1984, 18 U.S.C. § 1030, provides criminal and civil penalties for unauthorized access to computers. Originally passed in 1984, the statue was amended updated throughout the 1990s. Several states have similar statutes regarding the misuse of computers. As Orin Kerr notes:

> While no two statutes are identical, all share the common trigger of "access without authorization" or "unauthorized access" to computers, sometimes in tandem with its close cousin, "exceeding authorized access" to computers.[82]

Scope. The CFAA applies to all "protected computer[s]." A "protected computer" is any computer used in interstate commerce or communication. Whereas the Stored Communications Act of ECPA appears to apply only to ISPs, the CFAA applies to both ISPs and individual computers.

Criminal Penalties. The CFAA creates seven crimes. Among these, it imposes criminal penalties when a person or entity "intentionally accesses a computer without authorization or exceeds authorized access, and thereby obtains . . . information from any protected computer." § 1030(a)(2)(c). It criminalizes unauthorized access to "any nonpublic computer of a department or agency of the United States." § 1030(a)(3). The CFAA also criminalizes unauthorized access to computers "knowingly with intent to defraud" and the obtaining of "anything of value, unless the object of the fraud and the thing obtained consists only of the use of the computer and the value of such use is not more than $5,000 in any 1-year period." § 1030(a)(4). Yet another crime created by the CFAA prohibits knowingly transmitting "a program, information, code, or command" or "intentionally access[ing] a protected computer without authorization" that causes damage to a

---

[82] Orin S. Kerr, *Cybercrime's Scope: Interpreting "Access" and "Authorization" in Computer Misuse Statutes*, 78 N.Y.U. L. Rev. 1596, 1615 (2003).

protected computer. § 1030(5)(A)(i). Punishments range from fines to imprisonment for up to 20 years depending upon the provision violated.

Damage. The term "damage" means "any impairment to the integrity or availability of data, a program, a system, or information." § 1030(e). In many provisions in the CFAA, the damage must exceed $5,000 in a one-year period.

Civil Remedies. "Any person who suffers damage or loss by reason of a violation of this section may maintain a civil action against the violator to obtain compensatory damages or injunctive relief or other equitable relief." § 1030(g). "Damage" must cause a "loss aggregating at least $5,000 in value during any 1-year period to one or more individuals." § 1030(e).

Exceeding Authorized Access. Many provisions in the CFAA can be violated not just by unauthorized access, but also when one "exceeds authorized access." To exceed authorized access means "to access a computer with authorization and to use such access to obtain or alter information in the computer that the accesser is not entitled so to obtain and alter." § 1030(e)(6).

CREATIVE COMPUTING V. GETLOADED.COM LLC

386 F.3d 930 (9th Cir. 2004)

KLEINFELD, J. Truck drivers and trucking companies try to avoid dead heading. "Dead heading" means having to drive a truck, ordinarily on a return trip, without a revenue-producing load. If the truck is moving, truck drivers and their companies want it to be carrying revenue-producing freight. In the past, truckers and shippers used blackboards to match up trips and loads. Eventually television screens were used instead of blackboards, but the matching was still inefficient. Better information on where the trucks and the loads are — and quick, easy access to that information — benefits shippers, carriers, and consumers.

Creative Computing developed a successful Internet site, truckstop.com, which it calls "The Internet Truckstop," to match loads with trucks. The site is very easy to use. It has a feature called "radius search" that lets a truck driver in, say, Middletown, Connecticut, with some space in his truck, find within seconds all available loads in whatever mileage radius he likes (and of course lets a shipper post a load so that a trucker with space can find it). The site was created so early in Internet history and worked so well that it came to dominate the load-board industry.

Getloaded decided to compete, but not honestly. After Getloaded set up a load-matching site, it wanted to get a bigger piece of Creative's market. Creative wanted to prevent that, so it prohibited access to its site by competing loadmatching services. The Getloaded officers thought trucking companies would probably use the same login names and passwords on truckstop.com as they did on getloaded.com. Getloaded's president, Patrick Hull, used the login name and password of a Getloaded subscriber, in effect impersonating the trucking company, to sneak into truckstop.com. Getloaded's vice-president, Ken Hammond, accomplished the same thing by registering a defunct company, RFT Trucking, as a truckstop.com subscriber. ~~These tricks enabled them to see all of the information~~ available to Creative's bona fide customers.

Getloaded's officers also hacked into the code Creative used to operate its website. Microsoft had distributed a patch to prevent a hack it had discovered, but Creative Computing had not yet installed the patch on truckstop.com. Getloaded's president and vice-president hacked into Creative Computing's website through the back door that this patch would have locked. Once in, they examined the source code for the tremendously valuable radius-search feature. . . .

Getloaded argues that no action could lie under the Computer Fraud and Abuse Act because it requires a $5,000 floor for damages from each unauthorized access, and that Creative Computing submitted no evidence that would enable a jury to find that the floor was reached on any single unauthorized access. . . .

The briefs dispute which version of the statute we should apply — the one in effect when Getloaded committed the wrongs, or the one in effect when the case went to trial (which is still in effect). The old version of the statute made an exception to the fraudulent access provision if "the value of such use [unauthorized access to a protected computer] is not more than $5,000 in any 1-year period."[83] The new version, in effect now and during trial, says "loss . . . during any 1-year period . . . aggregating at least $5,000 in value."[84] These provisions are materially identical.

The old version of the statute defined "damage" as "any impairment to the integrity or availability of data, a program, a system, or information" that caused the loss of at least $5,000. It had no separate definition of "loss." The new version defines "damage" the same way, but adds a definition of loss. "Loss" is defined in the new version as "any reasonable cost to any victim, including the cost of responding to an offense, conducting a damage assessment, and restoring the data . . . and any revenue lost, cost incurred, or other consequential damages incurred because of interruption of service."

For purposes of this case, we need not decide which version of the Act applies, because Getloaded loses either way. Neither version of the statute supports a construction that would require proof of $5,000 of damage or loss from a single unauthorized access. The syntax makes it clear that in both versions, the $5,000 floor applies to how much damage or loss there is to the victim over a one-year period, not from a particular intrusion. Getloaded argues that "impairment" is singular, so the floor has to be met by a single intrusion. The premise does not lead to the conclusion. The statute (both the earlier and the current versions) says "damage" means "any impairment to the integrity or availability of data [etc.] . . . that causes loss aggregating at least $5,000." Multiple intrusions can cause a single impairment, and multiple corruptions of data can be described as a single

---

[83] 18 U.S.C. § 1030(a)(4) (2001) ("[Whoever] knowingly and with intent to defraud, accesses a protected computer without authorization, or exceeds authorized access, and by means of such conduct furthers the intended fraud and obtains anything of value, unless the object of the fraud and the thing obtained consists only of the use of the computer and the value of such use is not more than $5,000 in any 1-year period.").

[84] 18 U.S.C. § 1030(a)(5)(B)(i) ("[Whoever caused] loss to 1 or more persons during any 1-year period (and, for purposes of an investigation, prosecution, or other proceeding brought by the United States only, loss resulting from a related course of conduct affecting 1 or more other protected computers) aggregating at least $5,000 in value.").

"impairment" to the data. The statute does not say that an "impairment" has to result from a single intrusion, or has to be a single corrupted byte. A court construing a statute attributes a rational purpose to Congress. Getloaded's construction would attribute obvious futility to Congress rather than rationality, because a hacker could evade the statute by setting up thousands of $4,999 (or millions of $4.99) intrusions. As the First Circuit pointed out in the analogous circumstance of physical impairment, so narrow a construction of the $5,000 impairment requirement would merely "reward sophisticated intruders." The damage floor in the Computer Fraud and Abuse Act contains no "single act" requirement.

NOTES & QUESTIONS

1. ***The $5,000 Threshold.*** In *In re Doubleclick Inc. Privacy Litigation*, 154 F. Supp. 2d 497 (S.D.N.Y. 2001), the plaintiffs brought a CFAA claim and contended that collectively they suffered more than $5,000 in damages. But the court held that the plaintiffs could not add up their damages. Damages could only be combined "for a single act" against "a particular computer." Since the plaintiffs' CFAA claims concerned multiple acts against many different computers, they could not be aggregated to reach the $5,000 threshold.

2. ***Spyware.*** Spyware is a new kind of computer program that raises significant threats to privacy. Paul Schwartz distinguishes "spyware" from "adware" in terms of the notice provided to the user. He also explains how these programs come about through the linking of personal computers via the Internet: "Spyware draws on computer resources to create a network that can be used for numerous purposes, including collecting personal and nonpersonal information from computers and delivering adware or targeted advertisements to individuals surfing the Web. Adware is sometimes, but not always, delivered as part of spyware; the definitional line between the two depends on whether the computer user receives adequate notice of the program's installation."[85] Would the CFAA apply to a company that secretly installs spyware in a person's computer that transmits her personal data back to the company without her awareness? Would the Wiretap Act apply?

3. ***State Spyware Statutes.*** The state of Utah became the first state to pass legislation to regulate spyware. The original Spyware Control Act, Utah Code Ann. §§ 13-40-101 *et seq.*, prohibited the installation of spyware on another person's computer, limited the display of certain types of advertising, created a private right of action, and empowered the Utah Division of Consumer Protection to collect complaints. WhenU, an advertising network, challenged the Act in 2004, arguing that it violated the Commerce Clause of the U.S. Constitution, and it obtained a preliminary injunction against the statute. A revised bill was signed by the Utah governor on March 17, 2005. The revised Act defines "spyware" as "software on a computer of a user who resides in this state that . . . collects information about an Internet website at the time the

---

[85] Paul M. Schwartz, *Property, Privacy, and Personal Data*, 117 Harv. L. Rev. 2055 (2004).

Internet website is being viewed in this state, unless the Internet website is the Internet website of the person who provides the software; and . . . uses the information . . . contemporaneously to display pop-up advertising on the computer."

Following Utah's lead, California enacted a spyware bill, which was signed by Governor Arnold Schwarzenegger on September 28, 2004. The Consumer Protection Against Computer Spyware Act, SB 1426, prohibits a person from causing computer software to be installed on a computer and using the software to (1) take control of the computer; (2) modify certain settings relating to the computer's access to the Internet; (3) collect, through intentionally deceptive means, personally identifiable information; (4) prevent, without authorization, the authorized user's reasonable efforts to block the installation of or disable software; (5) intentionally misrepresent that the software will be uninstalled or disabled by the authorized user's action; or (6) through intentionally deceptive means, remove, disable, or render, inoperative security, anti-spyware, or antivirus software installed on the computer.

UNITED STATES V. DREW

259 F.R.D. 449 (C.D. Cal. 2009)

WU, J. This case raises the issue of whether (and/or when will) violations of an Internet website's terms of service constitute a crime under the Computer Fraud and Abuse Act ("CFAA"), 18 U.S.C. § 1030. . . .

In the Indictment, Drew was charged with one count of conspiracy in violation of 18 U.S.C. § 371 and three counts of violating a felony portion of the CFAA, *i.e.,* 18 U.S.C. §§ 1030(a)(2)(C) and 1030(c)(2)(B)(ii), which prohibit accessing a computer without authorization or in excess of authorization and obtaining information from a protected computer where the conduct involves an interstate or foreign communication and the offense is committed in furtherance of a crime or tortious act.

The Indictment included, *inter alia,* the following allegations (not all of which were established by the evidence at trial). Drew, a resident of O'Fallon, Missouri, entered into a conspiracy in which its members agreed to intentionally access a computer used in interstate commerce without (and/or in excess of) authorization in order to obtain information for the purpose of committing the tortious act of intentional infliction of emotional distress upon "M.T.M.," subsequently identified as Megan Meier ("Megan"). Megan was a 13 year old girl living in O'Fallon who had been a classmate of Drew's daughter Sarah. Pursuant to the conspiracy, on or about September 20, 2006, the conspirators registered and set up a profile for a fictitious 16 year old male juvenile named "Josh Evans" on the www. My Space. com website ("MySpace"), and posted a photograph of a boy without that boy's knowledge or consent. Such conduct violated My Space's terms of service. The conspirators contacted Megan through the MySpace network (on which she had her own profile) using the Josh Evans pseudonym and began to flirt with her over a number of days. On or about October 7, 2006, the conspirators had "Josh" inform Megan that he was moving away. On or about October 16, 2006, the conspirators had "Josh" tell Megan that he no longer liked her and that "the world would be a better place without her in it." Later on that same day, after learning that Megan had killed herself, Drew caused the Josh Evans MySpace account to be deleted.

At the trial, after consultation between counsel and the Court, the jury was instructed that, if they unanimously decided that they were not convinced beyond a reasonable doubt as to the Defendant's guilt as to the felony CFAA violations of 18 U.S.C. §§ 1030(a)(2)(C) and 1030(c)(2)(B)(ii), they could then consider whether the Defendant was guilty of the "lesser included" misdemeanor CFAA violation of 18 U.S.C. §§ 1030(a)(2)(C) and 1030(c)(2)(A). [The jury found Drew not guilty of the felony CFAA violations and guilty of the misdemeanor CFAA violation. Drew made a motion for judgment of acquittal under Fed. R. Crim. P. 29(c).]

As Jae Sung (Vice President of Customer Care at MySpace) testified at trial, MySpace is a "social networking" website where members can create "profiles" and interact with other members. . . .

In 2006, to become a member, one had to go to the sign-up section of the MySpace website and register by filling in personal information (such as name, email address, date of birth, country/state/postal code, and gender) and creating a password. In addition, the individual had to check on the box indicating that "You agree to the MySpace Terms of Service and Privacy Policy." The terms of service did not appear on the same registration page that contained this "check box" for users to confirm their agreement to those provisions. . . . A person could become a MySpace member without ever reading or otherwise becoming aware of the provisions and conditions of the MySpace terms of service [MSTOS] by merely clicking on the "check box" and then the "Sign Up" button without first accessing the "Terms" section.

The MSTOS prohibited the posting of a wide range of content on the website including (but not limited to) material that: a) "is potentially offensive and promotes racism, bigotry, hatred or physical harm of any kind against any group or individual"; b) "harasses or advocates harassment of another person"; c) "solicits personal information from anyone under 18"; d) "provides information that you know is false or misleading or promotes illegal activities or conduct that is abusive, threatening, obscene, defamatory or libelous"; e) "includes a photograph of another person that you have posted without that person's consent"; f) "involves commercial activities and/or sales without our prior written consent"; g) "contains restricted or password only access pages or hidden pages or images"; or h) "provides any phone numbers, street addresses, last names, URLs or email addresses. . . ."

[In 2006, the CFAA (18 U.S.C. § 1030) punished a person who "intentionally accesses a computer without authorization or exceeds authorized access, and thereby obtains . . . information from any protected computer."]

As used in the CFAA, the term "computer" "includes any data storage facility or communication facility directly related to or operating in conjunction with such device. . . ." 18 U.S.C. § 1030(e)(1). The term "protected computer" "means a computer—(A) exclusively for the use of a financial institution or the United States Government . . . ; or (B) which is used in interstate or foreign commerce or communication. . . ." *Id.* § 1030(e)(2). The term "exceeds authorized access" means "to access a computer with authorization and to use such access to obtain or alter information in the computer that the accesser is not entitled so to obtain or alter . . . ." *Id.* § 1030(e)(6).

In addition to providing criminal penalties for computer fraud and abuse, the CFAA also states that "[A]ny person who suffers damage or loss by reason of a violation of this section may maintain a civil action against the violator to obtain compensatory damages and injunctive relief or other equitable relief." 18 U.S.C. § 1030(g). Because of the availability of civil remedies, much of the law as to the meaning and scope of the CFAA has been developed in the context of civil cases.

During the relevant time period herein, the misdemeanor 18 U.S.C. § 1030(a)(2)(C) crime consisted of the following three elements:

First, the defendant intentionally [accessed without authorization] [exceeded authorized access of] a computer;

Second, the defendant's access of the computer involved an interstate or foreign communication; and

Third, by [accessing without authorization] [exceeding authorized access to] a computer, the defendant obtained information from a computer . . . [used in interstate or foreign commerce or communication] . . . .

As to the term "without authorization," the courts that have considered the phrase have taken a number of different approaches in their analysis. . . . [W]here the relationship between the parties is contractual in nature or resembles such a relationship, access has been held to be unauthorized where there has been an ostensible breach of contract. . . .

Within the breach of contract approach, most courts that have considered the issue have held that a conscious violation of a website's terms of service/use will render the access unauthorized and/or cause it to exceed authorization. *See, e.g., Southwest Airlines Co. v. Farechase, Inc.,* 318 F. Supp. 2d 435, 439-40 (N.D. Tex. 2004); *Nat'l Health Care Disc., Inc.,* 174 F. Supp. 2d at 899; *Register.com, Inc. v. Verio, Inc.,* 126 F. Supp. 2d 238, 247-51 (S.D.N.Y. 2000), *aff'd,* 356 F.3d 393 (2d Cir. 2004); *Am. Online, Inc. v. LCGM, Inc.,* 46 F. Supp. 2d 444, 450 (E.D. Va. 1998); *see also EF Cultural Travel BV v. Zefer Corp.,* 318 F.3d 58, 62-63 (1st Cir. 2003) ("A lack of authorization could be established by an explicit statement on the website restricting access. . . . [W]e think that the public website provider can easily spell out explicitly what is forbidden. . . ."). . . .

In this particular case, as conceded by the Government, the only basis for finding that Drew intentionally accessed MySpace's computer/servers without authorization and/or in excess of authorization was her and/or her co-conspirator's violations of the MSTOS by deliberately creating the false Josh Evans profile, posting a photograph of a juvenile without his permission and pretending to be a sixteen year old O'Fallon resident for the purpose of communicating with Megan. Therefore, if conscious violations of the My Space terms of service were not sufficient to satisfy the first element of the CFAA misdemeanor violation as per 18 U.S.C. §§ 1030(a)(2)(C) and 1030(b)(2)(A), Drew's Rule 29(c) motion would have to be granted on that basis alone. However, this Court concludes that an intentional breach of the MSTOS can potentially constitute accessing the MySpace computer/server without authorization and/or in excess of authorization under the statute. . . .

Justice Holmes observed that, as to criminal statutes, there is a "fair warning" requirement. . . .

The void-for-vagueness doctrine has two prongs: 1) a definitional/notice sufficiency requirement and, more importantly, 2) a guideline setting element to govern law enforcement. In *Kolender v. Lawson,* 461 U.S. 352 (1983), the Court explained that:

> As generally stated, the void-for-vagueness doctrine requires that a penal statute define the criminal offense with sufficient definiteness that ordinary people can understand what conduct is prohibited and in a manner that does not encourage arbitrary and discriminatory enforcement. . . .

To avoid contravening the void-for-vagueness doctrine, the criminal statute must contain "relatively clear guidelines as to prohibited conduct" and provide "objective criteria" to evaluate whether a crime has been committed. . . .

The pivotal issue herein is whether basing a CFAA misdemeanor violation as per 18 U.S.C. §§ 1030(a)(2)(C) and 1030(c)(2)(A) upon the conscious violation of a website's terms of service runs afoul of the void-for-vagueness doctrine. This Court concludes that it does primarily because of the absence of minimal guidelines to govern law enforcement, but also because of actual notice deficiencies. . . .

First, an initial inquiry is whether the statute, as it is written, provides sufficient notice. Here, the language of section 1030(a)(2)(C) does not explicitly state (nor does it implicitly suggest) that the CFAA has "criminalized breaches of contract" in the context of website terms of service. Normally, breaches of contract are not the subject of criminal prosecution. Thus, while "ordinary people" might expect to be exposed to civil liabilities for violating a contractual provision, they would not expect criminal penalties. . . .

Second, if a website's terms of service controls what is "authorized" and what is "exceeding authorization" — which in turn governs whether an individual's accessing information or services on the website is criminal or not, section 1030(a)(2)(C) would be unacceptably vague because it is unclear whether any or all violations of terms of service will render the access unauthorized, or whether only certain ones will. . . .

Third, by utilizing violations of the terms of service as the basis for the section 1030(a)(2)(C) crime, that approach makes the website owner — in essence — the party who ultimately defines the criminal conduct. This will lead to further vagueness problems. The owner's description of a term of service might itself be so vague as to make the visitor or member reasonably unsure of what the term of service covers. . . .

Fourth, because terms of service are essentially a contractual means for setting the scope of authorized access, a level of indefiniteness arises from the necessary application of contract law in general and/or other contractual requirements within the applicable terms of service to any criminal prosecution. . . .

Treating a violation of a website's terms of service, without more, to be sufficient to constitute "intentionally access[ing] a computer without authorization or exceed[ing] authorized access" would result in transforming section 1030(a)(2)(C) into an overwhelmingly overbroad enactment that would convert a multitude of otherwise innocent Internet users into misdemeanant criminals. . . .

One need only look to the MSTOS terms of service to see the expansive and elaborate scope of such provisions whose breach engenders the potential for criminal prosecution. Obvious examples of such breadth would include: 1) the lonely-heart who submits intentionally inaccurate data about his or her age, height and/or physical appearance, which contravenes the MSTOS prohibition against providing "information that you know is false or misleading"; 2) the student who posts candid photographs of classmates without their permission, which breaches the MSTOS provision covering "a photograph of another person that you have posted without that person's consent"; and/or 3) the exasperated parent who sends out a group message to neighborhood friends entreating them to purchase his or her daughter's girl scout cookies, which transgresses the MSTOS rule against "advertising to, or solicitation of, any Member to buy or sell any products or services through the Services." However, one need not consider hypotheticals to demonstrate the problem. In this case, Megan (who was then 13 years old) had her own profile on MySpace, which was in clear violation of the MSTOS which requires that users be "14 years of age or older." No one would seriously suggest that Megan's conduct was criminal or should be subject to criminal prosecution. . . .

In sum, if any conscious breach of a website's terms of service is held to be sufficient by itself to constitute intentionally accessing a computer without authorization or in excess of authorization, the result will be that section 1030(a)(2)(C) becomes a law "that affords too much discretion to the police and too little notice to citizens who wish to use the [Internet]."

NOTES & QUESTIONS

1. *The Implications of* **Drew.** Is the prosecutor's theory consistent with the CFAA's purpose? Suppose the court in *Drew* had reached the opposite conclusion. What effect would criminal liability for violating a website's terms of service have for people who use the Internet?

2. *Is the CFAA Unconstitutionally Vague?* The *Drew* court's holding is narrow, concluding only that the application of the CFAA to website terms of service violations would be unconstitutionally vague. More broadly, is the CFAA unconstitutionally vague on its face?

3. MARKETING

(a) The Telephone Consumer Protections Act

The Telephone Consumer Protections Act (TCPA) of 1991, Pub. L. No. 102-243, 47 U.S.C. § 227, requires the FCC to promulgate rules to "protect residential telephone subscribers' privacy rights and to avoid receiving telephone solicitations to which they object." § 227(c)(1). In addition, the FCC is authorized to require that a "single national database" be established of a "list of telephone numbers of residential subscribers who object to receiving telephone solicitations." § 227(c)(3).

Private Right of Action. The FCPA provides plaintiffs with a private right of action in small claims court against an entity for each call received after requesting to no longer receive calls from that entity. Plaintiffs can sue for an actual loss or up to $500 (whichever is greater), If telemarketer has acted "willfully or knowingly," then damages are trebled. § 227(c)(5).

Affirmative Defense. Telemarketers can offer as an affirmative defense that they established "reasonable practices and procedures to effectively prevent telephone solicitations in violation of the regulations prescribed under this subsection." § 227(c)(5).

Prohibition on Using Pre-Recorded Messages. The TCPA prohibits telemarketers from calling residences and using prerecorded messages without the consent of the called party. 47 U.S.C. § 227(b)(1)(B).

Fax Machines. The TCPA prohibits the use of a fax, computer, or other device to send an unsolicited advertisement to a fax machine. § 227(b)(1)(C).

State Enforcement. States may initiate actions against telemarketers "engaging in a pattern or practice of telephone calls or other transmissions to residents of that State" in violation of the TCPA. § 227(f)(1).

NOTES & QUESTIONS

1. ***First Amendment Limitations?*** In *Destination Ventures, Ltd. v. FCC,* 46 F.3d 54 (9th Cir. 1995), Destination Ventures challenged a provision of the TCPA banning unsolicited faxes that contained advertisements on First Amendment grounds. The court upheld the ban because it was designed to prevent shifting advertising costs to consumers, who would be forced to pay for the toner and paper to receive the ads.

2. ***A Do Not Track List.*** As a continuation of the "Do Not Call" list, a discussion is now emerging about "Do Not Track" (DNT) protection for the Internet. The idea of DNT turns on the use of an "opt-out header" in a Web browser.[86] The FTC has told Congress that it supports giving consumers a DNT option to give them a simple and easy way to control the fashion in which companies track them online.

   In contrast to "Do Not Call," considerable complexity exists around the concept of "tracking" on the Internet. The Center for Democracy and Technology (CDT) has defined tracking "as the collection and correlation of data about the Internet activities of a particular user, computer or device, over time and across non-commonly branded websites, for any purpose other than fraud prevention or compliance with law enforcement requests."[87] Thus, CDT considers behavioral advertising as "tracking."

---

[86] For more on the technology behind this policy proposal, see *Do Not Track,* at http://www.donottrack.us/.

[87] CDT, *What Does "Do Not Track" Mean?* (Jan. 31, 2011). For an approach that is largely in agreement with the CDT, see Electronic Frontier Foundation, *What Does the "Track" in "Do Not Track" Mean?* (Feb. 19, 2011).

CDT also argues that any "actively shared" data, such as information that data users provide in social networking profiles and Web forums or by registering for various accounts, should not fall within Do Not Track prohibitions.

Consider Omer Tene and Jules Polonetsky:

> The FTC put forth the following criteria to assess industry responses: DNT should be universal, that is, a single opt-out should cover all would-be trackers; easy to find, understand, and use; persistent, meaning that opt-out choices do not "vanish"; effective and enforceable, covering all tracking technologies; and controlling not only use of data but also their collection.[88] As discussed, the FTC has not yet taken a position on whether any legislation or rulemaking is necessary for DNT. It is clear, however, that regardless of the regulatory approach chosen, industry collaboration will remain key since the system will only work if websites and ad intermediaries respect users' preferences. . . .

> The debate raging around online behavioral tracking generally and DNT in particular is a smoke screen for a discussion that all parties hesitate to hold around deeper values and social norms. Which is more important — efficiency or privacy; law enforcement or individual rights; reputation or freedom of speech? Policymakers must engage with the underlying normative question: is online behavioral tracking a societal good, funding the virtue of the online economy and bringing users more relevant, personalized content and services; or is it an evil scheme for businesses to enrich themselves on account of ignorant users and for governments to create a foundation for pervasive surveillance? Policymakers cannot continue to sidestep these questions in the hope that "users will decide" for themselves.[89]

3. ***Revocation of Consent.*** In *Gager v. Dell Financial Services*, 727 F.3d 265 (3d Cir. 2013), the plaintiff applied for a credit line from Dell to purchase computer equipment. She listed her cell phone number. Dell began calling her cell phone using an automated telephone dialing system. The plaintiff wrote a letter to Dell requesting that it stop calling. Dell continued its calls, calling about 40 times over a three-week span. The plaintiff brought a TCPA action. Dell moved to dismiss claiming that the FTCPA did not provide a way for people to revoke prior consent. The court, however, concluded that "the absence of an express statutory authorization for revocation of prior express consent in the TCPA's provisions on autodialed calls to cellular phones does not tip the scales in favor of a position that no such right exists." The court reasoned that "the common law concept of consent shows that it is revocable" and that "in light of the TCPA's purpose, any silence in the statute as to the right of revocation should be construed in favor of consumers."

[88] Ed Felten, FTC Perspective, W3C Workshop on Web Tracking and User Privacy, Apr. 28-29, 2011, http://www.w3.org/2011/track-privacy/slides/Felten.pdf.

[89] Omer Tene & Jules Polonetsky, *To Track or "Do Not Track": Advancing Transparency and Individual Control in Online Behavioral Advertising*, available at http://www.futureofprivacy.org/tracking/.

(b) The CAN-SPAM Act

In 2003, Congress enacted the Controlling the Assault of Non-Solicited Pornography and Marketing (CAN-SPAM) Act, Pub. L. No. 108-187, 15 U.S.C. §§ 7701 *et seq.*, to address the problem of spam. Spam is a term to describe unsolicited commercial e-mail sent to individuals to advertise products and services.[90] Companies that send unsolicited e-mail are referred to as spammers. Spam is often mailed out in bulk to large lists of e-mail addresses. A recent practice has been to insert hidden HTML tags (also known as "pixel tags" or "Web bugs") into spam. This enables the sender of the e-mail to detect whether the e-mail was opened. It can also inform the sender about whether the e-mail message was forwarded, to what e-mail address it was forwarded, and sometimes, even comments added by a user when forwarding the e-mail. This only works if the recipient has an HTML-enabled e-mail reader rather than a text-only reader. HTML e-mail is e-mail that contains pictures and images rather than simply plain text.

Applicability. The CAN-SPAM Act applies to commercial e-mail, which it defines as a "message with the primary purpose of which is the commercial advertisement or promotion of a commercial product or service."

Prohibitions. The Act prohibits the knowing sending of commercial messages with the intent to deceive or mislead recipients.

Opt Out. The CAN-SPAM Act also requires that a valid opt-out option be made available to e-mail recipients. To make opt out possible, the Act requires senders of commercial e-mail to contain a return address "clearly and conspicuously displayed." Finally, it creates civil and criminal penalties for violations of its provisions. For example, the law allows the DOJ to seek criminal penalties, including imprisonment, for commercial e-mailers who engage in activities such as using a computer to relay or retransmit multiple commercial e-mail messages to receive or mislead recipients or an Internet access service about the message's origin and falsifying header information in multiple e-mail messages and initiate the transmission of these messages.

Enforcement. The CAN-SPAM Act is enforced by governmental and private entities. The chief enforcement entities are the Department of Justice (DOJ), the Federal Trade Commission (FTC), state attorney generals, and "Internet access services" (IAS). Unlike similar laws in other countries, such as Canada's Anti-Spam Legislation (CASL), the CAN-SPAM Act lacks a general private right of action.

The DOJ is charged with enforcing the Act's criminal provisions. These prohibit the unlawful transmission of sexually oriented unsolicited commercial e-mail as well as certain methods of sending commercial e-mail, such as zombie drones, materially false header information, and obtaining IP addresses through

---

[90] For more information on spam, see David E. Sorkin, *Technical and Legal Approaches to Unsolicited Electronic Mail*, 35 U.S.F. L. Rev. 325, 336 (2001).

fraudulent methods. The FTC and state attorney generals also have an enforcement role under the CAN-SPAM Act. The FTC has been involved both in litigation and settlement actions.

Finally, an IAS that has been adversely affected by violations of the CAN-SPAM Act has standing under the statute. The Act defines an IAS as "a service that enables users to access content, information, electronic mail, or other services over the Internet. . ." 47 U.S.C. § 231(e)(4) . Courts have found Internet Service Providers, social networking websites, and email providers to be an IAS.

Assessing the Act. A year after enactment of CAN-SPAM, media accounts faulted the law as ineffective. Indeed, reports stressed the increase in spam during this time. According to one anti-spam vendor, 67 percent of all e-mail was spam in February 2004, and 75 percent in November 2004. Some spammers employed new tactics after the passage of the Act, such as using "zombie networks," which involve hijacking computers with Trojan horse programs. Anti-spam activists faulted CAN-SPAM for preempting tougher state laws, failing to provide a general private right of action, and providing an opt-out option instead of an opt in.[91]

State Anti-Spam Laws. At least 20 states have anti-spam statutes. For example, Cal. Bus. & Professions Code § 17538.4 mandates that senders of spam include in the text of their e-mails a way through which recipients can request to receive no further e-mails. The sender must remove the person from its list. A provider of an e-mail service located within the state of California can request that spammers stop sending spam through its equipment. If the spammer continues to send e-mail, it can be liable for $50 per message up to a maximum of $25,000 per day. *See* § 17538.45.

A Critique of Anti-Spam Legislation. Consumers don't always dislike marketing messages. As Eric Goldman reminds us, "consumers want marketing when it creates personal benefits for them, and marketing also can have spillover benefits that improve social welfare." Goldman is worried that current legal regulation will block the kinds of filters that will improve the ability of consumers to manage information and receive information that will advance their interests. He points to anti-adware laws in Utah and Alaska as especially problematic; these statutes "prohibit client-side software from displaying pop-up ads triggered by the consumer's use of a third party trademark or domain name — even if the consumer has fully consented to the software." For Goldman, these statutes are flawed because they try to "ban or restrict matchmaking technologies." The ideal filter would be a "mind-reading wonder" that "could costlessly — but accurately — read consumers' minds, infer their expressed and latent preferences without the consumer bearing any disclosure costs, and act on the inferred preferences to screen out unwanted content and proactively seek out wanted content." Goldman is confident that such filtering technology is not only possible, but "inevitable —

[91] For a range of reform proposals, see David Lorentz, *Note: The Effectiveness of Litigation Under the CAN-SPAM Act*, 30 Rev. Litig. 559 (2011).

perhaps imminently."[92] What kind of regulatory approach would encourage development and adoption of Goldman's favored filters while also blocking existing SPAM technology? Will surrendering more privacy help better target marketing and thus clear out our inboxes of unwanted spam?

Spam and Speech. Is spam a form of speech, protected by the First Amendment? In *Cyber Promotions, Inc. v. America Online, Inc.,* 948 F. Supp. 436 (E.D. Pa. 1996), Cyber Promotions, Inc. sought a declaratory judgment that America Online (AOL) was prohibited under the First Amendment from denying it the ability to send AOL customers unsolicited e-mail. The court rejected Cyber Promotion's argument because of a lack of state action: "AOL is a private online company that is not owned in whole or part by the government." Today, the Internet is increasingly becoming a major medium of communication. Prior to modern communications media, individuals could express their views in traditional "public fora" — parks and street corners. These public fora are no longer the central place for public discourse. Perhaps the Internet is the modern public forum, the place where individuals come to speak and express their views. If this is the case, is it preferable for access to the Internet to be controlled by private entities?

International Approaches. Unlike the CAN-SPAM in the United States, most other countries favor an opt-in approach as a legal response to commercial unsolicited emails. For example, CASL in Canada generally permits the sending of commercial email only when there is consent.[93] CASL provides for strong administrative penalties as well as a private right of action.

This preference for an opt-in regime is also found in Australia's Spam Act of 2003 and New Zealand's Unsolicited Electronic Messages Act of 2007. In the European Union, the E-Privacy Directive, first enacted in 2002 and amended in 2009, states that the use of "electronic mail for the purposes of direct marketing may be only allowed in respect of subscribers who have given their prior consent."[94]

Within the EU, Germany is the country that may have the strictest regulation of spam. Its main provision prohibiting spam is Article 7 of the Act against Unfair Competition (UWG). This clause prohibits the sending of advertising emails that constitute an "unconscionable pestering." Clause 7(2) no.3 of this statute contains the critical language; it forbids advertising through email without "prior express consent" of the recipient. In German law, prior express consent requires a process termed "double opt-in." For example, a consumer might agree to receive commercial emails by checking a box, confirming the selection, and then opt-in

---

[92] Eric Goldman, *A Cosean Analysis of Marketing*, 2006 Wis. L. Rev. 1151, 1154-55, 1202, 1211-12.

[93] Bill C-28, Fighting Internet and Wireless Spam Act, 3rd Session, 40th Parl., 2010.

[94] Directive 2002/58/EC of the European Parliament and of the Council of 12 July 2002 concerning the processing of personal data and the protection of privacy in the electronic communications sector (Directive on privacy and electronic communications), L201, 2002-07-31, pp. 37-47 (2002); Directive 2009/136/EC of the European Parliament and of the Council of 25. November 2009, L337, 2009-12-18, pp. 11-36 (2009).

again by clicking on a link contained in the first email that she received after enrollment.[95]

Would an opt-in system be preferable to the current U.S. approach? Would there be benefits for the U.S. switching to opt-in to make regulations in this area of law more uniform internationally?

G. FIRST AMENDMENT LIMITATIONS ON PRIVACY REGULATION

Although the First Amendment protects privacy, privacy restrictions can come into conflict with the First Amendment. In particular, many privacy statutes regulate the disclosure of true information. The cases in this section explore the extent to which the First Amendment limits the privacy statutes. Before turning to the cases, some background about basic First Amendment jurisprudence is necessary. The cases in this section often focus on commercial speech, and the Court analyzes commercial speech differently than other forms of expression.

First Amendment Protection of Commercial Speech. For a while, the Court considered commercial speech as a category of expression that is not accorded First Amendment protection. However, in *Virginia State Board of Pharmacy v. Virginia Citizens Consumer Council, Inc.,* 425 U.S. 748 (1976), the Court held that commercial speech deserves constitutional protection. However, the Court held that commercial speech has a lower value than regular categories of speech and therefore is entitled to a lesser protection. *Ohralik v. Ohio State Bar Ass'n,* 436 U.S. 447 (1978).

Defining Commercial Speech. What is "commercial speech"? The Court has defined it as speech that "proposes a commercial transaction," *Virginia State Board,* 425 U.S. 748 (1976), and as "expression related solely to the economic interests of the speaker and its audience." *Central Hudson Gas & Electric Corp. v. Public Service Comm'n of New York,* 447 U.S. 557 (1980). The Court later held that neither of these are necessary requirements to define commercial speech; both are factors to be considered in determining whether speech is commercial. *See Bolger v. Youngs Drug Products Corp.,* 463 U.S. 60 (1983).

The **Central Hudson** *Test.* In *Central Hudson,* 447 U.S. 557 (1980), the Court established a four-part test for analyzing the constitutionality of restrictions on commercial speech:

> At the outset, we must determine whether the expression is protected by the First Amendment. For commercial speech to come within that provision, it at least must

---

[95] For German caselaw finding a requirement of double-opt in, see AG Düsseldorf, Decision of July 14, 2009 - 48 C 1911/09, BeckRS 2009, 25861; LG Essen, Decision of April 20, 2009 - 4 O 368/08, NJW-RR 2009, 1556; OLG Hamm, Decision of February 17, 2011 - I-4 U 174/10 (LG Dortmund) (rechtskräftig), MMR 2011, 539; OLG Jena, Decision of April 21, 2010 – 2 U 88/10, NJOZ 2011, 1164.

concern lawful activity and not be misleading. Next, we ask whether the asserted governmental interest is substantial. If both inquiries yield positive answers, we must determine whether the regulation directly advances the governmental interest asserted, and whether it is not more extensive than is necessary to serve that interest.

In *Board of Trustees of State University of New York v. Fox,* 492 U.S. 469 (1989), the Court revised the last part of the *Central Hudson* test — that speech "not [be] more extensive than is necessary to serve [the governmental] interest" — to a requirement that there be a "fit between the legislature's ends and the means chosen to accomplish the ends, . . . a fit that is not necessarily perfect, but reasonable."

In *Cincinnati v. Discovery Network, Inc.,* 507 U.S. 410 (1993), the Court, applying the commercial speech test in *Central Hudson* and *Fox,* struck down an ordinance that banned newsracks with "commercial handbills." The ordinance did not apply to newsracks for newspapers. The Court concluded that the ban was not a "reasonable fit" with the city's interest in aesthetics. Moreover, the Court concluded that the ordinance was not content-neutral. The Court held that Cincinnati "has enacted a sweeping ban on the use of newsracks that distribute 'commercial handbills,' but not 'newspapers.' Under the city's newsrack policy, whether any particular newsrack falls within the ban is determined by the content of the publication resting inside that newsrack. Thus, by any commonsense understanding of the term, the ban in this case is 'content based.' . . . [B]ecause the ban is predicated on the content of the publications distributed by the subject newsracks, it is not a valid time, place, or manner restriction on protected speech."

ROWAN V. UNITED STATES POST OFFICE DEPARTMENT
397 U.S. 728 (1970)

[A federal statute permitted individuals to require that entities sending unwanted mailings remove the individuals' names from their mailing lists and cease to send future mailings. A group of organizations challenged the statute on First Amendment grounds.]

BURGER, C.J. . . . The essence of appellants' argument is that the statute violates their constitutional right to communicate. . . . Without doubt the public postal system is an indispensable adjunct of every civilized society and communication is imperative to a healthy social order. But the right of every person "to be let alone" must be placed in the scales with the right of others to communicate.

In today's complex society we are inescapably captive audiences for many purposes, but a sufficient measure of individual autonomy must survive to permit every householder to exercise control over unwanted mail. To make the householder the exclusive and final judge of what will cross his threshold undoubtedly has the effect of impeding the flow of ideas, information, and arguments that, ideally, he should receive and consider. Today's merchandising methods, the plethora of mass mailings subsidized by low postal rates, and the growth of the sale of large mailing lists as an industry in itself have changed the mailman from a carrier of primarily private communications, as he was in a more leisurely day, and have made him an adjunct of the mass mailer who sends unsolicited and often unwanted mail into every home. It places no strain on the doctrine of judicial notice to observe that whether measured by pieces or pounds, Everyman's mail today is made up overwhelmingly of material he did not seek from persons he does not know. And all too often it is matter he finds offensive. . . .

The Court has traditionally respected the right of a householder to bar, by order or notice, solicitors, hawkers, and peddlers from his property. In this case the mailer's right to communicate is circumscribed only by an affirmative act of the addressee giving notice that he wishes no further mailings from that mailer.

To hold less would tend to license a form of trespass and would make hardly more sense than to say that a radio or television viewer may not twist the dial to cut off an offensive or boring communication and thus bar its entering his home. Nothing in the Constitution compels us to listen to or view any unwanted communication, whatever its merit; we see no basis for according the printed word or pictures a different or more preferred status because they are sent by mail. The ancient concept that "a man's home is his castle" into which "not even the king may enter" has lost none of its vitality, and none of the recognized exceptions includes any right to communicate offensively with another. . . .

If this prohibition operates to impede the flow of even valid ideas, the answer is that no one has a right to press even "good" ideas on an unwilling recipient. That we are often "captives" outside the sanctuary of the home and subject to objectionable speech and other sound does not mean we must be captives everywhere. The asserted right of a mailer, we repeat, stops at the outer boundary of every person's domain. . . .

MAINSTREAM MARKETING SERVICES, INC. V. FEDERAL TRADE COMMISSION
358 F.3d 1228 (10th Cir. 2004)

EBEL, J. . . . In 2003, two federal agencies—the Federal Trade Commission (FTC) and the Federal Communications Commission (FCC) — promulgated rules that together created the national do-not-call registry *See* 16 C.F.R. § 310.4(b)(1)(iii)(B) (FTC rule); 47 C.F.R. § 64.1200(c)(2) (FCC rule). The national do-not-call registry is a list containing the personal telephone numbers of telephone subscribers who have voluntarily indicated that they do not wish to receive unsolicited calls from commercial telemarketers. Commercial telemarketers are generally prohibited from calling phone numbers that have been placed on the do-not-call registry, and they must pay an annual fee to access the numbers on the registry so that they can delete those numbers from their telephone solicitation lists. So far, consumers have registered more than 50 million phone numbers on the national do-not-call registry.

The national do-not-call registry's restrictions apply only to telemarketing calls made by or on behalf of sellers of goods or services, and not to charitable or political fundraising calls. Additionally, a seller may call consumers who have signed up for the national registry if it has an established business relationship with the consumer or if the consumer has given that seller express written permission to call. Telemarketers generally have three months from the date on which a consumer signs up for the registry to remove the consumer's phone number from their call lists. Consumer registrations remain valid for five years, and phone numbers that are disconnected or reassigned will be periodically removed from the registry.

The national do-not-call registry is the product of a regulatory effort dating back to 1991 aimed at protecting the privacy rights of consumers and curbing the risk of telemarketing abuse. In the Telephone Consumer Protection Act of 1991 ("TCPA") — under which the FCC enacted its do-not-call rules — Congress found that for many consumers telemarketing sales calls constitute an intrusive invasion of privacy. . . . The TCPA therefore authorized the FCC to establish a national database of consumers who object to receiving "telephone solicitations," which the act defined as commercial sales calls. . . .

The national do-not-call registry's telemarketing restrictions apply only to commercial speech. Like most commercial speech regulations, the do-not-call rules draw a line between commercial and non-commercial speech on the basis of content. In reviewing commercial speech regulations, we apply the *Central Hudson* test. *Central Hudson Gas & Elec. Corp. v. Pub. Serv. Comm'n of N.Y.*, 447 U.S. 557 (1980).

Central Hudson established a three-part test governing First Amendment challenges to regulations restricting non-misleading commercial speech that relates to lawful activity. First, the government must assert a substantial interest to be achieved by the regulation. Second, the regulation must directly advance that governmental interest, meaning that it must do more than provide "only ineffective or remote support for the government's purpose." Third, although the regulation need not be the least restrictive measure available, it must be narrowly tailored not to restrict more speech than necessary. Together, these final two factors require that there be a reasonable fit between the government's objectives and the means it chooses to accomplish those ends. . . .

The government asserts that the do-not-call regulations are justified by its interests in 1) protecting the privacy of individuals in their homes, and 2) protecting consumers against the risk of fraudulent and abusive solicitation. Both of these justifications are undisputedly substantial governmental interests.

In *Rowan v. United States Post Office Dep't,* the Supreme Court upheld the right of a homeowner to restrict material that could be mailed to his or her house. The Court emphasized the importance of individual privacy, particularly in the context of the home, stating that "the ancient concept that 'a man's home is his castle' into which 'not even the king may enter' has lost none of its vitality." In *Frisby v. Schultz,* the Court [held] . . .

> One important aspect of residential privacy is protection of the unwilling listener. . . . [A] special benefit of the privacy all citizens enjoy within their own walls, which the State may legislate to protect, is an ability to avoid intrusions. Thus, we have repeatedly held that individuals are not required to welcome unwanted speech into their own homes and that the government may protect this freedom.

A reasonable fit exists between the do-not-call rules and the government's privacy and consumer protection interests if the regulation directly advances those interests and is narrowly tailored. . . .

These criteria are plainly established in this case. The do-not-call registry directly advances the government's interests by effectively blocking a significant number of the calls that cause the problems the government sought to redress. It is narrowly tailored because its opt-in character ensures that it does not inhibit any speech directed at the home of a willing listener.

The telemarketers assert that the do-not-call registry is unconstitutionally underinclusive because it does not apply to charitable and political callers. First Amendment challenges based on underinclusiveness face an uphill battle in the commercial speech context. As a general rule, the First Amendment does not require that the government regulate all aspects of a problem before it can make progress on any front. . . . The underinclusiveness of a commercial speech regulation is relevant only if it renders the regulatory framework so irrational that it fails materially to advance the aims that it was purportedly designed to further. . .

As discussed above, the national do-not-call registry is designed to reduce intrusions into personal privacy and the risk of telemarketing fraud and abuse that accompany unwanted telephone solicitation. The registry directly advances those goals. So far, more than 50 million telephone numbers have been registered on the do-not-call list, and the do-not-call regulations protect these households from receiving most unwanted telemarketing calls. According to the telemarketers' own estimate, 2.64 telemarketing calls per week — or more than 137 calls annually — were directed at an average consumer before the do-not-call list came into effect. *Cf.* 68 Fed. Reg. at 44152 (discussing the five-fold increase in the total number of telemarketing calls between 1991 and 2003). Accordingly, absent the do-not-call registry, telemarketers would call those consumers who have already signed up for the registry an estimated total of 6.85 *billion* times each year.

To be sure, the do-not-call list will not block all of these calls. Nevertheless, it will prohibit a substantial number of them, making it difficult to fathom how the registry could be called an "ineffective" means of stopping invasive or abusive calls, or a regulation that "furnish[es] only speculative or marginal support" for the government's interests. . . .

Finally, the type of unsolicited calls that the do-not-call list does prohibit—commercial sales calls — is the type that Congress, the FTC and the FCC have all determined to be most to blame for the problems the government is seeking to redress. According to the legislative history accompanying the TCPA, "[c]omplaint statistics show that unwanted commercial calls are a far bigger problem than unsolicited calls from political or charitable organizations." H.R. Rep. No. 102-317, at 16 (1991). Additionally, the FTC has found that commercial callers are more likely than non-commercial callers to engage in deceptive and abusive practices. . . . The speech regulated by the do-not-call list is therefore the speech most likely to cause the problems the government sought to alleviate in enacting that list, further demonstrating that the regulation directly advances the government's interests. . . .

Although the least restrictive means test is not the test to be used in the commercial speech context, commercial speech regulations do at least have to be "narrowly tailored" and provide a "reasonable fit" between the problem and the solution. Whether or not there are "numerous and obvious less-burdensome alternatives" is a relevant consideration in our narrow tailoring analysis. . . . We hold that the national do-not-call registry is narrowly tailored because it does not over-regulate protected speech; rather, it restricts only calls that are targeted at unwilling recipients. . . .

The Supreme Court has repeatedly held that speech restrictions based on private choice (i.e., an opt-in feature) are less restrictive than laws that prohibit speech directly. In *Rowan,* for example, the Court approved a law under which an individual could require a mailer to stop all future mailings if he or she received advertisements that he or she believed to be erotically arousing or sexually provocative. Although it was the government that empowered individuals to avoid materials they considered provocative, the Court emphasized that the mailer's right to communicate was circumscribed only by an affirmative act of a householder. . . .

Like the do-not-mail regulation approved in *Rowan,* the national do-not-call registry does not itself prohibit any speech. Instead, it merely "permits a citizen to erect a wall . . . that no advertiser may penetrate without his acquiescence." *See Rowan,* 397 U.S. at 738. Almost by definition, the do-not-call regulations only block calls that would constitute unwanted intrusions into the privacy of consumers who have signed up for the list. . . .

NOTES & QUESTIONS

1. ***The Do Not Call List and* Rowan.** To what extent is this case controlled by *Rowan*? Does the Do Not Call (DNC) list go beyond the statute in *Rowan*?
2. ***Charitable and Political Calls.*** The DNC list permits calls based on charitable or political purposes. There is no way to block such calls. Suppose that Congress decided that all calls could be included. Would a charity or political group have a First Amendment ground to overturn the DNC list?

U.S. WEST, INC. V. FEDERAL COMMUNICATIONS COMMISSION

182 F.3d 1224 (10th Cir. 1999)

TACHA, J. . . . U.S. West, Inc. petitions for review of a Federal Communication Commission ("FCC") order restricting the use and disclosure of and access to customer proprietary network information ("CPNI"). *See* 63 Fed. Reg. 20,326 (1998) ("CPNI Order"). [U.S. West argues that FCC regulations, implementing 47 U.S.C. § 222, among other things, violate the First Amendment. These regulations require telecommunications companies to ask consumers for approval (to "opt-in") before they can use a customer's personal information for marketing purposes.] . .

The dispute in this case involves regulations the FCC promulgated to implement provisions of 47 U.S.C. § 222, which was enacted as part of the Telecommunications Act of 1996. Section 222, entitled "Privacy of customer information," states generally that "[e]very telecommunications carrier has a duty to protect the confidentiality of proprietary information of, and relating to . . . customers." To effectuate that duty, § 222 places restrictions on the use, disclosure of, and access to certain customer information. At issue here are the FCC's regulations clarifying the privacy requirements for CPNI. The central provision of § 222 dealing with CPNI is § 222(c)(1), which states:

> Except as required by law or with the approval of the customer, a telecommunications carrier that receives or obtains customer proprietary network information by virtue of its provision of a telecommunications service shall only use, disclose, or permit access to individually identifiable customer proprietary network information in its provision of (A) the telecommunication service from which such information is derived, or (B) services necessary to, or used in, the provision of such telecommunications service, including the publishing of directories.

Section 222(d) provides three additional exceptions to the CPNI privacy requirements. [These exceptions permit the companies to use and disclose CPNI for billing purposes, to prevent fraud, and to provide services to the consumer if the consumer approves of the use of such information to provide the service. Any other uses or disclosures of CPNI not specifically permitted by § 222 require the consumer's consent. The regulations adopted by the CPNI Order implementing § 222 divides telecommunications services into three categories: (1) local, (2) long-distance, and (3) mobile or cellular. A telecommunications carrier can use or disclose CPNI to market products within one of these service categories if the customer already subscribes to that category of service. Carriers can't use or disclose CPNI to market categories of service to which the customer does not subscribe unless first obtaining the customer's consent. The regulations also prohibit using CPNI without consent to market other services such as voice mail or Internet access, to track customers that call competitors, or to try to regain the business of customers that switch carriers.] . . .

The regulations also describe the means by which a carrier must obtain customer approval. Section 222(c)(1) did not elaborate as to what form that approval should take. The FCC decided to require an "opt-in" approach, in which a carrier must obtain prior express approval from a customer through written, oral, or electronic means before using the customer's CPNI. The government acknowledged that the means of approval could have taken numerous other forms, including an "opt-out" approach, in which approval would be inferred from the customer-carrier relationship unless the customer specifically requested that his or her CPNI be restricted. . . .

Petitioner argues that the CPNI regulations interpreting 47 U.S.C. § 222 violate the First Amendment. . . .

Because petitioner's targeted speech to its customers is for the purpose of soliciting those customers to purchase more or different telecommunications services, it "does no more than propose a commercial transaction." Consequently, the targeted speech in this case fits soundly within the definition of commercial speech. It is well established that nonmisleading commercial speech regarding a lawful activity is a form of protected speech under the First Amendment, although it is generally afforded less protection than noncommercial speech. The parties do not dispute that the commercial speech based on CPNI is truthful and nonmisleading. Therefore, the CPNI regulations implicate the First Amendment by restricting protected commercial speech. . . .

We analyze whether a government restriction on commercial speech violates the First Amendment under the four-part framework set forth in *Central Hudson* [*Gas & Elec. Corp. v. Public Serv. Comm'n of N.Y.,* 477 U.S. 557 (1980)]. First, we must conduct a threshold inquiry regarding whether the commercial speech concerns lawful activity and is not misleading. If these requirements are not met, the government may freely regulate the speech. If this threshold requirement is met, the government may restrict the speech only if it proves: "(1) it has a substantial state interest in regulating the speech, (2) the regulation directly and materially advances that interest, and (3) the regulation is no more extensive than necessary to serve the interest." As noted above, no one disputes that the commercial speech based on CPNI is truthful and nonmisleading. We therefore proceed directly to whether the government has satisfied its burden under the remaining three prongs of the *Central Hudson* test. . . .

The respondents argue that the FCC's CPNI regulations advance two substantial state interests: protecting customer privacy and promoting competition. While, in the abstract, these may constitute legitimate and substantial interests, we have concerns about the proffered justifications in the context of this case. . . .

. . . Although we agree that privacy may rise to the level of a substantial state interest, the government cannot satisfy the second prong of the *Central Hudson* test by merely asserting a broad interest in privacy. It must specify the particular notion of privacy and interest served. Moreover, privacy is not an absolute good because it imposes real costs on society. Therefore, the specific privacy interest must be substantial, demonstrating that the state has considered the proper balancing of the benefits and harms of privacy. In sum, privacy may only constitute a substantial state interest if the government specifically articulates and properly justifies it.

In the context of a speech restriction imposed to protect privacy by keeping certain information confidential, the government must show that the dissemination of the information desired to be kept private would inflict specific and significant harm on individuals, such as undue embarrassment or ridicule, intimidation or harassment, or misappropriation of sensitive personal information for the purposes of assuming another's identity. Although we may feel uncomfortable knowing that our personal information is circulating in the world, we live in an open society where information may usually pass freely. A general level of discomfort from knowing that people can readily access information about us does not necessarily rise to the level of a substantial state interest under *Central Hudson* for it is not based on an identified harm.

Neither Congress nor the FCC explicitly stated what "privacy" harm § 222 seeks to protect against. The CPNI Order notes that "CPNI includes information that is extremely personal to customers . . . such as to whom, where, and when a customer places a call, as well as the types of service offerings to which the customer subscribes," and it summarily finds "call destinations and other details about a call . . . may be equally or more sensitive [than the content of the calls]." The government never states it directly, but we infer from this thin justification that disclosure of CPNI information could prove embarrassing to some and that the government seeks to combat this potential harm. . . .

Under the next prong of *Central Hudson,* the government must "demonstrate that the harms it recites are real and that its restriction will in fact alleviate them to a material degree.". . . On the record before us, the government fails to meet its burden.

The government presents no evidence showing the harm to either privacy or competition is real. Instead, the government relies on speculation that harm to privacy and competition for new services will result if carriers use CPNI. . . . While protecting against disclosure of sensitive and potentially embarrassing personal information may be important in the abstract, we have no indication of how it may occur in reality with respect to CPNI. Indeed, we do not even have indication that the disclosure might actually occur. The government presents no evidence regarding how and to whom carriers would disclose CPNI. . . . [T]he government has not explained how or why a carrier would disclose CPNI to outside parties, especially when the government claims CPNI is information that would give one firm a competitive advantage over another. This leaves us unsure exactly who would potentially receive the sensitive information. . . .

In order for a regulation to satisfy this final *Central Hudson* prong, there must be a fit between the legislature's means and its desired objective. . . .

. . . [O]n this record, the FCC's failure to adequately consider an obvious and substantially less restrictive alternative, an opt-out strategy, indicates that it did not narrowly tailor the CPNI regulations regarding customer approval. . . .

The respondents merely speculate that there are a substantial number of individuals who feel strongly about their privacy, yet would not bother to opt-out if given notice and the opportunity to do so. Such speculation hardly reflects the careful calculation of costs and benefits that our commercial speech jurisprudence requires. . . .

In sum, even assuming that respondents met the prior two prongs of *Central Hudson,* we conclude that based on the record before us, the agency has failed to satisfy its burden of showing that the customer approval regulations restrict no more speech than necessary to serve the asserted state interests. Consequently, we find that the CPNI regulations interpreting the customer approval requirement of 47 U.S.C. § 222(c) violate the First Amendment.

BRISCOE, J. dissenting. . . . After reviewing the CPNI Order and the administrative record, I am convinced the FCC's interpretation of § 222, more specifically its selection of the opt-in method for obtaining customer approval, is entirely reasonable. Indeed, the CPNI Order makes a strong case that, of the two options seriously considered by the FCC, the opt-in method is the only one that legitimately forwards Congress' goal of ensuring that customers give informed consent for use of their individually identifiable CPNI. . . .

. . . U.S. West suggests the CPNI Order unduly limits its ability to engage in commercial speech with its existing customers regarding new products and services it may offer. . . .

The problem with U.S. West's arguments is they are more appropriately aimed at the restrictions and requirements outlined in § 222 rather than the approval method adopted in the CPNI Order. As outlined above, it is the statute, not the CPNI Order, that prohibits a carrier from using, disclosing, or permitting access to individually identifiable CPNI without first obtaining informed consent from its customers. Yet U.S. West has not challenged the constitutionality of § 222, and this is not the proper forum for addressing such a challenge even if it was raised. . . .

The majority, focusing at this point on the CPNI Order rather than the statute, concludes the FCC failed to adequately consider the opt-out method, which the majority characterizes as "an obvious and substantially less restrictive alternative" than the opt-in method. Notably, however, the majority fails to explain why, in its view, the opt-out method is substantially less restrictive. Presumably, the majority is relying on the fact that the opt-out method typically results in a higher "approval" rate than the opt-in method. Were mere "approval" percentages the only factor relevant to our discussion, the majority would perhaps be correct. As the FCC persuasively concluded in the CPNI Order, however, the opt-out method simply does not comply with § 222's requirement of informed consent. In particular, the opt-out method, unlike the opt-in method, does not guarantee that a customer will make an informed decision about usage of his or her individually identifiable CPNI. To the contrary, the opt-out method creates the very real possibility of "uninformed" customer approval. In the end, I reiterate my point that the opt-in method selected by the FCC is the only method of obtaining approval that serves the governmental interests at issue while simultaneously complying with the express requirement of the statute (i.e., obtaining informed customer consent). . . .

In conclusion, I view U.S. West's petition for review as little more than a run-of-the-mill attack on an agency order "clothed by ingenious argument in the garb" of First Amendment issues. . . .

NOTES & QUESTIONS

1. *The Aftermath of* U.S. West: *The FCC and the D.C. Circuit.* The FCC responded to the *U.S. West* decision at length in its 2007 CPNI Order and largely rejected its holdings. FCC Report and Order, 07-22 (April 2, 2007). The one change that it made was to modify its 1998 Order at issue in *U.S. West* so that opt-in consent would be required only with respect to a carrier's sharing of customer information with third-party marketers.

The FCC also declared that the Tenth Circuit in *U.S. West* had based its decision "on a different record than the one compiled here" and in particular on premises that were no longer valid. First, the FCC reasoned, there was now ample evidence of disclosure of CPNI and the adverse effects it could have on customers. Second, there was now substantial evidence that an opt-out strategy would not adequately protect customer privacy "because most customers either do not read or do not understand carriers' opt-out notices." The FCC also stated that requiring opt-in consent from customers before sharing CPNI with joint venture partners and independent contractors for marketing purposes would pass First Amendment scrutiny.

The D.C. Circuit upheld the FCC's 2007 Report and Order. *National Cable and Telecommunications Association*, 555 F.3d 996 (D.C. Cir. 2009). It found that the government had a "substantial" interest, under the *Central Hudson* test, in "protecting the privacy of consumer credit information." In its analysis of the second part of the *Central Hudson* test, the D.C. Circuit found that the Commission's 2007 Order "directly advances" the government's interest:

[C]ommon sense supports the Commission's determination that the risk of unauthorized disclosure of customer information increases with the number of entities possessing it. The Commission therefore reasonably concluded that an opt-in consent requirement directly and materially advanced the interests in protecting customer privacy and in ensuring customer control over the information.

Finally, the court found that under *Central Hudson*'s final requirement the 2007 Report and Order easily met the standard of a regulation proportionate to the government's interest. The court reasoned that the difference between opt in and opt out is only a marginal one in the relative degree of burden on First Amendment interests. The D.C. Circuit found that the "Commission carefully considered the differences between the two regulatory approaches, and the evidence supports the Commission's decision to prefer opt-in consent."

If the *U.S. West* court were to examine the FCC's 2007 Report and Order, would it likely agree or disagree with the D.C. Circuit?

2. ***Is Opt In Narrowly Tailored?*** Is the opt-in system involved in *U.S. West* more restrictive than the do-not-mail list in *Rowan* or the DNC list in *Mainstream Marketing*? Is the privacy interest in *U.S. West* different than in *Rowan* and *Mainstream Marketing*?

3. ***Personal Information: Property, Contract, and Speech.*** Consider the following critique of *U.S. West* by Julie Cohen:

> The law affords numerous instances of regulation of the exchange of information as property or product. Securities markets, which operate entirely by means of information exchange, are subject to extensive regulation, and hardly anybody thinks that securities laws and regulations should be subjected to heightened or strict First Amendment scrutiny. Laws prohibiting patent, copyright, and trademark infringement, and forbidding the misappropriation of trade secrets, have as their fundamental purpose (and their undisputed effect) the restriction of information flows. The securities and intellectual property laws, moreover, are expressly content-based, and thus illustrate that (as several leading First Amendment scholars acknowledge) this characterization doesn't always matter. Finally, federal computer crime laws punish certain uses of information for reasons entirely unrelated to their communicative aspects. . . .
>
> The accumulation, use, and market exchange of personally-identified data don't fit neatly into any recognized category of "commercial speech" . . . because in the ways that matter, these activities aren't really "speech" at all. Although regulation directed at these acts may impose some indirect burden on direct-to-consumer communication, that isn't the primary objective of data privacy regulation. This suggests that, at most, data privacy regulation should be subject to the intermediate scrutiny applied to indirect speech regulation.[96]

4. ***Is Opt In Too Expensive?*** Michael Staten and Fred Cate have defended the *U.S. West* decision by noting the results of the testing of an opt-in system by U.S. West:

---

[96] Julie E. Cohen, *Examined Lives: Informational Privacy and the Subject as Object*, 52 Stan. L. Rev. 1373, 1416-18, 1421 (2000).

In 1997, U.S. West (now Qwest Communications), one of the largest telecommunications companies in the United States, conducted one of the few affirmative consent trials for which results are publicly available. In that trial, the company sought permission from its customers to utilize information about their calling patterns (e.g., volume of calls, time and duration of calls, etc.) to market new services to them. The direct mail appeal for permission received a positive response rate between 5 and 11 percent for residential customers (depending upon the size of a companion incentive offered by the company). Residential customers opted in at a rate of 28 percent when called about the service.

When U.S. West was actually communicating in person with the consumers, the positive response rate was three to six times higher than when it relied on consumers reading and responding to mail. But even with telemarketing, the task of reaching a customer is daunting. U.S. West determined that it required an average of 4.8 calls to each consumer household before they reached an adult who could grant consent. In one-third of households called, U.S. West never reached the customer, despite repeated attempts. In any case, many U.S. West customers received more calls than would have been the case in an opt-out system, and despite repeated contact attempts, one-third of their customers missed opportunities to receive new products and services. The approximately $20 cost per positive response in the telemarketing test and $29 to $34 cost per positive response in the direct mail test led the company to conclude that opt-in was not a viable business model because it was too costly, too difficult, and too time intensive.[97]

Robert Gellman, however, generally disputes the findings of industry studies about the costs of privacy protective measures. With regard to opt-in cost assessments, Gellman argues that industry studies often fail "to consider other ways [beyond direct mail and telemarketing] that business and charities can solicit individuals to replace any losses from opt-in requirements. Newspaper, Internet, radio, and television advertising may be effective substitutes for direct mail. There are other ways to approach individuals without the compilation of detailed personal dossiers. None of the alternatives is adequately considered."[98]

5. *Is Commercial Transaction Information Different from Other Speech?* Courts analyzing First Amendment challenges to regulation of data about commercial transactions have typically viewed the dissemination and use of such data as commercial speech, and they have applied the *Central Hudson* test. This test is less protective than regular First Amendment protection. Solveig Singleton contends that data about commercial transactions should be considered regular speech, not commercial speech:

Is commercial tracking essentially different from gossip? . . .

Gossip and other informal personal contacts serve an important function in advanced economies. In Nineteenth Century America, entrepreneurs would increase their sales by acquiring information about their customers. Customers

---

[97] Michael E. Staten & Fred H. Cate, *The Impact of Opt-In Privacy Rules on Retail Credit Markets: A Case Study of MBNA*, 52 Duke L.J. 745, 767-68 (2003).

[98] Robert Gellman, *Privacy, Consumers, and Costs: How the Lack of Privacy Costs Consumers and Why Business Studies of Privacy Costs Are Biased and Incomplete* (Mar. 2002), at http://www.epic.org/reports/dmfprivacy.html.

relied on their neighborhood banker, whom they knew since childhood, to grant them credit. They would return again and again to the same stores for personalized service. . . .

[E]conomic actors must develop new mechanisms of relaying information to each other about fraud, trust, and behavior of potential customers. Towards the end of the Nineteenth Century and throughout the Twentieth Century, formal credit reporting began to evolve out of gossip networks. . . .

The equivalence of gossip and consumer databases suggests that there is no need to treat the evolution of databases as a crisis. Those who argue for a new legal regime for privacy, however, view new uses of information as having crossed an "invisible line" between permissible gossip and violative information collection. While the use of new technology to collect information may make people uneasy, is there any reason to suppose that any harm that might result will amount to greater harm than the harm that could come from being a victim of vicious gossip?[99]

Singleton goes on to contend that information collected by businesses in databases is less pernicious than gossip because few people have access to it and it is "likely to be much more accurate than gossip." Is the information in computer databases merely gossip on a more systemic scale? Compare how the First Amendment regulates gossip with how it regulates commercial speech.

6. ***The Value of Privacy.*** What is the value of protecting the privacy of consumer information maintained by telecommunications companies? Is it more important than the economic benefits that the telecommunications companies gain by using that information for marketing? How should policymakers go about answering such questions? Consider James Nehf:

The choice of utilitarian reasoning — often reduced to cost-benefit analysis ("CBA") in policy debates — fixes the outcome in favor of the side that can more easily quantify results. In privacy debates, this generally favors the side arguing for more data collection and sharing. Although CBA can mean different things in various contexts, the term here means a strategy for making choices in which quantifiable weights are given to competing alternatives. . . .

We should openly acknowledge that non-economic values are legitimate in privacy debates, just as they have been recognized in other areas of fundamental importance. Decisions about the societal acceptance of disabled citizens, the codification of collective bargaining rights for workers, and the adoption of fair trial procedures for the accused did not depend entirely, or even primarily, on CBA outcomes. Difficulties in quantifying costs and benefits do not present insurmountable obstacles when policymakers address matters of basic human dignity. The protection of personal data should be viewed in a similar way, and CBA should play a smaller role in privacy debates. . . .

A similar phenomenon is at work in the formulation of public policy. Policymakers are often asked to compare incomparable alternatives. . . .

By converting all values to money, the incomparability problem is lessened, but only if we accept the legitimacy of money as the covering value. In the privacy debate, the legitimacy of monetizing individual privacy preferences is highly suspect. Benefits are often personal, emotional, intangible, and not

---

[99] Solveig Singleton, *Privacy Versus the First Amendment: A Skeptical Approach*, 11 Fordham Intell. Prop. Media & Ent. L.J. 97, 126-32 (2000).

readily quantifiable. Preferences on privacy matters are generally muddled, incoherent, and ill-informed. If privacy preferences are real but not sufficiently coherent to form a sound basis for valuation, any attempt to place a monetary value on them loses meaning. The choice of CBA as the model for justifying decisions fixes the end, because the chosen covering value will usually result in a decision favoring data proliferation over data protection. . . .

People make choices between seemingly incomparable things all the time, and they can do so rationally. A person is not acting irrationally by preferring a perceived notable value over an incomparable nominal value, even if she cannot state a normative theory to explain why the decision is right. A similar phenomenon may be seen in the formulation of public policy. Notable values may be preferred over nominal ones in the enactment of laws and the implementation of policies even if policymakers cannot explain why one alternative is better than the other. Moreover, by observing a number of such decisions over time, we may begin to see a pattern develop and covering values emerge that can serve as guides to later decisions that are closer to the margin.[100]

TRANS UNION CORP. V. FEDERAL TRADE COMMISSION

245 F.3d 809 (D.C. Cir. 2001)

TATEL, J. . . . Petitioner Trans Union sells two types of products. First, as a credit reporting agency, it compiles credit reports about individual consumers from credit information it collects from banks, credit card companies, and other lenders. It then sells these credit reports to lenders, employers, and insurance companies. Trans Union receives credit information from lenders in the form of "tradelines." A tradeline typically includes a customer's name, address, date   of birth, telephone number, Social Security number, account type, opening date of account, credit limit, account status, and payment history. Trans Union receives 1.4 to 1.6 billion records per month. The company's credit database contains information on 190 million adults.

Trans Union's second set of products — those at issue in this case — are known as target marketing products. These consist of lists of names and addresses of individuals who meet specific criteria such as possession of an auto loan, a department store credit card, or two or more mortgages. Marketers purchase these lists, then contact the individuals by mail or telephone to offer them goods and services. To create its target marketing lists, Trans Union maintains a database known as MasterFile, a subset of its consumer credit database. MasterFile consists of information about every consumer in the company's credit database who has (A) at least two tradelines with activity during the previous six months, or (B) one tradeline with activity during the previous six months plus an address confirmed by an outside source.   The company compiles target marketing lists by extracting from MasterFile the names and addresses of individuals with characteristics chosen by list purchasers. For example, a department store might buy a list of all individuals in a particular area code who have both a mortgage and a credit card with a $10,000 limit. Although target marketing lists contain only

---

[100] James P. Nehf, *Incomparability and the Passive Virtues of Ad Hoc Privacy Policy*, 76 U. Colo. L. Rev. 1, 29-36, 42 (2005).

names and addresses, purchasers know that every person on a list has the characteristics they requested because Trans Union uses those characteristics as criteria for culling individual files from its database. Purchasers also know that every individual on a target marketing list satisfies the criteria for inclusion in MasterFile.

The Fair Credit Reporting Act of 1970 ("FCRA"), 15 U.S.C. §§ 1681, 1681a-1681u, regulates consumer reporting agencies like Trans Union, imposing various obligations to protect the privacy and accuracy of credit information. The Federal Trade Commission, acting pursuant to its authority to enforce the FCRA, *see* 15 U.S.C. § 1681s(a), determined that Trans Union's target marketing lists were "consumer reports" subject to the Act's limitations. [The FTC concluded that targeted marketing was not an authorized use of consumer reports under the FCRA and ordered Trans Union to halt its sale of the lists.] . . .

. . . [Trans Union challenges the FTC's application of the FCRA as violative of the First Amendment.] Banning the sale of target marketing lists, the company says, amounts to a restriction on its speech subject to strict scrutiny. Again, Trans Union misunderstands our standard of review. In *Dun & Bradstreet, Inc. v. Greenmoss Builders, Inc.,* 472 U.S. 749 (1985), the Supreme Court held that a consumer reporting agency's credit report warranted reduced constitutional protection because it concerned "no public issue." "The protection to be accorded a particular credit report," the Court explained, "depends on whether the report's 'content, form, and context' indicate that it concerns a public matter." Like the credit report in *Dun & Bradstreet,* which the Supreme Court found "was speech solely in the interest of the speaker and its specific business audience," the information about individual consumers and their credit performance communicated by Trans Union target marketing lists is solely of interest to the company and its business customers and relates to no matter of public concern. Trans Union target marketing lists thus warrant "reduced constitutional protection."

We turn then to the specifics of Trans Union's First Amendment argument. The company first claims that neither the FCRA nor the Commission's Order advances a substantial government interest. The "Congressional findings and statement of purpose" at the beginning of the FCRA state: "There is a need to insure that consumer reporting agencies exercise their grave responsibilities with . . . respect for the consumer's right to privacy." 15 U.S.C. § 1681(a)(4). Contrary to the company's assertions, we have no doubt that this interest — protecting the privacy of consumer credit information — is substantial.

Trans Union next argues that Congress should have chosen a "less burdensome alternative," i.e., allowing consumer reporting agencies to sell credit information as long as they notify consumers and give them the ability to "opt out." Because the FCRA is not subject to strict First Amendment scrutiny, however, Congress had no obligation to choose the least restrictive means of accomplishing its goal.

Finally, Trans Union argues that the FCRA is underinclusive because it applies only to consumer reporting agencies and not to other companies that sell consumer information. But given consumer reporting agencies' unique "access to a broad range of continually-updated, detailed information about millions of consumers' personal credit histories," we think it not at all inappropriate for Congress to have singled out consumer reporting agencies for regulation. . . .

NOTES & QUESTIONS

1. **U.S. West *vs.* Trans Union.** Compare *U.S. West* with *Trans Union*. Are these cases consistent with each other? Which case's reasoning strikes you as more persuasive?

2. **Trans Union II.** In *Trans Union v. FTC*, 295 F.3d 42 (D.C. Cir. 2002) (*Trans Union II*), Trans Union sued to enjoin regulations promulgated pursuant to the Gramm-Leach-Bliley Act (GLBA), alleging, among other things, that they violated the First Amendment. Trans Union argued that these regulations would prevent it from selling credit headers, which consist of a consumer's name, address, Social Security number, and phone number. Trans Union contended that the sale of credit headers is commercial speech. The court concluded that Trans Union's First Amendment arguments were "foreclosed" by its earlier opinion in *Trans Union v. FTC,* which resolved that "the government interest in 'protecting the privacy of consumer credit information' 'is substantial.'"

3. ***Free Speech and the Fair Information Practices.*** Recall the discussion of the Fair Information Practices from Chapter 6. The Fair Information Practices provide certain limitations on the uses and disclosure of personal information. Eugene Volokh contends:

> I am especially worried about the normative power of the notion that the government has a compelling interest in creating "codes of fair information practices" restricting true statements made by nongovernmental speakers. The protection of free speech generally rests on an assumption that it's not for the government to decide which speech is "fair" and which isn't; the unfairnesses, excesses, and bad taste of speakers are something that current First Amendment principles generally require us to tolerate. Once people grow to accept and even like government restrictions on one kind of supposedly "unfair" communication of facts, it may become much easier for people to accept "codes of fair reporting," "codes of fair debate," "codes of fair filmmaking," "codes of fair political criticism," and the like. . . .[101]

Consider Paul Schwartz, who contends that free discourse is promoted by the protection of privacy:

> When the government requires fair information practices for the private sector, has it created a right to stop people from speaking about you? As an initial point, I emphasize that the majority of the core fair information practices do not involve the government preventing disclosure of personal information. [The fair information practices generally require: (1) the creation of a statutory fabric that defines obligations with respect to the use of personal information; (2) the maintenance of processing systems that are understandable to the concerned individual (transparency); (3) the assignment of limited procedural and substantive rights to the individual; and (4) the establishment of effective oversight of data use, whether through individual litigation (self-help), a government role (external oversight), or some combination of these approaches.] . . . [F]air information practices one, two, and four regulate the business practices of private entities without silencing their speech. No

---

[101] Eugene Volokh, *Freedom of Speech and Information Privacy: The Troubling Implications of a Right to Stop People from Speaking About You*, 52 Stan. L. Rev. 1049, 1090 (2000).

prevention of speech about anyone takes place, for example, when the Fair Credit Reporting Act of 1970 requires that certain information be given to a consumer when an "investigative consumer report" is prepared about her.

These nonsilencing fair information practices are akin to a broad range of other measures that regulate information use in the private sector and do not abridge the freedom of speech under any interpretation of the First Amendment. The First Amendment does not prevent the government from requiring product labels on food products or the use of "plain English" by publicly traded companies in reports sent to their investors or Form 10-Ks filed with the Securities and Exchange Commission. Nor does the First Amendment forbid privacy laws such as the Children's Online Privacy Protection Act, which assigns parents a right of access to their children's online data profiles. The ultimate merit of these laws depends on their specific context and precise details, but such experimentation by the State should be viewed as noncontroversial on free speech grounds.

Nevertheless, one subset of fair information practices does correspond to Volokh's idea of information privacy as the right to stop people from speaking about you. . . . [S]o long as [laws protecting personal information disclosure] are viewpoint neutral, these laws are a necessary element of safeguarding free communication in our democratic society. . . .

. . . [A] democratic order depends on both an underlying personal capacity for self-governance and the participation of individuals in community and democratic self-rule. Privacy law thus has an important role in protecting individual self-determination and democratic deliberation. By providing access to one's personal data, information about how it will be processed, and other fair information practices, the law seeks to structure the terms on which individuals confront the information demands of the community, private bureaucratic entities, and the State. Attention to these issues by the legal order is essential to the health of a democracy, which ultimately depends on individual communicative competence.[102]

SORRELL V. IMS HEALTH, INC.

131 S. Ct. 2653 (2011)

KENNEDY, J. Vermont law restricts the sale, disclosure, and use of pharmacy records that reveal the prescribing practices of individual doctors. Vt. Stat. Ann., Tit. 18, § 4631. Subject to certain exceptions, the information may not be sold, disclosed by pharmacies for marketing purposes, or used for marketing by pharmaceutical manufacturers. Vermont argues that its prohibitions safeguard medical privacy and diminish the likelihood that marketing will lead to prescription decisions not in the best interests of patients or the State. It can be assumed that these interests are significant. Speech in aid of pharmaceutical marketing, however, is a form of expression protected by the Free Speech Clause of the First Amendment. As a consequence, Vermont's statute must be subjected to heightened judicial scrutiny. The law cannot satisfy that standard. . . .

Pharmaceutical manufacturers promote their drugs to doctors through a process called "detailing." This often involves a scheduled visit to a doctor's office

---

[102] Paul M. Schwartz, *Free Speech vs. Information Privacy: Eugene Volokh's First Amendment Jurisprudence,* 52 Stan. L. Rev. 1559 (2000).

to persuade the doctor to prescribe a particular pharmaceutical. Detailers bring drug samples as well as medical studies that explain the "details" and potential advantages of various prescription drugs. Interested physicians listen, ask questions, and receive followup data. Salespersons can be more effective when they know the background and purchasing preferences of their clientele, and pharmaceutical salespersons are no exception. Knowledge of a physician's prescription practices—called "prescriber-identifying information"—enables a detailer better to ascertain which doctors are likely to be interested in a particular drug and how best to present a particular sales message. Detailing is an expensive undertaking, so pharmaceutical companies most often use it to promote high-profit brand-name drugs protected by patent. Once a brand-name drug's patent expires, less expensive bioequivalent generic alternatives are manufactured and sold.

Pharmacies, as a matter of business routine and federal law, receive prescriber-identifying information when processing prescriptions. Many pharmacies sell this information to "data miners," firms that analyze prescriber-identifying information and produce reports on prescriber behavior. Data miners lease these reports to pharmaceutical manufacturers subject to nondisclosure agreements. Detailers, who represent the manufacturers, then use the reports to refine their marketing tactics and increase sales.

In 2007, Vermont enacted the Prescription Confidentiality Law. The measure is also referred to as Act 80. It has several components. The central provision of the present case is § 4631(d).

> "A health insurer, a self-insured employer, an electronic transmission intermediary, a pharmacy, or other similar entity shall not sell, license, or exchange for value regulated records containing prescriber-identifiable information, nor permit the use of regulated records containing prescriber-identifiable information for marketing or promoting a prescription drug, unless the prescriber consents . . . . Pharmaceutical manufacturers and pharmaceutical marketers shall not use prescriber-identifiable information for marketing or promoting a prescription drug unless the prescriber consents. . . ."

The quoted provision has three component parts. The provision begins by prohibiting pharmacies, health insurers, and similar entities from selling prescriber-identifying information, absent the prescriber's consent. . . . The provision then goes on to prohibit pharmacies, health insurers, and similar entities from allowing prescriber-identifying information to be used for marketing, unless the prescriber consents. This prohibition in effect bars pharmacies from disclosing the information for marketing purposes. Finally, the provision's second sentence bars pharmaceutical manufacturers and pharmaceutical marketers from using prescriber-identifying information for marketing, again absent the prescriber's consent. The Vermont attorney general may pursue civil remedies against violators. § 4631(f). . . .

On its face, Vermont's law enacts content- and speaker-based restrictions on the sale, disclosure, and use of prescriber-identifying information. The provision first forbids sale subject to exceptions based in large part on the content of a purchaser's speech. For example, those who wish to engage in certain "educational communications," § 4631(e)(4), may purchase the information. The measure then bars any disclosure when recipient speakers will use the information for marketing.

Finally, the provision's second sentence prohibits pharmaceutical manufacturers from using the information for marketing. The statute thus disfavors marketing, that is, speech with a particular content. More than that, the statute disfavors specific speakers, namely pharmaceutical manufacturers. As a result of these content- and speaker-based rules, detailers cannot obtain prescriber-identifying information, even though the information may be purchased or acquired by other speakers with diverse purposes and viewpoints. . . . For example, it appears that Vermont could supply academic organizations with prescriber-identifying information to use in countering the messages of brand-name pharmaceutical manufacturers and in promoting the prescription of generic drugs. But § 4631(d) leaves detailers no means of purchasing, acquiring, or using prescriber-identifying information. The law on its face burdens disfavored speech by disfavored speakers. . . .

Act 80 is designed to impose a specific, content-based burden on protected expression. It follows that heightened judicial scrutiny is warranted. . . . Vermont's law does not simply have an effect on speech, but is directed at certain content and is aimed at particular speakers. The Constitution "does not enact Mr. Herbert Spencer's Social Statics." *Lochner v. New York*, 198 U.S. 45 (1905) (Holmes, J., dissenting). It does enact the First Amendment.

This Court has held that the creation and dissemination of information are speech within the meaning of the First Amendment. *See, e.g., Bartnicki* ("[I]f the acts of 'disclosing' and 'publishing' information do not constitute speech, it is hard to imagine what does fall within that category, as distinct from the category of expressive conduct"). Facts, after all, are the beginning point for much of the speech that is most essential to advance human knowledge and to conduct human affairs. There is thus a strong argument that prescriber-identifying information is speech for First Amendment purposes.

The State asks for an exception to the rule that information is speech, but there is no need to consider that request in this case. The State has imposed content- and speaker-based restrictions on the availability and use of prescriber-identifying information. So long as they do not engage in marketing, many speakers can obtain and use the information. But detailers cannot. Vermont's statute could be compared with a law prohibiting trade magazines from purchasing or using ink. As a consequence, this case can be resolved even assuming, as the State argues, that prescriber-identifying information is a mere commodity. . . .

The State's asserted justifications for § 4631(d) come under two general headings. First, the State contends that its law is necessary to protect medical privacy, including physician confidentiality, avoidance of harassment, and the integrity of the doctor-patient relationship. Second, the State argues that § 4631(d) is integral to the achievement of policy objectives—namely, improved public health and reduced healthcare costs. Neither justification withstands scrutiny.

Vermont argues that its physicians have a "reasonable expectation" that their prescriber-identifying information "will not be used for purposes other than . . . filling and processing" prescriptions. It may be assumed that, for many reasons, physicians have an interest in keeping their prescription decisions confidential. But § 4631(d) is not drawn to serve that interest. Under Vermont's law, pharmacies may share prescriber-identifying information with anyone for any reason save one: They must not allow the information to be used for marketing. . . .

Perhaps the State could have addressed physician confidentiality through "a more coherent policy." *Greater New Orleans Broadcasting*, [527 U.S. 173, 195 (1999)]. For instance, the State might have advanced its asserted privacy interest by allowing the information's sale or disclosure in only a few narrow and well-justified circumstances. *See, e.g.,* Health Insurance Portability and Accountability Act of 1996, 42 U.S.C. § 1320d–2; 45 CFR pts. 160 and 164. A statute of that type would present quite a different case than the one presented here. But the State did not enact a statute with that purpose or design. Instead, Vermont made prescriber-identifying information available to an almost limitless audience. The explicit structure of the statute allows the information to be studied and used by all but a narrow class of disfavored speakers. Given the information's widespread availability and many permissible uses, the State's asserted interest in physician confidentiality does not justify the burden that § 4631(d) places on protected expression.

. . . Section 4631(d) may offer a limited degree of privacy, but only on terms favorable to the speech the State prefers. Cf. *Rowan* (sustaining a law that allowed private parties to make "unfettered," "unlimited," and "unreviewable" choices regarding their own privacy). This is not to say that all privacy measures must avoid content-based rules. Here, however, the State has conditioned privacy on acceptance of a content-based rule that is not drawn to serve the State's asserted interest. To obtain the limited privacy allowed by § 4631(d), Vermont physicians are forced to acquiesce in the State's goal of burdening disfavored speech by disfavored speakers.

The State also contends that § 4631(d) protects doctors from "harassing sales behaviors." It is doubtful that concern for "a few" physicians who may have "felt coerced and harassed" by pharmaceutical marketers can sustain a broad content-based rule like § 4631(d). Many are those who must endure speech they do not like, but that is a necessary cost of freedom. In any event the State offers no explanation why remedies other than content-based rules would be inadequate. Physicians can, and often do, simply decline to meet with detailers, including detailers who use prescriber-identifying information. Doctors who wish to forgo detailing altogether are free to give "No Solicitation" or "No Detailing" instructions to their office managers or to receptionists at their places of work. . . .

Vermont argues that detailers' use of prescriber-identifying information undermines the doctor-patient relationship by allowing detailers to influence treatment decisions. . . . But the State does not explain why detailers' use of prescriber-identifying information is more likely to prompt these objections than many other uses permitted by § 4631(d). In any event, this asserted interest is contrary to basic First Amendment principles. . . . If pharmaceutical marketing affects treatment decisions, it does so because doctors find it persuasive. Absent circumstances far from those presented here, the fear that speech might persuade provides no lawful basis for quieting it.

The State contends that § 4631(d) advances important public policy goals by lowering the costs of medical services and promoting public health. If prescriber-identifying information were available for use by detailers, the State contends, then detailing would be effective in promoting brand-name drugs that are more expensive and less safe than generic alternatives. . . . While Vermont's stated policy goals may be proper, § 4631(d) does not advance them in a permissible way. . . . The State seeks to achieve its policy objectives through the indirect means of restraining certain speech by certain speakers—that is, by diminishing detailers' ability to influence prescription decisions. Those who seek to censor or burden free expression often assert that disfavored speech has adverse effects. But the "fear that people would make bad decisions if given truthful information" cannot justify content-based burdens on speech. . . .

It is true that content-based restrictions on protected expression are sometimes permissible, and that principle applies to commercial speech. . . . Here, however, Vermont has not shown that its law has a neutral justification.

The State nowhere contends that detailing is false or misleading within the meaning of this Court's First Amendment precedents. Nor does the State argue that the provision challenged here will prevent false or misleading speech. The State's interest in burdening the speech of detailers instead turns on nothing more than a difference of opinion. . . .

The capacity of technology to find and publish personal information, including records required by the government, presents serious and unresolved issues with respect to personal privacy and the dignity it seeks to secure. In considering how to protect those interests, however, the State cannot engage in content-based discrimination to advance its own side of a debate.

If Vermont's statute provided that prescriber-identifying information could not be sold or disclosed except in narrow circumstances then the State might have a stronger position. Here, however, the State gives possessors of the information broad discretion and wide latitude in disclosing the information, while at the same time restricting the information's use by some speakers and for some purposes, even while the State itself can use the information to counter the speech it seeks to suppress. Privacy is a concept too integral to the person and a right too essential to freedom to allow its manipulation to support just those ideas the government prefers. . . .

The State has burdened a form of protected expression that it found too persuasive. At the same time, the State has left unburdened those speakers whose messages are in accord with its own views. This the State cannot do. . . .

BREYER, J., joined by GINSBURG, J. and KAGAN, J., dissenting. The Vermont statute before us adversely affects expression in one, and only one, way. It deprives pharmaceutical and data-mining companies of data, collected pursuant to the government's regulatory mandate, that could help pharmaceutical companies create better sales messages. In my view, this effect on expression is inextricably related to a lawful governmental effort to regulate a commercial enterprise. The First Amendment does not require courts to apply a special "heightened" standard of review when reviewing such an effort. And, in any event, the statute meets the First Amendment standard this Court has previously applied when the government seeks to regulate commercial speech. For any or all of these reasons, the Court should uphold the statute as constitutional. . . .

In this case I would ask whether Vermont's regulatory provisions work harm to First Amendment interests that is disproportionate to their furtherance of legitimate regulatory objectives. . . .

[O]ur cases make clear that the First Amendment offers considerably less protection to the maintenance of a free marketplace for goods and services. And they also reflect the democratic importance of permitting an elected government to implement through effective programs policy choices for which the people's elected representatives have voted. . . .

Vermont's statute neither forbids nor requires anyone to say anything, to engage in any form of symbolic speech, or to endorse any particular point of view, whether ideological or related to the sale of a product. . . . Further, the statute's requirements form part of a traditional, comprehensive regulatory regime. The pharmaceutical drug industry has been heavily regulated at least since 1906. Longstanding statutes and regulations require pharmaceutical companies to engage in complex drug testing to ensure that their drugs are both "safe" and "effective." 21 U.S.C. §§ 355(b)(1), 355(d). Only then can the drugs be marketed, at which point drug companies are subject to the FDA's exhaustive regulation of the content of drug labels and the manner in which drugs can be advertised and sold.

Finally, Vermont's statute is directed toward information that exists only by virtue of government regulation. Under federal law, certain drugs can be dispensed only by a pharmacist operating under the orders of a medical practitioner. 21 U.S.C. § 355(b). Vermont regulates the qualifications, the fitness, and the practices of pharmacists themselves, and requires pharmacies to maintain a "patient record system" that, among other things, tracks who prescribed which drugs. But for these regulations, pharmacies would have no way to know who had told customers to buy which drugs (as is the case when a doctor tells a patient to take a daily dose of aspirin).

Regulators will often find it necessary to create tailored restrictions on the use of information subject to their regulatory jurisdiction. A car dealership that obtains credit scores for customers who want car loans can be prohibited from using credit data to search for new customers. *See* 15 U.S.C. § 1681b; *cf. Trans Union Corp. v. FTC,* 245 F.3d 809, *reh'g denied,* 267 F.3d 1138 (D.C. Cir. 2001). Medical specialists who obtain medical records for their existing patients cannot purchase those records in order to identify new patients. *See* 45 CFR § 164.508(a)(3). Or, speaking hypothetically, a public utilities commission that directs local gas distributors to gather usage information for individual customers might permit the distributors to share the data with researchers (trying to lower energy costs) but forbid sales of the data to appliance manufacturers seeking to sell gas stoves. . . . Thus, it is not surprising that, until today, this Court has *never* found that the First Amendment prohibits the government from restricting the use of information gathered pursuant to a regulatory mandate—whether the information rests in government files or has remained in the hands of the private firms that gathered it.

In short, the case law in this area reflects the need to ensure that the First Amendment protects the "marketplace of ideas," thereby facilitating the democratic creation of sound government policies without improperly hampering the ability of government to introduce an agenda, to implement its policies, and to favor them to the exclusion of contrary policies. To apply "heightened" scrutiny when the regulation of commercial activities (which often involve speech) is at issue is unnecessarily to undercut the latter constitutional goal. The majority's view of this case presents that risk. . . .

Moreover, given the sheer quantity of regulatory initiatives that touch upon commercial messages, the Court's vision of its reviewing task threatens to return us to a happily bygone era when judges scrutinized legislation for its interference with economic liberty. History shows that the power was much abused and resulted in the constitutionalization of economic theories preferred by individual jurists. *See Lochner v. New York,* 198 U.S. 45 (1905) (Holmes, J., dissenting). . . .

The statute threatens only modest harm to commercial speech. I agree that it withholds from pharmaceutical companies information that would help those entities create a more effective selling message. But I cannot agree with the majority that the harm also involves unjustified discrimination in that it permits "pharmacies" to "share prescriber-identifying information with anyone for any reason" (but marketing). Whatever the First Amendment relevance of such discrimination, there is no evidence that it exists in Vermont. The record contains no evidence that prescriber-identifying data is widely disseminated. . . .

The legitimate state interests that the statute serves are "substantial." *Central Hudson,* 447 U.S., at 564. . . . The protection of public health falls within the traditional scope of a State's police powers. The fact that the Court normally exempts the regulation of "misleading" and "deceptive" information even from the rigors of its "intermediate" commercial speech scrutiny testifies to the importance of securing "unbiased information," as does the fact that the FDA sets forth as a federal regulatory goal the need to ensure a "fair balance" of information about marketed drugs. As major payers in the health care system, health care spending is also of crucial state interest. And this Court has affirmed the importance of maintaining "privacy" as an important public policy goal—even in respect to information already disclosed to the public for particular purposes (but not others). *See Department of Justice v. Reporters Comm. for Freedom of Press,* 489 U.S. 749 (1989); *see also* Solove, *A Taxonomy of Privacy*, 154 U. Pa. L. Rev. 477, 520–522 (2006); *cf. NASA v. Nelson,* 131 S. Ct. 746 (2011) (discussing privacy interests in nondisclosure). . . .

The record also adequately supports the State's privacy objective. Regulatory rules in Vermont make clear that the confidentiality of an individual doctor's prescribing practices remains the norm. Exceptions to this norm are comparatively few.

. . . The prohibition against pharmaceutical firms using this prescriber-identifying information works no more than modest First Amendment harm; the prohibition is justified by the need to ensure unbiased sales presentations, prevent unnecessarily high drug costs, and protect the privacy of prescribing physicians. There is no obvious equally effective, more limited alternative. . . .

In sum, I believe that the statute before us satisfies the "intermediate" standards this Court has applied to restrictions on commercial speech. *A fortiori* it satisfies less demanding standards that are more appropriately applied in this kind of commercial regulatory case—a case where the government seeks typical regulatory ends (lower drug prices, more balanced sales messages) through the use of ordinary regulatory means (limiting the commercial use of data gathered pursuant to a regulatory mandate). The speech-related consequences here are indirect, incidental, and entirely commercial. . . .

Regardless, whether we apply an ordinary commercial speech standard or a less demanding standard, I believe Vermont's law is consistent with the First Amendment. And with respect, I dissent.

NOTES & QUESTIONS

1. *The Impact of* Sorrell. The Supreme Court takes an expansive view of commercial speech, which encompasses the sale and use of personal data. What kind of impact will this case likely have on other privacy laws regulating the trade of personal data? Does *Sorrell* affect *Mainstream Marketing Services, Inc. v. FTC* (excerpted above)? Does it affect the *Trans Union* cases (excerpted and discussed above)? What likely impact, if any, will it have?

2. *Narrow vs. Broad Laws.* Ironically, the Court's decision to strike down the law was based in part on how narrowly the law restricted the use or disclosure of personal data. How would you redraft the law to address the Court's concerns?

3. *HIPAA.* The *Sorrell* Court characterizes HIPAA as a law "allowing the information's sale or disclosure in only a few narrow and well-justified circumstances." Is this an accurate characterization of HIPAA? If HIPAA's restrictions pass muster, then can *Sorrell* be read as a narrow holding that applies only to laws that single out one particular use or one particular group of speakers?

4. *Is Information Speech?* Is the collection, use, and/or transfer of personal information a form of speech? Or is it merely trade in property?

    Eugene Volokh contends that such information processing constitutes speech:

    > Many . . . databases — for instance, credit history databases or criminal record databases — are used by people to help them decide whom it is safe to deal with and who is likely to cheat them. Other databases, which contain less incriminating information, such as a person's shopping patterns . . . [contain] data [that] is of direct daily life interest to its recipients, since it helps them find out with whom they should do business.[103]

    Further, Volokh contends: "[I]t is no less speech when a credit bureau sends credit information to a business. The owners and managers of a credit bureau are communicating information to decision-makers, such as loan officers, at the recipient business."[104]

    Daniel Solove recognizes that some forms of database information transfer and use can constitute speech:

    > There are no easy analytic distinctions as to what is or is not "speech." The "essence" of information is neither a good, nor is it speech, for information can be used in ways that make it akin to either one. It is the *use* of the information that determines what information is, not anything inherent in the information itself. If I sell you a book, I have engaged in a commercial transaction. I sold the book as a good. However, the book is also expressing something. Even

---

[103] Volokh, *Freedom of Speech, supra,* at 1093-94.
[104] *Id.* at 1083-84.

though books are sold as goods, the government cannot pass a law restricting the topics of what books can be sold. . . .

Volokh appears to view all information dissemination that is communicative as speech. Under Volokh's view, therefore, most forms of information dissemination would be entitled to equal First Amendment protection. . . .

However, Volokh's view would lead to severe conflicts with much modern regulation. Full First Amendment protection would apply to statements about a company's earnings and other information regulated by the SEC, insider trading, quid pro quo sexual harassment, fraudulent statements, perjury, bribery, blackmail, extortion, conspiracy, and so on. One could neatly exclude these examples from the category of speech, eliminating the necessity for First Amendment analysis. Although this seems the easiest approach, it is conceptually sloppy or even dishonest absent a meaningful way to argue that these examples do not involve communication. I contend that these examples of highly regulated forms of communication have not received the full rigor of standard First Amendment analysis because of policy considerations. Categorizing them as nonspeech conceals these policy considerations under the façade of an analytical distinction that thus far has not been persuasively articulated.

I am not eschewing all attempts at categorization between speech and nonspeech. To do so would make the First Amendment applicable to virtually anything that is expressive or communicative. Still, the distinction as currently constituted hides its ideological character. . . .

Dealing with privacy issues by categorizing personal information as nonspeech is undesirable because it cloaks the real normative reasons for why society wants to permit greater regulation of certain communicative activity. Rather than focusing on distinguishing between speech and nonspeech, the determination about what forms of information to regulate should center on policy considerations. These policy considerations should turn on the uses of the information rather than on notions about the inherent nature of the information.[105]

Solove goes on to argue that although transfers of personal information may be speech, they are of lower value than other forms of free speech, such as political speech. He contends that whereas speech of public concern is of high value, speech of private concern is given a lower constitutional value, and hence less stringent scrutiny, as is commercial speech and other lower-value categories of speech.

Neil Richards, however, contends that "most privacy regulation that interrupts information flows in the context of an express or implied commercial relationship is neither 'speech' within the current meaning of the First Amendment, nor should it be viewed as such." He criticizes Schwartz and Solove because "they grant too much ground to the First Amendment critique, and may ultimately prove to be underprotective of privacy interests, particularly in the database context." Richards finds Solove's contextual balancing approach too messy to "provide meaningfully increased protection for privacy in the courts." Richards argues instead for a categorical solution and contends

---

[105] Daniel J. Solove, *The Virtues of Knowing Less: Justifying Privacy Protections Against Disclosure,* 53 Duke L.J. 967, 979-80 (2003).

that much regulation of speech in the commercial context should be seen as falling entirely outside the scope of the heightened First Amendment scrutiny:

> This might be the case because the speech is threatening, obscene, or libelous, and thus part of the "established" categories of "unprotected speech." But it might also be the case because the speech is an insider trading tip, . . . an offer to create a monopoly in restraint of trade, or a breach of the attorney-client privilege. In either case, the speech would be outside the scope of the First Amendment and could be regulated as long as a rational basis existed for so doing. . . .
>
> [I]nformation disclosure rules that are the product of generally applicable laws fall outside the scope of the First Amendment. Where information is received by an entity in violation of some other legal rule — whether breach of contract, trespass, theft, or fraud — the First Amendment creates no barrier to the government's ability to prevent and punish disclosure. This is the case even if the information is newsworthy or otherwise of public concern. . . .
>
> From a First Amendment perspective, no such equivalently important social function [as dissemination of information by the press] . . . is played by database companies engaged in the trade of personal data. Indeed, a general law regulating the commercial trade in personal data by database, profiling, and marketing companies is far removed from the core speech protected by the First Amendment, and is much more like the "speech" outside the boundaries of heightened review.

Richards goes on to equate the First Amendment critique of privacy regulation to *Lochnerism,* where the Supreme Court in *Lochner v. New York,* 198 U.S. 45 (1905), struck down a statute regulating the hours bakers could work per week based on "freedom of contract." *Lochner* was, and remains, highly criticized for being an impediment to New Deal legislation by an activist ideological Court. Richards notes:

> [T]here are some fairly strong parallels between the traditional conception of *Lochner* and the First Amendment critique of data privacy legislation. Both theories are judicial responses to calls for legal regulation of the economic and social dislocations caused by rapid technological change. *Lochnerism* addressed a major socio-technological problem of the industrial age — the power differential between individuals and businesses in industrial working conditions, while the First Amendment critique is addressed to a major socio-technological problem of our information age — the power differential between individuals and businesses over information in the electronic environment. Both theories place a libertarian gloss upon the Constitution, interpreting it to mandate either "freedom of contract" or "freedom of information." Both theories seek to place certain forms of economic regulation beyond the power of legislatures to enact. And both theories are eagerly supported by business interests keen to immunize themselves from regulation under the aegis of Constitutional doctrine. To the extent that the First Amendment critique is similar to the traditional view of *Lochner,* then, its elevation of an economic right to first-order constitutional magnitude seems similarly dubious.[106]

---

[106] Neil Richards, *Reconciling Data Privacy and the First Amendment,* 52 UCLA L. Rev. 1149, 1169, 1180, 1172-73, 1206, 1212-13 (2005).

CHAPTER 10

DATA SECURITY

CHAPTER OUTLINE

A. INTRODUCTION

Consumers at Risk. In testimony to Congress in 2014, Edith Ramirez, the Chairwoman of the Federal Trade Commissioner, bluntly stated, "Consumers' data is at risk."[1] She also noted the critical importance of data security to consumers: "If companies do not protect the personal information they collect and store, that information could fall into the wrong hands, resulting in fraud, identity theft, and other harm, along with a potential loss of consumer confidence in the marketplace." Data security is more crucial than ever before, but more data breaches are taking places. The leaks involve Social Security numbers, payment card data, account passwords, health data, information about children, and many other types of personal information.

A data breach involving Target made worldwide headlines in 2013 and 2014. According to subsequent investigations, hackers using credentials from a HVAC vendor of the retailer entered into Target's computer network.[2] Once inside, the hackers installed malware that allowed them to steal credit card numbers from cashier stations in Target stores. The stolen information was temporarily stored within Target servers then sent to a hijacked "staging point" in the United States and then onward to the hackers in Russia. Target was obliged to announce the

---

[1] Edith Ramirez, Prepared Statement of the Federal Trade Commission on Data Breach on the Rise: Protecting Personal Information from Harm, Before the Committee on Homeland Security and Governmental Affairs, U.S. Senate (Apr. 2, 2014).

[2] Michael Riley et al., *Missed Alarms and 40 Million Stolen Credit Card Numbers: How Target Blew It*, Business Week (Mar. 13, 2014).

breach at perhaps the worst point possible in its sales year: December 15. By this point, 40 million credit card numbers had been stolen from the retailer. In August 2014, Target announced that it expected $148 million in expenses related to the breach.[3]

The problem of data security goes far beyond Target, and the dimensions of the problem are staggering. According to a Pew Research Poll from 2014, 18 percent of all online Americans report having had personal information stolen.[4] Separate studies by the Javelin Strategy and Research Group and by LexisNexis estimate that one-fourth of records involved in data breaches are used for fraudulent purposes, such as identity theft.[5] For a snapshot of the extent of data breaches today, two state reports are highly useful. Both California and New York require reporting of data breach notifications to state officials in their respective jurisdictions. In 2013, the California Department of Justice (DOJ) published its first review of these reports.[6] In 2012, it received reports of 131 data breaches, which put more than 2.5 million Californians at risk. Had the data in question only been encrypted, more than 1.4 million Californians would not have been put at risk and 28 percent of the breaches would not have required notification. The industries that reported the most data breaches in the state were the retail industry, followed by finance and insurance. Finally, more than half of the breaches involved Social Security numbers, which, according to the California DOJ, "pose the greatest risk of the most serious types of identity theft."

While California only mandated the filing of notices with state officials in 2011 and received its first reports in 2012, New York has been receiving breach notification reports since 2006. Its 2014 report was therefore able to analyze eight years of data breach notifications.[7] Between 2006 and 2013, the number of reported data security breaches more than tripled. As the Attorney General (AG) of New York, observes: "Over 22 million personal records have been exposed since 2006, jeopardizing the financial health and well-being of countless New Yorkers and costing the public and private sectors in New York — and around the world — billions of dollars." The report estimates the cost of data breaches for 2013 alone at more than $1.37 billion. It also found that five of the ten largest breaches affecting New York residents occurred in the past three years. Moreover, "mega-breaches" were responsible for nearly 80 percent of the personal records exposed in the state. Specifically, the New York State AG found that 28 mega-breaches exposed approximately 18.2 million personal records of New Yorkers.

---

[3] Michael Calia, *Target Lowers Outlook on Retail Softness, Data Breach Expenses*, Wall St. J. (Aug. 5, 2014).

[4] Mary Madden, Pew Research Center, More online Americans say they've experienced a personal data breach (Apr. 14, 2014).

[5] Lexis-Nexis True Cost of Fraud Study, Merchants Struggle Against an Onslaught of High-Cost Identity Fraud and Online Fraud 6 (2013).

[6] California Department of Justice, Data Breach Report 2012 (2013).

[7] New York State Attorney General, Information Exposed: Historical Examination of Data Breaches in New York State (2014).

Fines, Settlements, and High Financial Stakes. The stakes for consumers in data breaches are high. This area is equally important for organizations. Writing in *Computer World*, Jay Cline has tallied up the overall enforcement actions and fines for data privacy violations.[8] His conclusion: "Over the last 15 years, security breaches were the most likely to draw a large fine. They accounted for some 35% of the sizable penalties in our database." The top government- imposed fines for security flaws are against ChoicePoint, a database company, for $15 million (2006); LifeLock, an identity theft protection company, for $12 million (2010); CVS Caremark, a pharmacy chain, for $2.25 million (2009). The ChoicePoint settlement was with the FTC; the CVS Caremark settlement was with the U.S. Department of Health of Health and Human Services and the FTC; the LifeLock settlement was with the FTC and a group of 35 state attorneys general. In a tally from FTC Chairwoman Ramirez, this agency alone has settled more than 50 cases with businesses that it charged with failing to provide reasonable protection for the personal information of consumers.

Another reason that data security is a high-risk area for organizations is the threat of class action lawsuits. Data breach class action lawsuits have led to massive financial settlements. For example, in 2014, Sony agreed to a $15 million settlement of a class action lawsuit for the 2011 hacking of its PlayStation Network. The overall cost of cleaning up the breach, which caused a shut-down of the PlayStation Network for several weeks, has been estimated at $171 million. A data breach lawsuit in Florida against Avmed, Inc, a health care company, led to a $3 million settlement in 2013. The Eleventh Circuit's opinion in this case, *Resnick v. Avmed*, is excerpted below. Once the appellate court denied Avmed's motion for summary judgment, the company quickly settled.

B. DATA SECURITY BREACH NOTIFICATION STATUTES

California was the first state to require companies that maintain personal information to notify individuals in the event of a security breach where personal information is leaked or improperly accessed. The California statute was enacted in 2003. Pursuant to SB 1386, codified at Cal. Civ. Code § 1798.82(a):

> Any person or business that conducts business in California, and that owns or licenses computerized data that includes personal information, shall disclose any breach of the security of the system following discovery or notification of the breach in the security of the data to any resident of California whose unencrypted personal information was, or is reasonably believed to have been, acquired by an unauthorized person. The disclosure shall be made in the most expedient time possible and without unreasonable delay, consistent with the legitimate needs of law enforcement. . . .

---

[8] Jay Cline, U.S. takes the gold in doling out privacy fines, Computer World (Feb. 17, 2014).

The California security breach notice provision received national attention after the ChoicePoint data security breach in 2005. At the time, California was the only state with such a law. The security breach occurred because an identity theft crime ring set up fake businesses and then signed up to receive ChoicePoint's data. As a result, personal information, including names, addresses, and Social Security numbers of over 145,000 people, were improperly accessed. Over 700 of these individuals were victimized by some form of identity theft.

The fraud was discovered in October 2004 by ChoicePoint, but victims were not notified until February 2005 to avoid impeding the law enforcement investigation. When news of the breach was announced, it sparked considerable public attention. After angry statements by many state attorneys general and a public outcry, ChoicePoint decided to voluntarily notify all individuals affected by the breach, not just Californians.

Today, 48 states and the District of Columbia have such laws. Alabama and South Dakota are the remaining states without a breach notification law. Data breach notification statutes require governmental agencies and/or private companies to disclose security breaches involving personal information.[9] The resulting laws vary according to the following criteria: (1) the definition of covered information; (2) the trigger for notification; (3) any exceptions to the law's notification requirement; (4) a requirement of notification to a state agency or attorney general; (5) the presence or absence of a substantive requirement for data security; and (6) the presence or absence of a private right of action.[10]

Although the federal government has yet to enact a general federal data breach notification statute, in 2009, Congress enacted a data breach notification requirement for entities regulated by HIPAA as part of the HITECH Act.

The idea of data breach notification, born in California, has grown to achieve international popularity. The EU's ePrivacy Directive, as revised in 2009, requires telecommunication operators and Internet service providers to report "personal data breaches" to the respective national authority. When a breach is likely to adversely affect personal data, affected subscribers must be notified. More broadly, the Proposed General Data Protection Regulation of 2012 contains a requirement of notification of the supervisory authority within 24 hours of a breach. When a breach is likely to affect the privacy of an individual adversely, the data controller must inform this affected party without undue delay. Once enacted, the Data Protection Regulation will be immediately binding on all Member States and extend a breach notification requirement throughout the European Union.

Covered Information. The California data breach statute defines the underlying "notice-triggering information" as "first name or initial and last name" and any of the following list of other data: Social Security number; driver's license number; financial account number plus a password. In a 2013 amendment to the

[9] National Conference of State Legislatures, State Security Breach Notifications Laws, http://www.ncsl.org/programs/lis/cip/priv/breachlaws.htm (last visited July 16, 2008. For an analysis of data security breach laws, see Paul Schwartz & Edward Janger, *Notification of Data Security Breaches*, 105 Mich. L. Rev. 913, 924-25 (2007).

[10] For a chart examining these laws, state by state, see Daniel J. Solove & Paul M. Schwartz, *Privacy Law Fundamentals* 172-74 (2013).

statute, California became the first state to expand this definition to include user names or e-mail addresses in combination with a password or a security question and answer that would permit access to an online account. Florida, Georgia, and other states have followed this approach.

Like California, other states also define personal information as a party's name in conjunction with a list of other elements. For example, Maine has a data elements list that includes a broad savings clause to broaden the law beyond a person's name. Maine extends its data breach law to any of the listed data elements *without* a person's name "if the information if compromised would be sufficient to permit a person to fraudulently assume or attempt to assume the identity of the person whose information was compromised."

Trigger for Notification. Most states follow the California approach and rely on the "acquisition" standard for breach notification. These states generally require notification whenever there is a reasonable likelihood that an unauthorized party has "acquired" person information. A minority of states have adopted a higher standard. These states consider whether there is a reasonable likelihood of "misuse" of the information, or "material risk" of harm to the person. The idea is that a breach letter should not be sent to the affected public unless there is a more significant likelihood of harm.

Thus, California's breach notification law requires notification when "unencrypted personal information was, or is reasonably believed to have been, acquired by an unauthorized person." Cal. Civ. Code 17982(a). The California Office of Privacy Protection has issued a white paper with its recommendations regarding notification of security breaches.[11] In the white paper, it lists three factors to be considered, among others, in determining whether unencrypted notice-triggering information has been acquired:

1. Indications that the information is in the physical possession and control of an unauthorized person, such as a lost or stolen computer or other device ....

2. Indications that the information has been downloaded or copied.

3. Indications that the information was used by an unauthorized person, such as fraudulent accounts opened or instances of identity theft reported.

Other states have a stricter notification standard, that is, one that is further from the pro-notification side of the continuum than California. These states generally require notification only if "misuse" of a state resident's personal information has occurred or is reasonably likely to occur. States that use a misuse standard include Delaware and Kansas. Other states require a "risk of analysis" finding that misuse is *not* likely to occur. Such states include Maryland, Maine, and New Jersey. Which of these standards do you think is best?

---

[11] California Office of Privacy Protection, Recommended Practices on Notice of Security Breach Involving Personal Information (Jan. 2012).

Exceptions to Notification. Numerous states provide exceptions to the notification requirement if a risk of harm analysis shows that harm to a consumer will not result. Thus, Michigan does not require notification if the "person or agency determines that the security breach has not or is not likely to cause substantial loss or injury to, or result in identity theft with respect to, [one] or more residents." Me. Rev. Stat. tit. 10 § 1348(1)(B) (2014). North Carolina does not consider an acquisition of information a "security breach" if illegal use of the information did not occur or is not reasonably likely to occur, or does not "create[] a material risk of harm to a consumer." N.C. Gen. Stat. § 75-61(14) (2014). The New Jersey exception is for a business that establishes that "misuse of the information is not reasonably possible." N.J. Stat. § 56:8-163(a) (2014).

Florida has recently narrowed its risk analysis against possible misuse. Traditionally, it has not required notification if a data breach "has not and will not result in identity theft or other financial harm to the individual whose personal information has been acquired and accessed." Fla. Stat. § 817.5681(10)(a) (2013) (repealed 2014). However, the Florida Information Protection Act of 2014 (FIPA) requires "appropriate investigation and consultation with relevant federal, state, or local law enforcement agencies" before it can make a "no harm" determination, which it must provide to the Florida Department of Legal Affairs (FDLA). 2014 Fla. Laws ch. 189 § 3(4)(c). Moreover, the amendment requires notification to the FDLA of a breach affecting 500 or more individuals in Florida, without regard to likely harm. This notice is to include key details of the event, and the FDLA is authorized to request copies of the relevant police report, forensic report, and existing security policies of the affected entity.

Notification to State Agency or Attorney General. All the breach notification statutes require notification to the affected party. Writing in 2007, Paul Schwartz and Edward Janger argued that a critical need in the area of data security breaches was for a "coordinated response architecture," which would include a "coordinated response agent" (CRA) to help tailor notice content and supervise the decision whether to give notice.[12] The CRA was to help coordinate actions that companies take after a breach, tailor the content of the notification in light of the nature of the data breach, and help prepare comparative statistical information regarding data security events. Data breach notification laws that require notification to state entities are a strong step towards creation of such a "response architecture." Now states have information about the kinds of breaches that are occurring, whether notification has occurred, and indications of the kinds of potential harms to state residents. Notification also helps state entities decide whether to begin investigations and enforcement actions.

States that require notice to a state agency or attorney general include Alaska, California, Connecticut, Florida, Hawaii, Illinois, Indiana, Iowa, Maryland, Massachusetts, New York, North Carolina, South Carolina, Vermont, and Virginia. As noted above, attorney generals in California and New York have

---

[12] Paul M. Schwartz & Edward J. Janger, *Notification of Data Security Breaches,* 105 Mich. L. Rev. 913, 962-63 (2007).

drawn on the information received due to these notifications in preparing reports on data breaches in their respective states.

Substantive Data Security. Beyond data breach notification, a handful of states create a substantive duty to take reasonable steps to safeguard data. Typically, these statutes provide open-ended, general standards, such as California's requirement to provide "reasonable security procedures and practices appropriate to the nature of the information." Cal. Pub. Util. Code § 8381 (2014). Other states with such laws include Oregon and Nevada. The Massachusetts Standards for the Protection of Personal Information is considered to be the strictest state security law. It extends to any business, no matter where located, that processes personal information of a resident of Massachusetts. 201 Mass. Code Regs. 17.03 (2014). The statute requires the development of a "readily accessible . . . comprehensive information security program" that is "appropriate to (a) the size, scope, and type of business . . . (b) the amount of resources available to such person; (c) the amount of stored data; and (d) the need for security and confidentiality of both consumer and employee information."

Moreover, Massachusetts sets requirements beyond that of a security program. It calls for "the establishment and maintenance of a security system" that includes elements "to the extent technically feasible" including secure user authentication protocols, secure access control measures, and "encryption of all transmitted records and files containing personal information." An FAQ from the Office of Consumer Affairs and Business Regulation of Massachusetts warns that if it is not technically feasible to encrypt e-mail with personal information, the organization should "implement best practices by not sending unencrypted personal information in an email."[13]

Private Right of Action. Only a minority of the statutes provides a private right of action for individuals whose information has been breached. These states include Alaska, California, Maryland, Massachusetts, North Carolina, and Washington. In some states, the private right of action is found in the statute itself. In other states, the private right of action is located in the state's Unfair or Deceptive Trade Practices Act. State laws that do not have a private right of action generally assign their enforcement powers of the notification requirement to the attorney general.

Heightening Privacy Awareness Inside Corporations. Data breach notification laws have been found to play an important role in strengthening the "privacy function" in companies. According to Kenneth Bamberger and Deirdre Mulligan, the enactment of these statutes has been "an important driver of privacy in corporations."[14] In a series of interviews with leading privacy officials, Bamberger and Mulligan were told that corporate privacy officials were able to get

---

[13] Commonwealth of Massachusetts, Office of Consumer Affairs and Business Regulation, Frequently Asked Questions Regarding 201 CMR 17.00 (Nov. 3, 2009).

[14] Kenneth A. Bamberger & Deirdre K. Mulligan, *Privacy on the Ground* 71 (2015).

the attention of senior executives more easily because of these laws and found their roles enriched. In their summary, "Such laws . . . have served as a critical attention mechanism, transforming the effects of media coverage, and heightening consumer consciousness."[15]

C. CIVIL LIABILITY AND STANDING

In order to pursue a cause of action in federal court, plaintiffs must have standing. To establish standing, plaintiffs must show, among other things, that they have suffered an "injury in fact" that is "concrete and particularized" and "actual or imminent, not conjectural or hypothetical." *Friends of the Earth, Inc. v. Laidlaw Envtl. Sys. (TOC), Inc.,* 528 U.S. 167 (2000). If a plaintiff cannot establish standing, then a plaintiff's lawsuit cannot proceed forward in federal court.

REILLY V. CERIDIAN CORPORATION

664 F.3d 38 (3rd Cir. 2011)

ALDISERT, CJ. Kathy Reilly and Patricia Pluemacher, individually and on behalf of all others similarly situated, appeal from an order of the United States District Court for the District of New Jersey, which granted Ceridian Corporation's motion to dismiss for lack of standing, and alternatively, failure to state a claim. Appellants contend that (1) they have standing to bring their claims in federal court, and (2) they stated a claim that adequately alleged cognizable damage, injury, and ascertainable loss. We hold that Appellants lack standing and do not reach the merits of the substantive issue. We will therefore affirm.

Ceridian is a payroll processing firm with its principal place of business in Bloomington, Minnesota. To process its commercial business customers' payrolls, Ceridian collects information about its customers' employees. This information may include employees' names, addresses, social security numbers, dates of birth, and bank account information.

Reilly and Pluemacher were employees of the Brach Eichler law firm, a Ceridian customer, until September 2003. Ceridian entered into contracts with Appellants' employer and the employers of the proposed class members to provide payroll processing services.

On or about December 22, 2009, Ceridian suffered a security breach. An unknown hacker infiltrated Ceridian's Powerpay system and potentially gained access to personal and financial information belonging to Appellants and approximately 27,000 employees at 1,900 companies. It is not known whether the hacker read, copied, or understood the data.

Working with law enforcement and professional investigators, Ceridian determined what information the hacker may have accessed. On about January 29, 2010, Ceridian sent letters to the potential identity theft victims, informing them of the breach: "[S]ome of your personal information . . . may have been illegally

---

[15] Id. at 72.

accessed by an unauthorized hacker. . . . [T]he information accessed included your first name, last name, social security number and, in several cases, birth date and/or the bank account that is used for direct deposit." Ceridian arranged to provide the potentially affected individuals with one year of free credit monitoring and identity theft protection. Individuals had until April 30, 2010, to enroll in the free program, and Ceridian included instructions on how to do so within its letter.

Appellants' allegations of hypothetical, future injury do not establish standing under Article III. For the following reasons we will therefore affirm the District Court's dismissal.

Article III limits our jurisdiction to actual "cases or controversies." U.S. Const. art. III, § 2. One element of this "bedrock requirement" is that plaintiffs "must establish that they have standing to sue." *Raines v. Byrd,* 521 U.S. 811 (1997). It is the plaintiffs' burden, at the pleading stage, to establish standing. *See Lujan v. Defenders of Wildlife,* 504 U.S. 555 (1992).

We conclude that Appellants' allegations of hypothetical, future injury are insufficient to establish standing. Appellants' contentions rely on speculation that the hacker: (1) read, copied, and understood their personal information; (2) intends to commit future criminal acts by misusing the information; and (3) is able to use such information to the detriment of Appellants by making unauthorized transactions in Appellants' names. Unless and until these conjectures come true, Appellants have not suffered any injury; there has been no misuse of the information, and thus, no harm.

The requirement that an injury be "certainly impending" is best illustrated by *City of Los Angeles v. Lyons,* 461 U.S. 95 (1983). There, the Court held that a plaintiff lacked standing to enjoin the Los Angeles Police Department from using a controversial chokehold technique on arrestees. Although the plaintiff had already once been subjected to this maneuver, the future harm he sought to enjoin depended on the police again arresting and choking him. Appellants in this case have yet to suffer any harm, and their alleged increased risk of future injury is nothing more than speculation. As such, the alleged injury is not "certainly impending." *Lujan.*

Our Court, too, has refused to confer standing when plaintiffs fail to allege an imminent injury-in-fact.

In this increasingly digitized world, a number of courts have had occasion to decide whether the "risk of future harm" posed by data security breaches confers standing on persons whose information *may* have been accessed. Most courts have held that such plaintiffs lack standing because the harm is too speculative. *See Amburgy v. Express Scripts, Inc.,* 671 F. Supp. 2d 1046 (E.D. Mo. 2009); *see also Key v. DSW Inc.,* 454 F. Supp. 2d 684 (S.D. Ohio 2006). We agree with the holdings in those cases. Here, no evidence suggests that the data has been—or will ever be—misused. The present test is actuality, not hypothetical speculations concerning the possibility of future injury. Appellants' allegations of an increased risk of identity theft resulting from a security breach are therefore insufficient to secure standing. . . .

[Regarding comparisons of data-security-breach situations to defective-medical-device, toxic-substance-exposure, or environmental-injury cases, the Third Circuit stated, "These analogies do not persuade us, because defective-medical-device and toxic-substance-exposure cases confer standing based on two important factors not present in data breach cases."]

First, in those cases, an injury has undoubtedly occurred. In medical-device cases, a defective device has been implanted into the human body with a quantifiable risk of failure. Similarly, exposure to a toxic substance causes injury; cells are damaged and a disease mechanism has been introduced. Hence, the damage has been done; we just cannot yet quantify how it will manifest itself.

In data breach cases where no misuse is alleged, however, there has been no injury—indeed, no change in the status quo. Here, Appellants' credit card statements are exactly the same today as they would have been had Ceridian's database never been hacked. Moreover, there is no quantifiable risk of damage in the future. Any damages that may occur here are entirely speculative and dependent on the skill and intent of the hacker.

Second, standing in medical-device and toxic-tort cases hinges on human health concerns. . . . The deceased, after all, have little use for compensation. This case implicates none of these concerns. The hacker did not change or injure Appellants' bodies; any harm that may occur—if all of Appellants' stated fears are actually realized—may be redressed in due time through money damages after the harm occurs with no fear that litigants will be dead or disabled from the onset of the injury.

An analogy to environmental injury cases fails as well. [S]tanding is unique in the environmental context because monetary compensation may not adequately return plaintiffs to their original position. In a data breach case, however, there is no reason to believe that monetary compensation will not return plaintiffs to their original position completely—*if* the hacked information is actually read, copied, understood, and misused to a plaintiff's detriment. To the contrary, unlike priceless "mountains majesty," the thing feared lost here is simple cash, which is easily and precisely compensable with a monetary award. We therefore decline to analogize this case to those cases in the medical device, toxic tort or environmental injury contexts.

Finally, we conclude that Appellants' alleged time and money expenditures to monitor their financial information do not establish standing, because costs incurred to watch for a speculative chain of future events based on hypothetical future criminal acts are no more "actual" injuries than the alleged "increased risk of injury" which forms the basis for Appellants' claims.

RESNICK V. AVMED

693 F.3d 1317 (11th Cir. 2012)

WILSON, CJ. Juana Curry and William Moore (collectively "Plaintiffs") appeal the district court's dismissal of their Second Amended Complaint ("Complaint") for failure to state a claim upon which relief may be granted. The district court held that among its other deficiencies, the Complaint failed to state a cognizable injury. We find that the complaint states a cognizable injury for the purposes of standing and as a necessary element of injury in Plaintiffs' Florida law claims. We also conclude that the Complaint sufficiently alleges the causation element of negligence, negligence *per se*, breach of contract, breach of implied contract, breach of the implied covenant of good faith and fair dealing, and breach of fiduciary duty . . . . The Complaint similarly alleges facts sufficient to withstand a motion to dismiss on the restitution/unjust enrichment claim. However, the Complaint fails to allege entitlement to relief under Florida law for the claims of negligence *per se* and breach of the implied covenant of good faith and fair dealing. We therefore reverse in part, affirm in part, and remand the case to the district court for further proceedings.

AvMed, Inc. is a Florida corporation that delivers health care services through health plans and government-sponsored managed-care plans. AvMed has a corporate office in Gainesville, Florida, and in December 2009, two laptop computers were stolen from that office. Those laptops contained AvMed customers' sensitive information, which included protected health information, Social Security numbers, names, addresses, and phone numbers. AvMed did not take care to secure these laptops, so when they were stolen the information was readily accessible. The laptops were sold to an individual with a history of dealing in stolen property. The unencrypted laptops contained the sensitive information of approximately 1.2 million current and former AvMed members.

The laptops contained personal information of Juana Curry and William Moore. Plaintiffs are careful in guarding their sensitive information and had never been victims of identity theft before the laptops were stolen. Curry guards physical documents that contain her sensitive information and avoids storing or sharing her sensitive information digitally. Similarly, Moore guards physical documents that contain his sensitive information and is careful in the digital transmission of this information.

Notwithstanding their care, Plaintiffs have both become victims of identity theft. Curry's sensitive information was used by an unknown third party in October 2010—ten months after the laptop theft. Bank of America accounts were opened in Curry's name, credit cards were activated, and the cards were used to make unauthorized purchases. Curry's home address was also changed with the U.S. Postal Service. Moore's sensitive information was used by an unknown third party in February 2011 — fourteen months after the laptop theft. At that time, an account was opened in Moore's name with E*Trade Financial, and in April 2011, Moore was notified that the account had been overdrawn.

Prior to making an adjudication on the merits, we must assure ourselves that we have jurisdiction to hear the case before us. Litigants must show that their claim presents the court with a case or controversy under the Constitution and meets the "irreducible constitutional minimum of standing." *Lujan,* 504 U.S. at 560. To fulfill this requirement, a plaintiff must show that:

> (1) it has suffered an "injury in fact" that is (a) concrete and particularized and (b) actual or imminent, not conjectural or hypothetical; (2) the injury is fairly traceable to the challenged action of the defendant; and (3) it is likely, as opposed to merely speculative, that the injury will be redressed by a favorable decision.

Friends of the Earth, Inc. v. Laidlaw Envtl. Servs. (TOC), Inc., 528 U.S. 167 (2000). "At the pleading stage, general factual allegations of injury resulting from the defendant's conduct may suffice" to establish standing. *Lujan.*

Whether a party claiming actual identity theft resulting from a data breach has standing to bring suit is an issue of first impression in this Circuit. Plaintiffs allege that they have become victims of identity theft and have suffered monetary damages as a result. This constitutes an injury in fact under the law.[1]

We must next determine whether Plaintiffs' injury is fairly traceable to AvMed's actions. A showing that an injury is "fairly traceable" requires less than a showing of "proximate cause." *Focus on the Family v. Pinellas Suncoast Transit Auth.*, 344 F.3d 1263 (11th Cir. 2003). Even a showing that a plaintiff's injury is indirectly caused by a defendant's actions satisfies the fairly traceable requirement. Plaintiffs allege that AvMed failed to secure their information on company laptops, and that those laptops were subsequently stolen. Despite Plaintiffs' personal habits of securing their sensitive information, Plaintiffs became the victims of identity theft after the unencrypted laptops containing their sensitive information were stolen. For purposes of standing, these allegations are sufficient to "fairly trace" their injury to AvMed's failures.

Finally, Plaintiffs must show that a favorable resolution of the case in their favor could redress their alleged injuries. Plaintiffs allege a monetary injury and an award of compensatory damages would redress that injury. Plaintiffs have alleged sufficient facts to confer standing, and we now turn to the merits of their appeal. . . .

The complaint must contain enough facts to make a claim for relief plausible on its face; a party must plead "factual content that allows the court to draw the reasonable inference that the defendant is liable for the misconduct alleged."

. . . Plaintiffs brought seven counts against AvMed, all under Florida law. Of the seven causes of action alleged, Florida law requires a plaintiff to show that the defendant's challenged action *caused* the plaintiff's harm in six of them: negligence, negligence *per se,* breach of fiduciary duty, breach of contract, breach of contract implied in fact, and breach of the implied covenant of good faith and fair dealing. A negligence claim requires a plaintiff to show that (1) defendants owe plaintiffs a duty, (2) defendants breached the duty, (3) defendants' breach injured plaintiffs, and "(4) [plaintiffs'] damage [was] *caused by* the injury to the plaintiff as a result of the defendant's breach of duty." Similarly, under Florida law, an action for negligence *per se* requires a plaintiff to show "violation of a statute which establishes a duty to take precautions to protect a particular class of persons from a particularly injury or type of injury." As part of this showing, plaintiffs must establish "that the violation of the statute *was the proximate cause* of [their] injury." The elements of a cause of action for breach of fiduciary duty in Florida include "damages *flowing from* the breach."

The contract claims also require a showing of causation. In Florida, a breach of contract claim requires a party to show that *damages resulted from* the breach. Florida courts use breach of contract analysis to evaluate claims of breach of contract implied in fact and breach of the covenant of good faith and fair dealing.

We now consider the well-pleaded factual allegations relating to causation.... The complaint alleges that, prior to the data breach, neither Curry nor Moore had ever had their identities stolen or their sensitive information "compromised in any way." It further alleges that "Curry took substantial precautions to protect herself from identity theft," including not transmitting sensitive information over the Internet or any unsecured source; not storing her sensitive information on a computer or media device; storing sensitive information in a "safe and secure physical location;" and destroying "documents she receives in the mail that may contain any of her sensitive information, or that contain any information that could otherwise be used to steal her identity, such as credit card offers." Similarly, Moore alleges in the complaint that he "took substantial precautions to protect himself from identity theft," including not transmitting unencrypted sensitive information over the internet or any other source, storing documents containing sensitive information "in a safe and secure physical location and destroy[ing] any documents he receives in the mail" that include either sensitive information or information that "could otherwise be used to steal his identity." Plaintiffs became victims of identity theft for the first time in their lives ten and fourteen months after the laptops containing their sensitive information were stolen. Curry's sensitive information was used to open a Bank of America account and change her address with the United States Post Office, and Moore's sensitive information was used to open an E*Trade Financial account in his name.

Our task is to determine whether the pleadings contain "sufficient factual matter, accepted as true, to 'state a claim to relief that is plausible on its face.' " A claim is facially plausible when the court can draw "the reasonable inference that the defendant is liable for the misconduct alleged" from the pled facts. Taken as true, these factual allegations are consistent with Plaintiffs' conclusion that AvMed's failure to secure Plaintiffs' information caused them to become victims of identity theft. After thorough consideration, we conclude that the allegations are sufficient to cross the line from merely possible to plausible.

Generally, to prove that a data breach caused identity theft, the pleadings must include allegations of a nexus between the two instances beyond allegations of time and sequence. . . . Here, Plaintiffs allege a nexus between the two events that includes more than a coincidence of time and sequence: they allege that the sensitive information on the stolen laptop was the same sensitive information used to steal Plaintiffs' identity. Plaintiffs explicitly make this connection when they allege that Curry's identity was stolen by changing her address and that Moore's identity was stolen by opening an E*Trade Financial account in his name because in both of those allegations, Plaintiffs state that the identity thief used Plaintiffs' sensitive information. We understand Plaintiffs to make a similar allegation regarding the bank accounts opened in Curry's name even though they do not plead precisely that Curry's sensitive information was used to open the Bank of America account. The Complaint states that Curry's sensitive information was on the unencrypted stolen laptop, that her identity was stolen, and that the *stolen identity* was used to open unauthorized accounts. Considering the Complaint as a whole and applying common sense to our understanding of this allegation, we find that Plaintiffs allege that the same sensitive information that was stored on the stolen laptops was used to open the Bank of America account. Thus, Plaintiffs' allegations that the data breach caused their identities to be stolen move from the realm of the possible into the plausible. Had Plaintiffs alleged fewer facts, we doubt whether the Complaint could have survived a motion to dismiss. However, Plaintiffs have sufficiently alleged a nexus between the data theft and the identity theft and therefore meet the federal pleading standards. Because their contention that the data breach caused the identity theft is plausible under the facts pled, Plaintiffs meet the pleading standards for their allegations on the counts of negligence, negligence *per se,* breach of fiduciary duty, breach of contract, breach of implied contract, and breach of the implied covenant of good faith and fair dealing. . . .

To establish a cause of action for unjust enrichment/restitution, a Plaintiff must show that "1) the plaintiff has conferred a benefit on the defendant; 2) the defendant has knowledge of the benefit; 3) the defendant has accepted or retained the benefit conferred; and 4) the circumstances are such that it would be inequitable for the defendant to retain the benefit without paying fair value for it." *Della Ratta v. Della Ratta*, 927 So. 2d 1055, 1059 (Fla. Dist. Ct. App. 2006).

Plaintiffs allege that they conferred a monetary benefit on AvMed in the form of monthly premiums, that AvMed "appreciates or has knowledge of such benefit," that AvMed uses the premiums to "pay for the administrative costs of data management and security," and that AvMed "should not be permitted to retain the money belonging to Plaintiffs ... because [AvMed] failed to implement the data management and security measures that are mandated by industry standards." Plaintiffs also allege that AvMed either failed to implement or inadequately implemented policies to secure sensitive information, as can be seen from the data breach. Accepting these allegations as true, we find that Plaintiffs alleged sufficient facts to allow this claim to survive a motion to dismiss. . . .

AvMed argues that we can affirm the district court because the Complaint fails to allege an entitlement to relief under Florida law on each count. On review, we find that two of the pled causes of action do not allow Plaintiffs to recover under Florida law. We address only the two claims that fail: negligence *per se,* and breach of the covenant of good faith and fair dealing. . . .

[The Eleventh Circuit found that the negligence *per se* failed because the statutory section that the plaintiffs argued was contained in a chapter regulating the licensure, development, establishment, and minimum standard enforcement of hospitals, ambulatory surgical centers, and mobile surgical facilities. Fla. Stat. § 395.001. It stated: "Because AvMed is an integrated managed-care organization and not a hospital, ambulatory surgical center, or mobile surgical facility, AvMed is not subject to this statute."

The Eleventh Circuit also found that there was no violation of the implied covenant of good faith and fair dealing under Florida law by Avmed. Florida requires a "conscious act" to frustrate the common purpose of a contract and the Plaintiffs failed to allege "AvMed's shortcomings were conscious acts to frustrate the common purpose of the agreement."]

In this digital age, our personal information is increasingly becoming susceptible to attack. People with nefarious interests are taking advantage of the plethora of opportunities to gain access to our private information and use it in ways that cause real harm. Even though the perpetrators of these crimes often remain unidentified and the victims are left to clean up the damage caused by these identity thieves, cases brought by these victims are subject to the same pleading standards as are plaintiffs in all civil suits. Here, Plaintiffs have pled a cognizable injury and have pled sufficient facts to allow for a plausible inference that AvMed's failures in securing their data resulted in their identities being stolen. They have shown a sufficient nexus between the data breach and the identity theft beyond allegations of time and sequence.

PRYOR, CJ., dissenting. I agree with the majority opinion that Curry and Moore have standing to sue, but Curry and Moore's complaint should be dismissed for failure to state a claim. Their complaint fails to allege a plausible basis for finding that AvMed caused them to suffer identity theft, and their claim of unjust enrichment fails as a matter of law. . . .

The parties do not dispute that laptops containing the sensitive information of Curry and Moore was stolen from AvMed, but Curry and Moore's second amended complaint fails to plead enough facts to allow a factfinder to draw a reasonable inference that the sensitive information identity thieves used to open the fraudulent accounts in the plaintiffs' names was obtained from AvMed. In an attempt to bridge this gap, Curry and Moore allege that they have both been *very* careful to protect their sensitive information. But the manner in which Curry and Moore care for the sensitive information they receive from third parties tells us nothing about how the third parties care for that sensitive information before or after they send it to Curry and Moore.

Regarding the cause of the identity theft that Curry and Moore suffered it is conceivable that the unknown identity thieves used the sensitive information stolen from AvMed to open the fraudulent accounts, but it is equally conceivable, in the light of the facts alleged in the complaint, that the unknown identity thieves obtained the information from third parties. Curry and Moore do not allege any facts that make it plausible that the unknown identity thieves who opened the fraudulent accounts obtained the sensitive information necessary to do so from AvMed. . . .

The complaint also fails to state a claim of unjust enrichment under Florida law. "Florida courts have held that a plaintiff cannot pursue a quasi-contract claim for unjust enrichment if an express contract exists concerning the same subject matter." The parties do not dispute that they entered into an enforceable contract; they dispute whether the contract has been breached. In that circumstance, a claim of unjust enrichment cannot be maintained.

I respectfully dissent.

NOTES & QUESTIONS

1. *Harm? No Harm?* The stakes in data security breach litigation are high. Plaintiffs want companies to guard their information more carefully and are concerned about identity theft. Companies face considerable financial exposure. Consider that after the Eleventh Circuit allowed the lawsuit in *Resnick* to continue, AvMed negotiated a $3 million settlement quickly with the attorneys for the plaintiffs. That is a high cost for leaving two laptops unsecured in a corporate office.

   This high stakes litigation is also accompanied by legal uncertainty regarding the nature of the harm to plaintiffs and whether standing is present. *Reilly* and *Resnick* evaluated a different range of claims and reached sometimes contrary results. Analogies were attempted with toxic torts, defective medical devices, and environmental injury. Do you find any of these areas closer or farther from the concerns in data security? In *Resnick*, the plaintiffs were actual victims of identity theft occurring after the theft of the AvMed laptops. Why does that fact make a difference for the Eleventh Circuit?

2. ***Tort Negligence for Data Security Breaches.*** In tort law, under a general negligence theory, litigants might sue a company after a data security incident and seek to collect damages. In contrast to *Resnick*, however, many class action lawsuits following data breaches have been notably unsuccessful. Among other problems, claimants are facing trouble convincing courts that the data processing entities owe a duty to the individuals whose data are leaked, or that damages can be inferred from the simple fact of a data breach. For example, a South Carolina court declared in 2003 that "[t]he relationship, if any, between credit card issuers and potential victims of identity theft is far too attenuated to rise to the level of a duty between them." *Huggins v. Citibank*, 585 S.E.2d 275 (S.C. 2003).

3. ***Proving Injury from Data Security Breaches: Three Theories of Harm.*** Suppose a person has been notified that her personal information has been improperly accessed, but she has not yet suffered from identity theft. Should she be entitled to any form of compensation? Has she suffered an injury? One might argue that being made more vulnerable to future harm has made her worse off than before. The individual might live with greater unease knowing that she is less secure. On the other hand, no identity theft has occurred, and it may never occur. How should the law address this situation? Recognize a harm? If so, how should damages be assessed?

   For data security breaches, plaintiffs have generally advanced one or more of the following theories of harm:

   (1) *Emotional Distress.* The exposure of their data has caused them emotional distress.
   (2) *Increased Risk of Future Harm.* The exposure of their data has subjected them to an increased risk of harm from identity theft, fraud, or other injury.
   (3) *Expenditures to Reduce Risk of Future Harm.* The exposure of their data has resulted in their having to expend time and money to prevent future fraud, such as signing up for credit monitoring, contacting credit reporting agencies and placing fraud alerts on their accounts, and so on.

   Courts are divided on whether to recognize harm on these theories, but the majority of courts have dismissed all of these theories. According to Daniel Solove and Danielle Keats Citron, many courts take a "visceral and vested" approach to harm: "Courts insist that data harms be visceral—easy to see, measure, and quantify. They require harms to be vested—already materialized in the here and now. Plaintiffs must experience physical, monetary, or property damage or, at least, the damage must be imminent."

   Solove and Citron observe:

This cramped understanding of harm harkens back to early conceptions of the common law. Nineteenth-century tort claims required proof of physical injury or property loss. Financial losses could be recovered in tort actions if defendants owed plaintiffs a special duty of care. Along these lines, courts have recognized claims for privacy violations only where redress is sought for tangible financial losses. Courts have found a sufficient injury in data breach cases where the exposure of personal data has led to identity theft. But without proof of physical harm or financial loss, courts rarely recognize harm.

Requiring harm to be visceral and vested has severely restricted the recognition of data harms, which rarely have these qualities. Data breach harms are not easy to see, at least not in any physical way. They are not tangible like broken limbs and destroyed property. Instead, the harm is intangible. Data breaches increase a person's risk of identity theft or fraud and cause emotional distress as a result of that risk.[16]

4. ***Emotional Distress.*** The majority of courts are reluctant to recognize emotional distress as a harm stemming from a data breach. Solove and Citron explain why:

> A concern with recognizing emotional distress in data breach cases is that psychic distress can be readily manufactured. Arguments against the recognition of anxiety focus on the fact that claims of anxiety are easy to make and difficult to dispute. Plaintiffs will quickly learn to make poignant statements about their anguish, with statements exaggerating their distress. Defendants may have difficulty disproving plaintiffs' accounts of their own subjective mental states.[17]

However, Solove and Citron go on to note that in many other areas of law, courts readily move past these concerns to recognize pure emotional distress as a basis of harm:

> [T]he law has evolved to recognize emotional distress disconnected from physical or financial injury. In certain privacy cases, courts recognize pure emotional distress without hesitation, most likely, we posit, because courts recognize that most people would feel emotional distress in these situations. In essence, an unstated objective test to emotional distress seems to exist in privacy tort cases.

5. ***Increased Risk of Future Harm.*** In *Resnick*, the plaintiffs suffered identity fraud several months after the breach and the Eleventh Circuit concluded that their allegations were sufficient to "fairly trace" their injury to AvMed's information security failures. Would the court have reached the same conclusion if hackers had accessed data but there were no incidences of identity theft or fraud?

In *Krottner v. Starbucks Corp.*, 628 F.3d 1139 (9th Cir. 2010), the court concluded that increased vulnerability to identity theft could give rise to standing based upon the theft of a laptop containing unencrypted personal data:

---

[16] Daniel J. Solove & Danielle Keats Citron, *Risk and Anxiety: A Theory of Data Breach Harms,* 96 Tex. L. Rev. — (forthcoming 2017).
[17] *Id.*

Here, Plaintiffs–Appellants have alleged a credible threat of real and immediate harm stemming from the theft of a laptop containing their unencrypted personal data. Were Plaintiffs–Appellants' allegations more conjectural or hypothetical—for example, if no laptop had been stolen, and Plaintiffs had sued based on the risk that it would be stolen at some point in the future—we would find the threat far less credible. On these facts, however, Plaintiffs–Appellants have sufficiently alleged an injury-in-fact for purposes of Article III standing.

6. ***Expenditures to Reduce Risk of Future Harm.*** Why do most courts conclude that expenditures to reduce risks of future harm created by another are not recoverable? Suppose a company leaks a toxic chemical, causing a person to have an increased risk of cancer. The person sees a doctor and gets a prescription for a drug that will reduce the likelihood that the chemical will cause cancer. Would the expenses of seeing the doctor and purchasing the drug be recoverable? Is this hypothetical analogous to a data security breach?

7. ***The Impact of* Clapper**. A 2013 Supreme Court case involving a constitutional challenge to national security surveillance had become a key and contested precedent for the issue of standing in data breach cases. In *Clapper v. Amnesty International USA*, 133 S. Ct. (2013), a group of attorneys, journalists, and others contended that government surveillance under the Foreign Intelligence Surveillance Act (FISA) violated their constitutional rights. They could not establish that they were definitely under surveillance, but they had a legitimate reason to suspect that they were under surveillance because they represented or spoke to individuals who the government viewed as suspicious.

The Supreme Court held that the plaintiffs could not establish standing. The Court reasoned that "it is speculative whether the Government will imminently target communications to which respondents are parties."

The plaintiffs also contended that they were injured because they had to take measures to avoid the risk that they were under surveillance. "Respondents claim, for instance, that the threat of surveillance sometimes compels them to avoid certain e-mail and phone conversations, to 'tal[k] in generalities rather than specifics,' or to travel so that they can have in-person conversations." The Court rejected these costs as a basis for injury because "parties cannot manufacture standing by incurring costs in anticipation of non-imminent harm."

Many courts have used *Clapper* to deny standing to plaintiffs in data breach cases when plaintiffs claim injury due to an increased risk of future harm or expenditures to reduce the risk of future harm. Other courts have held that *Clapper* does not foreclose finding harm on these theories. Consider the cases that follow.

REMIJAS V. NEIMAN MARCUS CORP.
794 F.3d 688 (7th Cir. 2015)

WOOD, J. Sometime in 2013, hackers attacked Neiman Marcus, a luxury department store, and stole the credit card numbers of its customers. In December 2013, the company learned that some of its customers had found fraudulent charges on their cards. On January 10, 2014, it announced to the public that the cyberattack had occurred and that between July 16, 2013, and October 30, 2013, approximately 350,000 cards had been exposed to the hackers' malware. In the wake of those disclosures, several customers brought this action under the Class Action Fairness Act, 28 U.S.C. § 1332(d), seeking various forms of relief. The district court stopped the suit in its tracks, however, ruling that both the individual plaintiffs and the class lacked standing under Article III of the Constitution. This resulted in a dismissal of the complaint without prejudice. We conclude that the district court erred. The plaintiffs satisfy Article III's requirements based on at least some of the injuries they have identified. We thus reverse and remand for further proceedings. . . .

The plaintiffs . . . allege that they have standing based on two imminent injuries: an increased risk of future fraudulent charges and greater susceptibility to identity theft. We address the two alleged imminent injuries first and then the four asserted actual injuries.

Allegations of future harm can establish Article III standing if that harm is "certainly impending," but "allegations of possible future injury are not sufficient." *Clapper v. Amnesty Int'l USA*, 133 S.Ct. 1138 (2013). Here, the complaint alleges that everyone's personal data has already been stolen; it alleges that the 9,200 who already have incurred fraudulent charges have experienced harm. Those victims have suffered the aggravation and loss of value of the time needed to set things straight, to reset payment associations after credit card numbers are changed, and to pursue relief for unauthorized charges. The complaint also alleges a concrete risk of harm for the rest. The question is whether these allegations satisfy *Clapper*'s requirement that injury either already have occurred or be "certainly impending."

As for the 9,200 (including Frank and Farnoush), the plaintiffs concede that they were later reimbursed and that the evidence does not yet indicate that their identities (as opposed to the data) have been stolen. But as we already have noted, there are identifiable costs associated with the process of sorting things out. Neiman Marcus challenges the standing of these class members, but we see no merit in that point. What about the class members who contend that un-reimbursed fraudulent charges and identity theft may happen in the future, and that these injuries are likely enough that immediate preventive measures are necessary? Neiman Marcus contends that this is too speculative to serve as injury-in-fact. It argues that all of the plaintiffs would be reimbursed for fraudulent charges because (it asserts) that is the common practice of major credit card companies. The plaintiffs disagree with the latter proposition; they contend that they, like all consumers subject to fraudulent charges, must spend time and money replacing cards and monitoring their credit score, and that full reimbursement is not guaranteed. (It would not be enough to review one's credit card statements carefully every month, because the thieves might—and often do—acquire new credit cards unbeknownst to the victim.) This reveals a material factual dispute on such matters as the class members' experiences and both the content of, and the universality of, bank reimbursement policies.

Clapper does not, as the district court thought, foreclose any use whatsoever of future injuries to support Article III standing. In *Clapper*, the Supreme Court decided that human rights organizations did not have standing to challenge the

Foreign Intelligence Surveillance Act (FISA) because they could not show that their communications with suspected terrorists were intercepted by the government. The plaintiffs only suspected that such interceptions might have occurred. This, the Court held, was too speculative to support standing. In so ruling, however, it did not jettison the "substantial risk" standard. To the contrary, it stated that "[o]ur cases do not uniformly require plaintiffs to demonstrate that it is literally certain that the harms they identify will come about. In some instances, we have found standing based on a 'substantial risk' that the harm will occur, which may prompt plaintiffs to reasonably incur costs to mitigate or avoid that harm." . . . .

The plaintiffs allege that the hackers deliberately targeted Neiman Marcus in order to obtain their credit-card information. Whereas in *Clapper*, "there was no evidence that any of respondents' communications either had been or would be monitored," in our case there is "no need to speculate as to whether [the Neiman Marcus customers'] information has been stolen and what information was taken." . . . . [T]he Neiman Marcus customers should not have to wait until hackers commit identity theft or credit-card fraud in order to give the class standing, because there is an "objectively reasonable likelihood" that such an injury will occur. . . .

At this stage in the litigation, it is plausible to infer that the plaintiffs have shown a substantial risk of harm from the Neiman Marcus data breach. Why else would hackers break into a store's database and steal consumers' private information? Presumably, the purpose of the hack is, sooner or later, to make fraudulent charges or assume those consumers' identities. The plaintiffs are also careful to say that only 9,200 cards have experienced fraudulent charges so far; the complaint asserts that fraudulent charges and identity theft can occur long after a data breach. It cites a Government Accountability Office Report that finds that "stolen data may be held for up to a year or more before being used to commit identity theft. Further, once stolen data have been sold or posted on the Web, fraudulent use of that information may continue for years." U.S. Gov't Accountability Office, GAO-07-737, *Report to Congressional Requesters: Personal Information* 29 (2007). . . .

In addition to the alleged future injuries, the plaintiffs assert that they have already lost time and money protecting themselves against future identity theft and fraudulent charges. Mitigation expenses do not qualify as actual injuries where the harm is not imminent. *Clapper*, 133 S.Ct. at 1152 (concluding that "costs that they have incurred to avoid [injury]" are insufficient to confer standing). Plaintiffs "cannot manufacture standing by incurring costs in anticipation of non-imminent harm." *Id.* at 1155. . . .

Once again, however, it is important not to overread *Clapper*. *Clapper* was addressing speculative harm based on something that may not even have happened to some or all of the plaintiffs. In our case, Neiman Marcus does not contest the fact that the initial breach took place. An affected customer, having been notified by Neiman Marcus that her card is at risk, might think it necessary to subscribe to a service that offers monthly credit monitoring. It is telling in this connection that Neiman Marcus offered one year of credit monitoring and identity-theft protection to all customers for whom it had contact information and who had shopped at their stores between January 2013 and January 2014. It is unlikely that it did so because the risk is so ephemeral that it can safely be disregarded. These credit-monitoring services come at a price that is more than de minimis. For instance, Experian offers credit monitoring for $4.95 a month for the first month, and then $19.95 per month thereafter. That easily qualifies as a concrete injury. . . .

BECK V. MCDONALD
949 F.3d 262 (4th Cir. 2017)

DIAZ, J. The Plaintiffs in these consolidated appeals are veterans who received medical treatment and health care at the William Jennings Bryan Dorn Veterans Affairs Medical Center ("Dorn VAMC") in Columbia, South Carolina. After two data breaches at the Center compromised their personal information, the Plaintiffs brought separate actions against the Secretary of Veterans Affairs and Dorn VAMC officials ("Defendants"), alleging violations of the Privacy Act of 1974, 5 U.S.C. § 552a *et seq.* and the Administrative Procedure Act ("APA"), 5 U.S.C. § 701 *et seq.*

In both cases, the Plaintiffs sought to establish Article III standing based on the harm from the increased risk of future identity theft and the cost of measures to protect against it. The district court dismissed the actions for lack of subject-matter jurisdiction, holding that the Plaintiffs failed to establish a non-speculative, imminent injury-in-fact for purposes of Article III standing. We agree with the district court and therefore affirm.

The Beck case arises from a report that on February 11, 2013, a laptop connected to a pulmonary function testing device with a Velcro strip was misplaced or stolen from Dorn VAMC's Respiratory Therapy department. The laptop contains unencrypted personal information of approximately 7,400 patients, including names, birth dates, the last four digits of social security numbers, and physical descriptors (age, race, gender, height, and weight).

An internal investigation determined that the laptop was likely stolen and that Dorn VAMC failed to follow the policies and procedures for utilizing a non-encrypted laptop to store patient information. Dorn VAMC officials used medical appointment records to notify every patient tested using the missing laptop and offered one year of free credit monitoring. To date, the laptop has not been recovered.

Richard Beck and Lakreshia Jeffery (the "Beck plaintiffs") filed suit on behalf of a putative class of the approximately 7,400 patients whose information was stored on the missing laptop. Relevant to this appeal, the Beck plaintiffs sought declaratory relief and monetary damages under the Privacy Act, alleging that the "Defendants' failures" and "violations" of the Privacy Act "caused Plaintiffs . . . embarrassment, inconvenience, unfairness, mental distress, and the threat of current and future substantial harm from identity theft and other misuse of their Personal Information." J. They further allege that the "threat of identity theft" required them to frequently monitor their "credit reports, bank statements, health insurance reports, and other similar information, purchas[e] credit watch services, and [shift] financial accounts." . . . .

The district court granted the Defendants' motion to dismiss, holding, pursuant to *Clapper v. Amnesty International USA*, 133 S.Ct. 1138 (2013), that the Beck plaintiffs lacked standing under the Privacy Act because they had "not submitted evidence sufficient to create a genuine issue of material fact as to whether they face a 'certainly impending' risk of identity theft." . . . .

The Watson case arises from Dorn VAMC's July 2014 discovery that four boxes of pathology reports headed for long-term storage had been misplaced or stolen. The reports contain identifying information of over 2,000 patients, including names, social security numbers, and medical diagnoses. Dorn VAMC officials alerted those affected and, as they did following the laptop's disappearance, offered each of them one year of free credit monitoring. The boxes have not been recovered.

While the Beck litigation was pending, Beverly Watson brought a putative class-action lawsuit on behalf of the over 2,000 individuals whose pathology reports had gone missing. Watson sought money damages and declaratory and injunctive relief, alleging the same harm as did the Beck plaintiffs. The Defendants moved to dismiss the complaint for lack of subject-matter jurisdiction and for failure to state a claim.

The district court granted the Defendants' motion to dismiss for lack of subject-matter jurisdiction, relying on *Clapper* to hold that Watson lacked Article III standing under the Privacy Act because she "ha[d] not alleged that there ha[d] been any actual or attempted misuse of her personal information," thus rendering her allegation that her information "will eventually be misused as a result of the disappearance of the boxes . . . speculative." . . . .

We focus our inquiry on the first element of Article III standing: injury-in-fact. "To establish injury in fact, a plaintiff must show that he or she suffered 'an invasion of a legally protected interest' that is 'concrete and particularized' and 'actual or imminent, not conjectural or hypothetical.'" *Spokeo, Inc. v. Robins*, 136 S.Ct. 1540 (2016). . . .

Clapper's discussion of when a threatened injury constitutes an Article III injury-in-fact is controlling here. Before explaining why, we address the Plaintiffs' contention that the district court misread *Clapper* to require a new, heightened burden for proving an Article III injury-in-fact. To the contrary, *Clapper*'s iteration of the well-established tenet that a threatened injury must be "certainly impending" to constitute an injury-in-fact is hardly novel.

We also reject the Plaintiffs' claim that "emotional upset" and "fear [of] identity theft and financial fraud" resulting from the data breaches are "adverse effects" sufficient to confer Article III standing. . . .

Our sister circuits are divided on whether a plaintiff may establish an Article III injury-in-fact based on an increased risk of future identity theft. The Sixth, Seventh, and Ninth Circuits have all recognized, at the pleading stage, that plaintiffs can establish an injury-in-fact based on this threatened injury. *See Galaria v. Nationwide Mut. Ins. Co.*, 663 Fed.Appx. 384 (6th Cir. 2016) (plaintiff-customers' increased risk of future identity theft theory established injury-in-fact after hackers breached Nationwide Mutual Insurance Company's computer network and stole their sensitive personal information, because "[t]here is no need for speculation where Plaintiffs allege that their data has already been stolen and is now in the hands of ill-intentioned criminals"); *Remijas v. Neiman Marcus Grp., LLC*, 794 F.3d 688 (7th Cir. 2015) (plaintiff-customers' increased risk of future fraudulent charges and identity theft theory established "certainly impending" injury-in-fact and "substantial risk of harm" after hackers attacked Neiman Marcus with malware to steal credit card numbers, because "[p]resumably, the purpose of the hack is, sooner or later, to make fraudulent charges or assume those consumers' identities"); *Krottner v. Starbucks Corp.*, 628 F.3d 1139 (9th Cir. 2010) (plaintiff-employees' increased risk of future identity theft theory a "credible threat of harm" for Article III purposes after theft of a laptop containing the unencrypted names, addresses, and social security numbers of 97,000 Starbucks employees). . . .

By contrast, the First and Third Circuits have rejected such allegations. *See Katz v. Pershing, LLC*, 672 F.3d 64 (1st Cir. 2012) (brokerage account-holder's increased risk of unauthorized access and identity theft theory insufficient to constitute "actual or impending injury" after defendant failed to properly maintain an electronic platform containing her account information, because plaintiff failed to "identify any incident in which her data has ever been accessed by an unauthorized person"); *Reilly v. Ceridian Corp.*, 664 F.3d 38 (3d Cir. 2011) (plaintiff-employees' increased risk of identity theft theory too hypothetical and speculative to establish "certainly impending" injury-in-fact after unknown hacker penetrated payroll system firewall, because it was "not known whether the hacker read, copied, or understood" the system's information and no evidence suggested past or future misuse of employee data or that the "intrusion was intentional or malicious").

The Plaintiffs say that our sister circuits' decisions in *Krottner, Pisciotta*, and *Remijas* support their allegations of standing based on threatened injury of future identity theft. To the contrary, these cases demonstrate why the Plaintiffs' theory is too speculative to constitute an injury-in-fact.

Underlying the cases are common allegations that sufficed to push the threatened injury of future identity theft beyond the speculative to the sufficiently imminent. In *Galaria, Remijas*, and *Pisciotta*, for example, the data thief intentionally targeted the personal information compromised in the data breaches. . . . And, in *Remijas* and *Krottner*, at least one named plaintiff alleged misuse or access of that personal information by the thief.

Here, the Plaintiffs make no such claims. This in turn renders their contention of an enhanced risk of future identity theft too speculative. On this point, the data breaches in Beck and Watson occurred in February 2013 and July 2014, respectively. Yet, even after extensive discovery, the Beck plaintiffs have uncovered no evidence that the information contained on the stolen laptop has been accessed or misused or that they have suffered identity theft, nor, for that matter, that the thief stole the laptop with the intent to steal their private information. Watson's complaint suffers from the same deficiency with regard to the four missing boxes of pathology reports. Moreover, "as the breaches fade further into the past," the Plaintiffs' threatened injuries become more and more speculative.

The Plaintiffs counter that there is "no need to speculate" here because they have alleged—and in the Beck case the VA's investigation concluded—that the laptop and pathology reports had been stolen. We of course accept this allegation as true. But the mere theft of these items, without more, cannot confer Article III standing.

Indeed, for the Plaintiffs to suffer the harm of identity theft that they fear, we must engage with the same "attenuated chain of possibilities" rejected by the Court in *Clapper*. In both cases, we must assume that the thief targeted the stolen items for the personal information they contained. And in both cases, the thieves must then select, from thousands of others, the personal information of the named plaintiffs and attempt successfully to use that information to steal their identities. This "attenuated chain" cannot confer standing. . . .

Nonetheless, our inquiry on standing is not at an end, for we may also find standing based on a "substantial risk" that the harm will occur, which in turn may prompt a party to reasonably incur costs to mitigate or avoid that harm. But here too the Plaintiffs fall short of their burden.

The Plaintiffs allege that: (1) 33% of health-related data breaches result in identity theft; (2) the Defendants expend millions of dollars trying to avoid and mitigate those risks; and (3) by offering the Plaintiffs free credit monitoring, the VA effectively conceded that the theft of the laptop and pathology reports constituted a "reasonable risk of harm to those victimized" by the data breaches.

These allegations are insufficient to establish a "substantial risk" of harm. Even if we credit the Plaintiffs' allegation that 33% of those affected by Dorn VAMC data breaches will become victims of identity theft, it follows that over 66% of veterans affected will suffer no harm. This statistic falls far short of establishing a "substantial risk" of harm. *E.g., Khan v. Children's Nat'l Health Sys.*, 188 F.Supp.3d 524 (D. Md. 2016) ("general allegations . . . that data breach victims are 9.5 times more likely to suffer identity theft and that 19 percent of data breach victims become victims of identity theft" insufficient to establish "substantial risk" of harm); *In re Sci. Applications Int'l Corp. (SAIC) Backup Tape Data Theft Litig.*, 45 F.Supp.3d 14, 26 (D.D.C. 2014) (no "substantial risk" of harm where "[b]y Plaintiff's own calculations, then, injury is likely not impending for over 80% of victims").

The Plaintiffs' other allegations fare no better. Contrary to some of our sister circuits, we decline to infer a substantial risk of harm of future identity theft from an organization's offer to provide free credit monitoring services to affected individuals. To adopt such a presumption would surely discourage organizations from offering these services to data-breach victims, lest their extension of goodwill render them subject to suit. . . .

Next, we turn to the Plaintiffs' allegation that they have suffered an injury-in-fact because they have incurred or will in the future incur the cost of measures to guard against identity theft, including the costs of credit monitoring services. All Plaintiffs allege that they wish to enroll in, are enrolled in, or have purchased credit monitoring services. They also say that, as a consequence of the breaches, they have incurred the burden of monitoring their financial and credit information. Even accepting these allegations as true, they do not constitute an injury-in-fact.

As was the case in *Clapper*, the Plaintiffs here seek "to bring this action based on costs they incurred in response to a speculative threat," i.e. their fear of future identity theft based on the breaches at Dorn VAMC. But this allegation is merely "a repackaged version of [Plaintiffs'] first failed theory of standing." Simply put, these self-imposed harms cannot confer standing. . . ..

We acknowledge that the named plaintiffs have been victimized by "at least two admitted VA data breaches," and that Ms. Watson's information was compromised in both the 2013 laptop theft and the 2014 pathology reports theft. . . . The most that can be reasonably inferred from the Plaintiffs' allegations regarding the likelihood of another data breach at Dorn VAMC is that the Plaintiffs could be victimized by a future data breach. That alone is not enough.

NOTES & QUESTIONS

1. *A Circuit Split?* There appears to be a circuit split over the impact of *Clapper* on data breach cases. Are *Remijas* and *Beck* inconsistent? *Beck* distinguishes *Remijas* because in *Remijas*, there was evidence that the "data thief intentionally targeted the personal information compromised in the data breaches" and "at least one named plaintiff alleged misuse or access of that personal information by the thief." Would the *Remijas* court have reached the same conclusion as the *Beck* court had it faced the same facts as in *Beck*?

   Suppose hackers cause the data breach rather than the data simply being lost or stolen. Also suppose that there have been no incidents of identity theft or fraud. Under the reasoning of *Remijas,* would plaintiffs have standing? How about under the reasoning of *Beck*?

   Courts are divided under these circumstances. For example, in *Storm v. Paytime, Inc.*, 90 F.Supp.3d 359 (M.D.Pa. 2015), the court denied standing to plaintiffs whose data was improperly accessed by a hacker:

   > Plaintiffs do not allege that they have actually suffered any form of identity theft as a result of the data breach—to wit, they have not alleged that their bank accounts have been accessed, that credit cards have been opened in their names, or that unknown third parties have used their Social Security numbers to impersonate them and gain access to their accounts. See Reilly, 664 F.3d at 45. In sum, their credit information and bank accounts look the same today as they did prior to Paytime's data breach in April 2014.

   In *Peters v. St. Joseph Servs. Corp.*, 74 F.Supp.3d 847 (S.D.Tex.2015), a health care provider was hacked and data about 405,000 people was compromised. The court held:

   > Peters' alleged future injuries are speculative—even hypothetical—but certainly not imminent. . . . For example, Peters might be able to demonstrate harm if third parties become aware of her exposed information and reveal their interest in it; if they form an intent to misuse her information; and if they take steps to acquire and actually use her information to her detriment. The misuse of her information could take any number of forms, at any point in time. The risk of future harm is, no doubt, indefinite. It may even be impossible to determine whether the misused information was obtained from exposure caused by the Data Breach or from some other source. . . .
   >
   > Under *Clapper*, Peters must at least plausibly establish a "certainly impending" or "substantial" risk that she will be victimized. The allegation that risk has been increased does not transform that assertion into a cognizable injury. In fact, as one district court has observed, "*Clapper* seems rather plainly to reject the premise . . . that any marginal increase in risk is sufficient to confer standing." *Strautins v. Trustwave Holdings, Inc.,* 27 F.Supp.3d 871, 878 (N.D.Ill.2014). . .
   >
   > The Court recognizes that before Clapper, a split existed among the Third, Seventh and Ninth circuit courts over whether the increased risk of harm stemming from a data security breach constitutes imminent injury under Article III. The Seventh and Ninth Circuits held that such a risk was sufficient to confer standing. *Krottner*, 628 F.3d 1139; *Pisciotta*, 499 F.3d 629. The Third Circuit held that the risk fails the constitutional test. *Reilly*, 664 F.3d at 42–45.

Arguably, *Clapper* has resolved the circuit split. Its holding compels the conclusion that Peters lacks standing to bring her federal claims to the extent they are premised on the heightened risk of future identity theft/fraud.

Does *Clapper* resolve the circuit split? Would the courts in *Remijas* and *Beck* agree?

In contrast to *Storm* and *Peters,* consider *In re Adobe Sys., Inc. Privacy Litigation*, 66 F.Supp.3d 1197 (N.D.Cal.2014), where the court concluded that plaintiffs had standing when a hacker gathered their personal data from Adobe's servers for several weeks:

> Unlike in *Clappe*r, where respondents' claim that they would suffer future harm rested on a chain of events that was both "highly attenuated" and "highly speculative," the risk that Plaintiffs' personal data will be misused by the hackers who breached Adobe's network is immediate and very real. Plaintiffs allege that the hackers deliberately targeted Adobe's servers and spent several weeks collecting names, usernames, passwords, email addresses, phone numbers, mailing addresses, and credit card numbers and expiration dates. Plaintiffs' personal information was among the information taken during the breach. Thus, in contrast to *Clapper*, where there was no evidence that any of respondents' communications either had been or would be monitored under Section 702, here there is no need to speculate as to whether Plaintiffs' information has been stolen and what information was taken.
>
> Neither is there any need to speculate as to whether the hackers intend to misuse the personal information stolen in the 2013 data breach or whether they will be able to do so. Not only did the hackers deliberately target Adobe's servers, but Plaintiffs allege that the hackers used Adobe's own systems to decrypt customer credit card numbers. Some of the stolen data has already surfaced on the Internet, and other hackers have allegedly misused it to discover vulnerabilities in Adobe's products. Given this, the danger that Plaintiffs' stolen data will be subject to misuse can plausibly be described as "certainly impending." Indeed, the threatened injury here could be more imminent only if Plaintiffs could allege that their stolen personal information had already been misused. However, to require Plaintiffs to wait until they actually suffer identity theft or credit card fraud in order to have standing would run counter to the well-established principle that harm need not have already occurred or be "literally certain" in order to constitute injury-in-fact.

2. ***The Nature of Data Security Harms.*** Consider Solove and Citron:

> To the individuals whose personal data is leaked into the hands of thieves, the risk of harm is continuing. Hackers may not use the personal data in the near term to steal bank accounts and take out loans. Instead, they may wait until an illness befalls a family member and then use personal data to generate medical bills in a victim's name. They may use the personal data a year later but only use some individuals' personal information for fraud. Although not all of the personal data will be used for criminal ends, some will. In the meanwhile, the individuals worry that their information will be misused and expend time and resources to protect themselves from this possibility.
>
> Long-term risk is not a harmless wrong unlike the risky driver who does not hurt anyone. It is not negligence "in the air," which the law has long understood

as unworthy of a legal response.[18] There is an injury; it is not a regrettable close call like the reckless driver who hits no one. When an entity inadequately secures personal data and thieves steal it, the entity's unreasonable actions impact a sizeable number of users, often in the millions, and the excess risk of fraud is certain to take its toll on a number of those users. Over time, the risk will materialize for a percentage of those users. Although the eventual victims cannot be immediately identified, the entity cannot deny the reality of the loss it has inflicted.[19]

Ryan Calo has proposed a theory for how privacy harms should be understood:

> [T]he vast majority of privacy harms fall into just two categories — one subjective, the other objective. The subjective category of privacy harm is the perception of unwanted observation. This category describes unwelcome mental states — anxiety, for instance, or embarrassment — that accompany the belief that one is or will be watched or monitored. . . .
>
> The objective category of privacy harm is the unanticipated or coerced use of information concerning a person against that person. These are negative, external actions justified by reference to personal information. Examples include the unanticipated sale of a user's contact information that results in spam and the leaking of classified information that exposes an undercover intelligence agent.

How does Calo's theory apply to data security breaches? Consider his analysis:

> As an initial matter, data breaches register as subjective privacy harms. When a consumer receives a notice in the mail telling her that her personal information has leaked out into the open, she experiences the exact sort of apprehension and feeling of vulnerability the first category of privacy harm is concerned about. That is, she believes that there has been or could be unwanted sensing of her private information. The same is true, to a lesser degree, when any of us read about a data breach — we feel less secure in our privacy overall.
>
> But what if there is a data breach or other increased risk of adverse consequence and the "victim" never knows about it? Then there has been neither subjective nor objective privacy harm, unless or until the information is used. Worse still, it would appear on this analysis that breach notification is a net evil in that it creates (subjective) privacy harm where there would be none.
>
> Here I disagree with this premise. A risk of privacy harm is no more a privacy harm than a chance of a burn is a burn. They are conceptually distinct: one is the thing itself, the other the likelihood of that thing. A feeling of greater vulnerability can constitute privacy harm, just as the apprehension of battery can constitute a distinct tort. But there is no assault or battery without the elements of apprehension or unwanted contact. . . .

---

[18] See Rosenberg, *supra* note, at 883 (arguing that increased risk due to exposure to toxic materials is not negligence in the air but real harm due to excessive risk of diseased that is certain to take its toll on a percentage of those exposed).

[19] Daniel J. Solove & Danielle Keats Citron, *Risk and Anxiety: A Theory of Data Breach Harms*, 96 Tex. L. Rev. — (forthcoming 2017).

Similarly, it does not disparage the seriousness of a data breach, nor the inconvenience of having to protect against identity theft, to deny that any objective privacy harm has yet occurred. If anything, clarifying the nature of the harm at risk should help us protect against that harm actually occurring by selecting the appropriate remedy. The goal of some rules is to deter specific harms, for instance; others exist to empower the vulnerable or hinder the powerful in an effort to make harm less likely. Data breach notification laws fulfill both functions, even if they are technically the "but for" cause of one category of privacy harm.[20]

Daniel Solove examines why courts often fail to recognize harm in data breach cases:

One of the challenges with data harms is that they are often created by the aggregation of many dispersed actors over a long period of time. They are akin to a form of pollution where each particular infraction might, in and of itself, not cause much harm, but collectively, the infractions do create harm. . . .

The flip side of collective harm is what I call the "multiplier problem," which affects the companies that cause privacy and data security problems. A company might lose personal data, and these days, even a small company can have data on tens of millions of people. Judges are reluctant to recognize harm because it might mean bankrupting a company just to give each person a very tiny amount of compensation.

Today, organizations have data on so many people that when there's a leak, millions could be affected, and even a small amount of damages for each person might add up to insanely high liability. . . .

When each case is viewed in isolation, it seems quite harsh to annihilate a company for causing tiny harms to many people. . . . But that still leaves the collective harm problem. If we let it go all the time, then we have death by a thousand bee stings. . . .[21]

3. *Emotional Distress for Lost or Stolen Sensitive Data?* In *Beck,* the data about the Watson plaintiffs differs significantly from those about the Beck plaintiffs. In particular, the data about the Watson plaintiffs involves medical diagnoses. For these plaintiffs, is there a harm caused by the loss of this data regardless of whether there is any risk of future identity theft or fraud? If so, how would you characterize the nature of such a harm? Suppose the Watson plaintiffs sued under breach of confidentiality tort. Would they prevail?

4. *Class Actions.* Many of the lawsuits in the wake of data security breaches are class actions. Although many have been dismissed because courts do not recognize a harm from a mere data leak without more direct proof of injuries to plaintiffs, others have ended in multi-million dollar settlements. Defendants may choose to settle, among other reasons, due to the high expense of litigation.

Do these class actions serving a valuable purpose? The attorneys receive a large award for attorney's fees, and class members rarely get significant benefits from the settlement. One might view class actions for data security

---

[20] M. Ryan Calo, The Boundaries of Privacy Harm, 86 Ind. L.J. 1131, 1133, 1256-57 (2011).

[21] Daniel J. Solove, Why the Law Often Doesn't Recognize Privacy and Data Security Harms, LinkedIn (July 2, 2014), https://www.linkedin.com/today/post/article/20140702054230-2259773-why-the-law-often-doesn-t-recognize-privacy-and-data-security-harms.

breaches as a kind of opportunistic extortion of settlement money. On the other hand, class actions provide a strong incentive for companies to be careful with personal data and take measures to avoid data security breaches. The attorney's fees serve as an incentive for spurring lawyers to bring and litigate the case — a reward for serving as a kind of "private attorney general." If not class action litigation, is there a more appropriate mechanism to deter data security breaches?

5. ***Strict Liability for Data Security Breaches?*** Danielle Citron argues for strict liability for harms caused by data breaches. Computer databases of personal information, Citron contends, are akin to the water reservoirs of the early Industrial Age:

> The dynamics of the early Industrial Age, a time of great potential and peril, parallel those at the advent of the Information Age. Then, as now, technological change brought enormous wealth and comfort to society. Industry thrived as a result of machines powered by water reservoirs. But when the dams holding those reservoirs failed, the escaping water caused massive property and personal damage different from the interpersonal harms of the previous century. *Rylands v. Fletcher* provided the Industrial Age's strict-liability response to the accidents caused by the valuable reservoirs' escaping water. The history of *Rylands*'s reception in Britain and the United States reflects the tension between that era's desire for economic growth and its concern for security from industrial hazards.
>
> Computer databases are this century's reservoirs. . . . Much as water reservoirs drove the Industrial Age, computer databases fuel the Internet economy of our Information Age.

Citron argues that a strict liability regime is preferable to negligence tort liability:

> The rapidly changing nature of information technologies may create uncertainty as to what a negligence regime entails. . . .
>
> Due to the rapidly changing threats to information security, database operators will likely be uncertain as to what constitutes optimal care. Cyber-intruders employ increasingly innovative techniques to bypass security measures and steal personal data, thereby requiring an ever-changing information-security response to new threats, vulnerabilities, and technologies. . . .
>
> A negligence regime will fail to address the significant leaks that will occur despite database operators' exercise of due care over personal data. Security breaches are an inevitable byproduct of collecting sensitive personal information in computer databases. No amount of due care will prevent significant amounts of sensitive data from escaping into the hands of cyber-criminals. Such data leaks constitute the predictable residual risks of information reservoirs.
>
> Consequently, negligence will not efficiently manage the residual risks of hazardous databases. Negligence would neither induce database operators to change their activity level nor discourage marginal actors from collecting sensitive information because such operators need not pay for the accident costs of their residual risk. . . .

Classifying database collection as an ultrahazardous activity is a logical extension of Posner's analysis. Just as no clear safety standard governing the building and maintenance of water reservoirs had emerged in the 1850s, a stable set of information-security practices has not yet materialized today. . . .

In this analysis, strict liability has the potential to encourage a change in activity level respecting the storage of sensitive personal information, unless and until more information allows operators to better assess optimal precaution levels and to respond to the persistent problem of residual risk. Because strict liability would force database operators to internalize the full costs of their activities, marginally productive database operators might refrain from maintaining cyber-reservoirs of personal data. Strict liability also may decrease the collection of ultrasensitive data among those who are at greatest risk of security breaches. Moreover, as insurance markets develop in this emerging area, database operators that continue collecting sensitive information will be better positioned to assess the cost of residual risk and the extent to which they can spread the cost of such risk onto consumers.[22]

Are you convinced by the analogy between the database industry and reservoirs? Will strict liability lead to the correct level of investment in security by companies? Could it lead to over-investment in data security?

6. *Assessing the Federal Approach to Data Security.* As discussed above, after the ChoicePoint data security breach in 2005 — along with the numerous other breaches that followed — a majority of states have now passed data security breach legislation. Despite several proposed bills, the federal government has yet to pass a comprehensive data security law. However, some existing federal privacy laws protect data security in the context of particular industries. Consider Andrea Matwyshyn:

The current approach to information security, exemplified by statutes such as COPPA, HIPAA, and GLBA, attempts to regulate information security by creating legal "clusters" of entities based on the type of business they transact, the types of data they control, and that data's permitted and nonpermitted uses. In other words, the current regulatory approach has singled out a few points in the system for the creation of information security enclaves. . . .

The current approach ignores the fundamental tenet of security that a system is only as strong as its weakest links, not its strongest points. . . . It will not prove adequate to only ensure that a few points or clusters in the system are particularly well-secured. . . .

The biggest economic losses arise not out of illegal leveraging of these protected categories of data; rather, losses arise out of stolen personally identifiable information, such as credit card data and social security numbers, which are warehoused frequently by entities that are not regulated by COPPA, HIPAA or GLBA. Therefore, creating enclaves of superior data security for data related to children online, some financial information, and some health data

---

[22] Danielle Keats Citron, Reservoirs of Danger: The Evolution of Public and Private Law at the Dawn of the Information Age, 80 S. Cal. L. Rev. 241, 243-44, 263-67 (2007).

will not alleviate the weak information security in other parts of the system and
will not substantially diminish information crime. . . . [23]

D. FTC REGULATION

The Federal Trade Commission (FTC) has acted on numerous occasions to
penalize companies that fail to take reasonable measures to protect customer data.
There are several sources of authority that the FTC uses to regulate data security.

Section 5 of the FTC Act. Since the late 1990s, the FTC has concluded in more
than 50 enforcement actions that companies with inadequate data security are
engaging in "unfair or deceptive acts or practices" in violation of Section 5 of the
FTC Act, 15 U.S.C. § 45(a). Section 5 covers a very wide array of industries, but
there are a few carve outs where other statutes govern, specifically with certain
types of financial institutions, airlines, and telecommunications carriers. Nonprofit institutions are generally not covered by the FTC Act.

The FTC's initial enforcement actions for data security involved companies
that failed to live up to promises made about data security in their privacy policies.
The FTC has deemed the failure to follow statements made in a privacy policy to
be a deceptive act or practice. A deceptive act or practice is a material
"representation, omission or practice that is likely to mislead the consumer acting
reasonably in the circumstances, to the consumer's detriment."[24]

The FTC later started finding certain data security practices to be "unfair"
regardless of what was promised in the privacy policy. Under the FTC Act, a
practice is unfair if it "causes or is likely to cause substantial injury to consumers
which is not reasonably avoidable by consumers themselves and is not outweighed
by countervailing benefits to consumers or competition." 15 U.S.C.
§ 45(n).

In many cases, the FTC charges that a company's practices are both deceptive
and unfair.

Under Section 5, the FTC lacks the authority to issue fines. When a company
violates a consent decree previously entered into for a Section 5 violation, then the
FTC can issue fines. Although the FTC cannot issue fines under Section 5, when
it has authority under other statutes to regulate data security, some of these laws
grant the FTC the ability to seek monetary penalties. Under Section 5, though, the
FTC can still obtain injunctive relief. There is no private right of action for
violations of Section 5 — only the FTC can enforce.

The FTC does not have specific rulemaking authority under Section 5, but it
can make rules according to Magnuson-Moss rulemaking authority. This method
of making rules is so burdensome that the FTC has barely used it. Instead, the FTC
has focused its Section 5 efforts on enforcement.

---

[23] Andrea M. Matwyshyn, Material Vulnerabilities: Data Privacy, Corporate Information
Security, and Securities Regulation, 3 Berkeley Bus. L.J. 129, 169-70 (2005).

[24] Letter from James C. Miller III, Chairman, FTC, to Hon. John D. Dingell, Chairman, House
Comm. on Energy & Commerce (Oct. 14, 1983).

Gramm-Leach-Bliley Act. The FTC can also act pursuant to its specific authority, under statutes and rules, to oversee how businesses protect consumer data. For example, the FTC's has issued the Safeguards Rule pursuant to its authority under the Gramm-Leach-Bliley Act (GLBA). The Safeguards Rule mandates data security requirements for non-bank financial institutions.

Children's Online Privacy Protection Act. The Children's Online Privacy Protection Act (COPPA) requires reasonable security for children's information collected online, and the FTC has issued a rule specifying the kinds of security provisions that companies should develop. These security obligations extend to service parties and third parties that a company uses in processing the personal information of children.

Fair Credit Reporting Act. Inadequate data security can also lead to data being disclosed impermissibly under the Fair Credit Reporting Act (FCRA). The FTC used to have primary enforcement responsibility of the FCRA, but now the enforcement is shared with the Consumer Financial Protection Bureau (CFPB), which has primary enforcement power. Fines can be issued under FCRA.

One of the most dramatic of the FTC enforcement actions for data security involved ChoicePoint. In settling the FTC charges for violating FCRA and Section 5 of the FTC Act, ChoicePoint agreed in January 2006 to pay $10 million in civil penalties and $5 million into a consumer redress fund. ChoicePoint also promised changes to its business and improvements to its security practices.

The stipulated final judgment bars the company from furnishing consumer reports to customers without a permissible purpose and requires it to establish reasonable procedures to ensure that it will provide consumer reports only to those with a permissible purpose. One requirement placed on ChoicePoint is to verify the identity of businesses that apply to receive consumer reports by auditing subscribers' use of consumer reports and by making site visits to certain of its customers.

Finally, the settlement obligated ChoicePoint to establish and maintain a comprehensive information security program and to submit this program for two decades to outside independent audits. It agreed to "establish and implement, and thereafter maintain, a comprehensive information security program that is reasonably designed to protect the security, confidentiality, and integrity of personal information collected from or about consumers." In maintaining this "comprehensive information security program," ChoicePoint promised to engage in risk assessments and to design and implement regular testing of the effectiveness of its security program's key controls, systems, and procedures. It also agreed to obtain an initial and then biennial outside assessment of its data security safeguards from an independent third-party professional.

For nearly two decades, FTC Section 5 data security cases settled. But finally, a company challenged the FTC. Wyndham Worldwide Corporation, a hotel company, argued that the FTC lacked authority under Section 5 to regulate data security and could only do so pursuant to a specific statute. Consider the case below, where the court rules on the issue.

FTC v. WYNDHAM WORLDWIDE CORPORATION
799 F.3d 236 (3d Cir. 2015)

AMBRO, J. . . . On three occasions in 2008 and 2009 hackers successfully accessed Wyndham Worldwide Corporation's computer systems. In total, they stole personal and financial information for hundreds of thousands of consumers leading to over $10.6 million dollars in fraudulent charges. The FTC filed suit in federal District Court, alleging that Wyndham's conduct was an unfair practice and that its privacy policy was deceptive. The District Court denied Wyndham's motion to dismiss, and we granted interlocutory appeal on two issues: whether the FTC has authority to regulate cybersecurity under the unfairness prong of § 45(a); and, if so, whether Wyndham had fair notice its specific cybersecurity practices could fall short of that provision. We affirm the District Court.

Wyndham Worldwide is a hospitality company that franchises and manages hotels and sells timeshares through three subsidiaries. Wyndham licensed its brand name to approximately 90 independently owned hotels. Each Wyndham-branded hotel has a property management system that processes consumer information that includes names, home addresses, email addresses, telephone numbers, payment card account numbers, expiration dates, and security codes. Wyndham "manage[s]" these systems and requires the hotels to "purchase and configure" them to its own specifications. It also operates a computer network in Phoenix, Arizona, that connects its data center with the property management systems of each of the Wyndham-branded hotels.

The FTC alleges that, at least since April 2008, Wyndham engaged in unfair cybersecurity practices that, "taken together, unreasonably and unnecessarily exposed consumers' personal data to unauthorized access and theft." This claim is fleshed out as follows.

1. The company allowed Wyndham-branded hotels to store payment card information in clear readable text.

2. Wyndham allowed the use of easily guessed passwords to access the property management systems. For example, to gain "remote access to at least one hotel's system," which was developed by Micros Systems, Inc., the user ID and password were both "micros."

3. Wyndham failed to use "readily available security measures"—such as firewalls—to "limit access between [the] hotels' property management systems, . . . corporate network, and the Internet."

4. Wyndham allowed hotel property management systems to connect to its network without taking appropriate cybersecurity precautions. It did not ensure that the hotels implemented "adequate information security policies and procedures." Also, it knowingly allowed at least one hotel to connect to the Wyndham network with an out-of-date operating system that had not received a security update in over three years. It allowed hotel servers to connect to Wyndham's network even though "default user IDs and passwords were enabled .

.., which were easily available to hackers through simple Internet searches." And, because it failed to maintain an "adequate [ ] inventory [of] computers connected to [Wyndham's] network [to] manage the devices," it was unable to identify the source of at least one of the cybersecurity attacks.

5. Wyndham failed to "adequately restrict" the access of third-party vendors to its network and the servers of Wyndham-branded hotels. . . .

6. It failed to employ "reasonable measures to detect and prevent unauthorized access" to its computer network or to "conduct security investigations."

7. It did not follow "proper incident response procedures." The hackers used similar methods in each attack, and yet Wyndham failed to monitor its network for malware used in the previous intrusions. . . .

As noted, on three occasions in 2008 and 2009 hackers accessed Wyndham's network and the property management systems of Wyndham-branded hotels. In April 2008, hackers first broke into the local network of a hotel in Phoenix, Arizona, which was connected to Wyndham's network and the Internet. They then used the brute-force method—repeatedly guessing users' login IDs and passwords—to access an administrator account on Wyndham's network. This enabled them to obtain consumer data on computers throughout the network. In total, the hackers obtained unencrypted information for over 500,000 accounts, which they sent to a domain in Russia.

In March 2009, hackers attacked again, this time by accessing Wyndham's network through an administrative account. The FTC claims that Wyndham was unaware of the attack for two months until consumers filed complaints about fraudulent charges. Wyndham then discovered "memory-scraping malware" used in the previous attack on more than thirty hotels' computer systems. The FTC asserts that, due to Wyndham's "failure to monitor [the network] for the malware used in the previous attack, hackers had unauthorized access to [its] network for approximately two months." In this second attack, the hackers obtained unencrypted payment card information for approximately 50,000 consumers from the property management systems of 39 hotels.

Hackers in late 2009 breached Wyndham's cybersecurity a third time by accessing an administrator account on one of its networks. Because Wyndham "had still not adequately limited access between . . . the Wyndham-branded hotels' property management systems, [Wyndham's network], and the Internet," the hackers had access to the property management servers of multiple hotels. Wyndham only learned of the intrusion in January 2010 when a credit card company received complaints from cardholders. In this third attack, hackers obtained payment card information for approximately 69,000 customers from the property management systems of 28 hotels.

The FTC alleges that, in total, the hackers obtained payment card information from over 619,000 consumers, which (as noted) resulted in at least $10.6 million in fraud loss. It further states that consumers suffered financial injury through "unreimbursed fraudulent charges, increased costs, and lost access to funds or credit," and that they "expended time and money resolving fraudulent charges and mitigating subsequent harm." . . . .

Wyndham argues that a practice is only "unfair" if it is "not equitable" or is "marked by injustice, partiality, or deception." Whether these are requirements of an unfairness claim makes little difference here. A company does not act equitably when it publishes a privacy policy to attract customers who are concerned about data privacy, fails to make good on that promise by investing inadequate resources in cybersecurity, exposes its unsuspecting customers to substantial financial injury, and retains the profits of their business. . . .

Continuing on, Wyndham asserts that a business "does not treat its customers in an 'unfair' manner when the business itself is victimized by criminals." It offers no reasoning or authority for this principle, and we can think of none ourselves. Although unfairness claims "usually involve actual and completed harms . . . they may also be brought on the basis of likely rather than actual injury." And the FTC Act expressly contemplates the possibility that conduct can be unfair before actual injury occurs. 15 U.S.C. §45(n) ("[An unfair act or practice] causes or is *likely to cause* substantial injury" (emphasis added)). More importantly, that a company's conduct was not *the most* proximate cause of an injury generally does not immunize liability from foreseeable harms. . . .

We are therefore not persuaded by Wyndham's arguments that the alleged conduct falls outside the plain meaning of "unfair."

Wyndham next argues that, even if cybersecurity were covered by § 45(a) as initially enacted, three legislative acts since the subsection was amended in 1938 have reshaped the provision's meaning to exclude cybersecurity. A recent amendment to the Fair Credit Reporting Act directed the FTC and other agencies to develop regulations for the proper disposal of consumer data. The Gramm–Leach–Bliley Act required the FTC to establish standards for financial institutions to protect consumers' personal information. And the Children's Online Privacy Protection Act ordered the FTC to promulgate regulations requiring children's websites, among other things, to provide notice of "what information is collected from children . . ., how the operator uses such information, and the operator's disclosure practices for such information." Wyndham contends these "tailored grants of substantive authority to the FTC in the cybersecurity field would be inexplicable if the Commission already had general substantive authority over this field." Citing *FDA v. Brown & Williamson Tobacco Corp.*, 529 U.S. 120 (2000), Wyndham concludes that Congress excluded cybersecurity from the FTC's unfairness authority by enacting these measures.

We are not persuaded. The inference to congressional intent based on post-enactment legislative activity in *Brown & Williamson* was far stronger. There, the Food and Drug Administration had repeatedly disclaimed regulatory authority over tobacco products for decades. During that period, Congress enacted six statutes regulating tobacco. The FDA later shifted its position, claiming authority over tobacco products. The Supreme Court held that Congress excluded tobacco-related products from the FDA's authority in enacting the statutes. As tobacco products would necessarily be banned if subject to the FDA's regulatory authority, any interpretation to the contrary would contradict congressional intent to regulate rather than ban tobacco products outright. Wyndham does not argue that recent privacy laws *contradict* reading corporate cybersecurity into § 45(a). Instead, it merely asserts that Congress had no reason to enact them if the FTC could already regulate cybersecurity through that provision.

We disagree that Congress lacked reason to pass the recent legislation if the FTC already had regulatory authority over some cybersecurity issues. The Fair Credit Reporting Act requires (rather than authorizes) the FTC to issue regulations, and expands the scope of the FTC's authority. The Gramm–Leach–Bliley Act similarly requires the FTC to promulgate regulations and relieves some of the burdensome §45(n) requirements for declaring acts unfair. And the Children's Online Privacy Protection Act required the FTC to issue regulations and empowered it to do so under the procedures of the Administrative Procedure Act, rather than the more burdensome Magnuson–Moss procedures under which the FTC must usually issue regulations, 15 U.S.C. §57a. Thus none of the recent privacy legislation was "inexplicable" if the FTC already had some authority to regulate corporate cybersecurity through §45(a). . . .

A conviction or punishment violates the Due Process Clause of our Constitution if the statute or regulation under which it is obtained "fails to provide a person of ordinary intelligence fair notice of what is prohibited, or is so standardless that it authorizes or encourages seriously discriminatory enforcement." Wyndham claims that, notwithstanding whether its conduct was unfair under §45(a), the FTC failed to give fair notice of the specific cybersecurity standards the company was required to follow. . . .

Wyndham's position is unmistakable: the FTC has not yet declared that cybersecurity practices can be unfair; there is no relevant FTC rule, adjudication or document that merits deference; and the FTC is asking the federal courts to interpret §45(a) in the first instance to decide whether it prohibits the alleged conduct here. The implication of this position is similarly clear: if the federal courts are to decide whether Wyndham's conduct was unfair in the first instance under the statute without deferring to any FTC interpretation, then this case involves ordinary judicial interpretation of a civil statute, and the ascertainable certainty standard does not apply. The relevant question is not whether Wyndham had fair notice of the *FTC's interpretation* of the statute, but whether Wyndham had fair notice of what the *statute itself* requires. . . .

Having decided that Wyndham is entitled to notice of the meaning of the statute, we next consider whether the case should be dismissed based on fair notice principles. We do not read Wyndham's briefs as arguing the company lacked fair notice that cybersecurity practices can, as a general matter, form the basis of an unfair practice under §45(a). Wyndham argues instead it lacked notice of what specific cybersecurity practices are necessary to avoid liability. We have little trouble rejecting this claim.

To begin with, Wyndham's briefing focuses on the FTC's failure to give notice of its interpretation of the statute and does not meaningfully argue that the statute itself fails fair notice principles. We think it imprudent to hold a 100–year–old statute unconstitutional as applied to the facts of this case when we have not expressly been asked to do so.

Subsection 45(n) asks whether "the act or practice causes or is likely to cause substantial injury to consumers which is not reasonably avoidable by consumers themselves and not outweighed by countervailing benefits to consumers or to competition." While far from precise, this standard informs parties that the relevant inquiry here is a cost-benefit analysis that considers a number of relevant factors, including the probability and expected size of reasonably unavoidable harms to consumers given a certain level of cybersecurity and the costs to consumers that would arise from investment in stronger cybersecurity. We acknowledge there will be borderline cases where it is unclear if a particular company's conduct falls below the requisite legal threshold. But under a due process analysis a company is not entitled to such precision as would eliminate all close calls. Fair notice is satisfied here as long as the company can reasonably foresee that a court could construe its conduct as falling within the meaning of the statute. . . .

As the FTC points out in its brief, the complaint does not allege that Wyndham used weak firewalls, IP address restrictions, encryption software, and passwords. Rather, it alleges that Wyndham failed to use *any* firewall at critical network points, did not restrict specific IP addresses *at all*, did not use *any* encryption for certain customer files, and did not require some users to change their default or factory-setting passwords *at all*. Wyndham did not respond to this argument in its reply brief.

Wyndham's as-applied challenge is even weaker given it was hacked not one or two, but three, times. At least after the second attack, it should have been painfully clear to Wyndham that a court could find its conduct failed the cost-benefit analysis. That said, we leave for another day whether Wyndham's alleged cybersecurity practices do in fact fail, an issue the parties did not brief. We merely note that certainly after the second time Wyndham was hacked, it was on notice of the possibility that a court *could* find that its practices fail the cost-benefit analysis.

Several other considerations reinforce our conclusion that Wyndham's fair notice challenge fails. In 2007 the FTC issued a guidebook, *Protecting Personal Information: A Guide for Business*, which describes a "checklist[ ]" of practices that form a "sound data security plan." The guidebook does not state that any particular practice is required by §45(a), but it does counsel against many of the specific practices alleged here. . . .

Before the attacks, the FTC also filed complaints and entered into consent decrees in administrative cases raising unfairness claims based on inadequate corporate cybersecurity. The agency published these materials on its website and provided notice of proposed consent orders in the Federal Register. Wyndham responds that the complaints cannot satisfy fair notice principles because they are not "adjudications on the merits." But even where the "ascertainable certainty" standard applies to fair notice claims, courts regularly consider materials that are neither regulations nor "adjudications on the merits." That the FTC commissioners—who must vote on whether to issue a complaint—believe that alleged cybersecurity practices fail the cost-benefit analysis of §45(n) certainly helps companies with similar practices apprehend the possibility that their cybersecurity could fail as well. . . .

NOTES & QUESTIONS

1. *A Lack of Fair Notice?* One of Wyndham's arguments was that the FTC's method of enforcing data security — in a case-by-case fashion rather than a rulemaking—led to companies not being put on sufficient notice about the specific data security practices that were deemed inadequate.

   Daniel Solove and Woodrow Hartzog contend that the FTC's body of consent decrees constitutes a body of law similar to the common law with lawyers analyzing the settlements akin to the way they look at judicial decisions.[25]

In contrast, Berin Szoka and Geoffrey Manne argue that "neither this 'common law of consent decrees' nor the FTC's privacy reports constitute actual law. It's a flexible approach, but only in the worst sense: made by disposing of any legal constraints or due process."[26]

Gerard Stegmaier and Wendell Bartnick argue that a "standard based on 'reasonableness' grounded solely in settlements raises its own questions of whether constitutionally adequate fair notice was provided. Such a standard seems unfair and problematic to those tasked with assisting entities in avoiding unfair and deceptive trade practices."[27]

Hartzog and Solove contend:

> Many critics seem to want a "check list" of data security practices that will, in essence, provide a safe harbor in all contexts. Yet data security changes too quickly and is far too dependent upon context to be reduced to a one-size-fits-all checklist. Instead, the FTC has opted to defer to industry to set the appropriate standards for good data security practices by utilizing a "reasonableness" standard. . . .[28]

Hartzog and Solove point to many laws that require a reasonableness standard for data security. They further argue:

> In a common law system — or any system where matters are decided case-by-case and there is an attempt at maintaining consistency across decisions, any reasonableness standard will evolve into something more akin to a rule with specifics over time. Indeed, any broad standard will follow this evolutionary trajectory. Such a developmental pattern is inevitable if prior decisions have any kind of precedential effect or the functional equivalent of precedent. The standard will start out rather broadly, but each new case will bring a new application of that standard to a concrete situation. From these collected specific applications, the details start to accumulate around the standard's skeletal frame.[29]

2. Overlapping Regulatory Authority. After Wyndham brought its challenge, another company, LabMD, raised a similar objection to FTC authority. One of LabMD's contentions was that it is regulated by HIPAA and under the authority of the Department of Health and Human Services (HHS). Although HHS did not bring an action to enforce the HIPAA Security Rule, the FTC brought an action under Section 5 for inadequate data security. LabMD contended that

---

[25] Daniel J. Solove & Woodrow Hartzog, *The FTC and the New Common Law of Privacy,* 114 Colum. L. Rev. 583 (2014).

[26] Berin Szoka & Geoffrey Manne, *Now in Its 100th year, the FTC Has Become the Federal Technology Commission,* TechFreedom (Sept. 26, 2013), http://techfreedom.org/post/62344465210/now-in-its-100th-year-the-ftc-has-become-the-federal.

[27] Gerard M. Stegmaier & Wendell Bartnick, *Psychics, Russian Roulette, and Data Security: The FTC's Hidden Data-Security Requirements,* 20 Geo. Mason L. Rev. 673 (2013).

[28] Woodrow Hartzog & Daniel J. Solove, *The Scope and Potential of FTC Data Protection,* 83 Geo. Wash. L. Rev. ___ (forthcoming 2015), http://ssrn.com/abstract=2461096.

[29] *Id.*

because it was regulated by HIPAA, it should not fall under the FTC's Section 5 authority for data security. Assess the strength of LabMD's argument.

3. *FTC Data Security Enforcement Under Section 5.* Since it began enforcing Section 5 against companies for data security problems, the FTC has pursued more than 50 enforcement actions against companies for failure to provide reasonable security practices. Consider the following Congressional testimony by Woodrow Hartzog in 2014:

> The Privacy Rights Clearinghouse has reported that since 2005 there have been over 4300 data breaches made public with a total of over 868 million records breached. Yet the FTC has filed only 55 total data security-related complaints, averaging around five complaints a year since 2008.[30]

Is the number of actions sufficient? Should the FTC be more aggressively enforcing Section 5? Should a different approach be taken? Or is the FTC pursuing an appropriate amount of cases?

For example, these actions have led to settlements against Twitter, charged with bad password management practices (settlement in 2011); HTC America, charged with failure to take reasonable steps to secure tablet and phone software (settlement in 2013); and Fandago, charged with misrepresentation of its mobile applications (settlement in 2014). Consider the FTC's settlement in *Trendnet*, which involved a security camera that lacked security:

IN THE MATTER OF TRENDNET

(F.T.C. 2014)

[TRENDnet, Inc. sold a range of home networking devices. It has approximately 80 employees and $62 million in total revenue in 2012.

One of its products was a video camera that generated a live audio and video feed that users could view over an Internet connection. According to the FTC's Complaint, TRENDnet advertised the camera, named "SecurView," as a device to help consumers and small businesses monitor "babies at home, patients in the hospital, offices and banks, and more." The camera came with software that created a Web interface where the user could enter login credentials to view the live feed. The interface included an option to disable authentication, making the feed open to the public. TRENDnet also distributed Android apps that allowed users to access feeds from mobile devices.

TRENDnet had a software flaw that caused SecurView feeds to be publicly viewable even if the user had not disabled the access protections. According to the FTC Complaint, "[h]ackers could and did exploit" the vulnerability of the software. Specifically, a hacker on January 10, 2012 was able to access live feeds at Trendnet's website "without entering login credentials" and gain access to live feeds that were not intended to be public. This initial hacker posted information about the breach online and then other hackers posted links to live feeds for nearly 700 IP Cameras. The compromised live feeds allowed anyone to watch

---

[30] Woodrow Hartzog, *Prepared Testimony and Statement for the Record*, U.S. House of Representatives, Committee on Oversight and Government Reform (July 24, 2014).

"unauthorized surveillance of infants sleeping in their cribs, young children playing, and adults engaging in typical daily activities." News stories published images from the feeds alongside photos of the locations from which the feeds were broadcast (based on geolocation of the feeds' IP addresses). Researchers discovered other security vulnerabilities, including the transmission of unencrypted passwords. TRENDnet also had failed to perform ordinary security testing.

The FTC filed a complaint against TRENDnet on January 16, 2013, alleging that TRENDnet's claims of security constituted false or misleading representations because TRENDnet failed to provide reasonable security to prevent unauthorized access to the live feeds from its cameras. As the FTC's press release accompanying the settlement of January 17, 2014 stated, "This is the agency's first action against a marketer of an everyday product with interconnectivity to the Internet and other mobile devices—commonly referred to as the 'Internet of Things.' "]

AGREEMENT CONTAINING CONSENT ORDER

The respondent, its attorney, and counsel for the Commission having executed an Agreement Containing Consent Order ("Consent Agreement"), which includes: a statement by respondent that it neither admits nor denies any of the allegations in the draft complaint, except as specifically stated in the Consent Agreement, and, only for purposes of this action, admits the facts necessary to establish jurisdiction; and waivers and other provisions as required by the Commission's Rules. . . . .

IT IS ORDERED that respondent and its officers, agents, representatives, and employees, directly or through any corporation, subsidiary, division, website, other device, or an affiliate owned or controlled by respondent, in or affecting commerce, shall not misrepresent in any manner, expressly or by implication:

A. The extent to which respondent or its products or services maintain and protect:

1. The security of Covered Device Functionality;

2. The security, privacy, confidentiality, or integrity of any Covered Information; and

B. The extent to which a consumer can control the security of any Covered Information input into, stored on, captured with, accessed, or transmitted by a Covered Device. . . .

IT IS FURTHER ORDERED that respondent shall, no later than the date of service of this Order, establish and implement, and thereafter maintain, a comprehensive security program that is reasonably designed to (1) address security risks that could result in unauthorized access to or use of Covered Device Functionality, and (2) protect the security, confidentiality, and integrity of Covered Information, whether collected by respondent, or input into, stored on, captured with, accessed, or transmitted through a Covered Device. Such program, the content and implementation of which must be fully documented in writing, shall contain administrative, technical, and physical safeguards appropriate to respondent's size and complexity, the nature and scope of respondent's activities, and the sensitivity of the Covered Device Functionality or Covered Information, including:

A. The designation of an employee or employees to coordinate and be accountable for the security program;

B. The identification of material internal and external risks to the security of Covered Devices that could result in unauthorized access to or use of Covered Device Functionality, and assessment of the sufficiency of any safeguards in place to control these risks;

C. The identification of material internal and external risks to the security, confidentiality, and integrity of Covered Information that could result in the unauthorized disclosure, misuse, loss, alteration, destruction, or other compromise of such information, whether such information is in respondent's possession or is input into, stored on, captured with, accessed, or transmitted through a Covered Device, and assessment of the sufficiency of any safeguards in place to control these risks;

D. At a minimum, the risk assessments required by Subparts B and C should include consideration of risks in each area of relevant operation, including, but not limited to: (1) employee training and management; (2) product design, development, and research; (3) secure software design, development, and testing; and (4) review, assessment, and response to third-party security vulnerability reports;

E. The design and implementation of reasonable safeguards to control the risks identified through the risk assessments, including but not limited to reasonable and appropriate software security testing techniques, such as: (1) vulnerability and penetration testing; (2) security architecture reviews; (3) code reviews; and (4) other reasonable and appropriate assessments, audits, reviews, or other tests to identify potential security failures and verify that access to Covered Information is restricted consistent with a user's security settings;

F. Regular testing or monitoring of the effectiveness of the safeguards' key controls, systems, and procedures;

G. The development and use of reasonable steps to select and retain service providers capable of maintaining security practices consistent with this Order, and requiring service providers, by contract, to establish and implement, and thereafter maintain, appropriate safeguards consistent with this Order; and

H. The evaluation and adjustment of the security program in light of the results of the testing and monitoring required by Subpart F, any material changes to the respondent's operations or business arrangements, or any other circumstances that respondent knows or has reason to know may have a material impact on the effectiveness of its security program.

IT IS FURTHER ORDERED that, in connection with its compliance with Part II of this Order, respondent shall obtain initial and biennial assessments and reports ("Assessments") from a qualified, objective, independent third-party professional, who uses procedures and standards generally accepted in the profession. The reporting period for the Assessments shall cover: (1) the first one hundred eighty (180) days after service of the Order for the initial Assessment; and (2) each two (2) year period thereafter for twenty (20) years after service of the Order for the biennial Assessments.

IT IS FURTHER ORDERED that respondent shall:

A. Notify Affected Consumers, clearly and prominently, that their Cameras had a flaw that allowed third parties to access their Live Feed Information without inputting authentication credentials, despite their security setting choices; and provide instructions on how to remove this flaw. . . .

This Order will terminate on January 16, 2034, or [in] twenty (20) years. . . .

NOTES & QUESTIONS

1. ***The Terms of Settlement.*** This settlement illustrates the FTC's classic approach in its data security settlements of imposing long-term requirements for an information security program. Do you think that the settlement terms in *Trendnet* are appropriate? Does the FTC strike the correct balance in providing some flexibility to the companies in deciding the content of a reasonable security program? Is a 20-year enforcement period too long?

2. ***The Internet of Things***. Trendnet is the FTC's first security case involving the "Internet of Things." This term refers to Web-enabled devices that generate data, some of which can be linked to specific individuals. Cisco has already predicted 50 billion connected devices by 2020. Are there special legal challenges in regulating the privacy issues of the Internet of Things?

   A white paper by the Future of Privacy Forum (FPF), released in November 2013, argued that current implementations of Fair Information Practice Principles (FIPPs) were outdated in the new frontier of connected devices. In particular, Christopher Wolf and Jules Polonetsky, co-chairs of the FPF, point to difficulties in providing meaningful notice on devices that lack meaningful screens or user interfaces. They also question FIPPs that limit future usage of data as roadblocks to socially valuable uses of information discoverable only once data is collected. The paper proposes these new principles: (1) use anonymized data when practical; (2) respect the context in which personally identifiable information is collected; (3) be transparent about data use; (4) automate accountability mechanisms; (5) develop codes of conduct; and (6) provide individuals with reasonable access to personally identifiable information.

   Has the FPF developed principles that serve progress in information use? Or do you consider these concepts a watering-down of FIPPs?

3. ***M&A and Privacy.*** In a complaint against Reed Elsevier and its Seisint subsidiary, the FTC alleged that Reed Elsevier and Seisint failed to provide "reasonable and appropriate security to prevent authorized access" to sensitive consumer information. It argued, "In particular, respondents failed to establish or implement reasonable policies and procedures governing the creation and authentication of user credentials for authorized customers. . . ." Among other flawed practices, the FTC pointed to the companies' failure to establish or enforce rules that would make it difficult to guess user credentials. It permitted their customers to use the same word as both password and user ID. In addition, it allowed the sharing of user credentials among multiple users at a single customer firm, which lowered the likely detection of unauthorized services. Seisint also failed to mandate periodic changes of user credentials and did not implement simple, readily available defenses against common network attacks.

Reed Elsevier had acquired Seisint in September 2004 and operated it as a wholly owned subsidiary within LexisNexis, more widely known for providing legal information. The FTC privacy settlement followed in 2008. The timing of this enforcement action raises questions about merger and acquisitions for companies with possible privacy and security liability issues. What kinds of checklists should lawyers work with when advising companies that wish to merge or acquire new companies? Where do you think the greatest areas of liability are located in the privacy and security areas?

4. ***Data Leaks:* Eli Lilly.** In *FTC v. Eli Lilly*, No. 012-3214, the FTC charged Eli Lilly, a pharmaceutical company, with disclosing people's health data that it collected through its Prozac.com website. Prozac is a drug used for treating depression. Lilly offered customers an e-mail service that would send them e-mail messages to remind them to take or refill their medication. In June 2001, the company sent e-mail messages to all 669 users of the reminder service announcing that the service was terminated. However, this message contained the e-mail addresses of all subscribers in the "To" line of the message. The FTC alleged that the company's privacy policy promising confidentiality was deceptive because the company failed to establish adequate security protections for its consumers' data. Specifically, the FTC complaint alleged that Eli Lilly failed to

> provide appropriate training for its employees regarding consumer privacy and information security; provide appropriate oversight and assistance for the employee who sent out the e-mail, who had no prior experience in creating, testing, or implementing the computer program used; and implement appropriate checks and controls on the process, such as reviewing the computer program with experienced personnel and pretesting the program internally before sending out the e-mail.

In January 2002, Eli Lilly settled. The settlement required Eli Lilly to establish a new security program. It was compelled to designate personnel to oversee the program, identify and address various security risks, and conduct an annual review of the security program. FTC Commissioners voted 5–0 to approve the settlement.

Consider the settlements in this case and the ones described above. Do you think that these settlements are adequate to redress the rights of the individuals affected?

5. **Microsoft Passport *and* Guess*: Proactive FTC Enforcement?*** Microsoft launched Microsoft.NET Passport, an online authentication service. Passport allowed consumers to use a single username and password to access multiple websites. The goal of Passport was to serve as a universal sign-on service, eliminating the need to sign on to each website separately. A related service, Wallet, permitted users to submit credit card and billing information in order to make purchases at multiple websites without having to reenter the information on each site.

The FTC initiated an investigation of the Passport services following a July 2001 complaint from a coalition of consumer groups. In the petition to the FTC, the privacy groups raised questions about the collection, use, and disclosure of personal information that Passport would make possible, and asserted that Microsoft's representations about the security of the system were both unfair and deceptive. In its privacy policy, Microsoft promised that ".NET Passport is protected by powerful online security technology and a strict privacy policy." Further, Microsoft stated: "Your .NET Passport information is stored on secure .NET Passport servers that are protected in controlled facilities."

On August 8, 2002, the FTC found that Microsoft had violated § 5 of the FTC Act and announced a proposed settlement with the company. *See In the Matter of Microsoft Corp.,* No. 012-3240. The Commission found that Microsoft falsely represented that (1) it employs reasonable and appropriate measures under the circumstances to maintain and protect the privacy and confidentiality of consumers' personal information collected through its Passport and Wallet services; (2) purchases made with Passport Wallet are generally safer or more secure than purchases made at the same site without Passport Wallet when, in fact, most consumers received identical security at those sites regardless of whether they used Passport Wallet to complete their transactions; (3) Passport did not collect any personally identifiable information other than that described in its privacy policy when, in fact, Passport collected and held, for a limited time, a personally identifiable sign-in history for each user; and (4) the Kids Passport program provided parents control over what information participating websites could collect from their children.

Under the terms of the proposed consent order, Microsoft may not make any misrepresentations, expressly or by implication, of any of its information practices. Microsoft is further obligated to establish a "comprehensive information security program," and conduct an annual audit to assess the security practices. Microsoft is also required to make available to the FTC for a period of five years all documents relating to security practices as well as compliance with the orders. The order remains in place for 20 years.

The FTC took a similar approach in *In re Guess.com, Inc.,* No. 022-3260 (July 30, 2003). Guess, a clothing company, had promised that all personal information "including . . . credit card information and sign-in password, are stored in an unreadable, encrypted format at all times." This assertion of company policy was false, and the FTC initiated an action even before data was leaked or improperly accessed. The case was eventually settled.

In both *Microsoft* and *Guess,* the FTC brought an action before any data security breach had occurred. Is this a form of proactive enforcement? Suppose a company merely makes a general promise to "keep customer data secure." The FTC believes that the company is not providing adequate security and brings an action. How should the adequacy of a company's security practices be evaluated, especially in cases in which privacy policies are vague about the precise security measures taken?

6. ***The Gramm-Leach-Bliley Act and the FTC.*** Consider the following observation by Daniel Solove:

> [O]ne problem with the FTC's jurisdiction is that it is triggered when a company breaches its own privacy policy. But what if a company doesn't make explicit promises about security? One hopeful development is the Gramm-Leach-Bliley (GLB) Act. The GLB Act requires a number of agencies that regulate financial institutions to promulgate "administrative, technical, and physical safeguards for personal information." In other words, financial institutions must adopt a security system for their data, and the minimum specifications of this system are to be defined by government agencies. . . .[31]

Solove argues that the security practices of many financial institutions are quite lax, as such institutions often provide access to accounts if a person merely supplies her Social Security number. Based on the GLB Act, could the FTC use its enforcement powers to curtail such practices?

7. ***Cybersecurity and the Security and Exchange Commission (SEC).*** A new frontier for data security concerns disclosures within the context of federal security laws. A company subject to SEC requirements faces the issue of how much information to provide investors to allow them to understand the security risks that the enterprise faces. As an article by three experts in securities litigation advises: "Ultimately, the question is not whether a publicly held company should provide cybersecurity disclosures, but how it should do so effectively."[32]

Currently, there is no specific new federal disclosure standard or requirement from the SEC concerning cybersecurity disclosures. The most important policy document currently is an October 2011 Guidance from the SEC's Division of Corporation Finance. This staff guidance finds that there is no existing rule or regulation from the SEC that explicitly refers to cybersecurity risks, but a number of existing disclosure requirements may impose an obligation on SEC registrants to disclose risks and incidents. For example, in the filing of periodical reports with the SEC, such as the SEC's Regulation S-K, a registrant "should disclose the risk of cyber incidents if these issues are among the most significant factors that make an investment in the company speculative or risky."[33]

---

[31] Daniel J. Solove, The Digital Person: Technology and Privacy in the Information Age 107-08 (2004).

[32] Howard M. Privette et al., Practice Tips, Los Angeles Lawyer (forthcoming Sept. 2014).

[33] Division of Corporate Finance, SEC, CF Disclosure Guidance: Topic No: 2, Cybersecurity (Oct. 13, 2011).

CHAPTER **11**

EDUCATION PRIVACY

CHAPTER OUTLINE

A. SCHOOL SEARCHES AND SURVEILLANCE

B. DRUG TESTING

C. SCHOOL RECORDS

A. SCHOOL SEARCHES AND SURVEILLANCE

NEW JERSEY V. T.L.O.

469 U.S. 325 (1984)

WHITE, J. . . . On March 7, 1980, a teacher at Piscataway High School in Middlesex County, N.J., discovered two girls smoking in a lavatory. One of the two girls was the respondent T.L.O., who at that time was a 14-year-old high school freshman. Because smoking in the lavatory was a violation of a school rule, the teacher took the two girls to the Principal's office, where they met with Assistant Vice Principal Theodore Choplick. In response to questioning by Mr. Choplick, T.L.O.'s companion admitted that she had violated the rule. T.L.O., however, denied that she had been smoking in the lavatory and claimed that she did not smoke at all.

Mr. Choplick asked T.L.O. to come into his private office and demanded to see her purse. Opening the purse, he found a pack of cigarettes, which he removed from the purse and held before T.L.O. as he accused her of having lied to him. As he reached into the purse for the cigarettes, Mr. Choplick also noticed a package of cigarette rolling papers. In his experience, possession of rolling papers by high school students was closely associated with the use of marihuana. Suspecting that a closer examination of the purse might yield further evidence of drug use, Mr. Choplick proceeded to search the purse thoroughly. The search revealed a small amount of marihuana, a pipe, a number of empty plastic bags, a substantial quantity of money in one-dollar bills, an index card that appeared to be a list of students who owed T.L.O. money, and two letters that implicated T.L.O. in marihuana dealing.

Mr. Choplick notified T.L.O.'s mother and the police, and turned the evidence of drug dealing over to the police. At the request of the police, T.L.O.'s mother took her daughter to police headquarters, where T.L.O. confessed that she had been selling marihuana at the high school. On the basis of the confession and the evidence seized by Mr. Choplick, the State brought delinquency charges against T.L.O. in the Juvenile and Domestic Relations Court of Middlesex County. Contending that Mr. Choplick's search of her purse violated the Fourth Amendment, T.L.O. moved to suppress the evidence found in her purse as well as her confession, which, she argued, was tainted by the allegedly unlawful search. . . .

In determining whether the search at issue in this case violated the Fourth Amendment, we are faced initially with the question whether that Amendment's prohibition on unreasonable searches and seizures applies to searches conducted by public school officials. We hold that it does. . . .

. . . [T]he State of New Jersey has argued that the history of the Fourth Amendment indicates that the Amendment was intended to regulate only searches and seizures carried out by law enforcement officers; accordingly, although public school officials are concededly state agents for purposes of the Fourteenth Amendment, the Fourth Amendment creates no rights enforceable against them.

It may well be true that the evil toward which the Fourth Amendment was primarily directed was the resurrection of the pre-Revolutionary practice of using general warrants or "writs of assistance" to authorize searches for contraband by officers of the Crown. But this Court has never limited the Amendment's prohibition on unreasonable searches and seizures to operations conducted by the police. Rather, the Court has long spoken of the Fourth Amendment's strictures as restraints imposed upon "governmental action" — that is, "upon the activities of sovereign authority." Accordingly, we have held the Fourth Amendment applicable to the activities of civil as well as criminal authorities: building inspectors, Occupational Safety and Health Act inspectors, and even firemen entering privately owned premises to battle a fire, are all subject to the restraints imposed by the Fourth Amendment. As we observed in *Camara v. Municipal Court,* "[t]he basic purpose of this Amendment, as recognized in countless decisions of this Court, is to safeguard the privacy and security of individuals against arbitrary invasions by governmental officials." . . .

To hold that the Fourth Amendment applies to searches conducted by school authorities is only to begin the inquiry into the standards governing such searches. Although the underlying command of the Fourth Amendment is always that searches and seizures be reasonable, what is reasonable depends on the context within which a search takes place. The determination of the standard of reasonableness governing any specific class of searches requires "balancing the need to search against the invasion which the search entails." On one side of the balance are arrayed the individual's legitimate expectations of privacy and personal security; on the other, the government's need for effective methods to deal with breaches of public order.

We have recognized that even a limited search of the person is a substantial invasion of privacy. We have also recognized that searches of closed items of personal luggage are intrusions on protected privacy interests, for "the Fourth Amendment provides protection to the owner of every container that conceals its contents from plain view." A search of a child's person or of a closed purse or other bag carried on her person, no less than a similar search carried out on an adult, is undoubtedly a severe violation of subjective expectations of privacy.

. . . To receive the protection of the Fourth Amendment, an expectation of privacy must be one that society is "prepared to recognize as legitimate." The State of New Jersey has argued that because of the pervasive supervision to which children in the schools are necessarily subject, a child has virtually no legitimate expectation of privacy in articles of personal property "unnecessarily" carried into a school. This argument has two factual premises: (1) the fundamental incompatibility of expectations of privacy with the maintenance of a sound educational environment; and (2) the minimal interest of the child in bringing any items of personal property into the school. Both premises are severely flawed.

Although this Court may take notice of the difficulty of maintaining discipline in the public schools today, the situation is not so dire that students in the schools may claim no legitimate expectations of privacy. . . .

Nor does the State's suggestion that children have no legitimate need to bring personal property into the schools seem well anchored in reality. Students at a minimum must bring to school not only the supplies needed for their studies, but also keys, money, and the necessaries of personal hygiene and grooming. In addition, students may carry on their persons or in purses or wallets such nondisruptive yet highly personal items as photographs, letters, and diaries. Finally, students may have perfectly legitimate reasons to carry with them articles of property needed in connection with extracurricular or recreational activities. In short, schoolchildren may find it necessary to carry with them a variety of legitimate, noncontraband items, and there is no reason to conclude that they have necessarily waived all rights to privacy in such items merely by bringing them onto school grounds.

Against the child's interest in privacy must be set the substantial interest of teachers and administrators in maintaining discipline in the classroom and on school grounds. Maintaining order in the classroom has never been easy, but in recent years, school disorder has often taken particularly ugly forms: drug use and violent crime in the schools have become major social problems. . . . "Events calling for discipline are frequent occurrences and sometimes require immediate, effective action." Accordingly, we have recognized that maintaining security and order in the schools requires a certain degree of flexibility in school disciplinary procedures, and we have respected the value of preserving the informality of the student-teacher relationship.

How, then, should we strike the balance between the schoolchild's legitimate expectations of privacy and the school's equally legitimate need to maintain an environment in which learning can take place? It is evident that the school setting requires some easing of the restrictions to which searches by public authorities are ordinarily subject. The warrant requirement, in particular, is unsuited to the school environment: requiring a teacher to obtain a warrant before searching a child suspected of an infraction of school rules (or of the criminal law) would unduly interfere with the maintenance of the swift and informal disciplinary procedures needed in the schools. Just as we have in other cases dispensed with the warrant requirement when "the burden of obtaining a warrant is likely to frustrate the governmental purpose behind the search," we hold today that school officials need not obtain a warrant before searching a student who is under their authority.

The school setting also requires some modification of the level of suspicion of illicit activity needed to justify a search. Ordinarily, a search — even one that may permissibly be carried out without a warrant — must be based upon "probable cause" to believe that a violation of the law has occurred. However, "probable cause" is not an irreducible requirement of a valid search. The fundamental command of the Fourth Amendment is that searches and seizures be reasonable, and although "both the concept of probable cause and the requirement of a warrant bear on the reasonableness of a search, . . . in certain limited circumstances neither is required." Thus, we have in a number of cases recognized the legality of searches and seizures based on suspicions that, although "reasonable," do not rise to the level of probable cause. Where a careful balancing of governmental and private interests suggests that the public interest is best served by a Fourth Amendment standard of reasonableness that stops short of probable cause, we have not hesitated to adopt such a standard.

. . . [T]he legality of a search of a student should depend simply on the reasonableness, under all the circumstances, of the search. Determining the reasonableness of any search involves a twofold inquiry: first, one must consider "whether the . . . action was justified at its inception"; second, one must determine whether the search as actually conducted "was reasonably related in scope to the circumstances which justified the interference in the first place." Under ordinary circumstances, a search of a student by a teacher or other school official will be "justified at its inception" when there are reasonable grounds for suspecting that the search will turn up evidence that the student has violated or is violating either the law or the rules of the school. Such a search will be permissible in its scope when the measures adopted are reasonably related to the objectives of the search and not excessively intrusive in light of the age and sex of the student and the nature of the infraction.

This standard will, we trust, neither unduly burden the efforts of school authorities to maintain order in their schools nor authorize unrestrained intrusions upon the privacy of schoolchildren. By focusing attention on the question of reasonableness, the standard will spare teachers and school administrators the necessity of schooling themselves in the niceties of probable cause and permit them to regulate their conduct according to the dictates of reason and common sense. At the same time, the reasonableness standard should ensure that the interests of students will be invaded no more than is necessary to achieve the legitimate end of preserving order in the schools. . . .

There remains the question of the legality of the search in this case. . . . Our review of the facts surrounding the search leads us to conclude that the search was in no sense unreasonable for Fourth Amendment purposes. . . .

T.L.O. had been accused of smoking, and had denied the accusation in the strongest possible terms when she stated that she did not smoke at all. Surely it cannot be said that under these circumstances, T.L.O.'s possession of cigarettes would be irrelevant to the charges against her or to her response to those charges. T.L.O.'s possession of cigarettes, once it was discovered, would both corroborate the report that she had been smoking and undermine the credibility of her defense to the charge of smoking. . . . The relevance of T.L.O.'s possession of cigarettes to the question whether she had been smoking and to the credibility of her denial that she smoked supplied the necessary "nexus" between the item searched for and the infraction under investigation. Thus, if Mr. Choplick in fact had a reasonable suspicion that T.L.O. had cigarettes in her purse, the search was justified despite the fact that the cigarettes, if found, would constitute "mere evidence" of a violation. . . .

Mr. Choplick's suspicion that there were cigarettes in the purse was not an "inchoate and unparticularized suspicion or 'hunch'"; rather, it was the sort of "common-sense conclusio[n] about human behavior" upon which "practical people" — including government officials — are entitled to rely. . . .

STEVENS, J. joined by MARSHALL J. (and partially by BRENNAN, J.) concurring in part and dissenting in part. . . . Justice Brandeis was both a great student and a great teacher. It was he who wrote:

> Our Government is the potent, the omnipresent teacher. For good or for ill, it teaches the whole people by its example. Crime is contagious. If the Government becomes a lawbreaker, it breeds contempt for law; it invites every man to become a law unto himself; it invites anarchy. *Olmstead v. United States,* 277 U.S. 438, 485 (1928) (dissenting opinion).

Those of us who revere the flag and the ideals for which it stands believe in the power of symbols. We cannot ignore that rules of law also have a symbolic power that may vastly exceed their utility.

Schools are places where we inculcate the values essential to the meaningful exercise of rights and responsibilities by a self-governing citizenry. If the Nation's students can be convicted through the use of arbitrary methods destructive of personal liberty, they cannot help but feel that they have been dealt with unfairly. The application of the exclusionary rule in criminal proceedings arising from illegal school searches makes an important statement to young people that "our society attaches serious consequences to a violation of constitutional rights," and that this is a principle of "liberty and justice for all." . . .

. . . The majority holds that "a search of a student by a teacher or other school official will be 'justified at its inception' when there are reasonable grounds for suspecting that the search will turn up evidence that the student has violated or is violating either the law or the rules of the school." This standard will permit teachers and school administrators to search students when they suspect that the search will reveal evidence of even the most trivial school regulation or precatory guideline for student behavior. The Court's standard for deciding whether a search is justified "at its inception" treats all violations of the rules of the school as though they were fungible. For the Court, a search for curlers and sunglasses in order to enforce the school dress code is apparently just as important as a search for evidence of heroin addiction or violent gang activity. . . .

In this case, Mr. Choplick overreacted to what appeared to be nothing more than a minor infraction — a rule prohibiting smoking in the bathroom of the freshmen's and sophomores' building. . . . Because this conduct was neither unlawful nor significantly disruptive of school order or the educational process, the invasion of privacy associated with the forcible opening of T.L.O.'s purse was entirely unjustified at its inception. . . .

BRENNAN, J. joined by MARSHALL, J. concurring in part and dissenting in part. . . . I emphatically disagree with the Court's decision to cast aside the constitutional probable-cause standard when assessing the constitutional validity of a schoolhouse search. The Court's decision jettisons the probable-cause standard — the only standard that finds support in the text of the Fourth Amendment — on the basis of its Rohrschach-like "balancing test." Use of such a "balancing test" to determine the standard for evaluating the validity of a full-scale search represents a sizable innovation in Fourth Amendment analysis. This innovation finds support neither in precedent nor policy and portends a dangerous weakening of the purpose of the Fourth Amendment to protect the privacy and security of our citizens. Moreover, even if this Court's historic understanding of the Fourth Amendment were mistaken and a balancing test of some kind were appropriate, any such test that gave adequate weight to the privacy and security interests protected by the Fourth Amendment would not reach the preordained result the Court's conclusory analysis reaches today. Therefore, because I believe that the balancing test used by the Court today is flawed both in its inception and in its execution, I respectfully dissent.

NOTES & QUESTIONS

1. *After Columbine: The Privacy Implications.* On April 20, 1999, two high school students entered their school (Columbine High School) in Littleton, Colorado, armed with firearms and explosives. In a brutal rampage, they killed 12 students and 1 teacher and injured 23 others before killing themselves. As a result of the Columbine massacre and other shootings and violent threats in high schools across the country, school administrators began to adopt stricter safety measures to prevent violence. Such measures include the installation of metal detectors, surveillance cameras, routine backpack and locker searches by police officers, and requirements that students carry identification cards at all times while on school grounds. In one particularly controversial experiment in California, grade school children were to be required to wear RFID-enabled identity tags around their necks. After protests and national media attention, the school rescinded the proposed policy.

   What are the pros and cons of having students wear RFID identification tags? Some critics argue that adopting these measures will teach students that the only way to be secure is to live in a police state. Supporters contend that the loss of privacy is justified by additional security and protection. Under *T.L.O.,* are the new measures described above constitutional?

2. *Strip Searching.* In *Safford U.S. School Dist. No. 1 v. Redding,* 129 S. Ct. 2633 (2009), the U.S. Supreme Court set forth standards for when a strip search of a student is unconstitutional. Suspecting a student of having contraband (pain pills for distribution to other students), school officials removed a 13-year-old student's outer clothing and then made her pull out her bra and pull out the elastic on her underpants. The search partially exposed her breasts and pelvic region. The Supreme Court held that the search violated the Fourth Amendment. The Court did not conclude that strip searches were a per se

violation, but that they must be reasonably related to the justification for the search and "not excessively intrusive in light of the age and sex of the student and the nature of the infraction."

The school argued that students can easily hide contraband in their clothing, but the Court concluded that there was no evidence that the student was hiding contraband in her undergarments and there was no "indication of danger" to others from the student's alleged contraband. In other words, the Supreme Court concluded that barring clear and direct evidence that a student is hiding contraband in her undergarments or barring any need to search to promote immediate safety, a strip search is improper.

B. DRUG TESTING

VERNONIA SCHOOL DISTRICT V. ACTON

515 U.S. 646 (1995)

SCALIA, J. . . . Petitioner Vernonia School District 47J (District) operates one high school and three grade schools in the logging community of Vernonia, Oregon. As elsewhere in small-town America, school sports play a prominent role in the town's life, and student athletes are admired in their schools and in the community.

Drugs had not been a major problem in Vernonia schools. In the mid-to-late 1980's, however, teachers and administrators observed a sharp increase in drug use. Students began to speak out about their attraction to the drug culture, and to boast that there was nothing the school could do about it. Along with more drugs came more disciplinary problems. . . .

Not only were student athletes included among the drug users but, as the District Court found, athletes were the leaders of the drug culture. This caused the District's administrators particular concern, since drug use increases the risk of sports-related injury. Expert testimony at the trial confirmed the deleterious effects of drugs on motivation, memory, judgment, reaction, coordination, and performance. The high school football and wrestling coach witnessed a severe sternum injury suffered by a wrestler, and various omissions of safety procedures and misexecutions by football players, all attributable in his belief to the effects of drug use.

Initially, the District responded to the drug problem by offering special classes, speakers, and presentations designed to deter drug use. It even brought in a specially trained dog to detect drugs, but the drug problem persisted. . . .

At that point, District officials began considering a drug-testing program. They held a parent "input night" to discuss the proposed Student Athlete Drug Policy (Policy), and the parents in attendance gave their unanimous approval. The school board approved the Policy for implementation in the fall of 1989. Its expressed purpose is to prevent student athletes from using drugs, to protect their health and safety, and to provide drug users with assistance programs. . . .

The Policy applies to all students participating in interscholastic athletics. Students wishing to play sports must sign a form consenting to the testing and must obtain the written consent of their parents. Athletes are tested at the beginning of the season for their sport. In addition, once each week of the season the names of the athletes are placed in a "pool" from which a student, with the supervision of two adults, blindly draws the names of 10% of the athletes for random testing. Those selected are notified and tested that same day, if possible.

The student to be tested completes a specimen control form which bears an assigned number. Prescription medications that the student is taking must be identified by providing a copy of the prescription or a doctor's authorization. The student then enters an empty locker room accompanied by an adult monitor of the same sex. Each boy selected produces a sample at a urinal, remaining fully clothed with his back to the monitor, who stands approximately 12 to 15 feet behind the student. Monitors may (though do not always) watch the student while he produces the sample, and they listen for normal sounds of urination. Girls produce samples in an enclosed bathroom stall, so that they can be heard but not observed. After the sample is produced, it is given to the monitor, who checks it for temperature and tampering and then transfers it to a vial.

The samples are sent to an independent laboratory, which routinely tests them for amphetamines, cocaine, and marijuana. Other drugs, such as LSD, may be screened at the request of the District, but the identity of a particular student does not determine which drugs will be tested. The laboratory's procedures are 99.94% accurate. . . . Only the superintendent, principals, vice-principals, and athletic directors have access to test results, and the results are not kept for more than one year.

If a sample tests positive, a second test is administered as soon as possible to confirm the result. If the second test is negative, no further action is taken. If the second test is positive, the athlete's parents are notified, and the school principal convenes a meeting with the student and his parents, at which the student is given the option of (1) participating for six weeks in an assistance program that includes weekly urinalysis, or (2) suffering suspension from athletics for the remainder of the current season and the next athletic season. The student is then retested prior to the start of the next athletic season for which he or she is eligible. The Policy states that a second offense results in automatic imposition of option (2); a third offense in suspension for the remainder of the current season and the next two athletic seasons. . . .

In the fall of 1991, respondent James Acton, then a seventh grader, signed up to play football at one of the District's grade schools. He was denied participation, however, because he and his parents refused to sign the testing consent forms. The Actons filed suit, seeking declaratory and injunctive relief from enforcement of the Policy on the grounds that it violated the Fourth and Fourteenth Amendments to the United States Constitution and Article I, §9, of the Oregon Constitution. . . .

As the text of the Fourth Amendment indicates, the ultimate measure of the constitutionality of a governmental search is "reasonableness." . . . Where a search is undertaken by law enforcement officials to discover evidence of criminal wrongdoing, this Court has said that reasonableness generally requires the obtaining of a judicial warrant. Warrants cannot be issued, of course, without the showing of probable cause required by the Warrant Clause. But a warrant is not required to establish the reasonableness of *all* government searches; and when a warrant is not required (and the Warrant Clause therefore not applicable), probable cause is not invariably required either. A search unsupported by probable cause can be constitutional, we have said, "when special needs, beyond the normal need for law enforcement, make the warrant and probable-cause requirement impracticable."

We have found such "special needs" to exist in the public school context. There, the warrant requirement "would unduly interfere with the maintenance of the swift and informal disciplinary procedures [that are] needed," and "strict adherence to the requirement that searches be based upon probable cause" would undercut "the substantial need of teachers and administrators for freedom to maintain order in the schools." *T.L.O.,* 469 U.S., at 340. The school search we approved in *T.L.O.,* while not based on probable cause, *was* based on individualized *suspicion* of wrongdoing. . . .

The first factor to be considered is the nature of the privacy interest upon which the search here at issue intrudes. The Fourth Amendment does not protect all subjective expectations of privacy, but only those that society recognizes as "legitimate." What expectations are legitimate varies, of course, with context, depending, for example, upon whether the individual asserting the privacy interest is at home, at work, in a car, or in a public park. . . .

. . . [W]hile children assuredly do not "shed their constitutional rights . . . at the schoolhouse gate," the nature of those rights is what is appropriate for children in school.

Fourth Amendment rights, no less than First and Fourteenth Amendment rights, are different in public schools than elsewhere; the "reasonableness" inquiry cannot disregard the schools' custodial and tutelary responsibility for children. For their own good and that of their classmates, public school children are routinely required to submit to various physical examinations, and to be vaccinated against various diseases. . . . Particularly with regard to medical examinations and procedures, therefore, "students within the school environment have a lesser expectation of privacy than members of the population generally."

Legitimate privacy expectations are even less with regard to student athletes. School sports are not for the bashful. They require "suiting up" before each practice or event, and showering and changing afterwards. Public school locker rooms, the usual sites for these activities, are not notable for the privacy they afford. The locker rooms in Vernonia are typical: No individual dressing rooms are provided; shower heads are lined up along a wall, unseparated by any sort of partition or curtain; not even all the toilet stalls have doors. . . . [T]here is "an element of 'communal undress' inherent in athletic participation."

There is an additional respect in which school athletes have a reduced expectation of privacy. By choosing to "go out for the team," they voluntarily subject themselves to a degree of regulation even higher than that imposed on students generally. In Vernonia's public schools, they must submit to a preseason physical exam (James testified that his included the giving of a urine sample), they must acquire adequate insurance coverage or sign an insurance waiver, maintain a minimum grade point average, and comply with any "rules of conduct, dress, training hours and related matters as may be established for each sport by the head coach and athletic director with the principal's approval." Somewhat like adults who choose to participate in a "closely regulated industry," students who voluntarily participate in school athletics have reason to expect intrusions upon normal rights and privileges, including privacy. . . .

Having considered the scope of the legitimate expectation of privacy at issue here, we turn next to the character of the intrusion that is complained of. . . . Under the District's Policy, male students produce samples at a urinal along a wall. They remain fully clothed and are only observed from behind, if at all. Female students produce samples in an enclosed stall, with a female monitor standing outside listening only for sounds of tampering. These conditions are nearly identical to those typically encountered in public restrooms, which men, women, and especially schoolchildren use daily. Under such conditions, the privacy interests compromised by the process of obtaining the urine sample are in our view negligible.

The other privacy-invasive aspect of urinalysis is, of course, the information it discloses concerning the state of the subject's body, and the materials he has ingested. In this regard it is significant that the tests at issue here look only for drugs, and not for whether the student is, for example, epileptic, pregnant, or diabetic. Moreover, the drugs for which the samples are screened are standard, and do not vary according to the identity of the student. And finally, the results of the tests are disclosed only to a limited class of school personnel who have a need to know; and they are not turned over to law enforcement authorities or used for any internal disciplinary function.

Respondents argue, however, that the District's Policy is in fact more intrusive than this suggests, because it requires the students, if they are to avoid sanctions for a falsely positive test, to identify *in advance* prescription medications they are taking. We agree that this raises some cause for concern. . . . Nothing in the Policy [states that the school would not keep the information confidential], and when respondents choose, in effect, to challenge the Policy on its face, we will not assume the worst. Accordingly . . . the invasion of privacy was not significant. . . .

Finally, we turn to consider the nature and immediacy of the governmental concern at issue here, and the efficacy of this means for meeting it. . . . Is there a compelling state interest here? . . . .

That the nature of the concern is important — indeed, perhaps compelling — can hardly be doubted. Deterring drug use by our Nation's schoolchildren is at least as important as enhancing efficient enforcement of the Nation's laws against the importation of drugs. . . . [T]he effects of a drug-infested school are visited not just upon the users, but upon the entire student body and faculty, as the educational process is disrupted. . . .

As to the efficacy of this means for addressing the problem: It seems to us self-evident that a drug problem largely fueled by the "role model" effect of athletes' drug use, and of particular danger to athletes, is effectively addressed by making sure that athletes do not use drugs. Respondents argue that a "less intrusive means to the same end" was available, namely, "drug testing on suspicion of drug use." We have repeatedly refused to declare that only the "least intrusive" search practicable can be reasonable under the Fourth Amendment. Respondents' alternative entails substantial difficulties — if it is indeed practicable at all. It may be impracticable, for one thing, simply because the parents who are willing to accept random drug testing for athletes are not willing to accept accusatory drug testing for all students, which transforms the process into a badge of shame.

Respondents' proposal brings the risk that teachers will impose testing arbitrarily upon troublesome but not drug-likely students. It generates the expense of defending lawsuits that charge such arbitrary imposition, or that simply demand greater process before accusatory drug testing is imposed. And not least of all, it adds to the ever-expanding diversionary duties of schoolteachers the new function of spotting and bringing to account drug abuse, a task for which they are ill prepared, and which is not readily compatible with their vocation. In many respects, we think, testing based on "suspicion" of drug use would not be better, but worse. . . .

Taking into account all the factors we have considered above — the decreased expectation of privacy, the relative unobtrusiveness of the search, and the severity of the need met by the search — we conclude Vernonia's Policy is reasonable and hence constitutional. . . .

O'CONNOR, J. joined by STEVENS and SOUTER, JJ. dissenting. . . . The population of our Nation's public schools, grades 7 through 12, numbers around 18 million. By the reasoning of today's decision, the millions of these students who participate in interscholastic sports, an overwhelming majority of whom have given school officials no reason whatsoever to suspect they use drugs at school, are open to an intrusive bodily search.

. . . Blanket searches, because they can involve "thousands or millions" of searches, "pos[e] a greater threat to liberty" than do suspicion-based ones, which "affec[t] one person at a time." Searches based on individualized suspicion also afford potential targets considerable control over whether they will, in fact, be searched because a person can avoid such a search by not acting in an objectively suspicious way. And given that the surest way to avoid acting suspiciously is to avoid the underlying wrongdoing, the costs of such a regime, one would think, are minimal.

But whether a blanket search is "better" than a regime based on individualized suspicion is not a debate in which we should engage. In my view, it is not open to judges or government officials to decide on policy grounds which is better and which is worse. For most of our constitutional history, mass, suspicionless searches have been generally considered *per se* unreasonable within the meaning of the Fourth Amendment. And we have allowed exceptions in recent years only where it has been clear that a suspicion-based regime would be ineffectual. Because that is not the case here, I dissent. . . .

[H]aving misconstrued the fundamental role of the individualized suspicion requirement in Fourth Amendment analysis, the Court never seriously engages the practicality of such a requirement in the instant case. And that failure is crucial because nowhere is it *less* clear that an individualized suspicion requirement would be ineffectual than in the school context. In most schools, the entire pool of potential search targets — students — is under constant supervision by teachers and administrators and coaches, be it in classrooms, hallways, or locker rooms.

The record here indicates that the Vernonia schools are no exception. The great irony of this case is that most (though not all) of the evidence the District introduced to justify its suspicionless drug testing program consisted of first- or second-hand stories of particular, identifiable students acting in ways that plainly gave rise to reasonable suspicion of in-school drug use — and thus that would have justified a drug-related search under our *T.L.O.* decision. Small groups of students, for example, were observed by a teacher "passing joints back and forth" across the street at a restaurant before school and during school hours. Another group was caught skipping school and using drugs at one of the students' houses. Several students actually *admitted* their drug use to school officials (some of them being caught with marijuana pipes). One student presented himself to his teacher as "clearly obviously inebriated" and had to be sent home. Still another was observed dancing and singing at the top of his voice in the back of the classroom; when the teacher asked what was going on, he replied, "Well, I'm just high on life." To take a final example, on a certain road trip, the school wrestling coach smelled marijuana smoke in a motel room occupied by four wrestlers, an observation that (after some questioning) would probably have given him reasonable suspicion to test one or all of them.

In light of all this evidence of drug use by particular students, there is a substantial basis for concluding that a vigorous regime of suspicion-based testing (for which the District appears already to have rules in place) would have gone a long way toward solving Vernonia's school drug problem while preserving the Fourth Amendment rights of James Acton and others like him. And were there any doubt about such a conclusion, it is removed by indications in the record that suspicion-based testing could have been supplemented by an equally vigorous campaign to have Vernonia's parents encourage their children to submit to the District's *voluntary* drug testing program. In these circumstances, the Fourth Amendment dictates that a mass, suspicionless search regime is categorically unreasonable.

. . . [I]ntrusive, blanket searches of schoolchildren, most of whom are innocent, for evidence of serious wrongdoing are not part of any traditional school function of which I am aware. Indeed, many schools, like many parents, prefer to trust their children unless given reason to do otherwise. As James Acton's father said on the witness stand, "[suspicionless testing] sends a message to children that are trying to be responsible citizens . . . that they have to prove that they're innocent . . . , and I think that kind of sets a bad tone for citizenship." . . .

BOARD OF EDUCATION V. EARLS

536 U.S. 822 (2002)

THOMAS, J. . . . The city of Tecumseh, Oklahoma, is a rural community located approximately 40 miles southeast of Oklahoma City. The School District administers all Tecumseh public schools. In the fall of 1998, the School District adopted the Student Activities Drug Testing Policy (Policy), which requires all middle and high school students to consent to drug testing in order to participate in any extracurricular activity. In practice, the Policy has been applied only to competitive extracurricular activities sanctioned by the Oklahoma Secondary Schools Activities Association, such as the Academic Team, Future Farmers of America, Future Homemakers of America, band, choir, pom pom, cheerleading, and athletics. Under the Policy, students are required to take a drug test before participating in an extracurricular activity, must submit to random drug testing while participating in that activity, and must agree to be tested at any time upon reasonable suspicion. The urinalysis tests are designed to detect only the use of illegal drugs, including amphetamines, marijuana, cocaine, opiates, and barbiturates, not medical conditions or the presence of authorized prescription medications. . . .

In *Vernonia,* this Court held that the suspicionless drug testing of athletes was constitutional. The Court, however, did not simply authorize all school drug testing, but rather conducted a fact-specific balancing of the intrusion on the children's Fourth Amendment rights against the promotion of legitimate governmental interests. Applying the principles of *Vernonia* to the somewhat different facts of this case, we conclude that Tecumseh's Policy is also constitutional. . . .

We first consider the nature of the privacy interest allegedly compromised by the drug testing. . . . A student's privacy interest is limited in a public school environment where the State is responsible for maintaining discipline, health, and safety. Schoolchildren are routinely required to submit to physical examinations and vaccinations against disease. Securing order in the school environment sometimes requires that students be subjected to greater controls than those appropriate for adults.

Respondents argue that because children participating in nonathletic extracurricular activities are not subject to regular physicals and communal undress, they have a stronger expectation of privacy than the athletes tested in *Vernonia.* This distinction, however, was not essential to our decision in *Vernonia,* which depended primarily upon the school's custodial responsibility and authority.

In any event, students who participate in competitive extracurricular activities voluntarily subject themselves to many of the same intrusions on their privacy as do athletes. Some of these clubs and activities require occasional off-campus travel and communal undress. All of them have their own rules and requirements for participating students that do not apply to the student body as a whole. . . . We therefore conclude that the students affected by this Policy have a limited expectation of privacy. . . .

Next, we consider the character of the intrusion imposed by the Policy. Urination is "an excretory function traditionally shielded by great privacy." . . .

Under the Policy, a faculty monitor waits outside the closed restroom stall for the student to produce a sample and must "listen for the normal sounds of urination in order to guard against tampered specimens and to insure an accurate chain of custody." The monitor then pours the sample into two bottles that are sealed and placed into a mailing pouch along with a consent form signed by the student. This procedure is virtually identical to that reviewed in *Vernonia,* except that it additionally protects privacy by allowing male students to produce their samples behind a closed stall. Given that we considered the method of collection in *Vernonia* a "negligible" intrusion, the method here is even less problematic.

In addition, the Policy clearly requires that the test results be kept in confidential files separate from a student's other educational records and released to school personnel only on a "need to know" basis. Respondents nonetheless contend that the intrusion on students' privacy is significant because the Policy fails to protect effectively against the disclosure of confidential information and, specifically, that the school "has been careless in protecting that information: for example, the Choir teacher looked at students' prescription drug lists and left them where other students could see them." But the choir teacher is someone with a "need to know," because during off-campus trips she needs to know what medications are taken by her students. Even before the Policy was enacted the choir teacher had access to this information. In any event, there is no allegation that any other student did see such information. This one example of alleged carelessness hardly increases the character of the intrusion.

Moreover, the test results are not turned over to any law enforcement authority. Nor do the test results here lead to the imposition of discipline or have any academic consequences. Rather, the only consequence of a failed drug test is to limit the student's privilege of participating in extracurricular activities. Indeed, a student may test positive for drugs twice and still be allowed to participate in extracurricular activities. After the first positive test, the school contacts the student's parent or guardian for a meeting. The student may continue to participate in the activity if within five days of the meeting the student shows proof of receiving drug counseling and submits to a second drug test in two weeks. For the second positive test, the student is suspended from participation in all extracurricular activities for 14 days, must complete four hours of substance abuse counseling, and must submit to monthly drug tests. Only after a third positive test will the student be suspended from participating in any extracurricular activity for the remainder of the school year, or 88 school days, whichever is longer.

Given the minimally intrusive nature of the sample collection and the limited uses to which the test results are put, we conclude that the invasion of students' privacy is not significant.

Finally, this Court must consider the nature and immediacy of the government's concerns and the efficacy of the Policy in meeting them. . . . The drug abuse problem among our Nation's youth has hardly abated since *Vernonia* was decided in 1995. In fact, evidence suggests that it has only grown worse. . . . The health and safety risks identified in *Vernonia* apply with equal force to Tecumseh's children. Indeed, the nationwide drug epidemic makes the war against drugs a pressing concern in every school.

Additionally, the School District in this case has presented specific evidence of drug use at Tecumseh schools. Teachers testified that they had seen students who appeared to be under the influence of drugs and that they had heard students speaking openly about using drugs. A drug dog found marijuana cigarettes near the school parking lot. Police officers once found drugs or drug paraphernalia in a car driven by a Future Farmers of America member. And the school board president reported that people in the community were calling the board to discuss the "drug situation.". . .

GINSBURG, J. joined by STEVENS, O'CONNOR, and SOUTER, JJ.   dissenting. . . . The particular testing program upheld today is not reasonable, it is capricious, even perverse: Petitioners' policy targets for testing a student population least likely to be at risk from illicit drugs and their damaging effects. . . .

Vernonia cannot be read to endorse invasive and suspicionless drug testing of all students upon any evidence of drug use, solely because drugs jeopardize the life and health of those who use them. Many children, like many adults, engage in dangerous activities on their own time; that the children are enrolled in school scarcely allows government to monitor all such activities. If a student has a reasonable subjective expectation of privacy in the personal items she brings to school, see *T.L.O.,* surely she has a similar expectation regarding the chemical composition of her urine. Had the *Vernonia* Court agreed that public school attendance, in and of itself, permitted the State to test each student's blood or urine for drugs, the opinion in *Vernonia* could have saved many words.

The second commonality to which the Court points is the voluntary character of both interscholastic athletics and other competitive extracurricular activities. . .

The comparison is enlightening. While extracurricular activities are "voluntary" in the sense that they are not required for graduation, they are part of the school's educational program. . . . Participation in such activities is a key component of school life, essential in reality for students applying to college, and, for all participants, a significant contributor to the breadth and quality of the educational experience. Students "volunteer" for extracurricular pursuits in the same way they might volunteer for honors classes: They subject themselves to additional requirements, but they do so in order to take full advantage of the education offered them. . . .

Observing that students produce urine samples in a bathroom stall with a coach or teacher outside, *Vernonia* typed the privacy interests compromised by the process of obtaining samples "negligible." . . .

In this case, however, Lindsay Earls and her parents allege that the School District handled personal information collected under the policy carelessly, with little regard for its confidentiality. Information about students' prescription drug use, they assert, was routinely viewed by Lindsay's choir teacher, who left files containing the information unlocked and unsealed, where others, including students, could see them; and test results were given out to all activity sponsors whether or not they had a clear "need to know." . . .

The School District cites the dangers faced by members of the band, who must "perform extremely precise routines with heavy equipment and instruments in close proximity to other students," and by Future Farmers of America, who "are required to individually control and restrain animals as large as 1500 pounds." . . . Notwithstanding nightmarish images of out-of-control flatware, livestock run amok, and colliding tubas disturbing the peace and quiet of Tecumseh, the great majority of students the School District seeks to test in truth are engaged in activities that are not safety sensitive to an unusual degree. There is a difference between imperfect tailoring and no tailoring at all.

Even if students might be deterred from drug use in order to preserve their extracurricular eligibility, it is at least as likely that other students might forgo their extracurricular involvement in order to avoid detection of their drug use. Tecumseh's policy thus falls short doubly if deterrence is its aim: It invades the privacy of students who need deterrence least, and risks steering students at greatest risk for substance abuse away from extracurricular involvement that potentially may palliate drug problems.

NOTES & QUESTIONS

1. **Earls *vs.* Vernonia.** Do you agree with the Court's conclusion that the holding in this case flows logically from *Vernonia*? Why or why not?

2. ***Steroid Testing.*** Would a school be justified pursuant to *T.L.O., Vernonia,* and *Earls* to test for steroid abuse among student athletes? Among all students engaged in extracurricular activities?

3. ***Drug Testing for All Students?*** Suppose a school district decided to implement mandatory drug testing for *all* students. Based on the Supreme Court's reasoning, would this policy be constitutional? In other words, is the fact that the students tested are voluntarily engaged in extracurricular activities an essential element of the Court's holding?

4. ***Routine School Searches?*** Suppose, in response to concerns over violence and guns in school, a school district decides to engage in routine searches of the bags and backpacks of all students engaging in extracurricular activities. Based on *T.L.O., Vernonia,* and *Earls,* would this policy be constitutional?

5. ***Prescription Drugs.*** Note that the school in *Vernonia* collected from each student that it tested information about any prescription medication that the student was taking. Why did the school collect this information? Does such information add significantly to the privacy invasion in this case?

6. ***Searches and Symbolism.*** Consider the Supreme Court's holding in *Chandler v. Miller,* 520 U.S. 305 (1997), a case in which the Court struck down a drug testing requirement for candidates for public office. Writing for the Court, Justice Ginsburg said:

   > What is left, after close review of Georgia's scheme, is the image the State seeks to project. By requiring candidates for public office to submit to drug testing, Georgia displays its commitment to the struggle against drug abuse. . . . But Georgia asserts no evidence of a drug problem among the State's elected officials, those officials typically do not perform high-risk, safety-sensitive tasks, and the required certification immediately aids no interdiction effort. The need revealed, in short, is symbolic, not "special," as that term draws meaning from our case law. . . .
   >
   > However well meant, the candidate drug test Georgia has devised diminishes personal privacy for a symbol's sake. The Fourth Amendment shields society against that state action.

   At what point does drug testing of students become symbolic? Can *Earls* be reconciled with *Chandler*? We will consider *Chandler* in more detail in section C of this chapter.

7. ***State Constitutional Law: The California Approach.*** Many states have their own versions of the Fourth Amendment in their constitutions. Accordingly, the constitutions of some states may provide more privacy protection to students than the federal Constitution. In addition to provisions that resemble the Fourth Amendment, some state constitutions contain an explicit right to privacy. One of these states is California, and its constitution states:

   > All people are by nature free and independent and have inalienable rights. Among these are enjoying and defending life and liberty, acquiring, possessing, and protecting property, and pursuing and obtaining safety, happiness, and privacy. Cal. Const. Art I, §1.

In *Hill v. National Collegiate Athletic Ass'n,* 865 P.2d 633 (Cal. 1994), the National Collegiate Athletic Association (NCAA) randomly selected college athletes competing in postseason football games to provide urine samples to be tested for drugs. Student athletes attending Stanford University sued, contending that the NCAA drug testing violated their right to privacy. As we will discuss later in this chapter, the California Supreme Court found that this provision of the state constitution applied to the private sector. The California high court also rejected the challenge to the NCAA drug testing:

> By its nature, sports competition demands highly disciplined physical activity conducted in accordance with a special set of social norms. Unlike the general population, student athletes undergo frequent physical examinations, reveal their bodily and medical conditions to coaches and trainers, and often dress and undress in same-sex locker rooms. In so doing, they normally and reasonably forgo a measure of their privacy in exchange for the personal and professional benefits of extracurricular athletics.
>
> A student athlete's already diminished expectation of privacy is outweighed by the NCAA's legitimate regulatory objectives in conducting testing for proscribed drugs. As a sponsor and regulator of sporting events, the NCAA has self-evident interests in ensuring fair and vigorous competition, as well as protecting the health and safety of student athletes. These interests justify a set of drug testing rules reasonably calculated to achieve drug-free athletic competition. The NCAA's rules contain elements designed to accomplish this purpose, including: (1) advance notice to athletes of testing procedures and written consent to testing; (2) random selection of athletes actually engaged in competition; (3) monitored collection of a sample of a selected athlete's urine in order to avoid substitution or contamination; and (4) chain of custody, limited disclosure, and other procedures designed to safeguard the confidentiality of the testing process and its outcome. As formulated, the NCAA's regulations do not offend the legitimate privacy interests of student athletes.

C. SCHOOL RECORDS

THE FAMILY EDUCATIONAL RIGHTS AND PRIVACY ACT

The Family Educational Rights and Privacy Act (FERPA) of 1974, Pub. L. No. 93-380, 20 U.S.C. § 1232g, commonly known as the "Buckley Amendment," generally prohibits schools from releasing student "education records" without the authorization of the student and/or parent. Schools may release such "directory" information as names, addresses, dates of attendance, degrees earned, and activities unless the student and/or parent expressly indicates in writing that he or she wants it to remain confidential.

Education Records. "Education records" are "those records, files, documents, and other materials which contain information directly related to a student; and are maintained by an educational agency or institution." 20 U.S.C. § 1232g(a)(4)(A). "Law enforcement unit records" and certain medical treatment records maintained by school officials do not constitute education records, § 1232g(a)(4)(B).

FERPA covers only records and information from education records, not information per se. Thus, school authorities' personal knowledge and observations that are not part of a record are not covered. *See Frasca v. Andrews*, 463 F. Supp. 1043, 1050 (E.D.N.Y. 1979) ("Congress could not have constitutionally prohibited comment on, or discussion of, facts about a student which were learned independently of his school records."). As a result, FERPA does not apply to "personal knowledge derived from direct, personal experience with a student."[1] For example, an employee of an educational institution, such as a faculty or staff member, can share information with others if she "personally observes a student engaging in erratic and threatening behavior."[2]

Ownership of Rights. FERPA rights initially belong to the parents or guardians of a student. When a student *either* turns 18 or attends an institution of higher education that student becomes an "eligible student" and FERPA rights transfer from the parent to the student. At the college level, FERPA rights always belong to the student, regardless of age.

Rights. FERPA provides parents/guardians or eligible students with the following rights:

1. to review the student's education records;
2. to correct any inaccuracies or misleading information in those records;
3. to control certain disclosures of the information in those records;
4. to file a complaint with the U.S. Department of Education in the event of a violation of the above rights.

Notice. Schools must inform students and parents of their rights under FERPA.

Access and Ability to Correct Errors. Schools generally must provide parents/guardians or eligible students with access to their education records — a chance to review their records upon request. § 1232g(a)(1)(A). Schools must provide an opportunity for a hearing "to challenge the content of such student's education records, in order to insure that the records are not inaccurate, misleading, or otherwise in violation of the privacy or other rights of students, and to provide an opportunity for the correction or deletion of any inaccurate, misleading, or otherwise inappropriate data contained therein." § 1232g(a)(2).

Disclosure of Student Education Records. Pursuant to § 1232g(b), schools cannot disclose a student's education records without written consent. Certain disclosures are exempted from this rule, and schools may (but are not required to) disclose information without consent. For example, the school can disclose records to "school officials" with a "legitimate educational interest," to appropriate persons in order to protect health or safety of the student or others, as well as to a number of other entities and officials. § 1232g(b)(1).

---

[1] Nancy E. Tribbensee & Steven J. McDonald, *FERPA and Campus Safety*, 5 NACU Notes (No. 4, Aug. 6, 2007).

[2] *Id.*

Law Enforcement Records. Records that are both created and maintained by a separate law enforcement unit of a school (either commissioned police or public safety) at least in part for law enforcement purposes are not considered "education records" and are not subject to FERPA protections.

Treatment Records. These records are the medical or psychological records of a student 18 years or older who is being treated by a physician, psychiatrist, psychologist, or other related professional or paraprofessional. 34 C.F.R. § 99.3. They are not considered "education records" as long as they are not shared with others not involved in the student's treatment.

Directory Information. If the parent/guardian or eligible student does not opt out, a school may release to the public the student's name, address, telephone numbers, birth date, major, activities and sports, dates of attendance, degrees and awards received, and certain other such "directory" information. § 1232g(b)(5).

Enforcement. FERPA authorizes the Secretary of Education to end all federal funding if a school fails to comply with the statute. § 1232g(f). The Department of Education's Family Policy Compliance Office (FPCO) oversees the enforcement of FERPA.

Before the FPCO takes action, an individual must file a complaint against a school. The FPCO then investigates and if the school is found in violation of FERPA, the FPCO recommends specific steps that the institution must take to comply. *See* 34 C.F.R. § 99.66. If the school fails to comply, then funding can be stopped.

OWASSO INDEPENDENT SCHOOL DISTRICT V. FALVO

534 U.S. 426 (2002)

KENNEDY, J. Teachers sometimes ask students to score each other's tests, papers, and assignments as the teacher explains the correct answers to the entire class. Respondent contends this practice, which the parties refer to as peer grading, violates the Family Educational Rights and Privacy Act of 1974 (FERPA or Act), 88 Stat. 571, 20 U.S.C. § 1232g. We took this case to resolve the issue. . . .

Respondent claimed the peer grading embarrassed her children. She asked the school district to adopt a uniform policy banning peer grading and requiring teachers either to grade assignments themselves or at least to forbid students from grading papers other than their own. The school district declined to do so, and respondent brought a class action pursuant to 42 U.S.C. § 1983. Respondent alleged the school district's grading policy violated FERPA and other laws not relevant here. . . .

Petitioners, supported by the United States as amicus curiae, contend the definition covers only institutional records — namely, those materials retained in a permanent file as a matter of course. They argue that records "maintained by an educational agency or institution" generally would include final course grades, student grade point averages, standardized test scores, attendance records, counseling records, and records of disciplinary actions — but not student homework or classroom work. . . .

Two statutory indicators tell us that the Court of Appeals erred in concluding that an assignment satisfies the definition of education records as soon as it is graded by another student. First, the student papers are not, at that stage, "maintained" within the meaning of § 1232g(a)(4)(A). The ordinary meaning of the word "maintain" is "to keep in existence or continuance; preserve; retain." Random House Dictionary of the English Language 1160 (2d ed. 1987). Even assuming the teacher's grade book is an education record — a point the parties contest and one we do not decide here — the score on a student-graded assignment is not "contained therein," § 1232g(b)(1), until the teacher records it. The teacher does not maintain the grade while students correct their peers' assignments or call out their own marks. Nor do the student graders maintain the grades within the meaning of § 1232g(a)(4)(A). The word "maintain" suggests FERPA records will be kept in a filing cabinet in a records room at the school or on a permanent secure database, perhaps even after the student is no longer enrolled. The student graders only handle assignments for a few moments as the teacher calls out the answers. It is fanciful to say they maintain the papers in the same way the registrar maintains a student's folder in a permanent file. . . .

Respondent's construction of the term "education records" to cover student homework or classroom work would impose substantial burdens on teachers across the country. It would force all instructors to take time, which otherwise could be spent teaching and in preparation, to correct an assortment of daily student assignments. . . . At argument, counsel for respondent seemed to agree that if a teacher in any of the thousands of covered classrooms in the Nation puts a happy face, a gold star, or a disapproving remark on a classroom assignment, federal law does not allow other students to see it.

We doubt Congress meant to intervene in this drastic fashion with traditional state functions. Under the Court of Appeals' interpretation of FERPA, the federal power would exercise minute control over specific teaching methods and instructional dynamics in classrooms throughout the country. The Congress is not likely to have mandated this result, and we do not interpret the statute to require it. . . .

NOTES & QUESTIONS

1. *The Enforcement of FERPA.* In *Owasso,* the individual plaintiffs used 42 U.S.C. § 1983 to challenge the grading policy as an infringement of their FERPA rights. Section 1983 authorizes individuals to sue state officials for violations of federal law and the Constitution. Recall also that FERPA does not directly provide for a private cause of action; it is enforced by the Secretary of Education. The Court did not reach the issue of whether § 1983 was an appropriate vehicle for private parties to seek redress for violations of FERPA. Instead, the Court addressed the issue in a case decided later in the same term.

   In *Gonzaga University v. Doe,* 536 U.S. 273 (2002), a student at Gonzaga University was attempting to become a public elementary school teacher upon graduation. Gonzaga was currently investigating Doe for allegations of sexual misconduct. Gonzaga contacted the state agency for teacher certification and disclosed to the agency the allegations. The victim of the alleged sexual misconduct later denied the allegations and stated that Gonzaga officials were wrong in their assessment of her relationship with Doe. Doe sued Gonzaga under § 1983, alleging a violation of FERPA. Doe contended that FERPA conferred to him a right not to have his education records disclosed to unauthorized persons without his consent. A jury awarded him $1,155,000, including compensatory and punitive damages. The Court held that FERPA could not be enforced by a private right of action under § 1983: "[A] plaintiff must assert the violation of a federal *right,* not merely a violation of federal *law.*" A federal statute must provide for an "unambiguously conferred right to support a cause of action brought under § 1983." The court concluded:

> [I]f Congress wishes to create new rights enforceable under § 1983, it must do so in clear and unambiguous terms — no less and no more than what is required for Congress to create new rights enforceable under an implied private right of action. FERPA's nondisclosure provisions contain no rights-creating language, they have an aggregate, not individual, focus, and they serve primarily to direct the Secretary of Education's distribution of public funds to educational institutions. They therefore create no rights enforceable under § 1983.

Justices Stevens and Ginsburg dissented, contending that FERPA contains numerous references to rights, including the title of the statute: "The entire statutory scheme was designed to protect such rights."

Recall the other federal privacy statutes that do not explicitly create a private right of action, such as the Health Insurance Portability and Accountability Act (HIPAA) regulations and Children's Online Privacy Protection Act (COPPA). What are the implications of this case for private causes of action under § 1983 to enforce these other privacy laws?

2. ***FERPA and the Virginia Tech Shooter.*** On April 16, 2007, Seung Cho, a student at Virginia Tech, shot and killed 32 students and faculty, wounded many others, and then took his own life. In the immediate aftermath of the tragedy, the Governor of Virginia appointed a panel to review the events leading up to the shootings and the handling of the incidents. Among other topics, the report looked at FERPA and other privacy laws.

The Review Panel found that many people knew about Cho's mental instability yet did not share what they knew with others because of widespread (and often incorrect) beliefs that information privacy laws blocked such information sharing:

> While Cho was a student at Virginia Tech, his professors, fellow students, campus police, the Office of Judicial Affairs, the Care Team, and the Cook Counseling Center all had dealings with him that raised questions about his mental stability. There is no evidence that Cho's parents were ever told of these contacts, and they say they were unaware of his problems at school. Most significantly, there is no evidence that Cho's parents, his suitemates, and their parents were ever informed that he had been temporarily detained, put through a commitment hearing for involuntary admission, and found to be a danger to himself. Efforts to share this information were impeded by laws about privacy of information, according to several university officials and the campus police.

Indeed, the university's attorney, during one of the panel's open hearings and in private meetings, told the panel that the university could not share this information due to privacy laws.

The panel's review of information privacy laws governing mental health, law enforcement, and educational records and information revealed widespread lack of understanding, conflicting practice, and laws that were poorly designed to accomplish their goals. Information privacy laws are intended to strike a balance between protecting privacy and allowing information sharing that is necessary or desirable. Because of this difficult balance, the laws are often complex and hard to understand.

The widespread perception is that information privacy laws make it difficult to respond effectively to troubled students. This perception is only partly correct. Privacy laws can block some attempts to share information, but even more often may cause holders of such information to default to the nondisclosure option — even when laws permit the option to disclose. Sometimes this is done out of ignorance of the law, and sometimes intentionally because it serves the purposes of the individual or organization to hide behind the privacy law. A narrow interpretation of the law is the least risky course, notwithstanding the harm that may be done to others if information is not shared.

Among other recommendations, the Report of the Review Panel suggested:

> The provisions [of privacy law] should insulate a person or organization from liability (or loss of funding) for making a disclosure with a good faith belief that the disclosure was necessary to protect the health, safety, or welfare of the person involved or members of the general public. Laws protecting good-faith disclosure for health, safety, and welfare can help combat any bias toward nondisclosure.[3]

What are the costs and benefits of this recommendation? Are there viable alternatives? How should officials share the mental health information of troubled students?

Regarding FERPA more specifically, the Report noted that "FERPA does not address the differences between medical records and ordinary educational records such as grade transcripts. It is not clear whether FERPA preempts state law regarding medical records and confidentiality of medical information or merely adds another requirement on top of these records." The Report recommended that "FERPA should make explicit an exception regarding treatment records. Disclosure of treatment records from university clinics should be available to any health care provider without the student's consent when the records are needed for medical treatment, as they would be if covered under HIPAA." Additionally, it recommended that FERPA's exception for release of records in an emergency should be interpreted more flexibly.

A federal task force also reported to the President after the Virginia Tech shooting. Among its key findings were the presence of "substantial obstacles" to information sharing; the panel stated: "Education officials, healthcare providers, law enforcement personnel, and others are not fully informed about when they can share critical information on persons who are likely to be a

---

[3] Virginia Tech Review Panel, *Mass Shootings at Virginia Tech* 63, 68 (Aug. 2007), http://www.governor.virginia.gov/TempContent/techPanelReport.cfm.

danger to self or others, and the resulting confusion may chill legitimate information sharing." It observed that it had repeatedly heard of "information silos" within educational institutions. It called for an increase in information sharing and collaboration among state and local communities, educators, mental health officers and law enforcement. It also requested that federal agencies provide additional guidance as to how information can be legally shared under HIPAA and FERPA.

The U.S. Department of Education amended the FERPA regulations to clarify that student information could be disclosed in a health or safety emergency.

3. *A Comparison of FERPA and HIPAA.* As Daniel Solove contends:

> It is an interesting exercise to compare FERPA to the Health Insurance Portability and Accountability Act (HIPAA) regulations after the HITECH Act amendments. HIPAA is far from perfect, but it leaves FERPA in the dust when it comes to the strength of its privacy and security provisions. In at least four major areas, HIPAA is far more advanced than FERPA. First, in the area of data security, the HIPAA Security Rule has detailed requirements about data security. FERPA does not. Second, HIPAA requires training of personnel about the institution's policies and procedures. FERPA does not. Third, HIPAA requires that institutions have a privacy program and a privacy officer. FERPA does not. And fourth, HIPAA (especially after the HITECH Act amendments) gives the Department of Health and Human Services (HHS) potent enforcement powers – sanctions of up to $1.5 million. HHS also has the power to audit. It has direct enforcement power not only against covered entities but also business associates such as cloud computing providers. FERPA's enforcement is narrow and virtually meaningless.[4]

On FERPA's enforcement, Solove writes:

> FERPA's enforcement leaves a lot to be desired. FERPA's enforcement is quite minimal, lacking a private right of action and having a sanction so implausible it has never been imposed in the 35+ year history of the law. That sanction is a withdrawal of all federal funds. It will never happen. So many steps must occur between the violation and the ultimate sanction being imposed that a school would literally have to walk a plank that would stretch halfway across the Atlantic Ocean. A school must be beyond bad in a systematic way to be even close to having the sanction imposed – and probably then it will still fail.
>
> The Department of Education only has power over the schools and education agencies it funds. Cloud computing providers are not directly subject to this enforcement power. In some circumstances, they can be restricted from contracting with schools. But the vast bulk of the Department's enforcement is on the schools themselves, and that enforcement is virtually meaningless.[5]

4. *The Demise of inBloom.* In April 2014, inBloom, a non-profit data repository for student data, announced that it planned to close. Financed with $100 million, including support from the Bill and Melinda Gates Foundation,

---

[4] Daniel J. Solove, *FERPA and the Cloud: What FERPA Can Learn from HIPAA,* LinkedIn (Dec. 18, 2012), https://www.linkedin.com/today/post/article/20121218131535-2259773-ferpa-and-the-cloud-what-ferpa-can-learn-from-hipaa.

[5] *Id.*

inBloom sought to store student data in streamlined dashboards where teachers could track the progress of individual students. The inBloom database included more than 400 different data fields about students.[6] After backlash about privacy and security issues, the nine states that initially signed on to the services backed out of the venture.

In his analysis, Daniel Solove viewed the demise of inBloom as demonstrating "a fundamental problem with educational privacy."[7] He argues: "The problem is that education privacy is lagging so far behind other industries and is so poorly regulated and addressed." In his metaphor: "There is no privacy infrastructure in K-12 schools. This is akin to there being no roads, no running water, no electricity, no police system, no fire protection, and no hospitals. The lack of this infrastructure is what doomed inBloom."

Solove also concedes that K-12 schools are woefully underfunded. What would be the most critical elements of a privacy and security environment for these schools to develop before sharing student information with outside companies?

5. ***Education Data in the Cloud.*** Fordham Law School's Center on Law and Information Policy (CLIP) examined how school districts address privacy when they transfer student information to cloud service providers.[8] Fordham CLIP selected a national sample of school districts and requested all of the district's cloud service agreements, notices to parents, and computer use policies for teachers. These materials were then reviewed against a checklist of legal obligations and privacy norms. CLIP found that 95 percent of school districts used a computer cloud service or third-party vendor for a diverse range of functions, "including data mining related to student performance, support for classroom activities, student guidance, data hosting, as well as special services, such as cafeteria payments and transportation services." The study also showed that only 25 percent of the districts inform parents of their use of cloud services, and less than 7 percent had written contract provisions that would prohibit the sale of student data by vendors. CLIP summarized: "Cloud services are poorly understood, non-transparent, and weakly governed."

In response, Fordham CLIP recommended that the existence and identity of cloud services providers and the privacy protections for student data be made available on district websites. It also called for school district to provide notice to parents of these services and the types of student information shared with third parties. It also made recommendations regarding data governance, contracting practices, and contract terms.

6. ***The White House Big Data Study.*** In its May 2014 Report on Big Data, the White House noted, "Students and their families need robust protection against current and emerging harms, but they also deserve access to the learning advancements enabled by technology that promise to empower all students to

[6] Natasha Singer, *InBloom Student Data Repository to Close*, N.Y. Times (Apr. 21, 2014).

[7] Daniel Solove, *Why did inBloom Die? A Hard Lesson About Education Privacy*, Safe.gov (Apr. 28, 2014), at http://www.safegov.org/2014/4/28/why-did-inbloom-die-a-hard-lesson-about-education-privacy.

[8] Joel R. Reidenberg et al., *Privacy and Cloud Computing in Public Schools* (Dec. 12, 2013).

reach their full potential."[9] It recommended that the federal government "explore how to modernize the privacy regulatory framework under the Family Education Rights and Privacy Act and Children's Online Privacy Protection Act to ensure two complementary goals: 1) protecting students against their data being shared or used inappropriately, especially when that data is gathered in an educational context, and 2) ensuring that innovation in educational technology, including new approaches and businesses models, have ample opportunity to flourish." How should these two goals be balanced? What are the special risks and opportunities present in the educational context?

---

[9] Executive Office of the President, *Big Data: Seizing Opportunities, Preserving Values* 64 (May 2014).

CHAPTER 12

EMPLOYMENT PRIVACY

CHAPTER OUTLINE

Privacy in the workplace is a difficult and complex issue that continues to grow in importance as technology enables new forms of testing and monitoring of workers. Employer monitoring of workers is not new. For decades, employers have sought to keep close tabs on their employees. For example, in the early twentieth century, Ford Motor Company had its "Sociological Department" scrutinize employees to determine whether they gambled, drank, or conducted other frowned-upon activities. The purpose of the examination was to determine whether employees deserved bonuses.

Today, modern technology has enabled vastly more sophisticated forms of surveillance of workers. Employers routinely engage in a number of forms of investigation and monitoring of employees, such as conducting drug tests, obtaining credit reports and medical records, hiring private investigators to scrutinize employees, conducting psychological tests, administering polygraph examinations, requiring employees to fill out questionnaires containing detailed information about their personal lives, listening to telephone calls and voice mail, reading e-mail, monitoring computer use, searching offices and other employee work spaces, monitoring the number of keystrokes that an employee types, installing video surveillance devices to monitor workers, and even using electronic devices to track the location of workers.

Workplace monitoring is all but omnipresent. According to a 2007 survey by the American Management Association (AMA), 77.7 percent of major U.S. firms "record and review employee communications and activities on the job, including their phone calls, e-mail, Internet connections, and computer files." This figure had doubled since 1997.[1] A 2007 AMA survey found that "[e]mployers are primarily concerned about inappropriate Web surfing, with 66% monitoring Internet connections."[2] Employers use software to block connections to websites considered inappropriate (65 percent); use URL blocks to stop employees from visiting external blogs (18 percent); track content, keystrokes, and time spent at the keyboard (45 percent); store and review employees' computer files (43 percent); and monitor social networking sites (10 percent) and the blogosphere (12 percent) to observe comments about the company.

This survey also found that a wide majority of companies informed employees that they were being monitored. For example, "83% inform workers that the company is monitoring content, keystrokes, and time spent at the keyboard." Only 27 percent of employers addressed monitoring as part of their formal employee training, whereas 70 percent of employers used an employee handbook to tell workers of Internet and e-mail surveillance. Employers believe that they have good reason to engage in employee surveillance and testing. First, employers desire to hire competent workers who are not likely to cause workplace disruptions or be careless and reckless on the job, possibly exposing the employer to liability. Employers want workers who are not likely to have problems in their personal life or health that will cause absences from work or will decrease productivity. In certain professions, if an employee's troubled past comes to light, it could place the employer in a bad light (e.g., the staff of a politician). In other professions, such as child care, there is strong pressure for employers to scrutinize their employees' pasts and other aspects of their private lives to minimize the risk that the employee will engage in misconduct. Employers can be directly liable for negligent hiring.

Second, employers desire to monitor workers to force increased productivity and to curtail employee misconduct. Liability for sexual harassment has made employers more likely to investigate and monitor their employees to ensure that the workplace is free from harassment. The legal trend is to make employers more responsible for training and monitoring their workers and for ensuring that their workers are competent to perform their jobs, especially when their jobs affect the safety of others (e.g., truck drivers, train operators, pilots, mechanics, and so on). Employers can be vicariously liable if their employees commit a tort on the job. Employers can also be directly liable for inadequate supervision.

Third, employers may desire to search workers to investigate particular incidents of misconduct in the workplace. If items are being stolen or important secrets or documents are being leaked, the employer may want to engage in searches and surveillance to catch the offenders.

---

[1] American Management Association, *Workplace Monitoring & Surveillance: Policies and Practices* (2001), at http://www.amanet.org/research/pdfs/emsfu_short.pdf.

[2] AMA/ePolicy Institute Research, *2007 Electronic Monitoring & Surveillance Survey* (2008), at www.amanet.org/research/pdfs/electronic-monitoring-surveillance-survey08.pdf.

Thus, there are several reasons why employers may want to monitor their workers. Yet privacy in the workplace is also an important value. Today, people are spending increasingly more time at work, often well over a third of the day and over half of their time while awake. Also, more workers are "telecommuting" from home.

A wide spectrum of law governs the privacy of employees. To understand how this law applies, it is important to distinguish between public and private sector employees.

Public Sector Employees. The federal government is the largest employer in the United States. There are approximately 2.75 million federal civilian employees and 1.4 million employed in the armed forces. State and local governments employ millions of employees as well. Public sector employees are protected by a number of laws. The Fourth Amendment applies not just to the police, but to all government officials, including government employers. Public sector employees are thus protected by the Fourth Amendment, although, as you will see, in a rather limited way. The constitutional right to information privacy can protect against employer disclosures of information. In *Whalen v. Roe,* 429 U.S. 589 (1977), the Supreme Court held that the right to privacy encompasses the "individual interest in avoiding disclosure of personal matters." In many states, state constitutions also protect the privacy of public employees. Federal wiretap law applies to government employers and restricts their ability to conduct certain forms of electronic surveillance. State wiretap law may provide additional protection. The Americans with Disabilities Act (ADA) prohibits employers from asking certain questions about employees. The federal Privacy Act protects against disclosures by government entities and could apply to disclosures of information about federal government employees in certain circumstances. Employees can also sue employers for privacy invasions under the privacy torts — particularly for intrusion upon seclusion, public disclosure of private facts, and false light.

Private Sector Employees. Private sector employees enjoy some of the same protections as public sector employees, although the Fourth Amendment and most state constitutions do not apply to these employees. As you will see later in this chapter, however, in some states, federal and state constitutions can serve as a source of public policy for suits for wrongful termination in violation of public policy. Federal wiretap law applies not only to government employers but to private sector actors as well, including private sector employers. Additionally, the ADA, breach of contract, and privacy torts serve to protect the privacy of private sector employees.[3]

Depending upon the type of employment contract, employees may have additional contractual remedies. Pursuant to some types of employment contracts, employees can only be terminated for certain reasons, such as inadequate performance, unprofessional conduct, or disciplinary violations. If an employee is terminated and the reason is invalid, the employee can sue for wrongful

---

[3] For an overview of U.S. workplace privacy law and comparisons with the European Union, see Lothar Determann & Robert Sprague, *Intrusive Monitoring: Employee Privacy Expectations are Reasonable in Europe, Destroyed in the United States*, 26 Berkeley Tech. L.J. 979 (2011).

termination and breach of contract. In contrast, many employees are "at-will" employees and may be dismissed at the whim of the employer. Generally, an at-will employee cannot bring a wrongful termination action. However, in many jurisdictions, there is an exception to this rule when the employee was fired for a reason that violates public policy (e.g., when the reason is discriminatory or the employee is fired for refusing to commit a criminal act). Employees who are terminated because of a refusal to comply with privacy-invasive testing, questioning, or monitoring or who are terminated because of the facts revealed by such activities can sometimes sue for wrongful termination in violation of public policy.

A. WORKPLACE SEARCHES

O'CONNOR V. ORTEGA

480 U.S. 709 (1987)

O'CONNOR, J. (plurality opinion). This suit under 42 U.S.C. § 1983 presents two issues concerning the Fourth Amendment rights of public employees. First, we must determine whether the respondent, a public employee, had a reasonable expectation of privacy in his office, desk, and file cabinets at his place of work. Second, we must address the appropriate Fourth Amendment standard for a search conducted by a public employer in areas in which a public employee is found to have a reasonable expectation of privacy. . . .

Dr. Magno Ortega, a physician and psychiatrist, held the position of Chief of Professional Education at Napa State Hospital (Hospital) for 17 years, until his dismissal from that position in 1981. As Chief of Professional Education, Dr. Ortega had primary responsibility for training young physicians in psychiatric residency programs.

In July 1981, Hospital officials, including Dr. Dennis O'Connor, the Executive Director of the Hospital, became concerned about possible improprieties in Dr. Ortega's management of the residency program. In particular, the Hospital officials were concerned with Dr. Ortega's acquisition of an Apple II computer for use in the residency program. The officials thought that Dr. Ortega may have misled Dr. O'Connor into believing that the computer had been donated, when in fact the computer had been financed by the possibly coerced contributions of residents. Additionally, the Hospital officials were concerned with charges that Dr. Ortega had sexually harassed two female Hospital employees, and had taken inappropriate disciplinary action against a resident.

On July 30, 1981, Dr. O'Connor requested that Dr. Ortega take paid administrative leave during an investigation of these charges. . . . Dr. Ortega remained on administrative leave until the Hospital terminated his employment on September 22, 1981.

Dr. O'Connor selected several Hospital personnel to conduct the investigation, including an accountant, a physician, and a Hospital security officer. Richard Friday, the Hospital Administrator, led this "investigative team." At some point

during the investigation, Mr. Friday made the decision to enter Dr. Ortega's office. The specific reason for the entry into Dr. Ortega's office is unclear from the record.
. . .

The resulting search of Dr. Ortega's office was quite thorough. The investigators entered the office a number of times and seized several items from Dr. Ortega's desk and file cabinets, including a Valentine's Day card, a photograph, and a book of poetry all sent to Dr. Ortega by a former resident physician. These items were later used in a proceeding before a hearing officer of the California State Personnel Board to impeach the credibility of the former resident, who testified on Dr. Ortega's behalf. The investigators also seized billing documentation of one of Dr. Ortega's private patients under the California Medicaid program. . . .

Dr. Ortega commenced this action against petitioners in Federal District Court under 42 U.S.C. § 1983, alleging that the search of his office violated the Fourth Amendment. . . .

The strictures of the Fourth Amendment, applied to the States through the Fourteenth Amendment, have been applied to the conduct of governmental officials in various civil activities. *New Jersey v. T.L.O.,* 469 U.S. 325 (1985). Thus, we have held in the past that the Fourth Amendment governs the conduct of school officials, building inspectors, and Occupational Safety and Health Act inspectors. . . . Searches and seizures by government employers or supervisors of the private property of their employees, therefore, are subject to the restraints of the Fourth Amendment.

. . . Our cases establish that Dr. Ortega's Fourth Amendment rights are implicated only if the conduct of the Hospital officials at issue in this case infringed "an expectation of privacy that society is prepared to consider reasonable." We have no talisman that determines in all cases those privacy expectations that society is prepared to accept as reasonable. Instead, "the Court has given weight to such factors as the intention of the Framers of the Fourth Amendment, the uses to which the individual has put a location, and our societal understanding that certain areas deserve the most scrupulous protection from government invasion." *Oliver v. United States,* 466 U.S. 170, 178 (1984).

Because the reasonableness of an expectation of privacy, as well as the appropriate standard for a search, is understood to differ according to context, it is essential first to delineate the boundaries of the workplace context. The workplace includes those areas and items that are related to work and are generally within the employer's control. At a hospital, for example, the hallways, cafeteria, offices, desks, and file cabinets, among other areas, are all part of the workplace. These areas remain part of the workplace context even if the employee has placed personal items in them, such as a photograph placed in a desk or a letter posted on an employee bulletin board.

Not everything that passes through the confines of the business address can be considered part of the workplace context, however. An employee may bring closed luggage to the office prior to leaving on a trip, or a handbag or briefcase each workday. While whatever expectation of privacy the employee has in the existence and the outward appearance of the luggage is affected by its presence in the workplace, the employee's expectation of privacy in the *contents* of the luggage is not affected in the same way. The appropriate standard for a workplace search does not necessarily apply to a piece of closed personal luggage, a handbag or a briefcase that happens to be within the employer's business address.

Within the workplace context, this Court has recognized that employees may have a reasonable expectation of privacy against intrusions by police. . . .

Individuals do not lose Fourth Amendment rights merely because they work for the government instead of a private employer. The operational realities of the workplace, however, may make *some* employees' expectations of privacy unreasonable when an intrusion is by a supervisor rather than a law enforcement official. Public employees' expectations of privacy in their offices, desks, and file cabinets, like similar expectations of employees in the private sector, may be reduced by virtue of actual office practices and procedures, or by legitimate regulation. . . . The employee's expectation of privacy must be assessed in the context of the employment relation. An office is seldom a private enclave free from entry by supervisors, other employees, and business and personal invitees. Instead, in many cases offices are continually entered by fellow employees and other visitors during the workday for conferences, consultations, and other work-related visits. Simply put, it is the nature of government offices that others — such as fellow employees, supervisors, consensual visitors, and the general public — may have frequent access to an individual's office. . . . Given the great variety of work environments in the public sector, the question whether an employee has a reasonable expectation of privacy must be addressed on a case-by-case basis. . . .

. . . [W]e recognize that the undisputed evidence suggests that Dr. Ortega had a reasonable expectation of privacy in his desk and file cabinets. The undisputed evidence discloses that Dr. Ortega did not share his desk or file cabinets with any other employees. Dr. Ortega had occupied the office for 17 years and he kept materials in his office, which included personal correspondence, medical files, correspondence from private patients unconnected to the Hospital, personal financial records, teaching aids and notes, and personal gifts and mementos. The files on physicians in residency training were kept outside Dr. Ortega's office. . . .

. . . [A]s we have stated in *T.L.O.,* "[t]o hold that the Fourth Amendment applies to searches conducted by [public employers] is only to begin the inquiry into the standards governing such searches. . . . [W]hat is reasonable depends on the context within which a search takes place." Thus, we must determine the appropriate standard of reasonableness applicable to the search. A determination of the standard of reasonableness applicable to a particular class of searches requires "balanc[ing] the nature and quality of the intrusion on the individual's Fourth Amendment interests against the importance of the governmental interests alleged to justify the intrusion." In the case of searches conducted by a public employer, we must balance the invasion of the employees' legitimate expectations of privacy against the government's need for supervision, control, and the efficient operation of the workplace.

"[I]t is settled . . . that 'except in certain carefully defined classes of cases, a search of private property without proper consent is "unreasonable" unless it has been authorized by a valid search warrant.'" There are some circumstances, however, in which we have recognized that a warrant requirement is unsuitable. . . . [A]s Justice Blackmun stated in *T.L.O.,* "[o]nly in those exceptional circumstances in which special needs, beyond the normal need for law enforcement, make the warrant and probable-cause requirement impracticable." . .

The legitimate privacy interests of public employees in the private objects they bring to the workplace may be substantial. Against these privacy interests, however, must be balanced the realities of the workplace, which strongly suggest that a warrant requirement would be unworkable. While police, and even administrative enforcement personnel, conduct searches for the primary purpose of obtaining evidence for use in criminal or other enforcement proceedings, employers most frequently need to enter the offices and desks of their employees for legitimate work-related reasons wholly unrelated to illegal conduct. Employers and supervisors are focused primarily on the need to complete the government agency's work in a prompt and efficient manner. An employer may have need for correspondence, or a file or report available only in an employee's office while the employee is away from the office. Or, as is alleged to have been the case here, employers may need to safeguard or identify state property or records in an office in connection with a pending investigation into suspected employee misfeasance.

In our view, requiring an employer to obtain a warrant whenever the employer wished to enter an employee's office, desk, or file cabinets for a work-related purpose would seriously disrupt the routine conduct of business and would be unduly burdensome. Imposing unwieldy warrant procedures in such cases upon supervisors, who would otherwise have no reason to be familiar with such procedures, is simply unreasonable. In contrast to other circumstances in which we have required warrants, supervisors in offices such as at the Hospital are hardly in the business of investigating the violation of criminal laws. Rather, work-related searches are merely incident to the primary business of the agency. Under these circumstances, the imposition of a warrant requirement would conflict with "the common-sense realization that government offices could not function if every employment decision became a constitutional matter."

Whether probable cause is an inappropriate standard for public employer searches of their employees' offices presents a more difficult issue. . . .

The governmental interest justifying work-related intrusions by public employers is the efficient and proper operation of the workplace. Government agencies provide myriad services to the public, and the work of these agencies would suffer if employers were required to have probable cause before they entered an employee's desk for the purpose of finding a file or piece of office correspondence. Indeed, it is difficult to give the concept of probable cause, rooted as it is in the criminal investigatory context, much meaning when the purpose of a search is to retrieve a file for work-related reasons. Similarly, the concept of probable cause has little meaning for a routine inventory conducted by public employers for the purpose of securing state property. To ensure the efficient and proper operation of the agency, therefore, public employers must be given wide latitude to enter employee offices for work-related, noninvestigatory reasons.

We come to a similar conclusion for searches conducted pursuant to an investigation of work-related employee misconduct. Even when employers conduct an investigation, they have an interest substantially different from "the normal need for law enforcement." Public employers have an interest in ensuring that their agencies operate in an effective and efficient manner, and the work of these agencies inevitably suffers from the inefficiency, incompetence, mismanagement, or other work-related misfeasance of its employees. Indeed, in many cases, public employees are entrusted with tremendous responsibility, and the consequences of their misconduct or incompetence to both the agency and the public interest can be severe. . . . In our view, therefore, a probable cause requirement for searches of the type at issue here would impose intolerable burdens on public employers. . . . It is simply unrealistic to expect supervisors in most government agencies to learn the subtleties of the probable cause standard. . . . [W]e conclude that a reasonableness standard will permit regulation of the employer's conduct "according to the dictates of reason and common sense." . . .

. . . We hold, therefore, that public employer intrusions on the constitutionally protected privacy interests of government employees for noninvestigatory, work-related purposes, as well as for investigations of work-related misconduct, should be judged by the standard of reasonableness under all the circumstances. . . .

On remand . . . the District Court must determine the justification for the search and seizure, and evaluate the reasonableness of both the inception of the search and its scope. . . .

BLACKMUN, joined by BRENNAN, MARSHALL, and STEVENS, JJ. dissenting. . . . . [T]he reality of work in modern time, whether done by public or private employees, reveals why a public employee's expectation of privacy in the workplace should be carefully safeguarded and not lightly set aside. It is, unfortunately, all too true that the workplace has become another home for most working Americans. Many employees spend the better part of their days and much of their evenings at work. Consequently, an employee's private life must intersect with the workplace, for example, when the employee takes advantage of work or lunch breaks to make personal telephone calls, to attend to personal business, or to receive personal visitors in the office. As a result, the tidy distinctions (to which the plurality alludes) between the workplace and professional affairs, on the one hand, and personal possessions and private activities, on the other, do not exist in reality. Not all of an employee's private possessions will stay in his or her briefcase or handbag. . . .

Although the plurality mentions the "special need" step, it turns immediately to a balancing test to formulate its standard of reasonableness. This error is significant because, given the facts of this case, no "special need" exists here to justify dispensing with the warrant and probable-cause requirements. As observed above, the facts suggest that this was an investigatory search undertaken to obtain evidence of charges of mismanagement at a time when Dr. Ortega was on administrative leave and not permitted to enter the Hospital's grounds. There was no special practical need that might have justified dispensing with the warrant and probable-cause requirements. Without sacrificing their ultimate goal of maintaining an effective institution devoted to training and healing, to which the disciplining of Hospital employees contributed, petitioners could have taken any evidence of Dr. Ortega's alleged improprieties to a magistrate in order to obtain a warrant. . . .

Furthermore, this seems to be exactly the kind of situation where a neutral magistrate's involvement would have been helpful in curtailing the infringement upon Dr. Ortega's privacy. Petitioners would have been forced to articulate their exact reasons for the search and to specify the items in Dr. Ortega's office they sought, which would have prevented the general rummaging through the doctor's office, desk, and file cabinets. . . .

NOTES & QUESTIONS

1. ***The Case on Remand.*** The final resolution of this litigation occurred 11 years after the Supreme Court opinion in *O'Connor v. Ortega* and following two opinions from the Ninth Circuit. In the second of these opinions, *Ortega v. O'Connor,* 146 F.3d 119 (9th Cir. 1998), the Ninth Circuit upheld a jury award of $636,000 to Dr. Ortega. The appellate court found that the search and seizure could not be justified under the Fourth Amendment by the particular complaints of sexual harassment that had been raised against the doctor. The Ninth Circuit declared that the concept of "reasonableness" was to "be viewed in the context of the nature of the intrusion involved." In this case, there had been an indiscriminate search that led to the seizure of "*purely personal* belongings," including personal letters and mementoes. Moreover, the court concluded, there was no reason to suspect that particular evidence regarding the sexual harassment complaints would be found in the places that were searched. Finally, the court faulted the search for failing to be sufficiently limited in scope.

2. ***Is the Workplace Different?*** Why does the Court conclude that people's expectation of privacy is diminished in the workplace? Recall in *Katz* that the Court declared that privacy "protects people, not places." Is this declaration still true after *O'Connor v. Ortega*?

   Consider the observation of John Craig on the Court's decisions on workplace privacy:

   > A common element in the Court's constitutional workplace jurisprudence is the view that employment is a separate and unique context in which the Constitution operates less rigorously to restrain the state. The Court has clearly been concerned that imposing strict constitutional limitations on privacy-invasive practices will hamper the day-to-day operations of the public sector workplace, and thereby create inefficiencies.[4]

3. ***The Privacy-Maximizing Aspects of* Ortega.** William Stuntz contends that the result in *Ortega* was paradoxically protective of privacy:

   > . . . [I]f the law were to forbid these ordinary work-related entries, employers would have a substantial incentive to restructure the work environment to recover their ability to retrieve information. There are a number of ways of doing this. File cabinets can be moved from closed offices to open secretarial pools to make access easy; more records can be kept in the accounting department and fewer in individual employees' files; computer space can be arranged so that private (and secure) recordkeeping by individual employees is difficult.
   >
   > In short, the employer . . . has a fair degree of substantive power to reshape the rules of the workplace, in order to accomplish indirectly what he cannot do

---

[4] John D.R. Craig, *Privacy and Employment Law* 64-65 (1999).

directly. If information cannot be taken from offices, offices can be turned into places where little information is stored. . . .

Given this kind of authority, it is easy to imagine that employees might prefer a regime that gives their superiors broad discretion to enter presumptively private work areas. Such authority reduces the likelihood that sanctions (such as the failure to get a desired promotion or job assignment) will be imposed based on unverifiable, and possibly false, suspicions. More importantly, broad search authority vastly reduces the cost to government employers of creating private spaces for their employees. The Fourth Amendment issue is thus turned upside down: the rule that probably maximizes privacy (and thus the rule that search targets would probably want) is the rule that permits searches of work areas for any authentically work-related reason. That is the rule *Ortega* adopts.[5]

Had the Court in *Ortega* adopted a warrant and probable cause requirement, would employers likely restructure their workplaces in the privacy-reducing ways Stuntz suggests?

4. ***Reasonable Expectations of Privacy in One's Desk.*** In *Sheppard v. Beerman*, 18 F.3d 147, 152 (2d Cir. 1994), plaintiff Brian Sheppard served as a law clerk to Justice Leon Beerman of the Supreme Court of New York. In New York, the Supreme Court is a trial court. Sheppard alleged that Beerman, after speaking ex parte with the prosecutor in a murder case, requested that Sheppard draft a denial of the defendant's speedy trial motion. Sheppard voiced his objection to the judge that the denial was unfair to the defendant. The argument became heated, with Sheppard accusing the judge of engaging in other instances of misconduct and he called the judge "corrupt" and a "son of a bitch." Beerman subsequently fired Sheppard.

Sheppard subsequently sued, claiming, among other things a violation of his Fourth Amendment rights. The court held:

> Sheppard alleges that after the dismissal, Beerman searched his office, desk, and file cabinets in violation of his Fourth Amendment rights. . . .
>
> An "employee's expectation of privacy must be assessed in the context of the employment relation[ship]." *Ortega.* The working relationship between a judge and her law clerk, as noted by the district court, is unique. Unlike a typical employment relationship where an employer may limit the information she wants to share with her employees, in order for a judicial chambers to function efficiently, an absolute free flow of information between the clerk and the judge is usually necessary. Accordingly, the clerk has access to all the documents pertaining to a case. More importantly, clerks regularly have access to the judge's confidential thoughts on a case. The judge may discuss her feelings with her clerk, or may allow the clerk access to her personal notes. In turn, the judge necessarily has access to the files and papers kept by the clerk, which will often include the clerk's notes from discussions with the judge. Because of this distinctive open access to documents characteristic of judicial chambers, we agree with the district court's determination that Sheppard had "no reasonable

---

[5] William J. Stuntz, *Implicit Bargains, Government Power, and the Fourth Amendment*, 44 Stan. L. Rev. 553, 579 (1992).

expectation of privacy in chambers' appurtenances, embracing desks, file cabinets or other work areas."

5. *Waiver of Fourth Amendment Rights.* Can government employers require that their employees undergo unreasonable searches under the Fourth Amendment as a condition of employment? In short, the answer is no. *See Pickering v. Board of Education,* 391 U.S. 563 (1968). But if an employee voluntarily consents to the search, then such searches can be conducted. *See McDonell v. Hunter,* 809 F.2d 1302 (8th Cir. 1987).

K-MART CORP. V. TROTTI

677 S.W.2d 632 (Tex. Ct. App. 1984)

BULLOCK, J. K-Mart Corporation appeals from a judgment awarding the appellee, Trotti, $8,000.00 in actual damages and $100,000.00 in exemplary damages for [intrusion upon seclusion]. . . .

The appellee was an employee in the hosiery department at the appellants' store number 7441. Her supervisors had never indicated any dissatisfaction with her work nor any suspicion of her honesty.

The appellants provided their employees with lockers for the storage of personal effects during working hours. There was no assignment of any given locker to any individual employee. . . . The appellee, with appellants' knowledge, used one of these lockers and provided her own combination lock.

On October 31, 1981, the appellee placed her purse in her locker when she arrived for work. She testified that she snapped the lock closed and then pulled on it to make sure it was locked. When she returned to her locker during her afternoon break, she discovered the lock hanging open. Searching through her locker, the appellee further discovered her personal items in her purse in considerable disorder. Nothing was missing from either the locker or the purse. The store manager testified that, in the company of three junior administrators at the store, he had that afternoon searched the lockers because of a suspicion raised by the appellants' security personnel that an unidentified employee, not the appellee, had stolen a watch. The manager and his assistants were also searching for missing price-marking guns. The appellee further testified that, as she left the employee's locker area after discovering her locker open, she heard the manager suggest to his assistants, "Let's get busy again." The manager testified that none of the parties searched through employees' personal effects. . . .

The manager testified that during the initial hiring interviews, all prospective employees received verbal notification from personnel supervisors that it was the appellants' policy to conduct ingress-egress searches of employees and also to conduct unannounced searches of lockers. A personnel supervisor and an assistant manager, however, testified that, although locker searches did regularly occur, the personnel supervisors did not apprise prospective employees of this policy. . . .

We hold that the weight of the evidence indicates that the appellants' employees came upon a locker with a lock provided by an employee, disregarded the appellee's demonstration of her expectation of privacy, opened and searched the locker, and probably opened and searched her purse as well; and, in so holding, we consider it is immaterial whether the appellee actually securely locked her locker or not. It is sufficient that an employee in this situation, by having placed a lock on the locker at the employee's own expense and with the appellants' consent, has demonstrated a legitimate expectation to a right of privacy in both the locker itself and those personal effects within it. . . .

NOTES & QUESTIONS

1. *Public Disclosure and the Workplace.* Employers can be liable for public disclosure of private facts for revealing confidential information about their employees. For example, in *Levias v. United Airlines,* 500 N.E.2d 370 (Ohio Ct. App. 1985), the court held that a flight attendant had a viable public disclosure action when her employer disclosed medical information from her gynecologist to her supervisors and her husband. The disclosure of personal information by public sector employers can give rise to a § 1983 action for a violation of the constitutional right to information privacy.

B. WORKPLACE SURVEILLANCE

THOMPSON V. JOHNSON COUNTY COMMUNITY COLLEGE

930 F. Supp. 501 (D. Kan. 1996)

[The plaintiffs, a group of community college security personnel, sued the college for conducting video surveillance of their locker area. Among other things, the plaintiffs alleged that the surveillance violated federal wiretap law and the Fourth Amendment.]

VAN BEBBER, J. . . . Plaintiffs first claim that defendants violated Title I by conducting video surveillance in the workplace. Under Title I, "any person whose wire or oral communications is intercepted, disclosed or used in violation of [the Act] may in a civil action recover from the person or entity which engage in that violation such relief as may be appropriate." 18 U.S.C. § 2520. . . .

Virtually every circuit that has addressed the issue of silent video surveillance has held that Title I does not prohibit its use. . . .

On the other hand, the above cited cases implicitly imply that video surveillance that includes the capability to record audio conversations would violate Title I. In that situation, the video image captured by the surveillance camera is not what violates Title I. Rather, it is the interception of an oral communication that subjects the interceptor to liability.

In their current motion, defendants argue that they installed a silent video surveillance camera in the security personnel locker area. Defendants contend that, as a matter of law, they are entitled to summary judgment on this issue because silent video surveillance does not fall within the protection of Title I. The court agrees. . . .

In Count II, plaintiffs have brought a claim pursuant to 42 U.S.C. § 1983. They contend that defendants' warrantless video surveillance searches of the security personnel locker area violated their Fourth Amendment rights. The court disagrees.

Domestic silent video surveillance is subject to Fourth Amendment prohibitions against unreasonable searches. However, this does not mean that defendants' use of video surveillance automatically violated plaintiffs' Fourth Amendment rights. Rather, the court first must determine whether plaintiffs had a reasonable expectation of privacy in their locker area. If plaintiffs had no reasonable expectation of privacy in this area, there is "no fourth amendment violation regardless of the nature of the search." . . .

. . . [D]efendants assert that the security personnel locker area is similar to hallway lockers in a school. The security personnel locker area was part of a storage room that also housed the College's heating and air-conditioning equipment. Additionally, the College did not limit access to this storage room. Security personnel and other college employees, including maintenance and service personnel, had unfettered access to this storage room. Consequently, defendants argue that the open, public nature of the security personnel locker area defeats any reasonable expectation of privacy in this area. The court agrees.

. . . [V]ideo surveillance "in public places, such as banks, does not violate the fourth amendment; the police may record what they normally may view with the naked eye." In the employment context, the Supreme Court has held that "some government offices may be so open to fellow employees or the public that no expectation of privacy is reasonable." *O'Connor v. Ortega,* 480 U.S. 709 (1987). . . .

In the instant action, viewing the facts in a light most favorable to plaintiffs, the court finds that they did not have a reasonable expectation of privacy in the security personnel locker area. This area was not enclosed. Plaintiffs' activities could be viewed by anyone walking into or through the storage room/security personnel locker area. Additionally, plaintiffs cannot maintain that the security personnel locker area was reserved for their exclusive use considering that other college personnel also had regular access to this area. The court concludes that plaintiffs' lack of a reasonable expectation of privacy in the security personnel locker area defeats their claim that defendants violated their Fourth Amendment right to privacy.

NOTES & QUESTIONS

1. ***Intrusion upon Seclusion and Surveillance in the Workplace.*** In *Speer v. Ohio Department of Rehabilitation & Correction,* 624 N.E.2d 251 (Ohio Ct. App. 1993), rumors reached Leroy Payton, the supervisor of plaintiff Theresa Speer (a prison official), that Speer was being "too friendly" with two inmates. Payton launched an investigation and surveillance of Speer. In one instance, Payton hid in the ceiling of a co-ed staff rest room for over seven hours to spy on Speer. The trial court held that Payton's surveillance was pursuant to a broad policy of decision making and refused to second-guess Payton's choice of surveillance tactic. The court of appeals reversed, concluding that Payton's tactics were unreasonable and not defensible as a policy matter.

2. ***Intrusion upon Seclusion and Surveillance Outside the Workplace.*** In *Saldana v. Kelsey-Hayes,* 443 N.W.2d 382 (Mich. Ct. App. 1981), the plaintiff injured his back and arm from falling off a bicycle on the property of his employer, defendant Kelsey-Hayes Company. The defendant's property was comprised of different buildings, and plaintiff used his bicycle to travel from building to building. The plaintiff's employer suspected that the plaintiff was malingering and hired a private investigating firm to determine the extent of the plaintiff's injuries. The investigator observed the plaintiff's home from a parked car near his house, telephoned the plaintiff to determine whether he was home, walked passed the plaintiff's house and observed the plaintiff through an open window, used a powerful zoom lens to observe the plaintiff through the windows to his house, and posed as a process server in order to gain entry to the plaintiff's home and look around. According to the investigator, the plaintiff was able to move around freely. The plaintiff brought an action against his employer for intrusion upon seclusion. The court, however, concluded that the plaintiff's action should be dismissed:

> . . . [P]laintiff can show an intrusion. First, agents of defendants entered plaintiff's home under false pretenses. Also, agents of defendants observed plaintiff through the windows of his home by the naked eye and with a powerful camera lens. Other jurisdictions have held that "window-peeping" is actionable. Whether the intrusion is objectionable to a reasonable person is a factual question best determined by a jury. It may not be objectionable to peer through an open window where the curtains are not drawn, but the use of a powerful lens to observe the interior of a home or of a subterfuge to enter a home could be found objectionable to a reasonable person.
>
> However, even if we find that looking into plaintiff's window with the naked eye and with a powerful camera lens is an intrusion which would be objectionable to a reasonable person, plaintiff still cannot prevail. Plaintiff does not allege facts that show the intrusions were into matters which plaintiff had a right to keep private. . . . The defendants' duty to refrain from intrusion into another's private affairs is not absolute in nature, but rather is limited by those rights which arise from social conditions, *including the business relationship of the parties.* Defendants' surveillance of plaintiff at his home involved matters which defendants had a legitimate right to investigate. . . . Plaintiff's privacy was subject to the legitimate interest of his employer in investigating suspicions that plaintiff's work-related disability was a pretext. We conclude that plaintiff does not meet the second requirement of the intrusion into seclusion test. Defendant also has a right to investigate matters that are potential sources of legal liability.

The *Saldana* court apparently treated the surveillance of the plaintiff outside the workplace as equivalent to surveillance inside the workplace. Should an employer be permitted to spy on its employees when they are not at work?

3. ***Limits on Employee Consent.*** Some states have enacted laws prohibiting surveillance cameras in certain areas of the workplace, such as rest rooms. Some of these prohibitions have criminal penalties. For example, pursuant to Conn. Gen. Stat. § 31-48b(b):

No employer or agent or representative of an employer shall operate any electronic surveillance device or system, including but not limited to the recording of sound or voice or a closed circuit television system, or any combination thereof, for the purpose of recording or monitoring the activities of his employees in areas designed for the health or personal comfort of the employees or for safeguarding of their possessions, such as rest rooms, locker rooms or lounges.

Violations are punishable by fines; repeat violations (third and subsequent violations) are punishable by imprisonment for 30 days.

Can employees consent to video surveillance in such areas? Why would they give such consent freely? Recall from the notes following *O'Connor v. Ortega* that employees can consent to searches that would ordinarily be unreasonable under the Fourth Amendment. But what about consenting to violations of criminal statutes? For an answer, see *Cramer v. Consolidated Freightways, Inc.* in the notes following *Baggs v. Eagle-Pitcher Industries, Inc.*

4. ***United States vs. European Workplace Privacy Rights.*** For Matthew Finkin, employee privacy law sits on a continental divide. In European civil law systems, employers may limit employee privacy rights only to realize "legitimate, even necessary, business objectives."[6] These civil rights rest on a perception of employees as persons "who bear inalienable rights, assertable against their employers, including a right to privacy." In contrast, the U.S. common law "accords the employer near plenary power to govern the workplace; in fact, to govern the worker." Finkin concludes that the conception of the "employee as a person — the law's Menschenbild — in the civil and common law differs and sharply." Finkin finds that in the United States, the workplace is often not viewed as a shared life "where property rights and individual liberties have any need to be reconciled." Finkin ends his article by demanding: "[A]re we so very confident . . . [t]hat employees can make no claim whatsoever to any private space at work?" Do you agree that employee privacy rights in the United States are so restricted to allow the "employer near plenary power to govern the workplace"? How should the law reconcile the employer's ability to carry out legitimate business objectives and employees' privacy rights?

C. WORKPLACE DRUG TESTING

NATIONAL TREASURY EMPLOYEES UNION V. VON RAAB
489 U.S. 656 (1989)

KENNEDY, J. . . . The United States Customs Service, a bureau of the Department of the Treasury, is the federal agency responsible for processing persons, carriers, cargo, and mail into the United States, collecting revenue from imports, and

---

[6] Matthew W. Finkin, *Menschenbild: The Conception of the Employee as a Person in Western Law*, 23 Comp. Lab. L. & Pol'y J. 577 (2002).

enforcing customs and related laws. An important responsibility of the Service is the interdiction and seizure of contraband, including illegal drugs. . . . In the routine discharge of their duties, many Customs employees have direct contact with those who traffic in drugs for profit. Drug import operations, often directed by sophisticated criminal syndicates, may be effected by violence or its threat. As a necessary response, many Customs operatives carry and use firearms in connection with their official duties.

In December 1985, respondent, the Commissioner of Customs . . . announced his intention to require drug tests of employees who applied for, or occupied, certain positions within the Service. . . .

In May 1986, the Commissioner announced implementation of the drug-testing program. Drug tests were made a condition of placement or employment for positions that meet one or more of three criteria. The first is direct involvement in drug interdiction or enforcement of related laws, an activity the Commissioner deemed fraught with obvious dangers to the mission of the agency and the lives of Customs agents. The second criterion is a requirement that the incumbent carry firearms, as the Commissioner concluded that "[p]ublic safety demands that employees who carry deadly arms and are prepared to make instant life or death decisions be drug free." The third criterion is a requirement for the incumbent to handle "classified" material, which the Commissioner determined might fall into the hands of smugglers if accessible to employees who, by reason of their own illegal drug use, are susceptible to bribery or blackmail.

After an employee qualifies for a position covered by the Customs testing program, the Service advises him by letter that his final selection is contingent upon successful completion of drug screening. An independent contractor contacts the employee to fix the time and place for collecting the sample. On reporting for the test, the employee must produce photographic identification and remove any outer garments, such as a coat or a jacket, and personal belongings. The employee may produce the sample behind a partition, or in the privacy of a bathroom stall if he so chooses. To ensure against adulteration of the specimen, or substitution of a sample from another person, a monitor of the same sex as the employee remains close at hand to listen for the normal sounds of urination. Dye is added to the toilet water to prevent the employee from using the water to adulterate the sample. . . .

The laboratory tests the sample for the presence of marijuana, cocaine, opiates, amphetamines, and phencyclidine. . . .

Customs employees who test positive for drugs and who can offer no satisfactory explanation are subject to dismissal from the Service. Test results may not, however, be turned over to any other agency, including criminal prosecutors, without the employee's written consent. . . .

Petitioners, a union of federal employees and a union official, commenced this suit . . . on behalf of current Customs Service employees who seek covered positions. Petitioners alleged that the Custom Service drug-testing program violated, inter alia, the Fourth Amendment. . . .

It is clear that the Customs Service's drug-testing program is not designed to serve the ordinary needs of law enforcement. Test results may not be used in a criminal prosecution of the employee without the employee's consent. The purposes of the program are to deter drug use among those eligible for promotion to sensitive positions within the Service and to prevent the promotion of drug users to those positions. These substantial interests . . . present a special need that may justify departure from the ordinary warrant and probable-cause requirements. . . .

. . . [A] warrant would provide little or nothing in the way of additional protection of personal privacy. A warrant serves primarily to advise the citizen that an intrusion is authorized by law and limited in its permissible scope and to interpose a neutral magistrate between the citizen and the law enforcement officer "engaged in the often competitive enterprise of ferreting out crime." . . . A covered employee is simply not subject "to the discretion of the official in the field." The process becomes automatic when the employee elects to apply for, and thereafter pursue, a covered position. Because the Service does not make a discretionary determination to search based on a judgment that certain conditions are present, there are simply "no special facts for a neutral magistrate to evaluate." . . .

Even where it is reasonable to dispense with the warrant requirement in the particular circumstances, a search ordinarily must be based on probable cause. Our cases teach, however, that the probable-cause standard "'is peculiarly related to criminal investigations.'" In particular, the traditional probable-cause standard may be unhelpful in analyzing the reasonableness of routine administrative functions, especially where the Government seeks to prevent the development of hazardous conditions or to detect violations that rarely generate articulable grounds for searching any particular place or person. Our precedents have settled that, in certain limited circumstances, the Government's need to discover such latent or hidden conditions, or to prevent their development, is sufficiently compelling to justify the intrusion on privacy entailed by conducting such searches without any measure of individualized suspicion. We think the Government's need to conduct the suspicionless searches required by the Customs program outweighs the privacy interests of employees engaged directly in drug interdiction, and of those who otherwise are required to carry firearms. . . .

We think Customs employees who are directly involved in the interdiction of illegal drugs or who are required to carry firearms in the line of duty likewise have a diminished expectation of privacy in respect to the intrusions occasioned by a urine test. Unlike most private citizens or government employees in general, employees involved in drug interdiction reasonably should expect effective inquiry into their fitness and probity. Much the same is true of employees who are required to carry firearms. Because successful performance of their duties depends uniquely on their judgment and dexterity, these employees cannot reasonably expect to keep from the Service personal information that bears directly on their fitness. While reasonable tests designed to elicit this information doubtless infringe some privacy expectations, we do not believe these expectations outweigh the Government's compelling interests in safety and in the integrity of our borders.

. . . [P]etitioners argue that the program is unjustified because it is not based on a belief that testing will reveal any drug use by covered employees. In pressing this argument, petitioners point out that the Service's testing scheme was not implemented in response to any perceived drug problem among Customs employees, and that the program actually has not led to the discovery of a significant number of drug users. Counsel for petitioners informed us at oral argument that no more than 5 employees out of 3,600 have tested positive for drugs. Second, petitioners contend that the Service's scheme is not a "sufficiently productive mechanism to justify [its] intrusion upon Fourth Amendment interests," because illegal drug users can avoid detection with ease by temporary abstinence or by surreptitious adulteration of their urine specimens. These contentions are unpersuasive. . . .

We are unable, on the present record, to assess the reasonableness of the Government's testing program insofar as it covers employees who are required "to handle classified material." We readily agree that the Government has a compelling interest in protecting truly sensitive information from those who, "under compulsion of circumstances or for other reasons, . . . might compromise [such] information." We also agree that employees who seek promotions to positions where they would handle sensitive information can be required to submit to a urine test under the Service's screening program, especially if the positions covered under this category require background investigations, medical examinations, or other intrusions that may be expected to diminish their expectations of privacy in respect of a urinalysis test.

It is not clear, however, whether the category defined by the Service's testing directive encompasses only those Customs employees likely to gain access to sensitive information. Employees who are tested under the Service's scheme include those holding such diverse positions as "Accountant," "Accounting Technician," "Animal Caretaker," "Attorney (All)," "Baggage Clerk," "Co-op Student (All)," "Electric Equipment Repairer," "Mail Clerk/Assistant," and "Messenger." . . . [I]t is not evident that those occupying these positions are likely to gain access to sensitive information, and this apparent discrepancy raises in our minds the question whether the Service has defined this category of employees more broadly than is necessary to meet the purposes of the Commissioner's directive.

We cannot resolve this ambiguity on the basis of the record before us, and we think it is appropriate to remand the case to the Court of Appeals for such proceedings as may be necessary to clarify the scope of this category of employees subject to testing. Upon remand the Court of Appeals should examine the criteria used by the Service in determining what materials are classified and in deciding whom to test under this rubric. . . .

SCALIA, J. joined by STEVENS, J. dissenting. . . . Until today this Court had upheld a bodily search separate from arrest and without individualized suspicion of wrongdoing only with respect to prison inmates, relying upon the uniquely dangerous nature of that environment. . . .

The Court's opinion in the present case . . . will be searched in vain for real evidence of a real problem that will be solved by urine testing of Customs Service employees. . . . The only pertinent points, it seems to me, are supported by nothing but speculation, and not very plausible speculation at that. It is not apparent to me that a Customs Service employee who uses drugs is significantly more likely to be bribed by a drug smuggler, any more than a Customs Service employee who wears diamonds is significantly more likely to be bribed by a diamond smuggler — unless, perhaps, the addiction to drugs is so severe, and requires so much money to maintain, that it would be detectable even without benefit of a urine test. Nor is it apparent to me that Customs officers who use drugs will be appreciably less "sympathetic" to their drug-interdiction mission, any more than police officers who exceed the speed limit in their private cars are appreciably less sympathetic to their mission of enforcing the traffic laws. . . . Nor, finally, is it apparent to me that urine tests will be even marginally more effective in preventing gun-carrying agents from risking "impaired perception and judgment" than is their current knowledge that, if impaired, they may be shot dead in unequal combat with unimpaired smugglers — unless, again, their addiction is so severe that no urine test is needed for detection.

What is absent in the Government's justifications — notably absent, revealingly absent, and as far as I am concerned dispositively absent — is the recitation of even a single instance in which any of the speculated horribles actually occurred: an instance, that is, in which the cause of bribe-taking, or of poor aim, or of unsympathetic law enforcement, or of compromise of classified information, was drug use. Although the Court points out that several employees have in the past been removed from the Service for accepting bribes and other integrity violations, and that at least nine officers have died in the line of duty since 1974, there is no indication whatever that these incidents were related to drug use by Service employees. . . .

Today's decision would be wrong, but at least of more limited effect, if its approval of drug testing were confined to that category of employees assigned specifically to drug interdiction duties. Relatively few public employees fit that description. But in extending approval of drug testing to that category consisting of employees who carry firearms, the Court exposes vast numbers of public employees to this needless indignity. Logically, of course, if those who carry guns can be treated in this fashion, so can all others whose work, if performed under the influence of drugs, may endanger others — automobile drivers, operators of other potentially dangerous equipment, construction workers, school crossing guards. A similarly broad scope attaches to the Court's approval of drug testing for those with access to "sensitive information." Since this category is not limited to Service employees with drug interdiction duties, nor to "sensitive information" specifically relating to drug traffic, today's holding apparently approves drug testing for all federal employees with security clearances — or, indeed, for all federal employees with valuable confidential information to impart. Since drug use is not a particular problem in the Customs Service, employees throughout the Government are no less likely to violate the public trust by taking bribes to feed their drug habit, or by yielding to blackmail. Moreover, there is no reason why this super-protection against harms arising from drug use must be limited to public employees; a law requiring similar testing of private citizens who use dangerous instruments such as guns or cars, or who have access to classified information, would also be constitutional. . . .

NOTES & QUESTIONS

1. **Von Raab *on Remand*.** The Supreme Court in *Von Raab* remanded the case "to clarify the scope of this category of employees subject to testing." In *National Treasury v. Hallett*, 756 F. Supp. 947 (E.D. La. 1991), the district court decided the remaining issues in this case. It found that there was "no constitutional infirmity in Customs drug screening program for applicants for covered positions." The *Hallett* court rejected the plaintiffs' argument that it

distinguish between "Customs employees holding top secret security clearances and those holding secret or confidential clearances." It found a compelling interest at stake, which it broadly defined as the risk that "an employee with access to sensitive information may disclose such information through off duty intoxication, blackmail, or bribery." Moreover, each applicant for a covered position is required to undergo a background check, which meant Customs already had substantial information regarding her personal life and finances. The court added that "[s]uch disclosures significantly reduce an applicant's privacy expectations."

2. ***Skinner v. Railway Labor Executives' Ass'n.*** In *Skinner v. Railway Labor Executives' Ass'n,* 489 U.S. 602 (1989), decided on the same day as *Von Raab,* the Court upheld regulations mandating blood and urine tests of railroad employees who were involved in certain train accidents:

> The Government's interest in regulating the conduct of railroad employees to ensure safety, like its supervision of probationers or regulated industries, or its operation of a government office, school, or prison, "likewise presents 'special needs' beyond normal law enforcement that may justify departures from the usual warrant and probable-cause requirements." . . .
>
> . . . [T]he Government interest in testing without a showing of individualized suspicion is compelling. Employees subject to the tests discharge duties fraught with such risks of injury to others that even a momentary lapse of attention can have disastrous consequences. Much like persons who have routine access to dangerous nuclear power facilities, employees who are subject to testing under the FRA regulations can cause great human loss before any signs of impairment become noticeable to supervisors or others. . . .
>
> A requirement of particularized suspicion of drug or alcohol use would seriously impede an employer's ability to obtain this information, despite its obvious importance. Experience confirms the FRA's judgment that the scene of a serious rail accident is chaotic. Investigators who arrive at the scene shortly after a major accident has occurred may find it difficult to determine which members of a train crew contributed to its occurrence. Obtaining evidence that might give rise to the suspicion that a particular employee is impaired, a difficult endeavor in the best of circumstances, is most impracticable in the aftermath of a serious accident.

Justice Scalia was in the majority in *Skinner.* Is this consistent with his dissent in *Von Raab*? Consider Scalia's explanation:

> Today, in *Skinner,* we allow a less intrusive bodily search of railroad employees involved in train accidents. I joined the Court's opinion there because the demonstrated frequency of drug and alcohol use by the targeted class of employees, and the demonstrated connection between such use and grave harm, rendered the search a reasonable means of protecting society. I decline to join the Court's opinion in the present case because neither frequency of use nor connection to harm is demonstrated or even likely. In my view the Customs Service rules are a kind of immolation of privacy and human dignity in symbolic opposition to drug use.

3. **Vernonia *vs.* Von Raab.** Recall Justice Scalia's opinion for the majority in *Vernonia School District,* where the Court held that suspicionless drug testing

of student athletes passed constitutional muster. Can his majority opinion in *Vernonia School District* be reconciled with his dissent in *Von Raab*?

4. *Drug Testing.* Drug tests often do not merely test for current drug impairment on the job; they can detect the presence of drug use in urine even if the person is not currently under the influence of drugs. Indeed, drugs can be detected in urine several weeks after use. As one court has observed: "[U]rine testing — unaided by blood or breath testing — is a blunt instrument. A single positive urine test is silent as to when and how much of the drug was taken, the pattern of the employee's drug use, or whether the employee was intoxicated when the test was given." *National Federation of Federal Employees v. Cheney,* 884 F.2d 603 (D.C. Cir. 1989) (sustaining U.S. Army's drug testing program based on *Von Raab* and *Skinner*). Imagine a worker who uses marijuana while at home and never on the job. What is the justification for forcing that worker to be tested for drugs? An assumption behind drug testing programs is that a drug user will more likely be impaired at work. Is this assumption warranted? For the purposes of ensuring workers are not likely to be impaired on the job, is there any difference between the recreational pot smoker and the social drinker?[7]

CHANDLER V. MILLER

520 U.S. 305 (1997)

GINSBURG, J. [The State of Georgia required candidates for certain state offices to take a drug test in order to qualify for election.]

Our precedents establish that the proffered special need for drug testing must be substantial — important enough to override the individual's acknowledged privacy interest, sufficiently vital to suppress the Fourth Amendment's normal requirement of individualized suspicion. Georgia has failed to show, in justification of § 21-2-140, a special need of that kind.

Respondents' defense of the statute rests primarily on the incompatibility of unlawful drug use with holding high state office. The statute is justified, respondents contend, because the use of illegal drugs draws into question an official's judgment and integrity; jeopardizes the discharge of public functions, including antidrug law enforcement efforts; and undermines public confidence and trust in elected officials. The statute, according to respondents, serves to deter unlawful drug users from becoming candidates and thus stops them from attaining high state office. Notably lacking in respondents' presentation is any indication of a concrete danger demanding departure from the Fourth Amendment's main rule.

Nothing in the record hints that the hazards respondents broadly describe are real and not simply hypothetical for Georgia's polity. . . .

---

[7] For more background about drug testing in the workplace, see John Gilliom, *Surveillance, Privacy, and the Law: Employee Drug Testing and the Politics of Social Control* (1994); John B. Wefing, *Employer Drug Testing: Disparate Judicial and Legislative Responses,* 63 Alb. L. Rev. 799 (2000); Stephen M. Fogel et al., *Survey of the Law on Employee Drug Testing,* 42 U. Miami L. Rev. 553 (1988); Edward M. Chen, Pauline T. Kim & John M. True, *Common Law Privacy: A Limit on an Employer's Power to Test for Drugs,* 12 Geo. Mason U. L. Rev. 651 (1990).

In contrast to the effective testing regimes upheld in *Skinner, Von Raab,* and *Vernonia,* Georgia's certification requirement is not well designed to identify candidates who violate antidrug laws. Nor is the scheme a credible means to deter illicit drug users from seeking election to state office. The test date — to be scheduled by the candidate anytime within 30 days prior to qualifying for a place on the ballot — is no secret. As counsel for respondents acknowledged at oral argument, users of illegal drugs, save for those prohibitively addicted, could abstain for a pretest period sufficient to avoid detection. . . . Moreover, respondents have offered no reason why ordinary law enforcement methods would not suffice to apprehend such addicted individuals, should they appear in the limelight of a public stage. Section 21-2-140, in short, is not needed and cannot work to ferret out lawbreakers, and respondents barely attempt to support the statute on that ground.

Respondents and the United States as *amicus curiae* rely most heavily on our decision in *Von Raab,* which sustained a drug-testing program for Customs Service officers prior to promotion or transfer to certain high-risk positions, despite the absence of any documented drug abuse problem among Service employees. . . .

Hardly a decision opening broad vistas for suspicionless searches, *Von Raab* must be read in its unique context. As the Customs Service reported in announcing the testing program: "Customs employees, more than any other Federal workers, are routinely exposed to the vast network of organized crime that is inextricably tied to illegal drug use." . . .

Respondents overlook a telling difference between *Von Raab* and Georgia's candidate drug-testing program. In *Von Raab* it was "not feasible to subject employees [required to carry firearms or concerned with interdiction of controlled substances] and their work product to the kind of day-to-day scrutiny that is the norm in more traditional office environments." Candidates for public office, in contrast, are subject to relentless scrutiny — by their peers, the public, and the press. Their day-to-day conduct attracts attention notably beyond the norm in ordinary work environments.

What is left, after close review of Georgia's scheme, is the image the State seeks to project. By requiring candidates for public office to submit to drug testing, Georgia displays its commitment to the struggle against drug abuse. . . . But Georgia asserts no evidence of a drug problem among the State's elected officials, those officials typically do not perform high-risk, safety-sensitive tasks, and the required certification immediately aids no interdiction effort. The need revealed, in short, is symbolic, not "special," as that term draws meaning from our case law. . . .

BORSE V. PIECE GOODS SHOP

963 F.2d 611 (3d Cir. 1992)

BECKER, C.J. Plaintiff Sarah Borse brought suit against her former employer, Piece Goods Shop, Inc., in the district court for the Eastern District of Pennsylvania. She claimed that, by dismissing her when she refused to submit to urinalysis screening and personal property searches (conducted by her employer at the workplace pursuant to its drug and alcohol policy), the Shop violated a public policy that precludes employers from engaging in activities that violate their employees' rights to privacy and to freedom from unreasonable searches. Pursuant to Federal Rule of Civil Procedure 12(b)(6), the district court dismissed her complaint for failure to state a claim on which relief could be granted. This appeal requires us to decide whether an at-will employee who is discharged for refusing to consent to urinalysis screening for drug use and to searches of her personal property states a claim for wrongful discharge under Pennsylvania law. . . .

Borse was employed as a sales clerk by the Piece Goods Shop for almost fifteen years. In January 1990, the Shop adopted a drug and alcohol policy which required its employees to sign a form giving their consent to urinalysis screening for drug use and to searches of their personal property located on the Shop's premises.

Borse refused to sign the consent form. On more than one occasion, she asserted that the drug and alcohol policy violated her right to privacy and her right to be free from unreasonable searches and seizures as guaranteed by the United States Constitution. The Shop continued to insist that she sign the form and threatened to discharge her unless she did. On February 9, 1990, the Shop terminated Borse's employment.

The complaint alleges that Borse was discharged in retaliation for her refusal to sign the consent form and for protesting the Shop's drug and alcohol policy. It asserts that her discharge violated a public policy, embodied in the First and Fourth Amendments to the United States Constitution, which precludes employers from engaging in activities that violate their employees' rights to privacy and to freedom from unreasonable searches of their persons and property. Plaintiff seeks compensatory damages for emotional distress, injury to reputation, loss of earnings, and diminished earning capacity. She also alleges that the discharge was willful and malicious and, accordingly, seeks punitive damages. . . .

Ordinarily, Pennsylvania law does not provide a common-law cause of action for the wrongful discharge of an at-will employee. Rather, an employer "may discharge an employee with or without cause, at pleasure, unless restrained by some contract."

In *Geary v. United States Steel Corp.,* 319 A.2d 174 (Pa. 1974), however, the Pennsylvania Supreme Court recognized the possibility that an action for wrongful discharge might lie when the firing of an at-will employee violates public policy. . . .

In order to evaluate Borse's claim, we must attempt to "discern whether any public policy is threatened" by her discharge. As evidence of a public policy that precludes employers from discharging employees who refuse to consent to the practices at issue, Borse primarily relies upon the First and Fourth Amendments to the United States Constitution and the right to privacy included in the Pennsylvania Constitution. As will be seen, we reject her reliance on these constitutional provisions, concluding instead that, to the extent that her discharge implicates public policy, the source of that policy lies in Pennsylvania common law. . . .

In light of the narrowness of the public policy exception and of the Pennsylvania courts' continuing insistence upon the state action requirement, we predict that if faced with the issue, the Pennsylvania Supreme Court would not look to the First and Fourth Amendments as sources of public policy when there is no state action. . . .

Although we have rejected Borse's reliance upon constitutional provisions as evidence of a public policy allegedly violated by the Piece Goods Shop's drug and alcohol program, our review of Pennsylvania law reveals other evidence of a public policy that may, under certain circumstances, give rise to a wrongful discharge action related to urinalysis or to personal property searches. Specifically, we refer to the Pennsylvania common law regarding tortious invasion of privacy.

Pennsylvania recognizes a cause of action for tortious "intrusion upon seclusion." *Marks v. Bell Telephone Co.,* 331 A.2d 424 (Pa. 1975). The Restatement defines the tort as follows:

> One who intentionally intrudes, physically or otherwise, upon the solitude or seclusion of another or his private affairs or concerns, is subject to liability to the other for invasion of his privacy, if the intrusion would be highly offensive to a reasonable person. Restatement (Second) of Torts § 652B. . . .

We can envision at least two ways in which an employer's urinalysis program might intrude upon an employee's seclusion. First, the particular manner in which the program is conducted might constitute an intrusion upon seclusion as defined by Pennsylvania law. The process of collecting the urine sample to be tested clearly implicates "expectations of privacy that society has long recognized as reasonable." In addition, many urinalysis programs monitor the collection of the urine specimen to ensure that the employee does not adulterate it or substitute a sample from another person. Monitoring collection of the urine sample appears to fall within the definition of an intrusion upon seclusion because it involves the use of one's senses to oversee the private activities of another.

As the United States Supreme Court has observed:

> There are few activities in our society more personal or private than the passing of urine. Most people describe it by euphemisms if they talk about it at all. It is a function traditionally performed without public observation; indeed, its performance in public is generally prohibited by law as well as social custom.

Skinner, 109 S. Ct. at 1413. If the method used to collect the urine sample fails to give due regard to the employees' privacy, it could constitute a substantial and highly offensive intrusion upon seclusion.

Second, urinalysis "can reveal a host of private medical facts about an employee, including whether she is epileptic, pregnant, or diabetic." *Skinner,* 109 S. Ct. at 1413. A reasonable person might well conclude that submitting urine samples to tests designed to ascertain these types of information constitutes a substantial and highly offensive intrusion upon seclusion.

The same principles apply to an employer's search of an employee's personal property. If the search is not conducted in a discreet manner or if it is done in such a way as to reveal personal matters unrelated to the workplace, the search might well constitute a tortious invasion of the employee's privacy. See, for example, *K-Mart Corp. v. Trotti,* 677 S.W.2d 632 (Tex. App. 1984) (search of employee's locker). . . .

. . . [W]e believe that when an employee alleges that his or her discharge was related to an employer's invasion of his or her privacy, the Pennsylvania Supreme

Court would examine the facts and circumstances surrounding the alleged invasion of privacy. If the court determined that the discharge was related to a substantial and highly offensive invasion of the employee's privacy, we believe that it would conclude that the discharge violated public policy. . . .

In view of the foregoing analysis, we predict that the Pennsylvania Supreme Court would apply a balancing test to determine whether the Shop's drug and alcohol program (consisting of urinalysis and personal property searches) invaded Borse's privacy. . . . The test we believe that Pennsylvania would adopt balances the employee's privacy interest against the employer's interest in maintaining a drug-free workplace in order to determine whether a reasonable person would find the employer's program highly offensive. . . .

In sum, based on our prediction of Pennsylvania law, we hold that dismissing an employee who refused to consent to urinalysis testing and to personal property searches would violate public policy if the testing tortiously invaded the employee's privacy. . . .

NOTES & QUESTIONS

1. ***Sources of Public Policy.*** Do you agree with the reasoning of *Borse*'s distinction between constitutional law and tort law as sources of public policy in suits for wrongful termination in violation of public policy against private sector employers? For a contrasting view with regard to constitutional law, consider *Hennessey v. Coastal Eagle Point Oil Co.,* 609 A.2d 11 (N.J. 1992), where the New Jersey Supreme Court held that state constitutional law could be a source of public policy as applied in wrongful termination suits against private sector employers (for random urine testing). The court concluded:

> . . . [P]ersuasive precedent supports finding a clear mandate of public policy in privacy rights from several sources. Although one of those sources is the State Constitution, we emphasize that we are *not* finding in this opinion a constitutional right to privacy that governs the conduct of private actors. Rather, we find only that existing constitutional privacy protections may form the basis for a clear mandate of public policy supporting a wrongful-discharge claim. . .
> .
>
> In ascertaining whether an employee's individual rights constitute a "clear mandate of public policy," we must balance the public interest against the employee's right. If the employee's duties are so fraught with hazard that his or her attempts to perform them while in a state of drug impairment would pose a threat to co-workers, to the workplace, or to the public at large, then the employer must prevail.

For other states that follow a similar approach to *Hennessey,* see *Palmateer v. International Harvester Co.,* 421 N.E.2d 876 (Ill. 1981); *Cort v. Bristol-Myers Co.,* 431 N.E.2d 908 (Mass. Ct. App. 1982); *Twigg v. Hercules Corp.,* 406 S.E.2d 52 (W. Va. Ct. App. 1990); *Luedtke v. Nabors Alaska Drilling, Inc.,* 768 P.2d 1123 (Alaska 1989).

Consider Pauline Kim's argument that the privacy torts should serve as a source of public policy:

. . . [T]he public-policy exception is now widely recognized to apply in at least three types of situations: when an employee is discharged for refusing to commit an illegal act, for asserting an established job-related right (for example, by filing for workers' compensation benefits), or for fulfilling a public obligation (such as serving on jury duty). . . .

The common law privacy tort, by prohibiting unreasonable intrusions on the private concerns of another, also imposes a socially defined duty independent of any contractual relationship between the parties. Like participation in the jury system, respect for personal privacy is high on the scale of values in this society. And, as in the case of workers' compensation benefits, an employee's common law right of privacy is socially established independent of the terms of the employment relationship and should not be subject to waiver under threat of discharge. Because the interests it protects are at least as fundamental as others already found to warrant an exception to the at-will rule, the common law tort of invasion of privacy should be recognized as a public policy limiting an employer's authority to discharge.[8]

What other forms of information privacy law might serve as sources of public policy?

2. ***Direct Constitutional Liability for Private Sector Employers.*** In most states, and under the federal Constitution, constitutional provisions do not apply directly to private sector employers. As you have seen, however, state and federal constitutional law can serve in some jurisdictions as the source of public policy in a wrongful termination claim. Moreover, in California, as we have noted above, the California Constitution applies directly to private sector employers. The California Supreme Court has held that the right to privacy in Article I, § 1 of the California Constitution "creates a right of action against private as well as government entities." *Hill v. NCAA,* 865 P.2d 633 (Cal. 1994).

D. THE ISSUE OF CONSENT

BAGGS V. EAGLE-PICHER INDUSTRIES, INC.

750 F. Supp. 264 (W.D. Mich. 1990)

BELL, J. . . . This case arises out of surprise drug test conducted by defendant in August 1989. Defendant is an Ohio corporation with a division located in Kalkaska, Michigan. The Kalkaska plant is defendant's Trim Division which makes parts such as headliners and door panels for the automotive industry. Employees at defendant's plant work in teams in the assembly process. Some of the activities conducted by the teams are potentially hazardous such as hydraulic and electronic presses, forklifts and hot glue and adhesive.

Defendant employs approximately 230 people at its Kalkaska plant. [The employees were at-will employees and could be terminated without cause.]. . .

---

[8] Pauline T. Kim, *Privacy Rights, Public Policy, and the Employment Relationship*, 57 Ohio St. L.J. 671, 722, 724 (1996).

In 1988 and 1989, defendant's management became aware of a drug problem at its Kalkaska plant. . . . In response to this information, defendant posted a drug free workplace policy in April 1989. This policy prohibited employees from possessing, using or being under the influence of drugs while at work and provided that employees could be tested for drug use. Defendant also required all new applicants to submit to drug testing as a prerequisite to being hired.

In April 1989, defendant consulted with the Grand Traverse Narcotics Team and the Kalkaska County Sheriff and placed an undercover officer in the plant as an employee. . . . After the undercover officer finished his undercover work, he reported to defendant's management that he estimated that as many as 60% of defendant's employees used drugs at home, at work or both. . . .

On July 17, 1989 a new drug free workplace policy was posted. That policy stated:

> . . . In order to protect the well-being of our employees, our facilities and the community in which we live, each employee, as a condition of employment will be required, upon request of Company supervisory personnel, to submit to blood and/or urine tests for determining use of alcohol and/or illegal or illicit drugs. . .

On August 10 and 11, 1989, defendant announced that it was going to conduct drug testing on those days. Only three people in management knew about the tests ahead of time. The men and women employees were asked to go into the men and women's bathrooms respectively and produce urine samples. There was a nurse present in each bathroom (a male nurse in the men's bathroom and a female nurse in the women's). Employees were told that, if they did not want to take the test, they could leave the plant and they would be considered a voluntary quit. Some employees who are plaintiffs in this suit did leave and were considered as voluntary quits as of that date. . . . A number of the plaintiffs tested positive for marijuana, one tested positive for cocaine and one for propoxyphene. . . .

Count I of plaintiffs' third amended complaint alleges breach of contract for the failure of defendant to follow the progressive disciplinary stages set forth in the employee handbook in the drug testing and termination of employees. . . .

Defendant argues that Count I of plaintiffs' third amended complaint should be dismissed because defendant did not breach any contract with plaintiffs. Defendants argue that plaintiffs' employment was an at-will employment and that defendant was under no obligation to use the progressive disciplinary procedures set out in the handbook in this situation. . . .

. . . [T]he employees in the present case signed employment applications which contained language making their employment at-will and the handbook did not contain any language stating that employment with defendant would terminate only upon a showing of just cause. [Therefore, the defendant's motion for summary judgment as to Count I is granted.] . . .

Count III of plaintiffs' third amended complaint alleges invasion of privacy under the United States and Michigan constitutions. Defendant argues that plaintiffs have no cause of action for a constitutional violation because defendant is a private not a government actor. . . .

The Fourth Amendment to the United States Constitution does not protect against a search or seizure by a private party on its own initiative, even if the search or seizure is an arbitrary action. The Court knows of no such protection under the

Michigan Constitution and plaintiffs have provided no support for such protection. Plaintiffs are, therefore, left to their claims of the tort of [intrusion upon seclusion.] . . .

Plaintiffs in this case are divided into two classes. One class consists of plaintiffs who refused to participate in the testing and the other consists of those who tested positive for drugs. Those who did not participate cannot succeed on this count because there was no intrusion. Therefore, Count III will be dismissed as to those plaintiffs.

As to the remaining plaintiffs, the Court finds that the taking of urine samples is an intrusion in an area in which plaintiffs may have an expectation of privacy. However, in this case, the Court finds that plaintiffs had no expectation of privacy with regard to drug testing since they had been on notice since July 17, 1989 that they might be subjected to drug testing as a condition of employment. . . . [E]mployers have a right to investigate into areas which would normally be private if the investigation springs from the business relationship. In this case, the employer was concerned about the safety of its workers and the productivity of the plant. This was a justifiable concern since the work at defendant's plant included activity which could be hazardous to someone who was not in total control of his faculties. Defendant has stated that there were several activities at its plant which gave rise to concern. The combination of the notice and the business concerns leads this Court to find that plaintiffs did not have an expectation of privacy with regard to urinalysis under the law of Michigan.

The final element of the tort is that the intrusion be offensive to a reasonable person. The Court finds that plaintiffs cannot prove this third element. The testing was carried on in the bathroom with a nurse present and the nurse was of the appropriate gender. In addition, anyone who wanted the additional privacy of a stall in which to give the sample had just to ask. . . .

In conclusion, the Court finds that all of plaintiffs' claims are without merit and grants defendant's motion for summary judgment as to all counts of plaintiffs' third amended complaint. Plaintiffs' third amended complaint will be dismissed.

NOTES & QUESTIONS

1. ***The Effect of Consent on Employer Liability for Privacy Torts.*** In *Baggs,* do you agree that providing notice to employees that they will be subjected to drug testing eliminates their expectations of privacy? In a number of cases, courts have held that employers requiring employees to consent to drug testing (or to surveillance or monitoring) shield themselves from liability under the intrusion upon seclusion tort because the employees consented to the intrusion. For example, in *Jennings v. Minco Technology Labs,* 765 S.W.2d 497 (Tex. Ct. App. 1989), Minco Technology Labs initiated a random drug testing program requiring employees to consent before testing about 16 months after plaintiff Brenda Jennings had begun to work for the defendant. An at-will employee, Jennings was unwilling to accept the new terms of employment and sued for intrusion upon seclusion, arguing that she was permitted to continue her employment without agreeing to the drug tests. The Texas court concluded:

Jennings's employer threatens no *unlawful* invasion of any employee's privacy interest; therefore it threatens no act contrary to the public policy underlying the common-law right of privacy. The company's plan contemplates, rather, that an employee's urine will be taken and tested only if he consents. The plan therefore assumes, respects, and depends upon the central element of the right of privacy and its attendant public policy: the individual's exclusive right to determine the occasion, extent, and conditions under which he will disclose his private affairs to others. This consensual predicate to any test reduces Jennings's argument to her remaining contention.

Jennings contends finally that she is poor and needs her salary to maintain herself and her family. Consequently, any "consent" she may give, in submitting to urinalysis, will be illusory and not real. For that practical reason, she argues, the company's plan *does* threaten a non-consensual, and therefore unlawful, invasion of her privacy. We disagree with the theory. A competent person's legal rights and obligations, under the common law governing the making, interpretation, and enforcement of contracts, cannot vary according to his economic circumstances. There cannot be one law of contracts for the rich and another for the poor. We cannot imagine a theory more at war with the basic assumptions held by society and its law. Nothing would introduce greater disorder into both. Because Jennings may not be denied the legal rights others have under the common law of contracts, she may not be given greater rights than they. The law views her economic circumstances as neutral and irrelevant facts insofar as her contracts are concerned.

2. ***The Limits of Consent.*** What does "consent" mean? Given the disparate power relationship between employers and employees, are many employment conditions really consensual? If you view consent narrowly to exist only when power relationships are close to equal, then what is the effect on the ability for employers and employees to make contracts?

Consider *Feminist Women's Health Center v. Superior Court,* 61 Cal. Rptr. 2d 187 (Cal. Ct. App. 1997). The Feminist Women's Health Center hired the plaintiff for the position of "feminist health worker." One of the responsibilities in the job description was to demonstrate a cervical self-examination to other women. In front of a group of other women, the plaintiff was to insert a plastic speculum into her vagina. According to the Health Center, the reason for the demonstration "is to demystify and redefine the normal functions of a woman's body. Our unique and effective, although not strictly necessary tool to accomplish this is for women to visualize their own cervixes and vaginas, which are not usually seen with the naked eye without the use of a vaginal speculum." After being hired, the plaintiff refused to demonstrate the cervical self-examination, and she was terminated by the Health Center. She sued for wrongful termination in violation of public policy, as embodied in the California Constitution, art. I, § 1, which provides: "All people are by nature free and independent and have inalienable rights. Among these are enjoying and defending life and liberty, acquiring, possessing, and protecting property, and pursuing and obtaining safety, happiness, and privacy." The court held:

> . . . [W]e agree with plaintiff that the observation of the insertion of a speculum into plaintiff's vagina by fellow employees and female clients of the Center infringes a legally protected privacy interest. This invasion is at least as serious

as observing urination, and we do not question plaintiff's assertions that it was contrary to her religious and cultural beliefs. . .

The real issue is whether this type of cervical self-examination may reasonably be required of the Center's employees. In other words, the seriousness of the privacy invasion leads us to the third part of the *Hill* test: consideration of the Center's countervailing interests and the feasibility of the alternatives proposed by plaintiff.

. . . [C]ervical self-examination is important in advancing the Center's fundamental goal of educating women about the function and health of their reproductive systems. . . .

The Center also could reasonably conclude that the alternative methods of self-examination proposed by plaintiff would have stifled such candor. These alternatives, such as the use of mannequins, or the private use of the speculum followed by discussion, are pale imitations of uninhibited group cervical self-examination. . . .

In balancing these competing interests, we return to plaintiff's consent to demonstrate cervical self-examination as part of her employment agreement with the Center. The Center was not obligated to hire plaintiff, and consent remains a viable defense even in cases of serious privacy invasions. Therefore, we believe the facts as disclosed in the trial court give rise to the following inferences only: the requirement that health workers perform cervical self-examinations in front of other females is a reasonable condition of employment and does not violate the health worker's right to privacy where the plaintiff's written employment agreement evidences her knowledge of this condition and agreement to be bound by it. Where the employee thereafter refuses to abide by the agreement, the employee's wrongful termination claim based on a violation of the right to privacy is rendered infirm. Such is the case under the facts presented, and the superior court should have granted summary adjudication of this claim.

Many laws restrict an employee's freedom to contract. For example, an employee may not agree to work for below minimum wage, be exposed to certain toxic materials, or commit an illegal act. Upon what basis should legislatures and courts distinguish between those things to which people can and cannot consent?

3. ***Consenting to Violations of Privacy Law and Collective Bargaining.*** Should labor law prohibit employers from bargaining with a union over certain privacy rights? Consider *Cramer v. Consolidated Freightways, Inc.,* 255 F.3d 683 (9th Cir. 2001) (en banc). Consolidated Freightways, a large trucking company, installed concealed video cameras and audio listening devices behind two-way mirrors in its rest rooms in order to discover and prevent drug use by its drivers. Employees discovered the cameras when a mirror fell off the rest room wall. Consolidated employees brought several suits seeking damages for invasion of privacy and infliction of emotional distress. They also sought an injunction to stop the surveillance. These cases were consolidated into one action.

The employees' union had a collective bargaining agreement (CBA) with Consolidated. One of the central issues in the case turned on whether § 301 of the Labor Management Relations Act (LMRA), 29 U.S.C. § 185, preempted the plaintiffs' claims, an issue that turned on whether the CBA's provisions could be interpreted as addressing the issue of surreptitious videotaping. The court concluded that it did not. The court also concluded:

> Even if the CBA did expressly contemplate the use of two-way mirrors to facilitate detection of drug users, such a provision would be illegal under California law, and it is well established in California that illegal provisions of a contract are void and unenforceable. Section 653n of the California Penal Code makes the installation and maintenance of two-way mirrors permitting the observation of restrooms illegal without reference to the reasonable expectations of those so viewed. Determination of guilt under the statute is not dependent on context or subjective factors; use of the mirrors is a per se violation of the penal code, and an assumption that the mirrors will not be used is per se reasonable.
>
> Under settled Supreme Court precedent, "§ 301 does not grant the parties to a collective-bargaining agreement the ability to contract for what is illegal under state law." Consolidated was therefore required to abide by the provisions of California penal law, and its employees had a right to assume their employer would obey the law. This assumption is inherently reasonable. Indeed, any contrary assumption would be irrational, because illegal behavior is unreasonable. Even if the CBA purported to reduce or limit this expectation in some way, that reduction would be illegal and therefore unenforceable. Because installation of two-way mirrors is immutably illegal, and freedom from the illegality is a "nonnegotiable state-law right[ ]," a court reviewing plaintiffs' claims that their privacy rights were violated need not interpret the CBA to arrive at its conclusion. By definition, therefore, plaintiffs in this action were reasonable in expecting to be free of the two-way mirrors and hidden video cameras installed in the restrooms.

Under California Penal Code § 653n, "[a]ny person who installs or who maintains . . . any two-way mirror permitting observation of any restroom, toilet, bathroom, washroom, shower, locker room, fitting room, motel room, or hotel room, is guilty of a misdemeanor." Do you agree with the court that employers and the union cannot bargain around this law? Would your conclusion be different if the applicable provision were tort law rather than criminal law?

Under *Cramer,* even if the employees desired to sacrifice their privacy in return for higher wages or other benefits, they could not make this bargain under the reasoning of the court. Does this result prevent employees from having the freedom to contract? Would a default rule that such surveillance is improper, but nonetheless could be bargained around, be preferable? Or if the law could be bargained around, would employees be able to circumvent the law too easily by forcing employees to agree to the privacy invasion?

4. ***Is Notice and Consent Adequate to Protect Privacy in the Workplace?*** Many employers are now providing privacy policies to their employees informing them of the types of workplace monitoring. Does providing notice and obtaining consent adequately protect employee privacy in the workplace? Consider the following argument by Pauline Kim:

> Clearly, the right to fire at will is not absolute. It has come into conflict with fundamental public concerns before, and yielded. Almost all the states recognize an exception to the at-will rule based on public policy. Even the

staunchest defenders of employment at will acknowledge some legitimate exceptions to the rule, as when the performance of a public duty or the protection of a public right is threatened. . . .

. . . [E]mployment is not an all-encompassing relationship. Although some territorial boundaries are necessarily breached to make employment possible, this implicit waiver of territorial claims does not automatically extend to those areas recognized to be at the core of personal privacy. Because employer and employee enter into the relationship for a specific, limited purpose, any implied waiver only extends as far as necessary to achieve that purpose. To conclude otherwise would set the employment relationship apart among social relationships, for the individual who could expect — and enforce — limits on unjustified intrusions by the government or third parties on core areas of privacy would have no such expectation vis-à-vis her employer. Given that the interests at stake are the same regardless of the source of the intrusion, it would be anomalous to treat the employer's actions as uniquely privileged. When core areas of privacy — those central to the self — are threatened, employer intrusions should not be permitted unless essential to meet some business need.[9]
. . .

Suppose an employer wanted to film its employees all hours of the day. Should employees be permitted to consent to such monitoring? Isn't this what the "Big Brother" television show did? This television show placed individuals in a house that had cameras in every room, including the bathrooms. The show was filmed in California. Suppose a contestant sued for intrusion upon seclusion. Under the reasoning of *Cramer,* would the contestant be able to sue for intrusion?

5. ***The Limits of Consenting to Privacy Protection.*** In *Giannecchini v. Hospital of St. Raphael,* 780 A.2d 1006 (Conn. Super. 2000), the plaintiff, a nurse, was fired by the defendant hospital (Hospital of St. Raphael) for making serious medication errors and demonstrating below average ability and industry. With the help of an attorney, the plaintiff negotiated an agreement with the hospital that all references in the nurse's file to an involuntary termination of employment would be expunged and that in response to any inquiries or reference requests by prospective employers, the hospital would not disclose any information except the plaintiff's dates of service, title, position, and salary information. The plaintiff later applied for a position as a registered nurse with another hospital, which sent St. Raphael a letter requesting information about the plaintiff. St. Raphael responded by stating that the nurse had been discharged, had below average ability and industry, and made several serious medication errors. Among other things, the plaintiff sued for breach of contract.

St. Raphael argued that the confidentiality agreement that it entered into with the nurse violated public policy because it did not account for the interest of third parties (namely, the safety of the patients in the hospital planning to hire the nurse). The court concluded that public policy was against disclosure, and therefore, the agreement was valid and that St. Raphael had breached it. Should

---

[9] Pauline T. Kim, *Privacy Rights, Public Policy, and the Employment Relationship*, 57 Ohio St. L.J. 671, 682, 703 (1996).

public policy prohibit confidentiality agreements that restrict the disclosure of information that might be relevant to the health and safety of third parties?

E. TESTING, QUESTIONNAIRES, AND POLYGRAPHS

1. TESTING AND QUESTIONNAIRES

GREENAWALT V. INDIANA DEPARTMENT OF CORRECTIONS

397 F.3d 587 (7th Cir. 2005)

[Kristin Greenawalt, a research analyst at the Indiana Department of Corrections, was told that in order to retain her job, she would be required to undergo a psychological test. This occurred two years after she was hired. She underwent the test but then sued under 42 U.S.C. § 1983, alleging that the test was an unreasonable search under the Fourth Amendment. She requested damages as well as an injunction forcing the department to remove the results of the test from her file.]

POSNER, C.J. . . . Almost any quest for information that involves a physical touching, which a test does not, is nowadays deemed a "search" within the meaning of the Fourth Amendment, which the Fourteenth Amendment has been interpreted as making fully applicable to state action. Drawing a tiny amount of blood from an unconscious person to determine the level of alcohol in his blood is a search, and so even is administering a breathalyzer test, where physical contact is at its minimum — the subject's lips merely touch the breathalyzer. And so finally is a urine test, in which the subject is required merely to provide a urine sample, so that the test instrument does not touch the subject's body at all. The invasion of privacy caused by submitting to the kind of psychological test given to the plaintiff in this case may well have been more profound than the invasion caused by a blood test, a breathalyzer test, or a urine test, though we cannot say for sure; the test is not in the record — all we know is that, according to the complaint, "the battery of psychological tests examined Ms. Greenawalt's personality traits, psychological adjustments and health-related issues." It is true that she consented to take the test, but had she not done so she would have lost her job, which, if she had a constitutional right not to take the test, would place a heavy burden on the exercise of her constitutional rights. . . .

. . . [W]e do not think that the Fourth Amendment should be interpreted to reach the putting of questions to a person, even when the questions are skillfully designed to elicit what most people would regard as highly personal private information. The cases we have cited show, it is true, that a Fourth Amendment claim does not depend on the claimant's being able to establish an invasion of such interests that tort law traditionally protects as the interest in bodily integrity (protected by the tort of battery), in freedom of movement (protected by the tort of false imprisonment), and in property (protected by the torts of trespass and of conversion). But that is all they show, so far as bears on the issue in this case. The implications of extending the doctrine of those cases to one involving mere questioning would be strange. In a case involving sex or some other private matter, a government trial lawyer might be required to obtain a search warrant before being allowed to conduct a cross-examination — or the judge before being allowed to ask a question of the witness. Police might have to obtain search warrants or waivers before conducting routine inquiries, even of the complaining witness in a rape case, since they would be inquiring about the witness's sexual behavior. Questioning in a police inquiry or a background investigation or even a credit check would be in peril of being deemed a search of the person about whom the questions were asked. Psychological tests, widely used in a variety of sensitive employments, would be deemed forbidden by the Constitution if a judge thought them "unreasonable." . . .

Even though administering a lie-detector test involves placing sensors on the skin of the person being interrogated, the Supreme Court has suggested that because the objective is to obtain testimonial rather than physical evidence, the relevant constitutional amendment is not the Fourth but the Fifth. . . . The Fourth Amendment was not drafted, and has not been interpreted, with interrogations in mind. . . .

Our conclusion that the plaintiff has not stated a Fourth Amendment claim does not leave people in her position remediless — or indeed leave her remediless. States are free to protect privacy more comprehensively than the Fourth Amendment commands; and Greenawalt is free to continue to press her state-law claims in state court, where they belong. In most states if prison officials were to publicize highly personal information obtained from someone in Greenawalt's position by the kind of test of which she complains, she would have a state-law claim for invasion of her tort right of privacy. Indiana, it is true, has thus far refused to recognize this branch of the tort law of privacy. *Felsher v. University of Evansville,* 755 N.E.2d 589 (Ind. 2001). But the Fourth Amendment does not expand accordion-like to fill what may be a gap in the privacy law of a particular state. And there are other strings to the plaintiff's state-law bow; it is possible, though perhaps unlikely in light of *Cullison v. Medley,* 570 N.E.2d 27 (Ind. 1991), that Indiana recognizes "intrusion into a person's emotional solace" as an actionable invasion of privacy. *Branham v. Celadon Trucking Services, Inc.,* 744 N.E.2d 514 (Ind. App. 2001). Greenawalt may also be able to obtain mileage from cases, none however in Indiana, that hold that requiring a public employee to take a lie-detector test without good cause is an invasion of privacy. *Texas State Employees Union v. Texas Dept. of Mental Health & Mental Retardation,* 746 S.W.2d 203 (Tex. 1987); *Long Beach City Employees Ass'n v. City of Long Beach,* 719 P.2d 660 (Cal. 1986). She may also be able to prove intentional infliction of emotional distress.

NOTES & QUESTIONS

1. *Should Questioning Be a "Search" Under the Fourth Amendment?* Judge Posner argues that if the Fourth Amendment deemed questioning a search, then a warrant might be required for a cross-examination or for the police to question a rape victim about her rape. Do these implications necessarily follow from a

holding that the psychological test constitutes a Fourth Amendment search? Posner also argues that the plaintiff has other state law options for redress. Assess her likelihood of prevailing on these alternative grounds.

2. ***The Constitutional Right to Information Privacy.*** In *Norman-Bloodsaw v. Lawrence Berkeley Laboratory,* 135 F.3d 1260 (9th Cir. 1998), plaintiffs were offered employment at Lawrence Berkeley Laboratory, but their employment was conditioned on their undergoing a medical examination. In addition to a questionnaire, the blood and urine of the employees was tested for syphilis, sickle cell, and pregnancy. This was done without the plaintiffs' knowledge and consent. The court held that the plaintiffs had a viable case for violations of two constitutional rights. The first was the right to information privacy, which the Supreme Court first identified in *Whalen v. Roe,* 429 U.S. 589 (1977) (the right to privacy protects "the individual interest in avoiding disclosure of personal matters"). The second constitutional right implicated in *Norman-Bloodsaw* was the Fourth Amendment. The Ninth Circuit stated:

> The constitutionally protected privacy interest in avoiding disclosure of personal matters clearly encompasses medical information and its confidentiality. Although cases defining the privacy interest in medical information have typically involved its disclosure to "third" parties, rather than the collection of information by illicit means, it goes without saying that the *most basic* violation possible involves the performance of unauthorized tests — that is, the non-consensual retrieval of previously unrevealed medical information that may be unknown even to plaintiffs. These tests may also be viewed as searches in violation of Fourth Amendment rights that require Fourth Amendment scrutiny. The tests at issue in this case thus implicate rights protected under both the Fourth Amendment and the Due Process Clause of the Fifth or Fourteenth Amendments.
>
> Because it would not make sense to examine the collection of medical information under two different approaches, we generally "analyze [ ] [medical tests and examinations] under the rubric of [the Fourth] Amendment." Accordingly, we must balance the government's interest in conducting these particular tests against the plaintiffs' expectations of privacy. Furthermore, "application of the balancing test requires not only considering the degree of intrusiveness and the state's interests in requiring that intrusion, but also 'the efficacy of this [the state's] means for meeting' its needs." . . .
>
> One can think of few subject areas more personal and more likely to implicate privacy interests than that of one's health or genetic make-up. Furthermore, the facts revealed by the tests are highly sensitive, even relative to other medical information. With respect to the testing of plaintiffs for syphilis and pregnancy, it is well established in this circuit "that the Constitution prohibits unregulated, unrestrained employer inquiries into personal sexual matters that have no bearing on job performance." The fact that one has syphilis is an intimate matter that pertains to one's sexual history and may invite tremendous amounts of social stigma. Pregnancy is likewise, for many, an intensely private matter, which also may pertain to one's sexual history and often carries far-reaching societal implications. Finally, the carrying of sickle cell trait can pertain to sensitive information about family history and reproductive decisionmaking. Thus, the conditions tested for were aspects of one's health in which one enjoys the highest expectations of privacy.

NATIONAL AERONAUTICS AND SPACE ADMINISTRATION V. NELSON

131 S. Ct. 746 (2011)

ALITO, J. In two cases decided more than 30 years ago, this Court referred broadly to a constitutional privacy "interest in avoiding disclosure of personal matters." *Whalen v. Roe,* 429 U.S. 589, (1977); *Nixon v. Administrator of General Services,* 433 U.S. 425 (1977). Respondents in this case, federal contract employees at a Government laboratory, claim that two parts of a standard employment background investigation violate their rights under *Whalen* and *Nixon.* Respondents challenge a section of a form questionnaire that asks employees about treatment or counseling for recent illegal-drug use. They also object to certain open-ended questions on a form sent to employees' designated references.

We assume, without deciding, that the Constitution protects a privacy right of the sort mentioned in *Whalen* and *Nixon.* We hold, however, that the challenged portions of the Government's background check do not violate this right in the present case. The Government's interests as employer and proprietor in managing its internal operations, combined with the protections against public dissemination provided by the Privacy Act of 1974, 5 U.S.C. § 552a, satisfy any "interest in avoiding disclosure" that may "arguably ha[ve] its roots in the Constitution." *Whalen, supra.* . . .

One NASA facility, the Jet Propulsion Laboratory (JPL) in Pasadena, California, is staffed exclusively by contract employees. NASA owns JPL, but the California Institute of Technology (Cal Tech) operates the facility under a Government contract. . . .

Twenty-eight JPL employees are respondents here. Many of them have worked at the lab for decades, and none has ever been the subject of a Government background investigation. At the time when respondents were hired, background checks were standard only for federal civil servants. In some instances, individual contracts required background checks for the employees of federal contractors, but no blanket policy was in place.

The Government has recently taken steps to eliminate this two-track approach to background investigations. In 2004, a recommendation by the 9/11 Commission prompted the President to order new, uniform identification standards for "[f]ederal employees," including "contractor employees." The Department of Commerce implemented this directive by mandating that contract employees with long-term access to federal facilities complete a standard background check, typically the National Agency Check with Inquiries (NACI). . . .

The NACI process has long been the standard background investigation for prospective civil servants. The process begins when the applicant or employee fills out a form questionnaire. Employees who work in "non-sensitive" positions (as all respondents here do) complete Standard Form 85 (SF-85). . . .

Most of the questions on SF-85 seek basic biographical information: name, address, prior residences, education, employment history, and personal and professional references. The form also asks about citizenship, selective-service registration, and military service. The last question asks whether the employee has "used, possessed, supplied, or manufactured illegal drugs" in the last year. If the answer is yes, the employee must provide details, including information about "any treatment or counseling received." A "truthful response," the form notes, cannot be used as evidence against the employee in a criminal proceeding. . . .

Once a completed SF-85 is on file, the "agency check" and "inquiries" begin. The Government runs the information provided by the employee through FBI and other federal-agency databases. It also sends out form questionnaires to the former employers, schools, landlords, and references listed on SF-85. The particular form at issue in this case — the Investigative Request for Personal Information, Form 42 — goes to the employee's former landlords and references.

Form 42 is a two-page document that takes about five minutes to complete. . . . After several preliminary questions about the extent of the reference's associations with the employee, the form asks if the reference has "any reason to question" the employee's "honesty or trustworthiness." It also asks if the reference knows of any "adverse information" concerning the employee's "violations of the law," "financial integrity," "abuse of alcohol and/or drugs," "mental or emotional stability," "general behavior or conduct," or "other matters." If "yes" is checked for any of these categories, the form calls for an explanation in the space below. . . .

About two months before the October 2007 deadline for completing the NACI, respondents brought this suit, claiming, as relevant here, that the background-check process violates a constitutional right to informational privacy. . . .

[The U.S. Court of Appeals for the Ninth Circuit held that several "questions are designed to elicit a wide range of adverse, private information that 'is not generally disclosed by individuals to the public'; accordingly, they must be deemed to implicate the right to informational privacy." The court concluded that the questions were not narrowly tailored to meet any legitimate need, and that "the form invites the recipient to reveal *any* negative information of which he or she is aware." *Nelson v. National Aeronautics and Space Administration,* 512 F.3d 1134 (9th Cir. 2008).]

As noted, respondents contend that portions of SF-85 and Form 42 violate their "right to informational privacy." This Court considered a similar claim in *Whalen.* . . . In discussing that claim, the Court said that "[t]he cases sometimes characterized as protecting 'privacy'" actually involved "at least two different kinds of interests": one, an "interest in avoiding disclosure of personal matters"; the other, an interest in "making certain kinds of important decisions" free from government interference. . . .

Whalen acknowledged that the disclosure of "private information" to the State was an "unpleasant invasion of privacy," but the Court pointed out that the New York statute contained "security provisions" that protected against "public disclosure" of patients' information. This sort of "statutory or regulatory duty to avoid unwarranted disclosures" of "accumulated private data" was sufficient, in the Court's view, to protect a privacy interest that "arguably ha[d] its roots in the Constitution." . . .

As was our approach in *Whalen,* we will assume for present purposes that the Government's challenged inquiries implicate a privacy interest of constitutional significance. We hold, however, that, whatever the scope of this interest, it does not prevent the Government from asking reasonable questions of the sort included on SF-85 and Form 42 in an employment background investigation that is subject to the Privacy Act's safeguards against public disclosure. . . .

The questions challenged by respondents are part of a standard employment background check of the sort used by millions of private employers. The Government itself has been conducting employment investigations since the earliest days of the Republic. Since 1871, the President has enjoyed statutory authority to "ascertain the fitness of applicants" for the civil service "as to age, health, character, knowledge and ability for the employment sought." . . . Standard background investigations similar to those at issue here became mandatory for all candidates for the federal civil service in 1953. . . .

As this long history suggests, the Government has an interest in conducting basic employment background checks. Reasonable investigations of applicants and employees aid the Government in ensuring the security of its facilities and in employing a competent, reliable workforce. Courts must keep those interests in mind when asked to go line-by-line through the Government's employment forms and to scrutinize the choice and wording of the questions they contain. . . .

With these interests in view, we conclude that the challenged portions of both SF-85 and Form 42 consist of reasonable, employment-related inquiries that further the Government's interests in managing its internal operations. As to SF-85, the only part of the form challenged here is its request for information about "any treatment or counseling received" for illegal-drug use within the previous year. The "treatment or counseling" question, however, must be considered in context. It is a follow-up to SF-85's inquiry into whether the employee has "used, possessed, supplied, or manufactured illegal drugs" during the past year. The Government has good reason to ask employees about their recent illegal-drug use. Like any employer, the Government is entitled to have its projects staffed by reliable, law-abiding persons who will "'efficiently and effectively'" discharge their duties. Questions about illegal-drug use are a useful way of figuring out which persons have these characteristics.

In context, the follow-up question on "treatment or counseling" for recent illegal-drug use is also a reasonable, employment-related inquiry. The Government, recognizing that illegal-drug use is both a criminal and a medical issue, seeks to separate out those illegal-drug users who are taking steps to address and overcome their problems. The Government thus uses responses to the "treatment or counseling" question as a mitigating factor in determining whether to grant contract employees long-term access to federal facilities. . . .

We reject the argument that the Government, when it requests job-related personal information in an employment background check, has a constitutional burden to demonstrate that its questions are "necessary" or the least restrictive means of furthering its interests. So exacting a standard runs directly contrary to *Whalen*. The patients in *Whalen*, much like respondents here, argued that New York's statute was unconstitutional because the State could not "demonstrate the necessity" of its program. The Court quickly rejected that argument, concluding that New York's collection of patients' prescription information could "not be held unconstitutional simply because" a court viewed it as "unnecessary, in whole or in part." . . .

The Court of Appeals also held that the broad, "open-ended questions" on Form 42 likely violate respondents' informational-privacy rights. . . .

These open-ended inquiries, like the drug-treatment question on SF-85, are reasonably aimed at identifying capable employees who will faithfully conduct the

Government's business. Asking an applicant's designated references broad, open-ended questions about job suitability is an appropriate tool for separating strong candidates from weak ones. It would be a truly daunting task to catalog all the reasons why a person might not be suitable for a particular job, and references do not have all day to answer a laundry list of specific questions. . . .

The reasonableness of such open-ended questions is illustrated by their pervasiveness in the public and private sectors. Form 42 alone is sent out by the Government over 1.8 million times annually. In addition, the use of open-ended questions in employment background checks appears to be equally commonplace in the private sector. . . .

Not only are SF-85 and Form 42 reasonable in light of the Government interests at stake, they are also subject to substantial protections against disclosure to the public. Both *Whalen* and *Nixon* recognized that government "accumulation" of "personal information" for "public purposes" may pose a threat to privacy. But both decisions also stated that a "statutory or regulatory duty to avoid unwarranted disclosures" generally allays these privacy concerns. . . .

The Privacy Act, which covers all information collected during the background-check process, allows the Government to maintain records "about an individual" only to the extent the records are "relevant and necessary to accomplish" a purpose authorized by law. 5 U.S.C. § 552a(e)(1). The Act requires written consent before the Government may disclose records pertaining to any individual. § 552a(b). And the Act imposes criminal liability for willful violations of its nondisclosure obligations. § 552a(i)(1). . . . Like the protections against disclosure in *Whalen* and *Nixon,* they "evidence a proper concern" for individual privacy.

Notwithstanding these safeguards, respondents argue that statutory exceptions to the Privacy Act's disclosure bar, see §§ 552a(b)(1)-(12), leave its protections too porous to supply a meaningful check against "unwarranted disclosures." Respondents point in particular to what they describe as a "broad" exception for "routine use[s]," defined as uses that are "compatible with the purpose for which the record was collected." §§ 552a(b)(3), (a)(7).

Respondents' reliance on these exceptions rests on an incorrect reading of both our precedents and the terms of the Privacy Act. . . . [T]he mere fact that the Privacy Act's nondisclosure requirement is subject to exceptions does not show that the statute provides insufficient protection against public disclosure.

Nor does the substance of the "routine use" exception relied on by respondents create any undue risk of public dissemination. None of the authorized "routine use[s]" of respondents' background-check information allows for release to the public. . . .

Citing past violations of the Privacy Act, respondents note that it is possible that their personal information could be disclosed as a result of a similar breach. But data breaches are a possibility any time the Government stores information. As the Court recognized in *Whalen,* the mere possibility that security measures will fail provides no "proper ground" for a broad-based attack on government information-collection practices. . . .

In light of the protection provided by the Privacy Act's nondisclosure requirement, and because the challenged portions of the forms consist of reasonable inquiries in an employment background check, we conclude that the

Government's inquiries do not violate a constitutional right to informational privacy.

NOTES & QUESTIONS

1. ***Collection vs. Disclosure.*** In *Nelson,* what is the nature of the disclosure? In *Whalen v. Roe,* the Supreme Court articulated the right as "the individual interest in avoiding disclosure of personal matters." It appeared to view the right as one protecting against disclosure of personal information that the government had already collected, not as a right that would prevent the government's gathering of personal information. Could the Supreme Court have decided *Nelson* merely by concluding that questionnaires to collect information, without any evidence of disclosure, simply did not implicate the constitutional right to information privacy?

2. ***The Threat of Disclosure.*** *Whalen* suggested that whenever the government collects information, it has a duty to keep it secure. Failure to secure data might give rise to a violation of the constitutional right to information privacy even if no data were disclosed. The plaintiffs argued that the Privacy Act provided insufficient protection to their data, but the Court concluded otherwise. Recall the cases and materials regarding the Privacy Act from Chapter 6. Does the Privacy Act provide adequate protection? Note that it says little about specific security measures, and it provides liability for willful violations but not negligent ones. How weak do statutory protections have to be to trigger a legitimate security concern?

   Suppose there were no Privacy Act. Would the Court's conclusion be different? Consider *Fraternal Order of Police, Lodge No. 5 v. City of Philadelphia,* 812 F.2d 105 (3d Cir. 1987), a case decided many years before *Nelson.* A police union challenged the constitutionality of a questionnaire used by the police department to select candidates for a special investigations unit. Among other things, the questionnaire contained questions dealing with physical and mental conditions, behavior, and financial information. The court held that the questions about physical and mental conditions were necessary to determine the officers' fitness for their positions in the special investigations unit. The financial information was relevant because of the assumption that officers with large debts would be more susceptible to the temptations of corruption in narcotics investigations. Likewise, the behavior information (gambling and alcohol use) was relevant for this purpose. However, the court held that the city's safeguards against unnecessary disclosure of the information were inadequate:

   > Safeguards against disclosure of private material have been held to be adequate when there exists a statutory penalty for unauthorized disclosures; when there exist security provisions to prevent mishandling of files coupled with an express regulatory policy prohibiting disclosure; and in a unique situation when, even absent an explicit statutory or regulatory policy, the record supported the conclusion that those officials with private information would not disclose it.

In contrast, we find a complete absence of comparable protection of the confidential information to be disclosed in response to the SIU questionnaire. There is no directive limiting access to the responses to specific persons or specifying the handling and storage of the responses. . . . Apparently, there is no statute or regulation that penalizes officials with confidential information from disclosing it. . . .

3. *The Americans with Disabilities Act.* The Americans with Disabilities Act (ADA), 42 U.S.C. §§ 12112 *et seq.*, restricts the ability of employers to conduct medical examinations of job applicants. The ADA protects the rights of those with disabilities. A "disability" is defined as "a physical or mental impairment that substantially limits one or more of the major life activities of such individual." § 12102.

The ADA treats pre-employment and post-employment examinations and inquiries differently. Pursuant to § 12112(d):

(2) Preemployment.

(A) Prohibited examination or inquiry. Except as provided in paragraph (3), a covered entity shall not conduct a medical examination or make inquiries of a job applicant as to whether such applicant is an individual with a disability or as to the nature and severity of such disability.

(B) Acceptable injury. A covered entity may make preemployment inquiries into the ability of an applicant to perform job-related functions.

(3) Employment entrance examination. A covered entity may require a medical examination after an offer of employment has been made to a job applicant and prior to the commencement of the employment duties of such applicant, and may condition an offer of employment on the results of such examination, if—

(A) all entering employees are subjected to such an examination regardless of disability. . . .

Employers are more restricted in testing and making inquiries of employees once they are hired. Pursuant to § 12112(d)(4):

(4) Examination and inquiry

(A) Prohibited examinations and inquiries. A covered entity shall not require a medical examination and shall not make inquiries of an employee as to whether such employee is an individual with a disability or as to the nature and severity of the disability, unless such examination or inquiry is shown to be job-related and consistent with business necessity.

(B) Acceptable examinations and inquiries. A covered entity may conduct voluntary medical examinations, including voluntary medical histories, which are part of an employee health program available to employees at the work site. A covered entity may make inquiries into the ability of an employee to perform job-related functions.

Drug testing is not considered a "medical examination" under the ADA. § 12114(d).

4. *State Statutory Law.* Many states restrict certain forms of employment testing and questionnaires. For example, Wisconsin prohibits employers from requiring employees or applicants to undergo HIV testing:

> . . . [N]o employer or agent of an employer may directly or indirectly . . . [s]olicit or require as a condition of employment of any employee or prospective employee a test for the presence of HIV, antigen or nonantigenic products of HIV or an antibody to HIV. Wis. Stat. Ann. §103.15(2).

Massachusetts prohibits employers from asking prospective employees about arrests not leading to conviction, misdemeanor convictions, or any prior commitment to medical treatment facilities. *See* Mass. Gen. Laws ch. 151B § 4(9). Maryland restricts questions about disability or handicap unless it bears a direct and material relationship to the applicant's fitness for the job. *See* Md. Lab. & Empl. Code § 3-701. A number of states restrict genetic testing. *See, e.g.,* Cal. Govt. Code § 12940(o); Conn. Gen. Stat. Ann. § 46a-60(11)(A); Del. Code Ann. tit. 19 § 711(e); N.Y. Exec. Law § 296.19 (a)(1).

2. POLYGRAPH TESTING

The first lie detector was invented by William Marston around 1917. Marston claimed that his device could detect deception by measuring increases in systolic blood pressure. In *Frye v. United States,* 293 F. 1013 (D.C. Cir. 1923), a famous case in evidence law, a defendant wanted to offer evidence about his successful lie detector test, but the trial court refused to admit the evidence. The court of appeals concluded that "the systolic blood pressure deception test has not yet gained such standing and scientific recognition among physiological and psychological authorities as would justify the courts in admitting expert testimony deduced from the discovery, development, and experiments thus far made." In the 1930s, the prototype of the modern polygraph machine was developed. The modern polygraph device is a portable machine that uses moving paper and three styluses to record three physiological responses: galvanic skin response, relative blood pressure, and respiration. These responses are recorded by placing devices on the person's chest, abdomen, fingers, and arm.

The reliability of polygraphs is still subject to significant dispute. In his comprehensive history of the polygraph machine, Ken Adler argues:

> The proponents of lie detection have packaged their technique as a mechanical oracle that can read the body's hidden signs for evidence of deceit — while they sidestep the skeptical interpretative labor that scientists ordinarily demand of such claims. The lie detector and its progeny have been repeatedly denounced by respectable science — but since when has that stopped millions of Americans from believing in something, especially when the public media breathlessly extols its successes?[10]

According to Adler, the lie detector is "less a 'technology of truth' than a 'technology of truthiness.' "

---

[10] Ken Adler, *The Lie Detectors: The History of an American Obsession* 270-71 (2007).

Despite these concerns, polygraph use is at its highest level in two decades. Laurie Cohen argues that polygraph results should be considered as "good enough" in many settings. In particular, Cohen observes that the polygraph machine has become the "centerpiece in an expanding range of parole and probation programs that are designed to dissuade sex offenders and other felons from committing more crimes."[11] Adherents of the polygraph propose that the machine is useful even if its reliability levels are too low for many uses, because criminal offenders believe it works, which may deter them from committing new crimes.

Many courts continue to exclude polygraph evidence. A recent report from the National Research Council concluded that polygraph testing was too flawed for security screening. "Polygraph testing now rests on weak scientific underpinnings despite nearly a century of study," the report said. "And much of the available evidence for judging its validity lacks scientific rigor."[12]

Despite their questionable reliability, polygraphs are used by many employers when deciding whether to hire people or when investigating workplace misconduct. Polygraphs merely detect physiological responses to emotional arousal; they cannot detect thoughts or feelings directly. Are polygraphs more invasive to privacy than drug tests or written psychological exams?

In *Anderson v. City of Philadelphia,* 845 F.2d 1216 (3d Cir. 1988), a group of unsuccessful applicants for Philadelphia police and correctional officers claimed that the requirement of taking a polygraph test to obtain such jobs was unconstitutional. They argued that being forced to take a polygraph test violated their due process and equal protection rights. The court, however, concluded:

> In *Board of Regents v. Roth,* the Supreme Court made it clear that "[t]he requirements of procedural due process apply only to the deprivation of interests encompassed by the Fourteenth Amendment's protection of liberty and property." 408 U.S. 564, 569 (1972). . . .
>
> To demonstrate a property interest . . . these plaintiffs must show that under Pennsylvania law they had a legitimate claim of entitlement to employment as City police or prison officers.
>
> The plaintiffs here were never more than applicants for employment by the City. Although the plaintiffs occupied high positions on the civil service eligibility lists for the type of employment they sought, occupancy of these positions entitled the plaintiffs to nothing more than consideration for employment when openings occurred. . . .
>
> We therefore conclude that the plaintiffs' interest in the civil service positions they sought did not rise to the level of a property interest protected by the Constitution. . . .
>
> We next address the plaintiffs' argument that they have been denied equal protection of the law. . . . [We] will apply the "general rule . . . that legislation is presumed to be valid and will be sustained if the classification drawn by the statute is rationally related to a legitimate state interest." *City of Cleburne v. Cleburne Living Center, Inc.,* 473 U.S. 432 (1985). The plaintiffs bear the burden of proof on this issue, and so must show that the requirements imposed by law or regulation

---

[11] Laurie P. Cohen, *The Polygraph Paradox,* Wall St. J., A1 (Mar. 22-23, 2008).

[12] National Research Council, *The Polygraph and Lie Detection* (2002), available at http://www.nap.edu/books/0309084369/html/.

"so lack rationality that they constitute a constitutionally impermissible denial of equal protection." . . .

. . . [W]e think it rational for the departments to believe that the polygraph requirement results in fuller, more candid disclosures on the PDQ and thus provides additional information that is helpful in selecting qualified law enforcement officers. . . .

Accordingly, we conclude that in the absence of a scientific consensus, reasonable law enforcement administrators may choose to include a polygraph requirement in their hiring process without offending the equal protection clause.

. . .

In *States Employees Union v. Department of Mental Health,* 746 S.W.2d 203 (Tex. 1987), the Texas State Employees Union and several employees sued the Texas Department of Mental Health and Mental Retardation to invalidate the department's mandatory polygraph policy. Under the policy, employees were subject to "adverse personnel action" if they refused to submit to a polygraph examination to investigate patient abuse, theft, criminal activity, or health or safety threats. The court concluded:

We hold that the Texas Constitution protects personal privacy from unreasonable intrusion. This right to privacy should yield only when the government can demonstrate that an intrusion is reasonably warranted for the achievement of a compelling governmental objective that can be achieved by no less intrusive, more reasonable means. . . .

As justification for its polygraph policy, the Department asserts its interest in maintaining a safe environment for Department patients. This interest is in many respects compelling. The Department is not concerned solely with the smooth operation of its agency. It has been charged by the legislature with a unique responsibility towards its patients. . . . In its effort to achieve these goals, the Department must minimize incidents of employee misconduct. . . .

. . . The Department's objectives, important as they are, are not adequately compelling to warrant an intrusion into the privacy rights of the employees.

The polygraph policy itself undoubtedly implicates the privacy rights of the employees. The trial court found that "[the Department's] polygraph's intrusion is highly offensive to a regular person." Further, the trial court found that in light of its unreliability, a polygraph test was not a reasonable means of identifying miscreant employees.

We do not doubt that the Department is entitled to require employees to answer questions that are narrowly and specifically related to the performance of their job duties. The use of a lie detector, however, presents a qualitatively different question. The Department's asserted interests are inadequate to overcome the privacy interests impinged upon by the polygraph testing. We hold that the Department's polygraph policies impermissibly violate privacy rights protected by the Texas Constitution.

Can a public sector employer force its employees to engage in a polygraph examination as part of an investigation of employee misconduct? Under the Fourth Amendment, is a polygraph examination a "reasonable" search based on *O'Connor v. Ortega*?

THE EMPLOYEE POLYGRAPH PROTECTION ACT

In 1988, Congress passed the Employee Polygraph Protection Act (EPPA), Pub. L. No. 100-618, codified at 29 U.S.C. §§ 2001–2009. The EPPA applies only to private sector employers. It specifically exempts "the United States Government, any State or local government, or any political subdivision of a State or local government." § 2006(a).

Limitations on Polygraph Testing. Pursuant to 29 U.S.C. § 2002, it is unlawful for private sector employers:

(1) directly or indirectly, to require, request, suggest, or cause any employee or prospective employee to take or submit to any lie detector test;

(2) to use, accept, refer to, or inquire concerning the results of any lie detector test of any employee or prospective employee;

(3) to discharge, discipline, discriminate against in any manner, or deny employment or promotion to, or threaten to take any such action against

(A) any employee or prospective employee who refuses, declines, or fails to take or submit to any lie detector test, or

(B) any employee or prospective employee on the basis of the results of any lie detector test. . . .

Exception for Ongoing Investigations. However, there are certain exceptions where employers may use polygraphs:

(1) the test is administered in connection with an ongoing investigation involving economic loss or injury to the employer's business, such as theft, embezzlement, misappropriation, or an act of unlawful industrial espionage or sabotage;

(2) the employee had access to the property that is the subject of the investigation;

(3) the employer has a reasonable suspicion that the employee was involved in the incident or activity under investigation; and

(4) the employer executes a statement, provided to the examinee before the test, that [among other things, describes the particular incident being investigated and describes the basis of the employer's reasonable suspicion of the employee's involvement in the incident]. § 2006(d).

Exception for Security Services. Certain employers who engage in security services (e.g., armored car services, security alarm services, security personnel) are exempt. These security services must protect government interests such as nuclear power, water supply facilities, toxic waste disposal, and public transportation; or the services must protect "currency, negotiable securities, precious commodities or instruments, or proprietary information." § 2006(e).

When polygraphs are used under these exceptions, the test or the refusal to take the test cannot be the sole basis of any adverse employment action. § 2007(a). Further, the EPPA provides certain procedures, responsibilities, and restrictions on the use of polygraphs. For example, polygraph examiners cannot ask questions concerning beliefs regarding religion, racial matters, politics, sexual behavior, or union activities. § 2007(b). The EPPA limits the disclosure of polygraph information to people authorized by the examinee, the employer, or pursuant to a court order. § 2008.

Enforcement. Violations will result in a civil penalty of up to $10,000. The Secretary of Labor may bring an action to obtain restraining orders and injunctions to require compliance with the EPPA. Employers who violate the EPPA are liable to employees or prospective employees for legal and equitable relief including reinstatement, promotion, and payment of lost wages and benefits. § 2005.

Preemption. The EPPA does not preempt state law. About half of the states regulate the use of polygraphs by statute.

Waiver. The EPPA prohibits the waiver of rights and procedures provided by the Act except in the case of a written settlement, signed by the parties to the pending action or complaint under the Act. § 2005(d).

F. TELEPHONE MONITORING

Recall that federal electronic surveillance law (Chapter 3) applies not only to government and law enforcement officials but also to private parties as well. Thus, employers are subject to the restrictions of federal electronic surveillance law. However, three notable exceptions to electronic surveillance law are relevant to the employment context.

First, the Wiretap Act does not apply when one party to a communication consents to the interception. *See* 18 U.S.C. § 2511(2)(d).

Second, the providers of wire or electronic communications services are exempt from the Stored Communications Act's restrictions on accessing stored communications. *See* 18 U.S.C. § 2701(c)(1). Under the Wiretap Act, providers of wire or electronic communication services whose facilities are used in the transmission of such communications are permitted to intercept, disclose, or use that communication as a necessary incident to render the service or to protect the rights or property of the service. *See* 18 U.S.C. § 2511(2). The service provider exception is relevant in the employment context because many employers serve as the providers of certain communications services, such as Internet connections.

Third, under the "ordinary course of business" exception, the Wiretap Act does not apply when an employer uses certain intercepting devices "in the ordinary course of [the employer's] business." § 2510(5). The device must be furnished to the employer by the provider of the wire or electronic communication service. § 2510(5)(a)(i).

WATKINS V. L.M. BERRY & CO.

704 F.2d 577 (11th Cir. 1983)

SMITH, J. In this case appellant Watkins sued her employer, L.M. Berry & Company, and others, alleging violation of the federal wiretapping statute, title III of the Omnibus Crime Control and Safe Streets Act of 1968, 18 U.S.C. §§ 2510–

2520. The district court granted summary judgment on the merits against Watkins, and she now appeals. . . .

. . . Carmie Watkins was employed as a sales representative by L.M. Berry & Company (Berry Co.). Watkins' immediate supervisor was Martha Little, and Little's supervisor was Diane Wright. Berry Co. was under contract with South Central Bell to solicit Yellow Pages advertising from South Central Bell's present and prospective Yellow Pages advertisers. Much of this solicitation was done by telephone and Watkins was hired and trained to make those calls.

Berry Co. has an established policy, of which all employees are informed, of monitoring solicitation calls as part of its regular training program. The monitored calls are reviewed with employees to improve sales techniques. This monitoring is accomplished with a standard extension telephone, located in the supervisor's office, which shares lines with the telephones in the employees' offices. Employees are permitted to make personal calls on company telephones, and they are told that personal calls will not be monitored except to the extent necessary to determine whether a particular call is of a personal or business nature.

In April or May 1980, during her lunch hour, Watkins received a call in her office from a friend. At or near the beginning of the call (there are conflicting indications), the friend asked Watkins about an employment interview Watkins had had with another company (Lipton) the evening before. Watkins responded that the interview had gone well and expressed a strong interest in taking the Lipton job. Unbeknownst to Watkins, Little was monitoring the call from her office and heard the discussion of the interview.

After hearing the conversation (how much is unclear), Little told Wright about it. Later that afternoon Watkins was called into Wright's office and was told that the company did not want her to leave. Watkins responded by asking whether she was being fired. Upon discovering that her supervisors' questions were prompted by Little's interception of her call, Watkins became upset and tempers flared. The upshot was that Wright did fire Watkins the next day. However, Watkins complained to Wright's supervisor and was reinstated with apologies from Wright and Little. Within a week Watkins left Berry Co. to work for Lipton. . . .

Title III forbids the interception, without judicial authorization, of the contents of telephone calls. . . .

It is not disputed that Little's conduct violates section 2511(1)(b) unless it comes within an exemption "specifically provided in" title III (18 U.S.C. § 2511(1)). Appellees claim the applicability of two such exemptions. The first is the consent exemption set out in section 2511(2)(d):

> It shall not be unlawful under this chapter for a person not acting under color of law to intercept a wire or oral communication . . . where one of the parties to the communication has given prior consent to such interception. . . .

Appellees argue that, by using Berry Co.'s telephones and knowing that monitoring was possible, Watkins consented to the monitoring. The second is the business extension exemption in section 2510(5)(a)(i):

> "electronic, mechanical, or other device" [in §2511(1)(b)] means any device or apparatus which can be used to intercept a wire or oral communication other than

—

(a) any telephone or telegraph instrument, equipment or facility, or any component thereof, (i) furnished to the subscriber or user by a communications common carrier in the ordinary course of its business and being used by the subscriber or user *in the ordinary course of its business.* . . . [emphasis supplied].

"[E]quipment . . . furnished to the subscriber or user by a communications common carrier in the ordinary course of its business" means in this case simply a standard extension telephone. *See Briggs v. American Air Filter Co.,* 630 F.2d 414 (5th Cir. 1980). The issue is therefore whether the monitoring of this call was in the ordinary course of Berry Co.'s business. Appellees contend that it was and hence that the extension telephone was not a "device" within the statutory meaning (section 2511(1)(b)) of "interception."

Briggs v. American Air Filter Co., decided by the Fifth Circuit in 1980, provides the framework for interpreting these exemptions. The consent and business extension exemptions are analytically separate. Consent may be obtained for any interceptions, and the business or personal nature of the call is entirely irrelevant. Conversely, the business extension exemption operates without regard to consent. So long as the requisite business connection is demonstrated, the business extension exemption represents the "circumstances under which non-consensual interception" is not violative of section 2511(1)(b). Accordingly, in analyzing the present case we will first consider the scope of Watkins' consent to the monitoring of this call and then move to the question whether the interception was justified as being in the ordinary course of Berry Co.'s business, notwithstanding the absence of consent. . . .

Appellees argue that Watkins' acceptance of employment with Berry Co. with knowledge of the monitoring policy constituted her consent to the interception of this call. This is erroneous with respect to both Watkins' actual and implied consent.

It is clear, to start with, that Watkins did not actually consent to interception of *this* particular call. Furthermore, she did not consent to a *policy* of general monitoring. She consented to a policy of monitoring sales calls but not personal calls. This consent included the inadvertent interception of a personal call, but only for as long as necessary to determine the nature of the call. So, if Little's interception went beyond the point necessary to determine the nature of the call, it went beyond the scope of Watkins' actual consent.

Consent under title III is not to be cavalierly implied. Title III expresses a strong purpose to protect individual privacy by strictly limiting the occasions on which interception may lawfully take place. Stiff penalties are provided for its violation. It would thwart this policy if consent could routinely be implied from circumstances. Thus, knowledge of the *capability* of monitoring alone cannot be considered implied consent. . . .

If, as appears from the undisputed facts, there was no consent to interception of the call beyond what was initially required to determine its nature, appellees must rely on the business extension exemption to shield them from liability for any listening beyond that point. To prevail, they must show that the interception of the call beyond the initial period was in the ordinary course of business. It is not enough for Berry Co. to claim that its general policy is justifiable as part of the ordinary course of business. We have no doubt that it is. The question before us, rather, is whether the interception of *this* call was in the ordinary course of business.

Under *Briggs,* the general rule seems to be that if the intercepted call was a business call, then Berry Co.'s monitoring of it was in the ordinary course of business. If it was a personal call, the monitoring was probably, but not certainly, *not* in the ordinary course of business. The undisputed evidence strongly suggests that the intercepted call here was not a business call. Watkins received the call and so could not have been soliciting advertising; the caller was a personal friend; and the topics discussed were mainly social. To that extent this was certainly a personal call.

Appellees argue, however, that the signal topic was Watkins' interview with another employer. This was obviously of interest and concern to Berry Co., so, appellees argue, it was in the ordinary course of business to listen. . . .

The phrase "in the ordinary course of business" cannot be expanded to mean anything that interests a company. Such a broad reading "flouts the words of the statute and establishes an exemption that is without basis in the legislative history" of title III. Berry Co. might have been curious about Watkins' plans, but it had no legal interest in them. Watkins was at liberty to resign at will and so at liberty to interview with other companies. Her interview was thus a personal matter, neither in pursuit nor to the legal detriment of Berry Co.'s business. To expand the business extension exemption as broadly as appellees suggest would permit monitoring of obviously personal and very private calls on the ground, for example, that the company was interested in whether Watkins' friends were "nice" or not. We therefore conclude that the subject call was personal. . . .

We hold that a personal call may not be intercepted in the ordinary course of business under the exemption in section 2510(5)(a)(i), except to the extent necessary to guard against unauthorized use of the telephone or to determine whether a call is personal or not. In other words, a personal call may be intercepted in the ordinary course of business to determine its nature but never its contents. The limit of the exemption for Berry Co.'s business was the policy that Berry Co. in fact instituted. It thus appears that Little was justified in listening to that portion of the call which indicated that it was not a business call; beyond that, she was not. Determination of the relevant points in the call is for the trier of fact. . . .

A final issue remains with respect to both exemptions. *If* it turns out that Little was justified in listening to the beginning of the conversation, either to determine its nature or with consent, and *if* it turns out that during that portion of the conversation the interview was discussed, then we must decide whether Little was obliged to hang up or, having entered the conversation legally, could remain on the line indefinitely. We think that the conclusion is inescapable that these exemptions do not automatically justify interception of an entire call. The expectation of privacy in a conversation is not lost entirely because the privacy of part of it is violated. Under title III a law enforcement officer executing a wiretap order must minimize his intrusion to the extent possible. 18 U.S.C. § 2518(5). Therefore, Little was obliged to cease listening as soon as she had determined that the call was personal, regardless of the contents of the legitimately heard conversation.

The violation of section 2511(1)(b) is the intercepting itself, not the interception of particular material. It is not necessary to recovery of damages that the violator hear anything in particular; she need do no more than listen. Thus, the reinstatement of Watkins and her subsequent departure, while they may affect the amount of actual damages, do not moot or render *de minimis* her claim. Watkins' right to recover at least the minimum statutory damages flows from the interception, not from the actual damage caused. It is for the trier of fact to determine at what point the telephone should have been hung up. . . .

We hold that this case was not properly disposed of by summary judgment, as genuinely disputed issues of material fact remain. A detailed factual inquiry into the interception is necessary if the standards set forth above are to be adequately addressed. Among the factual questions that should be considered are: What was the monitoring policy to which Watkins consented? Did Little know that Watkins had received the call and if so did that necessarily indicate a personal call? How long was the call? When was the interview discussed? Were other subjects discussed? For how long did Little listen? How long does it take to discover that a call is personal, for example, is there an immediately recognizable pattern to a sales call? This list of questions is not exhaustive, but it is hoped that it points out the directions in which further inquiries should be pursued. . . .

DEAL V. SPEARS

980 F.2d 1153 (8th Cir. 1992)

BOWMAN, J. . . . Newell and Juanita Spears have owned and operated the White Oak Package Store near Camden, Arkansas, for about twenty years. The Spearses live in a mobile home adjacent to the store. The telephone in the store has an extension in the home, and is the only phone line into either location. The same phone line thus is used for both the residential and the business phones.

Sibbie Deal was an employee at the store from December 1988 until she was fired in August 1990. The store was burglarized in April 1990 and approximately $16,000 was stolen. The Spearses believed that it was an inside job and suspected that Deal was involved. Hoping to catch the suspect in an unguarded admission, Newell Spears purchased and installed a recording device on the extension phone in the mobile home. When turned on, the machine would automatically record all conversations made or received on either phone, with no indication to the parties using the phone that their conversation was being recorded. Before purchasing the recorder, Newell Spears told a sheriff's department investigator that he was considering this surreptitious monitoring and the investigator told Spears that he did not "see anything wrong with that."

Calls were taped from June 27, 1990, through August 13, 1990. During that period, Sibbie Deal, who was married to Mike Deal at the time, was having an extramarital affair with Calvin Lucas, then married to Pam Lucas. Deal and Lucas spoke on the telephone at the store frequently and for long periods of time while Deal was at work. (Lucas was on 100% disability so he was at home all day.) Based on the trial testimony, the District Court concluded that much of the conversation between the two was "sexually provocative." Deal also made or received numerous other personal telephone calls during her workday. Even before Newell Spears purchased the recorder, Deal was asked by her employers to cut down on her use of the phone for personal calls, and the Spearses told her they might resort to monitoring calls or installing a pay phone in order to curtail the abuse.

Newell Spears listened to virtually all twenty-two hours of the tapes he recorded, regardless of the nature of the calls or the content of the conversations, and Juanita Spears listened to some of them. Although there was nothing in the record to indicate that they learned anything about the burglary, they did learn, among other things, that Deal sold Lucas a keg of beer at cost, in violation of store policy. On August 13, 1990, when Deal came in to work the evening shift, Newell Spears played a few seconds of the incriminating tape for Deal and then fired her. Deal and Lucas filed this action on August 29, 1990 [alleging that the Spearses violated Federal Wiretap Law. The district court found the Spearses liable and assessed damages at a total of $40,000 — $10,000 to Deal and Lucas respectively assessed against Newell Spears and $10,000 to Deal and Lucas respectively assessed against Juanita Spears]. . . .

The Spearses challenge the court's finding of liability. They admit the taping but contend that the facts here bring their actions under two statutory exceptions to civil liability. Further, Juanita Spears alleges that she did not disclose information learned from the tapes, thus the statutory damages assessed against her on that ground were improper. For their part Deal and Lucas challenge the court's failure to award them punitive damages as permitted by statute.

The elements of a violation of the wire and electronic communications interception provisions (Title III) of the Omnibus Crime Control and Safe Streets Act of 1968 are set forth in the section that makes such interceptions a criminal offense. 18 U.S.C. § 2511 (1988). Under the relevant provisions of the statute, criminal liability attaches and a federal civil cause of action arises when a person intentionally intercepts a wire or electronic communication or intentionally discloses the contents of the interception. The successful civil plaintiff may recover actual damages plus any profits made by the violator. If statutory damages will result in a larger recovery than actual damages, the violator must pay the plaintiff "the greater of $100 a day for each day of violation or $10,000." Further, punitive damages, attorney fees, and "other litigation costs reasonably incurred" are allowed.

The Spearses first claim they are exempt from civil liability because Sibbie Deal consented to the interception of calls that she made from and received at the store. Under the statute, it is not unlawful "to intercept a wire, oral, or electronic communication . . . where one of the parties to the communication has given prior consent to such interception," 18 U.S.C. § 2511(2)(d), and thus no civil liability is incurred. The Spearses contend that Deal's consent may be implied because Newell Spears had mentioned that he might be forced to monitor calls or restrict telephone privileges if abuse of the store's telephone for personal calls continued. They further argue that the extension in their home gave actual notice to Deal that her calls could be overheard, and that this notice resulted in her implied consent to interception. We find these arguments unpersuasive. . . .

We do not believe that Deal's consent may be implied from the circumstances relied upon in the Spearses' arguments. The Spearses did not inform Deal that they were monitoring the phone, but only told her they might do so in order to cut down on personal calls. Moreover, it seems clear that the couple anticipated Deal would not suspect that they were intercepting her calls, since they hoped to catch her making an admission about the burglary, an outcome they would not expect if she knew her calls were being recorded. . . .

Given these circumstances, we hold as a matter of law that the Spearses have failed to show Deal's consent to the interception and recording of her conversations.

The Spearses also argue that they are immune from liability under what has become known as an exemption for business use of a telephone extension. The exception is actually a restrictive definition. Under Title III, a party becomes criminally and civilly liable when he or she "intercepts" wire communications. "'[I]ntercept' means the aural or other acquisition of the contents of any wire, electronic, or oral communication through the use of any electronic, mechanical, or other device[.]" Such a device is "any device or apparatus which can be used to intercept a wire, oral, or electronic communication" except when that device is a

> telephone . . . instrument, equipment or facility, or any component thereof, (i) furnished to the subscriber or user by a provider of wire or electronic communication service in the ordinary course of its business and being used by the subscriber or user in the ordinary course of its business or furnished by such subscriber or user for connection to the facilities of such service and used in the ordinary course of its business[.]

Thus there are two essential elements that must be proved before this becomes a viable defense: the intercepting equipment must be furnished to the user by the phone company or connected to the phone line, and it must be used in the ordinary course of business. The Spearses argue that the extension in their residence, to which the recorder was connected, meets the equipment requirement, and the listening-in was done in the ordinary course of business. We disagree. . . .

We hold that the recording device, and not the extension phone, intercepted the calls. But even if the extension phone intercepted the calls, we do not agree that the interception was in the ordinary course of business.

We do not quarrel with the contention that the Spearses had a legitimate business reason for listening in: they suspected Deal's involvement in a burglary of the store and hoped she would incriminate herself in a conversation on the phone. Moreover, Deal was abusing her privileges by using the phone for numerous personal calls even, by her own admission, when there were customers in the store. The Spearses might legitimately have monitored Deal's calls to the extent necessary to determine that the calls were personal and made or received in violation of store policy.

But the Spearses recorded twenty-two hours of calls, and Newell Spears listened to all of them without regard to their relation to his business interests. Granted, Deal might have mentioned the burglary at any time during the conversations, but we do not believe that the Spearses' suspicions justified the extent of the intrusion. We conclude that the scope of the interception in this case takes us well beyond the boundaries of the ordinary course of business. . . .

NOTES & QUESTIONS

1. *Postscript.* Following the court's decision, a number of other plaintiffs who were speaking with Deal while the conversations were being wiretapped filed

suit. Each new plaintiff sought damages of $10,000 and attorney's fees and costs. The court, however, declined to award damages, noting 18 U.S.C. § 2520(c)(2) provides that "the court *may* assess . . . statutory damages of . . . $10,000." Damages were thus at the discretion of the court, and the judge reasoned:

> [T]he plaintiffs suffered no actual damages; the privacy intrusion as to these plaintiffs appears to have been relatively minor as compared to the intrusion into the affairs of Sibbie and Calvin Lucas; the Spears have already paid approximately $60,000.00 for their unlawful acts; the Spears, who are now retired and in their seventies, have no source of income other than their accumulated wealth; and Newell Spears used the recorder solely for the purpose of discovering who robbed his business. Though the court notes that the Spears' accumulated wealth is substantial and would allow them to pay a significant judgment, this factor is outweighed by the others listed above, all of which counsel against an award of damages.

Reynolds v. Spears, 857 F. Supp. 1341 (W.D. Ark. 1994). The district court's judgment was affirmed in *Reynolds v. Spears,* 93 F.3d 428 (8th Cir. 1996).

2. ***Telephone Monitoring Policy.*** Suppose the Spearses had a policy that all calls, regardless of whether they were personal or business related, would be recorded and monitored. Would the Spearses still be liable under the Wiretap Act?

3. ***Other Means of Investigating.*** Would it be likely that Deal would speak about the burglary on a business-related call? If the Spearses could not listen to Deal's private calls, their investigation might be significantly limited. If you were the Spearses' attorney and they came to you, explained that they suspected Deal of the burglary, and wanted your advice about how they could legally investigate, how would you advise them?

G. COMPUTER MONITORING AND SEARCHES

1. E-MAIL

E-mail presents an interesting privacy problem in the workplace. Unlike regular mail, e-mail is less secure from prying eyes. Because e-mail travels through numerous computers to reach its final destination, it can be intercepted and copied at many points. E-mail goes through the employer's computer network. It may be stored by the employer as part of the routine system backup. E-mail is often stored on the employee's computer even after it is received and read. Employers can easily scan e-mail for certain words. At the same time, encryption techniques may enable employees to send messages so that at least the content is not easily accessible to employers. Given the nature of e-mail — especially e-mail correspondence at the workplace — how should we assess whether individuals have a reasonable expectation of privacy in e-mail?[13]

---

[13] For more background about e-mail and the workplace, see Michael S. Leib, *E-Mail and the Wiretap Laws: Why Congress Should Add Electronic Communications to Title II's Statutory Exclusionary Rule and Expressly Reject a "Good Faith" Exception,* 34 Harv. J. Legis. 393 (1997);

The answer to this question depends in part on how we analogize e-mail. Some view e-mail as akin to a letter — just one in electronic form rather than on paper. Should e-mail deserve the same legal protection and privacy expectations as regular letters? Others argue that without any encryption, e-mail is quite insecure and is more akin to a postcard than a letter. Another analogy is that e-mail should be understood as similar to a telephone call. E-mail often travels across phone lines, and e-mail correspondence is often conducted fairly rapidly with frequent responses and replies. Should e-mail be given the same legal protection and privacy expectations as telephone conversations? One might argue that given how insecure e-mail is from being intercepted by unauthorized individuals, it is more akin to a radio communication. The following cases examine the privacy of e-mail in the workplace:

SMYTH V. PILLSBURY CO.

914 F. Supp. 97 (E.D. Pa. 1996)

WEINER, J. In this diversity action, plaintiff, an at-will employee, claims he was wrongfully discharged from his position as a regional operations manager by the defendant. Presently before the court is the motion of the defendant to dismiss pursuant to Rule 12(b)(6) of the Federal Rules of Civil Procedure. For the reasons which follow, the motion is granted.

A claim may be dismissed under Fed. R. Civ. P. 12(b)(6) only if the plaintiff can prove no set of facts in support of the claim that would entitle him to relief. The reviewing court must consider only those facts alleged in the Complaint and accept all of the allegations as true. Applying this standard, we find that plaintiff has failed to state a claim upon which relief can be granted.

Defendant maintained an electronic mail communication system ("e-mail") in order to promote internal corporate communications between its employees. Defendant repeatedly assured its employees, including plaintiff, that all e-mail communications would remain confidential and privileged. Defendant further assured its employees, including plaintiff, that e-mail communications could not be intercepted and used by defendant against its employees as grounds for termination or reprimand.

In October 1994, plaintiff received certain e-mail communications from his supervisor over defendant's e-mail system on his computer at home. In reliance on defendant's assurances regarding defendant's e-mail system, plaintiff responded and exchanged e-mails with his supervisor. At some later date, contrary to the assurances of confidentiality made by defendant, defendant, acting through its agents, servants and employees, intercepted plaintiff's private e-mail messages made in October 1994. On January 17, 1995, defendant notified plaintiff that it was terminating his employment effective February 1, 1995, for transmitting what

---

Kevin P. Kopp, *Electronic Communications in the Workplace: E-Mail Monitoring and the Right of Privacy*, 8 Seton Hall Const. L.J. 861 (1998); Scott A. Sundstrom, *You've Got Mail (and the Government Knows It): Applying the Fourth Amendment to Workplace E-Mail Monitoring*, 73 N.Y.U. L. Rev. 2064 (1998).

it deemed to be inappropriate and unprofessional comments over defendant's e-mail system in October, 1994.

As a general rule, Pennsylvania law does not provide a common law cause of action for the wrongful discharge of an at-will employee such as plaintiff. . . . However, in the most limited of circumstances, exceptions have been recognized where discharge of an at-will employee threatens or violates a clear mandate of public policy. . . .

Plaintiff claims that his termination was in violation of "public policy which precludes an employer from terminating an employee in violation of the employee's right to privacy as embodied in Pennsylvania common law." . . . [O]ur Court of Appeals stated "our review of Pennsylvania law reveals other evidence of a public policy that may, under certain circumstances, give rise to a wrongful discharge action related to urinalysis or to personal property searches. Specifically, we refer to the Pennsylvania common law regarding tortious invasion of privacy."

The Court of Appeals . . . observed that one of the torts which Pennsylvania recognizes as encompassing an action for invasion of privacy is the tort of "intrusion upon seclusion." As noted by the Court of Appeals, the Restatement (Second) of Torts defines the tort as follows:

> One who intentionally intrudes, physically or otherwise, upon the solitude or seclusion of another or his private affairs or concerns, is subject to liability to the other for invasion of his privacy, if the intrusion would be highly offensive to a reasonable person.

Restatement (Second) of Torts § 652B.

Applying the Restatement definition of the tort of intrusion upon seclusion to the facts and circumstances of the case sub judice, we find that plaintiff has failed to state a claim upon which relief can be granted. In the first instance, unlike urinalysis and personal property searches, we do not find a reasonable expectation of privacy in e-mail communications voluntarily made by an employee to his supervisor over the company e-mail system notwithstanding any assurances that such communications would not be intercepted by management. Once plaintiff communicated the alleged unprofessional comments to a second person (his supervisor) over an e-mail system which was apparently utilized by the entire company, any reasonable expectation of privacy was lost. Significantly, the defendant did not require plaintiff, as in the case of an urinalysis or personal property search to disclose any personal information about himself. Rather, plaintiff voluntarily communicated the alleged unprofessional comments over the company e-mail system. We find no privacy interests in such communications.

In the second instance, even if we found that an employee had a reasonable expectation of privacy in the contents of his e-mail communications over the company e-mail system, we do not find that a reasonable person would consider the defendant's interception of these communications to be a substantial and highly offensive invasion of his privacy. Again, we note that by intercepting such communications, the company is not, as in the case of urinalysis or personal property searches, requiring the employee to disclose any personal information about himself or invading the employee's person or personal effects. Moreover, the company's interest in preventing inappropriate and unprofessional comments or even illegal activity over its e-mail system outweighs any privacy interest the employee may have in those comments.

In sum, we find that the defendant's actions did not tortiously invade the plaintiff's privacy and, therefore, did not violate public policy. As a result, the motion to dismiss is granted.

NOTES & QUESTIONS

1. *E-mail Monitoring by Employers: Weighing the Interests.* Employers contend that e-mail monitoring is important because the use of e-mail (and the Internet) can bring in viruses that can harm the employer's computer system. Employers are liable for defamation, copyright violations, and sexual harassment, which can take place over e-mail. Chevron Corporation was sued for hostile work environment when some employees sent around via e-mail a joke list called "Why beer is better than women." The case settled out of court for $2.2 million. Should employers be permitted to monitor e-mail? How would you balance the employees' interest in privacy against the employers' interests in monitoring?[14]

2. *The Rights of Third Parties.* The employees' privacy rights are not the only rights implicated here. The rights of third parties who mail employees or chat with them over the Internet are also implicated. Would a third party who e-mailed a private document to an employee, which was subsequently opened and inspected by that employee's employer, have an action for intrusion upon seclusion? Are there other theories or remedies, including self-help, available in this situation?

3. *E-mail Privacy Policies.* One of the troubling aspects of *Pillsbury* is that the employer promised that the e-mail would remain confidential. Suppose you were counsel to a company that wanted to establish an e-mail privacy policy. What elements would you include in the policy and why?

   Suppose that the employer had an e-mail privacy policy that stated: "The employer's e-mail system is the property of the employer. The employer reserves the right to monitor all e-mail communications over its e-mail system." First, should the employer be permitted to have such a blanket policy without a legitimate reason? Under such a policy, would the employee have a reasonable expectation of privacy in a private e-mail?

   Suppose that the e-mail policy stated: "The employer's e-mail system shall be used exclusively for business-related purposes. The use of e-mail for an employee's own private purposes is prohibited." Would such a policy eliminate any reasonable expectation of privacy in e-mail?

4. *Webmail.* Employees now have the ability to e-mail others while at work without using the employer's e-mail system. They can establish a webmail account such as Hotmail, Yahoo E-mail, or Gmail. To what extent should

---

[14] For a proposal of how to balance employer and employee interests, see Jay P. Kesan, *Cyber-Working or Cyber-Shirking?: A First Principles Examination of Electronic Privacy in the Workplace,* 54 Fla. L. Rev. 289 (2002). For a discussion of how sexual harassment law inappropriately threatens employee privacy, see Jeffrey Rosen, *The Unwanted Gaze: The Destruction of Privacy in America* (2000). For a critique of Rosen's view, see Anita L. Allen, *The Wanted Gaze: Accountability for Interpersonal Conduct at Work,* 89 Geo. L.J. 2013 (2001).

employers have the ability to control the use of e-mailing from an employee's own private webmail account at work? Consider the following two situations: (1) an employee accesses her Hotmail account from her employer's computer; and (2) an employee accesses her Hotmail account from her own laptop, Blackberry, or other device with the wireless Internet service that the employee herself pays for. Should the employer have the ability to monitor in (1) or (2) or both of these situations?

5. ***E-mail, Text Messages, and Workplace Privacy Policies.*** In *City of Ontario v. Quon,* 130 S. Ct. 2619 (2010), a city police department provided pagers to several of its employees. The department contracted with Arch Wireless Operating Company, Inc. to provide the wireless service. The department "had no official policy directed to text-messaging by use of the pagers." Its general policy regarding computer, Internet, and e-mail use was that they were not to be used for "personal benefit," that the city reserved the right to monitor all network activity, and that "[u]sers should have no expectation of privacy or confidentiality when using these resources." Jeff Quon exceeded his text messaging usage limits repeatedly, and the lieutenant billed him for the overages. Quon paid the city each time. Finally, after Quon exceeded his usage limits again, the city sought and obtained from Arch Wireless transcripts of Quon's texting. The transcripts revealed that many of his messages were personal and sexually explicit in nature.

Quon and several others sued, claiming that the city and Arch Wireless violated the Stored Communications Act (SCA) and the Fourth Amendment. The U.S. Court of Appeals for the Ninth Circuit concluded that Arch Wireless violated the SCA when it disclosed the messages to the city. The court then analyzed whether the officers had Fourth Amendment protection in the messages. First, the court reasoned that text messages should be treated as content information (similar to letters and e-mail text) rather than as envelope information (similar to pen registers or e-mail headers). Second, the court declared that although the city had a general Internet and e-mail usage policy, it was not the "operational reality" with regard to the pagers. The lieutenant stated that he would not monitor the text messages if officers paid for overages. Quon had exceeded his text character limit on several occasions before without his messages being reviewed. Thus, the court concluded:

> This demonstrated that the [police department] followed its "informal policy" and that Quon reasonably relied on it. Nevertheless, without warning, his text messages were audited by the Department. Under these circumstances, Quon had a reasonable expectation of privacy in the text messages archived on Arch Wireless's server.

The court then held that the search was unreasonable under the *O'Connor v. Ortega* approach.

The U.S. Supreme Court granted certiorari and considered only the Fourth Amendment issue. At the outset, the Court opted to avoid reaching the issue of whether Quon had a reasonable expectation of privacy:

The Court must proceed with care when considering the whole concept of privacy expectations in communications made on electronic equipment owned by a government employer. The judiciary risks error by elaborating too fully on the Fourth Amendment implications of emerging technology before its role in society has become clear. . . .

Prudence counsels caution before the facts in the instant case are used to establish far-reaching premises that define the existence, and extent, of privacy expectations enjoyed by employees when using employer-provided communication devices. . . .

A broad holding concerning employees' privacy expectations vis-à-vis employer-provided technological equipment might have implications for future cases that cannot be predicted. It is preferable to dispose of this case on narrower grounds.

The Court assumed for the purposes of argument that Quon had a reasonable expectation of privacy and concluded that the search was reasonable:

The City and [the Ontario Police Department] had a legitimate interest in ensuring that employees were not being forced to pay out of their own pockets for work-related expenses, or on the other hand that the City was not paying for extensive personal communications. . . .

Even if he could assume some level of privacy would inhere in his messages, it would not have been reasonable for Quon to conclude that his messages were in all circumstances immune from scrutiny. Quon was told that his messages were subject to auditing. As a law enforcement officer, he would or should have known that his actions were likely to come under legal scrutiny, and that this might entail an analysis of his on-the-job communications. Under the circumstances, a reasonable employee would be aware that sound management principles might require the audit of messages to determine whether the pager was being appropriately used. . . .

Because the search was motivated by a legitimate work-related purpose, and because it was not excessive in scope, the search was reasonable under the approach of the *O'Connor* plurality. . . .

Had the Court addressed the issue of whether Quon had a reasonable expectation of privacy in his text messages despite the department's general Internet and e-mail usage policy, what should have been the conclusion? If an employer with a monitoring policy does not monitor, does this create an expectation in employees that there is an informal policy of non-monitoring? Many employers have broad network monitoring policies yet might not routinely exercise their right to monitor or may tell employees that they generally won't be monitored. Can these informal statements and practices negate the employer's general policy? Is the Court correct in its conclusion that the search was reasonable?

The Court avoided reaching the issue about whether the search violated the Fourth Amendment rights of the people who sent text messages to Quon:

It is not necessary to resolve this question in order to dispose of the case, however. Respondents argue that because "the search was unreasonable as to Sergeant Quon, it was also unreasonable as to his correspondents." They make no corollary argument that the search, if reasonable as to Quon, could nonetheless be unreasonable as to Quon's correspondents. In light of this litigating position and the Court's conclusion that the search was reasonable as to Jeff Quon, it necessarily follows that these other respondents cannot prevail.

The Court seemed to seize the opportunity to avoid deciding this issue, perhaps because it is so complex. Consider Orin Kerr:

> The City of Ontario argues in its merits brief that the three plaintiffs didn't have any rights at stake because they should have known that they were communicating with someone who had no privacy rights in the text message service. . . .
>
> This is a pretty bad argument, I think. First, I have no idea how someone who sends a text message to a city employee is supposed to have such a detailed understanding of both Fourth Amendment law and the city's employment policies that they would know the recipient won't have Fourth Amendment rights in the message. . . .
>
> More broadly, even if the others did somehow know that Quon didn't have any privacy rights when he received the messages, it's not clearly how that matters for Fourth Amendment purposes. Is that some sort of consent to pre-delivery inspection of the messages, like you might have when you drive on to a military base and are held to have consented to an inspection for your car? If so, that's a fact question, and there are no relevant facts about this in the record.[15]

6. **_Mail vs. E-mail._** In *Vernars v. Young*, 539 F.2d 966 (3d Cir. 1976), a plaintiff sued her employer under the intrusion upon seclusion tort for opening and reading her mail that "was delivered to the corporation's office but was addressed to her and marked personal." The court concluded:

> Just as private individuals have a right to expect that their telephonic communications will not be monitored, they also have a reasonable expectation that their personal mail will not be opened and read by unauthorized persons. Recognition of a cause of action for violation of that expectation seems particularly fitting under the right of privacy doctrine.

Generally, private letters mailed to a workplace are monitored much less frequently than e-mail. Suppose an employer adopted a policy that all employees' mail will be opened and read. What legal recourse would employees objecting to this policy have?

7. **_Will the Market Establish the Proper Level of Workplace Privacy?_** Some might argue for a laissez-faire approach. Workers will choose to work for employers providing greater privacy. In this way, the market will decide the appropriate level of workplace privacy. Do you agree that the market is properly functioning to reach the appropriate level of workplace privacy? If not, for what reasons is the market failing?

8. **_Is There a Reasonable Expectation of Privacy in Workplace E-mail?_** Consider *United States v. Maxwell,* 45 M.J. 406 (U.S. Ct. App. Armed Forces 1996):

---

[15] Orin Kerr, *Communicating with Those Who Have No Privacy Rights: The Hard Question in City of Ontario v. Quon,* Volokh Conspiracy (Mar. 31, 2010), http://volokh.com/2010/03/31/communicating-with-those-who-have-no-privacy-rights-the-hard-question-in-city-of-ontario-v-quon/.

E-mail transmissions are not unlike other forms of modern communication. We can draw parallels from these other mediums. For example, if a sender of first-class mail seals an envelope and addresses it to another person, the sender can reasonably expect the contents to remain private and free from the eyes of the police absent a search warrant founded upon probable cause. However, once the letter is received and opened, the destiny of the letter then lies in the control of the recipient of the letter, not the sender, absent some legal privilege.

Similarly, the maker of a telephone call has a reasonable expectation that police officials will not intercept and listen to the conversation; however, the conversation itself is held with the risk that one of the participants may reveal what is said to others.

Drawing from these parallels, we can say that the transmitter of an e-mail message enjoys a reasonable expectation that police officials will not intercept the transmission without probable cause and a search warrant. However, once the transmissions are received by another person, the transmitter no longer controls its destiny. In a sense, e-mail is like a letter. It is sent and lies sealed in the computer until the recipient opens his or her computer and retrieves the transmission. The sender enjoys a reasonable expectation that the initial transmission will not be intercepted by the police. The fact that an unauthorized "hacker" might intercept an e-mail message does not diminish the legitimate expectation of privacy in any way.

There is, however, one major difference between an e-mail message which has been transmitted via a network such as AOL and a direct computer "real time" transmission. The former transmission is stored in a centralized computer until the recipient opens his or her network and retrieves the e-mail, while the latter is lost forever, unless one of the communicators chooses to download the conversation to a disk. This latter action would be much like clandestinely recording one's telephone conversation. Thus, while a user of an e-mail network may enjoy a reasonable expectation that his or her e-mail will not be revealed to police, there is the risk that an employee or other person with direct access to the network service will access the e-mail, despite any company promises to the contrary. One always bears the risk that a recipient of an e-mail message will redistribute the e-mail or an employee of the company will read e-mail against company policy. However, this is not the same as the police commanding an individual to intercept the message. . . .

Compare *Maxwell* to *Pillsbury*. How do the courts differ as to their view about whether there is a reasonable expectation of privacy in e-mail?

9. ***The Union Setting.*** In *The Guard Publishing Co. d/b/a The Register Guard*, 351 NLRB No. 70, 2007 WL 4540458 (N.L.R.B. 2007), the National Labor Relations Board (NLRB) found that a company could "lawfully bar employees' nonwork-related use of its e-mail system" unless it acted in a manner that discriminated against a worker's rights under Section 7 of the National Labor Relations Act. This section protects an employee's ability to engage in "concerted activities . . . for mutual aid or protection." It safeguards collective bargaining, and the right to form and join a union.

In a 3–2 decision, the NLRB upheld a company's Communications System Policy (CSP), which governed employee use of its communications systems, including e-mail. The CSP limited use of company communication systems to "assist in conducting" company business. The policy also stated:

"Communication systems are not to be used to solicit or proselytize for commercial ventures, religious or political causes, outside organizations, or other non-job-related solicitations." The majority of the NLRB found that the employer had a basic property right to regulate employee use of company property, and that, absent discrimination, employees had no statutory right under the NLRA to "use an employer's equipment or media for Section 7 communications." Since the CSP did not "on its face" discriminate against Section 7 activity, the NLRB upheld it.

In dissent, Members Wilma Liebman and Dennis Walsh accused the majority of turning the NRLB into the "Rip Van Winkle of administrative agencies." In their view: "Only a Board that has been asleep for the past 20 years could fail to recognize that e-mail has revolutionized communication both inside and outside the workplace." As a result, "[w]here, as here, an employer has given employees access to email for regular routine use in their work, we would find that banning all non-work related 'solicitations' is presumptively unlawful absent special circumstances." Employees had an affirmative right to engage in Section 7 communications in the workplace, even though the employee's "property" was involved. The dissent also noted that the company had failed to demonstrate any special circumstances in this case, and that it had consistently permitted employees, with its knowledge and tacit approval, to use e-mail for nonwork-related matters, including "baby announcements, party invitations, a request for a dog walker, and offers of sports tickets." It drew the line only at union related e-mails.

On appeal, the D.C. Circuit found that there was no substantial evidence to support the NLRB's finding that the employer lawfully disciplined the union president for the contested solicitation e-mails that had violated the employer's CSP. *See Guard Publishing Co v. NLRB,* 571 F.3d 53 (D.C. Cir. 2009). The court then remanded that issue back to the Board, which found that the employee had, in fact, violated the NLRB by disciplining the union president. *See The Guard Publishing Co.,* 357 NLRB No. 27 (N.L.R.B. July 26, 2011). As one analysis of this matter found, "the more important issue" in *Register-Guard* concerned the legality of an "employer computer use policy that restricts access to email systems." This matter was not appealed to the D.C. Circuit. By way of prediction, Christine Neylon O'Brien states that this case and its holding will be of diminished future importance: "Facebook, Twitter and smartphones make it less likely that employees will need to use their employers' computer and e-mail systems, or even workers' e-mail addresses, in order to communicate." In her view, the critical issue will be the amount of work time employees are allowed to spend on non-work activities.[16] Beyond the email issue, the NLRB has developed social media policies that protect certain work-related conversations conducted on social media. These policies will be discussed below.

10. ***The Service Provider Exception.*** Under federal electronic surveillance law, service providers (who provide e-mail service) are exempt under the Wiretap Act, 18 U.S.C. § 2511(2)(a)(i), "while engaged in any activity which is

---

[16] Christine Neylon O'Brien, *Employer E-mail Policies and the National Labor Relations Act,* 61 Lab. L.J. 5, 10 (2010).

necessary to provide the service, or to protect the rights or property of the provider." *See Bohach v. City of Reno*, 932 F. Supp. 1232 (D. Nev. 1996). In many workplaces — such as government workplaces, universities, and large corporations — the employers are also the service providers. Therefore, they would be exempt from intercepting e-mail under the Wiretap Act. Additionally, employers can have employees sign consent forms to the monitoring, and consent is an exception to federal wiretap law.

2. INTERNET USE

LEVENTHAL V. KNAPEK

266 F.3d 64 (2d Cir. 2001)

SOTOMAYOR, J. After receiving anonymous allegations that an employee reasonably suspected to be plaintiff-appellant Gary Leventhal was neglecting his duties in the Accounting Bureau of the New York State Department of Transportation ("DOT"), DOT investigators, without Leventhal's consent, printed out a list of the file names found on Leventhal's office computer. The list of file names contained evidence that certain non-standard software was loaded on Leventhal's computer. This led to additional searches confirming that Leventhal had a personal tax preparation program on his office computer and to disciplinary charges against Leventhal for misconduct. After settling the disciplinary charges, Leventhal sued defendants-appellees, challenging the legality of the searches and of two employment actions taken against him. . . .

Leventhal began his career at the DOT in 1974. At the time of the searches in question, Leventhal had risen to the position of Principal Accountant in the Accounting Bureau of the DOT, a grade 27 position. In 1996, and for several previous years, Leventhal maintained a private tax practice while employed at the DOT. He received DOT approval to make up on weekends or after normal work hours any time he missed because of his outside employment. In order to receive approval for this arrangement, Leventhal declared that his outside employment would "not interfere with the complete and proper execution of my duties with the Department of Transportation."

The DOT had a written policy prohibiting theft. The policy broadly defined theft to include:

> improper use of State equipment, material or vehicles. Examples include but are not limited to: conducting personal business on State time; using State equipment, material or vehicles for personal business; improper use of the mail, copiers, fax machines, personal computers, lincs codes or telephones and time spent on non-State business related activities during the workday.

During the DOT's interrogation of Leventhal after the searches of his office computer, Leventhal acknowledged that using DOT equipment for private purposes was "a violation of [DOT] policies."

The DOT also had an unwritten rule that only "standard" DOT software could be loaded on DOT computers. Although this rule was never officially promulgated as a DOT policy, Leventhal remarked during his interrogation that "the stated policy" was that employees were not to have personal software on a DOT computer "without permission." Nevertheless, it was known that the staff of the Accounting Bureau had loaded unlicensed copies of "non-standard" software on DOT computers and used the software to perform work-related activities due, at least in part, to the DOT's inability to purchase needed software for its employees. The DOT also had an official policy restricting office Internet access to DOT business.

In July 1996, the DOT circulated a memo from Ann Snow, the Network Administrator for the Budget and Finance Division, which stated that only original, licensed copies of software could be installed on DOT computers. Following the distribution of this memo, however, Leventhal's supervisors discussed their difficulties in complying with the memo because of the department's dependance upon the use of unlicensed software. Leventhal's immediate supervisor at the time, John Chevalier, instructed his subordinates, including Leventhal, that they could continue to use non-standard software for departmental business. . . .

On October 15, 1996, the New York State Office of the Inspector General referred to the DOT an anonymous letter it had received complaining of abuses at the DOT Accounting Bureau. This letter described specific employees by reference to their salary grades, genders, and job titles, without providing names. The letter made certain allegations concerning a grade 27 employee. Leventhal was the only grade 27 employee in the office at that time and, therefore, the DOT investigators inferred that the grade 27 employee described in the letter was Leventhal. The relevant portion of the letter states:

> The abuse of time and power is so far out of line with the intended functions of the bureau that to cite all specifics would be an endless task. The day to day operation of this bureau is a slap in the face to all good state workers. You have to see this place to believe it. I will cite a few examples. A grade 27 who is late everyday. The majority of his time is spent on non-DOT business related phone calls or talking to other personnel about personal computers. He is only in the office half the time he is either sick or on vacation. . . . [Half the time of a grade 23] is spent playing computer games and talking on the phone to his family or talking sports to one his subordinates, the guy who sleeps at his desk. . . . A grade 18 with an apparent alcohol problem who is so incompetent that his supervisor allows him to sleep at his desk. The grade 27 is aware of this problem. When [the grade 18] is not sleeping he is playing computer games or drafting up letters which are typed by [another] grade 18, who is barely able to function at an entry level clerical position. . . . And the sad part is that management knows what is going on although they would deny it if you asked them. . . . I think its [sic] time for some new leadership in the bureau.

Lawrence Knapek, the Assistant Commissioner of the DOT for the Office of Budget and Finance, met with John Samaniuk, the acting director of the Office of Internal Audit and Investigations, and Gary Cuyler, the chief investigator for that office, to discuss how to respond to the allegations made in the letter. They decided that the Office of Internal Audit and Investigation would conduct an investigation employing "such techniques as reviewing telephone records, reviewing computer records, Internet logs, that kind of thing." A "computer review" was ordered for all of the employees who could be identified from the letter. This involved printing out a list of file names found on these DOT computers to determine whether any contained non-standard software. After business hours on October 25, 1996, the investigators entered Leventhal's office through an open door, turned on his DOT computer, and reviewed the directories of files on the computer's hard drive. There was no power-on password to gain access to Leventhal's computer, but once the machine was turned on, some of the menu selections that appeared were password-protected. In order to perform their search, the investigators may have used a "boot-disk," a disk which allows the computer to start up without encountering the menus normally found there.

Having located the computer directories, the investigators printed out a list of the file names to enable the later identification of the programs loaded on Leventhal's computer without having to open each program. This included a printout of the names of the "hidden" files on Leventhal's computer. These "hidden" directories, the investigators found, contained "Morph," a type of drawing program and "PPU," a program suspected of containing tax software because of file names such as "TAX.FNT," and "CUSTTAX.DBF." On the non-"hidden" directories, the investigators found other non-standard software, including the programs Prodigy, Quicken, and Lotus Suite (although one part of Lotus Suite was standard DOT software at the time). . . .

In February 1997, DOT management and investigators met to examine the results from these searches. Assistant DOT Commissioner Knapek attended the meeting and, aware of Leventhal's private tax practice, was particularly interested in confirming the investigators' suspicion that Leventhal had loaded tax software on his DOT office computer. They decided to conduct a further search of Leventhal's computer to determine with greater certainty whether the "PPU" directory they had discovered during the first search was part of a tax preparation program. Investigators reexamined the computer in Leventhal's office once in February 1997 and twice in April 1997. During these subsequent searches, they copied the "Morph" and "PPU" directories onto a laptop computer, obtained additional printouts of the file directories, and opened a few files to examine their contents. In the first April search, an investigator noticed that some items had been added to the PPU directory since the previous search, indicating recent activity. The PPU directory was later identified as belonging to "Pencil Pushers," a tax preparation program. . . .

In September 1997, the DOT brought disciplinary charges against Leventhal under N.Y. Civ. Serv. Law § 75 charging six grounds of misconduct or incompetence. . . . Three months later, on October 18, 1999, Leventhal settled with the DOT. As part of the settlement, the DOT agreed to withdraw all disciplinary charges except that of lateness, to which Leventhal pleaded guilty. As a result, Leventhal was penalized thirty work days leave without pay. . . .

Four days after he settled the DOT disciplinary charges, Leventhal filed this action in United States District Court for the Northern District of New York. In his complaint, Leventhal alleged, under 42 U.S.C. § 1983 . . . Fourth Amendment violations arising out of the computer searches. . . .

"[T]he Fourth Amendment protects individuals from unreasonable searches conducted by the Government, even when the Government acts as an employer." *Nat'l Treasury Employees Union v. Von Raab,* 489 U.S. 656 (1989). The "special needs" of public employers may, however, allow them to dispense with the probable cause and warrant requirements when conducting workplace searches related to investigations of work-related misconduct. *See O'Connor v. Ortega,* 480 U.S. 709 (1987) (plurality opinion). In these situations, the Fourth Amendment's protection against "unreasonable" searches is enforced by "a careful balancing of governmental and private interests." *New Jersey v. T.L.O.,* 469 U.S. 325 (1985). A public employer's search of an area in which an employee had a reasonable expectation of privacy is "reasonable" when "the measures adopted are reasonably related to the objectives of the search and not excessively intrusive in light of" its purpose. *O'Connor,* 480 U.S. at 726.

We begin by inquiring whether "the conduct . . . at issue . . . infringed an expectation of privacy that society is prepared to consider reasonable." Without a reasonable expectation of privacy, a workplace search by a public employer will not violate the Fourth Amendment, regardless of the search's nature and scope. The workplace conditions can be such that an employee's expectation of privacy in a certain area is diminished.

We hold, based on the particular facts of this case, that Leventhal had a reasonable expectation of privacy in the contents of his office computer. We make this assessment "in the context of the employment relation, after considering what access other employees or the public had to Leventhal's office.

Leventhal occupied a private office with a door. He had exclusive use of the desk, filing cabinet, and computer in his office. Leventhal did not share use of his computer with other employees in the Accounting Bureau nor was there evidence that visitors or the public had access to his computer.

We are aware that "[p]ublic employees' expectations of privacy in their offices, desks, and file cabinets, like similar expectations of employees in the private sector, may be reduced by virtue of actual office practices and procedures, or by legitimate regulation." Construing the evidence in favor of Leventhal, as we must in reviewing this grant of summary judgment against him, we do not find that the DOT either had a general practice of routinely conducting searches of office computers or had placed Leventhal on notice that he should have no expectation of privacy in the contents of his office computer.

Viewing the DOT anti-theft policy in the light most favorable to Leventhal, we find that it did not prohibit the mere storage of personal materials in his office computer. Rather, the anti-theft policy prohibited "using" state equipment "for personal business" without defining further these terms. John Samaniuk, acting director of the DOT's Office of Internal Audits and Investigations, testified at Leventhal's disciplinary hearing that an employee would not violate state policies by keeping a personal checkbook in an office drawer, even though it would take up space there. Under the circumstances presented here, we cannot say that the same anti-theft policy prohibited Leventhal from storing personal items in his office computer.

Although the DOT technical support staff had access to all computers in the DOT offices, their maintenance of these computers was normally announced and the one example in the record of an unannounced visit to Leventhal's computer was only to change the name of a server. DOT personnel might also need, at times, to search for a document in an unattended computer, but there was no evidence that these searches were frequent, widespread, or extensive enough to constitute an atmosphere "so open to fellow employees or the public that no expectation of privacy is reasonable." This type of infrequent and selective search for maintenance purposes or to retrieve a needed document, justified by reference to the "special needs" of employers to pursue legitimate work-related objectives, does not destroy any underlying expectation of privacy that an employee could otherwise possess in the contents of an office computer. . . .

Even though Leventhal had some expectation of privacy in the contents of his office computer, the investigatory searches by the DOT did not violate his Fourth Amendment rights. An investigatory search for evidence of suspected work-related employee misfeasance will be constitutionally "reasonable" if it is "justified at its inception" and of appropriate scope. . . .

The initial consideration of the search's justification examines whether "there are reasonable grounds for suspecting that the search will turn up evidence that the employee is guilty of work-related misconduct." Here, there were reasonable grounds to believe that the searches would uncover evidence of misconduct. The specific allegations against the grade 27 employee, who was reasonably assumed to be Leventhal, were that (1) he was "late everyday"; (2) he spent "[t]he majority of his time . . . on non-DOT business related phone calls or talking to other personnel about personal computers"; and that (3) "[h]e is only in the office half the time[; the other half] he is either sick or on vacation." Probable cause is not necessary to conduct a search in this context, a plurality of the Court has explained, because "public employers have a direct and overriding interest in ensuring that the work of the agency is conducted in a proper and efficient manner." The individualized suspicion of misconduct in this case justified the DOT's decision to instigate some type of search.

The scope of a search will be appropriate if "reasonably related to the objectives of the search and not excessively intrusive in light of the nature of the misconduct." We conclude that the DOT search to identify whether Leventhal was using non-standard DOT software was "reasonably related" to the DOT's investigation of the allegations of Leventhal's workplace misconduct. Although the anonymous letter did not allege that the grade 27 employee was misusing DOT office computers, it did allege that the grade 27 employee was not attentive to his duties and spent a significant amount of work time discussing personal computers with other employees. Furthermore, the letter's allegations assumed that the DOT prohibition against misusing office computers was not rigorously enforced in the Accounting Bureau, remarking that a grade 18 employee "play[ed] computer games," that a grade 23 employee spent a substantial part of the day "playing computer games" or in non-work related conversations, and that another grade 23 employee "amuses himself by learning about computer software which have nothing to do with work." In view of the allegations of the misuse of DOT computers among other employees in the Accounting Bureau, Leventhal's alleged penchant for discussing personal computers during work hours, and Leventhal's general inattention to his duties which included, we presume, supervision of the computer use of others, we find that the searches of his computer were "reasonably related" to the DOT investigation of allegations of Leventhal's workplace misconduct.

Leventhal argues that a search for non-standard software would be irrelevant to charges of misconduct because the DOT had, *de facto,* approved of the use of non-standard software needed to conduct DOT business. Even assuming that this were true, the investigation was more broadly aimed at uncovering evidence that

Leventhal was using his office computer for non-DOT purposes. The searches accomplished this task by uncovering evidence that Leventhal had loaded a tax preparation program onto his office computer, a program that he later admitted he used to print out personal tax returns in his office. . . .

NOTES & QUESTIONS

1. *Applying the "Special Needs" Doctrine.* Did the anonymous letter focus enough on Leventhal's computer misuse to justify the search? Given the court's reasoning, would a search of Leventhal's desk drawers have been "reasonable"?

2. *Reasonable Expectations of Privacy in Workplace Computers.* In *United States v. Simons*, 206 F.3d 392 (4th Cir. 2000), Simons was employed at the Foreign Bureau of Information Services (FBIS) within the CIA. The FBIS had an Internet use policy that provided that employees were to use the Internet only for official government business. Furthermore, the policy provided, the "FBIS will periodically audit, inspect, and/or monitor the user's Internet access as deemed appropriate." FBIC contracted with an outside company to manage its computer network. One day, a manager at the company was testing the firewall database by entering the keyword "sex," and he discovered a "a large number of Internet 'hits' originating from Simons's computer." The manager informed FBIS, and a person from FBIS along with employees of the company remotely examined Simons's computer. They discovered more than 1,000 pornographic images. Among the pictures were images of child pornography. Criminal investigators then became involved. A company official entered Simons's office and swapped his hard drive with a copy. FBI Agent John Mesisca found over 50 images of child pornography on Simons's hard drive. Simons was indicted on one count of knowingly receiving child pornography and one count of knowingly possessing material containing images of child pornography. Simons moved to suppress the evidence, arguing that the searches of his office and computer violated the Fourth Amendment. The district court denied his motion. Simons was convicted and sentenced to 18 months' imprisonment.

   Simons contended that the search of his computer violated his Fourth Amendment rights. The court concluded that Simons lacked a reasonable expectation of privacy in his computer:

   > We first consider Simons's challenge to the warrantless searches of his computer and office by FBIS. We conclude that the remote searches of Simons's computer did not violate his Fourth Amendment rights because, in light of the Internet policy, Simons lacked a legitimate expectation of privacy in the files downloaded from the Internet. Additionally, we conclude that Simons's Fourth Amendment rights were not violated by FBIS' retrieval of Simons's hard drive from his office.
   >
   > Simons did not have a legitimate expectation of privacy with regard to the record or fruits of his Internet use in light of the FBIS Internet policy. The policy clearly stated that FBIS would "audit, inspect, and/or monitor" employees' use of the Internet, including all file transfers, all websites visited, and all e-mail

messages, "as deemed appropriate." This policy placed employees on notice that they could not reasonably expect that their Internet activity would be private. Therefore, regardless of whether Simons subjectively believed that the files he transferred from the Internet were private, such a belief was not objectively reasonable after FBIS notified him that it would be overseeing his Internet use. Accordingly, FBIS's actions in remotely searching and seizing the computer files Simons downloaded from the Internet did not violate the Fourth Amendment.

The court noted that the warrantless entry into Simons's office did trigger the Fourth Amendment, as he had a reasonable expectation of privacy in his office. However, the court concluded that the search was reasonable under the special needs doctrine:

> We have little trouble concluding that the warrantless entry of Simons's office was reasonable under the Fourth Amendment standard announced in *O'Connor*. At the inception of the search FBIS had "reasonable grounds for suspecting" that the hard drive would yield evidence of misconduct because FBIS was already aware that Simons had misused his Internet access to download over a thousand pornographic images, some of which involved minors. The search was also permissible in scope. The measure adopted, entering Simons's office, was reasonably related to the objective of the search, retrieval of the hard drive. And, the search was not excessively intrusive. Indeed, there has been no suggestion that Harper searched Simons's desk or any other items in the office; rather, Harper simply crossed the floor of Simons's office, switched hard drives, and exited.

Compare *Simons* with *Leventhal*. Why did Leventhal have a reasonable expectation of privacy in his computer but not Simons?

3. ***Telecommuting.*** Consider an employee working from home. What factors should be considered if a dispute arises concerning e-mail or use of the Internet? Would it matter if the computer or the e-mail service were provided by the employer? What if the computer is also for personal use?

4. ***Electronic Surveillance Law: Telephone Use vs. Internet Use.*** Consider Clifford Fishman:

> [W]hile the Wiretap Act presumes all phone conversations are protected and obliges the employer to demonstrate a legitimate business purpose to justify monitoring, the Stored Communications Act gives the employer/ISP the unrestricted right to make a post-transmission examination of employees' every e-mail and Web-surf. There is no logical reason for this dichotomy.[17]

5. ***Unauthorized Access to Password-Protected Websites.*** In *Konop v. Hawaiian Airlines, Inc.*, 302 F.3d 868 (9th Cir. 2002), Konop, a pilot for Hawaiian Airlines, maintained a website where he posted comments criticizing his employer. To access Konop's website, visitors had to log in with a user name and password. Moreover, users had to indicate that they accepted the website's terms and conditions of use, which prohibited any Hawaiian manager from

---

[17] Clifford S. Fishman, *Technology and the Internet: The Impending Destruction of Privacy by Betrayers, Grudgers, Snoops, Spammers, Corporations, and the Media*, 72 Geo. Wash. L. Rev. 1503, 1530 (2004).

viewing the website and restricted users in divulging the website's contents to others. Konop gave the password to a select group of people, primarily pilots and employees of the airline. Hawaiian Airlines vice president James Davis obtained the passwords of two pilots on Konop's list and accessed the website. The court held that there was no violation of the Wiretap Act because there was no interception. Relying on *Steve Jackson Games,* the court concluded that Konop's website postings were not acquired in transmission. Applying the Stored Communications Act, the court accepted the parties' stipulation that the content of the website was in "electronic storage" and subject to the Stored Communications Act. However, the Act states that a "user" can authorize a third party to access the communication. *See* 18 U.S.C. § 2701(c)(2). The court concluded that it was unclear from the record whether the two pilots were users because merely having the password was insufficient to establish the statutory definition of user, which requires that a user not only be authorized to use the communication service but also must actually use the service. Since there was no evidence that the pilots used Konop's website, the court refused to grant summary judgment to the defendants on this claim. Would Konop have a viable intrusion upon seclusion claim? Should an employer have any legal interest in finding out about statements workers are making about that employer outside the workplace?

6. ***Employer Demands for Social Media Passwords.*** Some employers demand that employees provide them with their social media passwords so employers can examine their postings to their friends. In addition to employers, a number of college and university athletic departments engaged in a similar practice regarding student athletes. News of these practices resulted in considerable public backlash, and a number of states passed statutes to prohibit such demands for passwords.

In *R.S. v. Minnewaska Area School District No. 2149*, 894 F. Supp. 2d 1128 (D. Min. 2012), school officials forced R.S. to provider her Facebook and e-mail passwords because she had a conversation related to sex outside of school. R.S., a 12-year-old student, through her mother S.S., sued the school for violating her First and Fourth Amendment rights among other things.

Regarding the First Amendment, the court concluded:

> The law on out-of-school statements by students can thus be summarized as follows: Such statements are protected under the First Amendment and not punishable by school authorities unless they are true threats or are reasonably calculated to reach the school environment *and* are so egregious as to pose a serious safety risk or other substantial disruption in that environment. R.S.'s Facebook wall postings were not true threats or threats of any kind. While her statements may have been reasonably calculated to reach a school audience, that possible fact is not sufficient to justify her punishment. The school defendants must also show that the statements posed a substantial disruptive effect.
>
> The content of R.S.'s wall postings are a far cry from the statements made by the students in cases in which courts have approved of school intervention. The Court notes that the Supreme Court reasoned in Tinker that black arm bands worn in opposition to the Vietnam War were not likely to cause the requisite substantial disruption to justify punishment. Based on the facts alleged in

Plaintiffs' complaint, a reasonable reader could not consider her statements likely to cause a substantial disruption to the school environment. R.S. stated that she "hated" a particular adult school employee because that employee was mean to her, and she then expressed salty curiosity about who had "told on her." Such statements were not likely to cause a substantial disruption to the school environment.

Regarding the Fourth Amendment, the court held that R.S. had a reasonable expectation of privacy to her private Facebook postings: "As with a private letter, the content of R.S.'s electronic correspondence was available only to her and her correspondent." The court also concluded that school officials lacked a "legitimate interest" in "perusing R.S.'s private communications" because this did not involve maintaining discipline on school grounds or "illegal behavior or violations of school policy."

Several states have passed laws to prohibit demanding social media passwords.[18] In many states, the law covers both employers and schools. But in some, the law only covers employers. Most states that have laws covering schools only cover higher education and do not cover K-12 schools. Michigan is one of the few exceptions, which covers both higher education and K-12.

In a number of states, the law covers only social media sites. For example, the law in New Mexico applies to an online service where individuals "construct a public or semi-public profile" and "create a list of other users with whom they share a connection within the system." N. M. Stat. § 50-4-34. Other states focus on all personal online accounts or are ambiguous about what types of accounts are covered. For example, Utah's law applies to any "personal Internet account[,]" which means "any online account that is used by an employee or applicant exclusively for personal communications unrelated to any business purpose of the employer." Utah Code § 34-48-101.

7. ***The NRLB and Social Media.*** The National Labor Relations Board has found that the National Labor Relations Act (NLRA) extends to certain work-related conversations conducted on social media. These interests relate to both union and non-union settings; the National Labor Relations Act's Section 7 protects the rights of employees, unionized or non-unionized, to engage in concerted activities for "mutual aid or protection." Moreover, an employer violates Section 8(a)(1) of the NLRA through maintenance of a work rule that would "reasonably tend to chill employees in the exercise of their Section 7 rights." *Lafayette Park Hotel*, 326 NLRB 824, 825 (1998), enfd. 203 F.3d 52 (D.C. Cir. 1999).

A social media case of the Board from 2012 found it to be unlawful for a non-profit organization to terminate five employees who posted on Facebook about a co-worker who intended to complain to management about their workplace performance. The Facebook communications "had a clear 'mutual aid' objective of preparing her coworkers for a group defense to those

---

[18] For a survey, see National Conference of State Legislatures, *Employer Access to Social Media Usernames and Passwords*, at http://www.ncsl.org/research/telecommunications-and-information-technology/employer-access-to-social-media-passwords-2013.aspx.

complaints." *Hispanics United of Buffalo, Inc. and Carlos Ortiz*, 359 NLRB no. 37, 1, 3 (Dec. 14, 2012). The NLRB has also issued guidance on permissible and impermissible social media policies for employers. NLRB, Office of the General Counsel, Division of Operations-Management, *Memorandum OM 12-59* (May 30, 2012).[19]

UNITED STATES V. ZIEGLER

474 F.3d 1184 (9th Cir. 2007)

O'SCANNLAIN, J. . . . Frontline Processing ("Frontline"), a company that services Internet merchants by processing on-line electronic payments, is located in Bozeman, Montana. On January 30, 2001, Anthony Cochenour, the owner of Frontline's Internet-service provider and the fiancé of a Frontline employee, contacted Special Agent James A. Kennedy, Jr. of the FBI with a tip that a Frontline employee had accessed child-pornographic websites from a workplace computer.

Agent Kennedy pursued the report that day, first contacting Frontline's Internet Technology ("IT") Administrator, John Softich. One of Softich's duties at Frontline was to monitor employee use of the workplace computers including their Internet access. He informed Kennedy that the company had in place a firewall, which permitted constant monitoring of the employees' Internet activities.

During the interview, Softich confirmed Cochenour's report that a Frontline employee had accessed child pornography via the Internet. Softich also reported that he had personally viewed the sites and confirmed that they depicted "very, very young girls in various states of undress." Softich further informed Kennedy that, according to the Internet Protocol address and log-in information, the offending sites were accessed from a computer in the office of Appellant Jeffrey Brian Ziegler, who had been employed by Frontline as director of operations since August 2000. Softich also informed Kennedy that the IT department had already placed a monitor on Ziegler's computer to record its Internet traffic by copying its cache files.

Agent Kennedy next interviewed William Schneider, Softich's subordinate in Frontline's IT department. Schneider confirmed that the IT department had placed a device in Ziegler's computer that would record his Internet activity. He reported that he had "spot checked" Ziegler's cache files and uncovered several images of child pornography. A review of Ziegler's "search engine cache information" also disclosed that he had searched for "things like 'preteen girls' and 'underage girls.'" Furthermore, according to Schneider, Frontline owned and routinely monitored all workplace computers. The employees were aware of the IT department's monitoring capabilities.

The parties dispute what happened next. According to testimony that Softich and Schneider provided to a federal grand jury, Agent Kennedy instructed them to make a copy of Ziegler's hard drive because he feared it might be tampered with

---

[19] For a discussion of the NLRB's decisions about acceptable social media policies, see Robert Sprague, *Facebook Meets the NLRB: Employee Online Communications and Unfair Labor Practices*, 14 U. Pa. J. Bus.L. 957 (2012).

before the FBI could make an arrest. Agent Kennedy, however, denied that he directed the Frontline employees to do anything. According to his testimony, his understanding was that the IT department had already made a backup copy of Ziegler's hard drive. As the government points out, his notes from the Softich interview say, "IT Dept has backed up JZ's hard drive to protect info." Thinking that the copy had already been made, Kennedy testified that he instructed Softich only to ensure that no one could tamper with the backup copy.

Whatever Agent Kennedy's actual instructions, the Frontline IT employees' subjective understanding of that conversation seems evident from their actions during the late evening of January 30, 2001. Around 10:00 P.M., Softich and Schneider obtained a key to Ziegler's private office from Ronald Reavis, the chief financial officer of Frontline, entered Ziegler's office, opened his computer's outer casing, and made two copies of the hard drive.

Shortly thereafter, Michael Freeman, Frontline's corporate counsel, contacted Agent Kennedy and informed him that Frontline would cooperate fully in the investigation. Freeman indicated that the company would voluntarily turn over Ziegler's computer to the FBI and thus explicitly suggested that a search warrant would be unnecessary. On February 5, 2001, Reavis delivered to Agent Kennedy Ziegler's computer tower (containing the original hard drive) and one of the hard drive copies made by Schneider and Softich. Schneider delivered the second copy sometime later. Forensic examiners at the FBI discovered many images of child pornography.

On May 23, 2003, a federal grand jury handed down a three-count indictment charging Ziegler with receipt of child pornography, in violation of 18 U.S.C. § 2252A(a)(2); possession of child pornography, in violation of 18 U.S.C. § 2252A(a)(5)(B); and receipt of obscene material, in violation of 18 U.S.C. § 1462. . . .

Ziegler's sole contention on appeal is that the January 30, 2001, entry into his private office to search his workplace computer violated the Fourth Amendment and, as such, the evidence contained on the computer's hard drive must be suppressed.

Ziegler argues that "[t]he district court erred in its finding that Ziegler did not have a legitimate expectation of privacy in his office and computer." He likens the workplace computer to the desk drawer or file cabinet given Fourth Amendment protection in cases such as *O'Connor v. Ortega,* 480 U.S. 709 (1987). Ziegler further contends that the Fourth Circuit's *Simons* case is inapposite. Whereas in *Simons* "the person conducting the search was a network administrator whose purpose was to search for evidence of employee misconduct," in this case "the search was conducted at the behest of Agent Kennedy who was undeniably seeking evidence of a crime."

The government, of course, views the matter quite differently. It contends that the district court's ruling was correct — Ziegler did not have an objectively reasonable expectation of privacy in his workplace computer. . . .

As we know, the Fourth Amendment protects people, not places. Although it is often true that "for most people, their computers are their most private spaces," the validity of that expectation depends entirely on its context.

In that vein, a criminal defendant may invoke the protections of the Fourth Amendment only if he can show that he had a *legitimate* expectation of privacy in the place searched or the item seized. . . .

The government does not contest Ziegler's claim that he had a subjective expectation of privacy in his office and the computer. The use of a password on his computer and the lock on his private office door are sufficient evidence of such expectation.

But Ziegler's expectation of privacy in his office and workplace computer must also have been objectively reasonable. The seminal case addressing the reasonable expectations of private employees in the workplace is *Mancusi v. DeForte,* 392 U.S. 364 (1968). In *Mancusi,* the Supreme Court addressed whether a union employee had a legitimate expectation of privacy, and therefore Fourth Amendment standing, in the contents of records that he stored in an office that he shared with several other union officials. The Court held that DeForte had standing to object to the search and that the search was unreasonable, noting that it was clear that "if DeForte had occupied a 'private' office in the union headquarters, and union records had been seized from a desk or a filing cabinet in that office, he would have had standing." That was so because he could expect that he would not be disturbed except by business or personal invitees and that the records would not be taken except with the permission of his supervisors. The Court thought the fact that the office was shared with a few other individuals to be of no constitutional distinction.

Mancusi compels us to recognize that in the private employer context, employees retain at least some expectation of privacy in their offices.

Furthermore, Ziegler's expectation of privacy in his office was reasonable on the facts of this case. His office was not shared by co-workers, and kept locked.

Because Ziegler had a reasonable expectation of privacy in his office, any search of that space and the items located therein must comply with the Fourth Amendment.

The next step is to inquire whether there was a search or seizure by the government. We need not dwell upon this matter too long. Given the district court's factual findings, we treat Softich and Schneider as de facto government agents. While the two Frontline employees may not have scoured the desk drawers and cabinets for evidence, as the agents did in *Mancusi,* they undoubtedly "searched" Ziegler's office when they entered to make a copy of the hard drive of his computer. . . .

The remaining question is whether the search of Ziegler's office and the copying of his hard drive were "unreasonable" within the meaning of the Fourth Amendment. As in *Mancusi,* the government does not deny that the search and seizure were without a warrant, and "it is settled for purposes of the Amendment that 'except in certain carefully defined classes of cases, a search of private property without proper consent is 'unreasonable' unless it has been authorized by a valid search warrant.'"

One well-settled exception is where valid consent is obtained by the government. In proving voluntary consent, the government "is not limited to proof that consent was given by the defendant, but may show that permission to search was obtained from a third party who possessed common authority over or other sufficient relationship to the premises or effects sought to be inspected." *United States v. Matlock,* 415 U.S. 164 (1974).

We first consider whether Frontline exercised common authority over the office and the workplace computer such that it could validly consent to a search. *Mancusi* is again instructive. In *Mancusi,* the Supreme Court recognized that in his office, DeForte retained an expectation "that records would not be taken [by the police] except with his permission or that of his union superiors." The Court continued: "It is, of course, irrelevant that the Union or some of its officials might validly have consented to a search of the area where the records were kept, regardless of DeForte's wishes, for it is not claimed that any such consent was given, either expressly or by implication." *Mancusi* thus establishes that even where a private employee retains an expectation that his private office will not be the subject of an unreasonable government search, such interest may be subject to the possibility of an employer's consent to a search of the premises which it owns.

We are also convinced that Frontline could give valid consent to a search of the contents of the hard drive of Ziegler's workplace computer because the computer is the type of workplace property that remains within the control of the employer "even if the employee has placed personal items in [it]." *O'Connor v. Ortega,* 480 U.S. 709 (1987). In *Ortega,* the Supreme Court offered an analogy that is helpful to our resolution of this question. The Court posited a situation where an employee brings a piece of personal luggage to work and places it within his office. The Court noted that "[w]hile . . . the outward appearance of the luggage is affected by its presence in the workplace, the employee's expectation of privacy in the *contents* of the luggage is not affected in the same way." The Court further explained that "[t]he appropriate standard for a workplace search does not necessarily apply to a piece of closed personal luggage, a handbag or a briefcase that happens to be within the employer's business address."

The workplace computer, however, is quite different from the piece of personal luggage which the Court described in *Ortega.* Although use of each Frontline computer was subject to an individual log-in, Schneider and other IT-department employees "had complete administrative access to anybody's machine." The company had also installed a firewall, which, according to Schneider, is "a program that monitors Internet traffic . . . from within the organization to make sure nobody is visiting any sites that might be unprofessional." Monitoring was routine, and the IT department reviewed the log created by the firewall "[o]n a regular basis," sometimes daily if Internet traffic was high enough to warrant it. Finally, upon their hiring, Frontline employees were apprised of the company's monitoring efforts through training and an employment manual, and they were told that the computers were company-owned and not to be used for activities of a personal nature.

In this context, Ziegler could not reasonably have expected that the computer was his personal property, free from any type of control by his employer. The contents of his hard drive, like the files in *Mancusi,* were work-related items that contained business information and which were provided to, or created by, the employee in the context of the business relationship. Ziegler's downloading of personal items to the computer did not destroy the employer's common authority. Thus, Frontline, as the employer, could consent to a search of the office and the computer that it provided to Ziegler for his work.

The remaining question is, given Frontline's *ability* to consent to a search, did it consent to a search of the office and the computer. We conclude that it did. The exact type of employer consent that was absent in *Mancusi* clearly exists in this case. While the district court found that Softich and Schneider acted at the direction of Agent Kennedy, the record shows that Softich and Schneider received consent to search the office and the keys to the office from the Chief Financial Officer of Frontline Ronald Reavis. . . .

Although Ziegler retained a legitimate expectation of privacy in his workplace office, Frontline retained the ability to consent to a search of Ziegler's office and his business computer. And because valid third party consent to search the office and computer located therein was given by his employer, the district court's order denying suppression of the evidence of child pornography existing on Ziegler's computer is affirmed.

NOTES & QUESTIONS

1. ***Public vs. Private Sector Employment.*** *Simons* involves a search of a public sector employee; *Ziegler* involves a search of a private sector employee. Does the Fourth Amendment apply differently in these settings? If so, how?

2. ***A Duty to Monitor Employees?*** In *Doe v. XYC Corp.*, 887 A.2d 1156 (N.J. Super. Ct. App. Div. 2005), XYC Corporation employed Jane Doe's husband as an accountant. The network administrator discovered that the employee was visiting porn sites. The employee's supervisors told him to stop, and the employee said he would. The employee, however, had been videotaping and photographing his ten-year-old stepdaughter, Jill Doe, in the nude and transmitted three pictures of Jill Doe from his workplace computer to gain access to a child porn website. Jane Doe sued XYC on behalf of Jill, alleging that it knew or should have known that her husband was using his computer to view child porn and that it had a duty to report the employee to the authorities. XYC moved for summary judgment, but the court sided with the plaintiff:

   > We hold that an employer who is on notice that one of its employees is using a workplace computer to access pornography, possibly child pornography, has a duty to investigate the employee's activities and to take prompt and effective action to stop the unauthorized activity, lest it result in harm to innocent third parties. No privacy interest of the employee stands in the way of this duty on the part of the employer. . . .
   >
   > In this case, defendant had an e-mail policy which stated that "all messages composed, sent or received on the e-mail system are and remain the property of the [defendant]. They are not the private property of any employee." Further, defendant reserved the "right to review, audit, access and disclose all messages created, received or sent over the e-mail system as deemed necessary by and at the sole discretion of [defendant]." Concerning the internet, the policy stated that employees were permitted to "access sites, which are of a business nature only" and provided that:
   >
   > > Any employees who discover a violation of this policy shall notify personnel. Any employee who violates this policy or uses the electronic mail or Internet system for improper purposes shall be subject to discipline, up to and including discharge.

The written e-mail policy contained an acknowledgement page to be signed by each employee. While the record does not contain a copy of such acknowledgement signed by Employee, there is no suggestion that he was not aware of the company policy. In addition, as we have noted, Employee's office, as with others in the same area, did not have a door and his computer screen was visible from the hallway, unless he took affirmative action to block it. Under those circumstances, we readily conclude that Employee had no legitimate expectation of privacy that would prevent his employer from accessing his computer to determine if he was using it to view adult or child pornography. As a result, we turn to whether defendant had reason to investigate Employee's use of his computer. . . .

Viewed in a light favorable to plaintiff, defendant was on notice of Employee's pornographic related computer activity by early 2000. By late March 2001, defendant had knowledge, through its supervisory personnel, that Employee had visited a variety of "porn sites" including one that suggested child pornography. Yet, despite being reported to high level management, no action was taken. A reasonable fact-finder could conclude that an appropriate investigation at that time would have revealed the extent of Employee's activities and, presumably, would have led to action to shut down those activities. It is true, as defendant contends, that Employee could still have possibly utilized a computer elsewhere, such as at home or at a library, to transmit Jill's photos. But that possibility does not negate proximate cause as a matter of law; it simply presents a contested issue for a jury.

Doe v. XYC Corp. suggests that if an employer has a policy of monitoring its employees' computer use, then that employer is responsible for harm resulting from failing to monitor or from failing to discipline employees who violate the underlying rules regarding computer use at work. What incentives does this create for employers? Is this case likely to be followed in other jurisdictions?

3. ***Minimal Expectations of Privacy?*** Lothar Determann and Robert Sprague summarize U.S. workplace privacy in negative terms, "employees should anticipate very minimal expectations of privacy in workplaces in the United States."[20] They also list the reasons why employers feel it is necessary to monitor their workers: employers wish to protect information and other IP assets; increase productivity; and avoid liability due to a hostile workplace environment or improper use of computers by employees, including copyright infringement. Has the right balance been struck in the United States between employer and employee interests in the workplace?

---

[20] Determann & Sprague, *Intrusive Monitoring, supra* at 1018.

CHAPTER 13

INTERNATIONAL PRIVACY LAW

CHAPTER OUTLINE

The study of information privacy provides an opportunity to understand privacy law in different countries. This chapter explores the European Union General Data Protection Regulation, important European privacy case law, Canadian privacy law, and other international privacy materials. It focuses on international legal developments that will have an impact in the United States as well as on texts that offer a comparative perspective on the U.S. privacy regime.

United States and foreign privacy regimes differ in some respects. Consider the standard description of privacy legislation in Europe as "omnibus" and privacy law in the United States as "sectoral." In Europe, one statute typically regulates the processing of personal information in public and private sectors alike. In the absence of more specific legislation, the general information privacy law in Europe sets the initial terms for the processing, storage, and transfer of personal information. The omnibus law is often accompanied, moreover, by more specific privacy laws. These typically regulate certain areas of data use such as telecommunications, health care, and social welfare programs. In the United States, in contrast, there are only sectoral laws. These statutes focus on specific sectors of the economy or certain technologies.[1]

Outside of Europe, other countries around the world are moving toward adopting comprehensive privacy legislation based on the European model. According to Graham Greenleaf, there are now 120 data privacy laws in the world.[2] In his assessment, the trend since the start of the 21st Century has been for enactment of laws in OECD countries in the Asia-Pacific region with activity in Latin America, Africa, the Middle East, and Central Asia as well. He notes, "Since 2010 the average number of new laws per year has increased to 5.5, double the 2.7 average over the whole 44 years" from enactment of the first national data protection law in Sweden in 1973.[3] Moreover, Greenleaf notes that a large portion of the laws of these countries reflect European standards. In his assessment,

---

[1] Joel R. Reidenberg, *Setting Standards for Fair Information Practice in the U.S. Private Sector*, 80 Iowa L. Rev. 497, 500 (1995).

[2] Graham Greenleaf, *Countries with Data Privacy Laws — by Year 1973-2016*, 146 Privacy Laws & Business Int'l Rep. 18 (2017).

[3] Id. For a comprehensive list of the world's data protection statutes, see Graham Greenleaf, Global Tables of Data Privacy Laws and Bills (5th ed. 2017, updated March 2017), 145 Privacy Laws & Business Int'l Rep. 14-26 (2017).

"[S]omething reasonably described as 'European standard' data privacy laws are becoming the norm in most parts of the world with data privacy laws."[4]

In Europe, privacy law is shaped by the Council of Europe and the European Union (EU) and entities within these institutions. It was Article 8 of the Council of Europe's Convention on Human Rights of 1950, which firmly established privacy protection as a critical human rights claim in postwar Europe. The Council of Europe, located in Strasbourg, France, is Europe's leading human rights organization. Forty-seven Member States belong to it; 28 of these belong to the EU as well.

The privacy provisions in Article 8 have been given effect both by the decisions of the European Court of Human Rights, which is located in Strasbourg, France, and by the Convention on Data Protection established by the Council of Europe in 1980. The counter-party in litigation under Article 8 is the respective Member State whose law or other activity is challenged as violative of privacy. An interpretation of Article 8 by the European Court of Human Rights can lead it to remand the case back to the judiciary in the Member State for a further proceeding in light of its ruling on the applicable law.

Beyond the European Convention of Human Rights, the EU has a Charter of Fundamental Rights, which contains key privacy protections. The Convention and Charter function as the two pillars of fundamental rights in Europe. The former is an international treaty; the latter is a key constitutional document of the EU.

In its Article 8, the Convention grants everyone a "right to respect for his private and family life, his home and his correspondence." The EU's Charter of Fundamental Rights has more detailed protection for privacy. Its Article 7 protects private life and family life. In its Article 8, however, the Charter more specifically articulates "a right to the protection of personal data concerning him or her." In addition, the EU's Lisbon Treaty of 2007 explicitly recognized a right to data protection and also made the Charter of Fundamental Rights a legally enforceable document within the EU. The highest court in the EU is the European Court of Justice. It is located in Luxembourg City, Luxembourg.

One of the most important areas of European privacy law for almost a decade has been the Data Protection Directive of the European Union. Enacted in 1995, the Data Protection Directive establishes a basic legislative framework for the processing of personal information in the European Union. The EU Data Protection Directive has exercised a profound effect on the development of privacy law, not only in Europe but around the world. The EU has now replaced the Directive with the General Data Protection Regulation, which takes effect on May 25, 2018.

In the view of Gregory Schaffer, there has been a "ratcheting up" effect in the relationship between the United States and Europe in the area of privacy policy.[5] As a consequence of laws in Europe that safeguard privacy, Schaffer predicted in 2000 that it was more likely that similar laws will be adopted in the United States

---

[4] GRAHAM GREENLEAF, ASIAN DATA PRIVACY LAWS 57 (2014). Moreover, as Greenleaf states, "One of the most-implemented 'European' principles outside Europe is 'Data export restrictions based on destination,' which could also be named the 'adequacy requirement' for data exports." Id.

[5] Gregory Shaffer, *Globalization and Social Protection: The Impact of EU and International Rules in the Ratcheting Up of U.S. Privacy Standards*, 25 Yale J. Int'l L. 1 (2000).

or at least that U.S. firms will improve their privacy protection. While there is no omnibus bill in the United States, there has been considerable regulatory activity. In addition, Kenneth Bamberger and Deirdre Mulligan attribute the rise of Chief Privacy Officers in U.S. corporations at least in part to their role "smoothing interactions with European regulators under the Safe Harbor Agreement."[6]

It is worth noting that the phrase "data protection" is frequently used to describe privacy protection in the European context. This term reflects the modern concept of privacy protection that emerged in the 1970s as computer systems were increasingly used to process information on citizens. At the same time, a concept of "privacy," sometimes referred to as that of private life or the private domain, continues to play an important role in the European conception of information privacy.

Beyond Europe, important international and regional agreements have helped shape the structure of national privacy law and influenced the development of privacy as a legal claim in particular countries. The Privacy Guidelines of the Organization for Economic Cooperation and Development (OECD), adopted in 1980, represent a consensus position of countries from North America, Europe, and East Asia as to the basic structure of privacy law. This non-binding framework was supplemented in 2013 by additional OECD privacy guidelines.

Other privacy laws follow from Article 12 of the Universal Declaration of Human Rights, adopted by the United Nations in 1948, which states that "[n]o one shall be subjected to arbitrary interference with his privacy, family, home or correspondence, nor to attacks upon his honor and reputation. Everyone has the right to the protection of the law against such interference or attacks."

A. THE OECD PRIVACY GUIDELINES

1. THE 1980 ORIGINAL GUIDELINES

On September 23, 1980, the Organization for Economic Cooperation and Development (OECD), a group of leading industrial countries concerned with global economic and democratic development, issued guidelines for privacy protection in the transfer of personal information across national borders. The United States is a member of the OECD, which has 34 member countries. Its 1980 document is the Guidelines on the Protection of Privacy and Transborder Flows of Personal Data (the Guidelines), which establish eight key principles for the protection of personal information. It creates a non-binding framework that is intended to influence policymaking about privacy throughout the world.

Scope. The Guidelines "apply to personal data, whether in the public or private sectors, which, because of the manner in which they are processed, or because of their nature or the context in which they are used, pose a danger to privacy and individual liberties." "Personal data" is defined as "any information relating to an

---

[6] Kenneth Bamberger & Deirdre Mulligan, *Privacy on the Books and on the Ground*, 63 Stan. L. Rev. 247, 262 (2014).

identified or identifiable individual (data subject)." § 1(b). The Guidelines provide a floor of protection; member countries can adopt more stringent protections. It is important to note, however, that the Guidelines are not binding on the member nations of the OECD. Rather, they offer suggestions to lead to a more uniform treatment throughout different countries of personal data processing and to a free international flow of information. Their goal is to promote and protect, by recommending the implementation of uniform principles across member states, "the fundamental values of privacy, individual liberties and the global free flow of information."[7]

Principles. The OECD Privacy Guidelines establish eight principles regarding the processing of personal data:

1. *Collection Limitation Principle.* There should be limits to the collection of personal data and any such data should be obtained by lawful and fair means and, where appropriate, with the knowledge or consent of the data subject.

2. *Data Quality Principle.* Personal data should be relevant to the purposes for which they are to be used, and, to the extent necessary for those purposes, should be accurate, complete and kept up-to-date.

3. *Purpose Specification Principle.* The purposes for which personal data are collected should be specified not later than at the time of data collection and the subsequent use limited to the fulfillment of those purposes or such others as are not incompatible with those purposes and as are specified on each occasion of change of purpose.

4. *Use Limitation Principle.* Personal data should not be disclosed, made available or otherwise used for purposes other than those specified in accordance with [the Purpose Specification Principle] except: a) with the consent of the data subject; or b) by the authority of law.

5. *Security Safeguards Principle.* Personal data should be protected by reasonable security safeguards against such risks as loss or unauthorised access, destruction, use, modification or disclosure of data.

6. *Openness Principle.* There should be a general policy of openness about developments, practices and policies with respect to personal data. Means should be readily available of establishing the existence and nature of personal data, and the main purposes of their use, as well as the identity and usual residence of the data controller.

7. *Individual Participation Principle.* An individual should have the right: (a) to obtain from a data controller, or otherwise, confirmation of whether or not the data controller has data relating to him; (b) to have communicated to him, data relating to him (i) within a reasonable time; (ii) at a charge, if any, that is not excessive; (iii) in a reasonable manner; and (iv) in a form that is readily intelligible to him; (c) to be given reasons if a request made under subparagraphs (a) and (b) is denied, and to be able to challenge such denial; and (d) to challenge data relating to him and, if the challenge is successful to have the data erased, rectified, completed or amended.

8. *Accountability Principle.* A data controller should be accountable for complying with measures which give effect to the principles stated above. . . .

---

[7] OECD, *Recommendation of the Council concerning Guidelines governing the Protection of Privacy and Transborder Flows of Personal Data (2013)*, C(80)58/FINAL, as amended on 11 July 2013 by C(2013)79, at 11.

Self-Regulation and International Data Flow. The OECD Guidelines stress the importance of self-regulation and the free flow of data on a global basis. They call in § 19(b) for Member countries to "in particular endeavor to . . . encourage and support self-regulation, whether in the form of codes of conduct or otherwise." Sections 15-18 establish the "basic principles" of "free flow" of personal data and of transborder data flow. For example, § 16 of the Guidelines states: "Member countries should take all reasonable and appropriate steps to ensure that transborder flows of personal data, including transit through a member country are uninterrupted and secure." Section 18 permits restriction on these flows, but seeks to limit the conditions under which these limits can be exercised. This section provides: "A Member country should refrain from restricting transborder flows of personal data between itself and another Member country except where the latter does not yet substantially observe these Guidelines or where the re-export of such data would circumvent its domestic privacy legislation."

The Worldwide Influence of the OECD Privacy Guidelines. As noted, the OECD Privacy Guidelines are non-binding on members of the OECD. Nonetheless, they have had a significant impact on the development of national law in North America, Europe, and East Asia.[8] For example, in the United States, the subscriber privacy provisions in the Cable Act of 1984 include many of the principles of the OECD Privacy Guidelines. In Australia, the Privacy Act of 1988 establishes 11 privacy principles based on the OECD Privacy Guidelines. New Zealand's 1993 Privacy Act, which regulates both the public and private sectors, adopts 12 principles based on the OECD Privacy Guidelines. South Korea's Act on the Protection of Personal Information Managed by Public Agencies of 1994 follows a number of the OECD Privacy Guidelines.

The Working Party on Information Security and Privacy (WPISP). WPISP is an important forum at the OECD for the development of policy options. It brings together both government and representatives of "[b]usiness, civil society, other international organizations and non-members." The WPISP has published white papers and guidances on policy and practices, including a paper on "Making privacy notices simple" and a "privacy policy statement generator."[9] It also played a key role in the formulation of the 2013 update to the 1980 Guidelines. It developed the Terms of Reference that served as a roadmap for the review process and delivered important preparatory work to the Expert Group that was formed to review the 1980 Guidelines.

2. THE 2013 OECD PRIVACY GUIDELINES

The OECD released a set of new guidelines in 2013 that update the 1980 Guidelines but do not replace them. A volunteer Expert Group led the revision

---

[8] For an analysis of privacy laws around the world, see EPIC & Privacy International, Privacy and Human Rights (2006).

[9] OECD, *What Is the Working Party on Information Security and Privacy (WPISP)?*, at http://www.oecd.org/document/46/0,3746,en_2649_34255_36862382_1_1_1_1,00.html.

process; it was chaired by Jennifer Stoddart, Privacy Commissioner of Canada. Omer Tene, an international privacy expert, served as rapporteur for the project.

New Concepts in the 2013 Guidelines. The new guidelines emphasize the need for multifaceted national privacy strategy, privacy management programs, and data security breach notification. The 2013 guidelines provide additional details about accountability in organizations, an idea already present in the 1980 Guidelines, and simplify and consolidate the OECD approach to transborder data flows.

Multifaceted National Privacy Strategies. National strategies should "reflect a coordinated approach across governmental bodies." Article 19(a). This approach should include establishment of "privacy enforcement authorities with the governance, resources and technical expertise necessary to exercise their powers effectively and to make decisions on an objective, impartial and consistent basis." Article 19(c).

Privacy Management Programs. A "data controller" is required to establish a privacy management program with a number of elements including the ability to give "effect to these Guidelines for all personal data under its control." Article 15(a). The Guidelines define a data controller as "a party who, according to national law, is competent to decide about the contents and use of personal data regardless of whether or not such data are collected, stored, processed or disseminated by that party or by an agent on its behalf." Article 1(a).

Data Security Breach Notification. Notification is to be given both to an authority and to the affected individual affected by the security breach. Article 15(c). Notice must be given to an authority only when a "significant security breach affecting personal data" occurs. Article 15(c). Notification to data subjects is required only where the breach "is likely to adversely affect" these persons. The *Supplementary Explanatory Memorandum to the Revised OECD Guidelines* explains that it seeks a "risk-based approach to notification." It seeks to curb excessive notifications, which can create an undue burden on data controllers and enforcement authorities as well as encourage affected individuals to ignore breach notices.

Expanding Accountability. The original OECD Guidelines already contained a principle of "accountability." The 2013 Guidelines provide more details about the steps that an accountable organization should take. These include establishment of a privacy management program, as discussed above, and being able to demonstrate that the management program is appropriate. Article 15(b).

Transborder Data Flows. Regarding international data flows, a data controller is "accountable for personal data under its control without regard to the location of the data." Article 16. As the Supplementary Explanatory Memorandum points out, this paragraph "restates the basic principle of accountability . . . in the context of transborder data flows." Article 17 establishes a principle of free flow of international data. It states:

A Member country should refrain from restricting transborder data flows . . . where (a) the other country substantially observes these Guidelines or (b) sufficient safeguards exist, including effective enforcement mechanisms and appropriate measures put in place by the data controller, to ensure a continuing level of protection consistent with these Guidelines.

Finally, Article 18 requires any restriction to transborder flows to be "proportionate to the risks presented, taking into account the sensitivity of the data, and the purpose and context of the processing."

NOTES & QUESTIONS

1. *The OECD Privacy Guidelines, Old and New, and the Fair Information Practices.* How do the 1980 OECD Privacy Guidelines compare with the 2013 Guidelines? What do the new areas of emphasis demonstrate about trends in information privacy law? Do the two OECD Guidelines compare favorably with the articulation of Fair Information Practices in the Department of Housing, Education, and Welfare (HEW) Report of 1973 (Chapter 7). Is either framework more comprehensive? More detailed? Which framework would be easier to comply with? To enforce?

B. PRIVACY PROTECTION IN EUROPE

1. DIVERGENCE OR CONVERGENCE?

JAMES Q. WHITMAN, *THE TWO WESTERN CULTURES OF PRIVACY: DIGNITY VERSUS LIBERTY*

113 Yale L.J. 1151 (2004)

Continental law is avidly protective of many kinds of "privacy" in many realms of life, whether the issue is consumer data, credit reporting, workplace privacy, discovery in civil litigation, the dissemination of nude images on the Internet, or shielding criminal offenders from public exposure. To people accustomed to the continental way of doing things, American law seems to tolerate relentless and brutal violations of privacy in all these areas of law. I have seen Europeans grow visibly angry, for example, when they learn about routine American practices like credit reporting. How, they ask, can merchants be permitted access to the entire credit history of customers who have never defaulted on their debts? Is it not obvious that this is a violation of privacy and personhood, which must be prohibited by law?

[Differences about privacy in the United States and Europe] are clashes in attitude that go well beyond the occasional social misunderstanding. In fact, they have provoked some tense and costly transatlantic legal and trade battles over the last decade and a half. Thus, the European Union and the United States slid into a major trade conflict over the protection of consumer data in the 1990s, only problematically resolved by a 2000 "safe harbor" agreement. Europeans still constantly complain that Americans do not accept the importance of protecting consumer privacy. Those tensions have only grown in the aftermath of September 11. . . .

For sensitive Europeans, indeed, a tour through American law may be an experience something like a visit to the latrines of Ephesus. Correspondingly, it has become common for Europeans to maintain that they respect a "fundamental right to privacy" that is either weak or wholly absent in the "cultural context" of the United States. Here, Europeans point with pride to Article 8 of the European Convention on Human Rights, which protects "the right to respect for private and family life," and to the European Union's new Charter of Fundamental Rights, which demonstratively features articles on both "Respect for Private and Family Life" and "Protection of Personal Data." By the standards of those great documents, American privacy law seems, from the European point of view, simply to have "failed.". . .

What we must acknowledge, instead, is that there are, on the two sides of the Atlantic, two different cultures of privacy, which are home to different intuitive sensibilities, and which have produced two significantly different laws of privacy. . . .

So why do these sensibilities differ? Why is it that French people won't talk about their salaries, but will take off their bikini tops? Why is it that Americans comply with court discovery orders that open essentially all of their documents for inspection, but refuse to carry identity cards? Why is it that Europeans tolerate state meddling in their choice of baby names? Why is it that Americans submit to extensive credit reporting without rebelling? . . .

At its conceptual core, the American right to privacy still takes much the form that it took in the eighteenth century: It is the right to freedom from intrusions by the state, especially in one's own home. The prime danger, from the American point of view, is that "the sanctity of [our] home[s]," in the words of a leading nineteenth-century Supreme Court opinion on privacy, will be breached by government actors. American anxieties thus focus comparatively little on the media. Instead, they tend to be anxieties about maintaining a kind of private sovereignty within our own walls.

Such is the contrast that lies at the base of our divergent sensibilities about what counts as a "privacy" violation. On the one hand, we have an Old World in which it seems fundamentally important not to lose public face; on the other, a New World in which it seems fundamentally important to preserve the home as a citadel of individual sovereignty. . . . When Americans seem to continental Europeans to violate norms of privacy, it is because they seem to display an embarrassing lack of concern for public dignity — whether the issue is the public indignity inflicted upon Monica Lewinsky by the media, or the self-inflicted indignity of an American who boasts about his salary. Conversely, when continental Europeans seem to Americans to violate norms of privacy, it is because they seem to show a supine lack of resistance to invasions of the realm of private sovereignty whose main citadel is the home — whether the issue is wiretapping or baby names. . . .

Where do the peculiar continental anxieties about "privacy" come from? To understand the continental law of privacy, we must start by recognizing how deeply "dignity" and "honor" matter in continental law more broadly. Privacy is not the only area in which continental law aims to protect people from shame and humiliation, from loss of public dignity. The law of privacy, in these continental countries, is only one member of a much wider class of legal protections for interpersonal respect. The importance of the value of respect in continental law is most familiar to Americans from one body of law in particular: the continental law of hate speech, which protects minorities against disrespectful epithets. But the continental attachment to norms of respect goes well beyond hate speech. Minorities are not the only ones protected against disrespectful epithets on the Continent. Everybody is protected against disrespect, through the continental law of "insult," a very old body of law that protects the individual right to "personal honor." Nor does it end there. Continental law protects the right of workers to respectful treatment by their bosses and coworkers, through what is called the law of "mobbing" or "moral harassment." This is law that protects employees against being addressed disrespectfully, shunned, or even assigned humiliating tasks like xeroxing. Continental law also protects the right of women to respectful treatment through its version of the law of sexual harassment. It even tries to protect the right of prison inmates to respectful treatment . . . to a degree almost unimaginable for Americans. . . .

If I may use a cosmological metaphor: American privacy law is a body caught in the gravitational orbit of liberty values, while European law is caught in the orbit of dignity. . . . Continental Europeans are consistently more drawn to problems touching on public dignity, while Americans are consistently more drawn to problems touching on the depredations of the state. . . .

Why does continental law work so hard to guarantee norms of "respect," "dignity," and "personal honor" in so many walks of life? This is a question to which I believe we must give a different answer from the one Europeans themselves commonly give. Europeans generally give a dramatic explanation for why dignity figures so prominently in their law: They assert that contemporary continental dignity is the product of a reaction against fascism, and especially against Nazism. Having experienced the horrific indignities of the 1930s and 1940s, continental societies, Europeans say, have mended their ways. Europe has dignity today because Europe was traumatized seventy years ago. . . .

In fact, the history of the continental law of dignity begins long before the postwar period. It begins in the eighteenth, and even the seventeenth, centuries. The continental societies that we see today are the descendants of the sharply hierarchical societies that existed two or two-and-a-half centuries ago — of the aristocratic and monarchical societies of which the France of Louis XIV was the model. In point of fact, continental law has enforced norms of respect and dignity for a very long time. In earlier centuries, though, only persons of high social status could expect their right to respect to be protected in court. Indeed, well into the twentieth century, only high-status persons could expect to be treated respectfully in the daily life of Germany or France, and only high-status persons could expect their "personal honor" to be protected in continental courts. . . .

What we see in continental law today is the result of a centuries-long, slow-maturing revolt against that style of status privilege. Over time, it has come to seem unacceptable that only certain persons should enjoy legal protections for their "dignity." Indeed, the rise of norms of respect for everybody — even minorities, even prison inmates — represents a great social transformation on the Continent. Everybody is now supposed to be treated in ways that only highly placed and wealthy people were treated a couple of centuries ago. . . .

The uncomfortable paradox . . . is that much of this leveling up took place during the fascist period, for fascist politics involved precisely the promise that all members of the nation-state would be equal in "honor" — that all racial Germans, for example, would be "masters." For that very reason, some of the fundamental institutions of the continental law of dignity experienced significant development under the star of fascism. In fact, the fascist period, seen in proper sociological perspective, was one stage in a continuous history of the extension of honor throughout all echelons of continental society.

This long-term secular leveling-up tendency has shaped continental law in a very fundamental way. Contemporary continental hate speech protections, for example, can be traced back to dueling law: In the nineteenth century, continental courts protected the right to respect only of the dueling classes. Today they protect everybody's right to respect; indeed, the rules of dueling have had a striking influence in the Continent, sometimes being imported bodily into the law. . . . As for Americans: They have their own concepts of personhood, their own traditions, and their own values. And the consequence is that there will always be practices that intuitively seem to represent obvious violations to Americans. Most especially, state action will raise American hackles much more often than European ones.

This is indeed almost too obvious to need describing for American readers. Suspicion of the state has always stood at the foundation of American privacy thinking, and American scholarly writing. . . .

What matters in America, over the long run, is liberty against the state within the privacy of one's home. This does not mean that the American approach to "privacy" is narrowly limited to Fourth Amendment search and seizure problems, of course. Lawyers do ingenious things, and the conception of privacy as liberty within the sanctity of the home can be extended in important ways. This has been notably true, of course, in the famous series of "constitutional privacy" decisions that began with *Griswold v. Connecticut*. . . .

Nevertheless, the fundamental limit on American thinking always remains: American "privacy" law, however ingenious its elaborations, always tends to imagine the home as the primary defense, and the state as the primary enemy. This gives American privacy law a distinctive coloration. Where American law perceives a threat to privacy, it is typically precisely because the state has become involved in the transaction. . . .

In truth, there is little reason to suppose that Americans will be persuaded to think of their world of values in a European way any time soon; American law simply does not endorse the general norm of personal dignity found in Europe. Nor is there any greater hope that Europeans will embrace the American ideal; the law of Europe does not recognize many of the antistatist concerns that Americans seem to take for granted. Of course we are all free to plead for a different kind of law — in Europe or in the United States. But pleading for privacy as such is not the way to do it. There is no such thing as privacy as such. The battle, if it is to be fought, will have to be fought over more fundamental values than that.

PAUL M. SCHWARTZ & KARL-NIKOLAUS PEIFER, *TRANSATLANTIC DATA PRIVACY LAW*
106 Georgetown L.J. — (forthcoming 2017)

Rights talk forms an essential part of the European project, and one that has become more central over time. As Fabbrini notes, there has been a "growth of a fundamental rights culture in Europe in the last few decades."[10] Data protection law is at the front ranks of this effort. The EU began as an economic trading zone, but has always been about more than rationalizing a trade in coal and steel or safeguarding the free movement of goods. Constructed in the aftermath of the destruction of World War II, the European Community rests on a desire for a new model of political cooperation with the goal of bringing lasting peace to Europe. Meeting this goal led to creation of a supranational authority, and one with "the power to bind its constituent member states."[11] Yet, the rise of these largely Brussels-based institutions has not been without challenges.

Of the considerable hurdles faced by the EU project, one of the most significant has been the "democratic deficit" of its institutions. The ordinary European citizen feels bound to her national government, but is likely to have a more distant relationship to the EU as a sovereign entity. Too often, the EU is considered a distant, inaccessible institution. There are complaints about its transparency, complexity, the dominance of its executive institutions, the inability of its citizens to replace important decision makers, and the lack of power for more democratic EU institutions.

One response has been to increase the power of the European Parliament. Starting in 1979, EU reforms have made it a directly elected body and assigned it more traditional kinds of legislative power. Nonetheless, as Paul Craig and Grainne de Búrca warn, "The problems of secrecy, impenetrability, accountability, and representativeness are not addressed simply by giving added powers to the European Parliament."[12] Another response to the democratic deficit in the EU has been made at the constitutional level.

The hope has been to create a sense of European citizenship through development and enforcement of European constitutional rights. Jürgen Habermas, the German philosopher, has emerged as one of the clearest voices for constitutionality as the key to Europe's future. In his analysis, the European Union is made up of citizens of the member states ("We the People") as well as the nations of Europe.[13] Each individual therefore participates in the EU in a double fashion: both as a European citizen and through a role in her home nation.

In turn, the EU must provide its citizens with constitutional guarantees of justice and freedom. Human dignity is the bedrock on which these guarantees rest. As the Charter of Fundamental Rights states in its Article 1: "Human dignity is inviolable. It must be respected and protected." Above all, Habermas stresses the need for construction of a "common public sphere" in which citizens of Europe

---

[10] Federico Fabbrini, Fundamental Rights in Europe 13 (2014).

[11] Paul Craig & Grainne de Búrca, EU Law: Texts, Cases, and Materials 5 (4th ed. 2008).

[12] *Id.* at 133.

[13] Jürgen Habermas, Zur Verfassung Europas 66 (2011).

will engage in democratic deliberation. Rather than as Croatians, Czechs, Frenchmen, or Italians, Europeans are to discuss issues that require transnational solutions in a new shared, deliberative space.

This new communicative area, Habermas' "common public sphere" for EU citizens, is far from established. But the EU is further along in development of a shared political identity based on common fundamental rights. The rights talk around data protection should be understood within this context. Here is the forward-looking focus of EU data protection; it seeks to create a constitutional basis for a pan-European identity. To be sure, there are other foundational elements for the EU's interest in privacy and data protection. The first element concerns integration of member states around a common market. As Abraham Newman argues, one goal of EU regulators has been to draw on their powers to further market integration.[14] Similarly, both the Directive and GDPR reflect, in part, such a market purpose.[15] Early caselaw of the European Court of Justice interpreting the Directive also emphasize this "market integration objective."[16]

The second element is the continent's terrible experience of fascism, totalitarianism, and authoritarianism. The experience with the data gathering of different kinds of secret police in Western and Eastern Europe alike has profoundly heightened sensitivities towards data protection throughout the EU. The rise of dignity and personality interests in European law after World War II played important part in the later development of information privacy rights.

To view EU data protection law, however, as resting only on the internal market and the lessons of the past, however crucial, would be to ignore its equally important role in a rights-oriented European project. As one German law professor has stated, Europe is no longer conversing in different languages when it comes to data protection law, but now speaks "European." The European language of data protection is now formed through the decisions of the European Court of Human Rights, the European Court of Justice, the GDPR, and a shared institutional structure, which includes the European Data Protection Board, the European Data Protection Supervisor, and national data protection authorities. Data protection is a critical part of the EU's development of European human rights law. In this regard, Fabbrini points to a 2014 decision of the European Court of Justice invalidating the EU's Data Retention Directive as the ruling that "crowns a decade of progressive jurisprudential developments in the field of human rights."[17]

III. The United States: Protecting the Privacy Consumer

U.S. privacy law situates the consumer within a marketplace for data trade. In it, the FTC has a central role through its policing data exchanges against the most

---

[14] ABRAHAM NEWMAN, PROTECTORS OF PRIVACY 75 (2008).

[15] ORLA LYNSKEY, THE FOUNDATIONS OF EU DATA PROTECTION LAW 8 (2015).

[16] Id. at 51-54.

[17] Federico Fabbrini, *Human Rights in the Digital Age: The European Court of Justice Ruling in the Data Retention Case and Its Lessons for Privacy and Surveillance in the United States*, 28 Harv. Hum. Rts. J. 65, 81 (2015). The 2014 case that Fabbrini points to as a turning point has been expanded by a subsequent 2016 data retention decision of the same court, Tele2 Sverige AB v. Post-och telestyreisen, ECLI:EU:C:2016:970 (Dec. 21, 2016) (Data Retention) [Editors' Note: This chapter contains an excerpt from Tele2 Sverige infra].

deceptive kinds of practices. There is considerable distance here from the EU's rights discourse about data subjects. There are equally important differences between the U.S. and EU regarding the comparative constitutional aspects of information privacy law and data protection law, and the incorporation of doctrines of contract and consent.

NOTES & QUESTIONS

1. ***U.S. vs. EU Privacy Regulation of the Private Sector.*** Is Whitman correct that the United States has little concern about privacy with regard to private actors? As you read this chapter, consider whether there are areas where U.S. information privacy regulation might exceed those of the Europeans.

2. ***The Rise of the European Union.*** Writing over a decade after Whitman, and taking a different approach to the question of U.S. and European privacy, Schwartz and Peifer situate privacy in a development that they call the "EU project." In their view, data protection rests on three elements. These are, first, the integration of EU member states around a common market. Second, there is "the continent's terrible experience of fascism, totalitarianism, and authoritarianism." Finally, data protection law has a central role in the development of a rights-oriented EU. How does this interpretation follow or differ from Whitman's concept of "two cultures" of privacy?

3. ***Regional Variation in Privacy Norms.*** How well does Whitman's analysis apply to regional diversities for privacy culture within the United States or Europe? Are individuals in New York City more likely to share the views of those in Paris or London, or those in a small town in South Carolina?

4. ***The U.S. Privacy Consumer.*** Rather than the "rights talk" in the EU, Schwartz and Peifer describe the U.S. as protecting a "privacy consumer." In their view, "the U.S. anchors its information privacy law in the marketplace." In their summary regarding the U.S., "[T]he rhetoric of bilateral self-interest holds sway." They state: "Personal information is another commodity in the market, and human flourishing is furthered to the extent that the individual can maximize her preferences regarding data trades. The focus of information privacy in the U.S. is policing fairness in exchanges of personal data." Does this summary seem to be a correct or complete assessment of U.S. privacy law?

5. ***Divergence or Convergence?*** Whitman describes a divergence between European and U.S. views toward privacy. In 1992, Colin Bennett, a Canadian political scientist, proposed that convergence was taking place between U.S. and European information privacy law. He argued:

> The process of policy making in the data protection area is clearly one where broad transnational forces for convergence have transcended variations in national characteristics. The background to the legislation is the rapid technological process that is commonly recognized to be restructuring individual, social, economic, and political relationships. . . .
>
> The technology, however, should not be regarded as an independent force that "causes" anything. The crucial variable is the common set of attitudes that developed about the technology. . . .

In this context, the salience of national factors as independent variables has been reduced. The partisan orientation of governments has been insignificant. . . . Fair information practice exposes the commonalities among the closely interlinked historical, cultural, and political developments of these societies.[18]

Subsequently, Bennett modified his views regarding convergence. In *The Governance of Privacy*, Bennett and Charles Raab identify a "decentering of privacy." In their view, "The governance of privacy is exercised through a variety of institutional forms — public and private, domestic and transnational, with the result that in certain contexts the government regulators are not necessarily the most important actors, and the laws they enact not necessarily the most important instruments." There is now a "fragmentation" with privacy regulation involving "a plurality of actors and a range of methods of operation and coordination." As a consequence, Bennett and Raab point to a lack of any single race to the bottom or top among different countries in different policy areas: "There are many races, many tops and many bottoms as a host of actors, public and private, use or resist the expanding repertoire of privacy instruments to encourage or obstruct the more responsible use of personal information within modern organizations."[19]

Compare Whitman's concluding paragraph to Bennett and Raab's argument that the many different policy areas and policy instruments throughout the world make any single comparison impossible. Is there an unbridgeable rift between the privacy laws in different countries based on different cultural values? Or is increasing globalization forcing countries to resolve these rifts?

6. ***Culture and Privacy Norms.*** As you go through the materials in this chapter, consider whether privacy claims vary in different parts of the world, and more generally, which factors contribute to the structuring of privacy norms. For example, is the concept of privacy determined by cultural traditions, trade requirements, legal developments, or technological influences?

2. EUROPEAN CONVENTION ON HUMAN RIGHTS, ARTICLE 8

The European Convention on Human Rights (ECHR), an international convention covering a wide range of civil and political rights, was adopted in 1950, shortly after the Universal Declaration of Human Rights of the United Nations. It was drafted under the auspices of the Council of Europe, an international organization composed today of over 40 European states, which was formed in 1949 as a result of a strong political willingness to unify European countries, to consolidate and stabilize its democracies after World War II, to prevent any future violations of human rights such as those that had taken place during the Nazi regime, and to establish a bulwark against Communism. The European Convention was intended to bring violations of human rights to the attention of the international community. As commentators have observed:

---

[18] Colin J. Bennett, *Regulating Privacy: Data Protection and Public Policy in Europe and the United States* 150-53 (1992).

[19] Colin J. Bennett & Charles D. Raab, *The Governance of Privacy: Policy Instruments in Global Perspective* 294 (2006).

In practice, this function of the ECHR, which imagines large-scale violations of human rights, has largely remained dormant. The ECHR has instead been used primarily to raise questions of isolated weaknesses in legal systems that basically conform to its requirements and which are representative of the "common heritage of political traditions, ideals, freedom and the rule of law" to which the Preamble to the ECHR refers.[20]

Protocol No. 11 to the Convention (1994) altered the path to the European Court of Human Rights.[21] Under the previous system, there had been a complicated system of referral to the Court involving the European Commission on Human Rights. Once Protocol No. 11 entered into force in November 1998, however, the Court was able to receive applications directly "from any person, non-governmental organization or group of individuals claiming to be a victim of a violation . . . of the rights set forth in the Convention and the protocols thereto." In addition, member countries are able to refer to the Court violations of the Convention and its protocols by another member country. Finally, the Committee of Ministers is permitted to request advisory opinions from the European Court of Human Rights.

The Court's judgment is binding upon the member state against which the application was brought. It is normally declaratory. If the Court finds that a breach of the Convention has occurred, it brings into operation the defendant state's obligation in international law to make reparation. However, the Court may always award "just satisfaction" to the injured if the internal law of the defendant state allows only partial reparation.

The whole procedure can take up to five years between the registration of the application and the Court's final ruling. Although this is a slow procedure, "the primary purpose of state and individual applications is not to offer an international remedy for individual victims of violations of the Convention but to bring to light violations of an inter-state guarantee."[22]

The role of the European Court is of particular importance for several reasons. First, the volume of cases brought to the Court has increased over the years and has raised more complex jurisprudential issues than those that came before the court in earlier years. Second, the Court is the longest standing international human rights court; it is considered the model against which other regional courts can be measured. Finally, the jurisprudence of the court has influenced the normative development of other parts of the international human rights system. The Convention itself has a fundamental role in the European legal system as it has gradually acquired the status of a "constitutional instrument of European public order in the field of human rights."[23]

The critical privacy provision in the European Convention on Human Rights is Article 8. The language in Article 8 of the ECHR is similar to Article 12 of the Universal Declaration of Human Rights.

---

[20] S.H. Bailey, D.J. Harris & B.L. Jones, *Civil Liberties — Cases and Materials* 749-50 (3d ed. 1991).

[21] Protocol No. 11 to the Convention for the Protection of Human Rights and Fundamental Freedoms, restructuring the control machinery established thereby (ETS No. 155) (11 May 1994).

[22] S.H. Bailey, D.J. Harris & B.L. Jones, *Civil Liberties: Cases and Materials* 761 (3d ed. 1991).

[23] J. Polakiewicz & V. Jacob-Foltzer, *The European Human Rights Convention in Domestic Law,* 12 Hum. Rts. L.J. 65, 125 (1991).

ECHR ARTICLE 8

Article 8 — Right to Respect for Private and Family Life

1. Everyone has the right to respect for his private and family life, his home and his correspondence.

2. There shall be no interference by a public authority with the exercise of this right except such as is in accordance with the law and is necessary in a democratic society in the interests of national security, public safety or the economic well-being of the country, for the prevention of disorder or crime, for the protection of health or morals, or for the protection of the rights and freedoms of others.

NOTES & QUESTIONS

1. *"In Accordance with Law."* As John Wadham describes it, a central requirement of Article 8 is "the rule of law":

> No matter how desirable the end to be achieved, no interference with a right protected under the Convention is permissible unless the citizen knows the basis for the interference because it is set out in an ascertainable law. In the absence of such detailed authorisation by the law, any interference, however justified, will violate the Convention. . . . No such interference can be permitted by executive rules alone.
>
> To be "prescribed by law" or "in accordance with law" means that there must be an ascertainable legal regime governing the interference in question. The Strasbourg court explained the concept in *Sunday Times v. United Kingdom* (1979) 2 EHRR 245 at paragraph 49: "Firstly, the law must be adequately accessible: the citizens must be able to have an indication that is adequate in the circumstances of the legal rules applicable to a given case. Secondly, a norm cannot be regarded as a 'law' unless it is formulated with sufficient precision to enable the citizen to regulate his conduct."
>
> The common law may be sufficiently clear for this purpose and statute law or regulation is not necessary. . . .
>
> It is not acceptable for an interference with a Convention right to occur without any legal regulation. . . .

Moreover, "any interference by a public authority with a Convention right must be directed towards an identified legitimate aim. . . . The sorts of aims which are legitimate are the interests of public safety, national security, the protection of health and morals and the economic well-being of the country or the protection of the rights and freedoms of others."[24]

2. *A Two-Stage Inquiry.* Orla Lynsky has provided an overview of the "non-exhaustive elements" that the ECHR uses in deciding whether there has been an interference with a protected interest under Article 8(1).[25] First, sometimes the mere storage of data relating to the private life of an individual may interfere

---

[24] John Wadham, *Human Rights and Privacy — The Balance,* speech given at Cambridge (Mar. 2000), http://www.liberty-human-rights.org.uk/mhrp6j.html.

[25] ORLY LYNSKEY, THE FOUNDATIONS OF EU DATA PROTECTION LAW 108-110 (2015).

with Article 8(1). Second, even for non-private information, a "systematic collection and storage of the information by a public authority" can be an activity that implicates this part of the Convention. Third, "the Court takes into consideration whether the use of information collected goes beyond that which was reasonably foreseeable by the applicant." Fourth, the Court has been more willing to find impingement of Article 8(1) "when the data concerned constitutes sensitive personal information." Finally, the Court considers whether consent was given for the processing.

If the ECJ finds an interference, with Article 8(1), it moves to the second stage of its inquiry, which concerns whether the action can be justified as in accordance with the law as well as necessary in a democratic society.

3. *"Necessary in a Democratic Society."* Wadham notes:

> Although a few rights in the Convention are absolute, most are not. The Convention approach is to decide whether a particular limitation from a right is justified in the sense of being "proportionate to the legitimate aim pursued."
>
> This means that even if a policy which interferes with a Convention right might be aimed at securing a legitimate aim of social policy, for example, the prevention of crime, this will not in itself justify the violation if the means adopted to secure the aim are excessive in the circumstances. . . .
>
> Where the Convention allows restrictions on rights it requires them to be justified by a legitimate aim and proportional to the need at hand, that is, "necessary in a democratic society." The case law interprets this to mean that there must be a "pressing social need" for the interference. . . . [T]he state's desire to protect a legitimate aim does not allow it to restrict the right of the individual disproportionately — the state cannot use a sledgehammer to crack a nut.[26]

4. ***The Council of Europe's Convention 108 on Privacy.*** Another important document for European privacy is the Council of Europe's Convention for the Protection of Individuals with Regard to Automatic Processing of Personal Data, ETS No. 108 (1981) (Convention 108). The convention is a "non-self-executing treaty." Its standards do not directly impose binding norms on signatory nations. It requires signatory nations to establish domestic data protection legislation that gives effect to the Convention's principles. These principles provide a common core of safeguards for the processing of personal data. Convention 108 permits domestic standards to exceed its basic safeguards.

Throughout the 1980s, the Convention was the most important European-wide agreement for privacy. Fifty-one nations have acceded to it. The members of the Council of Europe that have recently adopted the Convention include Armenia (2008), Monaco (2009), Azebaijan (2010), and the Ukraine (2011). Non-member nations that have adopted the Convention include Uruguay (2013), Senegal (2016), and Tunisia (2017).

---

[26] John Wadham, *Human Rights and Privacy — The Balance,* speech given at Cambridge (Mar. 2000), http://www.liberty-human-rights.org.uk/mhrp6j.html.

VON HANNOVER V. GERMANY [NO. 1]

59320/00 [2004] ECHR 294 (June 24, 2004)

1. The case originated in an application against the Federal Republic of Germany lodged with the Court under Article 34 of the Convention for the Protection of Human Rights and Fundamental Freedoms ("the Convention") by a national of Monaco, Caroline von Hannover ("the applicant"), on 6 June 2000.

2. The applicant alleged that the German court decisions in her case had infringed her right to respect for her private and family life as guaranteed by Article 8 of the Convention. . . .

THE FACTS

8. The applicant, who is the eldest daughter of Prince Rainier III of Monaco, was born in 1957. Her official residence is in Monaco but she lives in the Paris area most of the time. . . .

9. Since the early 1990s the applicant has been trying — often through the courts — in a number of European countries to prevent the publication of photos about her private life in the tabloid press.

10. The photos that were the subject of the proceedings described below were published by the publishing company Burda in the German magazines *Bunte* and *Freizeit Revue* and by the publishing company Heinrich Bauer in the German magazine *Neue Post*.

11. [Five photos in *Freizeit Revue* magazine] show her with the actor Vincent Lindon at the far end of a restaurant courtyard in Saint-Rémy-de-Provence. [Photos in the magazine *Bunte* show her riding on horseback, with her children Peter and Andrea, in a canoe with her daughter, in a restaurant, on a bicycle, shopping in a market, skiing, leaving her house, and playing tennis. Photos in *Neue Post* magazine show her at a beach club in a swimsuit and wrapped up in a bathing towel. In this sequence, she tripped over an obstacle and fell down. The photos, which were described as "quite blurred," were accompanied by an article entitled, "Prince Ernst August played fisticuffs and Princess Caroline fell flat on her face."]

. . .

[The regional court denied her application under German law, reasoning that she did not have a right to protection against photos taken in public places. The case was appealed to the German Federal Court of Justice, and then to the German Federal Constitutional Court.] . . .

25. In a landmark judgment of 15 December 1999, delivered after a hearing, the Constitutional Court allowed the applicant's appeal in part on the ground that the three photos that had appeared in the 32nd and 34th editions of *Bunte* magazine, dated 5 August 1993 and 19 August 1993, featuring the applicant with her children had infringed her right to the protection of her personality rights guaranteed by sections 2(1) and 1(1) of the Basic Law, reinforced by her right to family protection under section 6 of the Basic Law. It referred the case to the Federal Court of Justice on that point. However, the Constitutional Court dismissed the applicant's appeal regarding the other photos.

The relevant extract of the judgment reads as follows:

The fact that the press fulfils the function of forming public opinion does not exclude entertainment from the functional guarantee under the Basic Law. The formation of opinions and entertainment are not opposites. Entertainment also plays a role in the formation of opinions. It can sometimes even stimulate or influence the formation of opinions more than purely factual information. Moreover, there is a growing tendency in the media to do away with the distinction between information and entertainment both as regards press coverage generally and individual contributions, and to disseminate information in the form of entertainment or mix it with entertainment ("infotainment"). Consequently, many readers obtain information they consider to be important or interesting from entertaining coverage. . . .

Nor can mere entertainment be denied any role in the formation of opinions. That would amount to unilaterally presuming that entertainment merely satisfies a desire for amusement, relaxation, escapism or diversion. Entertainment can also convey images of reality and propose subjects for debate that spark a process of discussion and assimilation relating to philosophies of life, values and behaviour models. In that respect it fulfils important social functions. . . . When measured against the aim of protecting press freedom, entertainment in the press is neither negligible nor entirely worthless and therefore falls within the scope of application of fundamental rights. . . .

The same is true of information about people. Personalization is an important journalistic means of attracting attention. Very often it is this which first arouses interest in a problem and stimulates a desire for factual information. Similarly, interest in a particular event or situation is usually stimulated by personalised accounts. Additionally, celebrities embody certain moral values and lifestyles. Many people base their choice of lifestyle on their example. They become points of crystallisation for adoption or rejection and act as examples or counter-examples. This is what explains the public interest in the various ups and downs occurring in their lives. . . .

The public has a legitimate interest in being allowed to judge whether the personal behaviour of the individuals in question, who are often regarded as idols or role models, convincingly tallies with their behaviour on their official engagements. . . .

The decision of the Federal Court of Justice cannot be criticised under constitutional law regarding the photos of the appellant at a market, doing her market shopping accompanied by her bodyguard or dining with a male companion at a well-attended restaurant. The first two cases concerned an open location frequented by the general public. The third case admittedly concerned a well circumscribed location, spatially speaking, but one in which the appellant was exposed to the other people present.

It is for this reason, moreover, that the Federal Court of Justice deemed it legitimate to ban photos showing the applicant in a restaurant garden, which were the subject of the decision being appealed but are not the subject of the constitutional appeal.

The presence of the applicant and her companion there presented all the features of seclusion. The fact that the photographs in question were evidently taken from a distance shows that the applicant could legitimately have assumed that she was not exposed to public view.

Nor can the decision being appealed be criticised regarding the photos of the applicant alone on horseback or riding a bicycle. In the Federal Court of Justice's view, the appellant had not been in a secluded place, but in a public one. That finding cannot attract criticism under constitutional law. The applicant herself describes the photos in question as belonging to the intimacy of her private sphere merely because they manifest her desire to be alone. In accordance with the criteria set out above, the mere desire of the person concerned is not relevant in any way.

The three photos of the applicant with her children require a fresh examination, however, in the light of the constitutional rules set out above. We cannot rule out the possibility that the review that needs to be carried out in the light of the relevant criteria will lead to a different result for one or other or all the photos. The decision must therefore be set aside in that respect and remitted to the Federal Court of Justice for a fresh decision. . . .

39. The relevant provisions of the Basic Law are worded as follows:

Section 1(1) — "The dignity of human beings is inviolable. All public authorities have a duty to respect and protect it."

Section 2(1) — "Everyone shall have the right to the free development of their personality provided that they do not interfere with the rights of others or violate the constitutional order or moral law (*Sittengesetz*)."

Section 5(1) — "(1) Everyone shall have the right freely to express and disseminate his or her opinions in speech, writing and pictures and freely to obtain information from generally accessible sources. Freedom of the press and freedom of reporting on the radio and in films shall be guaranteed. There shall be no censorship. (2) These rights shall be subject to the limitations laid down by the provisions of the general laws and by statutory provisions aimed at protecting young people and to the obligation to respect personal honour (*Recht der persönlichen Ehre*)."

Section 6(1) and (2) — "(1) Marriage and the family enjoy the special protection of the State. (2) The care and upbringing of children is the natural right of parents and a duty primarily incumbent on them. The State community shall oversee the performance of that duty."

40. Section 22(1) of the Copyright (Arts Domain) Act provides that images can only be disseminated with the express approval of the person concerned.

41. Section 23(1) no. 1 of that Act provides for exceptions to that rule, particularly where the images portray an aspect of contemporary society (*Bildnisse aus dem Bereich der Zeitgeschichte*) on condition that publication does not interfere with a legitimate interest (*berechtigtes Interesse*) of the person concerned (section 23(2)). . . .

THE LAW

43. The applicant submitted that the German court decisions had infringed her right to respect for her private and family life guaranteed by Article 8 of the Convention. . . .

44. The applicant stated that she had spent more than ten years in unsuccessful litigation in the German courts trying to establish her right to the protection of her private life. She alleged that as soon as she left her house she was constantly hounded by paparazzi who followed her every daily movement, be it crossing the

road, fetching her children from school, doing her shopping, out walking, practising sport or going on holiday. In her submission, the protection afforded to the private life of a public figure like herself was minimal under German law because the concept of a "secluded place" as defined by the Federal Court of Justice and the Federal Constitutional Court was much too narrow in that respect. Furthermore, in order to benefit from that protection the onus was on her to establish every time that she had been in a secluded place. She was thus deprived of any privacy and could not move about freely without being a target for the paparazzi. She affirmed that in France her prior agreement was necessary for the publication of any photos not showing her at an official event. Such photos were regularly taken in France and then sold and published in Germany. The protection of private life from which she benefited in France was therefore systematically circumvented by virtue of the decisions of the German courts. On the subject of the freedom of the press the applicant stated that she was aware of the essential role played by the press in a democratic society in terms of informing and forming public opinion, but in her case it was just the entertainment press seeking to satisfy its readers' voyeuristic tendencies and make huge profits from generally anodyne photos showing her going about her daily business. Lastly, the applicant stressed that it was materially impossible to establish in respect of every photo whether or not she had been in a secluded place. As the judicial proceedings were generally held several months after publication of the photos, she was obliged to keep a permanent record of her every movement in order to protect herself from paparazzi who might photograph her. With regard to many of the photos that were the subject of this application it was impossible to determine the exact time and place at which they had been taken.

45. The Government submitted that German law, while taking account of the fundamental role of the freedom of the press in a democratic society, contained sufficient safeguards to prevent any abuse and ensure the effective protection of the private life of even public figures. In their submission, the German courts had in the instant case struck a fair balance between the applicant's rights to respect for her private life guaranteed by Article 8 and the freedom of the press guaranteed by Article 10, having regard to the margin of appreciation available to the State in this area. The courts had found in the first instance that the photos had not been taken in a secluded place and had, in the second instance, examined the limits on the protection of private life, particularly in the light of the freedom of the press and even where the publication of photos by the entertainment press were concerned. The protection of the private life of a figure of contemporary society "*par excellence*" did not require the publication of photos without his or her authorisation to be limited to showing the person in question engaged in their official duties. The public had a legitimate interest in knowing how the person behaved generally in public. The Government submitted that this definition of the freedom of the press by the Federal Constitutional Court was compatible with Article 10 and the European Court's relevant case-law. Furthermore, the concept of a secluded place was only one factor, albeit an important one, of which the domestic courts took account when balancing the protection of private life against the freedom of the press. Accordingly, while private life was less well protected where a public figure was photographed in a public place other factors could also be taken into consideration, such as the nature of the photos, for example, which

should not shock the public. Lastly, the Government reiterated that the decision of the Federal Court of Justice — which had held that the publication of photos of the applicant with the actor Vincent Lindon in a restaurant courtyard in Saint-Rémy-de-Provence were unlawful — showed that the applicant's private life was protected even outside her home. . . .

B. The Court's Assessment

50. The Court reiterates that the concept of private life extends to aspects relating to personal identity, such as a person's name or a person's picture.

Furthermore, private life, in the Court's view, includes a person's physical and psychological integrity; the guarantee afforded by Article 8 of the Convention is primarily intended to ensure the development, without outside interference, of the personality of each individual in his relations with other human beings. . . .

52. As regards photos, with a view to defining the scope of the protection afforded by Article 8 against arbitrary interference by public authorities, the Commission had regard to whether the photographs related to private or public matters and whether the material thus obtained was envisaged for a limited use or was likely to be made available to the general public.

53. In the present case there is no doubt that the publication by various German magazines of photos of the applicant in her daily life either on her own or with other people falls within the scope of her private life.

54. The Court notes that, in its landmark judgment of 15 December 1999, the Federal Constitutional Court interpreted sections 22 and 23 of the Copyright (Arts Domain) Act (see paragraphs 40-41 above) by balancing the requirements of the freedom of the press against those of the protection of private life, that is, the public interest in being informed against the legitimate interests of the applicant. In doing so the Federal Constitutional Court took account of two criteria under German law, one functional and the other spatial. It considered that the applicant, as a figure of contemporary society "*par excellence*", enjoyed the protection of her private life even outside her home but only if she was in a secluded place out of the public eye "to which the person concerned retires with the objectively recognisable aim of being alone and where, confident of being alone, behaves in a manner in which he or she would not behave in public". In the light of those criteria the Federal Constitutional Court held that the Federal Court of Justice's judgment of 19 December 1995 regarding publication of the photos in question was compatible with the Basic Law. The court attached decisive weight to the freedom of the press, even the entertainment press, and to the public interest in knowing how the applicant behaved outside her representative functions. . . .

56. In the present case the applicant did not complain of an action by the State, but rather of the lack of adequate State protection of her private life and her image.

57. The Court reiterates that although the object of Article 8 is essentially that of protecting the individual against arbitrary interference by the public authorities, it does not merely compel the State to abstain from such interference: in addition to this primarily negative undertaking, there may be positive obligations inherent in an effective respect for private or family life. These obligations may involve the adoption of measures designed to secure respect for private life even in the sphere of the relations of individuals between themselves. . . .

58. That protection of private life has to be balanced against the freedom of expression guaranteed by Article 10 of the Convention. In that context the Court reiterates that the freedom of expression constitutes one of the essential foundations of a democratic society. Subject to paragraph 2 of Article 10, it is applicable not only to "information" or "ideas" that are favourably received or regarded as inoffensive or as a matter of indifference, but also to those that offend, shock or disturb. Such are the demands of that pluralism, tolerance and broadmindedness without which there is no "democratic society."

In that connection the press plays an essential role in a democratic society. Although it must not overstep certain bounds, in particular in respect of the reputation and rights of others, its duty is nevertheless to impart — in a manner consistent with its obligations and responsibilities — information and ideas on all matters of public interest. . . .

59. Although freedom of expression also extends to the publication of photos, this is an area in which the protection of the rights and reputation of others takes on particular importance. The present case does not concern the dissemination of "ideas", but of images containing very personal or even intimate "information" about an individual. Furthermore, photos appearing in the tabloid press are often taken in a climate of continual harassment which induces in the person concerned a very strong sense of intrusion into their private life or even of persecution. . . .

61. The Court points out at the outset that in the present case the photos of the applicant in the various German magazines show her in scenes from her daily life, thus engaged in activities of a purely private nature such as practising sport, out walking, leaving a restaurant or on holiday. . . .

63. The Court considers that a fundamental distinction needs to be made between reporting facts — even controversial ones — capable of contributing to a debate in a democratic society relating to politicians in the exercise of their functions, for example, and reporting details of the private life of an individual who, moreover, as in this case, does not exercise official functions. While in the former case the press exercises its vital role of "watchdog" in a democracy by contributing to "impart[ing] information and ideas on matters of public interest, it does not do so in the latter case.

64. Similarly, although the public has a right to be informed, which is an essential right in a democratic society that, in certain special circumstances, can even extend to aspects of the private life of public figures, particularly where politicians are concerned, this is not the case here. The situation here does not come within the sphere of any political or public debate because the published photos and accompanying commentaries relate exclusively to details of the applicant's private life.

65. As in other similar cases it has examined, the Court considers that the publication of the photos and articles in question, of which the sole purpose was to satisfy the curiosity of a particular readership regarding the details of the applicant's private life, cannot be deemed to contribute to any debate of general interest to society despite the applicant being known to the public. . . .

68. The Court finds another point to be of importance: even though, strictly speaking, the present application concerns only the publication of these photos and articles by various German magazines, the context in which these photos were

taken — without the applicant's knowledge or consent — and the harassment endured by many public figures in their daily lives cannot be fully disregarded.

In the present case this point is illustrated in particularly striking fashion by the photos taken of the applicant at the Monte Carlo Beach Club tripping over an obstacle and falling down. . . .

69. The Court reiterates the fundamental importance of protecting private life from the point of view of the developments of every human being's personality. That protection . . . extends beyond the private family circle and also includes a social dimension. . . . [A]nyone, even if they are known to the general public, must be able to enjoy a "legitimate expectation" of protection of and respect for their private life.

74. The Court therefore considers that the criteria on which the domestic courts based their decisions were not sufficient to protect the applicant's private life effectively. As a figure of contemporary society *"par excellence"* she cannot — in the name of freedom of the press and the public interest — rely on protection of her private life unless she is in a secluded place out of the public eye and, moreover, succeeds in proving it (which can be difficult). Where that is not the case, she has to accept that she might be photographed at almost any time, systematically, and that the photos are then very widely disseminated even if, as was the case here, the photos and accompanying articles relate exclusively to details of her private life.

75. In the Court's view, the criterion of spatial isolation, although apposite in theory, is in reality too vague and difficult for the person concerned to determine in advance. In the present case merely classifying the applicant as a figure of contemporary society *"par excellence"* does not suffice to justify such an intrusion into her private life.

76. As the Court has stated above, it considers that the decisive factor in balancing the protection of private life against freedom of expression should lie in the contribution that the published photos and articles make to a debate of general interest. It is clear in the instant case that they made no such contribution since the applicant exercises no official function and the photos and articles related exclusively to details of her private life.

77. Furthermore, the Court considers that the public does not have a legitimate interest in knowing where the applicant is and how she behaves generally in her private life even if she appears in places that cannot always be described as secluded and despite the fact that she is well known to the public.

Even if such a public interest exists, as does a commercial interest of the magazines in publishing these photos and these articles, in the instant case those interests must, in the Court's view, yield to the applicant's right to the effective protection of her private life.

78. Lastly, in the Court's opinion the criteria established by the domestic courts were not sufficient to ensure the effective protection of the applicant's private life and she should, in the circumstances of the case, have had a "legitimate expectation" of protection of her private life.

79. Having regard to all the foregoing factors, and despite the margin of appreciation afforded to the State in this area, the Court considers that the German courts did not strike a fair balance between the competing interests.

80. There has therefore been a breach of Article 8 of the Convention. . . .

85. The Court considers the question of the application of Article 41 [providing for "just satisfaction to the injured party," i.e., damages] is not ready for decision. Accordingly, it shall be reserved and the subsequent procedure fixed having regard to any agreement which might be reached between the Government and the applicant.

NOTES & QUESTIONS

1. **Von Hannover's *Impact on German Law*.** *Von Hannover I* represents what one law professor has termed the European Court of Human Rights' (ECHR) "censure" of the German Constitutional Court, the highest German court, and its case law regarding the press and privacy.[27] For Andreas Heldrich, the European Court of Human Rights in its decision "overruled nearly point for point" the German Court's arguments in its decisions. Heldrich points in particular to the German court's need to change, after *Von Hannover I,* its existing jurisprudence, which had required "absolute persons of contemporary history" (*absolute Personen der Zeitgeschichte*) to accept being photographed anywhere outside of their homes as long as they did not retreat into a private place to be alone. In Heldrich's prediction, *Von Hannover I* means that in the future, "we will be able to enjoy colorful pictures from the private life of our celebrities only with their permission. Nonetheless, we need not worry. There will be enough of them left over."

   In contrast, Stefan Engels and Uwe Jürgens describe a path by which German courts might integrate *Von Hannover I* with existing case law. For them, the core of the decision of the European Court of Human Rights turns on whether there has been "constant annoyances that the affected party feels as a weighty invasion of her private life and even as a persecution."[28] Yet, not every such confrontation with the press will qualify under this proposed test. Engels and Jürgens argue that "prominent persons of public life" who jog by a river in Hamburg or leave a famous nightclub in Munich cannot claim that they have retreated to the private sphere. In their view, the law must accept that there is also a "reverse side" to fame, namely, public attention. The plaintiff must demonstrate that an image has been taken in the context of a "weighty persecution" by the press of her, and the court must evaluate the image in the context of the journalist's report that accompanies it. Do Engels and Jürgens or Heldrich make the more convincing case about the extent of the impact of *Von Hannover I* with existing German protection of the press?

2. **Von Hannover II *and* Von Hannover III.** Subsequent to *Von Hannover I*, the European Court of Human Rights issued opinions in two more cases brought by Princess Caroline, who lost both appeals.

   In *Von Hannover II*, Princess Caroline argued that a decision of the German Federal Constitutional Court from 2008 violated her Article 8 rights. Case of

---

[27] Andreas Heldrich, Persönlichkeitsschutz und Pressefreiheit nach der Europäischen Menschenrechtskonvention, NJW 2634 (2004).

[28] Stefan Engels & Uwe Jürgens, Auswirkungen der EGMR-Rechtsprechung zum Privatsphärenschutz-Möglichkeiten und Grenzen der Umsetzung des "Caroline"-Urteils im deutschen Recht, NJW 2517, 2521 (2007).

Von Hannover v. Germany (no. 2), no. 40660/08 and 60641/08, ECHR 228 (Feb. 7, 2012). She objected to the publication of photographs of her on vacation that were published in German magazines. The underlying case involved the German Federal Constitutional Court's review of a decision of the Federal Court of Justice (*Bundesgerichtshof*).[29] The Federal Court of Justice found that some of the photographs of Princess Caroline contributed to a debate of general interests and some did not. The photographs that contributed to the public debate were protected by freedom of the press, and Princess Caroline appealed this part of the decision to the Constitutional Court. The core issue for the Constitutional Court was "the question of the extent to which articles may be illustrated using photographs showing the private life of celebrities." For it, the key was whether a photograph, even one that showed a celebrity on vacation, "dealt with relevant factual topics that affect a democratic society."

The Constitutional Court found against Caroline, and agreed with the Federal Court of Justice, in holding that some of the contested photographs met this standard. Photographs were published, for example, of Princess Caroline on vacation with her husband in St. Moritz, a Swiss winter sport resort. The photograph accompanied an article about the illness of her father, Prince Rainier, that discussed how his children, including Caroline, were taking turns caring for him. The Constitutional Court stated that "the illness of the reigning Prince of Monaco constitutes an event of general public interest and . . . the press should also be allowed, in connection with such an event, to report on the way his children including [Caroline] were managing to reconcile their duties towards solidarity within the family with their legitimate interest in safeguarding the needs of their own private lives including the desire to go on holiday." Regarding the relevant European precedent, the Constitutional Court argued, "The European Court of Human Rights in its [*Von Hannover* opinion] did not categorically exclude the possibility that a report which contributes to the treatment of important factual issues that are of interest to the general public may also be illustrated using pictures taken from the everyday life of persons who are part of public or political life."

In *Von Hannover II*, the European Court of Human Rights decided that the German national courts did not violate the requirements of Article 8. It found that the national courts "explicitly took account of the [European Court of Human Right's] relevant case law." Indeed, the German Federal Constitutional Court had "undertaken a detailed analysis of the [European Court's] case-law in response to the applicants' complaints. . . ." The Court of Human Rights stated that it accepted "that the photos in question, considered in the light of the accompanying articles, did contribute, at least to some degree, to a debate of general interest." It added that the press had the task of imparting information and ideas on all matters of public interest, and the public had a right to receive the resulting information and ideas.

Von Hannover III concerned a further complaint by Princess Caroline against the German press. After losing her case in German courts, Princess

---

[29] Order of the First Senate of 26 February 2008, German Federal Constitutional Court (1 BcR 1602, 1606, 1626/07 (official English translation), at http://www.bverfg.de/entscheidungen/rs20080226_1bvr160207en.html.

Caroline again appealed and again lost before the European Court of Human Rights. *Affaire Von Hannover c. Allemagne* (No. 3) no. 8772/10, ECHR 835 (Sept. 19, 2013).[30] The photographs in question accompanied, among other articles in the popular press, one regarding a trend in which Hollywood stars and royalty rented out their vacation homes. The European Court of Human Rights found that it could accept the decision of the German courts that the photographs contributed to a debate of general interest.

3. ***Axel Springer.*** In *Von Hannover II* and *Von Hannover III*, the European Court of Justice found that the German courts had adequately balanced privacy and the freedom of the press. In *Case of Axel Springer v. Germany*, No. 39954, ECHR 227 (Feb. 7, 2012), it reached a different conclusion.

In *Springer*, German courts had placed restrictions on the publication in the *Bild Zeitung*, a daily newspaper, of articles about the arrest of "TV star X" for possession of cocaine at the Oktoberfest in Munich. Ironically, TV star X was famous for playing "a police superintendent, whose mission was law enforcement and crime prevention." Regarding X's role as a TV cop, the European Court of Human Rights stated: "The fact was such as to increase the public's interest in being informed of X's arrest for a criminal offence." It also noted that X "was arrested in public, in a tent at the beer festival in Munich." The Court of Human Rights found that the German courts failed to give adequate weight to the public interest in the publication. It added that, "The fact that the first article contained certain expressions which, to all intents and purposes, were designed to attract the public's attention cannot in itself raise an issue under the Court's case-law . . . ." The expressions in question included the article's headline: "TV star X caught in possession of cocaine. A bretzel (*Brezn*), a beer mug [containing a litre of beer — *Maß*] and a line of coke (*Koks*)."[31]

4. ***Privacy in Public.*** How would the *Von Hannover* cases and the *Axel Springer* case be decided under the American privacy torts? Is the ECHR's protection of privacy in public too strong? For Nicholas Nohlen, "German courts had long given too much weight to the freedom of the press (even protecting 'news' that was merely entertaining), to the disadvantage of the individual's right to protection of private life."[32] In contrast, Nohlen states that the ECHR emphasized that "the decisive factor for balancing the right to private life and freedom of the press lies in the contribution of the delivered information to a debate of general interest." In other words, the focus should now be placed on the value of the information that the press delivers.

How is a court to assess the whether information is connected to a "debate of general interest" (the ECHR's test)? Nohlen concedes:

---

[30] Only a French official version of the decision and an unofficial German translation of the decision are available.

[31] For two 2014 cases of the Court of Human Rights applying the *Von Hannover* criteria, see Case of Lillo-Stenberg and Saether v. Norway, No. 13258/09 (Apr. 16, 2014); Case of Ruusunen v. Finland, No. 73579/10, ECHR (Apr. 14, 2014).

[32] Nicholas Hohlen, Case Note: Von Hannover v. Germany, 100 Am. J. Int'l L. 196, 198 (2006).

The ECHR's criterion in *Von Hannover* remains unclear. The Court held that the decisive criterion in balancing the right to private life against freedom of the press is whether the published photos contribute to a debate of general interest. It did not then establish a criterion, however, for determining what is to be considered as contributing to such a debate.

Nohlen then proposes a series of examples of the kinds of press reports that would possibly contribute to such a debate of general interest: "published articles with photos showing a well-known musician, who was said to be a family man, secretly cheating on his wife, or of a young soccer star, who always appeared to be shy and reserved, involved in a street fight." As he notes, moreover, nothing in *Von Hannover I* limits the test of a "debate of general interest" to merely political topics.

Consider as well the reasoning of the German Constitutional Court, which noted that the "applicant herself describes the photos in question as belonging to the intimacy of her private sphere merely because they manifest her desire to be alone. . . . [T]he mere desire of the person concerned is not relevant in any way." Does the ECHR have a satisfactory answer to this objection—namely, that there must be more objective criteria to define what is private than merely an individual's desires? Does the ruling of the ECHR threaten to make privacy too subjective a matter by not relying as heavily upon the fact that at least some of the photographs of Princess Caroline were taken while she was in public places?

5. *Article 8 vs. Article 10.* Whereas Article 8 of the Convention protects privacy, Article 10 protects freedom of speech and press:

> 1. Everyone has the right to freedom of expression. This right shall include freedom to hold opinions and to receive and impart information and ideas without interference by public authority and regardless of frontiers. This article shall not prevent States from requiring the licensing of broadcasting, television or cinema enterprises.
> 2. The exercise of these freedoms, since it carries with it duties and responsibilities, may be subject to such formalities, conditions, restrictions or penalties as are prescribed by law and are necessary in a democratic society, in the interests of national security, territorial integrity or public safety, for the prevention of disorder or crime, for the protection of health or morals, for the protection of the reputation or rights of others, for preventing the disclosure of information received in confidence, or for maintaining the authority and impartiality of the judiciary.

How are Article 8 and Article 10 to be reconciled? In *Von Hannover,* how does the ECHR's balance between Articles 8 and 10 compare to the U.S. Supreme Court's analysis of privacy laws that conflict with the First Amendment right to freedom of speech and press? How does the ECHR differ from the German Constitutional Court on the scope of freedom of press?

Does *Von Hannover* strike the right balance between privacy and free speech? Consider Barbara McDonald:

> [E]ven in the case of public figures, the court's decision [in *Von Hannover*] indicates a greater respect for the notion that some aspects of their lives should remain private and free of intrusion even when they are in public. The

applicable tests — whether the information came within their "legitimate expectation" of privacy so as to invoke a need to be balanced with the right to freedom of expression, and if so, whether it contributes to a debate of general interest — is a fairly high bar for the media to overcome.[33]

IN THE CASE OF MOSLEY V. THE UNITED KINGDOM

48009/08 [2011] ECHR 774 (10 May 2011)

---

8. The applicant was born in 1940 and lives in Monaco.

9. On 30 March 2008, the *News of the World*, a Sunday newspaper owned by News Group Newspapers Limited, published on its front page an article headed "F1 boss has sick Nazi orgy with 5 hookers." The article opened with the sentence, "Formula 1 motor racing chief Max Mosley is today exposed as a secret sadomasochistic sex pervert." Several pages inside the newspaper were also devoted to the story, which included still photographs taken from video footage secretly recorded by one of the participants in the sexual activities, who was paid in advance to do so. An edited extract of the video as well as still images were also published on the newspaper's website and reproduced elsewhere on the internet. The print version of the newspaper invited readers to view the video, providing the website address of the newspaper. . . .

13. On 6 April 2008 a second series of articles on the applicant's sexual activities was published in the *News of the World*. . . .

22. On 24 July 2008 judgment was handed down in the privacy proceedings. . . .

25. Eady J concluded that the newspaper articles and images constituted a breach of the applicant's right to privacy. He found that there were no Nazi connotations in the applicant's sexual activities and that there was therefore no public interest or justification in the publication of the article about his personal life and the accompanying images.

26. On the question of damages, Eady J declined to award exemplary damages and limited the damages available to a compensatory award. He considered it questionable whether deterrence should have a distinct, as opposed to a merely incidental, role to play in the award of compensatory damages, noting that it was a notion more naturally associated with punishment. He further observed that if damages were paid to an individual for the purpose of deterring the defendant it would naturally be seen as an undeserved windfall. He added that if damages for deterrence were to have any prospect of success it would be necessary to take into account the means of the relevant defendant. Any award against the *News of the World* would have to be so large that it would fail the test of proportionality when seen as fulfilling a compensatory function and would risk having a "chilling effect" on freedom of expression.

27. Eady J recognized that the sum awarded would not constitute adequate redress, noting:

---

[33] Barbara McDonald, Privacy, Princesses, and Paparazzi, 50 N.Y. L. Sch. L. Rev. 205, 223 (2005).

"231. . . . it has to be accepted that an infringement of privacy cannot ever be effectively compensated by a monetary award. Judges cannot achieve what is, in the nature of things, impossible. That unpalatable fact cannot be mitigated by simply adding a few noughts to the number first thought of. Accordingly, it seems to me that the only realistic course is to select a figure which marks the fact that an unlawful intrusion has taken place while affording some degree of *solatium* to the injured party. . . ."[34]

28. The applicant was awarded GBP 60,000 in damages and recovered approximately GBP 420,000 in costs.[35] The judge noted that the applicant was hardly exaggerating when he said that his life was ruined. A final injunction was granted against the newspaper. . . .

65. The applicant complained that the United Kingdom had violated its positive obligations under Article 8 of the Convention . . . by failing to impose a legal duty on the *News of the World* to notify him in advance in order to allow him the opportunity to seek an interim injunction and thus prevent publication of material which violated his right to respect for his private life. The Government contested that argument.

a. General principles

i. Article 8

106. It is clear that the words "the right to respect for . . . private . . . life" which appear in Article 8 require not only that the State refrain from interfering with private life but also entail certain positive obligations on the State to ensure effective enjoyment of this right by those within its jurisdiction. Such an obligation may require the adoption of positive measures designed to secure effective respect for private life even in the sphere of the relations of individuals between themselves (see *Von Hannover v. Germany*).

107. The Court emphasises the importance of a prudent approach to the State's positive obligations to protect private life in general and of the need to recognise the diversity of possible methods to secure its respect. The choice of measures designed to secure compliance with that obligation in the sphere of the relations of individuals between themselves in principle falls within the Contracting States' margin of appreciation. However, this discretion goes hand in hand with European supervision.

108. The Court recalls that a number of factors must be taken into account when determining the breadth of the margin of appreciation to be accorded to the State in a case in which Article 8 of the Convention is engaged. First, the Court reiterates that the notion of "respect" in Article 8 is not clear-cut, especially as far as the positive obligations inherent in that concept are concerned: bearing in mind the diversity of the practices followed and the situations obtaining in the Contracting States, the notion's requirements will vary considerably from case to

---

[34] Editors' Note: In English law, *solatium* is a term used for general damages. It is given as compensation for suffering, loss, or injured feelings.

[35] Editors' Note: GBP 60,000 is approximately $100,000, and GBP 420,000 is approximately $700,000.

case. Thus Contracting Parties enjoy a wide margin of appreciation in determining the steps to be taken to ensure compliance with the Convention. . . .

109. Second, the nature of the activities involved affects the scope of the margin of appreciation. The Court has previously noted that a serious interference with private life can arise where the state of domestic law conflicts with an important aspect of personal identity. Thus, in cases concerning Article 8, where a particularly important facet of an individual's existence or identity is at stake, the margin allowed to the State is correspondingly narrowed.

110. Third, the existence or absence of a consensus across the Member States of the Council of Europe, either as to the relative importance of the interest at stake or as to the best means of protecting it, is also relevant to the extent of the margin of appreciation: where no consensus exists, the margin of appreciation afforded to States is generally a wide one.

111. Finally, in cases where measures which an applicant claims are required pursuant to positive obligations under Article 8 would have an impact on freedom of expression, regard must be had to the fair balance that has to be struck between the competing rights and interests arising under Article 8 and Article 10.

ii. Article 10

112. The Court emphasises the pre-eminent role of the press in informing the public and imparting information and ideas on matters of public interest in a State governed by the rule of law. Not only does the press have the task of imparting such information and ideas but the public also has a right to receive them. Were it otherwise, the press would be unable to play its vital role of "public watchdog." . . .

114. The Court also reiterates that there is a distinction to be drawn between reporting facts — even if controversial — capable of contributing to a debate of general public interest in a democratic society, and making tawdry allegations about an individual's private. In respect of the former, the pre-eminent role of the press in a democracy and its duty to act as a "public watchdog" are important considerations in favour of a narrow construction of any limitations on freedom of expression. However, different considerations apply to press reports concentrating on sensational and, at times, lurid news, intended to titillate and entertain, which are aimed at satisfying the curiosity of a particular readership regarding aspects of a person's strictly private life (*Von Hannover*). Such reporting does not attract the robust protection of Article 10 afforded to the press. . . . While confirming the Article 10 right of members of the public to have access to a wide range of publications covering a variety of fields, the Court stresses that in assessing in the context of a particular publication whether there is a public interest which justifies an interference with the right to respect for private life, the focus must be on whether the publication is in the interest of the public and not whether the public might be interested in reading it.

115. It is commonly acknowledged that the audiovisual media have often a much more immediate and powerful effect than the print media. Accordingly, although freedom of expression also extends to the publication of photographs, the Court recalls that this is an area in which the protection of the rights of others takes on particular importance, especially where the images contain very personal and

intimate "information" about an individual or where they are taken on private premises and clandestinely through the use of secret recording devices (see *Von Hannover*). . . .

117. Finally, the Court has emphasized that while Article 10 does not prohibit the imposition of prior restraints on publication, the dangers inherent in prior restraints are such that they call for the most careful scrutiny on the part of the Court. This is especially so as far as the press is concerned, for news is a perishable commodity and to delay its publication, even for a short period, may well deprive it of all its value and interest. The Court would, however, observe that prior restraints may be more readily justified in cases which demonstrate no pressing need for immediate publication and in which there is no obvious contribution to a debate of general public interest.

118. . . . The question for consideration in the present case is whether the specific measure called for by the applicant, namely a legally binding pre-notification rule, is required in order to discharge that obligation.

119. The Court observes at the outset that this is not a case where there are no measures in place to ensure protection of Article 8 rights. A system of self-regulation of the press has been established in the United Kingdom, with guidance provided in the Editors' Code and Codebook and oversight of journalists' and editors' conduct by the [Press Complaints Commission (PCC)]. While the PCC itself has no power to award damages, an individual may commence civil proceedings in respect of any alleged violation of the right to respect for private life which, if successful, can lead to a damages award in his favour. . . . The Court is of the view that such awards can reasonably be expected to have a salutary effect on journalistic practices. Further, if an individual is aware of a pending publication relating to his private life, he is entitled to seek an interim injunction preventing publication of the material. . . . Further protection for individuals is provided by the Data Protection Act 1998, which sets out the right to have unlawfully collected or inaccurate data destroyed or rectified.

120. The Court further observes that, in its examination to date of the measures in place at domestic level to protect Article 8 rights in the context of freedom of expression, it has implicitly accepted that *ex post facto* damages provide an adequate remedy for violations of Article 8 rights arising from the publication by a newspaper of private information. . . .

121. . . . While the specific facts of the applicant's case provide a backdrop to the Court's consideration of this question, the implications of any pre-notification requirement are necessarily far wider. However meritorious the applicant's own case may be, the Court must bear in mind the general nature of the duty called for. In particular, its implications for freedom of expression are not limited to the sensationalist reporting at issue in this case but extend to political reporting and serious investigative journalism. The Court recalls that the introduction of restrictions on the latter type of journalism requires careful scrutiny.

i. The margin of appreciation

122. The Court recalls, first, that the applicant's claim relates to the positive obligation under Article 8 and that the State in principle enjoys a wide margin of appreciation. It is therefore relevant that the respondent State has chosen to put in

place a system for balancing the competing rights and interests which excludes a pre-notification requirement. . . .

123.   Second, the Court notes that the applicant's case concerned the publication of intimate details of his sexual activities, which would normally result in a narrowing of the margin of appreciation. However, the highly personal nature of the information disclosed in the applicant's case can have no significant bearing on the margin of appreciation afforded to the State in this area given that any pre-notification requirement would have an impact beyond the circumstances of the applicant's own case.

124. Third, the Court highlights the diversity of practice among member States as to how to balance the competing interests of respect for private life and freedom of expression. Indeed the applicant has not cited a single jurisdiction in which a pre-notification requirement as such is imposed. In so far as any common consensus can be identified, it therefore appears that such consensus is against a pre-notification requirement rather than in favor of it. . . . The Court therefore concludes that the respondent State's margin of appreciation in the present case is a wide one.

ii. The clarity and effectiveness of a pre-notification requirement

126. . . . [T]he Court is persuaded that concerns regarding the effectiveness of a pre-notification duty in practice are not unjustified. Two considerations arise. First, it is generally accepted that any pre-notification obligation would require some form of "public interest" exception. Thus a newspaper could opt not to notify a subject if it believed that it could subsequently defend its decision on the basis of the public interest. The Court considers that in order to prevent a serious chilling effect on freedom of expression, a reasonable belief that there was a "public interest" at stake would have to be sufficient to justify non-notification, even if it were subsequently held that no such "public interest" arose. . . .

128. Second, and more importantly, any pre-notification requirement would only be as strong as the sanctions imposed for failing to observe it. A regulatory or civil fine, unless set at a punitively high level, would be unlikely to deter newspapers from publishing private material without pre-notification. . . .

129. Although punitive fines or criminal sanctions could be effective in encouraging compliance with any pre-notification requirement, the Court considers that these would run the risk of being incompatible with the requirements of Article 10 of the Convention. It reiterates in this regard the need to take particular care when examining restraints which might operate as a form of censorship prior to publication. . . .

iii. Conclusion

130. As noted above, the conduct of the newspaper in the applicant's case is open to severe criticism. Aside from publication of the articles detailing the applicant's sexual activities, the *News of the World* published photographs and video footage, obtained through clandestine recording, which undoubtedly had a far greater impact than the articles themselves. Despite the applicant's efforts in a number of jurisdictions, these images are still available on the Internet. The Court

can see no possible additional contribution made by the audiovisual material, which appears to have been included in the *News of the World*'s coverage merely to titillate the public and increase the embarrassment of the applicant. . . .

132. However, the Court has consistently emphasized the need to look beyond the facts of the present case and to consider the broader impact of a pre-notification requirement. The limited scope under Article 10 for restrictions on the freedom of the press to publish material which contributes to debate on matters of general public interest must be borne in mind. Thus, having regard to the chilling effect to which a pre-notification requirement risks giving rise, to the significant doubts as to the effectiveness of any pre-notification requirement and to the wide margin of appreciation in this area, the Court is of the view that Article 8 does not require a legally binding pre-notification requirement. Accordingly, the Court concludes that there has been no violation of Article 8 of the Convention by the absence of such a requirement in domestic law.

> FOR THESE REASONS, THE COURT UNANIMOUSLY
> 1. *Declares* the application admissible;
> 2. *Holds* that there has been no violation of Article 8 of the Convention.

NOTES & QUESTIONS

1. **Mosley:** *The European Court and "the Margin of Appreciation."* The European Court of Human Rights found that Article 8 did not require that the press engage in pre-notification of subjects before publishing articles about their private life. One of the most interesting aspects of the decision is the European Court's assessment of the extent to which it should grant deference to the way in which the legal system in the United Kingdom handled the case. The term for this principle is "the margin of appreciation" to be accorded the State. The European Court applied a multi-factor test for assessing the "breadth of the margin of appreciation to be accorded to the State in a case in which Article of the Convention is engaged." Is there any particular factor that proved especially important in this case?

2. **Mosley:** *The Decision of the U.K. High Court of Justice.* As the European Court of Human Rights noted in its opinion, the U.K. court found for Mosley. Much of its decision turned on an assessment of the contested events involving Mosley that the *News of the World* wrote about in multiple articles and that was captured in a video that it posted on its website. Specifically, the court felt obligated to consider whether the event involved "Nazi-themed or concentration camp role-play," or merely "sado-masochistic ('S and M') and some sexual activities."[36] Why did this distinction matter?

   For the U.K. court, "if it really were the case, as the newspaper alleged, that the Claimant had for entertainment and sexual gratification been 'mocking the humiliating ways the Jews were treated,' or 'parodying Holocaust horrors,' there could be a public interest in that being revealed at least to those in

---

[36] Max Mosley and News Group Newspapers Limited, Case No: HQ08X01303, [2008] EWHC 1777 (QB) (24 July 2008).

[Formula 1 auto racing, or FIA] to whom he is accountable." The privacy interest in Article 8 would not protect Mosley's participation in such activities from press revelation. The court noted of Mosley:

> He had to deal with many people of all races and religions and has spoken out against racism in the sport. If he really were behaving in the way I have just described, that would, for many people, call seriously into question his suitability for his FIA role. It would be information which people arguably should have the opportunity to know and evaluate. It is probably right to acknowledge that private fantasies should not in themselves be subjected to legal scrutiny by the courts, but when they are acted out that is not necessarily so.

In its judgment, however, the U.K. court decided that "[b]eatings, humiliation and the infliction of pain are inherent to S and M activities. So too is the enactment of domination, restraints, punishment and prison scenarios. Behavior of this kind, in itself, is in this context therefore merely neutral. It does not entail Nazism." It declared, "The fact a particular relationship happens to be adulterous, or that someone's tastes are unconventional or 'perverted,' does not give the media *carte blanche*."

Did the U.K. court locate a convincing distinction for line drawing as to where the public interest begins and ends?

3. ***Mosley v. Google: Germany and France.*** In 2014, Mosley won a decision against Google in the Regional Court of Hamburg. *Injunctive Relief Claim (Unterlassungsanspruch)*, LG Hamburg 24 Zivilkammer, Jan. 24, 2014. The German court decided that Google had an obligation to prevent the re-posting of images beyond "notice-and-take" down limited to specific URL's. Once it was informed of a violation of Mosley's personality right caused by publication of specific images, the search engine company was required to prevent future similar violations by making the offending images inaccessible at its site. The Hamburg court stated that Google had a legal duty to use filtering software to stop its search engine's future distribution of these images

In 2013, Mosley won a similar judgment in France. Mosley v. S.A.R.L. Google, Tribunal de Grande Instance de Paris, Nov. 6, 2013. The French court identified an obligation of Google to automate a procedure for blocking nine images that courts had found to represent a significant violation of Mosley privacy. With approval, the court referred to an expert opinion by Viktor Mayer-Schönberg, an Oxford University professor. Mayer-Schönberg had evaluated the cost and complexity of the development or use of filtering software that would automatically recognize these images and block of them from any Google "web images" result. He concluded that the task would cost little and be attainable by a "programmer of moderate expertise."

For more on the obligations of operators of search engines under European privacy law, see below for the European Court of Justice's *Google* decision (2014) and the Notes following it.

4. ***The English Breach of Confidence Tort.*** In England, courts have frequently considered and consistently rejected recognizing the Warren and Brandeis privacy torts. Instead, the tort of breach of confidence is the primary common law protection of privacy. The tort traces back to *Prince Albert v. Strange*,

(1848) 41 Eng. Rep. 1171 (Ch.), the case that Warren and Brandeis relied heavily upon in arguing that a basis for the privacy torts existed in the common law. Later on, in *Coco v. Clark,* [1969], R.P.C. 41 (U.K.), three elements for the tort were established: (1) the information must have "the necessary quality of confidence about it"; (2) the information "must have been imparted in circumstances importing an obligation of confidence"; and (3) there must be an "unauthorised use of that information to the detriment of the party communicating it."

The English breach of confidence tort is quite broad. Unlike the American version of the tort, which applies to doctors, bankers, and other professionals, the English tort also applies to friends and family. *See Stephens v. Avery,* (1988) 1 Ch. 449 (U.K.) (breach of confidence tort applies to friends); *Argyll v. Argyll,* (1967) 1 Ch. 302 (U.K.) (breach of confidence applies to spouses). The tort even applies to lovers, such as in the case of *Barrymore v. News Group Newspapers, Ltd.,* [1997] F.S.R. 600 (Ch.) (U.K.), where the court declared: "when people kiss and later one of them tells, that second person is almost certainly breaking a confidential arrangement." In *A v. B,* [2003] Q.B. 195, 207 (U.K.), the court explained the full scope of the tort:

> A duty of confidence will arise whenever the party subject to the duty is in a situation where he either knows or ought to know that the other person can reasonably expect his privacy to be protected. The range of situations in which protection can be provided is therefore extensive. Obviously, the necessary relationship can be expressly created. More often its existence will have to be inferred from the facts. Whether a duty of confidence does exist which courts can protect, if it is right to do so, will depend on all the circumstances of the relationship between the parties at the time of the threatened or actual breach of the alleged duty of confidence.

Parties who induce breaches of confidence or receive information based on another's a breach of confidence can also be liable. Similar third-party liability exists with the American breach of confidentiality tort. Some commentators have noted that the English tort has become too broad. Consider Joshua Rozenberg:

> The need for a formal relationship between two parties has become attenuated almost to the point of non-existence. Where information has the necessary quality of confidence about it, the courts are more than willing to infer an obligation of confidence from the surrounding facts. . . . That means they will hold that someone who has received confidential information is bound by a duty of confidence. Put bluntly, if the judges think something ought to remain private then they will find a way of making it so.[37]

Although the English breach of confidence tort is quite broad, it does not cover some of the actions that the privacy torts protect against. For example, in *Kay v. Robertson,* [1991] F.S.R. 62 (C.A.) (U.K.), a famous actor suffered a severe head injury. In the hospital where he was recovering, notices were placed in several locations near his room and on the room's door that only permitted individuals would be allowed to visit him. A journalist and photographer snuck

---

[37] Joshua Rozenberg, Privacy and the Press 15 (2004).

in, interviewed the actor, and took photographs of him and his room. He was eventually discovered by hospital security staff and ejected. The actor was not in a good condition to be interviewed and had no recollection of the events. The actor sought to stop the publication of an article about the interview and containing the photos. The court considered whether to recognize a common law protection of privacy but concluded that doing so would be a matter for Parliament:

> It is well-known that in English law there is no right to privacy, and accordingly there is no right of action for breach of a person's privacy. The facts of the present case are a graphic illustration of the desirability of Parliament considering whether and in what circumstances statutory provision can be made to protect the privacy of individuals. . . .

What Warren and Brandeis privacy tort(s) could apply in this case? Would the actor have a successful case under the tort(s)? The English breach of confidence tort was not among the causes of action considered in the case. Would it have provided protection? If so, under what theory would it have applied?

Neil Richards and Daniel Solove contrast the American privacy torts with the English breach of confidence tort and note several important differences. Many of the privacy torts contain a "highly offensive" requirement; the breach of confidence tort does not. The public disclosure tort requires "publicity" (widespread disclosure); the breach of confidence tort does not. The public disclosure tort also does not apply when the disclosure is newsworthy; the English tort contains no such restriction.

> In contrast to Warren and Brandeis's individualistic conception of privacy, the English law of confidentiality focuses on relationships rather than individuals. Far from a right to be let alone, confidentiality focuses on the norms of trust within relationships. Indeed, most of our personal information is known by other people, such as doctors, spouses, children, and friends, as well as institutions, such as ISPs, banks, merchants, insurance companies, phone companies, and other businesses. We need to share our secrets with select others, and when we tell others a secret, we still consider it to be a secret. We confide in others, we trust them with information that can make us vulnerable, and we expect them not to betray us. These norms are missing from the Warren and Brandeis conception of privacy.
>
> The key conceptual difference between the breach of confidence tort and public disclosure of private facts tort is the nature of what is protected. The public disclosure tort focuses on the nature of the information being made public. By contrast, the focus of the tort of breach of confidentiality is on the nature of the relationship.[38]

Under the Human Rights Act (HRA) of 1998, the United Kingdom now follows the European Convention on Human Rights. This means that courts must balance Article 8 with Article 10. The result has been a broader protection of privacy as well as of free speech. The HRA prompted English courts to once

---

[38] Neil M. Richards & Daniel J. Solove, *Privacy's Other Path: Recovering the Law of Confidentiality*, 96 Geo. L.J. 123, 174 (2007).

again consider whether to recognize the Warren and Brandeis privacy torts. Instead of doing so, the courts have thus far concluded that the breach of confidence tort can be stretched to include a wider range of privacy violations. As for incorporating Article 10, England does not have a First Amendment, so Article 10 purportedly increases protection for speech. Courts consider freedom of speech and the press as a factor in assessing whether a party ought to be liable under the breach of confidence tort.

5. ***Photos of J.K. Rowling's Son in Public.*** In *Murray v. Big Pictures Ltd.,* [2008] EWCA Civ 446, the England and Wales Court of Appeal concluded that David Murray (the son of J.K. Rowling, author of the Harry Potter book series) was entitled to privacy protection from being photographed in public. When David was less than two years old, a photographer secretly snapped a photograph of him with a zoom lens when he was out in public in Edinburgh with his parents. The photo captured nothing "embarrassing or untoward." The photo appeared in a magazine in 2005. David's parents sued on his behalf. The judge below dismissed "the claim based on breach of confidence or invasion of privacy . . . [because] on my understanding of the law including *Von Hannover* there remains an area of innocuous conduct in a public place which does not raise a reasonable expectation of privacy." The judge reasoned:

> It seems to me that a distinction can be drawn between a child (or an adult) engaged in family and sporting activities and something as simple as a walk down a street or a visit to the grocers to buy the milk. The first type of activity is clearly part of a person's private recreation time intended to be enjoyed in the company of family and friends. Publicity on the test deployed in *Von Hannover* is intrusive and can adversely affect the exercise of such social activities. But if the law is such as to give every adult or child a legitimate expectation of not being photographed without consent on any occasion on which they are not, so to speak, on public business then it will have created a right for most people to the protection of their image. If a simple walk down the street qualifies for protection then it is difficult to see what would not.

The appellate court, however, disagreed:

> It seems to us that, although the judges regarded the parents' concerns as overstated, the parents' wish, on behalf of their children, to protect the freedom of the children to live normal lives without the constant fear of media intrusion is (at least arguably) entirely reasonable and, other things being equal, should be protected by the law. It is true . . . that the photographs showed no more than could be seen by anyone in the street but, once published, they would be disseminated to a potentially large number of people on the basis that they were children of well-known parents, leading to the possibility of further intrusion in the future. . . .
>
> We do not share the predisposition . . . that routine acts such as a visit to a shop or a ride on a bus should not attract any reasonable expectation of privacy. All depends upon the circumstances. The position of an adult may be very different from that of a child. In this appeal we are concerned only with the question whether David, as a small child, had a reasonable expectation of privacy, not with the question whether his parents would have had such an expectation. Moreover, we are concerned with the context of this case, which

was not for example a single photograph taken of David which was for some reason subsequently published.

It seems to us that, subject to the facts of the particular case, the law should indeed protect children from intrusive media attention, at any rate to the extent of holding that a child has a reasonable expectation that he or she will not be targeted in order to obtain photographs in a public place for publication which the person who took or procured the taking of the photographs knew would be objected to on behalf of the child. That is the context in which the photographs of David were taken.

How broadly does the *Von Hannover* decision extend? Is there any way to avoid the slippery slope problem described by the judge below, that "[i]f a simple walk down the street qualifies for protection then it is difficult to see what would not"?

6. *Use of CCTV Footage by the Media.* In England, the government uses an extensive system of millions of public surveillance cameras that are monitored via closed circuit television, a system known as CCTV. The government frequently supplies the video to the media. Consider *Peck v. United Kingdom,* 44647/98 [2003] ECHR 44 (28 January 2003):

The present applicant was in a public street but he was not there for the purposes of participating in any public event and he was not a public figure. It was late at night, he was deeply perturbed and in a state of distress. While he was walking in public wielding a knife, he was not later charged with any offence. The actual suicide attempt was neither recorded nor therefore disclosed. However, footage of the immediate aftermath was recorded and disclosed by the Council directly to the public in its CCTV News publication. In addition, the footage was disclosed to the media for further broadcasting and publication purposes. Those media included the audiovisual media: Anglia Television broadcast locally to approximately 350,000 people and the BBC broadcast nationally, and it is "commonly acknowledged that the audiovisual media have often a much more immediate and powerful effect than the print media." The Yellow Advertiser was distributed in the applicant's locality to approximately 24,000 readers. The applicant's identity was not adequately, or in some cases not at all, masked in the photographs and footage so published and broadcast. He was recognised by certain members of his family and by his friends, neighbours and colleagues.

As a result, the relevant moment was viewed to an extent which far exceeded any exposure to a passer-by or to security observation . . . and to a degree surpassing that which the applicant could possibly have foreseen when he walked in Brentwood on 20 August 1995. . . .

[T]he Court appreciates the strong interest of the State in detecting and preventing crime. It is not disputed that the CCTV system plays an important role in these respects and that that role is rendered more effective and successful through advertising the CCTV system and its benefits.

However, the Court notes that the Council had other options available to it to allow it to achieve the same objectives. In the first place, it could have identified the applicant through enquiries with the police and thereby obtained his consent prior to disclosure. Alternatively, the Council could have masked the relevant images itself. A further alternative would have been to take the utmost care in ensuring that the media, to which the disclosure was made, masked those images. The Court notes that the Council did not explore the first and second options and considers that the steps taken by the Council in respect of the third were inadequate. . . .

In sum, the Court does not find that, in the circumstances of this case, there were relevant or sufficient reasons which would justify the direct disclosure by the Council to the public of stills from the footage in its own CCTV News article without the Council obtaining the applicant's consent or masking his identity, or which would justify its disclosures to the media without the Council taking steps to ensure so far as possible that such masking would be effected by the media. The crime-prevention objective and context of the disclosures demanded particular scrutiny and care in these respects in the present case. . . .

Accordingly, the Court considers that the disclosures by the Council of the CCTV material in the CCTV News and to the Yellow Advertiser, Anglia Television and the BBC were not accompanied by sufficient safeguards to prevent disclosure inconsistent with the guarantees of respect for the applicant' private life contained in Article 8. As such, the disclosure constituted a disproportionate and therefore unjustified interference with his private life and a violation of Article 8 of the Convention.

Could the English breach of confidentiality tort have provided an adequate remedy for the plaintiff?

As the *von Hannover* and *Mosley* decisions demonstrate, the Convention on Human Rights protects both privacy and freedom of expression. Its protection of the latter is found in Article 10, which states: "Everyone has the right to freedom of expression. This right shall include freedom to hold opinions and to receive and impart information and ideas without interference by public authority and regardless of frontiers." Article 10 also makes clear that this right is not absolute: "The exercise of these freedoms, since it carries with it duties and responsibilities, may be subject to such formalities, conditions, restrictions or penalties as are prescribed by law and are necessary in a democratic society. . . ." In the following decision, the ECHR seeks, in its words, "to retain the essence" of both Articles 8 (privacy) and Article 10 (freedom of expression).

SATUKUNNAN MARKKINAPÖRSSI OY AND SATAMEDIA OY V. FINLAND

ECHR, No. 931/13, Grand Chamber (June 22, 2017)

I. THE CIRCUMSTANCES OF THE CASE

A. Background to the case

1. Since 1994 the first applicant company, Satakunnan Markkinapörssi Oy collected data from the Finnish tax authorities for the purpose of publishing information about natural persons' taxable income and assets in the Veropörssi newspaper. Several other publishing and media companies also publish such data which, pursuant to Finnish law, are accessible to the public

2. In 2002 Veropörssi appeared 17 times, with each issue concentrating on a certain geographical area of the country. The data published comprised the surnames and forenames of approximately 1.2 million natural persons whose

annual taxable income exceeded certain thresholds, mainly from 60,000 to 80,000 Finnish marks (approximately 10,000 to 13,500 euros (EUR)), as well as the amount, to the nearest EUR 100, of their earned and unearned income and taxable net assets. When published in the newspaper, the data were set out in the form of an alphabetical list and organised according to municipality and income bracket.

3. The first applicant company worked in cooperation with the second applicant company, Satamedia Oy, and both were owned by the same shareholders. In 2003 the first applicant company started to transfer personal data published in Veropörssi, in the form of CD-ROM discs, to the second applicant company which, together with a mobile telephone operator, started a text-messaging service (SMS service). By sending a person's name to a service number, taxation information could be obtained concerning that person, on the requesting person's mobile telephone, if information was available in the database or register created by the second applicant company. This database was created using personal data already published in the newspaper and transferred in the form of CD-ROM discs to the second applicant company. From 2006 the second applicant company also published Veropörssi.

4. In September 2000 and November 2001, the applicant companies ordered taxation data from the Finnish National Board of Taxation (verohallitus, skattestyrelsen). Following the first order, the Board requested an opinion from the Data Protection Ombudsman, on the basis of which the Board invited the applicant companies to provide further information regarding their request and indicating that the data could not be disclosed if Veropörssi continued to be published in its usual form. The applicant companies subsequently cancelled their data request and paid people to collect taxation data manually at the local tax offices.

D. The Court's assessment

1. Preliminary remarks on the scope and context of the Court's assessment

5. The Court notes at the outset that the present case is unusual to the extent that the taxation data at issue were publicly accessible in Finland. Furthermore, as emphasised by the applicant companies, they were not alone amongst media outlets in Finland in collecting, processing and publishing taxation data such as the data which appeared in Veropörssi. Their publication differed from that of those other media outlets by virtue of the manner and the extent of the data published.

6. In addition, ... only a very small number of Council of Europe member States provide for public access to taxation data, a fact which raises issues regarding the margin of appreciation which Finland enjoys when providing and regulating public access to such data and reconciling that access with the requirements of data protection rules and the right to freedom of expression of the press.

7. Given this context and the fact that at the heart of the present case lies the question whether the correct balance was struck between that right and the right to privacy as embodied in domestic data protection and access to information legislation, it is necessary, at the outset, to outline some of the general principles deriving from the Court's case-law on Article 10 and press freedom, on the one

hand, and the right to privacy under Article 8 of the Convention in the particular context of data protection on the other.

8. Bearing in mind the need to protect the values underlying the Convention and considering that the rights under Articles 10 and 8 of the Convention deserve equal respect, it is important to remember that the balance to be struck by national authorities between those two rights must seek to retain the essence of both.

(a) Article 10 and press freedom

9. The Court has consistently held that freedom of expression constitutes one of the essential foundations of a democratic society and one of the basic conditions for its progress and for each individual's self-fulfilment. Subject to paragraph 2 of Article 10, it is applicable not only to "information" or "ideas" that are favourably received or regarded as inoffensive or as a matter of indifference, but also to those that offend, shock or disturb. Such are the demands of pluralism, tolerance and broadmindedness without which there is no "democratic society". As enshrined in Article 10, freedom of expression is subject to exceptions which must, however, be construed strictly, and the need for any restrictions must be established convincingly.

10. Although the press must not overstep certain bounds, regarding in particular protection of the reputation and rights of others, its task is nevertheless to impart – in a manner consistent with its obligations and responsibilities — information and ideas on all matters of public interest . . . .

(b) Article 8, the right to privacy and data protection

11. As regards whether, in the circumstances of the present case, the right to privacy under Article 8 of the Convention is engaged given the publicly accessible nature of the taxation data processed and published by the applicant companies, the Court has constantly reiterated that the concept of "private life" is a broad term not susceptible to exhaustive definition.

12. Leaving aside the numerous cases in which the Court has held that the right to privacy in Article 8 covers the physical and psychological integrity of a person, private life has also been held to include activities of a professional or business nature.

13. The fact that information is already in the public domain will not necessarily remove the protection of Article 8 of the Convention. Thus, in Von Hannover v. Germany (no. 59320/00, §§ 74-75 and 77, ECHR 2004 VI), concerning the publication of photographs which had been taken in public places of a known person who did not have any official function, the Court found that the interest in publication of that information had to be weighed against privacy considerations, even though the person's public appearance could be assimilated to "public information".

14. It follows from well-established case-law that where there has been compilation of data on a particular individual, processing or use of personal data or publication of the material concerned in a manner or degree beyond that normally foreseeable, private life considerations arise.

15. The protection of personal data is of fundamental importance to a person's enjoyment of his or her right to respect for private and family life, as guaranteed by Article 8 of the Convention. The domestic law must afford appropriate safeguards to prevent any such use of personal data as may be inconsistent with the guarantees of this Article. Article 8 of the Convention thus provides for the right to a form of informational self-determination, allowing individuals to rely on their right to privacy as regards data which, albeit neutral, are collected, processed and disseminated collectively and in such a form or manner that their Article 8 rights may be engaged.

16. In the light of the foregoing considerations and the Court's existing case-law on Article 8 of the Convention, it appears that the data collected, processed and published by the applicant companies in Veropörssi, providing details of the taxable earned and unearned income as well as taxable net assets, clearly concerned the private life of those individuals, notwithstanding the fact that, pursuant to Finnish law, that data could be accessed, in accordance with certain rules, by the public.

5. Necessary in a democratic society

17. The core question in the instant case, as indicated previously, is whether the interference with the applicant companies' right to freedom of expression was "necessary in a democratic society" and whether, in answering this question, the domestic courts struck a fair balance between that right and the right to respect for private life.

18. [T]he Court considers it useful to reiterate the criteria for balancing these two rights in the circumstances of a case such as the present one.

(a) General principles concerning the margin of appreciation and balancing of rights

19. According to the Court's established case-law, the test of necessity in a democratic society requires the Court to determine whether the interference complained of corresponded to a pressing social need, whether it was proportionate to the legitimate aim pursued and whether the reasons given by the national authorities to justify it are relevant and sufficient. The margin of appreciation left to the national authorities in assessing whether such a need exists and what measures should be adopted to deal with it is not, however, unlimited but goes hand in hand with European supervision by the Court, whose task it is to give a final ruling on whether a restriction is reconcilable with freedom of expression as protected by Article 10. As indicated above, when exercising its supervisory function, the Court's task is not to take the place of the national courts but rather to review, in the light of the case as a whole, whether the decisions they have taken pursuant to their power of appreciation are compatible with the provisions of the Convention relied on. Where the balancing exercise has been undertaken by the national authorities in conformity with the criteria laid down in the Court's case-law, the Court would require strong reasons to substitute its view for that of the domestic courts.

20. The Court has already had occasion to lay down the relevant principles which must guide its assessment — and, more importantly, that of domestic courts — of necessity. It has thus identified a number of criteria in the context of balancing the competing rights. The relevant criteria have thus far been defined as: contribution to a debate of public interest, the degree of notoriety of the person affected, the subject of the news report, the prior conduct of the person concerned, the content, form and consequences of the publication, and, where it arises, the circumstances in which photographs were taken. Where it examines an application lodged under Article 10, the Court will also examine the way in which the information was obtained and its veracity, and the gravity of the penalty imposed on the journalists or publishers.

(b) Application of the relevant general principles to the present case

(i) Contribution of the impugned publication to a debate of public interest

21. In order to ascertain whether a publication concerning an individual's private life is not intended purely to satisfy the curiosity of a certain readership, but also relates to a subject of general importance, it is necessary to assess the publication as a whole and have regard to the context in which it appears.

22. Public interest ordinarily relates to matters which affect the public to such an extent that it may legitimately take an interest in them, which attract its attention or which concern it to a significant degree, especially in that they affect the well-being of citizens or the life of the community. This is also the case with regard to matters which are capable of giving rise to considerable controversy, which concern an important social issue, or which involve a problem that the public would have an interest in being informed about. The public interest cannot be reduced to the public's thirst for information about the private life of others, or to an audience's wish for sensationalism or even voyeurism.

23. It is unquestionable that permitting public access to official documents, including taxation data, is designed to secure the availability of information for the purpose of enabling a debate on matters of public interest. Such access, albeit subject to clear statutory rules and restrictions, has a constitutional basis in Finnish law and has been widely guaranteed for many decades.

24. . . . . Taking the publication as a whole and in context and analysing it in the light of the above-mentioned case-law, the Court, like the Supreme Administrative Court, is not persuaded that publication of taxation data in the manner and to the extent done by the applicant companies contributed to such a debate or indeed that its principal purpose was to do so.

25. . . . . While the information might have enabled curious members of the public to categorise named individuals, who are not public figures, according to their economic status, this could be regarded as a manifestation of the public's thirst for information about the private life of others and, as such, a form of sensationalism, even voyeurism.

26. In the light of these considerations, the Court cannot but agree with the Supreme Administrative Court that the sole object of the impugned publication was not, as required by domestic and EU law, the disclosure to the public of information, opinions and ideas, a conclusion borne out by the layout of the

publication, its form, content and the extent of the data disclosed. Furthermore, it does not find that the impugned publication could be regarded as contributing to a debate of public interest or assimilated to the kind of speech, namely political speech, which traditionally enjoys a privileged position in its case-law, thus calling for strict Convention scrutiny and allowing little scope under Article 10 § 2 of the Convention for restrictions.

(ii) Subject of the impugned publication and how well-known were the persons concerned

27. The data published in Veropörssi comprised the surnames and names of natural persons whose annual taxable income exceeded certain thresholds (see paragraph 9 above). The data also comprised the amount, to the nearest EUR 100, of their earned and unearned income as well as details relating to their taxable net assets. When published in the newspaper, the data were set out in the form of an alphabetical list and were organised according to municipality and income bracket.

28. . . . Unlike other Finnish publications, the information published by the applicant companies did not pertain specifically to any particular category of persons such as politicians, public officials, public figures or others who belonged to the public sphere by dint of their activities or high earnings. As the Court has previously stated, such persons inevitably and knowingly lay themselves open to close scrutiny by both journalists and the public at large.

(iv) Content, form and consequences of the publication and related considerations

29. It is noteworthy that the CJEU has made clear . . . . that the public character of data processed does not exclude such data from the scope of the Data Protection Directive and the guarantees the latter lays down for the protection of privacy.

30. Whilst the taxation data in question were publicly accessible in Finland, they could only be consulted at the local tax offices and consultation was subject to clear conditions. The copying of that information on memory sticks was prohibited. Journalists could receive taxation data in digital format, but retrieval conditions also existed and only a certain amount of data could be retrieved. Journalists had to specify that the information was requested for journalistic purposes and that it would not be published in the form of a list. Therefore, while the information relating to individuals was publicly accessible, specific rules and safeguards governed its accessibility.

31. The fact that the data in question were accessible to the public under the domestic law did not necessarily mean that they could be published to an unlimited extent. Publishing the data in a newspaper, and further disseminating that data via an SMS service, rendered it accessible in a manner and to an extent not intended by the legislator.

32. As indicated previously, the gathering of information is an essential preparatory step in journalism and an inherent, protected part of press freedom. It is noteworthy that, in the instant case, the Supreme Administrative Court did not seek to interfere with the collection by the applicant companies of raw data, an

activity which goes to the heart of press freedom, but rather with the dissemination of data in the manner and to the extent outlined above.

    (v) Gravity of the sanction imposed on the journalists or publishers

    33. As indicated in the Chamber judgment, the applicant companies were not prohibited from publishing taxation data or from continuing to publish Veropörssi, albeit they had to do so in a manner consistent with Finnish and EU rules on data protection and access to information. The fact that, in practice, the limitations imposed on the quantity of the information to be published may have rendered some of their business activities less profitable is not, as such, a sanction within the meaning of the case-law of the Court.

    (vi) Conclusion

    34. In the light of the aforementioned considerations, the Court considers that, in assessing the circumstances submitted for their appreciation, the competent domestic authorities and, in particular, the Supreme Administrative Court gave due consideration to the principles and criteria as laid down by the Court's case-law for balancing the right to respect for private life and the right to freedom of expression. In so doing, the Supreme Administrative Court attached particular weight to its finding that the publication of the taxation data in the manner and to the extent described did not contribute to a debate of public interest and that the applicants could not in substance claim that it had been done solely for a journalistic purpose within the meaning of domestic and EU law. The Court discerns no strong reasons which would require it to substitute its view for that of the domestic courts and to set aside the balancing done by them. It is satisfied that the reasons relied upon were both relevant and sufficient to show that the interference complained of was "necessary in a democratic society" and that the authorities of the respondent State acted within their margin of appreciation in striking a fair balance between the competing interests at stake.

    35. The Court therefore concludes that there has been no violation of Article 10 of the Convention.

NOTES & QUESTIONS

1. ***The Holding.*** The publisher in *Satamedia Oy* gathered Finnish individuals' publicly-available tax data. It then collaborated with a service provider to send out tax information via text message following a customer's request. The ECHR found that such extensive publication of personal tax information violated Article 8. Although tax information was publicly available in Finland, the Finnish legislator had not intended to permit publication of this information "to an unlimited extent," such as via a text messaging service. The ECHR also found that the publication of this information did not enable "a debate of public interest." Hence, there was no violation of Article 10's protection of freedom of expression and press freedom.

2. ***Assessing the Public Interest.*** The ECHR built on its earlier decisions in *Satamedia Oy* concerning when a publication contributed to a debate of public interest. All publicly accessible information does not advance such a discussion; the ECHR spoke in negative terms of "the public's thirst for information about the private life of others," especially those who are not public figures, which it termed "a form of sensationalism, even voyeurism." *Satamedia Oy*, ¶ 22. In contrast, it defined the concept of "public interest" as "matters which affect the public to such an extent that it may legitimately take an interest in them, which attract its attention or which concern it to a significant degree, especially in that they affect the well-being of citizens or the life of the community." Id. How does this approach differ from that of U.S. courts when deciding newsworthiness? How does U.S. court typically assess the privacy impact of publicly-accessible information?

3. EUROPEAN UNION DATA PROTECTION

(a) The European Charter of Fundamental Rights, Articles 7 and 8

The European Union Data Protection Directive of 1995 established common rules for data protection among Member States of the European Union. The Directive was created in the early 1990s and formally adopted in 1995. The Directive will be replaced by the General Data Protection Regulation on May 25, 2018.

Another milestone in EU privacy law was the adoption of the European Charter of Fundamental Rights. In December 2000, the leaders of the institutions of the European Union gathered in Nice to sign this document.[39] The Charter of Fundamental Rights sets out in a single text, for the first time in the European Union's history, the whole range of civil, political, economic, and social rights of European citizens and all persons living in the European Union. It entrenches the rights found in the case law of the European Court of Justice; rights and freedoms enshrined in the European Convention on Human Rights; and other rights and principles developed through the common constitutional traditions of EU Member States and other international instruments. The Treaty of Lisbon of 2007 both specifically recognized data protection as a fundamental human right and made the Charter of Fundamental Rights a legally enforceable document within the EU. The cases from the European Court of Justice that follow will interpret both the Directive and the EU Charter of Fundamental Rights.

EU CHARTER OF FUNDAMENTAL RIGHTS, ARTICLES 7 AND 8

ARTICLE 7 — RESPECT FOR PRIVATE AND FAMILY LIFE

Everyone has the right to respect for his or her private and family life, home and communications.

---

[39] Available at http://www.europarl.eu.int/charter/default_en.htm.

ARTICLE 8 — PROTECTION OF PERSONAL DATA

1. Everyone has the right to the protection of personal data concerning him or her.

2. Such data must be processed fairly for specified purposes and on the basis of the consent of the person concerned or some other legitimate basis laid down by law. Everyone has the right of access to data which has been collected concerning him or her, and the right to have it rectified.

3. Compliance with these rules shall be subject to control by an independent authority.

(b) The Data Protection Directive

Although the General Data Protection Regulation will replace the Data Protection Directive in May 2018, it is still important to understand the Directive. First, the earlier document has played an important role in shaping the current contours of EU and world privacy. Second, important decisions of the European Court of Justice interpret and develop EU constitutional data protection through its framework. Finally, "what's past is prologue" (Shakespeare), and the development of the Directive has important lessons for the future of data protection law.

Prior to the adoption of the Directive, leading EU countries had national privacy legislation. As Abraham Newman has shown, different historically contingent factors had already smoothed the path to enactment of data protection statutes in the 1970s in France and Germany, two leaders in information privacy law.[40] For example, Newman demonstrates that French industry's potential opposition to the proposed French data protection legislation was muted by the past nationalization of many affected companies and the centralization of these industries, which minimized the impact of the statutes. As a further example, in Germany, a pro-privacy alliance benefited at a critical stage in the late 1970s from an "alignment of political actors at that time [who] neutralized key barriers to the passage of the policy."

The choice was also made in these key European nations to enact "omnibus" privacy laws. Recall that an omnibus law establishes regulatory standards for a broad area of information law. In contrast, a sectoral law regulates information use through attention only to narrower areas, such as the use of information in video rentals, or provision of cable television. After the initial choice in key European nations to enact omnibus law, the EU's "harmonizing" project in the field of data protection exercised a strong influence on other nations.[41] This term of European community law refers to formal regulatory attempts to increase the similarity of legal measures in member states. Specifically, European integration increased the sharing of data among EU Member Nations and created new demands for personal information. Due to this data sharing throughout the EU, nations with privacy statutes had incentives to advocate equivalent standards in all member nations. Without such shared levels of protection, previous efforts within individual nations

---

[40] Abraham L. Newman, Protectors of Privacy 60-69 (2008).
[41] Paul M. Schwartz, Preemption and Privacy, 118 Yale L.J. 902, 914-16 (2009).

to ensure privacy for their citizen's data would be for naught. The information could easily be transferred to other member states with weaker levels of data protection.

Thus, the Directive's purpose, somewhat paradoxically, was to facilitate the free flow of personal data within the EU by setting an equally high privacy level in all EU Member States. An increased harmonization of the privacy laws of various European nations would enable the free flow of goods and services, labor, and capital. The Directive also reinforced the preference in the EU for omnibus privacy laws. The benefit of an omnibus law is that it provides a relatively limited series of benchmarks and sets them within a single statute. In contrast, an exclusively sectoral approach would have caused far greater complexity for the EU in assessing the "equivalency" of data protection for each of the now 27 EU member states.

The Directive imposed obligations on the processors of personal data. It required technical security and the notification of individuals whose data was being collected, and outlined circumstances under which data transfer could occur. The Directive also gave individuals substantial rights to control the use of data about themselves. These rights included the right to be informed that their personal data was being transferred, the need to obtain "unambiguous" consent from the individual for the transfer of certain data, the opportunity to make corrections in the data, and the right to object to the transfer. Data regulatory authority, enforcement provisions, and sanctions were also key elements of the directive. Following passage of the Directive, the various national governments of the EU amended their own national data protection legislation to bring it into line with the Directive.

The Directive also extended privacy safeguards to personal data that was transferred outside of the European Union. Article 25 of the Directive stated that data could only be transferred to third countries that provided an "adequate level of data protection." As a result, implementation focused on both the adoption of national law within the European Union and the adoption of adequate methods for privacy protection in third party countries.[42]

Directives are a form of EU law that is binding for Member States, but only as to the result to be achieved. They allow the national authorities to choose the form and the methods of their implementation and generally fix a deadline for it. Therefore, the rules of law applicable in each Member State are the national laws implementing the directives and not the directive itself. However, the directive has a "direct effect" on individuals: it grants them rights that can be upheld by the national courts in their respective countries if their governments have not implemented the directive by the set deadline. A directive thus grants *rights* rather than creates obligations, and they are enforceable by *individuals* rather than by public authorities.

It is important to distinguish between vertical and horizontal effects. "Vertical effects" means that the rights established by a directive flow from the European

---

[42] For perspectives on the EU Directive, see Peter P. Swire & Robert E. Litan, None of Your Business: World Data Flows, Electronic Commerce, and the Europea*n Privacy Directive* (1998); Spiros Simitis, *From the Market to the Polis: The EU Directive on the Protection of Personal Data,* 80 Iowa L. Rev. 445 (1995); Symposium, *Data Protection Law and the European Union's Directive: The Challenge for the United States,* 80 Iowa L. Rev. 431 (1995).

Union to citizens of the EU. Where a violation occurs, citizens may petition EU institution and their national government that has adopted (or "transposed") a directive into national law. But this interest does not create a right for one citizen of the EU to bring an action against another citizen. For such an impact to occur ("horizontal effects") there must be national law or an EU regulation in place. Whereas the EU "regulations" or treaty provisions are able to confer rights on private individuals and impose obligations on them, directives can only confer rights on individuals against the State; they cannot impose on them obligations in favor of the State or other individuals. Directives are only capable of "vertical" direct effect, unlike treaty provisions and regulations, which are also capable of "horizontal" direct effect.

Directives are enacted in the context of the European Community (EC)'s competences, the EC being one of the legal entities that is part of the European Union. It means that their scope is limited to the area of competence of the EC. The EU Data Directive, as a result, does not cover activities, which fall outside the scope of EC law, such as the data processing operations concerning public security, defense, State security, and the activities of the State in areas of criminal law. *See, e.g.,* EU Data Directive, Article 3(2). In such cases, the only authorities that may promulgate enforceable legislation are the Member States. The European Union, however, can voice its concerns on privacy issues regarding policing and security through its "Justice and Home Affairs" branch. Under the direction of the EU Council,[43] the Justice and Home Affairs branch can take common positions defining the approach of the EU to a particular matter or even establish conventions, although each Member State can always oppose these decisions and not implement them into national law. The EU Council is the group of delegates of the Member States, each State being represented by a government minister who is authorized to commit his government.

NOTES & QUESTIONS

1. *Defining "Personal Data," Dynamic IP Addresses, and Graffiti Registers.* The EU Data Directive's definition of "personal data" (Art. 2(a)) is one of the keys to understanding the scope and application of the Directive as it only applies to the processing of personal data. The Directive defined "personal data" as "information relating to an identified or identifiable natural person." The GDPR adopts this same definition. The determination of the scope of "personal data" constitutes a crucial issue when enforcing data protection rules, particularly in the online context.

   Paul Schwartz and Daniel Solove argue that the EU has adopted an "expansionist approach" to defining the scope of "personal data."[44] As you read the following examples involving "dynamic IP addresses" and graffiti registers,

---

[43] The EU Council is the group of delegates of the Member States, each State being represented by a government minister who is authorized to commit his government.

[44] Paul M. Schwartz & Daniel J. Solove, *The PII Problem: Privacy and a New Concept of Personally Identifiable Information*, 86 N.Y.U. L. Rev. 1814 (2011). For additional analysis of the EU definition of "personal information," see Paul M. Schwartz & Daniel J. Solove, *Reconciling Personal Information in the EU and U.S.*, 102 Cal. L. Rev. 877 (2014).

consider whether these seem to indicate such a broad definitional approach at work. Compare these notions of "personal data" with the notion of "personally identifiable information" found in U.S. privacy laws. Are they identical?

In 2007, the Article 29 Working Party, the independent advisory body made up of data protection commissioners from EU Member States, issued an opinion concerning "the concept of personal data."[45] As the opinion states, "Working on a common definition of the notion of personal data is tantamount to defining what falls inside or outside the scope of data protection rules." For the Article 29 Party, dynamic IP addresses can be considered as personal data:

> [e]specially in those cases where the processing of IP addresses is carried out with the purpose of identifying the users of the computer (for instance, by Copyright holders in order to prosecute computer users for violation of intellectual property rights), the controller anticipates that the "means likely reasonably to be used" to identify the persons will be available e.g. through the courts appealed to (otherwise the collection of the information makes no sense).
>
> . . .

This view has been controversial. Some experts have argued that ISPs are generally unable to identify a specific user associated with an IP, but only tie an IP address with an account holder for it.

Another interesting hypothetical from this opinion concerns graffiti, and a transportation company choosing to create a register with information about the circumstances of damage to its passenger vehicles "as well as the images of the damaged items and of the 'tags' or 'signatures' of the author." When the register is created, the creator of the graffiti is unknown and may never be known. Nonetheless, "the purpose of the processing is precisely to identify individuals to whom the information relates as the authors of the damage, so as to be able to exercise legal claims against them." Hence, the processing is to be made "subject to data protection rules, which allow such processing as legitimate under certain circumstances and subject to certain safeguards."

2. ***The Underlying Philosophy of the EU Data Directive.*** Consider the following argument by Joel Reidenberg:

> The background and underlying philosophy of the European Directive differs in important ways from that of the United States. While there is a consensus among democratic states that information privacy is a critical element of civil society, the United States has, in recent years, left the protection of privacy to markets rather than law. In contrast, Europe treats privacy as a political imperative anchored in fundamental human rights. European democracies approach information privacy from the perspective of social protection. In European democracies, public liberty derives from the community of individuals, and law is the fundamental basis to pursue norms of social and citizen protection. This vision of governance generally regards the state as the necessary player to frame the social community in which individuals develop and in which information practices must serve individual identity. Citizen autonomy, in this view, effectively depends on a backdrop of legal rights. Law

---

[45] Article 29 Data Protection Working Party, Opinion 2/2007 on the concept of personal data (June 20, 2007).

thus enshrines prophylactic protection through comprehensive rights and responsibilities. Indeed, citizens trust government more than the private sector with personal information.[46]

As you examine the various provisions of the EU Data Directive and the OECD Privacy Guidelines throughout this chapter, consider how the overall approach of European democracies toward protecting differs from that of the United States. Are there ways in which the approaches are similar? To the extent that the approaches are different, think about why such differences exist.

3. ***Electronic Communication and the Processing of Personal Data.*** Personal data processed in connection with electronic communications are the subject of the ePrivacy Directive (Directive 2002/58/EC concerning the processing of personal data and the protection of privacy in the electronic communications sector). In turn, this document has been subject to two important amending directives. The later directives are the 2006 Data Retention Directive (Directive 2006/24) and a 2009 Amendment Directive (Directive 2009/136).

The ePrivacy Directive establishes specific protections covering electronic mail, telephone communications, traffic data, calling line identification, and unsolicited communications. Member states were required to transpose the Directive before October 31, 2002. Like the EU Data Protection Directive, the ePrivacy Directive is intended to harmonize national law in Europe. Article 5 of this Directive sets out a strong presumption in favor of communications privacy:

> Member States shall ensure the confidentiality of communications and the related traffic data by means of a public communications network and publicly available electronic communications services, through national legislation. In particular, they shall prohibit listening, tapping, storage or other kinds of interception or surveillance of communications and the related traffic data by persons other than users, without the consent of the users concerned, except when legally authorised to do so in accordance with Article 15(1). This paragraph shall not prevent technical storage which is necessary for the conveyance of a communication without prejudice to the principle of confidentiality.

The ePrivacy Directive directs Member States to permit unsolicited commercial telephone calls, e-mails, and faxes only with the subject's opt-in consent. It gives subscribers to communication services the right to be informed before they are included in any subscriber directory.

---

[46] Joel R. Reidenberg, *E-Commerce and Trans-Atlantic Privacy,* 38 Hous. L. Rev. 717, 730-31 (2001).

CRIMINAL PROCEEDINGS AGAINST BODIL LINDQVIST

European Court of Justice, 11/6/2003

1. By order of 23 February 2001, received at the Court on 1 March 2001, the Gota hovratt (Gota Court of Appeal) referred to the Court for a preliminary ruling under Article 234 EC seven questions concerning *inter alia* the interpretation of Directive 95/46/EC of the European Parliament and of the Council of 24 October 1995 on the protection of individuals with regard to the processing of personal data and on the free movement of such data.

2. Those questions were raised in criminal proceedings before that court against Mrs. Lindqvist, who was charged with breach of the Swedish legislation on the protection of personal data for publishing on her internet site personal data on a number of people working with her on a voluntary basis in a parish of the Swedish Protestant Church. . . .

12. In addition to her job as a maintenance worker, Mrs. Lindqvist worked as a catechist in the parish of Alseda (Sweden). She followed a data processing course on which she had *inter alia* to set up a home page on the internet. At the end of 1998, Mrs. Lindqvist set up internet pages at home on her personal computer in order to allow parishioners preparing for their confirmation to obtain information they might need. At her request, the administrator of the Swedish Church's website set up a link between those pages and that site.

13. The pages in question contained information about Mrs. Lindqvist and 18 colleagues in the parish, sometimes including their full names and in other cases only their first names. Mrs. Lindqvist also described, in a mildly humorous manner, the jobs held by her colleagues and their hobbies. In many cases family circumstances and telephone numbers and other matters were mentioned. She also stated that one colleague had injured her foot and was on half-time on medical grounds.

14. Mrs. Lindqvist had not informed her colleagues of the existence of those pages or obtained their consent, nor did she notify the Datainspektionen (supervisory authority for the protection of electronically transmitted data) of her activity. She removed the pages in question as soon as she became aware that they were not appreciated by some of her colleagues.

15. The public prosecutor brought a prosecution against Mrs. Lindqvist charging her with breach of the PUL [Personuppgiftslag, Swedish law on personal data] on the grounds that she had:

- processed personal data by automatic means without giving prior written notification to the Datainspektionen (Paragraph 36 of the PUL);
- processed sensitive personal data (injured foot and half-time on medical grounds) without authorisation (Paragraph 13 of the PUL);
- transferred processed personal data to a third country without authorisation (Paragraph 33 of the PUL).

16. Mrs. Lindqvist accepted the facts but disputed that she was guilty of an offence. Mrs. Lindqvist was fined by the Eksjo tingsratt (District Court) (Sweden) and appealed against that sentence to the referring court.

17. The amount of the fine was SEK 4000,[47] which was arrived at by multiplying the sum of SEK 100, representing Mrs. Lindqvist's financial position, by a factor of 40, reflecting the severity of the offence. Mrs. Lindqvist was also sentenced to pay SEK 300[48] to a Swedish fund to assist victims of crimes. . . .

19. . . . [T]he referring court asks whether the act of referring, on an internet page, to various persons and identifying them by name or by other means, for instance by giving their telephone number or information regarding their working conditions and hobbies, constitutes the processing of personal data wholly or partly by automatic means within the meaning of Article 3(1) of Directive 95/46. . . .

24. The term personal data used in Article 3(1) of Directive 95/46 covers, according to the definition in Article 2(a) thereof, any information relating to an identified or identifiable natural person. The term undoubtedly covers the name of a person in conjunction with his telephone coordinates or information about his working conditions or hobbies.

25. According to the definition in Article 2(b) of Directive 95/46, the term processing of such data used in Article 3(1) covers any operation or set of operations which is performed upon personal data, whether or not by automatic means. That provision gives several examples of such operations, including disclosure by transmission, dissemination or otherwise making data available. It follows that the operation of loading personal data on an internet page must be considered to be such processing.

27. . . . [T]he act of referring, on an internet page, to various persons and identifying them by name or by other means, for instance by giving their telephone number or information regarding their working conditions and hobbies, constitutes the processing of personal data wholly or partly by automatic means within the meaning of Article 3(1) of Directive 95/46. . . .

[The court concludes that neither the exception for the processing of personal data or for charitable and religious organizations in Article 3(2) apply in this case. Hence, the court affirmed the convictions for illegal processing of information and illegal disclosure of health information.]

37. Article 3(2) of Directive 95/46 provides for two exceptions to its scope.

38. The first exception concerns the processing of personal data in the course of an activity which falls outside the scope of Community law, such as those provided for by Titles V and VI of the Treaty on European Union, and in any case processing operations concerning public security, defence, State security (including the economic well-being of the State when the processing operation relates to State security matters) and the activities of the State in areas of criminal law.

39. As the activities of Mrs. Lindqvist which are at issue in the main proceedings are essentially not economic but charitable and religious, it is necessary to consider whether they constitute the processing of personal data in the course of an activity which falls outside the scope of Community law within the meaning of the first indent of Article 3(2) of Directive 95/46. . . .

43. The activities mentioned by way of example in the first indent of Article 3(2) of Directive 95/46 (in other words, the activities provided for by Titles V and

---

[47] Editors' Note: This sum is approximately $670.

[48] Editors' Note: This sum is approximately $50.

VI of the Treaty on European Union and processing operations concerning public security, defence, State security and activities in areas of criminal law) are, in any event, activities of the State or of State authorities and unrelated to the fields of activity of individuals.

44. It must therefore be considered that the activities mentioned by way of example in the first indent of Article 3(2) of Directive 95/46 are intended to define the scope of the exception provided for there, with the result that that exception applies only to the activities which are expressly listed there or which can be classified in the same category (*ejusdem generis*).

45. Charitable or religious activities such as those carried out by Mrs. Lindqvist cannot be considered equivalent to the activities listed in the first indent of Article 3(2) of Directive 95/46 and are thus not covered by that exception.

46. As regards the exception provided for in the second indent of Article 3(2) of Directive 95/46, the 12th recital in the preamble to that directive, which concerns that exception, cites, as examples of the processing of data carried out by a natural person in the exercise of activities which are exclusively personal or domestic, correspondence and the holding of records of addresses.

47. That exception must therefore be interpreted as relating only to activities which are carried out in the course of private or family life of individuals, which is clearly not the case with the processing of personal data consisting in publication on the internet so that those data are made accessible to an indefinite number of people.

48. The answer to the third question must therefore be that processing of personal data such as that described in the reply to the first question is not covered by any of the exceptions in Article 3(2) of Directive 95/46.

49. By its fourth question, the referring court seeks to know whether reference to the fact that an individual has injured her foot and is on half-time on medical grounds constitutes personal data concerning health within the meaning of Article 8(1) of Directive 95/46.

50. In the light of the purpose of the directive, the expression data concerning health used in Article 8(1) thereof must be given a wide interpretation so as to include information concerning all aspects, both physical and mental, of the health of an individual.

51. The answer to the fourth question must therefore be that reference to the fact that an individual has injured her foot and is on half-time on medical grounds constitutes personal data concerning health within the meaning of Article 8(1) of Directive 95/46.

65. For its part, Article 25 of Directive 95/46 imposes a series of obligations on Member States and on the Commission for the purposes of monitoring transfers of personal data to third countries in the light of the level of protection afforded to such data in each of those countries. . . .

69. If Article 25 of Directive 95/46 were interpreted to mean that there is transfer [of data] to a third country every time that personal data are loaded onto an internet page, that transfer would necessarily be a transfer to all the third countries where there are the technical means needed to access the internet. The special regime provided for by Chapter IV of the directive would thus necessarily become a regime of general application, as regards operations on the internet. Thus, if the Commission found, pursuant to Article 25(4) of Directive 95/46, that

even one third country did not ensure adequate protection, the Member States would be obliged to prevent any personal data being placed on the internet.

70. Accordingly, it must be concluded that Article 25 of Directive 95/46 is to be interpreted as meaning that operations such as those carried out by Mrs. Lindqvist do not as such constitute a transfer [of data] to a third country. It is thus unnecessary to investigate whether an individual from a third country has accessed the internet page concerned or whether the server of that hosting service is physically in a third country. . . .

72. . . . [T]he referring court seeks to know whether the provisions of Directive 95/46, in a case such as that in the main proceedings, bring about a restriction which conflicts with the general principles of freedom of expression or other freedoms and rights, which are applicable within the European Union and are enshrined in inter alia Article 10 of the ECHR.

86. . . . [F]undamental rights have a particular importance, as demonstrated by the case in the main proceedings, in which, in essence, Mrs. Lindqvist's freedom of expression in her work preparing people for Communion and her freedom to carry out activities contributing to religious life have to be weighed against the protection of the private life of the individuals about whom Mrs. Lindqvist has placed data on her internet site.

87. Consequently, it is for the authorities and courts of the Member States not only to interpret their national law in a manner consistent with Directive 95/46 but also to make sure they do not rely on an interpretation of it which would be in conflict with the fundamental rights protected by the Community legal order or with the other general principles of Community law, such as inter alia the principle of proportionality. . . .

90. The answer to the sixth question must therefore be that the provisions of Directive 95/46 do not, in themselves, bring about a restriction which conflicts with the general principles of freedom of expression or other freedoms and rights, which are applicable within the European Union and are enshrined inter alia in Article 10 of the ECHR. It is for the national authorities and courts responsible for applying the national legislation implementing Directive 95/46 to ensure a fair balance between the rights and interests in question, including the fundamental rights protected by the Community legal order.

91. By its seventh question, the referring court essentially seeks to know whether it is permissible for the Member States to provide for greater protection for personal data or a wider scope than are required under Directive 95/46.

95. Directive 95/46 is intended, as appears from the eighth recital in the preamble thereto, to ensure that the level of protection of the rights and freedoms of individuals with regard to the processing of personal data is equivalent in all Member States. The tenth recital adds that the approximation of the national laws applicable in this area must not result in any lessening of the protection they afford but must, on the contrary, seek to ensure a high level of protection in the Community.

96. The harmonisation of those national laws is therefore not limited to minimal harmonisation but amounts to harmonisation which is generally complete. It is upon that view that Directive 95/46 is intended to ensure free movement of personal data while guaranteeing a high level of protection for the rights and interests of the individuals to whom such data relate.

97. It is true that Directive 95/46 allows the Member States a margin for manoeuvre in certain areas and authorises them to maintain or introduce particular rules for specific situations as a large number of its provisions demonstrate. However, such possibilities must be made use of in the manner provided for by Directive 95/46 and in accordance with its objective of maintaining a balance between the free movement of personal data and the protection of private life.

98. On the other hand, nothing prevents a Member State from extending the scope of the national legislation implementing the provisions of Directive 95/46 to areas not included within the scope thereof, provided that no other provision of Community law precludes it.

99. In the light of those considerations, the answer to the seventh question must be that measures taken by the Member States to ensure the protection of personal data must be consistent both with the provisions of Directive 95/46 and with its objective of maintaining a balance between freedom of movement of personal data and the protection of private life. However, nothing prevents a Member State from extending the scope of the national legislation implementing the provisions of Directive 95/46 to areas not included in the scope thereof provided that no other provision of Community law precludes it.

THE COURT, in answer to the questions referred to it by the Gota hovratt by order of 23 February 2001, hereby rules:

1. The act of referring, on an internet page, to various persons and identifying them by name or by other means, for instance by giving their telephone number or information regarding their working conditions and hobbies, constitutes the processing of personal data. . . .

4. There is no transfer [of data] to a third country within the meaning of Article 25 of Directive 95/46 where an individual in a Member State loads personal data onto an internet page which is stored on an internet site on which the page can be consulted and which is hosted by a natural or legal person who is established in that State or in another Member State, thereby making those data accessible to anyone who connects to the internet, including people in a third country. . . .

NOTES & QUESTIONS

1. *A Sweeping Decision.* The *Lindqvist* court found that Mrs. Lindqvist's posting of her website on the Internet constituted the processing of data. It found that she had illegally processed personal information as well as health information. It read the Directive's provisions about personal data about health to extend even to a mention of a foot injury. Without the data subject's permission, such personal information could not be subject to processing. The court also found that Member States could enact data privacy protections beyond the areas specified within the Directive. It stated that "nothing prevents a Member State from extending the scope of the national legislation implementing the provisions of Directive 95/46 to areas not included within the scope thereof, provided that no other provision of Community law precludes it."

   In a negative reaction to this case, a student note in the United States argues: "The possibility of having each and every citizen claim that his or her privacy has been compromised by a use of information about him or her somewhere on the Internet is a monumental bureaucratic disaster, one which is difficult to imagine was the imagined intent of the drafters of the European Union's Data Protection Directive."[49] Do you agree that the decision is "draconian and abusive"?

2. **Lindqvist *in the United States?*** Imagine that Mrs. Lindqvist worked at the Lutheran Church in Lake Wobegon, Minnesota, and created a website similar to the one at stake in the above decision. Imagine you are an attorney and that an offended member of the church visits your office and seeks legal action against the Minnesota Mrs. Lindqvist. What are the available legal claims under U.S. law? Are they likely to be successful?

3. ***No Transfer of Information.*** The *Lindqvist* court also decided that she had not transferred the information on the site to a third country. Why did it reach this conclusion? Under what circumstances might a European court decide, to the contrary, that a website was transferring information to a third country? Would this decision have been decided differently if technology existed that could restrict access to a website based on the location of the viewer?

GOOGLE SPAIN SL, GOOGLE INC. V. AGENCIA ESPAÑOLA DE PROTECCIÓN DE DATOS (AEPD), MARIO COSTEJA GONZÁLEZ

European Court of Justice, Case C-131/12 (May 13, 2014)

---

14. On 5 March 2010, Mr Costeja González, a Spanish national resident in Spain, lodged with the AEPD a complaint against La Vanguardia Ediciones SL, which publishes a daily newspaper with a large circulation, in particular in Catalonia (Spain) ('La Vanguardia'), and against Google Spain and Google Inc. The complaint was based on the fact that, when an internet user entered Mr Costeja González's name in the search engine of the Google group ('Google Search'), he would obtain links to two pages of La Vanguardia's newspaper, of 19 January and 9 March 1998 respectively, on which an announcement mentioning Mr Costeja González's name appeared for a real-estate auction connected with attachment proceedings for the recovery of social security debts. . . .

Consideration of the questions referred

[Questions concerning material scope of the Directive]

26. As regards in particular the internet, the Court has already had occasion to state that the operation of loading personal data on an internet page must be considered to be such 'processing' within the meaning of Article 2(b) of Directive 95/46 (see Case C-101/01 *Lindqvist*). . . .

28. Therefore, it must be found that, in exploring the internet automatically, constantly and systematically in search of the information which is published there,

---

[49] Flora J. Garcia, *Bodil Lindqvist: A Swedish Churchgoer's Violation of the European Union's Data Protection Directive Should Be a Warning to U.S. Legislators*, 15 Fordham Intell. Prop. Media & Ent. L.J. 1206, 1232 (2005).

the operator of a search engine 'collects' such data which it subsequently 'retrieves', 'records' and 'organises' within the framework of its indexing programmes, 'stores' on its servers and, as the case may be, 'discloses' and 'makes available' to its users in the form of lists of search results. As those operations are referred to expressly and unconditionally in Article 2(b) of Directive 95/46, they must be classified as 'processing' within the meaning of that provision, regardless of the fact that the operator of the search engine also carries out the same operations in respect of other types of information and does not distinguish between the latter and the personal data.

29. Nor is the foregoing finding affected by the fact that those data have already been published on the internet and are not altered by the search engine. . . .

32. As to the question whether the operator of a search engine must be regarded as the 'controller' in respect of the processing of personal data that is carried out by that engine in the context of an activity such as that at issue in the main proceedings, it should be recalled that Article 2(d) of Directive 95/46 defines 'controller' as 'the natural or legal person, public authority, agency or any other body which alone or jointly with others determines the purposes and means of the processing of personal data'.

33. It is the search engine operator which determines the purposes and means of that activity and thus of the processing of personal data that it itself carries out within the framework of that activity and which must, consequently, be regarded as the 'controller' in respect of that processing pursuant to Article 2(d).

34. Furthermore, it would be contrary not only to the clear wording of that provision but also to its objective — which is to ensure, through a broad definition of the concept of 'controller', effective and complete protection of data subjects — to exclude the operator of a search engine from that definition on the ground that it does not exercise control over the personal data published on the web pages of third parties. . . .

36. Moreover, it is undisputed that that activity of search engines plays a decisive role in the overall dissemination of those data in that it renders the latter accessible to any internet user making a search on the basis of the data subject's name, including to internet users who otherwise would not have found the web page on which those data are published. . . .

[Questions concerning territorial scope of Directive]

42. . . . [T]he referring court seeks to establish whether it is possible to apply the national legislation transposing Directive 95/46 in circumstances such as those at issue in the main proceedings.

44 Specifically, the main issues raised by the referring court concern the notion of 'establishment', within the meaning of Article 4(1)(a) of Directive 95/46, and of 'use of equipment situated on the territory of the said Member State', within the meaning of Article 4(1)(c). . . .

55. In the light of that objective of Directive 95/46 and of the wording of Article 4(1)(a), it must be held that the processing of personal data for the purposes of the service of a search engine such as Google Search, which is operated by an undertaking that has its seat in a third State but has an establishment in a Member

State, is carried out 'in the context of the activities' of that establishment if the latter is intended to promote and sell, in that Member State, advertising space offered by the search engine which serves to make the service offered by that engine profitable.

56. In such circumstances, the activities of the operator of the search engine and those of its establishment situated in the Member State concerned are inextricably linked since the activities relating to the advertising space constitute the means of rendering the search engine at issue economically profitable and that engine is, at the same time, the means enabling those activities to be performed.

57. As has been stated in paragraphs 26 to 28 of the present judgment, the very display of personal data on a search results page constitutes processing of such data. Since that display of results is accompanied, on the same page, by the display of advertising linked to the search terms, it is clear that the processing of personal data in question is carried out in the context of the commercial and advertising activity of the controller's establishment on the territory of a Member State, in this instance Spanish territory.

58. That being so, it cannot be accepted that the processing of personal data carried out for the purposes of the operation of the search engine should escape the obligations and guarantees laid down by Directive 95/46, which would compromise the directive's effectiveness and the effective and complete protection of the fundamental rights and freedoms of natural persons which the directive seeks to ensure . . .

[Questions concerning the extent of the responsibility of the operator
of a search engine under the Directive]

80. It must be pointed out at the outset that . . . processing of personal data, such as that at issue in the main proceedings, carried out by the operator of a search engine is liable to affect significantly the fundamental rights to privacy and to the protection of personal data when the search by means of that engine is carried out on the basis of an individual's name, since that processing enables any internet user to obtain through the list of results a structured overview of the information relating to that individual that can be found on the internet — information which potentially concerns a vast number of aspects of his private life and which, without the search engine, could not have been interconnected or could have been only with great difficulty — and thereby to establish a more or less detailed profile of him. Furthermore, the effect of the interference with those rights of the data subject is heightened on account of the important role played by the internet and search engines in modern society, which render the information contained in such a list of results ubiquitous . . . .

81. In the light of the potential seriousness of that interference, it is clear that it cannot be justified by merely the economic interest which the operator of such an engine has in that processing. However, inasmuch as the removal of links from the list of results could, depending on the information at issue, have effects upon the legitimate interest of internet users potentially interested in having access to that information, in situations such as that at issue in the main proceedings a fair balance should be sought in particular between that interest and the data subject's fundamental rights under Articles 7 and 8 of the Charter. Whilst it is true that the

data subject's rights protected by those articles also override, as a general rule, that interest of internet users, that balance may however depend, in specific cases, on the nature of the information in question and its sensitivity for the data subject's private life and on the interest of the public in having that information, an interest which may vary, in particular, according to the role played by the data subject in public life. . . .

84. Given the ease with which information published on a website can be replicated on other sites and the fact that the persons responsible for its publication are not always subject to European Union legislation, effective and complete protection of data users could not be achieved if the latter had to obtain first or in parallel the erasure of the information relating to them from the publishers of websites.

85. Furthermore, the processing by the publisher of a web page consisting in the publication of information relating to an individual may, in some circumstances, be carried out 'solely for journalistic purposes' and thus benefit, by virtue of Article 9 of Directive 95/46, from derogations from the requirements laid down by the directive, whereas that does not appear to be so in the case of the processing carried out by the operator of a search engine. It cannot therefore be ruled out that in certain circumstances the data subject is capable of exercising the rights referred to in Article 12(b) and subparagraph (a) of the first paragraph of Article 14 of Directive 95/46 against that operator but not against the publisher of the web page. . . .

87. Indeed, since the inclusion in the list of results, displayed following a search made on the basis of a person's name, of a web page and of the information contained on it relating to that person makes access to that information appreciably easier for any internet user making a search in respect of the person concerned and may play a decisive role in the dissemination of that information, it is liable to constitute a more significant interference with the data subject's fundamental right to privacy than the publication on the web page.

88. In the light of all the foregoing considerations, . . . the operator of a search engine is obliged to remove from the list of results displayed following a search made on the basis of a person's name links to web pages, published by third parties and containing information relating to that person, also in a case where that name or information is not erased beforehand or simultaneously from those web pages, and even, as the case may be, when its publication in itself on those pages is lawful.

[Questions concerning the scope of the data subject's
rights guaranteed by the Directive]

89. By Question 3, the referring court asks, in essence, whether Article 12(b) and subparagraph (a) of the first paragraph of Article 14 of Directive 95/46 are to be interpreted as enabling the data subject to require the operator of a search engine to remove from the list of results displayed following a search made on the basis of his name links to web pages published lawfully by third parties and containing true information relating to him, on the ground that that information may be prejudicial to him or that he wishes it to be 'forgotten' after a certain time. . . .

94. Therefore, if it is found, following a request by the data subject pursuant to Article 12(b) of Directive 95/46, that the inclusion in the list of results displayed following a search made on the basis of his name of the links to web pages published lawfully by third parties and containing true information relating to him personally is, at this point in time, incompatible with Article 6(1)(c) to (e) of the directive because that information appears, having regard to all the circumstances of the case, to be inadequate, irrelevant or no longer relevant, or excessive in relation to the purposes of the processing at issue carried out by the operator of the search engine, the information and links concerned in the list of results must be erased. . . .

96. In the light of the foregoing, when appraising such requests made in order to oppose processing such as that at issue in the main proceedings, it should in particular be examined whether the data subject has a right that the information relating to him personally should, at this point in time, no longer be linked to his name by a list of results displayed following a search made on the basis of his name. In this connection, it must be pointed out that it is not necessary in order to find such a right that the inclusion of the information in question in the list of results causes prejudice to the data subject.

97. As the data subject may, in the light of his fundamental rights under Articles 7 and 8 of the Charter, request that the information in question no longer be made available to the general public by its inclusion in such a list of results, it should be held, as follows in particular from paragraph 81 of the present judgment, that those rights override, as a rule, not only the economic interest of the operator of the search engine but also the interest of the general public in finding that information upon a search relating to the data subject's name. However, that would not be the case if it appeared, for particular reasons, such as the role played by the data subject in public life, that the interference with his fundamental rights is justified by the preponderant interest of the general public in having, on account of inclusion in the list of results, access to the information in question.

98. As regards a situation such as that at issue in the main proceedings, which concerns the display, in the list of results that the internet user obtains by making a search by means of Google Search on the basis of the data subject's name, of links to pages of the on-line archives of a daily newspaper that contain announcements mentioning the data subject's name and relating to a real-estate auction connected with attachment proceedings for the recovery of social security debts, it should be held that, having regard to the sensitivity for the data subject's private life of the information contained in those announcements and to the fact that its initial publication had taken place 16 years earlier, the data subject establishes a right that that information should no longer be linked to his name by means of such a list. Accordingly, since in the case in point there do not appear to be particular reasons substantiating a preponderant interest of the public in having, in the context of such a search, access to that information, a matter which is, however, for the referring court to establish, the data subject may, by virtue of Article 12(b) and subparagraph (a) of the first paragraph of Article 14 of Directive 95/46, require those links to be removed from the list of results.

NOTES & QUESTIONS

1. ***The Logic of* Google Spain.** Citing *Lindqvist*, the European Court of Justice in *Google Spain* declared that the operator of search engines was a "processor" of data under the Data Protection Directive. The operator of the search engine could not justify its activity simply through its "economic interest" in the processing, and it was not protected, as a publisher of a Web page might be, by the language regarding journalism in Article 9 of the Directive. The Court also found that even when publication of the information may be lawful, the operator of the search engine could be required to remove links from a person's name in its search results. Do you agree with all, some, or none of these conclusions?

2. ***The Duty of a Search Engine Operator and "the Right to be Forgotten."*** The *Google Spain* Court notes that the referring court had asked whether a data subject could require the operator of a search engine operator to remove truthful information relating to him because it was "prejudicial to him or that he wishes it to be 'forgotten' after a certain time." The Court found that even if the information did not cause "prejudice" to the data subject, a data subject's under Articles 7 and 8 of the Charter generally were weightier than the economic interest of the operator of the search engine and the interest of the general public in access to information. In the case at hand, it specifically found an interest in the data subject in not having the information linked to him. What are the duties of Google and other search engine operators under *Google Spain*?

3. ***International Reactions.*** The *Google Spain* decision was widely commented and reported on throughout the world. In the United Kingdom, Christopher Graham, the data protection commissioner, was unconcerned about the logistical challenges now facing Google. He told the BBC, "Google is a massive commercial organization making millions and millions out of processing people's personal information. They're going to have to do some tidying up."[50]

   In contrast, Jimmy Wales, the founder of Wikipedia, worried about Internet search engines now being placed in charge of "censoring history."[51] In Germany, Sigmar Gabriel, the Minister for Economic Affairs and Energy and Chairman of the Social Democratic Party, warned against the "Information capitalism" of a handful of American Internet companies.[52] In an essay in the *Frankfurt Allgemeine Zeitung* he wrote, "Europe stands for the opposite of this totalitarian idea of making every detail of human behavior, human emotions and human thought into the object of a capitalistic marketing strategy." According to Minister Gabriel, the European emphasis was on protection of human dignity by safeguarding of an interest in self-determination over personal data.

---

[50] Rowena Mason, *Right to Be Forgotten*, The Guardian (July 25, 2014).

[51] *Id.*

[52] Sigmar Gabriel, *Unsere politischen Konsequenzen aus der Google-Debatte*, FAZ (May 16, 2014).

4. ***Commenting on Search Results***. Jonathan Zittrain considers the *Google Spain* decision to be a poor response to a significant policy issue: "[T]he Internet's ability to preserve indefinitely all its information about you" was a serious problem.[53] But Zittrain thought the decision "oddly narrow." It permitted the plaintiff to restrict the ability of search engines to list information, but not to have information removed from the Web or to restrict other Web pages— including articles about the decision itself—from listing the underlying information, such as the name of the plaintiff and the information that he viewed as objectionable. His proposed solution was for Google to re-introduce a feature, formerly found in its news aggregator, that allowed people to comment on information about them online. Such comments would provide context for search results.

5. ***Google Responds to the Court of Justice.*** In response to the decision, Google set up a Web page, "Search removal requests under data protection law in Europe."[54] It explains its approach there for compliance with the Court of Justice's opinion:

> When you make . . . a request, we will balance rights of the individual with the public's interest to know and the right to distribute information. When evaluating your request, we will look at whether the results include outdated information about you, as well as whether there's a public interest in the information – for example, we may decline to remove certain information about financial scams, professional malpractice, criminal convictions or public conduct of government information.

Does this language express the essence of the European Court of Justice's broad guidelines in the *Google Spain* decision?

In June 2014, Google then established an online form to allow those in the EU to request delisting of search requests that apply to them. It provides daily updates as to the statistics, country-by-country, regarding delisting requests and results. On July 30, 2017, it reported a total of 1.8 million delisting requests from the EU. It approved 43.2% of the contested URL's.[55] After first applying search result removals only to European domains, Google in 2016 began to apply these removal requests to all domains beyond Europe as long as the search engine was accessed within the EU. Google used the IP address to determine its location.

The ECJ now has a case before it regarding whether Google must de-list links not only within the EU, but globally. Such a decision would extend the ECJ decision in *Google Spain;* it would require Google to remove search results even for searches from the U.S. or other non-EU countries. In opposition to this measure, "Google argues that the extension of the right would pose a serious

---

[53] Jonathan Zittrain, *Don't Force Google to 'Forget,'* N.Y. Times (May 14, 2014).

[54] https://support.google.com/legal/contact/lr_eudpa?product=websearch&hl=en-GB

[55] Google, Search removals under European privacy law, https://transparencyreport.google.com/eu-privacy/overview.

risk that other countries with more egregious limitations on freedom of speech would similarly attempt to universalise their restrictions."[56]

6. ***Beyond* Google Spain: *Visual Images and Autocomplete.*** As noted above, courts in France and Germany have found for Max Mosley and required Google to automate a procedure for blocking images in advance once a court finds a photograph to violate a legal interest in privacy. Another privacy issue concerns Google's Autocomplete function. As Google explains Autocomplete, "As you type in the search box, you can find information quickly by seeing search predictions that might be similar to the search terms you're typing."[57] Autocomplete is "a reflection of the search activity of users and the content of web pages."

Germany's highest court for civil matters, the Federal Court of Justice (*Bundesgerichtshof)(*BGH*)*, has found that Google's Autocomplete can violate an individual's personality rights. In a 2013 case, the BGH found that the operator of a search engine was not generally required to check autocomplete suggestions in advance for violation of legal interests. BGH: Autocomplete, Az. VI ZR 269/12 (May 14, 2013). Rather, the search engine company became responsible once it had knowledge of a legal violation of a right of personality through an Autocomplete suggestion. Most importantly, the BGH found that an Autocomplete suggestion was Google's own content. Its software had generated the result. The Federal Court of Justice stated, "Untrue statements of facts do not have to be tolerated."

Once an affected party informed the software operator of an Autocomplete suggestion that violated a legal interest, the operator was required to prevent the software from generating this result. In its *Autocomplete* decision, the BGH had considered a plaintiff's claim that typing his first and last name in the Google search window lead to the search suggestion of "Scientology" and "Fraud." As the court noted, however, the plaintiff was neither a member of Scientology nor stood "in connection with a Fraud."

In a law review article published before this decision, Professor Niko Härtling argued against a finding against Google. In his view, no one who used a search engine on a regular basis would think that an Autocomplete search suggestion represented "the statement of a Google employee."[58] Rather, the suggestion was merely a truthful statement of already suggested language or concepts based on the activity of numerous Google users, who had typed certain words and not others into the search form.

How would you set a balance between freedom of expression and privacy when it comes to the matter of Autocomplete suggestions for search forms?

A few months before the European Court of Justice's *Google Spain* decision, the Court delivered another important privacy decision in *Digital Rights Ireland v.*

---

[56] Alex Hern, *ECJ to rule on whether 'right to be forgotten can search beyond EU*, Guardian (July 20, 2017). In June 2017, the Supreme Court of Canada did order Google "to de-index websites" of a distributor was unlawfully selling another company's intellectual property. Google Inc. v. Equustek Solutions, 2017 SCC 34 (Supreme Court of Canada, June 28, 2017).

[57] https://support.google.com/websearch/answer/106230?hl=en.

[58] Niko Härting, *Rotlichtgerüchte: Haftet Google?*, 10 Kommunikation und Recht 633 (2012).

Minister for Communications, Joined Cases C-293/12 and C-594/12 (April 8, 2014). In this decision, the European Court of Justice found that the Data Retention Directive failed to meet the necessary constitutional privacy standards.

The Directive did not create "any objective criterion by which to determine the limits of the access of the competent national authorities to the data and their subsequent us" of it. Moreover, it did not limit the access of the competent national authorities to "what is strictly necessary in the light of objective pursued" and did not require review of a request for access to a court or independent administrative entity. A final failing of the Data Retention Directive was its lack of sufficient safeguards for providers relating to the security of retained data.

In 2016 and 2017, the ECJ returned to the issue of data retention. First, in its *Tele2 Sverige* opinion, it considered the permissibility of national data retention legislation in light of the restrictions the ePrivacy Directive's Article 15 as well as the EU Charter's protections for privacy and data protection. It found the two national data retention laws before it in *Tele2 Sverige* to be invalid.

Second, in *Opinion 1/15*, the ECJ invalidated a proposed agreement between the EU and Canada to transfer passenger name record (PNR) data. The part of *Opinion 1/15* excerpted below concerns the agreement's data retention provisions. This opinion also develops the caselaw regarding the requirements of the EU for international data transfers, and this Chapter contains a further excerpt from *Opinion 1/15* in its section concerning that topic.

TELE2 SVERIGE AB V. POST- OCH TELESTYRELSEN & SEC'Y OF STATE FOR HOME DEPT V. WATSON (JOINED CASES)

ECHR, C: 2016: 970, Grand Chamber (Dec. 21, 2016)

62. By the first question in Case C 203/15, the Kammarrätten i Stockholm (Administrative Court of Appeal, Stockholm) seeks, in essence, to ascertain whether Article 15(1) of Directive 2002/58,[59] read in the light of Articles 7 and 8 and Article 52(1) of the Charter, must be interpreted as precluding national legislation such as that at issue in the main proceedings that provides, for the purpose of fighting crime, for general and indiscriminate retention of all traffic and location data of all subscribers and registered users with respect to all means of electronic communications.

63. That question arises, in particular, from the fact that Directive 2006/24,[60] which the national legislation at issue in the main proceedings was intended to transpose, was declared to be invalid by the *Digital Rights* judgment, though the parties disagree on the scope of that judgment and its effect on that legislation, given that it governs the retention of traffic and location data and access to that data by the national authorities.

102. Given the seriousness of the interference in the fundamental rights concerned represented by national legislation which, for the purpose of fighting

---

[59] Editors' Note: This Directive is termed the ePrivacy Directive.

[60] Editors' Note: This Directive is termed the Data Retention Directive.

crime, provides for the retention of traffic and location data, only the objective of fighting serious crime is capable of justifying such a measure

103. Further, while the effectiveness of the fight against serious crime, in particular organised crime and terrorism, may depend to a great extent on the use of modern investigation techniques, such an objective of general interest, however fundamental it may be, cannot in itself justify that national legislation providing for the general and indiscriminate retention of all traffic and location data . . .

104. In that regard, it must be observed, first, that the effect of such legislation, in the light of its characteristic features . . . , is that the retention of traffic and location data is the rule, whereas the system put in place by Directive 2002/58 requires the retention of data to be the exception.

105. Second, national legislation such as that at issue in the main proceedings, which covers, in a generalised manner, all subscribers and registered users and all means of electronic communication as well as all traffic data, provides for no differentiation, limitation or exception according to the objective pursued. It is comprehensive in that it affects all persons using electronic communication services, even though those persons are not, even indirectly, in a situation that is liable to give rise to criminal proceedings. It therefore applies even to persons for whom there is no evidence capable of suggesting that their conduct might have a link, even an indirect or remote one, with serious criminal offences. Further, it does not provide for any exception, and consequently it applies even to persons whose communications are subject, according to rules of national law, to the obligation of professional secrecy.

106. Such legislation does not require there to be any relationship between the data which must be retained and a threat to public security. In particular, it is not restricted to retention in relation to (i) data pertaining to a particular time period and/or geographical area and/or a group of persons likely to be involved, in one way or another, in a serious crime, or (ii) persons who could, for other reasons, contribute, through their data being retained, to fighting crime.

107. National legislation such as that at issue in the main proceedings therefore exceeds the limits of what is strictly necessary and cannot be considered to be justified, within a democratic society, as required by Article 15(1) of Directive 2002/58, read in the light of Articles 7, 8 and 11 and Article 52(1) of the Charter.

108. However, Article 15(1) of Directive 2002/58, read in the light of Articles 7, 8 and 11 and Article 52(1) of the Charter, does not prevent a Member State from adopting legislation permitting, as a preventive measure, the targeted retention of traffic and location data, for the purpose of fighting serious crime, provided that the retention of data is limited, with respect to the categories of data to be retained, the means of communication affected, the persons concerned and the retention period adopted, to what is strictly necessary.

109. In order to satisfy the requirements set out in the preceding paragraph of the present judgment, that national legislation must, first, lay down clear and precise rules governing the scope and application of such a data retention measure and imposing minimum safeguards, so that the persons whose data has been retained have sufficient guarantees of the effective protection of their personal data against the risk of misuse. That legislation must, in particular, indicate in what circumstances and under which conditions a data retention measure may, as a

preventive measure, be adopted, thereby ensuring that such a measure is limited to what is strictly necessary

110. Second, as regards the substantive conditions which must be satisfied by national legislation that authorises, in the context of fighting crime, the retention, as a preventive measure, of traffic and location data, if it is to be ensured that data retention is limited to what is strictly necessary, it must be observed that, while those conditions may vary according to the nature of the measures taken for the purposes of prevention, investigation, detection and prosecution of serious crime, the retention of data must continue nonetheless to meet objective criteria, that establish a connection between the data to be retained and the objective pursued. In particular, such conditions must be shown to be such as actually to circumscribe, in practice, the extent of that measure and, thus, the public affected.

111. As regard the setting of limits on such a measure with respect to the public and the situations that may potentially be affected, the national legislation must be based on objective evidence which makes it possible to identify a public whose data is likely to reveal a link, at least an indirect one, with serious criminal offences, and to contribute in one way or another to fighting serious crime or to preventing a serious risk to public security. Such limits may be set by using a geographical criterion where the competent national authorities consider, on the basis of objective evidence, that there exists, in one or more geographical areas, a high risk of preparation for or commission of such offences.

112. Having regard to all of the foregoing, the answer to the first question referred in Case C 203/15 is that Article 15(1) of Directive 2002/58, read in the light of Articles 7, 8 and 11 and Article 52(1) of the Charter, must be interpreted as precluding national legislation which, for the purpose of fighting crime, provides for the general and indiscriminate retention of all traffic and location data of all subscribers and registered users relating to all means of electronic communication.

The second question in Case C-203/15 and the first question in Case C-698/15

114. By the second question in Case C 203/15 and the first question in Case C 698/15, the referring courts seek, in essence, to ascertain whether Article 15(1) of Directive 2002/58, read in the light of Articles 7, 8 and Article 52(1) of the Charter, must be interpreted as precluding national legislation governing the protection and security of traffic and location data, and more particularly, the access of the competent national authorities to retained data, where that legislation does not restrict that access solely to the objective of fighting serious crime, where that access is not subject to prior review by a court or an independent administrative authority, and where there is no requirement that the data concerned should be retained within the European Union.

115. As regards objectives that are capable of justifying national legislation that derogates from the principle of confidentiality of electronic communications, it must be borne in mind that . . . . the list of objectives set out in the first sentence of Article 15(1) of Directive 2002/58 is exhaustive, access to the retained data must correspond, genuinely and strictly, to one of those objectives. Further, since the objective pursued by that legislation must be proportionate to the seriousness of the interference in fundamental rights that that access entails, it follows that, in the

area of prevention, investigation, detection and prosecution of criminal offences, only the objective of fighting serious crime is capable of justifying such access to the retained data.

116. As regards compatibility with the principle of proportionality, national legislation governing the conditions under which the providers of electronic communications services must grant the competent national authorities access to the retained data must ensure . . . . that such access does not exceed the limits of what is strictly necessary.

117. Further, since the legislative measures referred to in Article 15(1) of Directive 2002/58 must, in accordance with recital 11 of that directive, 'be subject to adequate safeguards', a data retention measure must, as follows from the case-law cited in paragraph 109 of this judgment, lay down clear and precise rules indicating in what circumstances and under which conditions the providers of electronic communications services must grant the competent national authorities access to the data. Likewise, a measure of that kind must be legally binding under domestic law.

118. In order to ensure that access of the competent national authorities to retained data is limited to what is strictly necessary, it is, indeed, for national law to determine the conditions under which the providers of electronic communications services must grant such access. . . . That national legislation must also lay down the substantive and procedural conditions governing the access of the competent national authorities to the retained data

119. Accordingly, and since general access to all retained data, regardless of whether there is any link, at least indirect, with the intended purpose, cannot be regarded as limited to what is strictly necessary, the national legislation concerned must be based on objective criteria in order to define the circumstances and conditions under which the competent national authorities are to be granted access to the data of subscribers or registered users. In that regard, access can, as a general rule, be granted, in relation to the objective of fighting crime, only to the data of individuals suspected of planning, committing or having committed a serious crime or of being implicated in one way or another in such a crime. However, in particular situations, where for example vital national security, defence or public security interests are threatened by terrorist activities, access to the data of other persons might also be granted where there is objective evidence from which it can be deduced that that data might, in a specific case, make an effective contribution to combating such activities.

120. In order to ensure, in practice, that those conditions are fully respected, it is essential that access of the competent national authorities to retained data should, as a general rule, except in cases of validly established urgency, be subject to a prior review carried out either by a court or by an independent administrative body, and that the decision of that court or body should be made following a reasoned request by those authorities submitted, inter alia, within the framework of procedures for the prevention, detection or prosecution of crime

121. Likewise, the competent national authorities to whom access to the retained data has been granted must notify the persons affected, under the applicable national procedures, as soon as that notification is no longer liable to jeopardise the investigations being undertaken by those authorities. That notification is, in fact, necessary to enable the persons affected to exercise, inter

alia, their right to a legal remedy, expressly provided for in Article 15(2) of Directive 2002/58, read together with Article 22 of Directive 95/46, where their rights have been infringed

122. . . . Given the quantity of retained data, the sensitivity of that data and the risk of unlawful access to it, the providers of electronic communications services must, in order to ensure the full integrity and confidentiality of that data, guarantee a particularly high level of protection and security by means of appropriate technical and organisational measures. In particular, the national legislation must make provision for the data to be retained within the European Union and for the irreversible destruction of the data at the end of the data retention period.

123. In any event, the Member States must ensure review, by an independent authority, of compliance with the level of protection guaranteed by EU law with respect to the protection of individuals in relation to the processing of personal data, that control being expressly required by Article 8(3) of the Charter and constituting, in accordance with the Court's settled case-law, an essential element of respect for the protection of individuals in relation to the processing of personal data. If that were not so, persons whose personal data was retained would be deprived of the right, guaranteed in Article 8(1) and (3) of the Charter, to lodge with the national supervisory authorities a claim seeking the protection of their data.

125. Having regard to all of the foregoing, the answer to the second question in Case C 203/15 and to the first question in Case C 698/15 is that Article 15(1) of Directive 2002/58, read in the light of Articles 7, 8 and 11 and Article 52(1) of the Charter, must be interpreted as precluding national legislation governing the protection and security of traffic and location data and, in particular, access of the competent national authorities to the retained data, where the objective pursued by that access, in the context of fighting crime, is not restricted solely to fighting serious crime, where access is not subject to prior review by a court or an independent administrative authority, and where there is no requirement that the data concerned should be retained within the European Union.

OPINION 1/15 OF THE COURT

European Court of Justice, Grand Chamber (July 26, 2017)

[A year after the *TeleSverige 2* decision, the ECJ in 2017 returned to the topic of data retention in its *Opinion 1/15*. This opinion considers the conditions under which international agreements with the EU may legalize international data transfers. As part of this assessment, it applied its caselaw regarding data retention to a situation in which the personal data of an EU citizen would be transferred and stored in a non-EU nation. The proposed EU-Canada agreement would permit storage of the data in Canada for five years. Under it, the PNR data of all passengers from the EU to Canada would be collected and retained.

As for the PNR data covered by the envisaged agreement, it was to includes "the name(s) of the air passenger(s), information necessary to the reservation, such as the dates of intended travel and the travel itinerary, information relating to tickets, groups of persons checked-in under the same reservation number, passenger contact information, information relating to the means of payment or billing, information concerning baggage and general remarks regarding the passengers."]

    (6)   The retention and use of PNR data

190. In order to ensure that the retention of the PNR data transferred, the access to that data by the Canadian authorities referred to in the envisaged agreement and the use of that data by those authorities is limited to what is strictly necessary, the envisaged agreement should, in accordance with the settled case-law of the Court cited in . . . this Opinion, lay down clear and precise rules indicating in what circumstances and under which conditions those authorities may retain, have access to and use such data.

191. So far as the retention of personal data is concerned, it must be pointed out that the legislation in question must, inter alia, continue to satisfy objective criteria that establish a connection between the personal data to be retained and the objective pursued (see, to that effect, judgments of 6 October 2015, Schrems, . . . and of 21 December 2016, Tele2 Sverige and Watson and Others).

    (i)   The retention and use of PNR data before the arrival of air passengers, during their stay in Canada and on their departure

196. The envisaged agreement accordingly permits, throughout the retention period, the use of the PNR data of all air passengers for the purposes referred to in Article 3 thereof.

197. As regards the retention of PNR data and its use up to the air passengers' departure from Canada, it should be noted that PNR data, inter alia, facilitates security checks and border control checks. Its retention and use for that purpose may not, on account of its very nature, be restricted to a particular circle of air passengers, nor can it be subject to prior authorisation by a court or by an independent administrative body. Consequently, . . . it must be held that, for as long as the air passengers are in Canada or are due to leave that non-member country, the necessary connection between that data and the objective pursued by that agreement exists, and the agreement therefore does not exceed the limits of what is strictly necessary merely because it permits the systematic retention and use of the PNR data of all air passengers.

198. Similarly, the systematic use of PNR data for the purpose of verifying the reliability and topicality of the pre-established models and criteria on which the automated processing of that data is based, . . . or of defining new models and criteria for such processing, is directly related to carrying out the checks referred to in the preceding paragraph of this Opinion, and must, therefore, also be considered to not exceed the limits of what is strictly necessary.

199. Furthermore, it must be pointed out that, during the air passengers' stay in Canada and irrespective of the results of the automated analysis of the PNR data carried out prior to their arrival in that non-member country, cases may arise in which the Canadian Competent Authority has information, collected during that

stay, indicating that use of their data might be necessary in order to combat terrorism and serious transnational crime.

200. As regards the use of PNR data in the situations referred to in the preceding paragraph, however, it should be pointed out that, since the air passengers have been allowed to enter the territory of that non-member country, following verification of their PNR data, the use of that data during their stay in Canada must be based on new circumstances justifying that use. That use therefore requires . . . rules laying down the substantive and procedural conditions governing that use in order, inter alia, to protect that data against the risk of abuse. Such rules must be based on objective criteria in order to define the circumstances and conditions under which the Canadian authorities referred to in the envisaged agreement are authorised to use that data.

201. In this connection, where there is objective evidence from which it may be inferred that the PNR data of one or more air passengers might make an effective contribution to combating terrorist offences and serious transnational crime, the use of that data does not exceed the limits of what is strictly necessary.

202. Furthermore, in order to ensure that, in practice, the conditions set out in the two preceding paragraphs are fully respected, it is essential that the use of retained PNR data, during the air passengers' stay in Canada, should, as a general rule, except in cases of validly established urgency, be subject to a prior review carried out either by a court, or by an independent administrative body, and that the decision of that court or body be made following a reasoned request by the competent authorities submitted, inter alia, within the framework of procedures for the prevention, detection or prosecution of crime.

203. In so far as the envisaged agreement does not meet the requirements set out in the two preceding paragraphs, that agreement does not ensure that the use of the PNR data of air passengers during their stay in Canada, by the Canadian authorities referred to in the agreement, will be limited to what is strictly necessary.

(ii) The retention and use of PNR data after the air passengers' departure from Canada

204. Air passengers who have left Canada have, as a general rule, been subject to checks on entry to and on departure from Canada. Similarly, their PNR data has been verified before their arrival in Canada and, as the case may be, during their stay and on their departure from that non-member country. . . . In any event, it is not apparent that all air passengers who have travelled to Canada would present, after their departure from that country, a higher risk than other persons who have not travelled to that country during the previous five years and in respect of whom Canada does not therefore hold PNR data.

205. Consequently, as regards air passengers in respect of whom no such risk has been identified on their arrival in Canada and up to their departure from that non-member country, there would not appear to be, once they have left, a connection — even a merely indirect connection — between their PNR data and the objective pursued by the envisaged agreement which would justify that data being retained. The considerations put forward before the Court, inter alia, by the Council and the Commission regarding the average lifespan of international serious crime networks and the duration and complexity of investigations relating

to those networks, do not justify the continued storage of the PNR data of all air passengers after their departure from Canada for the purposes of possibly accessing that data, regardless of whether there is any link with combating terrorism and serious transnational crime.

206. The continued storage of the PNR data of all air passengers after their departure from Canada is not therefore limited to what is strictly necessary.

207. However, in so far as, in specific cases, objective evidence is identified from which it may be inferred that certain air passengers may present a risk in terms of the fight against terrorism and serious transnational crime even after their departure from Canada, it seems permissible to store their PNR data beyond their stay in Canada.

208. As regards the use of PNR data so stored, such use should . . . be based on objective criteria in order to define the circumstances and conditions under which the Canadian authorities referred to in the envisaged agreement may have access to that data in order to use it. Similarly, that use should, except in cases of validly established urgency, be subject to a prior review carried out either by a court, or by an independent administrative body; the decision of that court or body authorising the use being made following a reasoned request by those authorities submitted, inter alia, within the framework of procedures for the prevention, detection or prosecution of crime.

209. As regards the period during which the PNR data of the air passengers . . . . may be retained, it should be observed that the general period, provided for in Article 16(1) of the envisaged agreement, has been extended by one and a half years by comparison with the period provided for in the 2006 Agreement. In this connection, it must nevertheless be accepted, in the light, inter alia, of the considerations put forward, in particular, by the Council and the Commission, mentioned in paragraph 205 of this Opinion, that the five-year retention period provided for in Article 16(1) of that agreement does not exceed the limits of what is strictly necessary for the purposes of combating terrorism and serious transnational crime.

210. Lastly, in so far as Article 9(2) of the envisaged agreement, which provides that Canada is to hold PNR data 'in a secure physical environment that is protected with access controls', means that that data has to be held in Canada, and in so far as Article 16(6) of that agreement, under which Canada is to destroy the PNR data at the end of the PNR data retention period, must be understood as requiring the irreversible destruction of that data, those provisions may be regarded as meeting the requirements as to clarity and precision.

211. Having regard to the considerations set out in paragraphs 204 to 206 and 208 of this Opinion, that agreement does not ensure that the retention and use of PNR data by the Canadian authorities after the air passengers' departure from Canada is limited to what is strictly necessary.

NOTES & QUESTIONS

1. **The Holding: Tele2 Sverige.** The *Tele2 Sverige* opinion invalidated national legislation on the grounds that these laws provided for general and indiscriminate data retention. Such an approach was incompatible with the

ePrivacy Directive as interpreted in light of EU Charter rights. More specifically, the ECJ in *Tele2 Sverige* found that legislation could not permit "retention of traffic and location data" as the rule since the ePrivacy Directive "requires the retention of data to be the exception. *Tele2 Sverige,* ¶104. This opinion required "a relationship between the data which must be retained and a threat to public security." Id. at ¶106.

2. *The Holding:* **Opinion 1/15.** In this judgment, the ECJ was responding to a request from the European Parliament to assess a proposed agreement with Canada that set conditions for transfer of PNR data. Regarding its provisions for data retention, the Court found in principle that the agreement's five-year retention period did not exceed the limits of what was strictly necessary. *Opinion 1/15* at ¶209. At the same time, it found numerous problematic aspects of the data retention aspects of the agreement. For example, the retention and use of PNR information after a passenger left Canada were not strictly necessary. Such data may only be stored in Canada where certain passengers present a risk of terrorism or serious transnational criminal activities. Moreover, it required that the use of the retained data would be subject to prior review by an independent body, such as a court. Id. at ¶¶202, 208.

3. *Strictly Necessary Data Retention.* What steps would national legislation have to take to meet the ECJ's standards set out in *Tele2 Sverige and Opinion 1/15*? How can a statute limit data retention to that which is "strictly necessary" under EU law? What are the critical benchmarks for the ECJ? *Opinion 1/15* speaks of a requirement for "rules laying down the substantive and procedural conditions government" use of data, such as how that data is to be used during a passenger's stay in Canada. *Opinion 1/15,* ¶200. What elements must such rules contain?

4. *Post-Departure Storage of PNR.* In *Opinion 1/15,* the ECJ found that PNR data of *all* EU passengers to Canada could not be retained in a blanket fashion post-departure. *Opinion 1/15,* ¶205. In particular, a justification regarding "the average lifespan of international serious crime networks" did not justify storage of information regarding all air passengers. In contrast, it would be permissible to store information post-departure about EU voyagers if "in specific cases," there was an identification of "objective evidence" relating to these individuals presenting "a risk in terms of the fight against terrorism and serious transnational crime even after their departure from Canada. Id. Do you agree with this approach? Should the ECJ defer to the assessment about blanket data retention from the Canadian and European negotiators of the PNR Agreement?

5. *Data Localization.* Among its mandated safeguards, the ECJ found it necessary, as part of a data retention law's protection of data security, that "the national legislation must make provision for the data to be retained within the European Union." *Tele2 Sverige,* ¶122. This part of the decision represents an important EU data localization requirement.

(c) The General Data Protection Regulation

The main reference point for European data protection law will soon be the General Data Protection Regulation (GDPR) of 2016. The GDPR takes effect on May 25, 2018, which will mark a decisive moment for international privacy law. The GDPR's influence will be felt throughout the world. As Jan Albrecht and Florian Jotzo observe, the GDPR on that date will "represent without any doubt the most important legal source for data protection."[61] In proof of this significance, Albrecht and Jotzo point to the Regulation's central role in "the largest domestic market in the world," the EU, as well as its future international impact.[62] Albrecht is in a good position to comment on the GDPR; a member of the Green party, he served for the EU Parliament as the influential Rapporteur of the Regulation.

The current key regulatory document, one that the GDPR will replace, is the European Data Protection Directive of 1995. The GDPR marks an important policy shift from a directive to a regulation. In EU law, while a directive requires harmonizing legislation, a regulation establishes directly enforceable standards. As Christopher Kuner explains, "a regulation leads to a greater degree of harmonization, since it immediately becomes part of a national legal system, without the need for adoption of separate national legislation; has legal effect independent of national law; and overrides contrary national laws."[63]

The EU's recourse to a regulation follows from its recognition of both privacy as a human right and the high status of the individual. As already noted in this Chapter, cornerstone documents of European integration safeguard privacy and data protection as human rights. In a reflection of the data subject's high status, the GDPR provides directly binding statutory protection in EU law. This choice marks a notable change with the established path of EU consumer protection law, where the usual path has been to enact directives and not regulations to protect citizens.

There was another reason for the EU's choice of a regulation instead of taking the path of a Data Protection Directive 2.0. The Directive was widely considered to have fallen short in harmonizing data protection throughout the EU. According to the Commission, for example, Member States were interpreting the rules for consent differently, and the Directive's grant of "room for manoeuvre in certain areas" and its permitting member states to issue "particular rules for specific situations" had created "additional cost[s] and administrative burden[s]" for private stakeholders.[64] Due to this absence of uniformity under the Directive, a regulation was needed to create legal certainty within the internal market and to assure a continuing role for the EU "in promoting high data protection standards worldwide."[65]

---

[61] Jan Philipp Albrecht & Florian Jotzo, *Das neue Datenschutzrecht der EU* 7 (2017).

[62] *Id.*

[63] Christopher Kuner, *The European Commission's Proposed Data Protection Regulation: A Copernican Revolution in European Data Protection Law*, 11 Privacy & Security L. Rep. 215, 217 (2012).

[64] Communication from the Commission to the European Parliament, the Council, the Economic and Social Committee and the Committee of the Regions, at 2, 8 COM (2010) 609 final (Nov. 11, 2010).

[65] *Id.* at 10.

Like the Directive, the GDPR contains strong protections for individual rights. It limits the sweep of individual content and restricts the processing of sensitive data and the use of "automated decision-making." Finally, it greatly increases the available enforcement tools, including fines, for violations of EU data protection law.

Limits on Data Processing. As an initial step in protecting individual rights, the Proposed Regulation requires a legal basis for the processing of personal data. The principles of the GDPR begin by requiring that information be: (1) "processed lawfully, fairly and in a transparent manner" (lawfulness, fairness, and transparency) and that it be (2) "collected for specified, explicit and legitimate purposes and not further processed in a manner that is incompatible with those purposes" (purpose limitation). Art. 5(1). The list continues with requirements of (3) data minimization; (4) data accuracy; (5) limited storage; (6) integrity; (7) data security; and (8) accountability for the data controller. Finally, in Article 51, the GDPR contains strong protections for (9) independent data protection authorities.

The Rights to Rectification and Erasure ("The Right to be Forgotten"). The GDPR provides a right of correction, termed a rectification interest, and imposes temporal limits on data use. The first interest permits the individual "to obtain from the controller without undue delay the rectification of inaccurate personal data concerning him or her." Art. 16. The controller is a person who or an organization which "determines the purposes and means of the processing of personal data." Art. 4(7). In addition, the individual shall the right to have incomplete personal data completed." Art. 16.

As a second important personal interest, the Proposed Regulation creates a a "right to erasure." Art. 17. In a parenthesis in its heading for this section, it refers to this individual interest as a "right to be forgotten." The right to erasure sets out a number of grounds that will trigger the controller's obligation to erase personal data. These begin with when "the personal data are no longer necessary in relation to the purposes for which they were collected or otherwise processed." Another erasure justification is when the individual withdraws her consent "and where there is no other legal ground for the processing." Other grounds for erasure include when the personal data are unlawfully processed, when a legal obligation in EU or Member State law require erasure, and when the data subject objects to processing and "there are no overriding legitimate grounds for the processing."

Consent. The GDPR strengthens individual rights in other ways. Among the most important of these measures are those that put in place strong restrictions on the use of consent requirements as a basis for processing personal data. As Christopher Kuner has observed, consent is an especially important concept in the EU because it is in "widespread use . . . as a legal basis for data processing."[66] The Directive required consent to be given "unambiguously." Directive, Art. 7(a). Strengthening this language, the GDPR requires that consent be "freely given,

---

[66] Christopher Kuner, *The European Commission's Proposed Data Protection Regulation: A Copernican Revolution in European Data Protection Law*, 11 Privacy & Security L. Rep. 215, 220 (2012).

specific, informed and unambiguous."[67] GDPR, Recital 32 notes: "Silence, pre-ticked boxes or inactivity should not . . . constitute consent." Thus, the GDPR clearly favors the use of affirmative steps to constitute consent, and disfavors inaction as indicating consent.

Mechanisms for gathering consent must also be understandable and transparent. If the data subject provides consent in a written declaration that concerns other matters, "the request for consent" must be made "in a manner which is clearly distinguishable from the other matters, in an intelligible and easily accessible form, using clear and plain language." Art. 7(2). Where consent involves the personal data of a child or sensitive data, there are additional enumerated conditions that must be met. Art. 8(1).

As a further restriction, consent can be withdrawn at any time. The GDPR states: "It shall be as easy to withdraw as to give consent." Moreover, the burden of demonstrating consent is placed squarely on "the controller."[68] Art. 12(5). The GDPR requires the controller to be able "to demonstrate that the data subject has consented to a processing of his or her personal data." Art. 7(1). "Data subject" is an EU term of art that refers to "an identified or identifiable natural person." Art 4(1).

Finally, the GDPR introduces an importance ban on "tying" in its Article 7(b). The idea is that the terms within a single contractual agreement cannot be extended, or "tied," to include processing of personal data beyond that which is necessary to the purpose of the contract.[69] Article 7(b) states that agreement to the "performance of a contract, including the provision of a service" is invalid if made "conditional on consent to the processing of personal data that is not necessary for the performance of that contract."[70] In other words, a contract cannot tie consent for an initial data processing operation to a second one. Indeed, Recital 43, GDPR notes, "Consent is presumed not to be freely given . . . if the performance of a contract, including the provision of a service, is dependent on the consent despite such consent not being necessary for such performance." The ban on tying consolidates restrictions in the GDPR regarding necessity and purpose limitation; in doing so, it takes aim at myriad new digital business models based around data trade. In the assessment of Ulrich Dammann, the GDPR's ban on tying is "unique in the entire world."[71]

Limits on Processing of Sensitive Data and Automated Decision-Making. The GDPR heightens the protections of the Directive for sensitive data and strengthens existing restrictions on automated decision-making. Article 9 provides a list of kinds of sensitive data, which it terms "special categories of personal data." The EU's attention to its "special categories" does not focus on risks from specific data processing operations, but singles out areas as being ex ante problematic for data processing. Following the Directive's approach, Article 9 flatly forbids the

[67] *Id.*

[68] *Id.* at art. 12(5).

[69] Ulrich Dammann, *Erfolge und Defizite der EU-Datenschutzgrundverordnung* 307, 311 ZEITSCHRIFT FÜR DATENSCHUTZ (2016).

[70] 2016 O.J. (L 119), art. 7.

[71] Dammann, *supra* note 155, at 311.

processing of "special categories" unless one of its specific exceptions is applicable.

The special categories in the GDPR are more extensive than in the Directive. The GDPR prohibits processing of personal data revealing: "racial or ethnic original political opinions, religious or philosophical beliefs, or trade union membership, and the processing of genetic data, biometric data for the purpose of uniquely identifying a natural person, data concerning health or data concerning a natural person's sex life or sexual orientation." Among the exceptions for processing such data are when the data subject has given "explicit consent" or the "processing is necessary for reasons of substantial public interest, on the basis of Union or Member State law." The latter exception further specifies that the law must "be proportionate to the aim pursued, respect the essence of the right to data protection and provide for suitable and specific measures to safeguard the fundamental rights and the interests of the data subject." Art. 9(g).

As for automated processing, the Regulation relates this concept to concerns about profiling. Article 22 states:

The data subject shall have the right not to be subject to a decision based solely on automated processing, including profiling, which produces legal effects concerning him or her or similarly significantly affects him or her. Art. 22(1).

An open question under the GDPR concerns the impact of this provision on certain contemporary forms of "automated processing," most notably analytics and "Big Data."

Monetary Fines. The GDPR increases the protection of individual rights by greatly increasing the size of monetary sanctions that are available for violations of it. Overall, administrative fines issued pursuant to the Regulation are to be "effective, proportionate and dissuasive." Art. 83(1). The Regulation grants to the power to levy such fines to the "supervisory authorities" of Member States. These entities are also called data protection commissions or commissioners.

Article 83(2) sets out a multi-factor test for calculation of administrative fines by the national data protection commissioners. The amount of the administrative fine in individual cases is required to take into account a long list of factors, including: "the nature, gravity and duration of the infringement taking into account the nature, scope, or purpose of the processing concerned as well as the number of data subjects affected and the level of damage suffered by them; [and] the intentional or negligent character of the infringement." The resulting yardstick provides a great measure of flexibility for a data protection commission in assessing penalties in individual cases.

Of special note, moreover, is that the GDPR permits fines under certain circumstances to reach as much as four percent of a company's worldwide revenues. Art. 83(1). At least on paper, this provision would permit penalties of as much as several hundred million dollars against companies. A fine of such magnitude might run afoul, however, of the Regulation's requirement that fines be "proportionate." Art. 83(1). Nonetheless, these penalty provisions demonstrate the EU's intention of ensuring compliance with its data protection rules.

Independent Supervisory Authorities. Much of the Proposed Regulation concerns the organization and practice of data protection within the EU. As Gerrit

Hornung already noted of the draft GDPR: "Institutional and organizational arrangements make up a significant part" of it.[72] Some of these measures have been received with general approval, such as the steps that the GDPR takes to guarantee the independence of data protection commissions within their member states.

Article 52 requires that each supervisory authority "act with complete independence in performing its tasks and exercising its powers in accordance with this Regulation." Art. 52(1). The Regulation further specifies that the members of each supervisory authority are to "remain free from external influence, whether direct or indirect, and shall neither seek nor take instruction from anybody." Art. 52(2). The GDPR also requires the Member States to provide each supervisory authority "with the human, technical and financial resources, premises and infrastructure necessary for the effective performance of its tasks and exercise of its powers." Art. 52(4).

The European Data Protection Board's Consistency Mechanism. The Regulation creates a new institution, the European Data Protection Board (EDPB). Art. 68. In so doing, the Proposed Regulation upgrades the status of the Article 29 Working Party, the existing panel of national supervisory authorities. The EDPB provides a useful forum in which national supervisory authorities can reach a consensus about important issues. The EDPB has the power to make both non-binding recommendations and binding decisions in individual cases. Art. 65. Its decision-making power extends, for example, to cases of conflict where multiple supervisory authorities are involved and are unable to reach consensus. Art. 65(1)(a); Art. 60(4).

The Adequacy Standard. Like the Directive, the Regulation requires "an adequate level of protection" before a transfer of data to a non-EU country. This Chapter examines the issue of international data transfers below.

NOTES & QUESTIONS

1. ***Evaluating the Proposed Regulation.*** Which aspects of the Proposed Data Protection Regulation do you think make the most decisive break with the past? Which aspects do you think are most different from current U.S. information privacy law?

2. ***Fundamental Protections versus Consent and Contract?*** It is important to note that the GDPR's fundamental protections cannot be overcome through individual consent or contract. Individuals cannot choose to "opt out" from core protections, such as purpose limitation, data minimization, data accuracy, limited storage, and so on. In the analysis of Niko Härting, for example, "Even if consent makes data processing legitimate," the "data minimization" principle of Article 6 "may make it unlawful."[73] Christopher Kuner makes a similar point in analyzing the EU's regulation of international transfers of data. These rules

---

[72] Gerrit Hornung, *Eine Datenschutz-Grundverordnung für Europa? Licht und Schatten im Kommissionsentwurf vom 25.1.2012*, 2012 Zeitschrift für Datenschutz 99, 104.

[73] Niko Härting, *Datenschutz-Grundverordnung* 26 (2016).

are secondary to the requirement of a legal basis for the processing of information. Kuner observes: "[C]ompanies become almost mesmerized with the mechanism to provide an adequate legal basis for the transfer, while neglecting to ask themselves what the legal basis is for the processing in the first place."[74] He adds: "Providing a legal basis for data processing is not a specific action, but rather an important principle that should be kept in mind at all stages of the company's compliance program."[75]

3. **Contracts and Consumer Law.** In evaluating the permissibility of contracts involving personal data, the GDPR draws on its consumer protection law. The GDPR requires a policing of the substantive terms of the contract as well as the form of its presentation. Concerning substance, the GDPR's Recital 42 references the Council Directive of 1993 on Unfair Terms in Consumer Contracts, which includes an expansive "black list" of unfair terms.[76] Its sweeping rule is that any contractual term which has not been individually negotiated is unfair if "it causes a significant imbalance in the parties' rights and obligations under the contract, to the detriment of the consumer."[77] The GDPR makes these protections part of the future DNA of EU privacy law.

C. INTERNATIONAL TRANSFERS OF DATA

We live today in a global economy that is becoming increasingly dependent upon information. The Internet has enabled a dramatic increase in international communication and commerce. As a result, personal information increasingly flows across the borders of different nations around the world. International data transfers can also occur pursuant to discovery requests in litigation in the United States that involves foreign parties.

Each nation has its own set of privacy laws and regulations. These differences raise at least two difficulties. First, differing levels of protection might interfere with the smooth and efficient flow of personal information between countries. Thus, there is a need for harmonization or convergence of approaches to regulating the processing of personal data. Second, countries seeking to protect the privacy of their citizens must depend upon the protections accorded by other countries since a vast amount of personal data flows out of its borders to these other countries.

The data flow can occur under many circumstances: One of the most important is when transnational litigation takes place. Gil Keteltas has pointed to significant underlying differences in the way that litigation takes place in most jurisdictions

---

[74] Christopher Kuner, *European Data Protection Law* 242 (2d ed. 2007) (emphasis removed).

[75] *Id.*

[76] 2016 O.J. (L 119), ¶ 42.

[77] 1993 O.J. (L 95). *See* Jane K. Winn & Mark Webber, *The Impact of EU Unfair Contract Terms Law on U.S. Business-to-Consumer Internet Merchants*, 62 Bus. Lawyer 6, 9 (2006) (analyzing the Unfair Terms Directive and its "non-exclusive list of terms that may be deemed unfair.").

outside the United States as opposed to within it.[78] In non-American court systems, "[p]retrial discovery is limited, with few documents changing hands." In contrast, "discovery in U.S. litigation is a right, and key information must be provided to an opponent even without a request from the opponent." Moreover, the Federal Rules of Civil Procedure permit discovery of all information relevant to a claim or defense and define relevancy broadly. Not surprisingly, the U.S. approach to discovery has led to collisions with the privacy laws in other jurisdictions.

1. INTERNATIONAL DATA TRANSFERS IN LITIGATION

VOLKSWAGEN, A.G. V. VALDEZ

909 S.W.2d 900 (Tex. 1995)

This mandamus action involves a conflict between Texas' discovery rules and Germany's privacy laws. We conclude that the trial court abused its discretion in failing to balance the competing interests of the parties and disregarding German law in its entirety. After balancing the respective parties' interests, we further conclude that the information sought should not be produced. Accordingly, we conditionally grant the writ of mandamus. . . .

The real parties in interest sued both Volkswagen of America and its German parent company, Volkswagen A.G. (VWAG), in products liability for personal injuries resulting from an accident involving their 1970 model Volkswagen. The real parties sought production of VWAG's current corporate telephone book to identify individuals who might have relevant information concerning defects in the automobile's door latches. This book contains the names, job titles, position within the company, and direct dial work numbers of more than 20,000 employees as well as the private home numbers of individuals in management positions. VWAG objected to this request on the basis of the German Federal Data Protection Act, which prohibits the dissemination of private information without the consent of the individuals. *Bundesdatenschutzgesetz*, BGBl, I, 2954 (1990) (FRG) (BDSG). The trial court overruled VWAG's objection and ordered it to produce the phone book.

When information sought for production is located in a foreign country, guidance is provided by the Restatement (Third) of Foreign Relations Law § 442 (1987). Section 442(1)(a) states:

A court or agency in the United States, when authorized by statute or rule of court, may order a person subject to its jurisdiction to produce documents, objects, or other information relevant to an action or investigation, even if the information or the person in possession of the information is outside the United States.

However, when the laws of the foreign sovereign protect relevant information from discovery, the interests of the domestic court or agency must be balanced with those of the foreign sovereign. The Restatement suggests:

[78] Gil Keteltas, *US E-discovery*, in *E-Discovery and Data Privacy: A Practical Guide* 3, 6 (2011).

> In deciding whether to issue an order directing production of information located abroad, and in framing such an order, a court or agency in the United States should take into account the importance to the investigation or litigation of the documents or other information requested; the degree of specificity of the request; whether the information originated in the United States; the availability of alternative means of securing the information; and the extent to which noncompliance with the request would undermine important interests of the United States, or compliance with the request would undermine important interests of the state [or country] where the information is located.

Restatement (Third) of Foreign Relations Law § 442(1)(c) (1987). Accordingly, only after a careful balancing of these interests should the trial court rule on a party's request for production.

Before the Restatement's balancing test may be applied, we must determine whether German and U.S. laws actually conflict. That a conflict exists is readily apparent after examination. Texas discovery rules allow an opposing party to discover evidence relevant to the subject matter in the pending action. Tex. R. Civ. P. 166b(2)(a). Germany's privacy laws protect from dissemination "personal data," which is defined as "information concerning the personal or material circumstances of an identified or identifiable individual." BDSG § 3(1). VWAG produced a plethora of authorities confirming its allegation that information contained in its current corporate phone book is, in fact, personal data. The affidavit of Horst-Gunther Bens explicitly acknowledges that VWAG's production of the book would violate the BDSG, while also explaining that privacy rights under German law are "equal in rank to the right of freedom of speech." Likewise, Paul Schwartz, a professor at the University of Arkansas School of Law and expert on German data protection law, opined that production of the book would be violative. This fact is also confirmed by Dr. Gerard Dronsch, the state commissioner for data protection for Lower Saxony, and the German Federal Ministry of Labor and Social Order. Additionally, the country of Germany submitted an amicus curiae brief, explicitly stating that production of the book would violate the BDSG. In the face of such overwhelming evidence, we have little doubt that German privacy laws conflict with the discovery laws of Texas.

As mentioned, the Restatement balancing test involves five factors. Two of the five factors are undisputed. First, as to the degree of specificity of the request, we note that the real parties' request is specific. All they seek is production of the one easily identifiable current corporate directory. Second, regarding where the document originated, VWAG is a German company and the book contains the names and other information of its German employees employed at its Wolfsburg plant and its facilities located in Brunswick, Emden, Kassel and Salzgitter, all within the country of Germany. The real parties do not contest that this book originated in Germany.

The remaining three factors deserve careful consideration. One, we must look to alternative discovery sources that are available. There are numerous alternative means that the real parties can and have used to obtain information which is the substantial equivalent of VWAG's current corporate phone book. VWAG produced its 1969 corporate phone book, and its United States subsidiary, Volkswagen of America, produced its current corporate phone book. Additionally, Erich Unterreiner, a current engineer for VWAG who also worked there in 1969, identified 29 past and present employees knowledgeable in the design of the 1970 model Volkswagen. He also provided a great deal of information about VWAG's organizational structure and identified Ernst Nockemann as "the man who did most of the design and development work in door latches." Therefore, there are adequate alternatives the real parties may use to discover the names of VWAG employees knowledgeable about the design of the subject vehicle.

Two, as to whether important interests of either this country or Germany are undermined, we conclude that, as asserted by Germany in its amicus curiae brief, its interests would be undermined if VWAG complied with the real parties' request for production. As we discussed, production of the book would violate German privacy laws. And, there is no evidence in the record suggesting that VWAG's failure to produce this phone book would undermine any important interest of this country, particularly when the record shows that alternative methods for obtaining the information exist.

Finally, VWAG's current corporate phone book bears little importance to the present litigation. The real parties already possess VWAG's 1969 corporate phone book that contains the names of the people who worked on the 1970 model Volkswagen. They have Volkswagen of America's current corporate phone book. And, they have the names of many VWAG employees directly responsible for the design and construction of the 1970 model Volkswagen. The plaintiffs simply desire to have the telephone book produced so they might double check the information provided in previous requests.

The trial court failed to balance the interests of the foreign sovereign with those of the real parties in any respect. In fact, the trial court rejected any consideration of German law. This was an abuse of discretion. Further, based on the record, we conclude that the trial court abused its discretion in ordering production of the book in question. VWAG's current corporate phone book should not be produced in contravention of German law. . . .

NOTES & QUESTIONS

1. *The Effects of Foreign Data Protection Law on the United States.* The *Valdez* case shows another way in which foreign data protection law can affect the United States. Prior to this opinion, a Texas trial court had ordered Volkwagen A.G. to turn over information located in Germany. In *Valdez*, the Texas Supreme Court reversed this lower court because its order would violate the legal obligation under U.S. Foreign Relations law to balance the interest of a foreign sovereign with those of the U.S. court. How well do you think the Texas High Court balanced the different interests involved? Why was the information in the corporate phone book considered to be personal data?

2. *Privacy Logs.* In *In re Vitamins Antitrust Litigation*, 2001 WL 1049433 (D.D.C. 2001), a U.S. district court allowed German defendants to maintain a "privacy log detailing exactly what requested information would be covered by the German privacy laws." This court felt that the protective order in the case provided some privacy protection, and also believed that the German defendants should "not be allowed to withhold information based upon minor inequivalencies between the Protective Order in this case and the [Federal Data

Protection statute of Germany].” But the court also noted that the German defendants appeared “to have some legitimate privacy law concerns and that the Protective Order in this case may not be sufficiently detailed to shield them for criminal liability in their own country.” Hence, to gain a better understanding of the information that was at stake and how necessary it would be to plaintiffs’ claims, the court decided to allow the use of a privacy log, which would allow a determination of the importance of the information that was sought and “whether there was a way to amend the Protective Order to safeguard defendants from liability in the production of this information.”

2. ADEQUATE LEVEL OF PROTECTION

Transborder Data Flows: An Adequacy Finding. Chapter V, Articles 44-50 of the GDPR establishes the rules for when Member States may permit the transfer of personal data to non-EU countries, or so-called “third countries.” The GDPR sets out the same “adequacy standard” as was found in the Data Protection Directive’s Article 25. One path to adequacy is through a formal adequacy finding by the Commission. At Article 45, the GDPR states:

1. A transfer of personal data to a third country or an international organisation may take place where the Commission has decided that the third country, a territory or one or more specified sectors within that third country, or the international organisation in question ensures an adequate level of protection. Such a transfer shall not require any specific authorisation.

2. When assessing the adequacy of the level of protection, the Commission shall, in particular, take account of the following elements:

(a) the rule of law, respect for human rights and fundamental freedoms, relevant legislation, both general and sectoral, including concerning public security, defence, national security and criminal law and the access of public authorities to personal data, as well as the implementation of such legislation, data protection rules, professional rules and security measures, including rules for the onward transfer of personal data to another third country or international organisation which are complied with in that country or international organisation, case-law, as well as effective and enforceable data subject rights and effective administrative and judicial redress for the data subjects whose personal data are being transferred;

(b) the existence and effective functioning of one or more independent supervisory authorities in the third country or to which an international organisation is subject, with responsibility for ensuring and enforcing compliance with the data protection rules, including adequate enforcement powers, for assisting and advising the data subjects in exercising their rights and for cooperation with the supervisory authorities of the Member States; and

(c) the international commitments the third country or international organisation concerned has entered into, or other obligations arising from legally binding conventions or instruments as well as from its participation in multilateral or regional systems, in particular in relation to the protection of personal data.

~~As under the Directive, the GDPR blocks~~ the transfer of personal information on European citizens processed in third-party countries that fails to meet the requirements of "adequacy." What do you think the reason is behind this requirement? Is this an example of an "extraterritorial" application of European law?

Transfers Subject to Appropriate Safeguards. Even without a formal finding of adequacy, the GDPR foresees other paths to ensure a data transfer with an adequate level of protection. These are set out in Article 46, and include Binding Corporate Rules (BCRs) and Standard Contract Clauses (SCCs). BCRs are to apply within an entire organization and must be legally binding as well as approved by the appropriate data protection commission. The GDPR's Article 47 sets out detailed requirements for this path to adequacy. As for the SCCs, the GDPR requires the Commission to approve these arrangements. Art. 46(2)(c).

Exceptions to the Adequacy Requirement. The GDPR provides for certain derogations, or exceptions, to its adequacy requirement. Transfers of personal data to a third-party country that do not ensure an adequate level of protection may still take place on condition that the data subject has explicitly consented; the transfer of data is "necessary for the performance of a contract between the data subject and the controller"; and the transfer is necessary for "important reasons of public interest." Article 49. There are several additional exceptions.

Adequate Level of Protection. As the ECJ's *Schrems* decision makes clear, adequate protection means "essentially equivalent" protection. The full list of adequacy determinations of the EU (with the date of the finding) are as follows:

- Andorra (2010)
- Argentina (2003)
- Australia: Passenger Name Records Agreement (2008)
- Canada (2001) (commercial organizations only)
- Balliwick of Guersney (2003)
- Balliwick of Jersey (2008)
- The Faeroe Islands (2010)
- Isle of Man (2004)
- Israel (2011)
- New Zealand (2012)
- Switzerland (2000)
- United States: Passenger Name Records Agreement (2000)
- United States: Privacy Shield (2016)
- Uruguay (2012)

This list consists of the names of countries or otherwise autonomous areas with three exceptions. This exception is for legal agreements: First, there is the Privacy Shield agreement between the EU and the United States. The United States has not been found to provide adequate protection, but the Privacy Shield does supply an adequate level for U.S. companies that comply with its requirements. Second, the United States has concluded a Passenger Names Record Agreement with the EU. This agreement permits the transfer of a broad range of information about passengers on flights from EU Member States to U.S. airports to be transferred to the U.S. Department of Homeland Security. Third, Australia concluded a similar agreement to permit information from passengers on flights from the EU to the Australian Customs and Border Protection Service.

The United States has never formally sought an adequacy determination from the European Commission for its entire legal system, as opposed to the more limited EU recognition of the Passenger Name Records Agreement and the Safe Harbor Principles. This reticence is likely due, according to Christopher Wolf, a leading D.C.-based privacy lawyer, "because of the well-understood outcome: request denied."[79] The Privacy Shield supplies an adequate level of data protection for U.S. companies that comply with its requirements.

Three countries are considered adequate due to their membership in the European Economic Area (EEA): Norway, Liechtenstein, and Iceland. Currently, the EU Commission is engaged in talks regarding an adequacy determination with Japan and South Korea.

3. FROM THE SAFE HARBOR TO PRIVACY SHIELD

By the late 1980s, European policymakers realized that their efforts to create strong safeguards for data protection necessitated transborder policies for the data of EU citizens. Because of global data flows already present in that pre-Internet age, legal regulatory efforts in the EU were doomed to failure if their reach ended at the territorial borders of Europe. From the EU perspective, moreover, permitting an abuse of European citizens' personal information *outside* of Europe would make a mockery out of the decades of work to create high levels of privacy *inside* Europe. Important efforts followed at the trans-European level and within member states to fashion a legal response to the perceived threat to privacy of international data transfers.

The resulting EU policy requirement then and now is an "adequate level of protection" in any non-EU recipient nation before a transfer of personal data from an EU member state. Both the Directive (1995) and the GDPR (2016) contain this "adequacy" requirement.[80] In consequence, data transfers from the EU to the U.S. have a questionable legal status.

This legal uncertainty follows from EU skepticism about the sufficiency of U.S. information privacy law. In 1999, the Article 29 Working Party, the influential group of national data protection commissioners, summed up the European view of the matter. It declared that the "current patchwork of narrowly focused sectoral laws and voluntary self-regulation in the U.S. is not adequate."[81] Yet, with so much valuable data trade between the EU and U.S., both sides had considerable incentives to find policy solutions to bridge their different legal approaches to data privacy. The most significant first-generation outcome of this

---

[79] Christopher Wolf, *Delusions of Adequacy?*, 43 Washington Univ. J.L. & Policy 227, 229 (2013).

[80] Directive, art. 56; GDPR, at art. 45.

[81] Working Party on the Protection of Individuals with regard to the Processing of Personal Data, *Opinion 1/99*, 2 DG MARKT Doc. 5092/98, WP 15 (Jan. 26, 1999).

policy effort was the Safe Harbor Agreement, a treaty negotiated by the U.S. Department of Commerce and the Commission of the EU.

In 1998, the U.S. Department of Commerce began negotiations with the EU Commission to formulate a "safe harbor" agreement to ensure that the United States met the EU Data Directive's "adequacy" requirement in Article 25. In July 2000, the negotiations yielded the Safe Harbor Arrangement as well as other supportive documents elaborating on the principles, such as letters and a list of Frequently Asked Questions.

The process for EU approval of the Safe Harbor agreement began with the EU Parliament, which issued a negative non-binding resolution about it. In this resolution, the EU Parliament condemned the Safe Harbor by a vote of 279 to 259 because of concerns over the adequacy of U.S. protections and the perception that the agreement had numerous loopholes.[82] The ultimate decision on whether the EU would approve the Safe Harbor agreement rested with the EU Commission, and on July 26, 2000, this entity approved it.

Decisions by organization to qualify for the Safe Harbor were voluntary, but once they joined it, they were required to publicly declare their compliance and to do so on a Department of Commerce website. The Safe Harbor represented a bold policy innovation: it transplanted EU data protection concepts into U.S. law in a fashion beyond the willingness of Congress or the ability of the FTC and other regulatory agencies. Its Principles were intended to be close enough to those of EU data protection so that the U.S. companies in following them would provide "adequate" data protection. Although U.S. companies needed only apply the Safe Harbor Principles to the personal data of Europeans, they were also free to bring all their data systems into compliance with it and apply these standards to U.S. citizens. In some instances, U.S. organizations decided to do so for reasons varying from managerial simplicity to policy leadership. In turn, the transplantation by the Safe Harbor of EU data protection onto U.S. territory proved politically palatable because decisions by U.S. companies to qualify for it were voluntary.

Another factor made the Safe Harbor acceptable in the U.S. As Paul Schwartz and Karl-Nikolaus Peifer have argued, "The Safe Harbor's negotiated standards weakened classic EU principles just enough to make the agreement tolerable on the American side of the Atlantic, but not too much to make them indefensible in Brussels."[83] At least, the EU at first did not view these standards as excessively watered down.[84]

Despite grumblings in the EU about the Safe Harbor, this treaty's future success seemed assured for the twenty-first century with over 5,000 U.S.

---

[82] Steven R. Salbu, The European Union Data Privacy Directive and International Relations, 35 Vand. J. Transnat'l L. 655, 678-79 (2002). There were 22 abstentions.

[83] Paul M. Schwartz & Karl-Nikolaus Peifer, Transatlantic Data Privacy, 106 Georgetown L.J. — (forthcoming 2017).

[84] Over time, the unhappiness in the EU with the Safe Harbor grew. For an indication of this evolving attitude see its commissioned reports from Galexia—an Australia consulting company—on the framework's weaknesses, Chris Connolly, *EU/US Safe Harbor—Effectiveness of the Framework in relation to National Security Surveillance*, GALEXIA (Oct 7, 2013), http://www.europarl.europa.eu/document/activities/cont/201310/20131008ATT72504/20131008A TT72504EN.pdf (testimony before the EU Parliament summarizing the 2008 and 2010 Galexia studies). For an analysis of the Galexia studies' strengths and weaknesses and further reflections on the "Unsafe Harbor," see THORSTEN HENNRICH, CLOUD COMPUTING 180–86 (2016).

companies entering it.[85] When the Commission and the Commerce Department began to consider improvements in a "Safe Harbor 2.0" in 2012, many in the U.S. expected only tinkering with the accepted formula. This expectation was, in turn, dashed by the Edward Snowden revelations, which began in June 2013. A former government analyst, Snowden leaked documents that detailed widespread collaboration by American companies with the NSA and called into doubt the "adequacy" of the protection in the U.S. Then on October 6, 2015, the European Court of Justice's opinion in *Schrems v. Data Protection Commissioner* ended any hope of only minor changes to the Safe Harbor. This judgment voided the Safe Harbor agreement and, thereby, strengthened the hand of EU negotiators in the ongoing discussions that would lead to the Privacy Shield.

SCHREMS V. DATA PROTECTION COMMISSIONER (JOINED BY DIGITAL RIGHTS IRELAND)

European Court of Justice, Case C-362/14 (6 October 2015)

2. The request has been made in proceedings between Mr Schrems and the Data Protection Commissioner ('the Commissioner') concerning the latter's refusal to investigate a complaint made by Mr Schrems regarding the fact that Facebook Ireland Ltd ('Facebook Ireland') transfers the personal data of its users to the United States of America and keeps it on servers located in that country.

The dispute in the main proceedings and the questions referred for a preliminary ruling

26. Mr Schrems, an Austrian national residing in Austria, has been a user of the Facebook social network ('Facebook') since 2008.

27. Any person residing in the European Union who wishes to use Facebook is required to conclude, at the time of his registration, a contract with Facebook Ireland, a subsidiary of Facebook Inc. which is itself established in the United States. Some or all of the personal data of Facebook Ireland's users who reside in the European Union is transferred to servers belonging to Facebook Inc. that are located in the United States, where it undergoes processing.

28. On 25 June 2013 Mr Schrems made a complaint to the Commissioner by which he in essence asked the latter to exercise his statutory powers by prohibiting Facebook Ireland from transferring his personal data to the United States. He contended in his complaint that the law and practice in force in that country did not ensure adequate protection of the personal data held in its territory against the surveillance activities that were engaged in there by the public authorities. Mr Schrems referred in this regard to the revelations made by Edward Snowden concerning the activities of the United States intelligence services, in particular those of the National Security Agency ('the NSA').

29. Since the Commissioner took the view that he was not required to investigate the matters raised by Mr Schrems in the complaint, he rejected it as

---

[85] The Department of Commerce continues to maintain the Safe Harbor List with its 5,457 entries. *See* U.S.–EU Safe Harbor List, Export, https://safeharbor.export.gov/list.aspx.

unfounded. The Commissioner considered that there was no evidence that Mr Schrems' personal data had been accessed by the NSA. He added that the allegations raised by Mr Schrems in his complaint could not be profitably put forward since any question of the adequacy of data protection in the United States had to be determined in accordance with Decision 2000/520 and the Commission had found in that decision that the United States ensured an adequate level of protection.

30. Mr Schrems brought an action before the High Court challenging the decision at issue in the main proceedings. After considering the evidence adduced by the parties to the main proceedings, the High Court found that the electronic surveillance and interception of personal data transferred from the European Union to the United States serve necessary and indispensable objectives in the public interest. However, it added that the revelations made by Edward Snowden had demonstrated a 'significant over-reach' on the part of the NSA and other federal agencies.

32. The High Court stated that Irish law precludes the transfer of personal data outside national territory save where the third country ensures an adequate level of protection for privacy and fundamental rights and freedoms. The importance of the rights to privacy and to inviolability of the dwelling, which are guaranteed by the Irish Constitution, requires that any interference with those rights be proportionate and in accordance with the law.

34. . . . . . [T]he High Court considers that this case concerns the implementation of EU law as referred to in Article 51 of the Charter and that the legality of the decision at issue in the main proceedings must therefore be assessed in the light of EU law. . . . .

35. The High Court further observes that in his action Mr Schrems in reality raises the legality of the safe harbour regime which was established by Decision 2000/520 and gives rise to the decision at issue in the main proceedings. . . .

Consideration of the questions referred

The powers of the national supervisory authorities, within the meaning of Article 28 of Directive 95/46, when the Commission has adopted a decision pursuant to Article 25(6) of that directive.

38. It should be recalled first of all that the provisions of Directive 95/46, inasmuch as they govern the processing of personal data liable to infringe fundamental freedoms, in particular the right to respect for private life, must necessarily be interpreted in the light of the fundamental rights guaranteed by the Charter.

41. The guarantee of the independence of national supervisory authorities is intended to ensure the effectiveness and reliability of the monitoring of compliance with the provisions concerning protection of individuals with regard to the processing of personal data and must be interpreted in the light of that aim. It was established in order to strengthen the protection of individuals and bodies affected by the decisions of those authorities. The establishment in Member States of independent supervisory authorities is therefore, as stated in recital 62 in the

preamble to Directive 95/46, an essential component of the protection of individuals with regard to the processing of personal data.

53. [A] Commission decision adopted pursuant to Article 25(6) of Directive 95/46, such as Decision 2000/520, cannot prevent persons whose personal data has been or could be transferred to a third country from lodging with the national supervisory authorities a claim, within the meaning of Article 28(4) of that directive, concerning the protection of their rights and freedoms in regard to the processing of that data. Likewise, ... , a decision of that nature cannot eliminate or reduce the powers expressly accorded to the national supervisory authorities by Article 8(3) of the Charter and Article 28 of the directive.

57. . . . . Article 28 of Directive 95/46 applies, by its very nature, to any processing of personal data. Thus, even if the Commission has adopted a decision pursuant to Article 25(6) of that directive, the national supervisory authorities, when hearing a claim lodged by a person concerning the protection of his rights and freedoms in regard to the processing of personal data relating to him, must be able to examine, with complete independence, whether the transfer of that data complies with the requirements laid down by the directive.

58. If that were not so, persons whose personal data has been or could be transferred to the third country concerned would be denied the right, guaranteed by Article 8(1) and (3) of the Charter, to lodge with the national supervisory authorities a claim for the purpose of protecting their fundamental rights.

59. A claim, within the meaning of Article 28(4) of Directive 95/46, by which a person whose personal data has been or could be transferred to a third country contends, as in the main proceedings, that, notwithstanding what the Commission has found in a decision adopted pursuant to Article 25(6) of that directive, the law and practices of that country do not ensure an adequate level of protection must be understood as concerning, in essence, whether that decision is compatible with the protection of the privacy and of the fundamental rights and freedoms of individuals.

66. Having regard to the foregoing considerations, the answer to the questions referred is that Article 25(6) of Directive 95/46, read in the light of Articles 7, 8 and 47 of the Charter, must be interpreted as meaning that a decision adopted pursuant to that provision, such as Decision 2000/520, by which the Commission finds that a third country ensures an adequate level of protection, does not prevent a supervisory authority of a Member State, within the meaning of Article 28 of that directive, from examining the claim of a person concerning the protection of his rights and freedoms in regard to the processing of personal data relating to him which has been transferred from a Member State to that third country when that person contends that the law and practices in force in the third country do not ensure an adequate level of protection.

The validity of Decision 2000/520

73. The word 'adequate' in Article 25(6) of Directive 95/46 admittedly signifies that a third country cannot be required to ensure a level of protection identical to that guaranteed in the EU legal order. However, as the Advocate General has observed in point 141 of his Opinion, the term 'adequate level of protection' must be understood as requiring the third country in fact to ensure, by

reason of its domestic law or its international commitments, a level of protection of fundamental rights and freedoms that is essentially equivalent to that guaranteed within the European Union by virtue of Directive 95/46 read in the light of the Charter. If there were no such requirement, the objective referred to in the previous paragraph of the present judgment would be disregarded. Furthermore, the high level of protection guaranteed by Directive 95/46 read in the light of the Charter could easily be circumvented by transfers of personal data from the European Union to third countries for the purpose of being processed in those countries.

74. It is clear from the express wording of Article 25(6) of Directive 95/46 that it is the legal order of the third country covered by the Commission decision that must ensure an adequate level of protection. . . .

75. Accordingly, when examining the level of protection afforded by a third country, the Commission is obliged to assess the content of the applicable rules in that country resulting from its domestic law or international commitments and the practice designed to ensure compliance with those rules, since it must, under Article 25(2) of Directive 95/46, take account of all the circumstances surrounding a transfer of personal data to a third country.

76. Also, in the light of the fact that the level of protection ensured by a third country is liable to change, it is incumbent upon the Commission, after it has adopted a decision pursuant to Article 25(6) of Directive 95/46, to check periodically whether the finding relating to the adequacy of the level of protection ensured by the third country in question is still factually and legally justified. Such a check is required, in any event, when evidence gives rise to a doubt in that regard.

78. In this regard, it must be stated that, in view of, first, the important role played by the protection of personal data in the light of the fundamental right to respect for private life and, secondly, the large number of persons whose fundamental rights are liable to be infringed where personal data is transferred to a third country not ensuring an adequate level of protection, the Commission's discretion as to the adequacy of the level of protection ensured by a third country is reduced, with the result that review of the requirements stemming from Article 25 of Directive 95/46, read in the light of the Charter, should be strict.

86. Thus, Decision 2000/520 lays down that 'national security, public interest, or law enforcement requirements' have primacy over the safe harbour principles, primacy pursuant to which self-certified United States organisations receiving personal data from the European Union are bound to disregard those principles without limitation where they conflict with those requirements and therefore prove incompatible with them.

87. In the light of the general nature of the derogation set out in the fourth paragraph of Annex I to Decision 2000/520, that decision thus enables interference, founded on national security and public interest requirements or on domestic legislation of the United States, with the fundamental rights of the persons whose personal data is or could be transferred from the European Union to the United States. To establish the existence of an interference with the fundamental right to respect for private life, it does not matter whether the information in question relating to private life is sensitive or whether the persons concerned have suffered any adverse consequences on account of that interference.

88. In addition, Decision 2000/520 does not contain any finding regarding the existence, in the United States, of rules adopted by the State intended to limit any

interference with the fundamental rights of the persons whose data is transferred from the European Union to the United States, interference which the State entities of that country would be authorised to engage in when they pursue legitimate objectives, such as national security.

89. Nor does Decision 2000/520 refer to the existence of effective legal protection against interference of that kind. . . .

92. Furthermore and above all, protection of the fundamental right to respect for private life at EU level requires derogations and limitations in relation to the protection of personal data to apply only in so far as is strictly necessary.

93. Legislation is not limited to what is strictly necessary where it authorises, on a generalised basis, storage of all the personal data of all the persons whose data has been transferred from the European Union to the United States without any differentiation, limitation or exception being made in the light of the objective pursued and without an objective criterion being laid down by which to determine the limits of the access of the public authorities to the data, and of its subsequent use, for purposes which are specific, strictly restricted and capable of justifying the interference which both access to that data and its use entail . . . .

94. In particular, legislation permitting the public authorities to have access on a generalised basis to the content of electronic communications must be regarded as compromising the essence of the fundamental right to respect for private life, as guaranteed by Article 7 of the Charter.

95. Likewise, legislation not providing for any possibility for an individual to pursue legal remedies in order to have access to personal data relating to him, or to obtain the rectification or erasure of such data, does not respect the essence of the fundamental right to effective judicial protection, as enshrined in Article 47 of the Charter. The first paragraph of Article 47 of the Charter requires everyone whose rights and freedoms guaranteed by the law of the European Union are violated to have the right to an effective remedy before a tribunal in compliance with the conditions laid down in that article. The very existence of effective judicial review designed to ensure compliance with provisions of EU law is inherent in the existence of the rule of law . . . .

102. The first subparagraph of Article 3(1) of Decision 2000/520 must . . . be understood as denying the national supervisory authorities the powers which they derive from Article 28 of Directive 95/46, where a person, in bringing a claim under that provision, puts forward matters that may call into question whether a Commission decision that has found, on the basis of Article 25(6) of the directive, that a third country ensures an adequate level of protection is compatible with the protection of the privacy and of the fundamental rights and freedoms of individuals.

103. The implementing power granted by the EU legislature to the Commission in Article 25(6) of Directive 95/46 does not confer upon it competence to restrict the national supervisory authorities' powers referred to in the previous paragraph of the present judgment

106. Having regard to all the foregoing considerations, it is to be concluded that Decision 2000/520 is invalid.

NOTES & QUESTIONS

1. **The *Shrems* Holding.** In *Schrems*, the ECJ struck down the Safe Harbor arrangement. This opinion also takes decisive steps to develop the EU constitutional law of data protection. First, the ECJ identified a violation of Article 7 of the Charter by the Safe Harbor's providing access to the U.S. government of the data of EU citizens. Second, it provided a constitutional analysis regarding the "adequacy" standard of the Directive. In *Schrems*, the Luxembourg Court observed that "an adequate level of protection" in any international data transfer meant "a level of protection of fundamental rights and freedoms that is *essentially equivalent* to that guaranteed within the European Union" (emphasis supplied). Finally, it found that the Charter's Article 8(1) and (3) safeguarded the "complete independence" of data protection commissioners.

2. ***Standard Contractual Clauses and Binding Corporate Rules.*** Beyond the Safe Harbor, the EU has approved two sets of Standard Contract Clauses (SCCs) to allow data transfers. Companies that follow these "off-the-rack" terms for a given data transfer will be considered to have met the EU's adequacy standard. In addition to the SCCs, the EU permits the use of Binding Corporate Rules (BCRs) as a means to meet the Directive's "adequacy test." BCRs can be used only when international data transfers occur within a single company or a group of affiliated companies. Companies that have gone through the EU approval process for a BCR include Accenture, BP, e-Bay, General Electric, HP, and Michelin.[86] The GDPR permits the use of BCRs as a way for a company to demonstrate adequate data protection for an international data transfer. Its Article 47 contains detailed rules for approval of BCRs by a supervisory authority.

3. ***The Same Fate for SCCs and BCRs?*** Soon after the *Schrems* decision, observers began to wonder if the same objections to Safe Harbor adequacy might not be made to SCCs and BCR's. The ECJ had found, after all, that the Safe Harbor did not provide adequate protection against access to information by U.S. intelligence agencies. The ECJ also called for a standard of "essentially equivalent" protection in looking at the totality of protection in the third-party nation.

    In follow-up litigation in Ireland, Max Schrems has challenged Model Contractual Clauses before the Irish High Court. As in *Schrems*, the issue before the Court is a transfer by Facebook from its Dublin headquarters to the U.S. A trial held before the Irish High Court concluded on March 15, 2017. It is to decide whether or not to refer the matter to the ECJ. In the litigation, the Data Protection Commissioner had supported referral to the ECJ. Commissioner Helen Dixon noted her "concerns as to the validity of the SCCs when considered in the light of a number of factors, [including] Articles 7, 8

---

[86] Francoise Gilbert, Binding Corporate Rules 451, 463-64 in I Eighth Annual Institute on Privacy and Security Law (Francoise Gilbert et al. eds., 2007).

and 47 of the Charter of Fundamental Rights of the European Union, and the CJEU's judgment in the first *Schrems* case."[87]

In the aftermath of *Schrems*, the ongoing negotiations between the Commission and U.S. Department of Commerce took on new urgency. "Safe Harbor 2.0" was a brand without a future. In its place, the two sides reached an agreement on a new treaty, which they called the "EU–U.S. Privacy Shield." The agreement took effect on August 1, 2016. Legal challenges have already been lodged against it.[88] As for the Safe Harbor, the European Court of Justice will be the ultimate arbiter of the constitutionality of the Privacy Shield.

EU-U.S. PRIVACY SHIELD FRAMEWORK PRINCIPLES ISSUED BY THE U.S. DEPARTMENT OF COMMERCE
(July 7, 2016)

I. OVERVIEW

1. While the United States and the European Union share the goal of enhancing privacy protection, the United States takes a different approach to privacy from that taken by the European Union. The United States uses a sectoral approach that relies on a mix of legislation, regulation, and self-regulation. Given those differences and to provide organizations in the United States with a reliable mechanism for personal data transfers to the United States from the European Union while ensuring that EU data subjects continue to benefit from effective safeguards and protection as required by European legislation with respect to the processing of their personal data when they have been transferred to non-EU countries, the Department of Commerce is issuing these Privacy Shield Principles, including the Supplemental Principles (collectively 'the Principles') under its statutory authority to foster, promote, and develop international commerce (15 U.S.C. § 1512). The Principles were developed in consultation with the European Commission, and with industry and other stakeholders, to facilitate trade and commerce between the United States and European Union. They are intended for use solely by organizations in the United States receiving personal data from the European Union for the purpose of qualifying for the Privacy Shield and thus benefitting from the European Commission's adequacy decision. . . .

2. In order to rely on the Privacy Shield to effectuate transfers of personal data from the EU, an organization must self-certify its adherence to the Principles to the Department of Commerce (or its designee) ('the Department'). While decisions by organizations to thus enter the Privacy Shield are entirely voluntary, effective compliance is compulsory: organizations that self-certify to the Department and

---

[87] Irish Data Protection Commissioner, Update on Litigation Involving Facebook and Maximilian Shrems (March 16, 2017), at https://www.dataprotection.ie/docs/16-03-2017-Update-on-Litigation-involving-Facebook-and-Maximilian-Schrems/1598.htm.

[88] Case T-670/16, Digital Rights Ireland v. Data Prot. Comm'r 2016 (General Court filed Sept. 16, 2016).

~~publicly declare their~~ commitment to adhere to the Principles must comply fully with the Principles. In order to enter the Privacy Shield, an organization must (a) be subject to the investigatory and enforcement powers of the Federal Trade Commission (the 'FTC'), the Department of Transportation or another statutory body that will effectively ensure compliance with the Principles (other U.S. statutory bodies recognized by the EU may be included as an annex in the future); (b) publicly declare its commitment to comply with the Principles; (c) publicly disclose its privacy policies in line with these Principles; and (d) fully implement them. An organization's failure to comply is enforceable under Section 5 of the Federal Trade Commission Act prohibiting unfair and deceptive acts in or affecting commerce (15 U.S.C. § 45(a)) or other laws or regulations prohibiting such acts.

3. The Department of Commerce will maintain and make available to the public an authoritative list of U.S. organizations that have self-certified to the Department and declared their commitment to adhere to the Principles ('the Privacy Shield List'). . . .

4. The Department will also maintain and make available to the public an authoritative record of U.S. organizations that had previously self-certified to the Department, but that have been removed from the Privacy Shield List. . . .

5. Adherence to these Principles may be limited: (a) to the extent necessary to meet national security, public interest, or law enforcement requirements; (b) by statute, government regulation, or case law that creates conflicting obligations or explicit authorizations, provided that, in exercising any such authorization, an organization can demonstrate that its non-compliance with the Principles is limited to the extent necessary to meet the overriding legitimate interests furthered by such authorization; or (c) if the effect of the Directive or Member State law is to allow exceptions or derogations, provided such exceptions or derogations are applied in comparable contexts. Consistent with the goal of enhancing privacy protection, organizations should strive to implement these Principles fully and transparently, including indicating in their privacy policies where exceptions to the Principles permitted by (b) above will apply on a regular basis. For the same reason, where the option is allowable under the Principles and/or U.S. law, organizations are expected to opt for the higher protection where possible.

8. Definitions:

   a. 'Personal data' and 'personal information' are data about an identified or identifiable individual that are within the scope of the Directive, received by an organization in the United States from the European Union, and recorded in any form.
   b. 'Processing' of personal data means any operation or set of operations which is performed upon personal data, whether or not by automated means, such as collection, recording, organization, storage, adaptation or alteration, retrieval, consultation, use, disclosure or dissemination, and erasure or destruction.

c. 'Controller' means a person or organization which, alone or jointly with others, determines the purposes and means of the processing of personal data.

II. PRINCIPLES

1. Notice

a. An organization must inform individuals about:
   i. its participation in the Privacy Shield and provide a link to, or the web address for, the Privacy Shield List,
   ii. the types of personal data collected and, where applicable, the entities or subsidiaries of the organization also adhering to the Principles,
   iii. its commitment to subject to the Principles all personal data received from the EU in reliance on the Privacy Shield,
   iv. the purposes for which it collects and uses personal information about them,
   v. how to contact the organization with any inquiries or complaints, including any relevant establishment in the EU that can respond to such inquiries or complaints,
   vi. the type or identity of third parties to which it discloses personal information, and the purposes for which it does so,
   vii. the right of individuals to access their personal data,
   viii. the choices and means the organization offers individuals for limiting the use and disclosure of their personal data,
   ix. the independent dispute resolution body designated to address complaints and provide appropriate recourse free of charge to the individual, and whether it is: (1) the panel established by DPAs, (2) an alternative dispute resolution provider based in the EU, or (3) an alternative dispute resolution provider based in the United States,
   x. being subject to the investigatory and enforcement powers of the FTC, the Department of Transportation or any other U.S. authorized statutory body,
   xi. the possibility, under certain conditions, for the individual to invoke binding arbitration,
   xii. the requirement to disclose personal information in response to lawful requests by public authorities, including to meet national security or law enforcement requirements, and
   xiii. its liability in cases of onward transfers to third parties.

b. This notice must be provided in clear and conspicuous language when individuals are first asked to provide personal information to the organization or as soon thereafter as is practicable, but in any event before the organization uses such information for a purpose other than that for which it was originally collected or processed by the transferring organization or discloses it for the first time to a third party.

2. Choice

    a. An organization must offer individuals the opportunity to choose (opt out) whether their personal information is (i) to be disclosed to a third party or (ii) to be used for a purpose that is materially different from the purpose(s) for which it was originally collected or subsequently authorized by the individuals. Individuals must be provided with clear, conspicuous, and readily available mechanisms to exercise choice.

    b. By derogation to the previous paragraph, it is not necessary to provide choice when disclosure is made to a third party that is acting as an agent to perform task(s) on behalf of and under the instructions of the organization. However, an organization shall always enter into a contract with the agent.

    c. For sensitive information (i.e., personal information specifying medical or health conditions, racial or ethnic origin, political opinions, religious or philosophical beliefs, trade union membership or information specifying the sex life of the individual), organizations must obtain affirmative express consent (opt in) from individuals if such information is to be (i) disclosed to a third party or (ii) used for a purpose other than those for which it was originally collected or subsequently authorized by the individuals through the exercise of opt-in choice. . . .

3. Accountability for Onward Transfer

    a. To transfer personal information to a third party acting as a controller, organizations must comply with the Notice and Choice Principles. Organizations must also enter into a contract with the third-party controller that provides that such data may only be processed for limited and specified purposes consistent with the consent provided by the individual and that the recipient will provide the same level of protection as the Principles and will notify the organization if it makes a determination that it can no longer meet this obligation. . . .

    b. To transfer personal data to a third party acting as an agent, organizations must: (i) transfer such data only for limited and specified purposes; (ii) ascertain that the agent is obligated to provide at least the same level of privacy protection as is required by the Principles; (iii) take reasonable and appropriate steps to ensure that the agent effectively processes the personal information transferred in a manner consistent with the organization's obligations under the Principles; (iv) require the agent to notify the organization if it makes a determination that it can no longer meet its obligation to provide the same level of protection as is required by the Principles; (v) upon notice, including under (iv), take reasonable and appropriate steps to stop and remediate unauthorized processing; and (vi) provide a summary or a representative copy of the relevant privacy provisions of its contract with that agent to the Department upon request.

4. Security

    a. Organizations creating, maintaining, using or disseminating personal information must take reasonable and appropriate measures to protect it from loss, misuse and unauthorized access, disclosure, alteration and destruction, taking into due account the risks involved in the processing and the nature of the personal data.

5. Data integrity and purpose limitation

    a. Consistent with the Principles, personal information must be limited to the information that is relevant for the purposes of processing. An organization may not process personal information in a way that is incompatible with the purposes for which it has been collected or subsequently authorized by the individual. To the extent necessary for those purposes, an organization must take reasonable steps to ensure that personal data is reliable for its intended use, accurate, complete, and current. An organization must adhere to the Principles for as long as it retains such information.

    b. Information may be retained in a form identifying or making identifiable the individual only for as long as it serves a purpose of processing within the meaning of 5a. This obligation does not prevent organizations from processing personal information for longer periods for the time and to the extent such processing reasonably serves the purposes of archiving in the public interest, journalism, literature and art, scientific or historical research, and statistical analysis. . . .

6. Access

    a. Individuals must have access to personal information about them that an organization holds and be able to correct, amend, or delete that information where it is inaccurate, or has been processed in violation of the Principles, except where the burden or expense of providing access would be disproportionate to the risks to the individual's privacy in the case in question, or where the rights of persons other than the individual would be violated.

7. Recourse, enforcement and liability

    a. Effective privacy protection must include robust mechanisms for assuring compliance with the Principles, recourse for individuals who are affected by non-compliance with the Principles, and consequences for the organization when the Principles are not followed. At a minimum such mechanisms must include:

        i. readily available independent recourse mechanisms by which each individual's complaints and disputes are investigated and expeditiously resolved at no cost to the individual and by reference to the Principles, and damages awarded where the applicable law or private-sector initiatives so provide;

ii. follow-up procedures for verifying that the attestations and assertions organizations make about their privacy practices are true and that privacy practices have been implemented as presented and, in particular, with regard to cases of non-compliance; and

iii. obligations to remedy problems arising out of failure to comply with the Principles by organizations announcing their adherence to them and consequences for such organizations. Sanctions must be sufficiently rigorous to ensure compliance by organizations. . . .

d. In the context of an onward transfer, a Privacy Shield organization has responsibility for the processing of personal information it receives under the Privacy Shield and subsequently transfers to a third party acting as an agent on its behalf. The Privacy Shield organization shall remain liable under the Principles if its agent processes such personal information in a manner inconsistent with the Principles, unless the organization proves that it is not responsible for the event giving rise to the damage. . . .

III. SUPPLEMENTAL PRINCIPLES

1. Sensitive Data
   a. An organization is not required to obtain affirmative express consent (opt in) with respect to sensitive data where the processing is:
      i. in the vital interests of the data subject or another person;
      ii. necessary for the establishment of legal claims or defenses;
      iii. required to provide medical care or diagnosis;
      iv. carried out in the course of legitimate activities by a foundation, association or any other non-profit body with a political, philosophical, religious or trade-union aim and on condition that the processing relates solely to the members of the body or to the persons who have regular contact with it in connection with its purposes and that the data are not disclosed to a third party without the consent of the data subjects;
      v. necessary to carry out the organization's obligations in the field of employment law; or
      vi. related to data that are manifestly made public by the individual.

2. Journalistic Exceptions

   a. Given U.S. constitutional protections for freedom of the press and the Directive's exemption for journalistic material, where the rights of a free press embodied in the First Amendment of the U.S. Constitution intersect with privacy protection interests, the First Amendment must govern the balancing of these interests with regard to the activities of U.S. persons or organizations.
   b. Personal information that is gathered for publication, broadcast, or other forms of public communication of journalistic material, whether used or not, as well as information found in previously published material disseminated from media archives, is not subject to the requirements of the Privacy Shield Principles. . . .

8. Access

   a. The Access Principle in Practice
       i.   Under the Privacy Shield Principles, the right of access is fundamental to privacy protection. In particular, it allows individuals to verify the accuracy of information held about them. The Access Principle means that individuals have the right to:
            1. obtain from an organization confirmation of whether or not the organization is processing personal data relating to them;
            2. have communicated to them such data so that they could verify its accuracy and the lawfulness of the processing; and
            3. have the data corrected, amended or deleted where it is inaccurate or processed in violation of the Principles. . . .
   b. Burden or Expense of Providing Access
       i.   The right of access to personal data may be restricted in exceptional circumstances where the legitimate rights of persons other than the individual would be violated or where the burden or expense of providing access would be disproportionate to the risks to the individual's privacy in the case in question. Expense and burden are important factors and should be taken into account but they are not controlling factors in determining whether providing access is reasonable.

PAUL M. SCHWARTZ & KARL-NIKOLAUS PEIFER, TRANSATLANTIC DATA PRIVACY LAW

106 Georgetown L. J. — (forthcoming 2017)

Like the Safe Harbor, the Privacy Shield is best understood as a mixture of EU and U.S. standards. Post-Snowden and *Schrems*, the EU could tug the resulting agreement closer to its fundamental principles. At the same time, the U.S. could sign it because it contained weaker versions of some of the core EU principles of data privacy. Moreover, many elements of the framework depend on future decisions as oversight mechanisms are deployed. Hence, U.S. negotiators could in good conscience agree to it and trust in future collaborative decision making with the EU. The four core Privacy Shield Principles concern "data integrity and purpose limitation," "choice," enforcement, and oversight. In assessing the Privacy Shield, we concentrate on those principles.

Data Integrity and Choice

The first key standard of the Privacy Shield is the "Data Integrity and Purpose Limitation Principle," which revisits the Safe Harbor's "Data Integrity Principle." The Privacy Shield adds language, front and center, regarding a requirement of "Purpose Limitation," which telegraphs its increased requirements around compatibility. The Principle also adds specific language, not found in the Safe Harbor, that emphasizes the existence of an "express prohibition on incompatible processing." U.S. companies must now pay greater attention to collection of personal information from EU citizens and the creation of limits to make only compatible uses of it. Moreover, the increased enforcement mechanisms of the Privacy Shield suggest greater pressure in the future from the EU on companies regarding incompatible uses of information.

"Data integrity and purpose limitation" are also bolstered within the Privacy Shield by a new requirement that restricts "onward transfers" of information. Such transfers to a third party must be for a limited and specified purpose and expressed in business-to-business agreements that provide the same level of protection as the Privacy Shield Principles. In this fashion, the European idea of a state protecting its citizens against bad decisions has been transplanted into international law and U.S. legal mechanisms. Here is a collective mechanism that places limits on individual privacy decision making.

From the perspective of U.S. negotiators, there is mixed news in this result. On the plus side, the language regarding a ban on incompatibility amounts to less than the full-blown EU concept. In EU law, a compatible use must be "specified, explicit, and legitimate."[89] Yet, the language of the Privacy Shield nonetheless moves U.S. companies, if taken seriously and enforced strongly, in a decisive direction towards the idea of "purpose specification."

The second key standard is "choice." The Privacy Shield establishes both opt-out and opt-in rights for the EU data subject whose personal information is being transferred to the U.S. It handles opt-in largely in the same fashion as the Safe Harbor. Before the processing of "sensitive data" of an EU citizen, organizations in the U.S. must obtain "the data subject's affirmative express consent." In other words, the Privacy Shield requires opt-in before processing such information. The concept of sensitive data is a long-established idea in EU data protection law, and a category that the GDPR expands further.[90] U.S. companies must make correct use of stringent EU consent mechanisms. In some instances, such as data processing involving sensitive information, the high requirements for consent will make problematic certain kinds of data transfers.[91]

As for opt-out, the Privacy Shield makes an important change to the Safe Harbor's regime. It creates a new category within compatibility, and one otherwise unknown to EU data protection law. It envisions a "materially changed, but still compatible" processing operation, which is made subject to an opt-out. This language represents an EU concession to the U.S.; it accepts the possibility that a "material" change in purpose may nonetheless still be close enough to the original purpose of collection not to require another round of individual consent. As for an *incompatible* use of information, the Privacy Shield explicitly forbids it without new consent. Under EU law, such consent must be specific, collected separately from the initial agreement to processing, and subject to a strict tying restriction.

---

[89] GDPR, at art. 5(1)(b).

[90] The GDPR refers to categories that include "personal data revealing racial or ethnic origin, political opinions, religious or philosophical beliefs, or trade union membership, and the processing of genetic data, biometric data for the purpose of uniquely identifying a natural person, data concerning health or data concerning a natural person's sex life or sexual orientation." GDPR, at art. 9(1).

[91] The health care sector in the U.S., for example, will face considerable challenges to use of the Privacy Shield and may choose to process personal data of EU citizens solely within the EU. This result follows in part from the strict standards for protecting sensitive data.

The Privacy Shield brings the "choice" principle into closer alignment with EU protections for the data subject than the Safe Harbor had done.[92] At the same time, the U.S. negotiators could craft a new category for opt-out, namely that of a material, yet compatible, change in use. Here is a source for future EU–U.S. discussions and possible conflict. The two data privacy regimes are far apart on questions regarding compatibility and purpose specification. In resolving disputes around this issue, mechanisms for enforcement and oversight are critical. They are critical because through these new processes the EU and U.S. will create new shared concepts regarding compatibility and purpose specification. We now turn to enforcement and oversight.

Enforcement

The third set of core principles regards enforcement, and, here, the Privacy Shield marks a considerable change from the Safe Harbor. Enforcement represents the area in the Privacy Shield with the greatest American concessions and the strongest moves in the EU direction. In the words of the European Commission, the Privacy Shield contains strong supervision mechanisms "to ensure that companies follow the rules that they submitted themselves to."[93] The new section concerning redress is termed, "Recourse, Enforcement and Liability Principle." Redress under the Privacy Shield consists of both general enforcement mechanisms and a subset relating only to U.S. intelligence agencies. The general enforcement mechanisms are extensive; the data subject may place a complaint with a Privacy Shield company in the U.S.; complain to their national data protection authority; use alternative dispute resolution if the U.S. company signs up for it; and make use of the "Privacy Shield Panel," an arbitration mechanism that permits binding decisions against U.S. companies.

After the Snowden revelations and the *Schrems* decision, the issue of U.S. government access to the data of EU citizens became a critical issue in Privacy Shield negotiations. The Privacy Shield creates important safeguards regarding U.S. government access to personal data of EU citizens. Among the important changes relating to enforcement is the creation of a U.S. Ombudsperson, who is independent from U.S. intelligence services. The Ombudsperson will respond to individual complaints from individuals who believe that their personal data has been misused by U.S. national security agencies. The Privacy Shield agreement also references important congressional and Executive Branch changes regarding regulation of foreign intelligence surveillance by U.S. agencies. The aim is to document factual changes compared to the record that had been before the *Schrems* court in 2015. The step is a prudent one, taken in anticipation of future litigation in the EU.

---

[92] From the U.S. perspective, the Safe Harbor contained weaker and, hence, more desirable language regarding consent.

[93] Communication from the Commission to the European Parliament and the Council—Transatlantic Data Flows: Restoring Trust through Strong Safeguards, COM (2016) 117 final (Feb. 29, 2016) [hereinafter Transatlantic Data Flows].

Oversight

The fourth set of core principles regards oversight. There is now supervision of enforcement procedures by the FTC and the Department of Commerce as well as a specified process to remove companies with insufficient procedures from the Privacy Shield list and to subject them to sanctions. There is also an annual joint review of the Privacy Shield by EU and U.S. officials. Although the Safe Harbor included a limited number of these concepts, the Privacy Shield adds to the oversight list and heightens the overall requirements. To be sure, however, these requirements take the form of political commitments in an agreement with the EU rather than firm statutory obligations through U.S. law. Nonetheless, in the aftermath of *Schrems*, the Privacy Shield necessarily provides strong oversight of the NSA and U.S. intelligence community and provides new ways for EU citizens to obtain redress from the U.S. government as well as private organizations. By comparison, the Safe Harbor did not address national security surveillance.

In sum, the Privacy Shield displays concessions by both sides regarding their own legal models for data privacy. Above all, the document moves the system for data transfers more in the direction of EU data protection law than the Safe Harbor did. At the same time, from the U.S. perspective, the bottom line for the free flow of data was acceptable. At the press conference in Brussels announcing the Privacy Shield, U.S. Commerce Secretary Penny Pritzker declared that a "free flow of data" was assured "[f]or businesses."[94] Secretary Pritzker added, "For consumers, the free flow of data means that you can take advantage of the latest, most innovative digital products and services, no matter where they originate."[95]

NOTES & QUESTIONS

1. ***FTC Enforcement.*** The FTC brought its first enforcement action based on a company's entering into the Safe Harbor in 2009. By the time of the demise of the Safe Harbor, it had brought thirty-nine enforcement actions pursuant to this agreement. These actions fall roughly into two groups.

   First, the FTC includes an allegation of violation of the Safe Harbor in a complaint that also claims violations of Section 5 of the FTC Act. Examples of such an enforcement action include the actions against Myspace (2012), Facebook (2011), and Google (2012).

   Second, the FTC has acted against companies who made false Safe Harbor certification claims. These actions do not allege substantive violations of the Safe Harbor principles, but rather that a company falsely, deceptively, or misleadingly claimed that it held a valid certification. Companies make these claims either through statements in a privacy policy or a Safe Harbor certification mark on their Website. Some of these organizations joined the Safe

---

[94] *Remarks by U.S. Secretary of Commerce Penny Pritzker at EU–U.S. Privacy Shield Framework Press Conference*, U.S. Dep't of Com. (July 12, 2016), https://www.commerce.gov/news/secretary-speeches/2016/07/remarks-us-secretary-commerce-penny-pritzker-eu-us-privacy-shield.
[95] *Id.*

Harbor, but failed to renew their annual certification while continuing to represent themselves as current members.

In October 2009, for example, the FTC announced settlement agreements with six companies over charges that they falsely claimed membership in the Safe Harbor. In January 2014, the FTC announced Safe Harbor settlements with 12 companies over the same kind of charges. These companies include three professional football teams: the Atlanta Falcons, Denver Broncos, and Tennessee Titans. The 2014 settlements were also with BitTorrent, Inc., a provider of the peer-to-peer file -sharing protocol; DataMotion, Inc, a provider of an encrypted e-mail platform; and Reynolds Consumer Products, Inc., the maker of aluminum foil and other consumer products.

As under the Safe Harbor, the FTC has important enforcement powers pursuant to the Privacy Shield. It has stated a commitment to four key areas: (1) referral prioritization and investigations; (2) addressed false or deceptive Privacy Shield claims; (3) continued order monitoring; and (4) enhanced engagement and enforcement cooperation with EU data protection authorities.[96]

In its *Opinion 1/15*, the ECJ returned to the question of "adequacy" for an international data transfer, which it had explored in *Schrems*. In *Schrems*, the mechanism for providing adequacy before the ECJ was the Safe Harbor, a U.S.-EU agreement. In *Opinion 1/15*, the mechanism was a proposed agreement between the EU and Canada for transferring PNR data of EU air passengers to Canada. An earlier section of this chapter excerpted sections from *Opinion 1/15* concerning data retention. The excerpt below concerns this decision's analysis of the "adequacy" standard in EU law and the failure of the proposed Canada-EU PNR to meet it.

OPINION 1/15 OF THE COURT

European Court of Justice, Grand Chamber (July 26, 2017)

[The ECJ first determined that the proposed PNR agreement furthered an "appropriate purpose," which was to protect public safety. It noted, "[T]he processing of PNR data has, amongst other results, enabled the arrest of 178 persons from among the 28 million travellers who flew between the European Union and Canada in the period from April 2014 to March 2015." At the same time, the ECJ found that the PNR data covered by the agreement was not specified in a "sufficiently precise" fashion. For example, the precise kind of "contact information" that was to be transferred was not set out. The ECJ then turned to the issue of whether "sensitive data" was included in PNR data and whether there would be automated processing of PNR data. The ECJ also examined issues such as the presence of sensitive data among the PNR data; the automated processing

---

[96] Letter from Chairwoman Edith Ramirez to Věra Jourová, Commissioner for Justice, Consumers and Gender Equality of the European Commission, Describing Federal Trade Commission Enforcement of the New EU-U.S. Privacy Shield Framework (July 7, 2016).

of this information; the purposes for which PNR data may be processed; and the disclosure of PNR data.]

(ii) Sensitive data

164. As regards the transfer of sensitive data within the meaning of Article 2(e) of the envisaged agreement, that provision defines such data as any information that reveals 'racial or ethnic origin, political opinions, religious or philosophical beliefs, trade-union membership', or concerning 'a person's health or sex life'. Although none of the 19 headings set out in Annex to that agreement expressly refers to data of that nature, as, inter alia, the Commission confirmed in its answer to the questions posed by the Court, such information could nevertheless fall within the scope of heading 17. Furthermore, the fact that Articles 8 and 16 of the envisaged agreement lay down specific rules relating to the use and retention of sensitive data necessarily implies that the parties to that agreement have accepted that such data may be transferred to Canada.

166. [I]t must be pointed out that the EU legislature has prohibited the processing of sensitive data in Article 6(4), Article 7(6) and Article 13(4) of Directive (EU) 2016/681 of the European Parliament and of the Council of 27 April 2016 on the use of passenger name record (PNR) data for the prevention, detection, investigation and prosecution of terrorist offences and serious crime (OJ 2016 L 119, p. 132).

167. Having regard to the assessments set out in the two preceding paragraphs, it must be held that Articles 7, 8 and 21 and Article 52(1) of the Charter preclude both the transfer of sensitive data to Canada and the framework negotiated by the European Union with that non-member State of the conditions concerning the use and retention of such data by the authorities of that non-member State.

(2)   The automated processing of the PNR data

169. The assessment of the risks to public security presented by air passengers is carried out . . . by means of automated analyses of the PNR data before the arrival of those air passengers in Canada. Since those analyses are carried out on the basis of unverified personal data and are based on pre-established models and criteria, they necessarily present some margin of error. . . .

170. As stated in point 30 of the Opinion of the EDPS on the draft Proposal for a Council Framework Decision on the use of Passenger Name Record (PNR) data for law enforcement purposes (OJ 2008 C 110, p. 1), to which the EDPS referred in his answer to the questions posed by the Court, that margin of error appears to be significant.

173. Furthermore, since the automated analyses of PNR data necessarily involve some margin of error, as stated in paragraph 169 of this Opinion, any positive result obtained following the automated processing of that data must, under Article 15 of the envisaged agreement, be subject to an individual re-examination by non-automated means before an individual measure adversely affecting the air passengers concerned is adopted. Consequently, such a measure may not, under Article 15, be based solely and decisively on the result of automated processing of PNR data.

174. Lastly, in order to ensure that, in practice, the pre-established models and criteria, the use that is made of them and the databases used are not discriminatory and are limited to that which is strictly necessary, the reliability and topicality of those pre-established models and criteria and databases used should, taking account of statistical data and results of international research, be covered by the joint review of the implementation of the envisaged agreement, provided for in Article 26(2) thereof.

(3) The purposes for which PNR data may be processed
(i)   The prevention, detection or prosecution of terrorist offences or serious transnational crime

175. Article 3(1) of the envisaged agreement provides that PNR data may be processed by the Canadian Competent Authority only for the purpose of preventing, detecting, investigating or prosecuting terrorist offences or serious transnational crime.

176. So far as the term 'terrorist offences' is concerned, Article 3(2) of that agreement defines in a clear and precise manner both the activities covered by that term and the persons, groups and organisations liable to be regarded as a 'terrorist entity'.

177. Similarly, as regards the term 'serious transnational crime', the first subparagraph of Article 3(3) of the envisaged agreement defines with clarity and precision the degree of seriousness of the offences concerned, by requiring that they be punishable by a maximum deprivation of liberty of at least four years or a more serious penalty. Furthermore, as regards the nature of those offences, that provision must also be regarded as being sufficiently precise inasmuch as it refers to offences defined by Canadian law. Lastly, the second subparagraph of Article 3(3) of that agreement sets out in a clear and precise manner the different situations in which a crime is considered to be transnational in nature.

178. In those circumstances, Article 3(1) to (3) of the envisaged agreement contains clear and precise rules limited to what is strictly necessary.

(ii) Other purposes

180. Since Article 3(4) of the envisaged agreement restricts the cases in which the Canadian Competent Authority may use PNR data collected under the agreement for purposes unconnected with those inherent in the envisaged agreement relating to combating terrorism and serious transnational crime to the protection of the vital interests of individuals, that provision defines in a clear and precise manner the cases in which such use is permissible. Moreover, in so far as Article 3(4) provides that it is only in exceptional cases that the Canadian Competent Authority is so authorised, it must be held that that provision contains rules that are limited to what is strictly necessary.

181. By contrast, the wording of the cases in which Canada may process PNR data under Article 3(5)(a) and (b) of the envisaged agreement is too vague and general to meet the requirements as to clarity and precision required. The rules set out in that provision are not therefore limited to what is strictly necessary to attain the objective pursued by that agreement.

(5)   The air passengers concerned

186. The envisaged agreement covers the PNR data of all air passengers flying between the European Union and Canada. The transfer of that data to Canada is to take place regardless of whether there is any objective evidence permitting the inference that the passengers are liable to present a risk to public security in Canada.

187. In this connection, it should be pointed out that . . . the PNR data is intended, inter alia, to be subject to automated processing. As several of the interveners have stated, that processing is intended to identify the risk to public security that persons, who are not, at that stage, known to the competent services, may potentially present, and who may, on account of that risk, be subject to further examination. In that respect, the automated processing of that data, before the arrival of the passengers in Canada, facilitates and expedites security checks, in particular at borders. Furthermore, the exclusion of certain categories of persons, or of certain areas of origin, would be liable to prevent the achievement of the objective of automated processing of PNR data, namely identifying, through verification of that data, persons liable to present a risk to public security from amongst all air passengers, and make it possible for that verification to be circumvented.

189. In those circumstances, the envisaged agreement does not exceed the limits of what is strictly necessary in so far as it permits the transfer of the PNR data of all air passengers to Canada.

(7)   The disclosure of PNR data
(i)   Disclosure of PNR data to government authorities

214. In this connection, it must be recalled that a transfer of personal data from the European Union to a non-member country may take place only if that country ensures a level of protection of fundamental rights and freedoms that is essentially equivalent to that guaranteed within the European Union. That same requirement applies in the case of the disclosure of PNR data by Canada to third countries, referred to in Article 19 of the envisaged agreement, in order to prevent the level of protection provided for in that agreement from being circumvented by transfers of personal data to third countries and to ensure the continuity of the level of protection afforded by EU law (see, by analogy, judgment of 6 October 2015, Schrems). In those circumstances, such disclosure requires the existence of either an agreement between the European Union and the non-member country concerned equivalent to that agreement, or a decision of the Commission, under Article 25(6) of Directive 95/46, finding that the third country ensures an adequate level of protection within the meaning of EU law and covering the authorities to which it is intended PNR data be transferred.

215. In so far as Articles 18 and 19 of the envisaged agreement do not meet the[se] requirements, that agreement does not ensure that the disclosure of PNR data by the Canadian Competent Authority to other Canadian government authorities or to government authorities of third countries will be limited to what is strictly necessary. [In particular, the ECJ found that the proposed agreement

conferred on Canada "a discretionary power to assess the level of protection" in countries outside of Canada before sharing the data further.]

(ii) Disclosure of PNR data to individuals

216. Article 12(3) of the envisaged agreement allows Canada to 'make any disclosure of information subject to reasonable legal requirements and limitations . . . with due regard for the legitimate interests of the individual concerned'. However, that agreement does not delimit the nature of the information that may be disclosed, nor the persons to whom such disclosure may be made, nor even the use that is to be made of that information.

217. Moreover, the envisaged agreement does not define the terms 'legal requirements and limitations' or the terms 'legitimate interests of the individual concerned', nor does it require that the disclosure of PNR data to an individual be linked to combating terrorism and serious transnational crime or that the disclosure be conditional on the authorisation of a judicial authority or an independent administrative body. In those circumstances, that provision exceeds the limits of what is strictly necessary.

3.   The individual rights of air passengers

[The ECJ noted flaws in the proposed agreement concerning the right to information, the right of access and the right to correction. It also identified flaws regarding the oversight of PNR data protection safeguards.]

IX.   Answer to the request for an Opinion

232. In the light of all the foregoing considerations, it must be held that:

(1) the Council decision on the conclusion of the envisaged agreement must be based jointly on Article 16(2) and Article 87(2)(a) TFEU;
(2) the envisaged agreement is incompatible with Articles 7, 8 and 21 and Article 52(1) of the Charter in so far as it does not preclude the transfer of sensitive data from the European Union to Canada and the use and retention of that data;
(3) the envisaged agreement must, in order to be compatible with Articles 7 and 8 and Article 52(1) of the Charter:
   (a) determine in a clear and precise manner the PNR data to be transferred from the European Union to Canada;
   (b) provide that the models and criteria used in the context of automated processing of PNR data will be specific and reliable and non-discriminatory; provide that the databases used will be limited to those used by Canada in relation to the fight against terrorism and serious transnational crime;
   (c) save in the context of verifications in relation to the pre-established models and criteria on which automated processing of PNR data is based, make the use of that data by the Canadian Competent Authority during the air passengers' stay in Canada and after their departure from

that country, and any disclosure of that data to other authorities, subject to substantive and procedural conditions based on objective criteria; make that use and that disclosure, except in cases of validly established urgency, subject to a prior review carried out either by a court or by an independent administrative body, the decision of that court or body authorising the use being made following a reasoned request by those authorities, inter alia, within the framework of procedures for the prevention, detection or prosecution of crime;

(d) limit the retention of PNR data after the air passengers' departure to that of passengers in respect of whom there is objective evidence from which it may be inferred that they may present a risk in terms of the fight against terrorism and serious transnational crime;

(e) make the disclosure of PNR data by the Canadian Competent Authority to the government authorities of a third country subject to the condition that there be either an agreement between the European Union and that third country equivalent to the envisaged agreement, or a decision of the Commission, under Article 25(6) of Directive 95/46, covering the authorities to which it is intended that PNR data be disclosed;

(f) provide for a right to individual notification for air passengers in the event of use of PNR data concerning them during their stay in Canada and after their departure from that country, and in the event of disclosure of that data by the Canadian Competent Authority to other authorities or to individuals; and

(g) guarantee that the oversight of the rules laid down in the envisaged agreement relating to the protection of air passengers with regard to the processing of PNR data concerning them will be carried out by an independent supervisory authority.

NOTES & QUESTIONS

1. *The Holding:* Opinion 1/15. In *Schrems*, the ECJ invalidated the Safe Harbor for its failure to meet the adequacy standard. In *Opinion 1/15*, the ECJ invalidated the proposed PNR agreement between the EU and Canada. For the ECJ, the proposed international agreement was unacceptable in its current form. Several of its elements failed to comport with the requirements of EU data protection. These included its failure: to provide sufficient protections for the transfer of sensitive data; to require non-automated individual re-examination of automated decisions that would adversely affect an air passenger; to limit transfers of data within Canada government or to government in other third countries; and to safeguard the individual privacy rights of air passengers.

2. *Future Impact of Decision.* The EU has concluded PNR agreements with Australia and the United States. These are used as the legal basis for international transfers of personal data from the EU to these countries. Challenges to the adequacy of these agreements may follow. The Privacy Shield will be evaluated as well according to the requirements that the ECJ articulates in *Opinion 1/15*. Of particular note in this regard are the

requirements to protect individual rights as well as to provide "oversight of the rules . . . carried out by an independent supervisory authority." Opinion 1/15, at ¶232(3)(g).

D. THE APEC PRIVACY FRAMEWORK

Asia-Pacific Economic Cooperation (APEC) is a cooperative of economies located along the Pacific Ocean. It includes the United States, China, Japan, the Russian Federation, China, Australia, New Zealand, Peru, Indonesia, Mexico, Singapore, Thailand, and Vietnam. APEC is a multilateral economic forum. Ministers of these countries adopted a privacy framework, based on the OECD Privacy Guidelines, on November 24, 2004 at a meeting in Santiago, Chile. Then U.S. Secretary of State Colin Powell stated, "The APEC Privacy Framework will establish a consistent approach to privacy across APEC member economies, while also avoiding the creation of unnecessary barriers to information flows."

The APEC Framework seeks to enable multinational businesses to implement uniform approaches to the use of personal data. Unlike the Data Protection Directive, the APEC Framework is not binding upon the APEC nations. In this regard, it resembles the non-binding OECD Guidelines. It explicitly states as well that member economies will vary in their implementation of their principles. It notes: "In view of the differences in social, cultural, economic and legal backgrounds of each member economy, there should be flexibility in implementing these Principles." APEC, Privacy Framework, Paragraph 12 (Nov. 2004). Moreover, exceptions to its principles are foreseen. To the extent that there are exceptions made by countries to its principles, these should be "limited and proportional to meeting the objectives to which the exceptions relate" and either publicly disclosed or made in accordance with law. Paragraph 13. Exceptions can be made on grounds of national sovereignty, national security, public safety or public policy.

The APEC Privacy Framework contains nine principles. These are: (1) preventing harm; (2) notice; (3) collection limitation; (4) use of personal information; (5) choice; (6) integrity; (7) security safeguards; (8) access and correction; and (9) accountability.

Of these nine principles, two should be explained further. The "use" principle specifies that personal information should be used "only to fulfil the purposes of collection and other compatible or related purposed," except when used with consent of the individual whose information is collected; to provide a product or service requested by the individual; or pursuant to legal authority. Section 19. The integrity principle calls for information to be completely up-to-date "to the extent necessary for the purposes of use." Paragraph 21.

The APEC Privacy Framework does not prohibit transfer of data to countries that do not comply with it. Its non-prescriptive approach is to recommend that member economies cooperate in investigation and enforcement as well as in development of cross-border privacy rules. Regarding the cooperative arrangements, the Privacy Framework states that its call for cross-border cooperation does not affect "the right of Member Economies to decline or limit cooperation on particular investigations or matters on the ground that compliance with a request for cooperation would be inconsistent with domestic laws, policies or priorities, or on the ground of resource constraints, or based on the absence of a mutual interest in the investigations in question." Paragraph 44.

In one view, the APEC rules establish "a practical middle ground" that establishes baseline principles while not unnecessarily restricting the flow of information.[97] On a less sanguine note, Graham Greenleaf views the APEC Privacy Framework as presenting "a relatively low set of privacy standards . . . , no requirements of any specific enforcement measures, and no substantive provisions concerning data exports."[98] He concludes, "In this sense it is the weakest international privacy standard yet developed."

In 2011, APEC released its system of voluntary cross-border privacy rules for the APEPC region. The CBPR website describes the Cross Border Privacy Rules (CBPR) as "a voluntary accountability-based system to facilitate privacy-respecting data flows among APEC economies." There are four elements of the CBPR system: (1) self-assessment; (2) compliance review; (3) recognition/acceptance; and (4) dispute resolution and enforcement. At present, there are three countries, Japan, the United States, and Mexico, participating in the CPBR system. Japan has applied for acceptance into the system. By July 2014, five companies have been awarded APEC certification, including IBM, the first company awarded certification, and Merck. In the United States, the FTC is the main enforcement agency for the CPBR.

CPBR Element 1, self-assessment, involves an organization's own evaluation of its data privacy policies and practices using an APEC-recognized questionnaire. This questionnaire is the submitted to an APEC-recognized Accountability Agent. An Accountability Agent is an organization that plays the role of certifying that a participating company is compliant with the requirements of the CPBR program. For the United States, APEC has named TRUSTe as an Accountability Agent.

CPBR Element 2, compliance review, requires the Accountability Agent to review an organization's privacy policies and practices as described in the self-assessment questionnaire. The official description of the CPBR system states, "An APEC-recognized Accountability Agent's assessment process may exceed [the CPBR program requirements] but may not fall below it." APEC Cross-Border Privacy Rules System: Policies, Rules and Guidelines (2011).

CPBR Element 3, recognition/acceptance, calls for development of a publicly accessible directory of organizations certified by Accountability Agents. Each organization's listing is to include the contact point information that consumers can use to contact the participating organization.

CPBR Element 4, dispute resolution and enforcement, makes the CPBR system enforceable by Accountability Agents and Privacy Enforcement Authorities. The Accountability Agents are to enforce program requirements through law or contract. The Privacy Enforcement Agent, notably the FTC in the

---

[97] Carla Budford, *Between East and West: the APEC Privacy Framework and the Balance of International Data Flows*, 3 I/S J.L. & Policy for Info. Society 705, 722 (2008).

[98] Graham Greenleaf, APEC Privacy Framework completed: No threat to privacy standards, Privacy Laws and Business, 11/8, 220 (2006).

United States, is to take enforcement actions under applicable domestic laws and regulations.

In March 2014, the EU's Article 29 Working Party and officials from the APEC member economies released a "data transfer interoperability map." This document seeks to compare, or map, the differences in the system and to find ways to move to interoperability. In particular, it provides "an informal pragmatic checklist for organizations applying for authorization of [Binding Corporate Rules] and/or certification of CBPR." The joint document, termed a "referential," does not represent a mutual recognition by the two systems for international data transfers. Rather, it seeks to streamline the process of double-certification.

NOTES & QUESTIONS

1. ***APEC and the EU Rules.*** How would you describe the similarities and differences between the APEC and EU approaches to international data transfers? Which system do you consider preferable?

E. PRIVACY PROTECTION IN NORTH AMERICA

1. CANADA

In 2001, a sweeping new privacy law became effective in Canada. This statute, the Personal Information Protection and Electronic Documents Act (PIPEDA), S.C. 2000 ch. 5 (Can.), governs all entities that collect personal information on Canadians.

PIPEDA extends to all "personal information" used in connection with any commercial activity. *Id.* § 4(1)–(2). The Act applies to all personal information collected prior to the enactment of PIPEDA, and it does not exempt non-Canadian entities. PIPEDA is based on the OECD Privacy Guidelines and, even more directly, the Canadian Standards Association (CSA) Model Code for the Protection of Personal Information, which articulate ten privacy principles.

PIPEDA requires that the individual must consent prior to the collection, use, or disclosure of personal data. *See id.* sched. 1, § 4.3. It also incorporates the OECD purpose specification principle, security safeguard principle, openness principle, accountability principle, and data quality principle, among others. PIPEDA has an unusual structure with its core found in its Schedule 1, which reprints most of the CSA Model Code.[99] PIPEDA's statutory text sometimes contradicts its Schedule 1, which creates an interpretive challenge for courts and the Privacy Commissioner. More follows about the role of the Privacy Commissioner below.

On December 20, 2001, the EU Commission issued a Decision that PIPEDA provides an adequate level of protection:

> The Canadian Act covers all the basic principles necessary for an adequate level of protection for natural persons, even if exceptions and limitations are also

---

[99] John Beardwood et al., Canadian Privacy Law, in Proskauer on Privacy 13-1, 13-5 (Kristin Mathews ed., 2011).

provided for in order to safeguard important public interests and to recognize certain information which exists in the public domain. The application of these standards is guaranteed by judicial remedy and by independent supervision carried out by the authorities, such as the Federal Privacy Commissioner invested with powers of investigation and intervention. Furthermore, the provisions of Canadian law regarding civil liability apply in the event of unlawful processing which is prejudicial to the persons concerned.[100]

PIPEDA may have substantial effects on transborder flows between Canada and the United States. According to some commentators:

> Although Canada's privacy laws certainly apply to covered organizations located in Canada, a more difficult question is raised when trying to determine their effects on companies located solely within the United States that happen to collect, use, or disclose the personal information of Canadians. . . . PIPEDA will certainly affect American companies. This is because of PIPEDA's secondary data transfer requirements which force Canadian companies to incorporate the Act's privacy requirements into all contracts which contemplate the transfer of Canadians' personal information to U.S. or other foreign companies. But to date Canadian law provides mixed guidance on how it will address the extraterritorial effects of the Act.[101]

Under PIPEDA, the Privacy Commissioner of Canada has the power to investigate citizen complaints and to conduct audits. The Commissioner can also publish information about personal information processing in the public and private sectors, and promote awareness and understanding of privacy issues. It also has an important ombudsman role in resolving complaints. Individuals are given a right under PIPEDA § 11(1) to file a complaint with the Privacy Commissioner. The Privacy Commissioner can also initiate a complaint, summon witnesses, and compel production of evidence. The Commissioner lacks power to make binding orders or impose penalties for violations of PIPEDA. The results of a complaint investigation by the Commissioner can be appealed to federal court, which under PIPEDA does have the power to order an organization to correct its practices, and to award damages.

Like the United States, Canada has a law that regulates the use of information by federal government institutions. As in the United States, this law is called the Privacy Act. It limits the collection, use, and disclosure of information by federal government entities and vests powers on the Privacy Commissioner to receive and investigate complaints, initiate an investigation on its own initiative, and to make findings and recommendations to government institutions.

In 2010, Canada enacted a strict anti-spam law, which finally came into force on July 1, 2014. Among its core provisions, Canada's Anti-Spam Law (CASL)

---

[100] Commission Decision of 20 December 2001 Pursuant to Directive 95/46/EC of the European Parliament and of the Council on the Adequate Protection of Personal Data Provided by the Canadian Personal Information Protection and Electronic Documents Act, C(2001) 4539, available at http://www.europa.eu.int/comm/internal_market/en/dataprot/adequacy/index.htm.

[101] Juliana M. Spaeth, Mark J. Plotkin & Sandra C. Sheets, *Privacy, Eh!: The Impact of Canada's Personal Information Protection and Electronic Documents Act on Transnational Business*, 4 Vand. J. Ent. L. & Prac. 29 (2002). For a detailed analysis of PIPEDA, see Stephanie Perrin, Heather H. Black, David H. Flaherty & T. Murray Rankin, *The Personal Information Protection and Electronic Documents Act: An Annotated Guide* (2001).

prohibits sending unsolicited commercial emails. As a general matter, CASL requires express consent from a recipient before sending commercial emails. CASL does recognize, however, implied consent in situations where sender and recipient have an existing business relationship.

Beyond its anti-spam provisions, CASL forbids the unsolicited installing of a computer program on another person's computer or causing an e-mail to be sent by such a computer with the installed computer program and collecting personal information by means of unauthorized access to computer systems. It provides for administrative monetary penalties and a private right of action.

NOTES & QUESTIONS

1. ***The PIPEDA Approach to Privacy Protection.*** PIPEDA seeks to regulate privacy through fairly broad principles, many of which are very flexible in order to establish a balance between privacy and business interests. Is PIPEDA too vague and broad? What are the pros and cons of a generalized principle-based approach to protecting privacy as opposed to a more detailed set of specific regulations? How does PIPEDA compare with the U.S. approach to regulating the private sector? Does it seem closer to the U.S. or European approach to information privacy?

2. MEXICO

The constitution of Mexico has a bill of rights that guarantees a broad series of fundamental rights and freedoms. These constitutional guarantees include a right to due process, and a right not to be disturbed in one's person, domicile, or documents without written order by competent authority. Since 1996, the Mexican constitution contains an explicit guarantee of the privacy of private communications.

In addition to a law that regulates credit bureaus and a Freedom of Information Act, Mexico enacted a general information privacy law, the Federal Data Protection Act (FDPA) of 2010. The FDPA is an omnibus law, following the EU model, that requires a lawful basis for collecting, processing, and disclosing personal information. It requires that all personal data be kept accurate and updated and used only for the purposes for which it was collected. Any person or company that manages personal data is required to designate a person for managing this information and provide privacy notices to the person to whom the data refers.

Unlike the EU model, however, the statute embodies the "habeas data" concept that several South American countries embrace. The idea is that the individual to whom the data refers is treated as a "data owner" with legal rights, such as those of access, that derive from this status. Habeas data itself is a special judicial measure that permits any person to know the content and purpose of the data pertaining to her in public records or in certain private records. This legal mechanism permits an individual to find out what information is held about her and to gain certain traditional information privacy rights with respect to that data. Under the FDPA, "data owners" have rights to initiate claims and procedures pursuant to the statute beginning 18 months after its enactment (July 15, 2010).

In 2013, Mexico's Privacy Notice Guidelines went into effect. The Guidelines establish requirements for obtaining consent and providing data privacy notices before information is collected from a person, whether directly or through electronic means, such as cookies. The Guidelines provide a framework for full notice, simplified notice and short notice depending on the circumstances of information collection.

F. PRIVACY PROTECTION IN SOUTH AMERICA

1. ARGENTINA

In 2000, Argentina became the first country in South America to adopt a comprehensive data protection law. The Law for the Protection of Personal Data is based on the European Union Data Protection Directive, several provisions of the Argentine constitution, and earlier national laws. It contains provisions relating to general data protection principles, the rights of data subjects, the obligations of data controllers and data users, the supervisory authority, sanctions, and rules of procedure in seeking "habeas data" as a judicial remedy. Habeas data is a special, simplified, and quick judicial remedy for the protection of personal data. Enshrined in the constitution, the habeas rule permits any person to know the content and purpose of the data pertaining to her in public records, or in certain private records. The Argentina data protection law also prohibits international transfers of personal information to countries without adequate protection.

The Commission of the European Community decided in 2003 that Argentina provided an adequate level of protection for personal data.[102] It thereby meets the standards of the EU Data Protection Directive. The adequacy finding means that all transborder data flows between Argentina and the European Union are presumptively in compliance with the EU Data Directive. Argentina is the first and thus far only country in Latin America to obtain a finding of adequacy.

2. BRAZIL

The constitution of Brazil explicitly protects privacy in its Article 5. Like Mexico, it also contains a constitutional right to habeas data. Two experts in international privacy law consider it "more watered-down" than Argentina's similar right.[103] Also like Mexico, Brazil lacks a general information privacy statute. It does, however, contain some sectoral privacy laws. These include a consumer protection law from 1990 that sets out regulations for personal data recordkeeping and a federal law from 1996 that regulates wiretapping.

---

[102] Commission Decision of 30/06/2003, Brussels C(2003) 1731 final.
[103] Dowling & Mittman, *International Privacy Law*, at 14-43.

G. PRIVACY PROTECTION IN AFRICA AND THE MIDDLE EAST

1. AFRICA

Where it once represented a "privacy free-for-all," Africa has now "radically transformed its privacy regime.[104] Angola, Benin, Burkina Faso, Cape Verde, the Cote D'Ivoire, Gabon, Ghana, Senegal, and South Africa all have data protection statutes.

Of these nations, South Africa has the most recent comprehensive information privacy law. Already, the 1996 Constitution of South Africa grants a right to privacy, which includes protections for the person, home, and communications. The South African Constitutional Court's "interpretation of the right is a mixture of U.S. and European jurisprudence."[105] The court emphasizes both human dignity and the need to protect reasonable expectations of privacy. In 2013, South Africa approved the Protection of Personal Information Act (Nov. 26, 2013).

2. THE MIDDLE EAST

The constitutions of several Arab countries mention privacy. For example, Article 10 of Jordan's constitution provides: "Dwelling houses shall be inviolable and shall not be entered except in the circumstances and in the manner prescribed by law." Saudi Arabia's constitution, Article 37, declares: "The home is sacrosanct and shall not be entered without the permission of the owner or be searched except in cases specified by statutes." Article 44 of Egypt's constitution protects the privacy of the home, and Article 45 contains a broader protection of privacy:

> The law shall protect the inviolability of the private life of citizens. Correspondence, wires, telephone calls an other means of communication shall have their own sanctity and secrecy and may not be confiscated or monitored except by a causal judicial warrant and for a definite period according to the provisions of the law.

In 2002, Dubai's Electronic Transactions and Commerce Law, No. 2/2002, restricted ISPs from disclosing customer data.

According to Jacqueline Klosek:

> Privacy rights were not very well developed in the Middle East even before September 11. Generally, the region is well known for being a territory in which the government exercises great level of control over the conduct, including, without limitation, the Internet-related activity of their users. Cultural issues may also play a role in the stagnant development of privacy rights in the region. Indeed, Arabic law has no equivalent to the English word "privacy" — some may say that the closest is the term *khususi* meaning "personal." According to one author, in the Arab world, the connotation of privacy does not relate to "personal" or "secret," as it does in other cultures. Rather, it concerns two specific spheres:

---

[104] Cynthia Rich, *Privacy Laws in Africa and the Middle East*, BNA Privacy & Sec. Law Rep. 717 (Apr. 28, 2014).
[105] EPIC & Privacy International, Privacy and Human Rights 865 (2006).

women and the family. Another author goes even further, claiming: "There is no concept of privacy among Arabs. In translation, the Arabic world that comes closest to 'privacy' means loneliness!"[106]

Israel provides stronger protections of privacy than many other Middle Eastern countries. It lacks a formal constitution, but its Basic Law, Article 7, provides for a right to privacy:

> (a) All persons have the right to privacy and to intimacy.
> (b) There shall be no entry into the private premises of a person who has not consented thereto.
> (c) No search shall be conducted on the private premises of a person, nor in the body or personal effects.
> (d) There shall be no violation of the confidentiality of conversation, or of the writings or records of a person.

Israel also has a data protection law, the Privacy Protection Act of 1981. Along the lines of a European omnibus statute, it regulates public and private organizations alike. It requires that certain databases be formally registered and prohibits the use or transfer of information in such a database for a purpose other than the one for which it was established. The Privacy Protection Act also requires that a person can inspect information about her that is kept in a database and also request correction or amendment of her information.

In 2011, the European Commission found that Israel provides an adequate level of protection for personal information. *See* Commission Decision of 31 January 2011 (2011/61/EU).

H. PRIVACY PROTECTION IN ASIA-PACIFIC

1. AUSTRALIA

The primary protection of privacy in Australia is the Privacy Act of 1988, which establishes 11 Information Privacy Principles based on the OECD Privacy Guidelines. The 1988 statute only applied to the public sector. In 2000, the Privacy Amendment Act created ten new privacy principles that extend to private sector entities. These principles are known as the National Privacy Principles (NPPs).

The 2000 law also established a "co-regulatory" scheme. Companies can apply to the Privacy Commissioner to substitute their own privacy practice standards if they are an "overall equivalent" to the NPPs. It also exempts "small businesses" entirely from its privacy rules. A further exemption exists for employment records.

Amendments to the Privacy Act passed in December 2012 and came into force on March 2014. The Privacy Amendment (Enhancing Privacy Protection) Act creates a set of 13 new privacy principles that regulate the handling of personal information. These principles are termed the Australian Privacy Principles (APP). The 2012 amendments also enhance the power of the Office of the Australian Information Commissioner and include new credit reporting provisions.

---

[106] Jacqueline Klosek, *The War on Privacy* 62 (2007).

2. JAPAN

The Japanese Diet enacted the Personal Data Protection Act in May 2003.[107] The law came into effect on April 1, 2005. According to an ordinance-cabinet order issued under the statute, the law covers all businesses with databases containing information on more than 5,000 individuals. It specifically excludes a number of entities, including broadcast and other reporting media, "individuals who are writers by trade," scholarly research, religious organizations, and political organizations.

The Japanese Personal Data Protection Act requires strong Fair Information Practices. Before collecting personal information, a business must articulate a "purpose of use." No business can process personal information beyond its stated purpose of use. A business that collects personal information must inform an individual of the planned purpose of use.

Businesses are forbidden from sharing personal information with any third party without the individual's consent unless pursuant to a law or ordinance, or necessary to protect human life, or subject to certain other exceptions.

Subject to certain exceptions, an individual has a right to ask a business to disclose his stored personal information to him. An individual has a right to correct, supplement, or delete his stored personal information if it is incorrect. Certain government ministers, termed "competent ministers," are responsible for supervision and enforcement under the Act.

3. CHINA AND HONG KONG

The Chinese constitution has several protections for privacy, including a protection against defamation, against intrusions into the home, and against monitoring of correspondence. However, the Chinese government engages in extensive surveillance and searches of its citizens:

> China has had a long-standing policy — dating back to the 4th Century B.C. — of keeping close track of its citizens. . . .
>
> China's law states that the "freedom of privacy of correspondence of citizens are protected by law." Furthermore, warrants are required before law enforcement officials can search premises. However, this requirement is frequently ignored; moreover, the Public Security Bureau and prosecutors can issue search warrants on their own authority without judicial consent, review, or consideration.[108]

According to Lü Yao-Huai, Chinese law and culture have long eschewed privacy, but are gradually moving toward an increased recognition of its value:

> Though many common Chinese still link privacy with *Yinsi* (shameful secret) — to a large extent, at least in the relevant discussion of many contemporary Chinese scholars, the concept of privacy is no longer limited to the earlier, narrower sense of [*Yinsi*], but now includes all personal information (i.e., whether shameful or not) that people do not want others to know. Such a concept is gradually exerting

---

[107] For an English translation of the law, see Japan's Personal Information Protection Act, 2003 Law No. 57, http://www.privacyexchange.org/japan/japanindex.html.

[108] Electronic Privacy Information Center & Privacy International, *Privacy and Human Rights* 338 (2006).

influence on the average Chinese. This expanding scope of "privacy" is apparently based, at least in part, on the expansion of physical personal space in contemporary China. . . .

[S]ince China entered the World Trade Organization, the problem of data privacy has caused more extensive concern. On the one hand, more and more foreign enterprises enter China to produce and market goods and services, which further inspires the Chinese consumer's request for protection for data privacy; on the other hand, more and more Chinese enterprises will go abroad, which requires that they must adopt the privacy rules for members of the WTO. The supra-regional and international character of the Internet and WTO make contemporary Chinese ideas of privacy break through the earlier limits of native culture, and to some degree, Chinese ideas are probably coming to more closely resemble common foreign ideas of privacy. . . .

Up until now, there has been no general data protection law in China, with the exception of some local laws involving data protection. Therefore, the protection of data privacy is a very urgent problem. . . .

[T]he protection of privacy in contemporary China, compared with its past, has relatively increased consideration of personal benefits, but still takes social benefits as the center of gravity, and the protection of personal privacy is obviously limited by the social benefits and national interest. Compared with Western countries, the protection of a right to privacy in China is still limited.[109]

In January 2011, government administrators in China released draft *Information Security Technology Guidelines for Information Privacy Protection.* The Guidelines were issued by the General Administration of Quality Supervision, Inspection, and Quarantine in consultation with the Ministry of Industry and Information Technology. The draft Guidelines grant data subjects broad rights in relation to their personal information held by data processors.

In contrast, Hong Kong enacted an information privacy statute in 1996. It has been termed an "Asian Privacy Pioneer."[110] Its Personal Data Ordinance regulates entities in both the public and private sector through a series of Fair Information Practices. This statute also establishes an Office of the Privacy Commissioner. The Privacy Commissioner explains the Ordinance in these terms:

The Ordinance gives rights to data subjects. They have the right to confirm with data users whether their personal data are held, to obtain a copy of such data, and to have personal data corrected. Any charge for providing a copy of personal data to a data subject may not be excessive. They may complain to the Privacy Commissioner for Personal Data about a suspected breach of the Ordinance's requirements and claim compensation for damage caused to them as a result of a contravention of the Ordinance through civil proceedings.

The Privacy Commissioner has wide-ranging authority under the law, including direct enforcement powers. These powers include providing guidance on compliance with the Ordinance, investigating violations of the Ordinance, and examining requests from data users who desire to conduct automated matching of personal information.

[109] Lü Yao-Huai, *Privacy and Data Privacy Issues in Contemporary China*, 7 Ethics & Info. Tech. 15, (2005).
[110] Warren B. Chik, *The Lion, the Dragon and the Wardrobe Guarding the Doorway to Information and Communications Privacy on the Internet*, 14 Int'l J.L. & Info. Tech. 47, 91 (2005).

Revisions to the Personal Data Ordinance took effect in April 2013. These amendments require consent prior to the use of personal data in targeted marketing as well as opt-out rights. These provisions also provide for strong maximum penalties for contraventions of the direct marketing requirements.

4. SOUTH KOREA

South Korea enacted a data protection law, the Personal Information Protection Act (PIPA), in March 2011. After a grace period, the law came into full effect in March 2012. This statute extends to both public and private sectors. It establishes a 15-member Data Protection Commission and requires most businesses and government agencies to have Privacy Compliance officers.

According to Graham Greenleaf and Whon-il Park, PIPA is "Asia's toughest data privacy law."[111] As proof, they point to PIPA's requirements that there be no denial of service because of a person's refusal to provide information that is legally unnecessary, that only the minimum collection of personal information occur, that sensitive data cannot be processed without consent, and that notification to the data subject occur when personal information collected from third parties. PIPA also requires data breach notification to data subjects. In sum, Greenleaf and Park warn, "Businesses need to take very seriously its compliance requirements."[112]

5. INDIA

India has a constitutional right to privacy, which the Indian Supreme Court identified as part of the constitution's protection in its Article 21 of individual liberty. This right of privacy applies only to the public sector.[113]

In April 2011, India issued the Information Technology (Electronic Service Delivery) Rules (Privacy Rules).[114] These implemented a 2008 IT Security Act law. The Privacy Rules serve to create the first data privacy law for India. Under them, organizations are required to establish a privacy policy that sets out their practices and policies, identifies any sensitive privacy policy collected and processed, explains the purposes for which data is collected and used, and provides for reasonable security practices. Additional restrictions are placed on sensitive personal data; for such information, prior written consent from an individual is needed before it can be processed. The Privacy Rules also give individuals rights of access and correction "as feasible."

---

[111] Graham Greenleaf & Whon-il Park, Korea's new Act: Asia's toughest data privacy law, Privacy Laws & Business International Report (Issue 117) (June 2012). On the statute's requirements for outsourcing and cross-border transfers, see Sung-Hey Park, South Korea's New Data Protection Act: Cross-Border Transfer Issues Examined in Relation to the Outsourcing Clause and the Relevant Regulatory Framework, 11 Bloomberg BNA World Data Protection Report 6 (Sept. 23, 2011).

[112] *Id.*

[113] Dowling & Mittman, International Privacy Law, in *Proskauer on Privacy*, 14-56 (Kristin Mathews, ed. 2011).

[114] Government of India, Ministry of Communications and Information Technology, *Information Technology (Electronic Service Delivery) Rules*, 2011 (New Delhi, 2011), at http://www.mit.gov.in/sites/upload_files/dit/files/RNUS_CyberLaw_15411.pdf.

INDEX